BAD DOINGS & BIG IDEAS

A **BILL WILLINGHAM** DELUXE EDITION

BILL WILLINGHAM
writer

Mark Buckingham • Ross Campbell • Zander Cannon • Richard Corben
Duncan Fegredo • Peter Gross • Paul Guinan • Niko Henrichon • Adam Hughes
Phil Jimenez • Michael Wm. Kaluta • Marc Laming • Jason Little
Shawn McManus • Linda Medley • Albert Monteys • Kevin Nowlan • Andrew Pepoy
David Petersen • Paul Pope • Eric Powell • Ron Randall • John Stokes
Jill Thompson • Daniel Torres • Bill Willingham • Bernie Wrightson
artists

Lee Loughridge • Pamela Rambo • James Sinclair • Daniel Vozzo
colorists

Phil Balsman • John Costanza • Todd Klein • Rob Leigh • Nick J. Napolitano
letterers

John Bolton • Dave McKean • Tara McPherson • Kevin Nowlan
original series covers

James Bennett
cover art

PROPOSITION PLAYER created by Bill Willingham
THE SANDMAN created by Neil Gaiman, Sam Kieth and Mike Dringenberg
THESSALY created by Neil Gaiman and Shawn McManus
THE DREAMING created by Neil Gaiman

DEDICATION

This massive collection of oddities is dedicated to my mom, Mrs. Hazel May Willingham, née Horner, veteran of WWII (working at the Hanford Atomics Plant as a member of the Manhattan Project — about which she never spilled any details), a lifetime reader, a novelist who ran out of days before she could bring it in, and a world traveler who could never afford to leave the farm. Somewhere along the line she managed to turn me into the same (including the bit with the nuclear weapons — but that's a story for another time).

— BILL WILLINGHAM
August 2011

SHELLY BOND, ALISA KWITNEY, ANGELA RUFINO *Editors - Original Series* • WILL DENNIS, MARIAH HUEHNER, JENNIFER LEE, BRANDON MONTCLARE *Assistant Editors - Original Series* • IAN SATTLER *Director - Editorial, Special Projects and Archival Editions* • SCOTT NYBAKKEN *Editor* ROBBIN BROSTERMAN *Design Director - Books* • BRAINCHILD STUDIOS/NYC *Publication Design* • KAREN BERGER *Senior VP - Executive Editor, Vertigo* BOB HARRAS *VP - Editor-in-Chief* • DIANE NELSON *President* • DAN DIDIO and JIM LEE *Co-Publishers* • GEOFF JOHNS *Chief Creative Officer* JOHN ROOD *Executive VP - Sales, Marketing and Business Development* • AMY GENKINS *Senior VP - Business and Legal Affairs* • NAIRI GARDINER *Senior VP - Finance* • JEFF BOISON *VP - Publishing Operations* • MARK CHIARELLO *VP - Art Direction and Design* • JOHN CUNNINGHAM *VP - Marketing* TERRI CUNNINGHAM *VP - Talent Relations and Services* • ALISON GILL *Senior VP - Manufacturing and Operations* • DAVID HYDE *VP - Publicity* HANK KANALZ *Senior VP - Digital* JAY KOGAN *VP - Business and Legal Affairs, Publishing* • JACK MAHAN *VP - Business Affairs, Talent* • NICK NAPOLITANO *VP - Manufacturing Administration* SUE POHJA *VP - Book Sales* • COURTNEY SIMMONS *Senior VP - Publicity* • BOB WAYNE *Senior VP - Sales*

BAD DOINGS AND BIG IDEAS: A BILL WILLINGHAM DELUXE EDITION

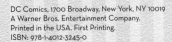

Table of Contents

Introduction by Bill Willingham. 5

PROPOSITION PLAYER
Part One: A New Player 7
Part Two: High Stakes Game 31
Part Three: An Open Seat 55
Part Four: House Rules. 79
Part Five: Full House 102
Part Six: Stacking the Deck 125

It Takes a Village. 150
From FLINCH #7

The Further Adventures of Danny Nod, Heroic Library Assistant. 159
From THE DREAMING #55

Merv Pumpkinhead, Agent of D.R.E.A.M. 183

Everything You Always Wanted to Know
About Dreams... But Were Afraid to Ask 233

THE THESSALIAD
Part One: The Daughters of Garm. 273
Part Two: The Long Crawl 297
Part Three: Necromancer. 320
Part Four: Soul Food 343

THESSALY — WITCH FOR HIRE
Part One: My Girl. 367
Part Two: Ghostraker. 391
Part Three: Something the Cat Dragged In 415
Part Four: The Last Full Measure. 439

The Hollows 462
From HOUSE OF MYSTERY #1

In Too Deep 467
From HOUSE OF MYSTERY #2

The War. 473
From HOUSE OF MYSTERY #7

Gothic Romance 479
From HOUSE OF MYSTERY #9

The Lace Anniversary 486
From HOUSE OF MYSTERY #13

The Hounds of Titus Roan 494
From HOUSE OF MYSTERY #16

High Spirits. 505
From HOUSE OF MYSTERY HALLOWEEN ANNUAL #1

An Introduction by BILL WILLINGHAM

BIG DOINGS

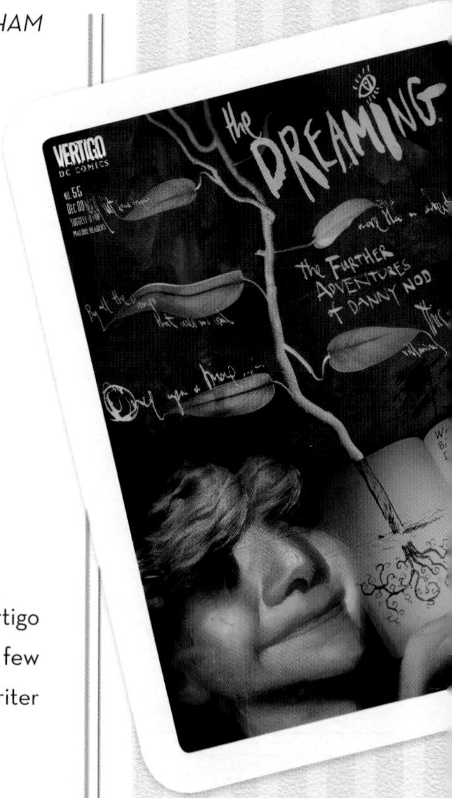
VERTIGO
DC COMICS
No. 55
Dec 00
the DREAMING
The Further Adventures of Danny Nod

Yikes, but this is a big book.

For the most part, it's a collection of everything I've written for Vertigo Comics (so far), not including the FABLES stories. With a rare few exceptions, I'm pleased with everything you're about to find here. No writer can look back at his previous work without a few regrets: wincing over the line I wish I'd written better, the joke that it turns out only I — in all the universe — thought was funny, the clunky bit in the middle that could have had a page trimmed out of it, and so on. That said, I've a fondness for these tales and hope you do too.

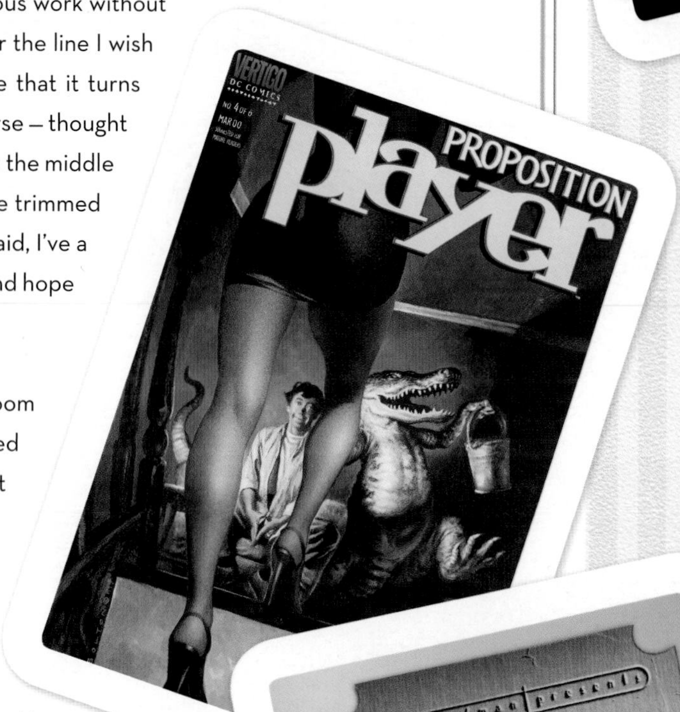
VERTIGO
DC COMICS
NO 4 OF 6
MAR 00
PROPOSITION
player

Since we have a bit of room to play with, I've added a thought or two about each of the stories you have here, but most of it is nonsense. Certainly none of it is so important that you have to read it. Feel free to skip the text pieces and go straight to the fun parts. After all, just because I've suffered for my art, it doesn't mean that you have to as well.

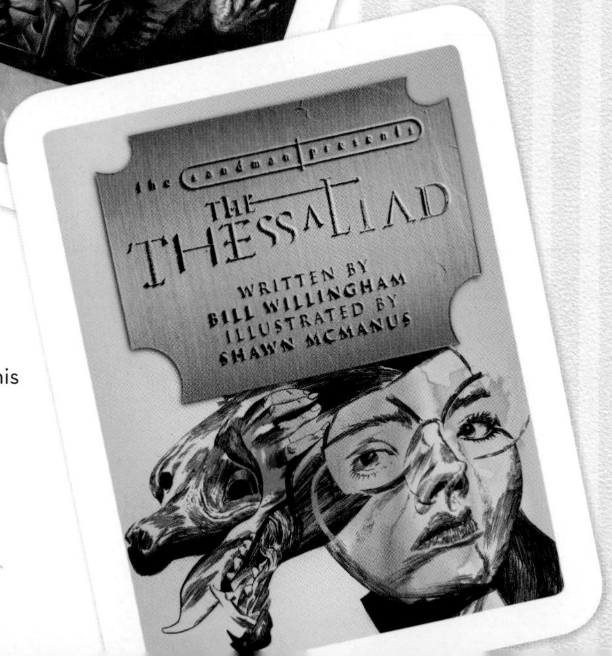
the sandman presents
THE THESSALIAD
WRITTEN BY
BILL WILLINGHAM
ILLUSTRATED BY
SHAWN McMANUS

Thank you for shelling out the big bucks for this big volume of stuff.

BAD DOINGS
& BIG IDEAS

A BILL WILLINGHAM DELUXE EDITION

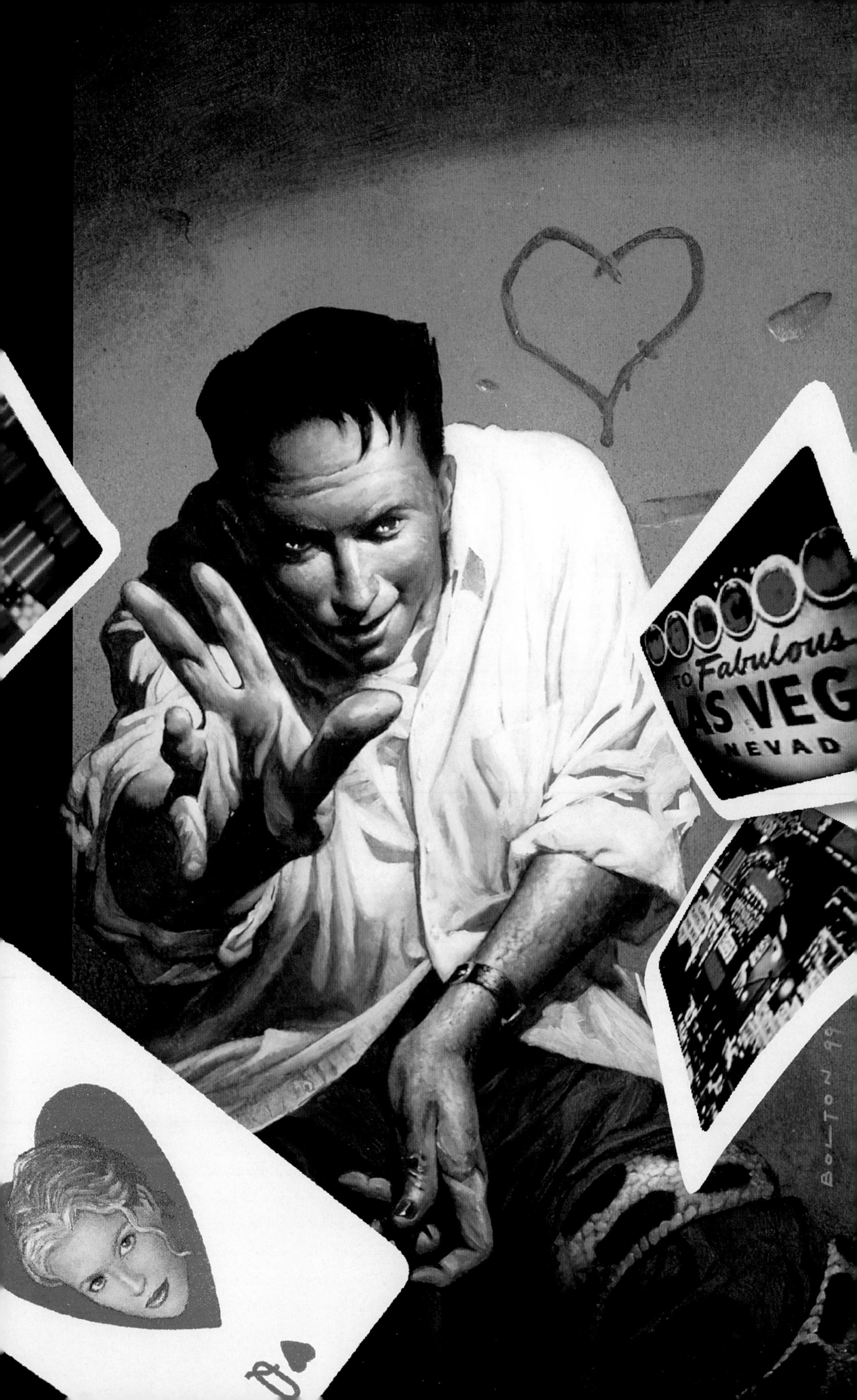
TO Fabulous
AS VEG
NEVAD

THIS WASN'T MY FIRST WORK FOR DC COMICS, but it was my first writing work. Up until this project, DC had ever only trusted me (and even then not often) to draw the occasional funnybook.

PROPOSITION PLAYER happened, circa 1999, because Vertigo editor Shelly Roeberg (now Shelly Bond) had once been, long ago in the distant past, Comico editor Shelly Roeberg – Comico being the same company that published *Elementals*, my middlingly successful super-hero series. It seems that she had maintained a fondness for those dusty old days and wanted to work with me again. "Come up with an idea and pitch it to me," she said. So, after some argument and foot-dragging, I did.

At that time I had recently been employed as a proposition player (something like a shill, but not really) at a run-down, wrong-side-of-the-tracks Las Vegas casino called the El Cortez. Since then I'd been nursing a desire to write about some of the oddities of the professional poker world – but not the top-of-the-mountain, big stakes poker world that we can see on TV. I wanted to write about the low stakes, bottom-of-the-barrel, degenerate gamblers – the grim, if-you-don't-win-today-you-don't-eat-today sub-basement of the professional poker world. That was the world I took a year off from funnybook-making to become a brief part of.

I wanted to write about poker and the extreme superstitions of those who play it, day in and day out.

And so I did.

A surprising amount of what you're about to read here is true – more, in fact, than I suspect you'd believe in a yarn about angels, devils, old gods and alligator attacks. Since I'm loath to spill private beans about some folks still living, you'll just have to take my word for it.

Paul Guinan was a wonderful artist to collaborate with, once it became clear that I couldn't keep up the pace of both writing and illustrating this series. He had (and I assume still has) just the right sense of absurdity this story needed. More important, he had the ability to translate that absurdity to every page. He's since gone on to bigger and better things – something the truly talented tend to do.

One final note: PROPOSITION PLAYER was originally designed to be an ongoing series, but, even though it garnered some positive critical attention, it sold roughly in the high dozens. Basically, we couldn't give it away with free medical coverage. By the third issue we knew we were doomed. Bless, then, the stalwarts at Vertigo and DC who were willing to take enough of a bath on this show to let me at least go six issues and bring the story to some sort of conclusion. It's for this reason that we probably won't visit the world of Joey Martin (a character name derived from two members of the infamous Rat Pack) and his weird friends again.

Too bad, huh?

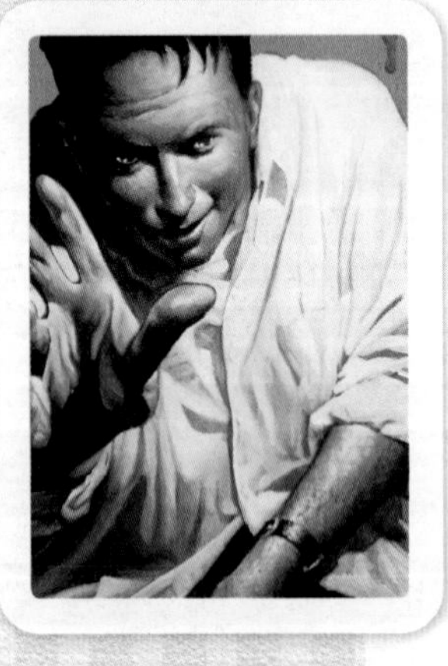

PROPOSITION PLAYER

PENCILS BY
Paul Guinan and
Bill Willingham

INKS BY
Ron Randall and
Bill Willingham

COLORS BY
James Sinclair

LETTERS BY
John Costanza

COVER ART BY
John Bolton

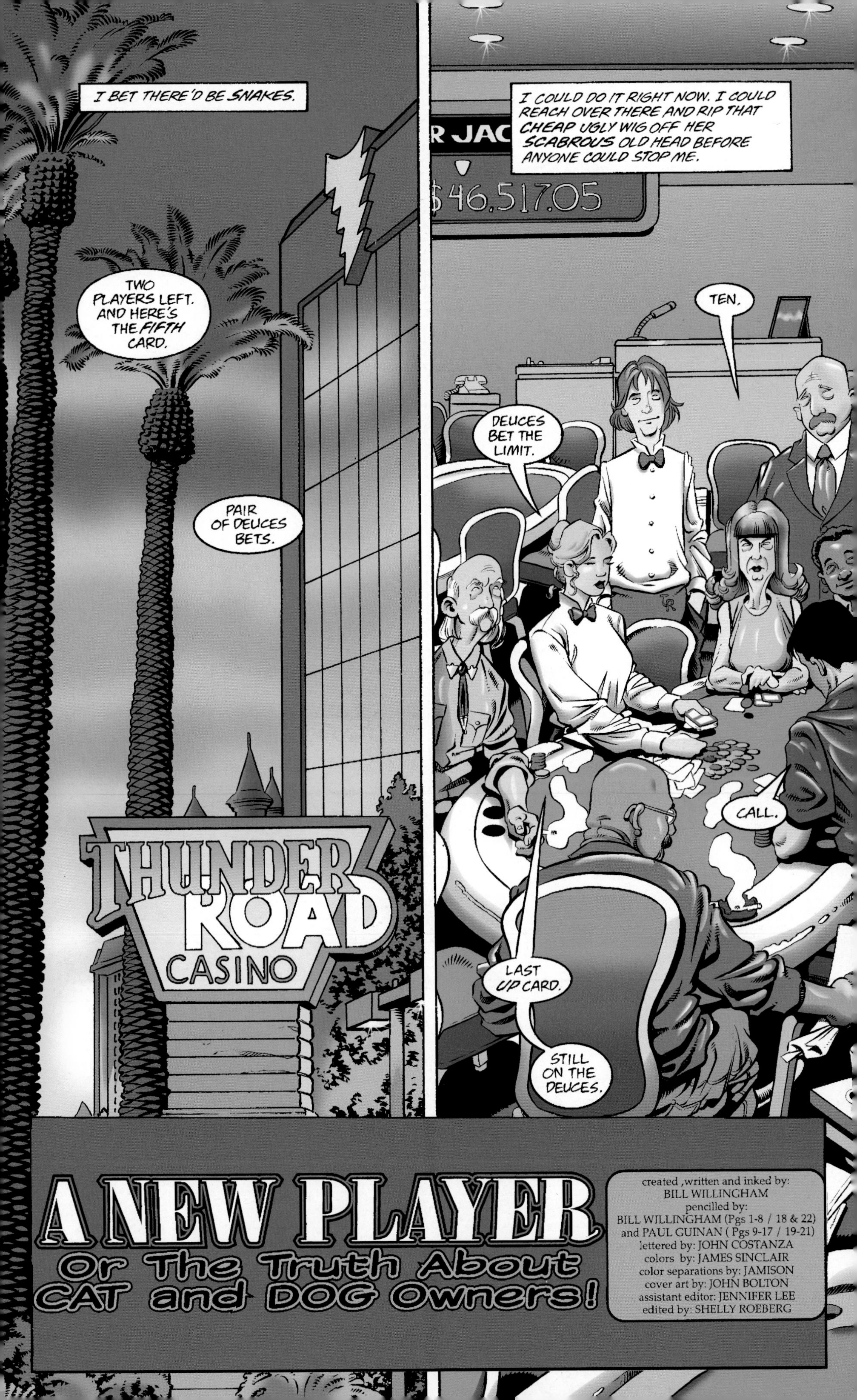

I BET THERE'D BE SNAKES.
TWO PLAYERS LEFT. AND HERE'S THE FIFTH CARD.
PAIR OF DEUCES BETS.
THUNDER ROAD CASINO
I COULD DO IT RIGHT NOW. I COULD REACH OVER THERE AND RIP THAT CHEAP UGLY WIG OFF HER SCABROUS OLD HEAD BEFORE ANYONE COULD STOP ME.
R JAC
$46,517.05
TEN.
DEUCES BET THE LIMIT.
CALL.
LAST UP CARD.
STILL ON THE DEUCES.
A NEW PLAYER
Or The Truth About CAT and DOG Owners!
created ,written and inked by: BILL WILLINGHAM
pencilled by: BILL WILLINGHAM (Pgs 1-8 / 18 & 22) and PAUL GUINAN (Pgs 9-17 / 19-21)
lettered by: JOHN COSTANZA
colors by: JAMES SINCLAIR
color separations by: JAMISON
cover art by: JOHN BOLTON
assistant editor: JENNIFER LEE
edited by: SHELLY ROEBERG

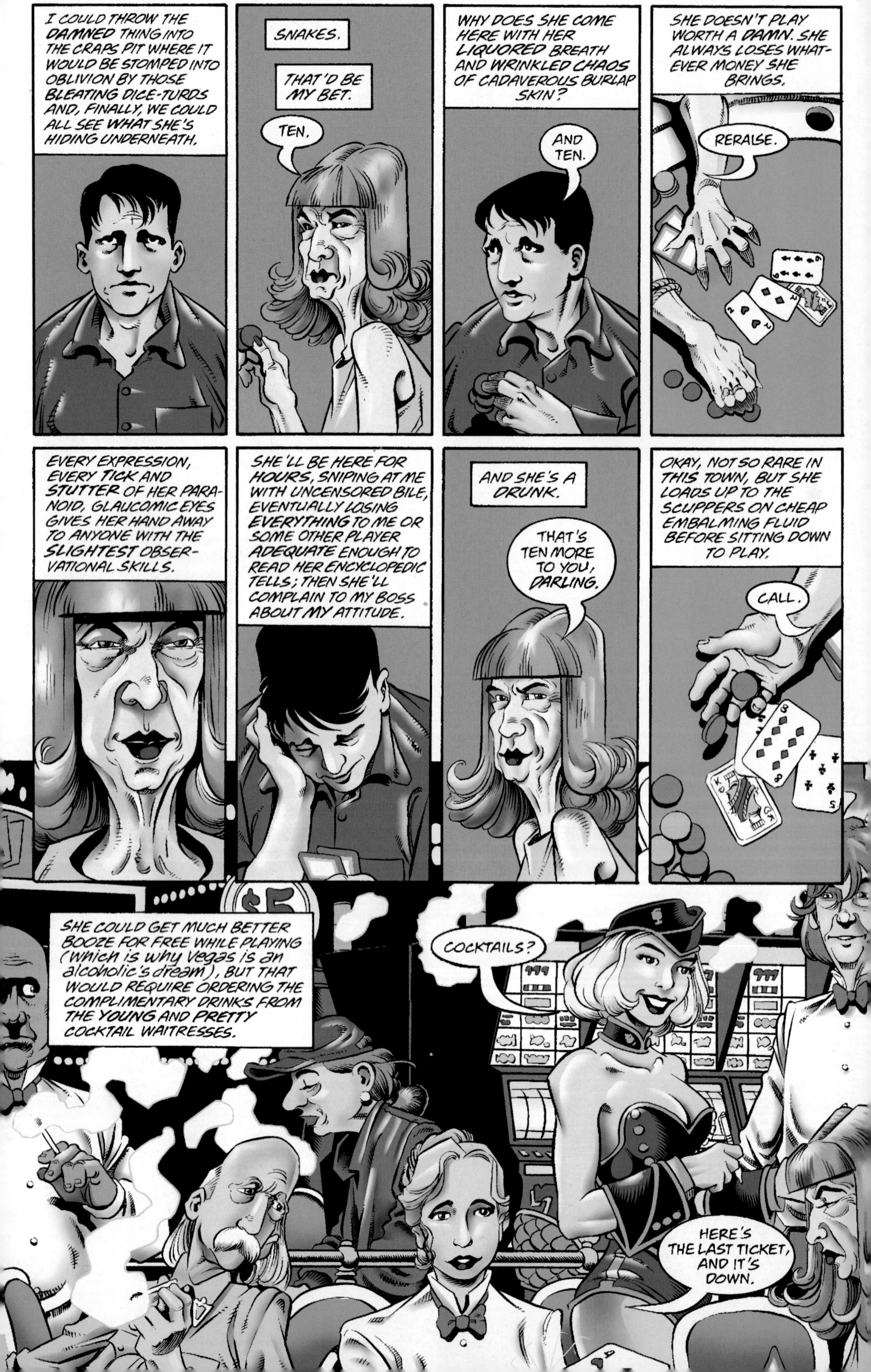
I COULD THROW THE DAMNED THING INTO THE CRAPS PIT WHERE IT WOULD BE STOMPED INTO OBLIVION BY THOSE BLEATING DICE-TURDS AND, FINALLY, WE COULD ALL SEE WHAT SHE'S HIDING UNDERNEATH.
SNAKES.
THAT'D BE MY BET.
TEN.
WHY DOES SHE COME HERE WITH HER LIQUORED BREATH AND WRINKLED CHAOS OF CADAVEROUS BURLAP SKIN?
AND TEN.
SHE DOESN'T PLAY WORTH A DAMN. SHE ALWAYS LOSES WHATEVER MONEY SHE BRINGS.
RERAISE.
EVERY EXPRESSION, EVERY TICK AND STUTTER OF HER PARANOID, GLAUCOMIC EYES GIVES HER HAND AWAY TO ANYONE WITH THE SLIGHTEST OBSERVATIONAL SKILLS.
SHE'LL BE HERE FOR HOURS, SNIPING AT ME WITH UNCENSORED BILE, EVENTUALLY LOSING EVERYTHING TO ME OR SOME OTHER PLAYER ADEQUATE ENOUGH TO READ HER ENCYCLOPEDIC TELLS; THEN SHE'LL COMPLAIN TO MY BOSS ABOUT MY ATTITUDE.
AND SHE'S A DRUNK.
THAT'S TEN MORE TO YOU, DARLING.
OKAY, NOT SO RARE IN THIS TOWN, BUT SHE LOADS UP TO THE SCUPPERS ON CHEAP EMBALMING FLUID BEFORE SITTING DOWN TO PLAY.
CALL.
$5
SHE COULD GET MUCH BETTER BOOZE FOR FREE WHILE PLAYING (which is why Vegas is an alcoholic's dream), BUT THAT WOULD REQUIRE ORDERING THE COMPLIMENTARY DRINKS FROM THE YOUNG AND PRETTY COCKTAIL WAITRESSES.
COCKTAILS?
HERE'S THE LAST TICKET, AND IT'S DOWN.

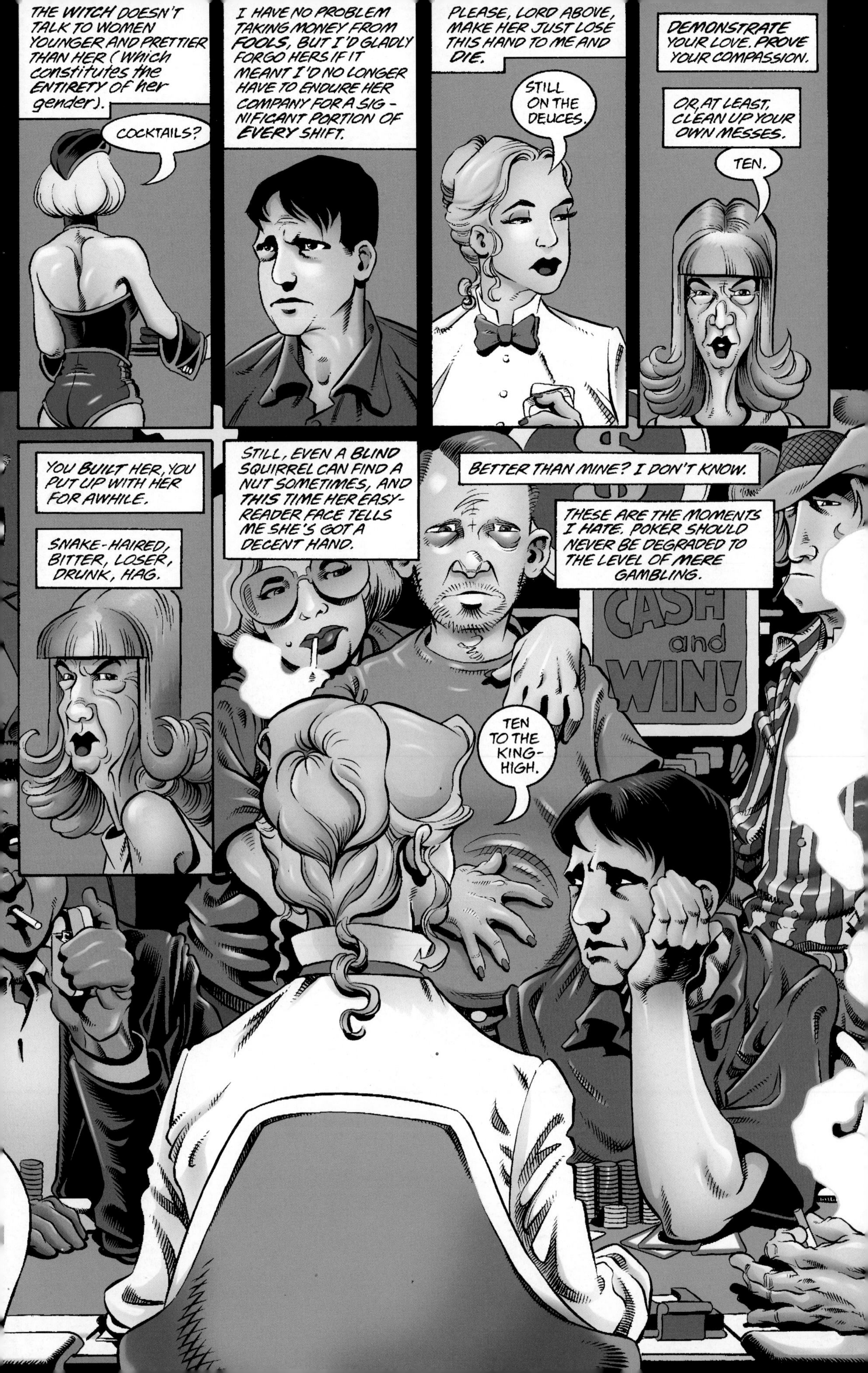
THE WITCH DOESN'T TALK TO WOMEN YOUNGER AND PRETTIER THAN HER (which constitutes the ENTIRETY of her gender).
COCKTAILS?
I HAVE NO PROBLEM TAKING MONEY FROM FOOLS, BUT I'D GLADLY FORGO HERS IF IT MEANT I'D NO LONGER HAVE TO ENDURE HER COMPANY FOR A SIG-NIFICANT PORTION OF EVERY SHIFT.
PLEASE, LORD ABOVE, MAKE HER JUST LOSE THIS HAND TO ME AND DIE.
STILL ON THE DEUCES.
DEMONSTRATE YOUR LOVE. PROVE YOUR COMPASSION.
OR, AT LEAST, CLEAN UP YOUR OWN MESSES.
TEN.
YOU BUILT HER, YOU PUT UP WITH HER FOR AWHILE.
SNAKE-HAIRED, BITTER, LOSER, DRUNK, HAG.
STILL, EVEN A BLIND SQUIRREL CAN FIND A NUT SOMETIMES, AND THIS TIME HER EASY-READER FACE TELLS ME SHE'S GOT A DECENT HAND.
BETTER THAN MINE? I DON'T KNOW.
THESE ARE THE MOMENTS I HATE. POKER SHOULD NEVER BE DEGRADED TO THE LEVEL OF MERE GAMBLING.
CASH and WIN!
TEN TO THE KING-HIGH.

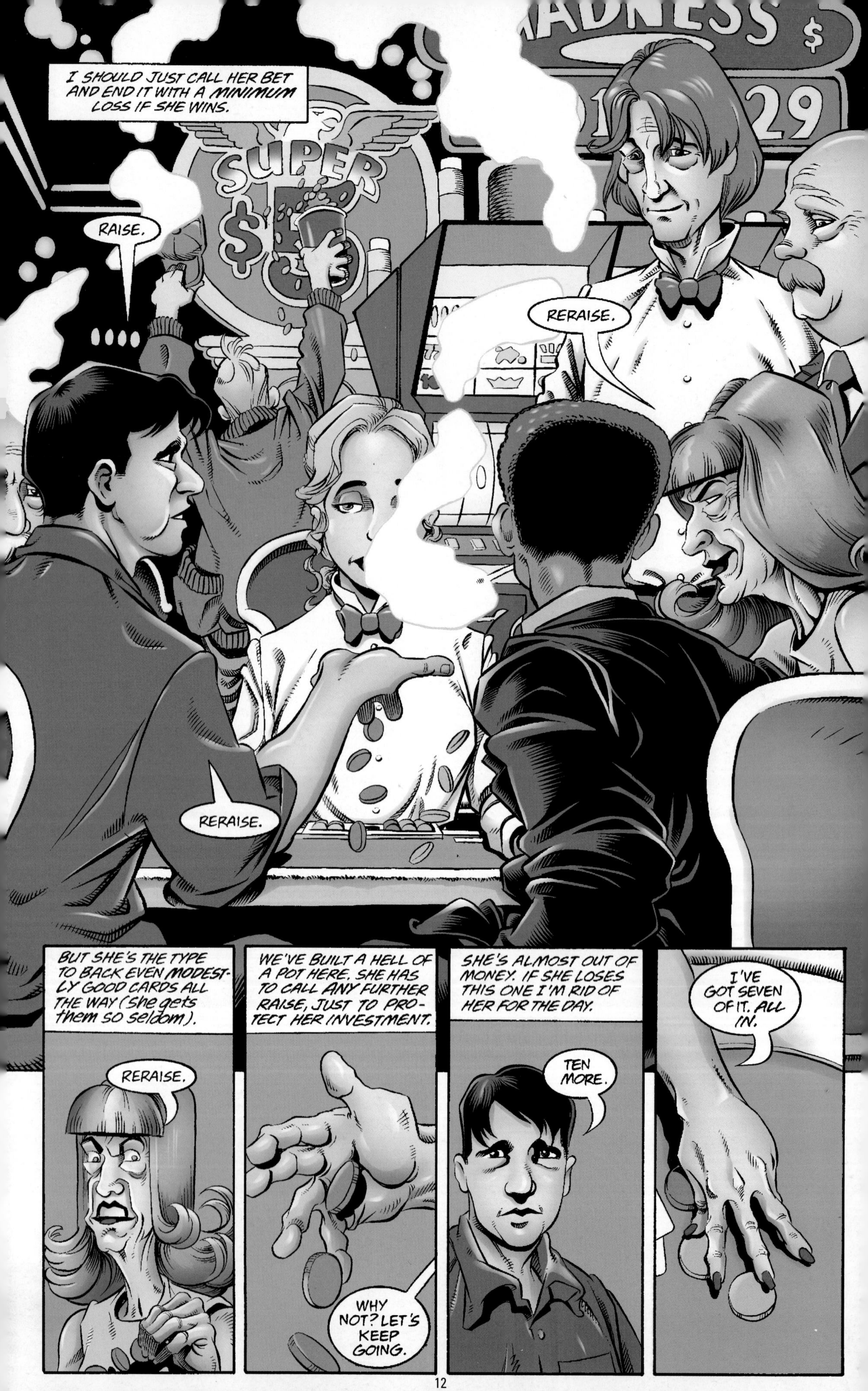
I SHOULD JUST CALL HER BET AND END IT WITH A MINIMUM LOSS IF SHE WINS.
SUPER $5
ADNESS $
RAISE.
RERAISE.
RERAISE.
BUT SHE'S THE TYPE TO BACK EVEN MODESTLY GOOD CARDS ALL THE WAY (She gets them so seldom).
RERAISE.
WE'VE BUILT A HELL OF A POT HERE. SHE HAS TO CALL ANY FURTHER RAISE, JUST TO PROTECT HER INVESTMENT.
WHY NOT? LET'S KEEP GOING.
SHE'S ALMOST OUT OF MONEY. IF SHE LOSES THIS ONE I'M RID OF HER FOR THE DAY.
TEN MORE.
I'VE GOT SEVEN OF IT. ALL IN.

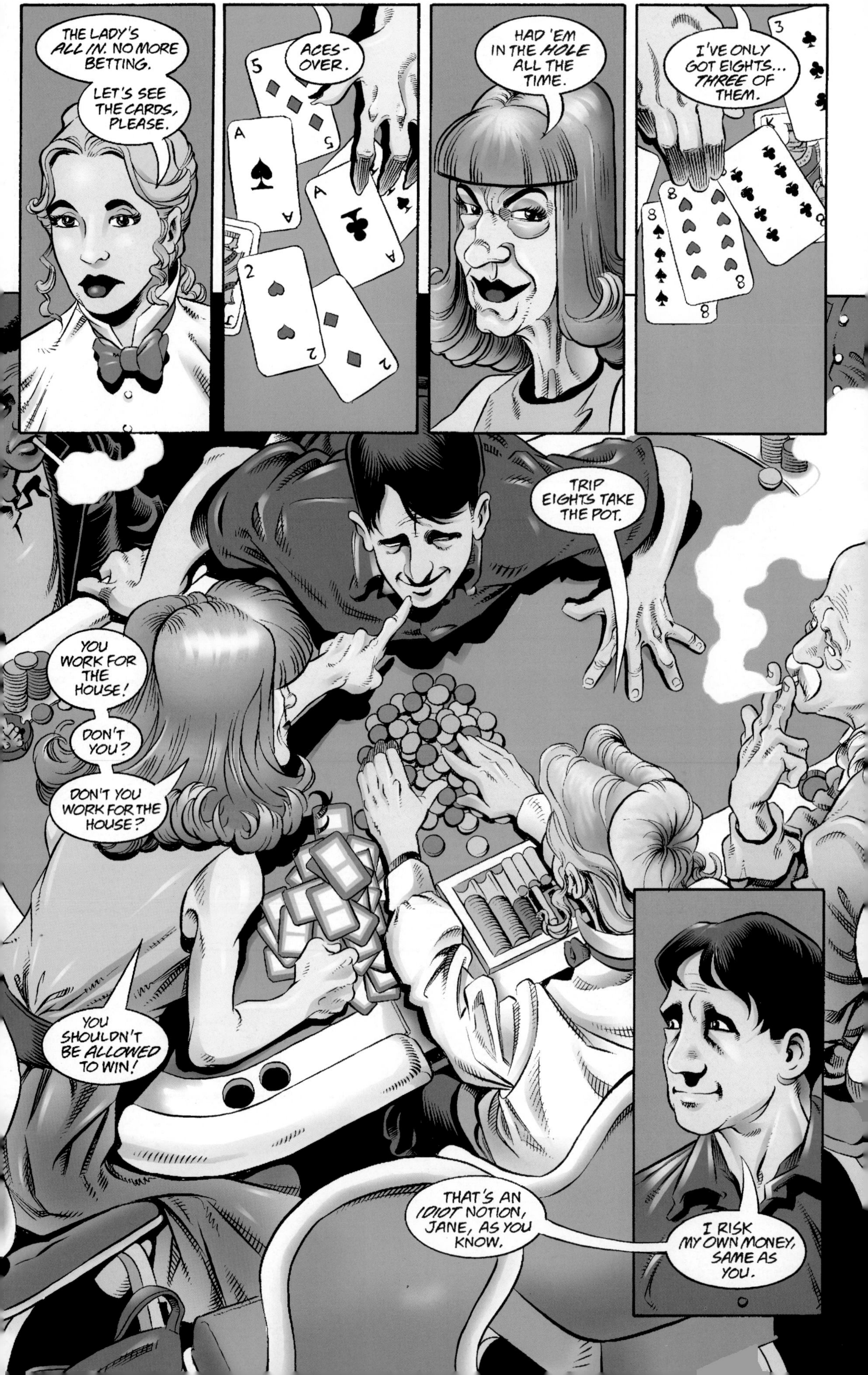
THE LADY'S ALL IN. NO MORE BETTING.
LET'S SEE THE CARDS, PLEASE.
ACES-OVER.
HAD 'EM IN THE HOLE ALL THE TIME.
I'VE ONLY GOT EIGHTS... THREE OF THEM.
TRIP EIGHTS TAKE THE POT.
YOU WORK FOR THE HOUSE!
DON'T YOU?
DON'T YOU WORK FOR THE HOUSE?
YOU SHOULDN'T BE ALLOWED TO WIN!
THAT'S AN IDIOT NOTION, JANE, AS YOU KNOW.
I RISK MY OWN MONEY, SAME AS YOU.

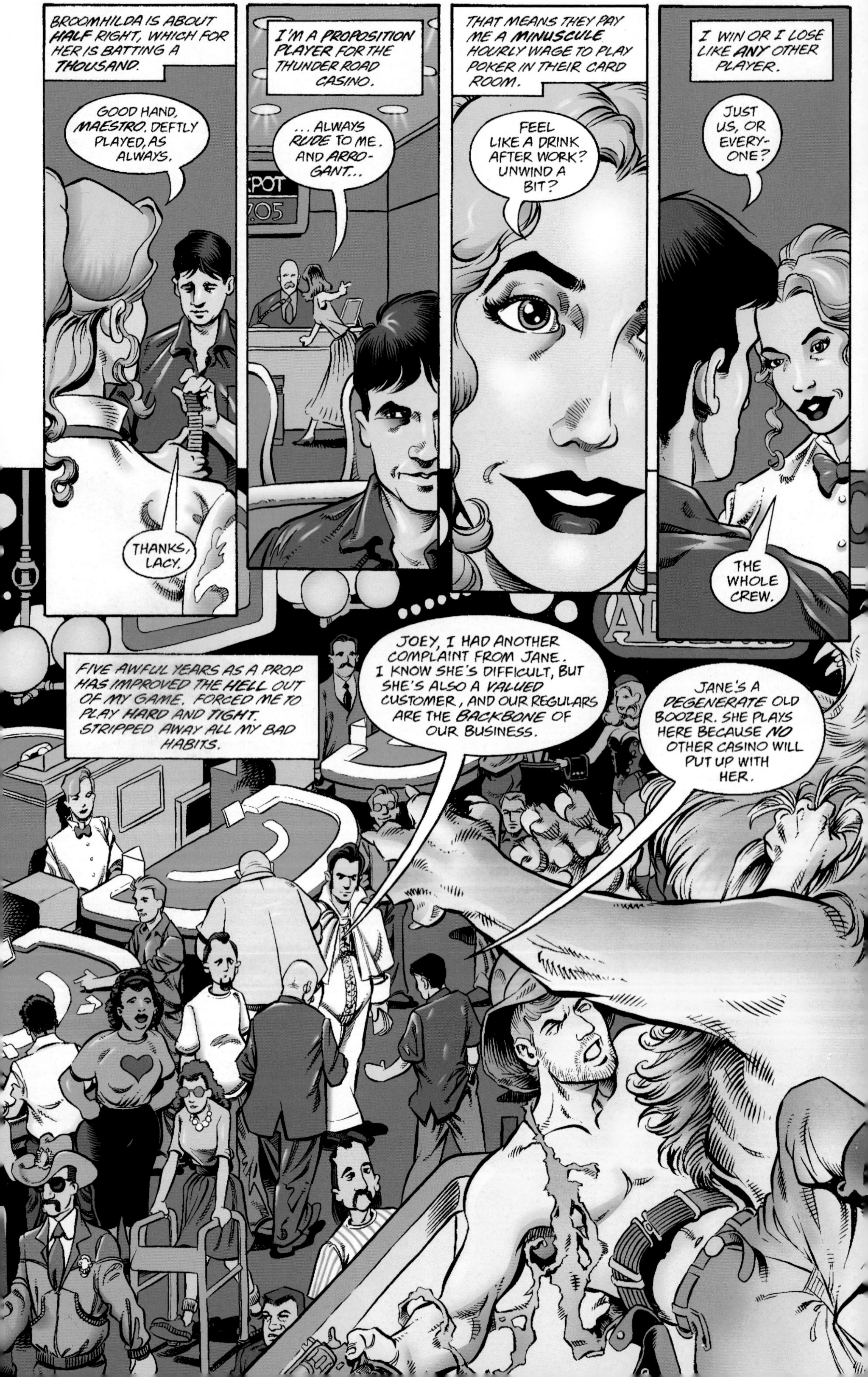
BROOMHILDA IS ABOUT HALF RIGHT, WHICH FOR HER IS BATTING A THOUSAND.
GOOD HAND, MAESTRO. DEFTLY PLAYED, AS ALWAYS.
THANKS, LACY.
I'M A PROPOSITION PLAYER FOR THE THUNDER ROAD CASINO.
... ALWAYS RUDE TO ME. AND ARRO-GANT...
THAT MEANS THEY PAY ME A MINUSCULE HOURLY WAGE TO PLAY POKER IN THEIR CARD ROOM.
FEEL LIKE A DRINK AFTER WORK? UNWIND A BIT?
I WIN OR I LOSE LIKE ANY OTHER PLAYER.
JUST US, OR EVERY-ONE?
THE WHOLE CREW.
FIVE AWFUL YEARS AS A PROP HAS IMPROVED THE HELL OUT OF MY GAME. FORCED ME TO PLAY HARD AND TIGHT. STRIPPED AWAY ALL MY BAD HABITS.
JOEY, I HAD ANOTHER COMPLAINT FROM JANE. I KNOW SHE'S DIFFICULT, BUT SHE'S ALSO A VALUED CUSTOMER, AND OUR REGULARS ARE THE BACKBONE OF OUR BUSINESS.
JANE'S A DEGENERATE OLD BOOZER. SHE PLAYS HERE BECAUSE NO OTHER CASINO WILL PUT UP WITH HER.

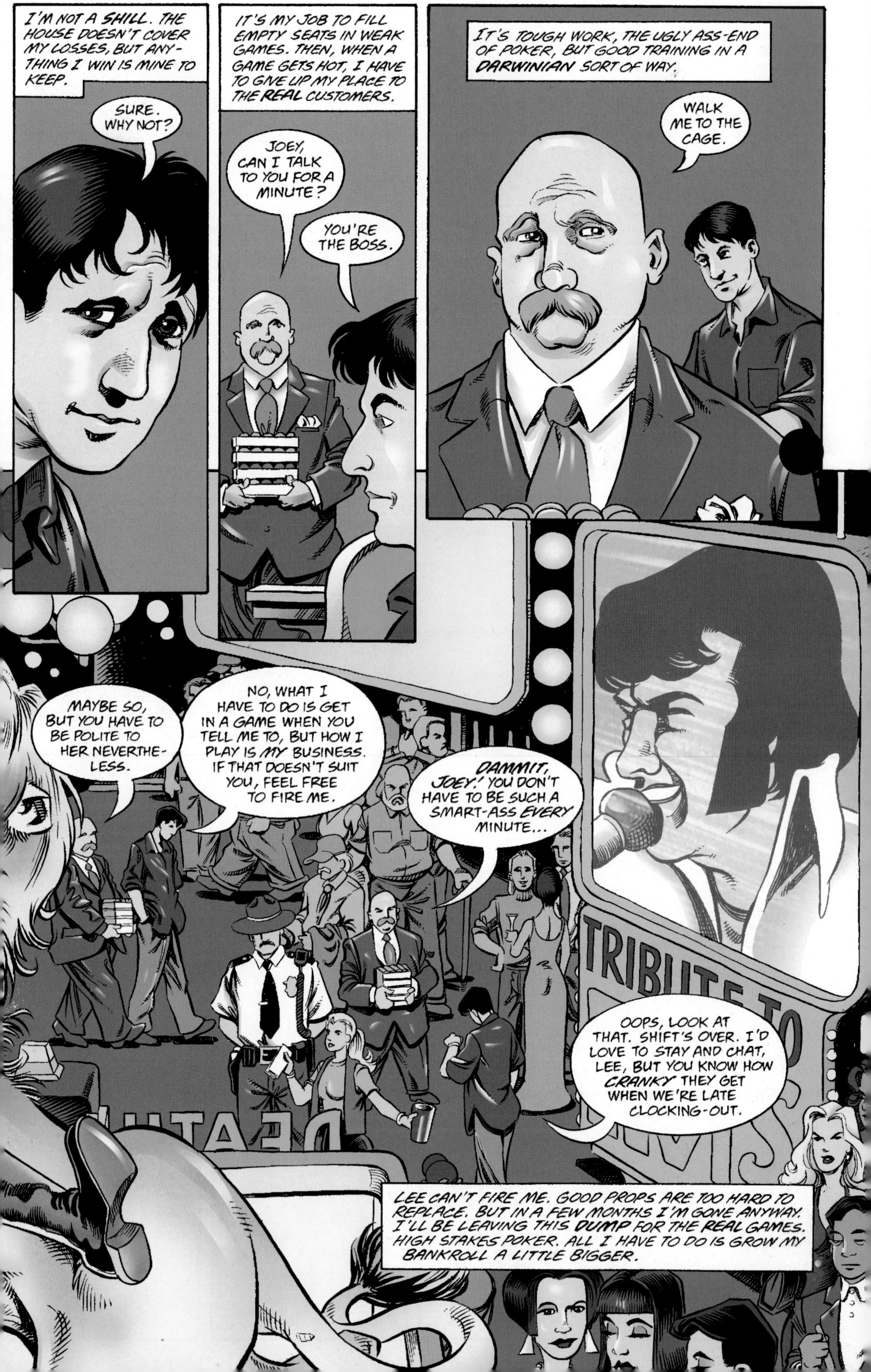

I'M NOT A SHILL. THE HOUSE DOESN'T COVER MY LOSSES, BUT ANYTHING I WIN IS MINE TO KEEP.
SURE. WHY NOT?
IT'S MY JOB TO FILL EMPTY SEATS IN WEAK GAMES. THEN, WHEN A GAME GETS HOT, I HAVE TO GIVE UP MY PLACE TO THE REAL CUSTOMERS.
JOEY, CAN I TALK TO YOU FOR A MINUTE?
YOU'RE THE BOSS.
IT'S TOUGH WORK, THE UGLY ASS-END OF POKER, BUT GOOD TRAINING IN A DARWINIAN SORT OF WAY.
WALK ME TO THE CAGE.
MAYBE SO, BUT YOU HAVE TO BE POLITE TO HER NEVERTHELESS.
NO, WHAT I HAVE TO DO IS GET IN A GAME WHEN YOU TELL ME TO, BUT HOW I PLAY IS MY BUSINESS. IF THAT DOESN'T SUIT YOU, FEEL FREE TO FIRE ME.
DAMMIT, JOEY! YOU DON'T HAVE TO BE SUCH A SMART-ASS EVERY MINUTE...
TRIBUTE TO
OOPS, LOOK AT THAT. SHIFT'S OVER. I'D LOVE TO STAY AND CHAT, LEE, BUT YOU KNOW HOW CRANKY THEY GET WHEN WE'RE LATE CLOCKING-OUT.
LEE CAN'T FIRE ME. GOOD PROPS ARE TOO HARD TO REPLACE. BUT IN A FEW MONTHS I'M GONE ANYWAY. I'LL BE LEAVING THIS DUMP FOR THE REAL GAMES. HIGH STAKES POKER. ALL I HAVE TO DO IS GROW MY BANKROLL A LITTLE BIGGER.

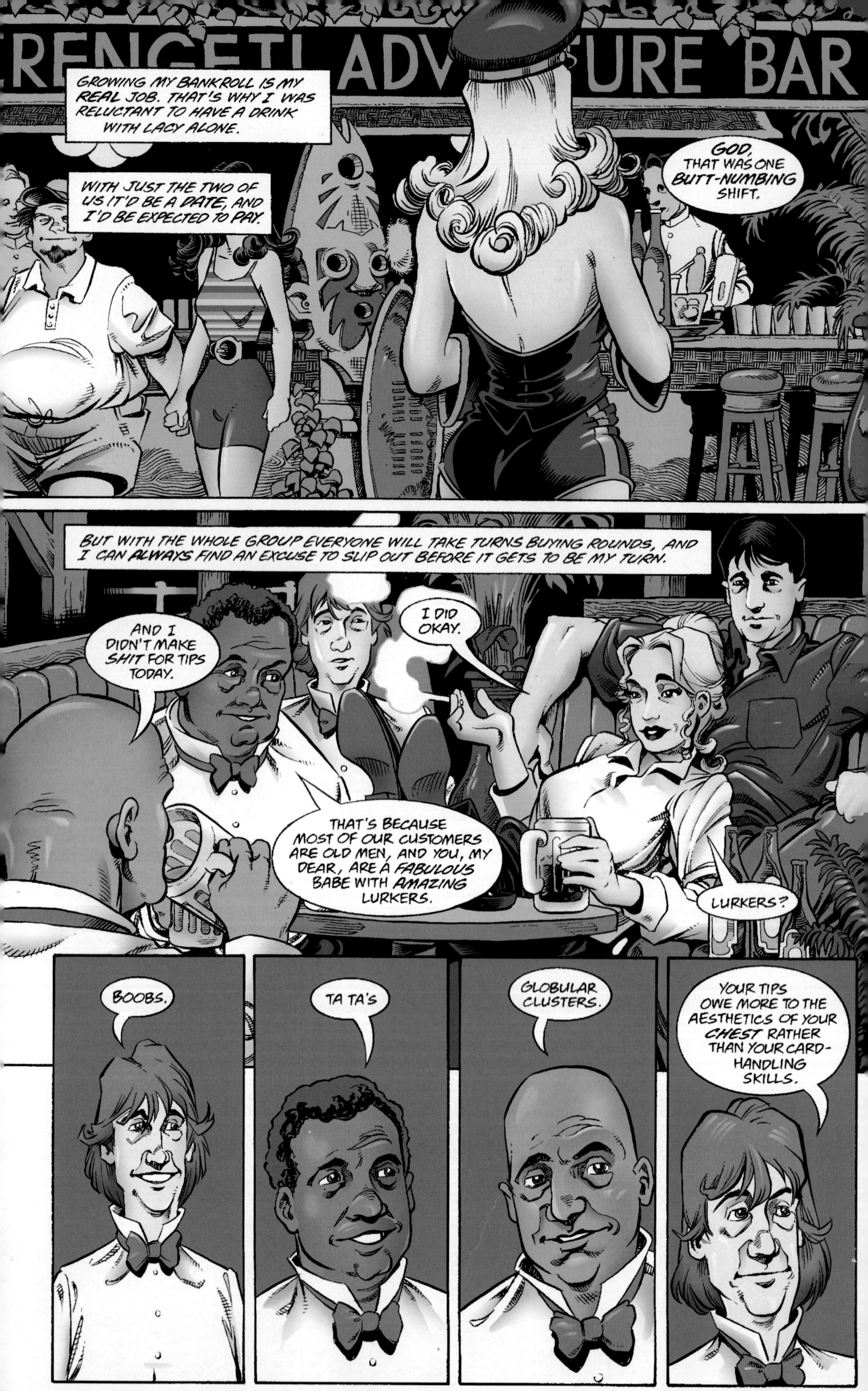
RENGETI ADVENTURE BAR
GROWING MY BANKROLL IS MY REAL JOB. THAT'S WHY I WAS RELUCTANT TO HAVE A DRINK WITH LACY ALONE.
WITH JUST THE TWO OF US IT'D BE A DATE, AND I'D BE EXPECTED TO PAY.
GOD. THAT WAS ONE BUTT-NUMBING SHIFT.
BUT WITH THE WHOLE GROUP EVERYONE WILL TAKE TURNS BUYING ROUNDS, AND I CAN ALWAYS FIND AN EXCUSE TO SLIP OUT BEFORE IT GETS TO BE MY TURN.
AND I DIDN'T MAKE SHIT FOR TIPS TODAY.
I DID OKAY.
THAT'S BECAUSE MOST OF OUR CUSTOMERS ARE OLD MEN, AND YOU, MY DEAR, ARE A FABULOUS BABE WITH AMAZING LURKERS.
LURKERS?
BOOBS.
TA TA'S
GLOBULAR CLUSTERS.
YOUR TIPS OWE MORE TO THE AESTHETICS OF YOUR CHEST RATHER THAN YOUR CARD-HANDLING SKILLS.

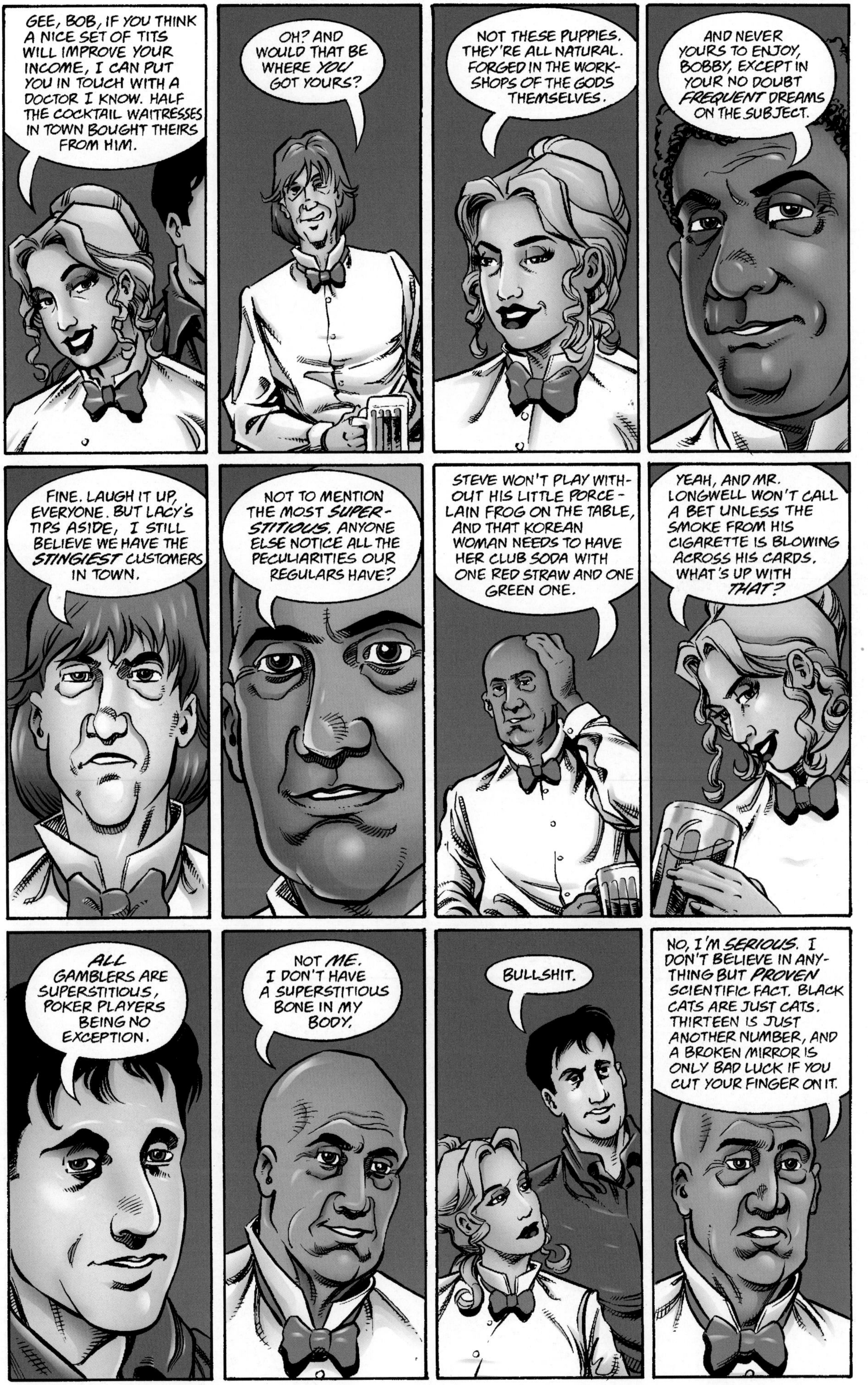
GEE, BOB, IF YOU THINK A NICE SET OF TITS WILL IMPROVE YOUR INCOME, I CAN PUT YOU IN TOUCH WITH A DOCTOR I KNOW. HALF THE COCKTAIL WAITRESSES IN TOWN BOUGHT THEIRS FROM HIM.
OH? AND WOULD THAT BE WHERE YOU GOT YOURS?
NOT THESE PUPPIES. THEY'RE ALL NATURAL. FORGED IN THE WORK-SHOPS OF THE GODS THEMSELVES.
AND NEVER YOURS TO ENJOY, BOBBY, EXCEPT IN YOUR NO DOUBT FREQUENT DREAMS ON THE SUBJECT.
FINE. LAUGH IT UP, EVERYONE. BUT LACY'S TIPS ASIDE, I STILL BELIEVE WE HAVE THE STINGIEST CUSTOMERS IN TOWN.
NOT TO MENTION THE MOST SUPER-STITIOUS. ANYONE ELSE NOTICE ALL THE PECULIARITIES OUR REGULARS HAVE?
STEVE WON'T PLAY WITH-OUT HIS LITTLE PORCE-LAIN FROG ON THE TABLE, AND THAT KOREAN WOMAN NEEDS TO HAVE HER CLUB SODA WITH ONE RED STRAW AND ONE GREEN ONE.
YEAH, AND MR. LONGWELL WON'T CALL A BET UNLESS THE SMOKE FROM HIS CIGARETTE IS BLOWING ACROSS HIS CARDS. WHAT'S UP WITH THAT?
ALL GAMBLERS ARE SUPERSTITIOUS, POKER PLAYERS BEING NO EXCEPTION.
NOT ME. I DON'T HAVE A SUPERSTITIOUS BONE IN MY BODY.
BULLSHIT.
NO, I'M SERIOUS. I DON'T BELIEVE IN ANY-THING BUT PROVEN SCIENTIFIC FACT. BLACK CATS ARE JUST CATS. THIRTEEN IS JUST ANOTHER NUMBER, AND A BROKEN MIRROR IS ONLY BAD LUCK IF YOU CUT YOUR FINGER ON IT.

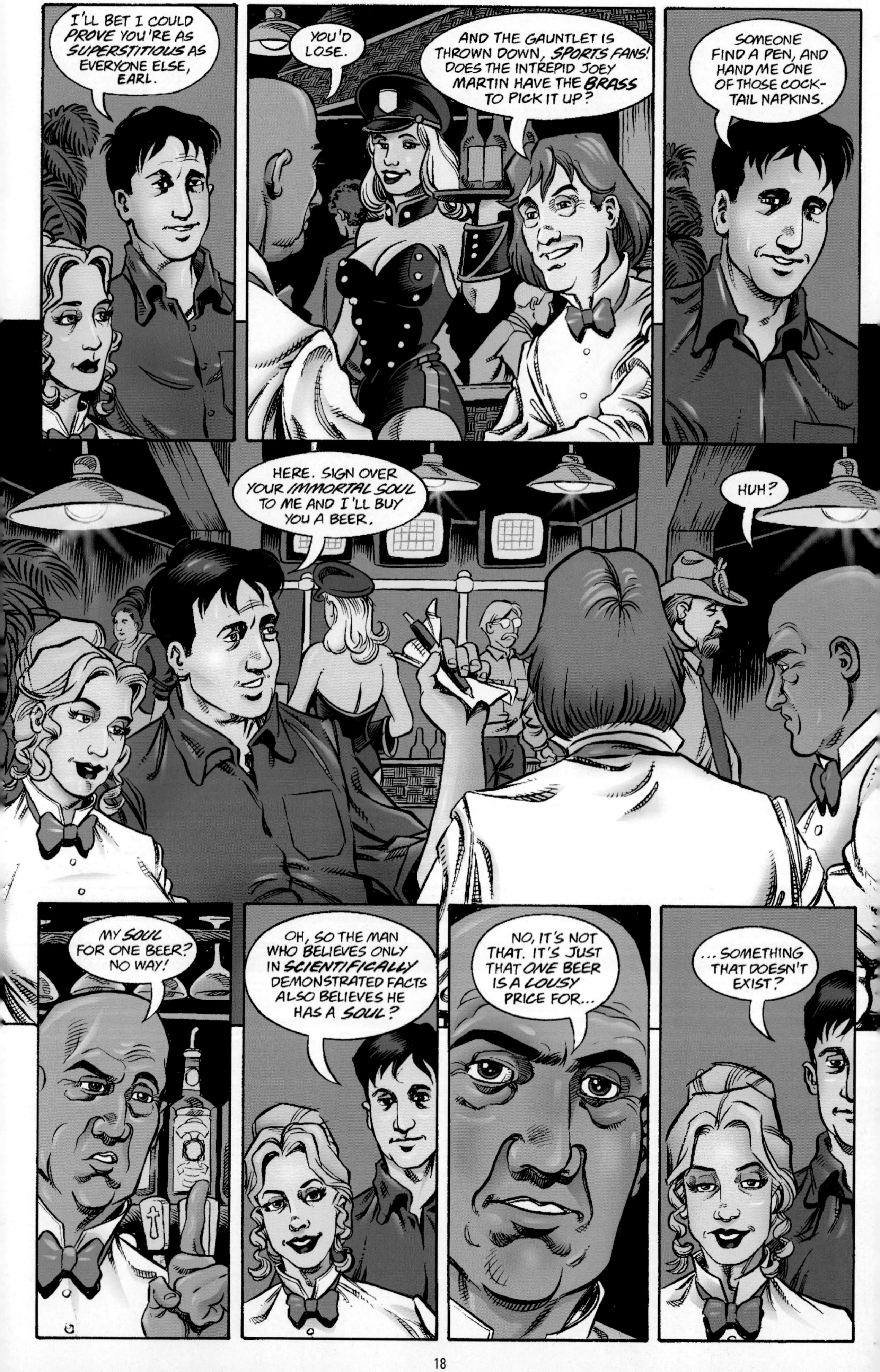
I'LL BET I COULD PROVE YOU'RE AS SUPERSTITIOUS AS EVERYONE ELSE, EARL.
YOU'D LOSE.
AND THE GAUNTLET IS THROWN DOWN, SPORTS FANS! DOES THE INTREPID JOEY MARTIN HAVE THE BRASS TO PICK IT UP?
SOMEONE FIND A PEN, AND HAND ME ONE OF THOSE COCK-TAIL NAPKINS.
HERE. SIGN OVER YOUR IMMORTAL SOUL TO ME AND I'LL BUY YOU A BEER.
HUH?
MY SOUL FOR ONE BEER? NO WAY!
OH, SO THE MAN WHO BELIEVES ONLY IN SCIENTIFICALLY DEMONSTRATED FACTS ALSO BELIEVES HE HAS A SOUL?
NO, IT'S NOT THAT. IT'S JUST THAT ONE BEER IS A LOUSY PRICE FOR...
...SOMETHING THAT DOESN'T EXIST?

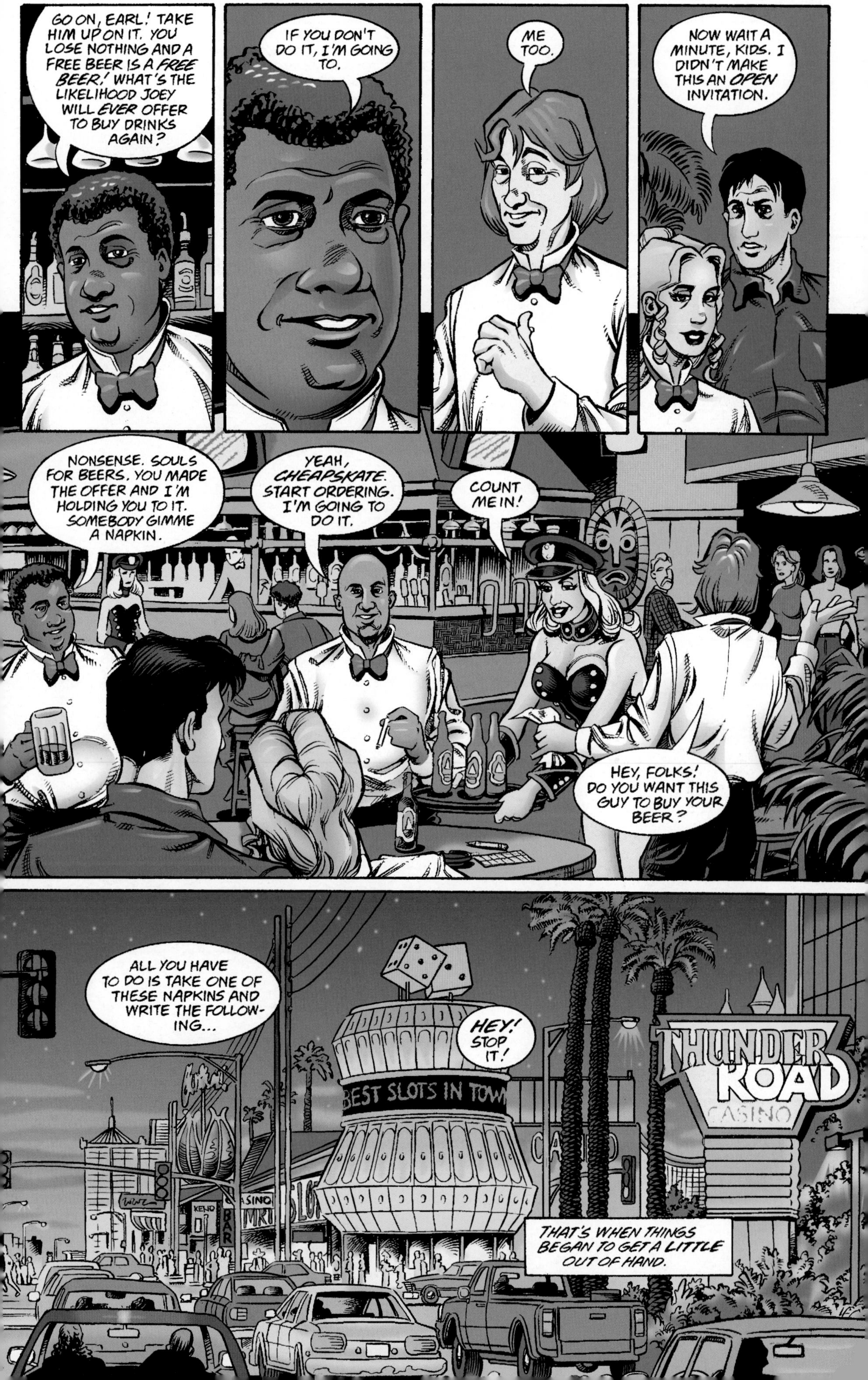
GO ON, EARL! TAKE HIM UP ON IT. YOU LOSE NOTHING AND A FREE BEER IS A FREE BEER! WHAT'S THE LIKELIHOOD JOEY WILL EVER OFFER TO BUY DRINKS AGAIN?
IF YOU DON'T DO IT, I'M GOING TO.
ME TOO.
NOW WAIT A MINUTE, KIDS. I DIDN'T MAKE THIS AN OPEN INVITATION.
NONSENSE. SOULS FOR BEERS. YOU MADE THE OFFER AND I'M HOLDING YOU TO IT. SOMEBODY GIMME A NAPKIN.
YEAH, CHEAPSKATE. START ORDERING. I'M GOING TO DO IT.
COUNT ME IN!
HEY, FOLKS! DO YOU WANT THIS GUY TO BUY YOUR BEER?
ALL YOU HAVE TO DO IS TAKE ONE OF THESE NAPKINS AND WRITE THE FOLLOWING...
HEY! STOP IT!
BEST SLOTS IN TOWN
THUNDER ROAD
CASINO
THAT'S WHEN THINGS BEGAN TO GET A LITTLE OUT OF HAND.

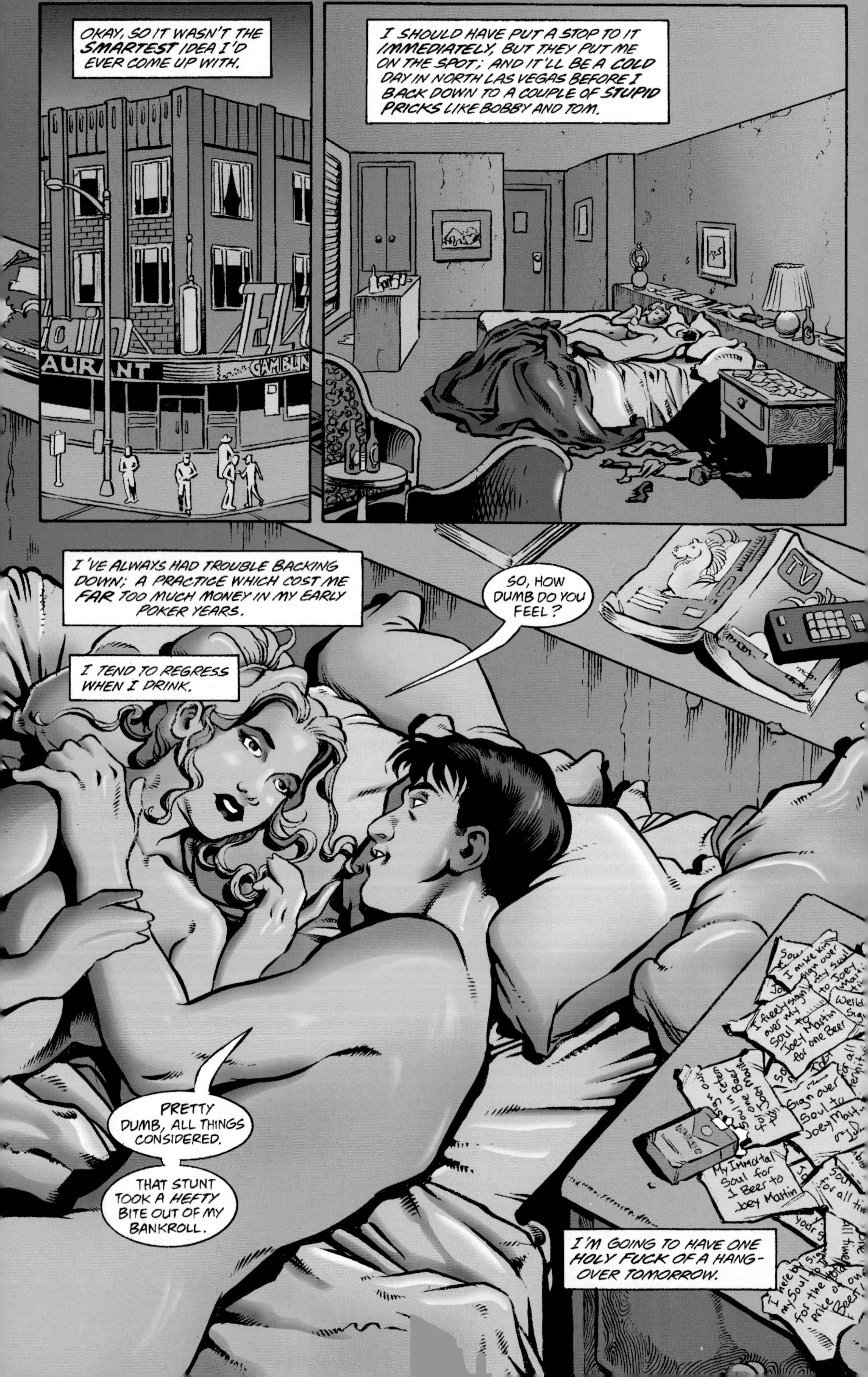
OKAY, SO IT WASN'T THE SMARTEST IDEA I'D EVER COME UP WITH.
AURANT
GAMBLIN
I SHOULD HAVE PUT A STOP TO IT IMMEDIATELY, BUT THEY PUT ME ON THE SPOT; AND IT'LL BE A COLD DAY IN NORTH LAS VEGAS BEFORE I BACK DOWN TO A COUPLE OF STUPID PRICKS LIKE BOBBY AND TOM.
I'VE ALWAYS HAD TROUBLE BACKING DOWN; A PRACTICE WHICH COST ME FAR TOO MUCH MONEY IN MY EARLY POKER YEARS.
SO, HOW DUMB DO YOU FEEL?
TV
I TEND TO REGRESS WHEN I DRINK.
PRETTY DUMB, ALL THINGS CONSIDERED.
THAT STUNT TOOK A HEFTY BITE OUT OF MY BANKROLL.
I freely sign over my Soul to Joey Martin for one Beer
My Immortal Soul for 1 Beers to Joey Martin
I'M GOING TO HAVE ONE HOLY FUCK OF A HANG-OVER TOMORROW.

AND IT LOOKS LIKE LACY'S BURROWING IN FOR THE NIGHT.

DON'T FEEL *TOO* BAD, SWEETIE. IT'S NOT ALL YOUR FAULT.

TOM AND BOBBY DID THEIR SHARE TO *EXACERBATE* THE SITUATION.

WHY CAN'T WOMEN GO HOME AFTER SEX, LIKE GUYS?

IT WAS A MISTAKE BRINGING HER HERE. WE SHOULD'VE GONE TO HER PLACE.

FILTER CO CIGARETTE

I NEVER HAVE TROUBLE THINKING OF AN EXCUSE TO LEAVE, AFTERWARDS.

THEY DIDN'T REALLY NEED TO INVITE ALL THOSE OTHER CUSTOMERS IN ON THE DEAL.

YES THEY DID.

WE'VE BEEN TOGETHER FOR AWHILE. DOESN'T SHE REALIZE BY NOW I'M GOING TO BE IN A SHITTY MOOD WHEN I WAKE UP?

ONCE THEY HAD ME ON THE SPOT, THEY HAD TO TAKE IT AS FAR AS THEY COULD.

IT'S IN THE RULES.

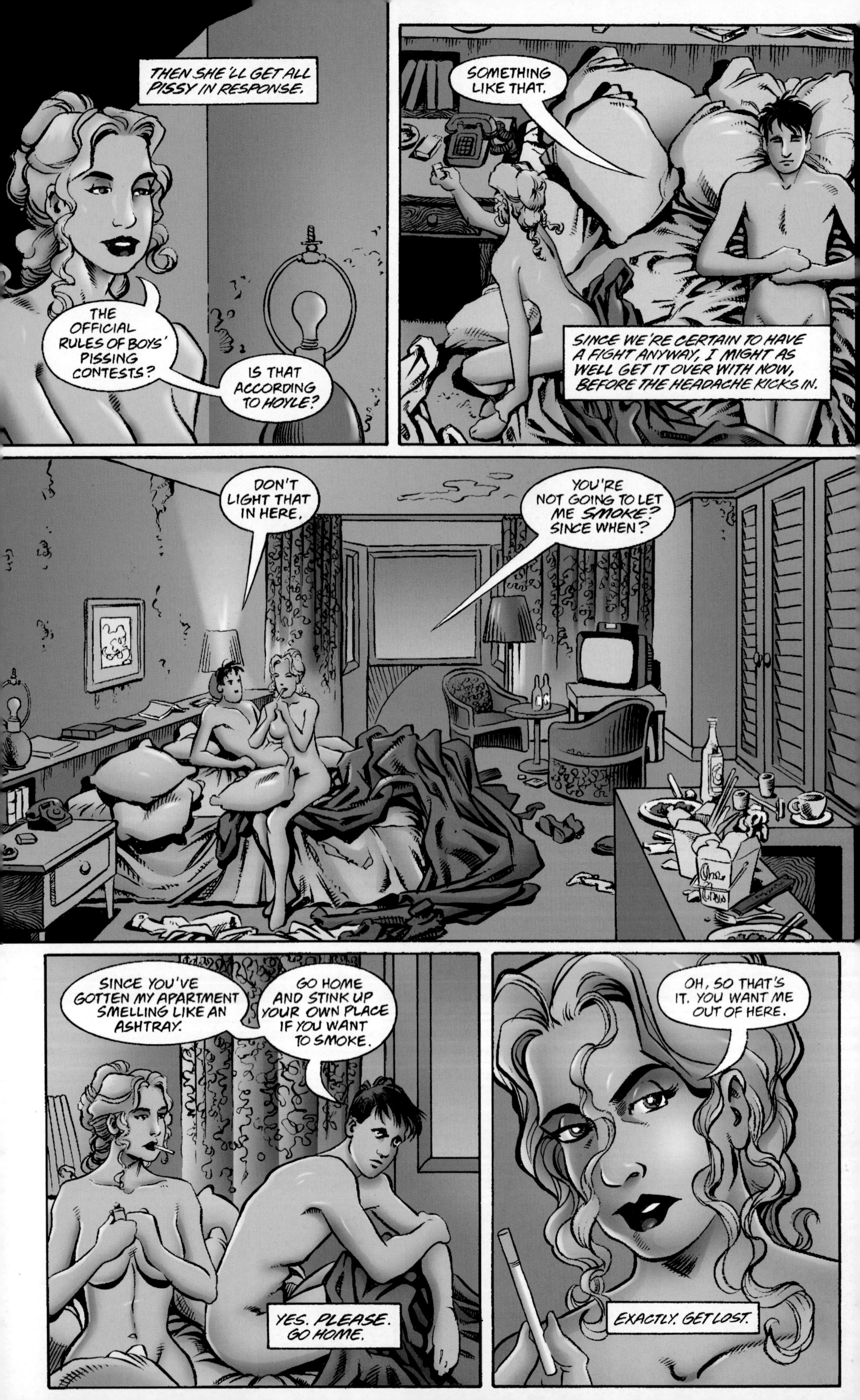
THEN SHE'LL GET ALL PISSY IN RESPONSE.
THE OFFICIAL RULES OF BOYS' PISSING CONTESTS?
IS THAT ACCORDING TO HOYLE?
SOMETHING LIKE THAT.
SINCE WE'RE CERTAIN TO HAVE A FIGHT ANYWAY, I MIGHT AS WELL GET IT OVER WITH NOW, BEFORE THE HEADACHE KICKS IN.
DON'T LIGHT THAT IN HERE.
YOU'RE NOT GOING TO LET ME SMOKE? SINCE WHEN?
SINCE YOU'VE GOTTEN MY APARTMENT SMELLING LIKE AN ASHTRAY.
GO HOME AND STINK UP YOUR OWN PLACE IF YOU WANT TO SMOKE.
YES. PLEASE. GO HOME.
OH, SO THAT'S IT. YOU WANT ME OUT OF HERE.
EXACTLY. GET LOST.

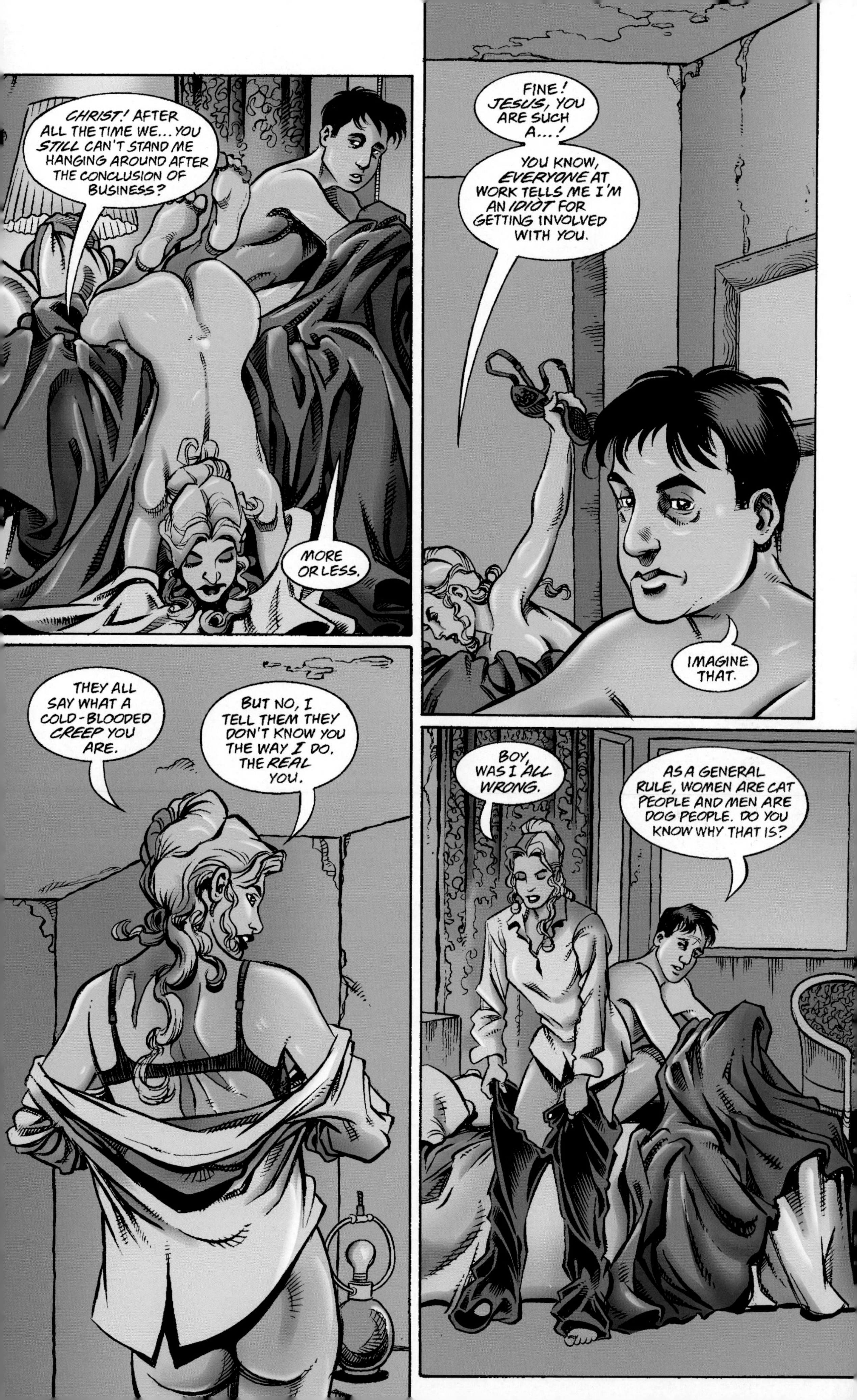
CHRIST! AFTER ALL THE TIME WE... YOU STILL CAN'T STAND ME HANGING AROUND AFTER THE CONCLUSION OF BUSINESS?
MORE OR LESS.
FINE! JESUS, YOU ARE SUCH A...!
YOU KNOW, EVERYONE AT WORK TELLS ME I'M AN IDIOT FOR GETTING INVOLVED WITH YOU.
IMAGINE THAT.
THEY ALL SAY WHAT A COLD-BLOODED CREEP YOU ARE.
BUT NO, I TELL THEM THEY DON'T KNOW YOU THE WAY I DO. THE REAL YOU.
BOY, WAS I ALL WRONG.
AS A GENERAL RULE, WOMEN ARE CAT PEOPLE AND MEN ARE DOG PEOPLE. DO YOU KNOW WHY THAT IS?

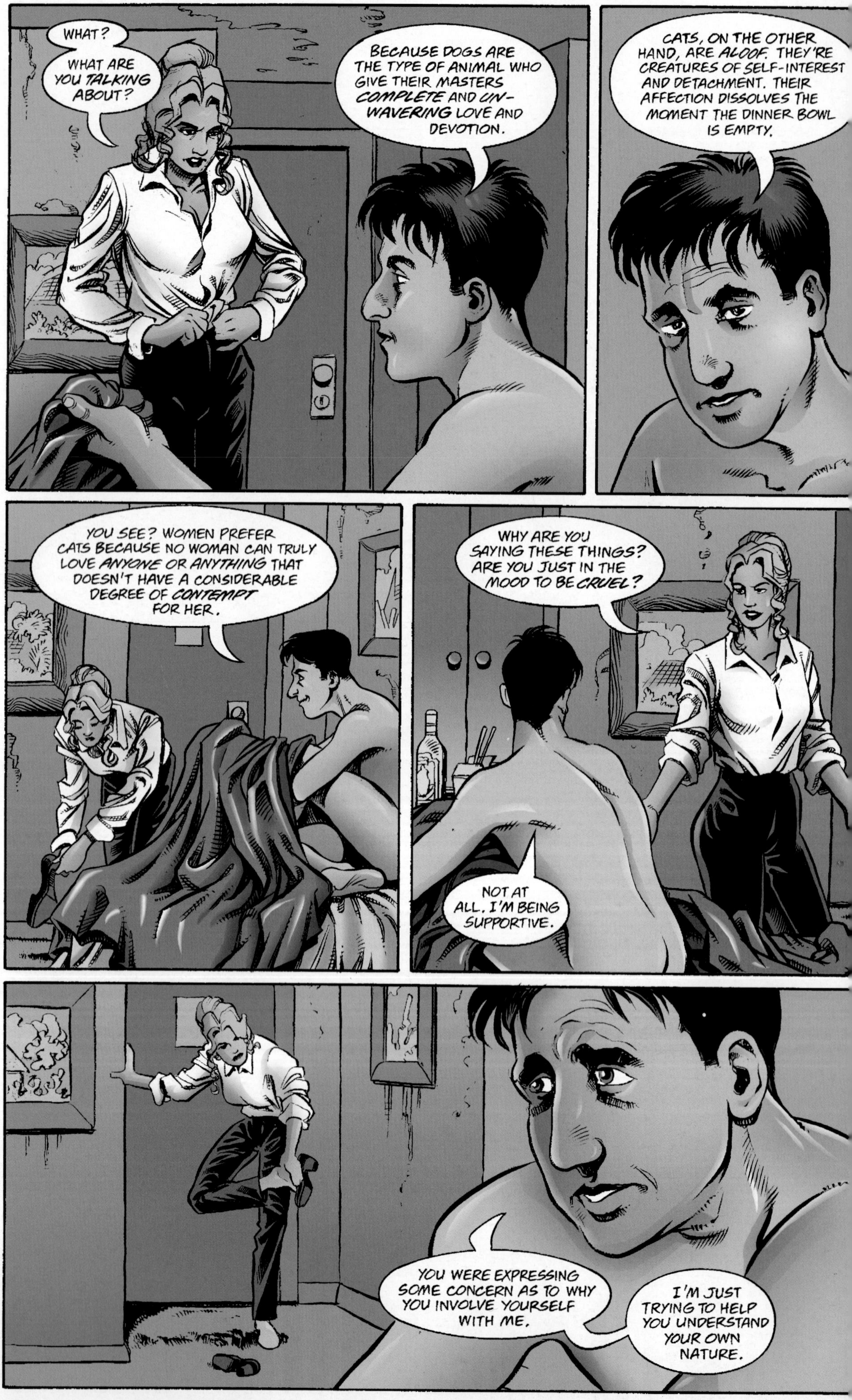
WHAT? WHAT ARE YOU TALKING ABOUT?
BECAUSE DOGS ARE THE TYPE OF ANIMAL WHO GIVE THEIR MASTERS COMPLETE AND UNWAVERING LOVE AND DEVOTION.
CATS, ON THE OTHER HAND, ARE ALOOF. THEY'RE CREATURES OF SELF-INTEREST AND DETACHMENT. THEIR AFFECTION DISSOLVES THE MOMENT THE DINNER BOWL IS EMPTY.
YOU SEE? WOMEN PREFER CATS BECAUSE NO WOMAN CAN TRULY LOVE ANYONE OR ANYTHING THAT DOESN'T HAVE A CONSIDERABLE DEGREE OF CONTEMPT FOR HER.
WHY ARE YOU SAYING THESE THINGS? ARE YOU JUST IN THE MOOD TO BE CRUEL?
NOT AT ALL. I'M BEING SUPPORTIVE.
YOU WERE EXPRESSING SOME CONCERN AS TO WHY YOU INVOLVE YOURSELF WITH ME.
I'M JUST TRYING TO HELP YOU UNDERSTAND YOUR OWN NATURE.

YOU KNOW WHAT? THE PEOPLE AT WORK *WERE* ALL WRONG ABOUT YOU!

YOU'RE NOT A *CREEP*, OR A *JERK*, OR ANYTHING LIKE THAT!

YOU'RE *EVIL*, JOEY MARTIN.

OKAY, THAT WAS A LITTLE MORE *SEVERE* THAN ONE OF OUR USUAL "YOU LEFT THE TOILET SEAT UP AGAIN" FIGHTS.

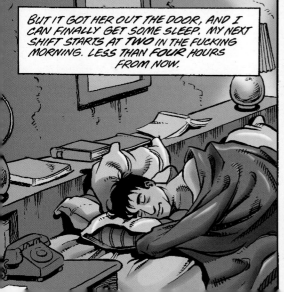

BUT IT GOT HER OUT THE DOOR, AND I CAN FINALLY GET SOME SLEEP. MY NEXT SHIFT STARTS AT *TWO* IN THE FUCKING MORNING. LESS THAN *FOUR* HOURS FROM NOW.

HELLO?

ANYBODY HOME?

JESUS!

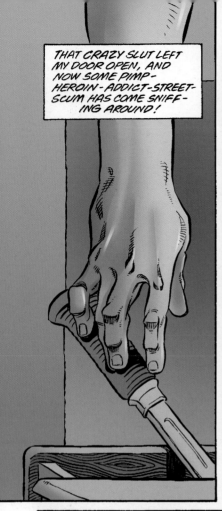

THAT CRAZY SLUT LEFT MY DOOR OPEN, AND NOW SOME PIMP-HEROIN-ADDICT-STREET-SCUM HAS COME SNIFF-ING AROUND!

HUH?

OH.

THERE YOU ARE, PARTNER.

HI. YOU MUST BE JOEY, RIGHT?

JOEY MARTIN?

HELL, YOU LOOK LIKE HIM, AND YOU'RE WEARING HIS PANTS, SO I'LL BET YOU'RE HIM.

YOU...? WHAT...?

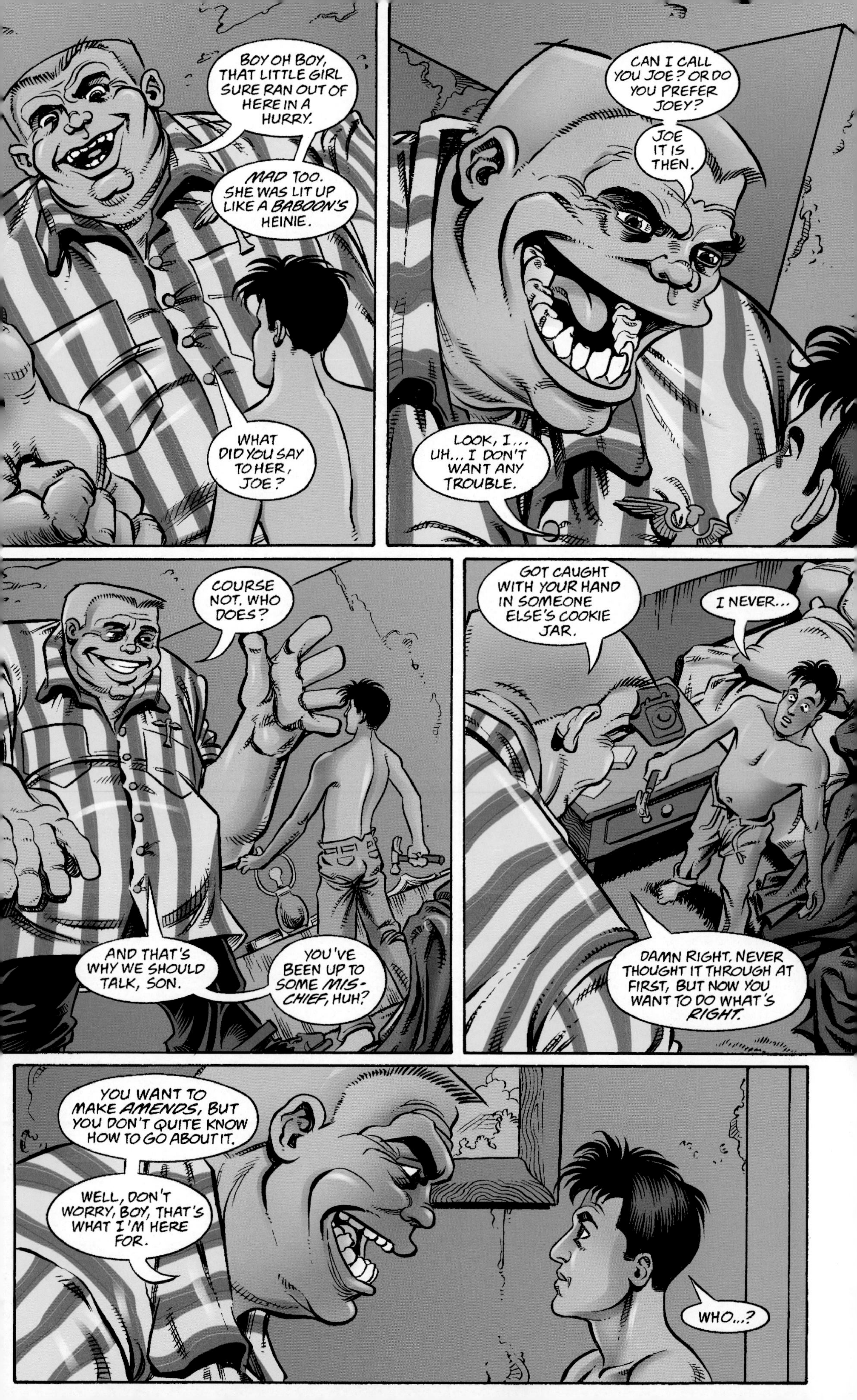
BOY OH BOY, THAT LITTLE GIRL SURE RAN OUT OF HERE IN A HURRY.
MAD TOO. SHE WAS LIT UP LIKE A BABOON'S HEINIE.
WHAT DID YOU SAY TO HER, JOE?
CAN I CALL YOU JOE? OR DO YOU PREFER JOEY?
JOE IT IS THEN.
LOOK, I... UH... I DON'T WANT ANY TROUBLE.
COURSE NOT. WHO DOES?
AND THAT'S WHY WE SHOULD TALK, SON.
YOU'VE BEEN UP TO SOME MIS-CHIEF, HUH?
GOT CAUGHT WITH YOUR HAND IN SOMEONE ELSE'S COOKIE JAR.
I NEVER...
DAMN RIGHT. NEVER THOUGHT IT THROUGH AT FIRST, BUT NOW YOU WANT TO DO WHAT'S RIGHT.
YOU WANT TO MAKE AMENDS, BUT YOU DON'T QUITE KNOW HOW TO GO ABOUT IT.
WELL, DON'T WORRY, BOY, THAT'S WHAT I'M HERE FOR.
WHO...?

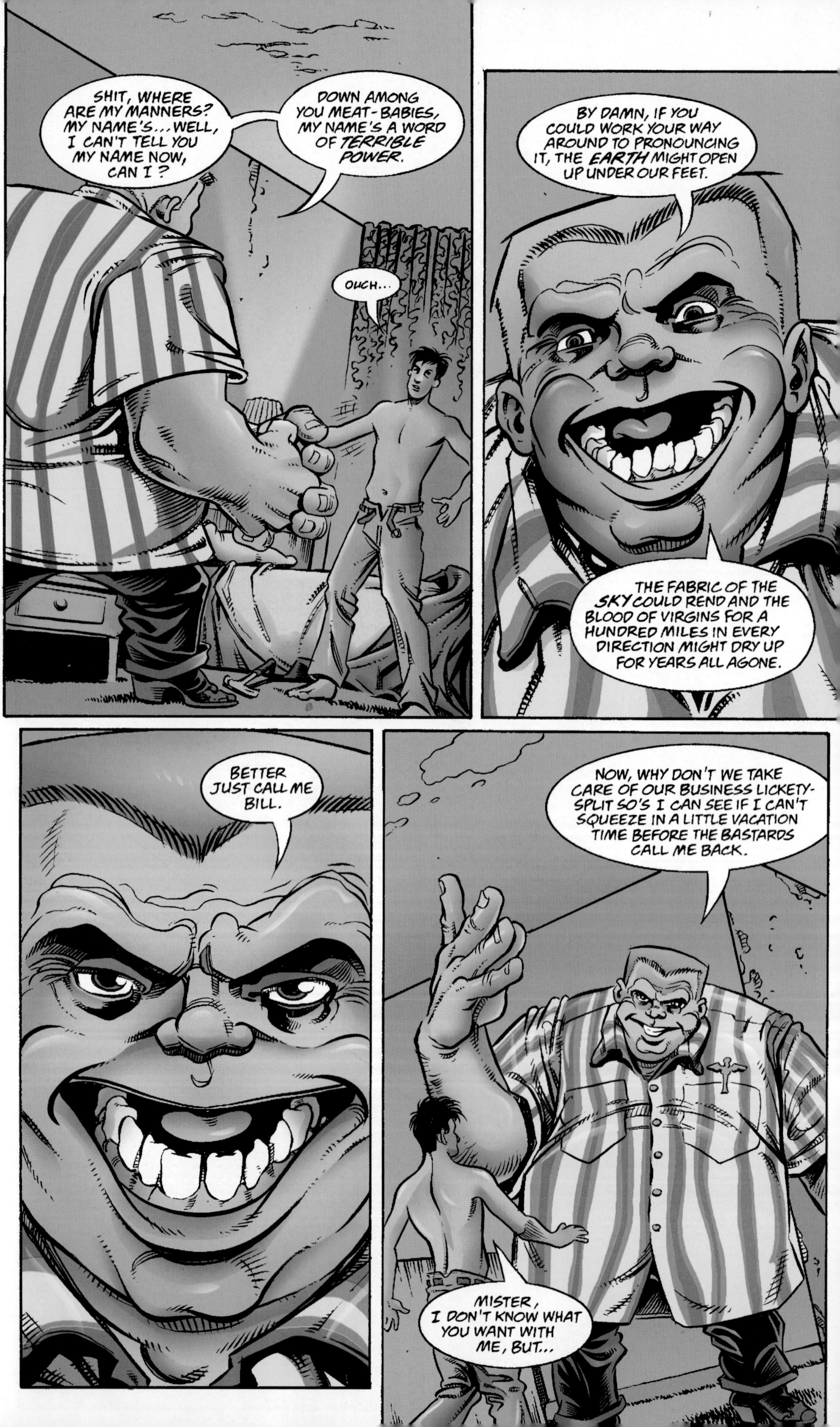
SHIT, WHERE ARE MY MANNERS? MY NAME'S... WELL, I CAN'T TELL YOU MY NAME NOW, CAN I?
DOWN AMONG YOU MEAT-BABIES, MY NAME'S A WORD OF TERRIBLE POWER.
OUCH...
BY DAMN, IF YOU COULD WORK YOUR WAY AROUND TO PRONOUNCING IT, THE EARTH MIGHT OPEN UP UNDER OUR FEET.
THE FABRIC OF THE SKY COULD REND AND THE BLOOD OF VIRGINS FOR A HUNDRED MILES IN EVERY DIRECTION MIGHT DRY UP FOR YEARS ALL AGONE.
BETTER JUST CALL ME BILL.
NOW, WHY DON'T WE TAKE CARE OF OUR BUSINESS LICKETY-SPLIT SO'S I CAN SEE IF I CAN'T SQUEEZE IN A LITTLE VACATION TIME BEFORE THE BASTARDS CALL ME BACK.
MISTER, I DON'T KNOW WHAT YOU WANT WITH ME, BUT...

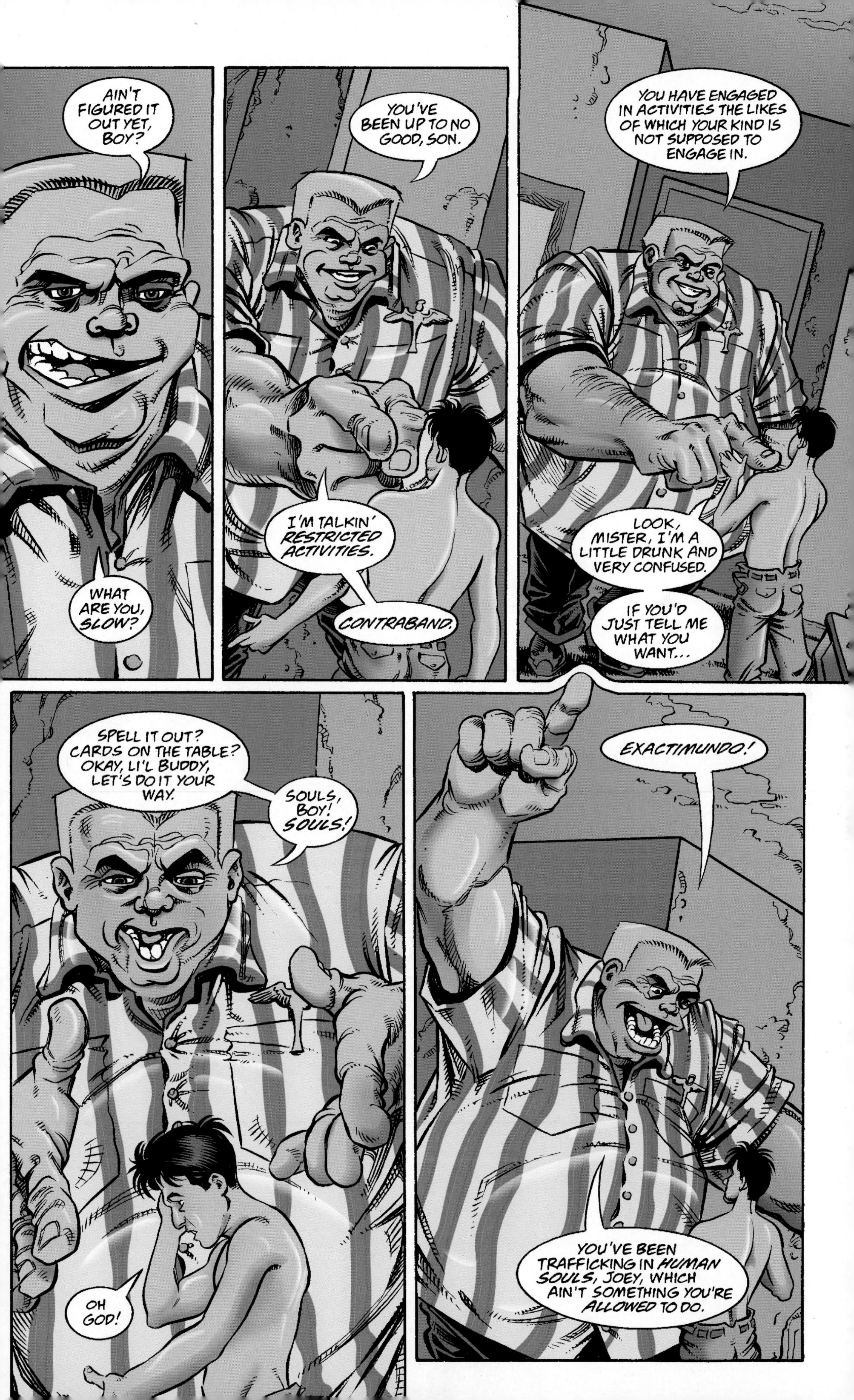
AIN'T FIGURED IT OUT YET, BOY?
WHAT ARE YOU, SLOW?
YOU'VE BEEN UP TO NO GOOD, SON.
I'M TALKIN' RESTRICTED ACTIVITIES.
CONTRABAND.
YOU HAVE ENGAGED IN ACTIVITIES THE LIKES OF WHICH YOUR KIND IS NOT SUPPOSED TO ENGAGE IN.
LOOK, MISTER, I'M A LITTLE DRUNK AND VERY CONFUSED.
IF YOU'D JUST TELL ME WHAT YOU WANT...
SPELL IT OUT? CARDS ON THE TABLE? OKAY, LI'L BUDDY, LET'S DO IT YOUR WAY.
SOULS, BOY! SOULS!
OH GOD!
EXACTIMUNDO!
YOU'VE BEEN TRAFFICKING IN HUMAN SOULS, JOEY, WHICH AIN'T SOMETHING YOU'RE ALLOWED TO DO.

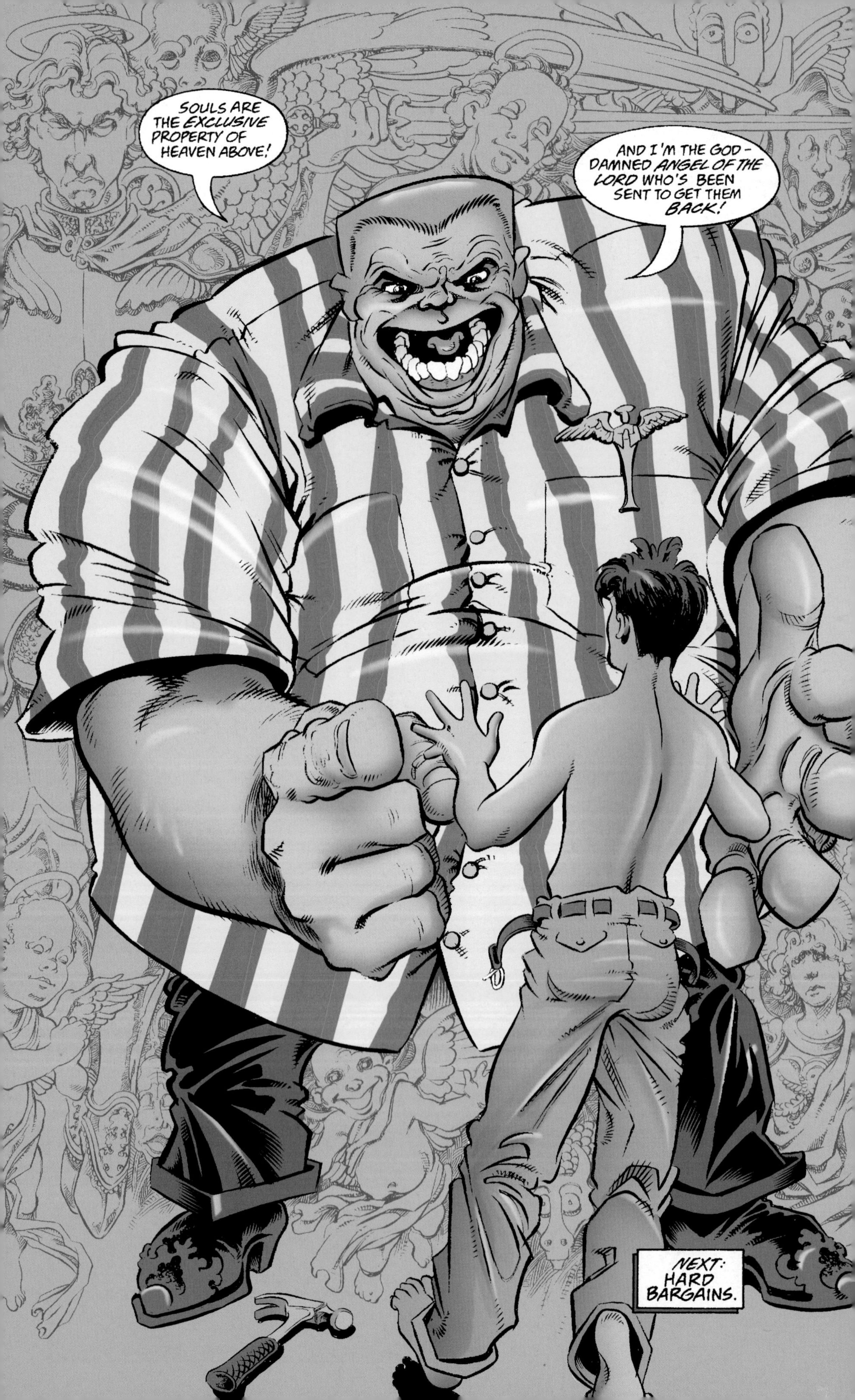
SOULS ARE THE *EXCLUSIVE* PROPERTY OF HEAVEN ABOVE!
AND I'M THE GOD-DAMNED *ANGEL OF THE LORD* WHO'S BEEN SENT TO GET THEM *BACK!*
NEXT: HARD BARGAINS.

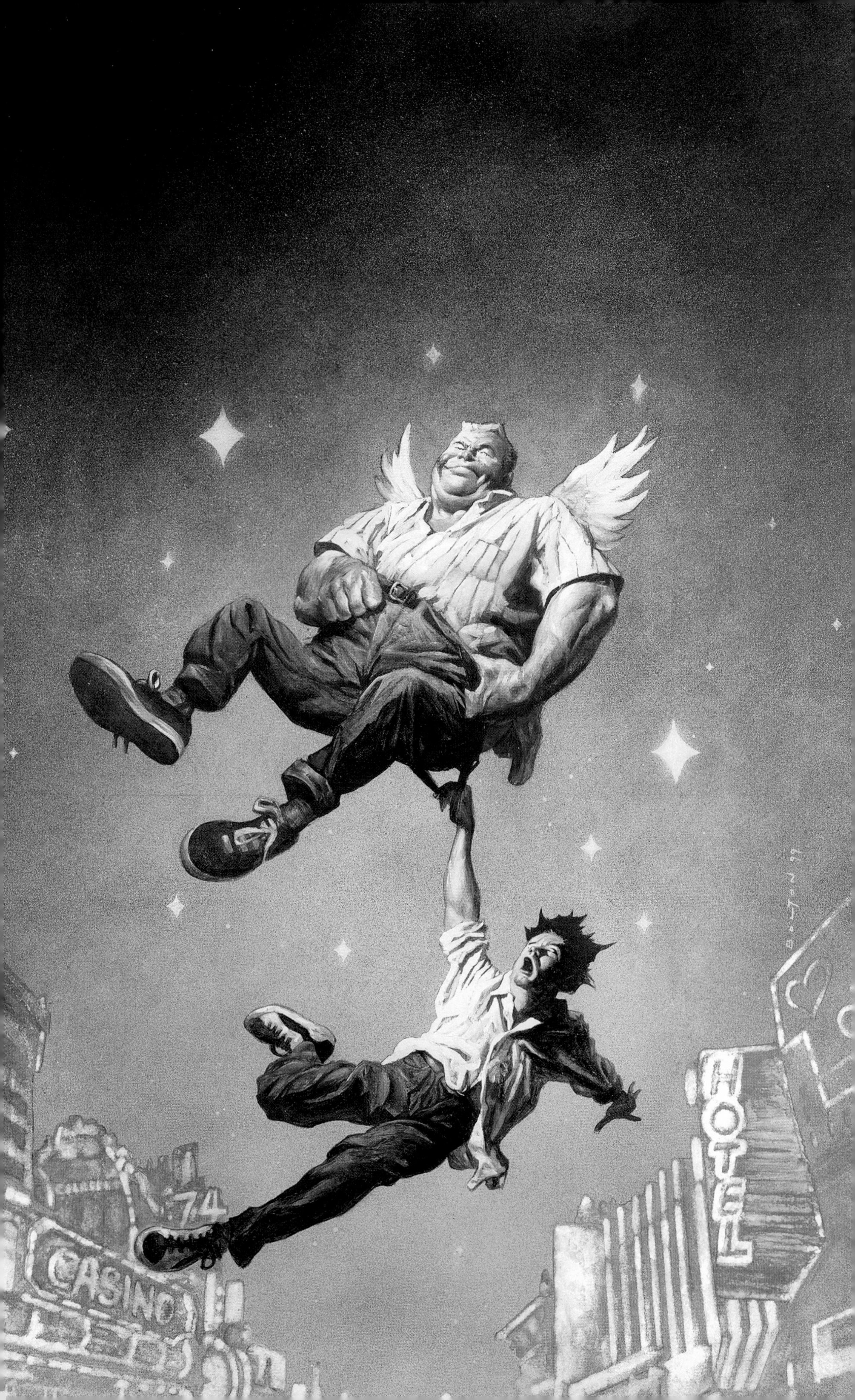
74
CASINO
HOTEL

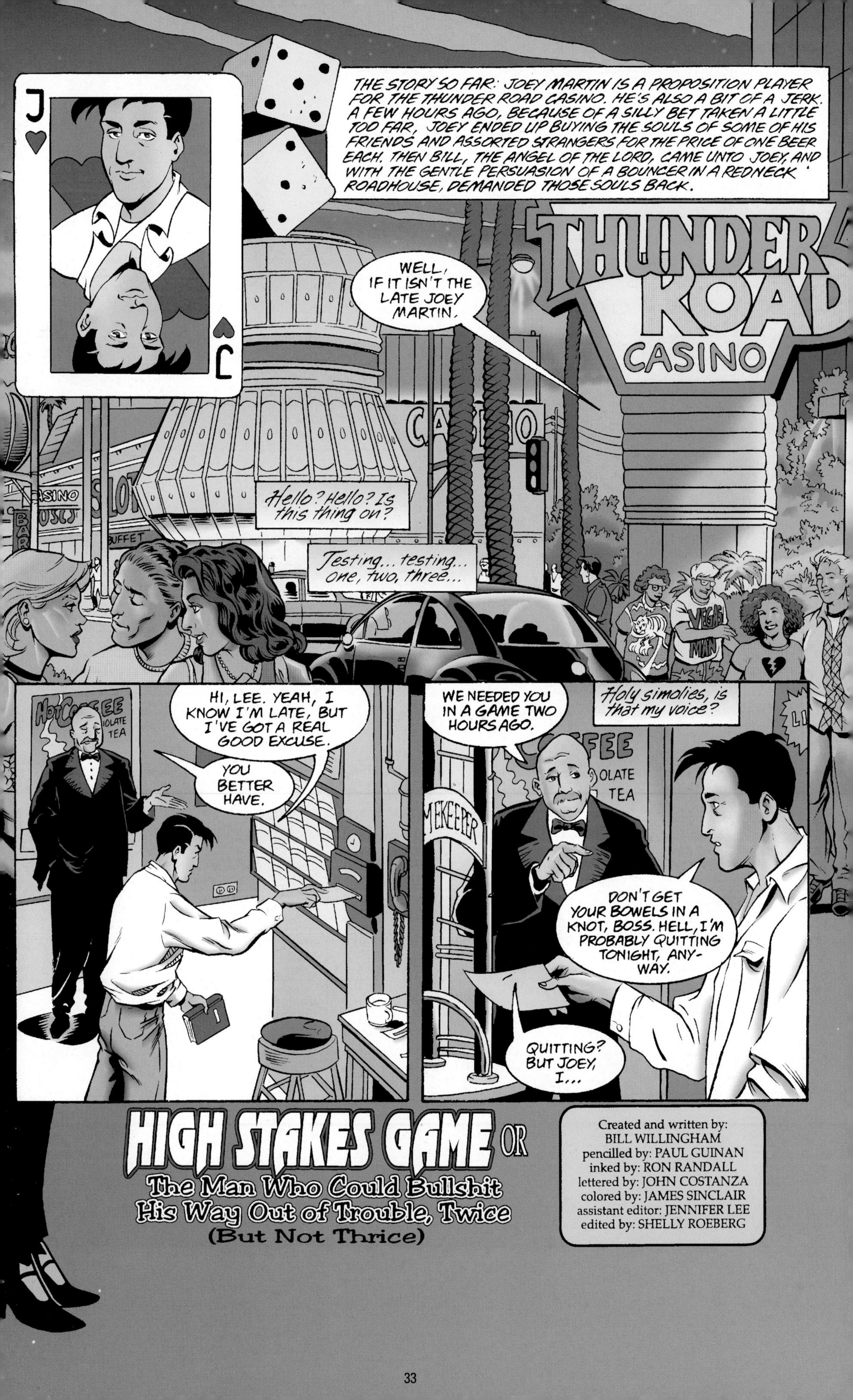
THE STORY SO FAR: JOEY MARTIN IS A PROPOSITION PLAYER FOR THE THUNDER ROAD CASINO. HE'S ALSO A BIT OF A JERK. A FEW HOURS AGO, BECAUSE OF A SILLY BET TAKEN A LITTLE TOO FAR, JOEY ENDED UP BUYING THE SOULS OF SOME OF HIS FRIENDS AND ASSORTED STRANGERS FOR THE PRICE OF ONE BEER EACH. THEN BILL, THE ANGEL OF THE LORD, CAME UNTO JOEY, AND WITH THE GENTLE PERSUASION OF A BOUNCER IN A REDNECK ROADHOUSE, DEMANDED THOSE SOULS BACK.
THUNDER ROAD CASINO
WELL, IF IT ISN'T THE LATE JOEY MARTIN.
Hello? Hello? Is this thing on?
Testing... testing... one, two, three...
HI, LEE. YEAH, I KNOW I'M LATE, BUT I'VE GOT A REAL GOOD EXCUSE.
YOU BETTER HAVE.
WE NEEDED YOU IN A GAME TWO HOURS AGO.
Holy simolies, is that my voice?
DON'T GET YOUR BOWELS IN A KNOT, BOSS. HELL, I'M PROBABLY QUITTING TONIGHT, ANYWAY.
QUITTING? BUT JOEY, I...

HIGH STAKES GAME OR

The Man Who Could Bullshit His Way Out of Trouble, Twice (But Not Thrice)

Created and written by: BILL WILLINGHAM
pencilled by: PAUL GUINAN
inked by: RON RANDALL
lettered by: JOHN COSTANZA
colored by: JAMES SINCLAIR
assistant editor: JENNIFER LEE
edited by: SHELLY ROEBERG

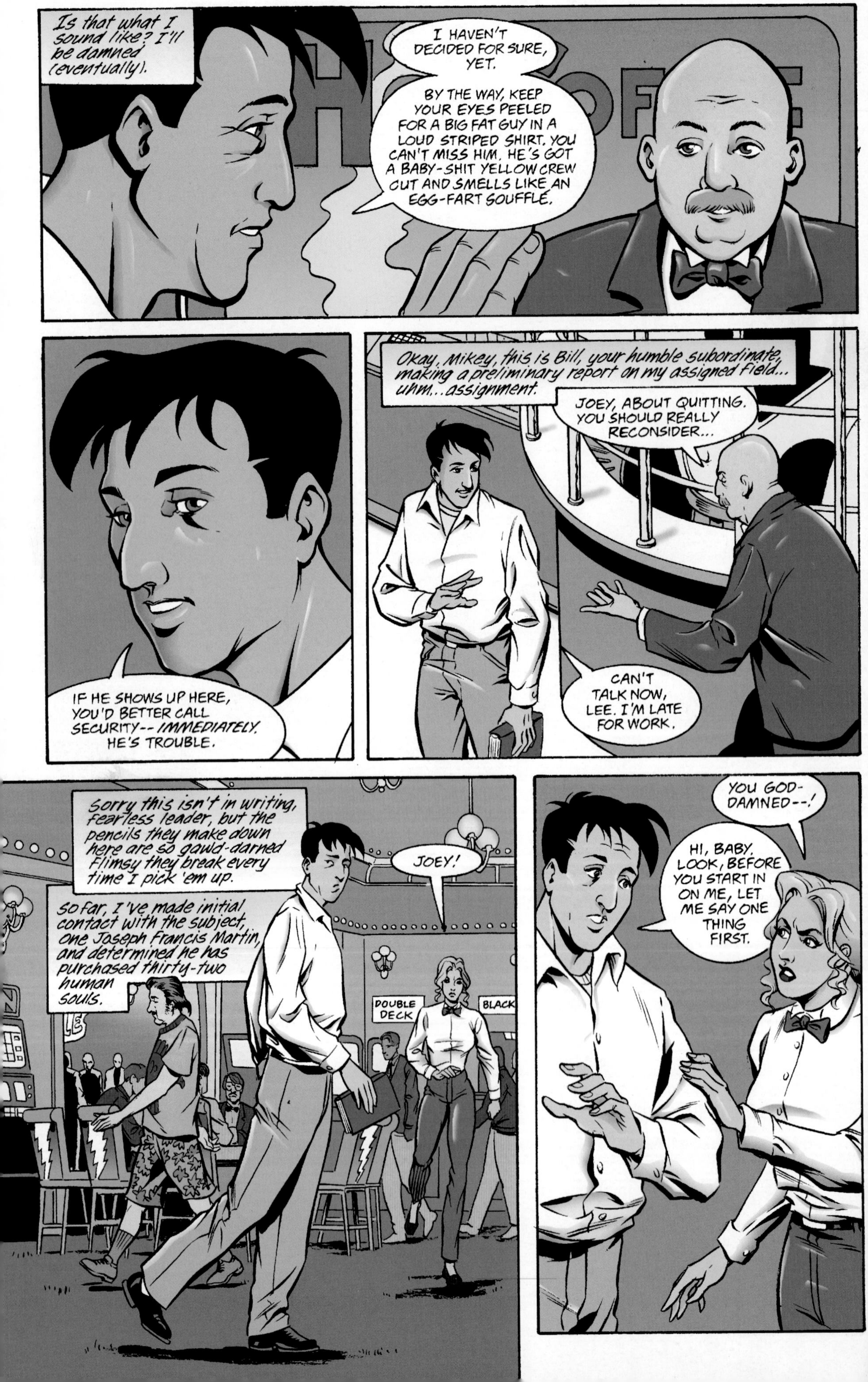
Is that what I sound like? I'll be damned (eventually).
I HAVEN'T DECIDED FOR SURE, YET.
BY THE WAY, KEEP YOUR EYES PEELED FOR A BIG FAT GUY IN A LOUD STRIPED SHIRT. YOU CAN'T MISS HIM. HE'S GOT A BABY-SHIT YELLOW CREW CUT AND SMELLS LIKE AN EGG-FART SOUFFLÉ.
IF HE SHOWS UP HERE, YOU'D BETTER CALL SECURITY-- IMMEDIATELY. HE'S TROUBLE.
Okay, Mikey, this is Bill, your humble subordinate, making a preliminary report on my assigned field... uhm...assignment.
JOEY, ABOUT QUITTING. YOU SHOULD REALLY RECONSIDER...
CAN'T TALK NOW, LEE. I'M LATE FOR WORK.
Sorry this isn't in writing, fearless leader, but the pencils they make down here are so gawd-darned flimsy they break every time I pick 'em up.
So far, I've made initial contact with the subject, one Joseph Francis Martin, and determined he has purchased thirty-two human souls.
JOEY!
DOUBLE DECK
BLACK
YOU GOD-DAMNED--!
HI, BABY. LOOK, BEFORE YOU START IN ON ME, LET ME SAY ONE THING FIRST.

I TREATED YOU LIKE SHIT EARLIER AND I'M SORRY.

I've also visually ascertained the existence of the purchase contracts in Mr. Martin's apartment.

I'VE GOT NO EXCUSE, AND I WON'T BLAME YOU IF YOU NEVER TALK TO ME AGAIN; BUT I WAS DRINKING AND...

DRINKING'S NO EXCUSE.

YOU'RE RIGHT, BUT... OH, HERE, BEFORE I FORGET. I GOT YOU THIS.

RIGHT.

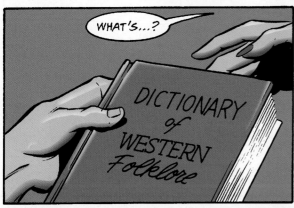

WHAT'S...?

DICTIONARY of WESTERN Folklore

A DICTIONARY OF WESTERN FOLKLORE?

However, as we suspected, I was unable to physically touch said documents, thus confirming their authenticity and celestial recognition of their new ownership.

IT'S FULL OF UNICORNS AND MYTHOLOGY AND ALL THAT KIND OF SHIT YOU LIKE.

OH, JOEY, IT'S PERFECT. IT'S...

WAIT A MINUTE.

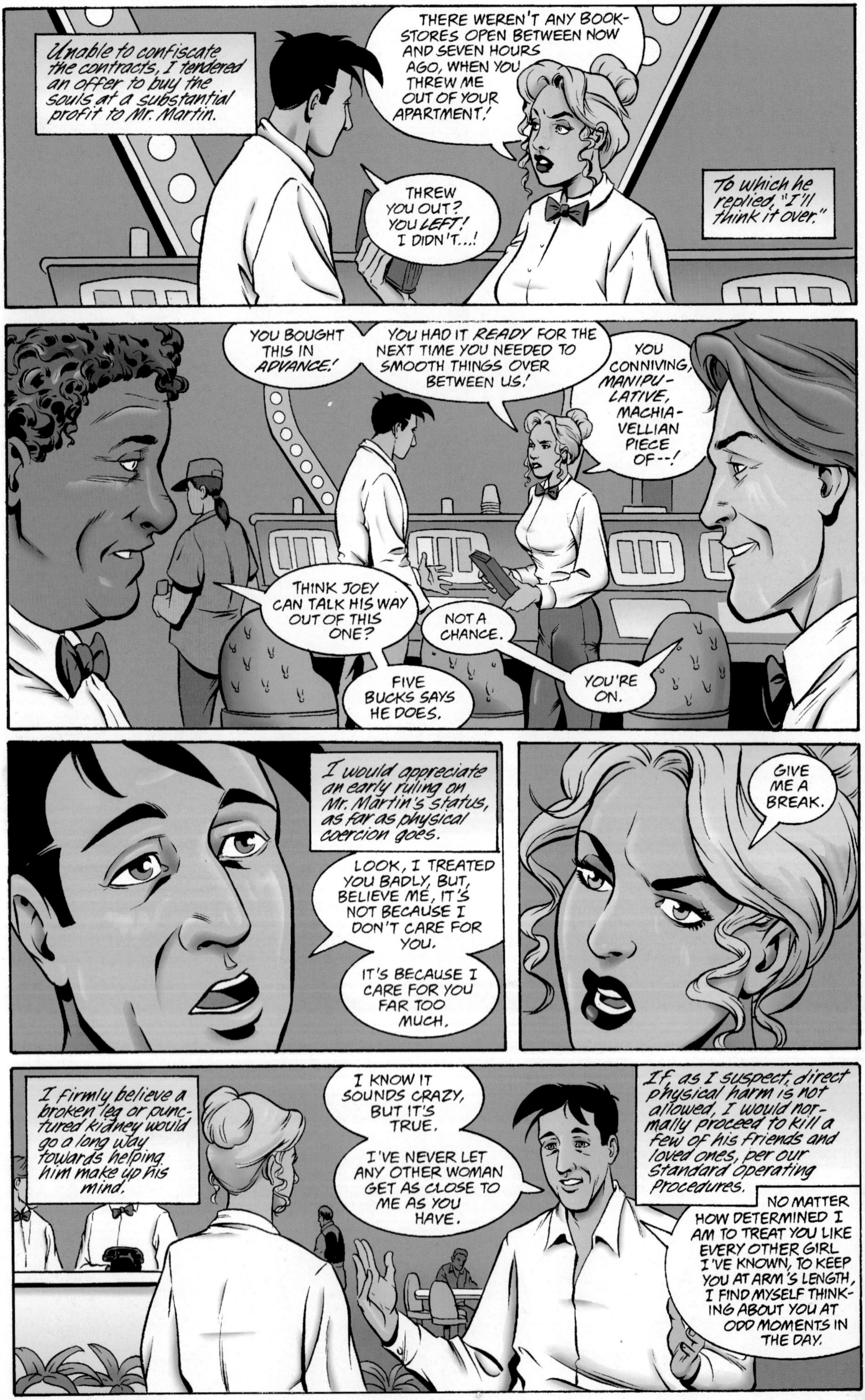
Unable to confiscate the contracts, I tendered an offer to buy the souls at a substantial profit to Mr. Martin.
THERE WEREN'T ANY BOOK-STORES OPEN BETWEEN NOW AND SEVEN HOURS AGO, WHEN YOU THREW ME OUT OF YOUR APARTMENT!
THREW YOU OUT? YOU LEFT! I DIDN'T...!
To which he replied, "I'll think it over."
YOU BOUGHT THIS IN ADVANCE!
YOU HAD IT READY FOR THE NEXT TIME YOU NEEDED TO SMOOTH THINGS OVER BETWEEN US!
YOU CONNIVING, MANIPU-LATIVE, MACHIA-VELLIAN PIECE OF--!
THINK JOEY CAN TALK HIS WAY OUT OF THIS ONE?
NOT A CHANCE.
FIVE BUCKS SAYS HE DOES.
YOU'RE ON.
I would appreciate an early ruling on Mr. Martin's status, as far as physical coercion goes.
LOOK, I TREATED YOU BADLY, BUT, BELIEVE ME, IT'S NOT BECAUSE I DON'T CARE FOR YOU.
IT'S BECAUSE I CARE FOR YOU FAR TOO MUCH.
GIVE ME A BREAK.
I firmly believe a broken leg or punctured kidney would go a long way towards helping him make up his mind.
I KNOW IT SOUNDS CRAZY, BUT IT'S TRUE.
I'VE NEVER LET ANY OTHER WOMAN GET AS CLOSE TO ME AS YOU HAVE.
If, as I suspect, direct physical harm is not allowed, I would normally proceed to kill a few of his friends and loved ones, per our Standard Operating Procedures.
NO MATTER HOW DETERMINED I AM TO TREAT YOU LIKE EVERY OTHER GIRL I'VE KNOWN, TO KEEP YOU AT ARM'S LENGTH, I FIND MYSELF THINKING ABOUT YOU AT ODD MOMENTS IN THE DAY.

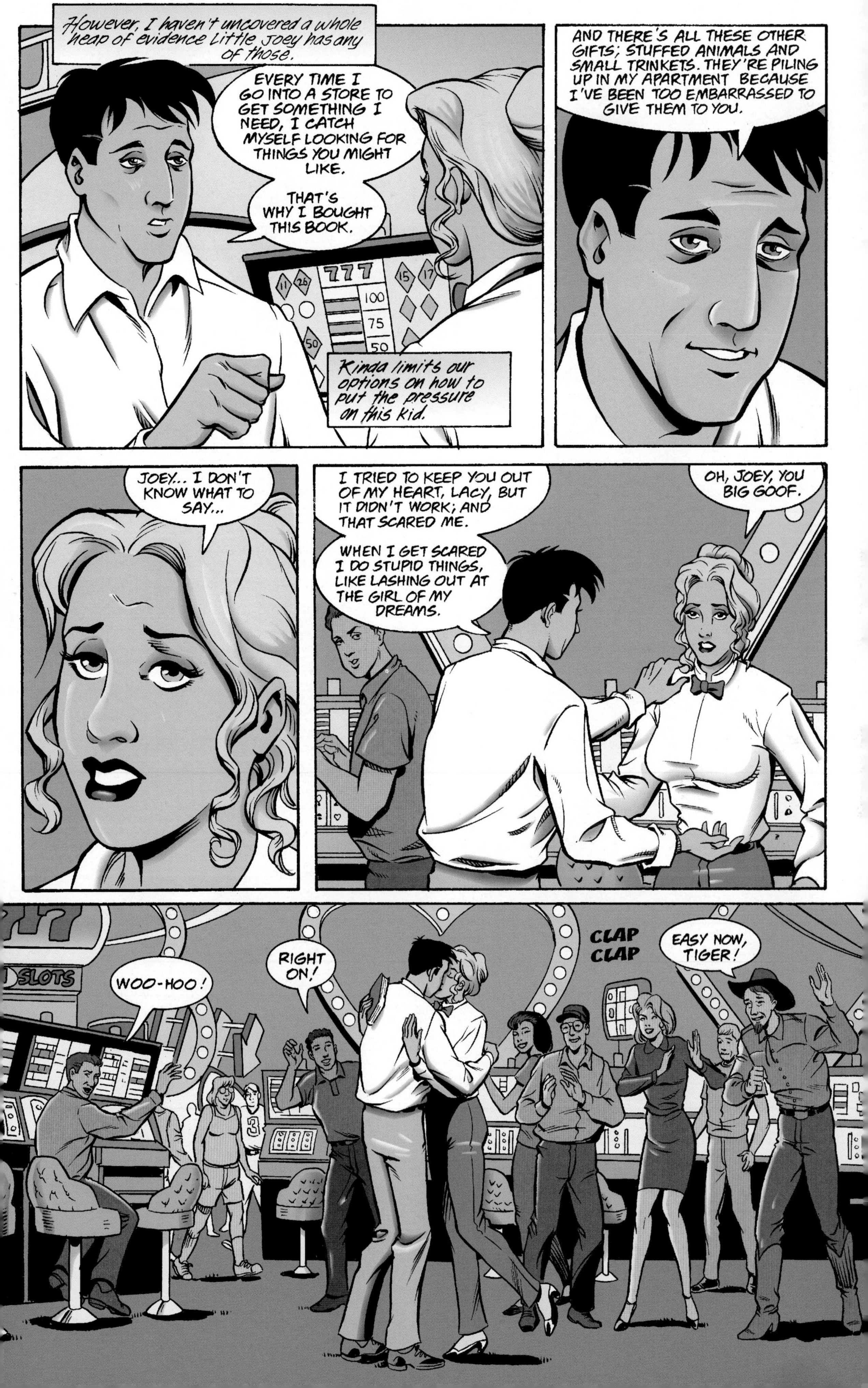

However, I haven't uncovered a whole heap of evidence Little Joey has any of those.
EVERY TIME I GO INTO A STORE TO GET SOMETHING I NEED, I CATCH MYSELF LOOKING FOR THINGS YOU MIGHT LIKE.
THAT'S WHY I BOUGHT THIS BOOK.
777
100
75
50
Kinda limits our options on how to put the pressure on this kid.
AND THERE'S ALL THESE OTHER GIFTS; STUFFED ANIMALS AND SMALL TRINKETS. THEY'RE PILING UP IN MY APARTMENT BECAUSE I'VE BEEN TOO EMBARRASSED TO GIVE THEM TO YOU.
JOEY... I DON'T KNOW WHAT TO SAY...
I TRIED TO KEEP YOU OUT OF MY HEART, LACY, BUT IT DIDN'T WORK; AND THAT SCARED ME.
WHEN I GET SCARED I DO STUPID THINGS, LIKE LASHING OUT AT THE GIRL OF MY DREAMS.
OH, JOEY, YOU BIG GOOF.
SLOTS
WOO-HOO!
RIGHT ON!
CLAP CLAP
EASY NOW, TIGER!

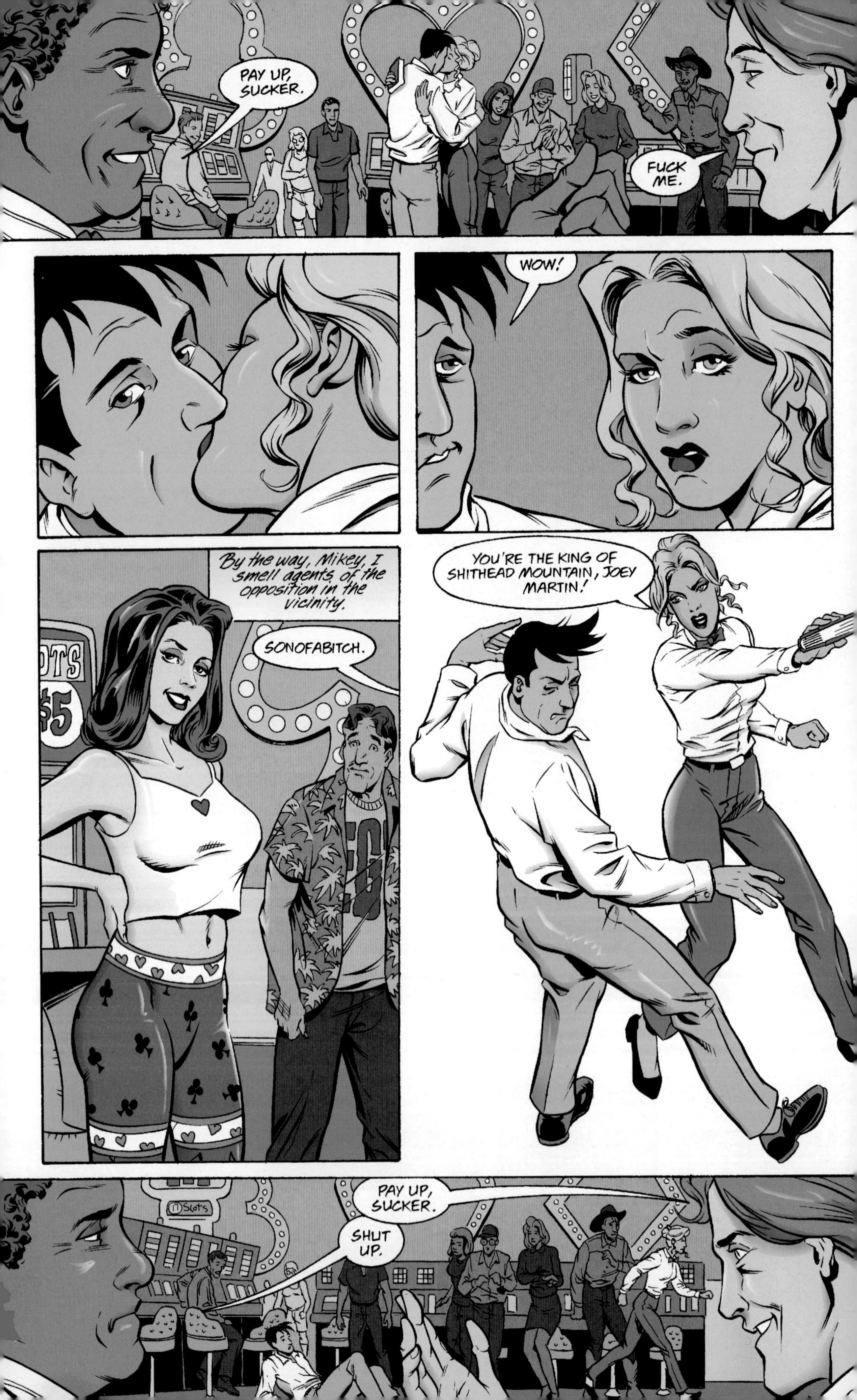
PAY UP, SUCKER.
FUCK ME.
WOW!
By the way, Mikey, I smell agents of the opposition in the vicinity.
SONOFABITCH.
YOU'RE THE KING OF SHITHEAD MOUNTAIN, JOEY MARTIN!
PAY UP, SUCKER.
SHUT UP.

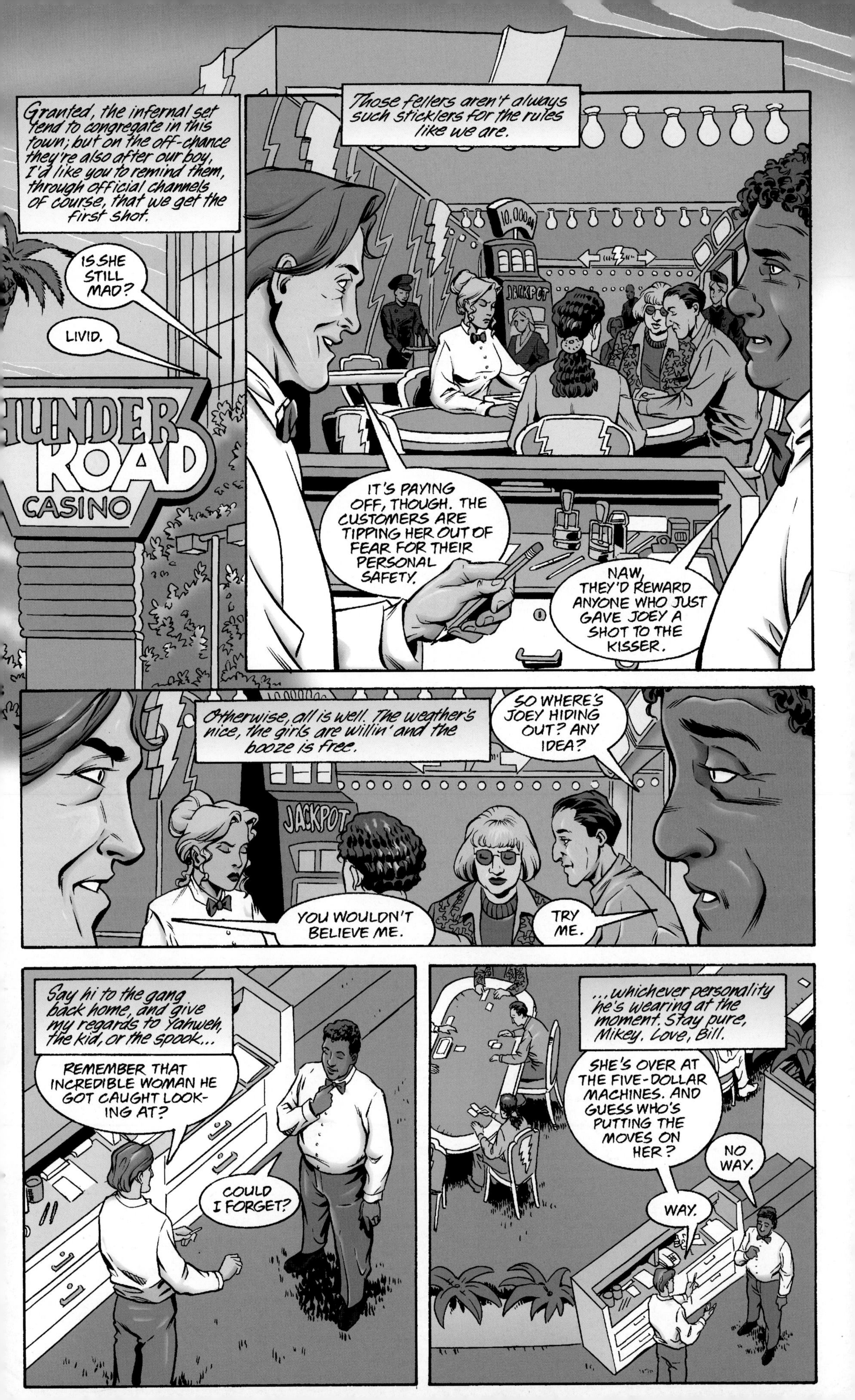
Granted, the infernal set tend to congregate in this town; but on the off-chance they're also after our boy, I'd like you to remind them, through official channels of course, that we get the first shot.
IS SHE STILL MAD?
LIVID.
HUNDER ROAD CASINO
Those fellers aren't always such sticklers for the rules like we are.
JACKPOT
IT'S PAYING OFF, THOUGH. THE CUSTOMERS ARE TIPPING HER OUT OF FEAR FOR THEIR PERSONAL SAFETY.
NAW, THEY'D REWARD ANYONE WHO JUST GAVE JOEY A SHOT TO THE KISSER.
Otherwise, all is well. The weather's nice, the girls are willin' and the booze is free.
SO WHERE'S JOEY HIDING OUT? ANY IDEA?
JACKPOT
YOU WOULDN'T BELIEVE ME.
TRY ME.
Say hi to the gang back home, and give my regards to Yahweh, the kid, or the spook...
REMEMBER THAT INCREDIBLE WOMAN HE GOT CAUGHT LOOKING AT?
COULD I FORGET?
...whichever personality he's wearing at the moment. Stay pure, Mikey. Love, Bill.
SHE'S OVER AT THE FIVE-DOLLAR MACHINES. AND GUESS WHO'S PUTTING THE MOVES ON HER?
NO WAY.
WAY.

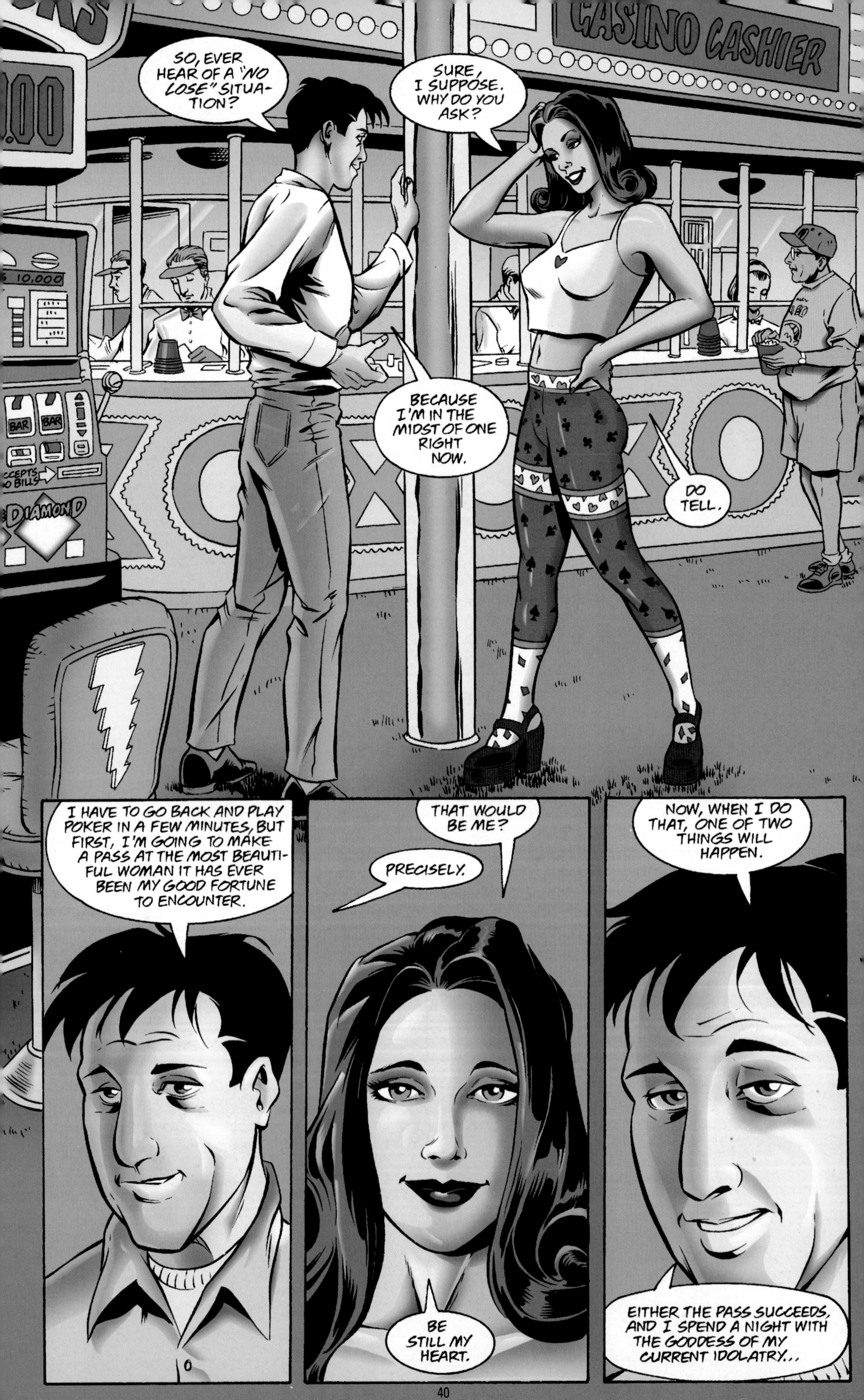
CASINO CASHIER
SO, EVER HEAR OF A "NO LOSE" SITUATION?
SURE, I SUPPOSE. WHY DO YOU ASK?
BECAUSE I'M IN THE MIDST OF ONE RIGHT NOW.
DO TELL.
I HAVE TO GO BACK AND PLAY POKER IN A FEW MINUTES, BUT FIRST, I'M GOING TO MAKE A PASS AT THE MOST BEAUTIFUL WOMAN IT HAS EVER BEEN MY GOOD FORTUNE TO ENCOUNTER.
THAT WOULD BE ME?
PRECISELY.
BE STILL MY HEART.
NOW, WHEN I DO THAT, ONE OF TWO THINGS WILL HAPPEN.
EITHER THE PASS SUCCEEDS, AND I SPEND A NIGHT WITH THE GODDESS OF MY CURRENT IDOLATRY...

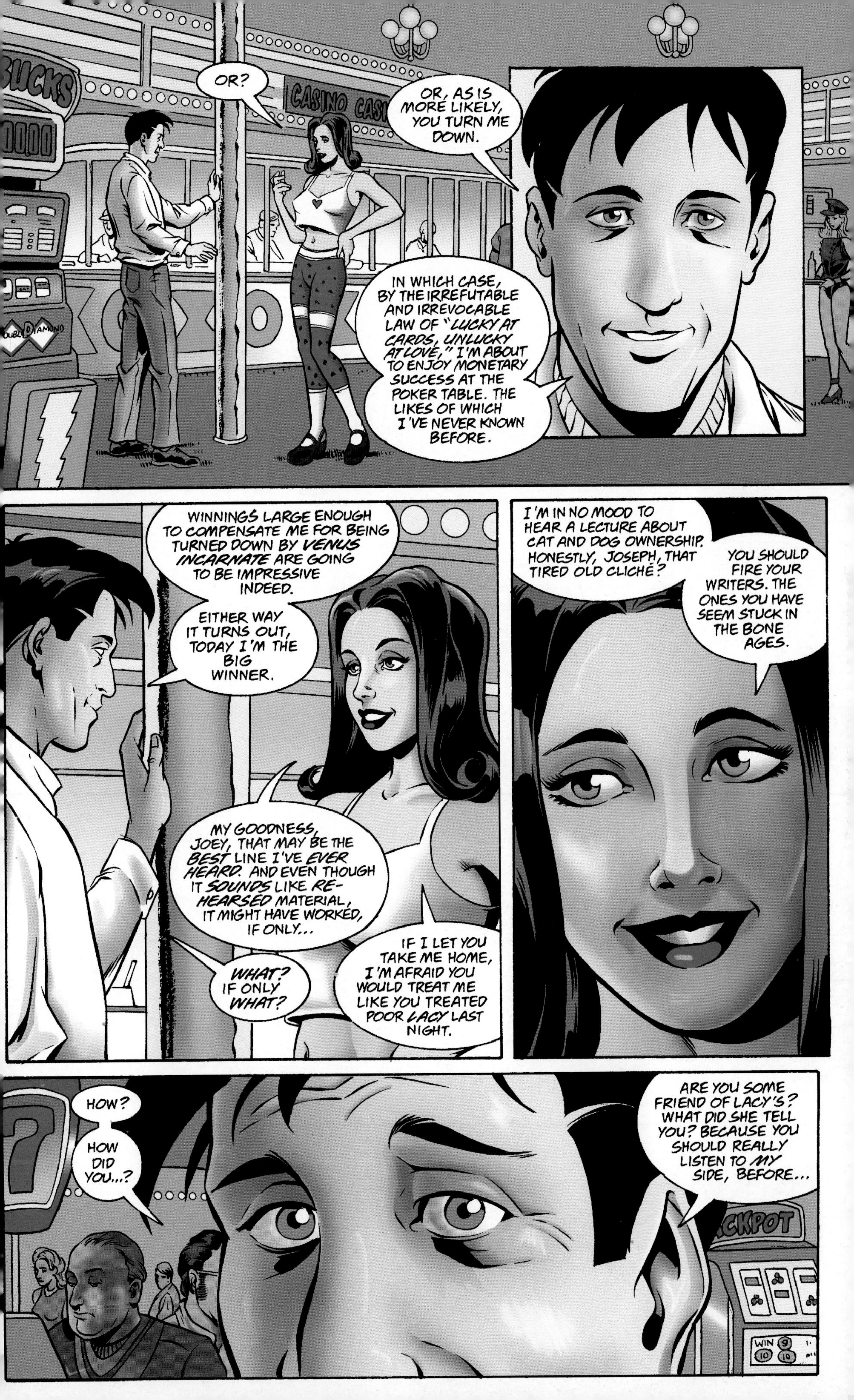
BUCKS
CASINO CASI
OR?
OR, AS IS MORE LIKELY, YOU TURN ME DOWN.
IN WHICH CASE, BY THE IRREFUTABLE AND IRREVOCABLE LAW OF "LUCKY AT CARDS, UNLUCKY AT LOVE," I'M ABOUT TO ENJOY MONETARY SUCCESS AT THE POKER TABLE. THE LIKES OF WHICH I'VE NEVER KNOWN BEFORE.
WINNINGS LARGE ENOUGH TO COMPENSATE ME FOR BEING TURNED DOWN BY VENUS INCARNATE ARE GOING TO BE IMPRESSIVE INDEED.
EITHER WAY IT TURNS OUT, TODAY I'M THE BIG WINNER.
MY GOODNESS, JOEY, THAT MAY BE THE BEST LINE I'VE EVER HEARD. AND EVEN THOUGH IT SOUNDS LIKE RE-HEARSED MATERIAL, IT MIGHT HAVE WORKED, IF ONLY...
WHAT? IF ONLY WHAT?
IF I LET YOU TAKE ME HOME, I'M AFRAID YOU WOULD TREAT ME LIKE YOU TREATED POOR LACY LAST NIGHT.
I'M IN NO MOOD TO HEAR A LECTURE ABOUT CAT AND DOG OWNERSHIP. HONESTLY, JOSEPH, THAT TIRED OLD CLICHÉ?
YOU SHOULD FIRE YOUR WRITERS. THE ONES YOU HAVE SEEM STUCK IN THE BONE AGES.
HOW?
HOW DID YOU...?
ARE YOU SOME FRIEND OF LACY'S? WHAT DID SHE TELL YOU? BECAUSE YOU SHOULD REALLY LISTEN TO MY SIDE, BEFORE...
ACKPOT
WIN

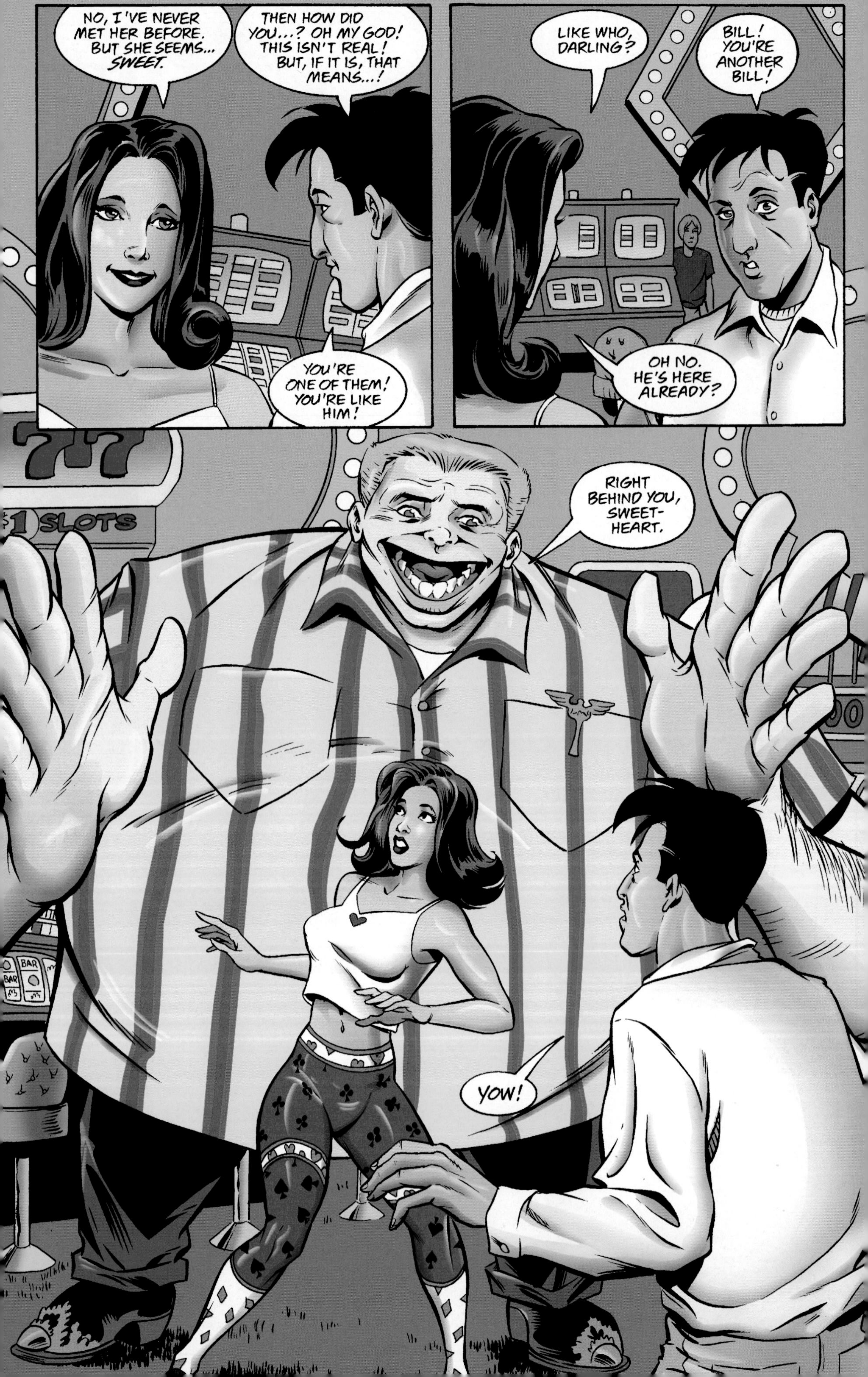
NO, I'VE NEVER MET HER BEFORE. BUT SHE SEEMS... SWEET.
THEN HOW DID YOU...? OH MY GOD! THIS ISN'T REAL! BUT, IF IT IS, THAT MEANS...!
YOU'RE ONE OF THEM! YOU'RE LIKE HIM!
LIKE WHO, DARLING?
BILL! YOU'RE ANOTHER BILL!
OH NO. HE'S HERE ALREADY?
777
$1 SLOTS
RIGHT BEHIND YOU, SWEET-HEART.
BAR
BAR
YOW!

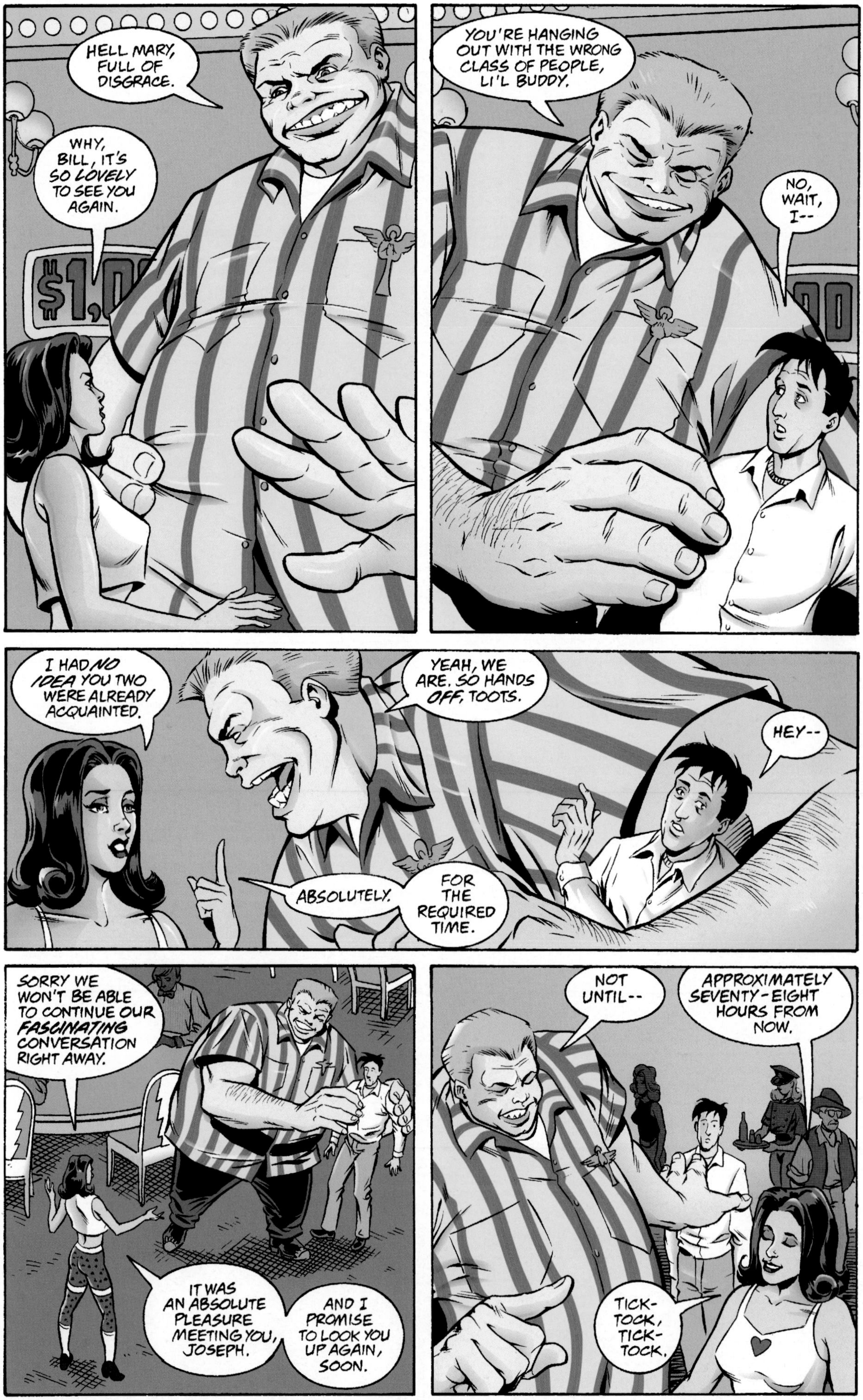
HELL MARY, FULL OF DISGRACE.
WHY, BILL, IT'S SO LOVELY TO SEE YOU AGAIN.
YOU'RE HANGING OUT WITH THE WRONG CLASS OF PEOPLE, LI'L BUDDY.
NO, WAIT, I--
I HAD NO IDEA YOU TWO WERE ALREADY ACQUAINTED.
YEAH, WE ARE. SO HANDS OFF, TOOTS.
HEY--
ABSOLUTELY.
FOR THE REQUIRED TIME.
SORRY WE WON'T BE ABLE TO CONTINUE OUR FASCINATING CONVERSATION RIGHT AWAY.
IT WAS AN ABSOLUTE PLEASURE MEETING YOU, JOSEPH.
AND I PROMISE TO LOOK YOU UP AGAIN, SOON.
NOT UNTIL--
APPROXIMATELY SEVENTY-EIGHT HOURS FROM NOW.
TICK-TOCK, TICK-TOCK.

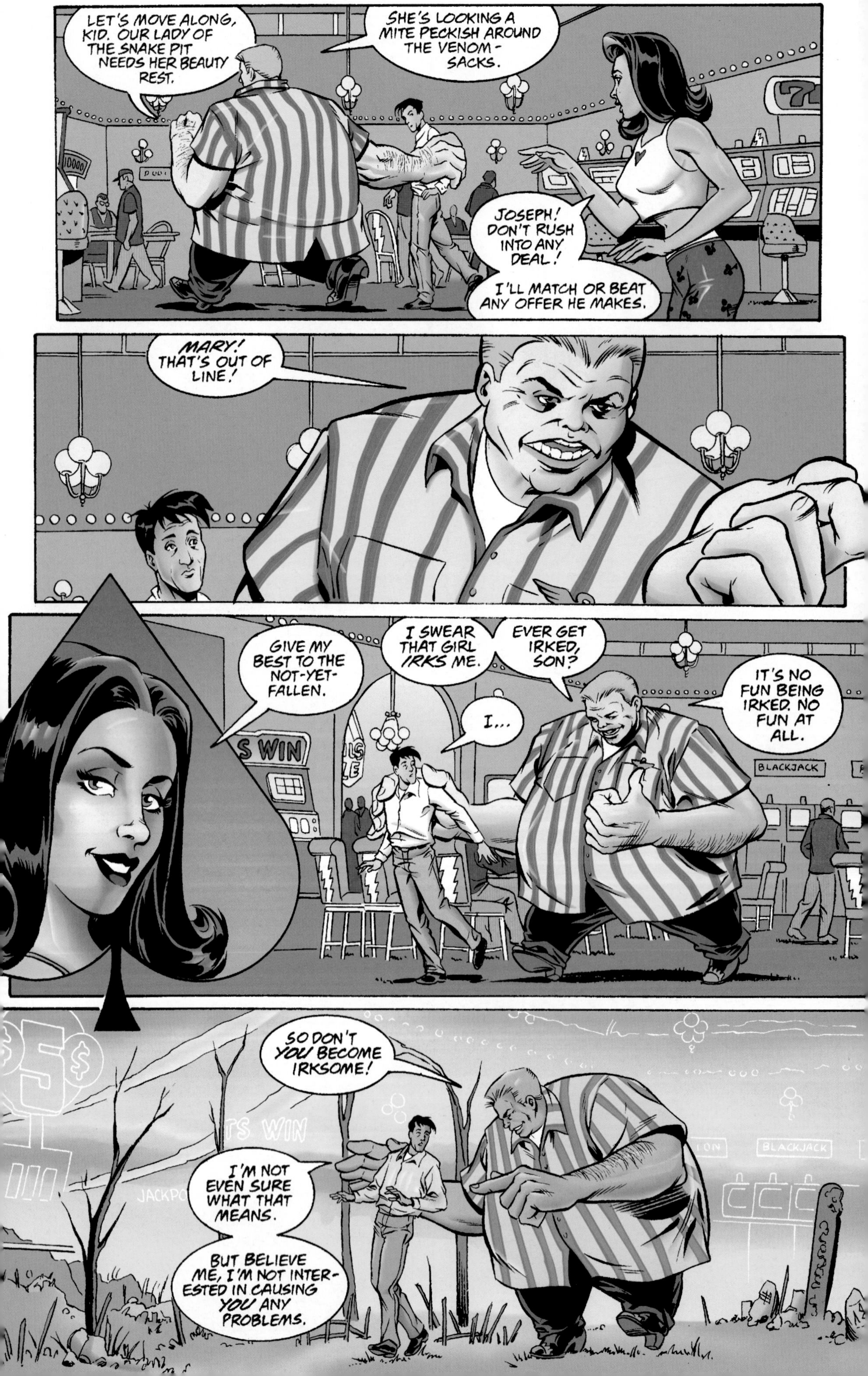
LET'S MOVE ALONG, KID. OUR LADY OF THE SNAKE PIT NEEDS HER BEAUTY REST.
SHE'S LOOKING A MITE PECKISH AROUND THE VENOM-SACKS.
JOSEPH! DON'T RUSH INTO ANY DEAL!
I'LL MATCH OR BEAT ANY OFFER HE MAKES.
MARY! THAT'S OUT OF LINE!
GIVE MY BEST TO THE NOT-YET-FALLEN.
I SWEAR THAT GIRL IRKS ME.
EVER GET IRKED, SON?
I...
IT'S NO FUN BEING IRKED. NO FUN AT ALL.
S WIN
BLACKJACK
SO DON'T YOU BECOME IRKSOME!
I'M NOT EVEN SURE WHAT THAT MEANS.
BUT BELIEVE ME, I'M NOT INTERESTED IN CAUSING YOU ANY PROBLEMS.
BLACKJACK

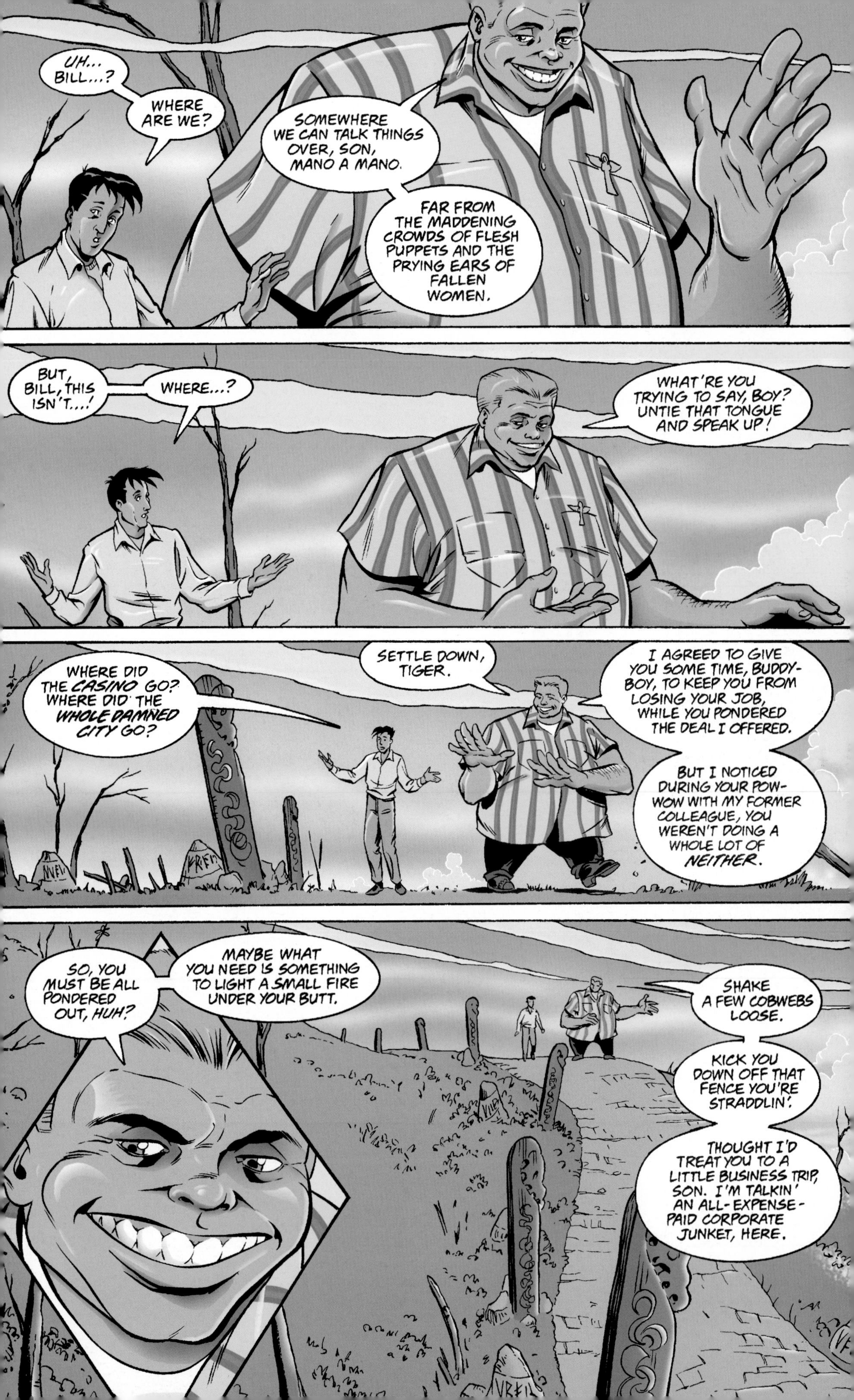
UH... BILL...?
WHERE ARE WE?
SOMEWHERE WE CAN TALK THINGS OVER, SON, MANO A MANO.
FAR FROM THE MADDENING CROWDS OF FLESH PUPPETS AND THE PRYING EARS OF FALLEN WOMEN.
BUT, BILL, THIS ISN'T...!
WHERE...?
WHAT'RE YOU TRYING TO SAY, BOY? UNTIE THAT TONGUE AND SPEAK UP!
WHERE DID THE CASINO GO? WHERE DID THE WHOLE DAMNED CITY GO?
SETTLE DOWN, TIGER.
I AGREED TO GIVE YOU SOME TIME, BUDDY-BOY, TO KEEP YOU FROM LOSING YOUR JOB, WHILE YOU PONDERED THE DEAL I OFFERED.
BUT I NOTICED DURING YOUR POW-WOW WITH MY FORMER COLLEAGUE, YOU WEREN'T DOING A WHOLE LOT OF NEITHER.
SO, YOU MUST BE ALL PONDERED OUT, HUH?
MAYBE WHAT YOU NEED IS SOMETHING TO LIGHT A SMALL FIRE UNDER YOUR BUTT.
SHAKE A FEW COBWEBS LOOSE.
KICK YOU DOWN OFF THAT FENCE YOU'RE STRADDLIN'.
THOUGHT I'D TREAT YOU TO A LITTLE BUSINESS TRIP, SON. I'M TALKIN' AN ALL-EXPENSE-PAID CORPORATE JUNKET, HERE.

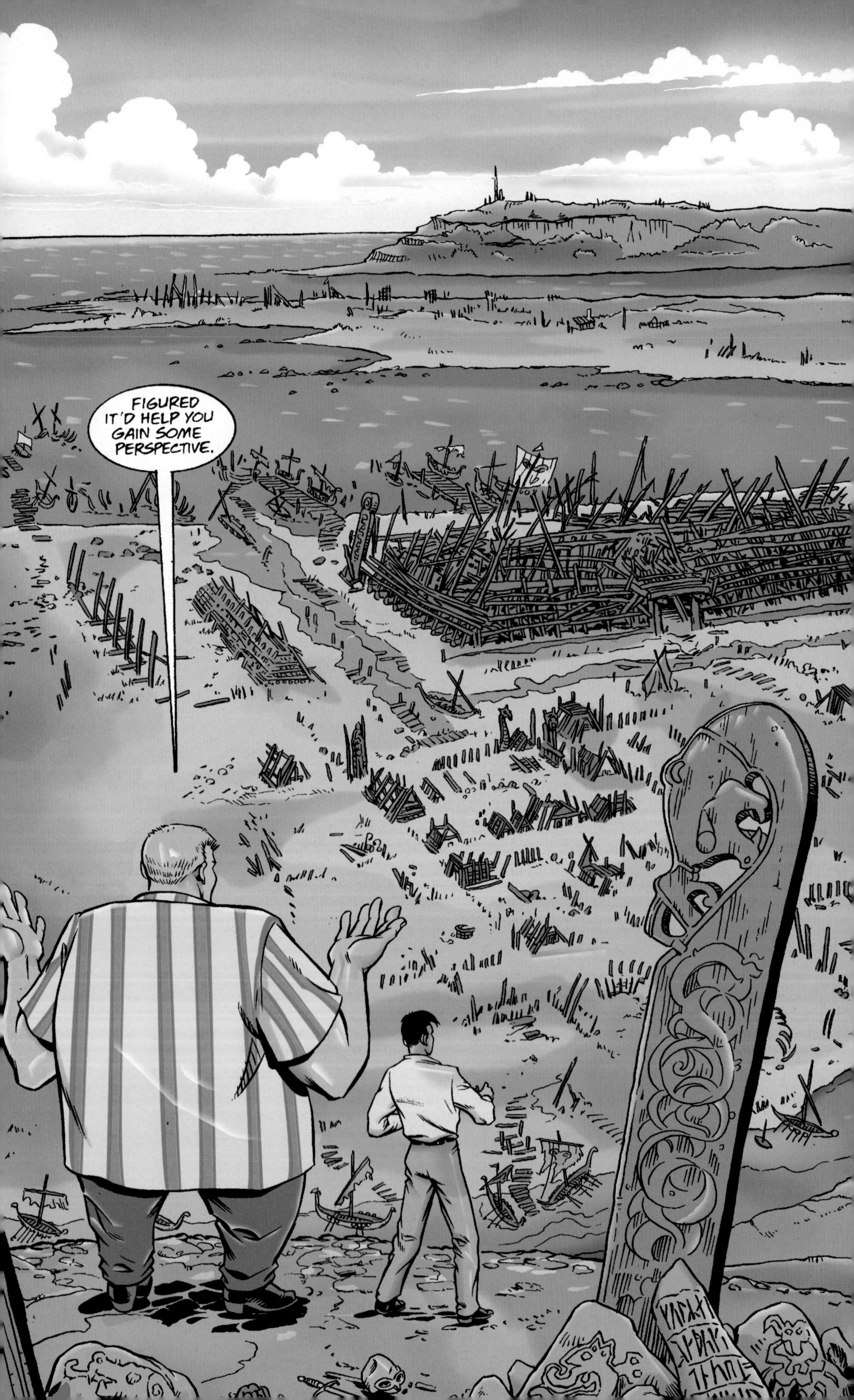
FIGURED IT'D HELP YOU GAIN SOME PERSPECTIVE.

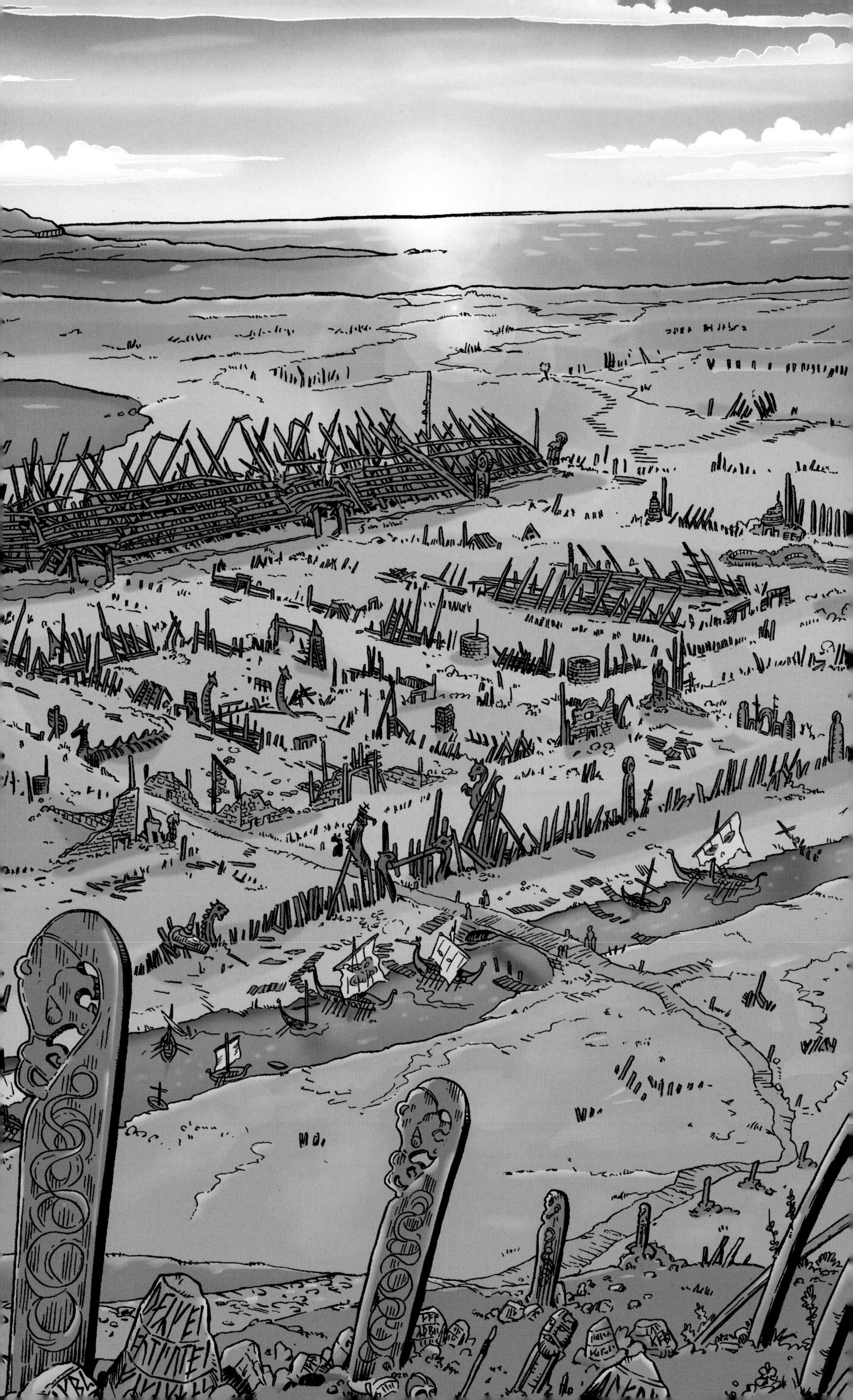

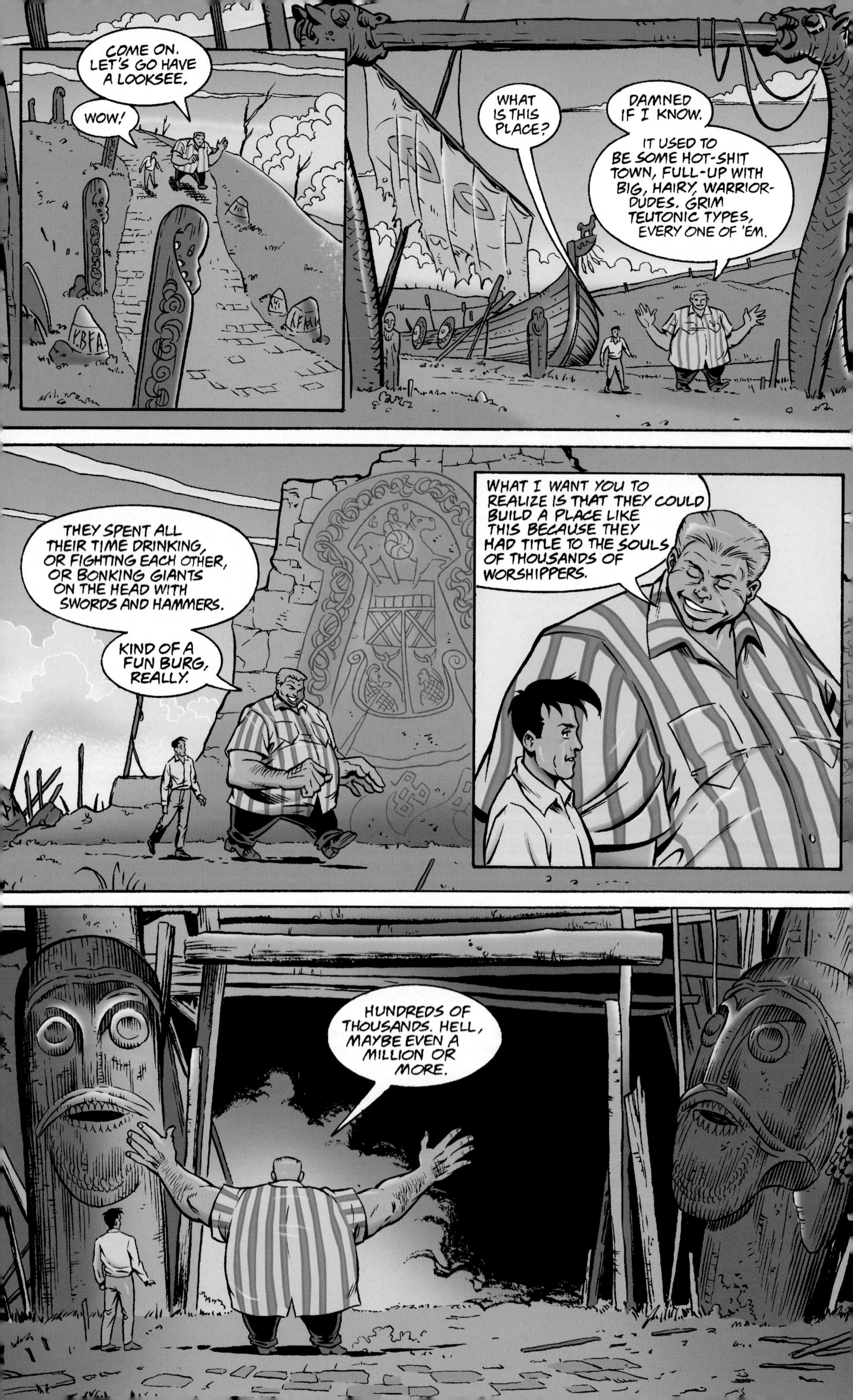
COME ON. LET'S GO HAVE A LOOKSEE.
WOW!
WHAT IS THIS PLACE?
DAMNED IF I KNOW.
IT USED TO BE SOME HOT-SHIT TOWN, FULL-UP WITH BIG, HAIRY, WARRIOR-DUDES. GRIM TEUTONIC TYPES, EVERY ONE OF 'EM.
THEY SPENT ALL THEIR TIME DRINKING, OR FIGHTING EACH OTHER, OR BONKING GIANTS ON THE HEAD WITH SWORDS AND HAMMERS.
KIND OF A FUN BURG, REALLY.
WHAT I WANT YOU TO REALIZE IS THAT THEY COULD BUILD A PLACE LIKE THIS BECAUSE THEY HAD TITLE TO THE SOULS OF THOUSANDS OF WORSHIPPERS.
HUNDREDS OF THOUSANDS. HELL, MAYBE EVEN A MILLION OR MORE.

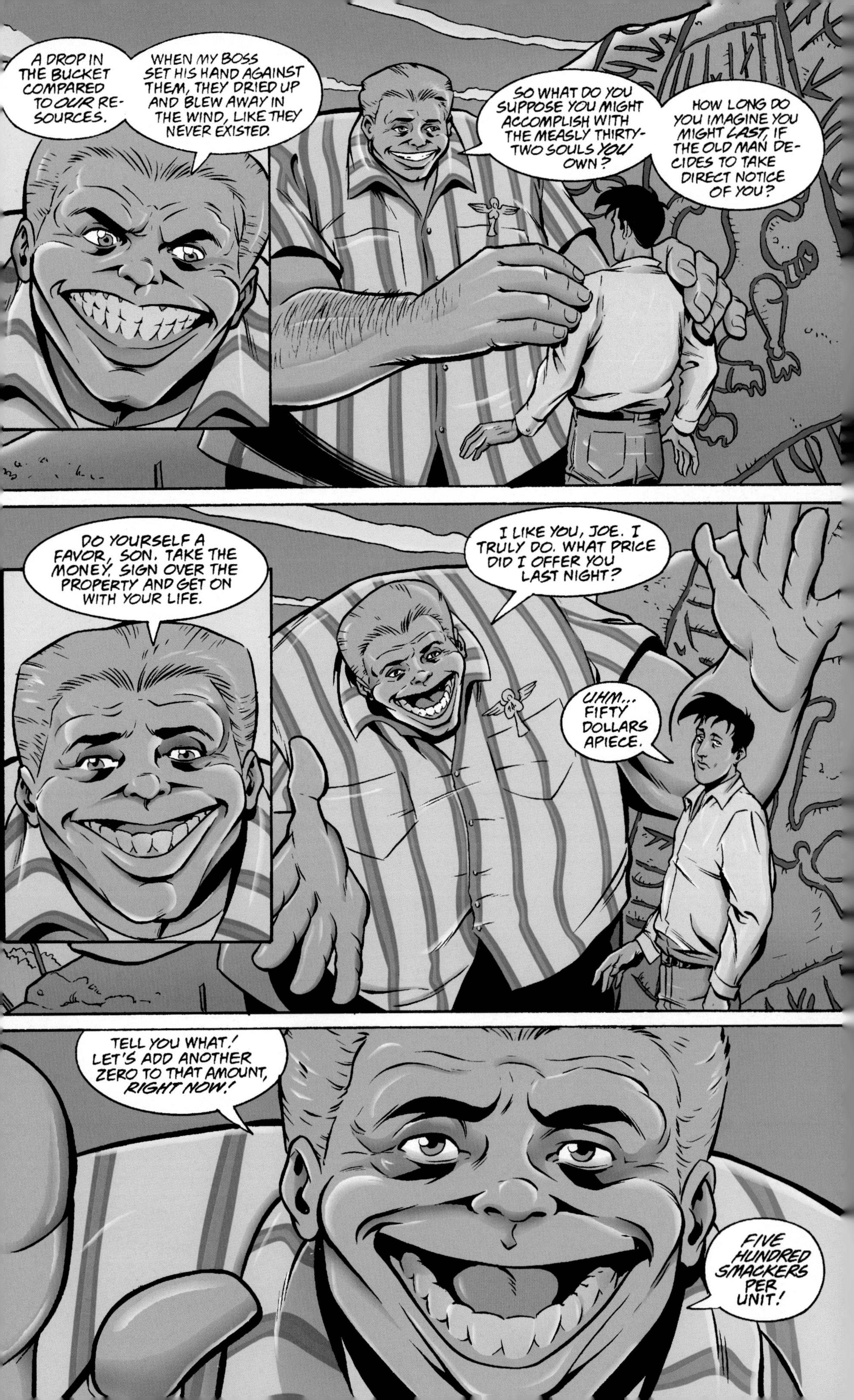
A DROP IN THE BUCKET COMPARED TO OUR RESOURCES.
WHEN MY BOSS SET HIS HAND AGAINST THEM, THEY DRIED UP AND BLEW AWAY IN THE WIND, LIKE THEY NEVER EXISTED.
SO WHAT DO YOU SUPPOSE YOU MIGHT ACCOMPLISH WITH THE MEASLY THIRTY-TWO SOULS YOU OWN?
HOW LONG DO YOU IMAGINE YOU MIGHT LAST, IF THE OLD MAN DECIDES TO TAKE DIRECT NOTICE OF YOU?
DO YOURSELF A FAVOR, SON. TAKE THE MONEY, SIGN OVER THE PROPERTY AND GET ON WITH YOUR LIFE.
I LIKE YOU, JOE. I TRULY DO. WHAT PRICE DID I OFFER YOU LAST NIGHT?
UHM... FIFTY DOLLARS APIECE.
TELL YOU WHAT! LET'S ADD ANOTHER ZERO TO THAT AMOUNT, RIGHT NOW!
FIVE HUNDRED SMACKERS PER UNIT!

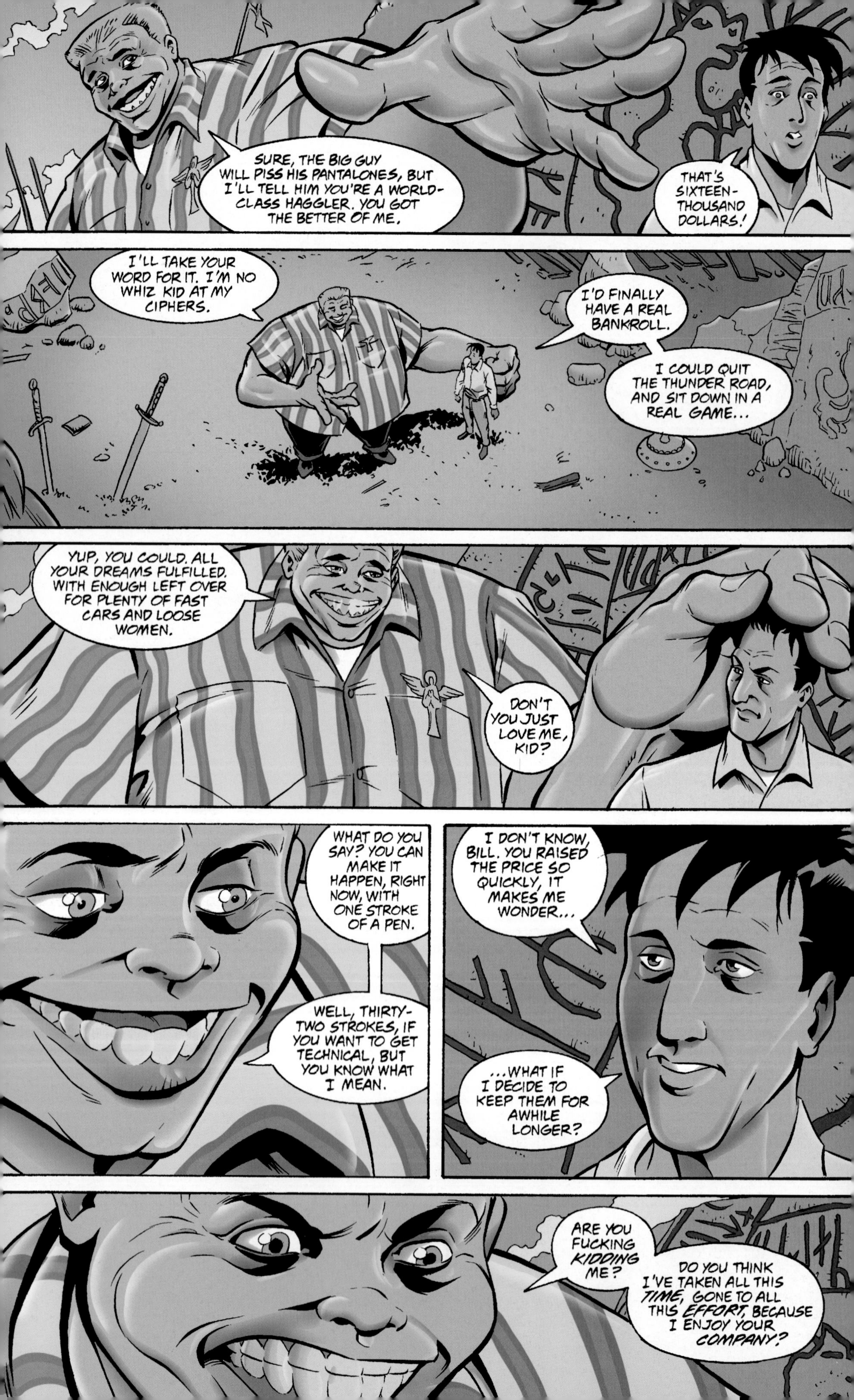
SURE, THE BIG GUY WILL PISS HIS PANTALONES, BUT I'LL TELL HIM YOU'RE A WORLD-CLASS HAGGLER. YOU GOT THE BETTER OF ME.
THAT'S SIXTEEN-THOUSAND DOLLARS!
I'LL TAKE YOUR WORD FOR IT. I'M NO WHIZ KID AT MY CIPHERS.
I'D FINALLY HAVE A REAL BANKROLL.
I COULD QUIT THE THUNDER ROAD, AND SIT DOWN IN A REAL GAME...
YUP, YOU COULD. ALL YOUR DREAMS FULFILLED. WITH ENOUGH LEFT OVER FOR PLENTY OF FAST CARS AND LOOSE WOMEN.
DON'T YOU JUST LOVE ME, KID?
WHAT DO YOU SAY? YOU CAN MAKE IT HAPPEN, RIGHT NOW, WITH ONE STROKE OF A PEN.
WELL, THIRTY-TWO STROKES, IF YOU WANT TO GET TECHNICAL, BUT YOU KNOW WHAT I MEAN.
I DON'T KNOW, BILL. YOU RAISED THE PRICE SO QUICKLY, IT MAKES ME WONDER...
...WHAT IF I DECIDE TO KEEP THEM FOR AWHILE LONGER?
ARE YOU FUCKING *KIDDING* ME?
DO YOU THINK I'VE TAKEN ALL THIS *TIME*, GONE TO ALL THIS *EFFORT*, BECAUSE I ENJOY YOUR *COMPANY*?

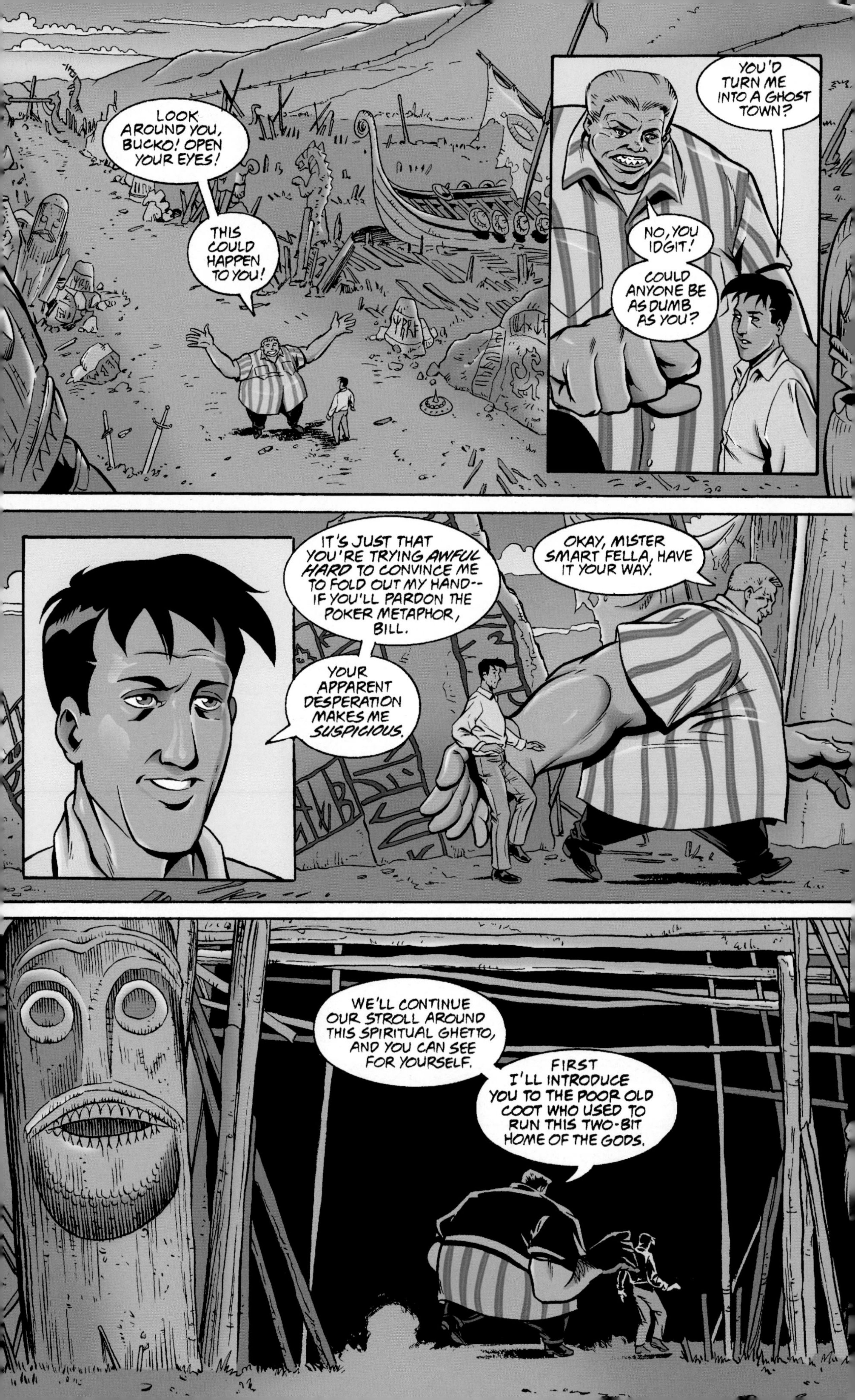
LOOK AROUND YOU, BUCKO! OPEN YOUR EYES!
THIS COULD HAPPEN TO YOU!
YOU'D TURN ME INTO A GHOST TOWN?
NO, YOU IDGIT!
COULD ANYONE BE AS DUMB AS YOU?
IT'S JUST THAT YOU'RE TRYING *AWFUL HARD* TO CONVINCE ME TO FOLD OUT MY HAND--IF YOU'LL PARDON THE POKER METAPHOR, BILL.
YOUR APPARENT DESPERATION MAKES ME *SUSPICIOUS.*
OKAY, MISTER SMART FELLA, HAVE IT YOUR WAY.
WE'LL CONTINUE OUR STROLL AROUND THIS SPIRITUAL GHETTO, AND YOU CAN SEE FOR YOURSELF.
FIRST I'LL INTRODUCE YOU TO THE POOR OLD COOT WHO USED TO RUN THIS TWO-BIT HOME OF THE GODS.

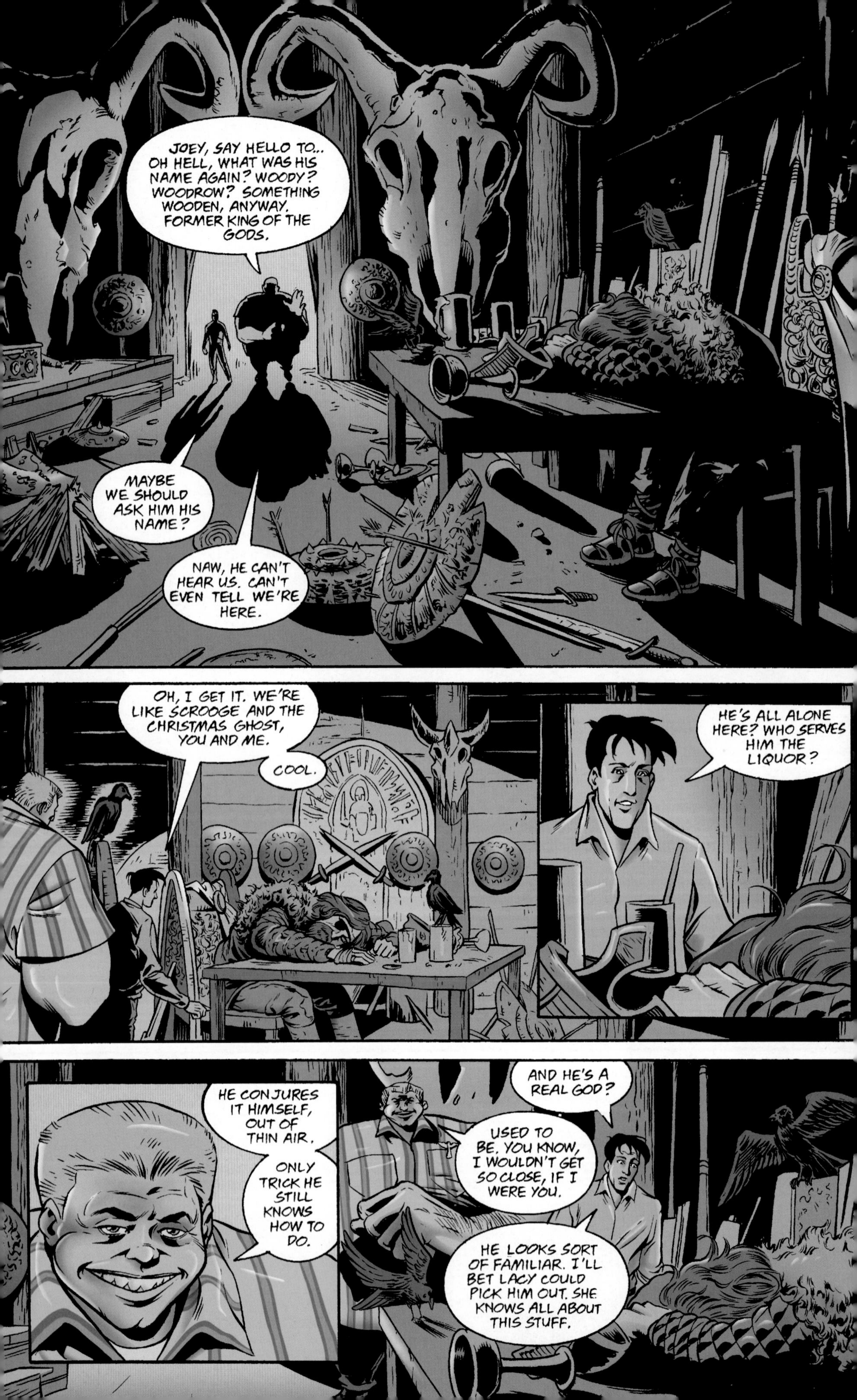
JOEY, SAY HELLO TO... OH HELL, WHAT WAS HIS NAME AGAIN? WOODY? WOODROW? SOMETHING WOODEN, ANYWAY. FORMER KING OF THE GODS.
MAYBE WE SHOULD ASK HIM HIS NAME?
NAW, HE CAN'T HEAR US. CAN'T EVEN TELL WE'RE HERE.
OH, I GET IT. WE'RE LIKE SCROOGE AND THE CHRISTMAS GHOST, YOU AND ME.
COOL.
HE'S ALL ALONE HERE? WHO SERVES HIM THE LIQUOR?
HE CONJURES IT HIMSELF, OUT OF THIN AIR.
ONLY TRICK HE STILL KNOWS HOW TO DO.
AND HE'S A REAL GOD?
USED TO BE. YOU KNOW, I WOULDN'T GET SO CLOSE, IF I WERE YOU.
HE LOOKS SORT OF FAMILIAR. I'LL BET LACY COULD PICK HIM OUT. SHE KNOWS ALL ABOUT THIS STUFF.

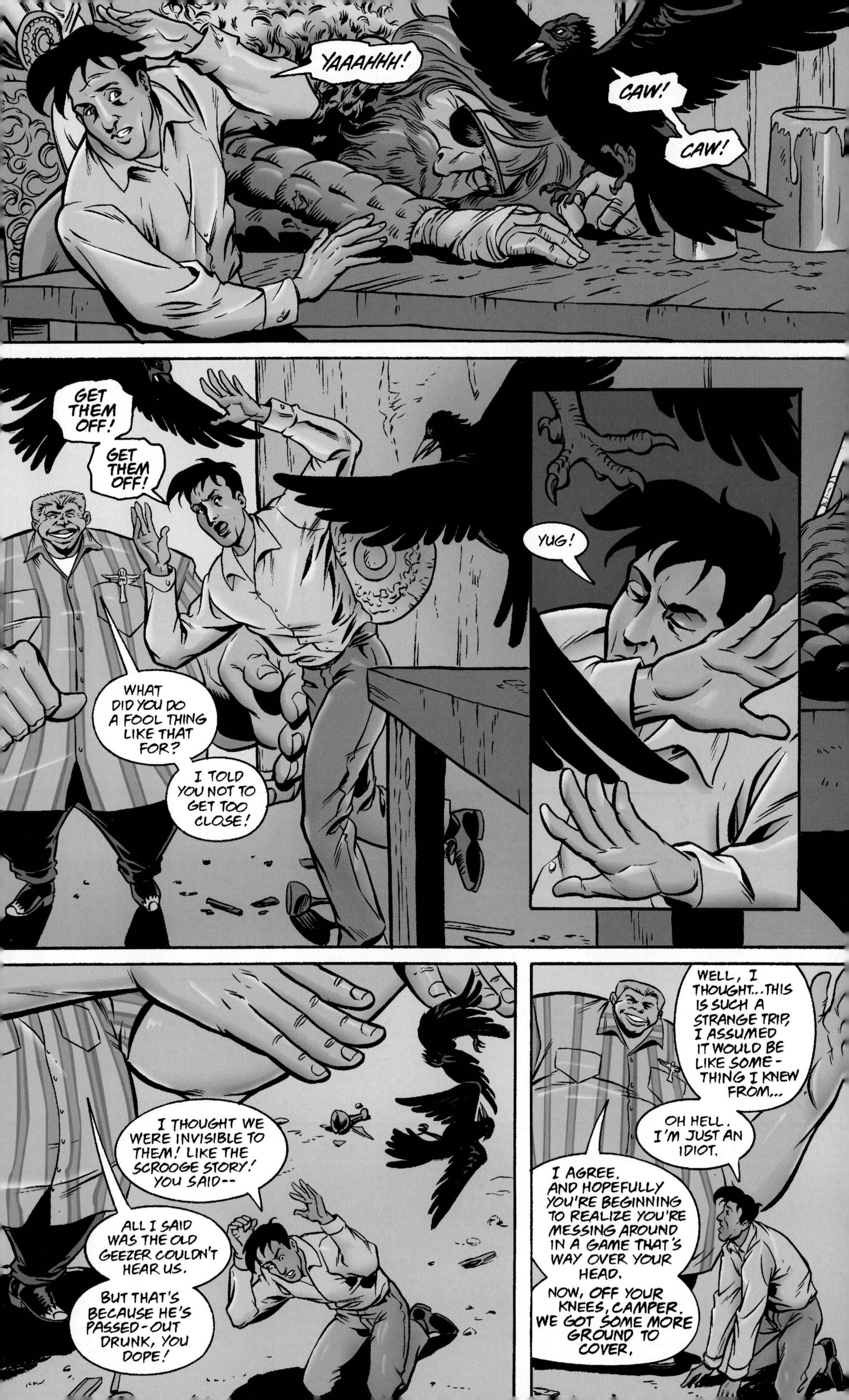
YAAAHHH!
CAW!
CAW!
GET THEM OFF!
GET THEM OFF!
WHAT DID YOU DO A FOOL THING LIKE THAT FOR?
I TOLD YOU NOT TO GET TOO CLOSE!
YUG!
I THOUGHT WE WERE INVISIBLE TO THEM! LIKE THE SCROOGE STORY! YOU SAID--
ALL I SAID WAS THE OLD GEEZER COULDN'T HEAR US.
BUT THAT'S BECAUSE HE'S PASSED-OUT DRUNK, YOU DOPE!
WELL, I THOUGHT...THIS IS SUCH A STRANGE TRIP, I ASSUMED IT WOULD BE LIKE SOME-THING I KNEW FROM...
OH HELL. I'M JUST AN IDIOT.
I AGREE. AND HOPEFULLY YOU'RE BEGINNING TO REALIZE YOU'RE MESSING AROUND IN A GAME THAT'S WAY OVER YOUR HEAD.
NOW, OFF YOUR KNEES, CAMPER. WE GOT SOME MORE GROUND TO COVER.

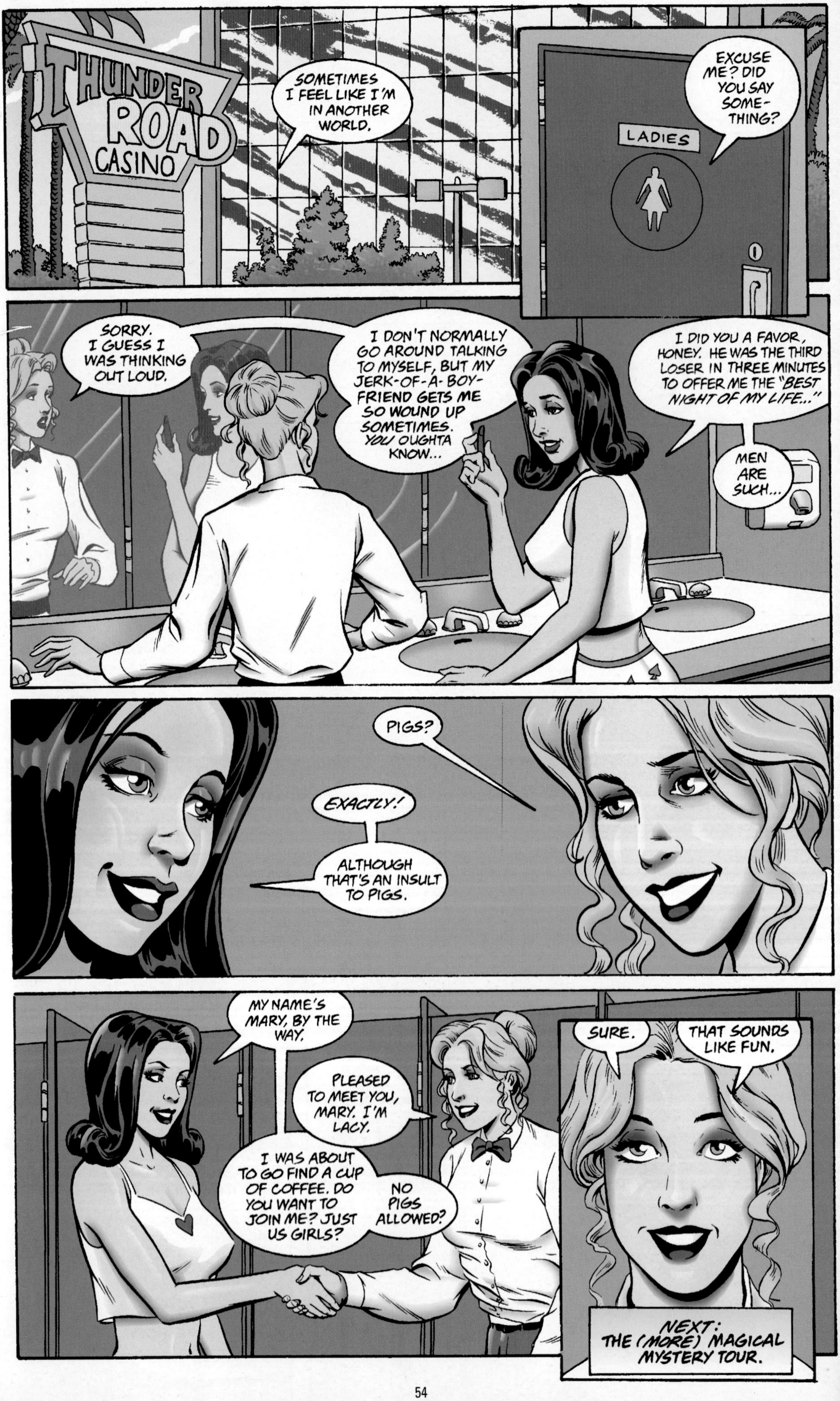
THUNDER ROAD CASINO
SOMETIMES I FEEL LIKE I'M IN ANOTHER WORLD.
LADIES
EXCUSE ME? DID YOU SAY SOME-THING?
SORRY. I GUESS I WAS THINKING OUT LOUD.
I DON'T NORMALLY GO AROUND TALKING TO MYSELF, BUT MY JERK-OF-A-BOY-FRIEND GETS ME SO WOUND UP SOMETIMES. YOU OUGHTA KNOW...
I DID YOU A FAVOR, HONEY. HE WAS THE THIRD LOSER IN THREE MINUTES TO OFFER ME THE "BEST NIGHT OF MY LIFE..."
MEN ARE SUCH...
PIGS?
EXACTLY!
ALTHOUGH THAT'S AN INSULT TO PIGS.
MY NAME'S MARY, BY THE WAY.
PLEASED TO MEET YOU, MARY. I'M LACY.
I WAS ABOUT TO GO FIND A CUP OF COFFEE. DO YOU WANT TO JOIN ME? JUST US GIRLS?
NO PIGS ALLOWED?
SURE.
THAT SOUNDS LIKE FUN.
NEXT: THE (MORE) MAGICAL MYSTERY TOUR.

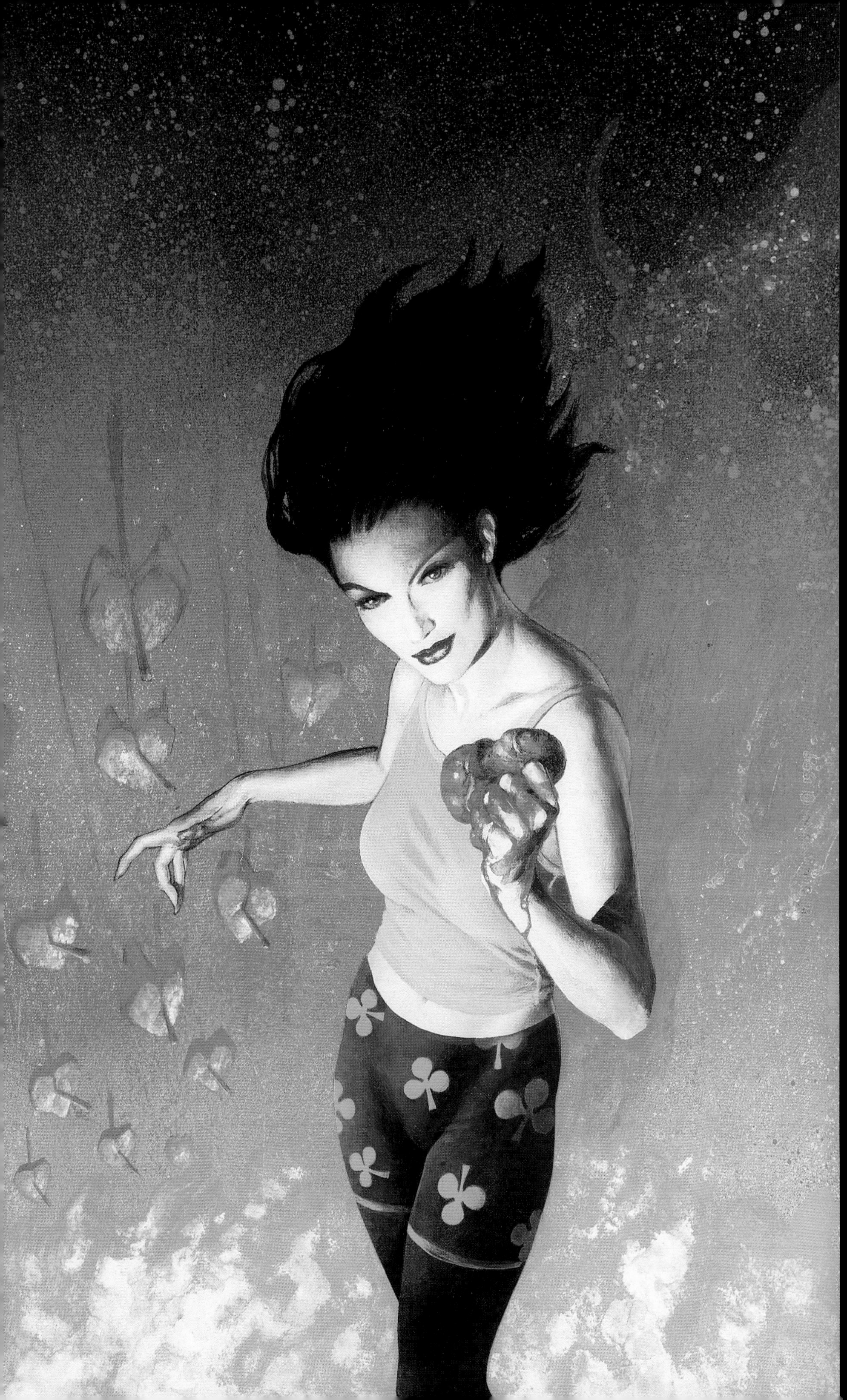

THE STORY SO FAR: IN THE COMPANY OF BILL, THE ANGEL OF THE LORD, JOEY BEGAN A TOUR OF STRANGE OTHER LANDS, FAR FROM ANY PART OF OUR OWN WORLD. BILL'S JOB IS TO FORCE JOEY TO SIGN OVER HIS THIRTY-TWO SOULS BY SHOWING HIM WHAT HAPPENS TO THOSE WHO GO AGAINST THE WISHES OF HIS HEAVENLY BOSSES. MEANWHILE, HELL MARY, AN AGENT OF THE INFERNAL REALM, AND BILL'S DIRECT COUNTERPART IN THIS ASSIGNMENT, HAS ENTERED THE SCENE. THE CELESTIAL RULES OF ENGAGEMENT REQUIRE THAT SHE LET BILL HAVE AN UNHINDERED FIRST SHOT AT THEIR QUARRY. BUT THE HOURS ARE PASSING EVER CLOSER TO THE TIME WHEN SHE, TOO, CAN HAVE HER CHANCE TO WIN, STEAL OR BUY JOEY'S SMALL TREASURE OF CONTRABAND SOULS. AND WHILE HELL MARY WAITS HER TURN, SHE GETS "CHUMMY" WITH JOEY'S (EX?) GIRLFRIEND...

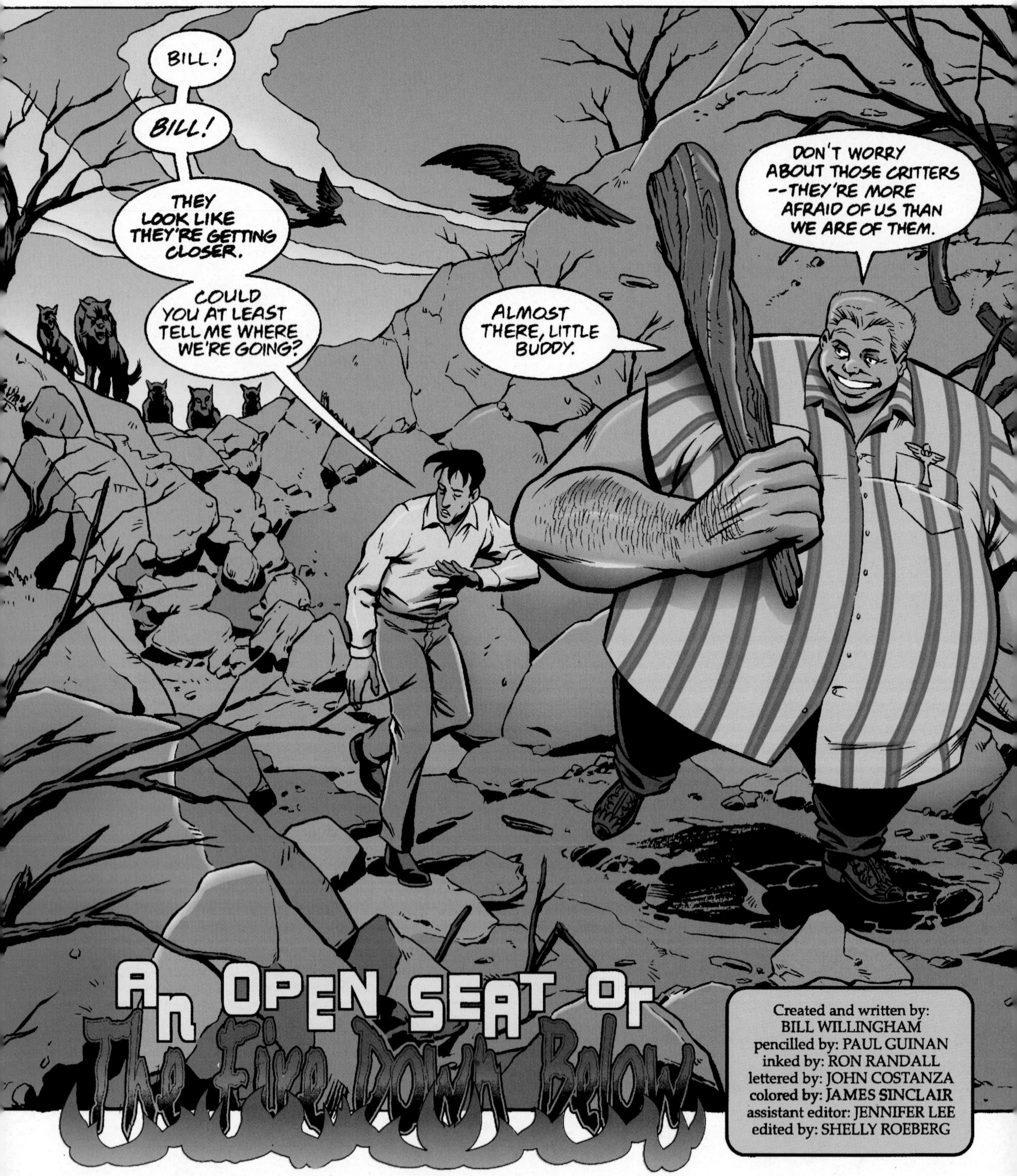
BILL!
BILL!
THEY LOOK LIKE THEY'RE GETTING CLOSER.
COULD YOU AT LEAST TELL ME WHERE WE'RE GOING?
ALMOST THERE, LITTLE BUDDY.
DON'T WORRY ABOUT THOSE CRITTERS --THEY'RE MORE AFRAID OF US THAN WE ARE OF THEM.
An OPEN SEAT or
The Fire Down Below
Created and written by: BILL WILLINGHAM
pencilled by: PAUL GUINAN
inked by: RON RANDALL
lettered by: JOHN COSTANZA
colored by: JAMES SINCLAIR
assistant editor: JENNIFER LEE
edited by: SHELLY ROEBERG

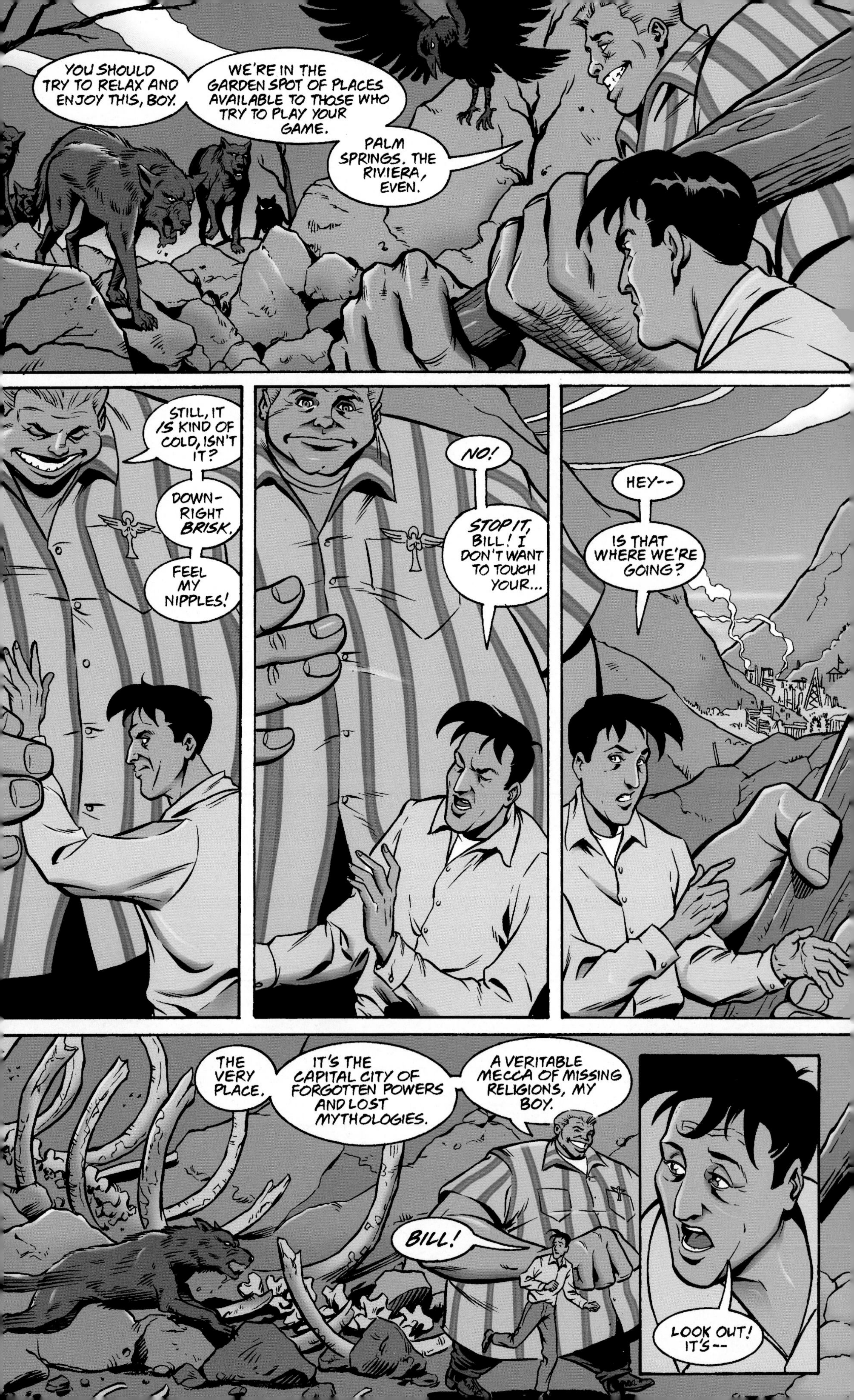
YOU SHOULD TRY TO RELAX AND ENJOY THIS, BOY.
WE'RE IN THE GARDEN SPOT OF PLACES AVAILABLE TO THOSE WHO TRY TO PLAY YOUR GAME.
PALM SPRINGS. THE RIVIERA, EVEN.
STILL, IT IS KIND OF COLD, ISN'T IT?
DOWN-RIGHT BRISK.
FEEL MY NIPPLES!
NO!
STOP IT, BILL! I DON'T WANT TO TOUCH YOUR...
HEY--
IS THAT WHERE WE'RE GOING?
THE VERY PLACE.
IT'S THE CAPITAL CITY OF FORGOTTEN POWERS AND LOST MYTHOLOGIES.
A VERITABLE MECCA OF MISSING RELIGIONS, MY BOY.
BILL!
LOOK OUT! IT'S--

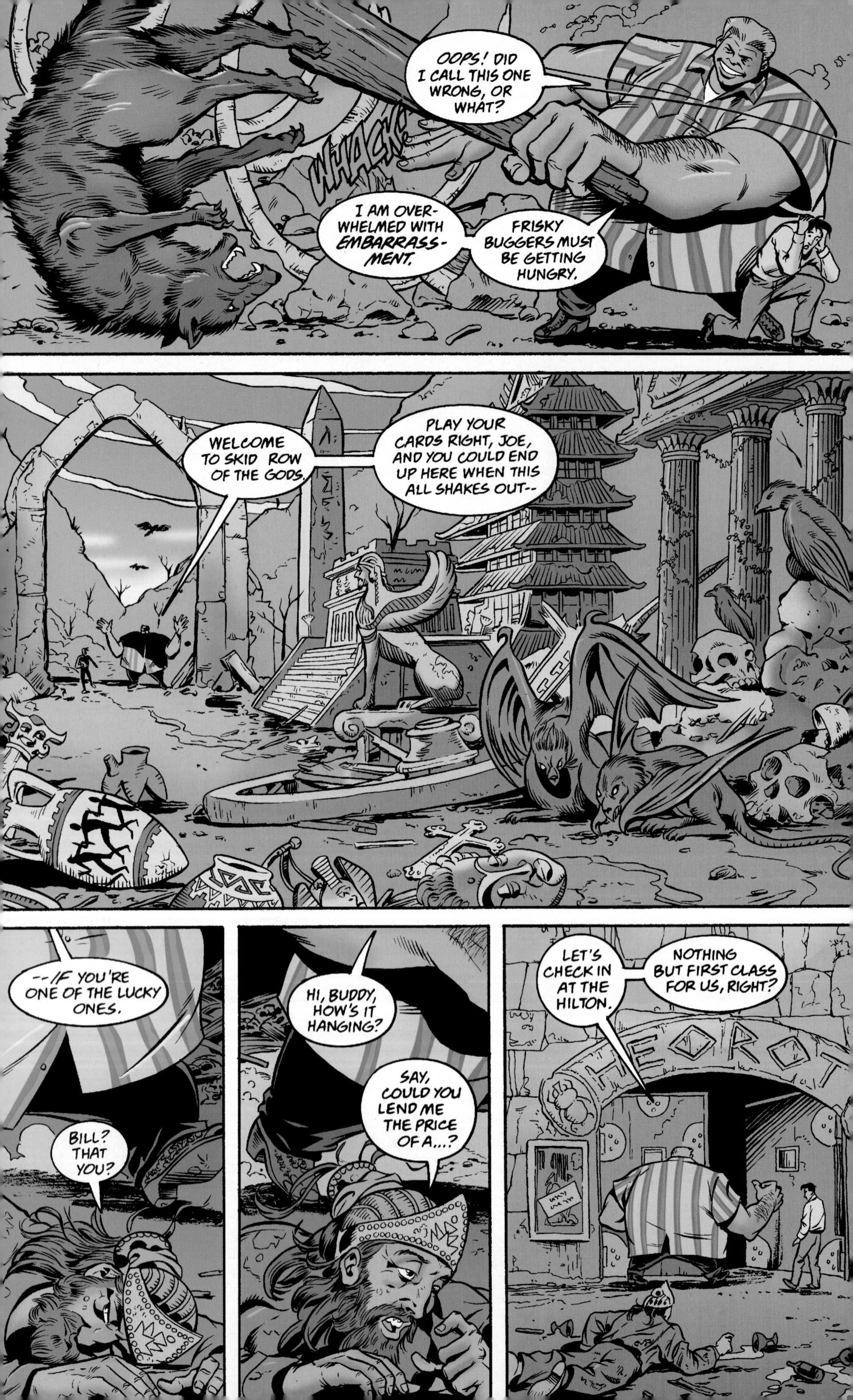
OOPS! DID I CALL THIS ONE WRONG, OR WHAT?
WHACK!
I AM OVER-WHELMED WITH *EMBARRASS-MENT.*
FRISKY BUGGERS MUST BE GETTING HUNGRY.
WELCOME TO SKID ROW OF THE GODS.
PLAY YOUR CARDS RIGHT, JOE, AND YOU COULD END UP HERE WHEN THIS ALL SHAKES OUT--
--*IF* YOU'RE ONE OF THE LUCKY ONES.
BILL? THAT YOU?
HI, BUDDY, HOW'S IT HANGING?
SAY, COULD YOU LEND ME THE PRICE OF A...?
LET'S CHECK IN AT THE HILTON.
NOTHING BUT FIRST CLASS FOR US, RIGHT?
HEOROT

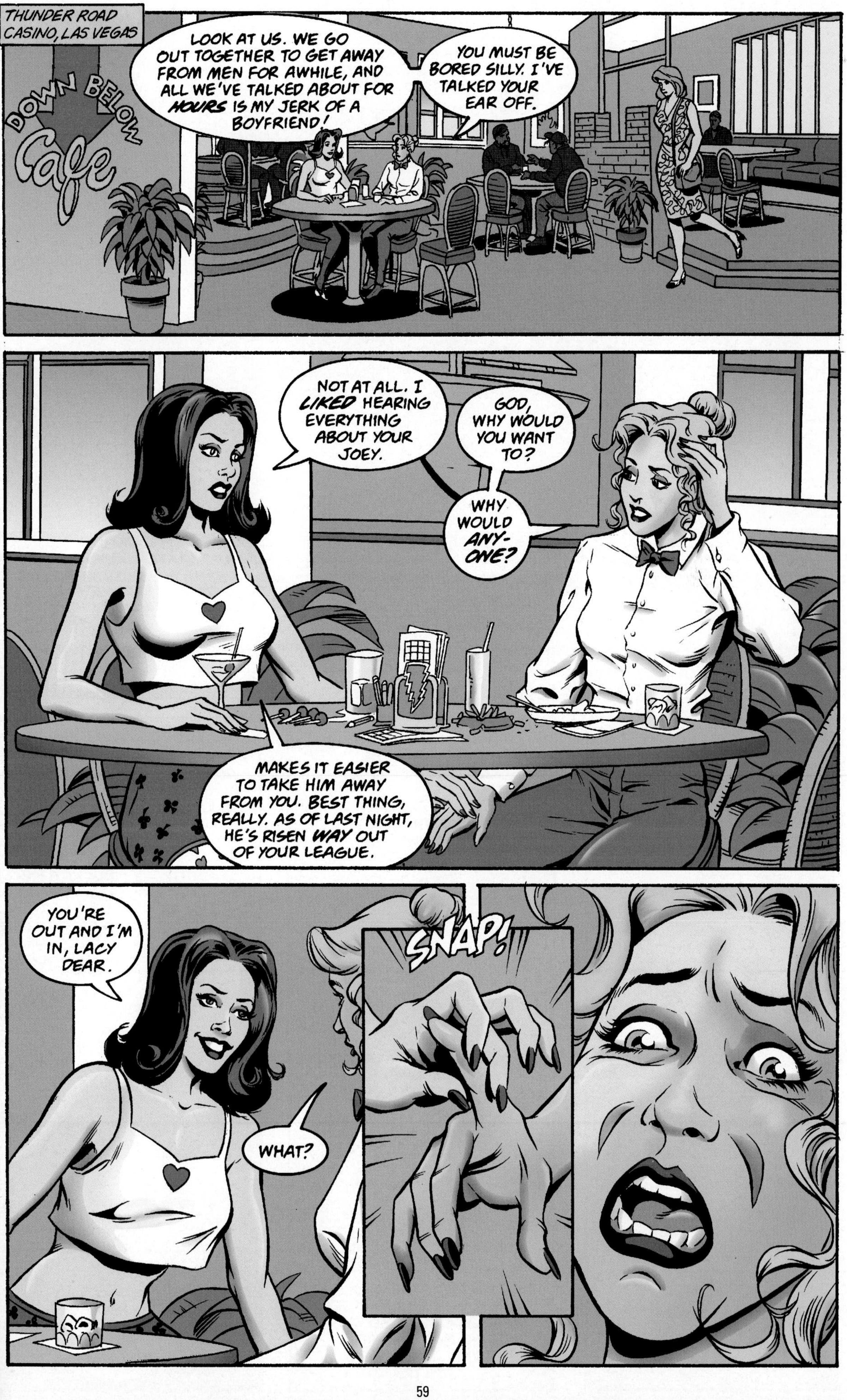
THUNDER ROAD CASINO, LAS VEGAS
DOWN BELOW Cafe
LOOK AT US. WE GO OUT TOGETHER TO GET AWAY FROM MEN FOR AWHILE, AND ALL WE'VE TALKED ABOUT FOR HOURS IS MY JERK OF A BOYFRIEND!
YOU MUST BE BORED SILLY. I'VE TALKED YOUR EAR OFF.
NOT AT ALL. I LIKED HEARING EVERYTHING ABOUT YOUR JOEY.
GOD, WHY WOULD YOU WANT TO?
WHY WOULD ANY-ONE?
MAKES IT EASIER TO TAKE HIM AWAY FROM YOU. BEST THING, REALLY. AS OF LAST NIGHT, HE'S RISEN WAY OUT OF YOUR LEAGUE.
YOU'RE OUT AND I'M IN, LACY DEAR.
WHAT?
SNAP!

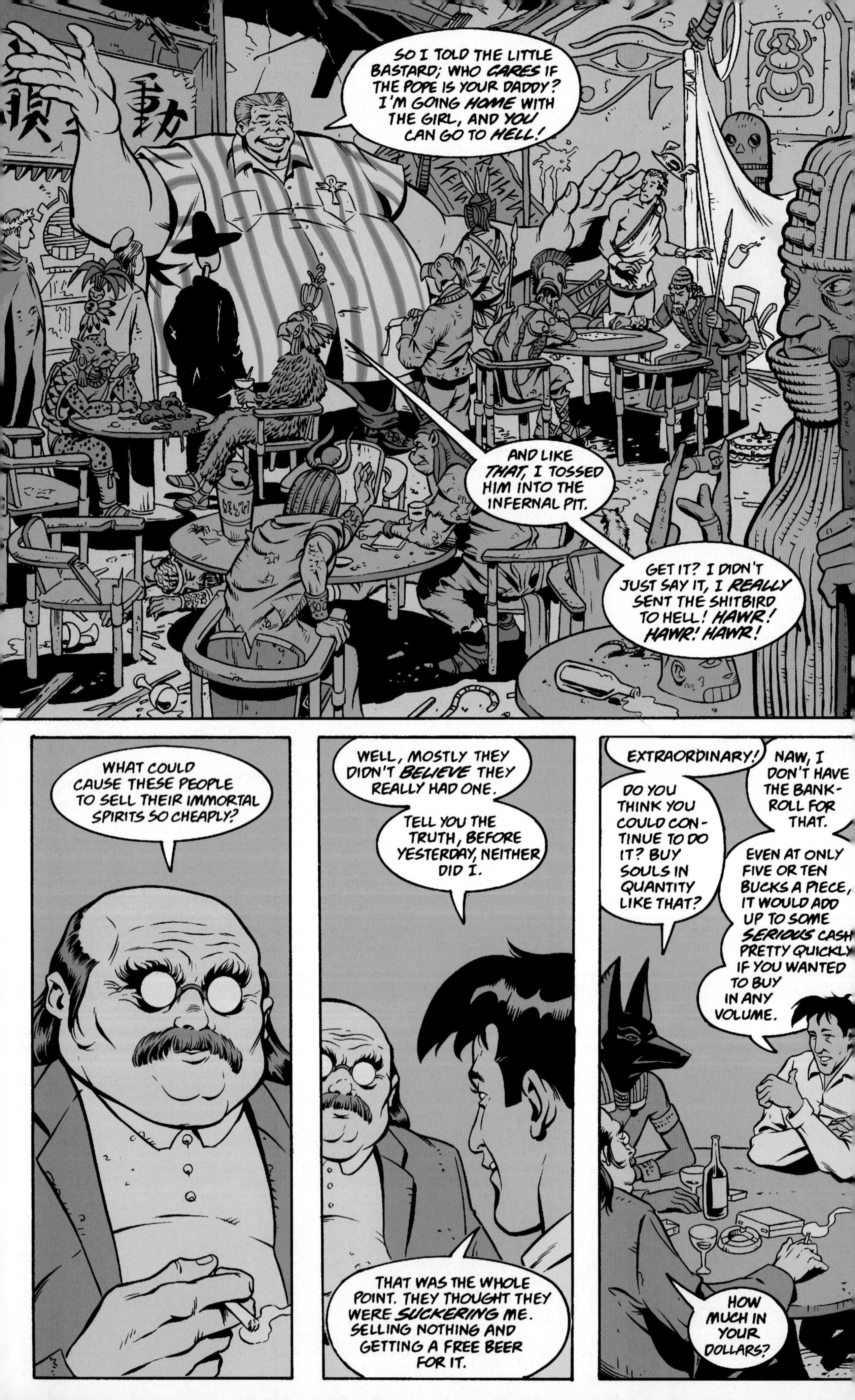
SO I TOLD THE LITTLE BASTARD; WHO *CARES* IF THE POPE IS YOUR DADDY? I'M GOING *HOME* WITH THE GIRL, AND *YOU* CAN GO TO *HELL*!
AND LIKE *THAT*, I TOSSED HIM INTO THE INFERNAL PIT.
GET IT? I DIDN'T JUST SAY IT, I *REALLY* SENT THE SHITBIRD TO HELL! *HAWR! HAWR! HAWR!*
WHAT COULD CAUSE THESE PEOPLE TO SELL THEIR IMMORTAL SPIRITS SO CHEAPLY?
WELL, MOSTLY THEY DIDN'T *BELIEVE* THEY REALLY HAD ONE.
TELL YOU THE TRUTH, BEFORE YESTERDAY, NEITHER DID I.
THAT WAS THE WHOLE POINT. THEY THOUGHT THEY WERE *SUCKERING ME*. SELLING NOTHING AND GETTING A FREE BEER FOR IT.
EXTRAORDINARY!
DO YOU THINK YOU COULD CON-TINUE TO DO IT? BUY SOULS IN QUANTITY LIKE THAT?
NAW, I DON'T HAVE THE BANK-ROLL FOR THAT.
EVEN AT ONLY FIVE OR TEN BUCKS A PIECE, IT WOULD ADD UP TO SOME *SERIOUS* CASH PRETTY QUICKLY IF YOU WANTED TO BUY IN ANY VOLUME.
HOW MUCH IN YOUR DOLLARS?

YOU ACTUALLY BOUGHT THE HUMAN SOULS FOR NO MORE THAN ONE BEER A PIECE? IN THE SPAN OF ONLY A FEW *HOURS?*

WELL, IT WAS JUST SUPPOSED TO BE A JOKE, BUT YEAH.

AMAZING... I HAD TO SPEND TERRIFIC EFFORT, CAREFULLY CULTIVATING EACH SOUL OVER THE SPAN OF THE SUBJECT'S *LIFETIME* IN ORDER TO REAP ITS BENEFIT.

WELL, YOU KNOW, A THOUSAND DOLLARS FOR A HUNDRED SOULS; TEN THOUSAND DOLLARS PER THOUSAND SOULS.

WHO'S GOT THAT KIND OF MONEY TO THROW AWAY?

WHAT?

WHY ARE YOU GRINNING LIKE THAT?

WHAT DID I SAY?

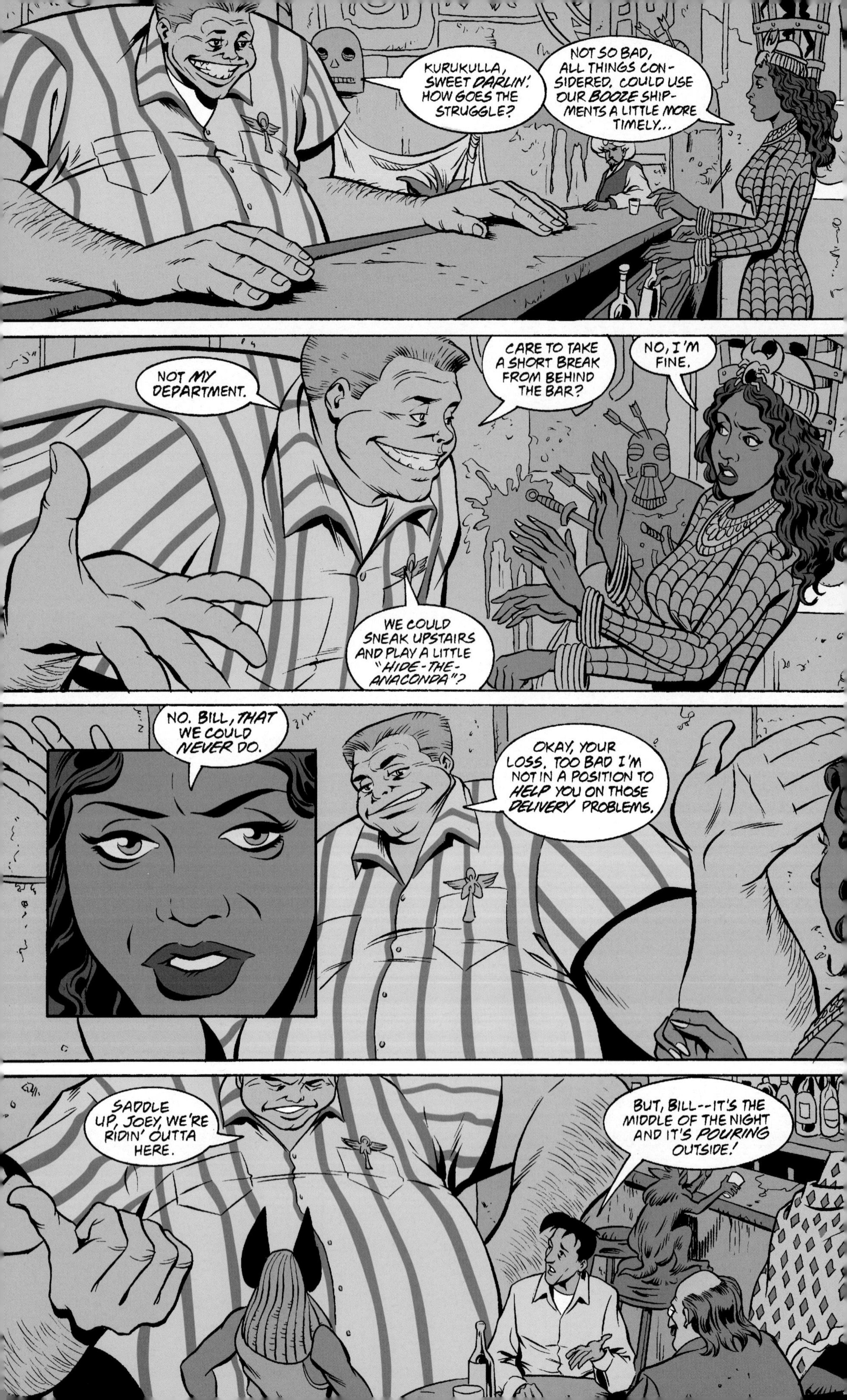
KURUKULLA, SWEET DARLIN'! HOW GOES THE STRUGGLE?
NOT SO BAD, ALL THINGS CONSIDERED. COULD USE OUR BOOZE SHIPMENTS A LITTLE MORE TIMELY...
NOT MY DEPARTMENT.
CARE TO TAKE A SHORT BREAK FROM BEHIND THE BAR?
NO, I'M FINE.
WE COULD SNEAK UPSTAIRS AND PLAY A LITTLE "HIDE-THE-ANACONDA"?
NO. BILL, THAT WE COULD NEVER DO.
OKAY, YOUR LOSS. TOO BAD I'M NOT IN A POSITION TO HELP YOU ON THOSE DELIVERY PROBLEMS.
SADDLE UP, JOEY, WE'RE RIDIN' OUTTA HERE.
BUT, BILL--IT'S THE MIDDLE OF THE NIGHT AND IT'S POURING OUTSIDE!

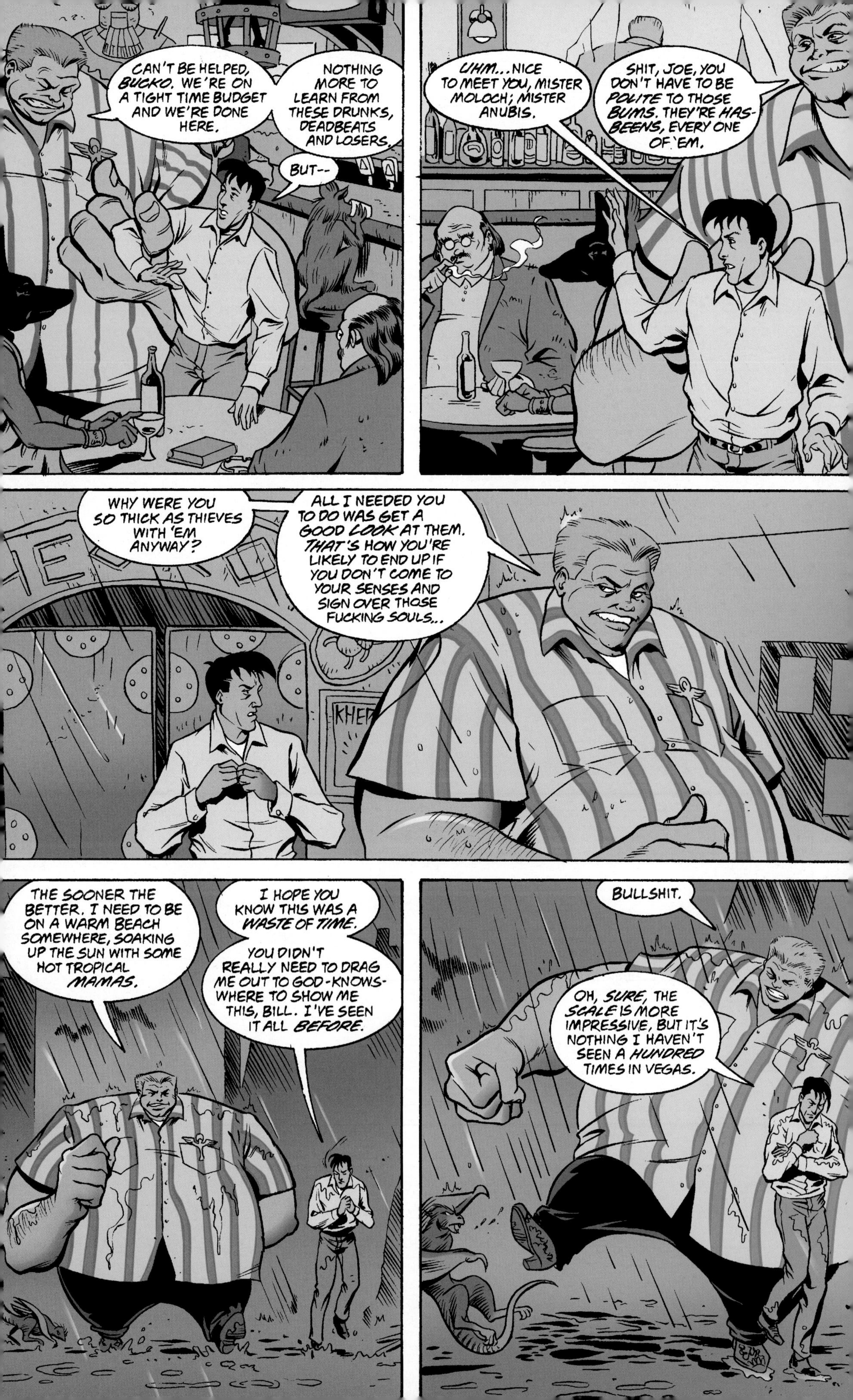
CAN'T BE HELPED, BUCKO. WE'RE ON A TIGHT TIME BUDGET AND WE'RE DONE HERE.
NOTHING MORE TO LEARN FROM THESE DRUNKS, DEADBEATS AND LOSERS.
BUT--
UHM... NICE TO MEET YOU, MISTER MOLOCH; MISTER ANUBIS.
SHIT, JOE, YOU DON'T HAVE TO BE POLITE TO THOSE BUMS. THEY'RE HAS-BEENS, EVERY ONE OF 'EM.
WHY WERE YOU SO THICK AS THIEVES WITH 'EM ANYWAY?
ALL I NEEDED YOU TO DO WAS GET A GOOD LOOK AT THEM. THAT'S HOW YOU'RE LIKELY TO END UP IF YOU DON'T COME TO YOUR SENSES AND SIGN OVER THOSE FUCKING SOULS...
THE SOONER THE BETTER. I NEED TO BE ON A WARM BEACH SOMEWHERE, SOAKING UP THE SUN WITH SOME HOT TROPICAL MAMAS.
I HOPE YOU KNOW THIS WAS A WASTE OF TIME.
YOU DIDN'T REALLY NEED TO DRAG ME OUT TO GOD-KNOWS-WHERE TO SHOW ME THIS, BILL. I'VE SEEN IT ALL BEFORE.
BULLSHIT.
OH, SURE, THE SCALE IS MORE IMPRESSIVE, BUT IT'S NOTHING I HAVEN'T SEEN A HUNDRED TIMES IN VEGAS.

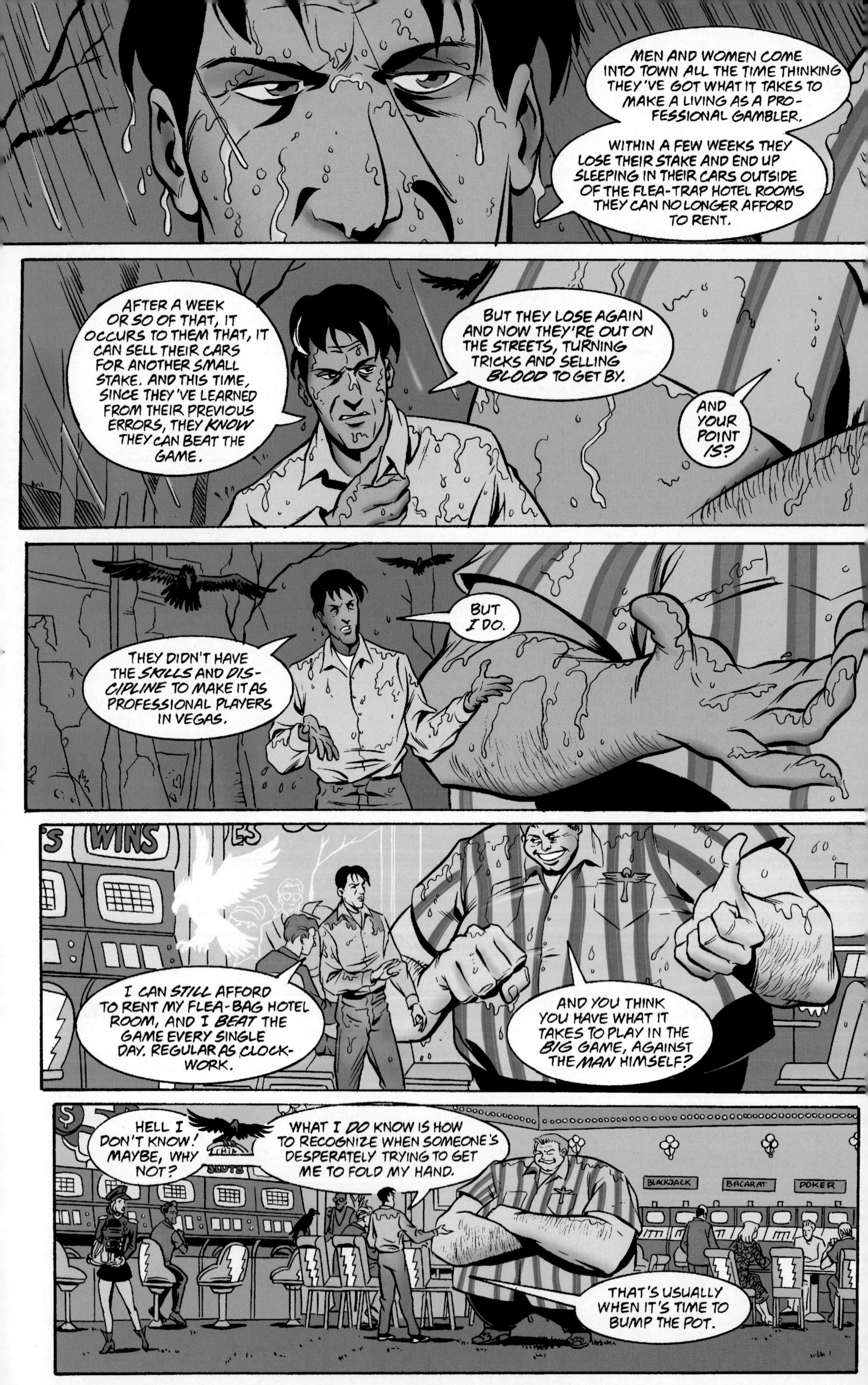
MEN AND WOMEN COME INTO TOWN ALL THE TIME THINKING THEY'VE GOT WHAT IT TAKES TO MAKE A LIVING AS A PROFESSIONAL GAMBLER.
WITHIN A FEW WEEKS THEY LOSE THEIR STAKE AND END UP SLEEPING IN THEIR CARS OUTSIDE OF THE FLEA-TRAP HOTEL ROOMS THEY CAN NO LONGER AFFORD TO RENT.
AFTER A WEEK OR SO OF THAT, IT OCCURS TO THEM THAT, IT CAN SELL THEIR CARS FOR ANOTHER SMALL STAKE. AND THIS TIME, SINCE THEY'VE LEARNED FROM THEIR PREVIOUS ERRORS, THEY *KNOW* THEY CAN BEAT THE GAME.
BUT THEY LOSE AGAIN AND NOW THEY'RE OUT ON THE STREETS, TURNING TRICKS AND SELLING *BLOOD* TO GET BY.
AND YOUR POINT *IS?*
THEY DIDN'T HAVE THE *SKILLS* AND *DISCIPLINE* TO MAKE IT AS PROFESSIONAL PLAYERS IN VEGAS.
BUT *I DO.*
WINS
I CAN *STILL* AFFORD TO RENT MY FLEA-BAG HOTEL ROOM, AND I *BEAT* THE GAME EVERY SINGLE DAY. REGULAR AS CLOCKWORK.
AND YOU THINK YOU HAVE WHAT IT TAKES TO PLAY IN THE *BIG GAME*, AGAINST THE *MAN* HIMSELF?
HELL I DON'T KNOW! MAYBE, WHY NOT?
WHAT I *DO* KNOW IS HOW TO RECOGNIZE WHEN SOMEONE'S DESPERATELY TRYING TO GET ME TO FOLD MY HAND.
SLOTS
BLACKJACK
BACARAT
POKER
THAT'S USUALLY WHEN IT'S TIME TO BUMP THE POT.

SORRY, BILL, BUT I'M GOING TO NEED MORE TIME TO THINK IT OVER BEFORE I DECIDE.

LOOK, MOMMY. CROWS. THEY GOT *CROWS* HERE.

WHY YOU UN-GRATEFUL LITTLE--

BILLY, JOSEPH, WHAT A PLEASURE TO SEE YOU BOTH AGAIN.

MARY!

BEEN OUT AT THE POOL, BOYS?

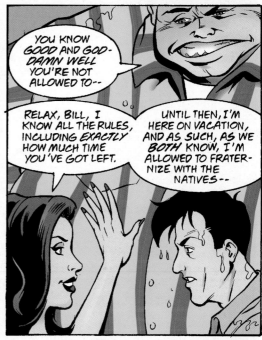

YOU KNOW *GOOD* AND *GOD-DAMN* WELL YOU'RE NOT ALLOWED TO--

RELAX, BILL, I KNOW ALL THE RULES, INCLUDING *EXACTLY* HOW MUCH TIME YOU'VE GOT LEFT.

UNTIL THEN, I'M HERE ON VACATION, AND AS SUCH, AS WE *BOTH* KNOW, I'M ALLOWED TO FRATER-NIZE WITH THE NATIVES--

--ON A PURELY SOCIAL LEVEL.

WHAT DO YOU SAY, JOEY? WANT TO GET *SOCIAL*?

UHM... I...?

WAIT A *MINUTE!* YOU CAN'T GET AWAY WITH THAT!

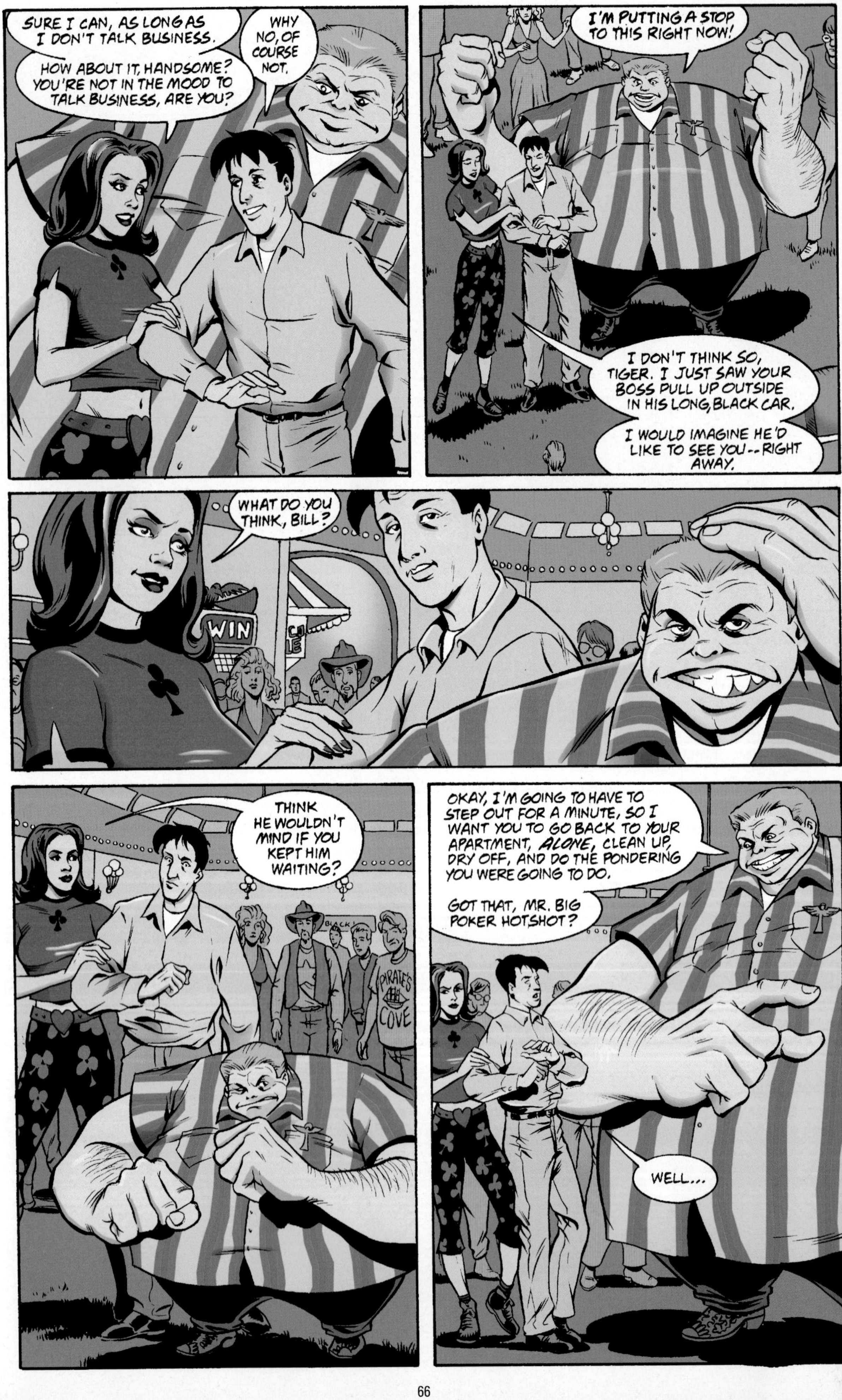
SURE I CAN, AS LONG AS I DON'T TALK BUSINESS.
HOW ABOUT IT, HANDSOME? YOU'RE NOT IN THE MOOD TO TALK BUSINESS, ARE YOU?
WHY NO, OF COURSE NOT.
I'M PUTTING A STOP TO THIS RIGHT NOW!
I DON'T THINK SO, TIGER. I JUST SAW YOUR BOSS PULL UP OUTSIDE IN HIS LONG, BLACK CAR.
I WOULD IMAGINE HE'D LIKE TO SEE YOU -- RIGHT AWAY.
WHAT DO YOU THINK, BILL?
WIN
THINK HE WOULDN'T MIND IF YOU KEPT HIM WAITING?
PIRATE'S COVE
OKAY, I'M GOING TO HAVE TO STEP OUT FOR A MINUTE, SO I WANT YOU TO GO BACK TO YOUR APARTMENT, ALONE, CLEAN UP, DRY OFF, AND DO THE PONDERING YOU WERE GOING TO DO.
GOT THAT, MR. BIG POKER HOTSHOT?
WELL...

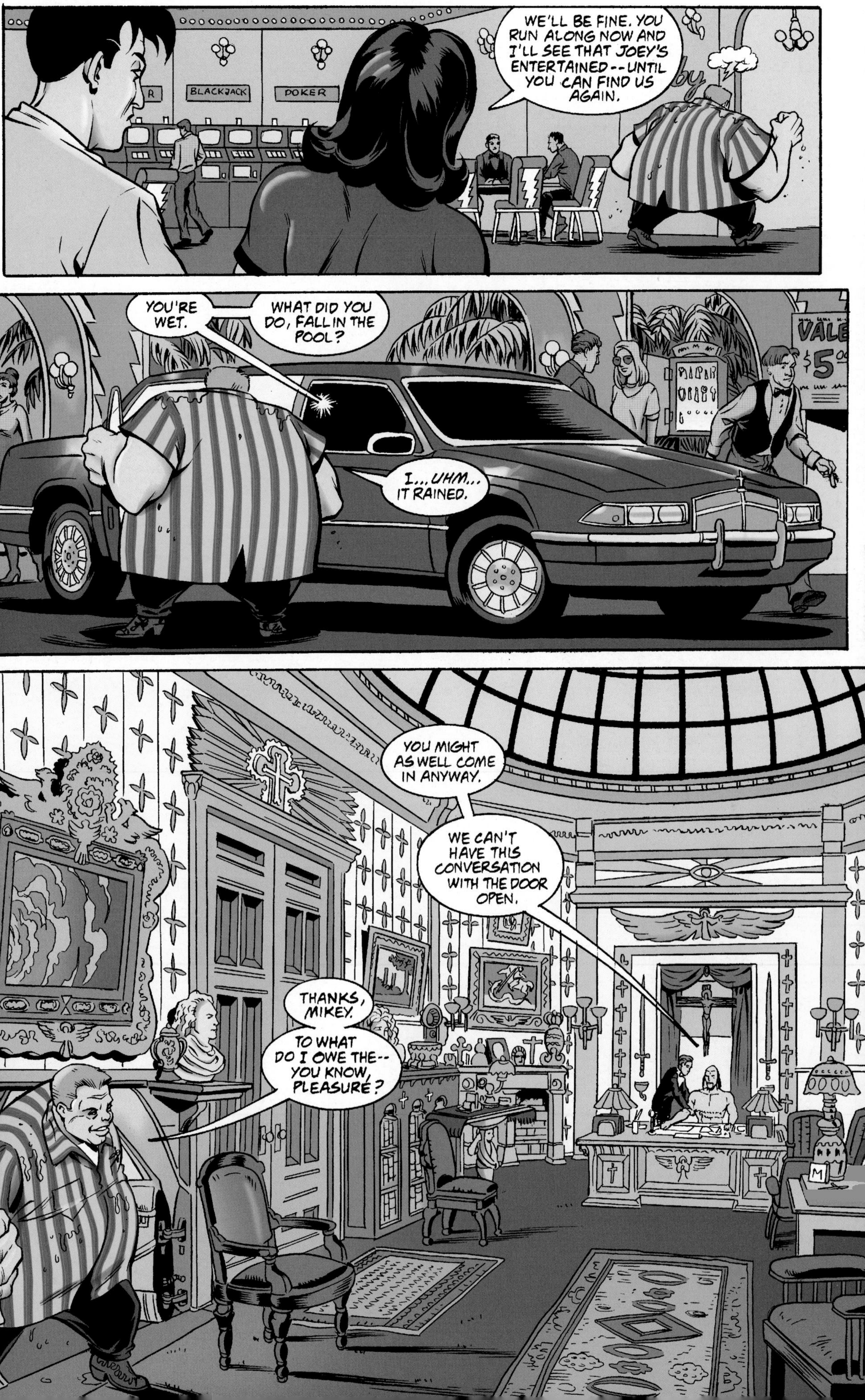

R
BLACKJACK
POKER
WE'LL BE FINE. YOU RUN ALONG NOW AND I'LL SEE THAT JOEY'S ENTERTAINED--UNTIL YOU CAN FIND US AGAIN.
YOU'RE WET.
WHAT DID YOU DO, FALL IN THE POOL?
VALE
$5
I...UHM... IT RAINED.
YOU MIGHT AS WELL COME IN ANYWAY.
WE CAN'T HAVE THIS CONVERSATION WITH THE DOOR OPEN.
THANKS, MIKEY.
TO WHAT DO I OWE THE--YOU KNOW, PLEASURE?
M

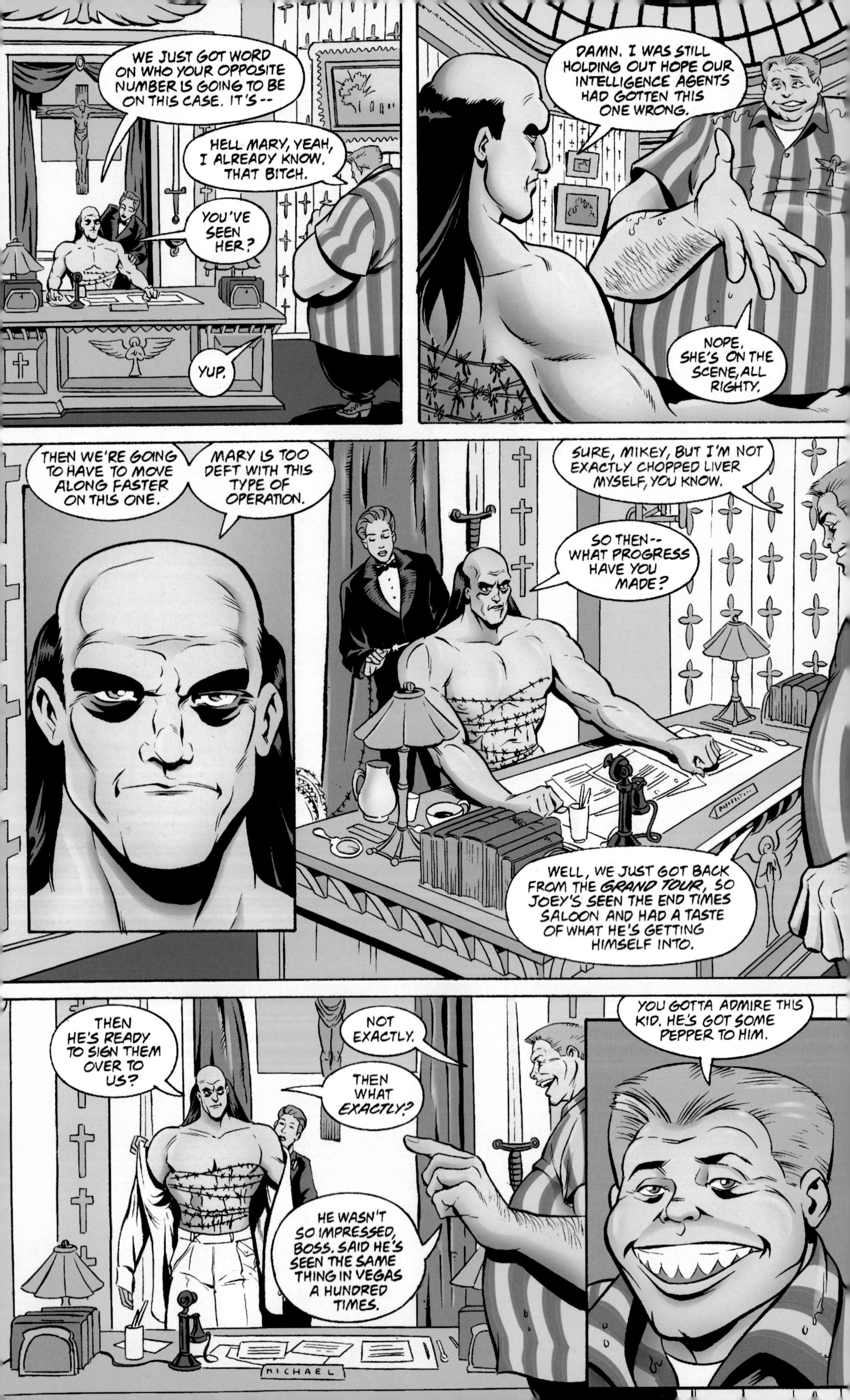
WE JUST GOT WORD ON WHO YOUR OPPOSITE NUMBER IS GOING TO BE ON THIS CASE. IT'S --
HELL MARY, YEAH, I ALREADY KNOW. THAT BITCH.
YOU'VE SEEN HER?
YUP.
DAMN. I WAS STILL HOLDING OUT HOPE OUR INTELLIGENCE AGENTS HAD GOTTEN THIS ONE WRONG.
NOPE. SHE'S ON THE SCENE, ALL RIGHTY.
THEN WE'RE GOING TO HAVE TO MOVE ALONG FASTER ON THIS ONE.
MARY IS TOO DEFT WITH THIS TYPE OF OPERATION.
SURE, MIKEY, BUT I'M NOT EXACTLY CHOPPED LIVER MYSELF, YOU KNOW.
SO THEN-- WHAT PROGRESS HAVE YOU MADE?
WELL, WE JUST GOT BACK FROM THE GRAND TOUR, SO JOEY'S SEEN THE END TIMES SALOON AND HAD A TASTE OF WHAT HE'S GETTING HIMSELF INTO.
THEN HE'S READY TO SIGN THEM OVER TO US?
NOT EXACTLY.
THEN WHAT EXACTLY?
HE WASN'T SO IMPRESSED, BOSS. SAID HE'S SEEN THE SAME THING IN VEGAS A HUNDRED TIMES.
YOU GOTTA ADMIRE THIS KID. HE'S GOT SOME PEPPER TO HIM.
MICHAEL

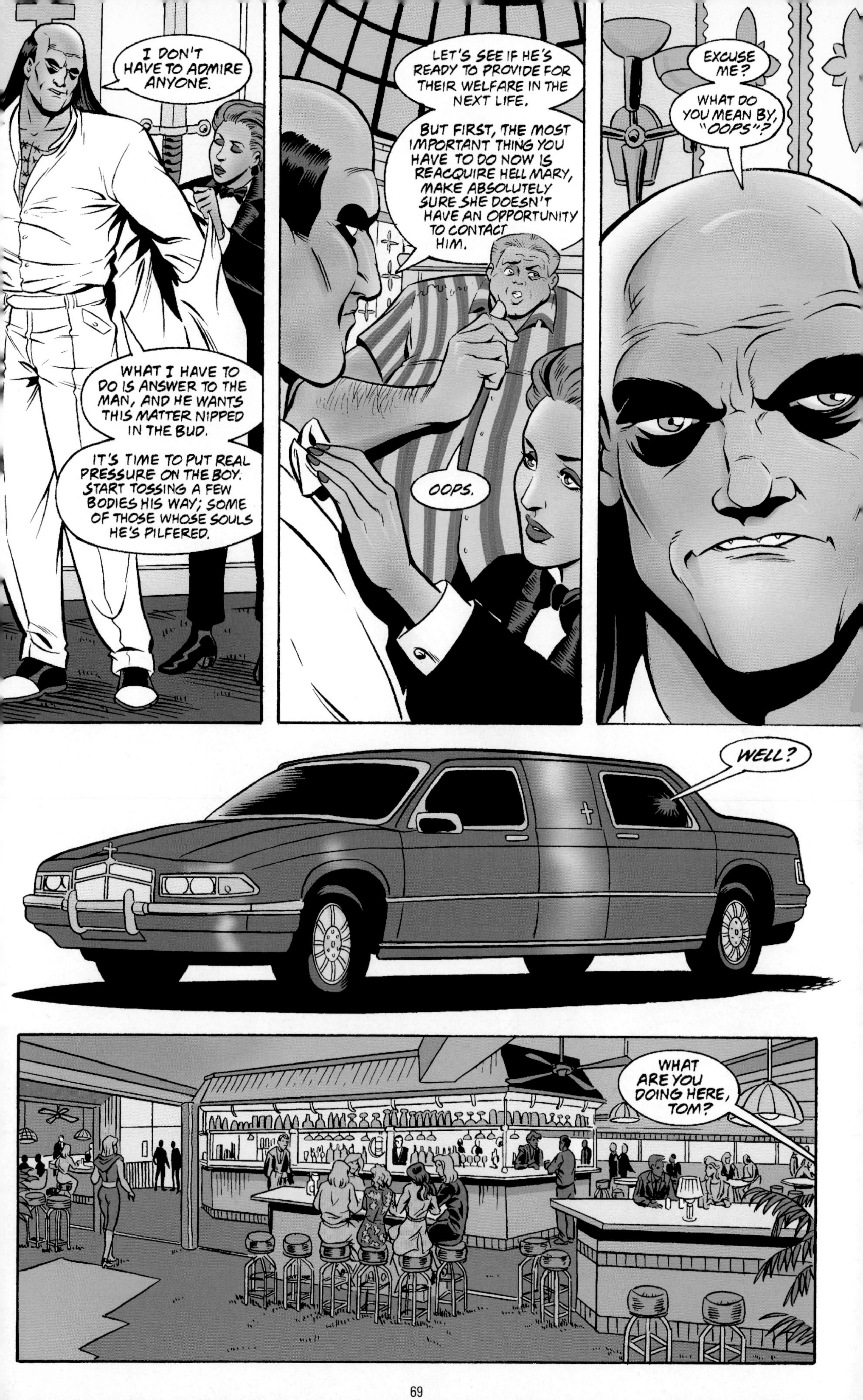
I DON'T HAVE TO ADMIRE ANYONE.
WHAT I HAVE TO DO IS ANSWER TO THE MAN, AND HE WANTS THIS MATTER NIPPED IN THE BUD.
IT'S TIME TO PUT REAL PRESSURE ON THE BOY. START TOSSING A FEW BODIES HIS WAY; SOME OF THOSE WHOSE SOULS HE'S PILFERED.
LET'S SEE IF HE'S READY TO PROVIDE FOR THEIR WELFARE IN THE NEXT LIFE.
BUT FIRST, THE MOST IMPORTANT THING YOU HAVE TO DO NOW IS REACQUIRE HELL MARY, MAKE ABSOLUTELY SURE SHE DOESN'T HAVE AN OPPORTUNITY TO CONTACT HIM.
OOPS.
EXCUSE ME?
WHAT DO YOU MEAN BY, "OOPS"?
WELL?
WHAT ARE YOU DOING HERE, TOM?

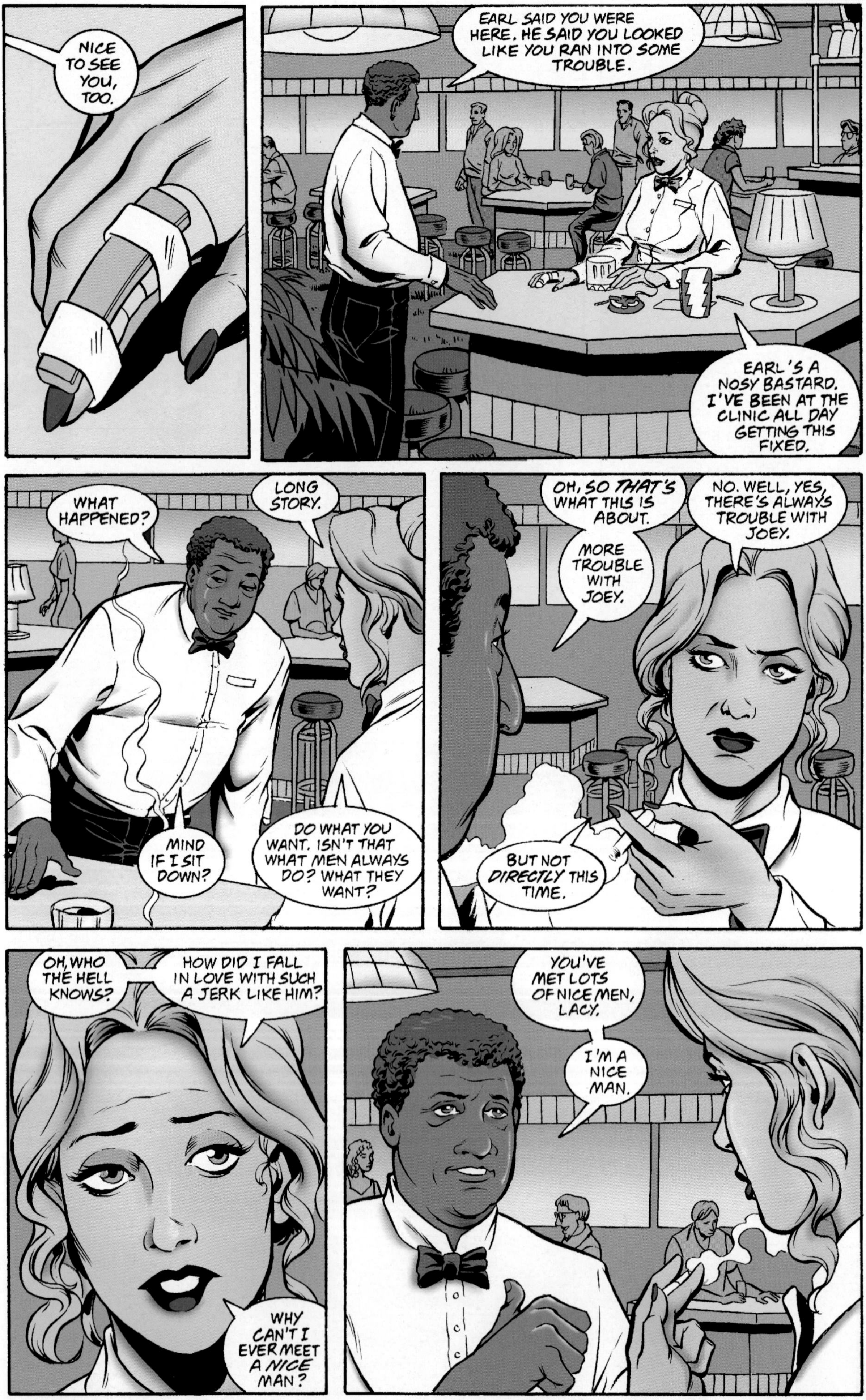
NICE TO SEE YOU, TOO.
EARL SAID YOU WERE HERE. HE SAID YOU LOOKED LIKE YOU RAN INTO SOME TROUBLE.
EARL'S A NOSY BASTARD. I'VE BEEN AT THE CLINIC ALL DAY GETTING THIS FIXED.
WHAT HAPPENED?
LONG STORY.
MIND IF I SIT DOWN?
DO WHAT YOU WANT. ISN'T THAT WHAT MEN ALWAYS DO? WHAT THEY WANT?
OH, SO THAT'S WHAT THIS IS ABOUT.
MORE TROUBLE WITH JOEY.
NO. WELL, YES, THERE'S ALWAYS TROUBLE WITH JOEY.
BUT NOT DIRECTLY THIS TIME.
OH, WHO THE HELL KNOWS?
HOW DID I FALL IN LOVE WITH SUCH A JERK LIKE HIM?
WHY CAN'T I EVER MEET A NICE MAN?
YOU'VE MET LOTS OF NICE MEN, LACY.
I'M A NICE MAN.

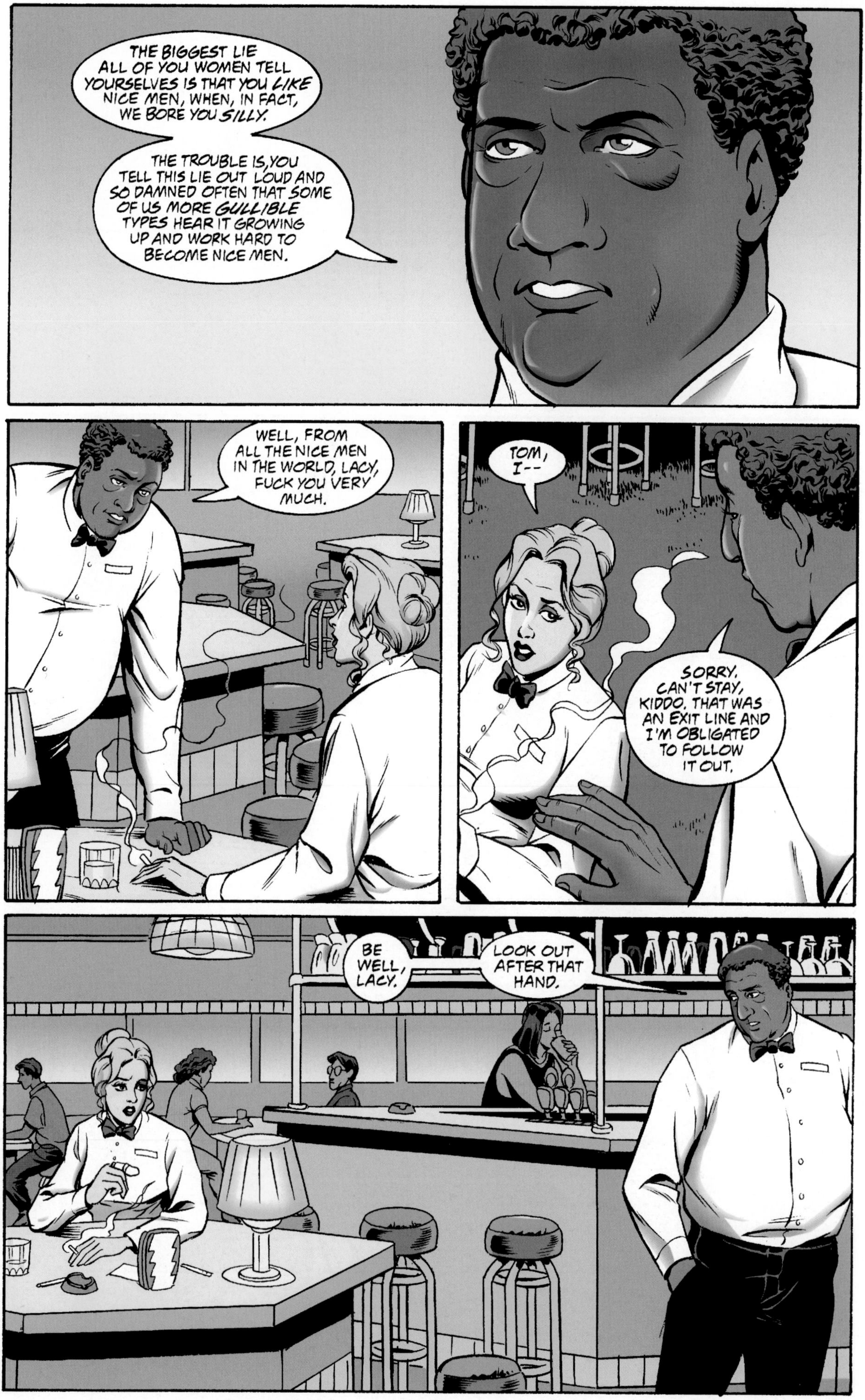
THE BIGGEST LIE ALL OF YOU WOMEN TELL YOURSELVES IS THAT YOU LIKE NICE MEN, WHEN, IN FACT, WE BORE YOU SILLY.
THE TROUBLE IS, YOU TELL THIS LIE OUT LOUD AND SO DAMNED OFTEN THAT SOME OF US MORE GULLIBLE TYPES HEAR IT GROWING UP AND WORK HARD TO BECOME NICE MEN.
WELL, FROM ALL THE NICE MEN IN THE WORLD, LACY, FUCK YOU VERY MUCH.
TOM, I--
SORRY, CAN'T STAY, KIDDO. THAT WAS AN EXIT LINE AND I'M OBLIGATED TO FOLLOW IT OUT.
BE WELL, LACY.
LOOK OUT AFTER THAT HAND.

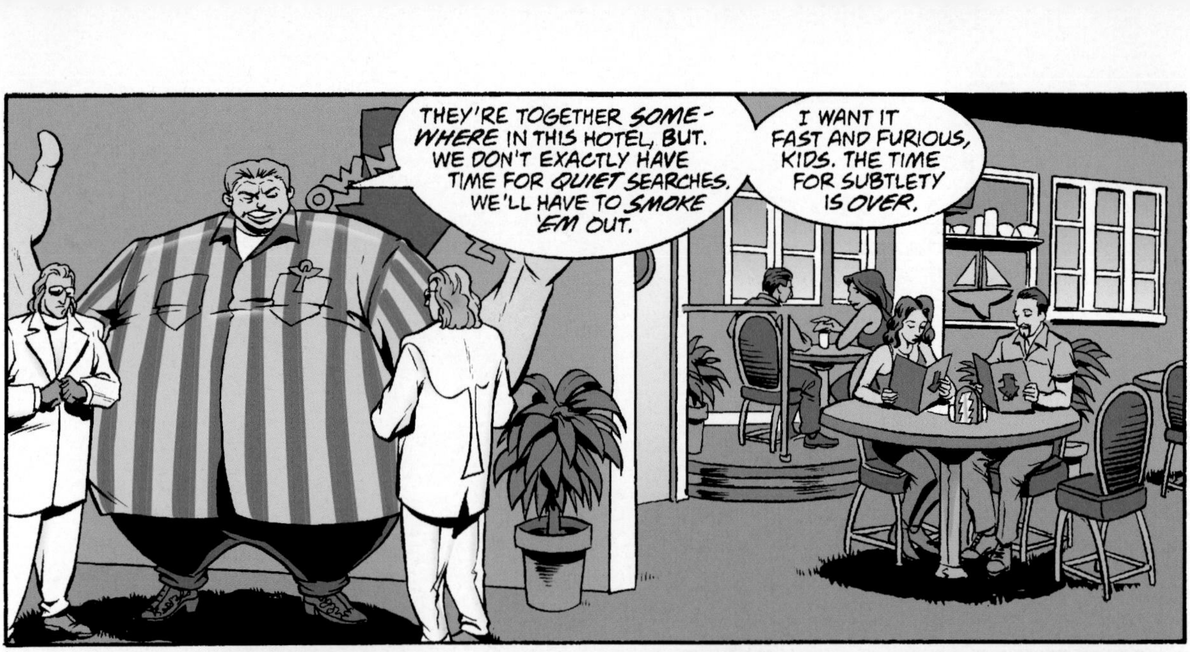
THEY'RE TOGETHER SOME-WHERE IN THIS HOTEL, BUT. WE DON'T EXACTLY HAVE TIME FOR QUIET SEARCHES. WE'LL HAVE TO SMOKE 'EM OUT.
I WANT IT FAST AND FURIOUS, KIDS. THE TIME FOR SUBTLETY IS OVER.

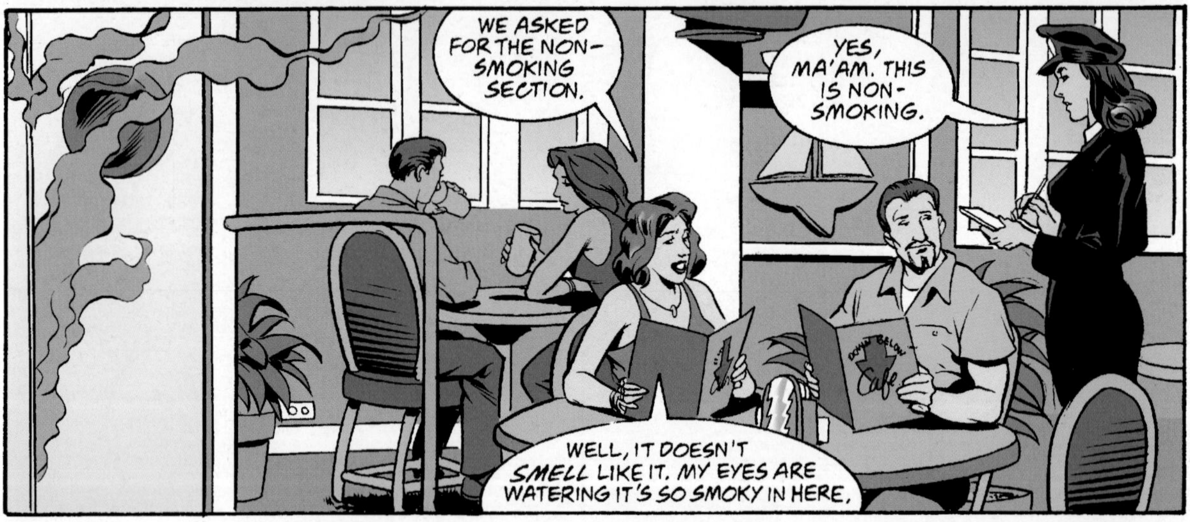
WE ASKED FOR THE NON-SMOKING SECTION.
YES, MA'AM. THIS IS NON-SMOKING.
WELL, IT DOESN'T SMELL LIKE IT. MY EYES ARE WATERING IT'S SO SMOKY IN HERE.

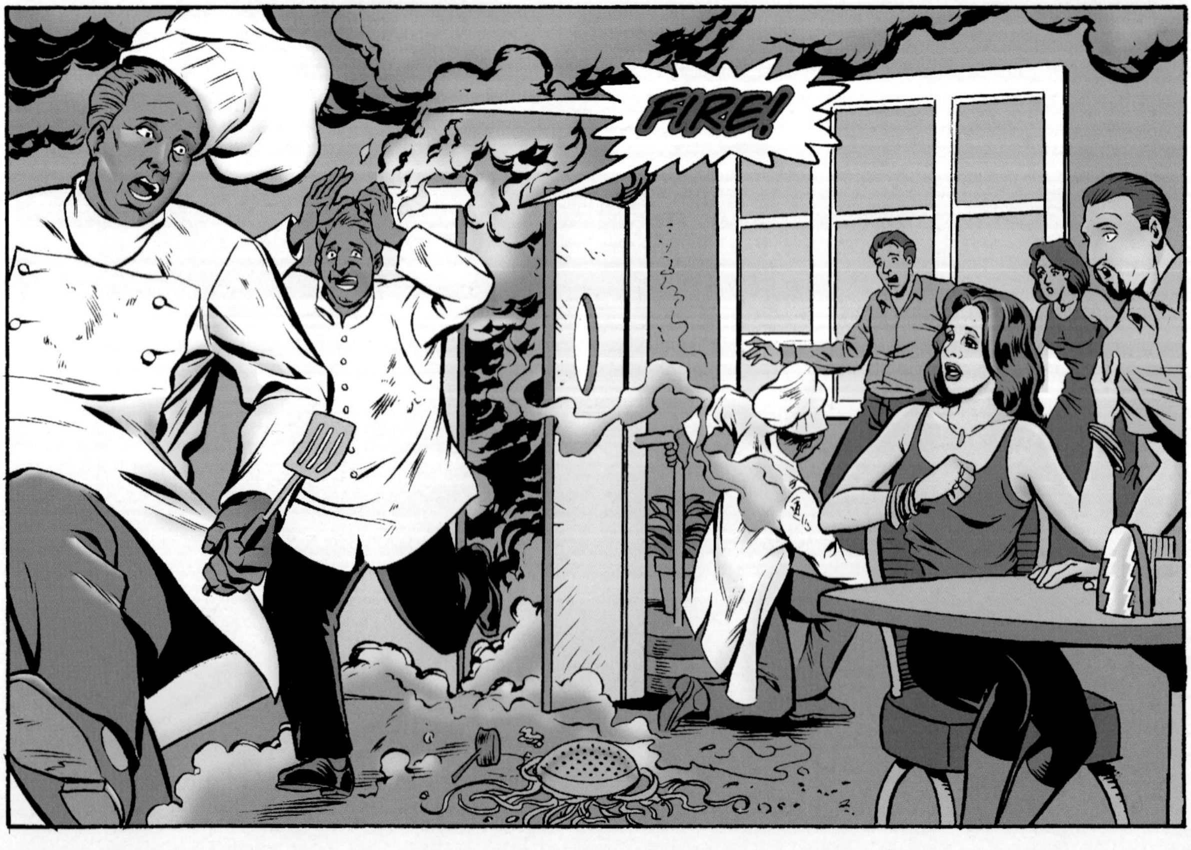
FIRE!

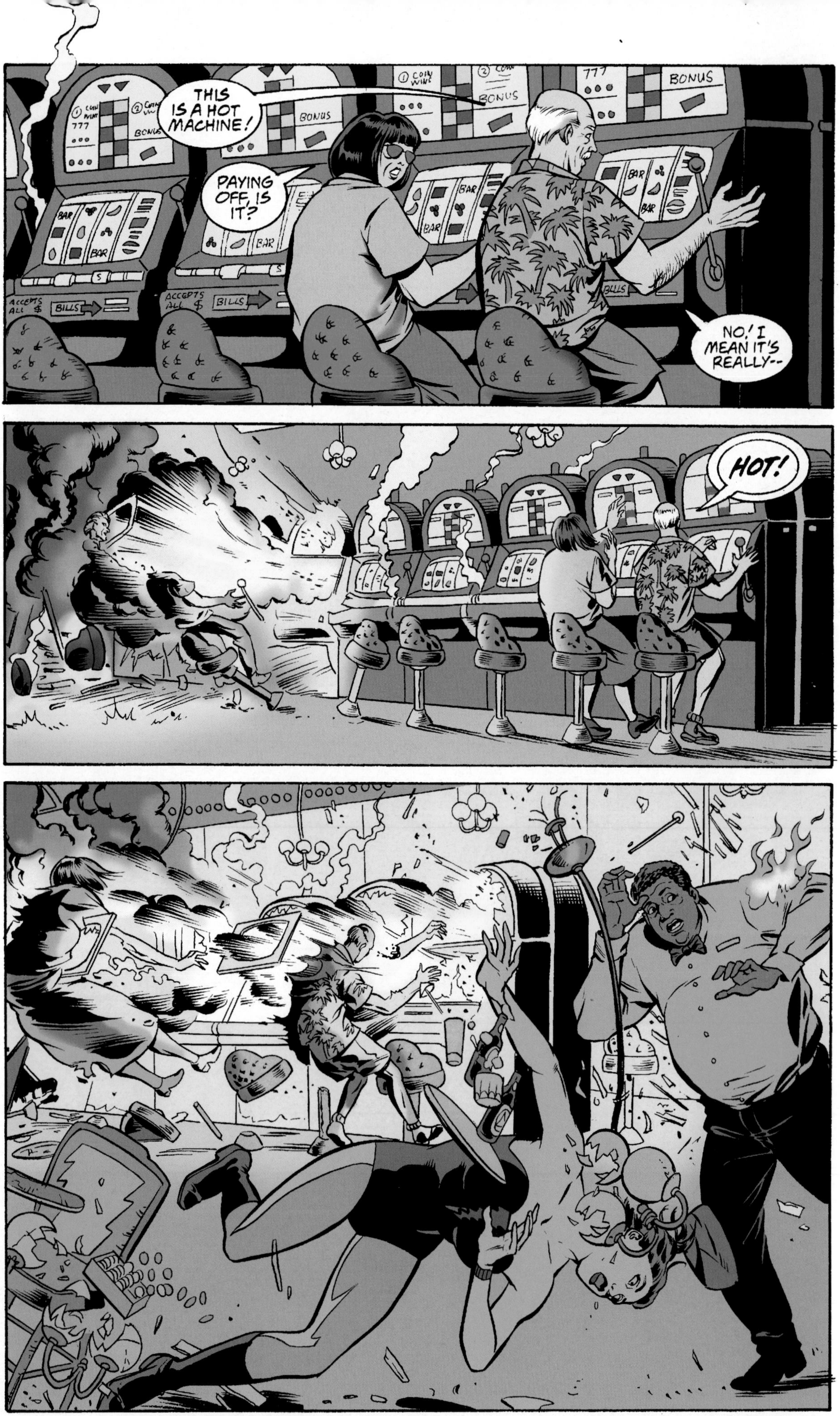
THIS IS A HOT MACHINE!
PAYING OFF, IS IT?
NO! I MEAN IT'S REALLY--
HOT!

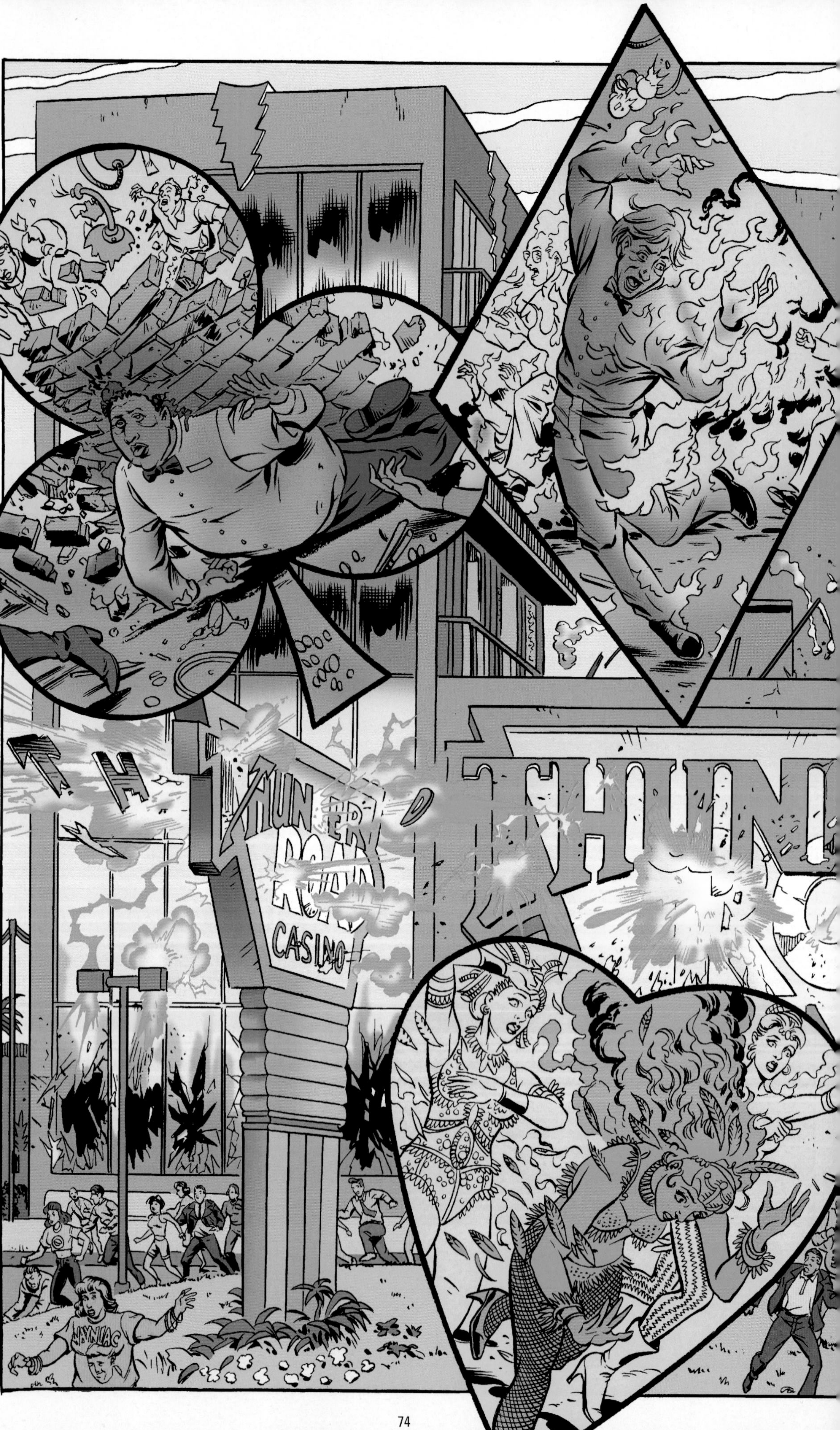
CASINO
THUN
WAYNIAC

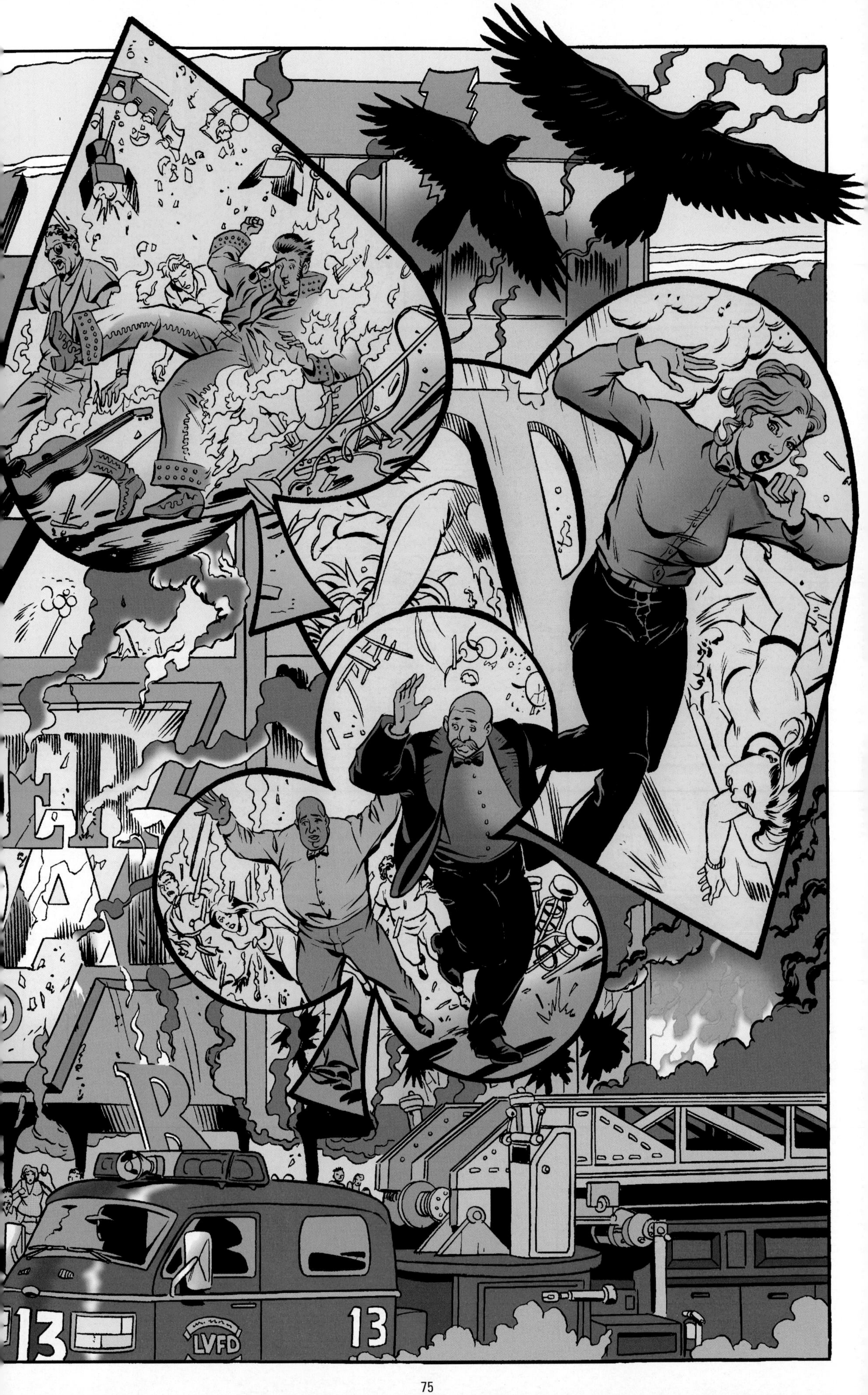
13
LVFD
13

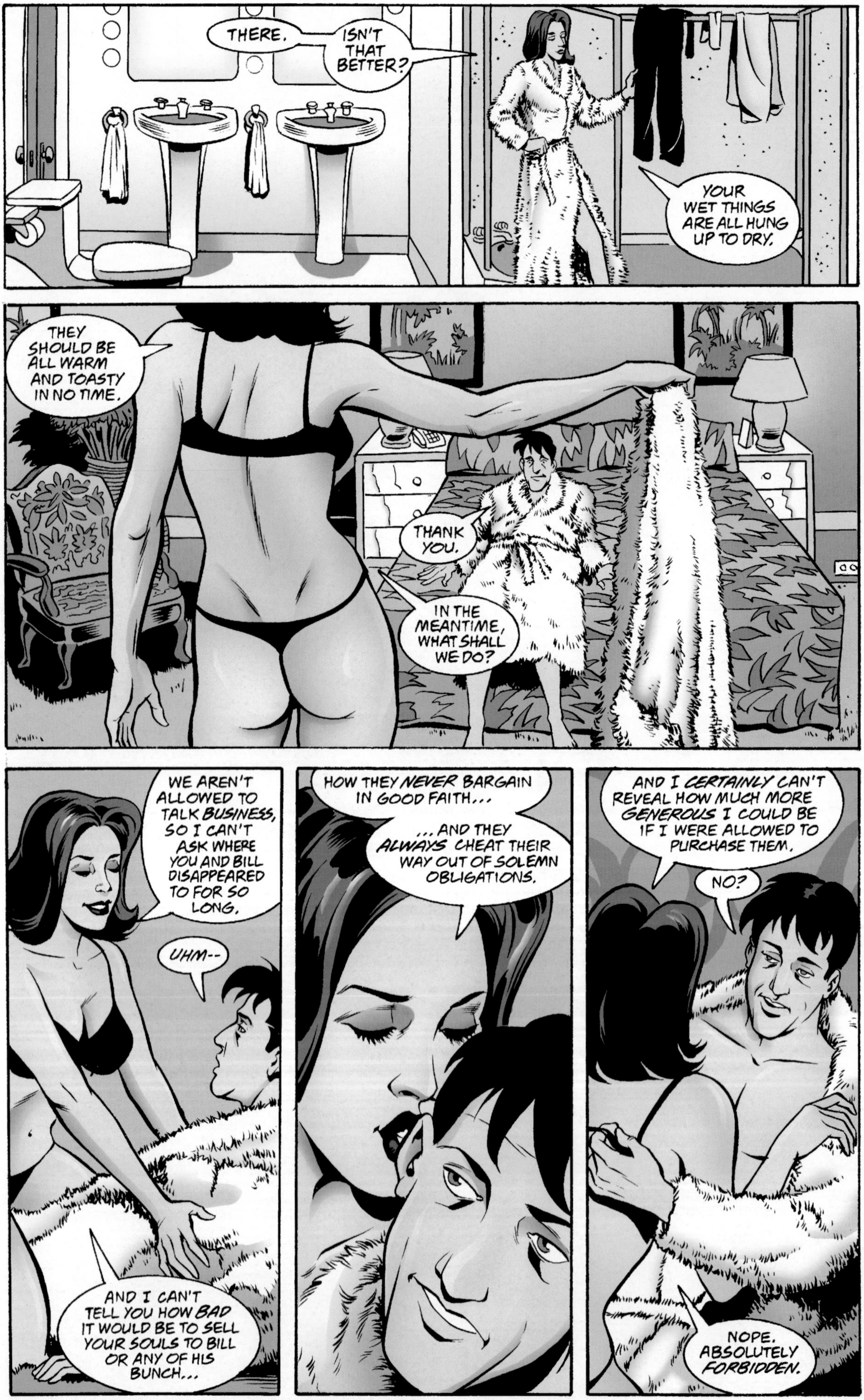
THERE.
ISN'T THAT BETTER?
YOUR WET THINGS ARE ALL HUNG UP TO DRY.
THEY SHOULD BE ALL WARM AND TOASTY IN NO TIME.
THANK YOU.
IN THE MEANTIME, WHAT SHALL WE DO?
WE AREN'T ALLOWED TO TALK *BUSINESS*, SO I CAN'T ASK WHERE YOU AND BILL DISAPPEARED TO FOR SO LONG.
UHM--
AND I CAN'T TELL YOU HOW *BAD* IT WOULD BE TO SELL YOUR SOULS TO BILL OR ANY OF HIS BUNCH...
HOW THEY *NEVER* BARGAIN IN GOOD FAITH...
...AND THEY *ALWAYS* CHEAT THEIR WAY OUT OF SOLEMN OBLIGATIONS.
AND I *CERTAINLY* CAN'T REVEAL HOW MUCH MORE *GENEROUS* I COULD BE IF I WERE ALLOWED TO PURCHASE THEM.
NO?
NOPE. ABSOLUTELY *FORBIDDEN*.

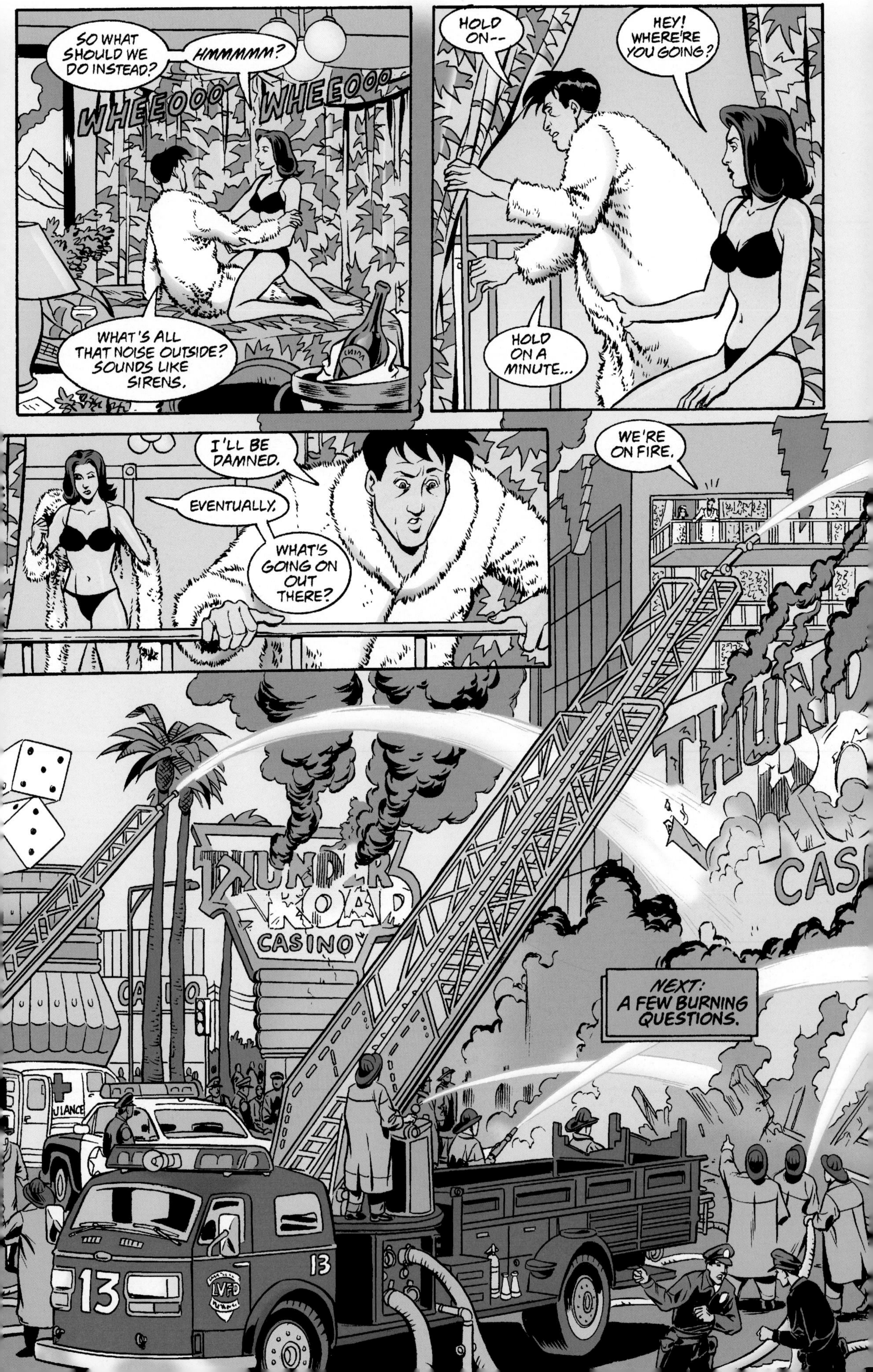
SO WHAT SHOULD WE DO INSTEAD?
HMMMMM?
WHEEOOO WHEEOOO
WHAT'S ALL THAT NOISE OUTSIDE? SOUNDS LIKE SIRENS.
HOLD ON--
HEY! WHERE'RE YOU GOING?
HOLD ON A MINUTE...
I'LL BE DAMNED.
EVENTUALLY.
WHAT'S GOING ON OUT THERE?
WE'RE ON FIRE.
THUNDER ROAD CASINO
CASINO
NEXT: A FEW BURNING QUESTIONS.
13
LVFD

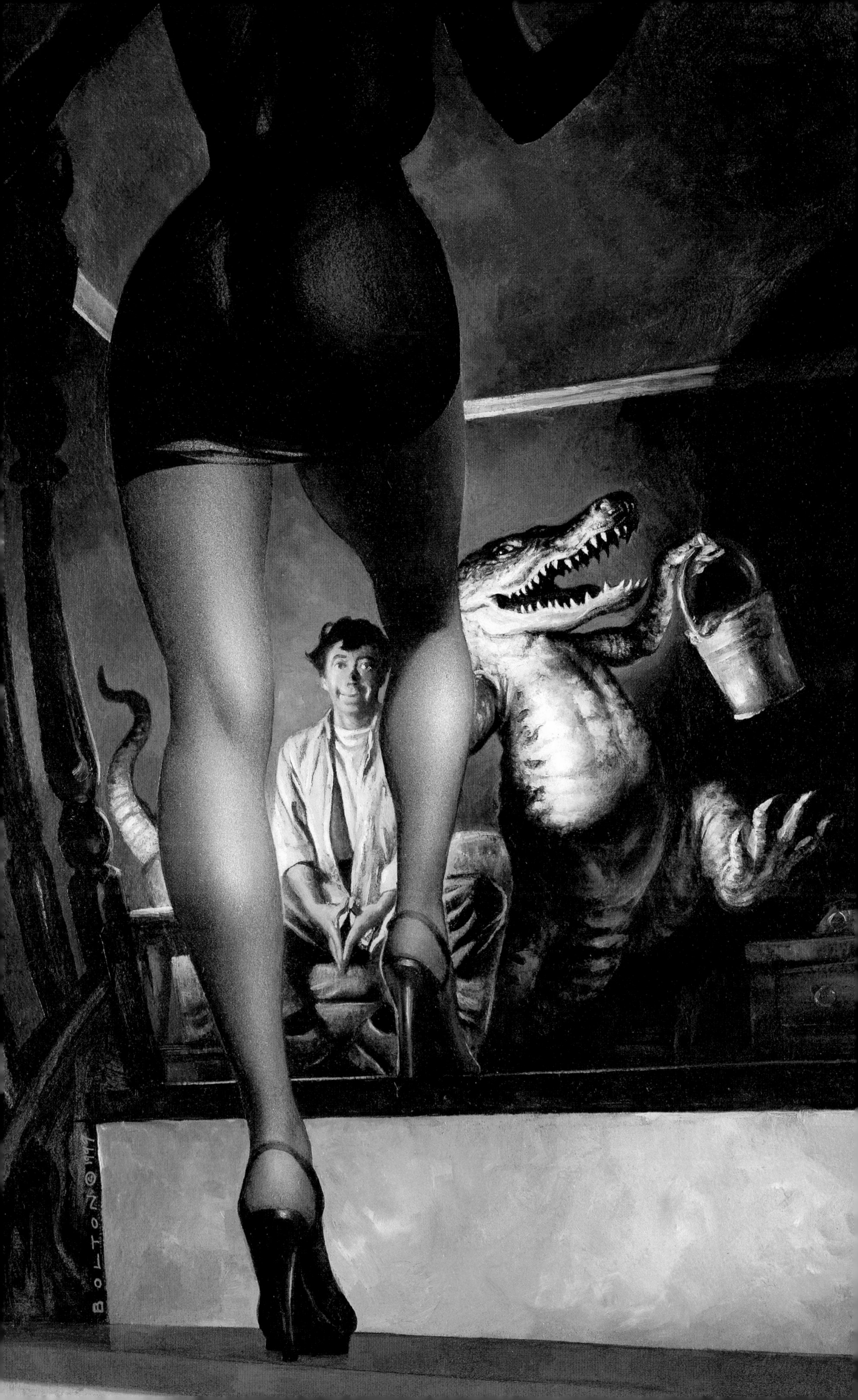
BOLTON © 1997

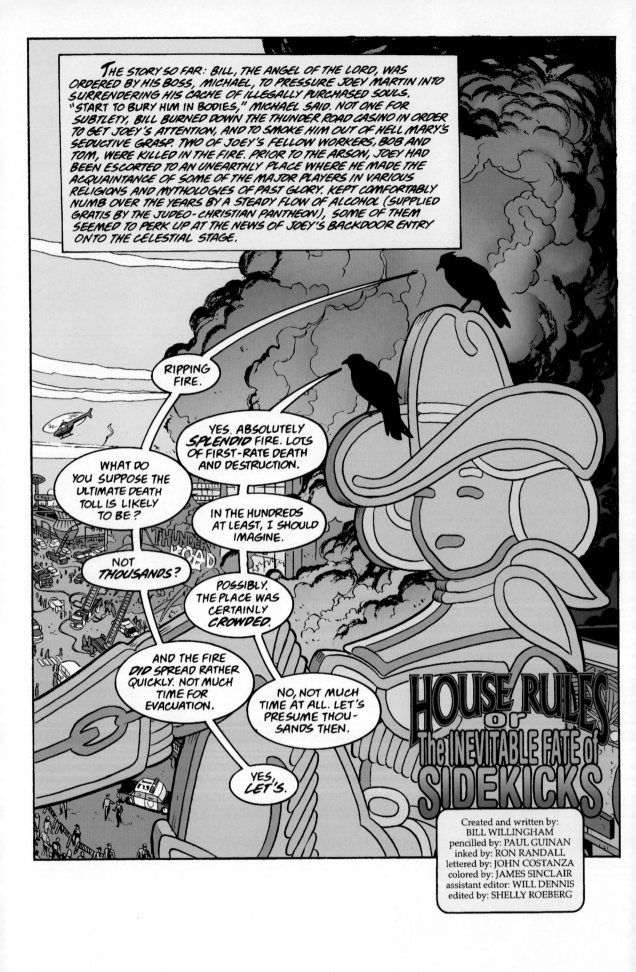

THE STORY SO FAR: BILL, THE ANGEL OF THE LORD, WAS ORDERED BY HIS BOSS, MICHAEL, TO PRESSURE JOEY MARTIN INTO SURRENDERING HIS CACHE OF ILLEGALLY PURCHASED SOULS. "START TO BURY HIM IN BODIES," MICHAEL SAID. NOT ONE FOR SUBTLETY, BILL BURNED DOWN THE THUNDER ROAD CASINO IN ORDER TO GET JOEY'S ATTENTION, AND TO SMOKE HIM OUT OF HELL MARY'S SEDUCTIVE GRASP. TWO OF JOEY'S FELLOW WORKERS, BOB AND TOM, WERE KILLED IN THE FIRE. PRIOR TO THE ARSON, JOEY HAD BEEN ESCORTED TO AN UNEARTHLY PLACE WHERE HE MADE THE ACQUAINTANCE OF SOME OF THE MAJOR PLAYERS IN VARIOUS RELIGIONS AND MYTHOLOGIES OF PAST GLORY. KEPT COMFORTABLY NUMB OVER THE YEARS BY A STEADY FLOW OF ALCOHOL (SUPPLIED GRATIS BY THE JUDEO-CHRISTIAN PANTHEON), SOME OF THEM SEEMED TO PERK UP AT THE NEWS OF JOEY'S BACKDOOR ENTRY ONTO THE CELESTIAL STAGE.

RIPPING FIRE.

YES. ABSOLUTELY *SPLENDID* FIRE. LOTS OF FIRST-RATE DEATH AND DESTRUCTION.

WHAT DO YOU SUPPOSE THE ULTIMATE DEATH TOLL IS LIKELY TO BE?

IN THE HUNDREDS AT LEAST, I SHOULD IMAGINE.

NOT *THOUSANDS*?

POSSIBLY. THE PLACE WAS CERTAINLY *CROWDED*.

AND THE FIRE *DID* SPREAD RATHER QUICKLY. NOT MUCH TIME FOR EVACUATION.

NO, NOT MUCH TIME AT ALL. LET'S PRESUME THOUSANDS THEN.

YES, LET'S.

HOUSE RULES or The INEVITABLE FATE of SIDEKICKS

Created and written by:
BILL WILLINGHAM
pencilled by: PAUL GUINAN
inked by: RON RANDALL
lettered by: JOHN COSTANZA
colored by: JAMES SINCLAIR
assistant editor: WILL DENNIS
edited by: SHELLY ROEBERG

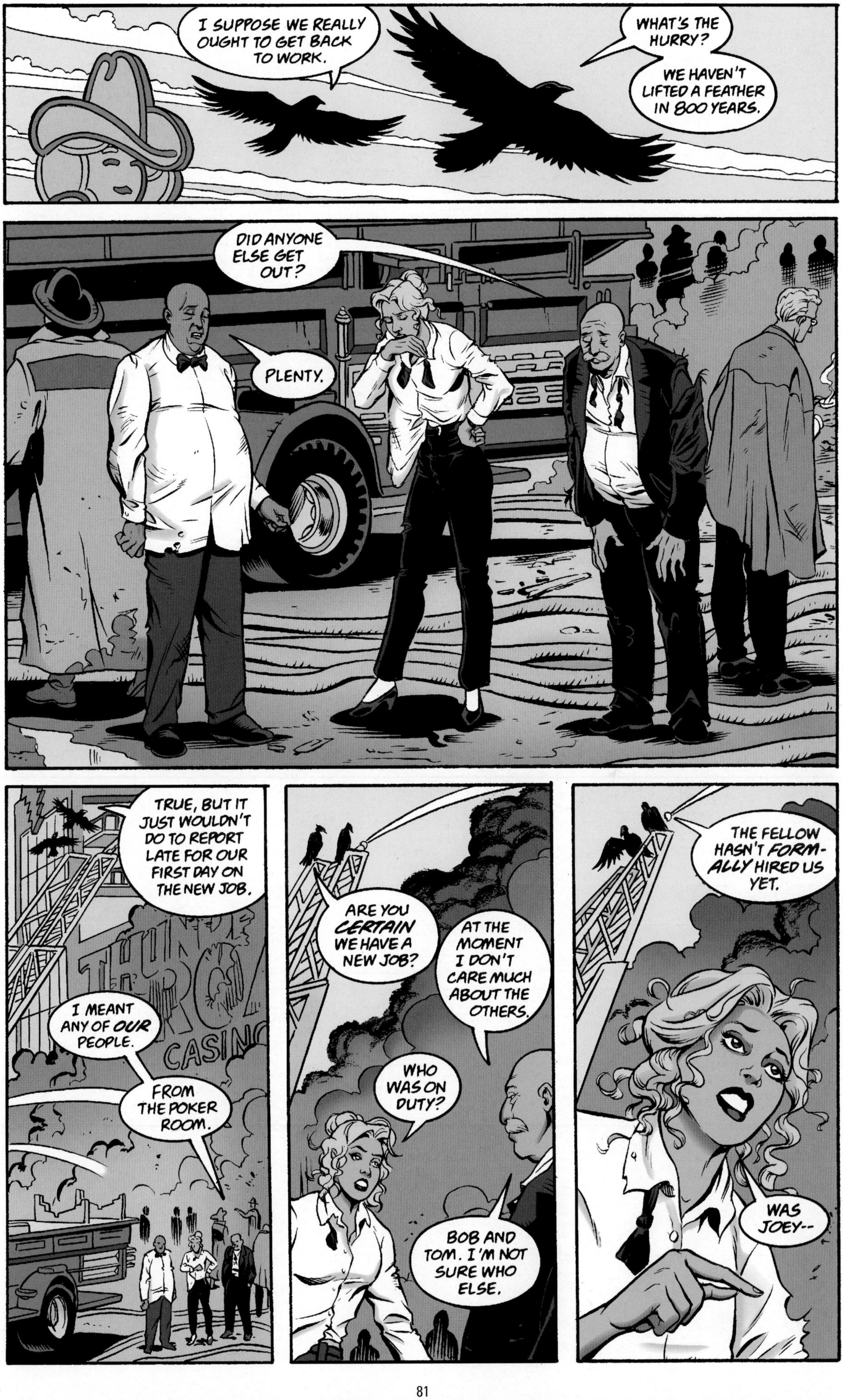
I SUPPOSE WE REALLY OUGHT TO GET BACK TO WORK.
WHAT'S THE HURRY?
WE HAVEN'T LIFTED A FEATHER IN 800 YEARS.
DID ANYONE ELSE GET OUT?
PLENTY.
TRUE, BUT IT JUST WOULDN'T DO TO REPORT LATE FOR OUR FIRST DAY ON THE NEW JOB.
CASINO
I MEANT ANY OF OUR PEOPLE.
FROM THE POKER ROOM.
ARE YOU CERTAIN WE HAVE A NEW JOB?
AT THE MOMENT I DON'T CARE MUCH ABOUT THE OTHERS.
WHO WAS ON DUTY?
BOB AND TOM. I'M NOT SURE WHO ELSE.
THE FELLOW HASN'T FORMALLY HIRED US YET.
WAS JOEY--

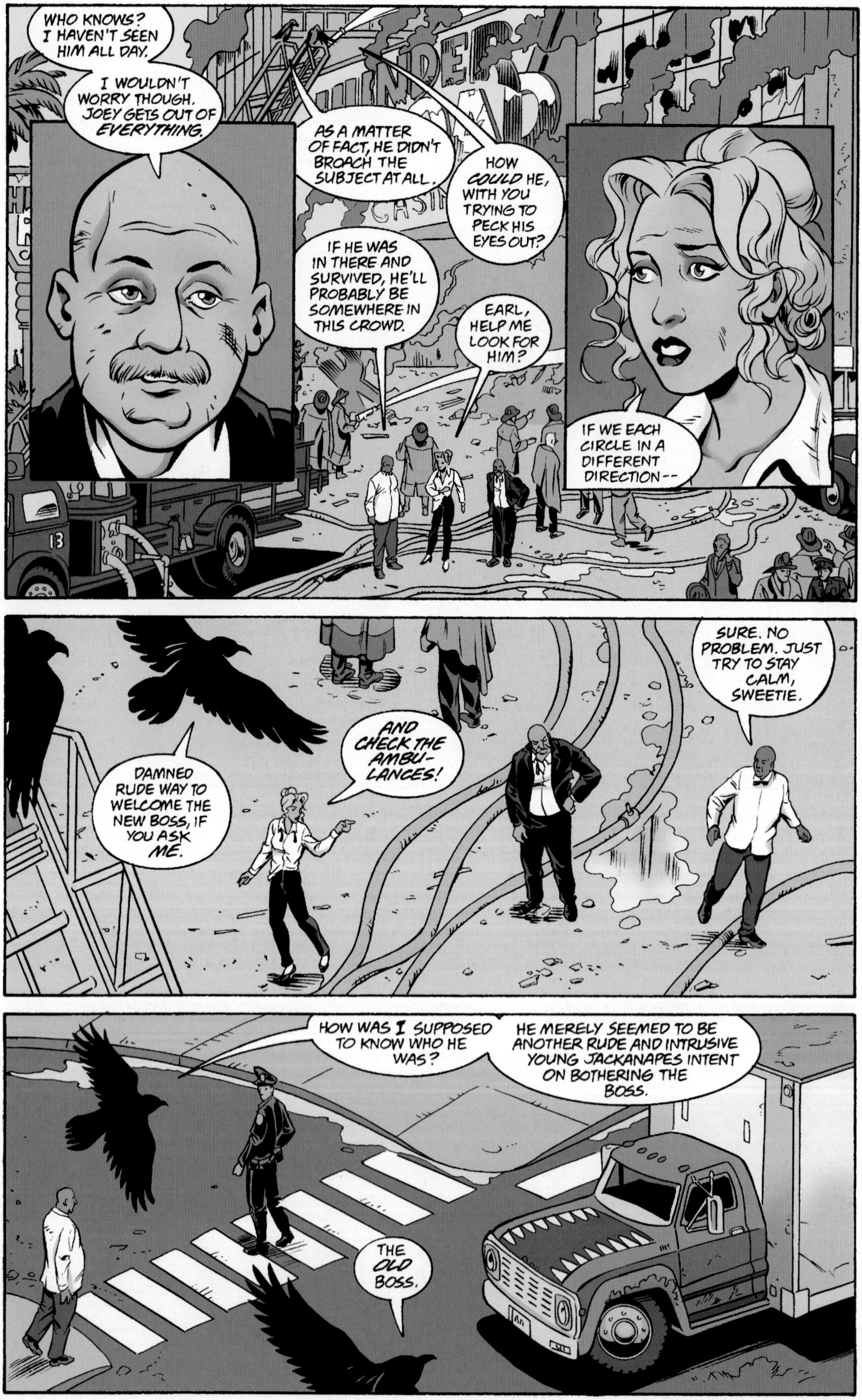
WHO KNOWS? I HAVEN'T SEEN HIM ALL DAY.
I WOULDN'T WORRY THOUGH. JOEY GETS OUT OF *EVERYTHING*.
AS A MATTER OF FACT, HE DIDN'T BROACH THE SUBJECT AT ALL.
HOW *COULD* HE, WITH YOU TRYING TO PECK HIS EYES OUT?
IF HE WAS IN THERE AND SURVIVED, HE'LL PROBABLY BE SOMEWHERE IN THIS CROWD.
EARL, HELP ME LOOK FOR HIM?
IF WE EACH CIRCLE IN A DIFFERENT DIRECTION--
DAMNED RUDE WAY TO WELCOME THE NEW BOSS, IF YOU ASK *ME*.
AND CHECK THE AMBU-LANCES!
SURE. NO PROBLEM. JUST TRY TO STAY CALM, SWEETIE.
HOW WAS **I** SUPPOSED TO KNOW WHO HE WAS?
HE MERELY SEEMED TO BE ANOTHER RUDE AND INTRUSIVE YOUNG JACKANAPES INTENT ON BOTHERING THE BOSS.
THE *OLD* BOSS.

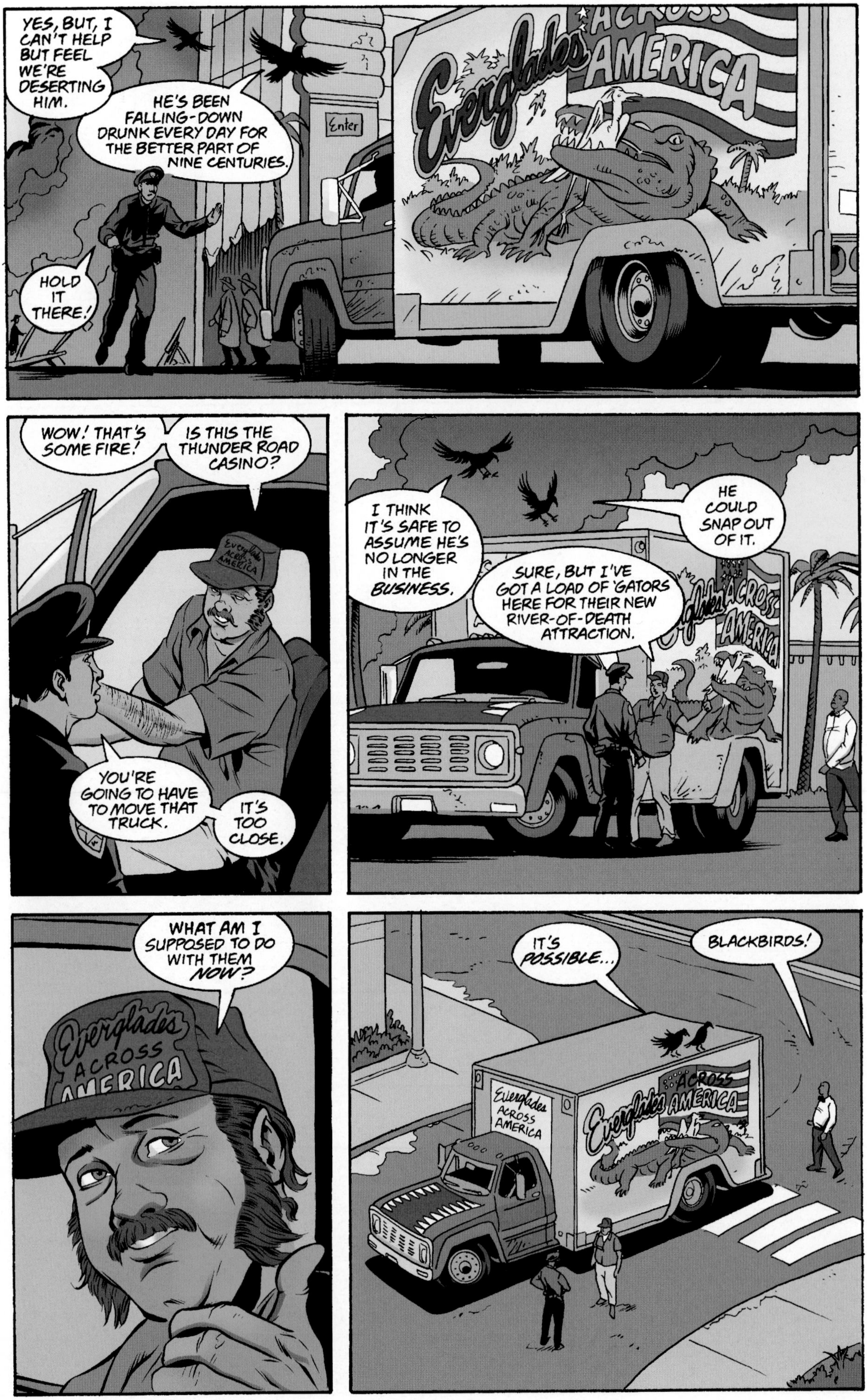
YES, BUT, I CAN'T HELP BUT FEEL WE'RE DESERTING HIM.
Enter
HE'S BEEN FALLING-DOWN DRUNK EVERY DAY FOR THE BETTER PART OF NINE CENTURIES.
Everglades ACROSS AMERICA
HOLD IT THERE!
WOW! THAT'S SOME FIRE!
IS THIS THE THUNDER ROAD CASINO?
YOU'RE GOING TO HAVE TO MOVE THAT TRUCK.
IT'S TOO CLOSE.
I THINK IT'S SAFE TO ASSUME HE'S NO LONGER IN THE BUSINESS.
HE COULD SNAP OUT OF IT.
SURE, BUT I'VE GOT A LOAD OF 'GATORS HERE FOR THEIR NEW RIVER-OF-DEATH ATTRACTION.
WHAT AM I SUPPOSED TO DO WITH THEM NOW?
Everglades ACROSS AMERICA
IT'S POSSIBLE...
BLACKBIRDS!
Everglades ACROSS AMERICA

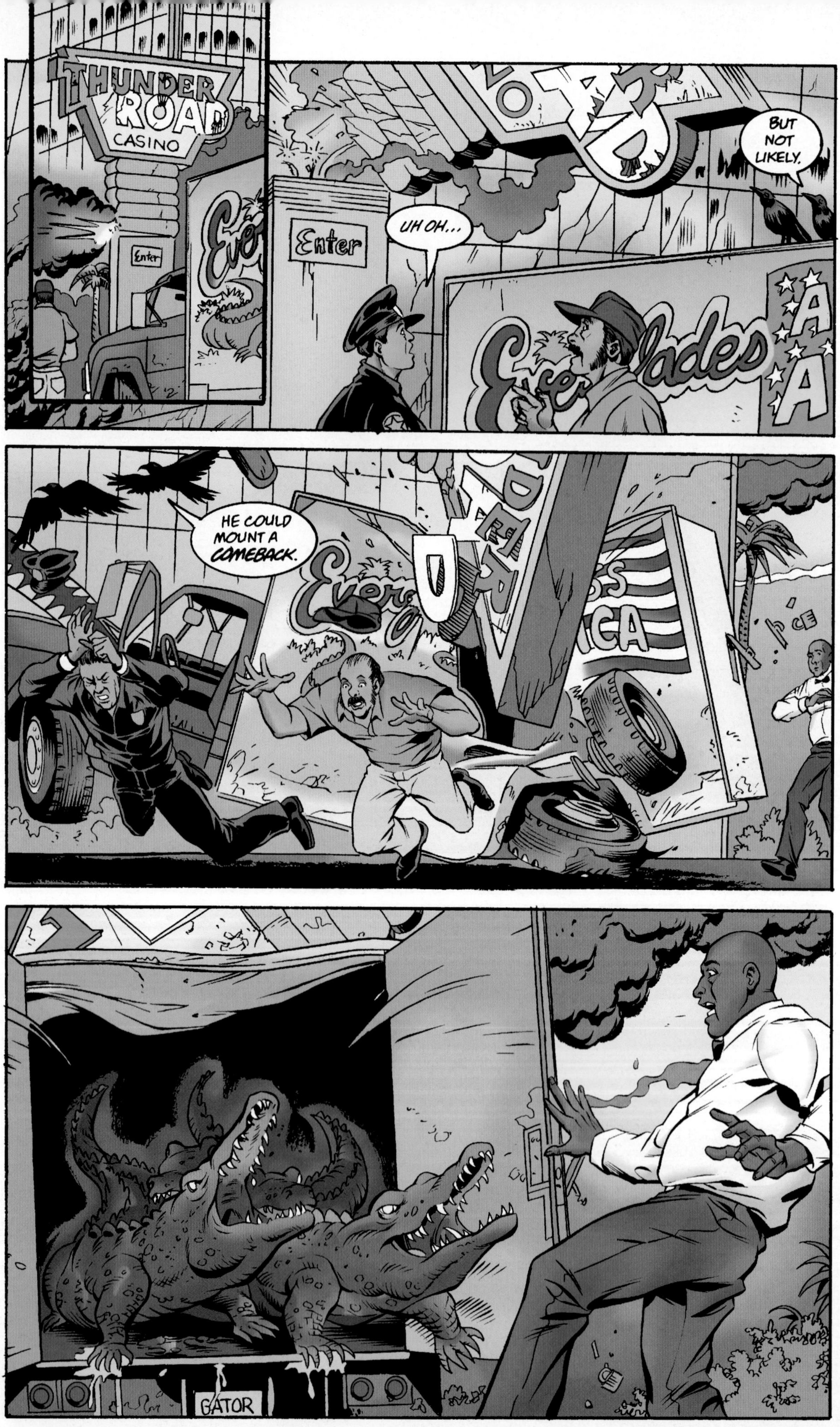
THUNDER ROAD CASINO
Enter
Enter
UH OH...
BUT NOT LIKELY.
HE COULD MOUNT A COMEBACK.
GATOR

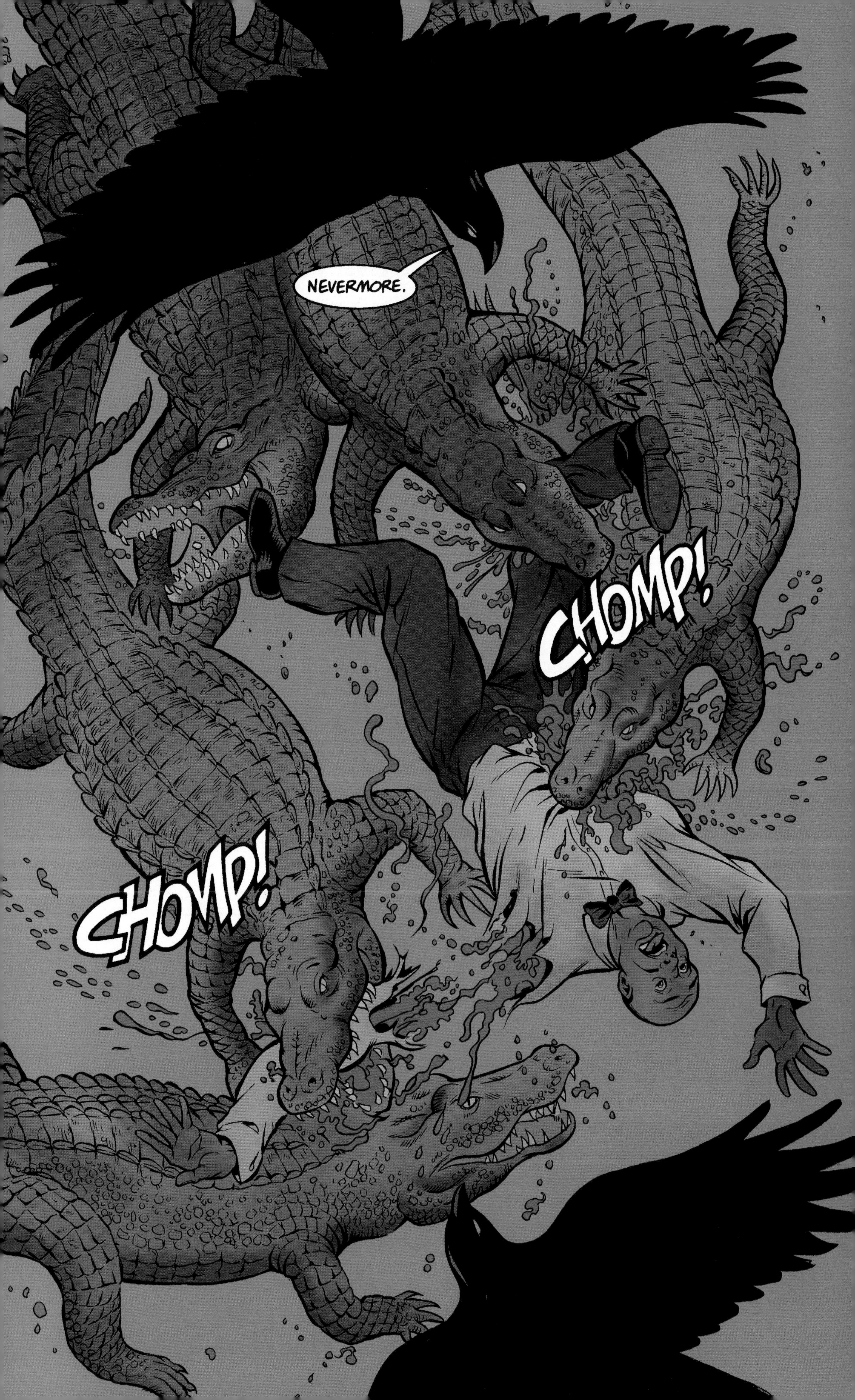
NEVERMORE.
CHOMP!
CHOMP!

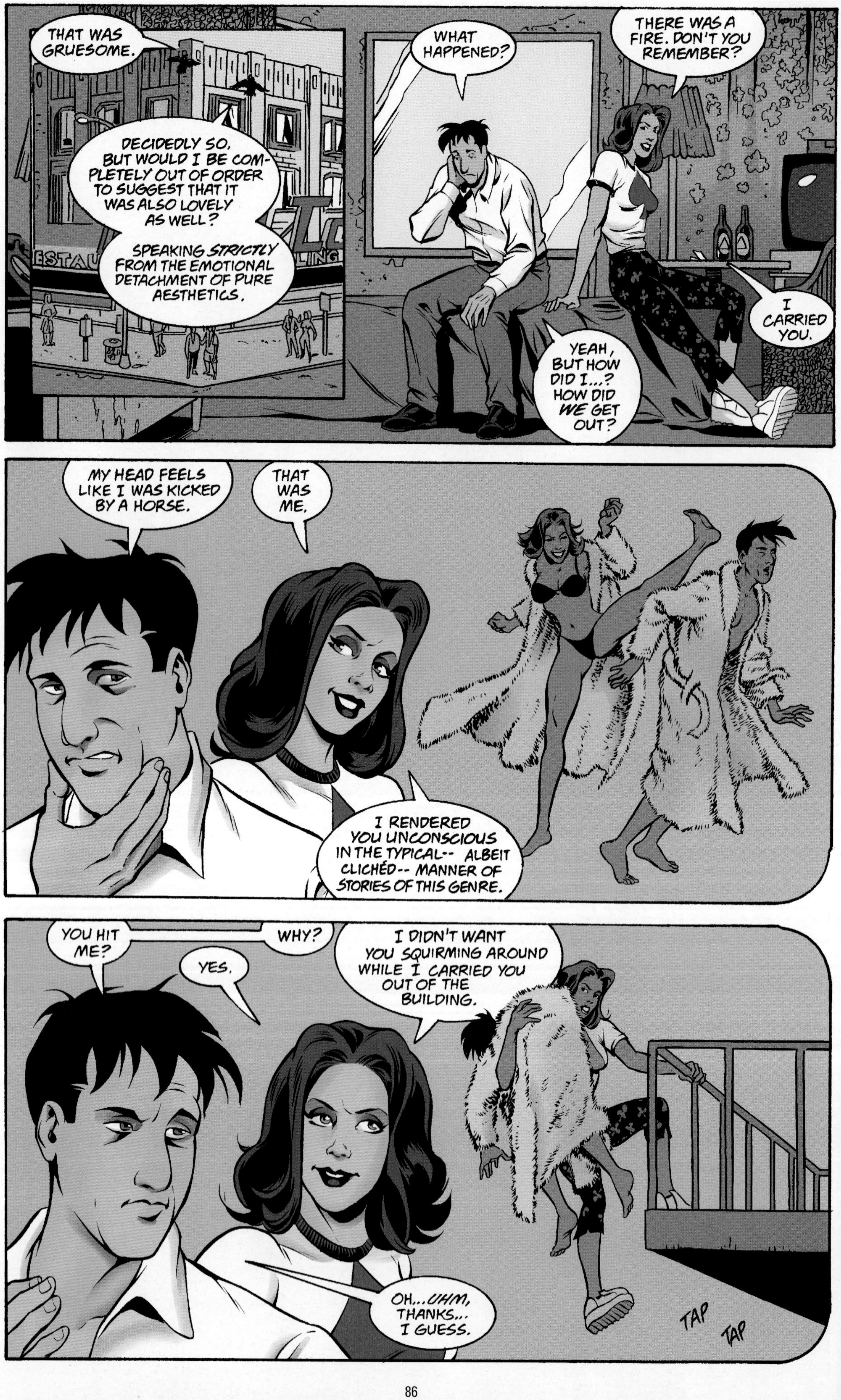
THAT WAS GRUESOME.
DECIDEDLY SO. BUT WOULD I BE COMPLETELY OUT OF ORDER TO SUGGEST THAT IT WAS ALSO LOVELY AS WELL?
SPEAKING STRICTLY FROM THE EMOTIONAL DETACHMENT OF PURE AESTHETICS.
WHAT HAPPENED?
THERE WAS A FIRE. DON'T YOU REMEMBER?
YEAH, BUT HOW DID I...? HOW DID WE GET OUT?
I CARRIED YOU.
MY HEAD FEELS LIKE I WAS KICKED BY A HORSE.
THAT WAS ME.
I RENDERED YOU UNCONSCIOUS IN THE TYPICAL-- ALBEIT CLICHÉD-- MANNER OF STORIES OF THIS GENRE.
YOU HIT ME?
YES.
WHY?
I DIDN'T WANT YOU SQUIRMING AROUND WHILE I CARRIED YOU OUT OF THE BUILDING.
OH...UHM, THANKS... I GUESS.
TAP
TAP

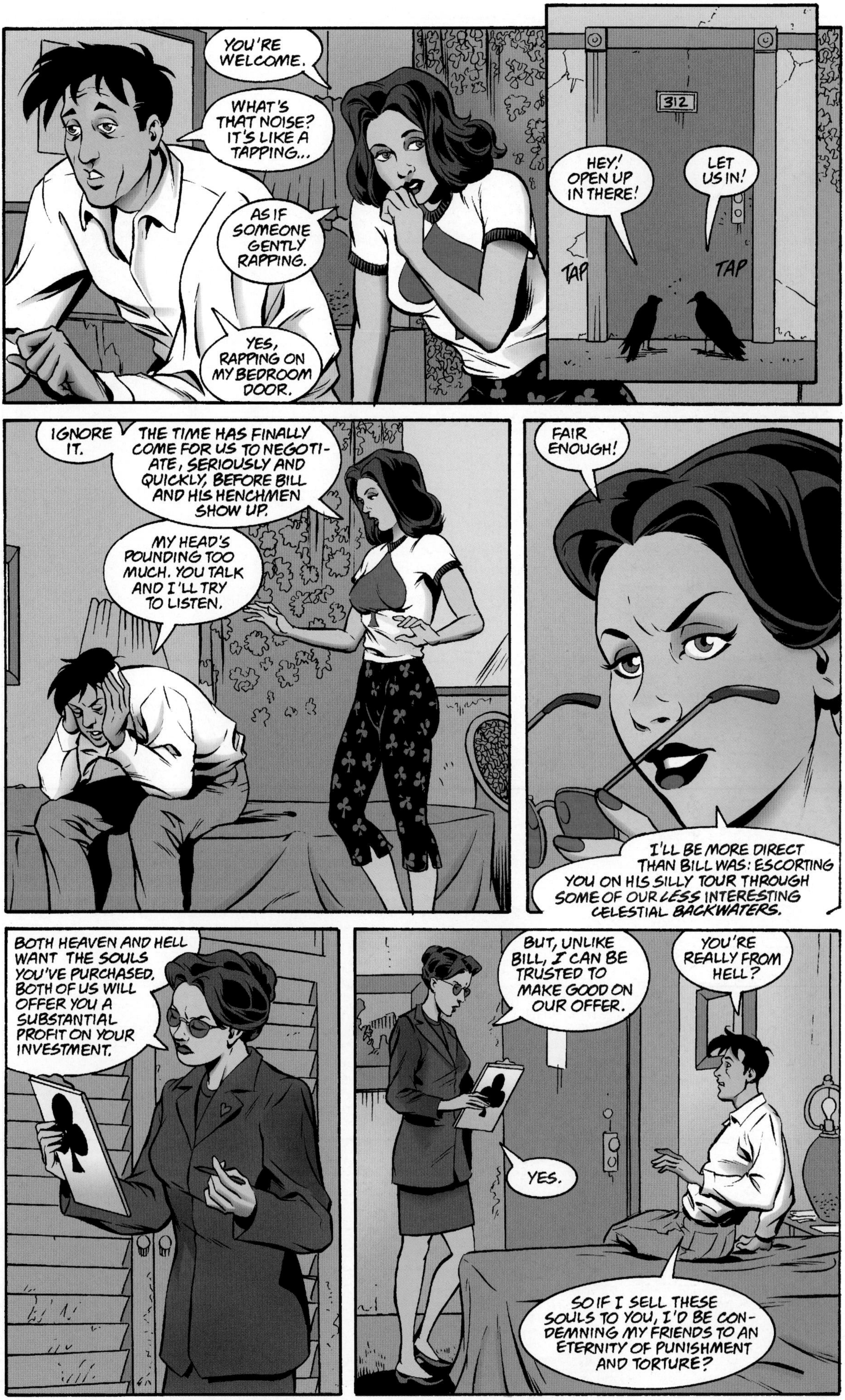
YOU'RE WELCOME.
WHAT'S THAT NOISE? IT'S LIKE A TAPPING...
AS IF SOMEONE GENTLY RAPPING.
YES, RAPPING ON MY BEDROOM DOOR.
312
HEY! OPEN UP IN THERE!
LET US IN!
TAP
TAP
IGNORE IT.
THE TIME HAS FINALLY COME FOR US TO NEGOTI-ATE, SERIOUSLY AND QUICKLY, BEFORE BILL AND HIS HENCHMEN SHOW UP.
MY HEAD'S POUNDING TOO MUCH. YOU TALK AND I'LL TRY TO LISTEN.
FAIR ENOUGH!
I'LL BE MORE DIRECT THAN BILL WAS: ESCORTING YOU ON HIS SILLY TOUR THROUGH SOME OF OUR *LESS* INTERESTING CELESTIAL *BACKWATERS*.
BOTH HEAVEN AND HELL WANT THE SOULS YOU'VE PURCHASED, BOTH OF US WILL OFFER YOU A SUBSTANTIAL PROFIT ON YOUR INVESTMENT.
BUT, UNLIKE BILL, *I* CAN BE TRUSTED TO MAKE GOOD ON OUR OFFER.
YOU'RE REALLY FROM HELL?
YES.
SO IF I SELL THESE SOULS TO YOU, I'D BE CON-DEMNING MY FRIENDS TO AN ETERNITY OF PUNISHMENT AND TORTURE?

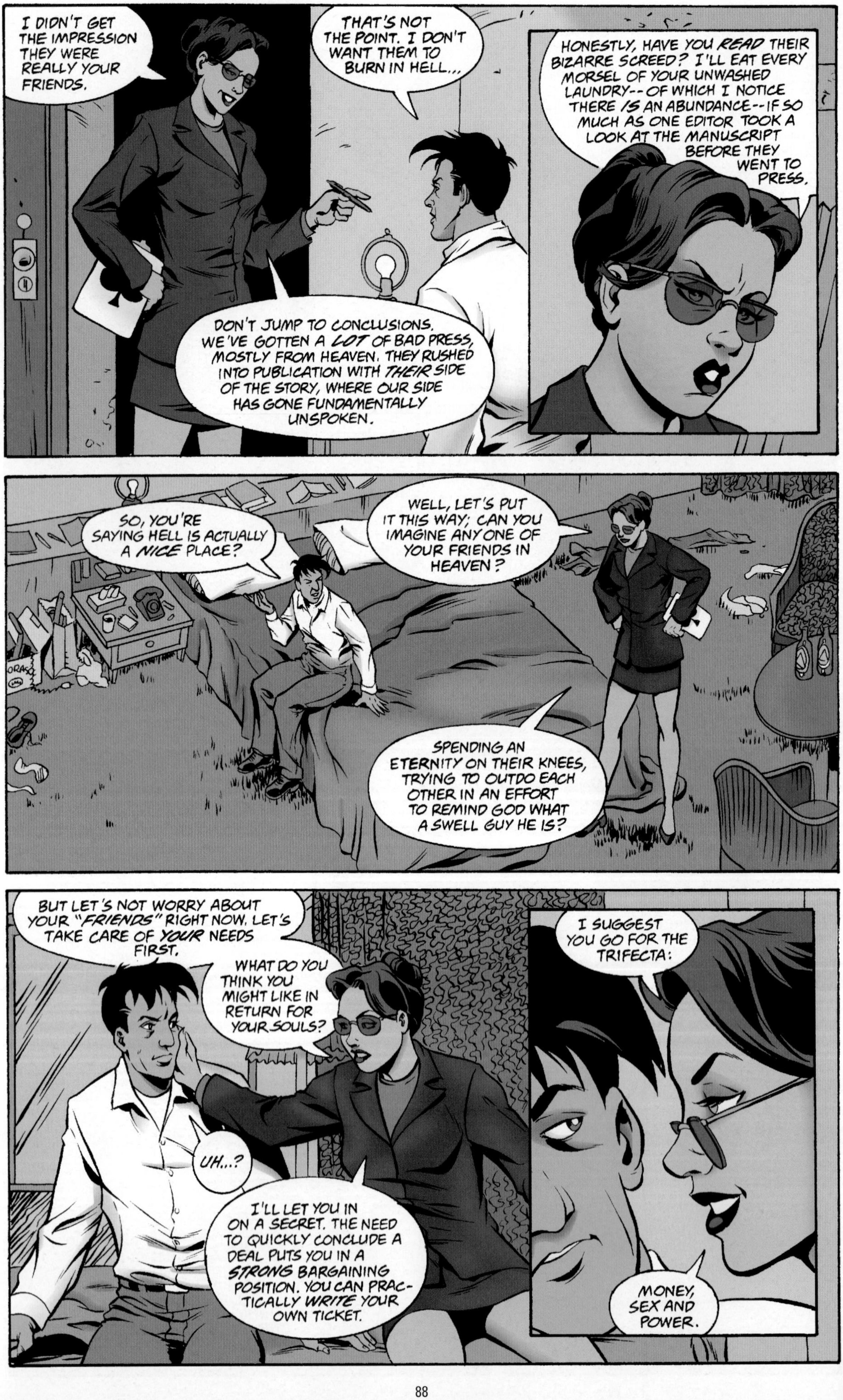
I DIDN'T GET THE IMPRESSION THEY WERE REALLY YOUR FRIENDS.
THAT'S NOT THE POINT. I DON'T WANT THEM TO BURN IN HELL...
DON'T JUMP TO CONCLUSIONS. WE'VE GOTTEN A LOT OF BAD PRESS, MOSTLY FROM HEAVEN. THEY RUSHED INTO PUBLICATION WITH THEIR SIDE OF THE STORY, WHERE OUR SIDE HAS GONE FUNDAMENTALLY UNSPOKEN.
HONESTLY, HAVE YOU READ THEIR BIZARRE SCREED? I'LL EAT EVERY MORSEL OF YOUR UNWASHED LAUNDRY-- OF WHICH I NOTICE THERE IS AN ABUNDANCE--IF SO MUCH AS ONE EDITOR TOOK A LOOK AT THE MANUSCRIPT BEFORE THEY WENT TO PRESS.
SO, YOU'RE SAYING HELL IS ACTUALLY A NICE PLACE?
WELL, LET'S PUT IT THIS WAY; CAN YOU IMAGINE ANY ONE OF YOUR FRIENDS IN HEAVEN?
SPENDING AN ETERNITY ON THEIR KNEES, TRYING TO OUTDO EACH OTHER IN AN EFFORT TO REMIND GOD WHAT A SWELL GUY HE IS?
BUT LET'S NOT WORRY ABOUT YOUR "FRIENDS" RIGHT NOW. LET'S TAKE CARE OF YOUR NEEDS FIRST.
WHAT DO YOU THINK YOU MIGHT LIKE IN RETURN FOR YOUR SOULS?
UH...?
I'LL LET YOU IN ON A SECRET. THE NEED TO QUICKLY CONCLUDE A DEAL PUTS YOU IN A STRONG BARGAINING POSITION. YOU CAN PRACTICALLY WRITE YOUR OWN TICKET.
I SUGGEST YOU GO FOR THE TRIFECTA:
MONEY, SEX AND POWER.

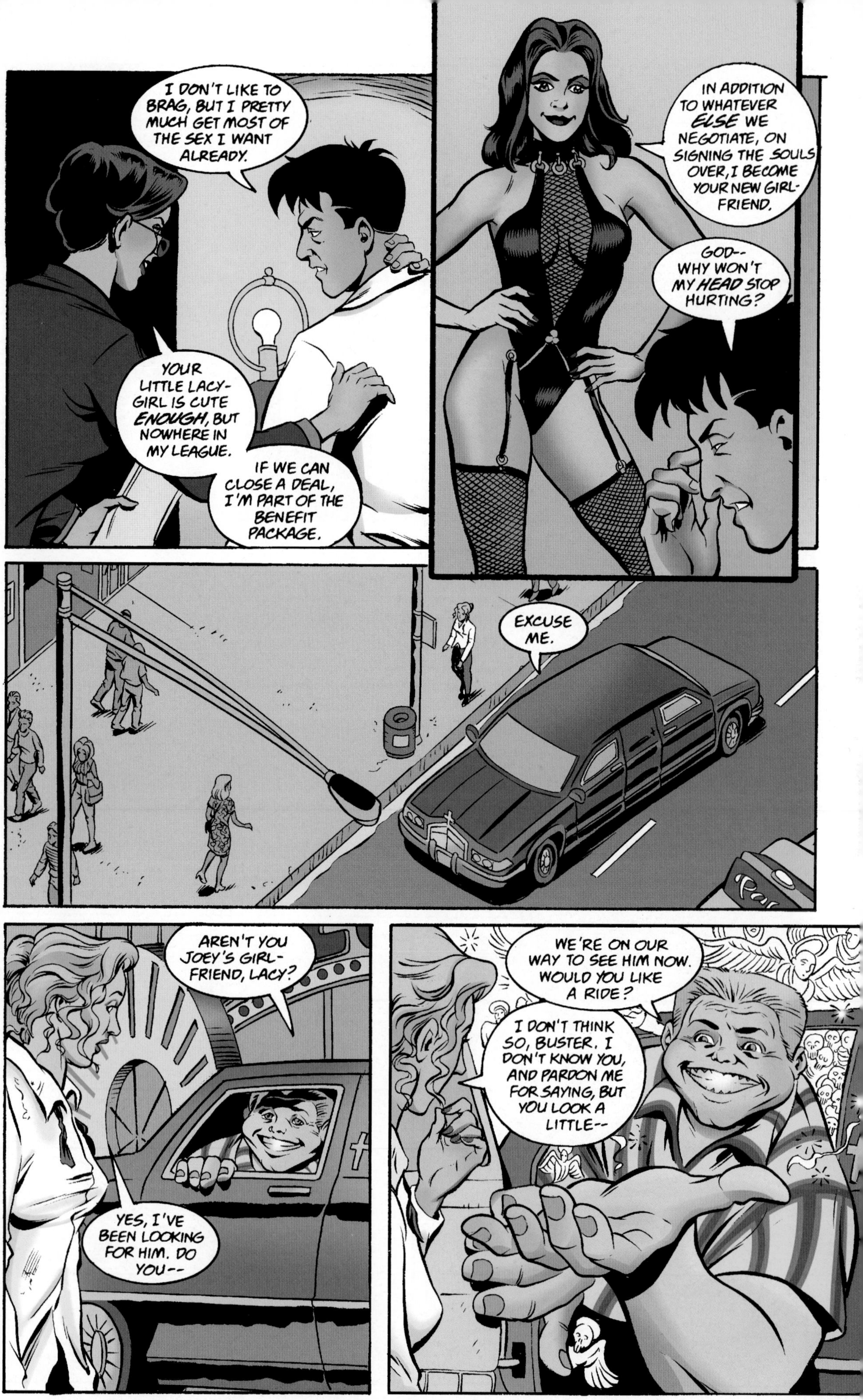
I DON'T LIKE TO BRAG, BUT I PRETTY MUCH GET MOST OF THE SEX I WANT ALREADY.
YOUR LITTLE LACY-GIRL IS CUTE ENOUGH, BUT NOWHERE IN MY LEAGUE.
IF WE CAN CLOSE A DEAL, I'M PART OF THE BENEFIT PACKAGE.
IN ADDITION TO WHATEVER ELSE WE NEGOTIATE, ON SIGNING THE SOULS OVER, I BECOME YOUR NEW GIRL-FRIEND.
GOD-- WHY WON'T MY HEAD STOP HURTING?
EXCUSE ME.
AREN'T YOU JOEY'S GIRL-FRIEND, LACY?
YES, I'VE BEEN LOOKING FOR HIM. DO YOU--
WE'RE ON OUR WAY TO SEE HIM NOW. WOULD YOU LIKE A RIDE?
I DON'T THINK SO, BUSTER. I DON'T KNOW YOU, AND PARDON ME FOR SAYING, BUT YOU LOOK A LITTLE--

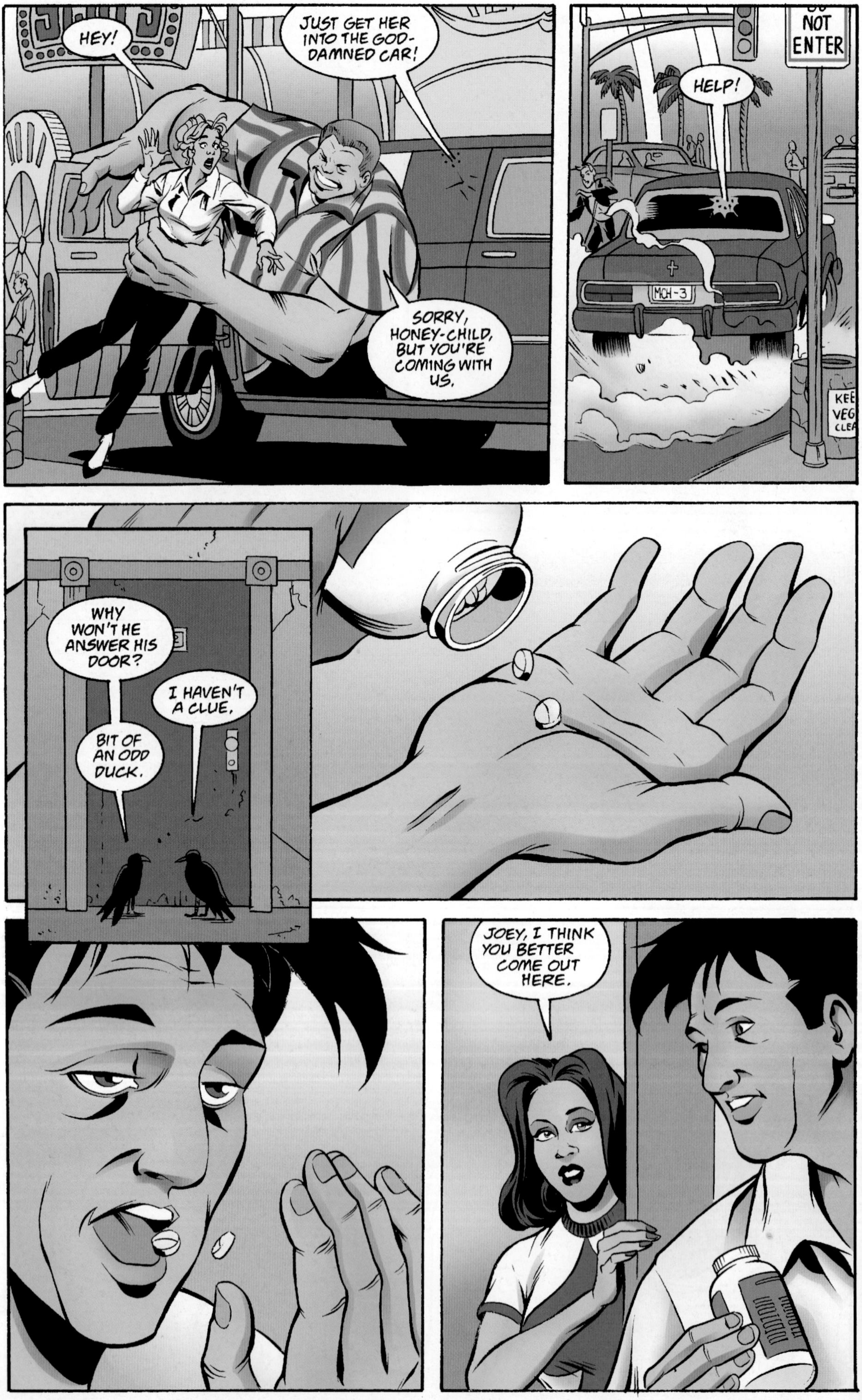
HEY!
JUST GET HER INTO THE GOD-DAMNED CAR!
SORRY, HONEY-CHILD, BUT YOU'RE COMING WITH US.
NOT ENTER
HELP!
MCH-3
WHY WON'T HE ANSWER HIS DOOR?
I HAVEN'T A CLUE.
BIT OF AN ODD DUCK.
JOEY, I THINK YOU BETTER COME OUT HERE.

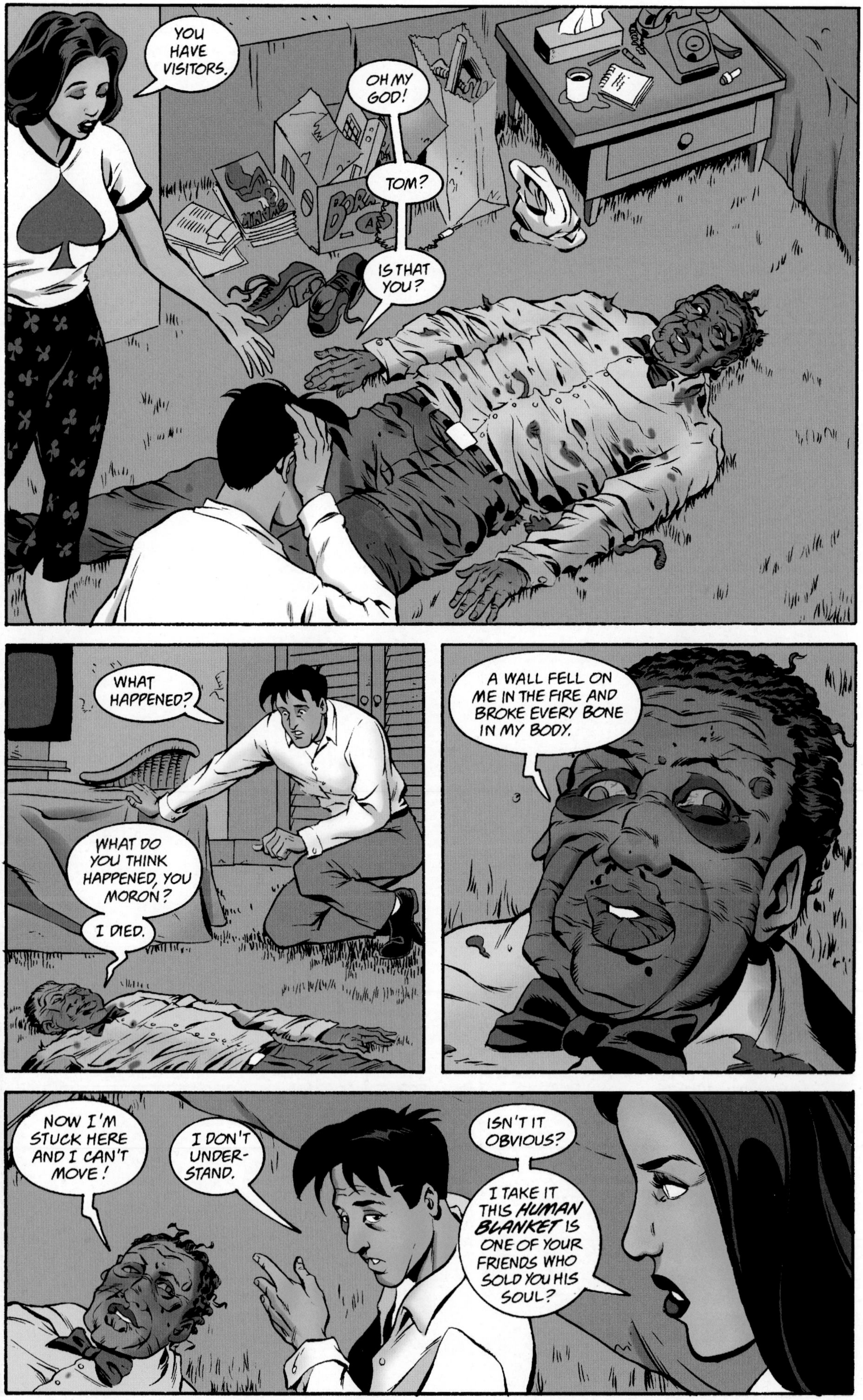
YOU HAVE VISITORS.
OH MY GOD!
TOM?
IS THAT YOU?
WHAT HAPPENED?
WHAT DO YOU THINK HAPPENED, YOU MORON?
I DIED.
A WALL FELL ON ME IN THE FIRE AND BROKE EVERY BONE IN MY BODY.
NOW I'M STUCK HERE AND I CAN'T MOVE!
I DON'T UNDER-STAND.
ISN'T IT OBVIOUS?
I TAKE IT THIS *HUMAN BLANKET* IS ONE OF YOUR FRIENDS WHO SOLD YOU HIS SOUL?

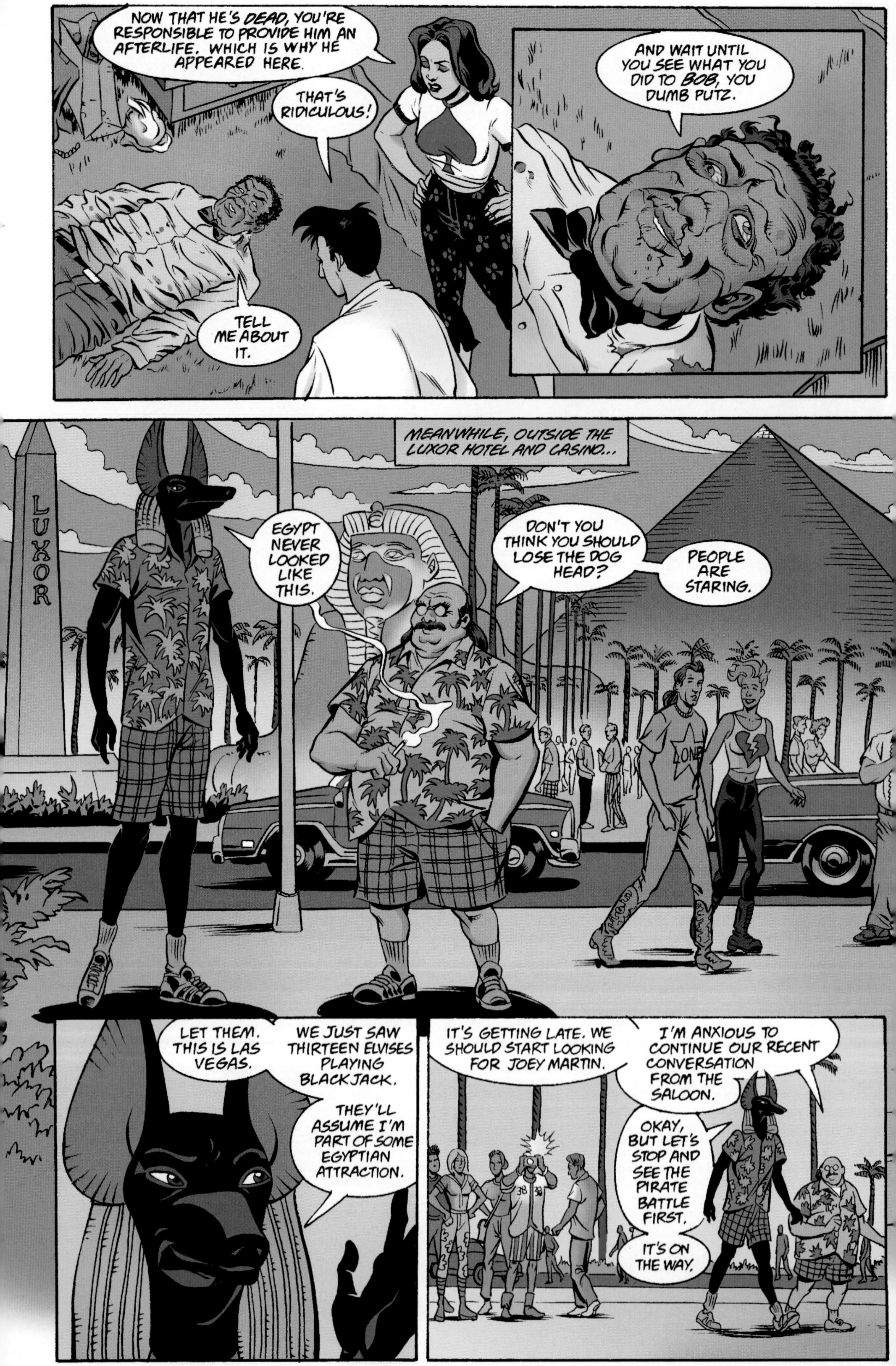
NOW THAT HE'S DEAD, YOU'RE RESPONSIBLE TO PROVIDE HIM AN AFTERLIFE. WHICH IS WHY HE APPEARED HERE.
THAT'S RIDICULOUS!
TELL ME ABOUT IT.
AND WAIT UNTIL YOU SEE WHAT YOU DID TO BOB, YOU DUMB PUTZ.
MEANWHILE, OUTSIDE THE LUXOR HOTEL AND CASINO...
LUXOR
EGYPT NEVER LOOKED LIKE THIS.
DON'T YOU THINK YOU SHOULD LOSE THE DOG HEAD?
PEOPLE ARE STARING.
LET THEM. THIS IS LAS VEGAS.
WE JUST SAW THIRTEEN ELVISES PLAYING BLACKJACK.
THEY'LL ASSUME I'M PART OF SOME EGYPTIAN ATTRACTION.
IT'S GETTING LATE. WE SHOULD START LOOKING FOR JOEY MARTIN.
I'M ANXIOUS TO CONTINUE OUR RECENT CONVERSATION FROM THE SALOON.
OKAY, BUT LET'S STOP AND SEE THE PIRATE BATTLE FIRST.
IT'S ON THE WAY.

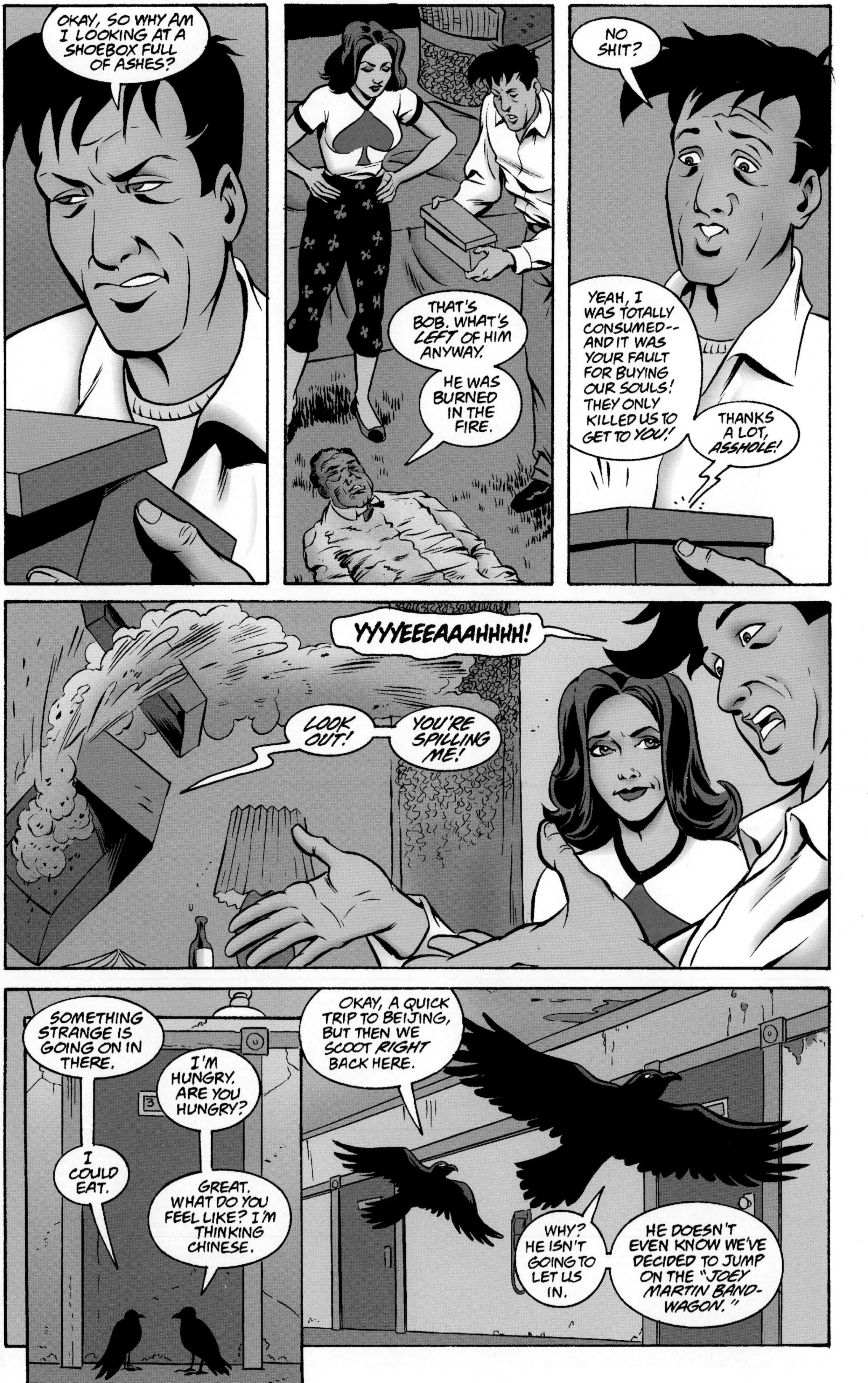
OKAY, SO WHY AM I LOOKING AT A SHOEBOX FULL OF ASHES?
THAT'S BOB. WHAT'S LEFT OF HIM ANYWAY.
HE WAS BURNED IN THE FIRE.
NO SHIT?
YEAH, I WAS TOTALLY CONSUMED-- AND IT WAS YOUR FAULT FOR BUYING OUR SOULS! THEY ONLY KILLED US TO GET TO YOU!
THANKS A LOT, ASSHOLE!
YYYYEEEAAAHHHH!
LOOK OUT!
YOU'RE SPILLING ME!
SOMETHING STRANGE IS GOING ON IN THERE.
I'M HUNGRY. ARE YOU HUNGRY?
I COULD EAT.
GREAT. WHAT DO YOU FEEL LIKE? I'M THINKING CHINESE.
OKAY, A QUICK TRIP TO BEIJING, BUT THEN WE SCOOT RIGHT BACK HERE.
WHY? HE ISN'T GOING TO LET US IN.
HE DOESN'T EVEN KNOW WE'VE DECIDED TO JUMP ON THE "JOEY MARTIN BAND-WAGON."

YOU SHOULD REALLY BE MORE CAREFUL, JOEY.

YOU ALMOST SCATTERED POOR BOB.

I THINK SOME OF ME SPILLED UNDER THE BED.

CHRIST, YOU WON'T BELIEVE SOME OF THE THINGS HE HAS GROWING UNDER THERE!

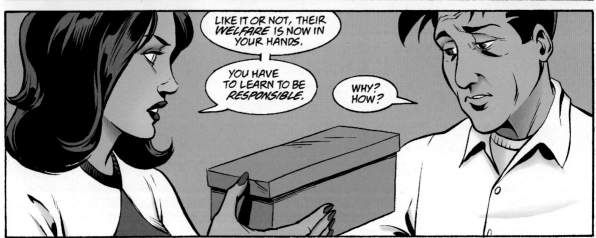

LIKE IT OR NOT, THEIR WELFARE IS NOW IN YOUR HANDS.

YOU HAVE TO LEARN TO BE RESPONSIBLE.

WHY? HOW?

YOU'RE BABBLING, DEAR.

I DON'T SUPPOSE ANYONE'S WILLING TO PICK ME UP OFF THE FLOOR?

HOW COME THEY'RE LIKE THIS, MARY?

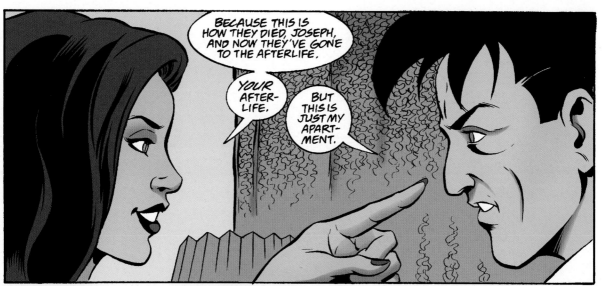

BECAUSE THIS IS HOW THEY DIED, JOSEPH, AND NOW THEY'VE GONE TO THE AFTERLIFE.

YOUR AFTER-LIFE.

BUT THIS IS JUST MY APART-MENT--

YEAH, IT'S NOT *MUCH*, BUT IT SEEMS TO BE ALL YOU'VE GOT. YOU SHOULD HAVE MADE A DEAL MORE QUICKLY.

NOW, NO MATTER WHAT ELSE HAPPENS, NO MATTER WHAT BARGAINS ARE MADE, YOU'RE *STUCK* WITH THESE TWO *FOREVER.*

THAT'S NOT *FAIR!*

DON'T JIGGLE THE BOX!

HE'S GOING TO SPILL ME AGAIN!

ON THE CONTRARY, IT'S *ENTIRELY* FAIR.

MAYBE YOU SHOULD SELL THE OTHERS TO ME BEFORE MORE OF THEM SHOW UP. IT COULD GET MIGHTY *CROWDED*--

TOO LATE.

EARL JUST ARRIVED.

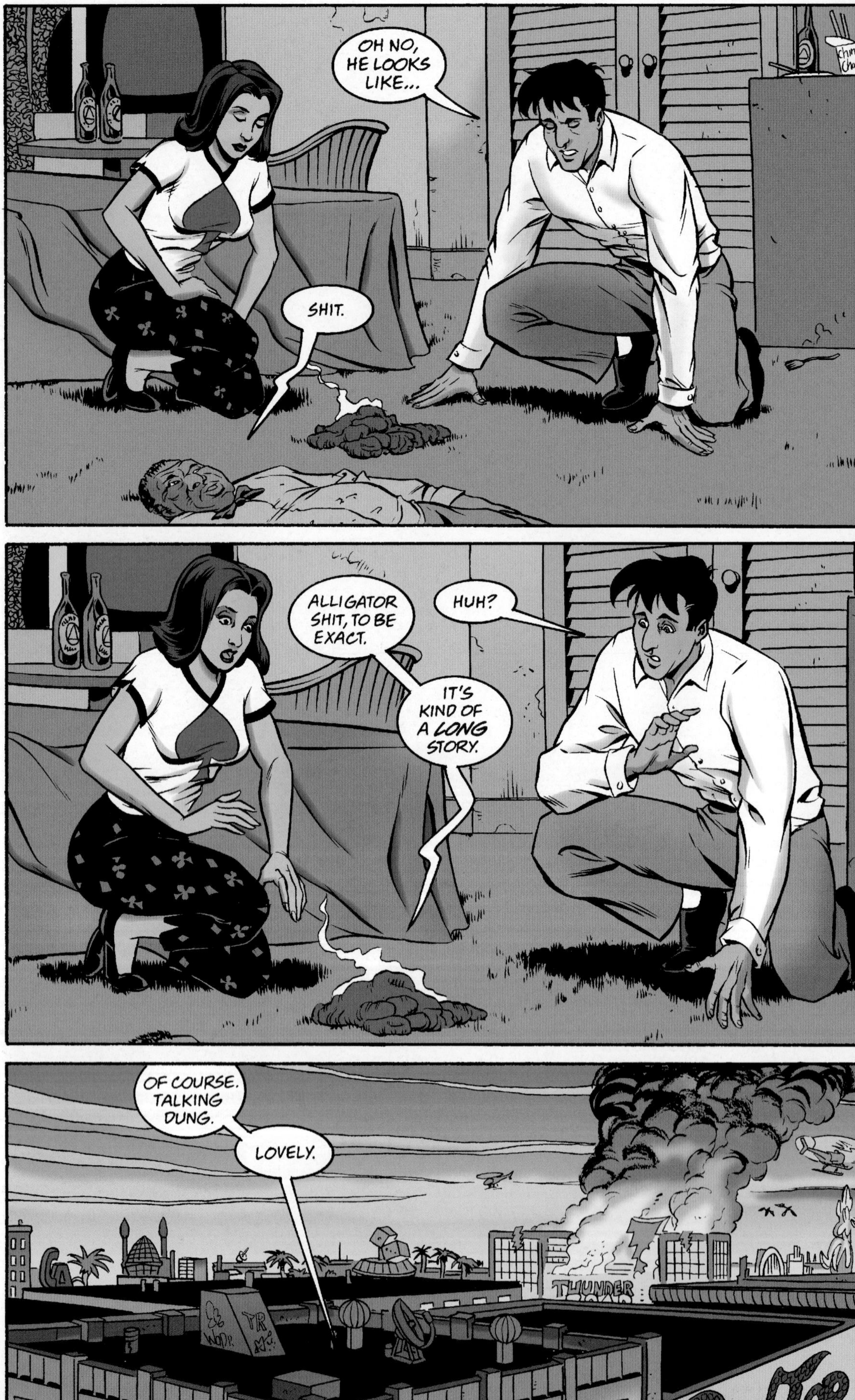
OH NO, HE LOOKS LIKE...
SHIT.
ALLIGATOR SHIT, TO BE EXACT.
HUH?
IT'S KIND OF A LONG STORY.
OF COURSE. TALKING DUNG.
LOVELY.
THUNDER
Red Top

GRANTED, THE MOOSHU MIGHT HAVE BEEN A TOUCH OVERLY TART...

TOO MUCH GARLIC.

OH NO, I QUITE DISAGREE. I CAN'T IMAGINE SUCH A THING AS TOO MUCH GARLIC.

WHICH IS WHY YOU DON'T DATE MUCH.

OH HOW DROLL. YOU-- HELLO, WHAT'S THIS?

DO YOU SEE WHAT I SEE?

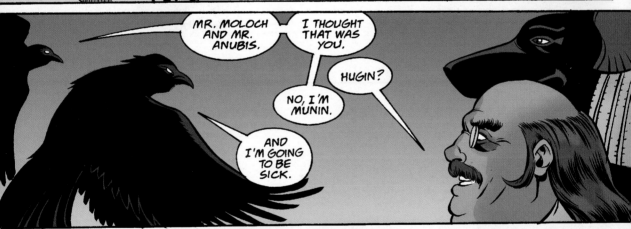

MR. MOLOCH AND MR. ANUBIS.

I THOUGHT THAT WAS YOU.

HUGIN?

NO, I'M MUNIN.

AND I'M GOING TO BE SICK.

WHAT'S WRONG WITH HIM?

WHAT'S ALWAYS WRONG WITH HIM?

I ATE TOO MUCH.

I HAVE TO SAY, I'M SURPRISED TO FIND YOU TWO HERE.

LIKEWISE.

WE UNDER-STOOD YOUR LORD AND MASTER WAS A BIT--UNDER THE WEATHER.

HE STILL IS. WE CHANGED EMPLOY-MENT.

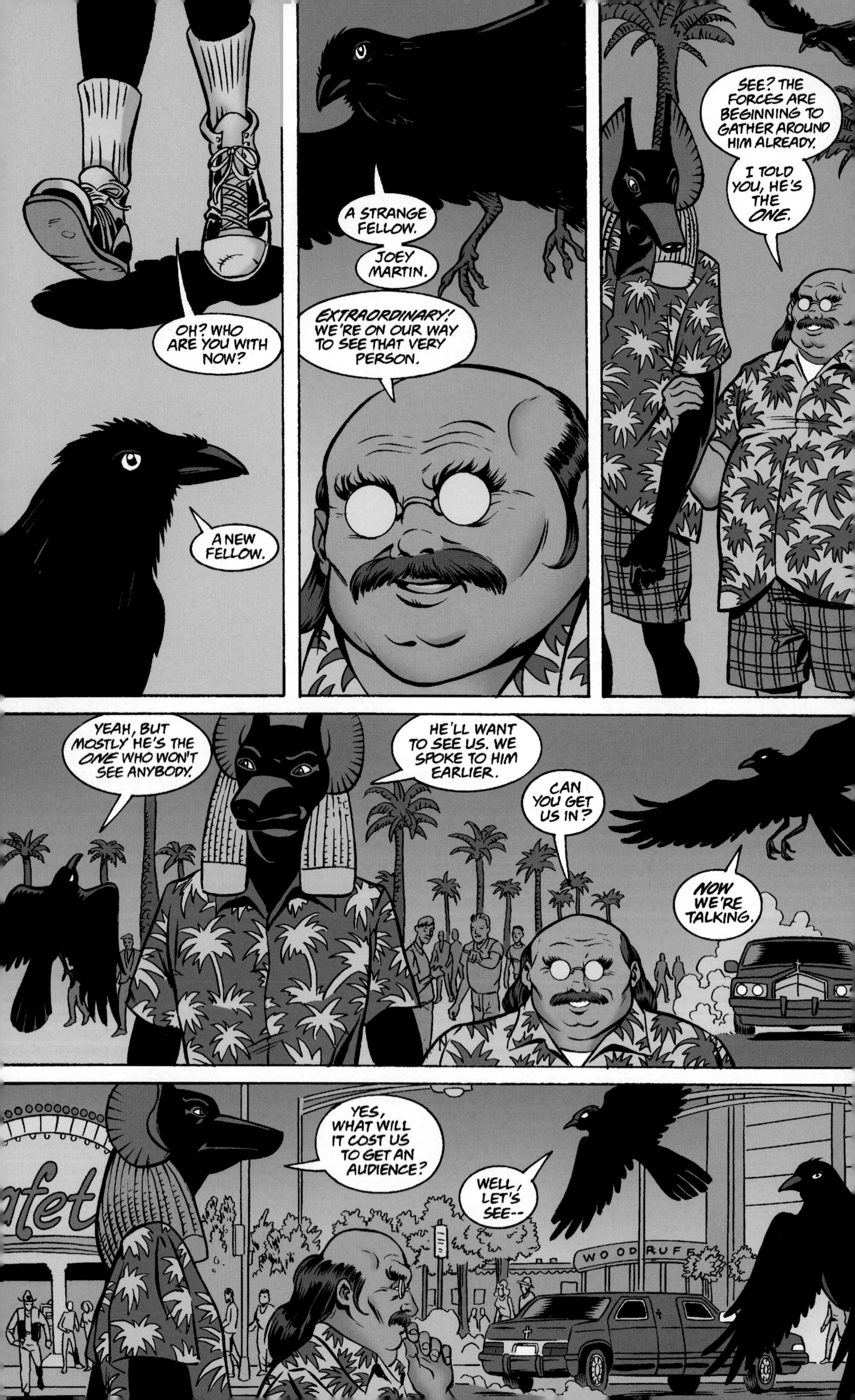
OH? WHO ARE YOU WITH NOW?
A NEW FELLOW.
A STRANGE FELLOW.
JOEY MARTIN.
EXTRAORDINARY! WE'RE ON OUR WAY TO SEE THAT VERY PERSON.
SEE? THE FORCES ARE BEGINNING TO GATHER AROUND HIM ALREADY.
I TOLD YOU, HE'S THE *ONE*.
YEAH, BUT MOSTLY HE'S THE *ONE* WHO WON'T SEE ANYBODY.
HE'LL WANT TO SEE US. WE SPOKE TO HIM EARLIER.
CAN YOU GET US IN?
NOW WE'RE TALKING.
YES, WHAT WILL IT COST US TO GET AN AUDIENCE?
WELL, LET'S SEE--

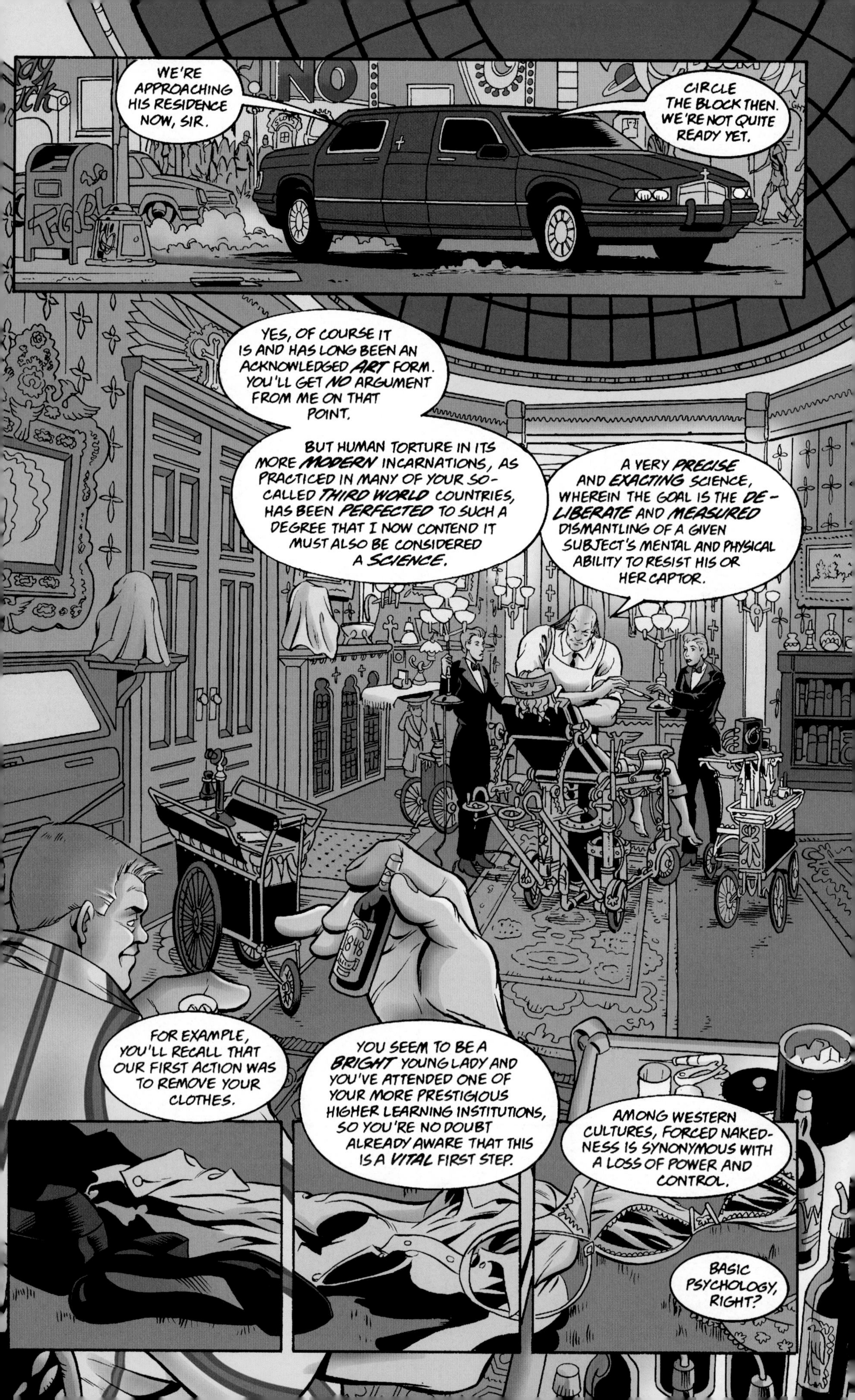
WE'RE APPROACHING HIS RESIDENCE NOW, SIR.
CIRCLE THE BLOCK THEN. WE'RE NOT QUITE READY YET.
YES, OF COURSE IT IS AND HAS LONG BEEN AN ACKNOWLEDGED ART FORM. YOU'LL GET NO ARGUMENT FROM ME ON THAT POINT.
BUT HUMAN TORTURE IN ITS MORE MODERN INCARNATIONS, AS PRACTICED IN MANY OF YOUR SO-CALLED THIRD WORLD COUNTRIES, HAS BEEN PERFECTED TO SUCH A DEGREE THAT I NOW CONTEND IT MUST ALSO BE CONSIDERED A SCIENCE.
A VERY PRECISE AND EXACTING SCIENCE, WHEREIN THE GOAL IS THE DE-LIBERATE AND MEASURED DISMANTLING OF A GIVEN SUBJECT'S MENTAL AND PHYSICAL ABILITY TO RESIST HIS OR HER CAPTOR.
FOR EXAMPLE, YOU'LL RECALL THAT OUR FIRST ACTION WAS TO REMOVE YOUR CLOTHES.
YOU SEEM TO BE A BRIGHT YOUNG LADY AND YOU'VE ATTENDED ONE OF YOUR MORE PRESTIGIOUS HIGHER LEARNING INSTITUTIONS, SO YOU'RE NO DOUBT ALREADY AWARE THAT THIS IS A VITAL FIRST STEP.
AMONG WESTERN CULTURES, FORCED NAKED-NESS IS SYNONYMOUS WITH A LOSS OF POWER AND CONTROL.
BASIC PSYCHOLOGY, RIGHT?

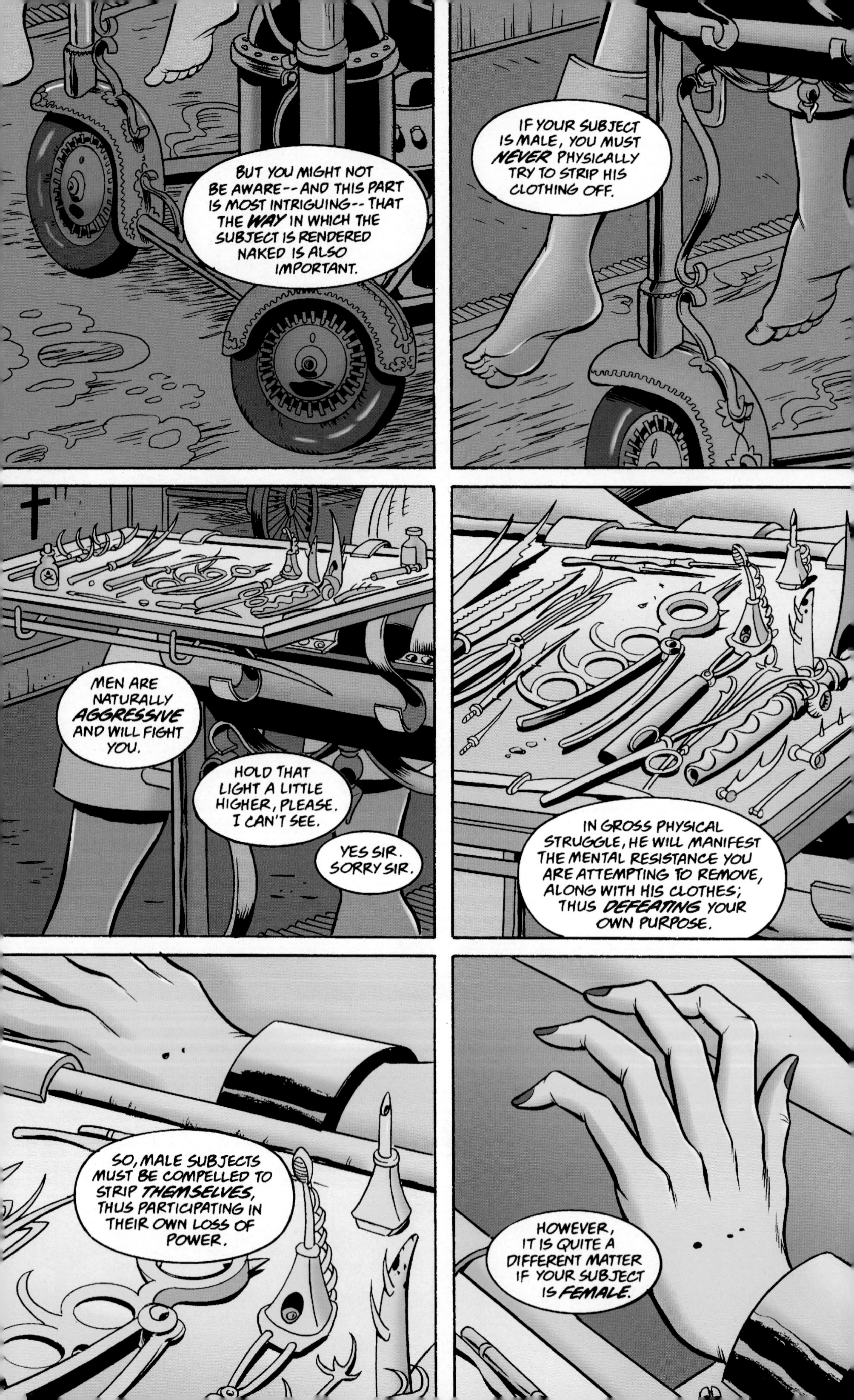

BUT YOU MIGHT NOT BE AWARE-- AND THIS PART IS MOST INTRIGUING-- THAT THE WAY IN WHICH THE SUBJECT IS RENDERED NAKED IS ALSO IMPORTANT.
IF YOUR SUBJECT IS MALE, YOU MUST NEVER PHYSICALLY TRY TO STRIP HIS CLOTHING OFF.
MEN ARE NATURALLY AGGRESSIVE AND WILL FIGHT YOU.
HOLD THAT LIGHT A LITTLE HIGHER, PLEASE. I CAN'T SEE.
YES SIR. SORRY SIR.
IN GROSS PHYSICAL STRUGGLE, HE WILL MANIFEST THE MENTAL RESISTANCE YOU ARE ATTEMPTING TO REMOVE, ALONG WITH HIS CLOTHES; THUS DEFEATING YOUR OWN PURPOSE.
SO, MALE SUBJECTS MUST BE COMPELLED TO STRIP THEMSELVES, THUS PARTICIPATING IN THEIR OWN LOSS OF POWER.
HOWEVER, IT IS QUITE A DIFFERENT MATTER IF YOUR SUBJECT IS FEMALE.

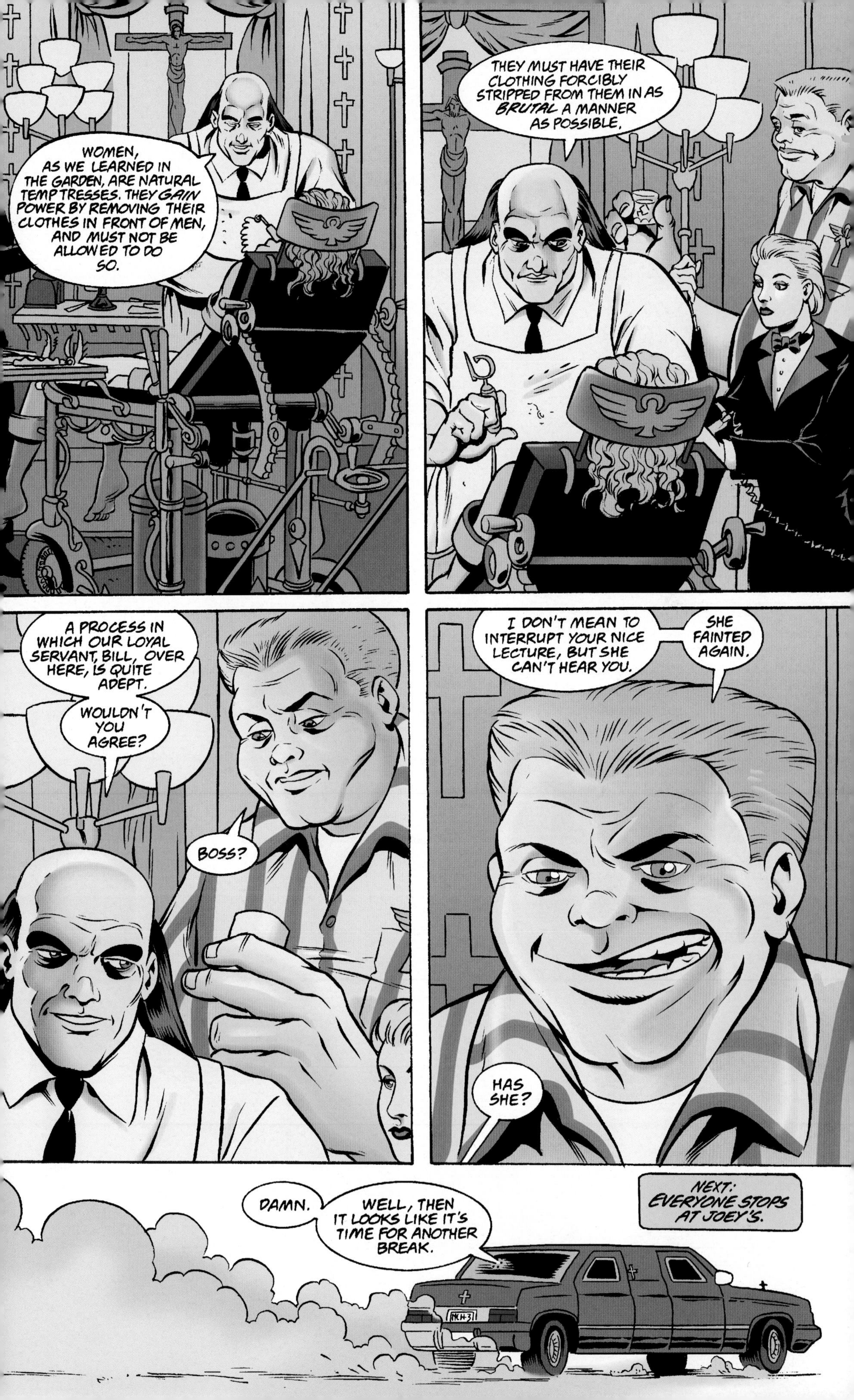
WOMEN, AS WE LEARNED IN THE GARDEN, ARE NATURAL TEMPTRESSES. THEY GAIN POWER BY REMOVING THEIR CLOTHES IN FRONT OF MEN, AND MUST NOT BE ALLOWED TO DO SO.
THEY MUST HAVE THEIR CLOTHING FORCIBLY STRIPPED FROM THEM IN AS BRUTAL A MANNER AS POSSIBLE.
A PROCESS IN WHICH OUR LOYAL SERVANT, BILL, OVER HERE, IS QUITE ADEPT.
WOULDN'T YOU AGREE?
BOSS?
I DON'T MEAN TO INTERRUPT YOUR NICE LECTURE, BUT SHE CAN'T HEAR YOU.
SHE FAINTED AGAIN.
HAS SHE?
DAMN.
WELL, THEN IT LOOKS LIKE IT'S TIME FOR ANOTHER BREAK.
NEXT: EVERYONE STOPS AT JOEY'S.

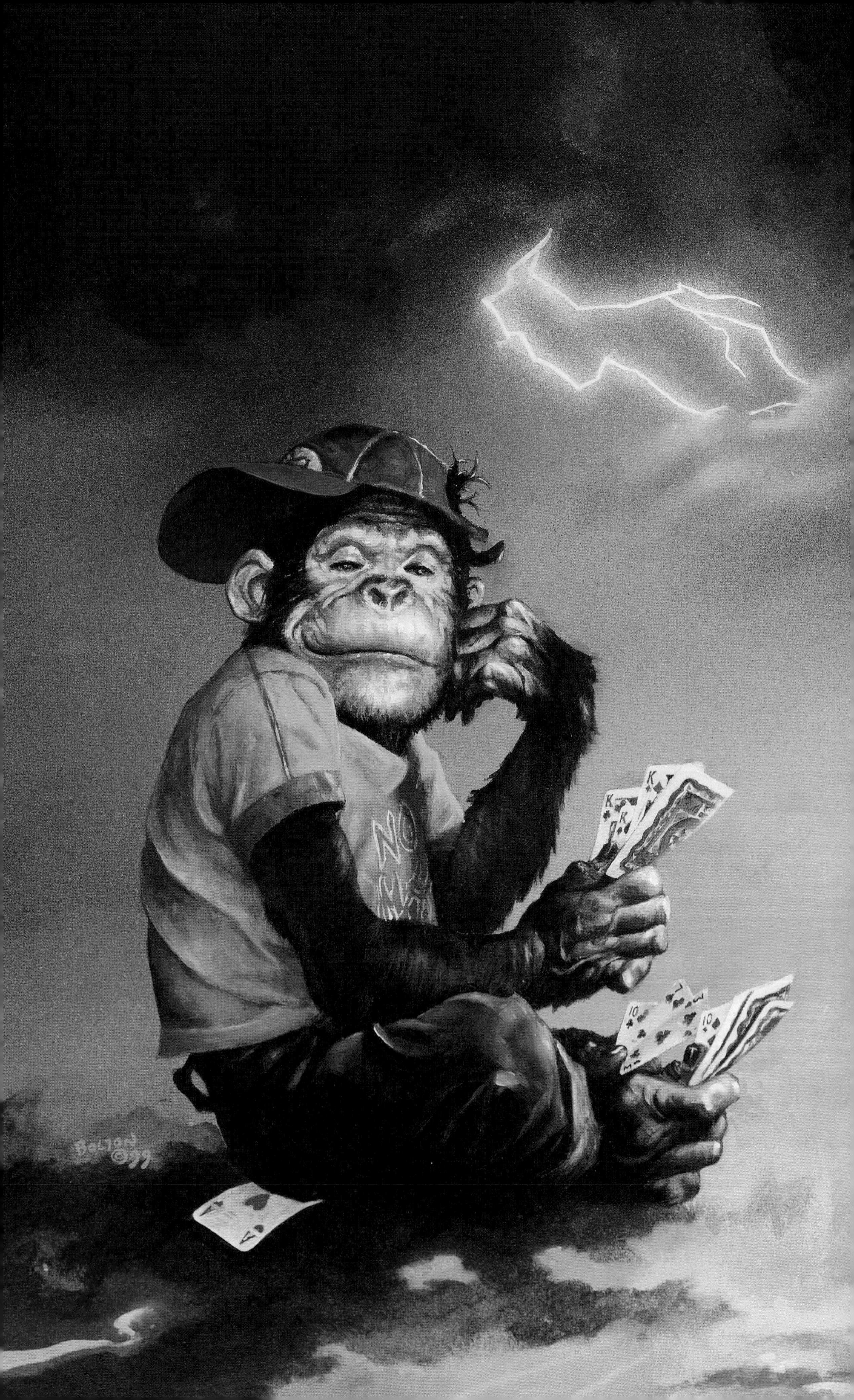
BOLTON
©99

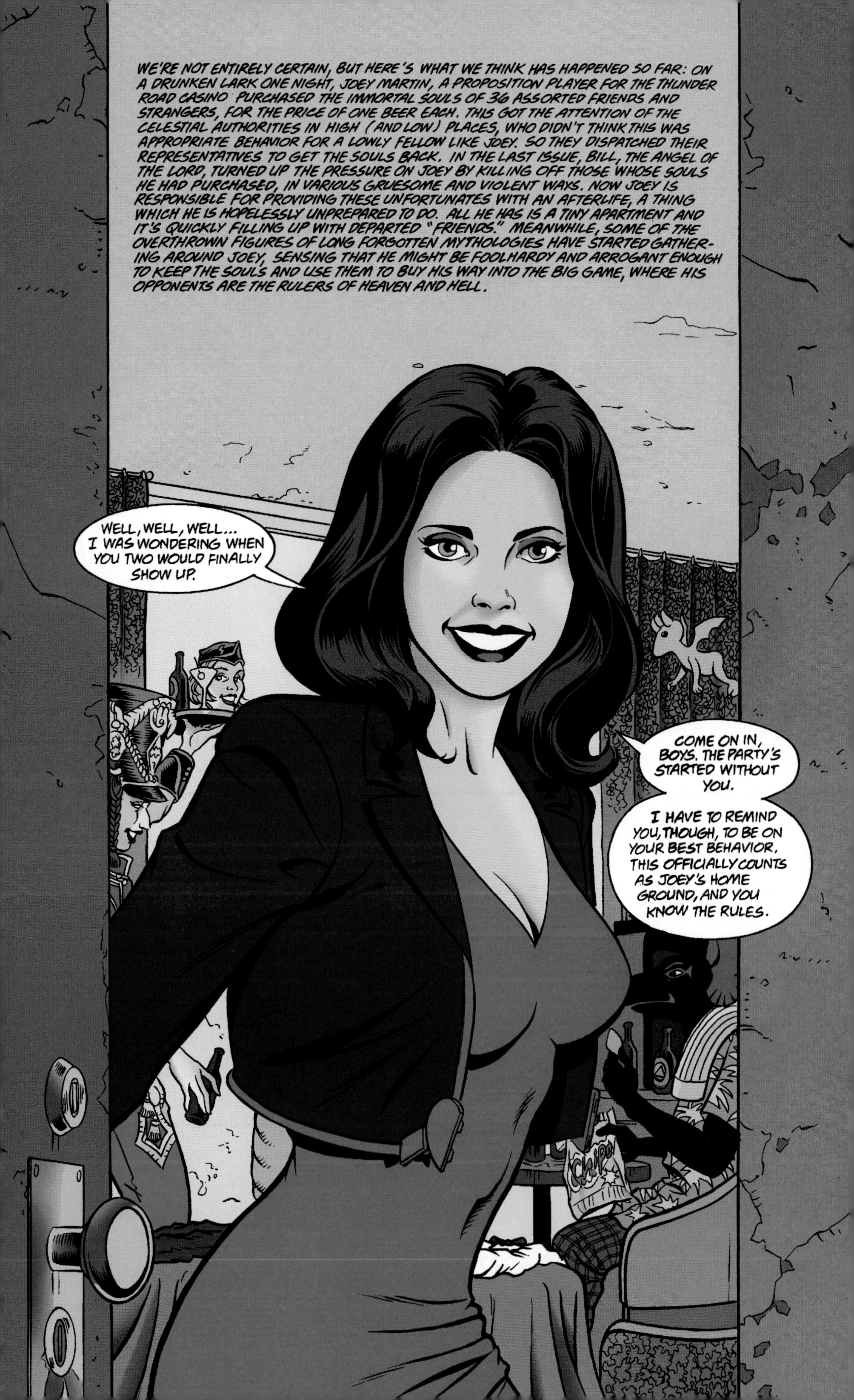
WE'RE NOT ENTIRELY CERTAIN, BUT HERE'S WHAT WE THINK HAS HAPPENED SO FAR: ON A DRUNKEN LARK ONE NIGHT, JOEY MARTIN, A PROPOSITION PLAYER FOR THE THUNDER ROAD CASINO PURCHASED THE IMMORTAL SOULS OF 36 ASSORTED FRIENDS AND STRANGERS, FOR THE PRICE OF ONE BEER EACH. THIS GOT THE ATTENTION OF THE CELESTIAL AUTHORITIES IN HIGH (AND LOW) PLACES, WHO DIDN'T THINK THIS WAS APPROPRIATE BEHAVIOR FOR A LOWLY FELLOW LIKE JOEY. SO THEY DISPATCHED THEIR REPRESENTATIVES TO GET THE SOULS BACK. IN THE LAST ISSUE, BILL, THE ANGEL OF THE LORD, TURNED UP THE PRESSURE ON JOEY BY KILLING OFF THOSE WHOSE SOULS HE HAD PURCHASED, IN VARIOUS GRUESOME AND VIOLENT WAYS. NOW JOEY IS RESPONSIBLE FOR PROVIDING THESE UNFORTUNATES WITH AN AFTERLIFE, A THING WHICH HE IS HOPELESSLY UNPREPARED TO DO. ALL HE HAS IS A TINY APARTMENT AND IT'S QUICKLY FILLING UP WITH DEPARTED "FRIENDS." MEANWHILE, SOME OF THE OVERTHROWN FIGURES OF LONG FORGOTTEN MYTHOLOGIES HAVE STARTED GATHERING AROUND JOEY, SENSING THAT HE MIGHT BE FOOLHARDY AND ARROGANT ENOUGH TO KEEP THE SOULS AND USE THEM TO BUY HIS WAY INTO THE BIG GAME, WHERE HIS OPPONENTS ARE THE RULERS OF HEAVEN AND HELL.
WELL, WELL, WELL... I WAS WONDERING WHEN YOU TWO WOULD FINALLY SHOW UP.
COME ON IN, BOYS. THE PARTY'S STARTED WITHOUT YOU.
I HAVE TO REMIND YOU, THOUGH, TO BE ON YOUR BEST BEHAVIOR. THIS OFFICIALLY COUNTS AS JOEY'S HOME GROUND, AND YOU KNOW THE RULES.
CHIPS

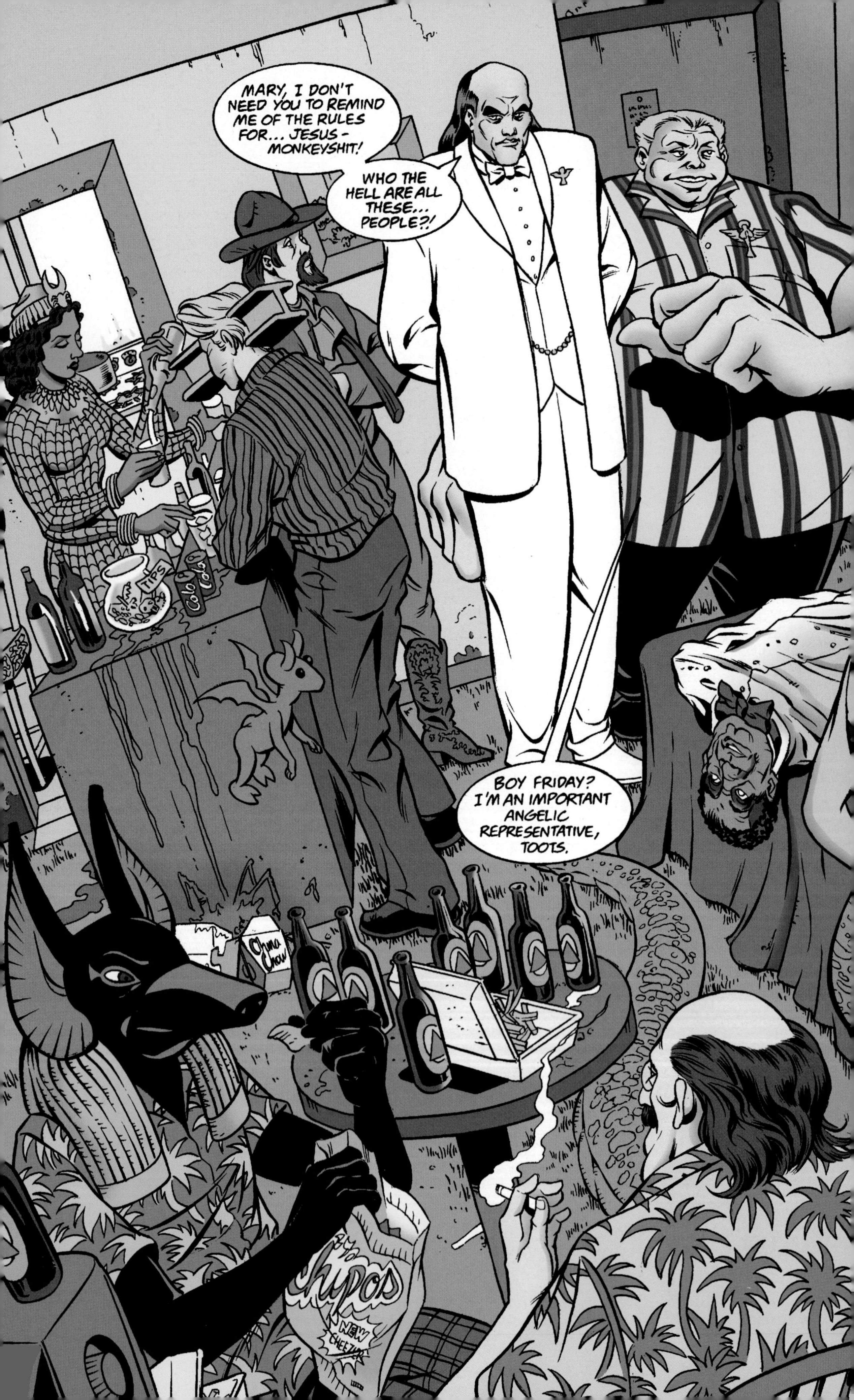
MARY, I DON'T NEED YOU TO REMIND ME OF THE RULES FOR... JESUS-MONKEYSHIT!
WHO THE HELL ARE ALL THESE... PEOPLE?!
BOY FRIDAY? I'M AN IMPORTANT ANGELIC REPRESENTATIVE, TOOTS.
TIPS
Cola
Cola
China Chow
Chipos
NEW

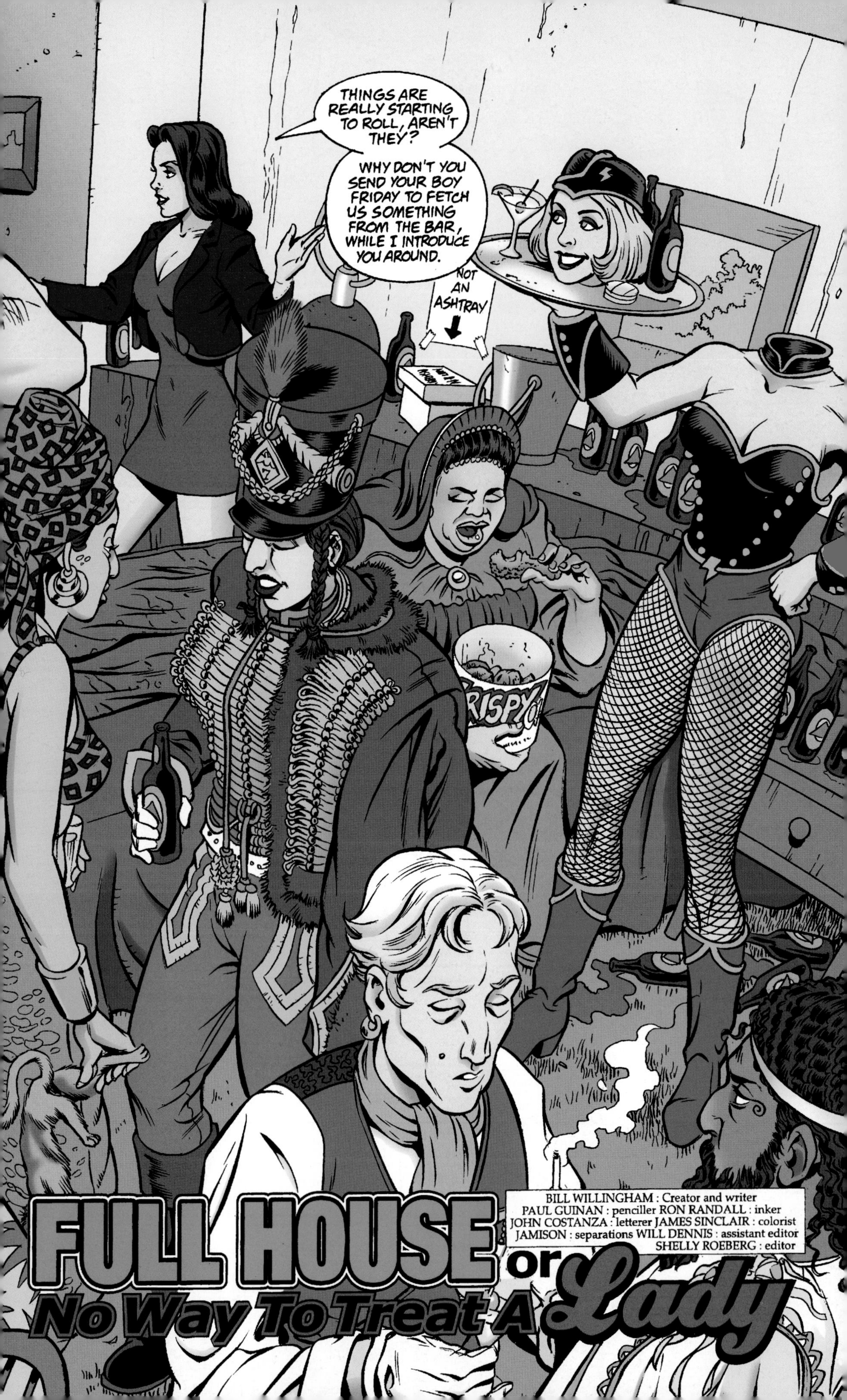
THINGS ARE REALLY STARTING TO ROLL, AREN'T THEY?
WHY DON'T YOU SEND YOUR BOY FRIDAY TO FETCH US SOMETHING FROM THE BAR, WHILE I INTRODUCE YOU AROUND.
NOT AN ASHTRAY
CRISPY
FULL HOUSE
or
No Way To Treat A Lady
BILL WILLINGHAM : Creator and writer
PAUL GUINAN : penciller RON RANDALL : inker
JOHN COSTANZA : letterer JAMES SINCLAIR : colorist
JAMISON : separations WILL DENNIS : assistant editor
SHELLY ROEBERG : editor

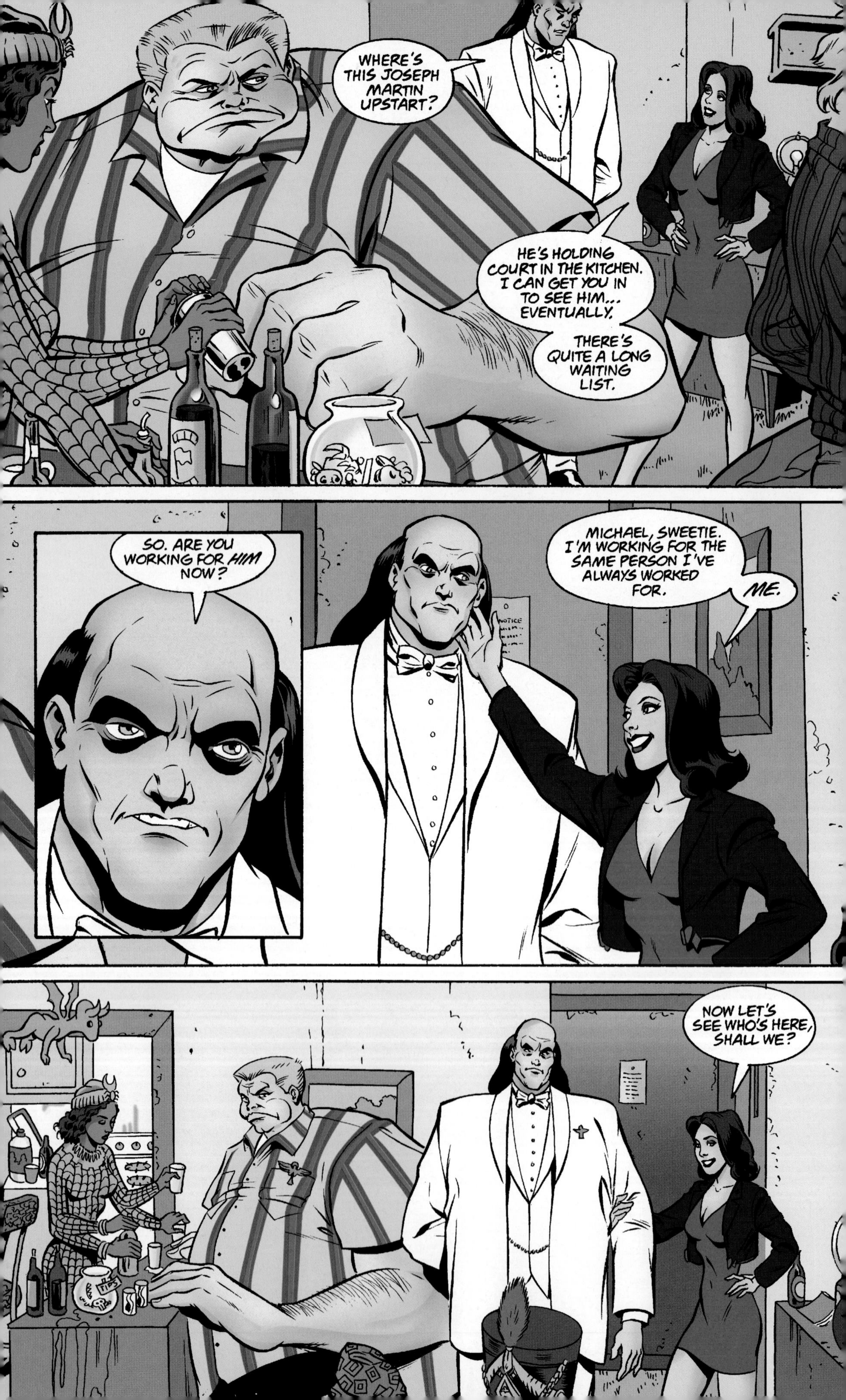
WHERE'S THIS JOSEPH MARTIN UPSTART?
HE'S HOLDING COURT IN THE KITCHEN. I CAN GET YOU IN TO SEE HIM... EVENTUALLY.
THERE'S QUITE A LONG WAITING LIST.
SO. ARE YOU WORKING FOR HIM NOW?
MICHAEL, SWEETIE. I'M WORKING FOR THE SAME PERSON I'VE ALWAYS WORKED FOR.
ME.
NOW LET'S SEE WHO'S HERE, SHALL WE?

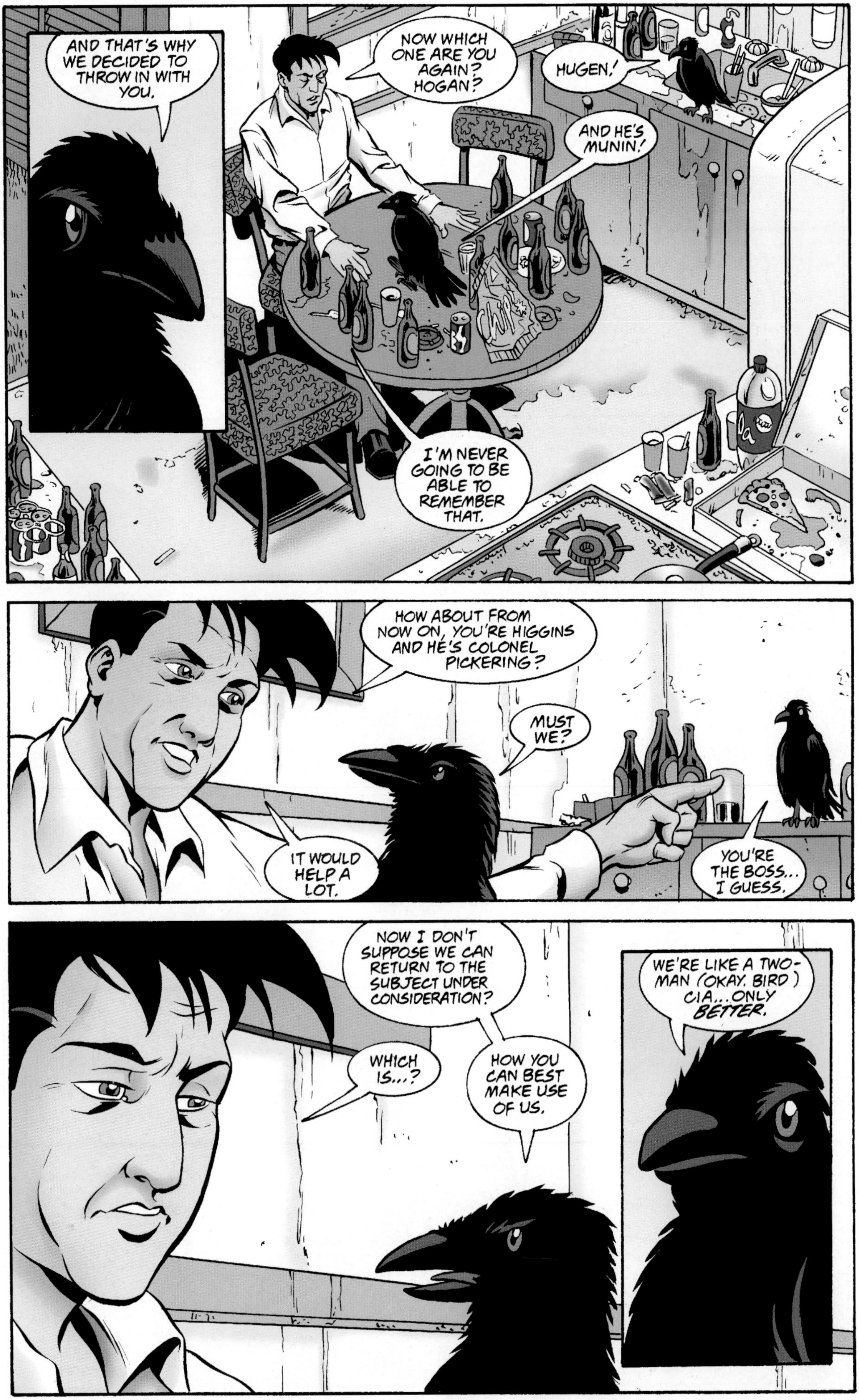
AND THAT'S WHY WE DECIDED TO THROW IN WITH YOU.
NOW WHICH ONE ARE YOU AGAIN? HOGAN?
HUGEN!
AND HE'S MUNIN!
I'M NEVER GOING TO BE ABLE TO REMEMBER THAT.
HOW ABOUT FROM NOW ON, YOU'RE HIGGINS AND HE'S COLONEL PICKERING?
MUST WE?
IT WOULD HELP A LOT.
YOU'RE THE BOSS... I GUESS.
NOW I DON'T SUPPOSE WE CAN RETURN TO THE SUBJECT UNDER CONSIDERATION?
WHICH IS...?
HOW YOU CAN BEST MAKE USE OF US.
WE'RE LIKE A TWO-MAN (OKAY, BIRD) CIA...ONLY BETTER.

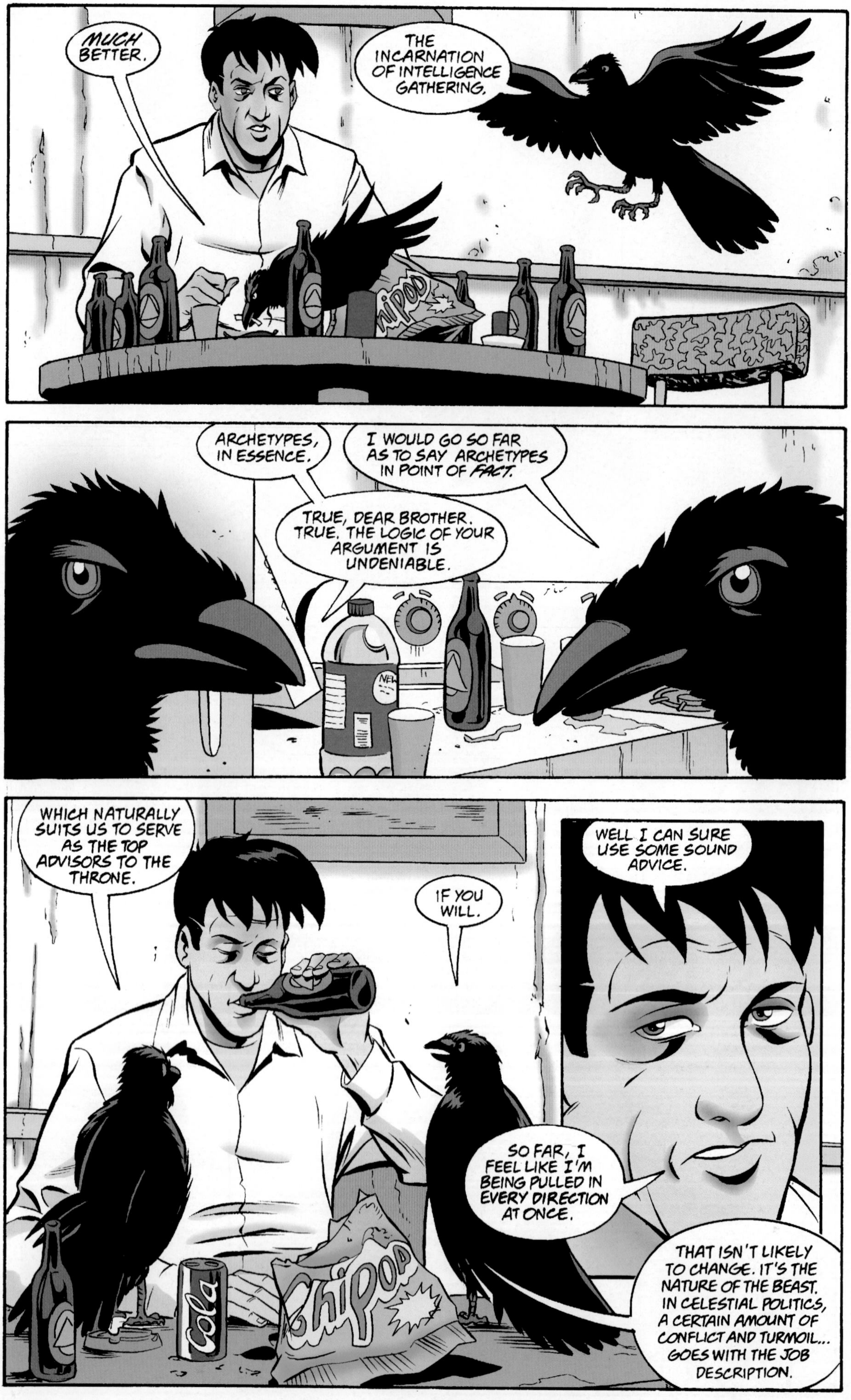
MUCH BETTER.
THE INCARNATION OF INTELLIGENCE GATHERING.
ARCHETYPES, IN ESSENCE.
I WOULD GO SO FAR AS TO SAY ARCHETYPES IN POINT OF FACT.
TRUE, DEAR BROTHER. TRUE. THE LOGIC OF YOUR ARGUMENT IS UNDENIABLE.
WHICH NATURALLY SUITS US TO SERVE AS THE TOP ADVISORS TO THE THRONE.
IF YOU WILL.
WELL I CAN SURE USE SOME SOUND ADVICE.
SO FAR, I FEEL LIKE I'M BEING PULLED IN EVERY DIRECTION AT ONCE.
THAT ISN'T LIKELY TO CHANGE. IT'S THE NATURE OF THE BEAST. IN CELESTIAL POLITICS, A CERTAIN AMOUNT OF CONFLICT AND TURMOIL... GOES WITH THE JOB DESCRIPTION.

NOW *THERE'S* A GOOD PLACE TO START.

WHAT *IS* MY JOB DESCRIP-TION?

NO ONE'S EXPLAINED THAT TO YOU YET?

NOT AS SUCH, NO. AT LEAST NOT IN ANY WAY I CAN UNDERSTAND.

WELL, SIR. NOT TO MINCE WORDS...

...ASSUMING YOU DECIDE TO CARRY ON...

...FOLLOW THROUGH, IF YOU WILL...

...YOU BECOME GOD.

GOD?

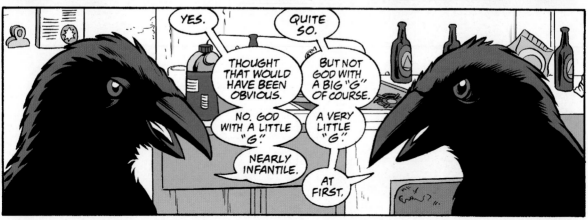

YES.

QUITE SO.

THOUGHT THAT WOULD HAVE BEEN OBVIOUS.

BUT NOT GOD WITH A BIG "G" OF COURSE.

NO. GOD WITH A LITTLE "G."

A VERY LITTLE "G."

NEARLY INFANTILE.

AT FIRST.

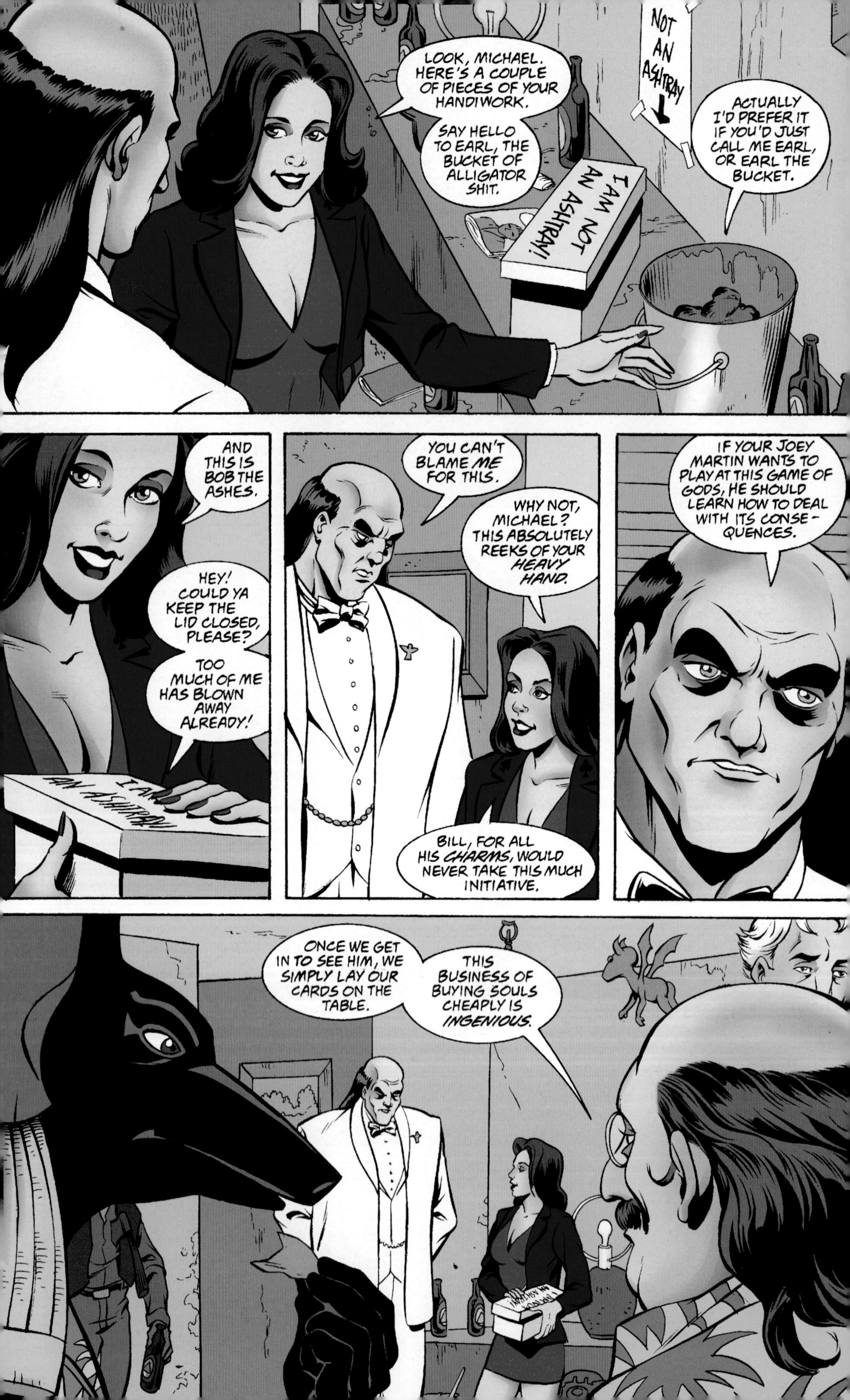
NOT AN ASHTRAY
LOOK, MICHAEL. HERE'S A COUPLE OF PIECES OF YOUR HANDIWORK.
SAY HELLO TO EARL, THE BUCKET OF ALLIGATOR SHIT.
I AM NOT AN ASHTRAY!
ACTUALLY I'D PREFER IT IF YOU'D JUST CALL ME EARL, OR EARL THE BUCKET.
AND THIS IS BOB THE ASHES.
HEY! COULD YA KEEP THE LID CLOSED, PLEASE?
TOO MUCH OF ME HAS BLOWN AWAY ALREADY!
I AM NOT AN ASHTRAY!
YOU CAN'T BLAME *ME* FOR THIS.
WHY NOT, MICHAEL? THIS ABSOLUTELY REEKS OF YOUR *HEAVY HAND.*
BILL, FOR ALL HIS *CHARMS,* WOULD NEVER TAKE THIS MUCH INITIATIVE.
IF YOUR JOEY MARTIN WANTS TO PLAY AT THIS GAME OF GODS, HE SHOULD LEARN HOW TO DEAL WITH ITS CONSE-QUENCES.
ONCE WE GET IN TO SEE HIM, WE SIMPLY LAY OUR CARDS ON THE TABLE.
THIS BUSINESS OF BUYING SOULS CHEAPLY IS *INGENIOUS.*

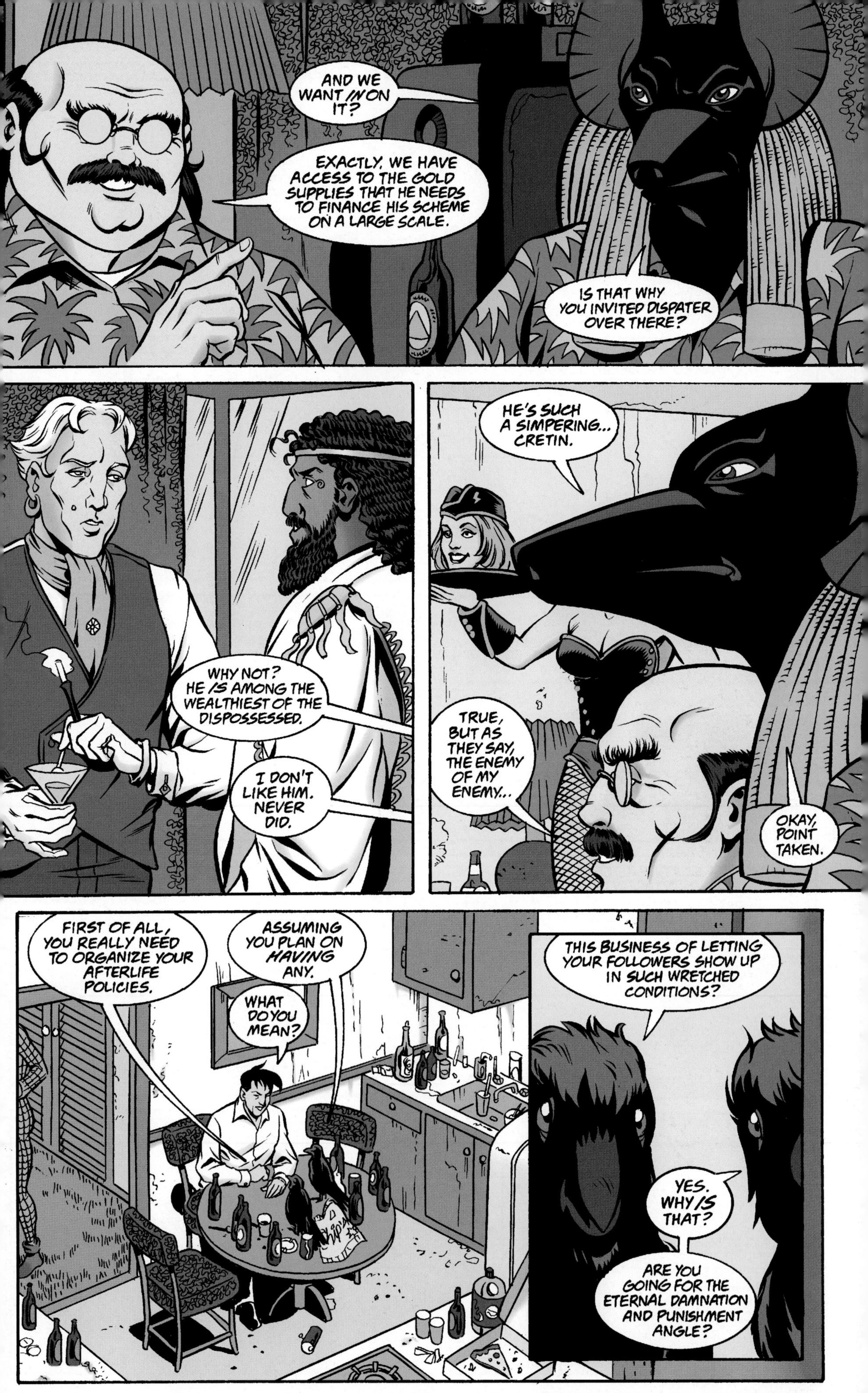
AND WE WANT IN ON IT?
EXACTLY, WE HAVE ACCESS TO THE GOLD SUPPLIES THAT HE NEEDS TO FINANCE HIS SCHEME ON A LARGE SCALE.
IS THAT WHY YOU INVITED DISPATER OVER THERE?
WHY NOT? HE IS AMONG THE WEALTHIEST OF THE DISPOSSESSED.
I DON'T LIKE HIM. NEVER DID.
HE'S SUCH A SIMPERING... CRETIN.
TRUE, BUT AS THEY SAY, THE ENEMY OF MY ENEMY...
OKAY, POINT TAKEN.
FIRST OF ALL, YOU REALLY NEED TO ORGANIZE YOUR AFTERLIFE POLICIES.
ASSUMING YOU PLAN ON HAVING ANY.
WHAT DO YOU MEAN?
THIS BUSINESS OF LETTING YOUR FOLLOWERS SHOW UP IN SUCH WRETCHED CONDITIONS?
YES. WHY IS THAT?
ARE YOU GOING FOR THE ETERNAL DAMNATION AND PUNISHMENT ANGLE?

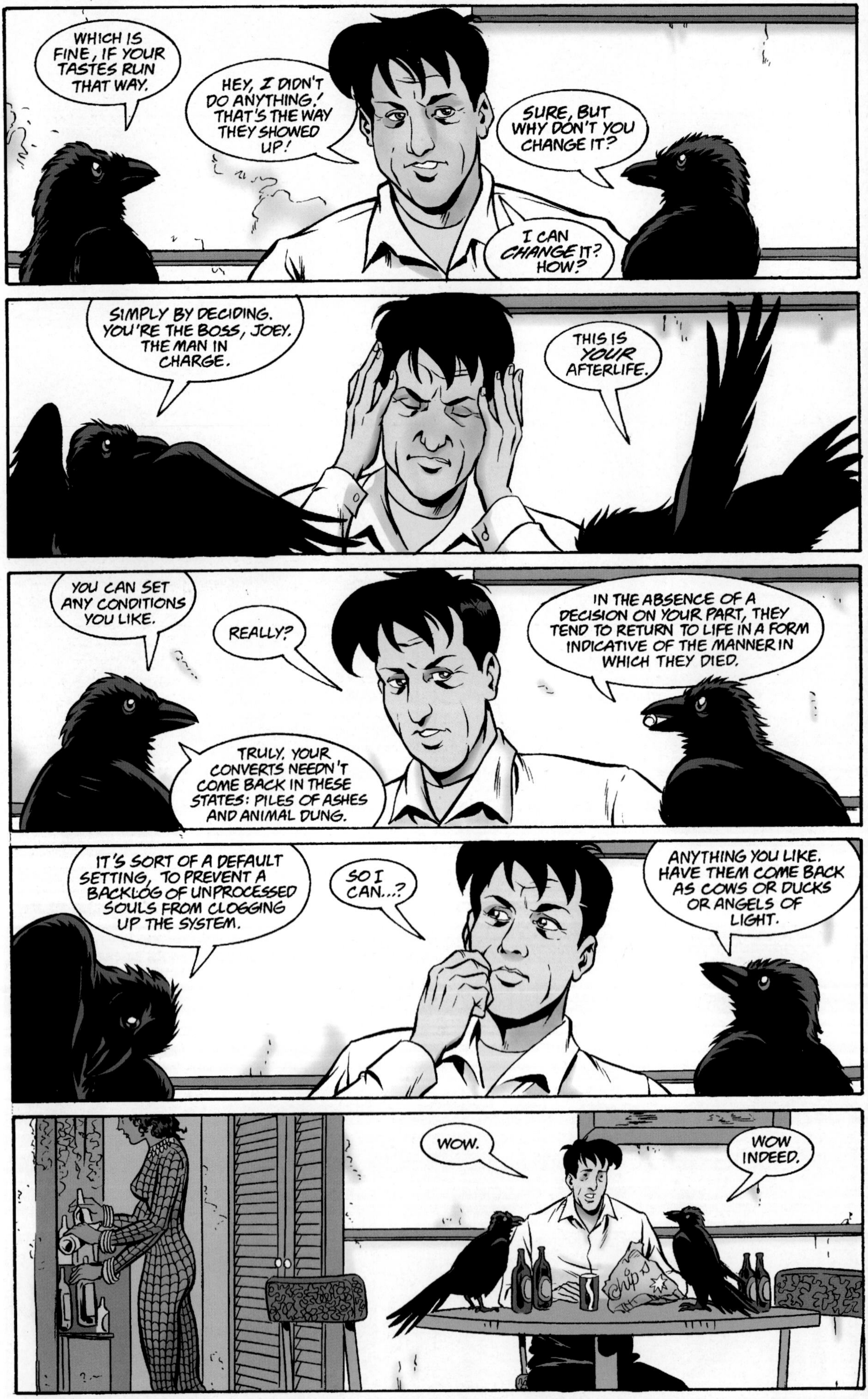
WHICH IS FINE, IF YOUR TASTES RUN THAT WAY.
HEY, I DIDN'T DO ANYTHING! THAT'S THE WAY THEY SHOWED UP!
SURE, BUT WHY DON'T YOU CHANGE IT?
I CAN CHANGE IT? HOW?
SIMPLY BY DECIDING. YOU'RE THE BOSS, JOEY. THE MAN IN CHARGE.
THIS IS YOUR AFTERLIFE.
YOU CAN SET ANY CONDITIONS YOU LIKE.
REALLY?
IN THE ABSENCE OF A DECISION ON YOUR PART, THEY TEND TO RETURN TO LIFE IN A FORM INDICATIVE OF THE MANNER IN WHICH THEY DIED.
TRULY, YOUR CONVERTS NEEDN'T COME BACK IN THESE STATES: PILES OF ASHES AND ANIMAL DUNG.
IT'S SORT OF A DEFAULT SETTING, TO PREVENT A BACKLOG OF UNPROCESSED SOULS FROM CLOGGING UP THE SYSTEM.
SO I CAN...?
ANYTHING YOU LIKE. HAVE THEM COME BACK AS COWS OR DUCKS OR ANGELS OF LIGHT.
WOW.
WOW INDEED.

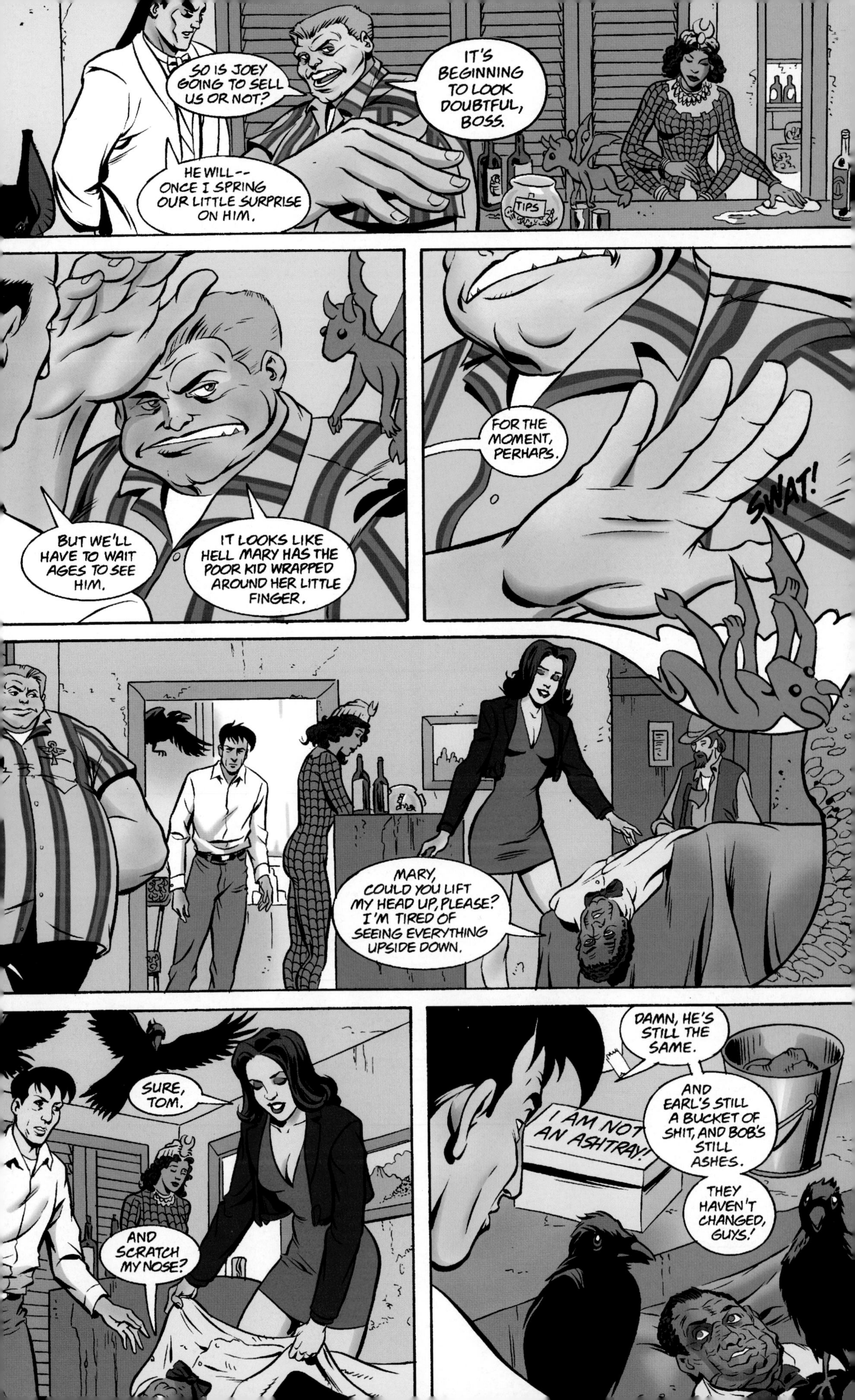
SO IS JOEY GOING TO SELL US OR NOT?
IT'S BEGINNING TO LOOK DOUBTFUL, BOSS.
HE WILL-- ONCE I SPRING OUR LITTLE SURPRISE ON HIM.
TIPS
BUT WE'LL HAVE TO WAIT AGES TO SEE HIM.
IT LOOKS LIKE HELL MARY HAS THE POOR KID WRAPPED AROUND HER LITTLE FINGER.
FOR THE MOMENT, PERHAPS.
SWAT!
MARY, COULD YOU LIFT MY HEAD UP, PLEASE? I'M TIRED OF SEEING EVERYTHING UPSIDE DOWN.
SURE, TOM.
AND SCRATCH MY NOSE?
DAMN, HE'S STILL THE SAME.
I AM NOT AN ASHTRAY!
AND EARL'S STILL A BUCKET OF SHIT, AND BOB'S STILL ASHES.
THEY HAVEN'T CHANGED, GUYS!

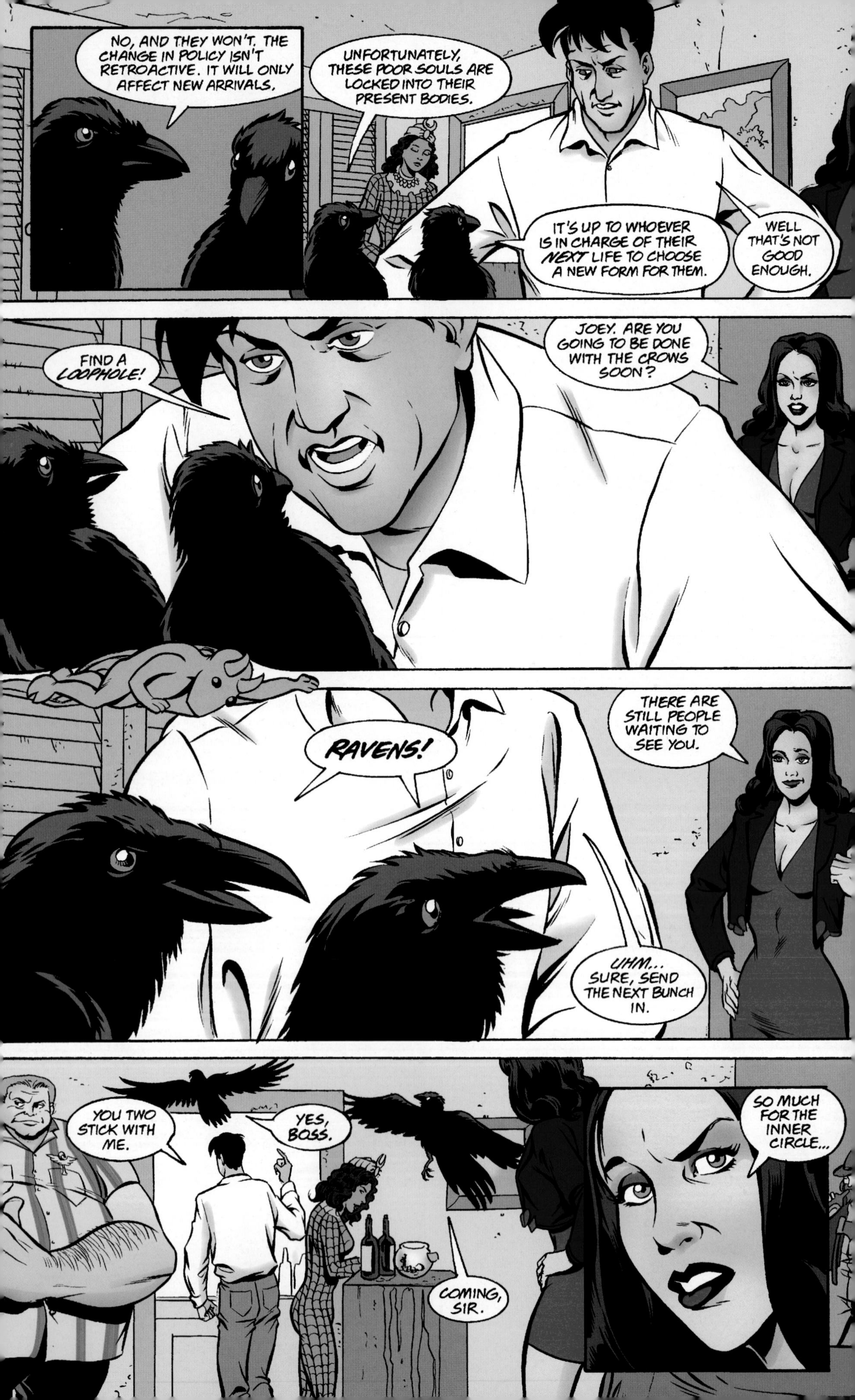
NO, AND THEY WON'T. THE CHANGE IN POLICY ISN'T RETROACTIVE. IT WILL ONLY AFFECT NEW ARRIVALS.
UNFORTUNATELY, THESE POOR SOULS ARE LOCKED INTO THEIR PRESENT BODIES.
IT'S UP TO WHOEVER IS IN CHARGE OF THEIR NEXT LIFE TO CHOOSE A NEW FORM FOR THEM.
WELL THAT'S NOT GOOD ENOUGH.
FIND A LOOPHOLE!
JOEY. ARE YOU GOING TO BE DONE WITH THE CROWS SOON?
RAVENS!
THERE ARE STILL PEOPLE WAITING TO SEE YOU.
UHM... SURE, SEND THE NEXT BUNCH IN.
YOU TWO STICK WITH ME.
YES, BOSS.
COMING, SIR.
SO MUCH FOR THE INNER CIRCLE...

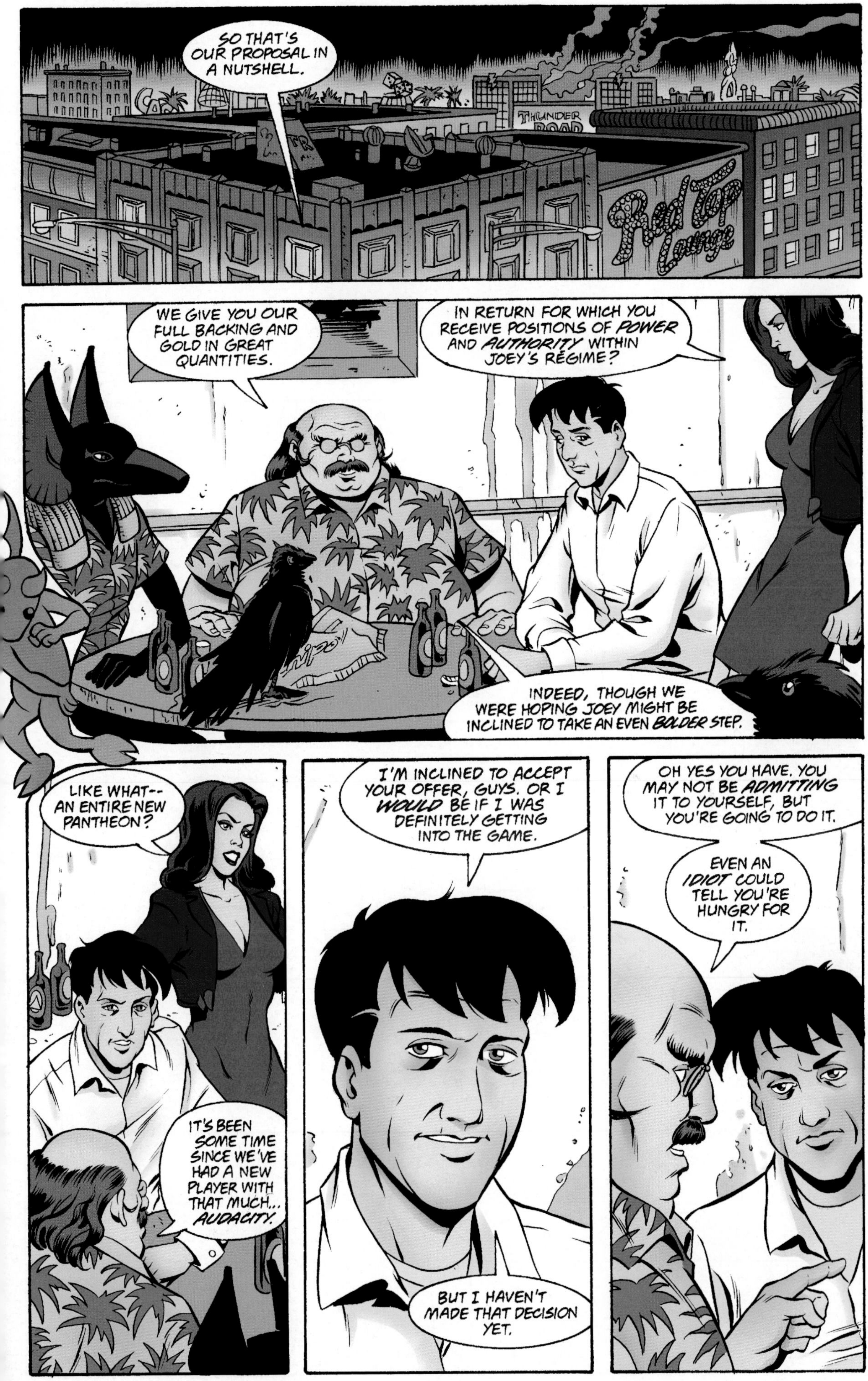
SO THAT'S OUR PROPOSAL IN A NUTSHELL.
THUNDER ROAD
Red Top Lounge
WE GIVE YOU OUR FULL BACKING AND GOLD IN GREAT QUANTITIES.
IN RETURN FOR WHICH YOU RECEIVE POSITIONS OF POWER AND AUTHORITY WITHIN JOEY'S RÉGIME?
INDEED, THOUGH WE WERE HOPING JOEY MIGHT BE INCLINED TO TAKE AN EVEN BOLDER STEP.
LIKE WHAT-- AN ENTIRE NEW PANTHEON?
IT'S BEEN SOME TIME SINCE WE'VE HAD A NEW PLAYER WITH THAT MUCH... AUDACITY.
I'M INCLINED TO ACCEPT YOUR OFFER, GUYS. OR I WOULD BE IF I WAS DEFINITELY GETTING INTO THE GAME.
BUT I HAVEN'T MADE THAT DECISION YET.
OH YES YOU HAVE. YOU MAY NOT BE ADMITTING IT TO YOURSELF, BUT YOU'RE GOING TO DO IT.
EVEN AN IDIOT COULD TELL YOU'RE HUNGRY FOR IT.

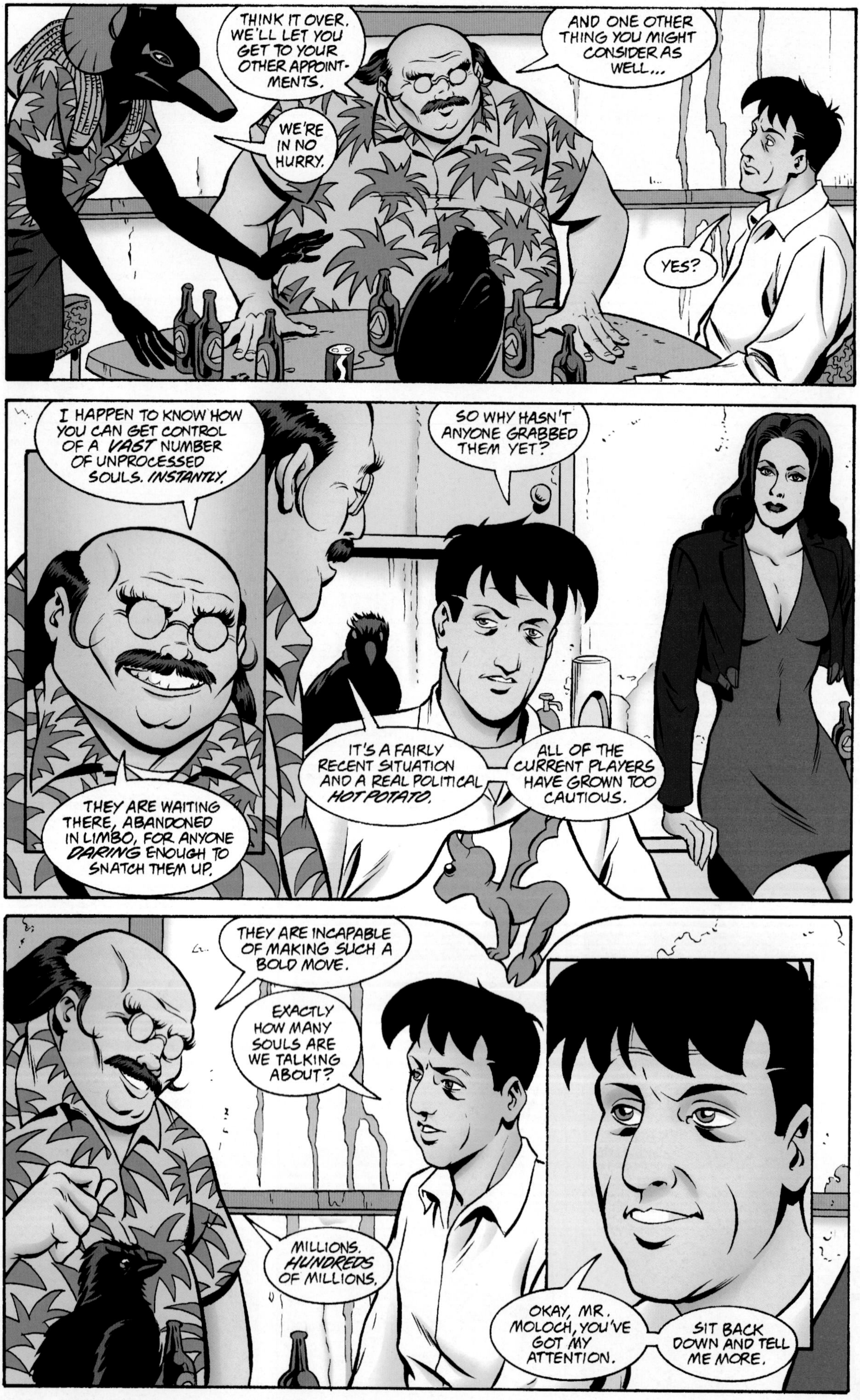
THINK IT OVER. WE'LL LET YOU GET TO YOUR OTHER APPOINTMENTS.
WE'RE IN NO HURRY.
AND ONE OTHER THING YOU MIGHT CONSIDER AS WELL...
YES?
I HAPPEN TO KNOW HOW YOU CAN GET CONTROL OF A *VAST* NUMBER OF UNPROCESSED SOULS. *INSTANTLY.*
THEY ARE WAITING THERE, ABANDONED IN LIMBO, FOR ANYONE *DARING* ENOUGH TO SNATCH THEM UP.
SO WHY HASN'T ANYONE GRABBED THEM YET?
IT'S A FAIRLY RECENT SITUATION AND A REAL POLITICAL *HOT POTATO.*
ALL OF THE CURRENT PLAYERS HAVE GROWN TOO CAUTIOUS.
THEY ARE INCAPABLE OF MAKING SUCH A BOLD MOVE.
EXACTLY HOW MANY SOULS ARE WE TALKING ABOUT?
MILLIONS. *HUNDREDS* OF MILLIONS.
OKAY, MR. MOLOCH, YOU'VE GOT MY ATTENTION.
SIT BACK DOWN AND TELL ME MORE.

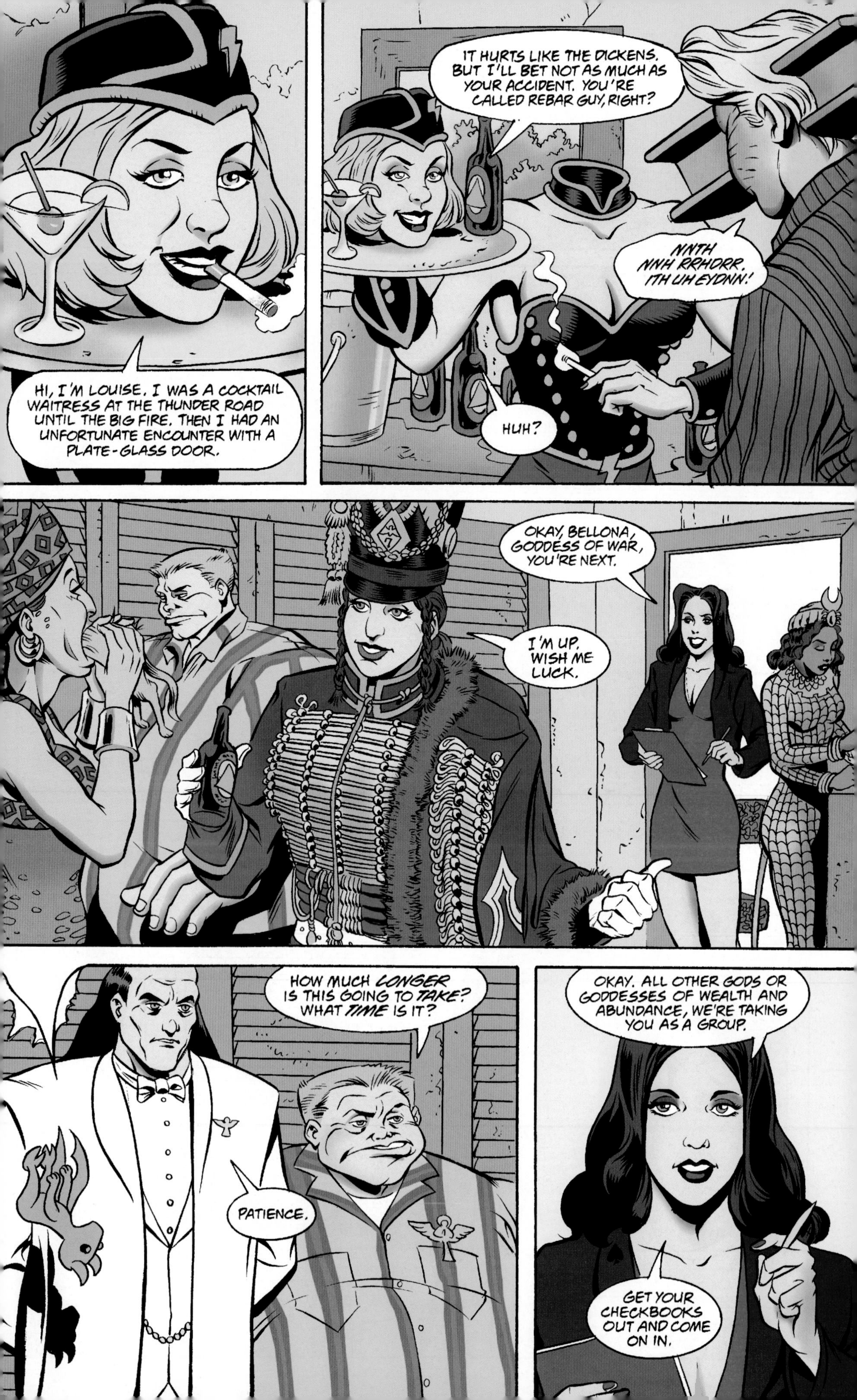
HI, I'M LOUISE. I WAS A COCKTAIL WAITRESS AT THE THUNDER ROAD UNTIL THE BIG FIRE. THEN I HAD AN UNFORTUNATE ENCOUNTER WITH A PLATE-GLASS DOOR.
IT HURTS LIKE THE DICKENS. BUT I'LL BET NOT AS MUCH AS YOUR ACCIDENT. YOU'RE CALLED REBAR GUY, RIGHT?
NNTH NNH RRHORR. ITH UH EYDNN!
HUH?
OKAY, BELLONA, GODDESS OF WAR, YOU'RE NEXT.
I'M UP. WISH ME LUCK.
HOW MUCH *LONGER* IS THIS GOING TO *TAKE*? WHAT *TIME* IS IT?
PATIENCE.
OKAY. ALL OTHER GODS OR GODDESSES OF WEALTH AND ABUNDANCE, WE'RE TAKING YOU AS A GROUP.
GET YOUR CHECKBOOKS OUT AND COME ON IN.

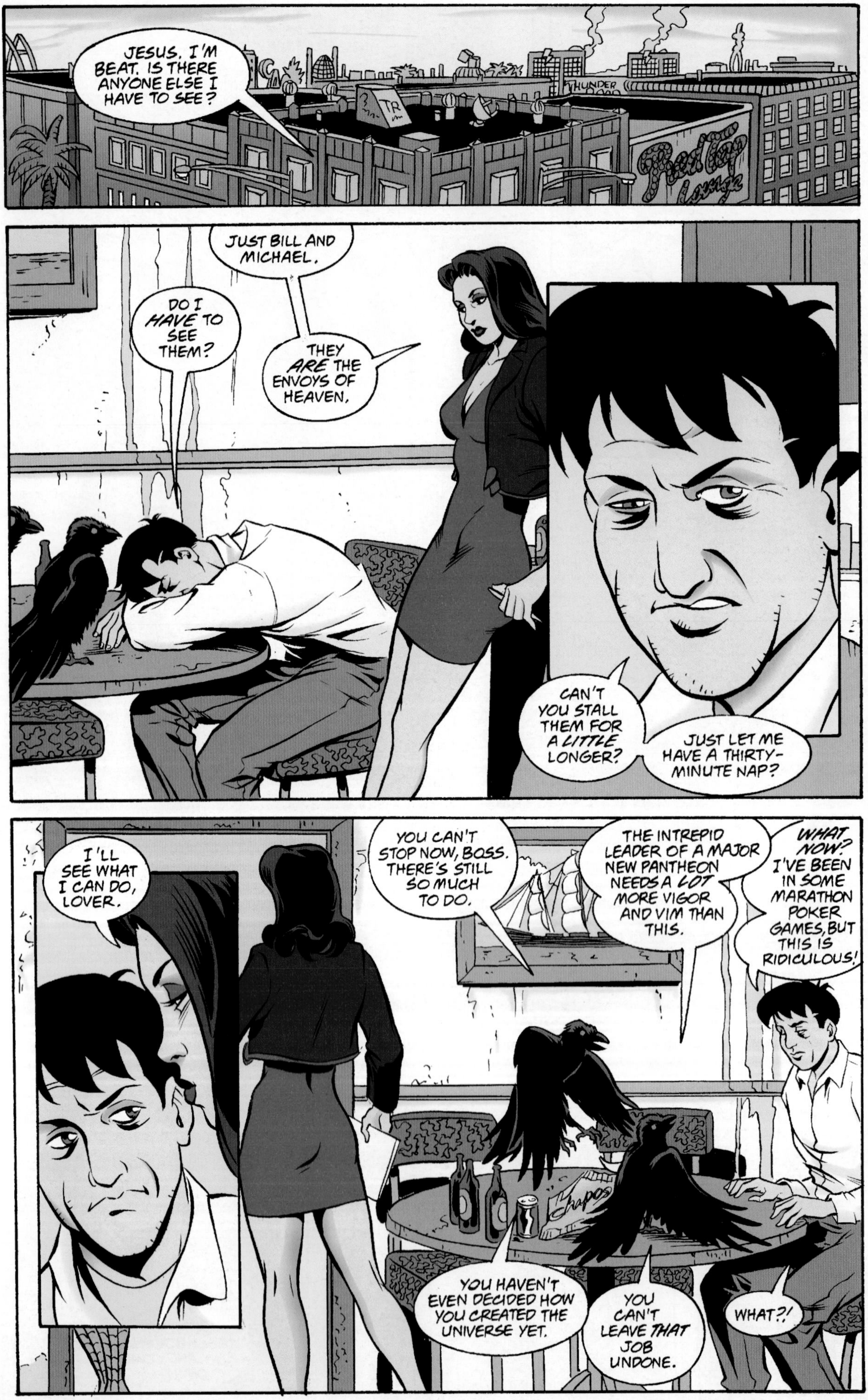
JESUS. I'M BEAT. IS THERE ANYONE ELSE I HAVE TO SEE?
THUNDER
Red Top Lounge
JUST BILL AND MICHAEL.
DO I HAVE TO SEE THEM?
THEY ARE THE ENVOYS OF HEAVEN.
CAN'T YOU STALL THEM FOR A LITTLE LONGER?
JUST LET ME HAVE A THIRTY-MINUTE NAP?
I'LL SEE WHAT I CAN DO, LOVER.
YOU CAN'T STOP NOW, BOSS. THERE'S STILL SO MUCH TO DO.
THE INTREPID LEADER OF A MAJOR NEW PANTHEON NEEDS A LOT MORE VIGOR AND VIM THAN THIS.
WHAT NOW? I'VE BEEN IN SOME MARATHON POKER GAMES, BUT THIS IS RIDICULOUS!
Chapos
YOU HAVEN'T EVEN DECIDED HOW YOU CREATED THE UNIVERSE YET.
YOU CAN'T LEAVE THAT JOB UNDONE.
WHAT?!

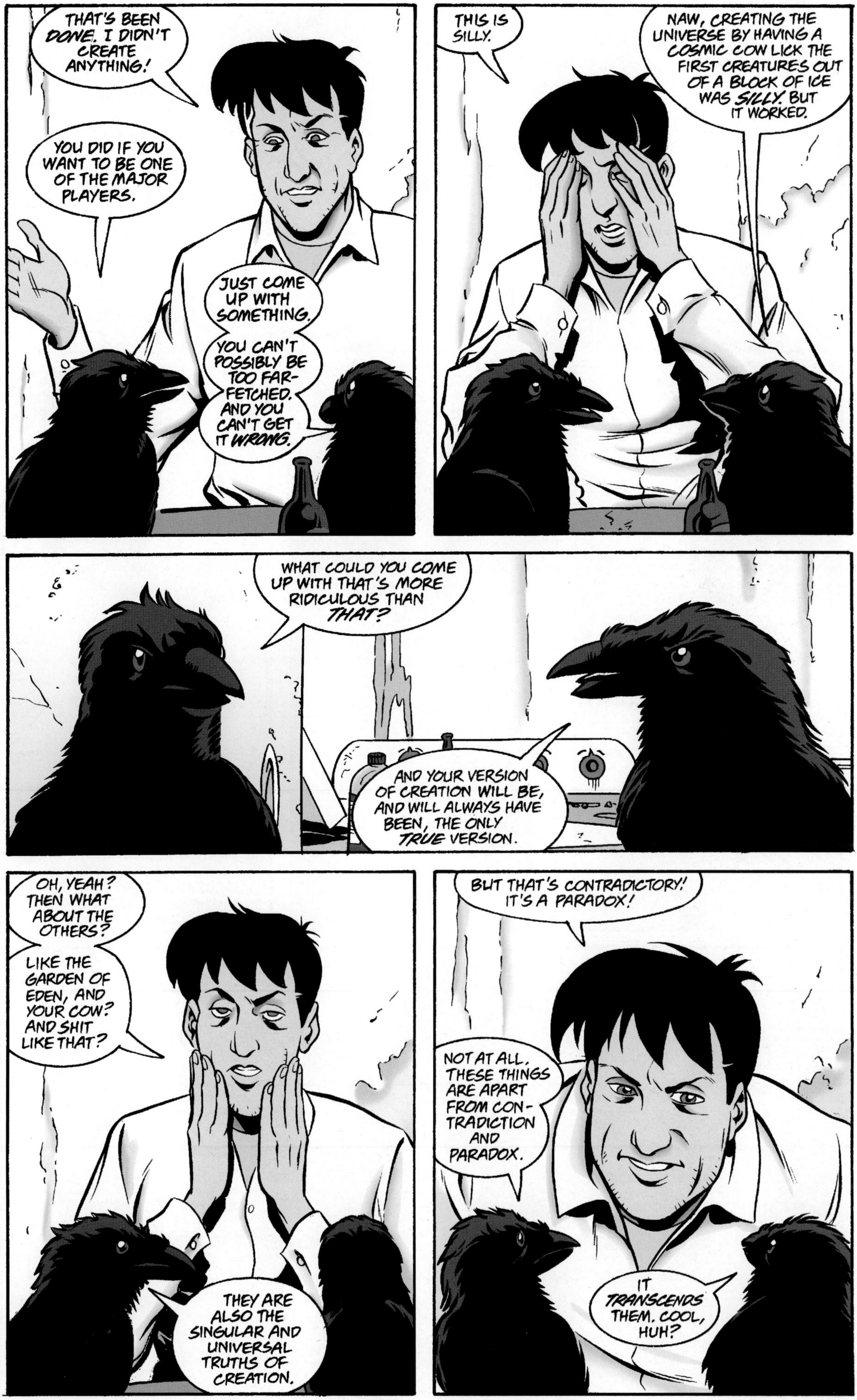
THAT'S BEEN DONE. I DIDN'T CREATE ANYTHING!
YOU DID IF YOU WANT TO BE ONE OF THE MAJOR PLAYERS.
JUST COME UP WITH SOMETHING.
YOU CAN'T POSSIBLY BE TOO FAR-FETCHED. AND YOU CAN'T GET IT WRONG.
THIS IS SILLY.
NAW, CREATING THE UNIVERSE BY HAVING A COSMIC COW LICK THE FIRST CREATURES OUT OF A BLOCK OF ICE WAS SILLY. BUT IT WORKED.
WHAT COULD YOU COME UP WITH THAT'S MORE RIDICULOUS THAN THAT?
AND YOUR VERSION OF CREATION WILL BE, AND WILL ALWAYS HAVE BEEN, THE ONLY TRUE VERSION.
OH, YEAH? THEN WHAT ABOUT THE OTHERS?
LIKE THE GARDEN OF EDEN, AND YOUR COW? AND SHIT LIKE THAT?
THEY ARE ALSO THE SINGULAR AND UNIVERSAL TRUTHS OF CREATION.
BUT THAT'S CONTRADICTORY! IT'S A PARADOX!
NOT AT ALL. THESE THINGS ARE APART FROM CONTRADICTION AND PARADOX.
IT TRANSCENDS THEM. COOL, HUH?

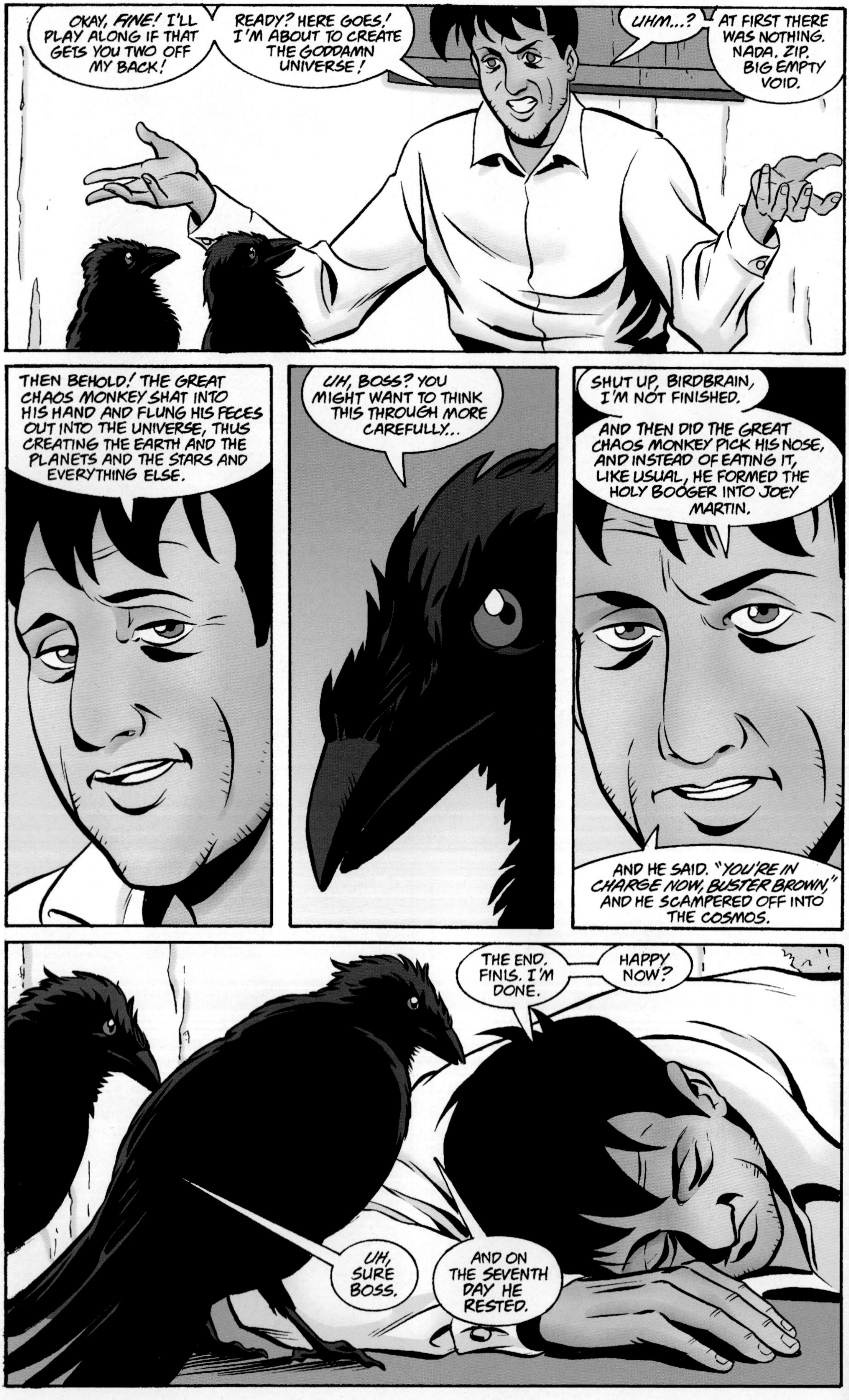
OKAY, FINE! I'LL PLAY ALONG IF THAT GETS YOU TWO OFF MY BACK!
READY? HERE GOES! I'M ABOUT TO CREATE THE GODDAMN UNIVERSE!
UHM...?
AT FIRST THERE WAS NOTHING. NADA. ZIP. BIG EMPTY VOID.
THEN BEHOLD! THE GREAT CHAOS MONKEY SHAT INTO HIS HAND AND FLUNG HIS FECES OUT INTO THE UNIVERSE, THUS CREATING THE EARTH AND THE PLANETS AND THE STARS AND EVERYTHING ELSE.
UH, BOSS? YOU MIGHT WANT TO THINK THIS THROUGH MORE CAREFULLY...
SHUT UP, BIRDBRAIN, I'M NOT FINISHED.
AND THEN DID THE GREAT CHAOS MONKEY PICK HIS NOSE, AND INSTEAD OF EATING IT, LIKE USUAL, HE FORMED THE HOLY BOOGER INTO JOEY MARTIN.
AND HE SAID. "YOU'RE IN CHARGE NOW, BUSTER BROWN," AND HE SCAMPERED OFF INTO THE COSMOS.
THE END. FINIS. I'M DONE.
HAPPY NOW?
UH, SURE BOSS.
AND ON THE SEVENTH DAY HE RESTED.

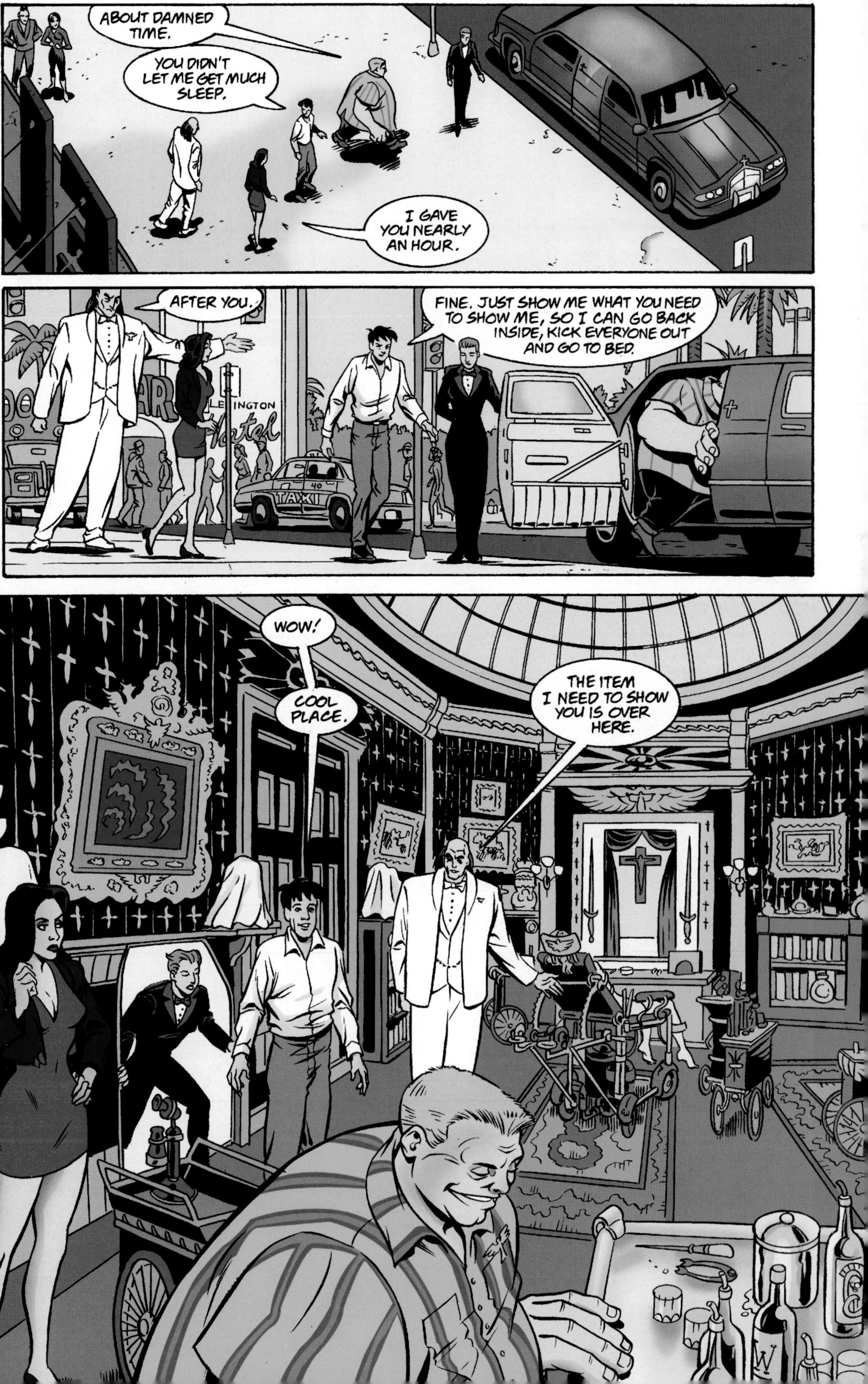
ABOUT DAMNED TIME.
YOU DIDN'T LET ME GET MUCH SLEEP.
I GAVE YOU NEARLY AN HOUR.
AFTER YOU.
FINE. JUST SHOW ME WHAT YOU NEED TO SHOW ME, SO I CAN GO BACK INSIDE, KICK EVERYONE OUT AND GO TO BED.
TAXI
WOW!
COOL PLACE.
THE ITEM I NEED TO SHOW YOU IS OVER HERE.

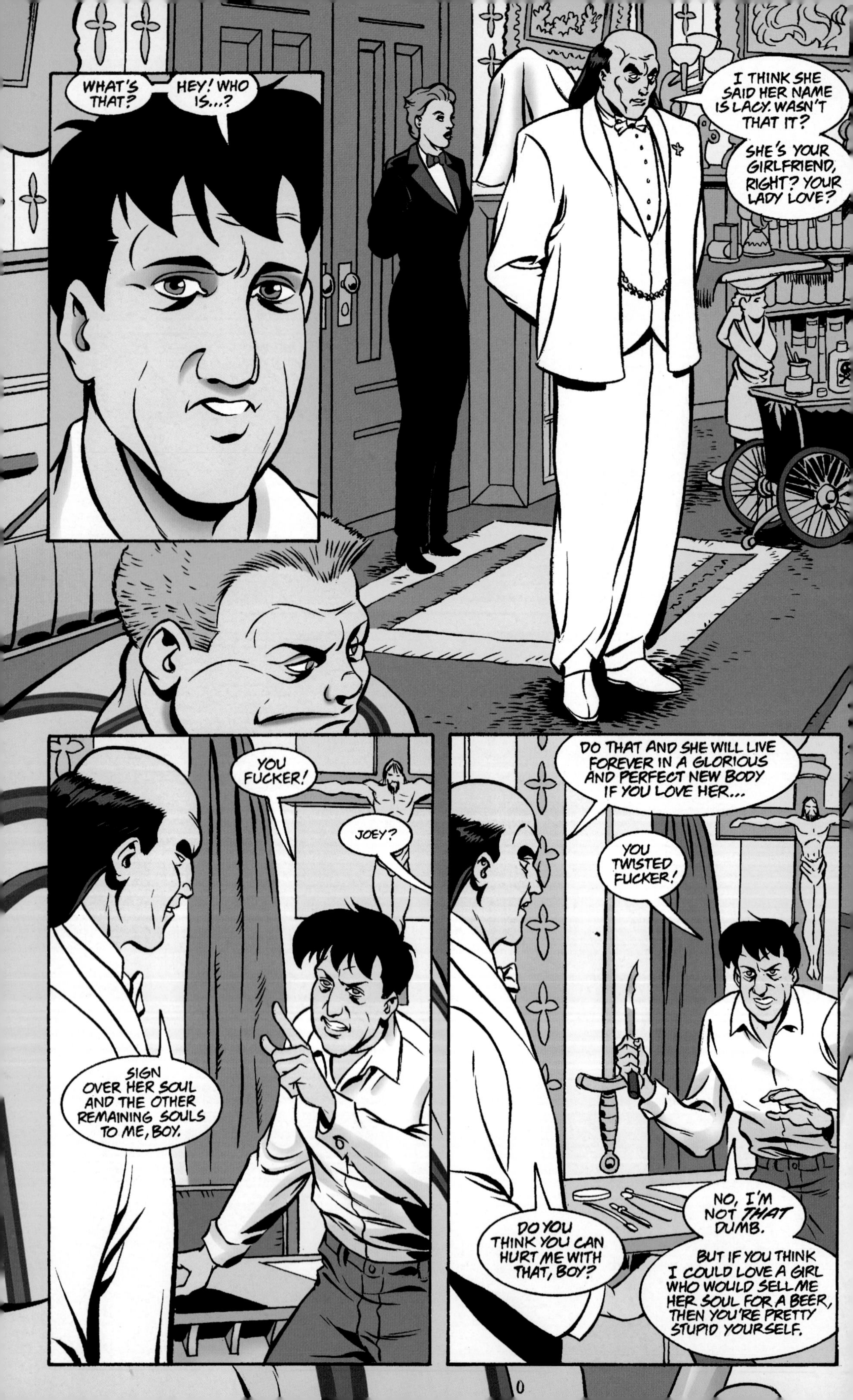
WHAT'S THAT?
HEY! WHO IS...?
I THINK SHE SAID HER NAME IS LACY. WASN'T THAT IT?
SHE'S YOUR GIRLFRIEND, RIGHT? YOUR LADY LOVE?
YOU FUCKER!
JOEY?
SIGN OVER HER SOUL AND THE OTHER REMAINING SOULS TO ME, BOY.
DO THAT AND SHE WILL LIVE FOREVER IN A GLORIOUS AND PERFECT NEW BODY IF YOU LOVE HER...
YOU TWISTED FUCKER!
DO YOU THINK YOU CAN HURT ME WITH THAT, BOY?
NO, I'M NOT THAT DUMB.
BUT IF YOU THINK I COULD LOVE A GIRL WHO WOULD SELL ME HER SOUL FOR A BEER, THEN YOU'RE PRETTY STUPID YOURSELF.

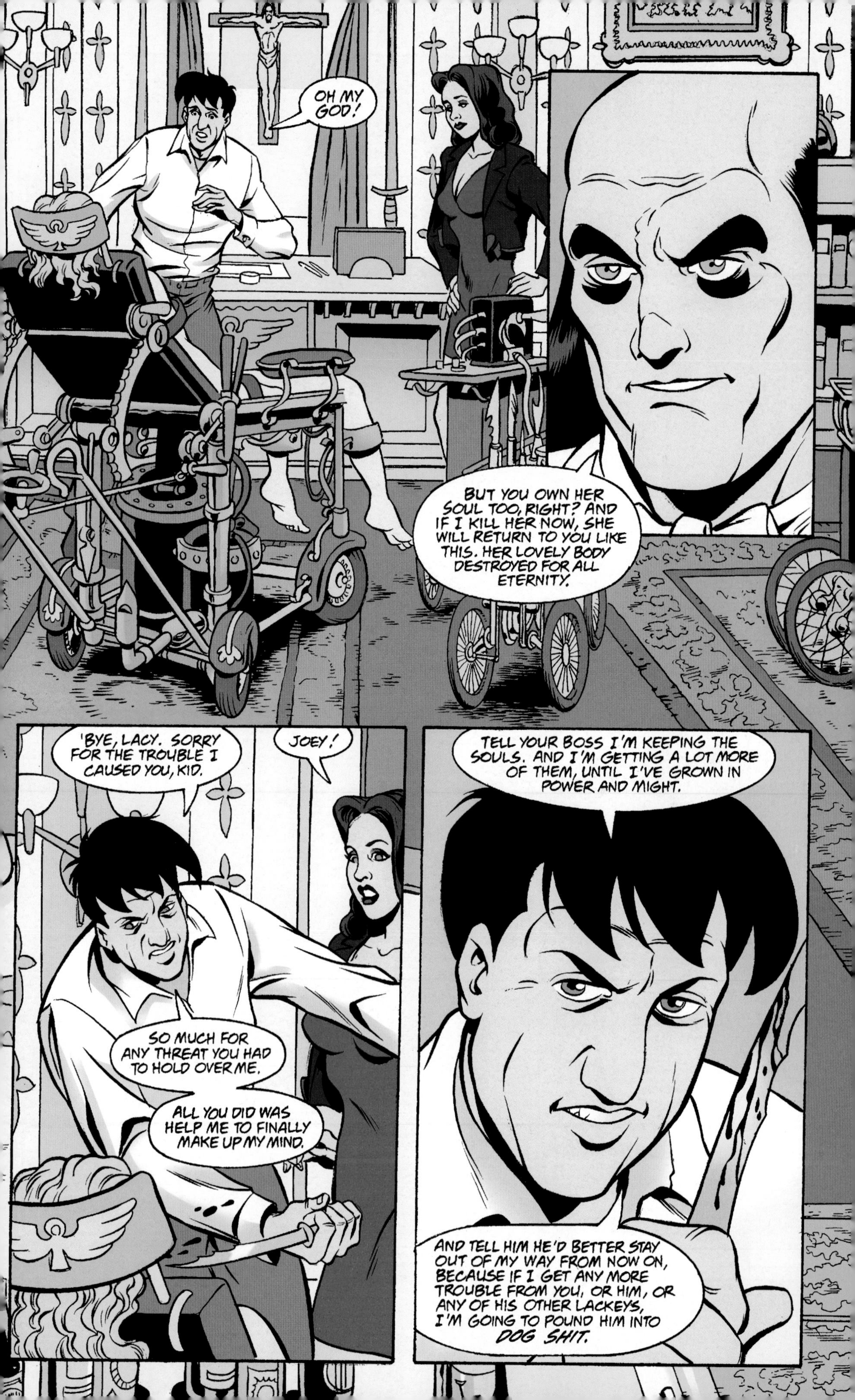
OH MY GOD!
BUT YOU OWN HER SOUL TOO, RIGHT? AND IF I KILL HER NOW, SHE WILL RETURN TO YOU LIKE THIS. HER LOVELY BODY DESTROYED FOR ALL ETERNITY.
'BYE, LACY. SORRY FOR THE TROUBLE I CAUSED YOU, KID.
JOEY!
SO MUCH FOR ANY THREAT YOU HAD TO HOLD OVER ME.
ALL YOU DID WAS HELP ME TO FINALLY MAKE UP MY MIND.
TELL YOUR BOSS I'M KEEPING THE SOULS. AND I'M GETTING A LOT MORE OF THEM, UNTIL I'VE GROWN IN POWER AND MIGHT.
AND TELL HIM HE'D BETTER STAY OUT OF MY WAY FROM NOW ON, BECAUSE IF I GET ANY MORE TROUBLE FROM YOU, OR HIM, OR ANY OF HIS OTHER LACKEYS, I'M GOING TO POUND HIM INTO *DOG SHIT.*

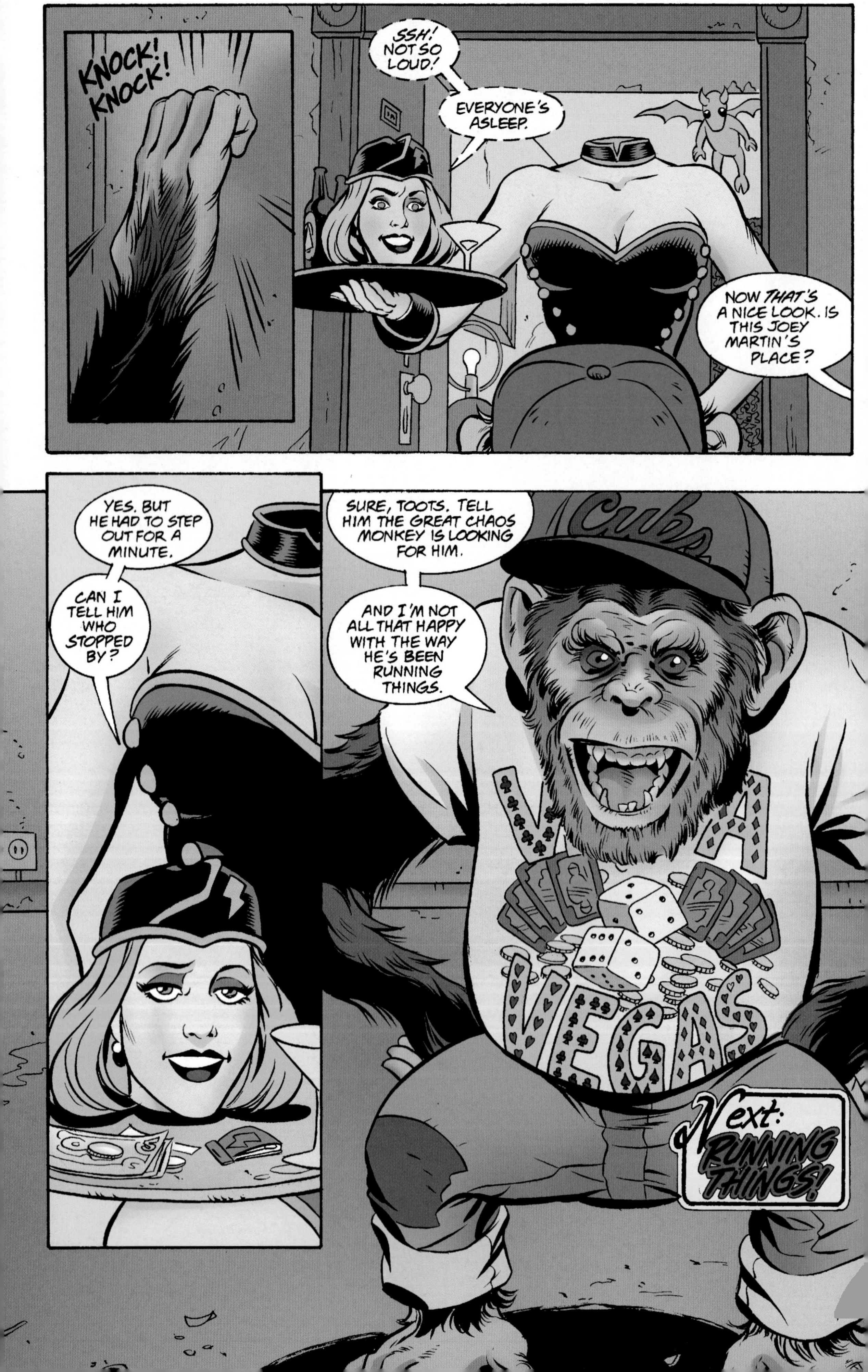
KNOCK! KNOCK!
SSH! NOT SO LOUD!
EVERYONE'S ASLEEP.
NOW THAT'S A NICE LOOK. IS THIS JOEY MARTIN'S PLACE?
YES. BUT HE HAD TO STEP OUT FOR A MINUTE.
CAN I TELL HIM WHO STOPPED BY?
SURE, TOOTS. TELL HIM THE GREAT CHAOS MONKEY IS LOOKING FOR HIM.
AND I'M NOT ALL THAT HAPPY WITH THE WAY HE'S BEEN RUNNING THINGS.
VEGAS
Next: RUNNING THINGS!

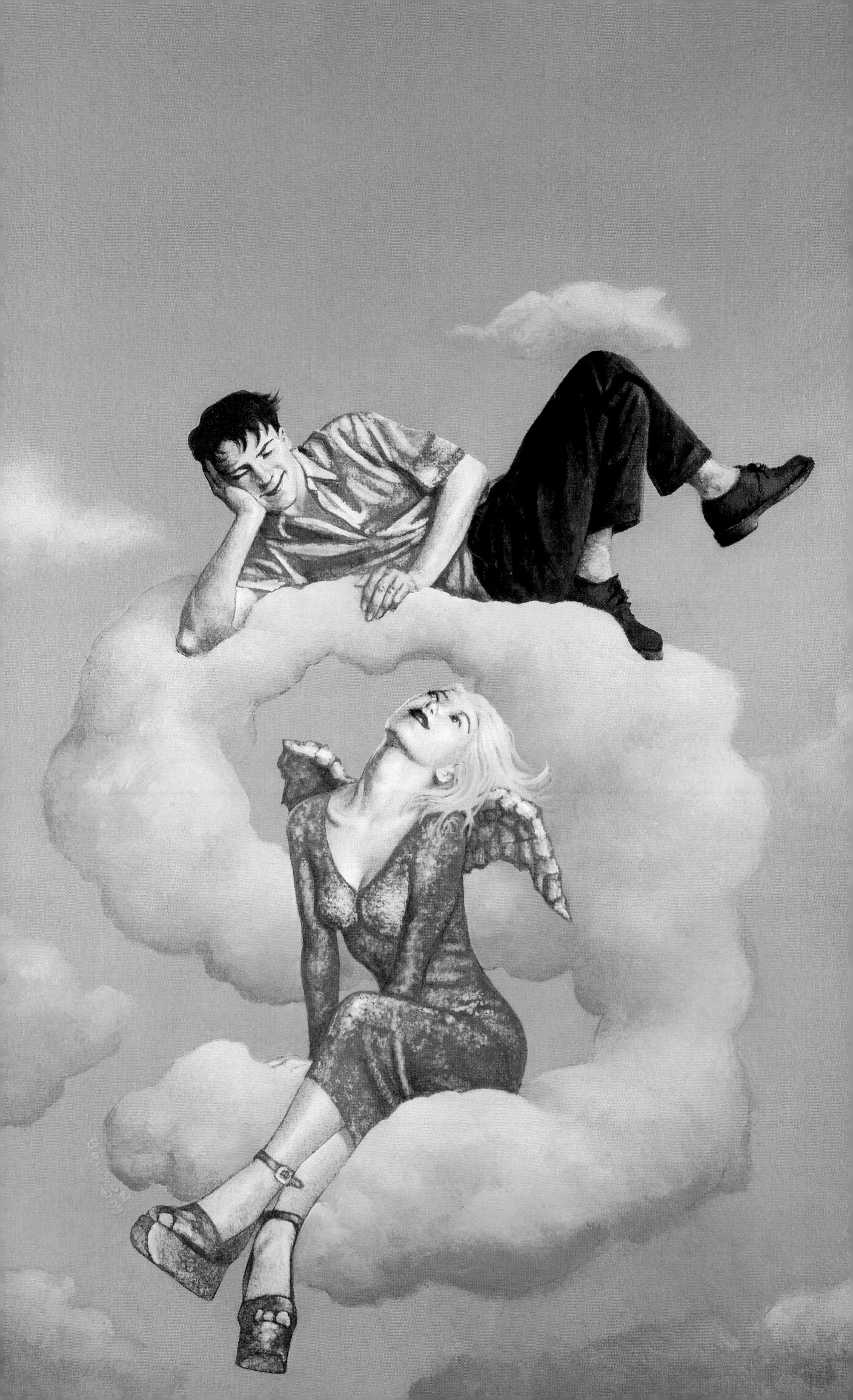

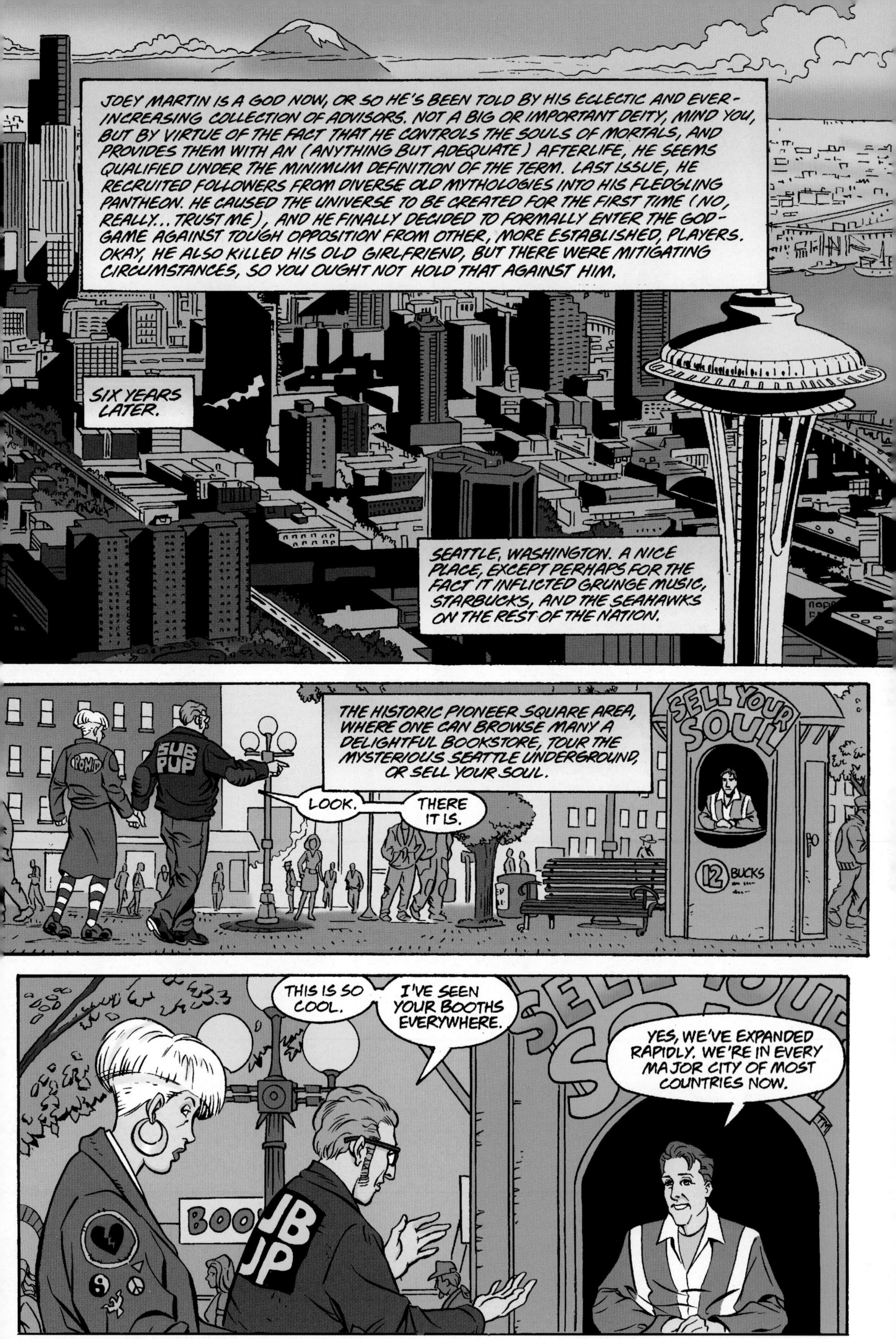
JOEY MARTIN IS A GOD NOW, OR SO HE'S BEEN TOLD BY HIS ECLECTIC AND EVER-INCREASING COLLECTION OF ADVISORS. NOT A BIG OR IMPORTANT DEITY, MIND YOU, BUT BY VIRTUE OF THE FACT THAT HE CONTROLS THE SOULS OF MORTALS, AND PROVIDES THEM WITH AN (ANYTHING BUT ADEQUATE) AFTERLIFE, HE SEEMS QUALIFIED UNDER THE MINIMUM DEFINITION OF THE TERM. LAST ISSUE, HE RECRUITED FOLLOWERS FROM DIVERSE OLD MYTHOLOGIES INTO HIS FLEDGLING PANTHEON. HE CAUSED THE UNIVERSE TO BE CREATED FOR THE FIRST TIME (NO, REALLY... TRUST ME), AND HE FINALLY DECIDED TO FORMALLY ENTER THE GOD-GAME AGAINST TOUGH OPPOSITION FROM OTHER, MORE ESTABLISHED, PLAYERS. OKAY, HE ALSO KILLED HIS OLD GIRLFRIEND, BUT THERE WERE MITIGATING CIRCUMSTANCES, SO YOU OUGHT NOT HOLD THAT AGAINST HIM.
SIX YEARS LATER.
SEATTLE, WASHINGTON. A NICE PLACE, EXCEPT PERHAPS FOR THE FACT IT INFLICTED GRUNGE MUSIC, STARBUCKS, AND THE SEAHAWKS ON THE REST OF THE NATION.
THE HISTORIC PIONEER SQUARE AREA, WHERE ONE CAN BROWSE MANY A DELIGHTFUL BOOKSTORE, TOUR THE MYSTERIOUS SEATTLE UNDERGROUND, OR SELL YOUR SOUL.
SUB PUP
SELL YOUR SOUL
LOOK.
THERE IT IS.
12 BUCKS
THIS IS SO COOL.
I'VE SEEN YOUR BOOTHS EVERYWHERE.
YES, WE'VE EXPANDED RAPIDLY. WE'RE IN EVERY MAJOR CITY OF MOST COUNTRIES NOW.

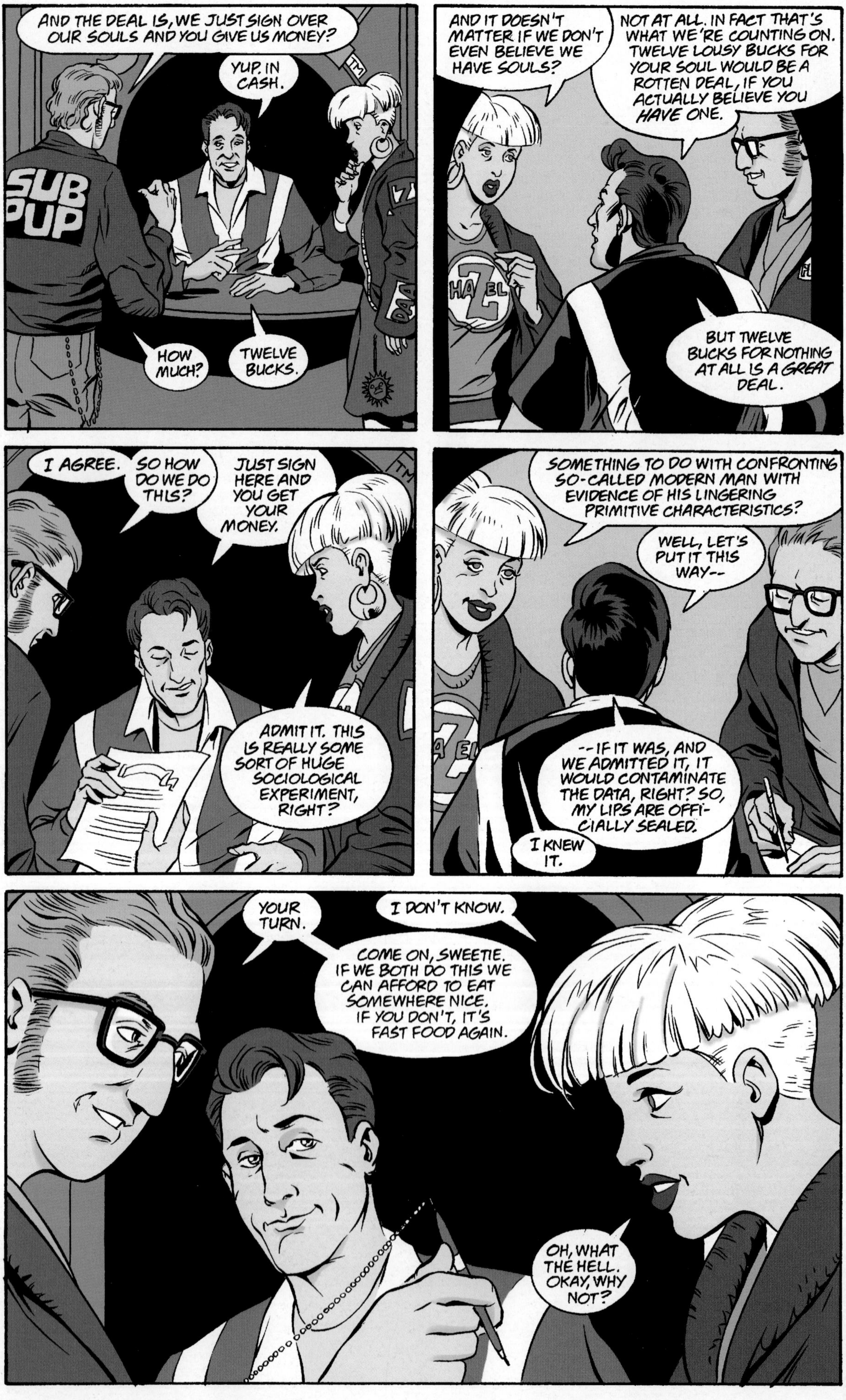
AND THE DEAL IS, WE JUST SIGN OVER OUR SOULS AND YOU GIVE US MONEY?
YUP. IN CASH.
SUB PUP
HOW MUCH?
TWELVE BUCKS.
AND IT DOESN'T MATTER IF WE DON'T EVEN BELIEVE WE HAVE SOULS?
NOT AT ALL. IN FACT THAT'S WHAT WE'RE COUNTING ON. TWELVE LOUSY BUCKS FOR YOUR SOUL WOULD BE A ROTTEN DEAL, IF YOU ACTUALLY BELIEVE YOU *HAVE* ONE.
BUT TWELVE BUCKS FOR NOTHING AT ALL IS A *GREAT* DEAL.
I AGREE.
SO HOW DO WE DO THIS?
JUST SIGN HERE AND YOU GET YOUR MONEY.
ADMIT IT. THIS IS REALLY SOME SORT OF HUGE SOCIOLOGICAL EXPERIMENT, RIGHT?
SOMETHING TO DO WITH CONFRONTING SO-CALLED MODERN MAN WITH EVIDENCE OF HIS LINGERING PRIMITIVE CHARACTERISTICS?
WELL, LET'S PUT IT THIS WAY--
--IF IT WAS, AND WE ADMITTED IT, IT WOULD CONTAMINATE THE DATA, RIGHT? SO, MY LIPS ARE OFFICIALLY SEALED.
I KNEW IT.
YOUR TURN.
I DON'T KNOW.
COME ON, SWEETIE. IF WE BOTH DO THIS WE CAN AFFORD TO EAT SOMEWHERE NICE. IF YOU DON'T, IT'S FAST FOOD AGAIN.
OH, WHAT THE HELL. OKAY, WHY NOT?

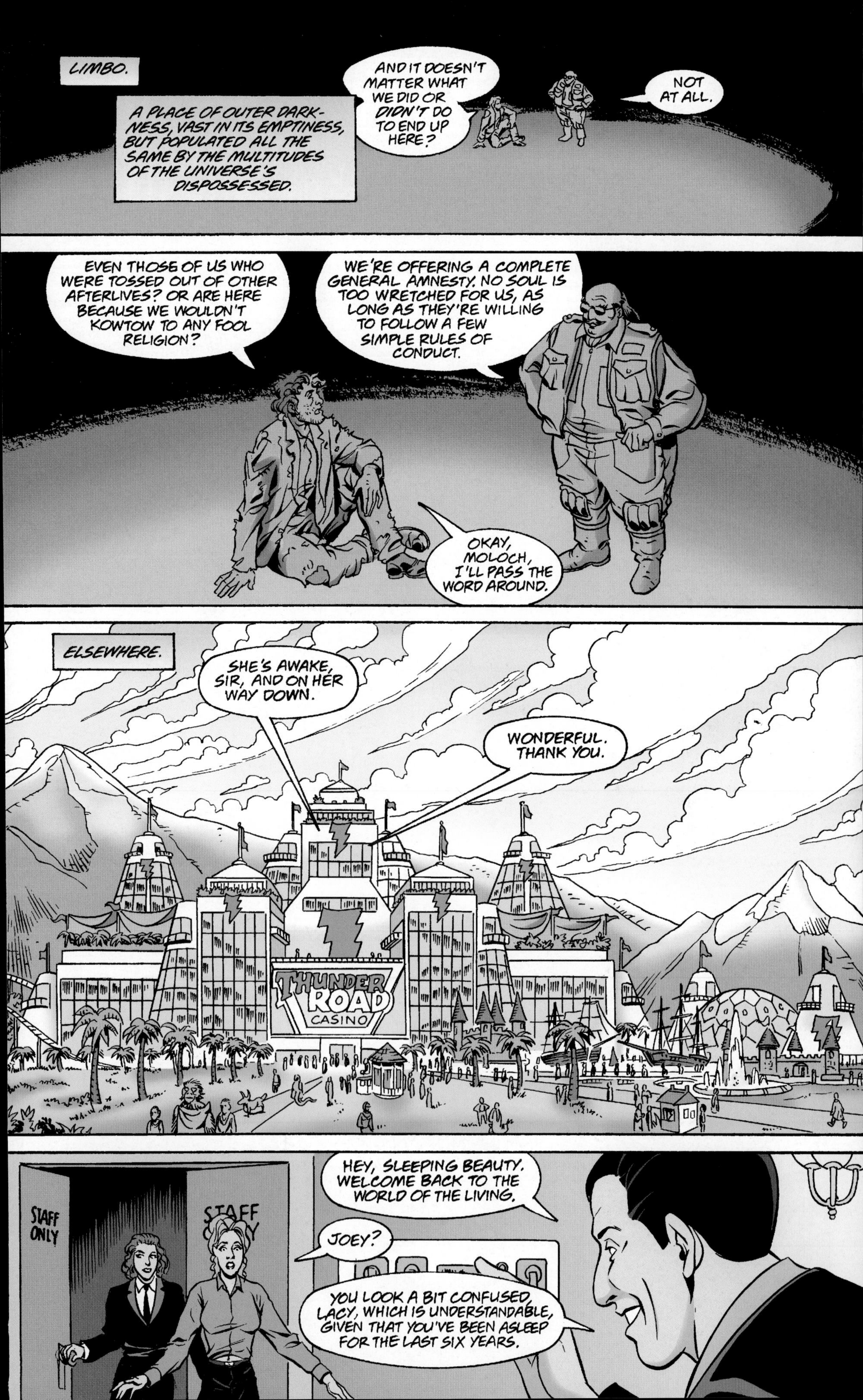
LIMBO.
A PLACE OF OUTER DARKNESS, VAST IN ITS EMPTINESS, BUT POPULATED ALL THE SAME BY THE MULTITUDES OF THE UNIVERSE'S DISPOSSESSED.
AND IT DOESN'T MATTER WHAT WE DID OR DIDN'T DO TO END UP HERE?
NOT AT ALL.
EVEN THOSE OF US WHO WERE TOSSED OUT OF OTHER AFTERLIVES? OR ARE HERE BECAUSE WE WOULDN'T KOWTOW TO ANY FOOL RELIGION?
WE'RE OFFERING A COMPLETE GENERAL AMNESTY. NO SOUL IS TOO WRETCHED FOR US, AS LONG AS THEY'RE WILLING TO FOLLOW A FEW SIMPLE RULES OF CONDUCT.
OKAY, MOLOCH, I'LL PASS THE WORD AROUND.
ELSEWHERE.
SHE'S AWAKE, SIR, AND ON HER WAY DOWN.
WONDERFUL. THANK YOU.
THUNDER ROAD CASINO
STAFF ONLY
STAFF ONLY
HEY, SLEEPING BEAUTY. WELCOME BACK TO THE WORLD OF THE LIVING.
JOEY?
YOU LOOK A BIT CONFUSED, LACY, WHICH IS UNDERSTANDABLE, GIVEN THAT YOU'VE BEEN ASLEEP FOR THE LAST SIX YEARS.

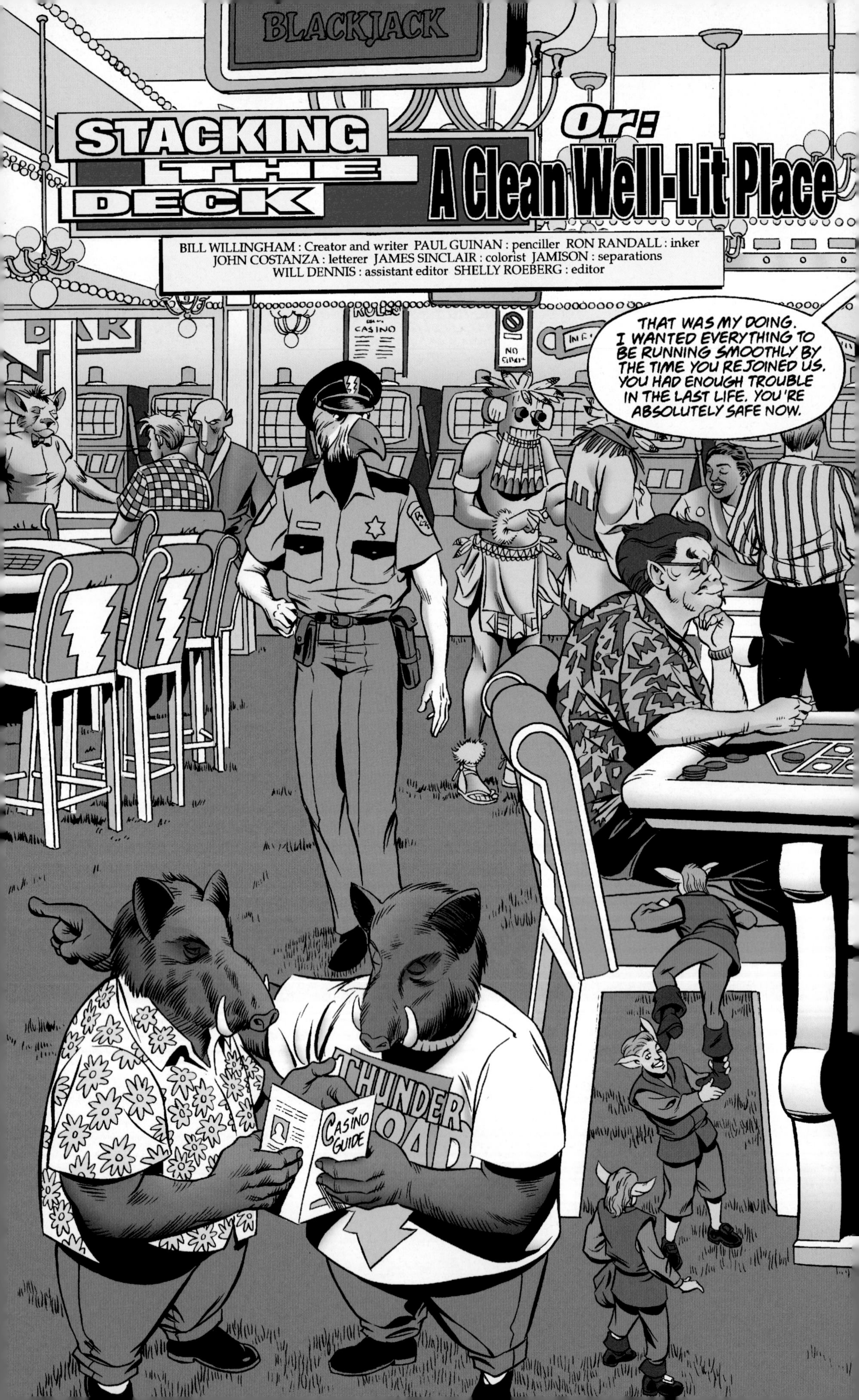
BLACKJACK
STACKING THE DECK
Or:
A Clean Well-Lit Place
BILL WILLINGHAM : Creator and writer PAUL GUINAN : penciller RON RANDALL : inker
JOHN COSTANZA : letterer JAMES SINCLAIR : colorist JAMISON : separations
WILL DENNIS : assistant editor SHELLY ROEBERG : editor
THAT WAS MY DOING. I WANTED EVERYTHING TO BE RUNNING SMOOTHLY BY THE TIME YOU REJOINED US. YOU HAD ENOUGH TROUBLE IN THE LAST LIFE. YOU'RE ABSOLUTELY SAFE NOW.
CASINO GUIDE

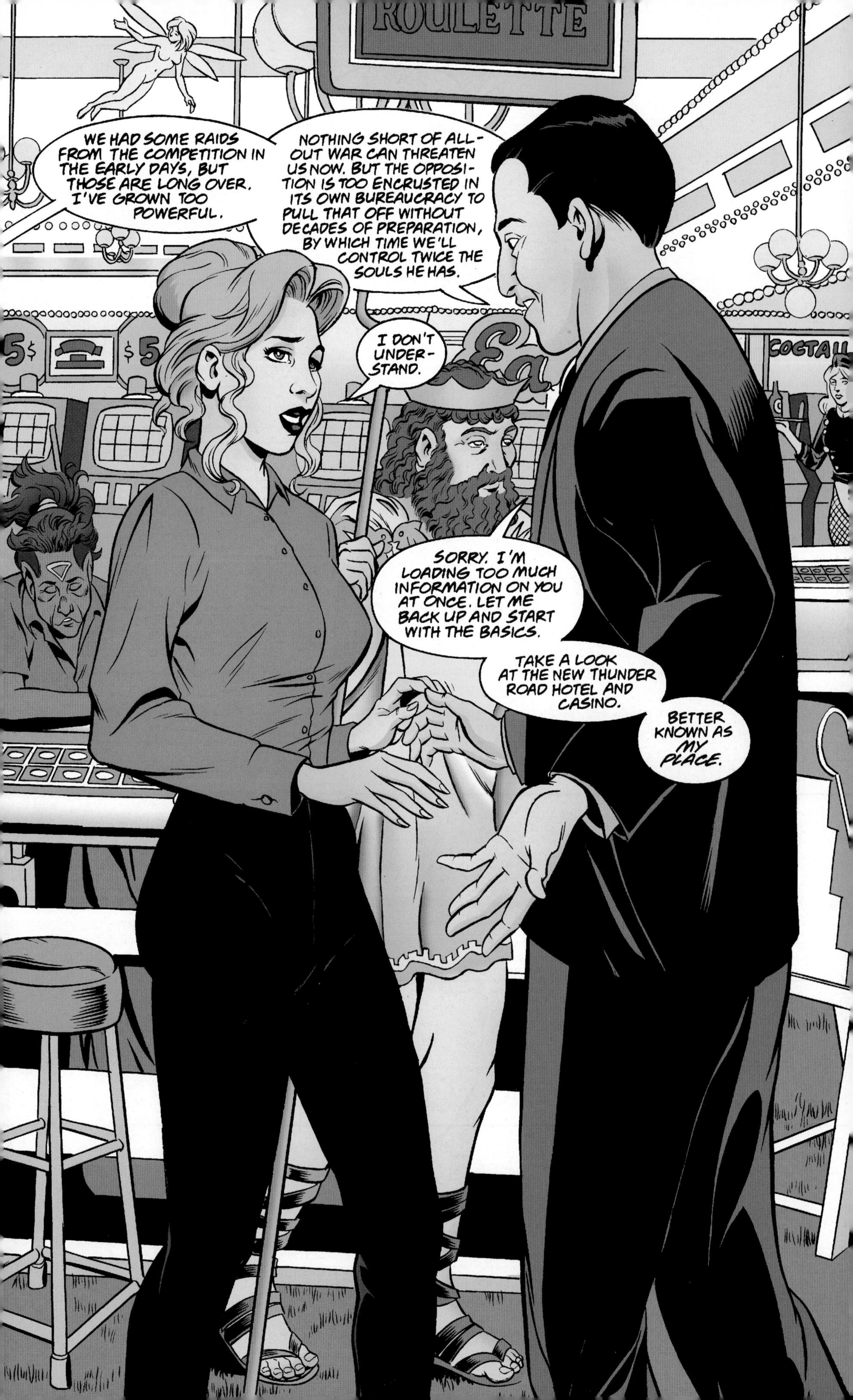
ROULETTE
WE HAD SOME RAIDS FROM THE COMPETITION IN THE EARLY DAYS, BUT THOSE ARE LONG OVER. I'VE GROWN TOO POWERFUL.
NOTHING SHORT OF ALL-OUT WAR CAN THREATEN US NOW. BUT THE OPPOSITION IS TOO ENCRUSTED IN ITS OWN BUREAUCRACY TO PULL THAT OFF WITHOUT DECADES OF PREPARATION, BY WHICH TIME WE'LL CONTROL TWICE THE SOULS HE HAS.
I DON'T UNDERSTAND.
SORRY. I'M LOADING TOO MUCH INFORMATION ON YOU AT ONCE. LET ME BACK UP AND START WITH THE BASICS.
TAKE A LOOK AT THE NEW THUNDER ROAD HOTEL AND CASINO.
BETTER KNOWN AS *MY PLACE*.

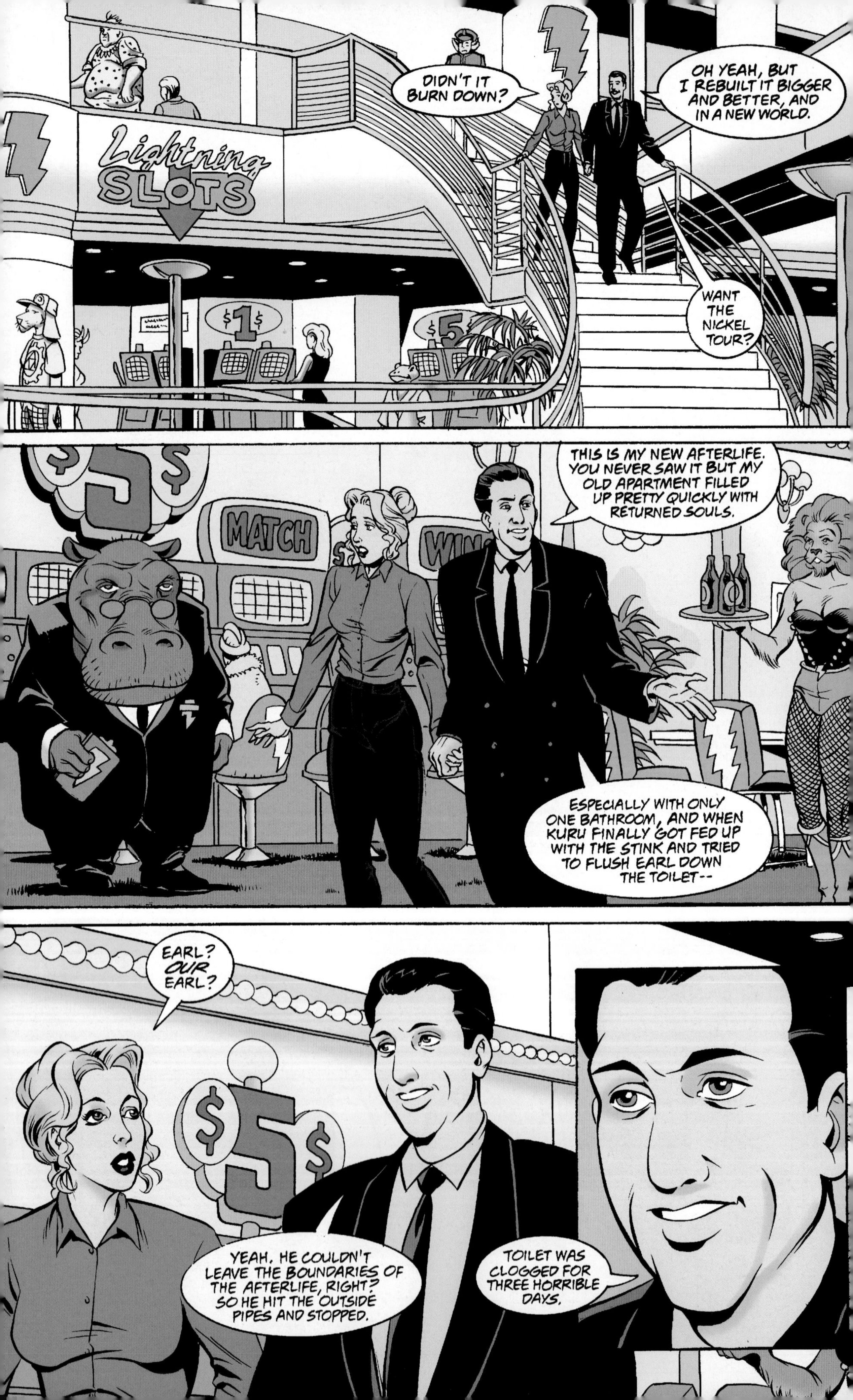
Lightning SLOTS
DIDN'T IT BURN DOWN?
OH YEAH, BUT I REBUILT IT BIGGER AND BETTER, AND IN A NEW WORLD.
WANT THE NICKEL TOUR?
THIS IS MY NEW AFTERLIFE. YOU NEVER SAW IT BUT MY OLD APARTMENT FILLED UP PRETTY QUICKLY WITH RETURNED SOULS.
MATCH
ESPECIALLY WITH ONLY ONE BATHROOM, AND WHEN KURU FINALLY GOT FED UP WITH THE STINK AND TRIED TO FLUSH EARL DOWN THE TOILET--
EARL? *OUR* EARL?
YEAH. HE COULDN'T LEAVE THE BOUNDARIES OF THE AFTERLIFE, RIGHT? SO HE HIT THE OUTSIDE PIPES AND STOPPED.
TOILET WAS CLOGGED FOR THREE HORRIBLE DAYS.

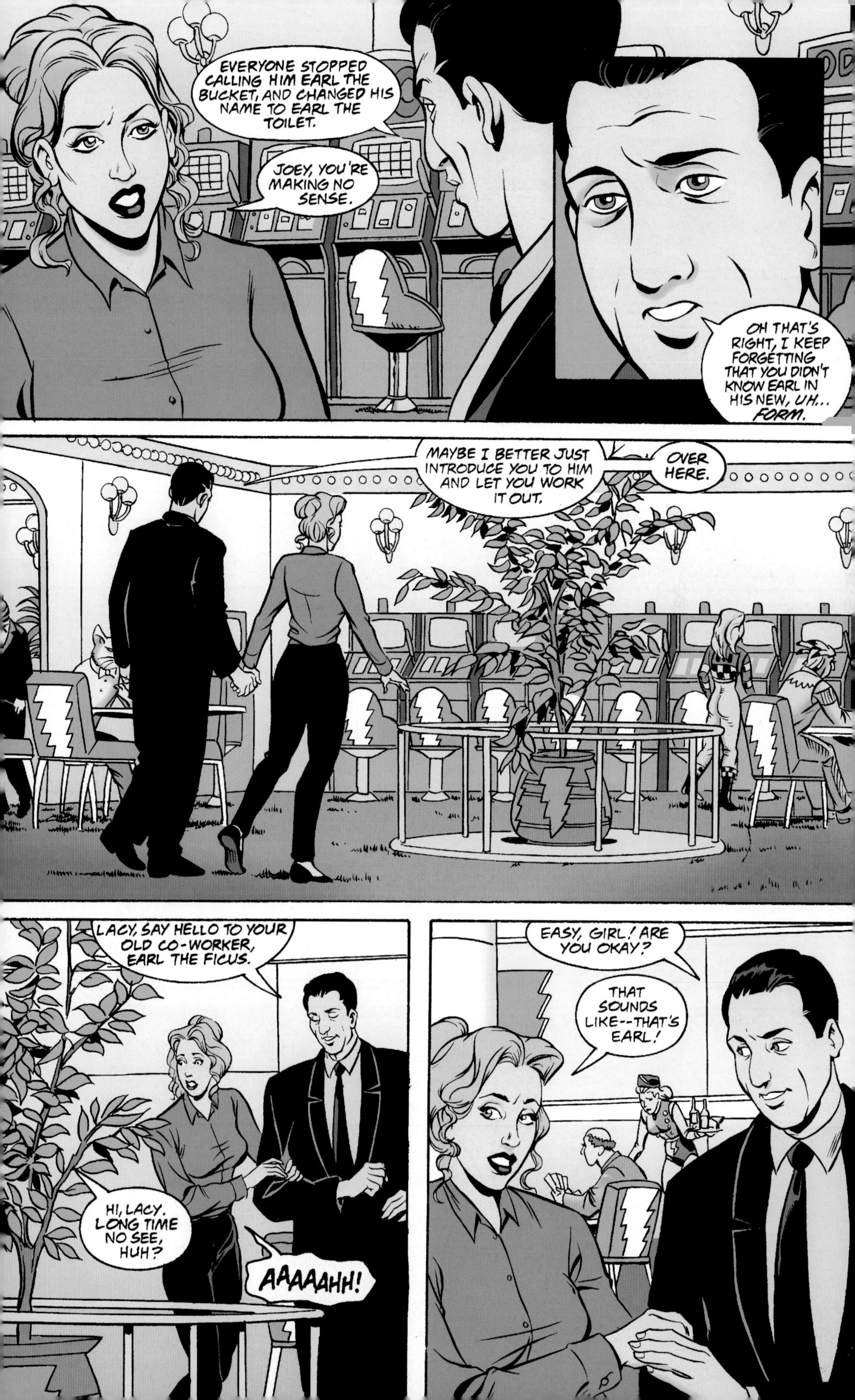
EVERYONE STOPPED CALLING HIM EARL THE BUCKET, AND CHANGED HIS NAME TO EARL THE TOILET.
JOEY, YOU'RE MAKING NO SENSE.
OH THAT'S RIGHT, I KEEP FORGETTING THAT YOU DIDN'T KNOW EARL IN HIS NEW, UH... FORM.
MAYBE I BETTER JUST INTRODUCE YOU TO HIM AND LET YOU WORK IT OUT.
OVER HERE.
LACY, SAY HELLO TO YOUR OLD CO-WORKER, EARL THE FICUS.
HI, LACY. LONG TIME NO SEE, HUH?
AAAAAHH!
EASY, GIRL! ARE YOU OKAY?
THAT SOUNDS LIKE--THAT'S EARL!

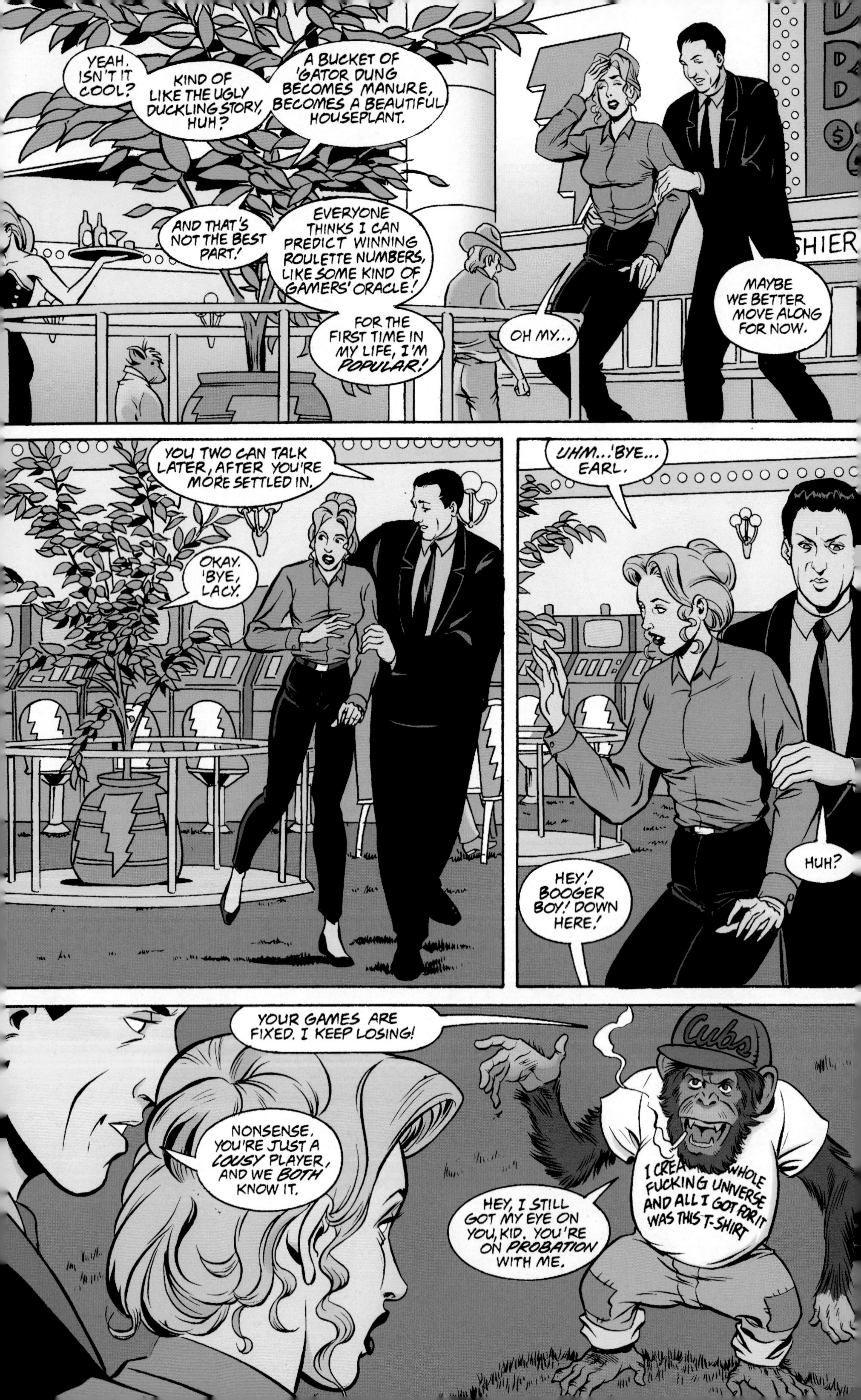
YEAH. ISN'T IT COOL?
KIND OF LIKE THE UGLY DUCKLING STORY, HUH?
A BUCKET OF 'GATOR DUNG BECOMES MANURE, BECOMES A BEAUTIFUL HOUSEPLANT.
AND THAT'S NOT THE BEST PART!
EVERYONE THINKS I CAN PREDICT WINNING ROULETTE NUMBERS, LIKE SOME KIND OF GAMERS' ORACLE!
FOR THE FIRST TIME IN MY LIFE, I'M *POPULAR!*
OH MY...
MAYBE WE BETTER MOVE ALONG FOR NOW.
YOU TWO CAN TALK LATER, AFTER YOU'RE MORE SETTLED IN.
OKAY. 'BYE, LACY.
UHM... 'BYE... EARL.
HEY! BOOGER BOY! DOWN HERE!
HUH?
YOUR GAMES ARE FIXED. I KEEP LOSING!
NONSENSE, YOU'RE JUST A *LOUSY* PLAYER, AND WE *BOTH* KNOW IT.
Cubs
HEY, I STILL GOT MY EYE ON YOU, KID. YOU'RE ON *PROBATION* WITH ME.
FUCKING UNIVERSE AND ALL I GOT FOR IT WAS THIS T-SHIRT

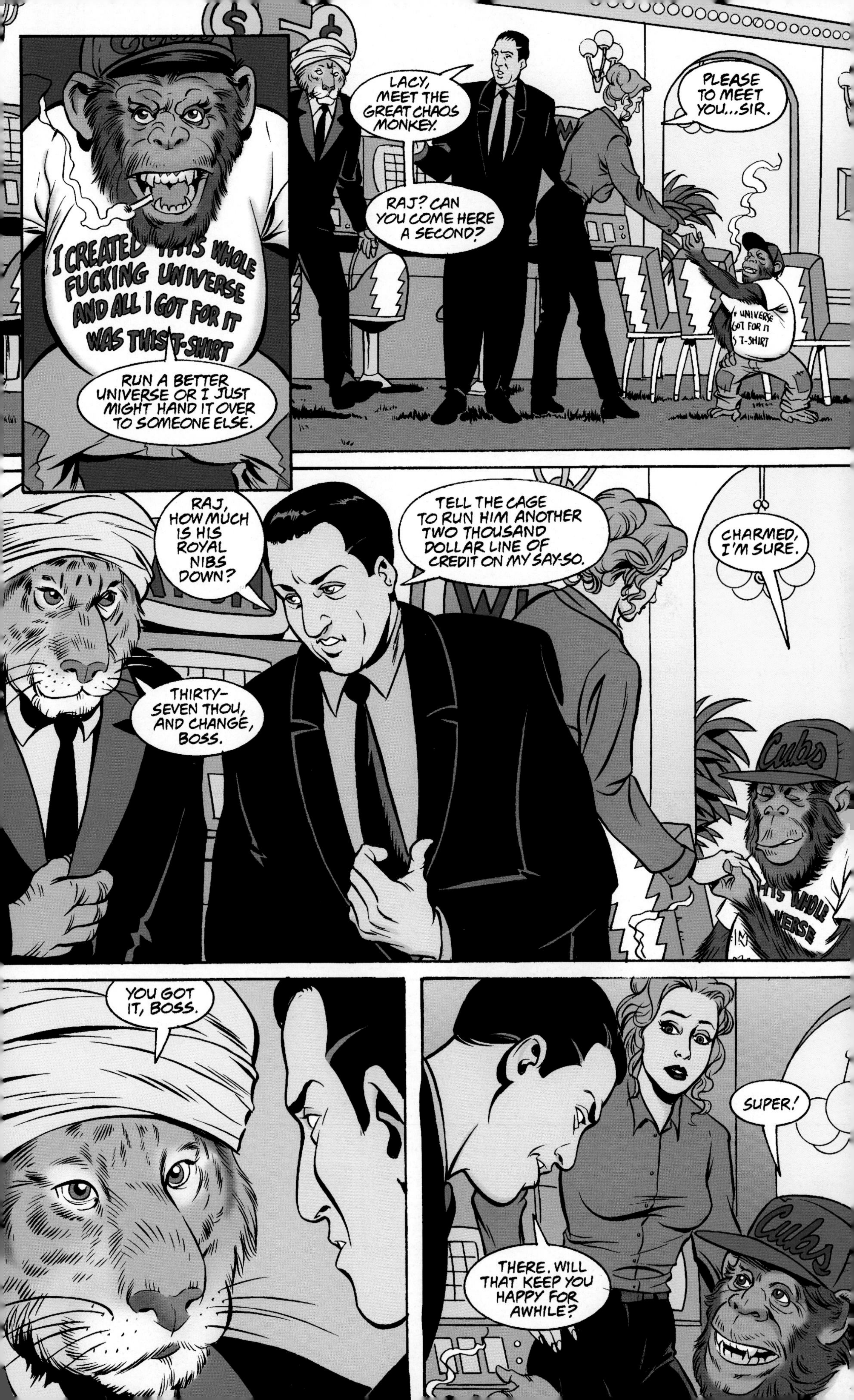
I CREATED THIS WHOLE FUCKING UNIVERSE AND ALL I GOT FOR IT WAS THIS T-SHIRT
RUN A BETTER UNIVERSE OR I JUST MIGHT HAND IT OVER TO SOMEONE ELSE.
LACY, MEET THE GREAT CHAOS MONKEY.
RAJ? CAN YOU COME HERE A SECOND?
PLEASE TO MEET YOU...SIR.
RAJ, HOW MUCH IS HIS ROYAL NIBS DOWN?
THIRTY-SEVEN THOU, AND CHANGE, BOSS.
TELL THE CAGE TO RUN HIM ANOTHER TWO THOUSAND DOLLAR LINE OF CREDIT ON MY SAY-SO.
CHARMED, I'M SURE.
Cubs
YOU GOT IT, BOSS.
SUPER!
THERE. WILL THAT KEEP YOU HAPPY FOR AWHILE?
Cubs

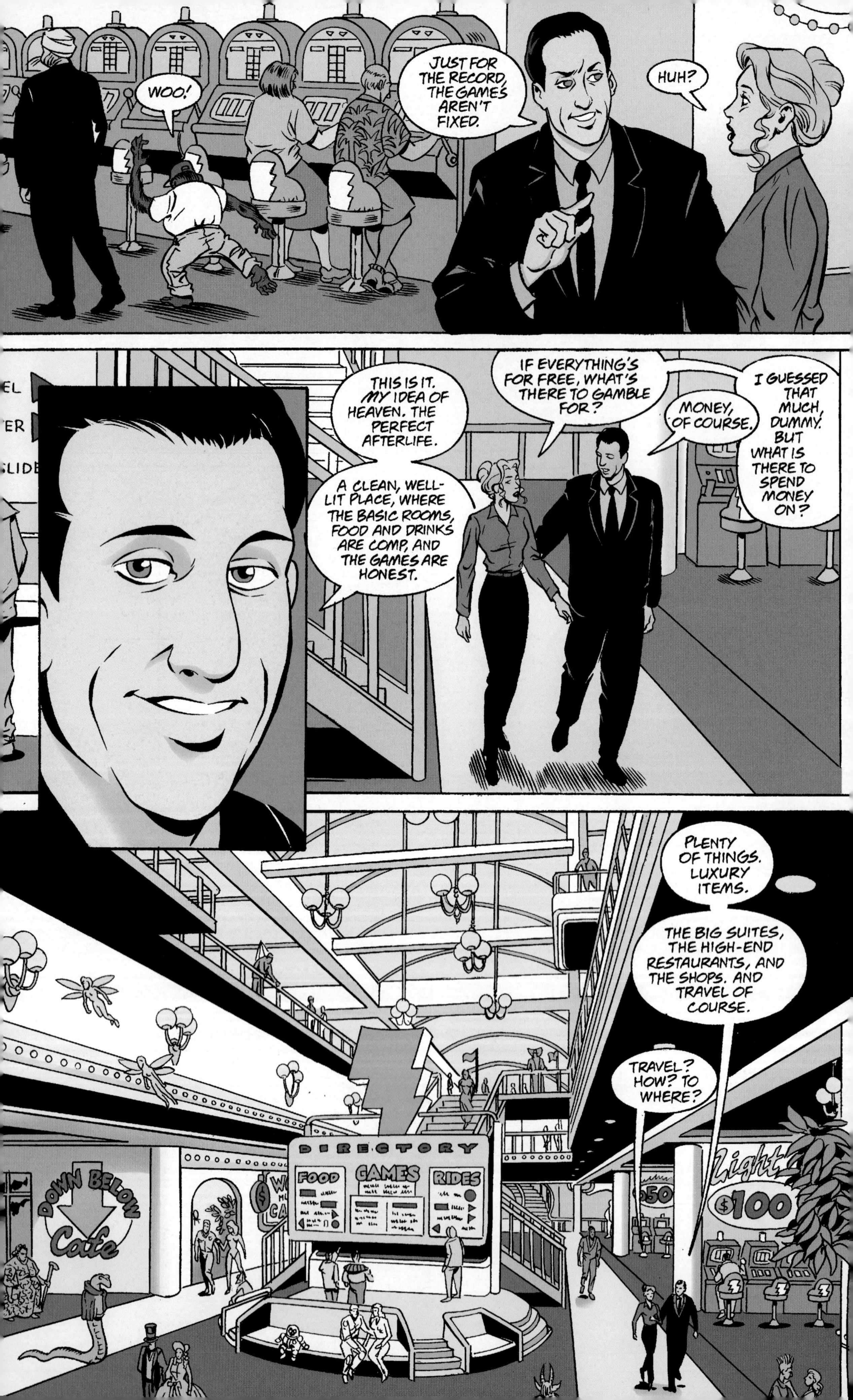
WOO!
JUST FOR THE RECORD, THE GAMES AREN'T FIXED.
HUH?
THIS IS IT. *MY* IDEA OF HEAVEN. THE PERFECT AFTERLIFE.
A CLEAN, WELL-LIT PLACE, WHERE THE BASIC ROOMS, FOOD AND DRINKS ARE COMP, AND THE GAMES ARE HONEST.
IF EVERYTHING'S FOR FREE, WHAT'S THERE TO GAMBLE FOR?
MONEY, OF COURSE.
I GUESSED THAT MUCH, DUMMY. BUT WHAT IS THERE TO SPEND MONEY ON?
PLENTY OF THINGS. LUXURY ITEMS.
THE BIG SUITES, THE HIGH-END RESTAURANTS, AND THE SHOPS. AND TRAVEL OF COURSE.
TRAVEL? HOW? TO WHERE?
DIRECTORY
FOOD
GAMES
RIDES
DOWN BELOW
Cafe
$100

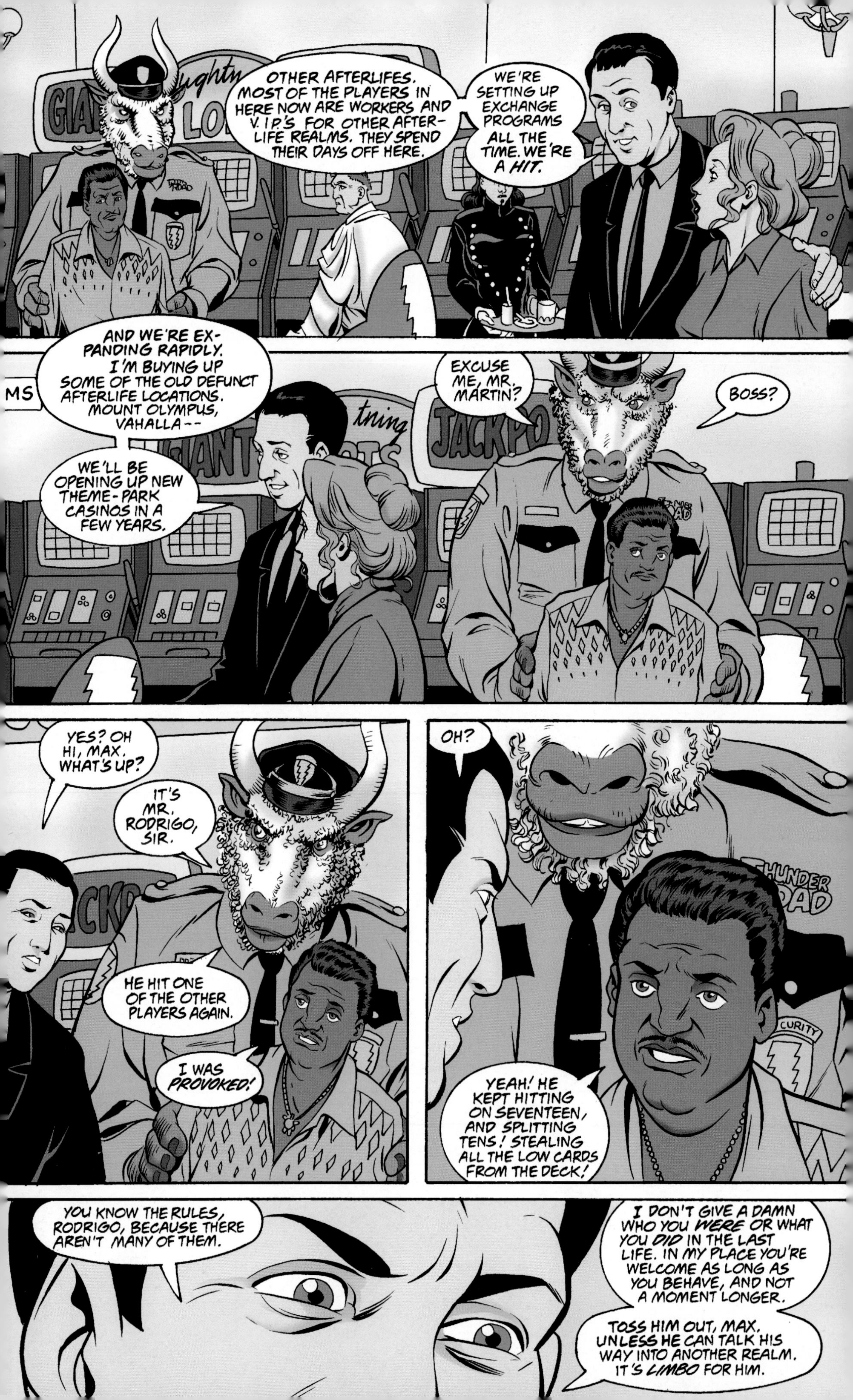
GIANT
LO
ughty
OTHER AFTERLIFES. MOST OF THE PLAYERS IN HERE NOW ARE WORKERS AND V.I.P.'S FOR OTHER AFTER-LIFE REALMS. THEY SPEND THEIR DAYS OFF HERE.
WE'RE SETTING UP EXCHANGE PROGRAMS ALL THE TIME. WE'RE A *HIT*.
MS
AND WE'RE EX-PANDING RAPIDLY. I'M BUYING UP SOME OF THE OLD DEFUNCT AFTERLIFE LOCATIONS. MOUNT OLYMPUS, VAHALLA--
WE'LL BE OPENING UP NEW THEME-PARK CASINOS IN A FEW YEARS.
tning
JACKPO
EXCUSE ME, MR. MARTIN?
BOSS?
YES? OH HI, MAX. WHAT'S UP?
IT'S MR. RODRIGO, SIR.
HE HIT ONE OF THE OTHER PLAYERS AGAIN.
I WAS *PROVOKED!*
OH?
THUNDER ROAD
CURITY
YEAH! HE KEPT HITTING ON SEVENTEEN, AND SPLITTING TENS! STEALING ALL THE LOW CARDS FROM THE DECK!
YOU KNOW THE RULES, RODRIGO, BECAUSE THERE AREN'T MANY OF THEM.
I DON'T GIVE A DAMN WHO YOU *WERE* OR WHAT YOU *DID* IN THE LAST LIFE. IN MY PLACE YOU'RE WELCOME AS LONG AS YOU BEHAVE, AND NOT A MOMENT LONGER.
TOSS HIM OUT, MAX. UNLESS HE CAN TALK HIS WAY INTO ANOTHER REALM. IT'S *LIMBO* FOR HIM.

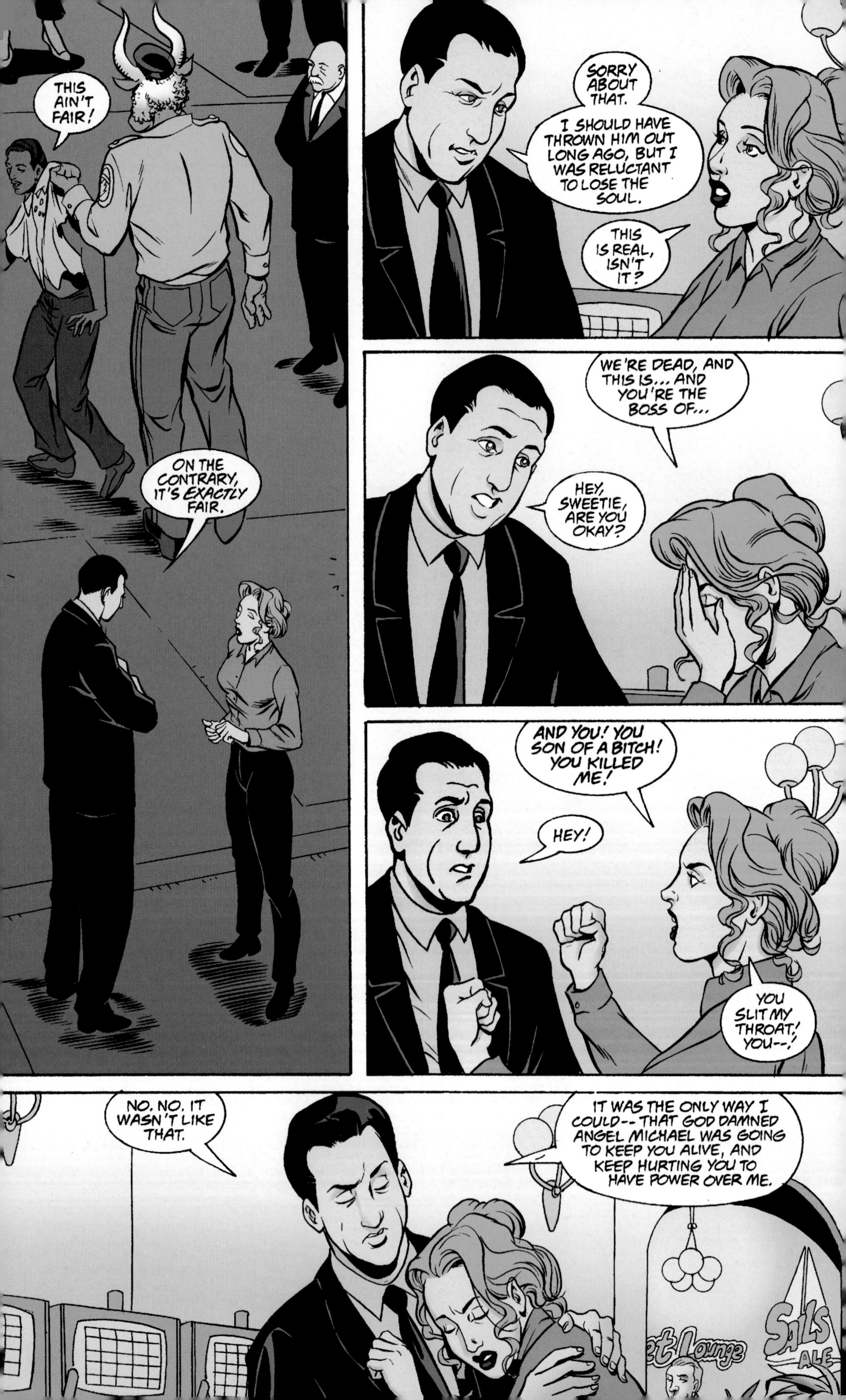
THIS AIN'T FAIR!
ON THE CONTRARY, IT'S EXACTLY FAIR.
SORRY ABOUT THAT.
I SHOULD HAVE THROWN HIM OUT LONG AGO, BUT I WAS RELUCTANT TO LOSE THE SOUL.
THIS IS REAL, ISN'T IT?
WE'RE DEAD, AND THIS IS... AND YOU'RE THE BOSS OF...
HEY, SWEETIE, ARE YOU OKAY?
AND YOU! YOU SON OF A BITCH! YOU KILLED ME!
HEY!
YOU SLIT MY THROAT! YOU--!
NO. NO. IT WASN'T LIKE THAT.
IT WAS THE ONLY WAY I COULD-- THAT GOD DAMNED ANGEL MICHAEL WAS GOING TO KEEP YOU ALIVE, AND KEEP HURTING YOU TO HAVE POWER OVER ME.

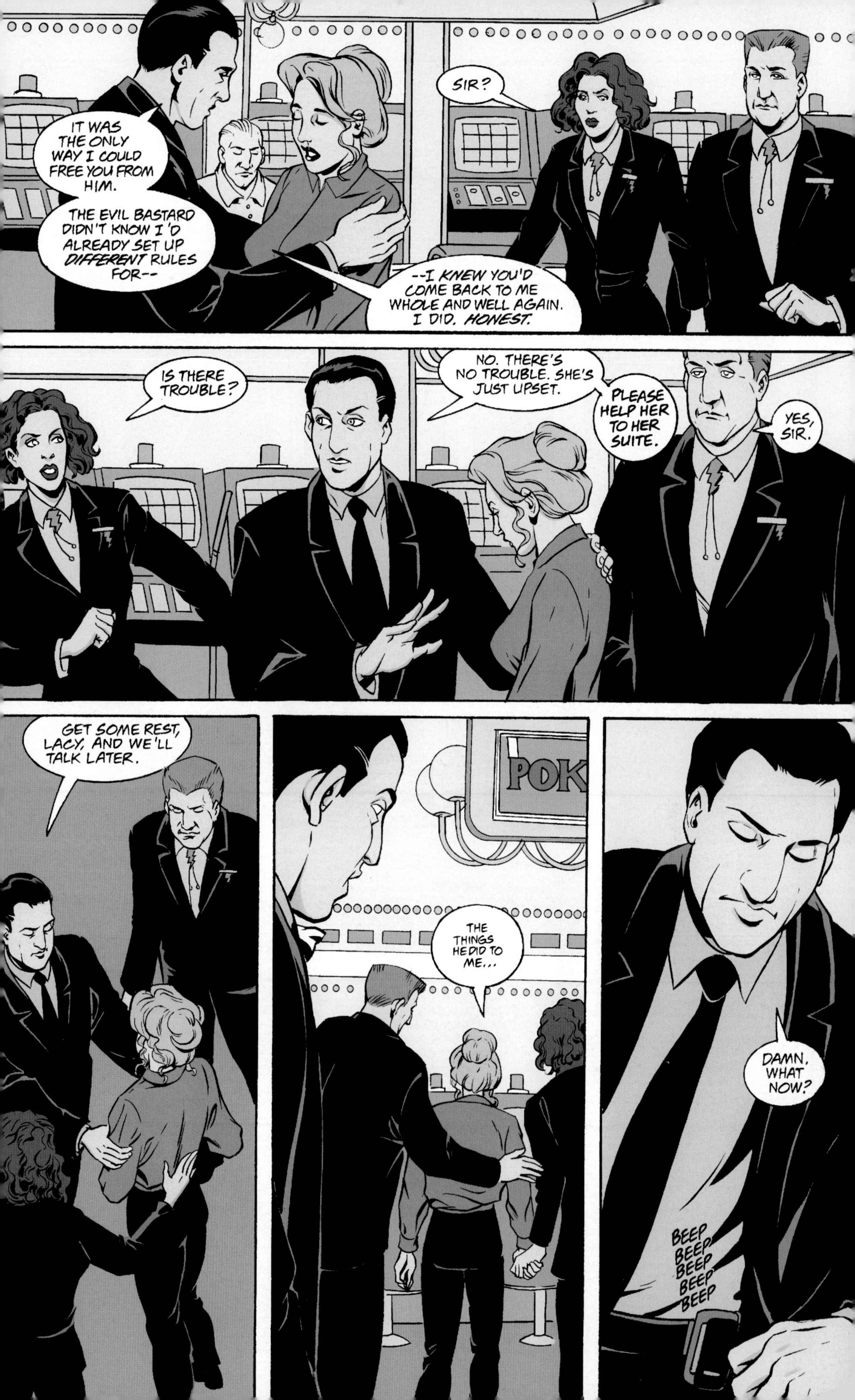
IT WAS THE ONLY WAY I COULD FREE YOU FROM HIM.
THE EVIL BASTARD DIDN'T KNOW I'D ALREADY SET UP DIFFERENT RULES FOR--
SIR?
--I KNEW YOU'D COME BACK TO ME WHOLE AND WELL AGAIN. I DID. HONEST.
IS THERE TROUBLE?
NO. THERE'S NO TROUBLE. SHE'S JUST UPSET.
PLEASE HELP HER TO HER SUITE.
YES, SIR.
GET SOME REST, LACY, AND WE'LL TALK LATER.
POK
THE THINGS HE DID TO ME...
DAMN. WHAT NOW?
BEEP BEEP BEEP BEEP BEEP

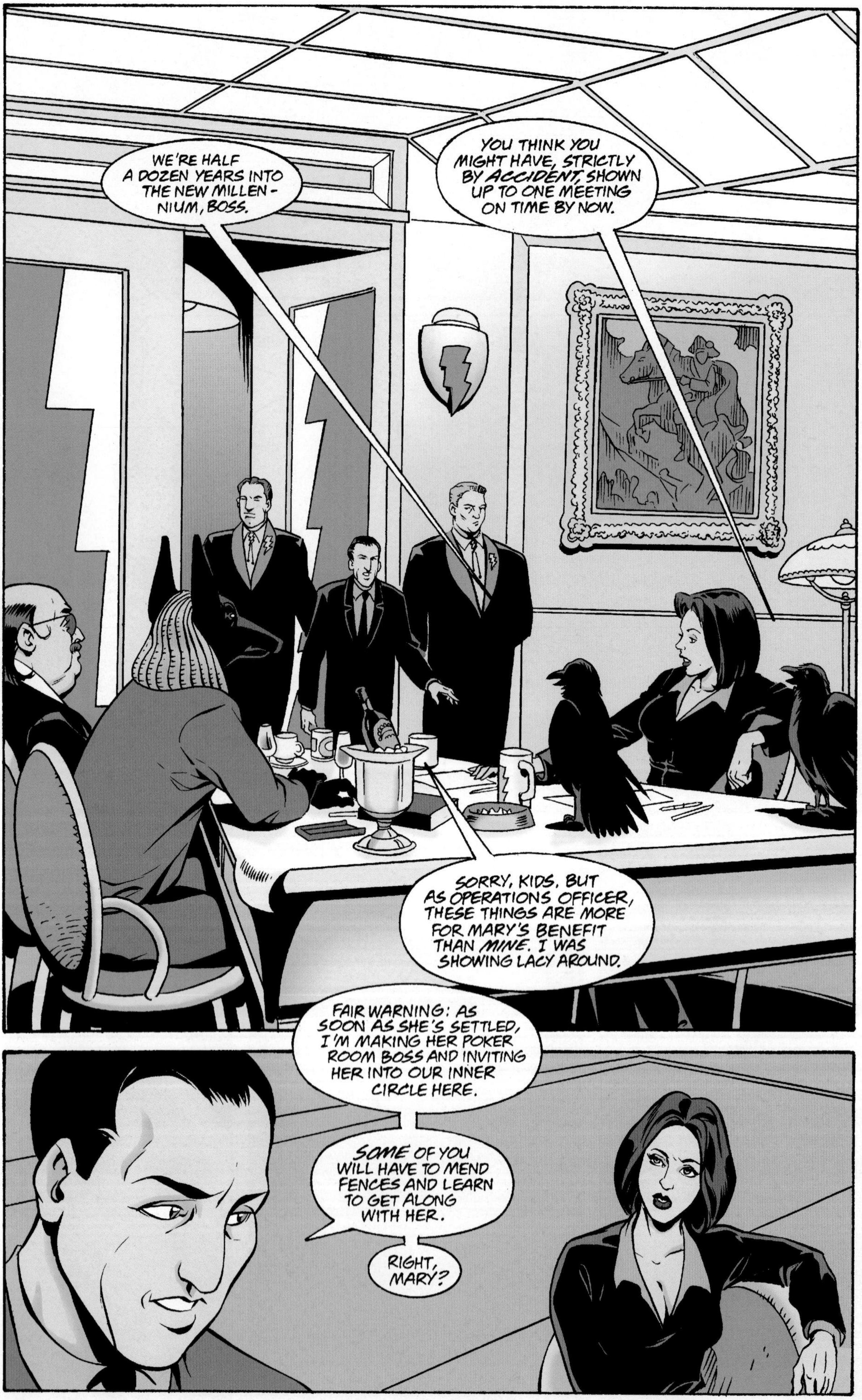
WE'RE HALF A DOZEN YEARS INTO THE NEW MILLEN-NIUM, BOSS.
YOU THINK YOU MIGHT HAVE, STRICTLY BY ACCIDENT, SHOWN UP TO ONE MEETING ON TIME BY NOW.
SORRY, KIDS, BUT AS OPERATIONS OFFICER, THESE THINGS ARE MORE FOR MARY'S BENEFIT THAN MINE. I WAS SHOWING LACY AROUND.
FAIR WARNING: AS SOON AS SHE'S SETTLED, I'M MAKING HER POKER ROOM BOSS AND INVITING HER INTO OUR INNER CIRCLE HERE.
SOME OF YOU WILL HAVE TO MEND FENCES AND LEARN TO GET ALONG WITH HER.
RIGHT, MARY?

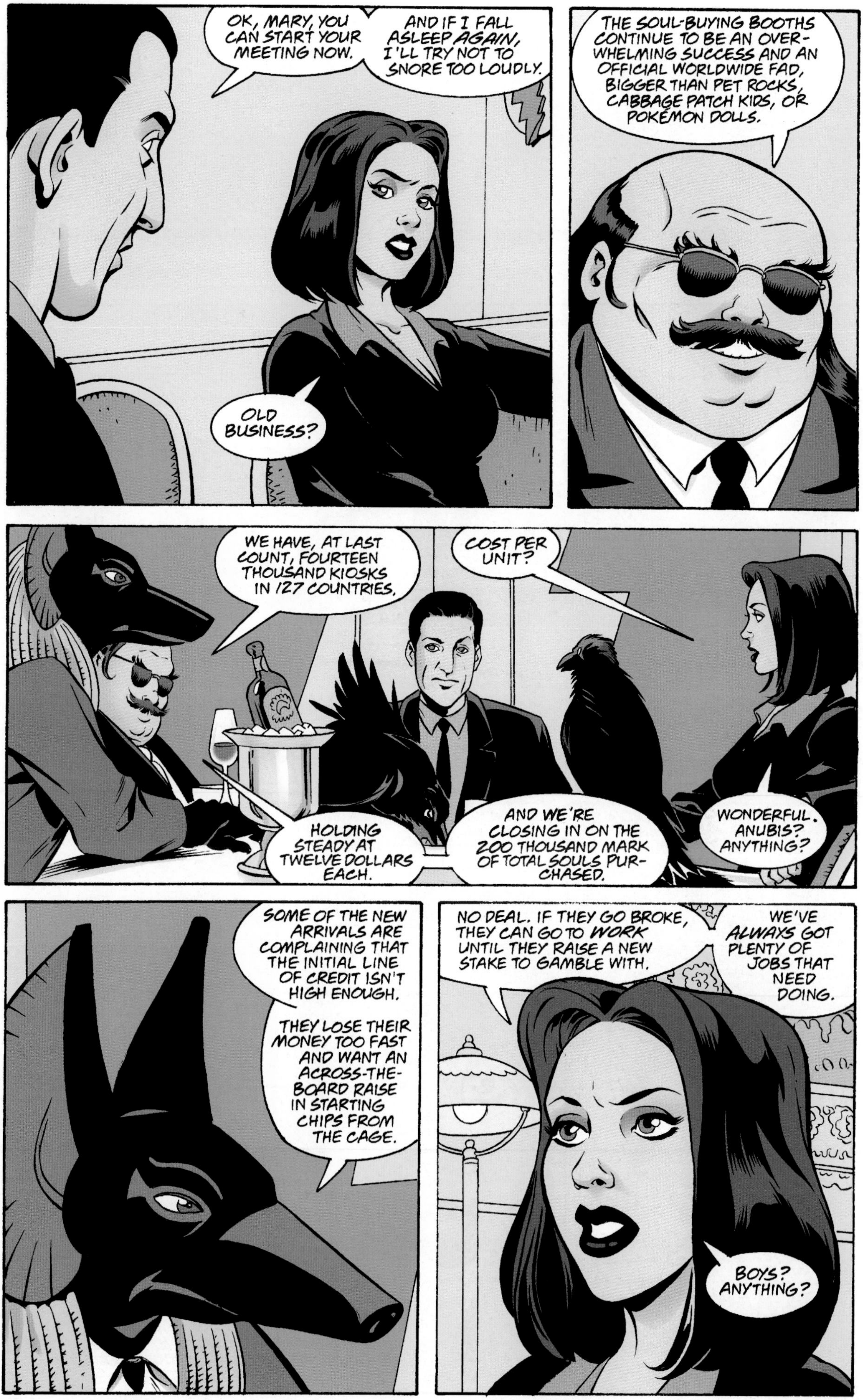
OK, MARY, YOU CAN START YOUR MEETING NOW.
AND IF I FALL ASLEEP AGAIN, I'LL TRY NOT TO SNORE TOO LOUDLY.
OLD BUSINESS?
THE SOUL-BUYING BOOTHS CONTINUE TO BE AN OVER-WHELMING SUCCESS AND AN OFFICIAL WORLDWIDE FAD, BIGGER THAN PET ROCKS, CABBAGE PATCH KIDS, OR POKÉMON DOLLS.
WE HAVE, AT LAST COUNT, FOURTEEN THOUSAND KIOSKS IN 127 COUNTRIES.
COST PER UNIT?
HOLDING STEADY AT TWELVE DOLLARS EACH.
AND WE'RE CLOSING IN ON THE 200 THOUSAND MARK OF TOTAL SOULS PUR-CHASED.
WONDERFUL. ANUBIS? ANYTHING?
SOME OF THE NEW ARRIVALS ARE COMPLAINING THAT THE INITIAL LINE OF CREDIT ISN'T HIGH ENOUGH.
THEY LOSE THEIR MONEY TOO FAST AND WANT AN ACROSS-THE-BOARD RAISE IN STARTING CHIPS FROM THE CAGE.
NO DEAL. IF THEY GO BROKE, THEY CAN GO TO WORK UNTIL THEY RAISE A NEW STAKE TO GAMBLE WITH.
WE'VE ALWAYS GOT PLENTY OF JOBS THAT NEED DOING.
BOYS? ANYTHING?

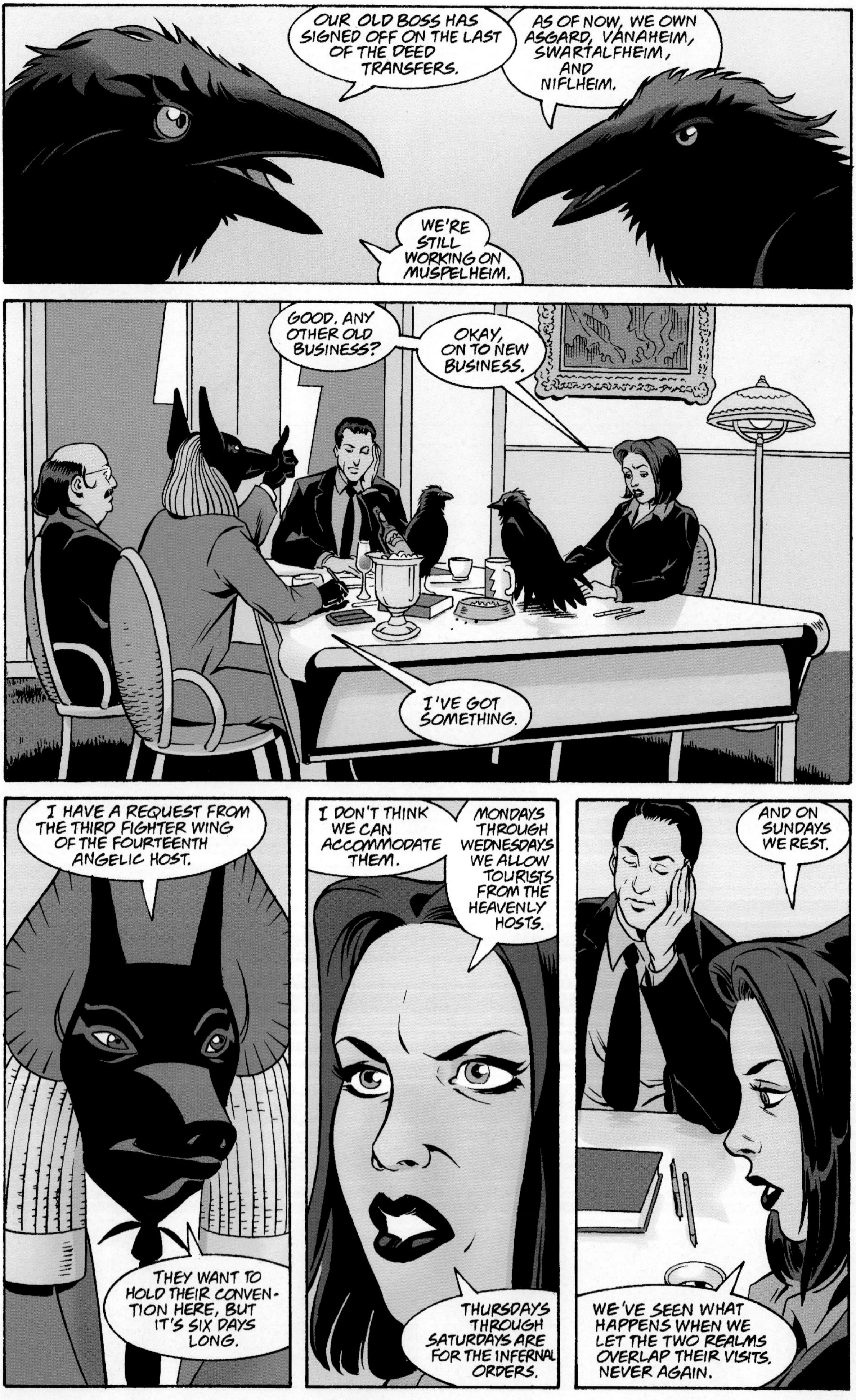

OUR OLD BOSS HAS SIGNED OFF ON THE LAST OF THE DEED TRANSFERS.
AS OF NOW, WE OWN ASGARD, VANAHEIM, SWARTALFHEIM, AND NIFLHEIM.
WE'RE STILL WORKING ON MUSPELHEIM.
GOOD. ANY OTHER OLD BUSINESS?
OKAY, ON TO NEW BUSINESS.
I'VE GOT SOMETHING.
I HAVE A REQUEST FROM THE THIRD FIGHTER WING OF THE FOURTEENTH ANGELIC HOST.
THEY WANT TO HOLD THEIR CONVEN-TION HERE, BUT IT'S SIX DAYS LONG.
I DON'T THINK WE CAN ACCOMMODATE THEM.
MONDAYS THROUGH WEDNESDAYS WE ALLOW TOURISTS FROM THE HEAVENLY HOSTS.
THURSDAYS THROUGH SATURDAYS ARE FOR THE INFERNAL ORDERS.
AND ON SUNDAYS WE REST.
WE'VE SEEN WHAT HAPPENS WHEN WE LET THE TWO REALMS OVERLAP THEIR VISITS. NEVER AGAIN.

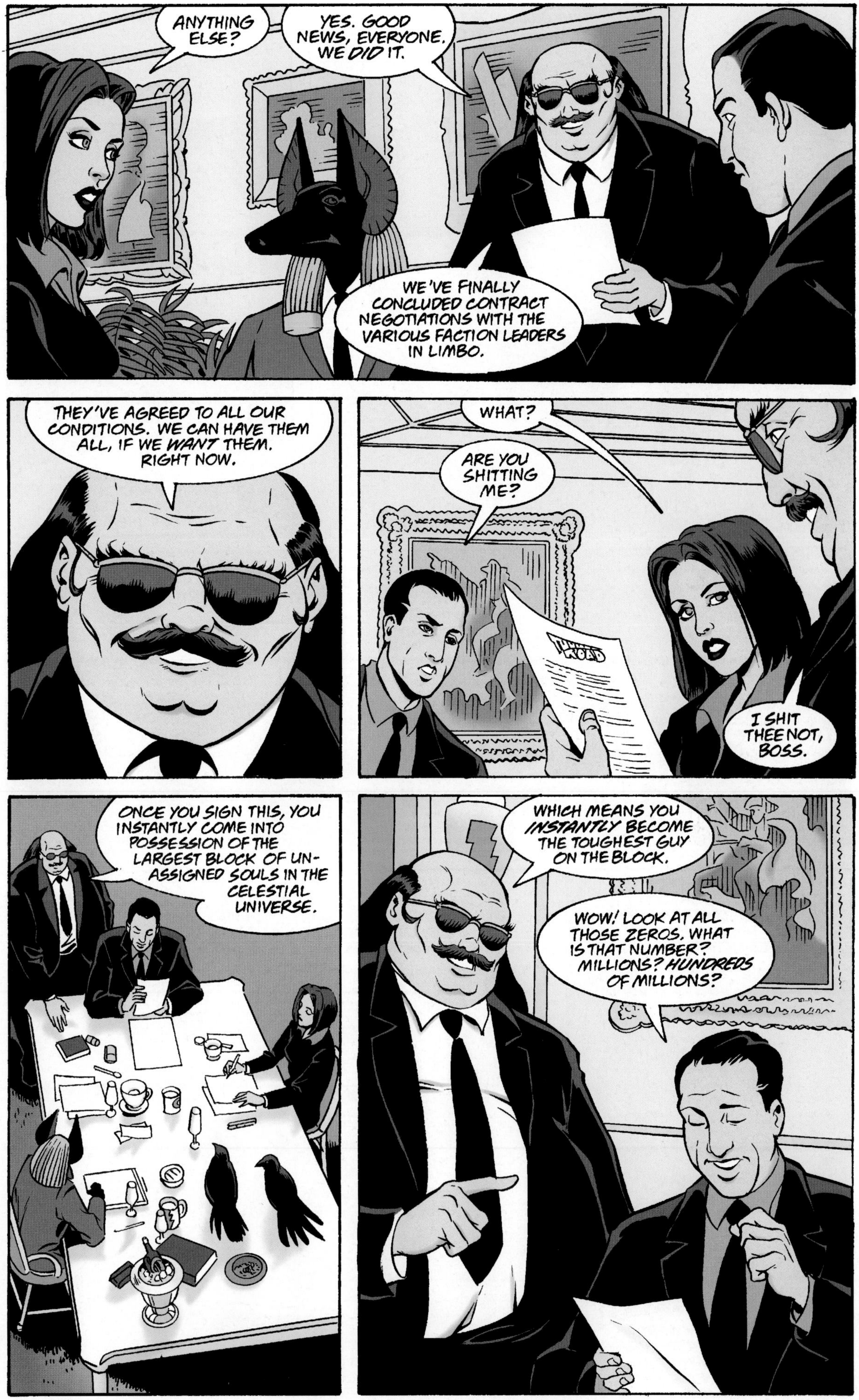
ANYTHING ELSE?
YES. GOOD NEWS, EVERYONE. WE DID IT.
WE'VE FINALLY CONCLUDED CONTRACT NEGOTIATIONS WITH THE VARIOUS FACTION LEADERS IN LIMBO.
THEY'VE AGREED TO ALL OUR CONDITIONS. WE CAN HAVE THEM ALL, IF WE WANT THEM. RIGHT NOW.
WHAT?
ARE YOU SHITTING ME?
I SHIT THEE NOT, BOSS.
ONCE YOU SIGN THIS, YOU INSTANTLY COME INTO POSSESSION OF THE LARGEST BLOCK OF UN-ASSIGNED SOULS IN THE CELESTIAL UNIVERSE.
WHICH MEANS YOU INSTANTLY BECOME THE TOUGHEST GUY ON THE BLOCK.
WOW! LOOK AT ALL THOSE ZEROS. WHAT IS THAT NUMBER? MILLIONS? HUNDREDS OF MILLIONS?

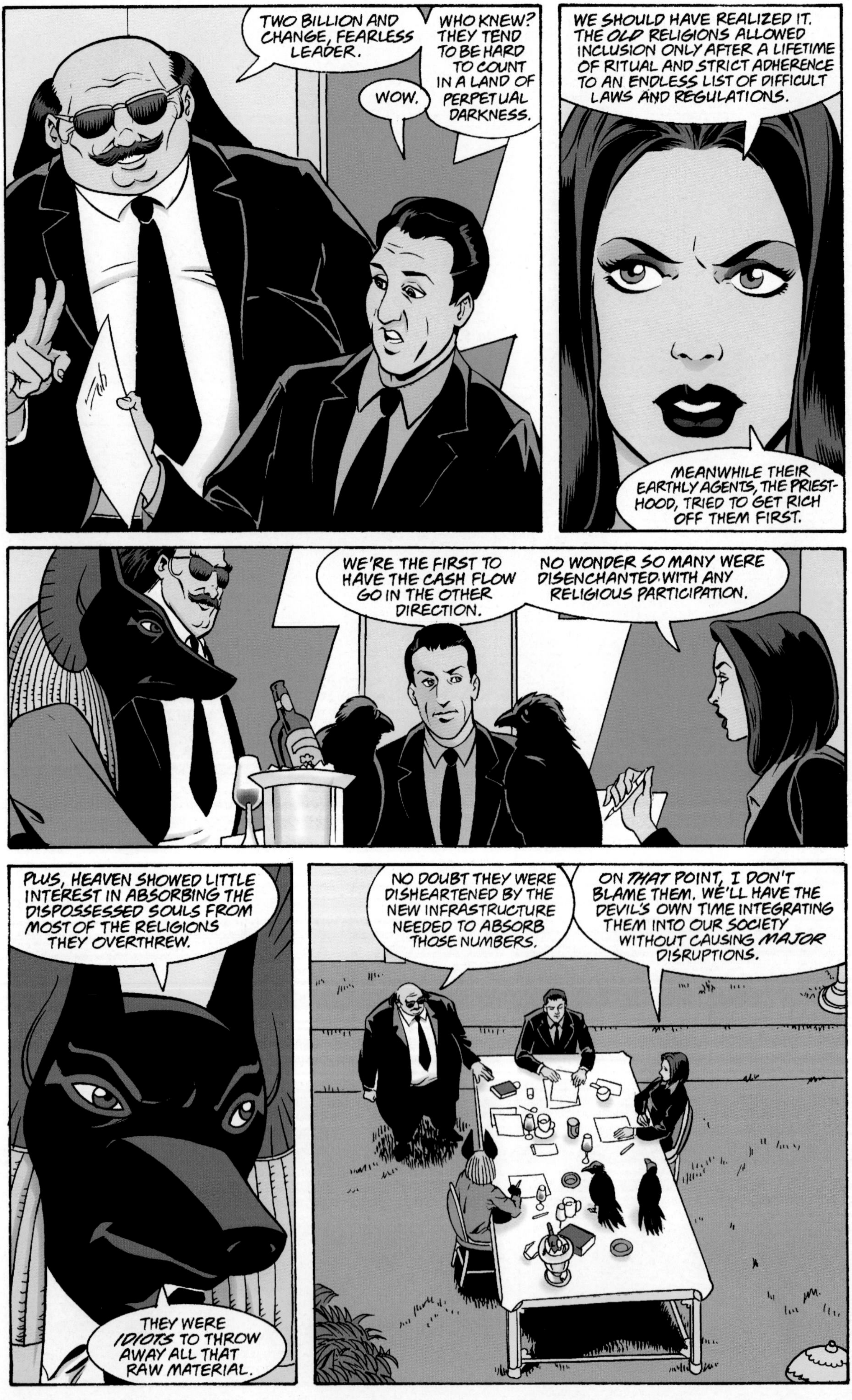
TWO BILLION AND CHANGE, FEARLESS LEADER.
WOW.
WHO KNEW? THEY TEND TO BE HARD TO COUNT IN A LAND OF PERPETUAL DARKNESS.
WE SHOULD HAVE REALIZED IT. THE OLD RELIGIONS ALLOWED INCLUSION ONLY AFTER A LIFETIME OF RITUAL AND STRICT ADHERENCE TO AN ENDLESS LIST OF DIFFICULT LAWS AND REGULATIONS.
MEANWHILE THEIR EARTHLY AGENTS, THE PRIESTHOOD, TRIED TO GET RICH OFF THEM FIRST.
WE'RE THE FIRST TO HAVE THE CASH FLOW GO IN THE OTHER DIRECTION.
NO WONDER SO MANY WERE DISENCHANTED WITH ANY RELIGIOUS PARTICIPATION.
PLUS, HEAVEN SHOWED LITTLE INTEREST IN ABSORBING THE DISPOSSESSED SOULS FROM MOST OF THE RELIGIONS THEY OVERTHREW.
THEY WERE IDIOTS TO THROW AWAY ALL THAT RAW MATERIAL.
NO DOUBT THEY WERE DISHEARTENED BY THE NEW INFRASTRUCTURE NEEDED TO ABSORB THOSE NUMBERS.
ON THAT POINT, I DON'T BLAME THEM. WE'LL HAVE THE DEVIL'S OWN TIME INTEGRATING THEM INTO OUR SOCIETY WITHOUT CAUSING MAJOR DISRUPTIONS.

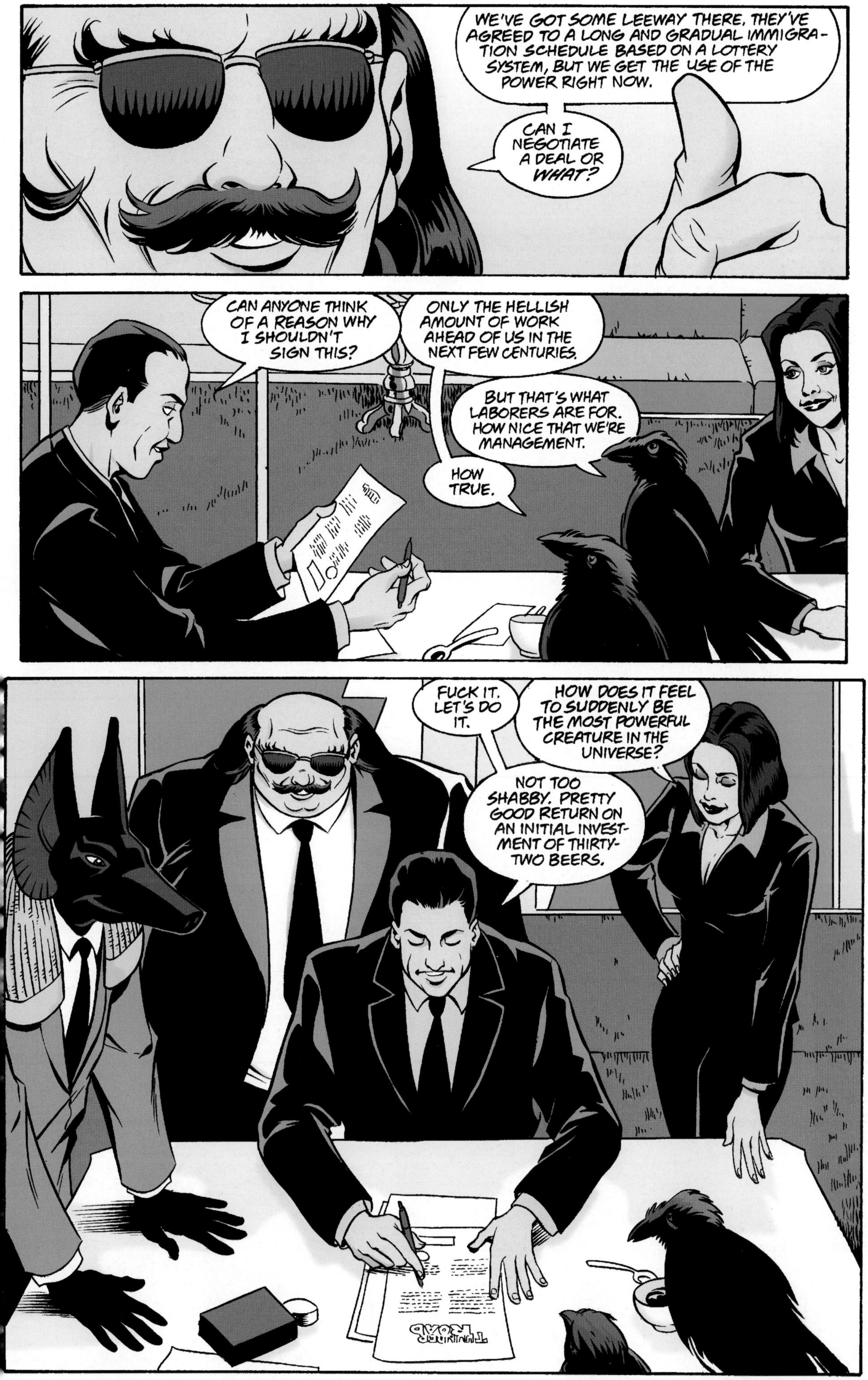
WE'VE GOT SOME LEEWAY THERE. THEY'VE AGREED TO A LONG AND GRADUAL IMMIGRATION SCHEDULE BASED ON A LOTTERY SYSTEM, BUT WE GET THE USE OF THE POWER RIGHT NOW.
CAN I NEGOTIATE A DEAL OR *WHAT?*
CAN ANYONE THINK OF A REASON WHY I SHOULDN'T SIGN THIS?
ONLY THE HELLISH AMOUNT OF WORK AHEAD OF US IN THE NEXT FEW CENTURIES.
BUT THAT'S WHAT LABORERS ARE FOR. HOW NICE THAT WE'RE MANAGEMENT.
HOW TRUE.
FUCK IT. LET'S DO IT.
HOW DOES IT FEEL TO SUDDENLY BE THE MOST POWERFUL CREATURE IN THE UNIVERSE?
NOT TOO SHABBY. PRETTY GOOD RETURN ON AN INITIAL INVESTMENT OF THIRTY-TWO BEERS.

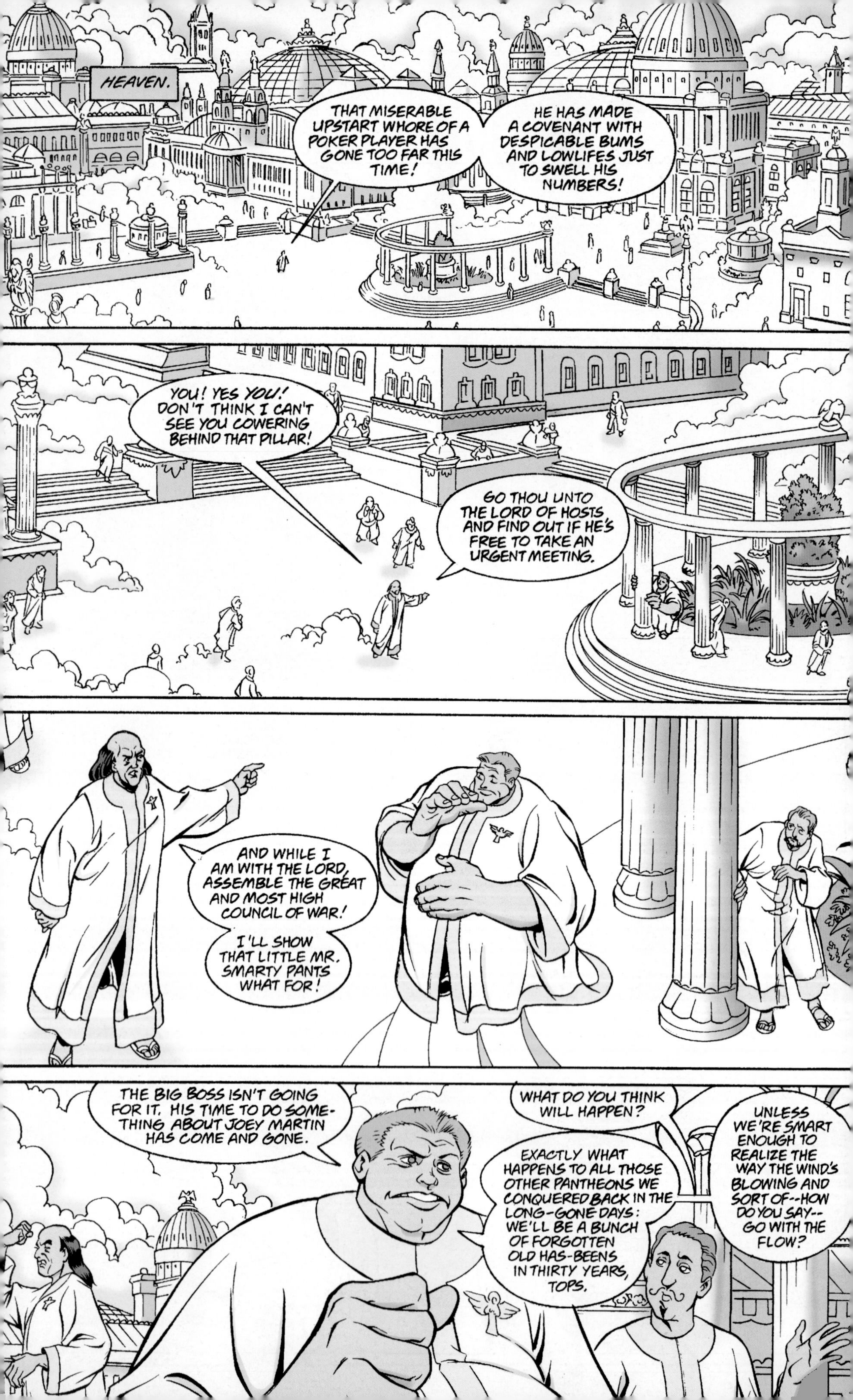
HEAVEN.
THAT MISERABLE UPSTART WHORE OF A POKER PLAYER HAS GONE TOO FAR THIS TIME!
HE HAS MADE A COVENANT WITH DESPICABLE BUMS AND LOWLIFES JUST TO SWELL HIS NUMBERS!
YOU! YES YOU! DON'T THINK I CAN'T SEE YOU COWERING BEHIND THAT PILLAR!
GO THOU UNTO THE LORD OF HOSTS AND FIND OUT IF HE'S FREE TO TAKE AN URGENT MEETING.
AND WHILE I AM WITH THE LORD, ASSEMBLE THE GREAT AND MOST HIGH COUNCIL OF WAR!
I'LL SHOW THAT LITTLE MR. SMARTY PANTS WHAT FOR!
THE BIG BOSS ISN'T GOING FOR IT. HIS TIME TO DO SOMETHING ABOUT JOEY MARTIN HAS COME AND GONE.
WHAT DO YOU THINK WILL HAPPEN?
EXACTLY WHAT HAPPENS TO ALL THOSE OTHER PANTHEONS WE CONQUERED BACK IN THE LONG-GONE DAYS: WE'LL BE A BUNCH OF FORGOTTEN OLD HAS-BEENS IN THIRTY YEARS, TOPS.
UNLESS WE'RE SMART ENOUGH TO REALIZE THE WAY THE WIND'S BLOWING AND SORT OF--HOW DO YOU SAY--GO WITH THE FLOW?

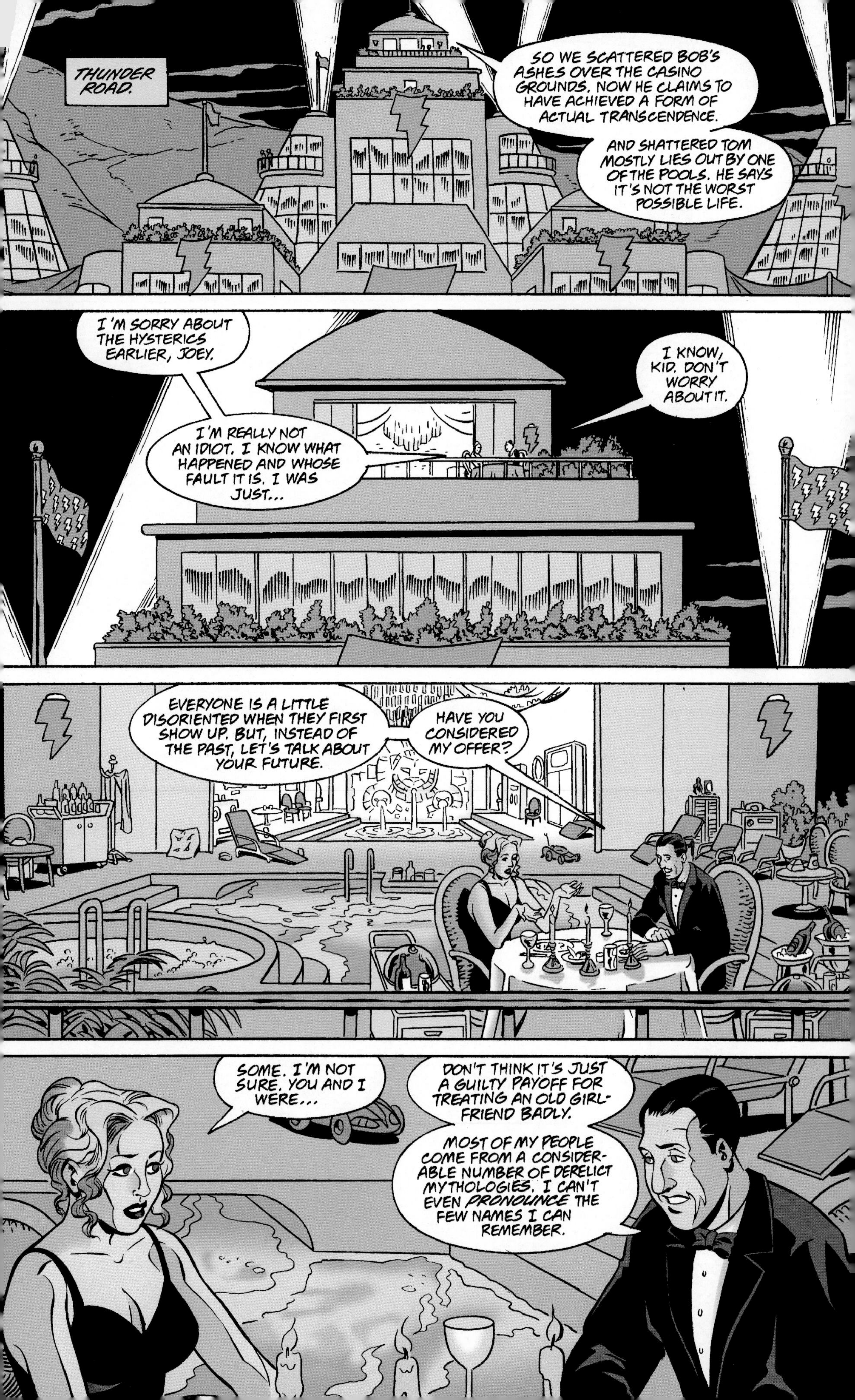
THUNDER ROAD.
SO WE SCATTERED BOB'S ASHES OVER THE CASINO GROUNDS. NOW HE CLAIMS TO HAVE ACHIEVED A FORM OF ACTUAL TRANSCENDENCE.
AND SHATTERED TOM MOSTLY LIES OUT BY ONE OF THE POOLS. HE SAYS IT'S NOT THE WORST POSSIBLE LIFE.
I'M SORRY ABOUT THE HYSTERICS EARLIER, JOEY.
I'M REALLY NOT AN IDIOT. I KNOW WHAT HAPPENED AND WHOSE FAULT IT IS. I WAS JUST...
I KNOW, KID. DON'T WORRY ABOUT IT.
EVERYONE IS A LITTLE DISORIENTED WHEN THEY FIRST SHOW UP. BUT, INSTEAD OF THE PAST, LET'S TALK ABOUT YOUR FUTURE.
HAVE YOU CONSIDERED MY OFFER?
SOME. I'M NOT SURE. YOU AND I WERE...
DON'T THINK IT'S JUST A GUILTY PAYOFF FOR TREATING AN OLD GIRL-FRIEND BADLY.
MOST OF MY PEOPLE COME FROM A CONSIDER-ABLE NUMBER OF DERELICT MYTHOLOGIES. I CAN'T EVEN *PRONOUNCE* THE FEW NAMES I CAN REMEMBER.

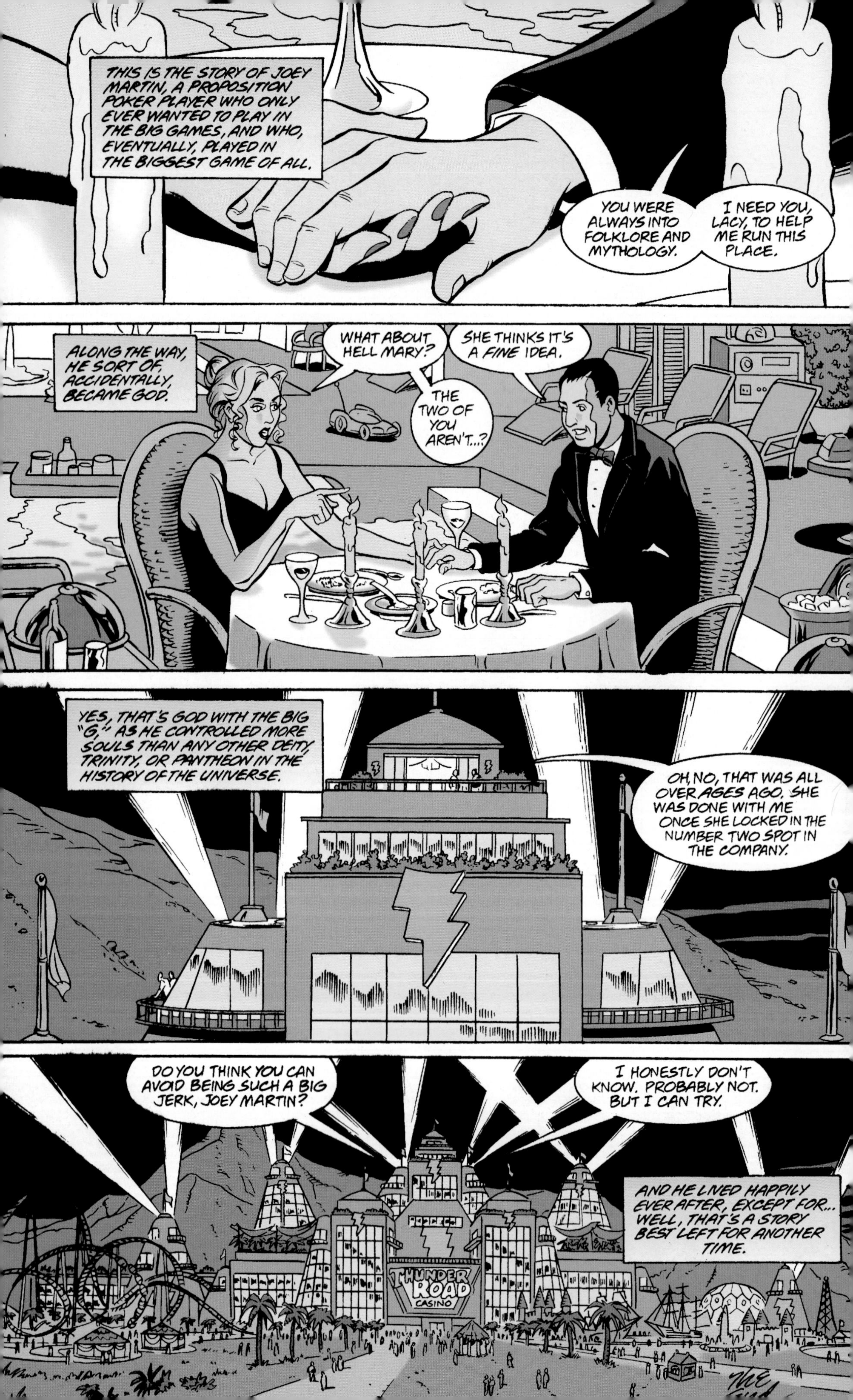
THIS IS THE STORY OF JOEY MARTIN, A PROPOSITION POKER PLAYER WHO ONLY EVER WANTED TO PLAY IN THE BIG GAMES, AND WHO, EVENTUALLY, PLAYED IN THE BIGGEST GAME OF ALL.
YOU WERE ALWAYS INTO FOLKLORE AND MYTHOLOGY.
I NEED YOU, LACY, TO HELP ME RUN THIS PLACE.
ALONG THE WAY, HE SORT OF, ACCIDENTALLY, BECAME GOD.
WHAT ABOUT HELL MARY?
SHE THINKS IT'S A FINE IDEA.
THE TWO OF YOU AREN'T...?
YES, THAT'S GOD WITH THE BIG "G," AS HE CONTROLLED MORE SOULS THAN ANY OTHER DEITY, TRINITY, OR PANTHEON IN THE HISTORY OF THE UNIVERSE.
OH, NO, THAT WAS ALL OVER AGES AGO. SHE WAS DONE WITH ME ONCE SHE LOCKED IN THE NUMBER TWO SPOT IN THE COMPANY.
DO YOU THINK YOU CAN AVOID BEING SUCH A BIG JERK, JOEY MARTIN?
I HONESTLY DON'T KNOW. PROBABLY NOT. BUT I CAN TRY.
AND HE LIVED HAPPILY EVER AFTER, EXCEPT FOR... WELL, THAT'S A STORY BEST LEFT FOR ANOTHER TIME.
THUNDER ROAD CASINO

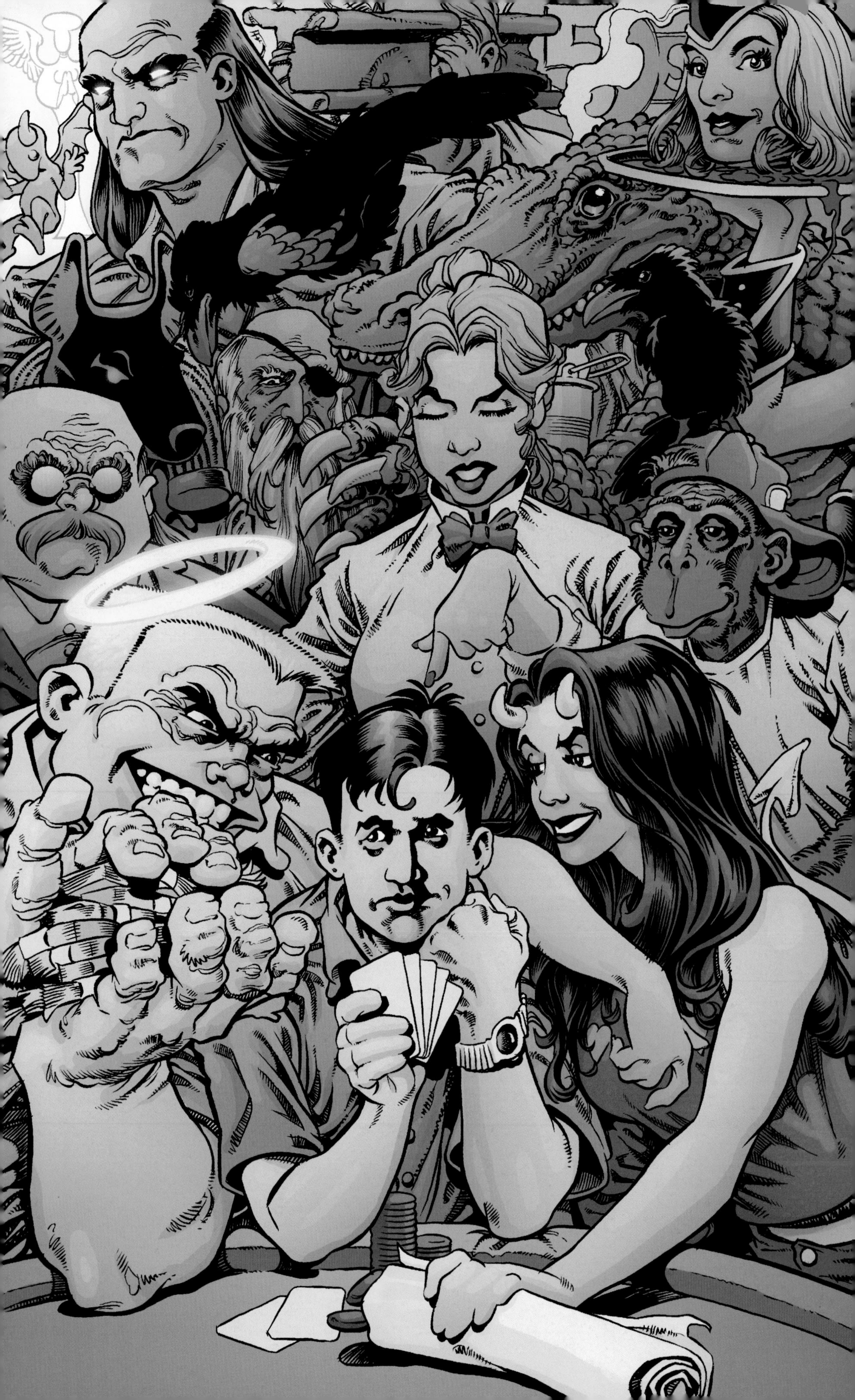

THIS STORY FIRST APPEARED IN A SHORT-LIVED VERTIGO HORROR ANTHOLOGY SERIES CALLED *FLINCH*. It was supposed to feature only truly horrific, disturbing stories, but at the time I didn't think I had any truly horrific stories in me (turns out I was wrong, as you'll see a bit further on in this tome), the sort of thing that might make a reader actually flinch. But I did like funny stories about monsters, so I tried one of those, and the editors of the series kindly let me get away with it.

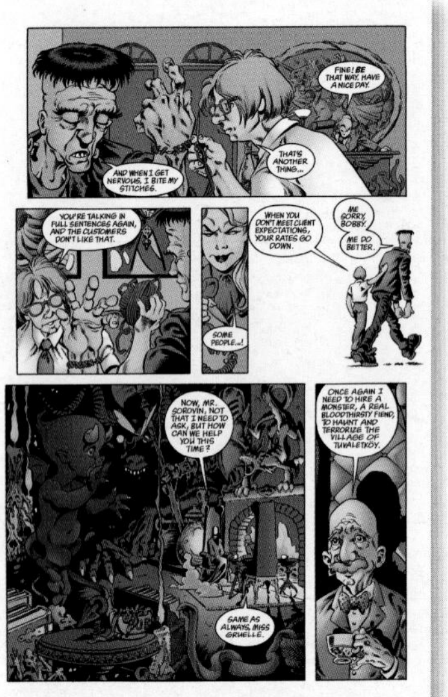
AND WHEN I GET NERVOUS, I BITE MY STITCHES.
THAT'S ANOTHER THING...
FINE! BE THAT WAY. HAVE A NICE DAY.
YOU'RE TALKING IN FULL SENTENCES AGAIN, AND THE CUSTOMERS DON'T LIKE THAT.
SOME PEOPLE...!
WHEN YOU DON'T MEET CLIENT EXPECTATIONS, YOUR RATES GO DOWN.
ME SORRY, BOBBY.
ME DO BETTER.
NOW, MR. SOROVIN, NOT THAT I NEED TO ASK, BUT HOW CAN WE HELP YOU THIS TIME?
SAME AS ALWAYS, MISS GRUELLE.
ONCE AGAIN I NEED TO HIRE A MONSTER, A REAL BLOODTHIRSTY FIEND, TO HAUNT AND TERRORIZE THE VILLAGE OF TUVALETKÖY.

Technically DC/Vertigo owns these characters, since all stories in this anthology were done as "work for hire." But I'm secretly planning to steal the lovely Mrs. Gruelle away from them someday to eventually appear in FABLES. (Shhhh, don't tell them.) I can easily imagine the Monsters for All Occasions shop existing right around the corner from Fabletown. In my mind, that's the fictional world she calls home.

I wrote, drew and inked this one, a hat trick that was becoming more and more of a rarity for me by this stage of my career. I think it only happened on this occasion because I had lots of time. The jobs were few and far between in those days. That was about to change.

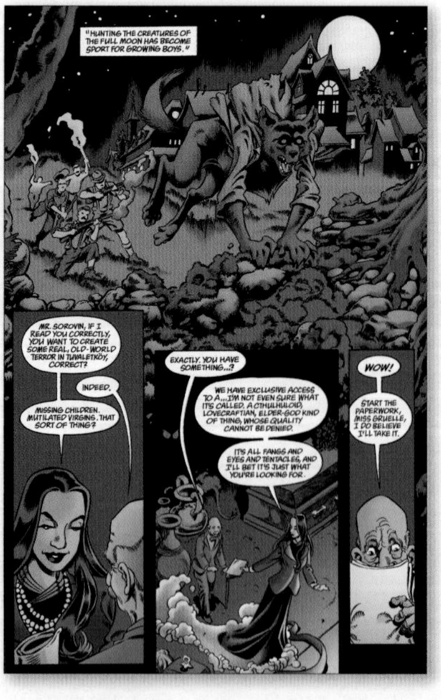
"HUNTING THE CREATURES OF THE FULL MOON HAS BECOME SPORT FOR GROWING BOYS."
MR. SOROVIN, IF I READ YOU CORRECTLY, YOU WANT TO CREATE SOME REAL, OLD-WORLD TERROR IN TUVALETKÖY, CORRECT?
INDEED.
MISSING CHILDREN. MUTILATED VIRGINS. THAT SORT OF THING?
EXACTLY. YOU HAVE SOMETHING...?
WE HAVE EXCLUSIVE ACCESS TO A...I'M NOT EVEN SURE WHAT IT'S CALLED. A CTHULHULOID, LOVECRAFTIAN, ELDER-GOD KIND OF THING, WHOSE QUALITY CANNOT BE DENIED.
IT'S ALL FANGS AND EYES AND TENTACLES, AND I'LL BET IT'S JUST WHAT YOU'RE LOOKING FOR.
WOW!
START THE PAPERWORK, MISS GRUELLE, I DO BELIEVE I'LL TAKE IT.

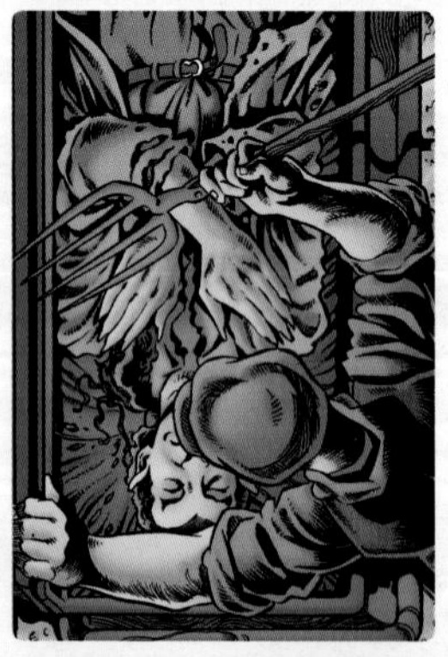

IT TAKES A VILLAGE

STORY AND ART BY
Bill Willingham

COLORS BY
Pamela Rambo

LETTERS BY
Todd Klein

Previous Page:
Cover art for the PROPOSITION PLAYER trade paperback collection by Bill Willingham (colors by James Sinclair).

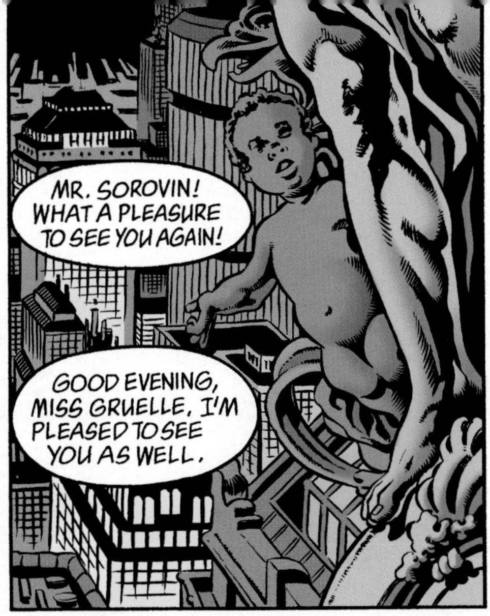
MR. SOROVIN! WHAT A PLEASURE TO SEE YOU AGAIN!
GOOD EVENING, MISS GRUELLE. I'M PLEASED TO SEE YOU AS WELL.

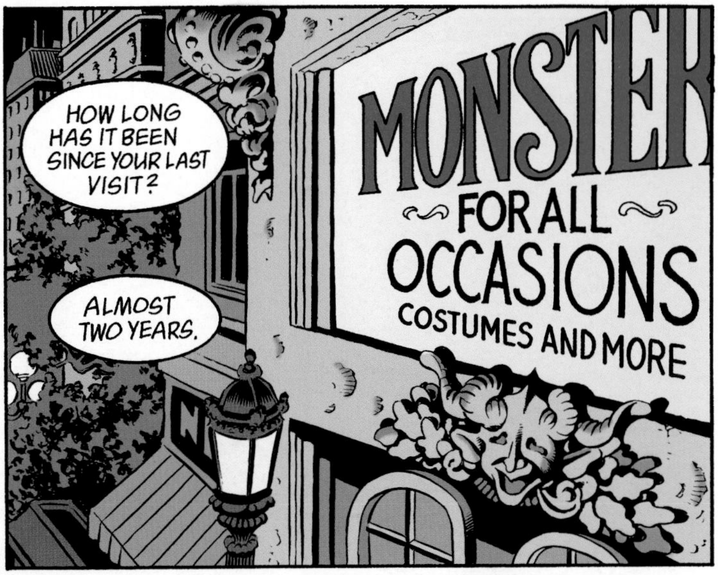
HOW LONG HAS IT BEEN SINCE YOUR LAST VISIT?
ALMOST TWO YEARS.
MONSTER
FOR ALL OCCASIONS
COSTUMES AND MORE

IT TAKES A VILLAGE

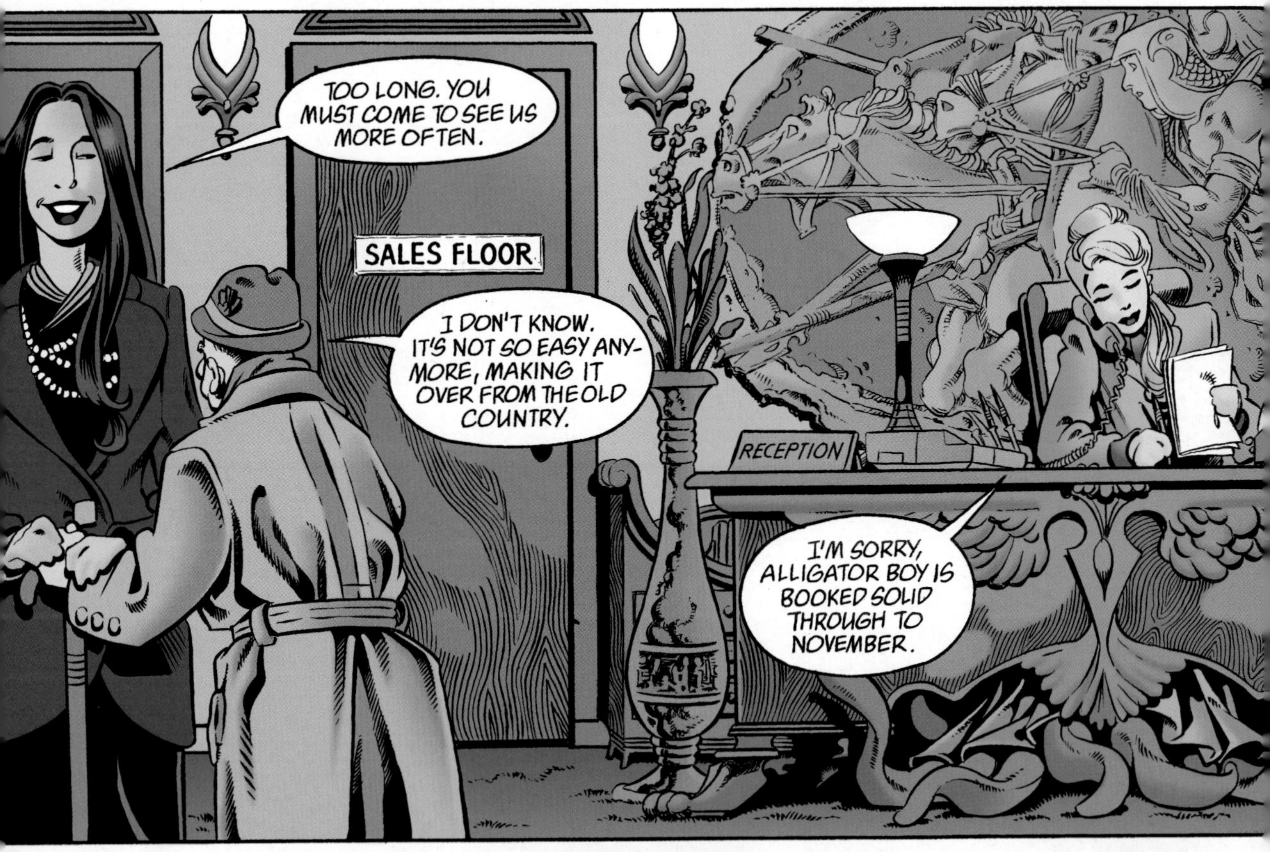
TOO LONG. YOU MUST COME TO SEE US MORE OFTEN.
SALES FLOOR
I DON'T KNOW. IT'S NOT SO EASY ANY-MORE, MAKING IT OVER FROM THE OLD COUNTRY.
RECEPTION
I'M SORRY, ALLIGATOR BOY IS BOOKED SOLID THROUGH TO NOVEMBER.

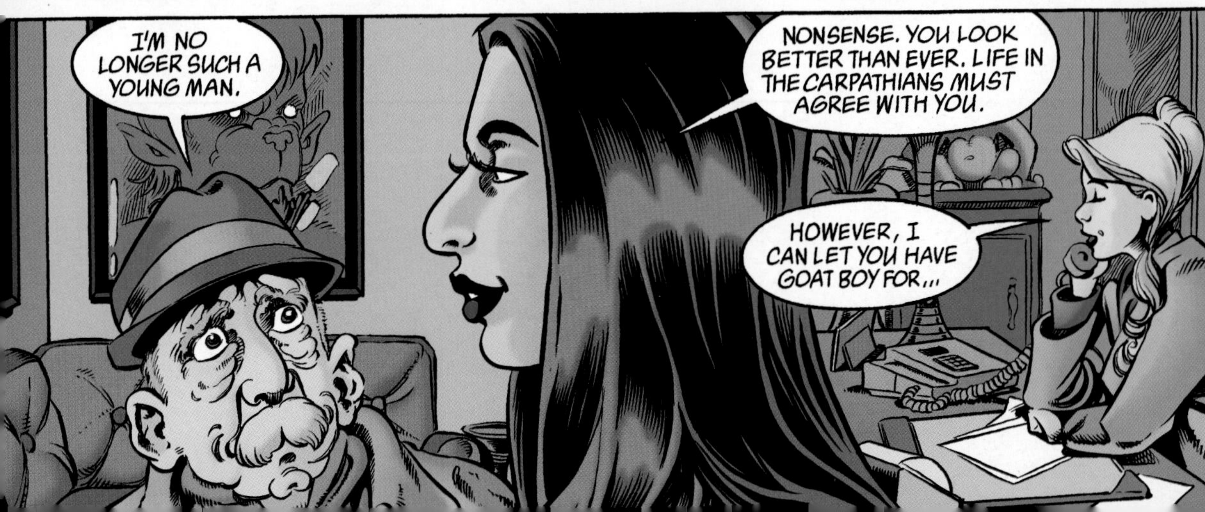
I'M NO LONGER SUCH A YOUNG MAN.
NONSENSE. YOU LOOK BETTER THAN EVER. LIFE IN THE CARPATHIANS MUST AGREE WITH YOU.
HOWEVER, I CAN LET YOU HAVE GOAT BOY FOR...

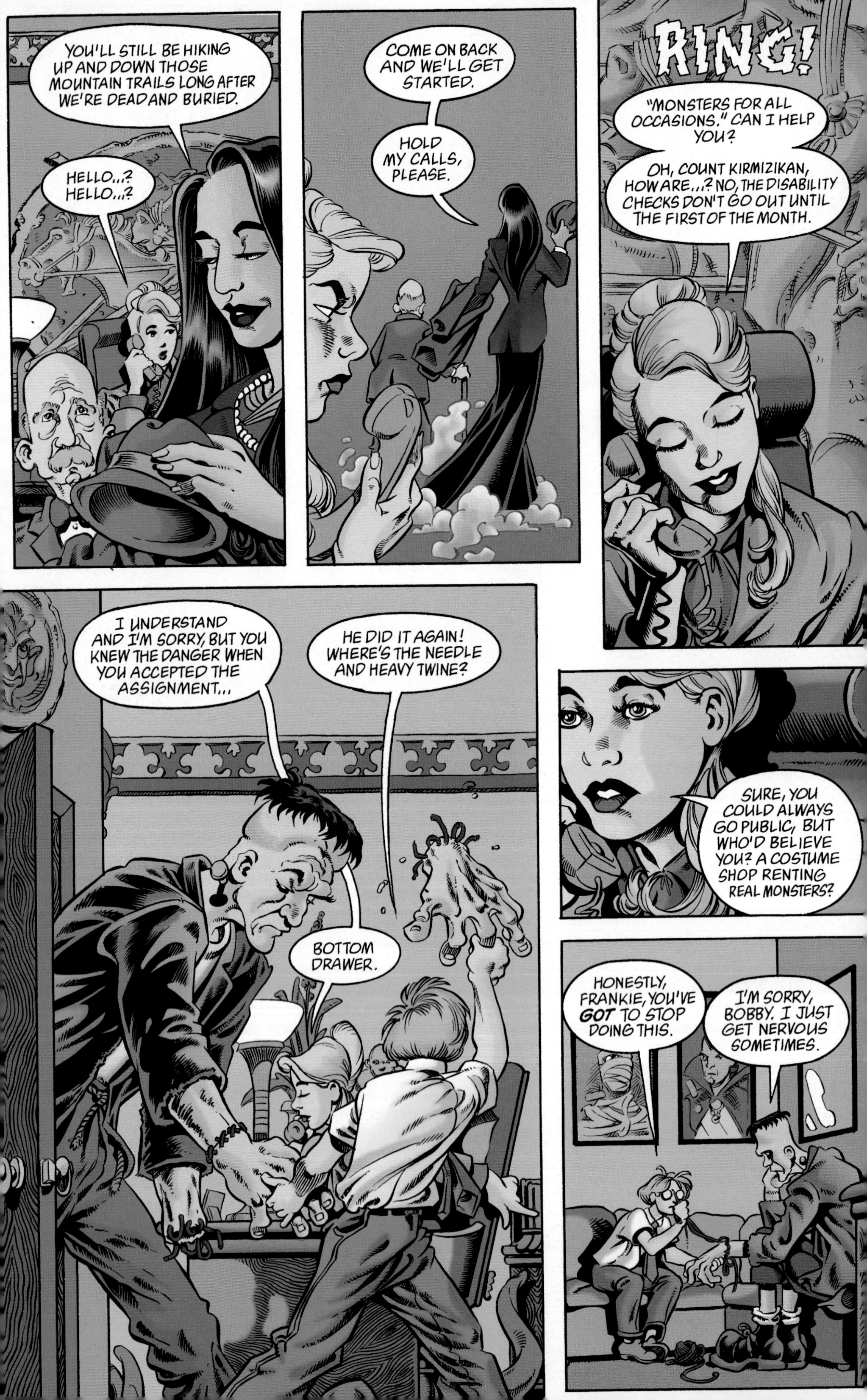
YOU'LL STILL BE HIKING UP AND DOWN THOSE MOUNTAIN TRAILS LONG AFTER WE'RE DEAD AND BURIED.
HELLO...? HELLO...?
COME ON BACK AND WE'LL GET STARTED.
HOLD MY CALLS, PLEASE.
RING!
"MONSTERS FOR ALL OCCASIONS." CAN I HELP YOU?
OH, COUNT KIRMIZIKAN, HOW ARE...? NO, THE DISABILITY CHECKS DON'T GO OUT UNTIL THE FIRST OF THE MONTH.
I UNDERSTAND AND I'M SORRY, BUT YOU KNEW THE DANGER WHEN YOU ACCEPTED THE ASSIGNMENT...
HE DID IT AGAIN! WHERE'S THE NEEDLE AND HEAVY TWINE?
BOTTOM DRAWER.
SURE, YOU COULD ALWAYS GO PUBLIC, BUT WHO'D BELIEVE YOU? A COSTUME SHOP RENTING REAL MONSTERS?
HONESTLY, FRANKIE, YOU'VE **GOT** TO STOP DOING THIS.
I'M SORRY, BOBBY. I JUST GET NERVOUS SOMETIMES.

AND WHEN I GET NERVOUS, I BITE MY STITCHES.

THAT'S ANOTHER THING...

FINE! **BE** THAT WAY. HAVE A NICE DAY.

YOU'RE TALKING IN FULL SENTENCES AGAIN, AND THE CUSTOMERS DON'T LIKE THAT.

SOME PEOPLE...!

WHEN YOU DON'T MEET CLIENT EXPECTATIONS, YOUR RATES GO DOWN.

ME SORRY, BOBBY.

ME DO BETTER.

NOW, MR. SOROVIN, NOT THAT I NEED TO ASK, BUT HOW CAN WE HELP YOU THIS TIME?

SAME AS ALWAYS, MISS GRUELLE.

ONCE AGAIN I NEED TO HIRE A MONSTER, A REAL BLOODTHIRSTY FIEND, TO HAUNT AND TERRORIZE THE VILLAGE OF TUVALETKÖY.

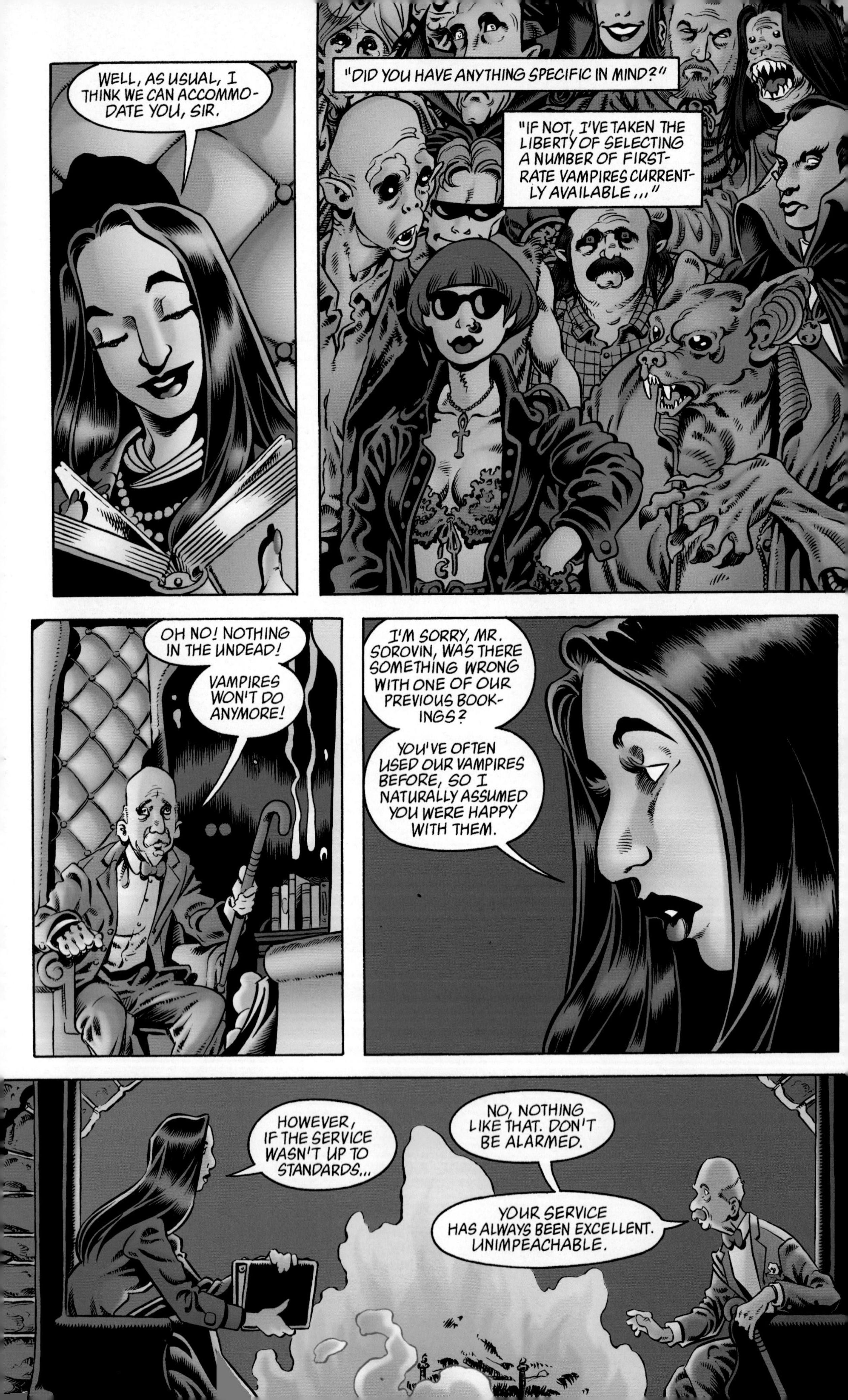
WELL, AS USUAL, I THINK WE CAN ACCOMMODATE YOU, SIR.
"DID YOU HAVE ANYTHING SPECIFIC IN MIND?"
"IF NOT, I'VE TAKEN THE LIBERTY OF SELECTING A NUMBER OF FIRST-RATE VAMPIRES CURRENTLY AVAILABLE..."
OH NO! NOTHING IN THE UNDEAD!
VAMPIRES WON'T DO ANYMORE!
I'M SORRY, MR. SOROVIN, WAS THERE SOMETHING WRONG WITH ONE OF OUR PREVIOUS BOOKINGS?
YOU'VE OFTEN USED OUR VAMPIRES BEFORE, SO I NATURALLY ASSUMED YOU WERE HAPPY WITH THEM.
HOWEVER, IF THE SERVICE WASN'T UP TO STANDARDS...
NO, NOTHING LIKE THAT. DON'T BE ALARMED.
YOUR SERVICE HAS ALWAYS BEEN EXCELLENT. UNIMPEACHABLE.

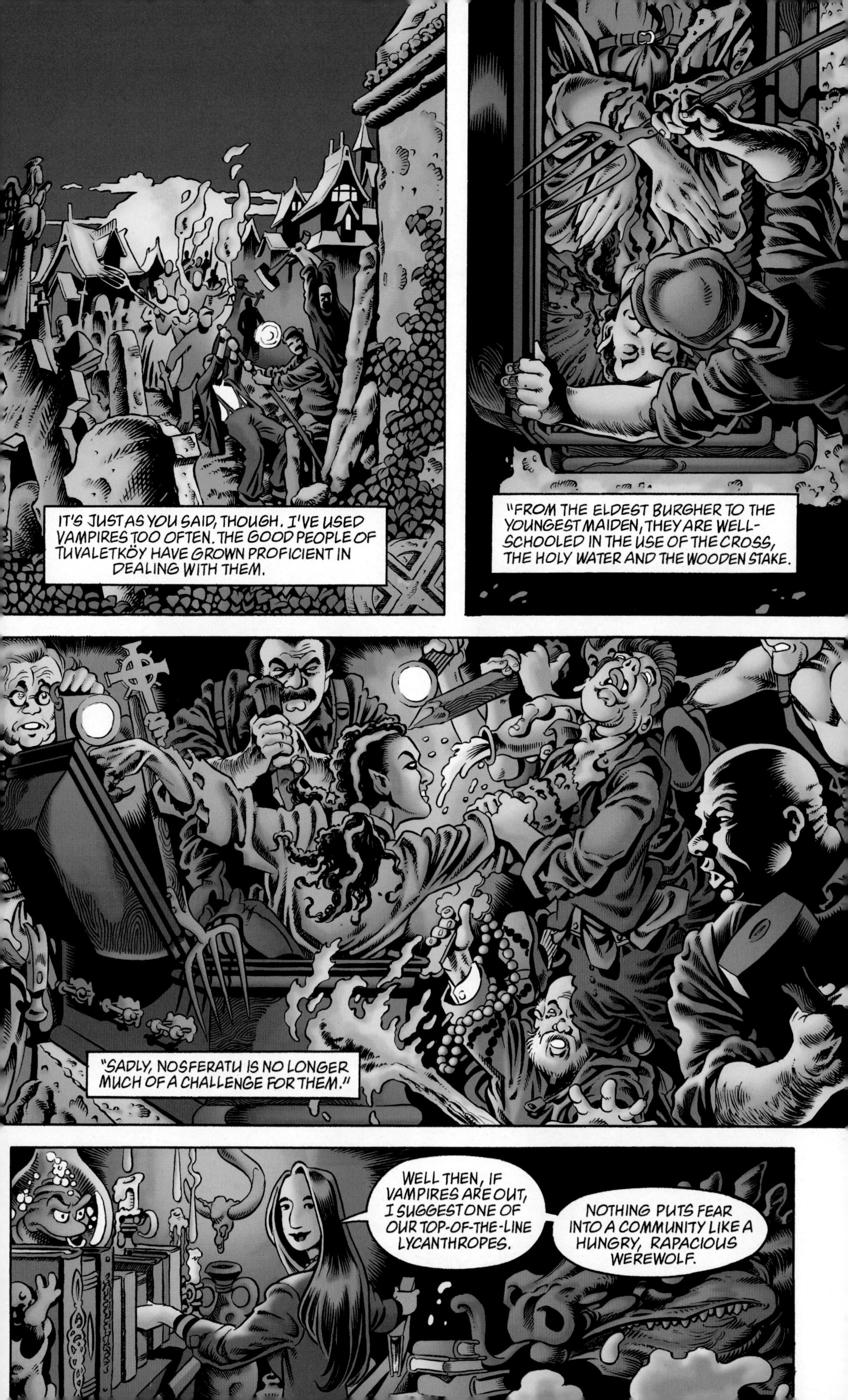
IT'S JUST AS YOU SAID, THOUGH. I'VE USED VAMPIRES TOO OFTEN. THE GOOD PEOPLE OF TUVALETKÖY HAVE GROWN PROFICIENT IN DEALING WITH THEM.
"FROM THE ELDEST BURGHER TO THE YOUNGEST MAIDEN, THEY ARE WELL-SCHOOLED IN THE USE OF THE CROSS, THE HOLY WATER AND THE WOODEN STAKE.
"SADLY, NOSFERATU IS NO LONGER MUCH OF A CHALLENGE FOR THEM."
WELL THEN, IF VAMPIRES ARE OUT, I SUGGEST ONE OF OUR TOP-OF-THE-LINE LYCANTHROPES.
NOTHING PUTS FEAR INTO A COMMUNITY LIKE A HUNGRY, RAPACIOUS WEREWOLF.

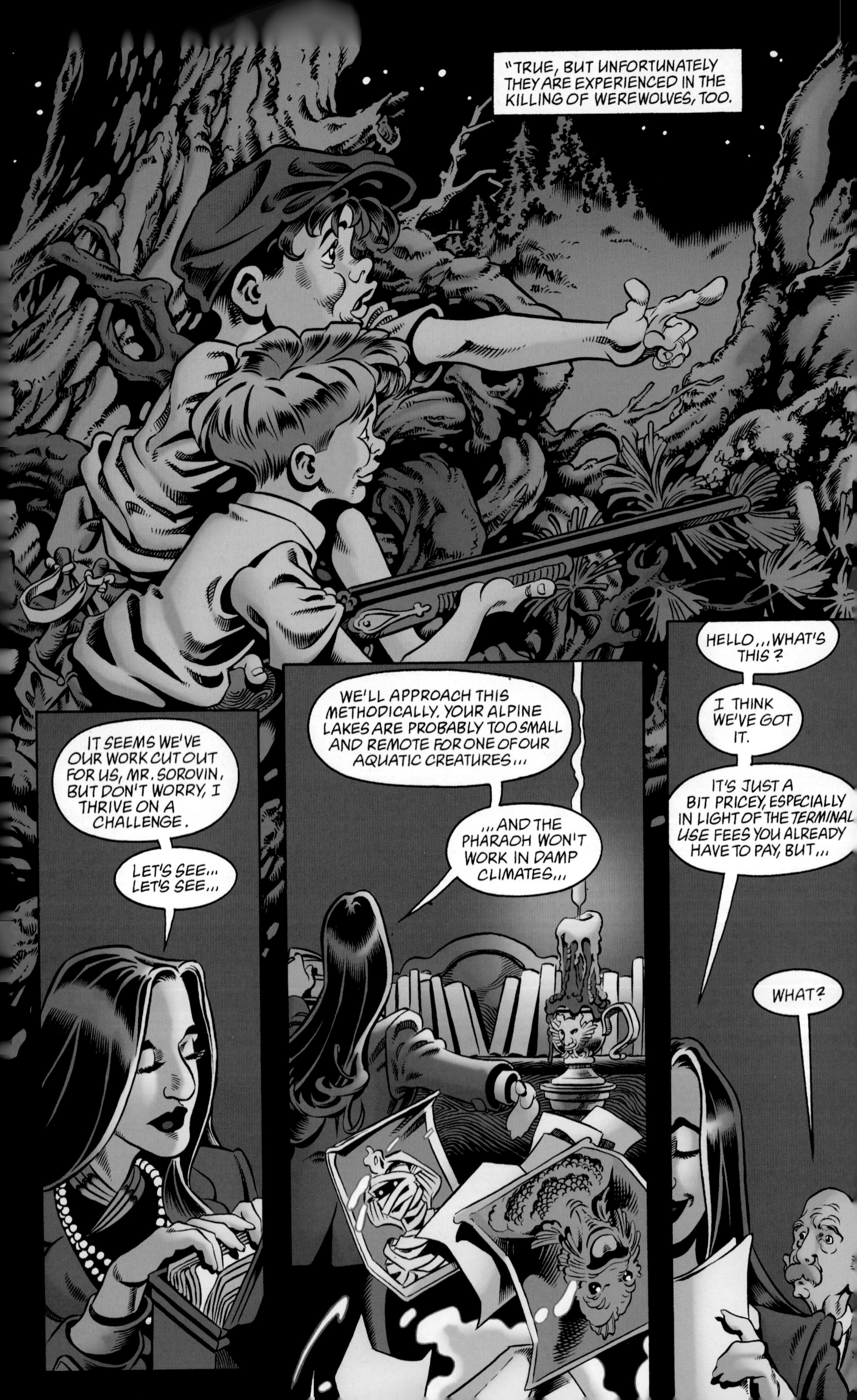
"TRUE, BUT UNFORTUNATELY THEY ARE EXPERIENCED IN THE KILLING OF WEREWOLVES, TOO.
IT SEEMS WE'VE OUR WORK CUT OUT FOR US, MR. SOROVIN, BUT DON'T WORRY, I THRIVE ON A CHALLENGE.
LET'S SEE... LET'S SEE...
WE'LL APPROACH THIS METHODICALLY. YOUR ALPINE LAKES ARE PROBABLY TOO SMALL AND REMOTE FOR ONE OF OUR AQUATIC CREATURES...
...AND THE PHARAOH WON'T WORK IN DAMP CLIMATES...
HELLO... WHAT'S THIS?
I THINK WE'VE GOT IT.
IT'S JUST A BIT PRICEY, ESPECIALLY IN LIGHT OF THE TERMINAL USE FEES YOU ALREADY HAVE TO PAY, BUT...
WHAT?

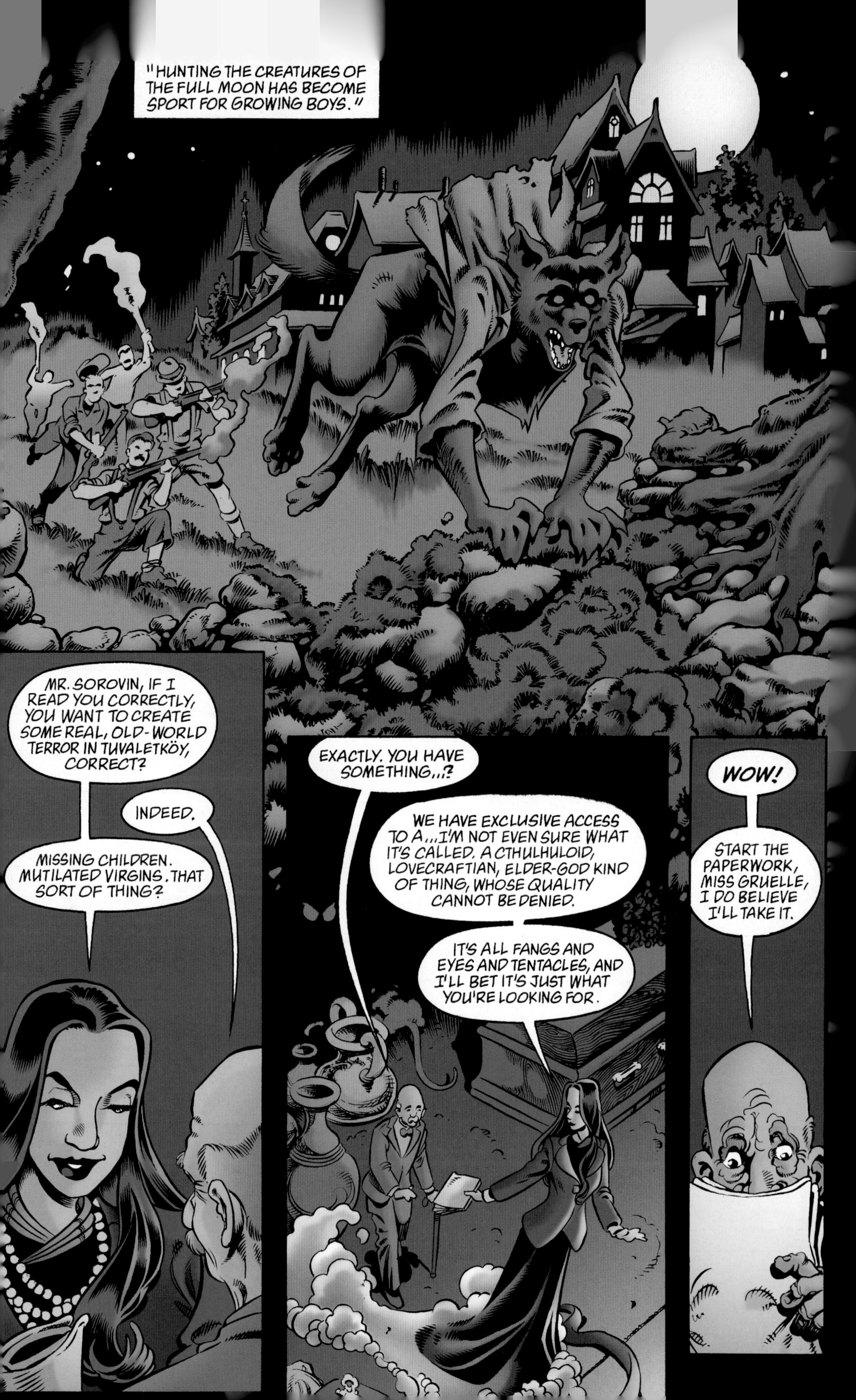
"HUNTING THE CREATURES OF THE FULL MOON HAS BECOME SPORT FOR GROWING BOYS."
MR. SOROVIN, IF I READ YOU CORRECTLY, YOU WANT TO CREATE SOME REAL, OLD-WORLD TERROR IN TUVALETKÖY, CORRECT?
INDEED.
MISSING CHILDREN. MUTILATED VIRGINS. THAT SORT OF THING?
EXACTLY. YOU HAVE SOMETHING...?
WE HAVE EXCLUSIVE ACCESS TO A...I'M NOT EVEN SURE WHAT IT'S CALLED. A CTHULHULOID, LOVECRAFTIAN, ELDER-GOD KIND OF THING, WHOSE QUALITY CANNOT BE DENIED.
IT'S ALL FANGS AND EYES AND TENTACLES, AND I'LL BET IT'S JUST WHAT YOU'RE LOOKING FOR.
WOW!
START THE PAPERWORK, MISS GRUELLE, I DO BELIEVE I'LL TAKE IT.

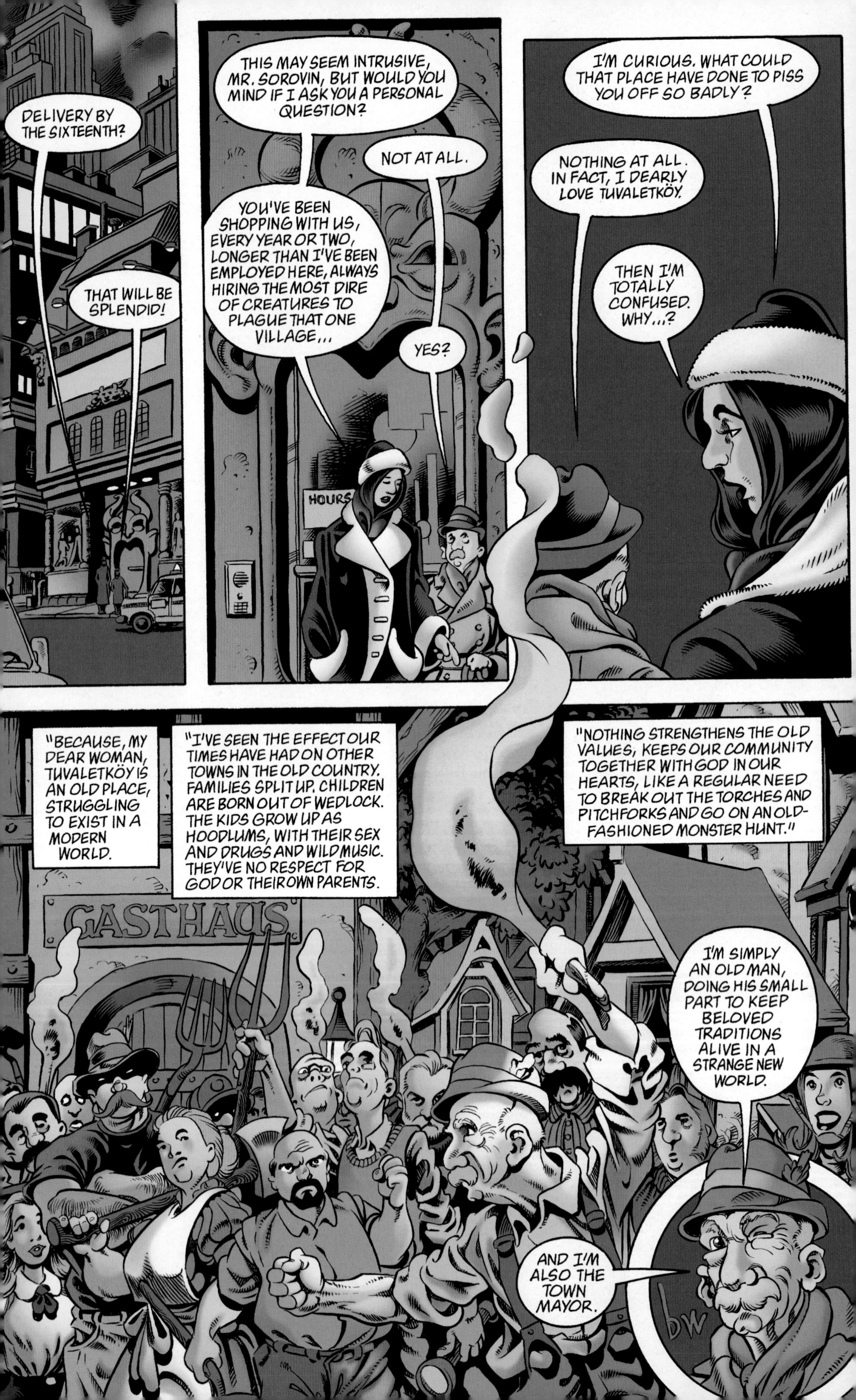
DELIVERY BY THE SIXTEENTH?
THAT WILL BE SPLENDID!
THIS MAY SEEM INTRUSIVE, MR. SOROVIN, BUT WOULD YOU MIND IF I ASK YOU A PERSONAL QUESTION?
NOT AT ALL.
YOU'VE BEEN SHOPPING WITH US, EVERY YEAR OR TWO, LONGER THAN I'VE BEEN EMPLOYED HERE, ALWAYS HIRING THE MOST DIRE OF CREATURES TO PLAGUE THAT ONE VILLAGE...
YES?
HOURS
I'M CURIOUS. WHAT COULD THAT PLACE HAVE DONE TO PISS YOU OFF SO BADLY?
NOTHING AT ALL. IN FACT, I DEARLY LOVE TUVALETKÖY.
THEN I'M TOTALLY CONFUSED. WHY...?
"BECAUSE, MY DEAR WOMAN, TUVALETKÖY IS AN OLD PLACE, STRUGGLING TO EXIST IN A MODERN WORLD.
"I'VE SEEN THE EFFECT OUR TIMES HAVE HAD ON OTHER TOWNS IN THE OLD COUNTRY. FAMILIES SPLIT UP. CHILDREN ARE BORN OUT OF WEDLOCK. THE KIDS GROW UP AS HOODLUMS, WITH THEIR SEX AND DRUGS AND WILD MUSIC. THEY'VE NO RESPECT FOR GOD OR THEIR OWN PARENTS.
"NOTHING STRENGTHENS THE OLD VALUES, KEEPS OUR COMMUNITY TOGETHER WITH GOD IN OUR HEARTS, LIKE A REGULAR NEED TO BREAK OUT THE TORCHES AND PITCHFORKS AND GO ON AN OLD-FASHIONED MONSTER HUNT."
GASTHAUS
I'M SIMPLY AN OLD MAN, DOING HIS SMALL PART TO KEEP BELOVED TRADITIONS ALIVE IN A STRANGE NEW WORLD.
AND I'M ALSO THE TOWN MAYOR.
bw

the DREAMING
The Further Adventures of Danny Nod
Written by
Bill Willingham
Illustrated by
Peter Gross
Daniel Torres
Paul Pope
Michael Kaluta
Phil Jimenez
Adam Hughes
Linda Medley
Bill Willingham
Marc Laming
John Stokes
Zander Cannon
Albert Monteys

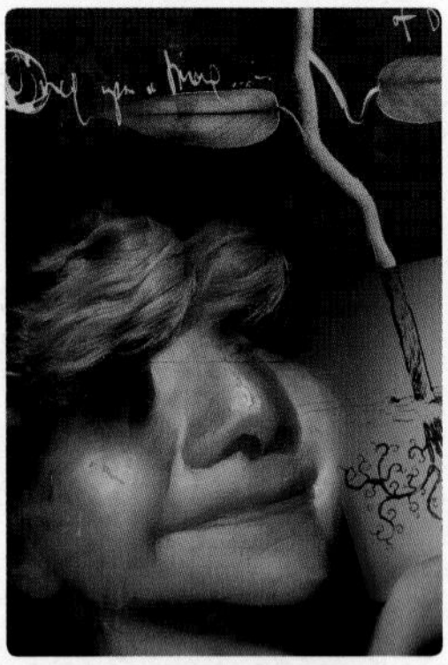

THE FURTHER ADVENTURES OF DANNY NOD, HEROIC LIBRARY ASSISTANT

ART BY
Peter Gross
(pages 161-162, 182)

Daniel Torres
(pages 163-164)

Paul Pope
(pages 165-167)

Michael Wm. Kaluta
(page 168)

Phil Jimenez
(page 169)

Adam Hughes
(pages 170-171)

Linda Medley
(pages 172-173)

Marc Laming
(pencils, pages 174-176, 181)

John Stokes
(inks, pages 174-176, 181)

Zander Cannon
(pages 177-179)

Albert Monteys
(page 180)

COLORS BY
Daniel Vozzo

LETTERS BY
Todd Klein

COVER ART BY
Dave McKean

TRUTH BE TOLD, THERE WERE NO PREVIOUS ADVENTURES OF DANNY NOD. I chose the title simply to imply that the boy had been at this for some time, and that this was just a typical day in the life of a very strange young fellow. But the title confused some readers into thinking they'd missed a previous story. Some readers spent valuable time trying to track down a comic book that never existed (which, come to think of it, has some poetic resonance in a tale about a library of books that never existed). I'm sorry. *Mea maxima culpa.* I never intended to send any of you on a wild-goose chase.

I liked this story enough to pitch it as an ongoing series to Vertigo. They politely declined, doing me a big favor (though I didn't see it that way at the time), since many of the ideas presented here eventually found their way into FABLES.

Shortly after this story came out and Vertigo nixed any idea of doing more of them, I took some of the original concepts that I'd contributed, stripped them out of the fictional world of The Dreaming, and repackaged them in another series proposal called TOMERAKER (terrible title — though I was taken with it at the time) about action characters who work in a magical, archetypal library and who enter the worlds of its books to have thrilling adventures. The Vertigo folks passed on this one too, and, with utmost discretion and tact, asked me to quit coming up with ideas about folks physically entering the world of books.

Years later they accepted a charming series by Mike Carey and Peter Gross called THE UNWRITTEN. The lesson here? It's not about the ideas, it's about the execution. Or, to put it more plainly: to do it right, it must also be done well. Vertigo was right to wait until the idea had been done well.

And I can't complain, since most of the ideas in the aborted TOMERAKER series, including the Page surnames of the main characters, translated quite nicely into the main villains of the JACK OF FABLES series.

Careful readers will note that Danny Nod still lives on, in a small way, having lent his name to the bookstore Nod's Books (and Comic Nook) in Fabletown.

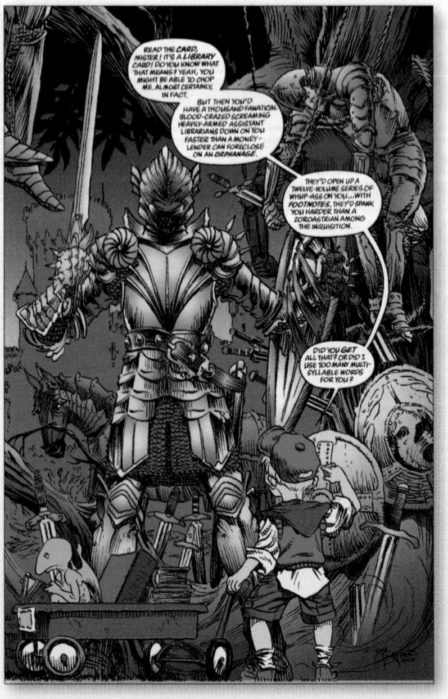
READ THE CARD, MISTER! IT'S A LIBRARY CARD! DO YOU KNOW WHAT THAT MEANS? YEAH, YOU MIGHT BE ABLE TO CHOP ME. ALMOST CERTAINLY, IN FACT.
BUT THEN YOU'D HAVE A THOUSAND FANATICAL BLOOD-CRAZED SCREAMING HEAVILY-ARMED ASSISTANT LIBRARIANS DOWN ON YOU FASTER THAN A MONEY-LENDER CAN FORECLOSE ON AN ORPHANAGE.
THEY'D OPEN UP A TWELVE-VOLUME SERIES OF WHUP-ASS ON YOU... WITH FOOTNOTES. THEY'D SPANK YOU HARDER THAN A ZOROASTRIAN AMONG THE INQUISITION.
DID YOU GET ALL THAT? OR DID I USE TOO MANY MULTI-SYLLABLE WORDS FOR YOU?

The Further Adventures of Danny Nod
–Heroic Library Assistant–

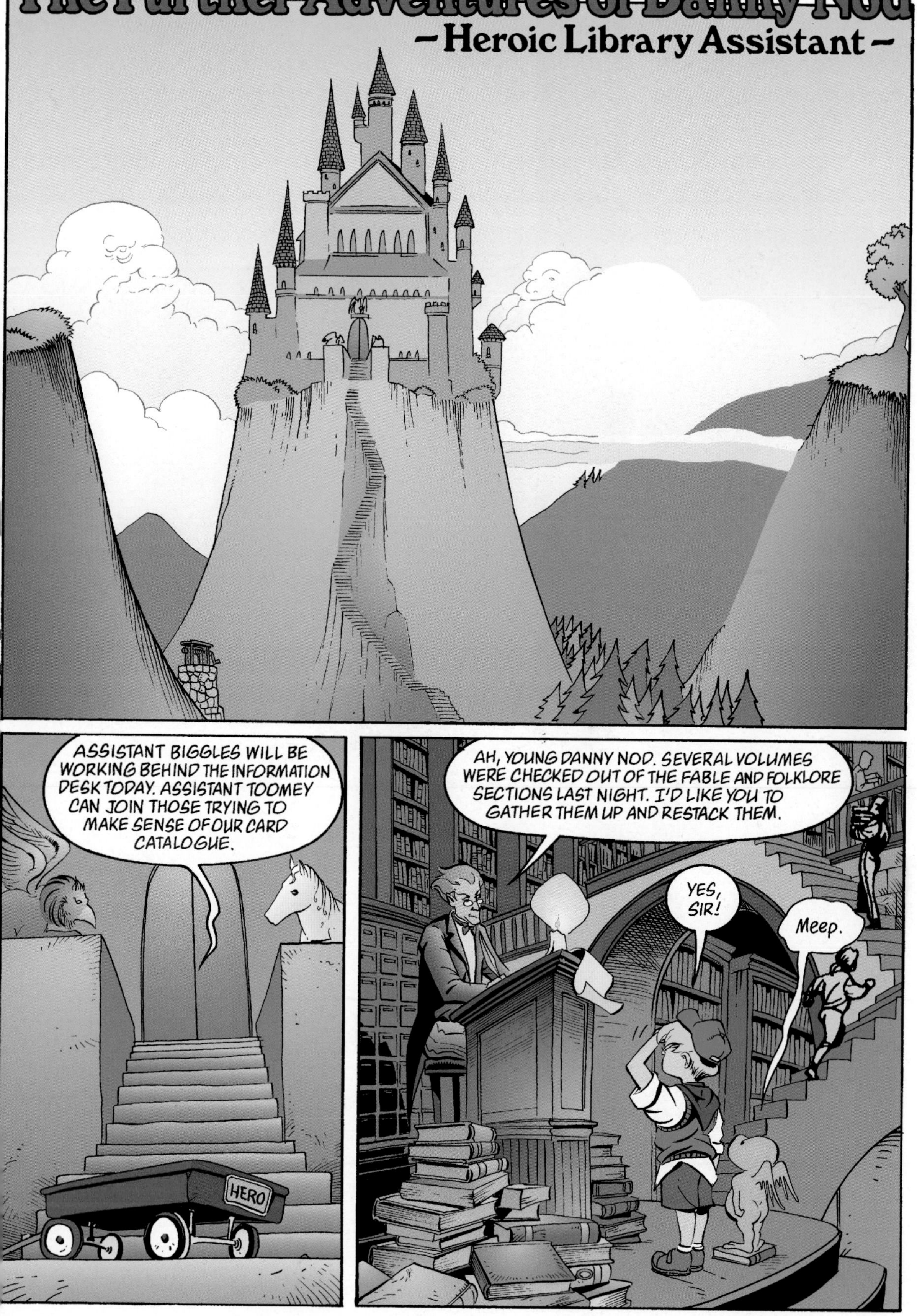
ASSISTANT BIGGLES WILL BE WORKING BEHIND THE INFORMATION DESK TODAY. ASSISTANT TOOMEY CAN JOIN THOSE TRYING TO MAKE SENSE OF OUR CARD CATALOGUE.
HERO
AH, YOUNG DANNY NOD. SEVERAL VOLUMES WERE CHECKED OUT OF THE FABLE AND FOLKLORE SECTIONS LAST NIGHT. I'D LIKE YOU TO GATHER THEM UP AND RESTACK THEM.
YES, SIR!
Meep.

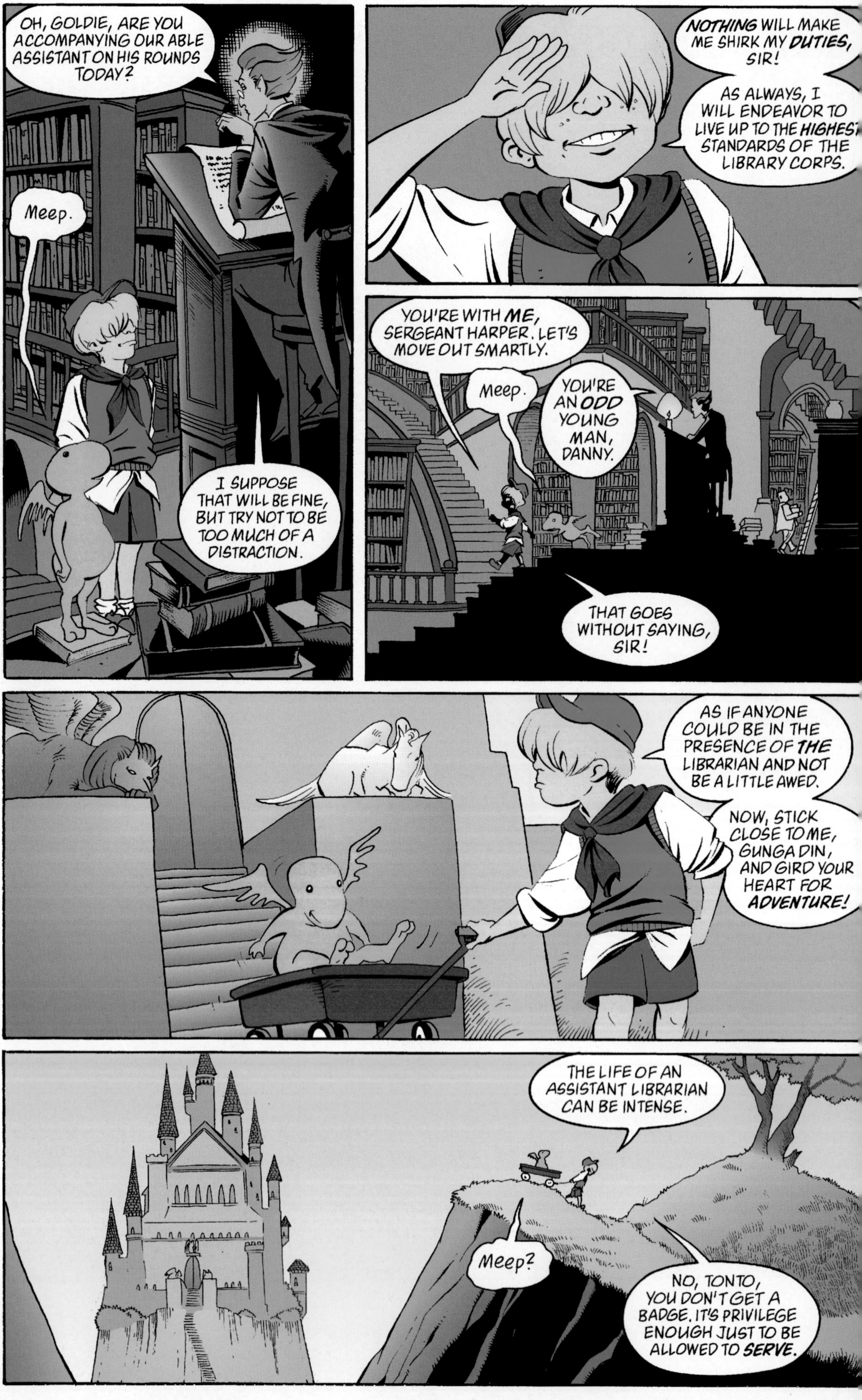
OH, GOLDIE, ARE YOU ACCOMPANYING OUR ABLE ASSISTANT ON HIS ROUNDS TODAY?
Meep.
I SUPPOSE THAT WILL BE FINE, BUT TRY NOT TO BE TOO MUCH OF A DISTRACTION.
NOTHING WILL MAKE ME SHIRK MY DUTIES, SIR!
AS ALWAYS, I WILL ENDEAVOR TO LIVE UP TO THE HIGHEST STANDARDS OF THE LIBRARY CORPS.
YOU'RE WITH ME, SERGEANT HARPER. LET'S MOVE OUT SMARTLY.
Meep.
YOU'RE AN ODD YOUNG MAN, DANNY.
THAT GOES WITHOUT SAYING, SIR!
AS IF ANYONE COULD BE IN THE PRESENCE OF THE LIBRARIAN AND NOT BE A LITTLE AWED.
NOW, STICK CLOSE TO ME, GUNGA DIN, AND GIRD YOUR HEART FOR ADVENTURE!
THE LIFE OF AN ASSISTANT LIBRARIAN CAN BE INTENSE.
Meep?
NO, TONTO, YOU DON'T GET A BADGE. IT'S PRIVILEGE ENOUGH JUST TO BE ALLOWED TO SERVE.

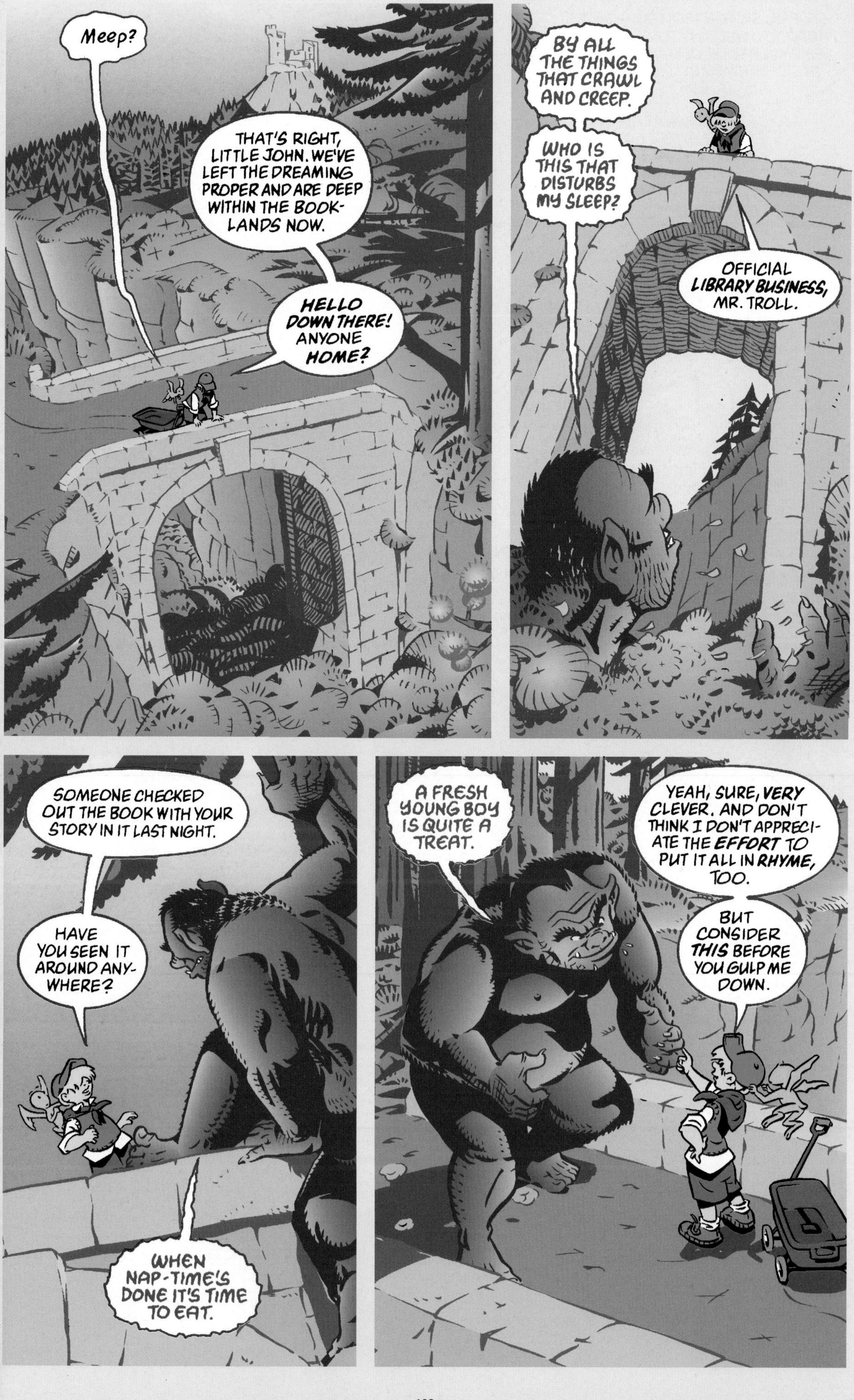
Meep?
THAT'S RIGHT, LITTLE JOHN. WE'VE LEFT THE DREAMING PROPER AND ARE DEEP WITHIN THE BOOK-LANDS NOW.
HELLO DOWN THERE! ANYONE HOME?
BY ALL THE THINGS THAT CRAWL AND CREEP.
WHO IS THIS THAT DISTURBS MY SLEEP?
OFFICIAL LIBRARY BUSINESS, MR. TROLL.
SOMEONE CHECKED OUT THE BOOK WITH YOUR STORY IN IT LAST NIGHT.
HAVE YOU SEEN IT AROUND ANY-WHERE?
WHEN NAP-TIME'S DONE IT'S TIME TO EAT.
A FRESH YOUNG BOY IS QUITE A TREAT.
YEAH, SURE, VERY CLEVER. AND DON'T THINK I DON'T APPRECI-ATE THE EFFORT TO PUT IT ALL IN RHYME, TOO.
BUT CONSIDER THIS BEFORE YOU GULP ME DOWN.

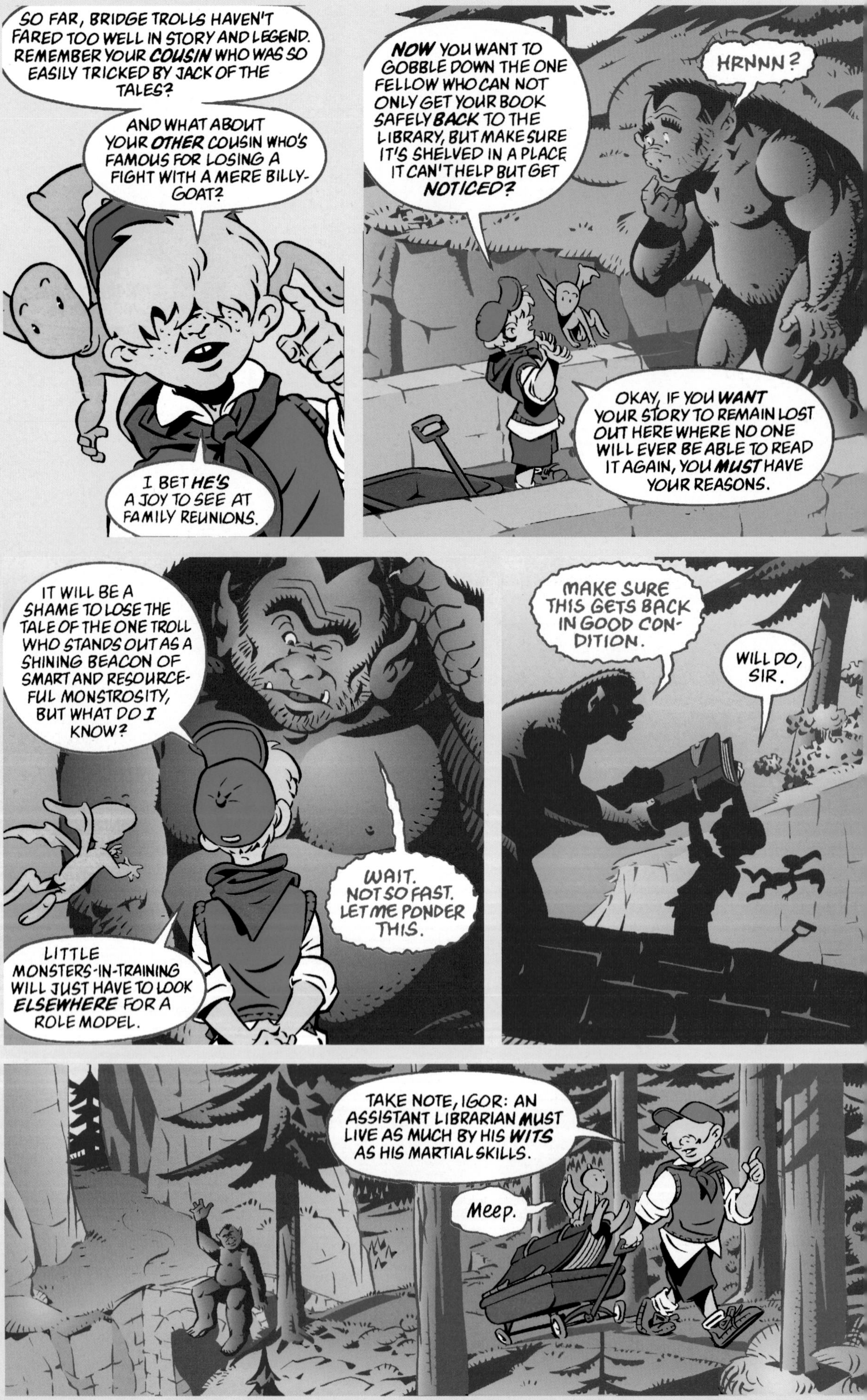
SO FAR, BRIDGE TROLLS HAVEN'T FARED TOO WELL IN STORY AND LEGEND. REMEMBER YOUR COUSIN WHO WAS SO EASILY TRICKED BY JACK OF THE TALES?
AND WHAT ABOUT YOUR OTHER COUSIN WHO'S FAMOUS FOR LOSING A FIGHT WITH A MERE BILLY-GOAT?
I BET HE'S A JOY TO SEE AT FAMILY REUNIONS.
NOW YOU WANT TO GOBBLE DOWN THE ONE FELLOW WHO CAN NOT ONLY GET YOUR BOOK SAFELY BACK TO THE LIBRARY, BUT MAKE SURE IT'S SHELVED IN A PLACE IT CAN'T HELP BUT GET NOTICED?
HRNNN?
OKAY, IF YOU WANT YOUR STORY TO REMAIN LOST OUT HERE WHERE NO ONE WILL EVER BE ABLE TO READ IT AGAIN, YOU MUST HAVE YOUR REASONS.
IT WILL BE A SHAME TO LOSE THE TALE OF THE ONE TROLL WHO STANDS OUT AS A SHINING BEACON OF SMART AND RESOURCE-FUL MONSTROSITY, BUT WHAT DO I KNOW?
LITTLE MONSTERS-IN-TRAINING WILL JUST HAVE TO LOOK ELSEWHERE FOR A ROLE MODEL.
WAIT. NOT SO FAST. LET ME PONDER THIS.
MAKE SURE THIS GETS BACK IN GOOD CON-DITION.
WILL DO, SIR.
TAKE NOTE, IGOR: AN ASSISTANT LIBRARIAN MUST LIVE AS MUCH BY HIS WITS AS HIS MARTIAL SKILLS.
Meep.

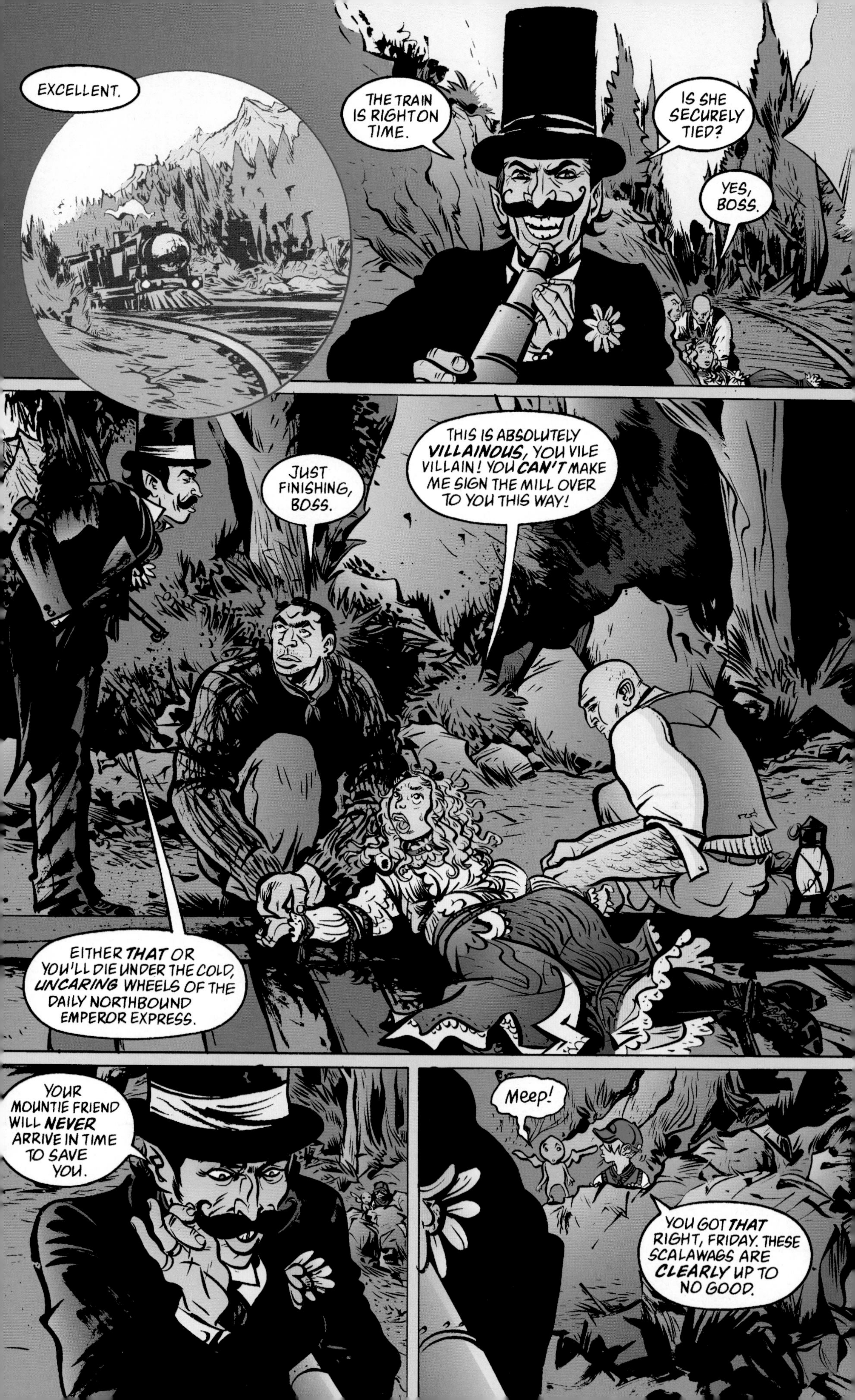
EXCELLENT.
THE TRAIN IS RIGHT ON TIME.
IS SHE SECURELY TIED?
YES, BOSS.
JUST FINISHING, BOSS.
THIS IS ABSOLUTELY **VILLAINOUS**, YOU VILE VILLAIN! YOU **CAN'T** MAKE ME SIGN THE MILL OVER TO YOU THIS WAY!
EITHER **THAT** OR YOU'LL DIE UNDER THE COLD, **UNCARING** WHEELS OF THE DAILY NORTHBOUND EMPEROR EXPRESS.
YOUR MOUNTIE FRIEND WILL **NEVER** ARRIVE IN TIME TO SAVE YOU.
Meep!
YOU GOT **THAT** RIGHT, FRIDAY. THESE SCALAWAGS ARE **CLEARLY** UP TO NO GOOD.

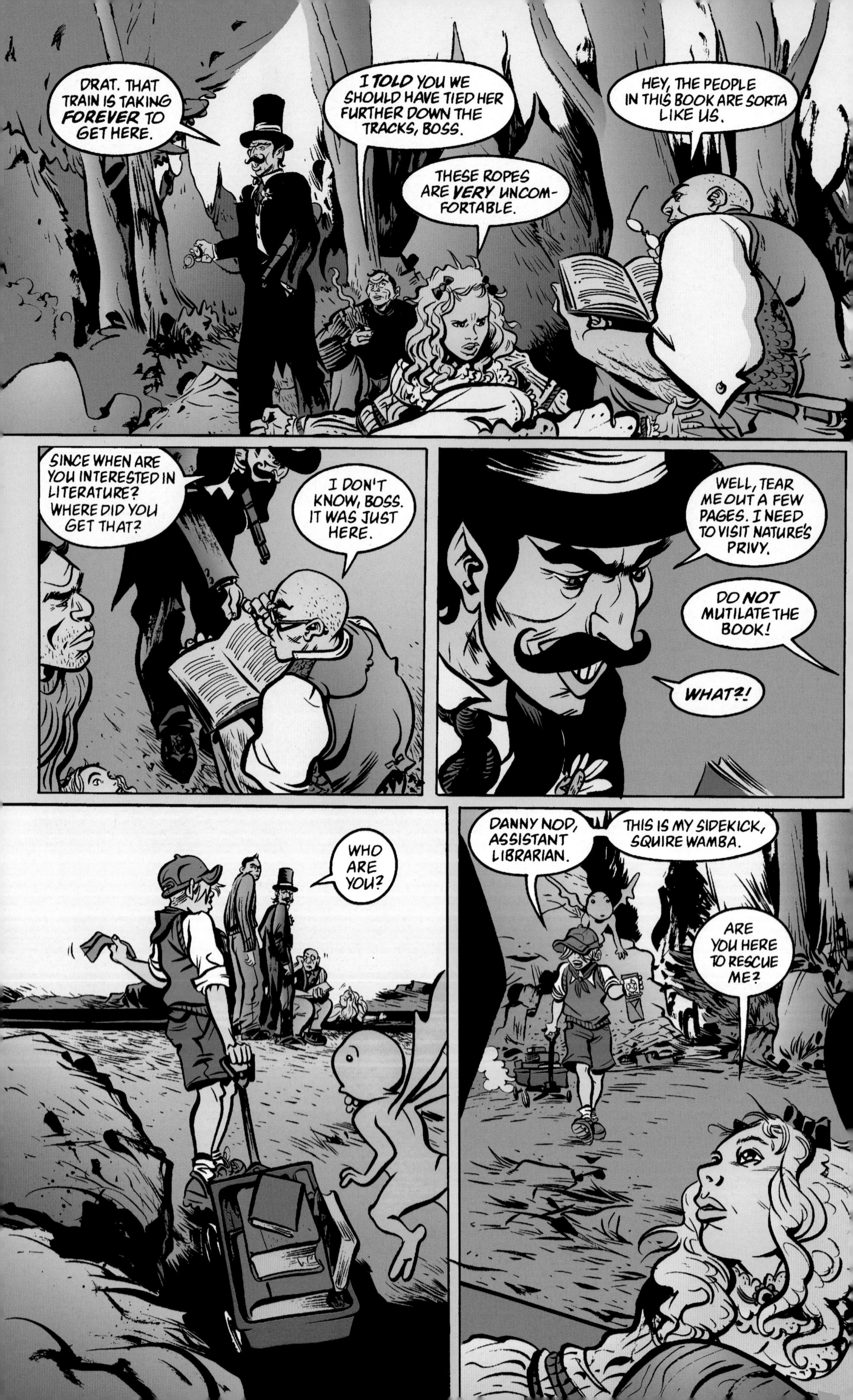
DRAT. THAT TRAIN IS TAKING FOREVER TO GET HERE.
I TOLD YOU WE SHOULD HAVE TIED HER FURTHER DOWN THE TRACKS, BOSS.
THESE ROPES ARE VERY UNCOMFORTABLE.
HEY, THE PEOPLE IN THIS BOOK ARE SORTA LIKE US.
SINCE WHEN ARE YOU INTERESTED IN LITERATURE? WHERE DID YOU GET THAT?
I DON'T KNOW, BOSS. IT WAS JUST HERE.
WELL, TEAR ME OUT A FEW PAGES. I NEED TO VISIT NATURE'S PRIVY.
DO NOT MUTILATE THE BOOK!
WHAT?!
WHO ARE YOU?
DANNY NOD, ASSISTANT LIBRARIAN.
THIS IS MY SIDEKICK, SQUIRE WAMBA.
ARE YOU HERE TO RESCUE ME?

NO, MA'AM. I'M HERE TO RESCUE THE *BOOK*.

BUT DON'T FRET. YOU GET SAVED IN THE NEXT CHAPTER.

AND MAY I SAY, MA'AM, YOU LOOK *LOVELY* IN THE AFTERNOON LIGHT.

ANOTHER IMPORTANT CODE OF THE LIBRARIAN CORPS, RENFIELD: *ALWAYS BE COMPLIMENTARY TO THE LADIES.*

WHAT IS THE *MEANING* OF THIS INTRUSION?

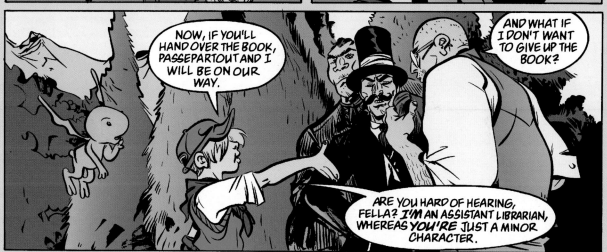

NOW, IF YOU'LL HAND OVER THE BOOK, PASSEPARTOUT AND I WILL BE ON OUR WAY.

AND WHAT IF I DON'T WANT TO GIVE UP THE BOOK?

ARE YOU HARD OF HEARING, FELLA? *I'M* AN ASSISTANT LIBRARIAN, WHEREAS *YOU'RE* JUST A MINOR CHARACTER.

WHEN I SAY *JUMP*, MERE WRITERS AND EDITORS ASK ME *HOW HIGH?*

KEEP UP THIS BOLD TALK AND I JUST MAY HAVE YOU COMPLETELY *WRITTEN OUT* IN THE NEXT DRAFT.

YOU WANT *THAT?*

UHM...NOT REALLY.

REMEMBER THAT GREAT AUTHORITY COMES HAND-IN-HAND WITH GREAT RESPONSIBILITY, PLANCHET.

DON'T BE AFRAID TO USE IT. THIS JOB ISN'T FOR THE TIMID.

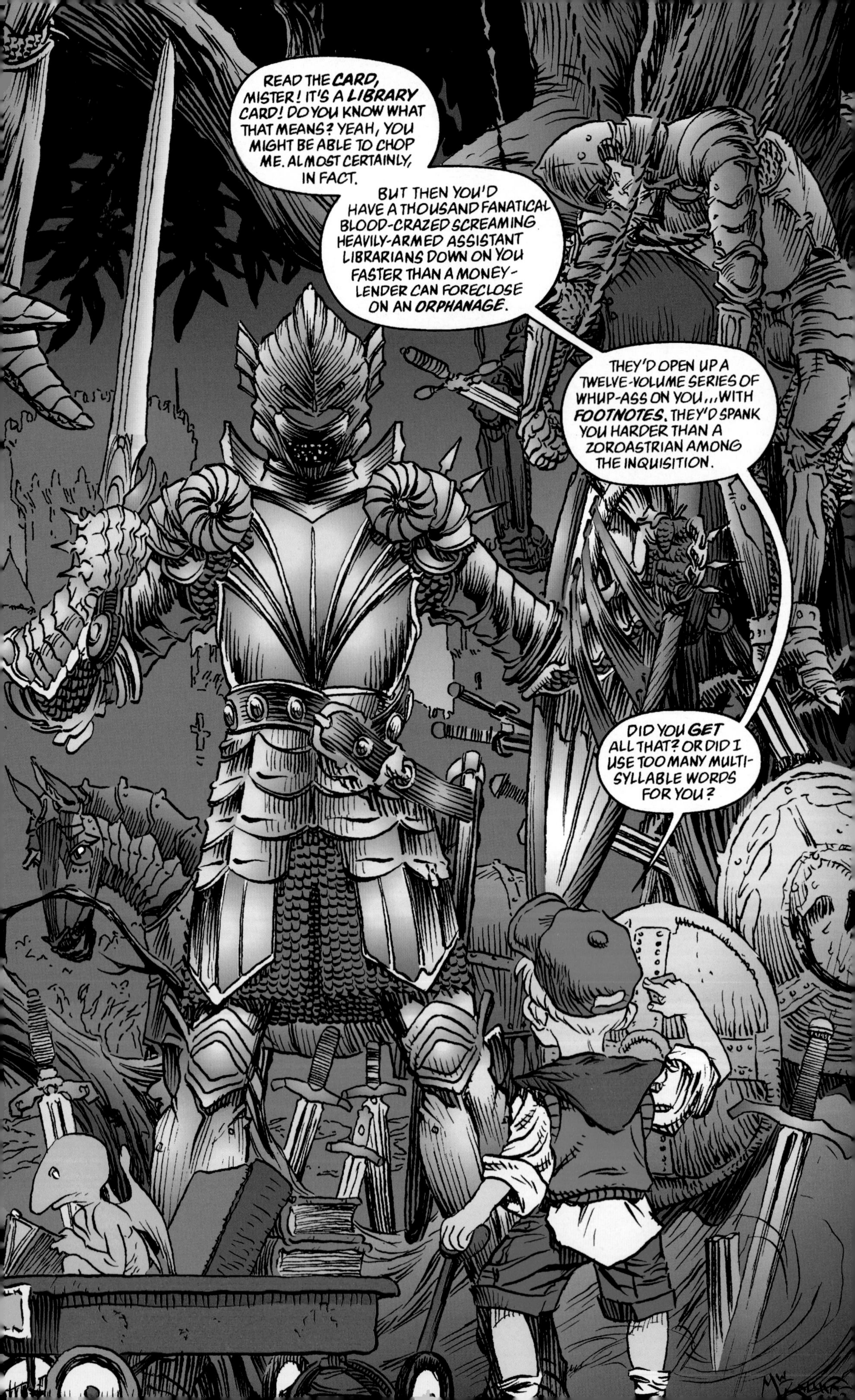
READ THE CARD, MISTER! IT'S A LIBRARY CARD! DO YOU KNOW WHAT THAT MEANS? YEAH, YOU MIGHT BE ABLE TO CHOP ME. ALMOST CERTAINLY, IN FACT.
BUT THEN YOU'D HAVE A THOUSAND FANATICAL BLOOD-CRAZED SCREAMING HEAVILY-ARMED ASSISTANT LIBRARIANS DOWN ON YOU FASTER THAN A MONEY-LENDER CAN FORECLOSE ON AN ORPHANAGE.
THEY'D OPEN UP A TWELVE-VOLUME SERIES OF WHUP-ASS ON YOU... WITH FOOTNOTES. THEY'D SPANK YOU HARDER THAN A ZOROASTRIAN AMONG THE INQUISITION.
DID YOU GET ALL THAT? OR DID I USE TOO MANY MULTI-SYLLABLE WORDS FOR YOU?

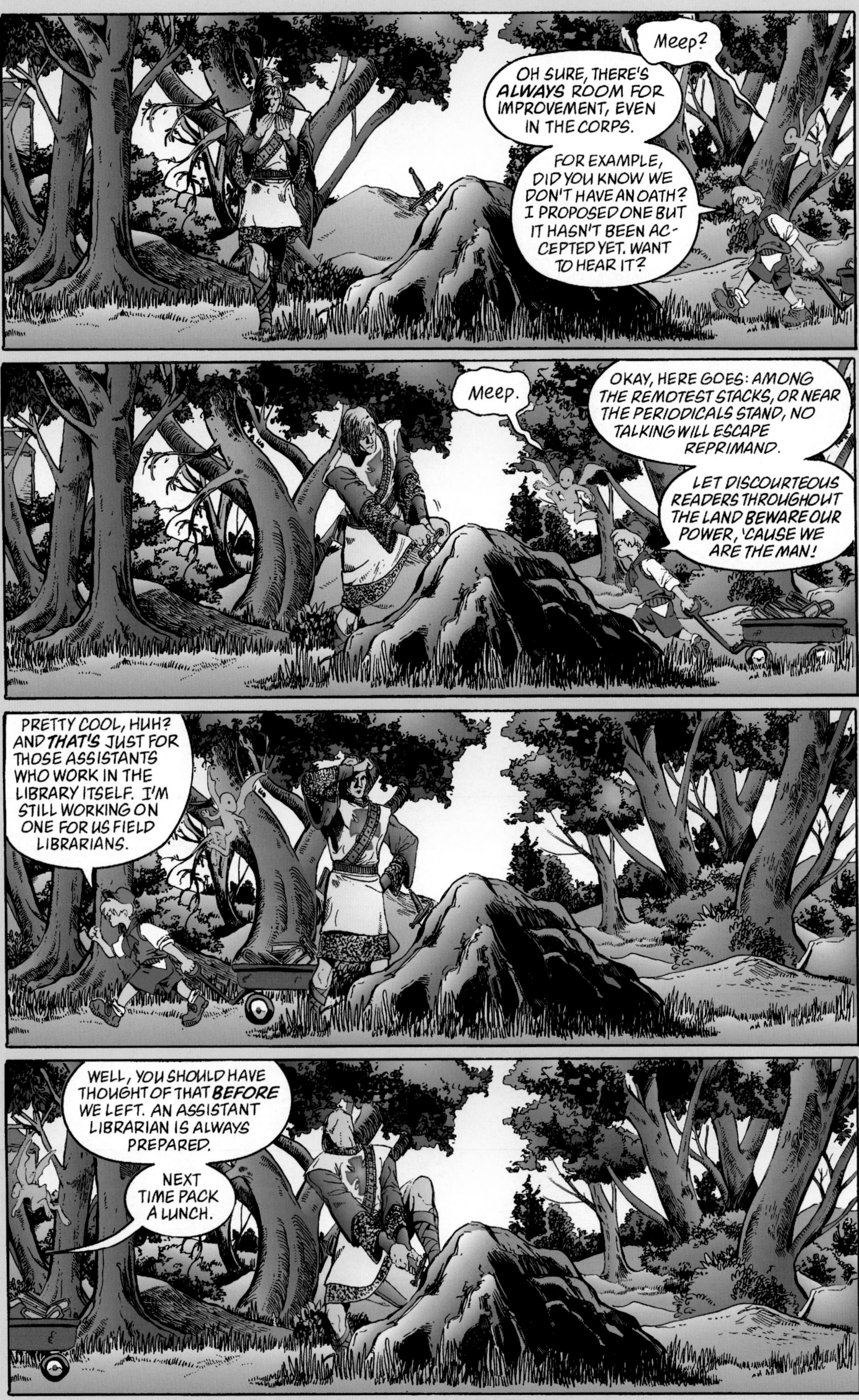
Meep?
OH SURE, THERE'S ALWAYS ROOM FOR IMPROVEMENT, EVEN IN THE CORPS.
FOR EXAMPLE, DID YOU KNOW WE DON'T HAVE AN OATH? I PROPOSED ONE BUT IT HASN'T BEEN AC-CEPTED YET. WANT TO HEAR IT?
Meep.
OKAY, HERE GOES: AMONG THE REMOTEST STACKS, OR NEAR THE PERIODICALS STAND, NO TALKING WILL ESCAPE REPRIMAND.
LET DISCOURTEOUS READERS THROUGHOUT THE LAND BEWARE OUR POWER, 'CAUSE WE ARE THE MAN!
PRETTY COOL, HUH? AND THAT'S JUST FOR THOSE ASSISTANTS WHO WORK IN THE LIBRARY ITSELF. I'M STILL WORKING ON ONE FOR US FIELD LIBRARIANS.
WELL, YOU SHOULD HAVE THOUGHT OF THAT BEFORE WE LEFT. AN ASSISTANT LIBRARIAN IS ALWAYS PREPARED.
NEXT TIME PACK A LUNCH.

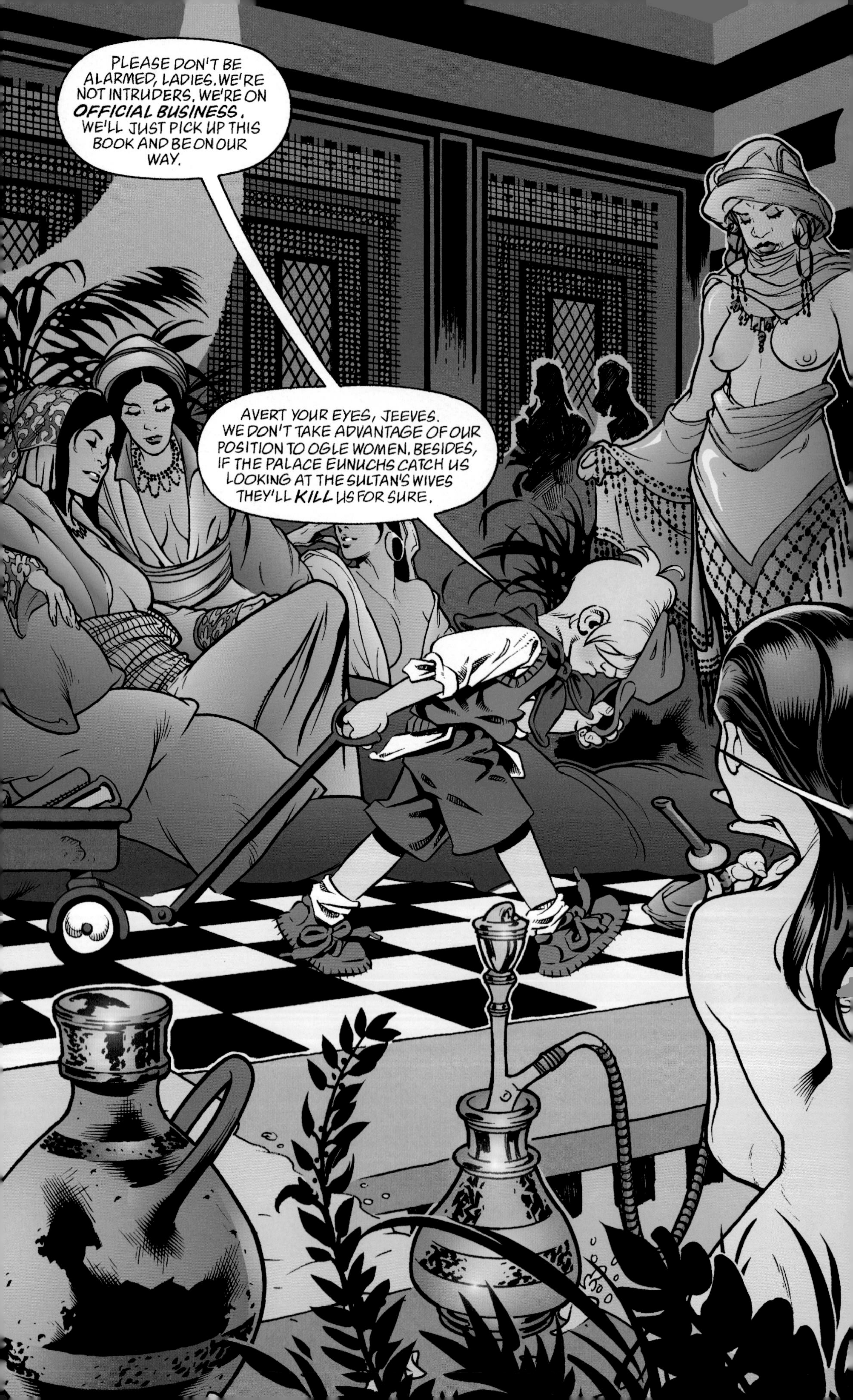
PLEASE DON'T BE ALARMED, LADIES. WE'RE NOT INTRUDERS. WE'RE ON **OFFICIAL BUSINESS.** WE'LL JUST PICK UP THIS BOOK AND BE ON OUR WAY.
AVERT YOUR EYES, JEEVES. WE DON'T TAKE ADVANTAGE OF OUR POSITION TO OGLE WOMEN. BESIDES, IF THE PALACE EUNUCHS CATCH US LOOKING AT THE SULTAN'S WIVES THEY'LL **KILL** US FOR SURE.

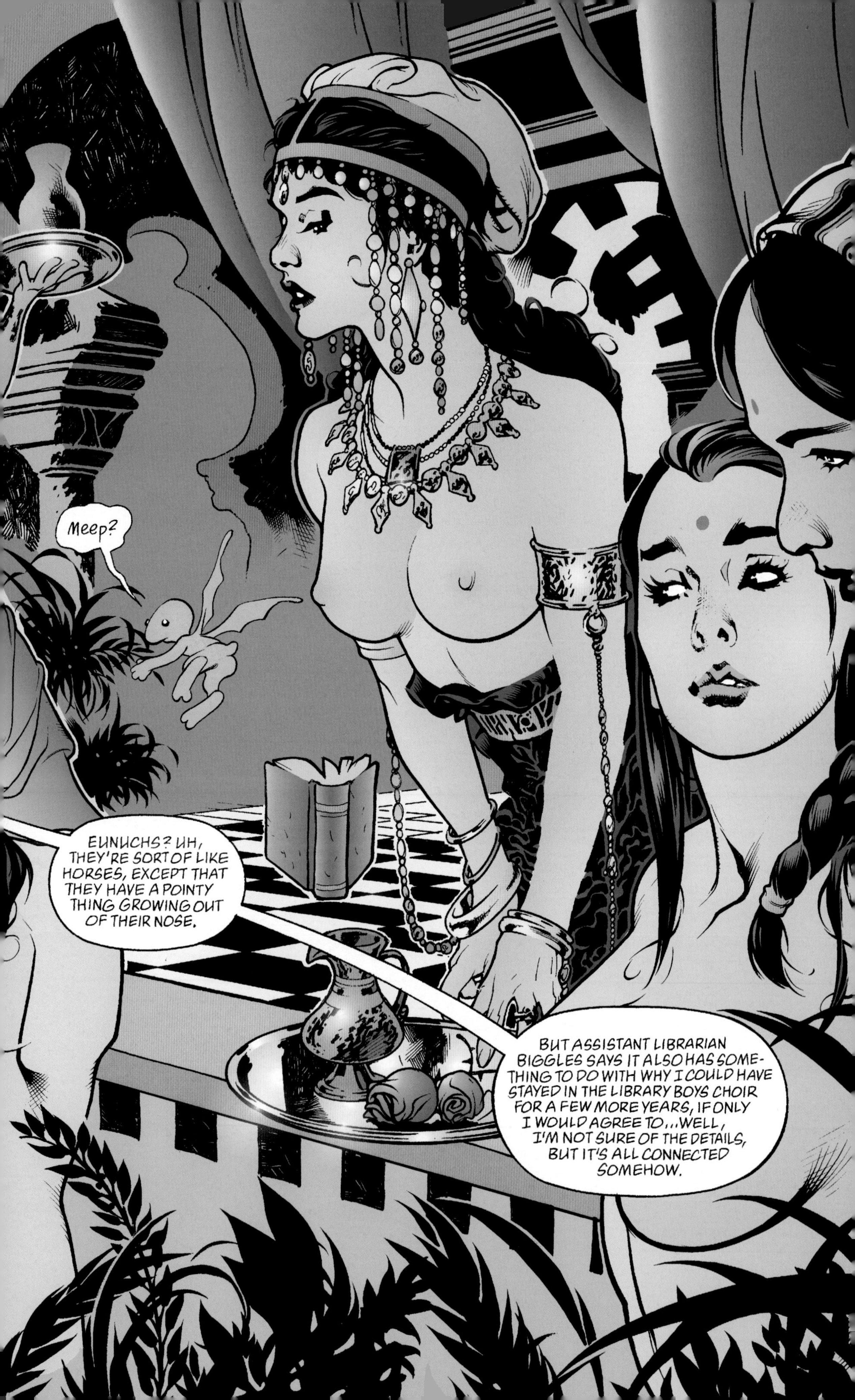
Meep?
EUNUCHS? UH, THEY'RE SORT OF LIKE HORSES, EXCEPT THAT THEY HAVE A POINTY THING GROWING OUT OF THEIR NOSE.
BUT ASSISTANT LIBRARIAN BIGGLES SAYS IT ALSO HAS SOME-THING TO DO WITH WHY I COULD HAVE STAYED IN THE LIBRARY BOYS CHOIR FOR A FEW MORE YEARS, IF ONLY I WOULD AGREE TO...WELL, I'M NOT SURE OF THE DETAILS, BUT IT'S ALL CONNECTED SOMEHOW.

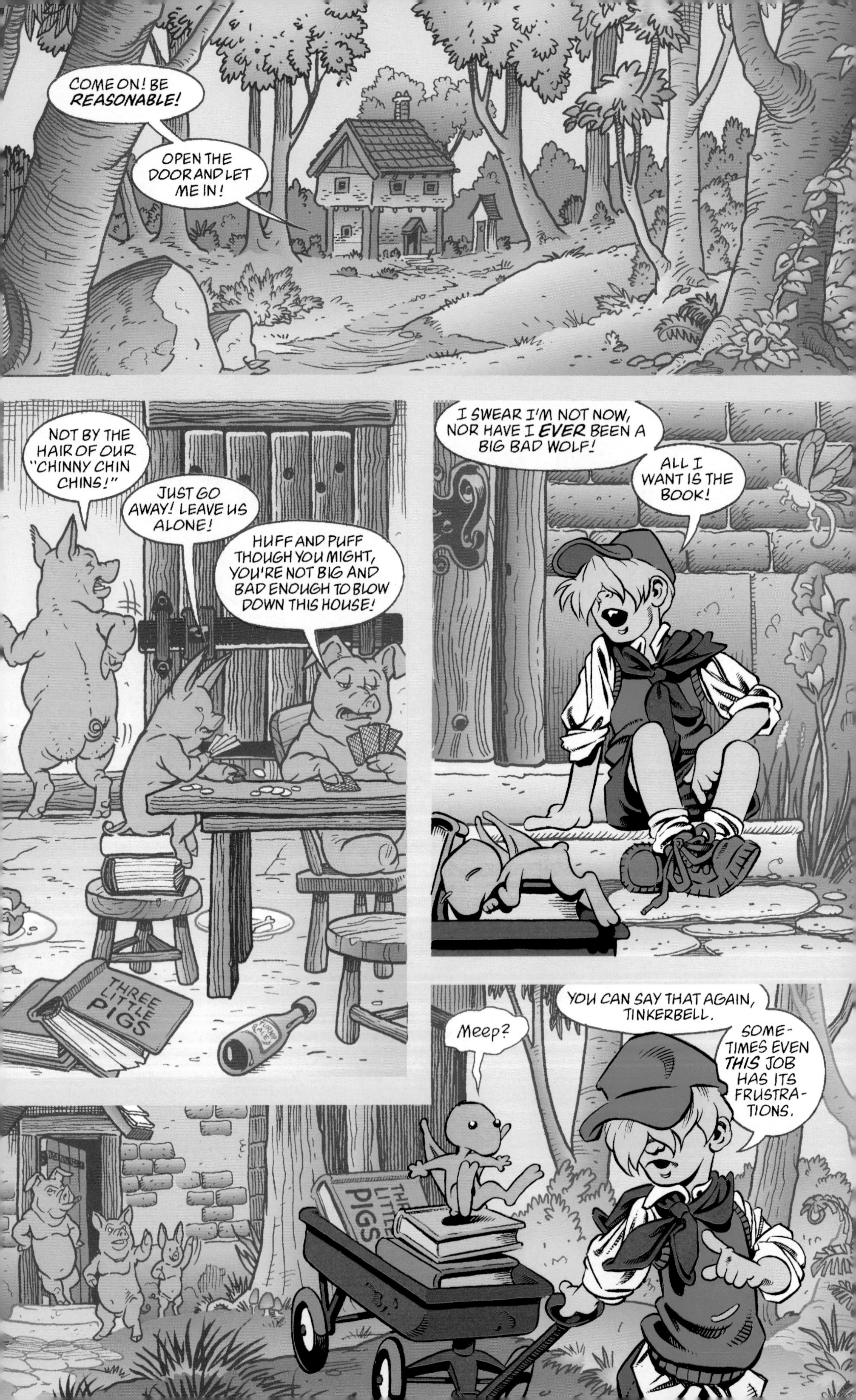
COME ON! BE *REASONABLE!*
OPEN THE DOOR AND LET ME IN!
NOT BY THE HAIR OF OUR "CHINNY CHIN CHINS!"
JUST GO AWAY! LEAVE US ALONE!
HUFF AND PUFF THOUGH YOU MIGHT, YOU'RE NOT BIG AND BAD ENOUGH TO BLOW DOWN THIS HOUSE!
THREE LITTLE PIGS
I SWEAR I'M NOT NOW, NOR HAVE I *EVER* BEEN A BIG BAD WOLF!
ALL I WANT IS THE BOOK!
Meep?
YOU CAN SAY THAT AGAIN, TINKERBELL.
SOMETIMES EVEN *THIS* JOB HAS ITS FRUSTRATIONS.

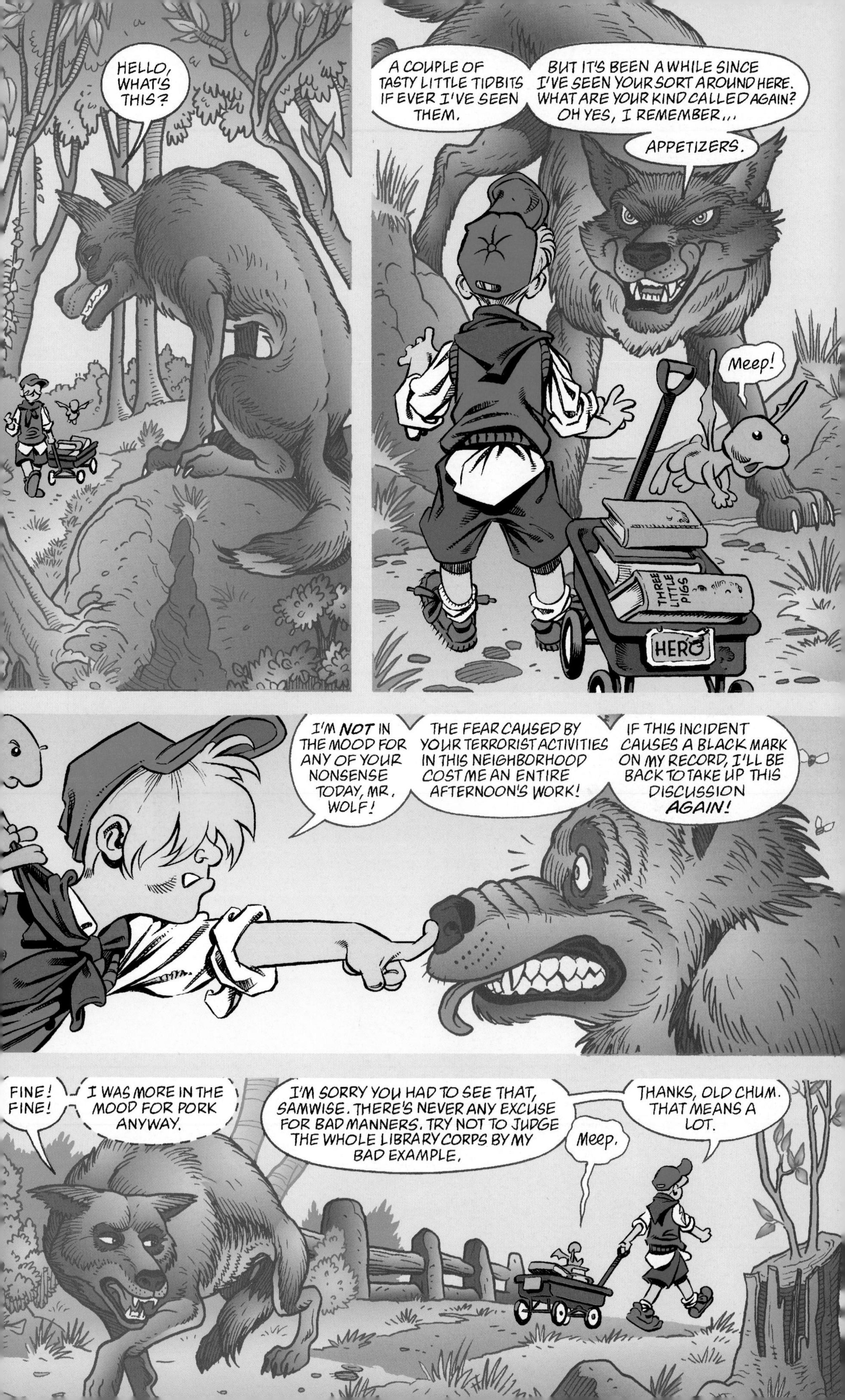
HELLO, WHAT'S THIS?
A COUPLE OF TASTY LITTLE TIDBITS IF EVER I'VE SEEN THEM.
BUT IT'S BEEN A WHILE SINCE I'VE SEEN YOUR SORT AROUND HERE. WHAT ARE YOUR KIND CALLED AGAIN? OH YES, I REMEMBER...
APPETIZERS.
Meep!
THREE LITTLE PIGS
HERO
I'M **NOT** IN THE MOOD FOR ANY OF YOUR NONSENSE TODAY, MR. WOLF!
THE FEAR CAUSED BY YOUR TERRORIST ACTIVITIES IN THIS NEIGHBORHOOD COST ME AN ENTIRE AFTERNOON'S WORK!
IF THIS INCIDENT CAUSES A BLACK MARK ON MY RECORD, I'LL BE BACK TO TAKE UP THIS DISCUSSION **AGAIN!**
FINE! FINE!
I WAS MORE IN THE MOOD FOR PORK ANYWAY.
I'M SORRY YOU HAD TO SEE THAT, SAMWISE. THERE'S NEVER ANY EXCUSE FOR BAD MANNERS. TRY NOT TO JUDGE THE WHOLE LIBRARY CORPS BY MY BAD EXAMPLE.
Meep.
THANKS, OLD CHUM. THAT MEANS A LOT.

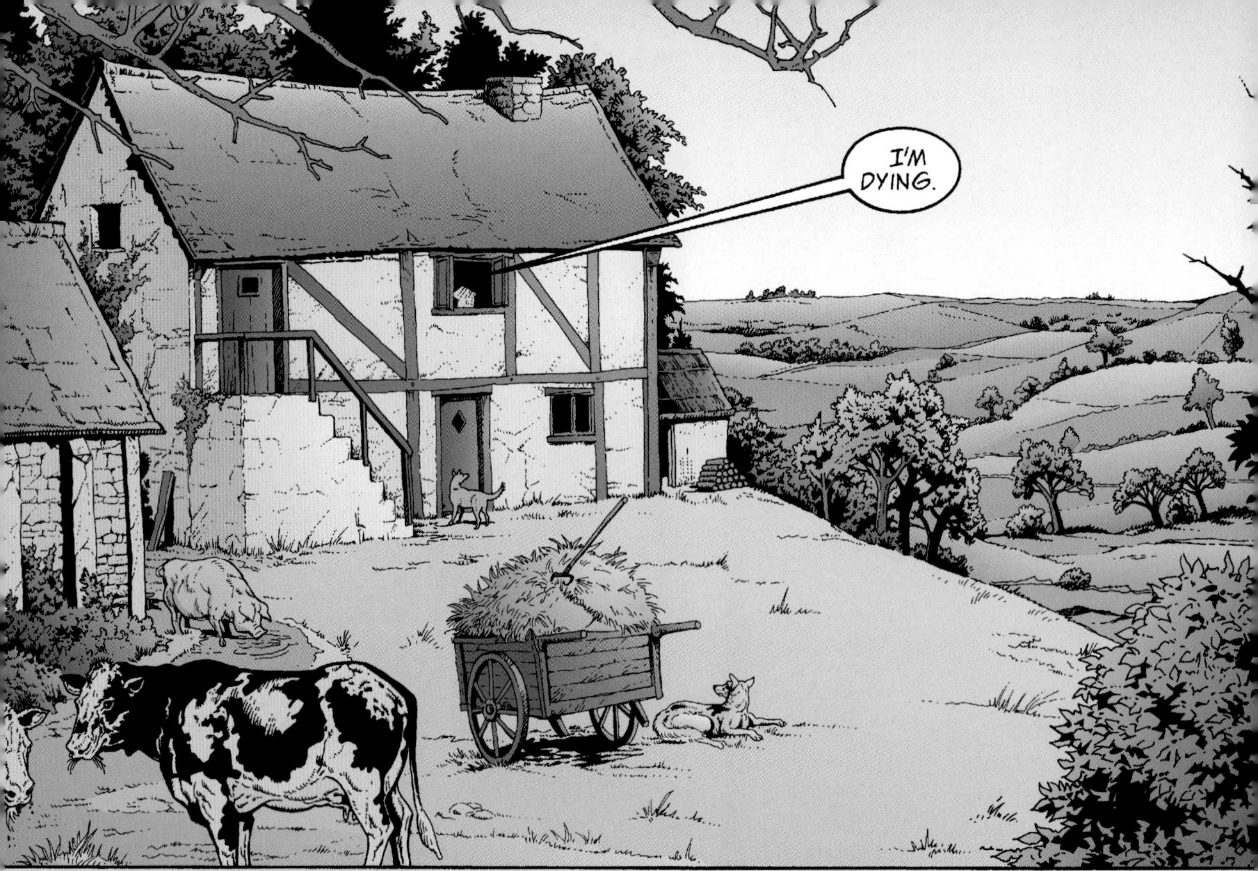
I'M DYING.
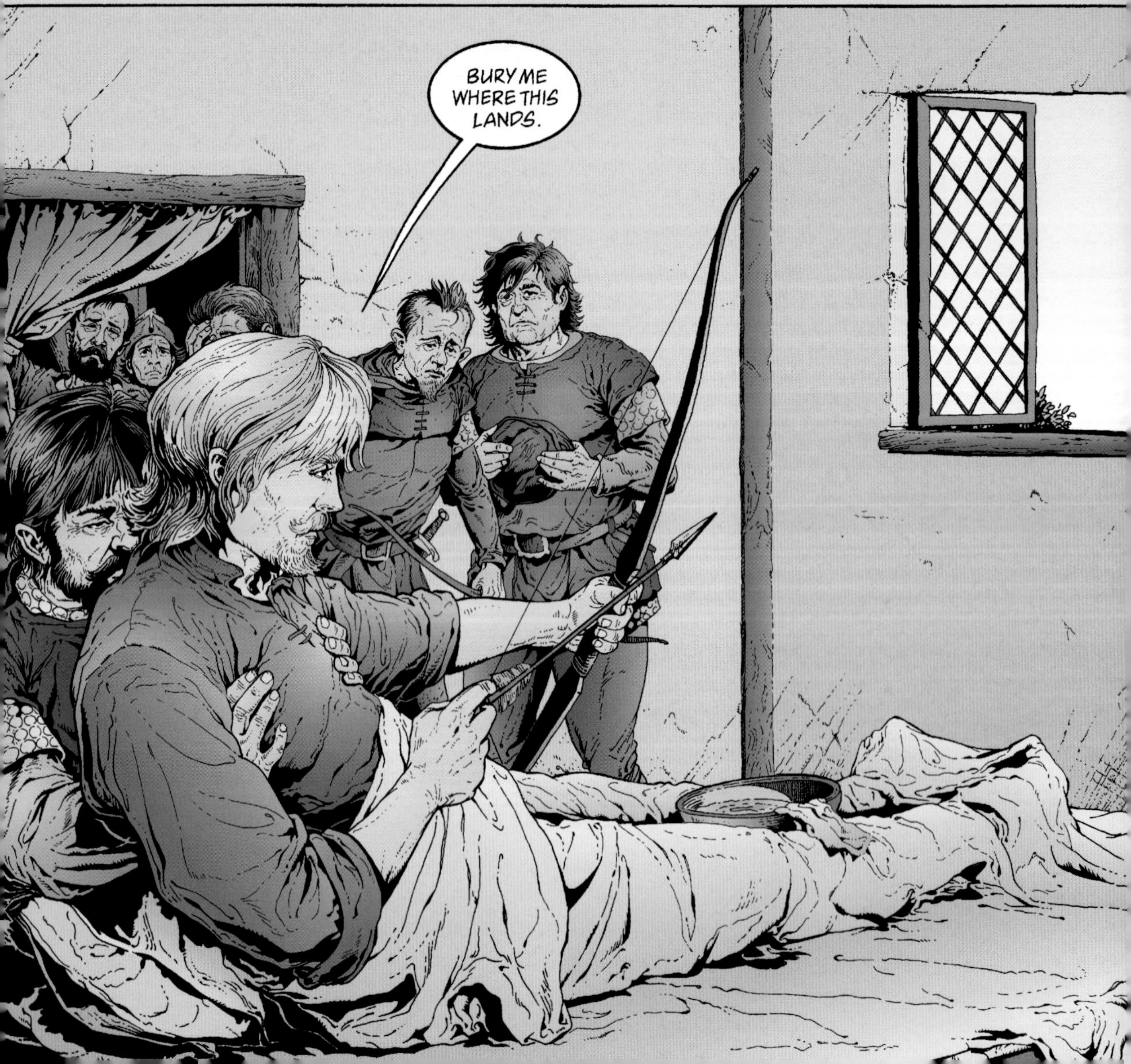
BURY ME WHERE THIS LANDS.

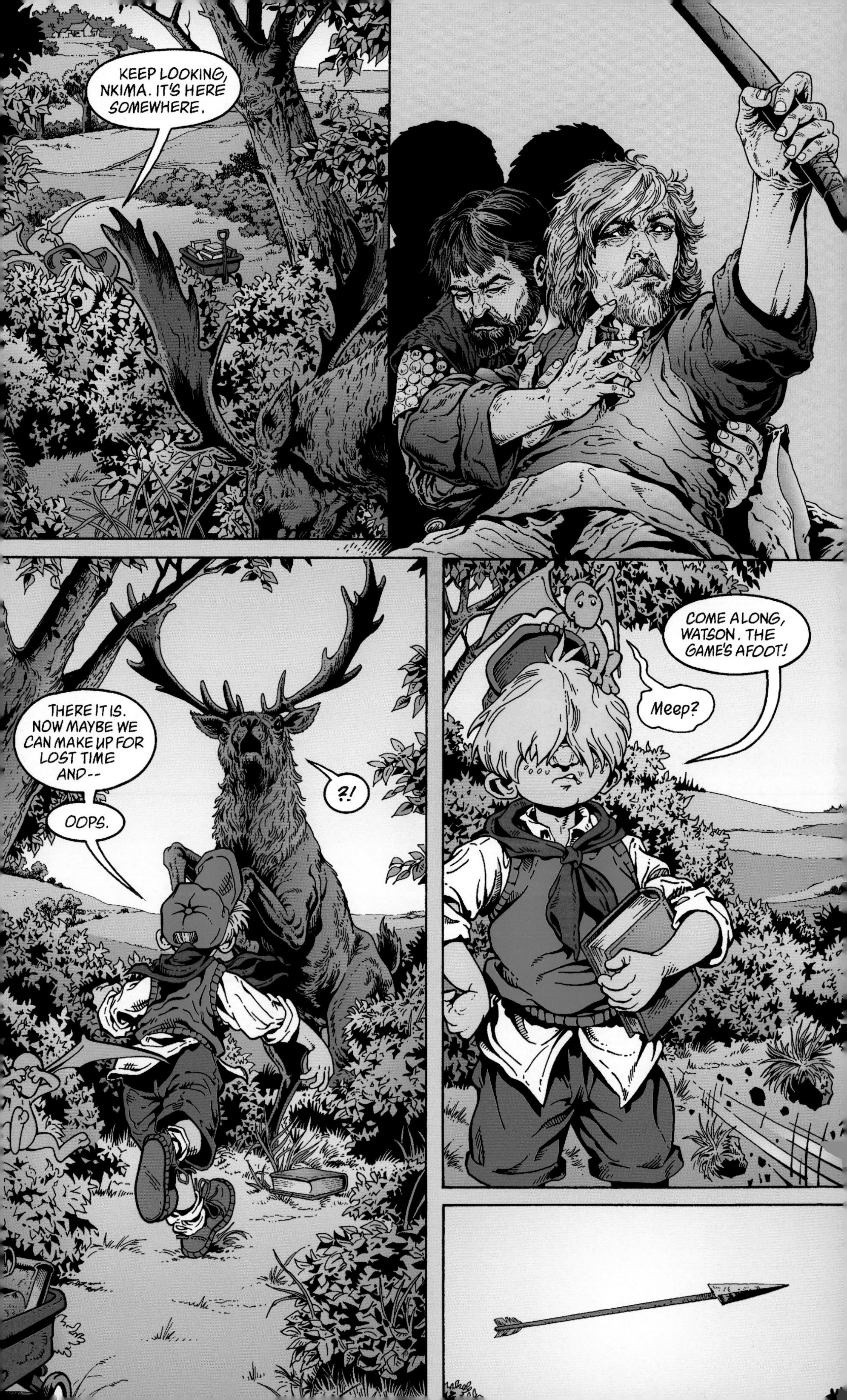
KEEP LOOKING, NKIMA. IT'S HERE SOMEWHERE.
THERE IT IS. NOW MAYBE WE CAN MAKE UP FOR LOST TIME AND--
OOPS.
?!
COME ALONG, WATSON. THE GAME'S AFOOT!
Meep?

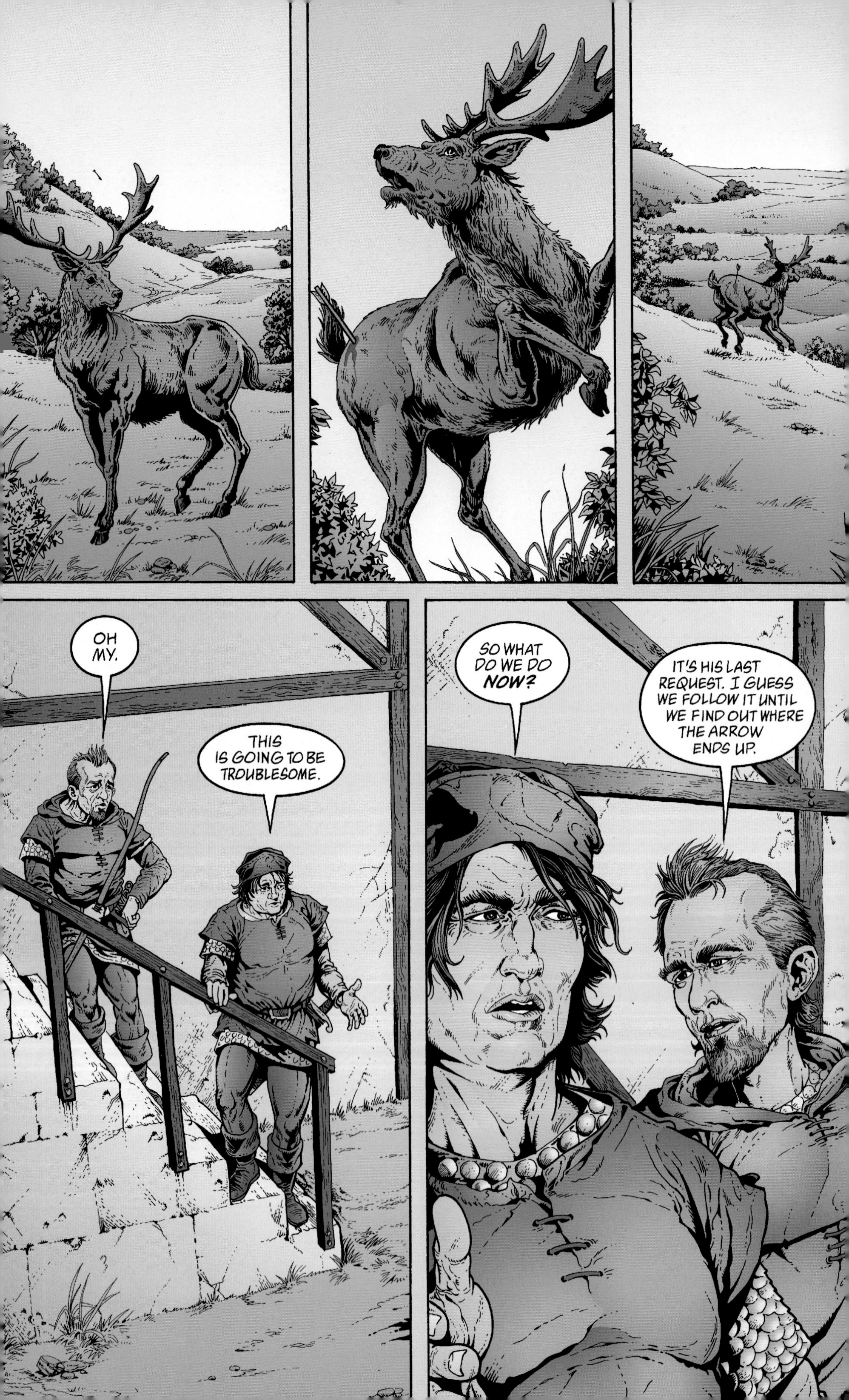
OH MY.
THIS IS GOING TO BE TROUBLESOME.
SO WHAT DO WE DO NOW?
IT'S HIS LAST REQUEST. I GUESS WE FOLLOW IT UNTIL WE FIND OUT WHERE THE ARROW ENDS UP.

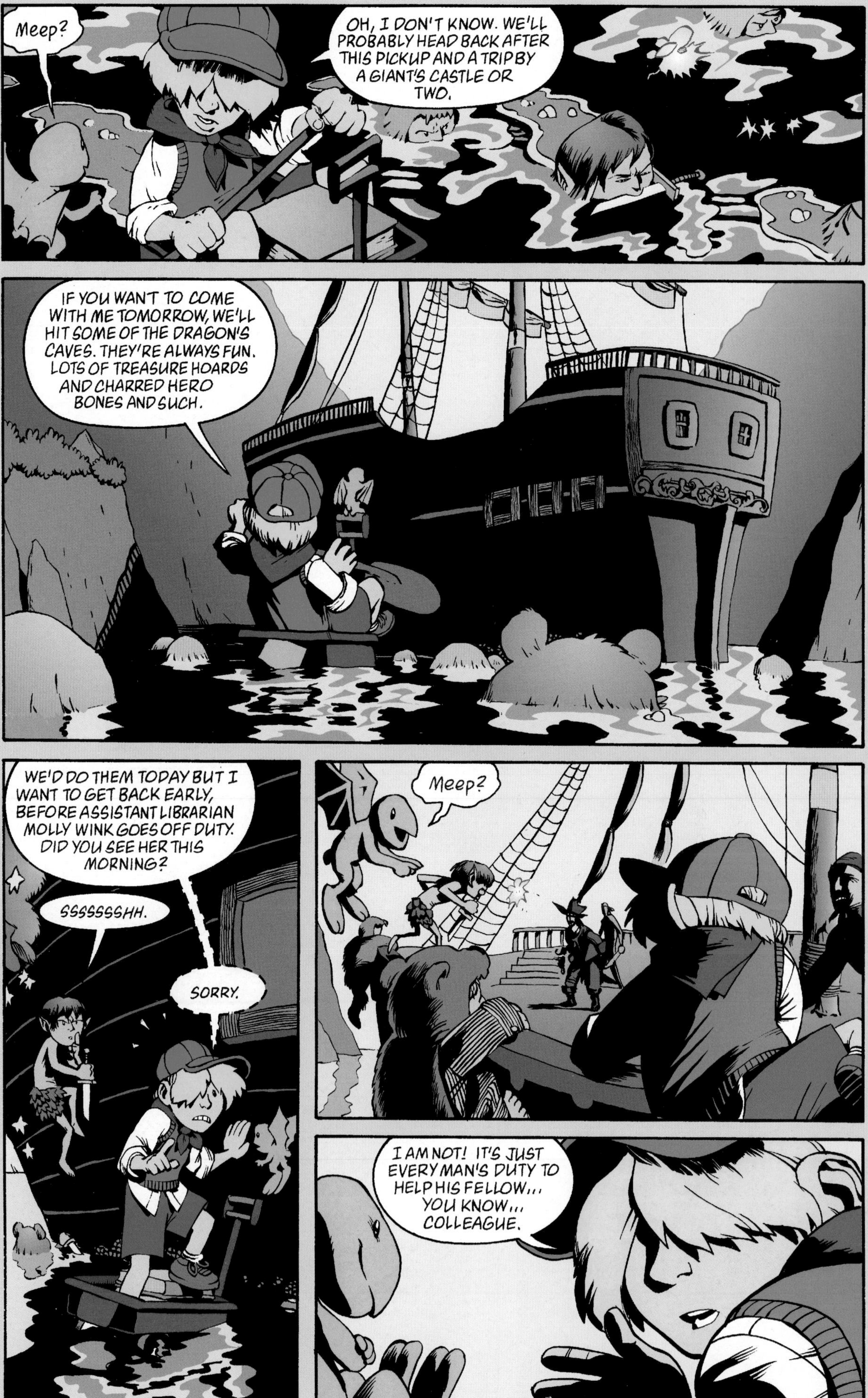
Meep?
OH, I DON'T KNOW. WE'LL PROBABLY HEAD BACK AFTER THIS PICKUP AND A TRIP BY A GIANT'S CASTLE OR TWO.
IF YOU WANT TO COME WITH ME TOMORROW, WE'LL HIT SOME OF THE DRAGON'S CAVES. THEY'RE ALWAYS FUN. LOTS OF TREASURE HOARDS AND CHARRED HERO BONES AND SUCH.
WE'D DO THEM TODAY BUT I WANT TO GET BACK EARLY, BEFORE ASSISTANT LIBRARIAN MOLLY WINK GOES OFF DUTY. DID YOU SEE HER THIS MORNING?
SSSSSSSHH.
SORRY.
Meep?
I AM NOT! IT'S JUST EVERY MAN'S DUTY TO HELP HIS FELLOW... YOU KNOW... COLLEAGUE.

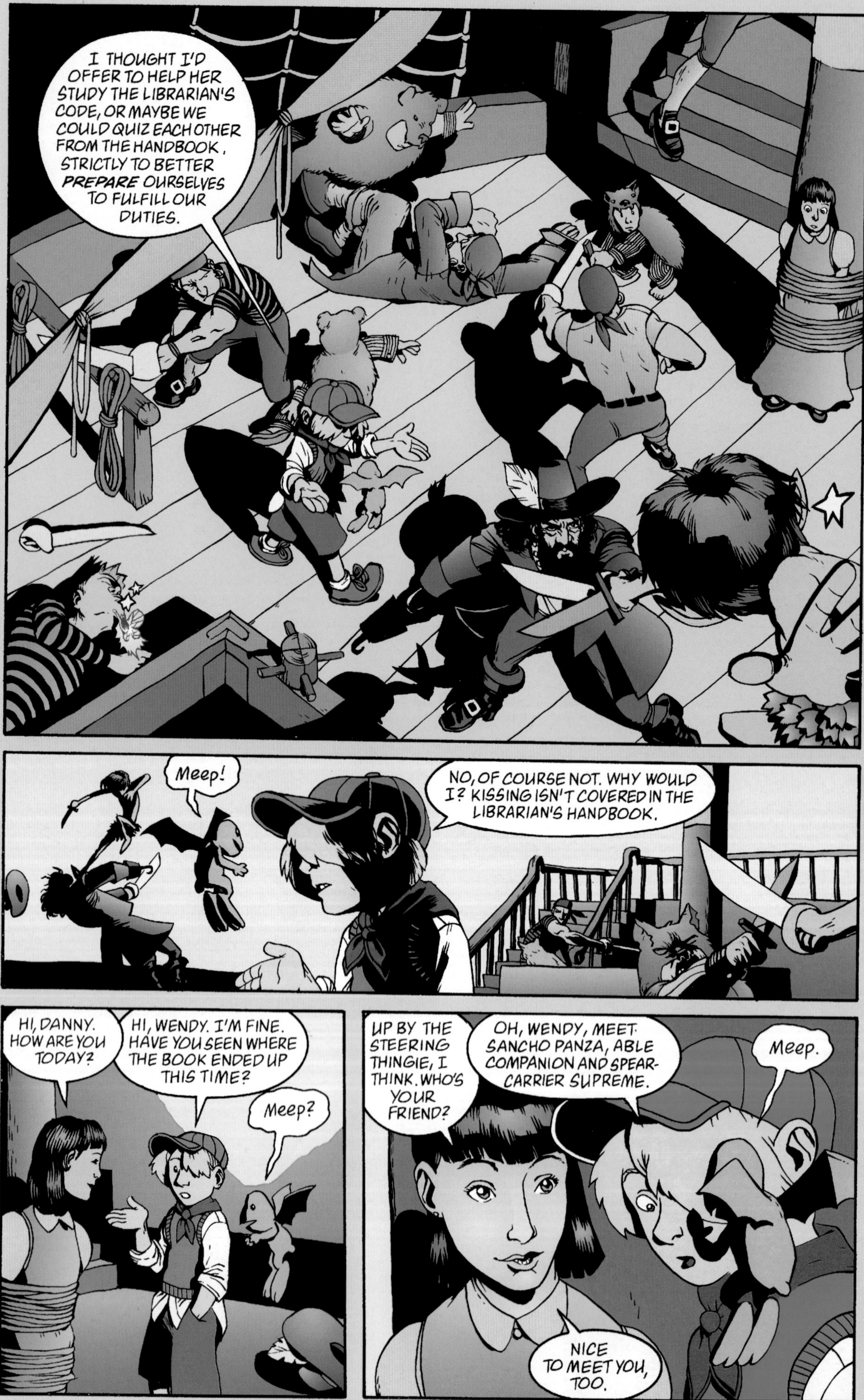
I THOUGHT I'D OFFER TO HELP HER STUDY THE LIBRARIAN'S CODE, OR MAYBE WE COULD QUIZ EACH OTHER FROM THE HANDBOOK, STRICTLY TO BETTER *PREPARE* OURSELVES TO FULFILL OUR DUTIES.
Meep!
NO, OF COURSE NOT. WHY WOULD I? KISSING ISN'T COVERED IN THE LIBRARIAN'S HANDBOOK.
HI, DANNY. HOW ARE YOU TODAY?
HI, WENDY. I'M FINE. HAVE YOU SEEN WHERE THE BOOK ENDED UP THIS TIME?
Meep?
UP BY THE STEERING THINGIE, I THINK. WHO'S YOUR FRIEND?
OH, WENDY, MEET SANCHO PANZA, ABLE COMPANION AND SPEAR-CARRIER SUPREME.
Meep.
NICE TO MEET YOU, TOO.

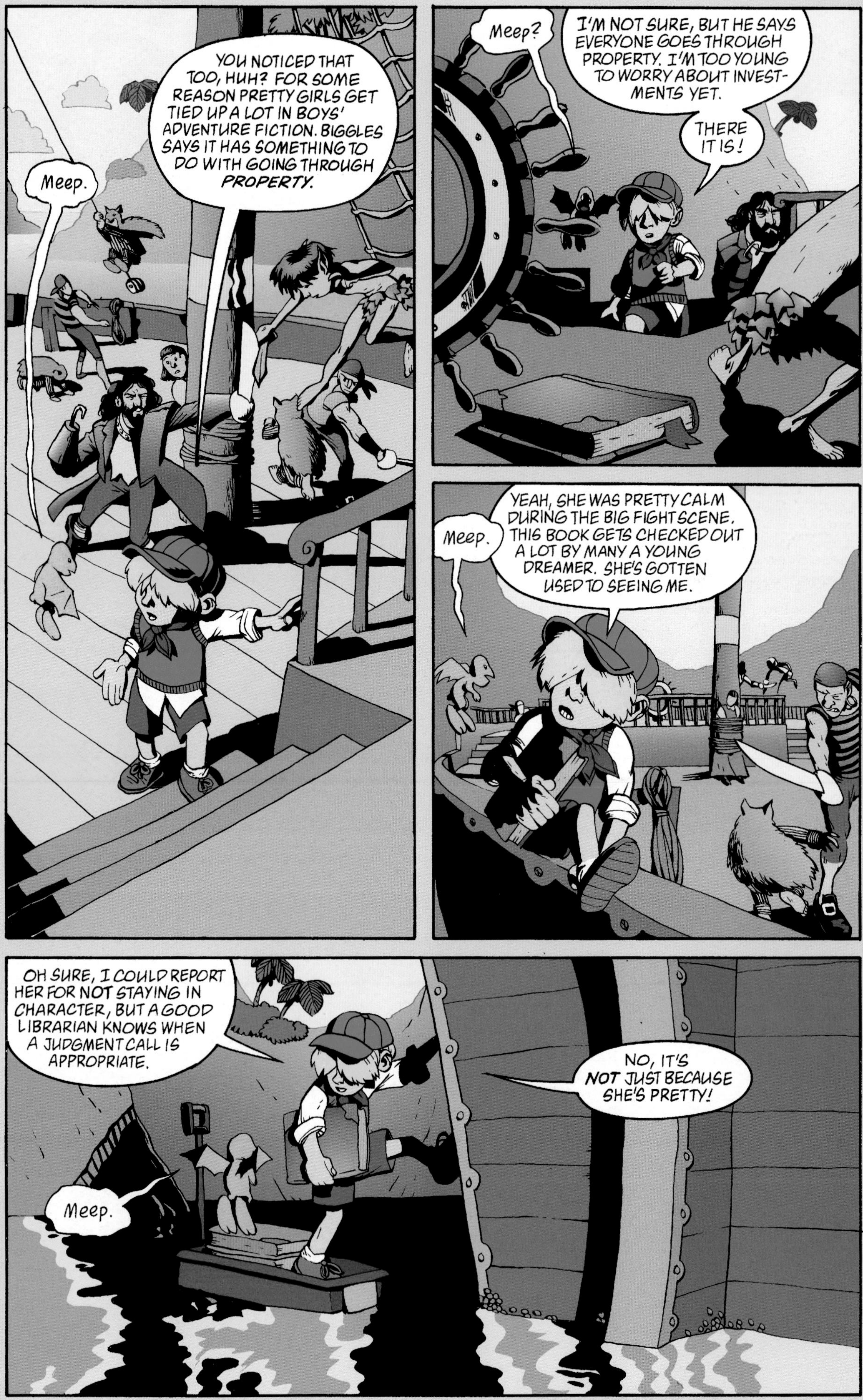
YOU NOTICED THAT TOO, HUH? FOR SOME REASON PRETTY GIRLS GET TIED UP A LOT IN BOYS' ADVENTURE FICTION. BIGGLES SAYS IT HAS SOMETHING TO DO WITH GOING THROUGH PROPERTY.
Meep.
Meep?
I'M NOT SURE, BUT HE SAYS EVERYONE GOES THROUGH PROPERTY. I'M TOO YOUNG TO WORRY ABOUT INVEST-MENTS YET.
THERE IT IS!
Meep.
YEAH, SHE WAS PRETTY CALM DURING THE BIG FIGHT SCENE. THIS BOOK GETS CHECKED OUT A LOT BY MANY A YOUNG DREAMER. SHE'S GOTTEN USED TO SEEING ME.
OH SURE, I COULD REPORT HER FOR NOT STAYING IN CHARACTER, BUT A GOOD LIBRARIAN KNOWS WHEN A JUDGMENT CALL IS APPROPRIATE.
NO, IT'S NOT JUST BECAUSE SHE'S PRETTY!
Meep.

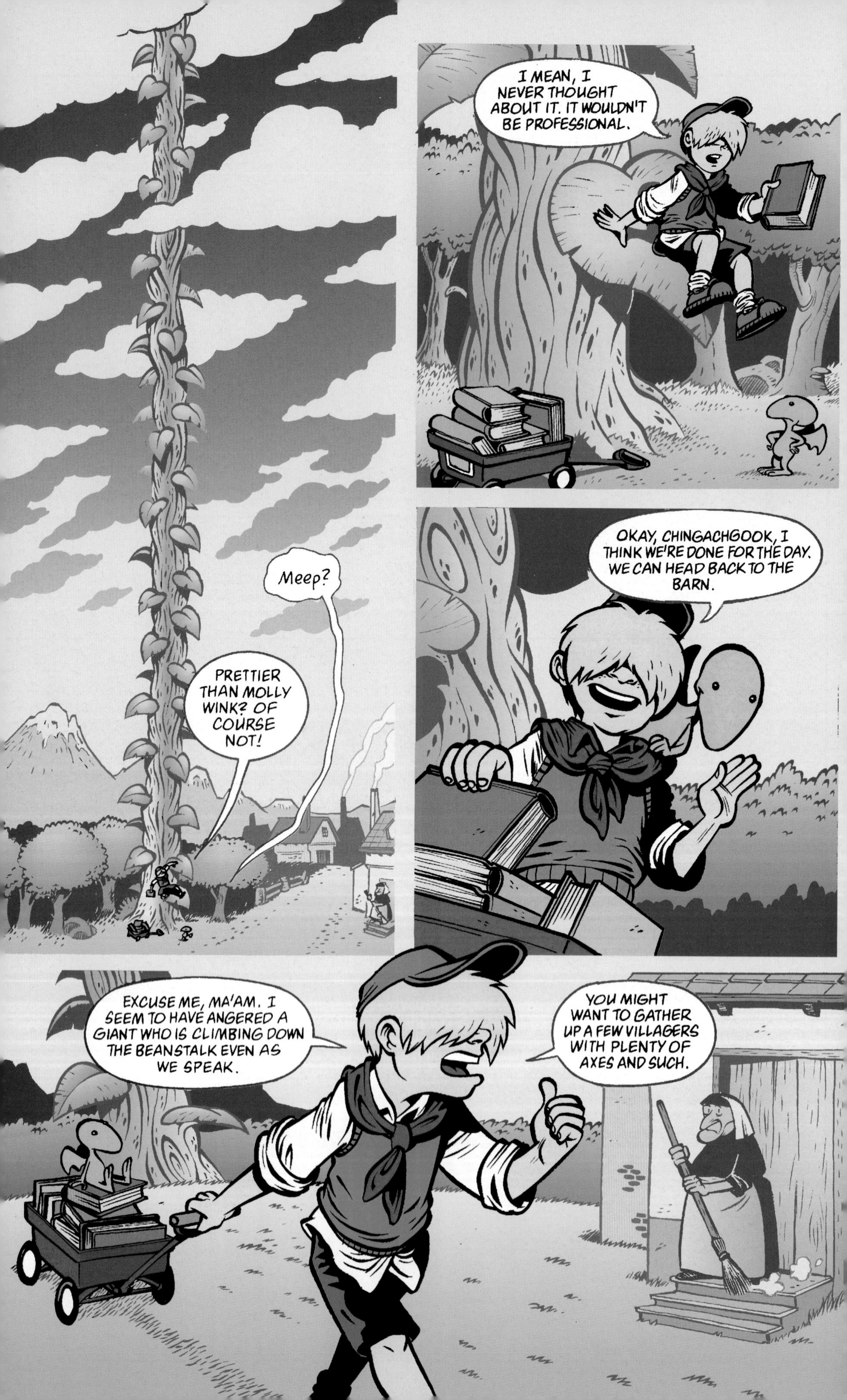
PRETTIER THAN MOLLY WINK? OF COURSE NOT!
Meep?
I MEAN, I NEVER THOUGHT ABOUT IT. IT WOULDN'T BE PROFESSIONAL.
OKAY, CHINGACHGOOK, I THINK WE'RE DONE FOR THE DAY. WE CAN HEAD BACK TO THE BARN.
EXCUSE ME, MA'AM. I SEEM TO HAVE ANGERED A GIANT WHO IS CLIMBING DOWN THE BEANSTALK EVEN AS WE SPEAK.
YOU MIGHT WANT TO GATHER UP A FEW VILLAGERS WITH PLENTY OF AXES AND SUCH.

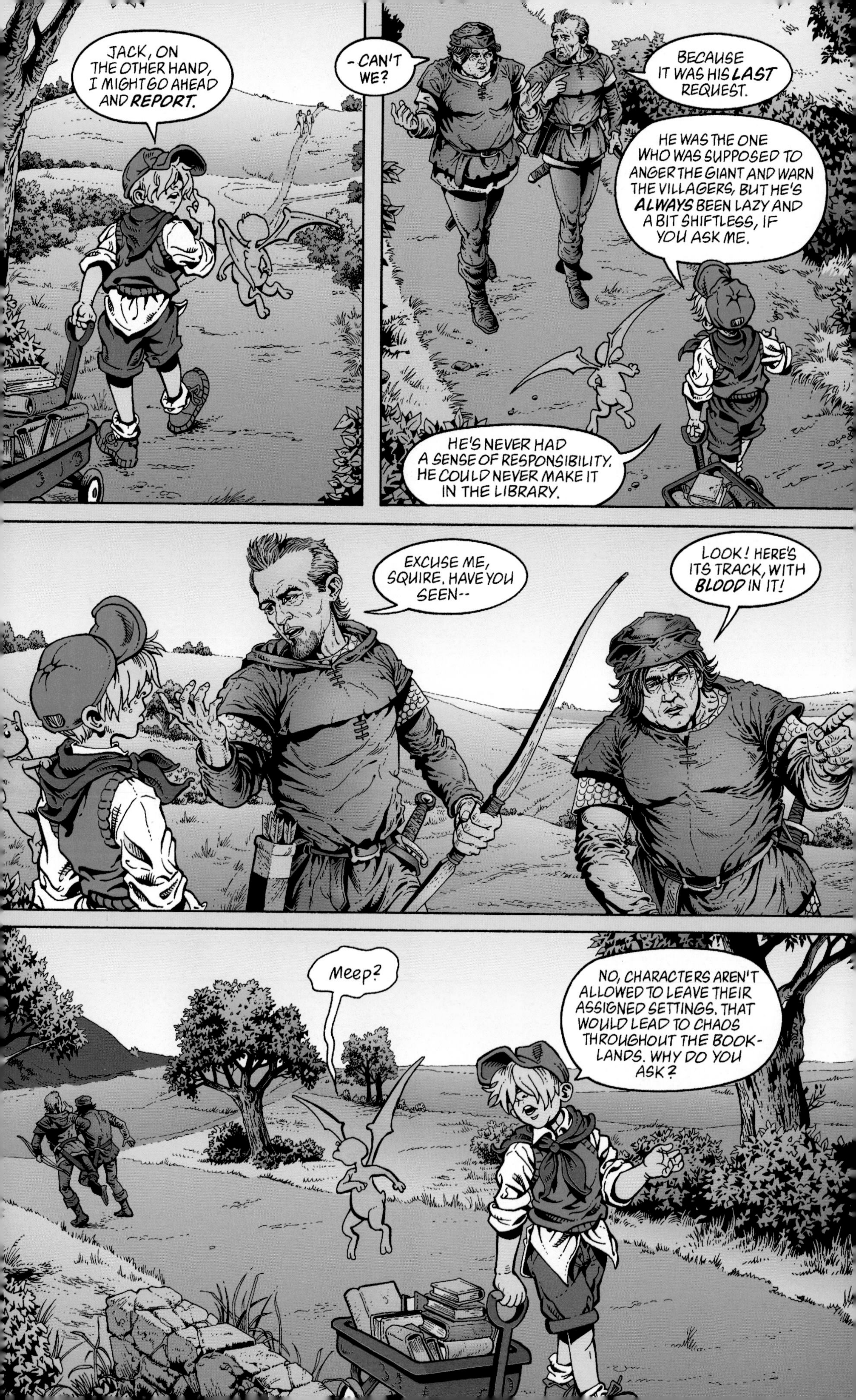
JACK, ON THE OTHER HAND, I MIGHT GO AHEAD AND **REPORT.**
- CAN'T WE?
BECAUSE IT WAS HIS **LAST** REQUEST.
HE WAS THE ONE WHO WAS SUPPOSED TO ANGER THE GIANT AND WARN THE VILLAGERS, BUT HE'S **ALWAYS** BEEN LAZY AND A BIT SHIFTLESS, IF YOU ASK ME.
HE'S NEVER HAD A SENSE OF RESPONSIBILITY. HE COULD NEVER MAKE IT IN THE LIBRARY.
EXCUSE ME, SQUIRE. HAVE YOU SEEN--
LOOK! HERE'S ITS TRACK, WITH **BLOOD** IN IT!
Meep?
NO, CHARACTERS AREN'T ALLOWED TO LEAVE THEIR ASSIGNED SETTINGS. THAT WOULD LEAD TO CHAOS THROUGHOUT THE BOOK-LANDS. WHY DO YOU ASK?

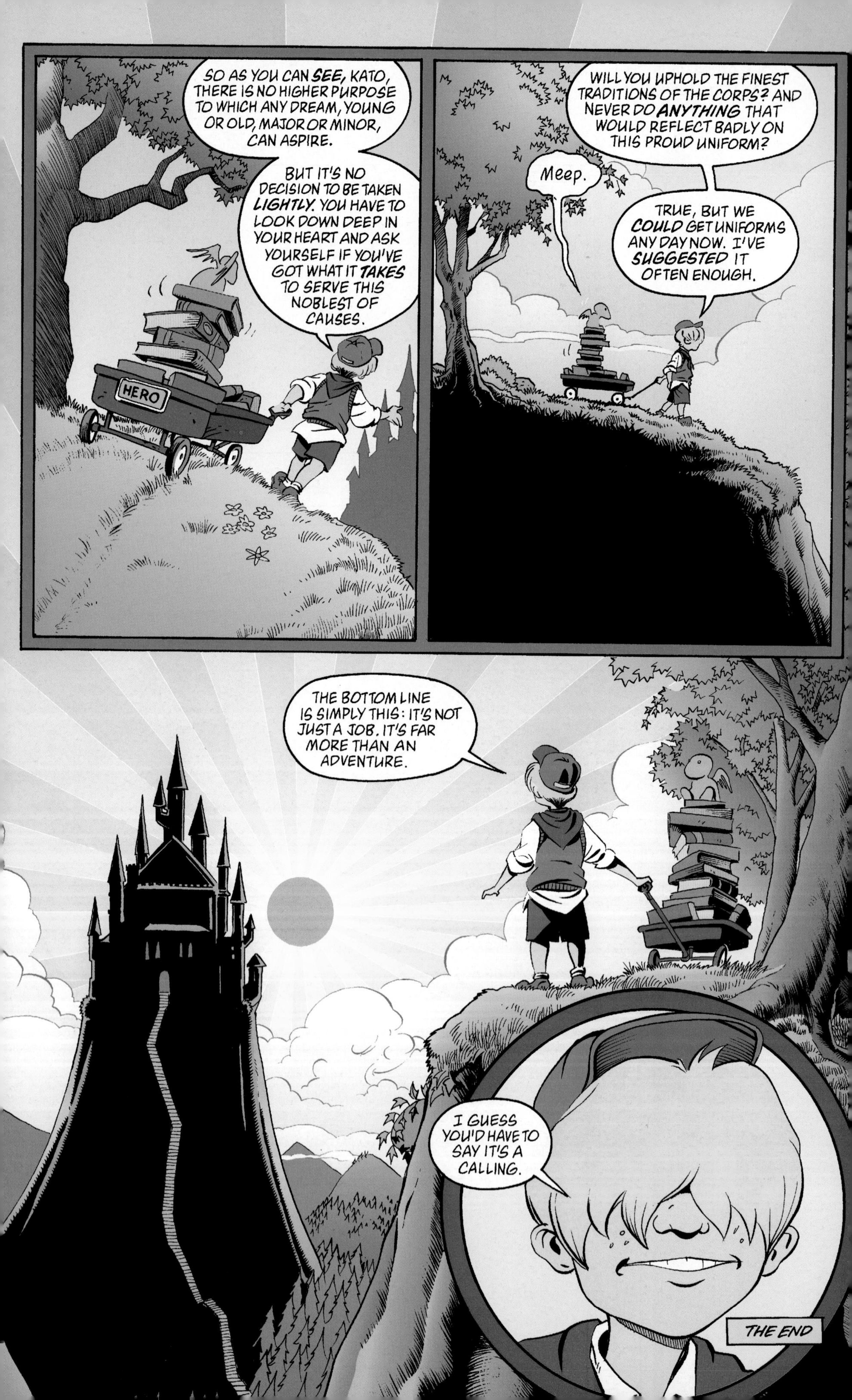
SO AS YOU CAN SEE, KATO, THERE IS NO HIGHER PURPOSE TO WHICH ANY DREAM, YOUNG OR OLD, MAJOR OR MINOR, CAN ASPIRE.
BUT IT'S NO DECISION TO BE TAKEN LIGHTLY. YOU HAVE TO LOOK DOWN DEEP IN YOUR HEART AND ASK YOURSELF IF YOU'VE GOT WHAT IT TAKES TO SERVE THIS NOBLEST OF CAUSES.
HERO
WILL YOU UPHOLD THE FINEST TRADITIONS OF THE CORPS? AND NEVER DO ANYTHING THAT WOULD REFLECT BADLY ON THIS PROUD UNIFORM?
Meep.
TRUE, BUT WE COULD GET UNIFORMS ANY DAY NOW. I'VE SUGGESTED IT OFTEN ENOUGH.
THE BOTTOM LINE IS SIMPLY THIS: IT'S NOT JUST A JOB. IT'S FAR MORE THAN AN ADVENTURE.
I GUESS YOU'D HAVE TO SAY IT'S A CALLING.
THE END

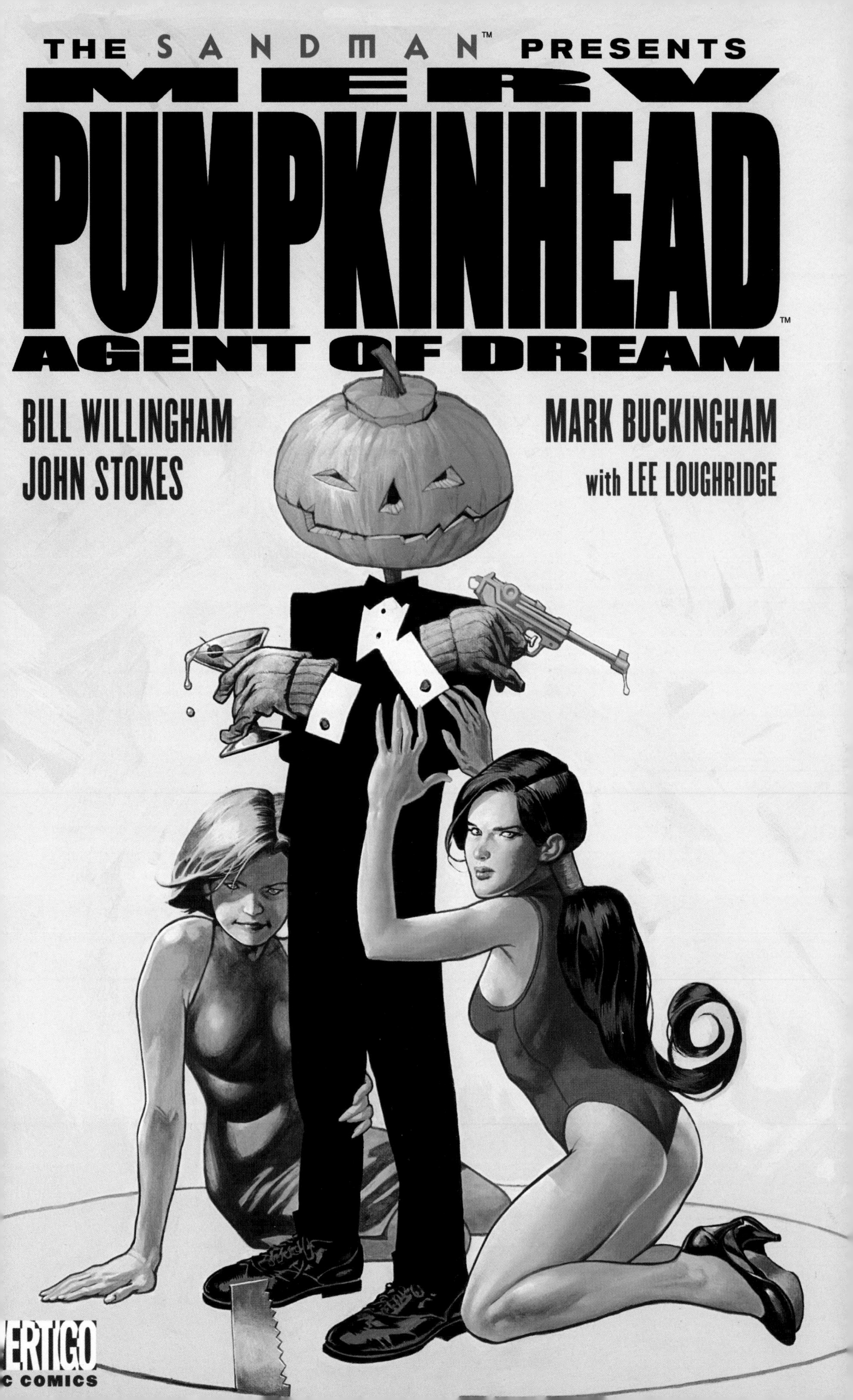
THE SANDMAN™ PRESENTS
MERV
PUMPKINHEAD™
AGENT OF DREAM
BILL WILLINGHAM
JOHN STOKES
MARK BUCKINGHAM
with LEE LOUGHRIDGE

THIS STORY ACTUALLY STARTED WITH SHELLY (still Roeberg at the time, as the suave and dashing Philip Bond had yet to sweep her off her tap shoes) asking me, in one of our marathon phone sessions, "What if Merv Pumpkinhead was James Bond?" With that the ideas started flooding in, and we were off to the races.

You've heard of stories that practically write themselves? That never actually happens, but this one came as close as any.

This is also the story that made my career, because it's the first time I got to work with Mark Buckingham. Shelly offered him as one of a list of possibilities to draw the story. I'll never know whose name was next on her list, since I immediately shouted, "Yes, if we can get him, get him!" I didn't know Mark — had never met him, even in passing — but I recalled an article in *The Comics Journal* praising the man. Its title was something like "The Best Artist in Comics Nobody Knows," and whoever wrote it must have made his case quite well, since that was why I knew he'd be a great choice for the story.

"...my favorite opening line of all opening lines kicks off this tale: 'Dreams are frisky.'"

Merv Pumpkinhead made my career because Mark Buckingham said yes to drawing it, which led to him a few years later saying yes to FABLES. I'll always appreciate the old melonhead for that. And because it was such a fun farce to tell, too. In fact, my favorite opening line of all opening lines kicks off this tale: "Dreams are frisky."

If this story had sold just a wee bit better at the time, our next idea was to bring Merv back as an Indiana Jones type of adventurer, and after that (at Neil Gaiman's request) as the protagonist in a dark and *noir*-ish Hong Kong style crime flick.

Missed opportunities, huh?

MERV PUMPKINHEAD, AGENT OF D.R.E.A.M.

PENCILS BY
Mark Buckingham

INKS BY
John Stokes

COLORS BY
Lee Loughridge

LETTERS BY
Todd Klein

COVER ART BY
Kevin Nowlan

CHAPTER ONE

ON HIS MAJESTY'S SLEEPING SERVICE

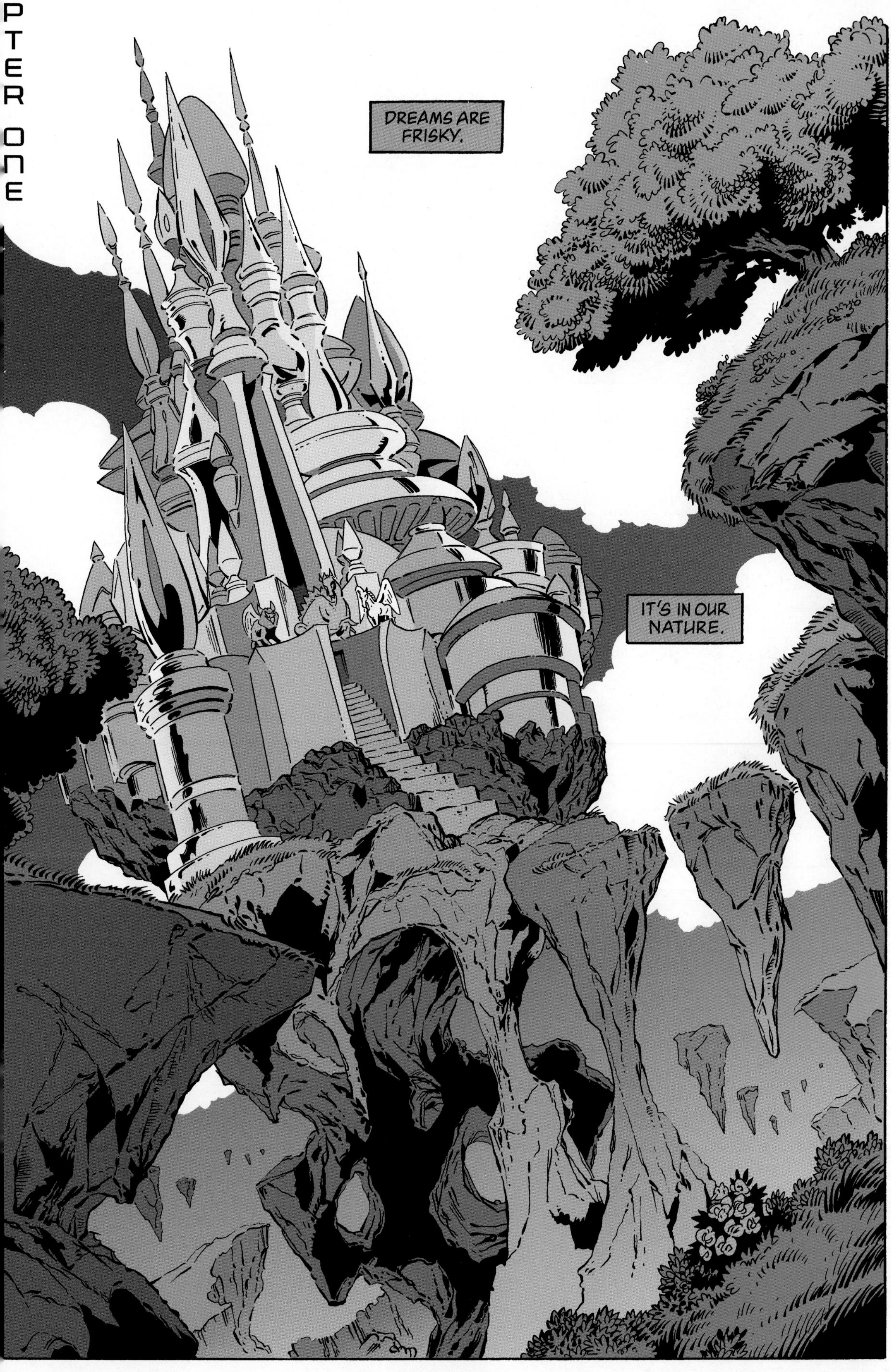
DREAMS ARE FRISKY.
IT'S IN OUR NATURE.

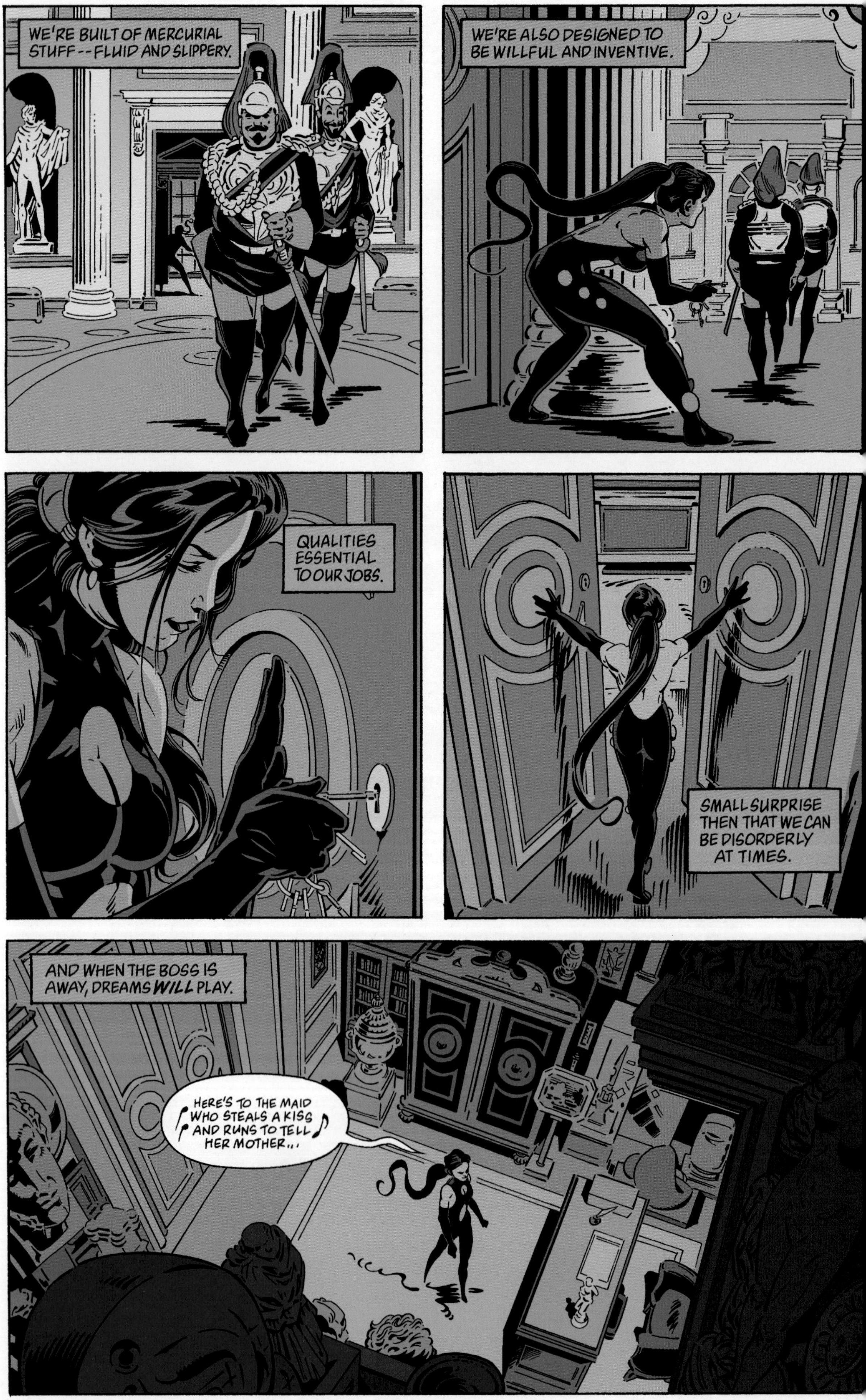
WE'RE BUILT OF MERCURIAL STUFF--FLUID AND SLIPPERY.
WE'RE ALSO DESIGNED TO BE WILLFUL AND INVENTIVE.
QUALITIES ESSENTIAL TO OUR JOBS.
SMALL SURPRISE THEN THAT WE CAN BE DISORDERLY AT TIMES.
AND WHEN THE BOSS IS AWAY, DREAMS **WILL** PLAY.
♪ HERE'S TO THE MAID WHO STEALS A KISS AND RUNS TO TELL HER MOTHER... ♪

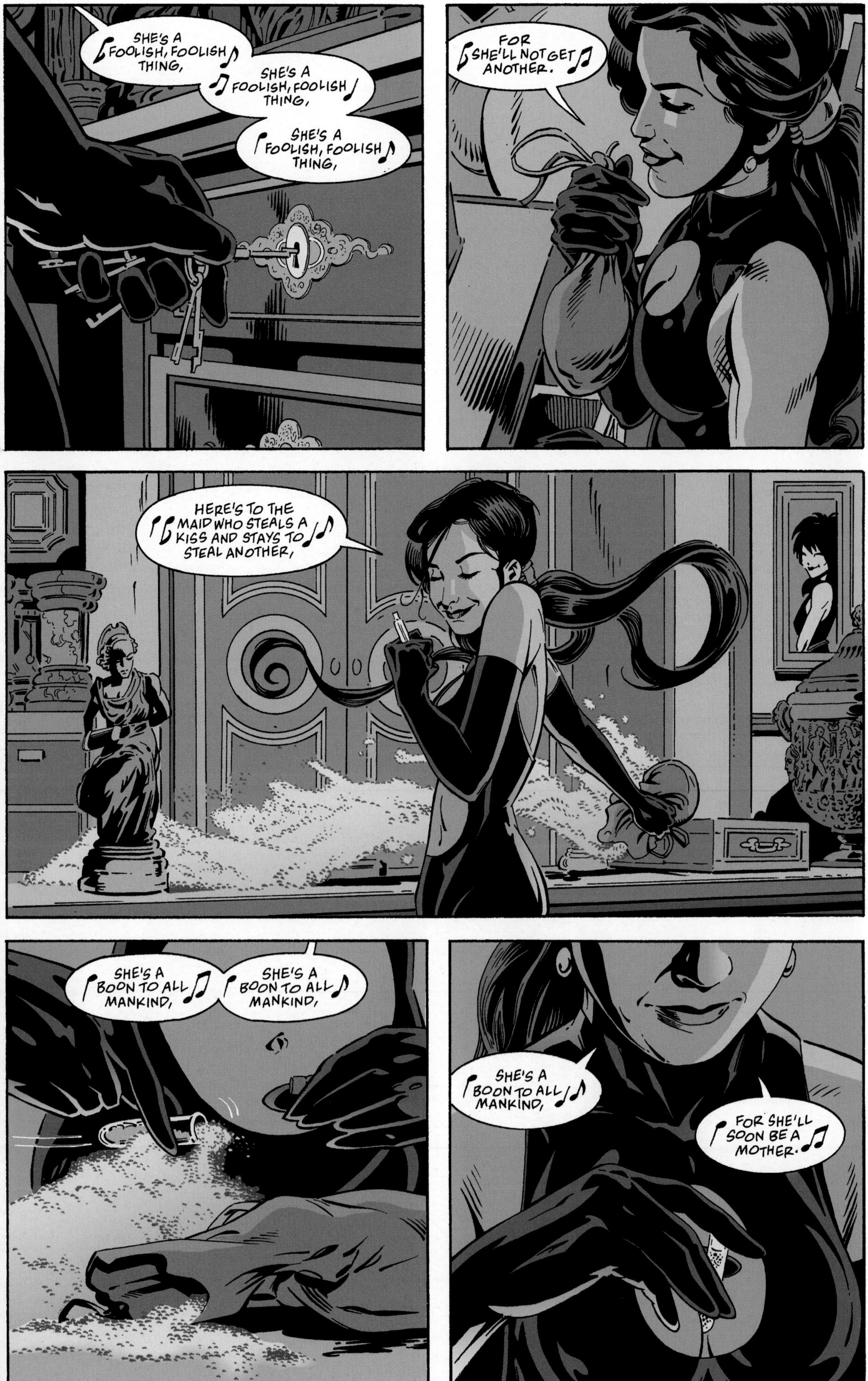
SHE'S A FOOLISH, FOOLISH THING,
SHE'S A FOOLISH, FOOLISH THING,
SHE'S A FOOLISH, FOOLISH THING,
FOR SHE'LL NOT GET ANOTHER.
HERE'S TO THE MAID WHO STEALS A KISS AND STAYS TO STEAL ANOTHER,
SHE'S A BOON TO ALL MANKIND,
SHE'S A BOON TO ALL MANKIND,
SHE'S A BOON TO ALL MANKIND,
FOR SHE'LL SOON BE A MOTHER.

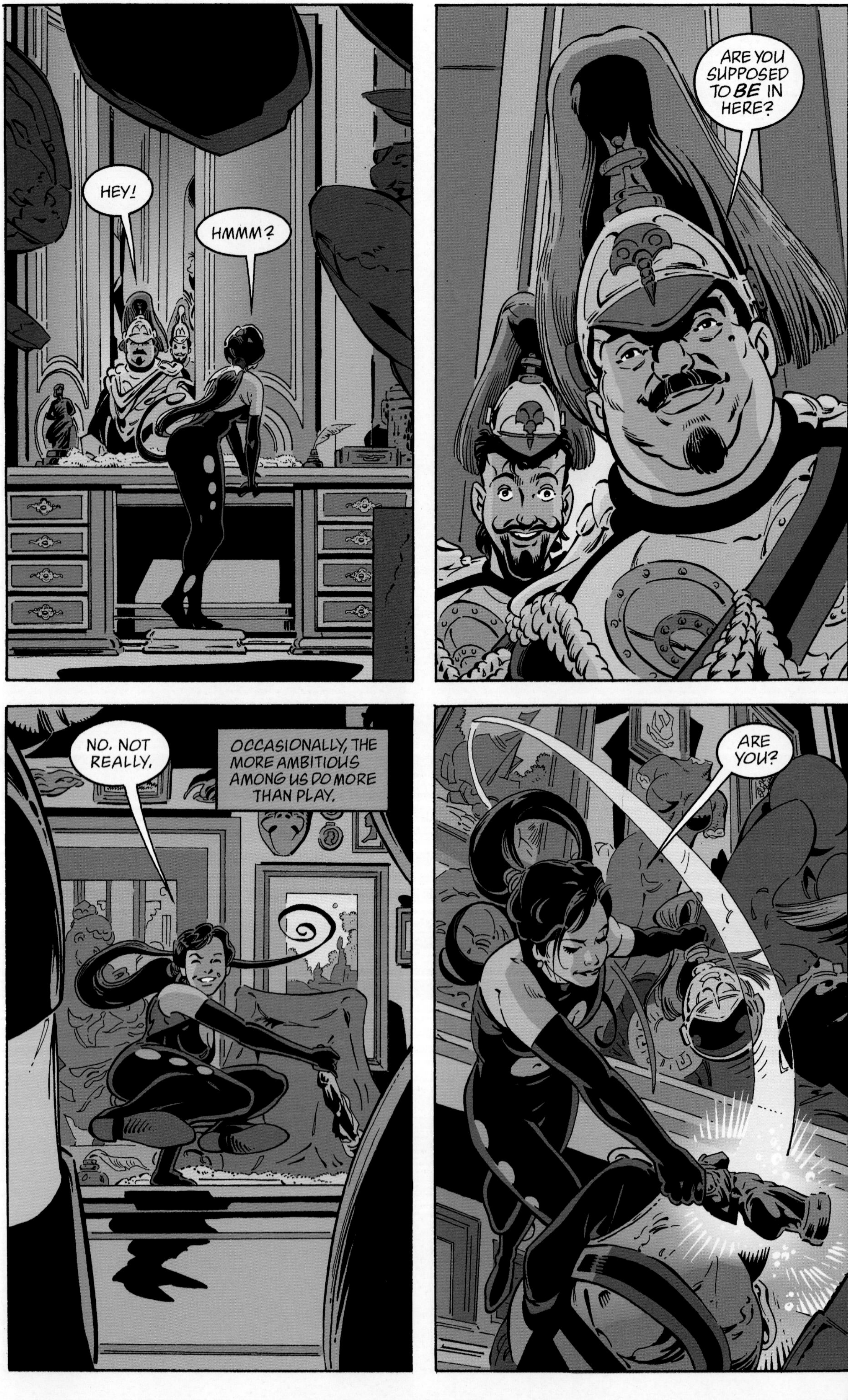
HEY!
HMMM?
ARE YOU SUPPOSED TO BE IN HERE?
NO. NOT REALLY.
OCCASIONALLY, THE MORE AMBITIOUS AMONG US DO MORE THAN PLAY.
ARE YOU?

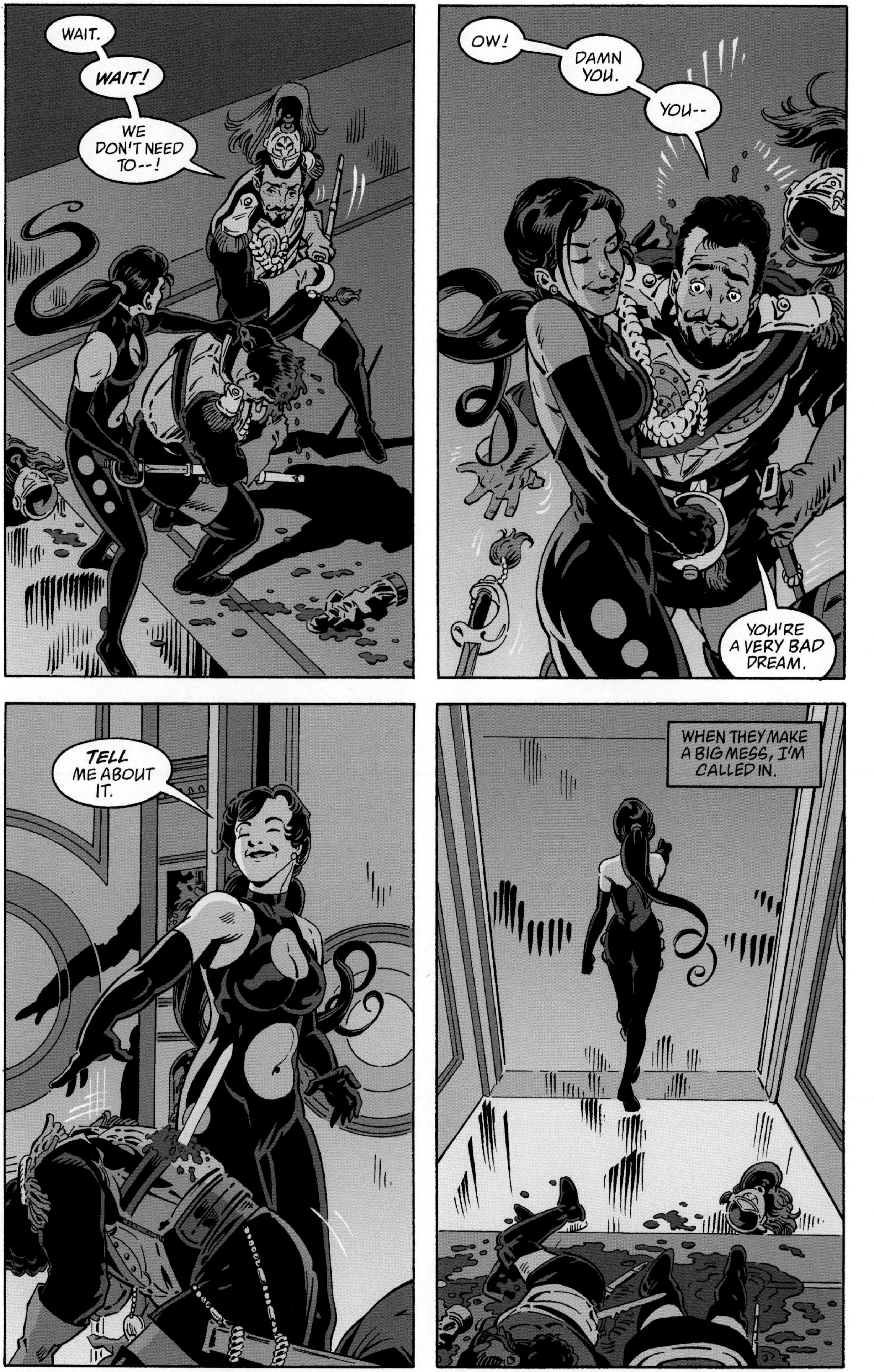
WAIT.
WAIT!
WE DON'T NEED TO--!
OW!
DAMN YOU.
YOU--
YOU'RE A VERY BAD DREAM.
TELL ME ABOUT IT.
WHEN THEY MAKE A BIG MESS, I'M CALLED IN.

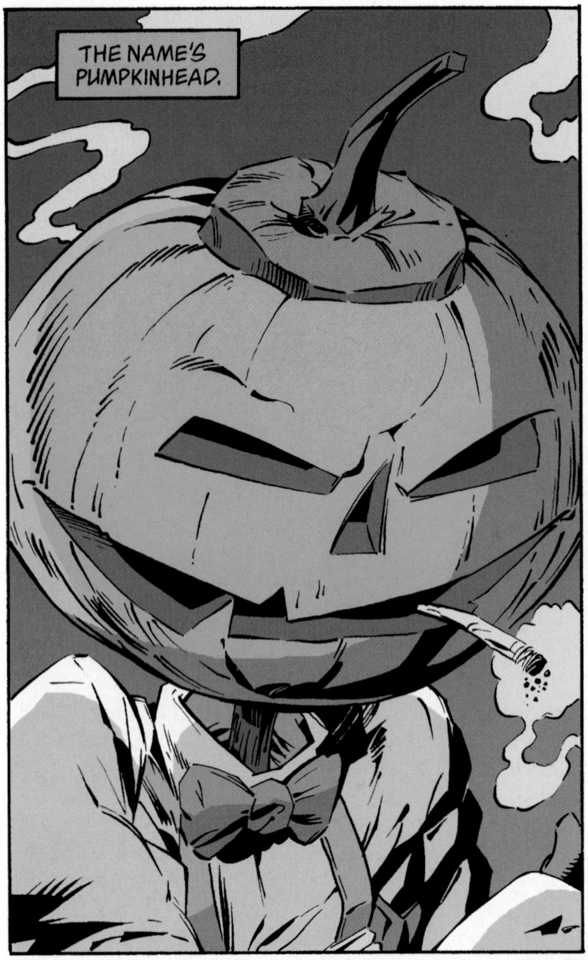
THE NAME'S PUMPKINHEAD.
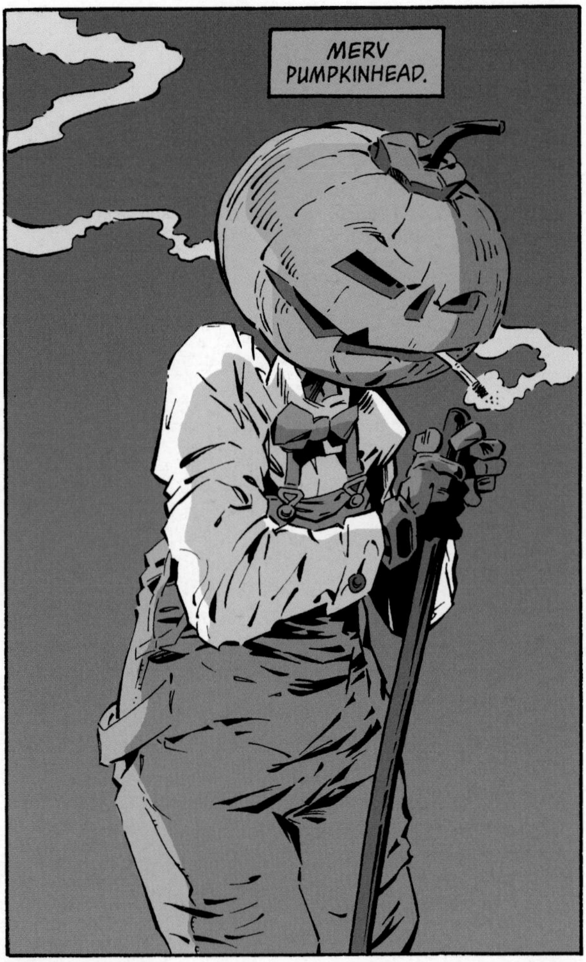
MERV PUMPKINHEAD.
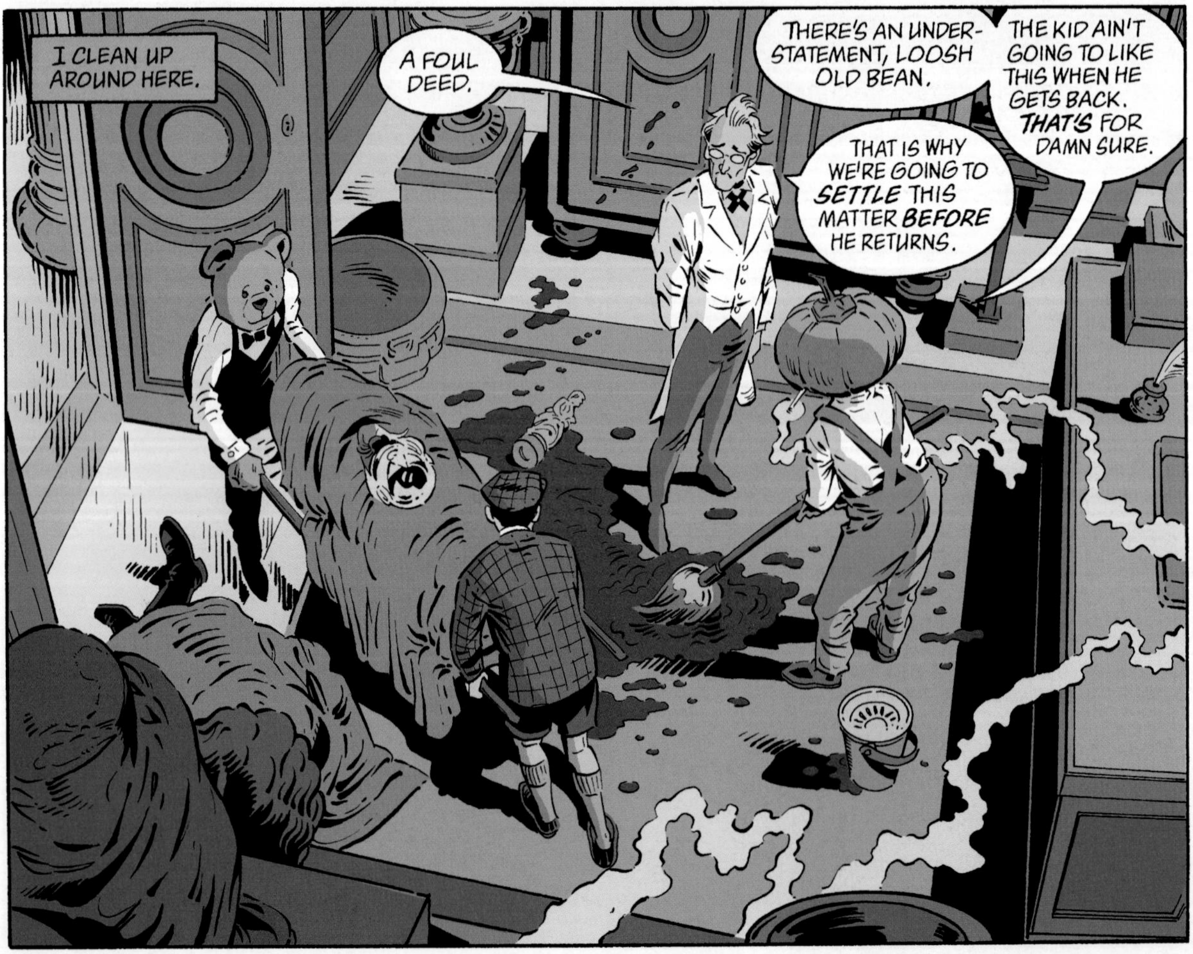
I CLEAN UP AROUND HERE.
A FOUL DEED.
THERE'S AN UNDER-STATEMENT, LOOSH OLD BEAN.
THAT IS WHY WE'RE GOING TO SETTLE THIS MATTER BEFORE HE RETURNS.
THE KID AIN'T GOING TO LIKE THIS WHEN HE GETS BACK. THAT'S FOR DAMN SURE.

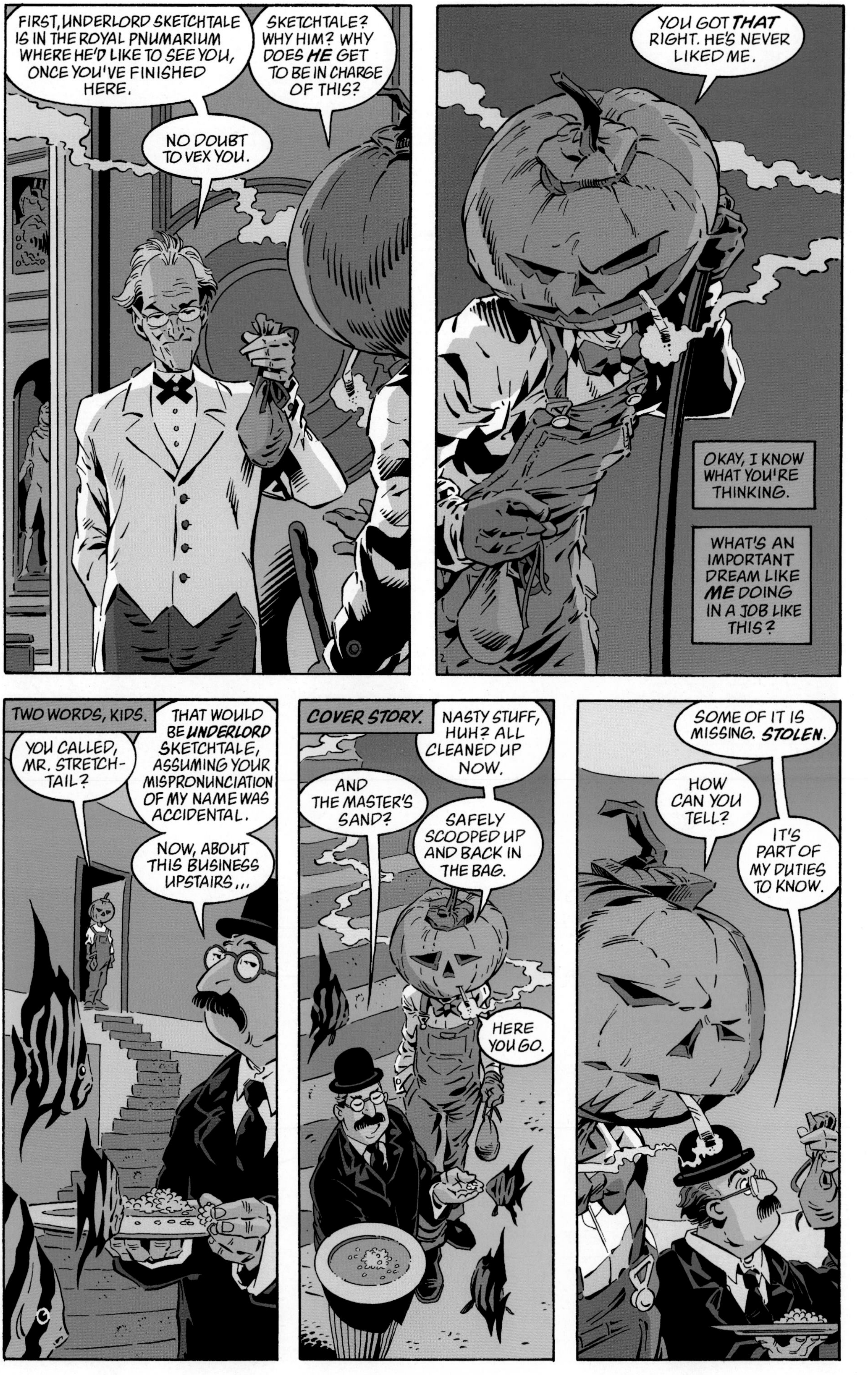
FIRST, UNDERLORD SKETCHTALE IS IN THE ROYAL PNUMARIUM WHERE HE'D LIKE TO SEE YOU, ONCE YOU'VE FINISHED HERE.
SKETCHTALE? WHY HIM? WHY DOES HE GET TO BE IN CHARGE OF THIS?
NO DOUBT TO VEX YOU.
YOU GOT THAT RIGHT. HE'S NEVER LIKED ME.
OKAY, I KNOW WHAT YOU'RE THINKING.
WHAT'S AN IMPORTANT DREAM LIKE ME DOING IN A JOB LIKE THIS?
TWO WORDS, KIDS.
YOU CALLED, MR. STRETCH-TAIL?
THAT WOULD BE UNDERLORD SKETCHTALE, ASSUMING YOUR MISPRONUNCIATION OF MY NAME WAS ACCIDENTAL.
NOW, ABOUT THIS BUSINESS UPSTAIRS...
COVER STORY.
NASTY STUFF, HUH? ALL CLEANED UP NOW.
AND THE MASTER'S SAND?
SAFELY SCOOPED UP AND BACK IN THE BAG.
HERE YOU GO.
SOME OF IT IS MISSING. STOLEN.
HOW CAN YOU TELL?
IT'S PART OF MY DUTIES TO KNOW.

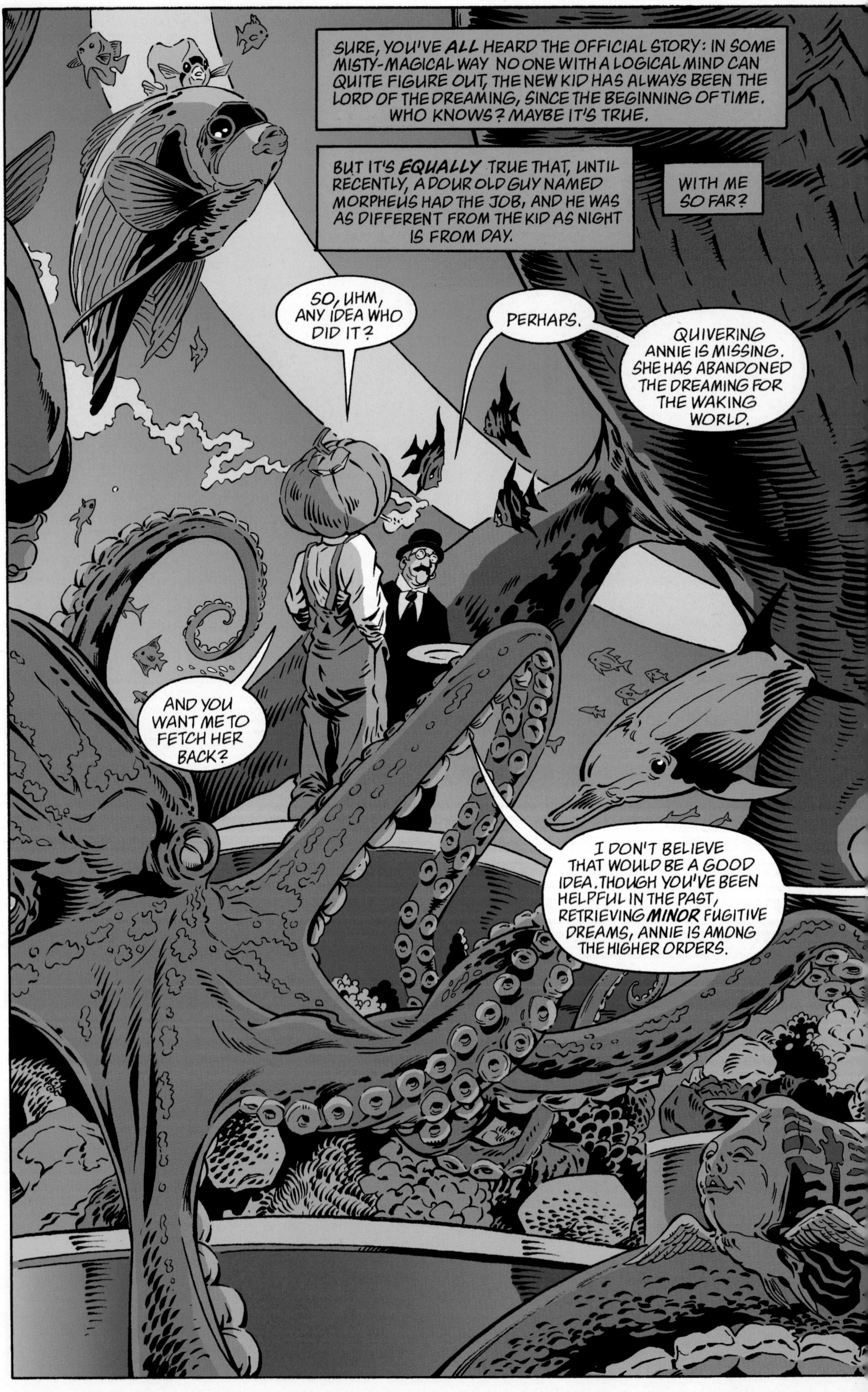
SURE, YOU'VE ALL HEARD THE OFFICIAL STORY: IN SOME MISTY-MAGICAL WAY NO ONE WITH A LOGICAL MIND CAN QUITE FIGURE OUT, THE NEW KID HAS ALWAYS BEEN THE LORD OF THE DREAMING, SINCE THE BEGINNING OF TIME. WHO KNOWS? MAYBE IT'S TRUE.
BUT IT'S EQUALLY TRUE THAT, UNTIL RECENTLY, A DOUR OLD GUY NAMED MORPHEUS HAD THE JOB, AND HE WAS AS DIFFERENT FROM THE KID AS NIGHT IS FROM DAY.
WITH ME SO FAR?
SO, UHM, ANY IDEA WHO DID IT?
PERHAPS.
QUIVERING ANNIE IS MISSING. SHE HAS ABANDONED THE DREAMING FOR THE WAKING WORLD.
AND YOU WANT ME TO FETCH HER BACK?
I DON'T BELIEVE THAT WOULD BE A GOOD IDEA. THOUGH YOU'VE BEEN HELPFUL IN THE PAST, RETRIEVING MINOR FUGITIVE DREAMS, ANNIE IS AMONG THE HIGHER ORDERS.

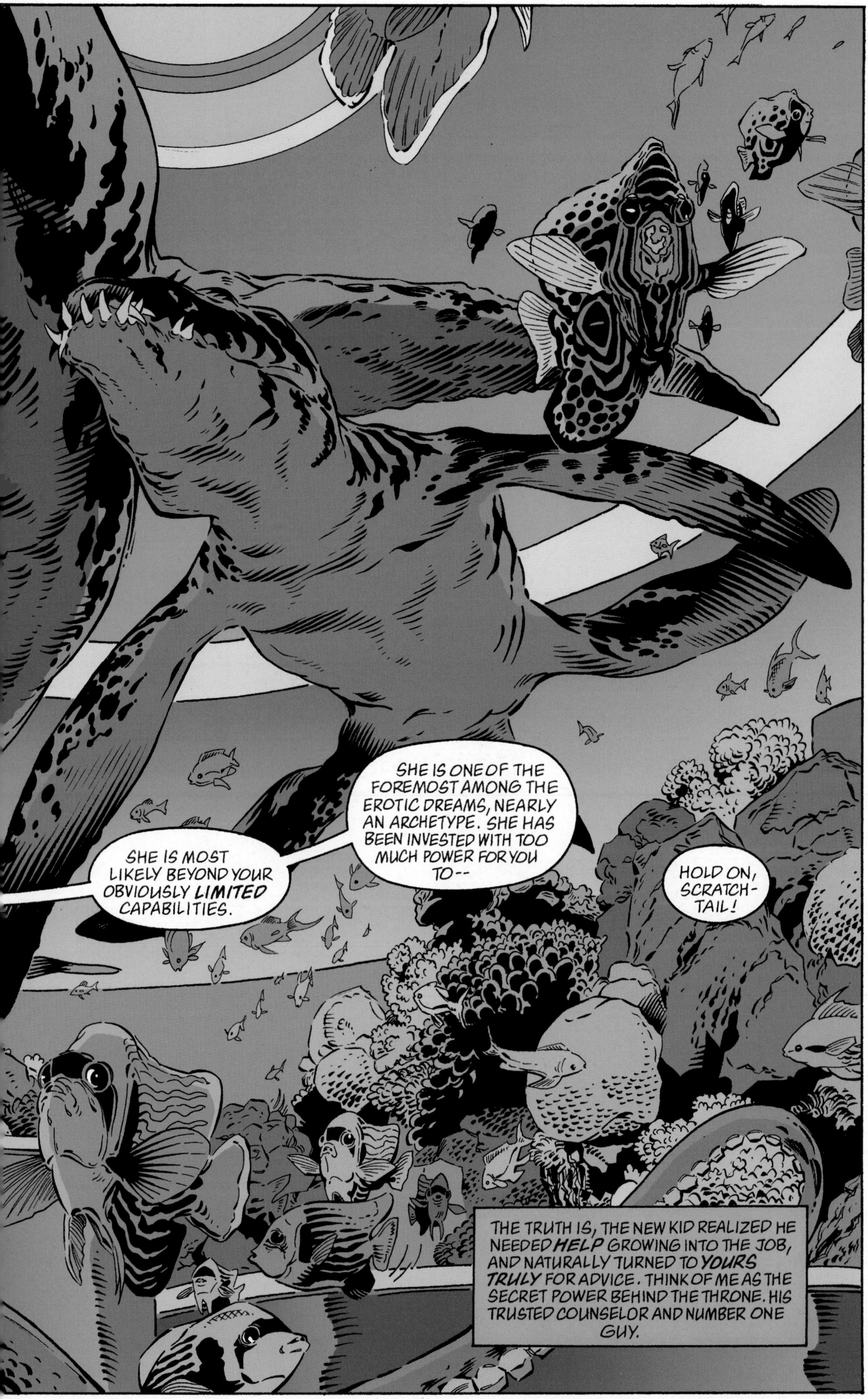
SHE IS MOST LIKELY BEYOND YOUR OBVIOUSLY LIMITED CAPABILITIES.
SHE IS ONE OF THE FOREMOST AMONG THE EROTIC DREAMS, NEARLY AN ARCHETYPE. SHE HAS BEEN INVESTED WITH TOO MUCH POWER FOR YOU TO--
HOLD ON, SCRATCH-TAIL!
THE TRUTH IS, THE NEW KID REALIZED HE NEEDED HELP GROWING INTO THE JOB, AND NATURALLY TURNED TO YOURS TRULY FOR ADVICE. THINK OF ME AS THE SECRET POWER BEHIND THE THRONE. HIS TRUSTED COUNSELOR AND NUMBER ONE GUY.

TRUTH IS, THE KID WON'T MAKE A **MOVE** WITHOUT CONSULTING ME FIRST. IT'S EVERYTHING I CAN **DO** TO KEEP THE POOR LI'L FELLA FROM DRAGGING ME ALONG TO FAMILY MEETINGS.

JUST GIVE ME A CHANCE!

I'M TOUGH!

I'M SMART!

YOU'RE A JANITOR.

I'M THE GUY WHO REALLY RUNS THIS PLACE. NO BRAG, JUST **FACT.** ME AND THE KID COOKED UP THE JANITOR COVER AS A BIT O' WHADDAYA-CALLIT? MISDIRECTION?

I CAN DO THE JOB! I **KNOW** I CAN!

TRUST ME!

GET UP, YOU DAMNED FOOL. YOU LOOK **RIDICULOUS.**

ALL THE OTHER DREAMS WOULD GET JEALOUS IF IT WERE COMMONLY KNOWN THAT I WAS **EL DREEMO SUPREEMO** (NUMERO DOSE) AROUND HERE.

IF I WERE TO LET YOU TRY THIS--

HOT **DAMN!**

--PROMISE ME YOU'LL CALL FOR HELP THE MOMENT YOU FIND YOURSELF IN OVER YOUR HEAD.

THEY'RE A MOROSE COLLECTION OF SULKY BASTARDS AS IT IS. IMAGINE IF THEY **KNEW** THAT **I'M** THE GUY WHO REALLY CALLS THE **SHOTS** AROUND HERE.

YOU WON'T REGRET THIS, SKRUNCH-TOIL!

I ALREADY DO.

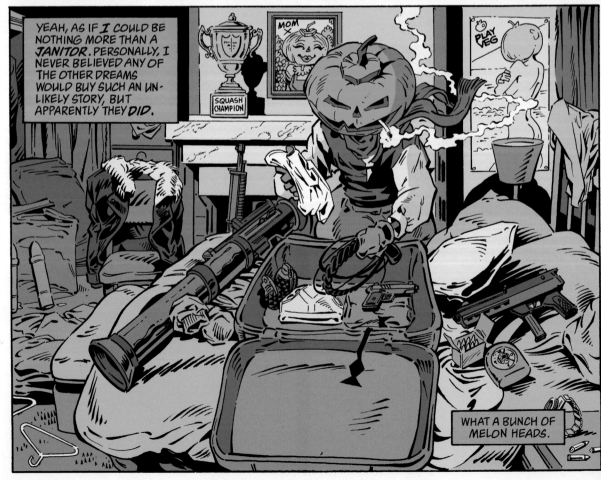

YEAH, AS IF **I** COULD BE NOTHING MORE THAN A **JANITOR.** PERSONALLY, I NEVER BELIEVED ANY OF THE OTHER DREAMS WOULD BUY SUCH AN UNLIKELY STORY, BUT APPARENTLY THEY **DID.**

SQUASH CHAMPION

MOM

PLAY VEG

WHAT A BUNCH OF MELON HEADS.

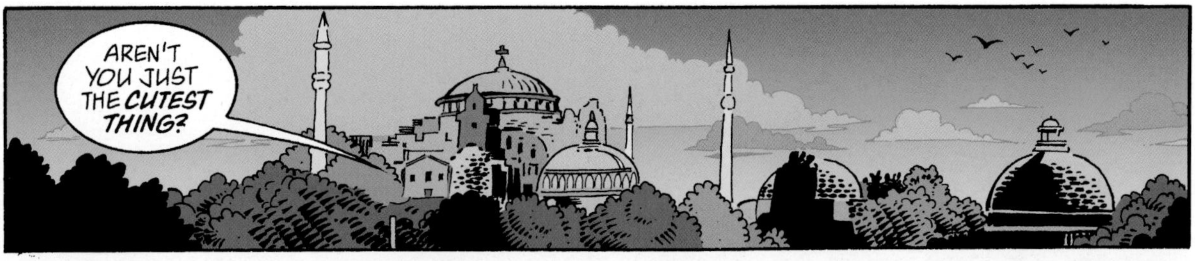
AREN'T YOU JUST THE CUTEST THING?

CHAPTER TWO: DOCTOR CROW

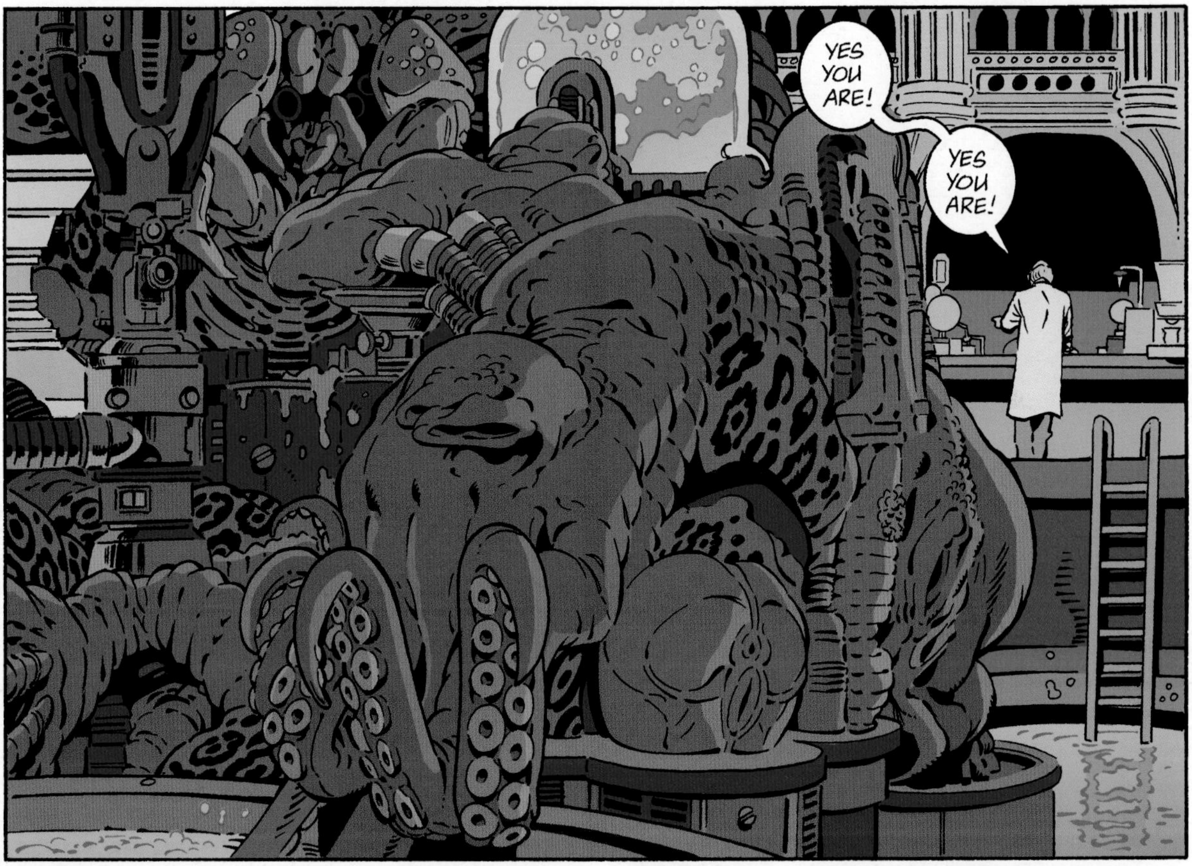
YES YOU ARE!
YES YOU ARE!

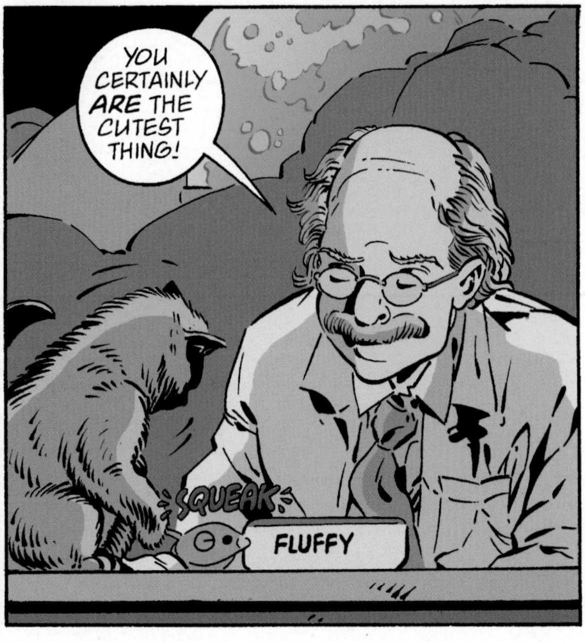
YOU CERTAINLY ARE THE CUTEST THING!
SQUEAK
FLUFFY

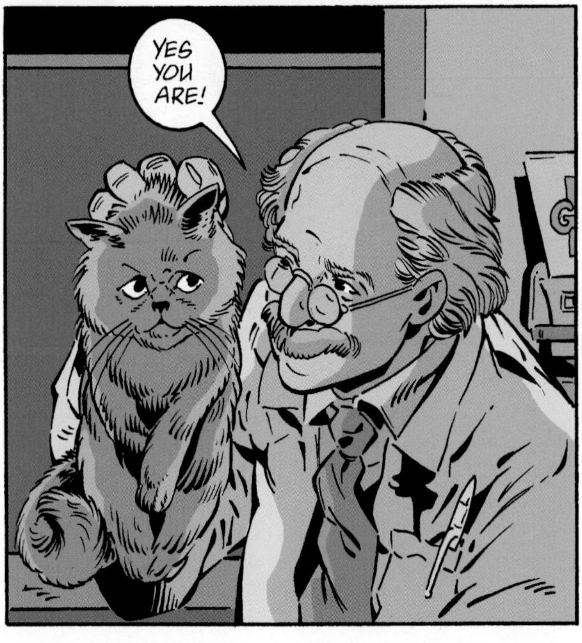
YES YOU ARE!

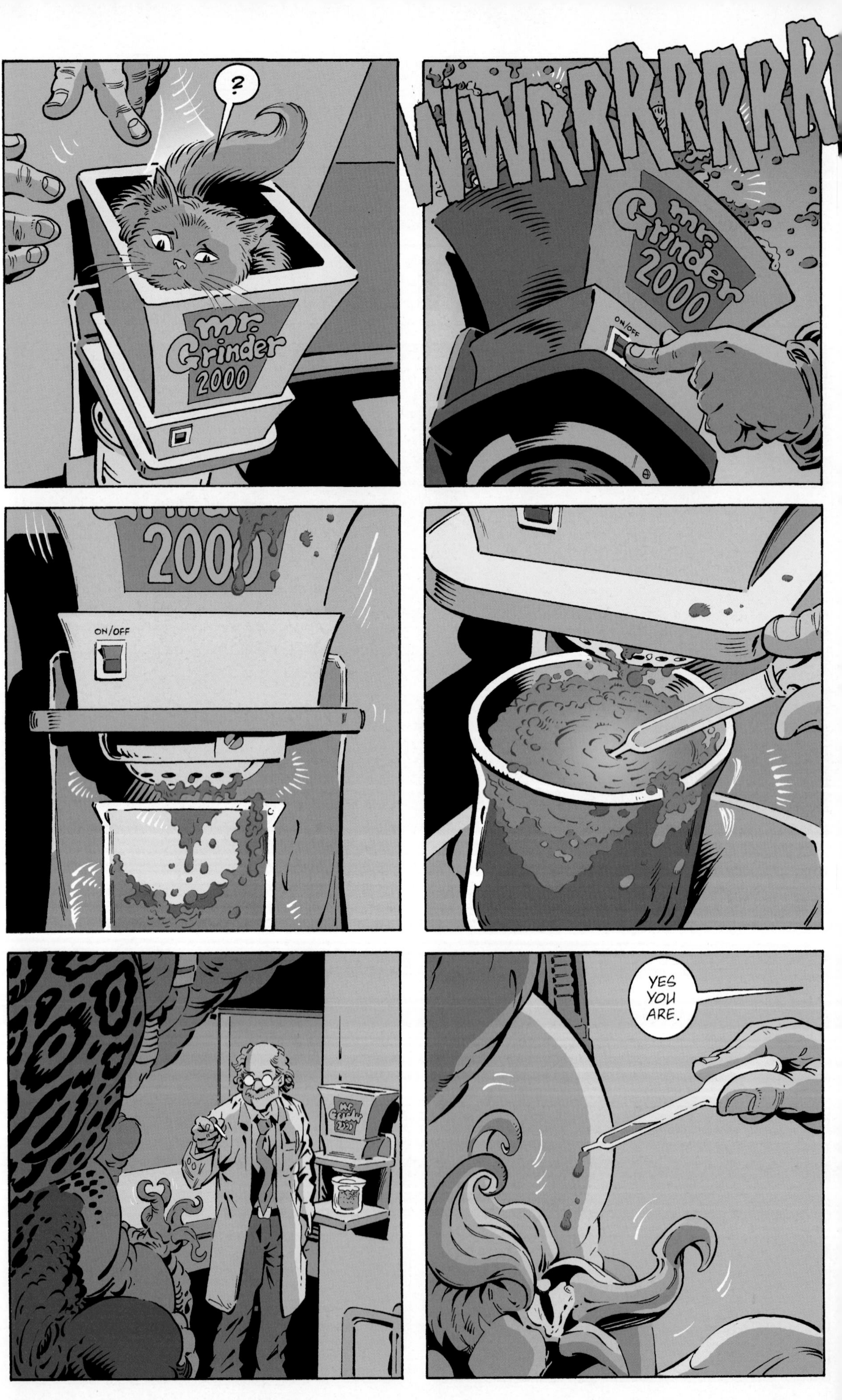
?
mr. Grinder 2000
WWRRRRRRRR
mr. Grinder 2000
ON/OFF
2000
ON/OFF
YES YOU ARE.

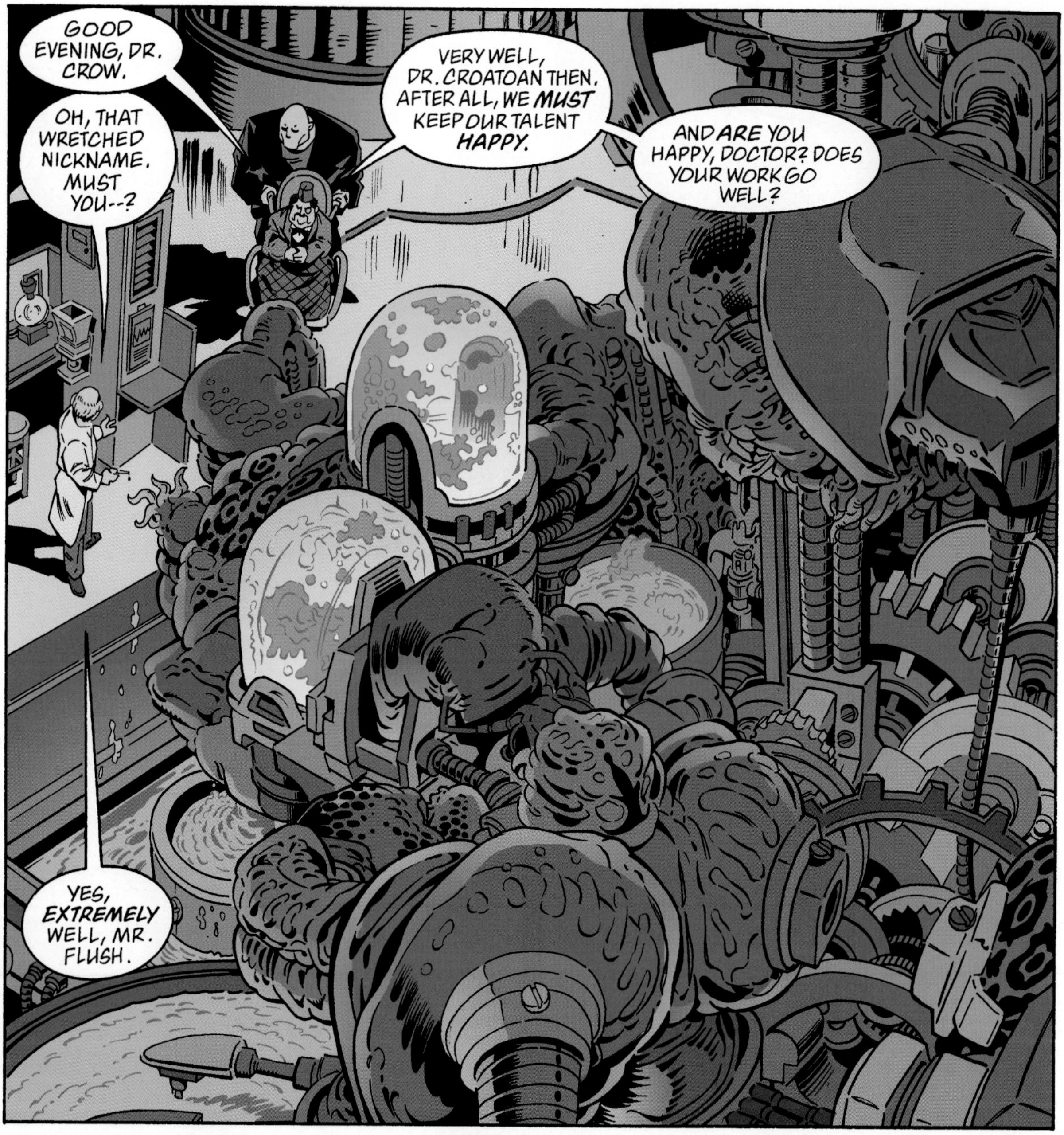
GOOD EVENING, DR. CROW.
OH, THAT WRETCHED NICKNAME. MUST YOU--?
VERY WELL, DR. CROATOAN THEN. AFTER ALL, WE MUST KEEP OUR TALENT HAPPY.
AND ARE YOU HAPPY, DOCTOR? DOES YOUR WORK GO WELL?
YES, EXTREMELY WELL, MR. FLUSH.
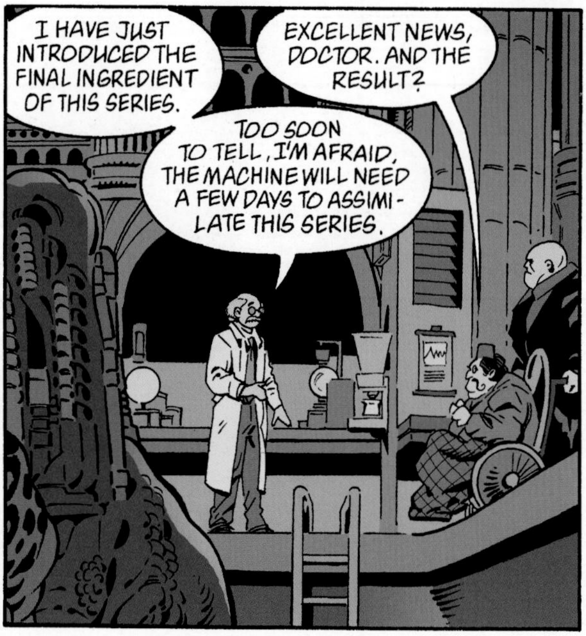
I HAVE JUST INTRODUCED THE FINAL INGREDIENT OF THIS SERIES.
EXCELLENT NEWS, DOCTOR. AND THE RESULT?
TOO SOON TO TELL, I'M AFRAID, THE MACHINE WILL NEED A FEW DAYS TO ASSIMI-LATE THIS SERIES.
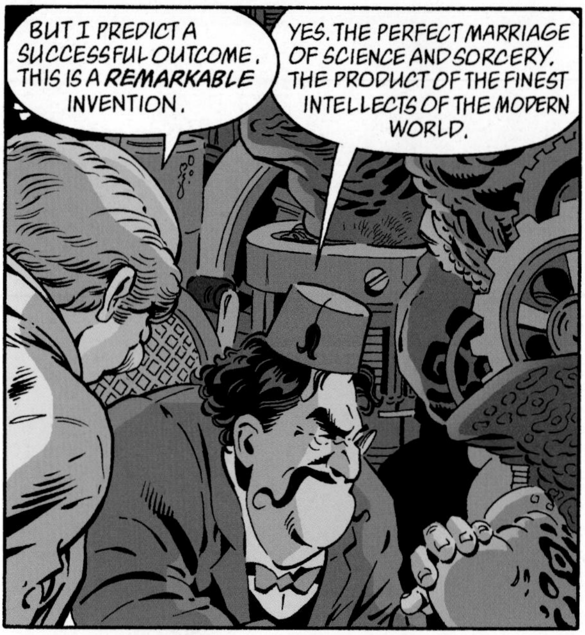
BUT I PREDICT A SUCCESSFUL OUTCOME. THIS IS A REMARKABLE INVENTION.
YES. THE PERFECT MARRIAGE OF SCIENCE AND SORCERY. THE PRODUCT OF THE FINEST INTELLECTS OF THE MODERN WORLD.

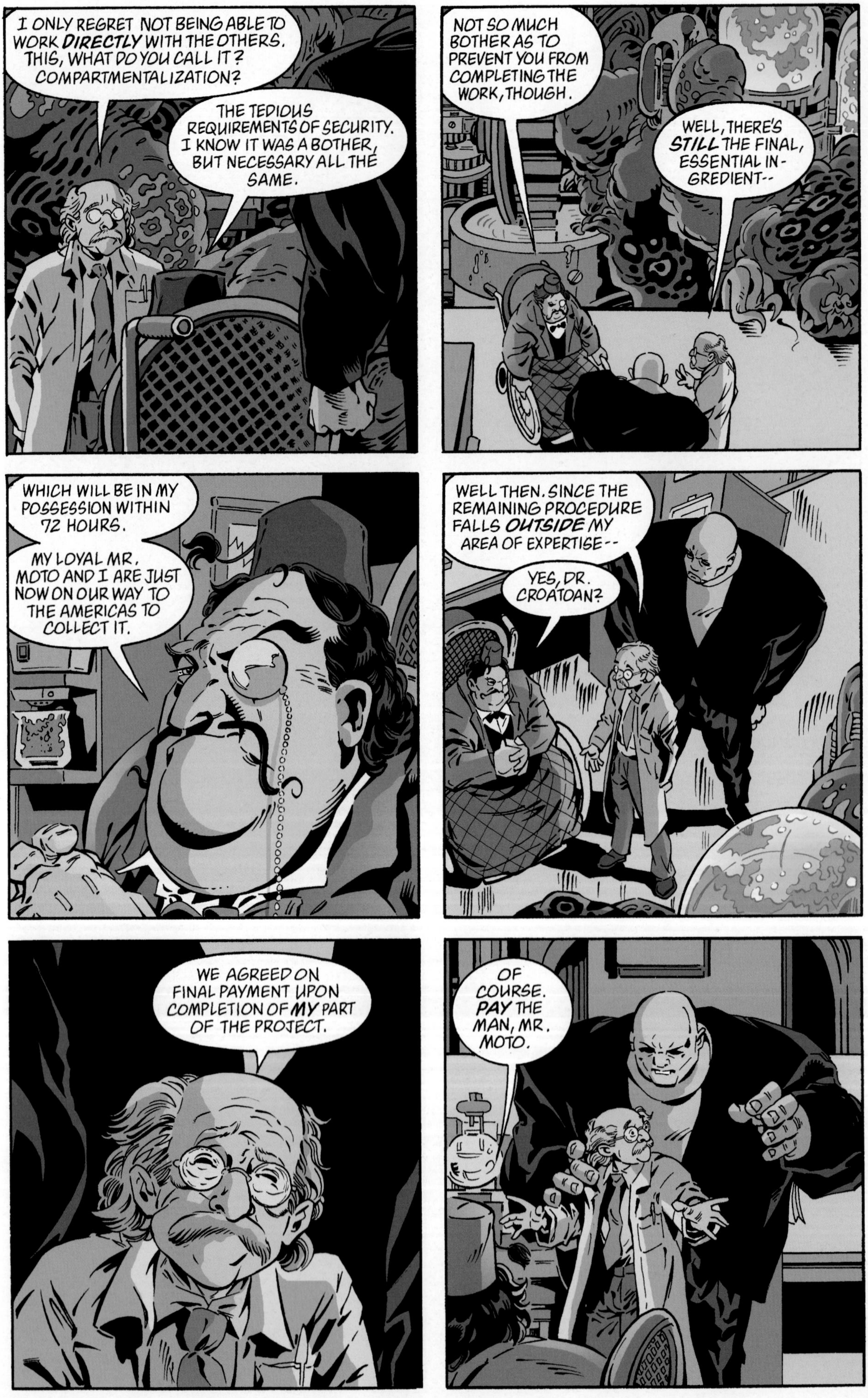
I ONLY REGRET NOT BEING ABLE TO WORK DIRECTLY WITH THE OTHERS. THIS, WHAT DO YOU CALL IT? COMPARTMENTALIZATION?
THE TEDIOUS REQUIREMENTS OF SECURITY. I KNOW IT WAS A BOTHER, BUT NECESSARY ALL THE SAME.
NOT SO MUCH BOTHER AS TO PREVENT YOU FROM COMPLETING THE WORK, THOUGH.
WELL, THERE'S STILL THE FINAL, ESSENTIAL IN-GREDIENT--
WHICH WILL BE IN MY POSSESSION WITHIN 72 HOURS.
MY LOYAL MR. MOTO AND I ARE JUST NOW ON OUR WAY TO THE AMERICAS TO COLLECT IT.
WELL THEN. SINCE THE REMAINING PROCEDURE FALLS OUTSIDE MY AREA OF EXPERTISE--
YES, DR. CROATOAN?
WE AGREED ON FINAL PAYMENT UPON COMPLETION OF MY PART OF THE PROJECT.
OF COURSE. PAY THE MAN, MR. MOTO.

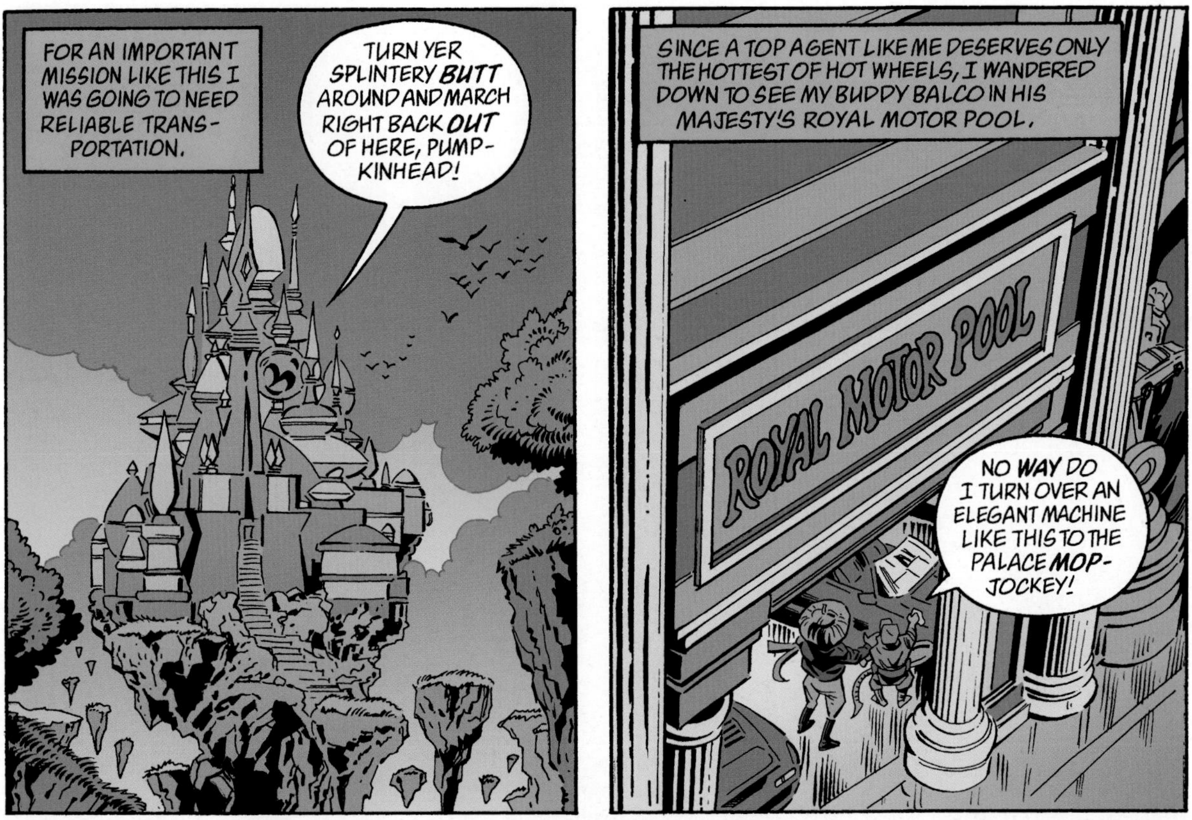
FOR AN IMPORTANT MISSION LIKE THIS I WAS GOING TO NEED RELIABLE TRANS-PORTATION.
TURN YER SPLINTERY BUTT AROUND AND MARCH RIGHT BACK OUT OF HERE, PUMP-KINHEAD!
SINCE A TOP AGENT LIKE ME DESERVES ONLY THE HOTTEST OF HOT WHEELS, I WANDERED DOWN TO SEE MY BUDDY BALCO IN HIS MAJESTY'S ROYAL MOTOR POOL.
ROYAL MOTOR POOL
NO WAY DO I TURN OVER AN ELEGANT MACHINE LIKE THIS TO THE PALACE MOP-JOCKEY!

CHAPTER THREE: FROM the DREAMING with LOVE

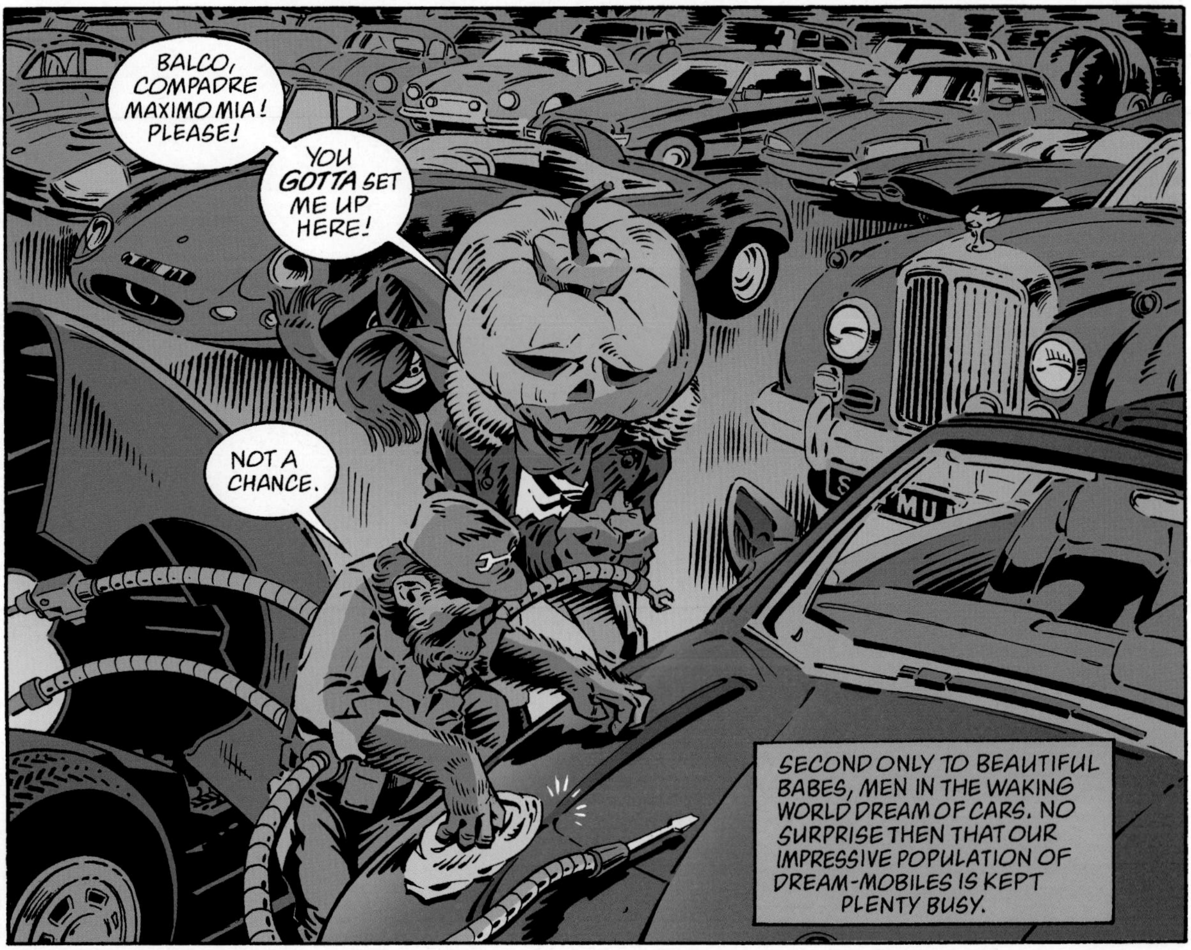
BALCO, COMPADRE MAXIMO MIA! PLEASE!
YOU GOTTA SET ME UP HERE!
NOT A CHANCE.
SECOND ONLY TO BEAUTIFUL BABES, MEN IN THE WAKING WORLD DREAM OF CARS. NO SURPRISE THEN THAT OUR IMPRESSIVE POPULATION OF DREAM-MOBILES IS KEPT PLENTY BUSY.

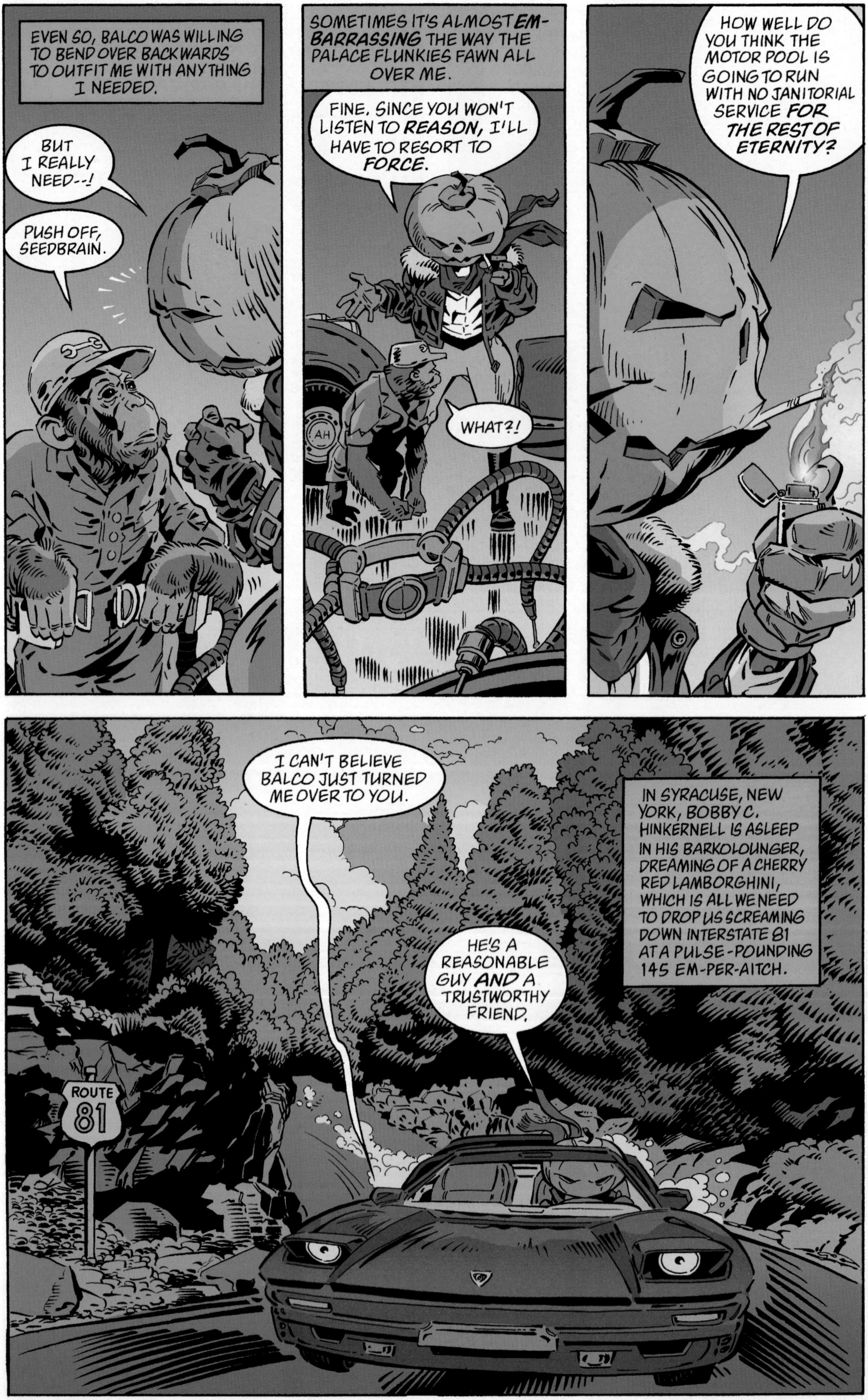
EVEN SO, BALCO WAS WILLING TO BEND OVER BACKWARDS TO OUTFIT ME WITH ANYTHING I NEEDED.
BUT I REALLY NEED--!
PUSH OFF, SEEDBRAIN.
SOMETIMES IT'S ALMOST EMBARRASSING THE WAY THE PALACE FLUNKIES FAWN ALL OVER ME.
FINE. SINCE YOU WON'T LISTEN TO REASON, I'LL HAVE TO RESORT TO FORCE.
WHAT?!
HOW WELL DO YOU THINK THE MOTOR POOL IS GOING TO RUN WITH NO JANITORIAL SERVICE FOR THE REST OF ETERNITY?
I CAN'T BELIEVE BALCO JUST TURNED ME OVER TO YOU.
IN SYRACUSE, NEW YORK, BOBBY C. HINKERNELL IS ASLEEP IN HIS BARKOLOUNGER, DREAMING OF A CHERRY RED LAMBORGHINI, WHICH IS ALL WE NEED TO DROP US SCREAMING DOWN INTERSTATE 81 AT A PULSE-POUNDING 145 EM-PER-AITCH.
HE'S A REASONABLE GUY AND A TRUSTWORTHY FRIEND.
ROUTE 81

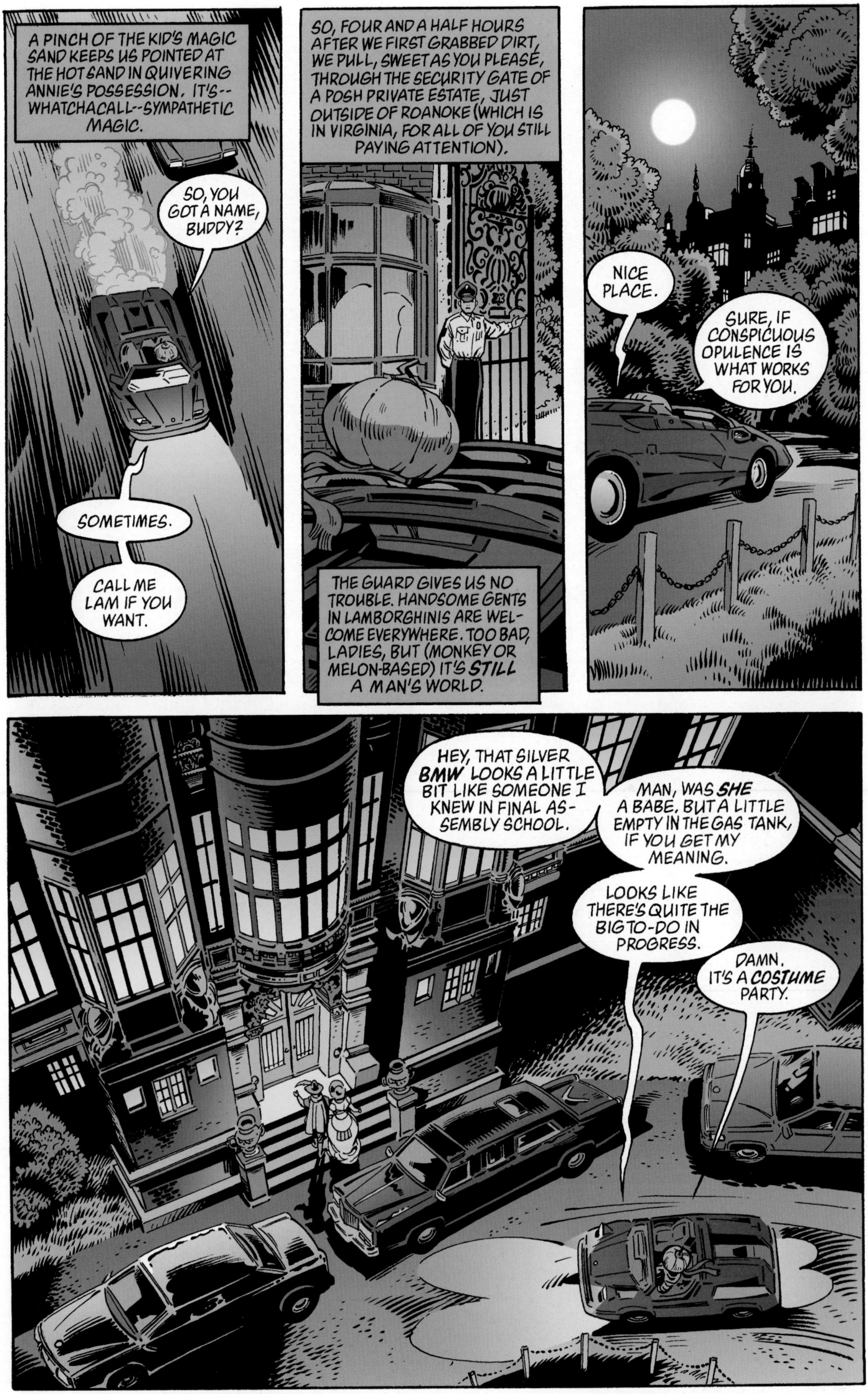
A PINCH OF THE KID'S MAGIC SAND KEEPS US POINTED AT THE HOT SAND IN QUIVERING ANNIE'S POSSESSION. IT'S--WHATCHACALL--SYMPATHETIC MAGIC.
SO, YOU GOT A NAME, BUDDY?
SOMETIMES.
CALL ME LAM IF YOU WANT.
SO, FOUR AND A HALF HOURS AFTER WE FIRST GRABBED DIRT, WE PULL, SWEET AS YOU PLEASE, THROUGH THE SECURITY GATE OF A POSH PRIVATE ESTATE, JUST OUTSIDE OF ROANOKE (WHICH IS IN VIRGINIA, FOR ALL OF YOU STILL PAYING ATTENTION).
THE GUARD GIVES US NO TROUBLE. HANDSOME GENTS IN LAMBORGHINIS ARE WELCOME EVERYWHERE. TOO BAD, LADIES, BUT (MONKEY OR MELON-BASED) IT'S **STILL** A MAN'S WORLD.
NICE PLACE.
SURE, IF CONSPICUOUS OPULENCE IS WHAT WORKS FOR YOU.
HEY, THAT SILVER **BMW** LOOKS A LITTLE BIT LIKE SOMEONE I KNEW IN FINAL ASSEMBLY SCHOOL.
MAN, WAS **SHE** A BABE, BUT A LITTLE EMPTY IN THE GAS TANK, IF YOU GET MY MEANING.
LOOKS LIKE THERE'S QUITE THE BIG TO-DO IN PROGRESS.
DAMN. IT'S A **COSTUME** PARTY.

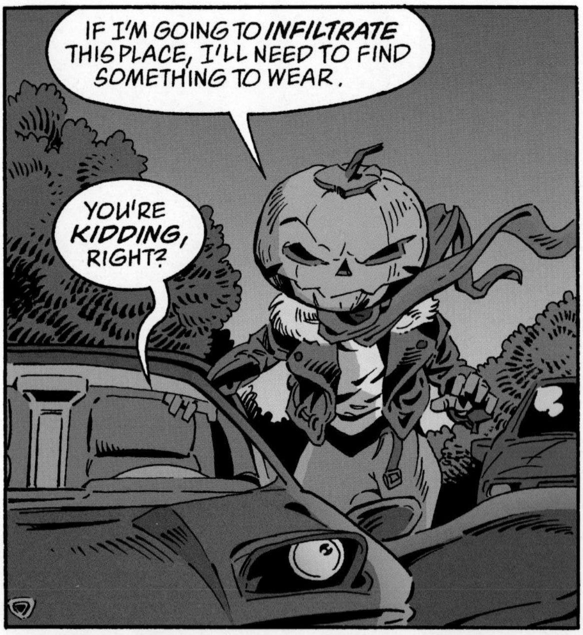
IF I'M GOING TO *INFILTRATE* THIS PLACE, I'LL NEED TO FIND SOMETHING TO WEAR.
YOU'RE *KIDDING*, RIGHT?

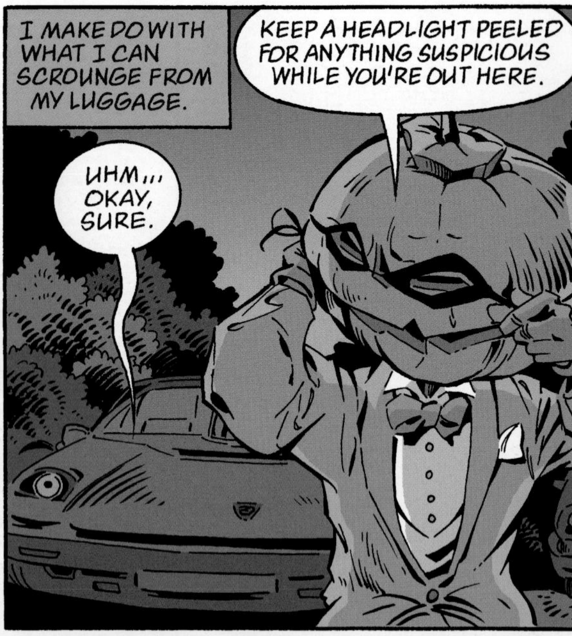
I MAKE DO WITH WHAT I CAN SCROUNGE FROM MY LUGGAGE.
KEEP A HEADLIGHT PEELED FOR ANYTHING SUSPICIOUS WHILE YOU'RE OUT HERE.
UHM... OKAY, SURE.

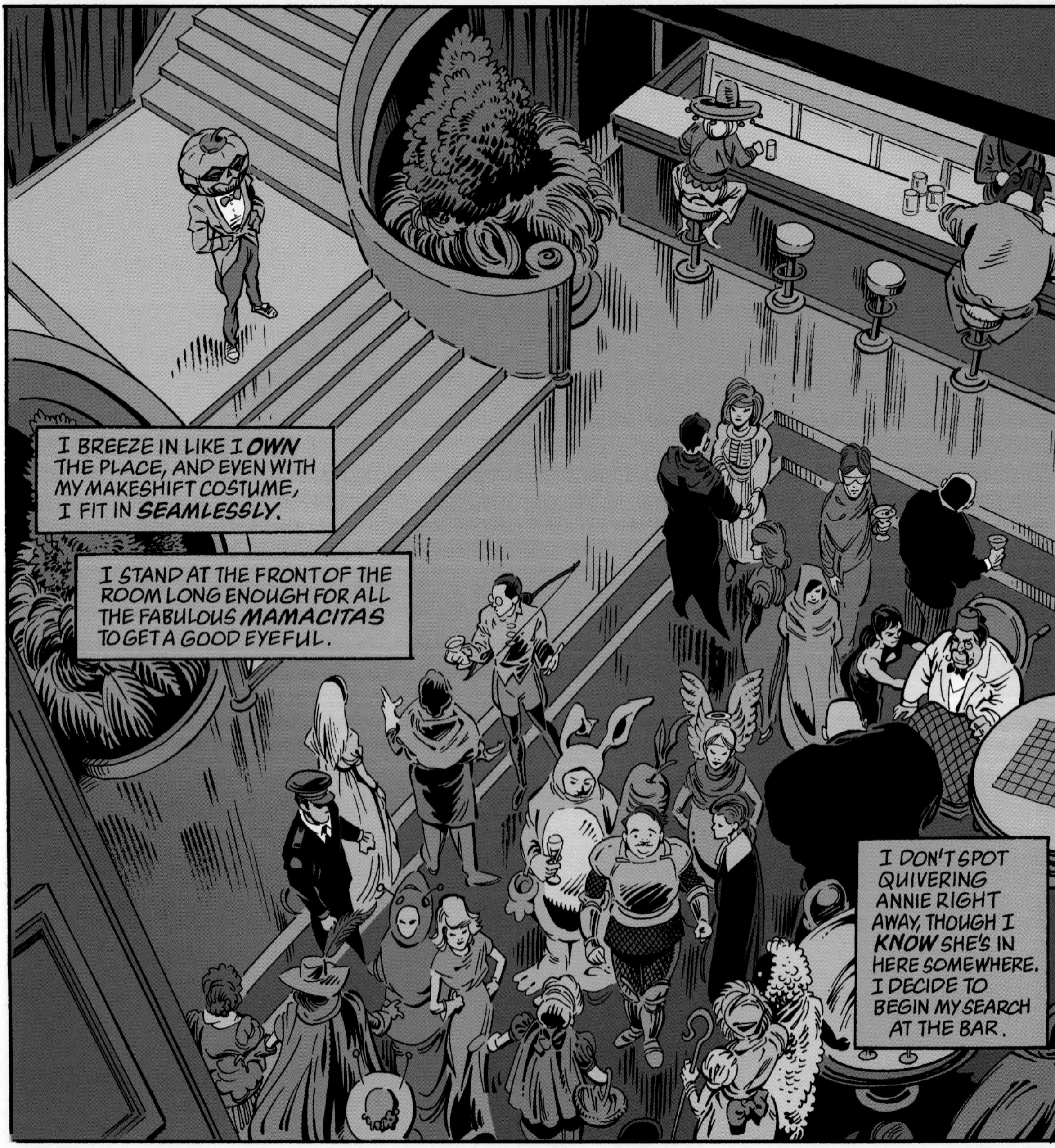
I BREEZE IN LIKE I *OWN* THE PLACE, AND EVEN WITH MY MAKESHIFT COSTUME, I FIT IN *SEAMLESSLY*.
I STAND AT THE FRONT OF THE ROOM LONG ENOUGH FOR ALL THE FABULOUS *MAMACITAS* TO GET A GOOD EYEFUL.
I DON'T SPOT QUIVERING ANNIE RIGHT AWAY, THOUGH I *KNOW* SHE'S IN HERE SOMEWHERE. I DECIDE TO BEGIN MY SEARCH AT THE BAR.

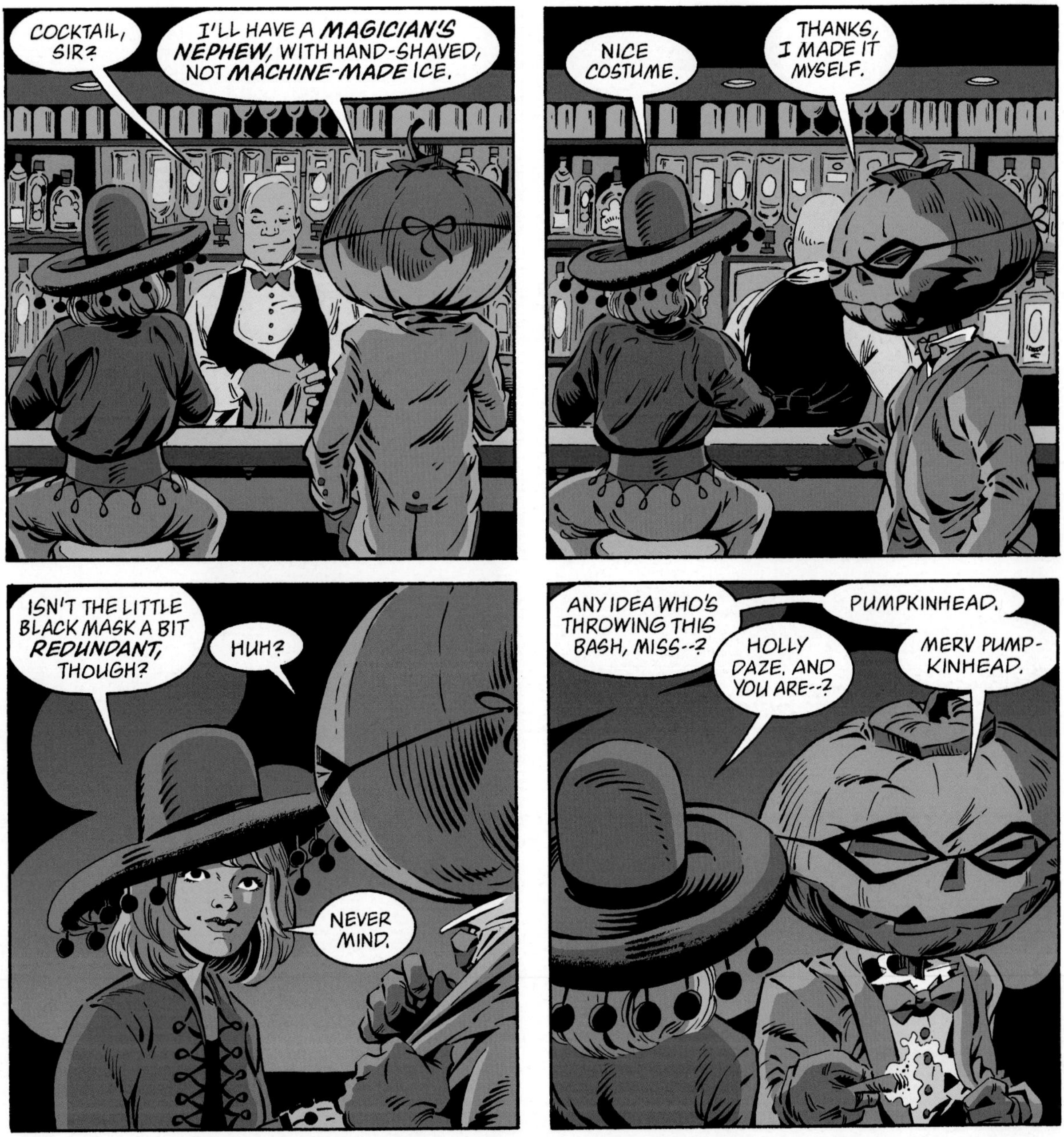
COCKTAIL, SIR?
I'LL HAVE A MAGICIAN'S NEPHEW, WITH HAND-SHAVED, NOT MACHINE-MADE ICE.
NICE COSTUME.
THANKS, I MADE IT MYSELF.
ISN'T THE LITTLE BLACK MASK A BIT REDUNDANT, THOUGH?
HUH?
NEVER MIND.
ANY IDEA WHO'S THROWING THIS BASH, MISS--?
HOLLY DAZE. AND YOU ARE--?
PUMPKINHEAD.
MERV PUMPKINHEAD.

CHAPTER FOUR: UNDERBALL

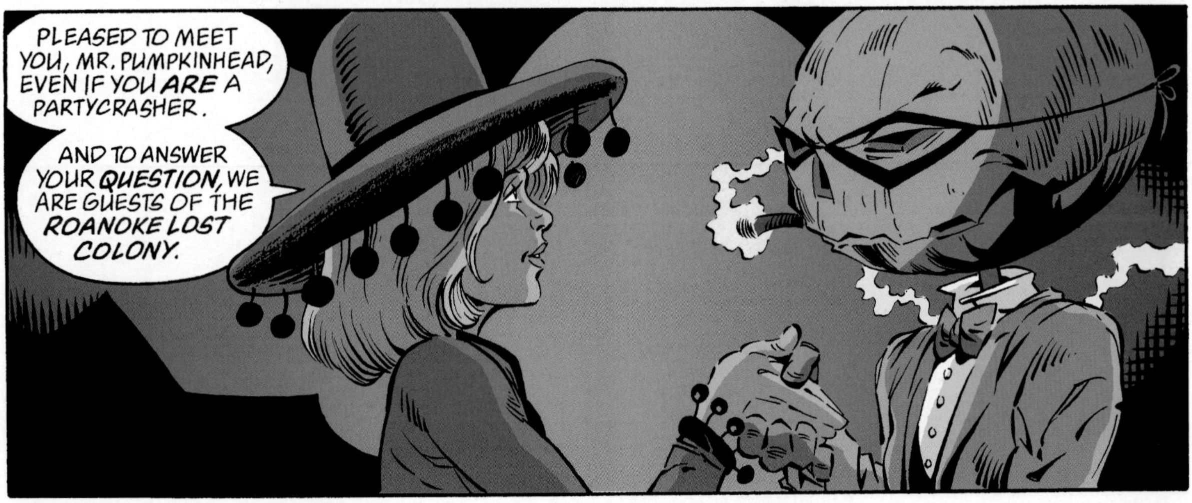
PLEASED TO MEET YOU, MR. PUMPKINHEAD, EVEN IF YOU ARE A PARTYCRASHER.
AND TO ANSWER YOUR QUESTION, WE ARE GUESTS OF THE ROANOKE LOST COLONY.

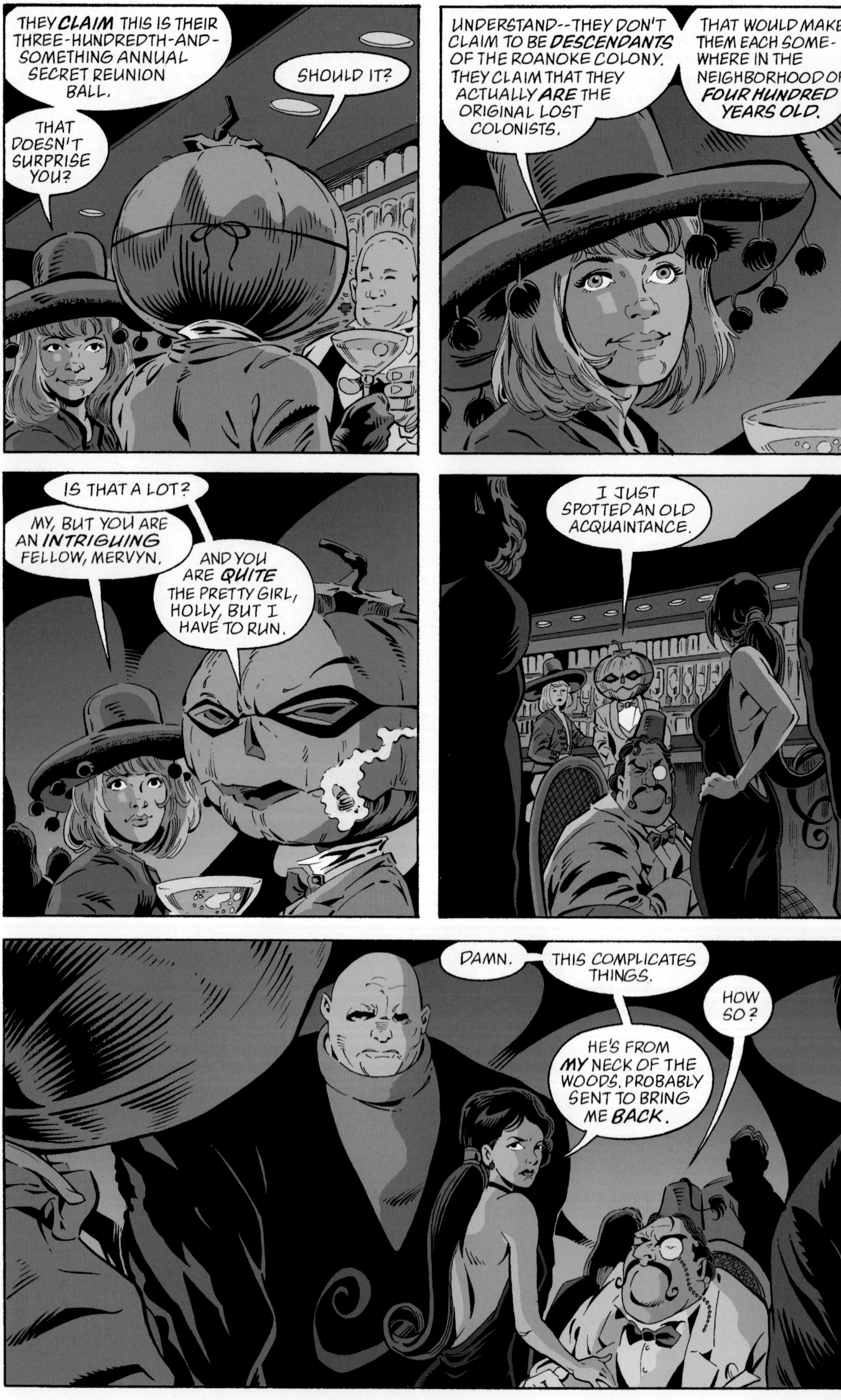
THEY CLAIM THIS IS THEIR THREE-HUNDREDTH-AND-SOMETHING ANNUAL SECRET REUNION BALL.
SHOULD IT?
THAT DOESN'T SURPRISE YOU?
UNDERSTAND--THEY DON'T CLAIM TO BE DESCENDANTS OF THE ROANOKE COLONY. THEY CLAIM THAT THEY ACTUALLY ARE THE ORIGINAL LOST COLONISTS.
THAT WOULD MAKE THEM EACH SOMEWHERE IN THE NEIGHBORHOOD OF FOUR HUNDRED YEARS OLD.
IS THAT A LOT?
MY, BUT YOU ARE AN INTRIGUING FELLOW, MERVYN.
AND YOU ARE QUITE THE PRETTY GIRL, HOLLY, BUT I HAVE TO RUN.
I JUST SPOTTED AN OLD ACQUAINTANCE.
DAMN.
THIS COMPLICATES THINGS.
HOW SO?
HE'S FROM MY NECK OF THE WOODS, PROBABLY SENT TO BRING ME BACK.

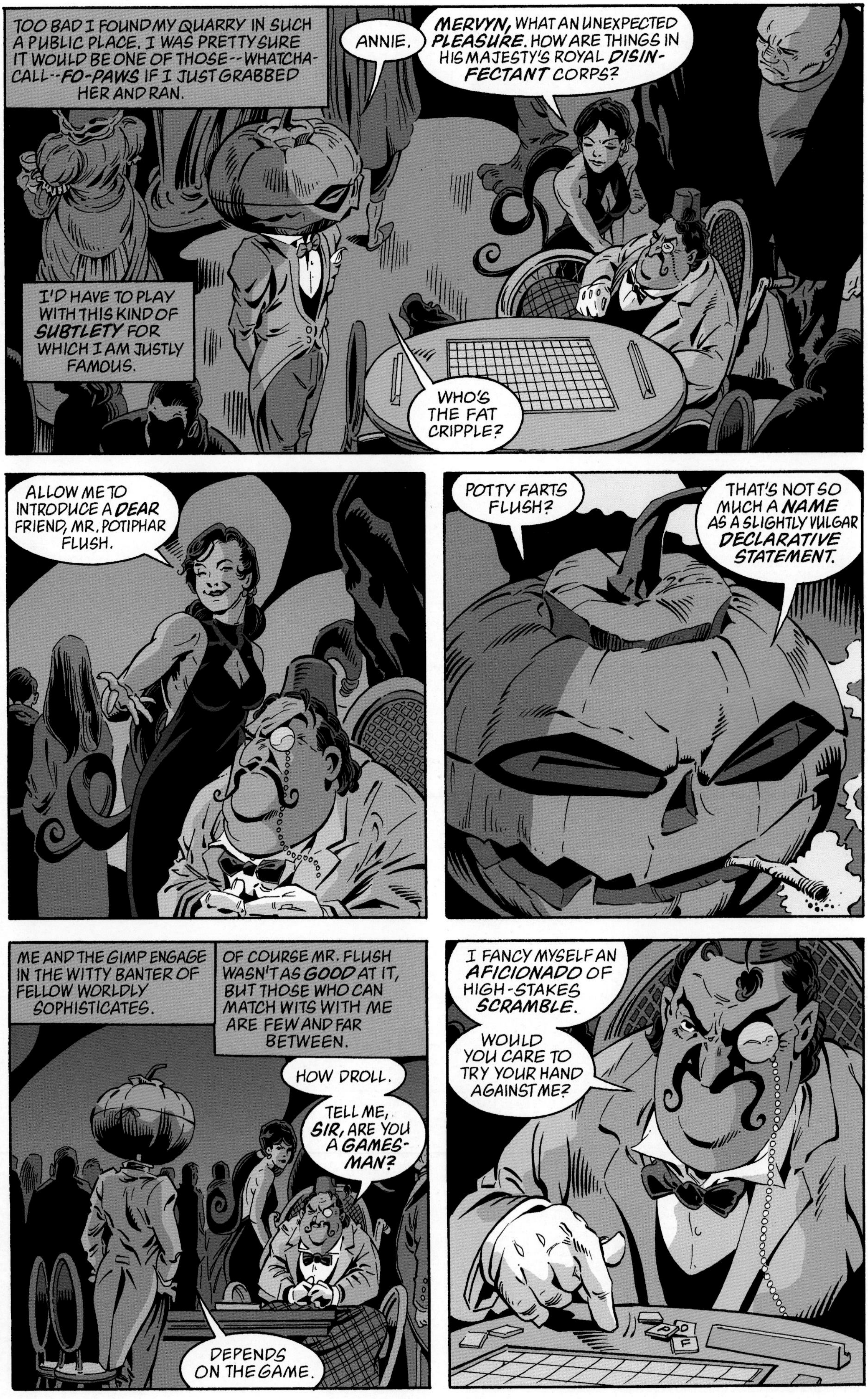
TOO BAD I FOUND MY QUARRY IN SUCH A PUBLIC PLACE. I WAS PRETTY SURE IT WOULD BE ONE OF THOSE--WHATCHA-CALL--FO-PAWS IF I JUST GRABBED HER AND RAN.
ANNIE.
MERVYN, WHAT AN UNEXPECTED PLEASURE. HOW ARE THINGS IN HIS MAJESTY'S ROYAL DISIN-FECTANT CORPS?
I'D HAVE TO PLAY WITH THIS KIND OF SUBTLETY FOR WHICH I AM JUSTLY FAMOUS.
WHO'S THE FAT CRIPPLE?
ALLOW ME TO INTRODUCE A DEAR FRIEND, MR. POTIPHAR FLUSH.
POTTY FARTS FLUSH?
THAT'S NOT SO MUCH A NAME AS A SLIGHTLY VULGAR DECLARATIVE STATEMENT.
ME AND THE GIMP ENGAGE IN THE WITTY BANTER OF FELLOW WORLDLY SOPHISTICATES.
OF COURSE MR. FLUSH WASN'T AS GOOD AT IT, BUT THOSE WHO CAN MATCH WITS WITH ME ARE FEW AND FAR BETWEEN.
HOW DROLL.
TELL ME, SIR, ARE YOU A GAMES-MAN?
DEPENDS ON THE GAME.
I FANCY MYSELF AN AFICIONADO OF HIGH-STAKES SCRAMBLE.
WOULD YOU CARE TO TRY YOUR HAND AGAINST ME?

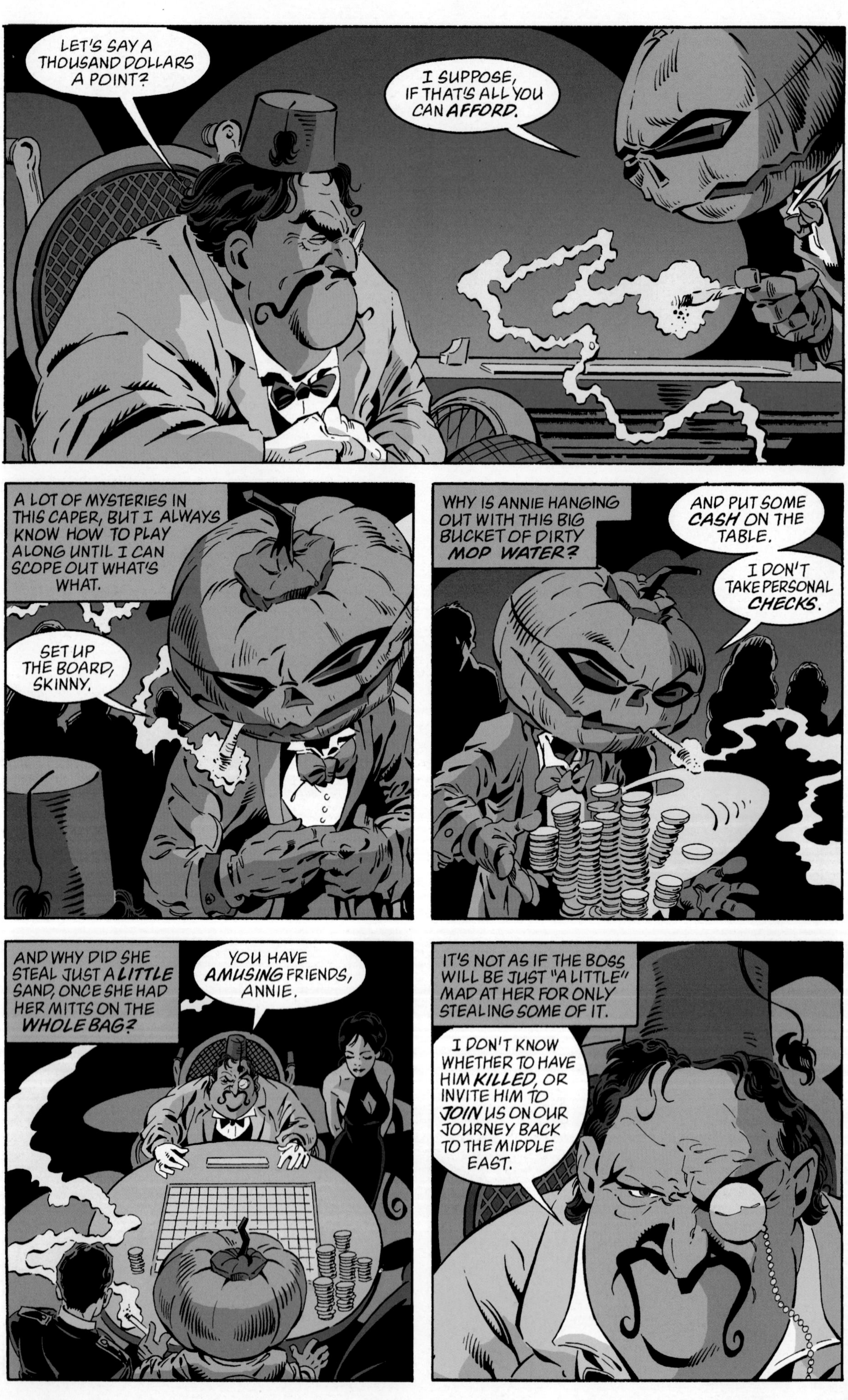
LET'S SAY A THOUSAND DOLLARS A POINT?
I SUPPOSE, IF THAT'S ALL YOU CAN AFFORD.
A LOT OF MYSTERIES IN THIS CAPER, BUT I ALWAYS KNOW HOW TO PLAY ALONG UNTIL I CAN SCOPE OUT WHAT'S WHAT.
SET UP THE BOARD, SKINNY.
WHY IS ANNIE HANGING OUT WITH THIS BIG BUCKET OF DIRTY MOP WATER?
AND PUT SOME CASH ON THE TABLE.
I DON'T TAKE PERSONAL CHECKS.
AND WHY DID SHE STEAL JUST A LITTLE SAND, ONCE SHE HAD HER MITTS ON THE WHOLE BAG?
YOU HAVE AMUSING FRIENDS, ANNIE.
IT'S NOT AS IF THE BOSS WILL BE JUST "A LITTLE" MAD AT HER FOR ONLY STEALING SOME OF IT.
I DON'T KNOW WHETHER TO HAVE HIM KILLED, OR INVITE HIM TO JOIN US ON OUR JOURNEY BACK TO THE MIDDLE EAST.

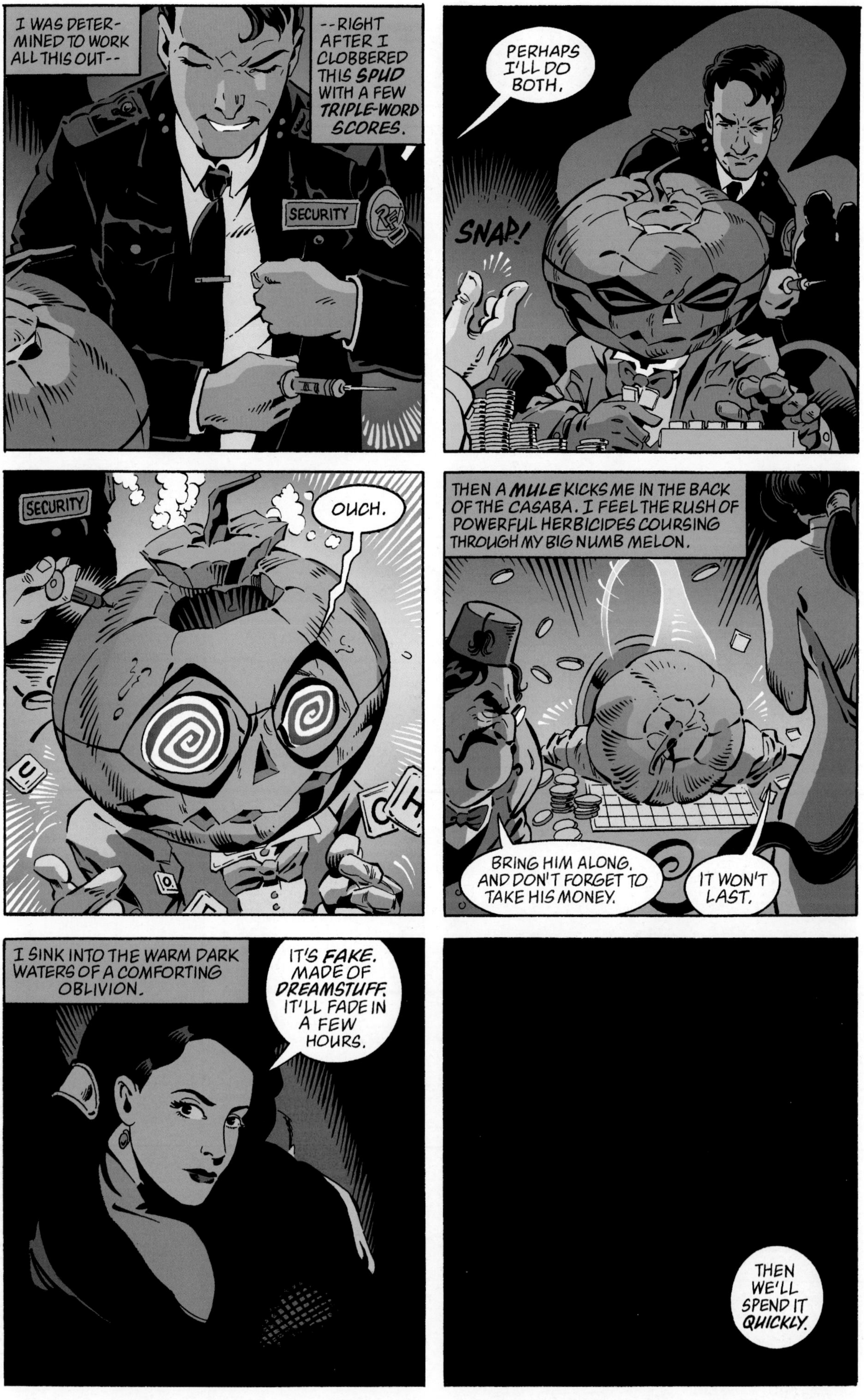
I WAS DETERMINED TO WORK ALL THIS OUT--
--RIGHT AFTER I CLOBBERED THIS SPUD WITH A FEW TRIPLE-WORD SCORES.
SECURITY
PERHAPS I'LL DO BOTH.
SNAP!
SECURITY
OUCH.
THEN A MULE KICKS ME IN THE BACK OF THE CASABA. I FEEL THE RUSH OF POWERFUL HERBICIDES COURSING THROUGH MY BIG NUMB MELON.
BRING HIM ALONG, AND DON'T FORGET TO TAKE HIS MONEY.
IT WON'T LAST.
I SINK INTO THE WARM DARK WATERS OF A COMFORTING OBLIVION.
IT'S FAKE. MADE OF DREAMSTUFF. IT'LL FADE IN A FEW HOURS.
THEN WE'LL SPEND IT QUICKLY.

CHAPTER FIVE: GOURDFINGER

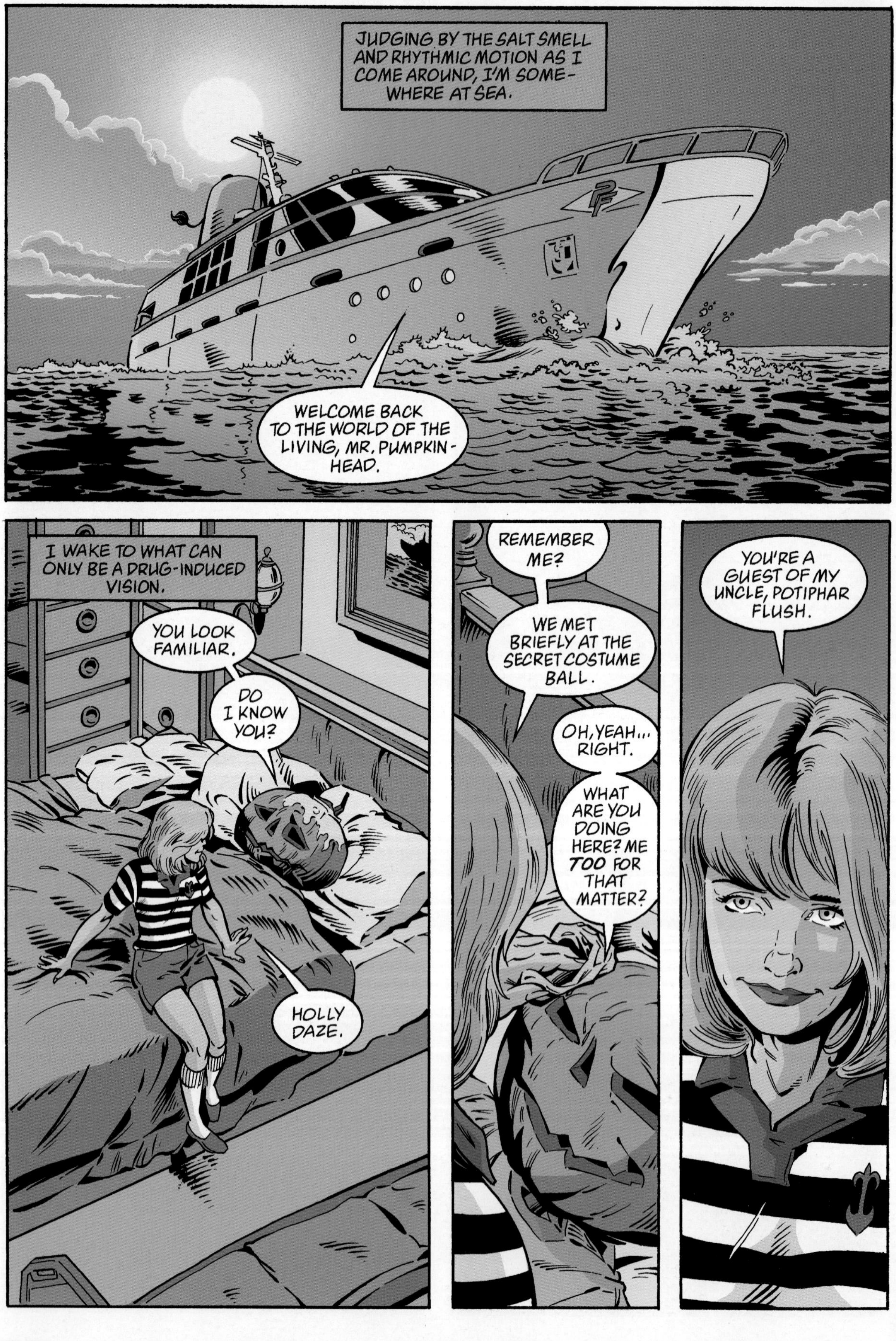
JUDGING BY THE SALT SMELL AND RHYTHMIC MOTION AS I COME AROUND, I'M SOMEWHERE AT SEA.
WELCOME BACK TO THE WORLD OF THE LIVING, MR. PUMPKINHEAD.
I WAKE TO WHAT CAN ONLY BE A DRUG-INDUCED VISION.
YOU LOOK FAMILIAR.
DO I KNOW YOU?
HOLLY DAZE.
REMEMBER ME?
WE MET BRIEFLY AT THE SECRET COSTUME BALL.
OH, YEAH... RIGHT.
WHAT ARE YOU DOING HERE? ME *TOO* FOR THAT MATTER?
YOU'RE A GUEST OF MY UNCLE, POTIPHAR FLUSH.

WHAT?! AN INNOCENT, WHOLESOME YOUNG BABE LIKE *YOU* IS RELATED TO *THAT* CORPULENT TUBER?

OH, BE NICE. AND *NO*, WE'RE NOT ACTUALLY RELATED.

HE SORT OF ADOPTED ME, AFTER MY PARENTS DIED IN A FREAK *CUSTARD-FILLING* ACCIDENT.

OH?

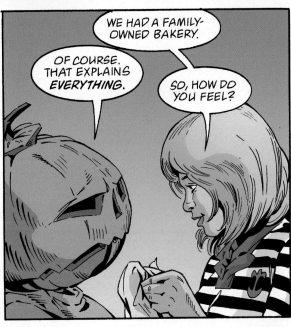

WE HAD A FAMILY-OWNED BAKERY.

OF COURSE. THAT EXPLAINS *EVERYTHING.*

SO, HOW DO YOU FEEL?

A LITTLE SHAKEN, BUT HARDLY STIRRED.

HOW LONG HAVE I BEEN OUT?

A FEW DAYS.

I WAS BEGINNING TO WORRY, UNTIL THAT ANNIE WOMAN TOLD ME WHAT SORT OF *CREATURE* YOU ARE.

IF YOU'RE REALLY A LIVING DREAM, DO YOU ALSO DREAM WHILE YOU SLEEP?

I DON'T KNOW. THIS IS THE FIRST TIME I'VE EVER BEEN ASLEEP, AND SO FAR I'M NOT *CRAZY* ABOUT IT.

DOES IT HURT THIS MUCH FOR *EVERYONE?*

PROBABLY NOT--

--DEPENDING ON THE LIFE YOU LIVE.

OPERATION "BIG SLEEP" PROCEEDS ON SCHEDULE.

THE BABE SEEMS DETERMINED TO STICK AROUND, SO WE *SMALL-TALK* (WHILE I SIFT THROUGH THE SEEDS TO THE MYSTERY AT LARGE).

I'M SO DAMNED CHARMING THAT THE SWEET KID SPILLS HER *GUTS,* NOT REALIZING THE VITAL INFORMATION SHE GIVES UP.

THE ROANOKE GROUP IS POISED TO MOVE AS SOON AS THE MACHINE IS ACTIVATED.

MOST OF THEIR MEMBERSHIP IS ALREADY PLACED IN KEY LEADER-SHIP POSITIONS THROUGH-OUT THE U.S. GOVERN-MENT AND INDUSTRY.

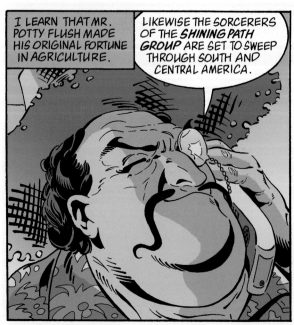

I LEARN THAT MR. POTTY FLUSH MADE HIS ORIGINAL FORTUNE IN AGRICULTURE.

LIKEWISE THE SORCERERS OF THE *SHINING PATH GROUP* ARE SET TO SWEEP THROUGH SOUTH AND CENTRAL AMERICA.

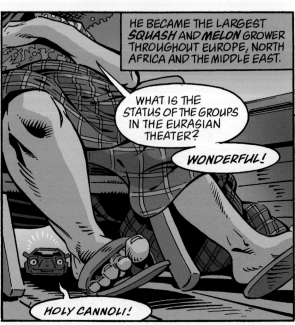

HE BECAME THE LARGEST *SQUASH* AND *MELON* GROWER THROUGHOUT EUROPE, NORTH AFRICA AND THE MIDDLE EAST.

WHAT IS THE STATUS OF THE GROUPS IN THE EURASIAN THEATER?

WONDERFUL!

HOLY CANNOLI!

GOURDFINGER, THEY CALL HIM. KING OF THE WORLD'S GOURD GROWERS.

I EXPECT TO RECEIVE CONFIRMATION FROM THE AFRICAN AND AUSTRALIAN GROUP LEADERS WITHIN THE HOUR.

MERVYN NEEDS TO HEAR ABOUT THIS.

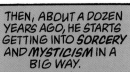

THEN, ABOUT A DOZEN YEARS AGO, HE STARTS GETTING INTO SORCERY AND MYSTICISM IN A BIG WAY.

HE USES HIS MONEY TO FINANCE ANY MAGIC-RELATED ORGANIZATION WILLING TO GIVE HIM THE TIME OF DAY.

CONSTANTLY WEEDING OUT THE FRAUDS AND FAKERS, WHILE ORGANIZING THE REAL ONES.

HALF A DOZEN BOTTLES OF CHAMPAGNE KEPT THE LADY'S TONGUE LOOSE. SHE HAD A CONSIDERABLE THIRST FOR SUCH A PETITE GIRL.

WANT ME TO GO GET US ANOTHER BOTTLE?

NOPE.

I'M FINE AND TOASTY.

BONK!

OW!

211

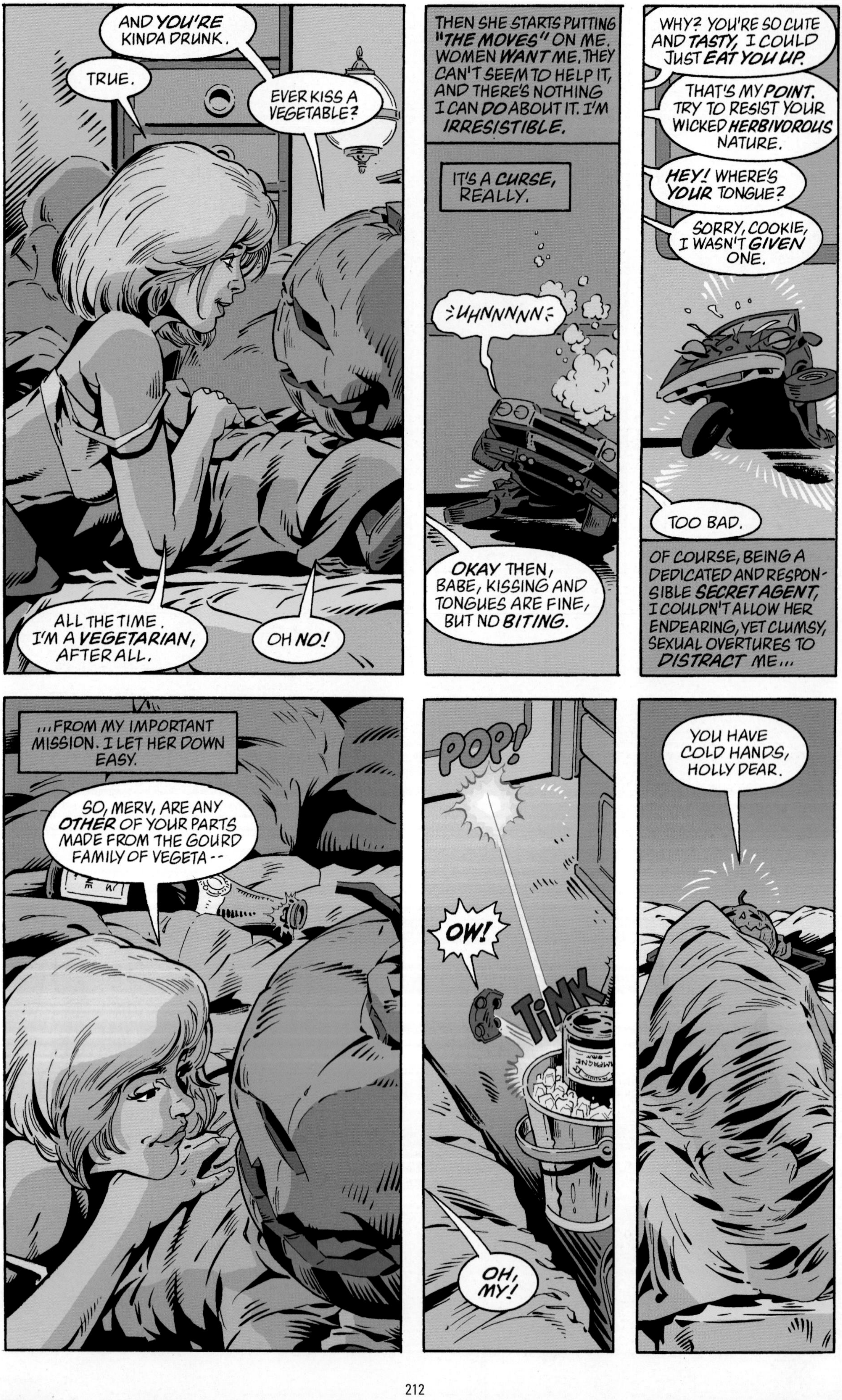
AND YOU'RE KINDA DRUNK.
TRUE.
EVER KISS A VEGETABLE?
ALL THE TIME. I'M A VEGETARIAN, AFTER ALL.
OH NO!
THEN SHE STARTS PUTTING "THE MOVES" ON ME. WOMEN WANT ME. THEY CAN'T SEEM TO HELP IT, AND THERE'S NOTHING I CAN DO ABOUT IT. I'M IRRESISTIBLE.
IT'S A CURSE, REALLY.
UHHNNNN
OKAY THEN, BABE, KISSING AND TONGUES ARE FINE, BUT NO BITING.
WHY? YOU'RE SO CUTE AND TASTY, I COULD JUST EAT YOU UP.
THAT'S MY POINT. TRY TO RESIST YOUR WICKED HERBIVOROUS NATURE.
HEY! WHERE'S YOUR TONGUE?
SORRY, COOKIE, I WASN'T GIVEN ONE.
TOO BAD.
OF COURSE, BEING A DEDICATED AND RESPONSIBLE SECRET AGENT, I COULDN'T ALLOW HER ENDEARING, YET CLUMSY, SEXUAL OVERTURES TO DISTRACT ME...
...FROM MY IMPORTANT MISSION. I LET HER DOWN EASY.
SO, MERV, ARE ANY OTHER OF YOUR PARTS MADE FROM THE GOURD FAMILY OF VEGETA--
POP!
OW!
TINK
OH, MY!
YOU HAVE COLD HANDS, HOLLY DEAR.

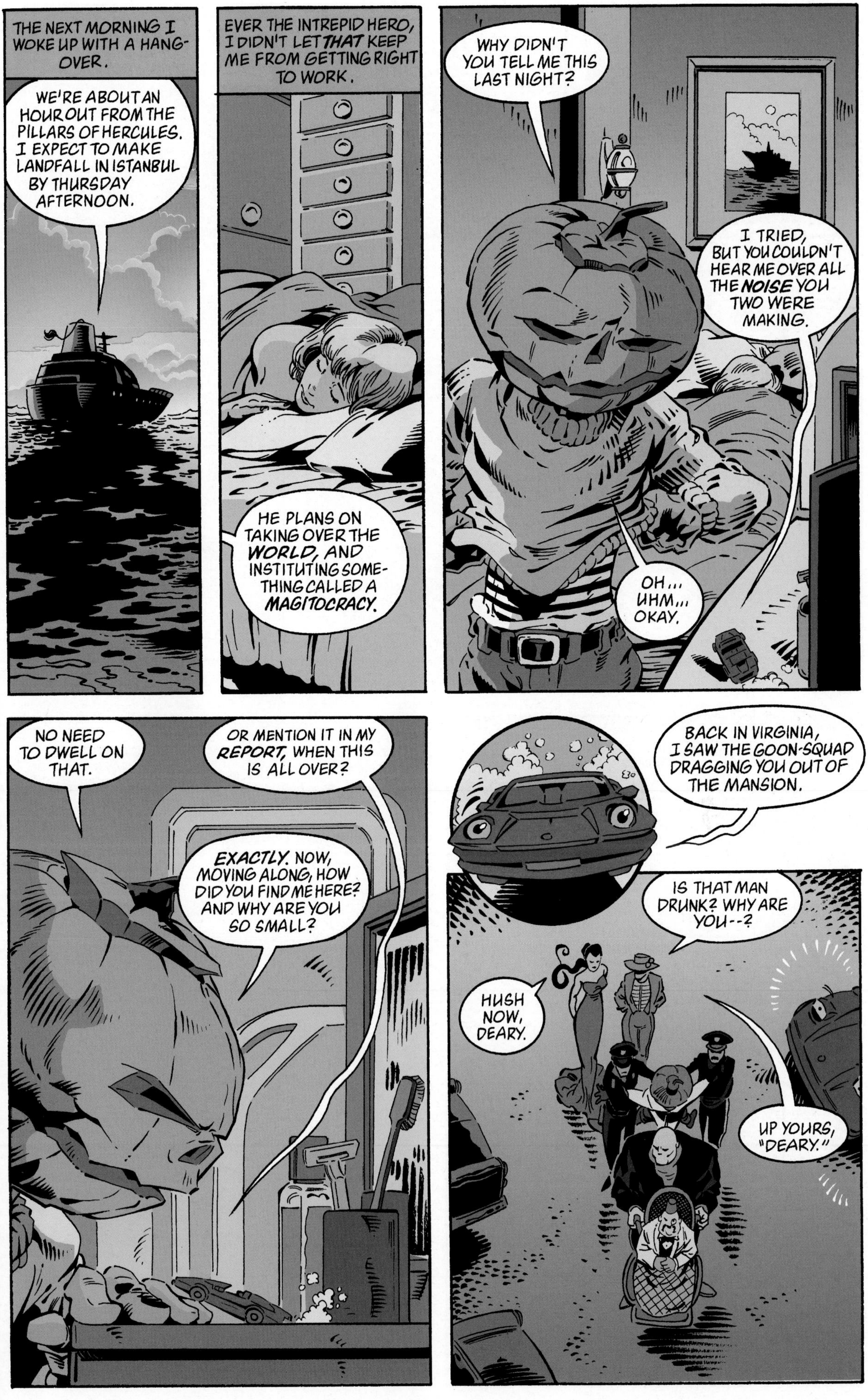

THE NEXT MORNING I WOKE UP WITH A HANG-OVER.
WE'RE ABOUT AN HOUR OUT FROM THE PILLARS OF HERCULES. I EXPECT TO MAKE LANDFALL IN ISTANBUL BY THURSDAY AFTERNOON.
EVER THE INTREPID HERO, I DIDN'T LET THAT KEEP ME FROM GETTING RIGHT TO WORK.
HE PLANS ON TAKING OVER THE WORLD, AND INSTITUTING SOME-THING CALLED A MAGITOCRACY.
WHY DIDN'T YOU TELL ME THIS LAST NIGHT?
I TRIED, BUT YOU COULDN'T HEAR ME OVER ALL THE NOISE YOU TWO WERE MAKING.
OH... UHM... OKAY.
NO NEED TO DWELL ON THAT.
OR MENTION IT IN MY REPORT, WHEN THIS IS ALL OVER?
EXACTLY. NOW, MOVING ALONG, HOW DID YOU FIND ME HERE? AND WHY ARE YOU SO SMALL?
BACK IN VIRGINIA, I SAW THE GOON-SQUAD DRAGGING YOU OUT OF THE MANSION.
IS THAT MAN DRUNK? WHY ARE YOU--?
HUSH NOW, DEARY.
UP YOURS, "DEARY."

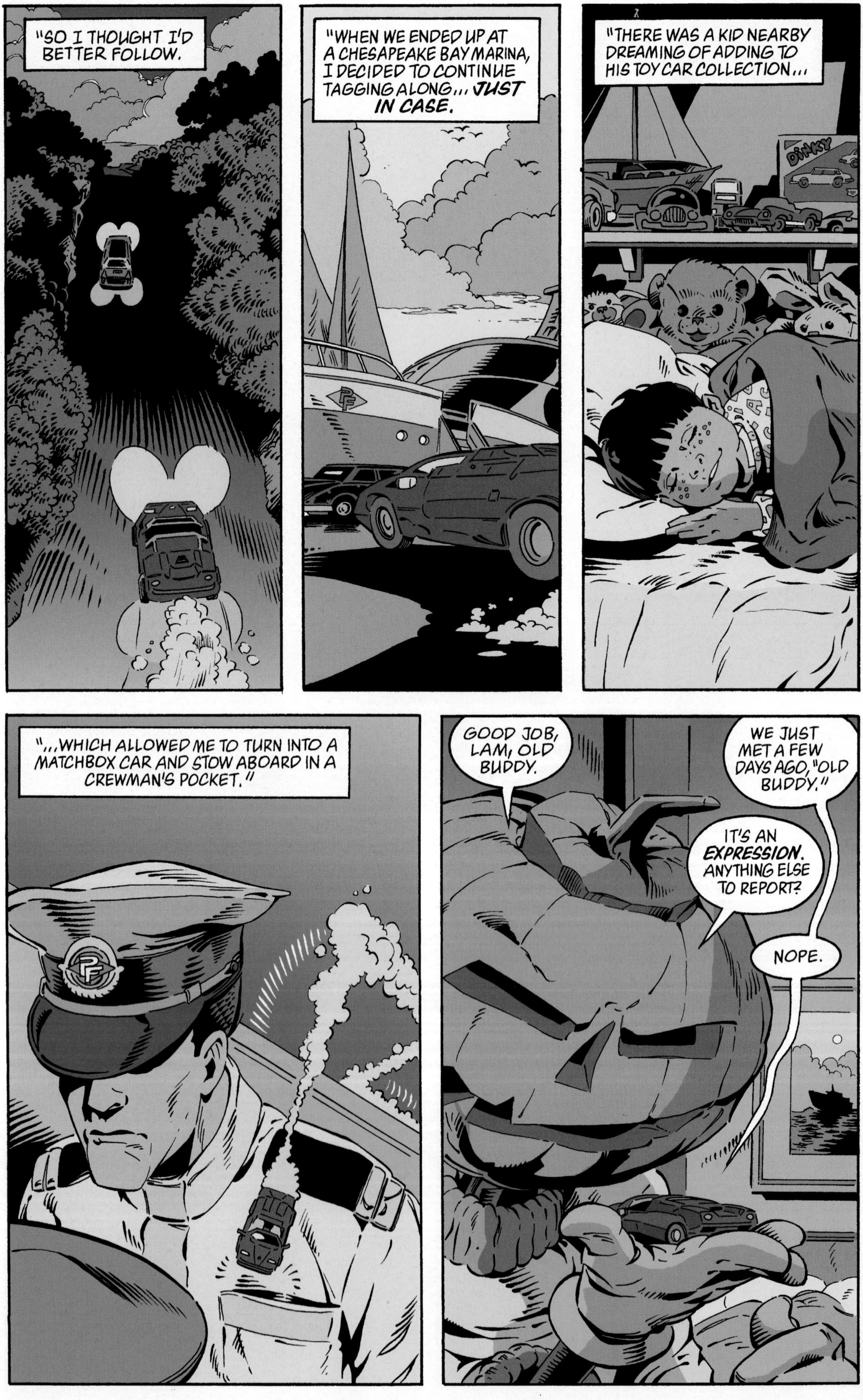
"SO I THOUGHT I'D BETTER FOLLOW.
"WHEN WE ENDED UP AT A CHESAPEAKE BAY MARINA, I DECIDED TO CONTINUE TAGGING ALONG... JUST IN CASE.
"THERE WAS A KID NEARBY DREAMING OF ADDING TO HIS TOY CAR COLLECTION...
DINKY
"...WHICH ALLOWED ME TO TURN INTO A MATCHBOX CAR AND STOW ABOARD IN A CREWMAN'S POCKET."
GOOD JOB, LAM, OLD BUDDY.
WE JUST MET A FEW DAYS AGO, "OLD BUDDY."
IT'S AN EXPRESSION. ANYTHING ELSE TO REPORT?
NOPE.

IT WAS TIME FOR THE SCENE WHERE THE HERO CONFRONTS THE VILLAINS AGAIN. TIME FOR THIS CASE TO GET WRAPPED UP, TOO.

BETTER STICK WITH *ME* FROM NOW ON.

OH, JOY.

SINISTER MOJO EMANATED FROM EVERY *BOLT* ON THE DOOMED VESSEL, BUT I STAYED THE COURSE, UNDAUNTED.

HEY, WHERE'S YOUR FEARLESS LEADER?

THE MAIN MAN? THE BIG, *REALLY BIG*, KAHUNA?

QUÉ?

NO DAUNTS HERE.

NEVER MIND.

I'LL FIND HIM.

MADRE DE DIOS.

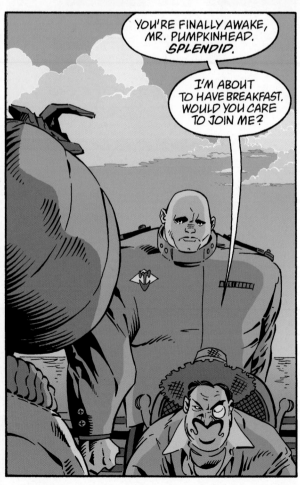

YOU'RE FINALLY AWAKE, MR. PUMPKINHEAD. *SPLENDID.*

I'M ABOUT TO HAVE BREAKFAST. WOULD YOU CARE TO JOIN ME?

NO THANKS, FLUSH. I'M TOO HUNG OVER TO EAT. I'D *RUTZ* ALL OVER YOUR OGRE FRIEND.

A MORNING COCKTAIL THEN?

HAIR OF THE PROVERBIAL *DOG?*

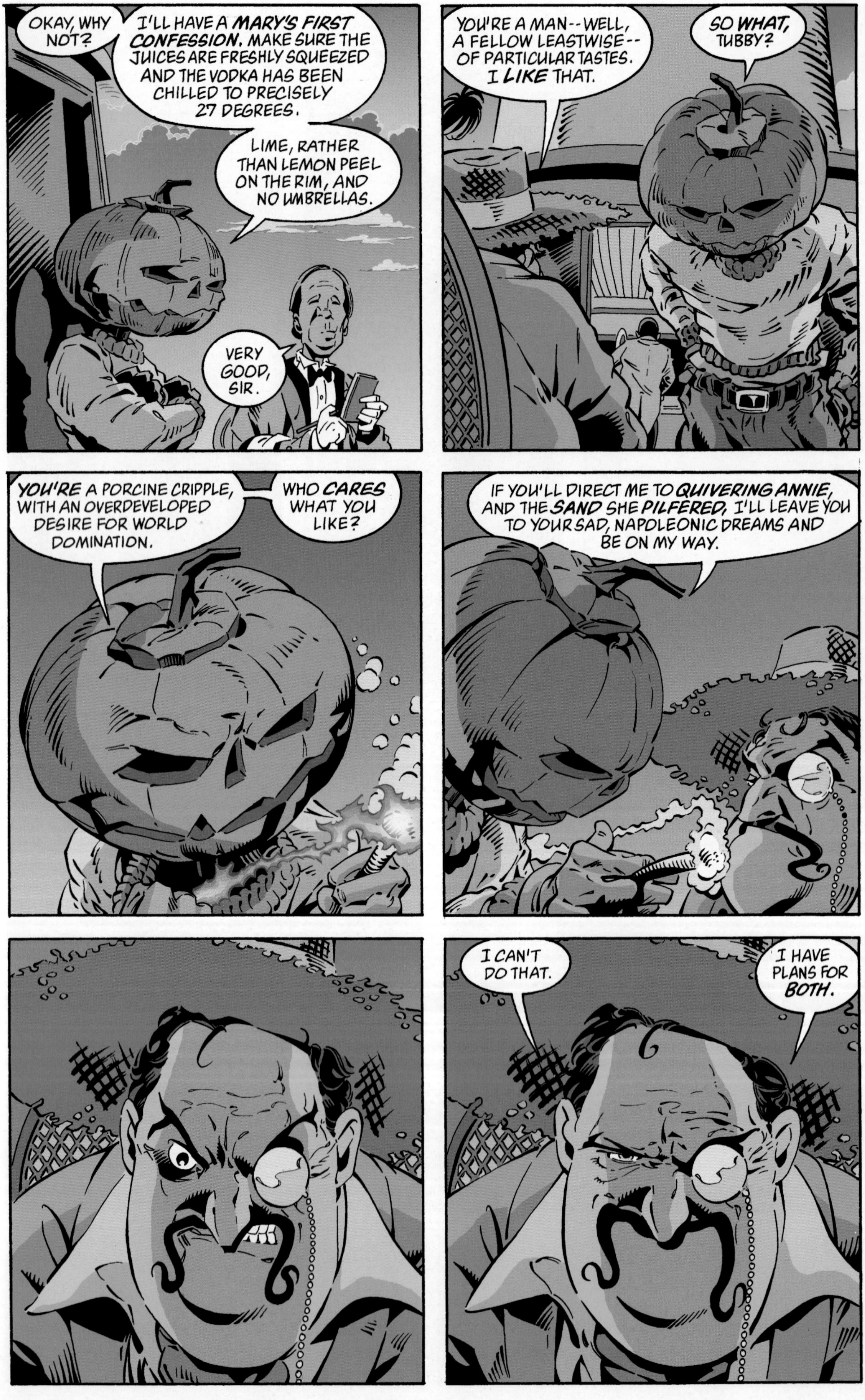
OKAY, WHY NOT?
I'LL HAVE A MARY'S FIRST CONFESSION. MAKE SURE THE JUICES ARE FRESHLY SQUEEZED AND THE VODKA HAS BEEN CHILLED TO PRECISELY 27 DEGREES.
LIME, RATHER THAN LEMON PEEL ON THE RIM, AND NO UMBRELLAS.
VERY GOOD, SIR.
YOU'RE A MAN--WELL, A FELLOW LEASTWISE--OF PARTICULAR TASTES. I LIKE THAT.
SO WHAT, TUBBY?
YOU'RE A PORCINE CRIPPLE, WITH AN OVERDEVELOPED DESIRE FOR WORLD DOMINATION.
WHO CARES WHAT YOU LIKE?
IF YOU'LL DIRECT ME TO QUIVERING ANNIE, AND THE SAND SHE PILFERED, I'LL LEAVE YOU TO YOUR SAD, NAPOLEONIC DREAMS AND BE ON MY WAY.
I CAN'T DO THAT.
I HAVE PLANS FOR BOTH.

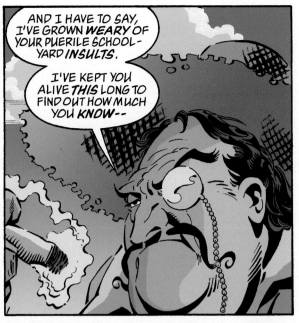

AND I HAVE TO SAY, I'VE GROWN *WEARY* OF YOUR *PUERILE* SCHOOL-YARD *INSULTS.*

I'VE KEPT YOU ALIVE *THIS* LONG TO FIND OUT HOW MUCH YOU *KNOW--*

ABOUT PROJECT: *BIG SLEEP?*

I KNOW THE WHOLE *SORDID PLAN,* FLUSHY.

GOOD?

GOOD.

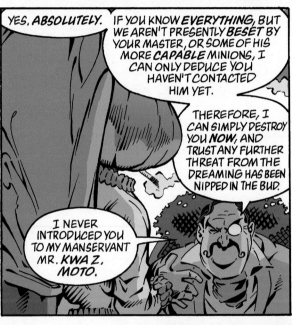

YES, *ABSOLUTELY.* IF YOU KNOW *EVERYTHING,* BUT WE AREN'T PRESENTLY *BESET* BY YOUR MASTER, OR SOME OF HIS MORE *CAPABLE* MINIONS, I CAN ONLY DEDUCE YOU HAVEN'T CONTACTED HIM YET.

THEREFORE, I CAN SIMPLY DESTROY YOU *NOW,* AND TRUST ANY FURTHER THREAT FROM THE *DREAMING* HAS BEEN NIPPED IN THE BUD.

I NEVER INTRODUCED YOU TO MY MANSERVANT MR. *KWA Z, MOTO.*

THROW THIS CLOWN TO THE *SHARKS,* MR. MOTO.

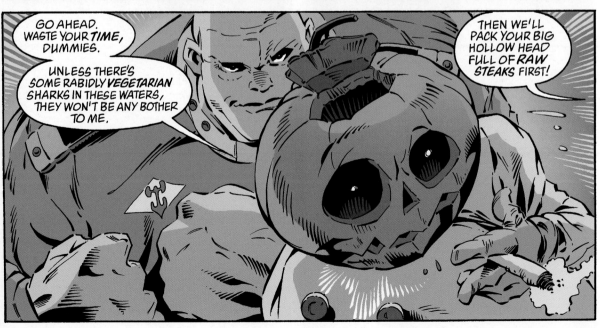

GO AHEAD. WASTE YOUR *TIME,* DUMMIES.

UNLESS THERE'S SOME RABIDLY *VEGETARIAN* SHARKS IN THESE WATERS, THEY WON'T BE ANY BOTHER TO ME.

THEN WE'LL PACK YOUR BIG HOLLOW HEAD FULL OF *RAW STEAKS* FIRST!

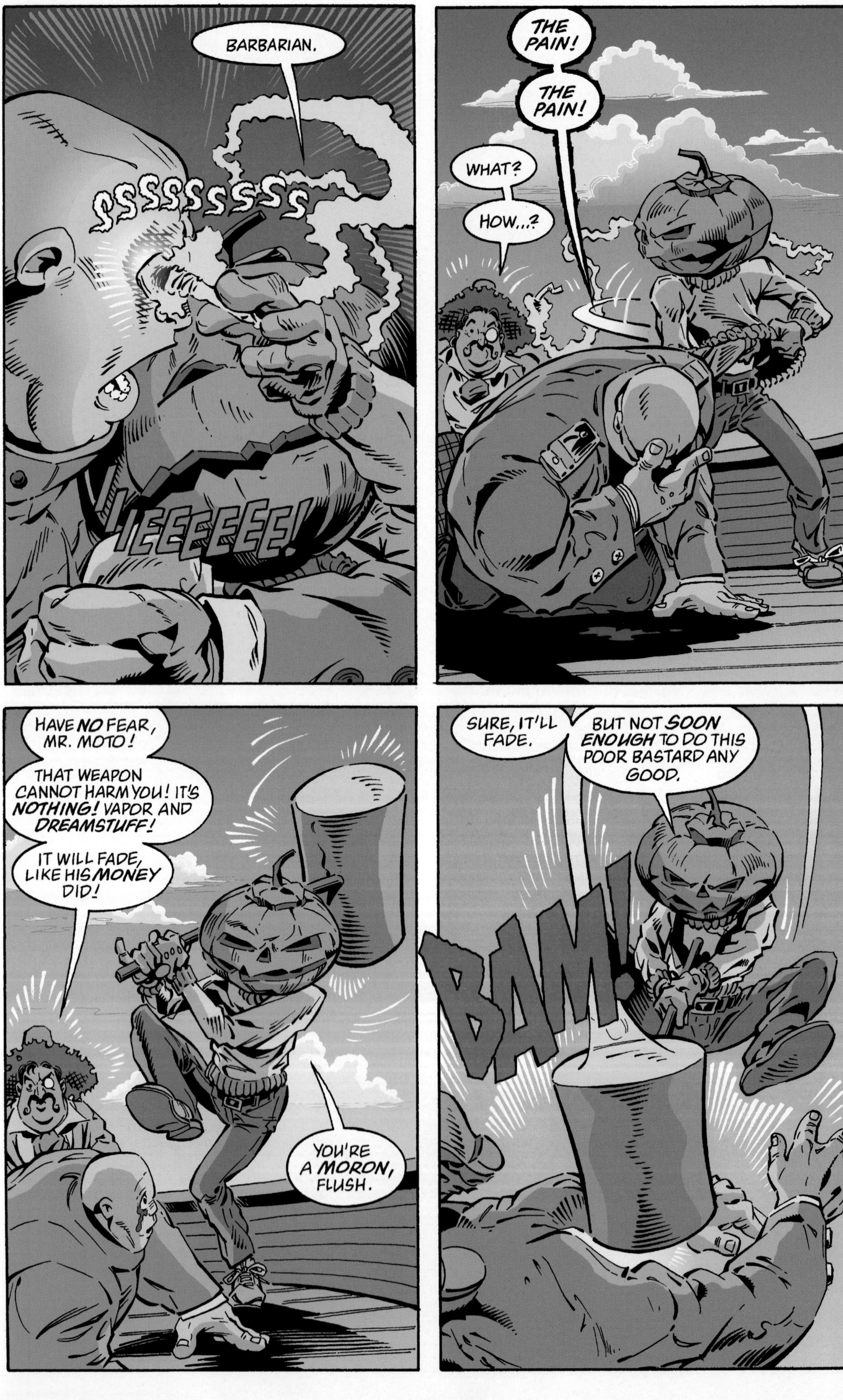
BARBARIAN.
SSSSSSSSS
IEEEEEEE!
THE PAIN!
THE PAIN!
WHAT?
HOW...?
HAVE NO FEAR, MR. MOTO!
THAT WEAPON CANNOT HARM YOU! IT'S NOTHING! VAPOR AND DREAMSTUFF!
IT WILL FADE, LIKE HIS MONEY DID!
YOU'RE A MORON, FLUSH.
SURE, IT'LL FADE.
BUT NOT SOON ENOUGH TO DO THIS POOR BASTARD ANY GOOD.
BAM!

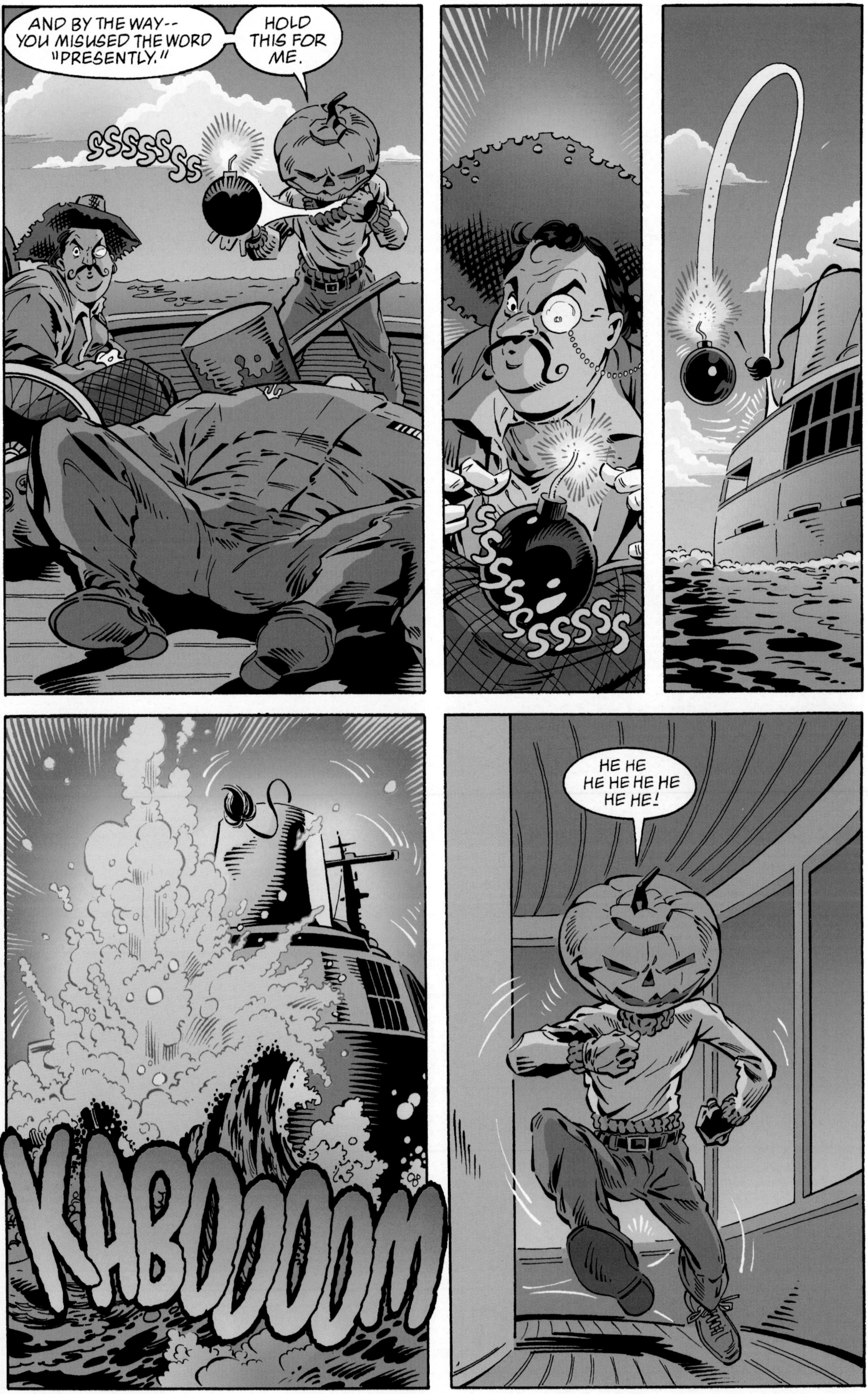
AND BY THE WAY-- YOU MISUSED THE WORD "PRESENTLY."
HOLD THIS FOR ME.
SSSSSSS
SSSSSSSSSS
KABOOOOM
HE HE HE HE HE HE HE HE!

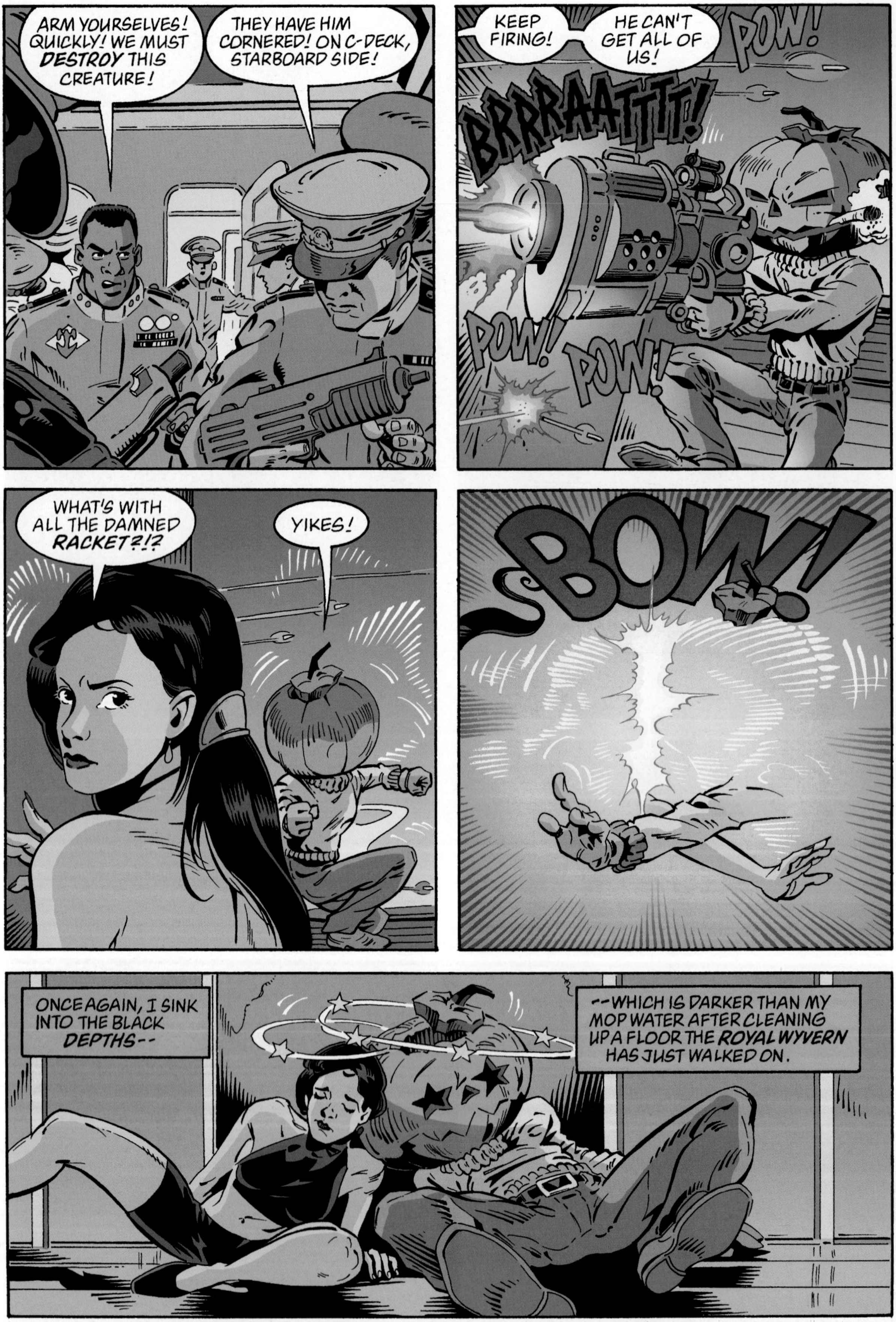
ARM YOURSELVES! QUICKLY! WE MUST DESTROY THIS CREATURE!
THEY HAVE HIM CORNERED! ON C-DECK, STARBOARD SIDE!
KEEP FIRING!
HE CAN'T GET ALL OF US!
POW!
BRRRAATTTT!
POW!
POW!
WHAT'S WITH ALL THE DAMNED RACKET?!?
YIKES!
BOW!
ONCE AGAIN, I SINK INTO THE BLACK DEPTHS--
--WHICH IS DARKER THAN MY MOP WATER AFTER CLEANING UP A FLOOR THE ROYAL WYVERN HAS JUST WALKED ON.

CHAPTER SIX: YOU ONLY SLEEP TWICE

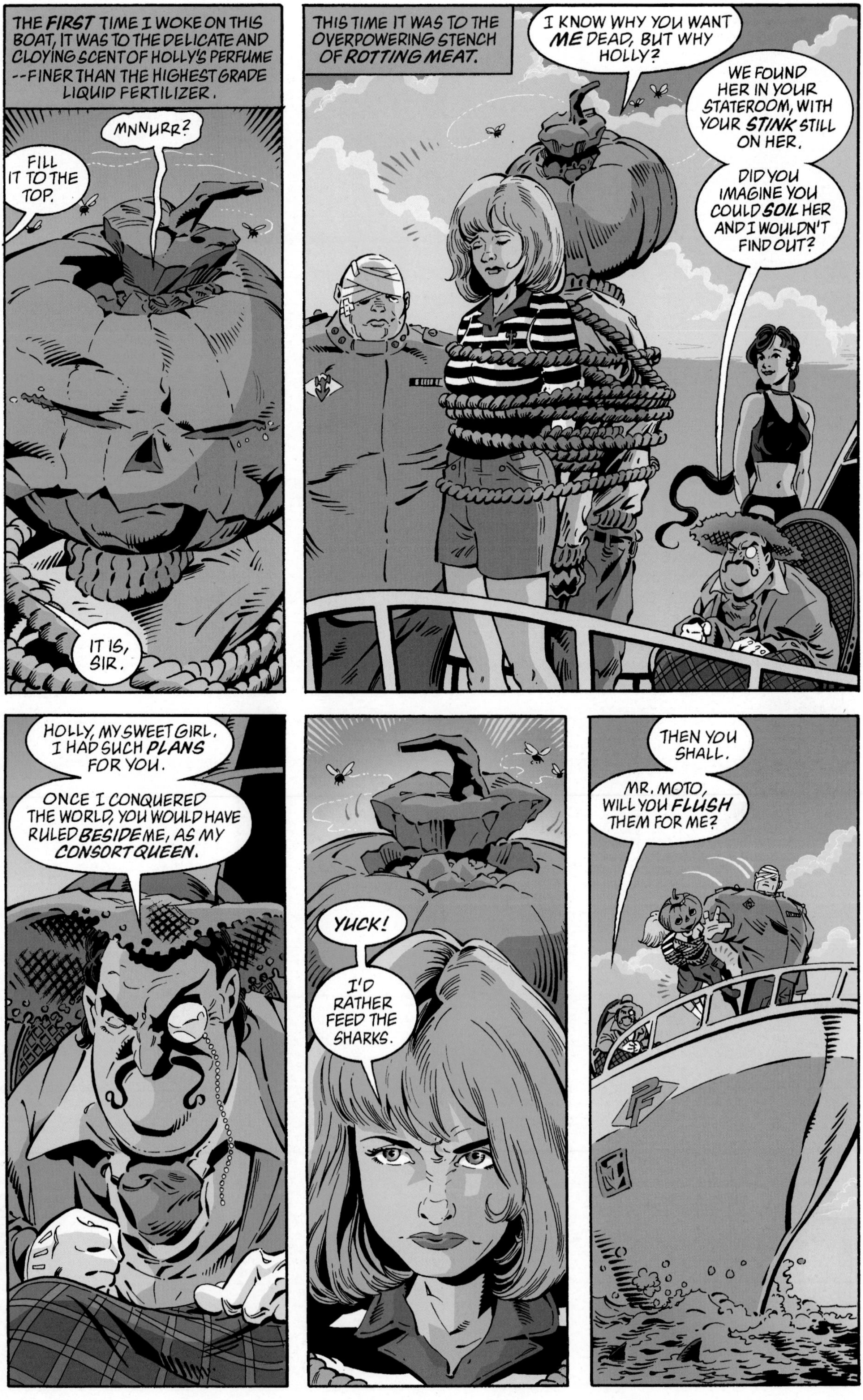
THE FIRST TIME I WOKE ON THIS BOAT, IT WAS TO THE DELICATE AND CLOYING SCENT OF HOLLY'S PERFUME --FINER THAN THE HIGHEST GRADE LIQUID FERTILIZER.
MNNURR?
FILL IT TO THE TOP.
IT IS, SIR.
THIS TIME IT WAS TO THE OVERPOWERING STENCH OF ROTTING MEAT.
I KNOW WHY YOU WANT ME DEAD, BUT WHY HOLLY?
WE FOUND HER IN YOUR STATEROOM, WITH YOUR STINK STILL ON HER.
DID YOU IMAGINE YOU COULD SOIL HER AND I WOULDN'T FIND OUT?
HOLLY, MY SWEET GIRL. I HAD SUCH PLANS FOR YOU.
ONCE I CONQUERED THE WORLD, YOU WOULD HAVE RULED BESIDE ME, AS MY CONSORT QUEEN.
YUCK!
I'D RATHER FEED THE SHARKS.
THEN YOU SHALL.
MR. MOTO, WILL YOU FLUSH THEM FOR ME?

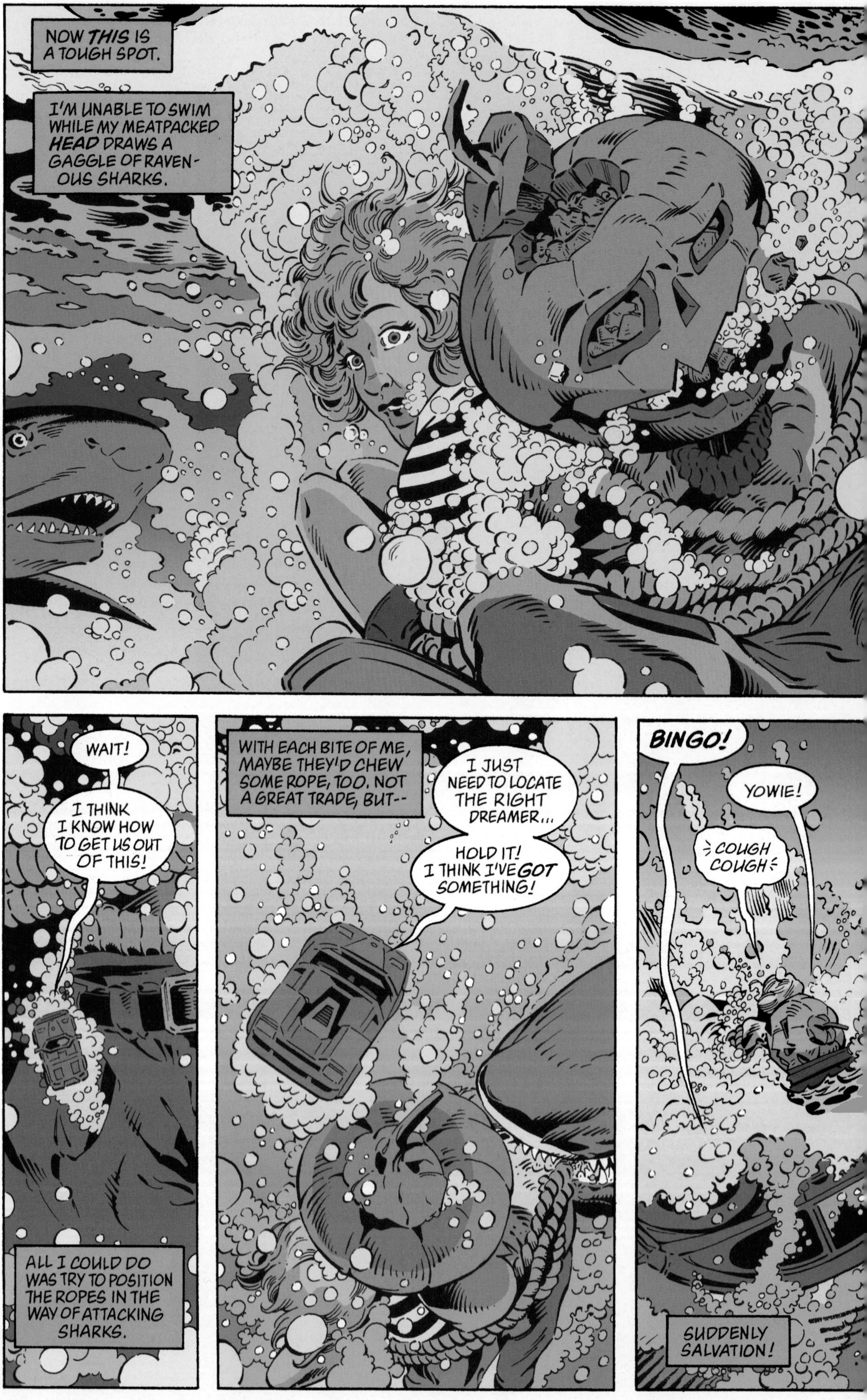
NOW THIS IS A TOUGH SPOT.
I'M UNABLE TO SWIM WHILE MY MEATPACKED HEAD DRAWS A GAGGLE OF RAVEN-OUS SHARKS.
WAIT!
I THINK I KNOW HOW TO GET US OUT OF THIS!
ALL I COULD DO WAS TRY TO POSITION THE ROPES IN THE WAY OF ATTACKING SHARKS.
WITH EACH BITE OF ME, MAYBE THEY'D CHEW SOME ROPE, TOO. NOT A GREAT TRADE, BUT--
I JUST NEED TO LOCATE THE RIGHT DREAMER...
HOLD IT! I THINK I'VE GOT SOMETHING!
BINGO!
YOWIE!
COUGH COUGH
SUDDENLY SALVATION!

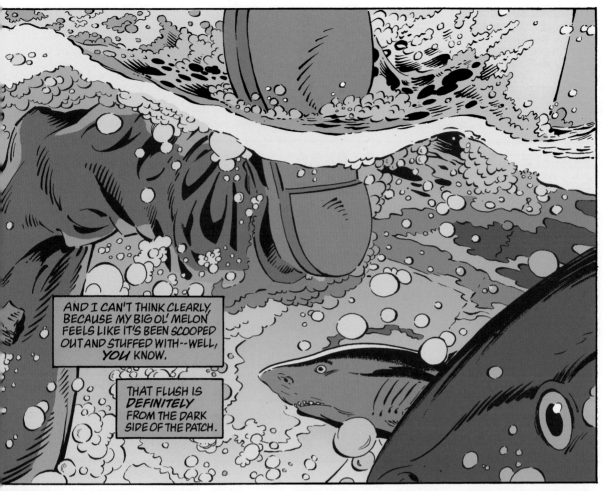

AND I CAN'T THINK CLEARLY, BECAUSE MY BIG OL' MELON FEELS LIKE IT'S BEEN *SCOOPED OUT* AND STUFFED WITH--WELL, *YOU* KNOW.

THAT FLUSH IS *DEFINITELY* FROM THE DARK SIDE OF THE PATCH.

I ALWAYS HEARD THESE THINGS WOULD FLOAT!

GOOD JOB, LITTLE BUDDY, YOU SAVED US.

DAMN *RIGHT* I DID.

SAVED, BUT *MILES* AWAY FROM ANYWHERE!

WHAT NOW, COWBOY?

WE FIND A WAY OUT OF HERE.

LAM, I DON'T SUPPOSE YOU CAN DO BOATS?

NOPE, JUST CARS. BUT DON'T WORRY. ALL I NEED TO DO IS FIND SOMEONE IN ISTANBUL DREAMING OF A CAR AND THEN, *BAM!* WE'RE THERE!

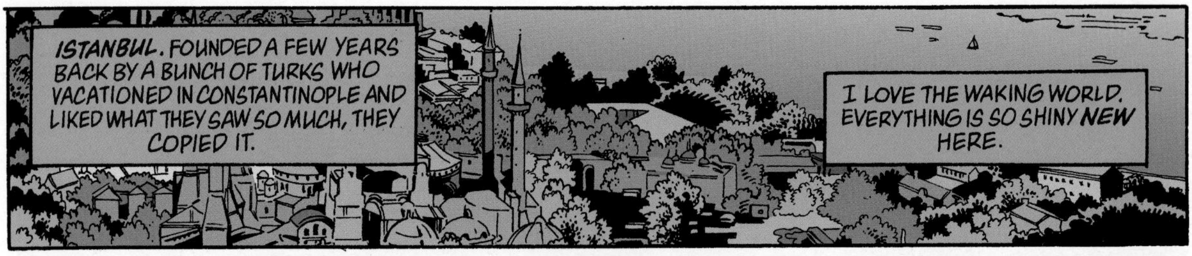
ISTANBUL. FOUNDED A FEW YEARS BACK BY A BUNCH OF TURKS WHO VACATIONED IN CONSTANTINOPLE AND LIKED WHAT THEY SAW SO MUCH, THEY COPIED IT.
I LOVE THE WAKING WORLD. EVERYTHING IS SO SHINY NEW HERE.

CHAPTER SEVEN: PUMPKINS ARE FOREVER

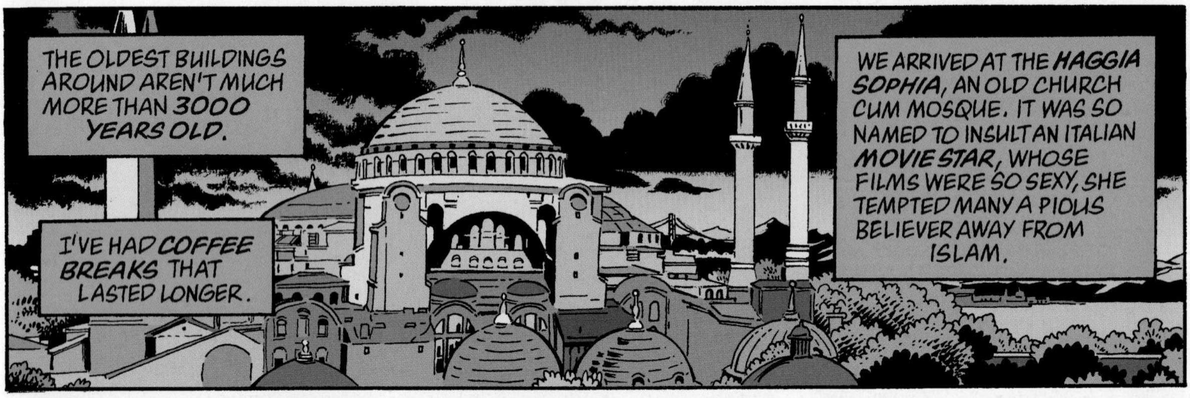
THE OLDEST BUILDINGS AROUND AREN'T MUCH MORE THAN 3000 YEARS OLD.
I'VE HAD COFFEE BREAKS THAT LASTED LONGER.
WE ARRIVED AT THE HAGGIA SOPHIA, AN OLD CHURCH CUM MOSQUE. IT WAS SO NAMED TO INSULT AN ITALIAN MOVIE STAR, WHOSE FILMS WERE SO SEXY, SHE TEMPTED MANY A PIOUS BELIEVER AWAY FROM ISLAM.

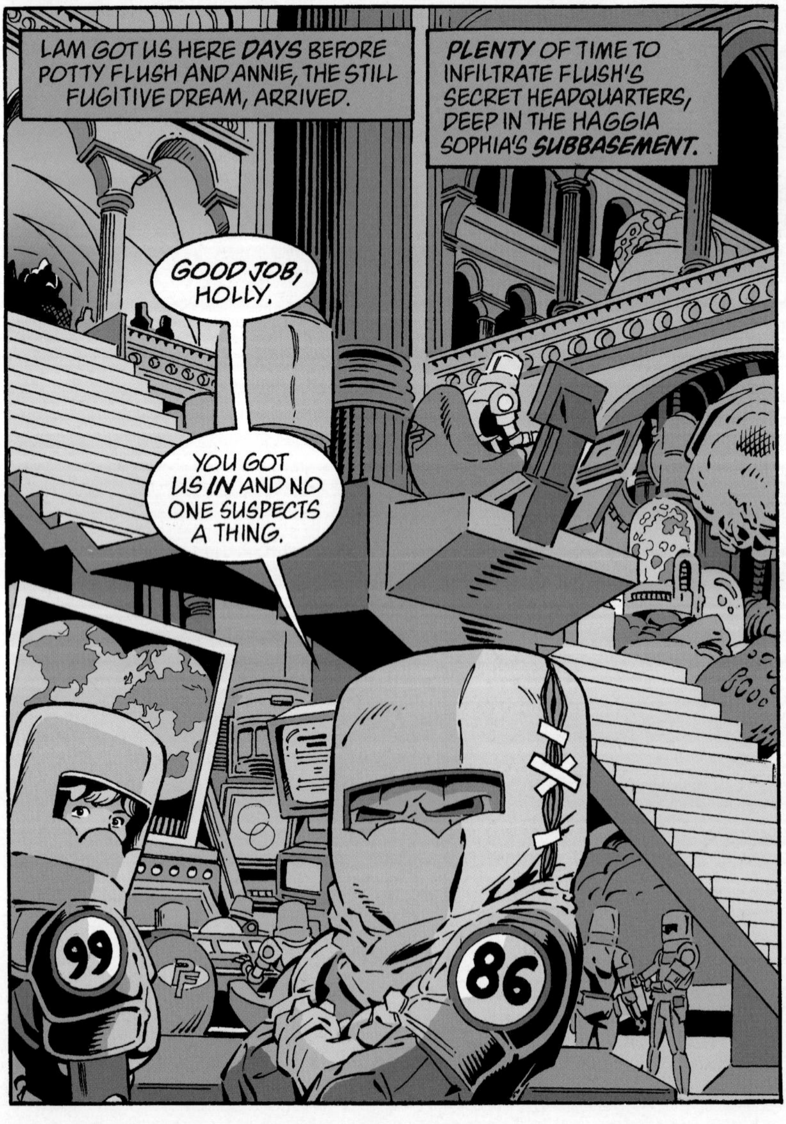
LAM GOT US HERE DAYS BEFORE POTTY FLUSH AND ANNIE, THE STILL FUGITIVE DREAM, ARRIVED.
PLENTY OF TIME TO INFILTRATE FLUSH'S SECRET HEADQUARTERS, DEEP IN THE HAGGIA SOPHIA'S SUBBASEMENT.
GOOD JOB, HOLLY.
YOU GOT US IN AND NO ONE SUSPECTS A THING.
99
86

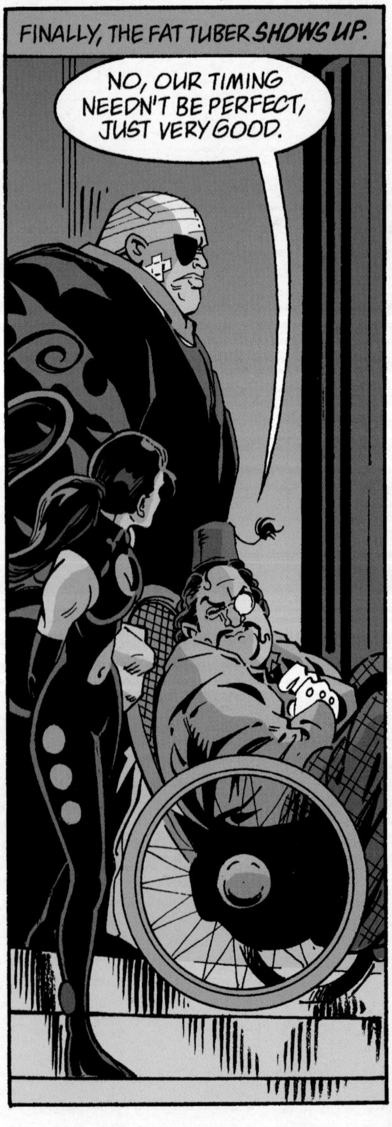
FINALLY, THE FAT TUBER SHOWS UP.
NO, OUR TIMING NEEDN'T BE PERFECT, JUST VERY GOOD.

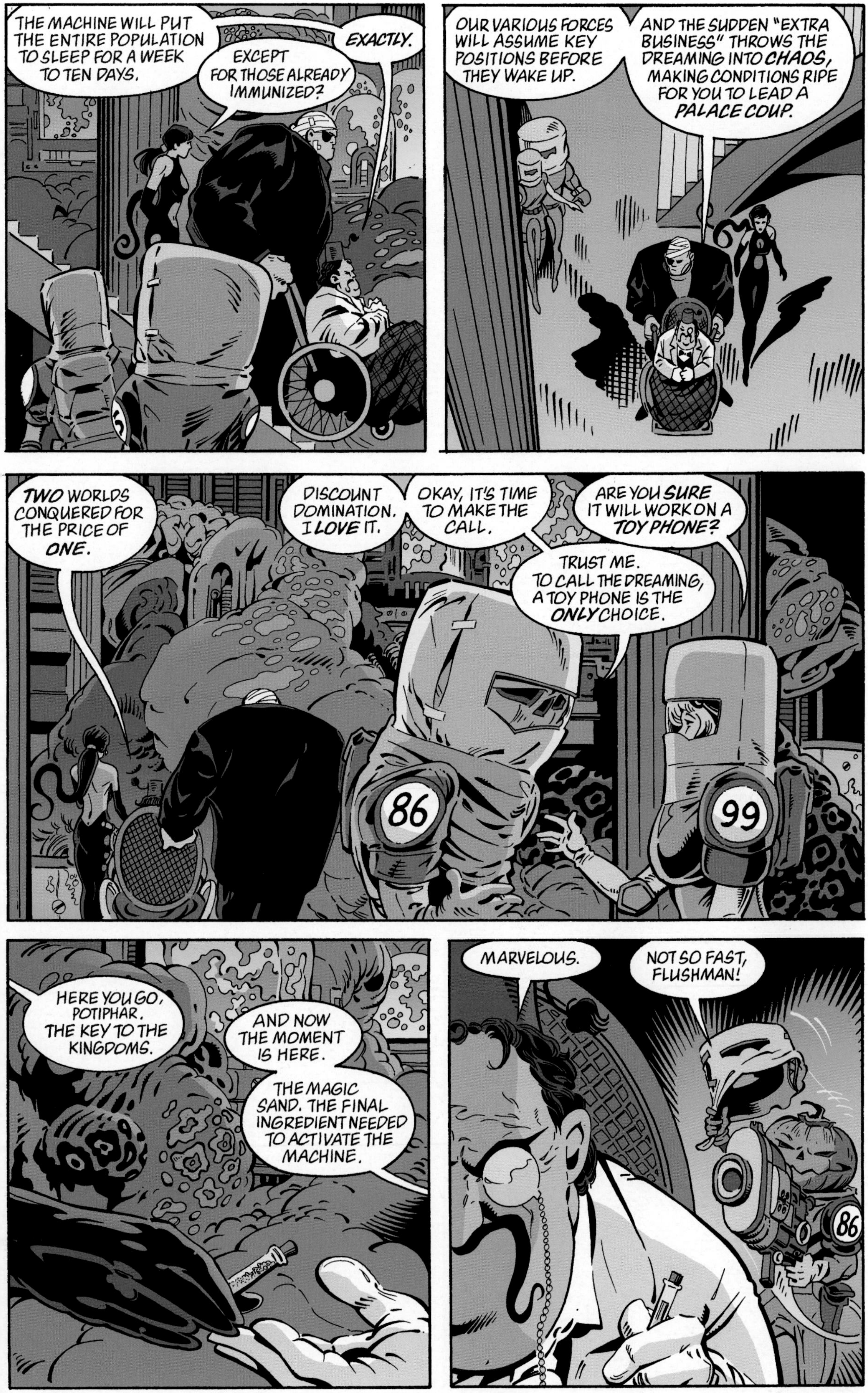
THE MACHINE WILL PUT THE ENTIRE POPULATION TO SLEEP FOR A WEEK TO TEN DAYS.
EXCEPT FOR THOSE ALREADY IMMUNIZED?
EXACTLY.
OUR VARIOUS FORCES WILL ASSUME KEY POSITIONS BEFORE THEY WAKE UP.
AND THE SUDDEN "EXTRA BUSINESS" THROWS THE DREAMING INTO CHAOS, MAKING CONDITIONS RIPE FOR YOU TO LEAD A PALACE COUP.
TWO WORLDS CONQUERED FOR THE PRICE OF ONE.
DISCOUNT DOMINATION. I LOVE IT.
OKAY, IT'S TIME TO MAKE THE CALL.
ARE YOU SURE IT WILL WORK ON A TOY PHONE?
TRUST ME. TO CALL THE DREAMING, A TOY PHONE IS THE ONLY CHOICE.
86
99
HERE YOU GO, POTIPHAR. THE KEY TO THE KINGDOMS.
AND NOW THE MOMENT IS HERE.
THE MAGIC SAND. THE FINAL INGREDIENT NEEDED TO ACTIVATE THE MACHINE.
MARVELOUS.
NOT SO FAST, FLUSHMAN!
86

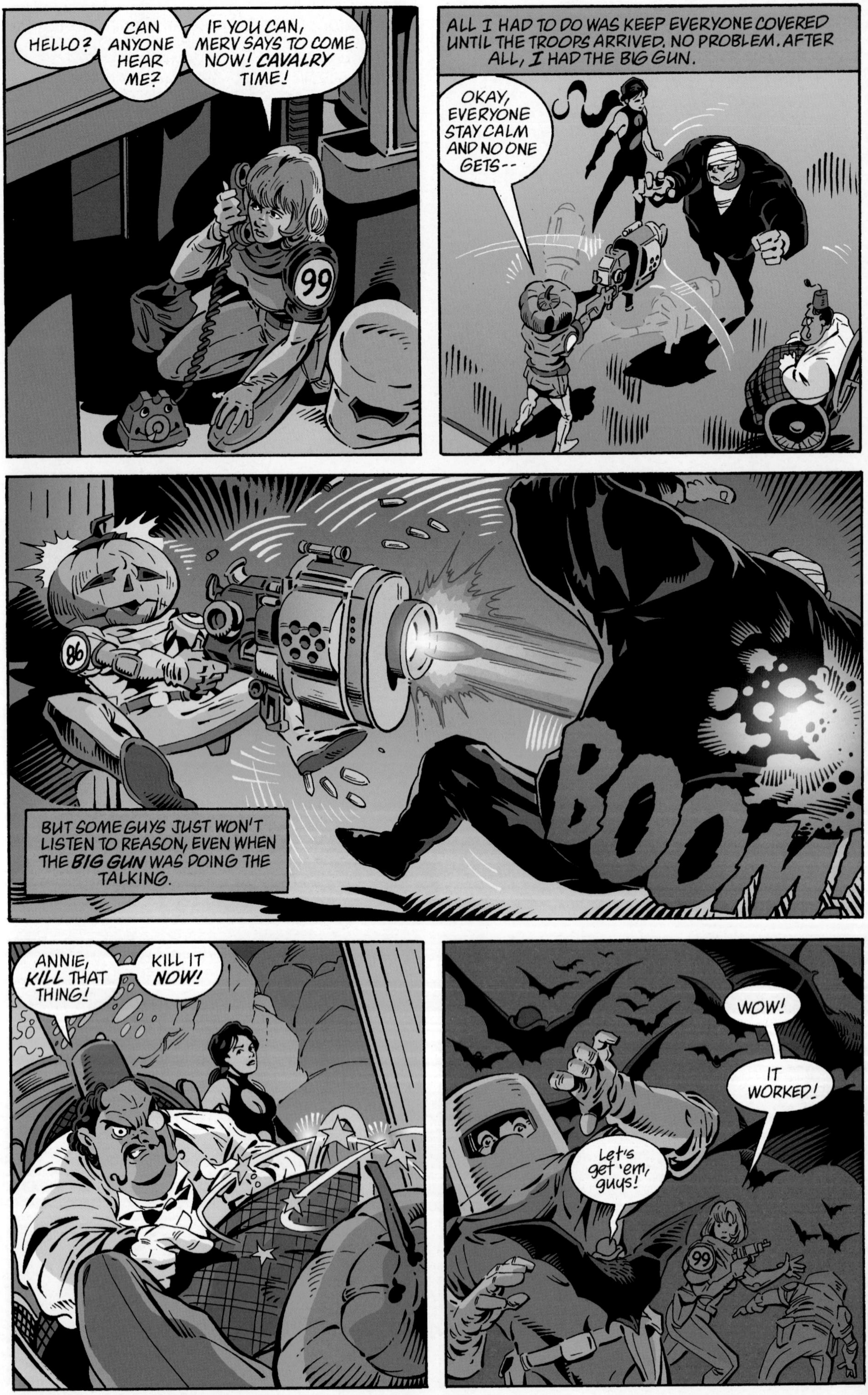
HELLO?
CAN ANYONE HEAR ME?
IF YOU CAN, MERV SAYS TO COME NOW! CAVALRY TIME!
ALL I HAD TO DO WAS KEEP EVERYONE COVERED UNTIL THE TROOPS ARRIVED. NO PROBLEM. AFTER ALL, I HAD THE BIG GUN.
OKAY, EVERYONE STAY CALM AND NO ONE GETS--
BUT SOME GUYS JUST WON'T LISTEN TO REASON, EVEN WHEN THE BIG GUN WAS DOING THE TALKING.
BOOM!
ANNIE, KILL THAT THING!
KILL IT NOW!
WOW!
IT WORKED!
Let's get 'em, guys!

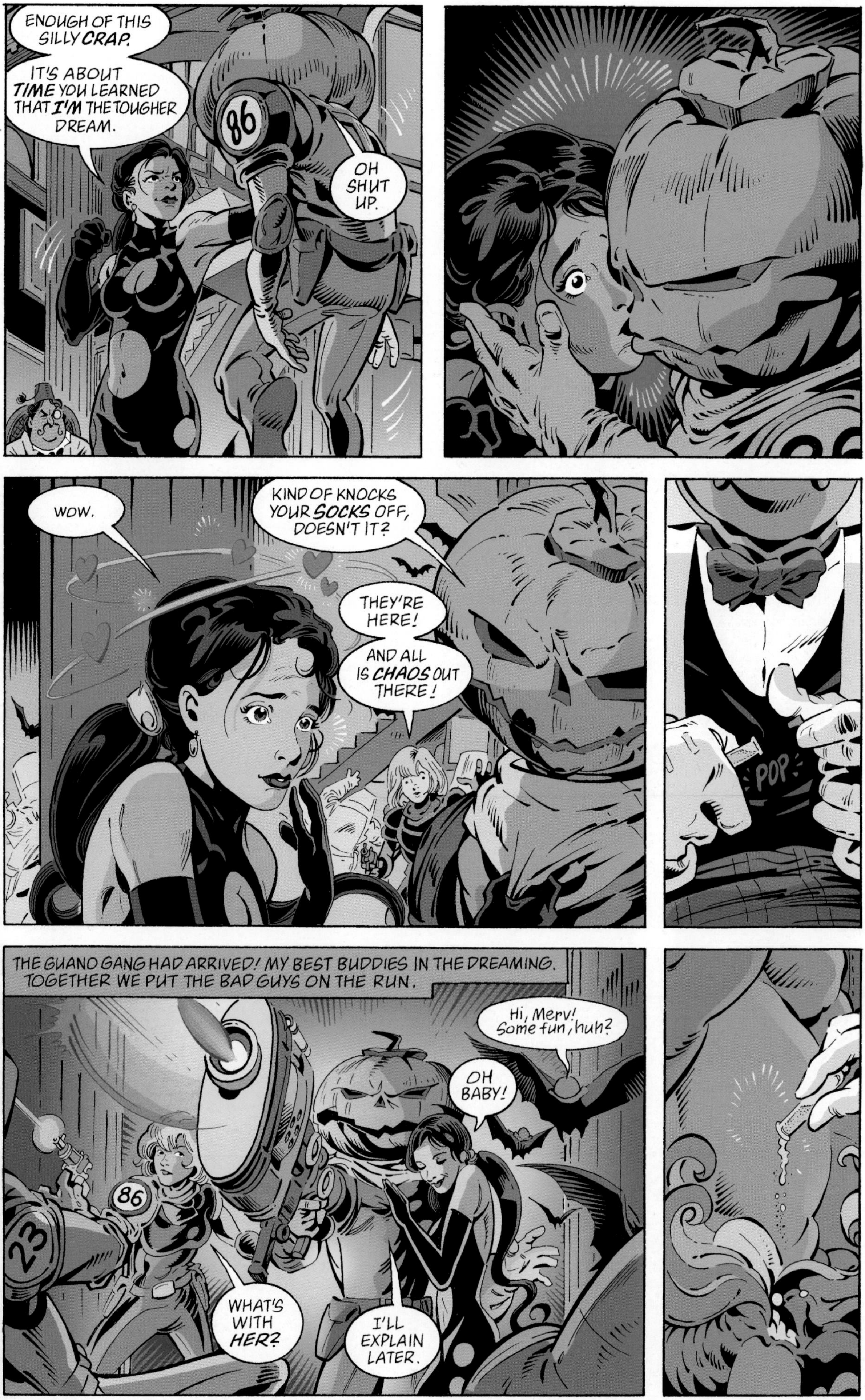
ENOUGH OF THIS SILLY *CRAP.*
IT'S ABOUT *TIME* YOU LEARNED THAT *I'M* THE TOUGHER DREAM.
OH SHUT UP.
WOW.
KIND OF KNOCKS YOUR *SOCKS* OFF, DOESN'T IT?
THEY'RE HERE!
AND ALL IS *CHAOS* OUT THERE!
POP
THE GUANO GANG HAD ARRIVED! MY BEST BUDDIES IN THE DREAMING. TOGETHER WE PUT THE BAD GUYS ON THE RUN.
Hi, Merv! Some fun, huh?
OH BABY!
86
23
WHAT'S WITH *HER?*
I'LL EXPLAIN LATER.

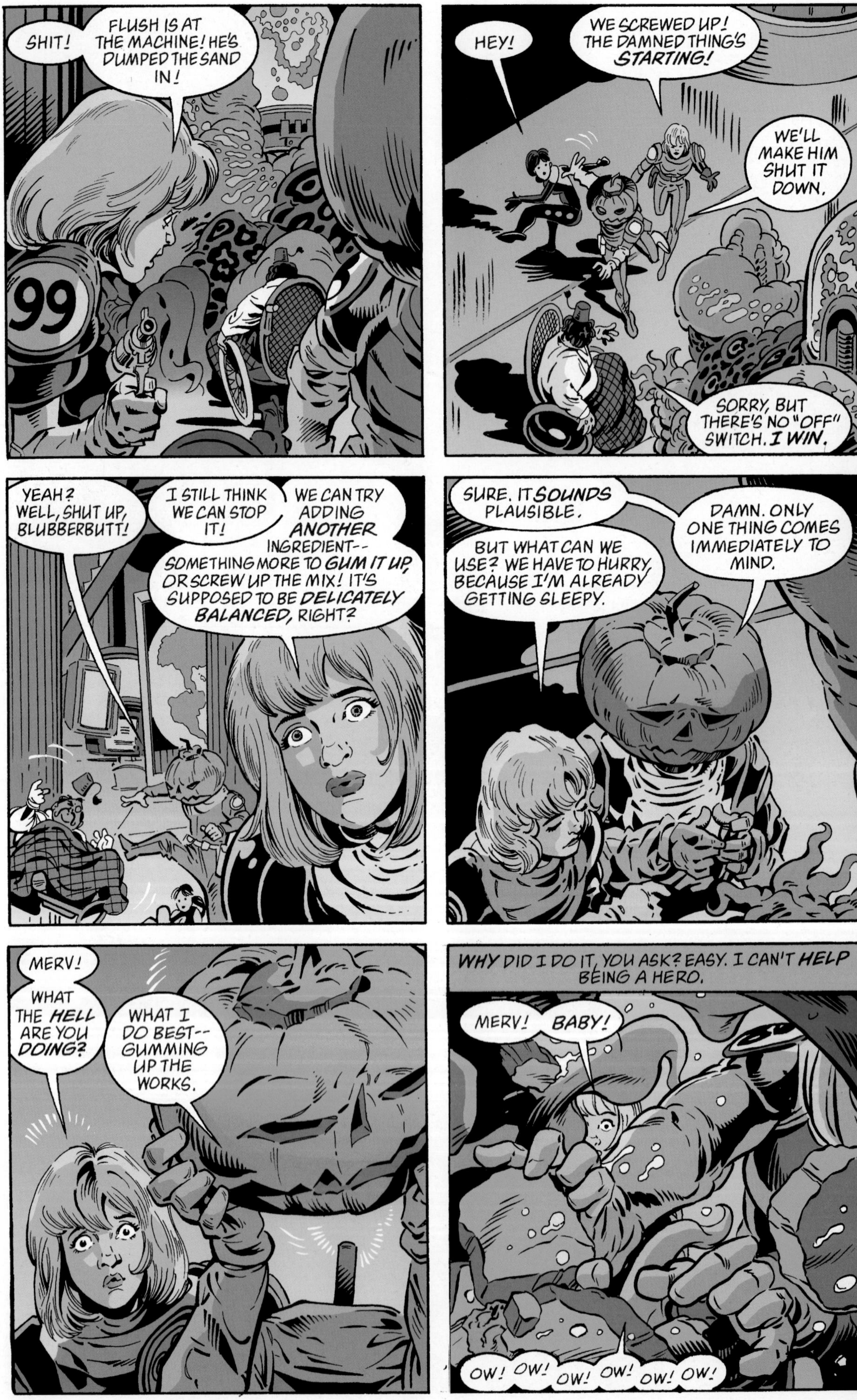
SHIT!
FLUSH IS AT THE MACHINE! HE'S DUMPED THE SAND IN!
HEY!
WE SCREWED UP! THE DAMNED THING'S STARTING!
WE'LL MAKE HIM SHUT IT DOWN.
SORRY, BUT THERE'S NO "OFF" SWITCH. I WIN.
YEAH? WELL, SHUT UP, BLUBBERBUTT!
I STILL THINK WE CAN STOP IT!
WE CAN TRY ADDING ANOTHER INGREDIENT-- SOMETHING MORE TO GUM IT UP, OR SCREW UP THE MIX! IT'S SUPPOSED TO BE DELICATELY BALANCED, RIGHT?
SURE. IT SOUNDS PLAUSIBLE.
BUT WHAT CAN WE USE? WE HAVE TO HURRY, BECAUSE I'M ALREADY GETTING SLEEPY.
DAMN. ONLY ONE THING COMES IMMEDIATELY TO MIND.
MERV!
WHAT THE HELL ARE YOU DOING?
WHAT I DO BEST-- GUMMING UP THE WORKS.
WHY DID I DO IT, YOU ASK? EASY. I CAN'T HELP BEING A HERO.
MERV!
BABY!
OW! OW! OW! OW! OW! OW!

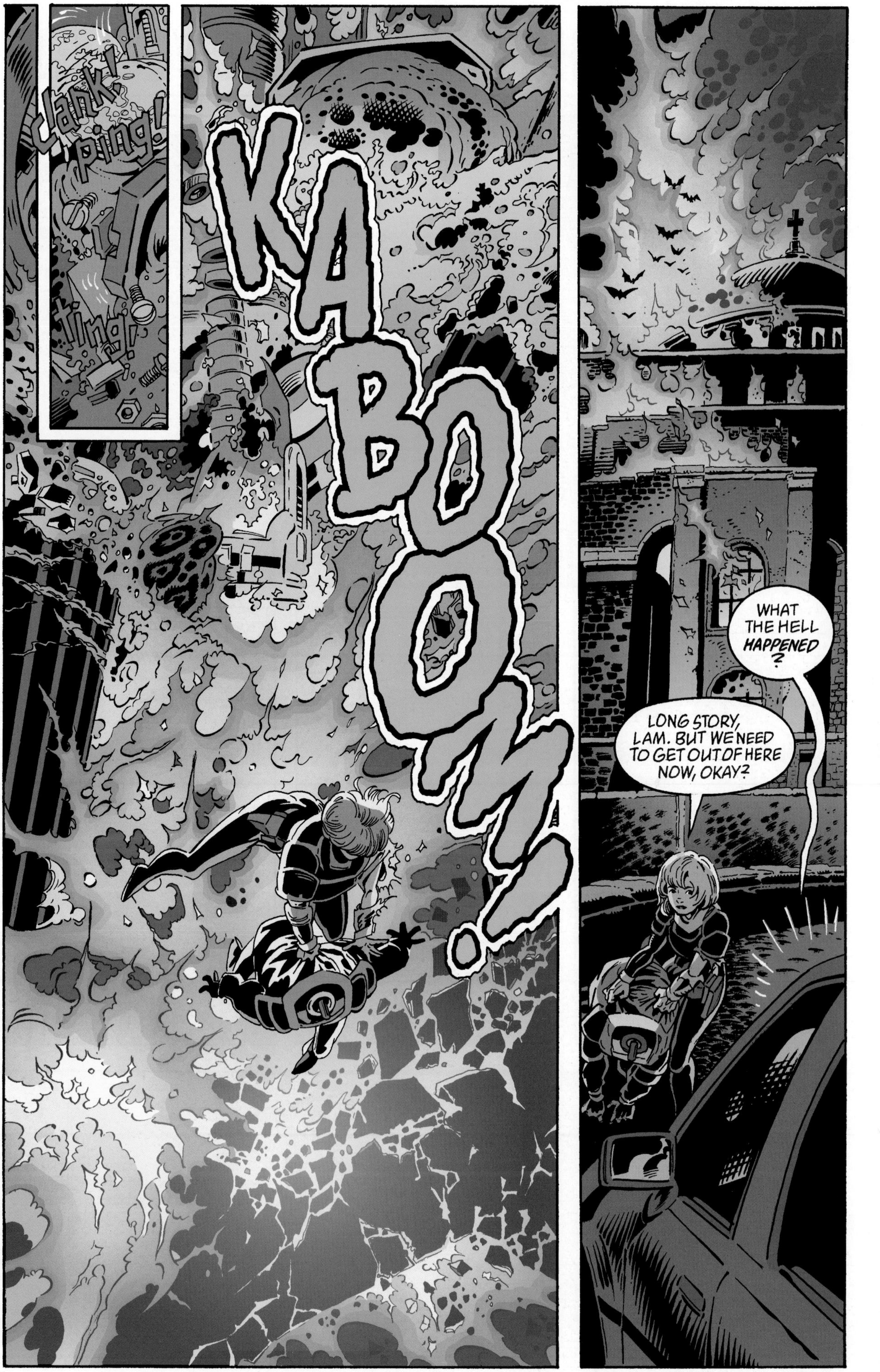
clank!
ping!
ting!
KABOOM!
WHAT THE HELL HAPPENED?
LONG STORY, LAM. BUT WE NEED TO GET OUT OF HERE NOW, OKAY?

EPILOGUE: THE PIE WHO LOVED ME

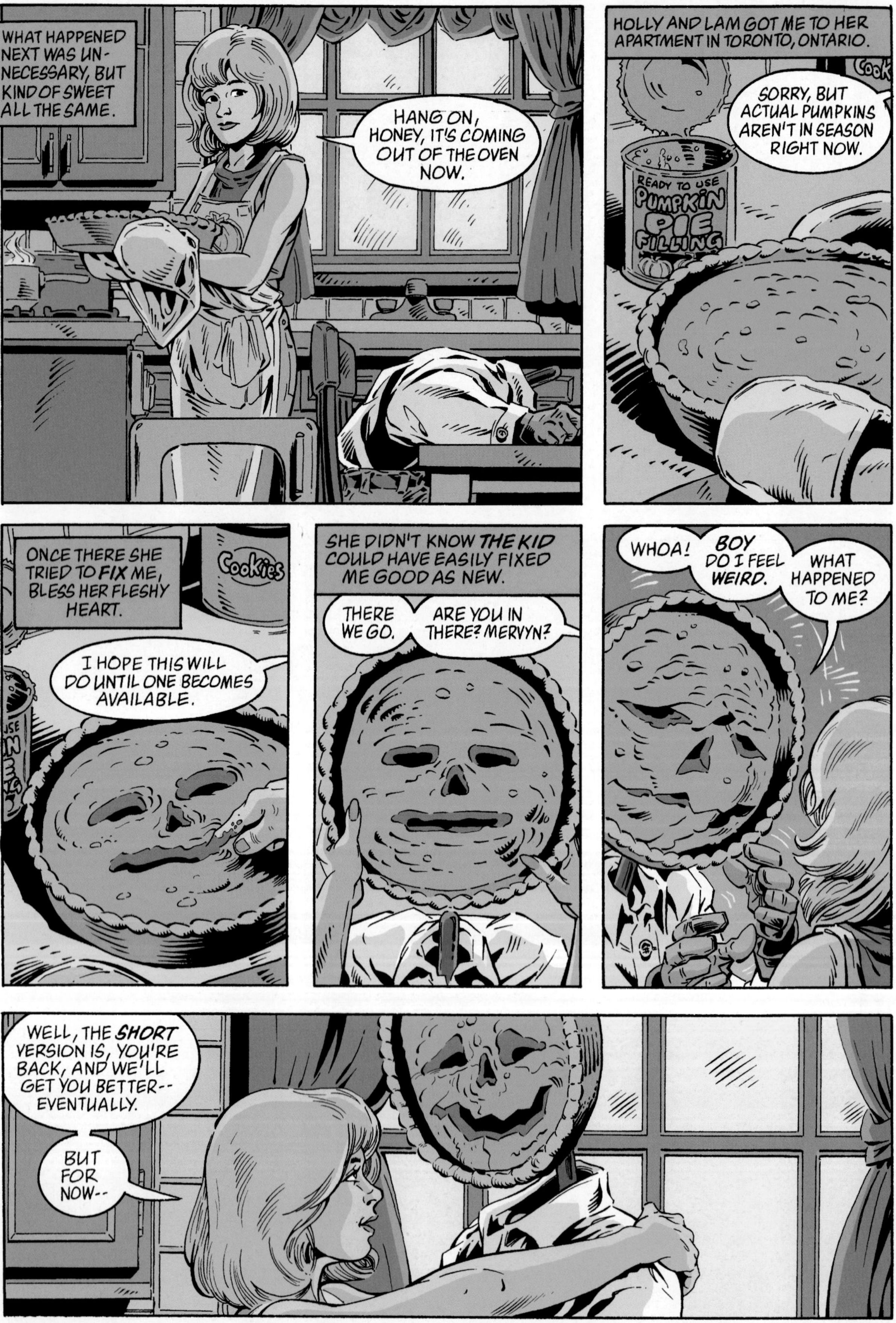
WHAT HAPPENED NEXT WAS UN-NECESSARY, BUT KIND OF SWEET ALL THE SAME.
HANG ON, HONEY, IT'S COMING OUT OF THE OVEN NOW.
HOLLY AND LAM GOT ME TO HER APARTMENT IN TORONTO, ONTARIO.
READY TO USE PUMPKIN PIE FILLING
COOKIES
SORRY, BUT ACTUAL PUMPKINS AREN'T IN SEASON RIGHT NOW.
ONCE THERE SHE TRIED TO FIX ME, BLESS HER FLESHY HEART.
COOKIES
I HOPE THIS WILL DO UNTIL ONE BECOMES AVAILABLE.
SHE DIDN'T KNOW THE KID COULD HAVE EASILY FIXED ME GOOD AS NEW.
THERE WE GO.
ARE YOU IN THERE? MERVYN?
WHOA!
BOY DO I FEEL WEIRD.
WHAT HAPPENED TO ME?
WELL, THE SHORT VERSION IS, YOU'RE BACK, AND WE'LL GET YOU BETTER-- EVENTUALLY.
BUT FOR NOW--

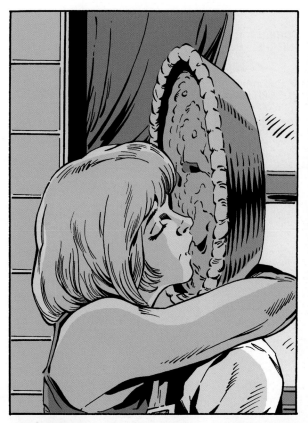

OKAY, WE NEED TO WORK ON THAT PART-- MERVYN PIEFACE.

UH, HOLLY? I THINK I SHOULD TELL YOU...

WELL, YOU KNOW HOW THIS ENDS.

DANIEL TRACKED ME DOWN, GAVE ME BACK MY OLD, HANDSOME HEAD, AND ESCORTED ME BACK TO THE DREAMING.

AND *THAT*, MORE OR LESS, IS HOW I SAVED BOTH THE DREAMING AND THE WAKING WORLD.

RIGHT.

V-VERY N-NICE SSSSTORY, MUM MUM MERVYN.

YES, TERRIFIC YARN. IT IS, OF COURSE, A BIG PILE OF *SHEEP DUNG*, BUT ENTERTAINING NONETHELESS.

NOT AS GOOD A TALE AS *I* COULD TELL, MIND YOU, BUT MILDLY AMUSING IN A *PEDES-TRIAN* SORT OF WAY.

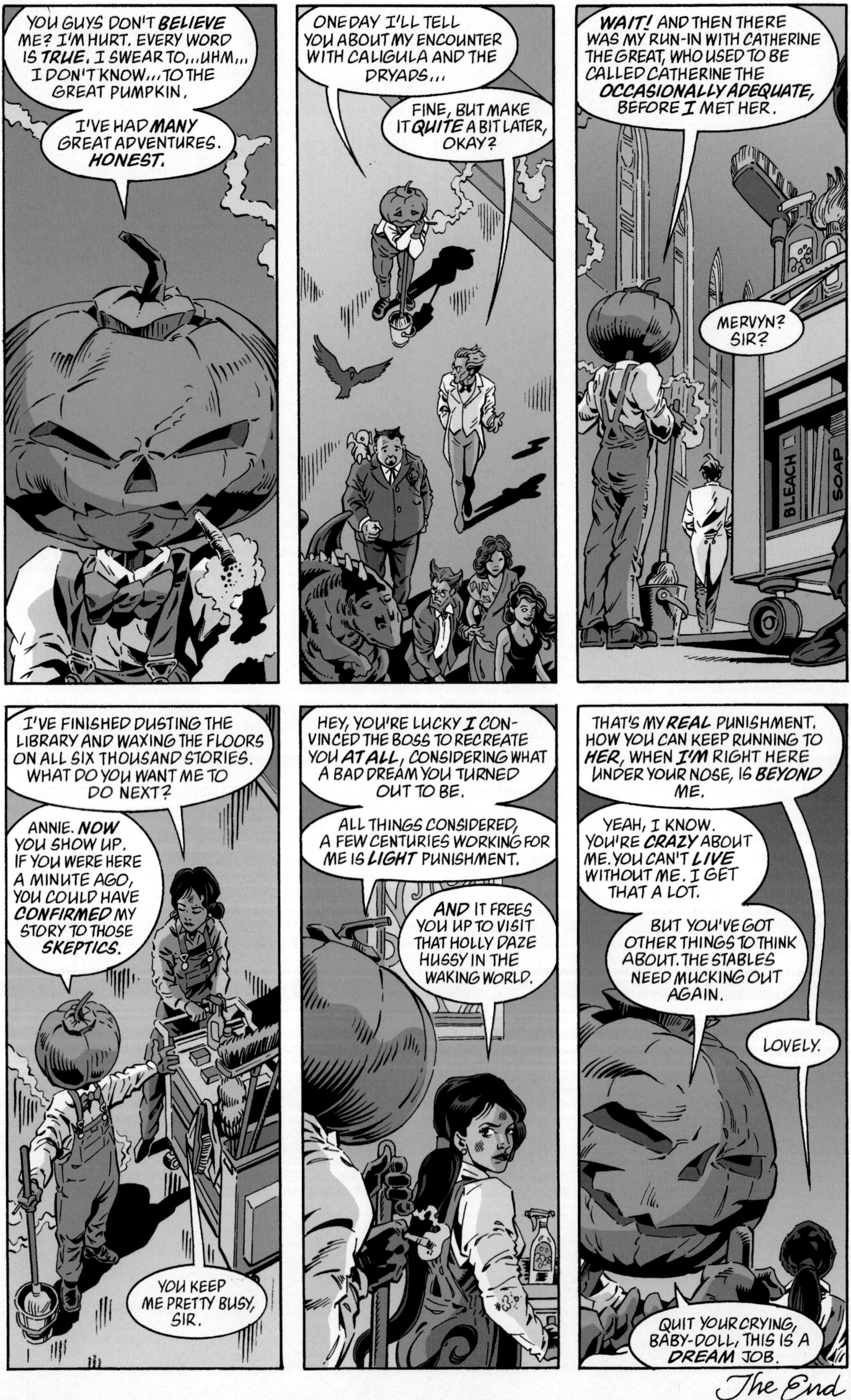
YOU GUYS DON'T BELIEVE ME? I'M HURT. EVERY WORD IS TRUE. I SWEAR TO... UHM... I DON'T KNOW... TO THE GREAT PUMPKIN.
I'VE HAD MANY GREAT ADVENTURES. HONEST.
ONE DAY I'LL TELL YOU ABOUT MY ENCOUNTER WITH CALIGULA AND THE DRYADS...
FINE, BUT MAKE IT QUITE A BIT LATER, OKAY?
WAIT! AND THEN THERE WAS MY RUN-IN WITH CATHERINE THE GREAT, WHO USED TO BE CALLED CATHERINE THE OCCASIONALLY ADEQUATE, BEFORE I MET HER.
MERVYN? SIR?
BLEACH
SOAP
I'VE FINISHED DUSTING THE LIBRARY AND WAXING THE FLOORS ON ALL SIX THOUSAND STORIES. WHAT DO YOU WANT ME TO DO NEXT?
ANNIE. NOW YOU SHOW UP. IF YOU WERE HERE A MINUTE AGO, YOU COULD HAVE CONFIRMED MY STORY TO THOSE SKEPTICS.
YOU KEEP ME PRETTY BUSY, SIR.
HEY, YOU'RE LUCKY I CONVINCED THE BOSS TO RECREATE YOU AT ALL, CONSIDERING WHAT A BAD DREAM YOU TURNED OUT TO BE.
ALL THINGS CONSIDERED, A FEW CENTURIES WORKING FOR ME IS LIGHT PUNISHMENT.
AND IT FREES YOU UP TO VISIT THAT HOLLY DAZE HUSSY IN THE WAKING WORLD.
THAT'S MY REAL PUNISHMENT. HOW YOU CAN KEEP RUNNING TO HER, WHEN I'M RIGHT HERE UNDER YOUR NOSE, IS BEYOND ME.
YEAH, I KNOW. YOU'RE CRAZY ABOUT ME. YOU CAN'T LIVE WITHOUT ME. I GET THAT A LOT.
BUT YOU'VE GOT OTHER THINGS TO THINK ABOUT. THE STABLES NEED MUCKING OUT AGAIN.
LOVELY.
QUIT YOUR CRYING, BABY-DOLL, THIS IS A DREAM JOB.

The End

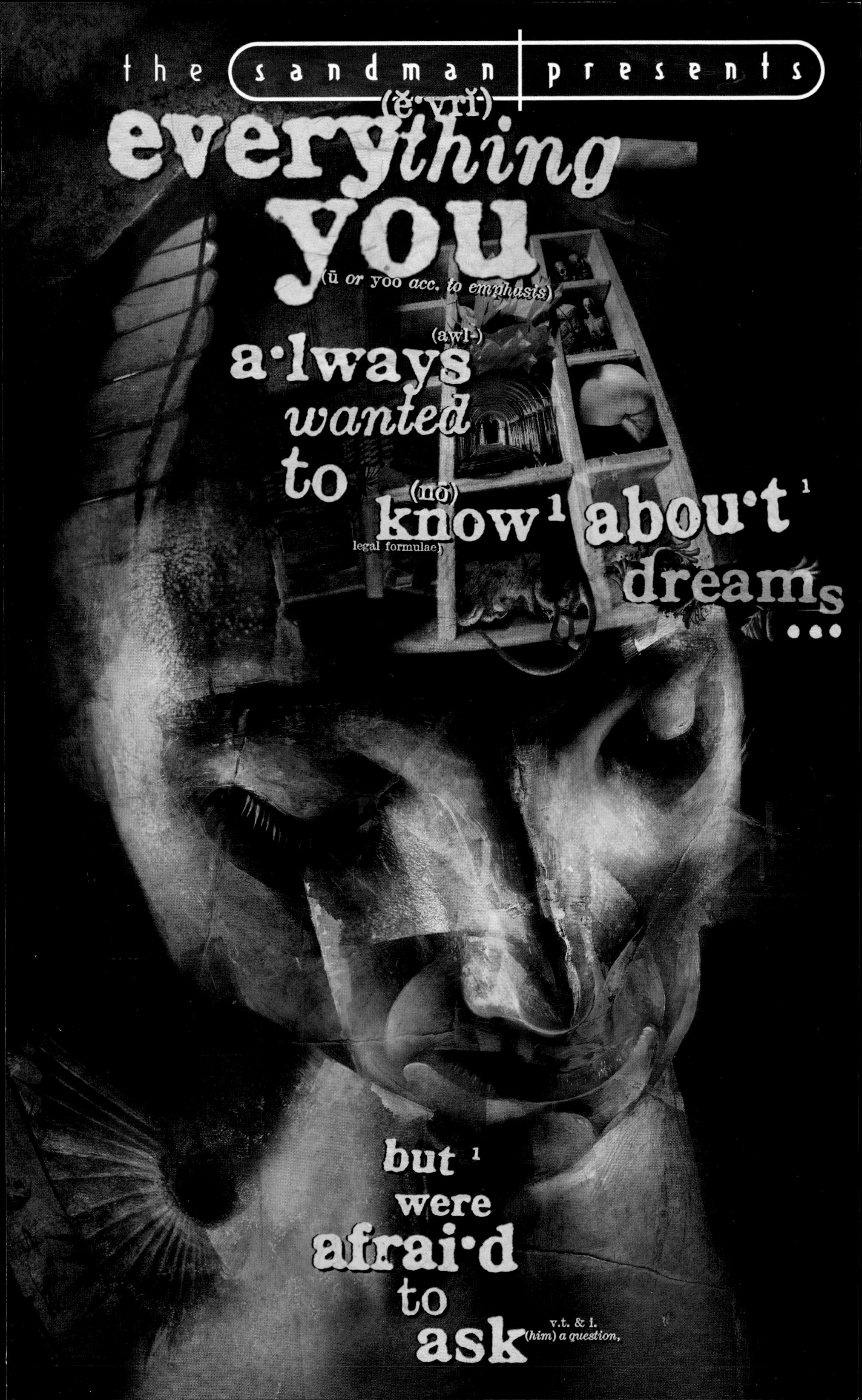
the sandman presents
(ĕ'vrĭ)
everything
you
(ū or yoo acc. to emphasis)
(awl·)
a·lways
wanted
to
(nō)
know 1
legal formulae)
about·t 1
dreams
...
but 1
were
afrai·d
to
ask
v.t. & i.
(him) a question,

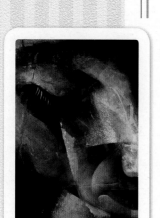

I CAN'T SEE ANYTHING ABOUT THIS SET OF TALL TALES THAT ISN'T SELF-EXPLANATORY. It's a silly look behind the scenes at how dreams are designed, built and performed each night, and the strange folk who are employed in doing it.

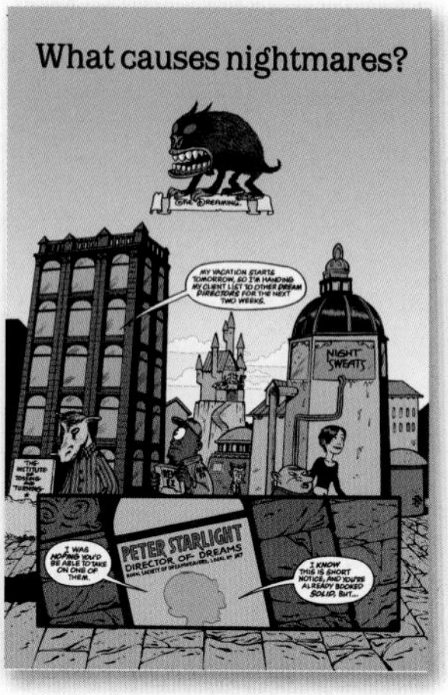
What causes nightmares?
NIGHT SWEATS
PETER STARLIGHT
DIRECTOR OF DREAMS

With this project I got to cross off one of the names on my wish list of artists I dearly wanted to work with someday. Every comics writer has such a list — if they say otherwise, they're lying. In this case, the name belonged to one Kevin Nowlan, Esquire. Sure, he'd just provided the cover art for the MERV PUMPKINHEAD one-shot special, so that sort of counted, but doing a cover isn't the same as getting down in the muck and filth, side by side with the writer in the dirty trenches of panel-by-panel storytelling, so this was quite a treat. Also, Mark Buckingham came back to do another Merv story — a second small step towards a lifetime (ten years so far and counting, knock wood) collaboration.

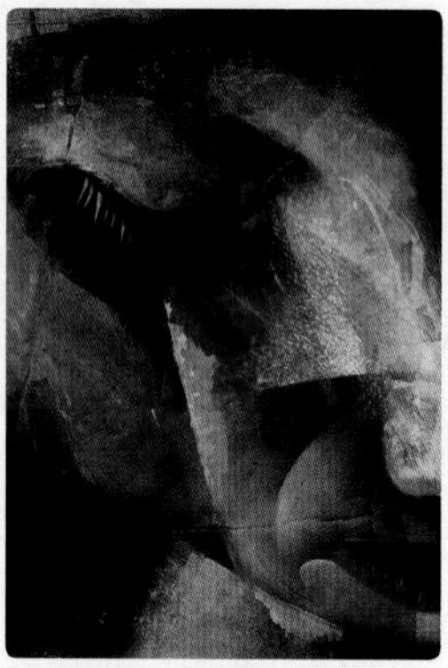

EVERYTHING YOU ALWAYS WANTED TO KNOW ABOUT DREAMS... BUT WERE AFRAID TO ASK

ART BY
Albert Monteys
(pages 235-240)
Duncan Fegredo
(pages 241-247)
Kevin Nowlan
(pages 248-249)
Jason Little
(pages 250-253, 263-264, 271-272)
Mark Buckingham
(pages 254-262)
Niko Henrichon
(pages 265-270)

COLORS BY
Daniel Vozzo

LETTERS BY
Todd Klein

COVER ART BY
Dave McKean

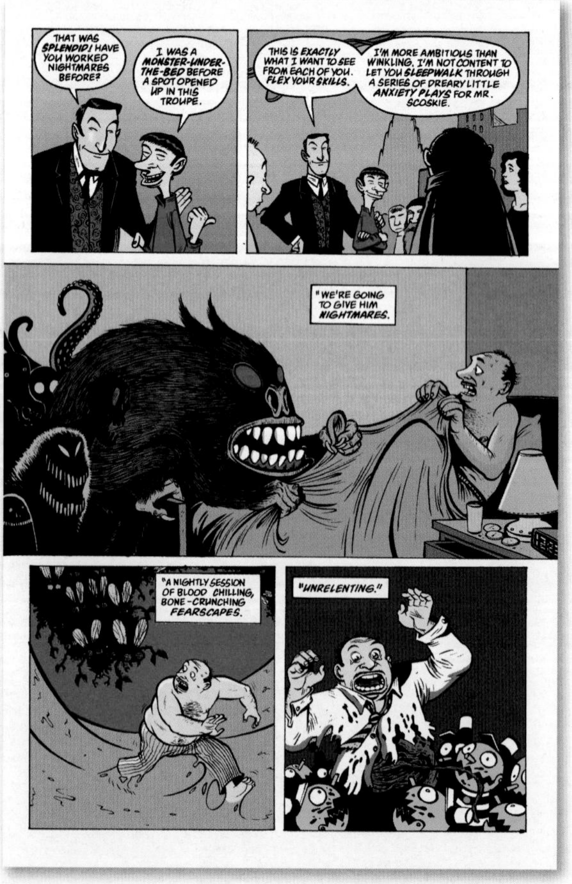
THAT WAS SPLENDID! HAVE YOU WORKED NIGHTMARES BEFORE?
I WAS A MONSTER-UNDER-THE-BED BEFORE A SPOT OPENED UP IN THIS TROUPE.
THIS IS EXACTLY WHAT I WANT TO SEE FROM EACH OF YOU. FLEX YOUR SKILLS.
I'M MORE AMBITIOUS THAN WINKLING. I'M NOT CONTENT TO LET YOU SLEEPWALK THROUGH A SERIES OF DREARY LITTLE ANXIETY PLAYS FOR MR. SCOSKIE.
"WE'RE GOING TO GIVE HIM NIGHTMARES.
"A NIGHTLY SESSION OF BLOOD CHILLING, BONE-CRUNCHING FEARSCAPES.
"UNRELENTING."

What causes nightmares?

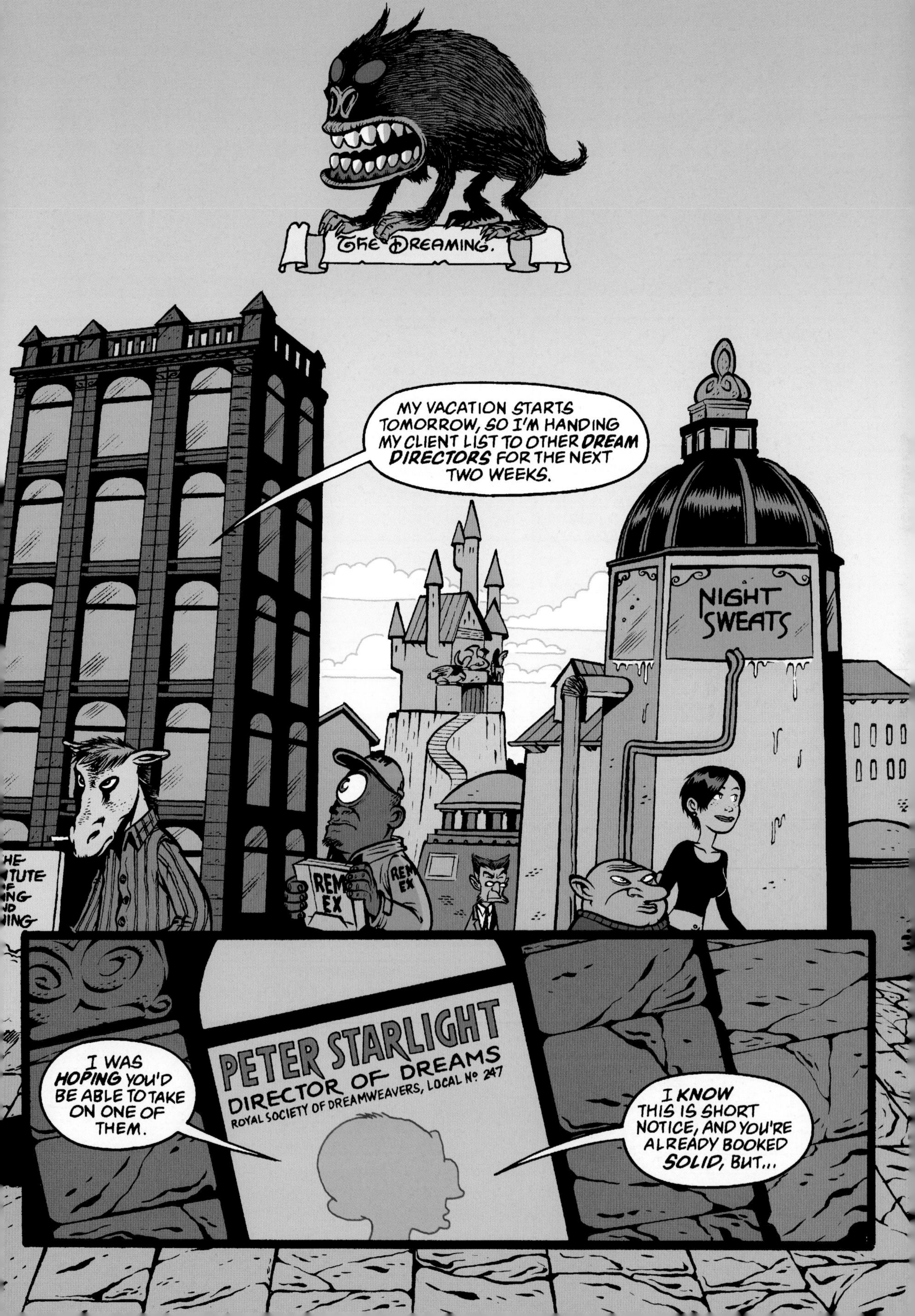
THE DREAMING.
MY VACATION STARTS TOMORROW, SO I'M HANDING MY CLIENT LIST TO OTHER DREAM DIRECTORS FOR THE NEXT TWO WEEKS.
NIGHT SWEATS
REM EX
I WAS HOPING YOU'D BE ABLE TO TAKE ON ONE OF THEM.
PETER STARLIGHT
DIRECTOR OF DREAMS
ROYAL SOCIETY OF DREAMWEAVERS, LOCAL Nº 247
I KNOW THIS IS SHORT NOTICE, AND YOU'RE ALREADY BOOKED SOLID, BUT...

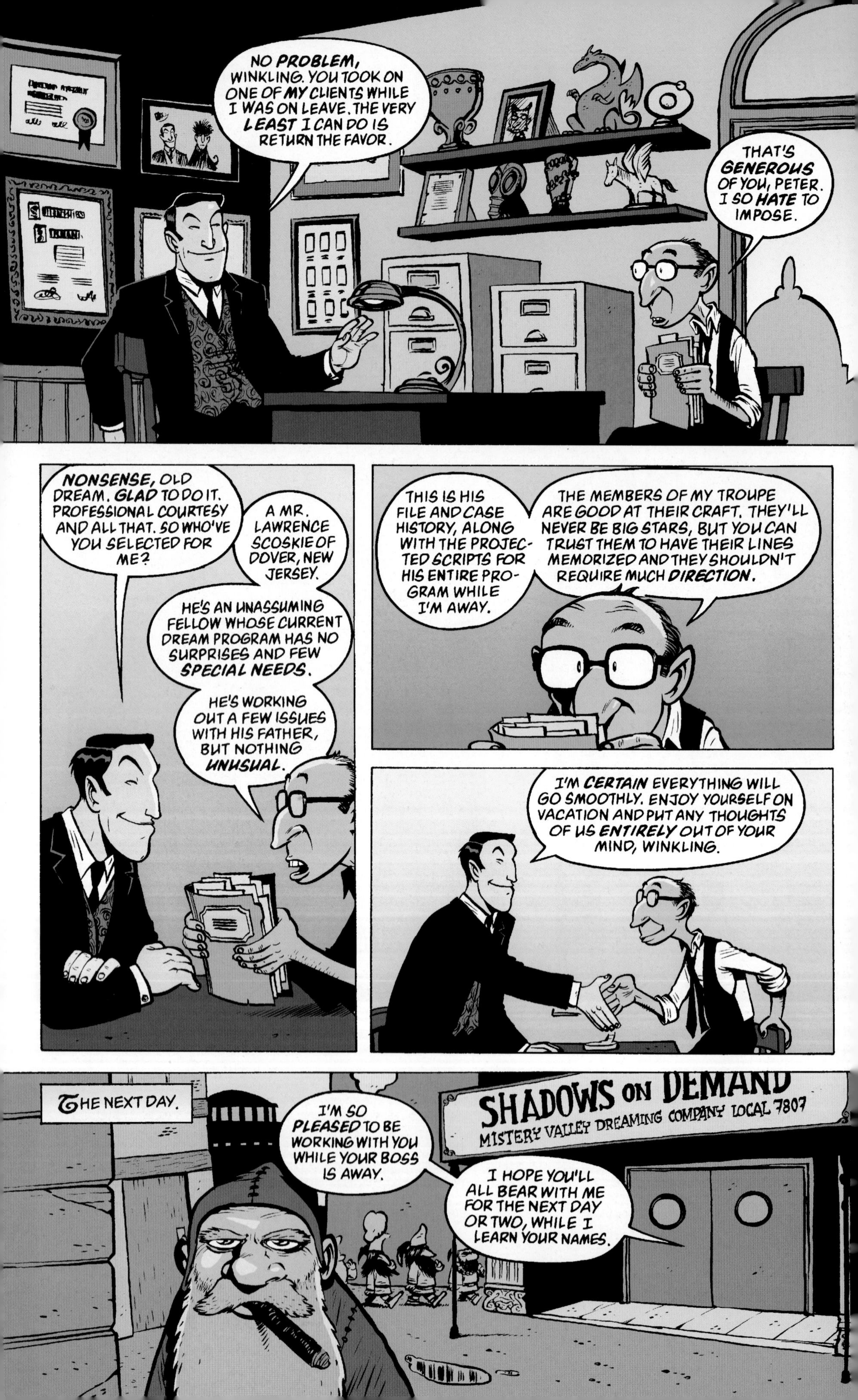
NO PROBLEM, WINKLING. YOU TOOK ON ONE OF MY CLIENTS WHILE I WAS ON LEAVE. THE VERY LEAST I CAN DO IS RETURN THE FAVOR.
THAT'S GENEROUS OF YOU, PETER. I SO HATE TO IMPOSE.
NONSENSE, OLD DREAM. GLAD TO DO IT. PROFESSIONAL COURTESY AND ALL THAT. SO WHO'VE YOU SELECTED FOR ME?
A MR. LAWRENCE SCOSKIE OF DOVER, NEW JERSEY.
HE'S AN UNASSUMING FELLOW WHOSE CURRENT DREAM PROGRAM HAS NO SURPRISES AND FEW SPECIAL NEEDS.
HE'S WORKING OUT A FEW ISSUES WITH HIS FATHER, BUT NOTHING UNUSUAL.
THIS IS HIS FILE AND CASE HISTORY, ALONG WITH THE PROJECTED SCRIPTS FOR HIS ENTIRE PROGRAM WHILE I'M AWAY.
THE MEMBERS OF MY TROUPE ARE GOOD AT THEIR CRAFT. THEY'LL NEVER BE BIG STARS, BUT YOU CAN TRUST THEM TO HAVE THEIR LINES MEMORIZED AND THEY SHOULDN'T REQUIRE MUCH DIRECTION.
I'M CERTAIN EVERYTHING WILL GO SMOOTHLY. ENJOY YOURSELF ON VACATION AND PUT ANY THOUGHTS OF US ENTIRELY OUT OF YOUR MIND, WINKLING.
THE NEXT DAY.
SHADOWS ON DEMAND
MISTERY VALLEY DREAMING COMPANY LOCAL 7807
I'M SO PLEASED TO BE WORKING WITH YOU WHILE YOUR BOSS IS AWAY.
I HOPE YOU'LL ALL BEAR WITH ME FOR THE NEXT DAY OR TWO, WHILE I LEARN YOUR NAMES.

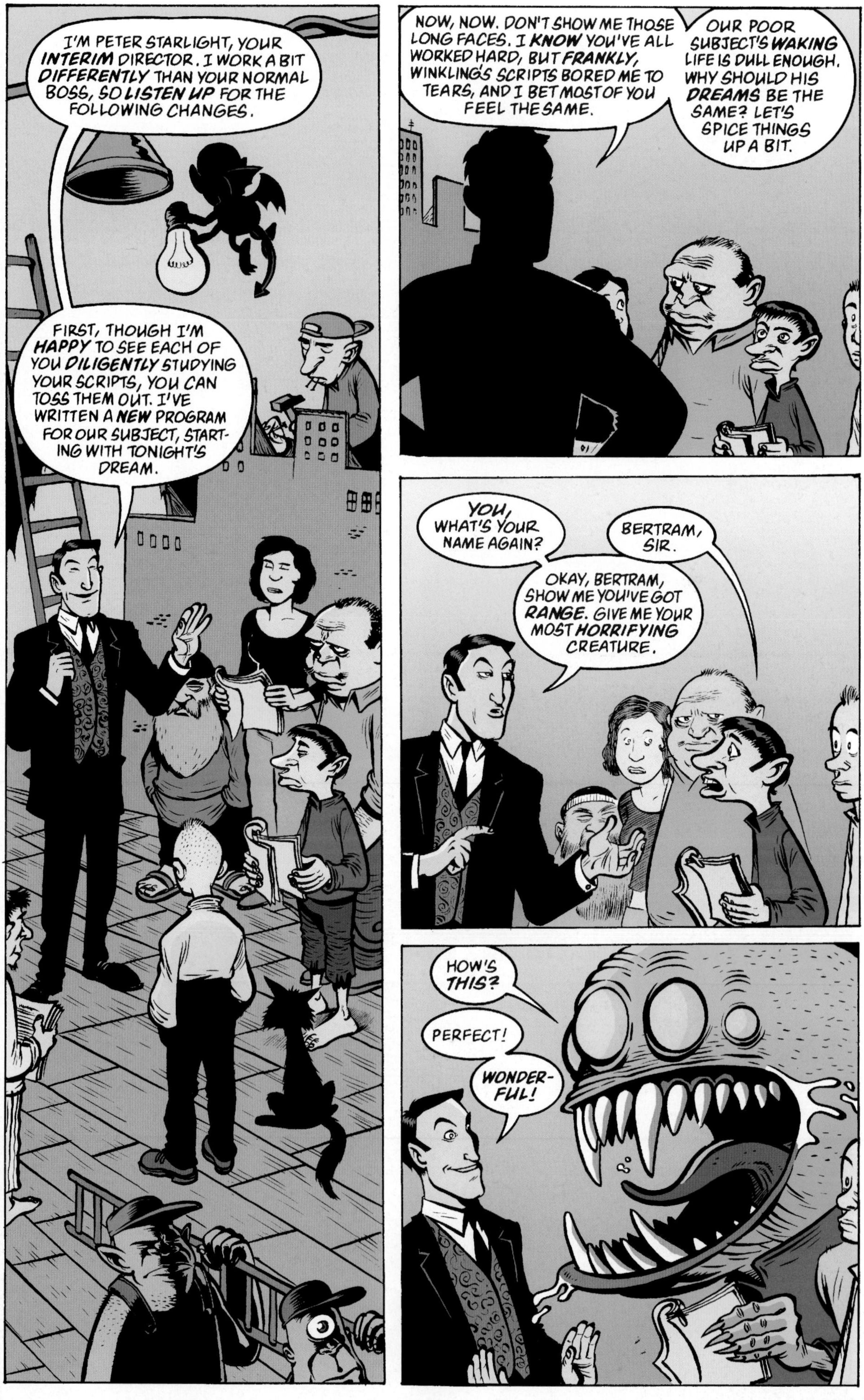
I'M PETER STARLIGHT, YOUR INTERIM DIRECTOR. I WORK A BIT DIFFERENTLY THAN YOUR NORMAL BOSS, SO LISTEN UP FOR THE FOLLOWING CHANGES.
FIRST, THOUGH I'M HAPPY TO SEE EACH OF YOU DILIGENTLY STUDYING YOUR SCRIPTS, YOU CAN TOSS THEM OUT. I'VE WRITTEN A NEW PROGRAM FOR OUR SUBJECT, STARTING WITH TONIGHT'S DREAM.
NOW, NOW. DON'T SHOW ME THOSE LONG FACES. I KNOW YOU'VE ALL WORKED HARD, BUT FRANKLY, WINKLING'S SCRIPTS BORED ME TO TEARS, AND I BET MOST OF YOU FEEL THE SAME.
OUR POOR SUBJECT'S WAKING LIFE IS DULL ENOUGH. WHY SHOULD HIS DREAMS BE THE SAME? LET'S SPICE THINGS UP A BIT.
YOU, WHAT'S YOUR NAME AGAIN?
BERTRAM, SIR.
OKAY, BERTRAM, SHOW ME YOU'VE GOT RANGE. GIVE ME YOUR MOST HORRIFYING CREATURE.
HOW'S THIS?
PERFECT!
WONDERFUL!

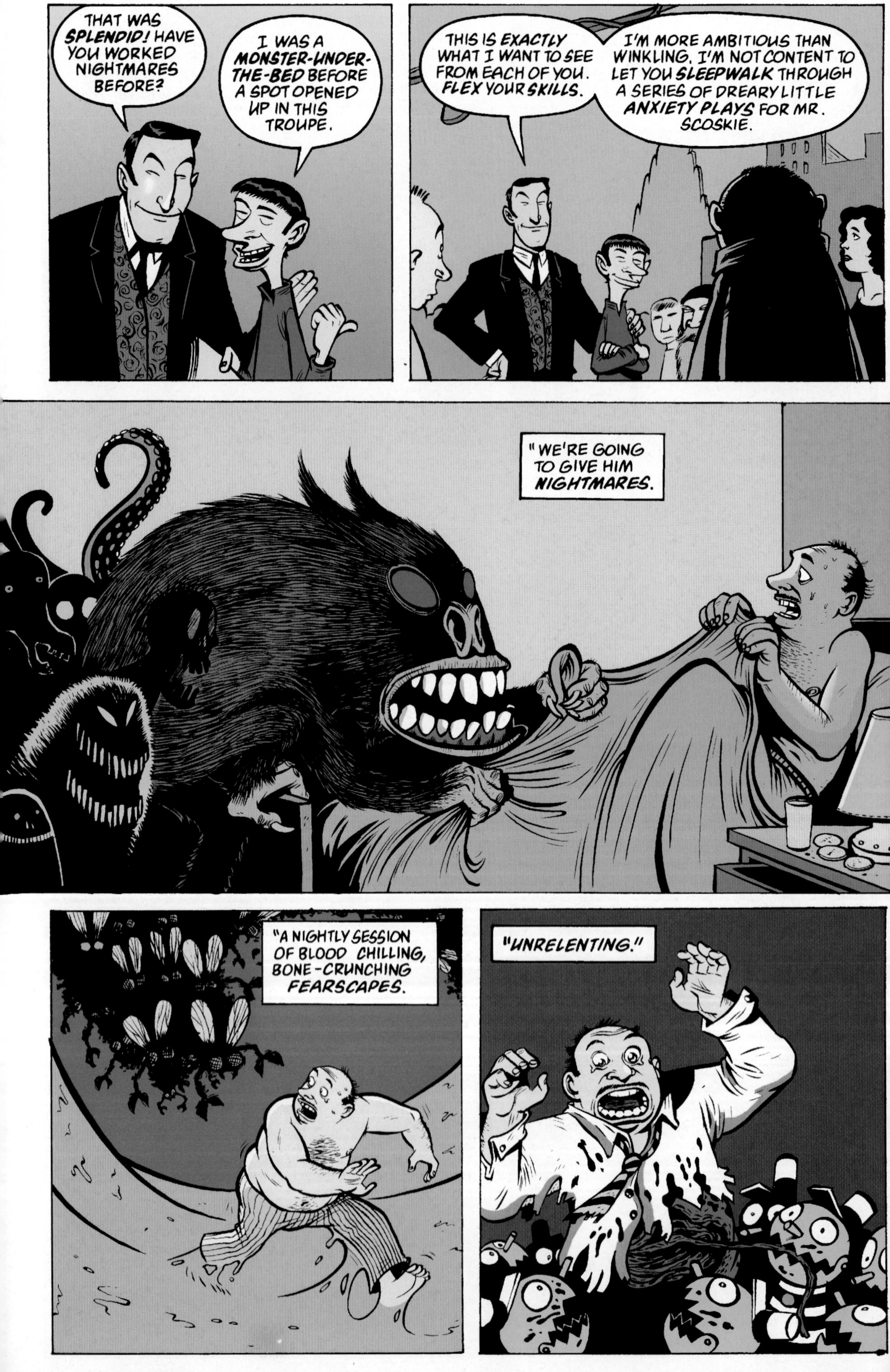
THAT WAS SPLENDID! HAVE YOU WORKED NIGHTMARES BEFORE?
I WAS A MONSTER-UNDER-THE-BED BEFORE A SPOT OPENED UP IN THIS TROUPE.
THIS IS EXACTLY WHAT I WANT TO SEE FROM EACH OF YOU. FLEX YOUR SKILLS.
I'M MORE AMBITIOUS THAN WINKLING. I'M NOT CONTENT TO LET YOU SLEEPWALK THROUGH A SERIES OF DREARY LITTLE ANXIETY PLAYS FOR MR. SCOSKIE.
"WE'RE GOING TO GIVE HIM NIGHTMARES.
"A NIGHTLY SESSION OF BLOOD CHILLING, BONE-CRUNCHING FEARSCAPES.
"UNRELENTING."

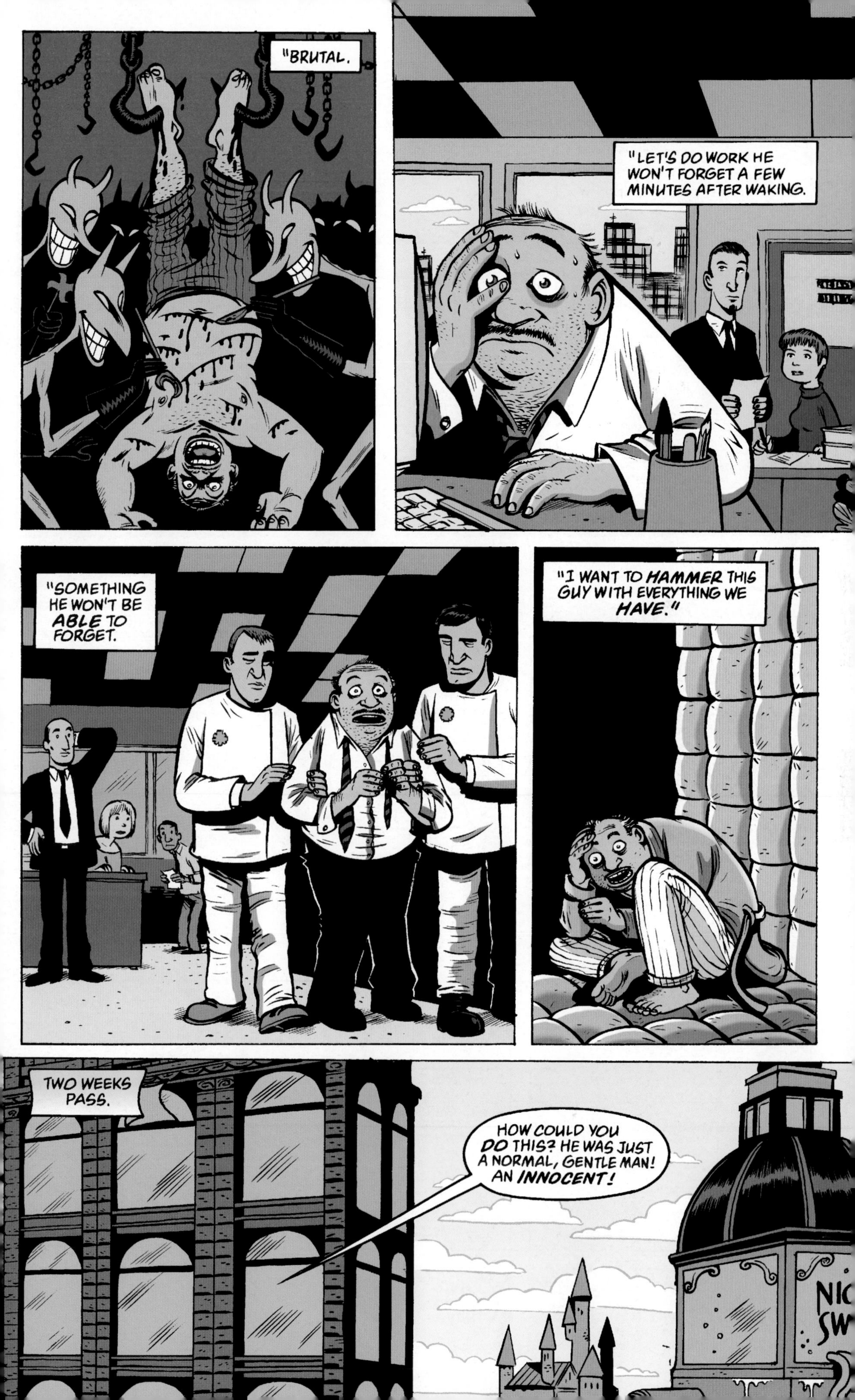
"BRUTAL.
"LET'S DO WORK HE WON'T FORGET A FEW MINUTES AFTER WAKING.
"SOMETHING HE WON'T BE *ABLE* TO FORGET.
"I WANT TO *HAMMER* THIS GUY WITH EVERYTHING WE *HAVE*."
TWO WEEKS PASS.
HOW COULD YOU *DO* THIS? HE WAS JUST A NORMAL, GENTLE MAN! AN *INNOCENT*!

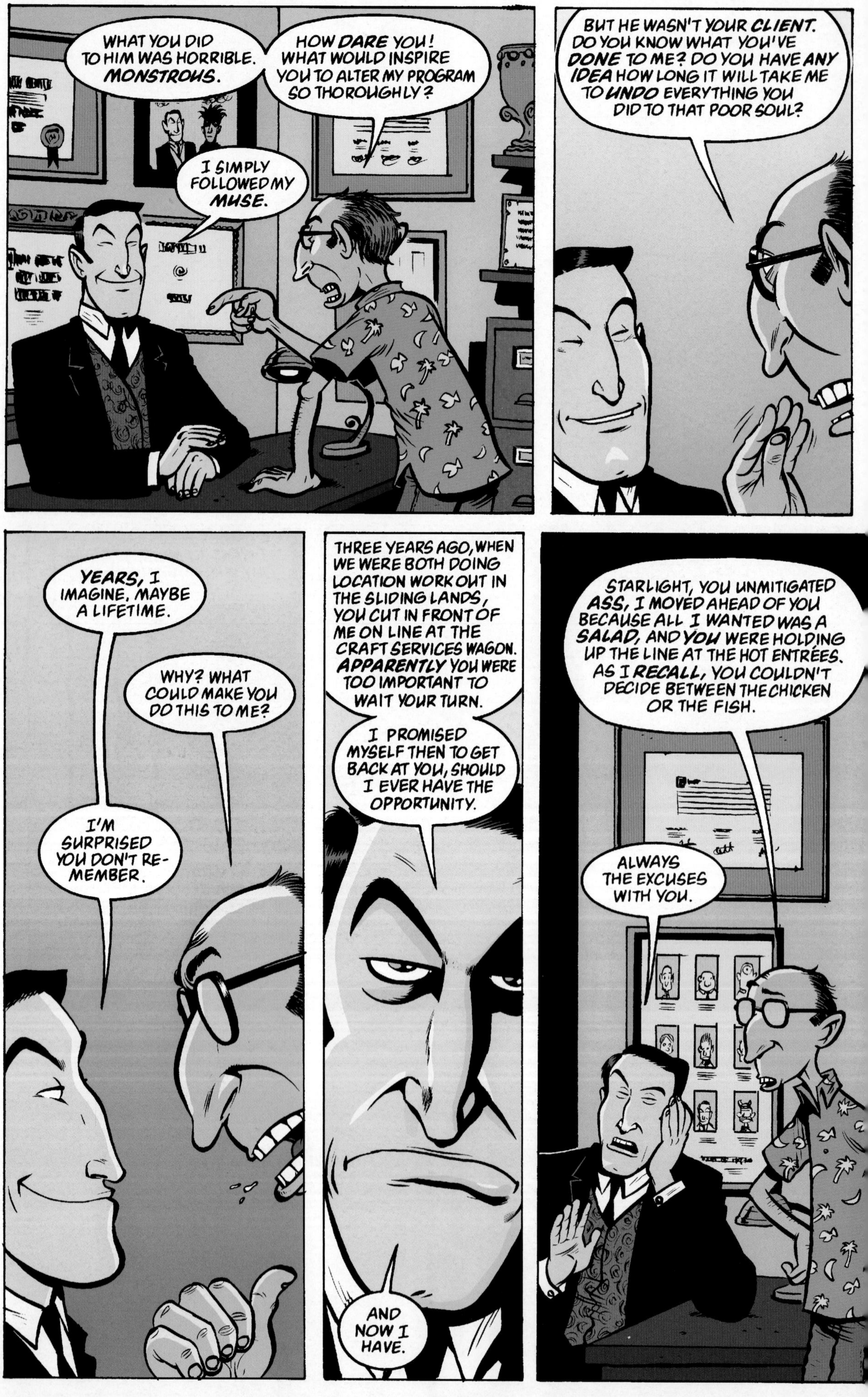
WHAT YOU DID TO HIM WAS HORRIBLE. MONSTROUS.
HOW DARE YOU! WHAT WOULD INSPIRE YOU TO ALTER MY PROGRAM SO THOROUGHLY?
I SIMPLY FOLLOWED MY MUSE.
BUT HE WASN'T YOUR CLIENT. DO YOU KNOW WHAT YOU'VE DONE TO ME? DO YOU HAVE ANY IDEA HOW LONG IT WILL TAKE ME TO UNDO EVERYTHING YOU DID TO THAT POOR SOUL?
YEARS, I IMAGINE, MAYBE A LIFETIME.
WHY? WHAT COULD MAKE YOU DO THIS TO ME?
I'M SURPRISED YOU DON'T RE-MEMBER.
THREE YEARS AGO, WHEN WE WERE BOTH DOING LOCATION WORK OUT IN THE SLIDING LANDS, YOU CUT IN FRONT OF ME ON LINE AT THE CRAFT SERVICES WAGON. APPARENTLY YOU WERE TOO IMPORTANT TO WAIT YOUR TURN.
I PROMISED MYSELF THEN TO GET BACK AT YOU, SHOULD I EVER HAVE THE OPPORTUNITY.
AND NOW I HAVE.
STARLIGHT, YOU UNMITIGATED ASS, I MOVED AHEAD OF YOU BECAUSE ALL I WANTED WAS A SALAD, AND YOU WERE HOLDING UP THE LINE AT THE HOT ENTRÉES. AS I RECALL, YOU COULDN'T DECIDE BETWEEN THE CHICKEN OR THE FISH.
ALWAYS THE EXCUSES WITH YOU.

Do dreams sleep and have other dreams of their own?

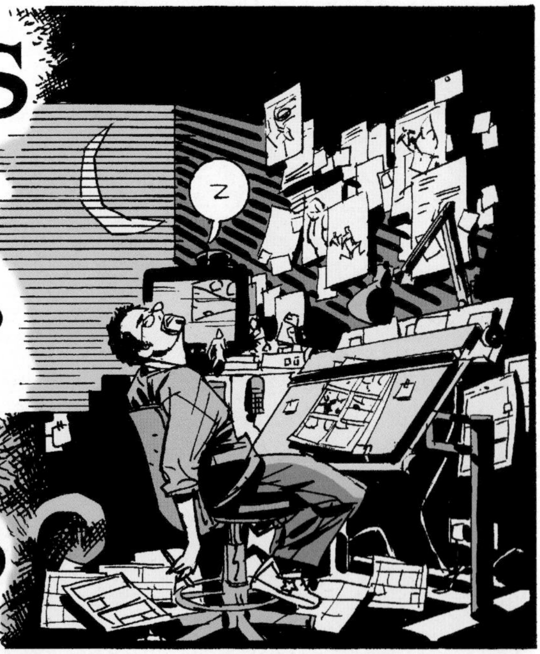
Z

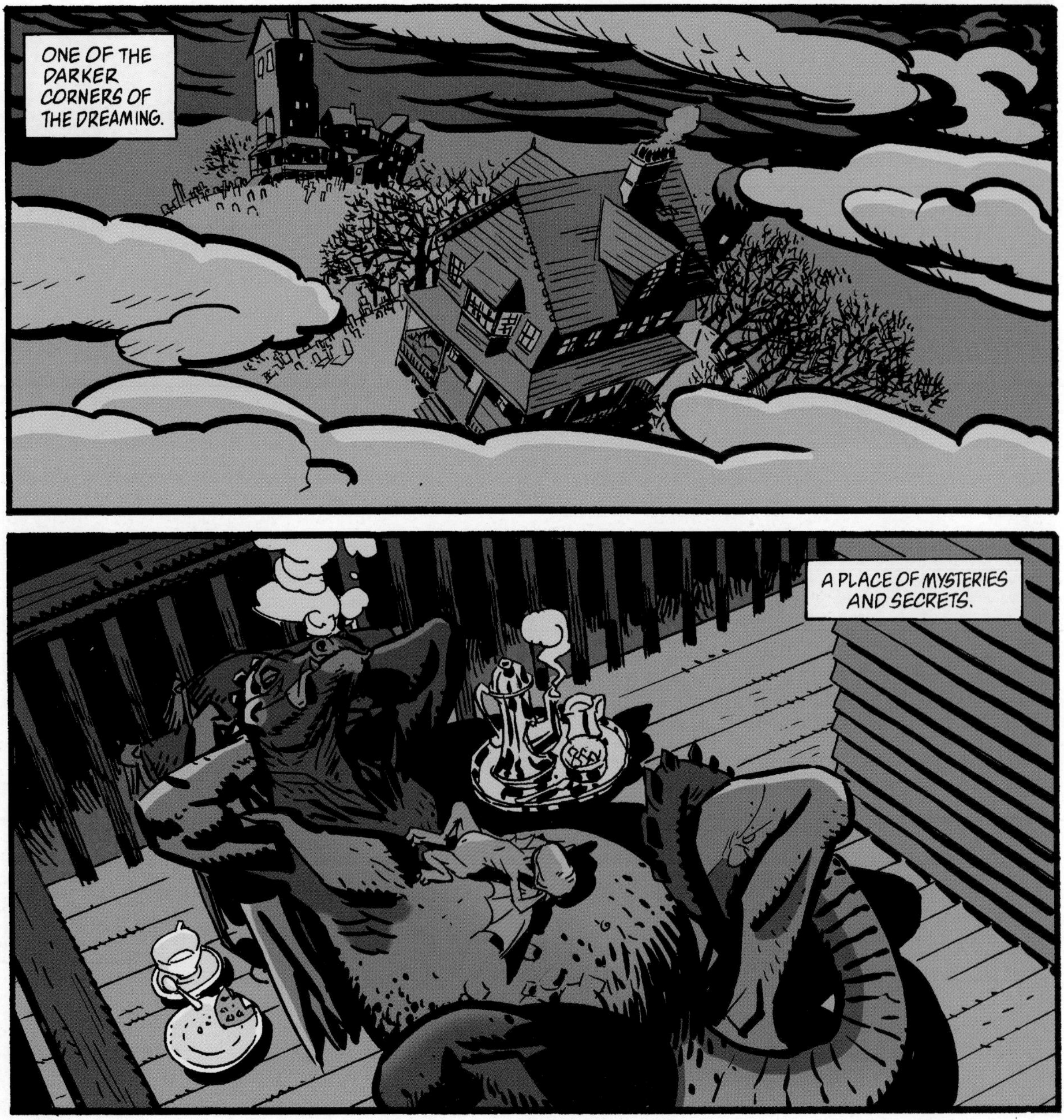
ONE OF THE DARKER CORNERS OF THE DREAMING.
A PLACE OF MYSTERIES AND SECRETS.

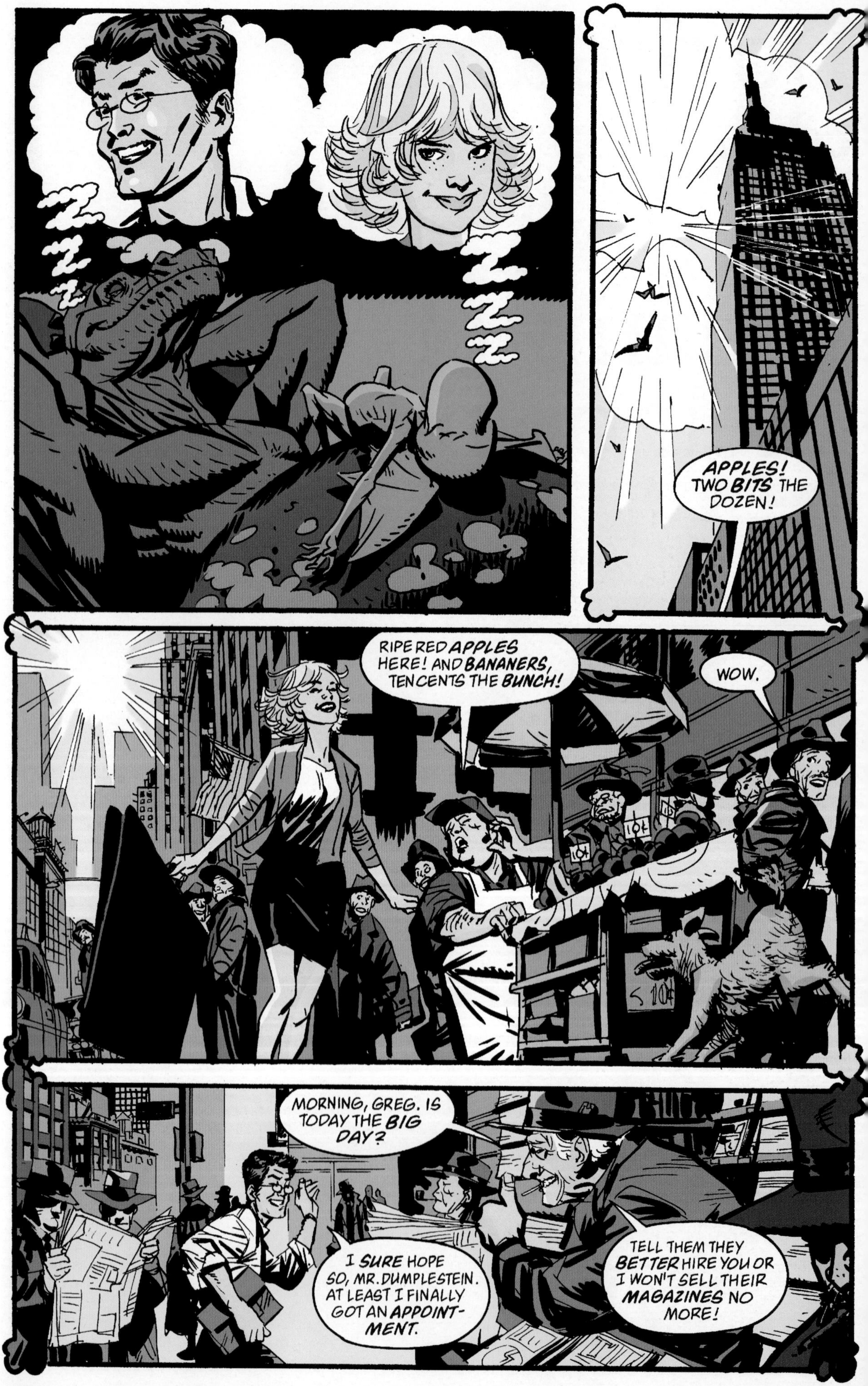
APPLES! TWO BITS THE DOZEN!
RIPE RED APPLES HERE! AND BANANERS, TEN CENTS THE BUNCH!
WOW.
10¢
10¢
MORNING, GREG. IS TODAY THE BIG DAY?
I SURE HOPE SO, MR. DUMPLESTEIN. AT LEAST I FINALLY GOT AN APPOINT-MENT.
TELL THEM THEY BETTER HIRE YOU OR I WON'T SELL THEIR MAGAZINES NO MORE!

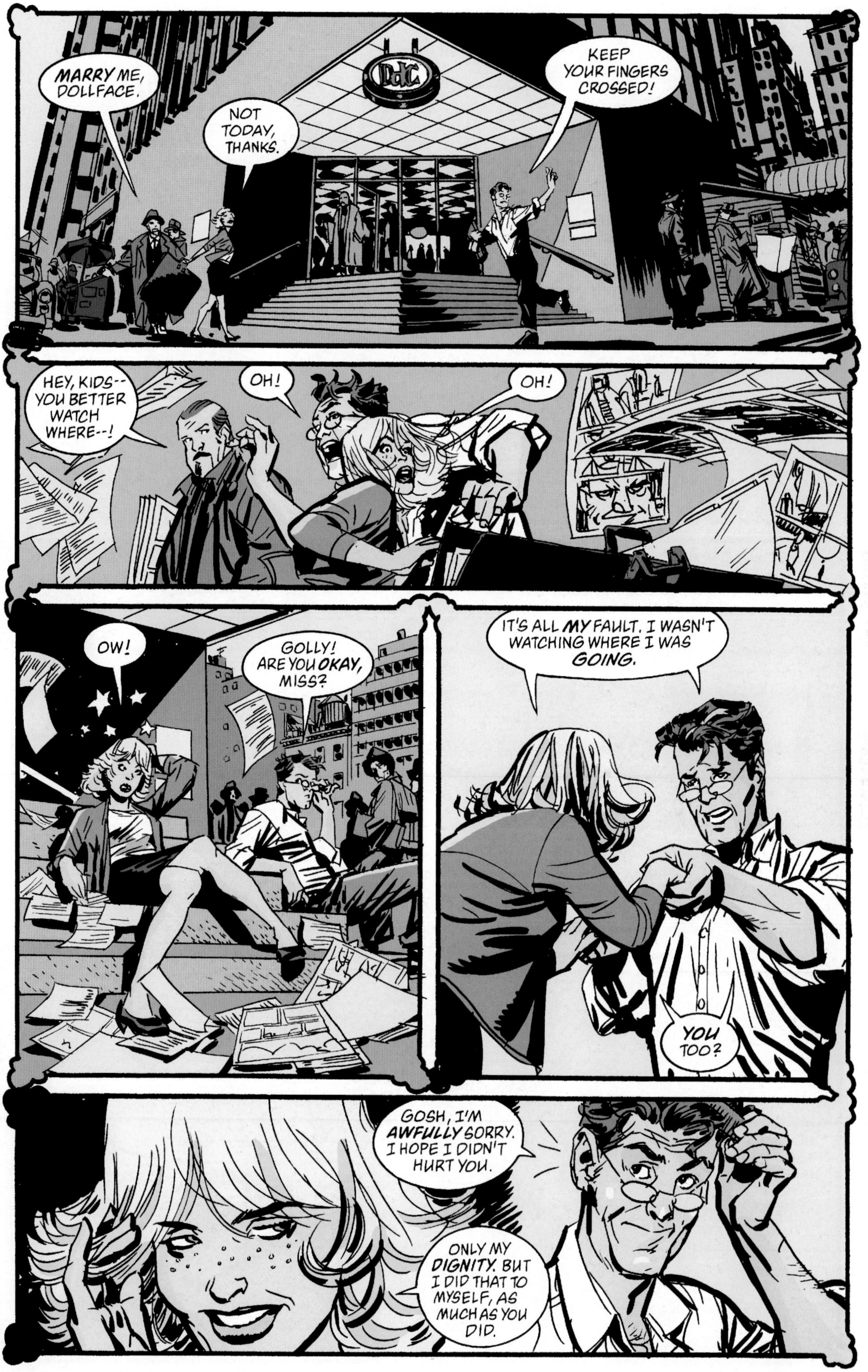
MARRY ME, DOLLFACE.
NOT TODAY, THANKS.
KEEP YOUR FINGERS CROSSED!
HEY, KIDS-- YOU BETTER WATCH WHERE--!
OH!
OH!
OW!
GOLLY! ARE YOU OKAY, MISS?
IT'S ALL MY FAULT. I WASN'T WATCHING WHERE I WAS GOING.
YOU TOO?
GOSH, I'M AWFULLY SORRY. I HOPE I DIDN'T HURT YOU.
ONLY MY DIGNITY. BUT I DID THAT TO MYSELF, AS MUCH AS YOU DID.

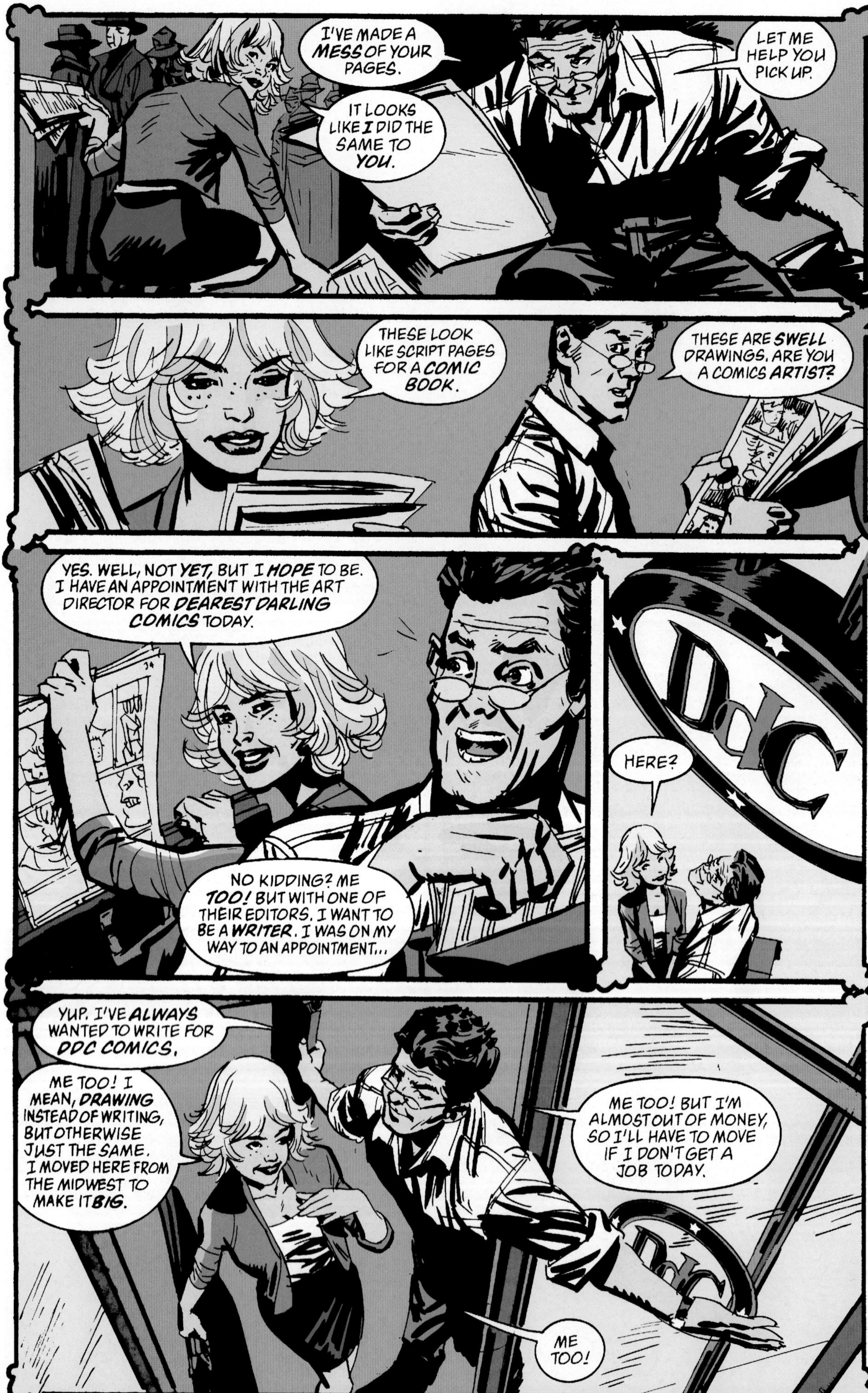
I'VE MADE A MESS OF YOUR PAGES.
IT LOOKS LIKE I DID THE SAME TO YOU.
LET ME HELP YOU PICK UP.
THESE LOOK LIKE SCRIPT PAGES FOR A COMIC BOOK.
THESE ARE SWELL DRAWINGS. ARE YOU A COMICS ARTIST?
YES. WELL, NOT YET, BUT I HOPE TO BE. I HAVE AN APPOINTMENT WITH THE ART DIRECTOR FOR DEAREST DARLING COMICS TODAY.
NO KIDDING? ME TOO! BUT WITH ONE OF THEIR EDITORS. I WANT TO BE A WRITER. I WAS ON MY WAY TO AN APPOINTMENT...
HERE?
DdC
YUP. I'VE ALWAYS WANTED TO WRITE FOR DDC COMICS.
ME TOO! I MEAN, DRAWING INSTEAD OF WRITING, BUT OTHERWISE JUST THE SAME. I MOVED HERE FROM THE MIDWEST TO MAKE IT BIG.
ME TOO! BUT I'M ALMOST OUT OF MONEY, SO I'LL HAVE TO MOVE IF I DON'T GET A JOB TODAY.
ME TOO!

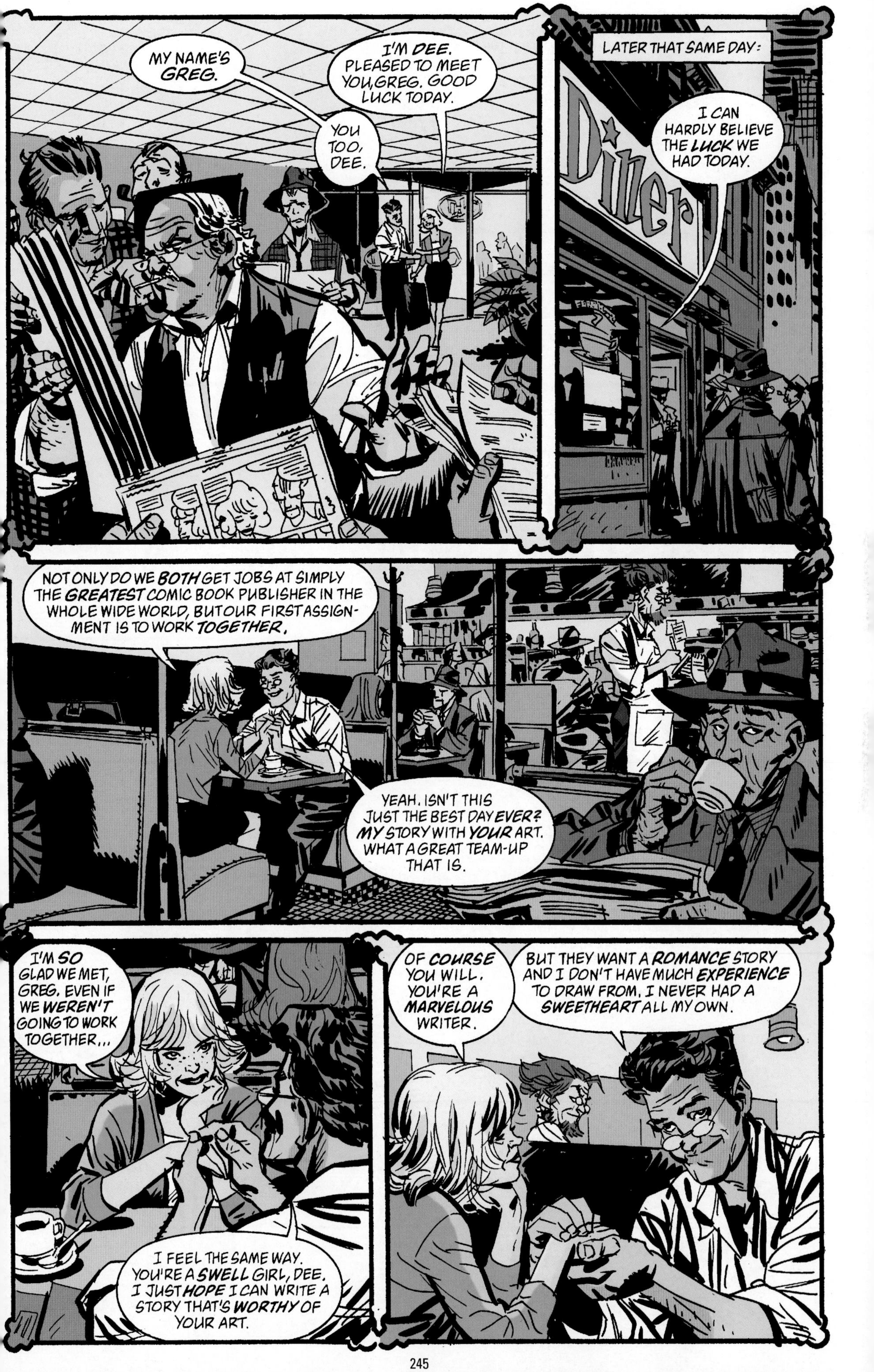
MY NAME'S GREG.
I'M DEE. PLEASED TO MEET YOU, GREG. GOOD LUCK TODAY.
YOU TOO, DEE.
LATER THAT SAME DAY:
I CAN HARDLY BELIEVE THE LUCK WE HAD TODAY.
NOT ONLY DO WE BOTH GET JOBS AT SIMPLY THE GREATEST COMIC BOOK PUBLISHER IN THE WHOLE WIDE WORLD, BUT OUR FIRST ASSIGNMENT IS TO WORK TOGETHER.
YEAH. ISN'T THIS JUST THE BEST DAY EVER? MY STORY WITH YOUR ART. WHAT A GREAT TEAM-UP THAT IS.
I'M SO GLAD WE MET, GREG. EVEN IF WE WEREN'T GOING TO WORK TOGETHER...
I FEEL THE SAME WAY. YOU'RE A SWELL GIRL, DEE. I JUST HOPE I CAN WRITE A STORY THAT'S WORTHY OF YOUR ART.
OF COURSE YOU WILL. YOU'RE A MARVELOUS WRITER.
BUT THEY WANT A ROMANCE STORY AND I DON'T HAVE MUCH EXPERIENCE TO DRAW FROM. I NEVER HAD A SWEETHEART ALL MY OWN.

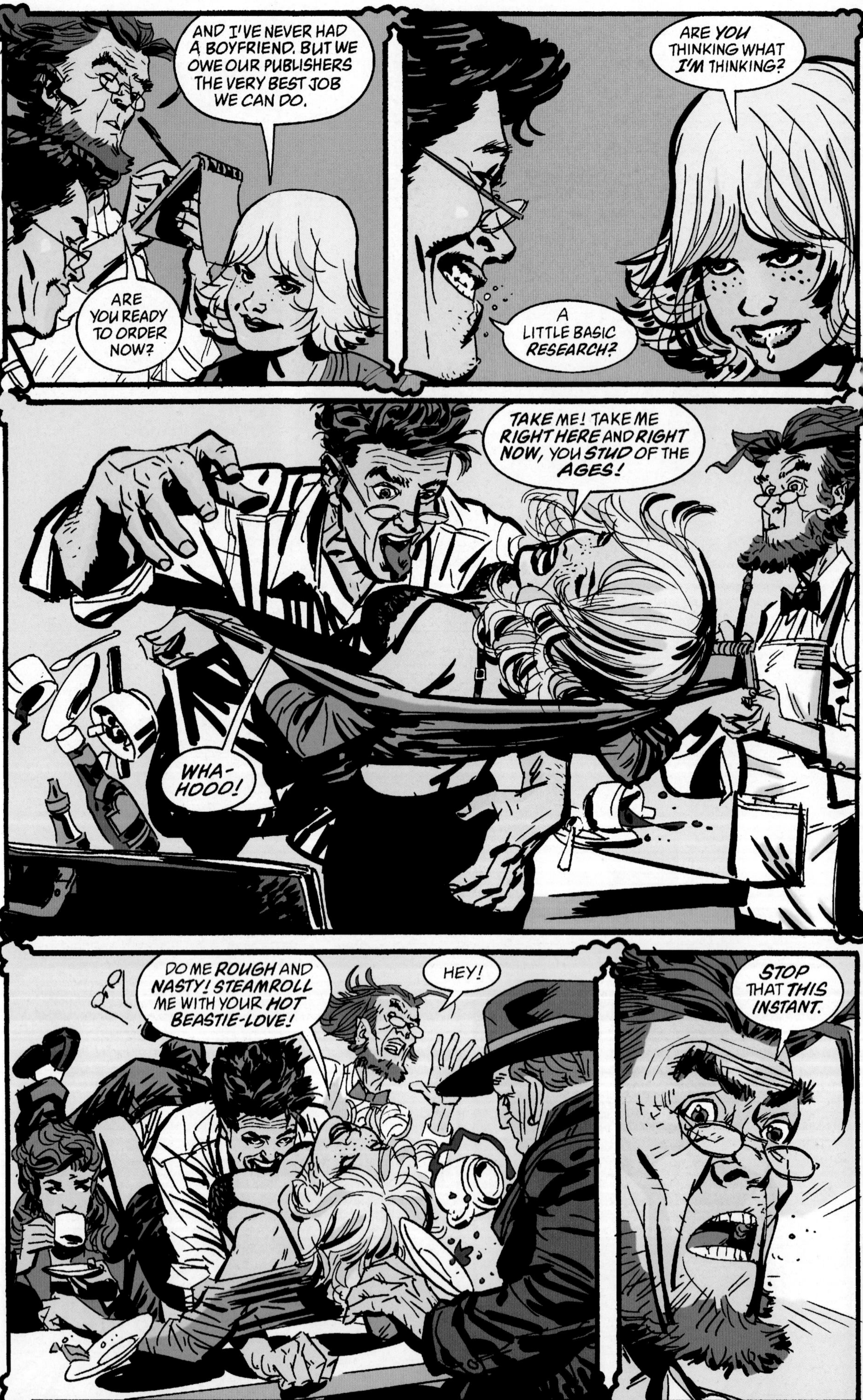
AND I'VE NEVER HAD A BOYFRIEND. BUT WE OWE OUR PUBLISHERS THE VERY BEST JOB WE CAN DO.
ARE YOU READY TO ORDER NOW?
ARE YOU THINKING WHAT I'M THINKING?
A LITTLE BASIC RESEARCH?
TAKE ME! TAKE ME RIGHT HERE AND RIGHT NOW, YOU STUD OF THE AGES!
WHA-HOOO!
DO ME ROUGH AND NASTY! STEAMROLL ME WITH YOUR HOT BEASTIE-LOVE!
HEY!
STOP THAT THIS INSTANT.

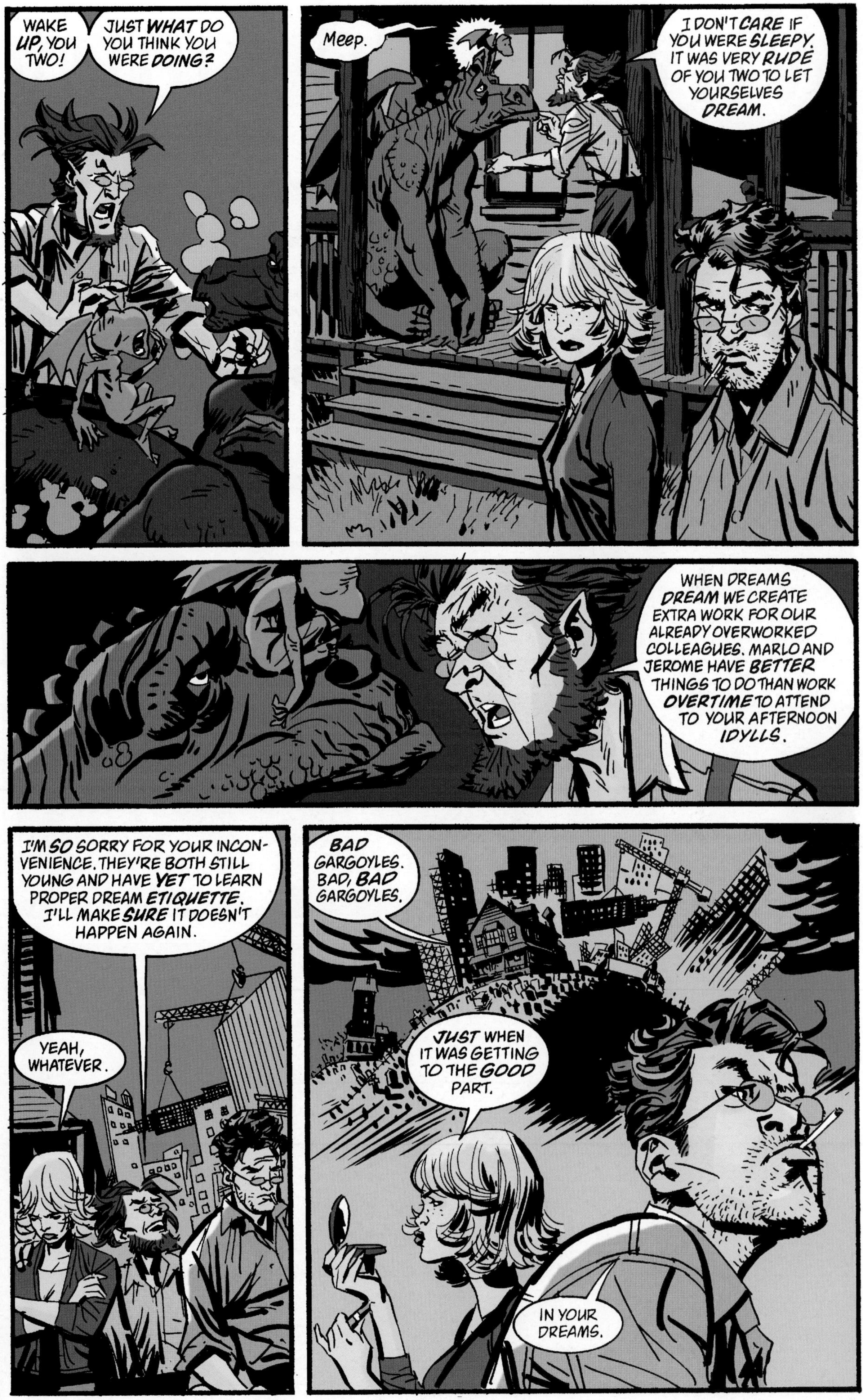
WAKE UP, YOU TWO!
JUST WHAT DO YOU THINK YOU WERE DOING?
Meep.
I DON'T CARE IF YOU WERE SLEEPY. IT WAS VERY RUDE OF YOU TWO TO LET YOURSELVES DREAM.
WHEN DREAMS DREAM WE CREATE EXTRA WORK FOR OUR ALREADY OVERWORKED COLLEAGUES. MARLO AND JEROME HAVE BETTER THINGS TO DO THAN WORK OVERTIME TO ATTEND TO YOUR AFTERNOON IDYLLS.
I'M SO SORRY FOR YOUR INCONVENIENCE. THEY'RE BOTH STILL YOUNG AND HAVE YET TO LEARN PROPER DREAM ETIQUETTE. I'LL MAKE SURE IT DOESN'T HAPPEN AGAIN.
YEAH, WHATEVER.
BAD GARGOYLES. BAD, BAD GARGOYLES.
JUST WHEN IT WAS GETTING TO THE GOOD PART.
IN YOUR DREAMS.

Why are so many dreams sexual in nature?

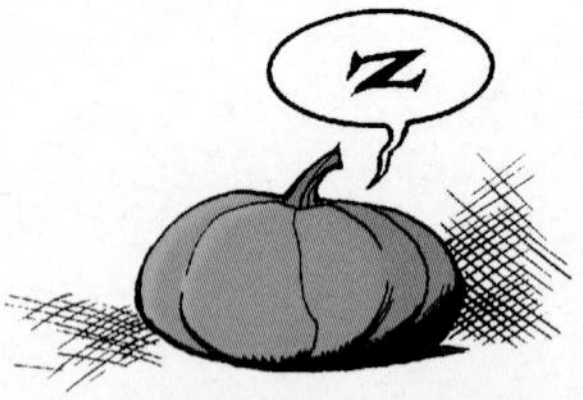
Z

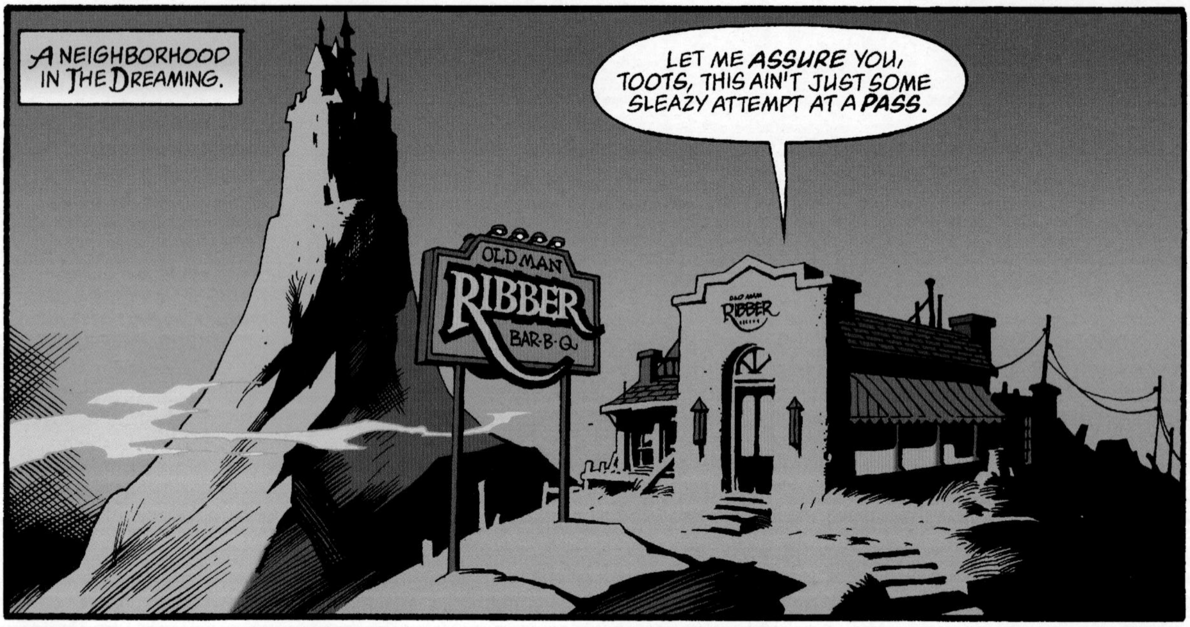
A NEIGHBORHOOD IN THE DREAMING.
LET ME ASSURE YOU, TOOTS, THIS AIN'T JUST SOME SLEAZY ATTEMPT AT A PASS.
OLD MAN RIBBER BAR-B-Q
OLD MAN RIBBER

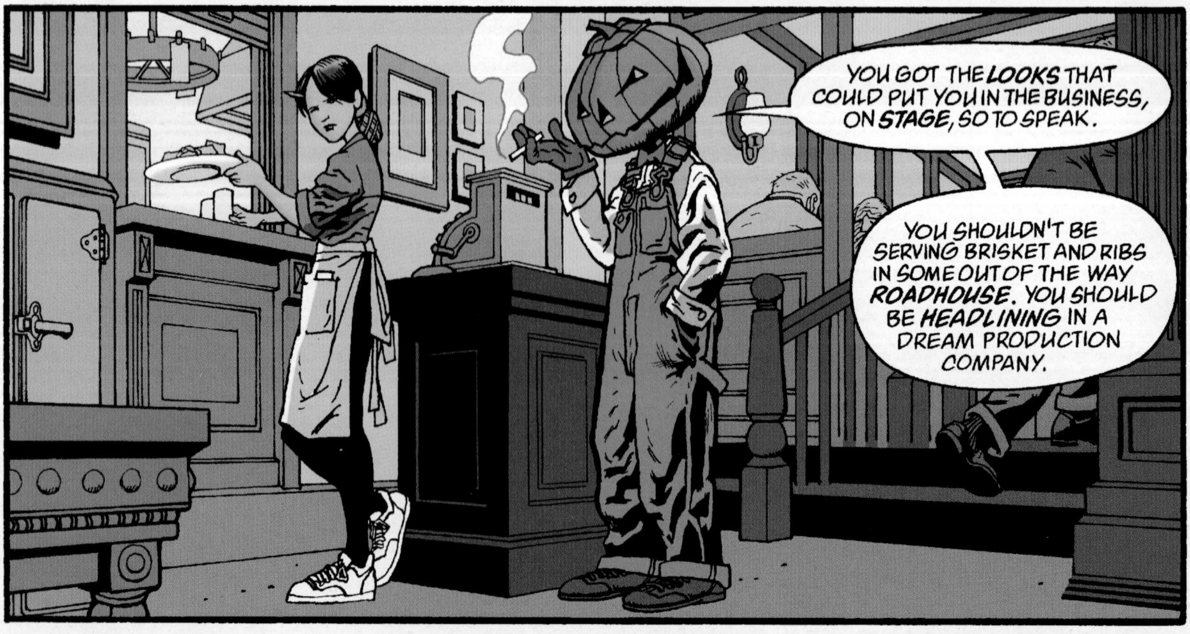
YOU GOT THE LOOKS THAT COULD PUT YOU IN THE BUSINESS, ON STAGE, SO TO SPEAK.
YOU SHOULDN'T BE SERVING BRISKET AND RIBS IN SOME OUT OF THE WAY ROADHOUSE. YOU SHOULD BE HEADLINING IN A DREAM PRODUCTION COMPANY.

TO TELL YOU THE TRUTH, I WAS *WORKING* HERE JUST UNTIL I COULD BREAK INTO THE DREAMS. I ALWAYS FELT I COULD BE A BIG *DREAMSTAR* SOMEDAY. IS THAT TERRIBLY *VAIN?*

NOT THE WAY *YOU* LOOK. HOW LONG YOU BEEN TRYING?

ONLY A FEW CENTURIES. SOMEDAY THE RIGHT CASTING AGENT WILL WALK IN HERE AND...

NOT *SOMEDAY,* SWEETHEART. *TODAY.* I'M *BIG* IN THE DREAM-ING. I RUN THE *PALACE.* I'M NOT A CASTING AGENT *PER SE,* BUT THERE'S NOT A ONE OF THEM THAT DOESN'T OWE ME, *BIG-TIME.*

AND YOU COULD GET ME AN *AUDITION?*

EASILY.

HAND ME YOUR PAD AND PENCIL. I'LL WRITE DOWN THE DIRECTIONS.

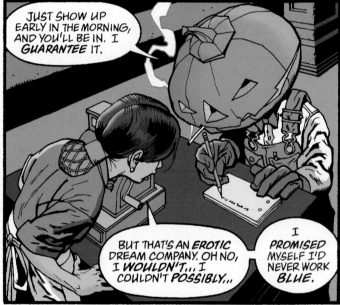

JUST SHOW UP EARLY IN THE MORNING, AND YOU'LL BE IN. I *GUARANTEE* IT.

BUT THAT'S AN *EROTIC* DREAM COMPANY. OH NO, I *WOULDN'T*... I COULDN'T *POSSIBLY*...

I *PROMISED* MYSELF I'D NEVER WORK *BLUE.*

OKAY, I *UNDERSTAND,* AND I DON'T *BLAME* YOU ONE *BIT.* TOO BAD THEY'RE THE ONLY ONES CAST-ING THESE DAYS. BUT I'LL BE BACK THIS WAY IN ANOTHER *CENTURY* OR TWO. I'M *SURE* SOMETHING ELSE WILL OPEN UP BY THEN.

WAIT! HOLD IT! COME *BACK!*

AS LONG AS IT'S *TASTEFUL* AND NOT *OVERLY* GRATUITOUS...

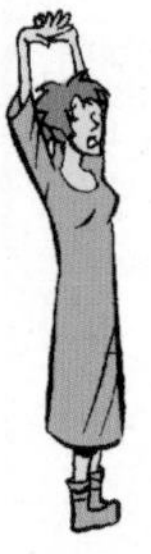

Why do some people dream in color and others in black & white?

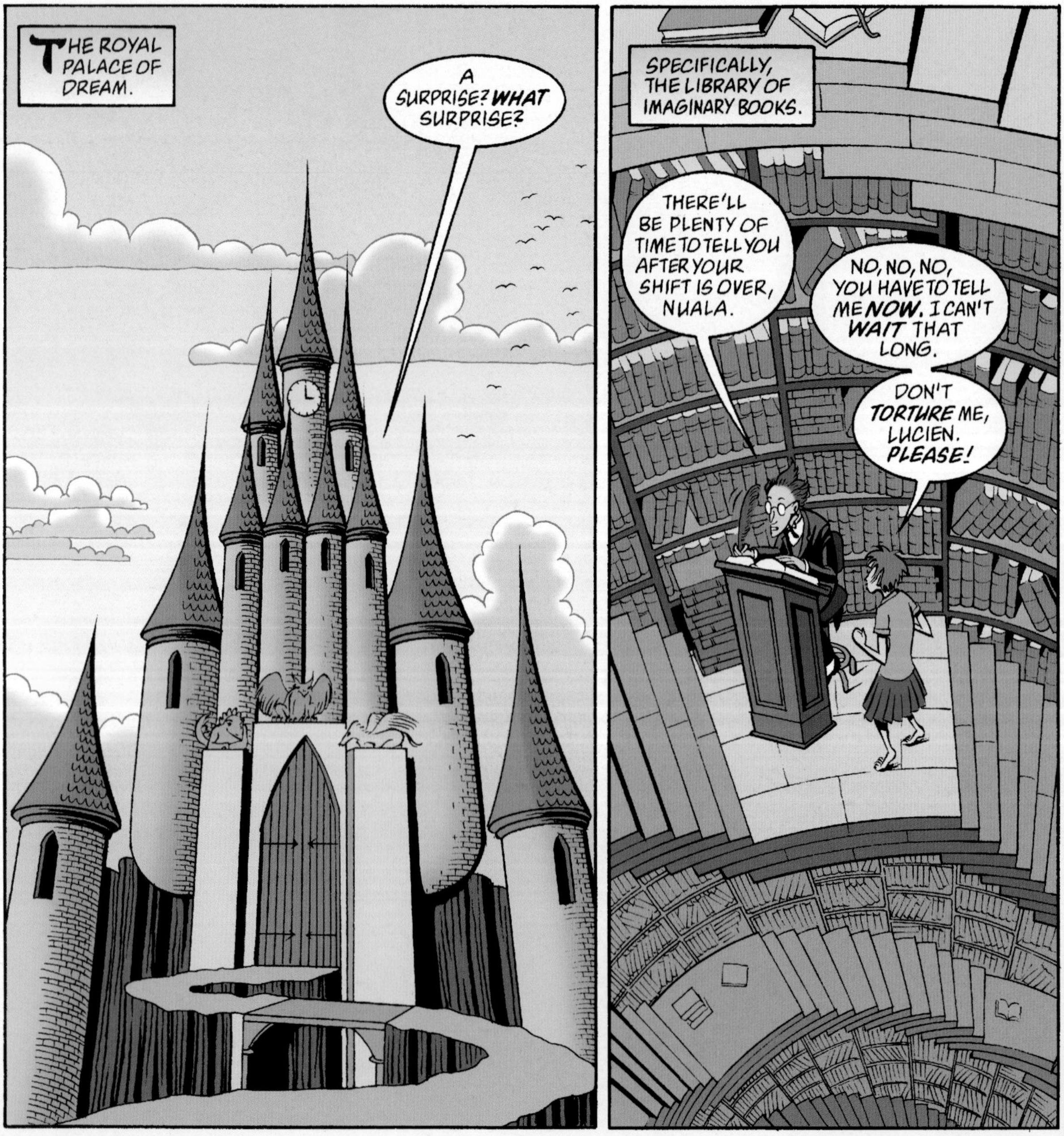
THE ROYAL PALACE OF DREAM.
A SURPRISE? WHAT SURPRISE?
SPECIFICALLY, THE LIBRARY OF IMAGINARY BOOKS.
THERE'LL BE PLENTY OF TIME TO TELL YOU AFTER YOUR SHIFT IS OVER, NUALA.
NO, NO, NO, YOU HAVE TO TELL ME NOW. I CAN'T WAIT THAT LONG.
DON'T TORTURE ME, LUCIEN. PLEASE!

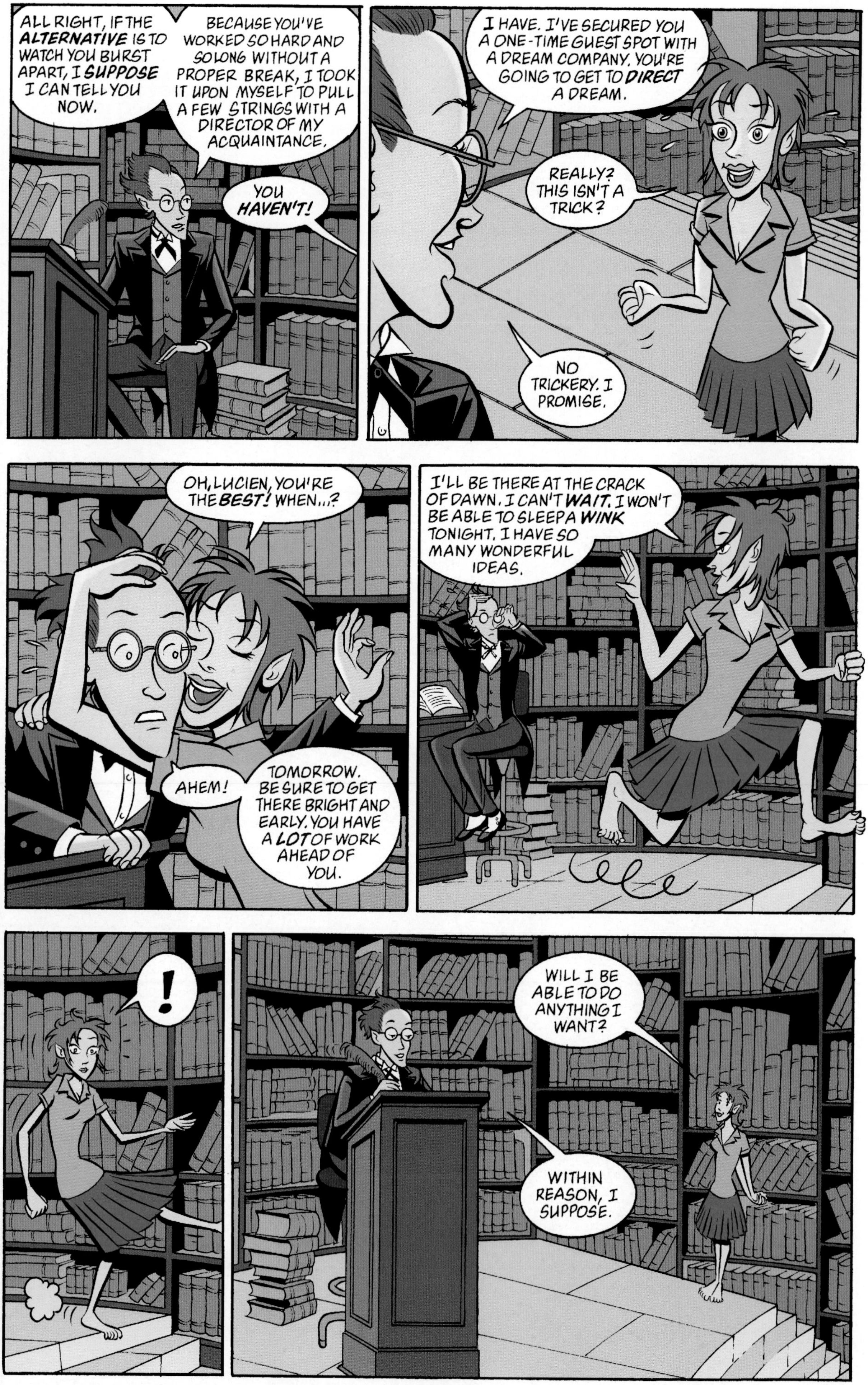
ALL RIGHT, IF THE **ALTERNATIVE** IS TO WATCH YOU BURST APART, I **SUPPOSE** I CAN TELL YOU NOW.
BECAUSE YOU'VE WORKED SO HARD AND SO LONG WITHOUT A PROPER BREAK, I TOOK IT UPON MYSELF TO PULL A FEW STRINGS WITH A DIRECTOR OF MY ACQUAINTANCE.
YOU **HAVEN'T!**
I HAVE. I'VE SECURED YOU A ONE-TIME GUEST SPOT WITH A DREAM COMPANY. YOU'RE GOING TO GET TO **DIRECT** A DREAM.
REALLY? THIS ISN'T A TRICK?
NO TRICKERY. I PROMISE.
OH, LUCIEN, YOU'RE THE **BEST!** WHEN...?
AHEM!
TOMORROW. BE SURE TO GET THERE BRIGHT AND EARLY. YOU HAVE A **LOT** OF WORK AHEAD OF YOU.
I'LL BE THERE AT THE CRACK OF DAWN. I CAN'T **WAIT**. I WON'T BE ABLE TO SLEEP A **WINK** TONIGHT. I HAVE SO MANY WONDERFUL IDEAS.
!
WILL I BE ABLE TO DO ANYTHING I WANT?
WITHIN REASON, I SUPPOSE.

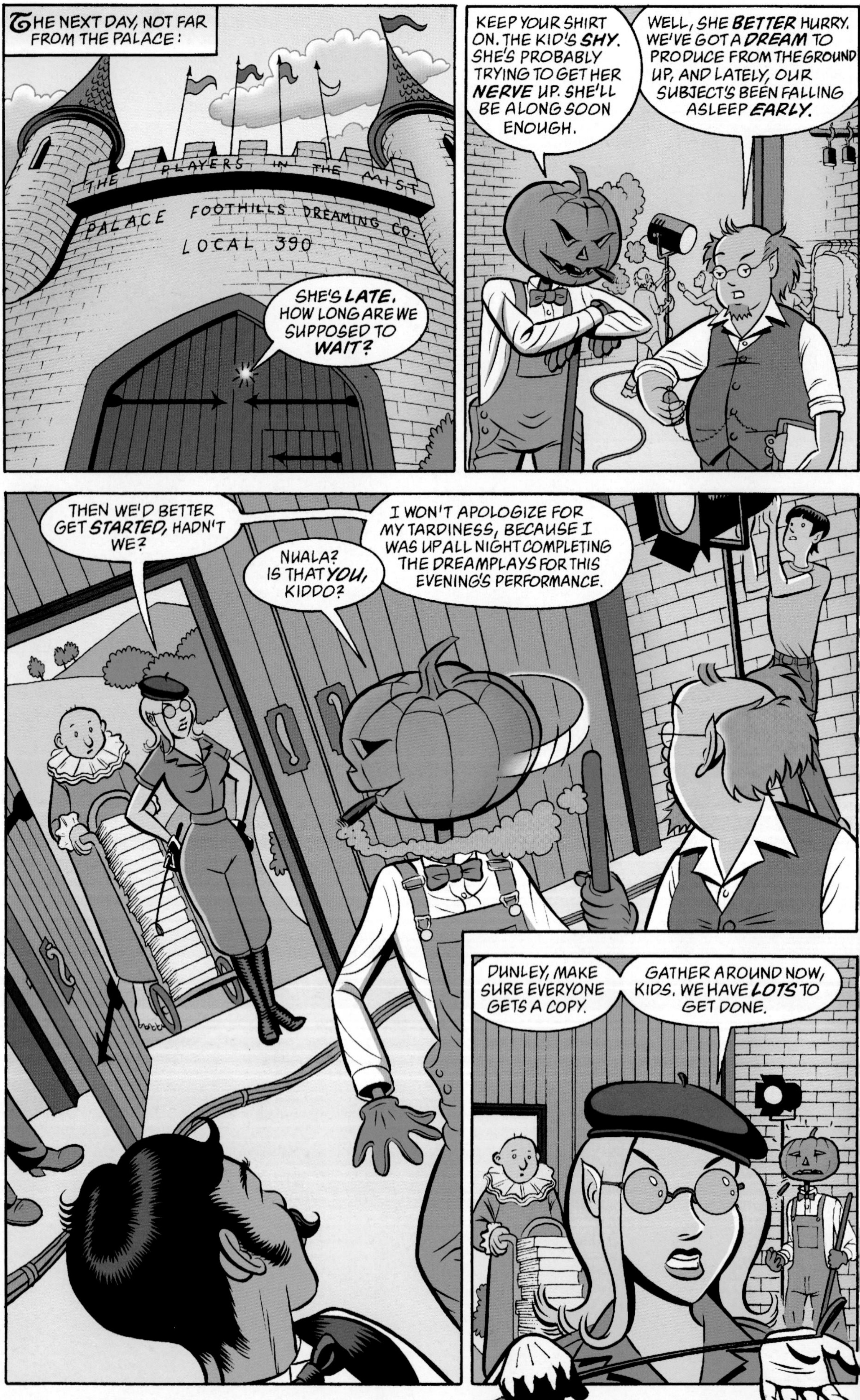
THE NEXT DAY, NOT FAR FROM THE PALACE:
THE PLAYERS IN THE MIST
PALACE FOOTHILLS DREAMING CO.
LOCAL 390
SHE'S LATE. HOW LONG ARE WE SUPPOSED TO WAIT?
KEEP YOUR SHIRT ON. THE KID'S SHY. SHE'S PROBABLY TRYING TO GET HER NERVE UP. SHE'LL BE ALONG SOON ENOUGH.
WELL, SHE BETTER HURRY. WE'VE GOT A DREAM TO PRODUCE FROM THE GROUND UP, AND LATELY, OUR SUBJECT'S BEEN FALLING ASLEEP EARLY.
THEN WE'D BETTER GET STARTED, HADN'T WE?
NUALA? IS THAT YOU, KIDDO?
I WON'T APOLOGIZE FOR MY TARDINESS, BECAUSE I WAS UP ALL NIGHT COMPLETING THE DREAMPLAYS FOR THIS EVENING'S PERFORMANCE.
DUNLEY, MAKE SURE EVERYONE GETS A COPY.
GATHER AROUND NOW, KIDS. WE HAVE LOTS TO GET DONE.

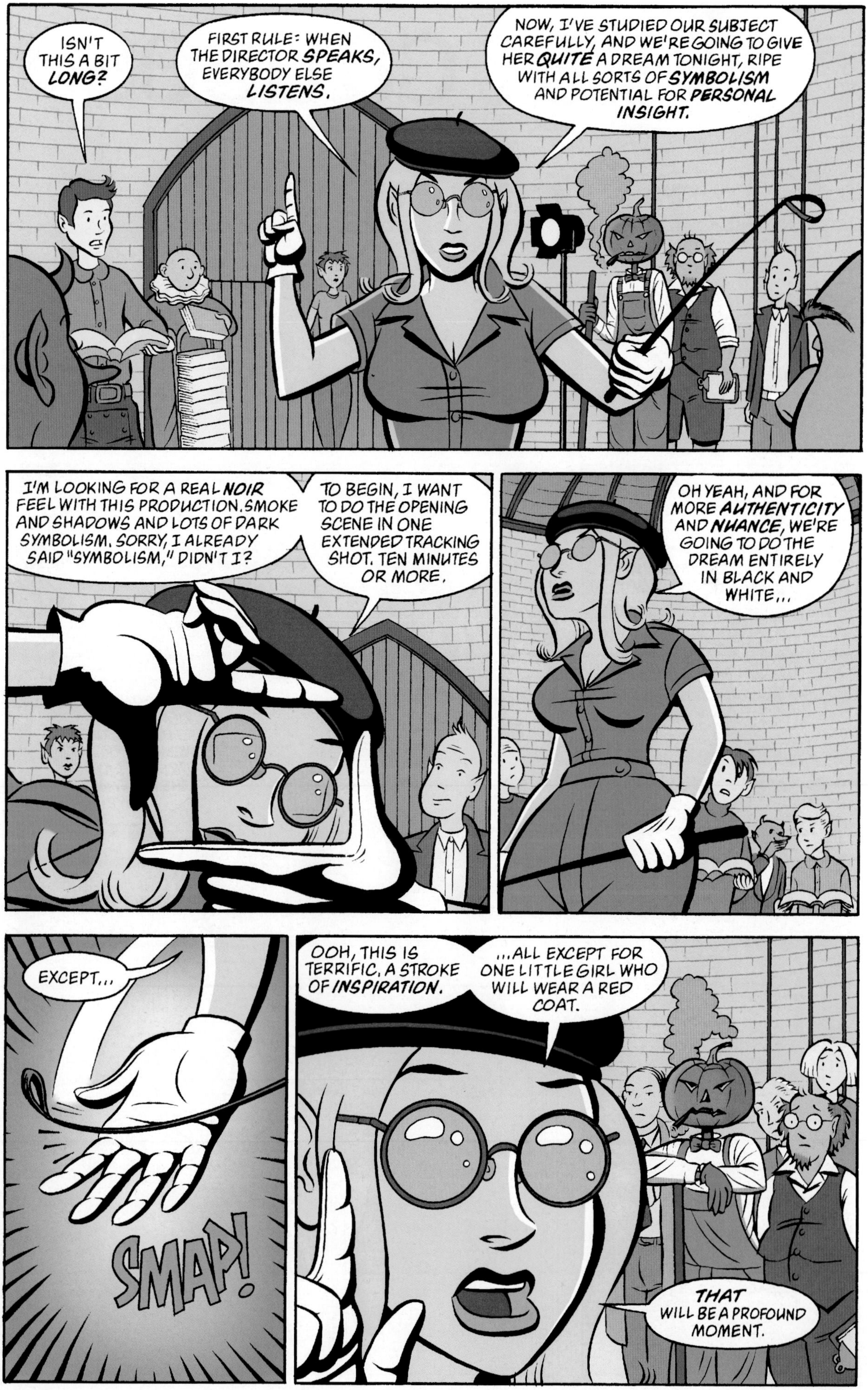
ISN'T THIS A BIT LONG?
FIRST RULE: WHEN THE DIRECTOR SPEAKS, EVERYBODY ELSE LISTENS.
NOW, I'VE STUDIED OUR SUBJECT CAREFULLY, AND WE'RE GOING TO GIVE HER QUITE A DREAM TONIGHT, RIPE WITH ALL SORTS OF SYMBOLISM AND POTENTIAL FOR PERSONAL INSIGHT.
I'M LOOKING FOR A REAL NOIR FEEL WITH THIS PRODUCTION. SMOKE AND SHADOWS AND LOTS OF DARK SYMBOLISM. SORRY, I ALREADY SAID "SYMBOLISM," DIDN'T I?
TO BEGIN, I WANT TO DO THE OPENING SCENE IN ONE EXTENDED TRACKING SHOT. TEN MINUTES OR MORE.
OH YEAH, AND FOR MORE AUTHENTICITY AND NUANCE, WE'RE GOING TO DO THE DREAM ENTIRELY IN BLACK AND WHITE...
EXCEPT...
SMAP!
OOH, THIS IS TERRIFIC. A STROKE OF INSPIRATION.
...ALL EXCEPT FOR ONE LITTLE GIRL WHO WILL WEAR A RED COAT.
THAT WILL BE A PROFOUND MOMENT.

What causes recurring dreams?

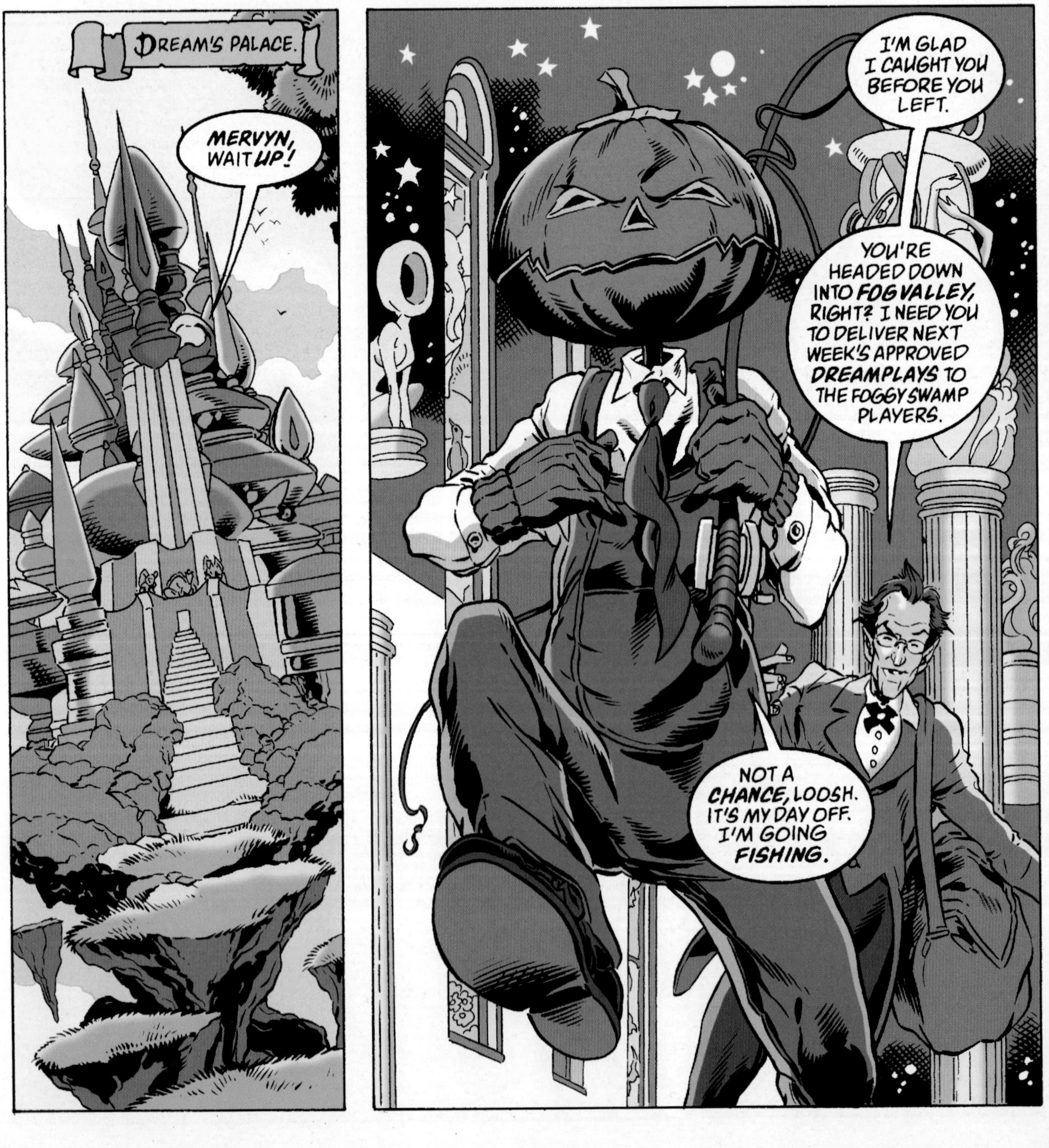
DREAM'S PALACE.
MERVYN, WAIT UP!
I'M GLAD I CAUGHT YOU BEFORE YOU LEFT.
YOU'RE HEADED DOWN INTO FOG VALLEY, RIGHT? I NEED YOU TO DELIVER NEXT WEEK'S APPROVED DREAMPLAYS TO THE FOGGY SWAMP PLAYERS.
NOT A CHANCE, LOOSH. IT'S MY DAY OFF. I'M GOING FISHING.

IT'S ON YOUR WAY, AND THESE SCRIPTS ARE *SERIOUSLY* LATE. ONE OF THEIR TROUPE WILL MEET YOU ON MIRKROAD, SO IT WON'T TAKE AN EXTRA *MINUTE* OF YOUR TIME.

HOW LATE, EXACTLY?

THEY SHOULD HAVE GONE OUT TWO DAYS AGO, BUT THEY GOT *MISFILED.*

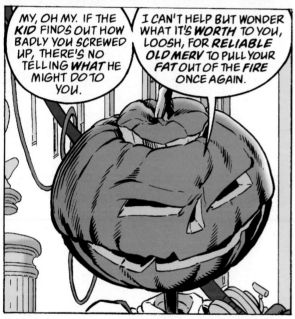

MY, OH MY. IF THE *KID* FINDS OUT HOW BADLY YOU *SCREWED* UP, THERE'S NO TELLING *WHAT* HE MIGHT DO TO YOU.

I CAN'T HELP BUT WONDER WHAT IT'S *WORTH* TO YOU, LOOSH, FOR *RELIABLE OLD MERV* TO PULL YOUR *FAT* OUT OF THE *FIRE* ONCE AGAIN.

"ONCE AGAIN"?

"ONCE AGAIN"?

WELL, IF *THAT'S* THE TONE YOU'RE GOING TO TAKE WITH *ME*...

NOT SO FAST, MR. PUMPKINHEAD. YOU ASKED A *QUESTION* WHICH DESERVES AN *ANSWER.* I'LL TELL YOU *EXACTLY* WHAT IT'S WORTH TO ME.

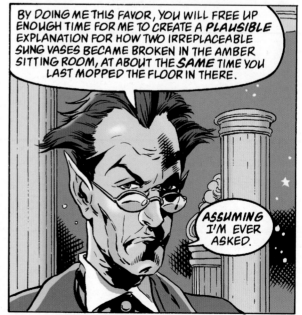

BY *DOING* ME THIS FAVOR, YOU WILL FREE UP ENOUGH TIME FOR ME TO CREATE A *PLAUSIBLE* EXPLANATION FOR HOW TWO IRREPLACEABLE SUNG VASES BECAME BROKEN IN THE AMBER SITTING ROOM, AT ABOUT THE *SAME* TIME YOU LAST MOPPED THE FLOOR IN THERE.

ASSUMING I'M EVER ASKED.

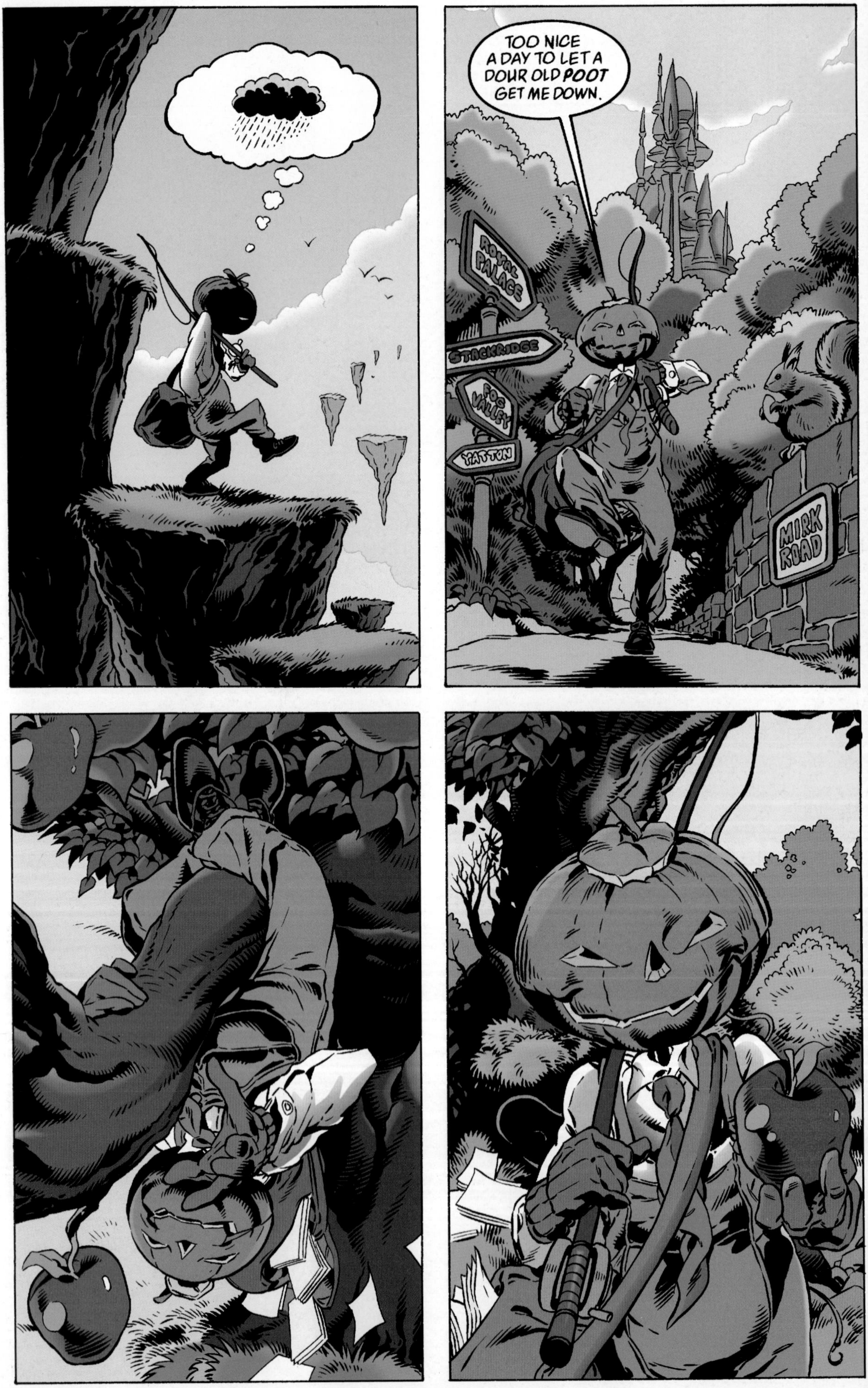
TOO NICE A DAY TO LET A DOUR OLD **POOT** GET ME DOWN.
ROYAL PALACE
STACKRIDGE
FOG VALLEY
PATTON
MIRK ROAD

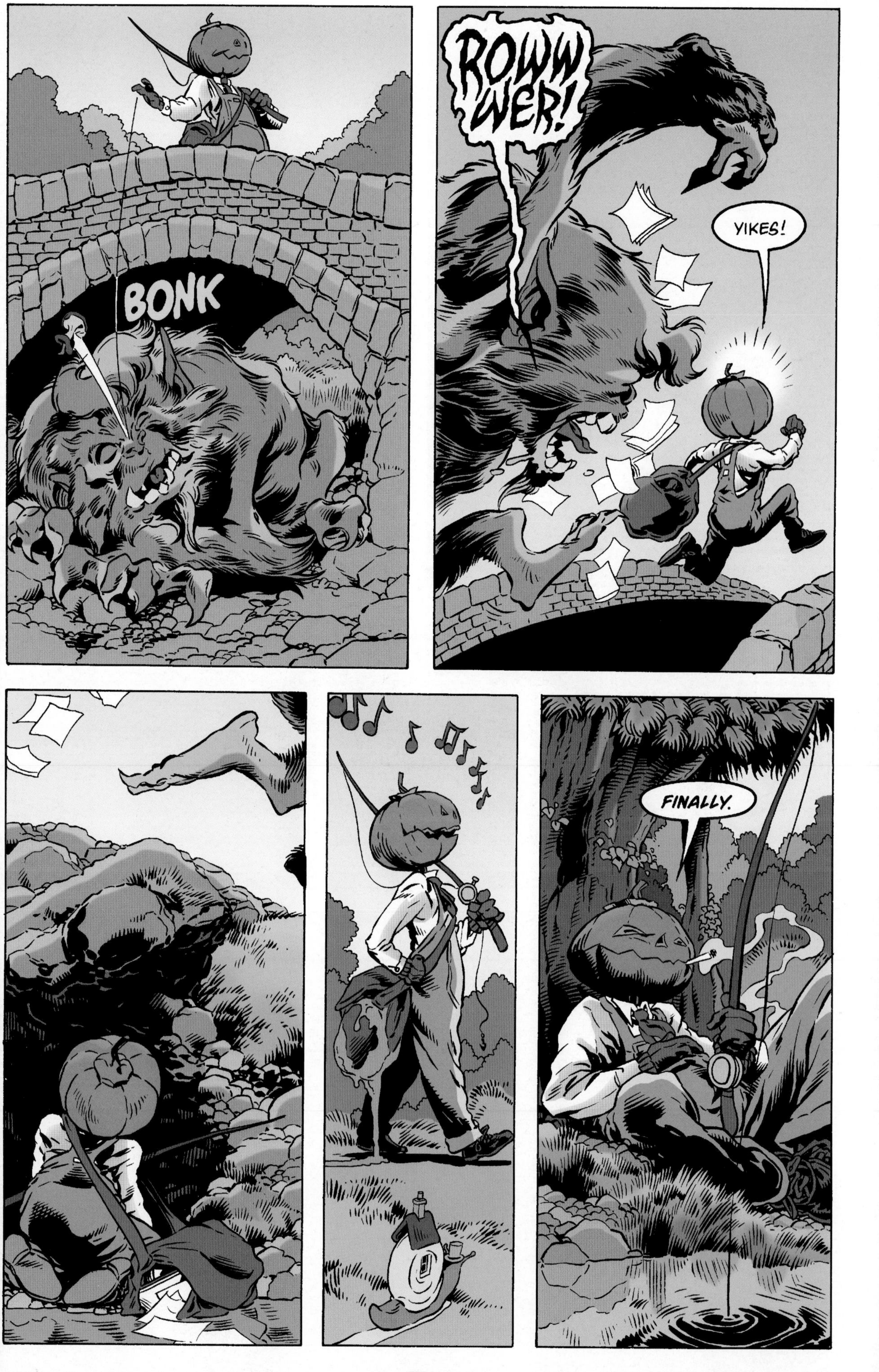
BONK
ROWW WER!
YIKES!
FINALLY.

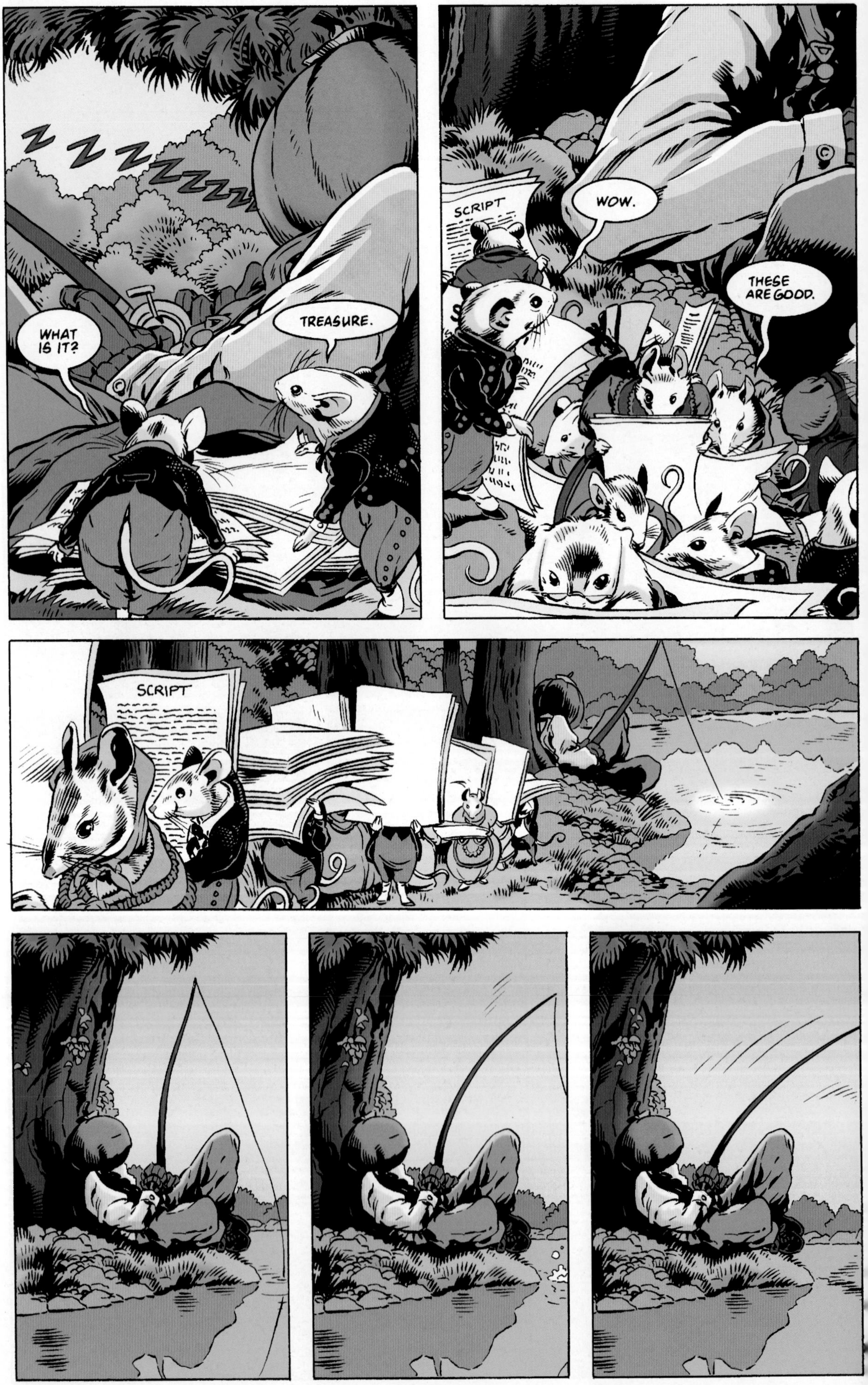
ZZZZZZZZZZ
WHAT IS IT?
TREASURE.
SCRIPT
WOW.
THESE ARE GOOD.
SCRIPT

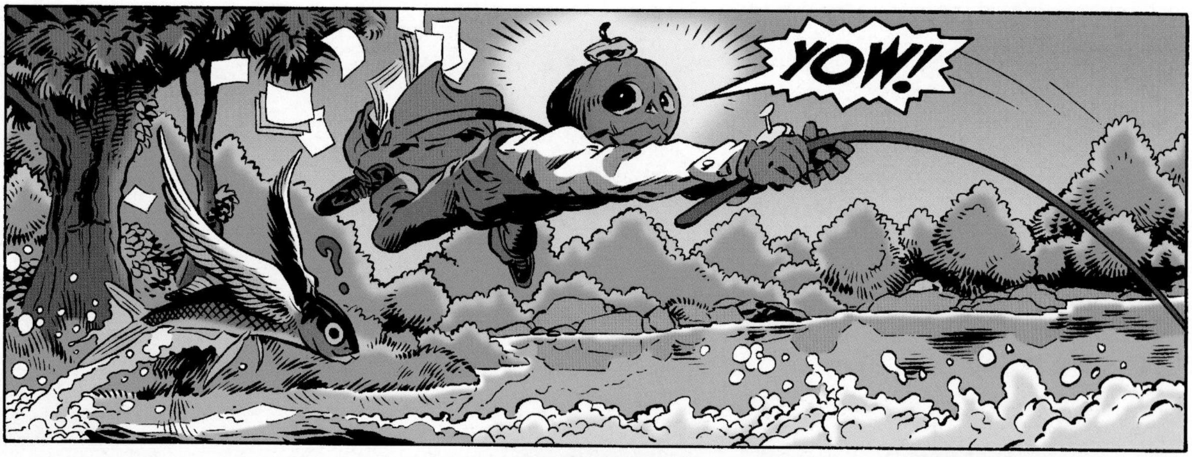
YOW!
?

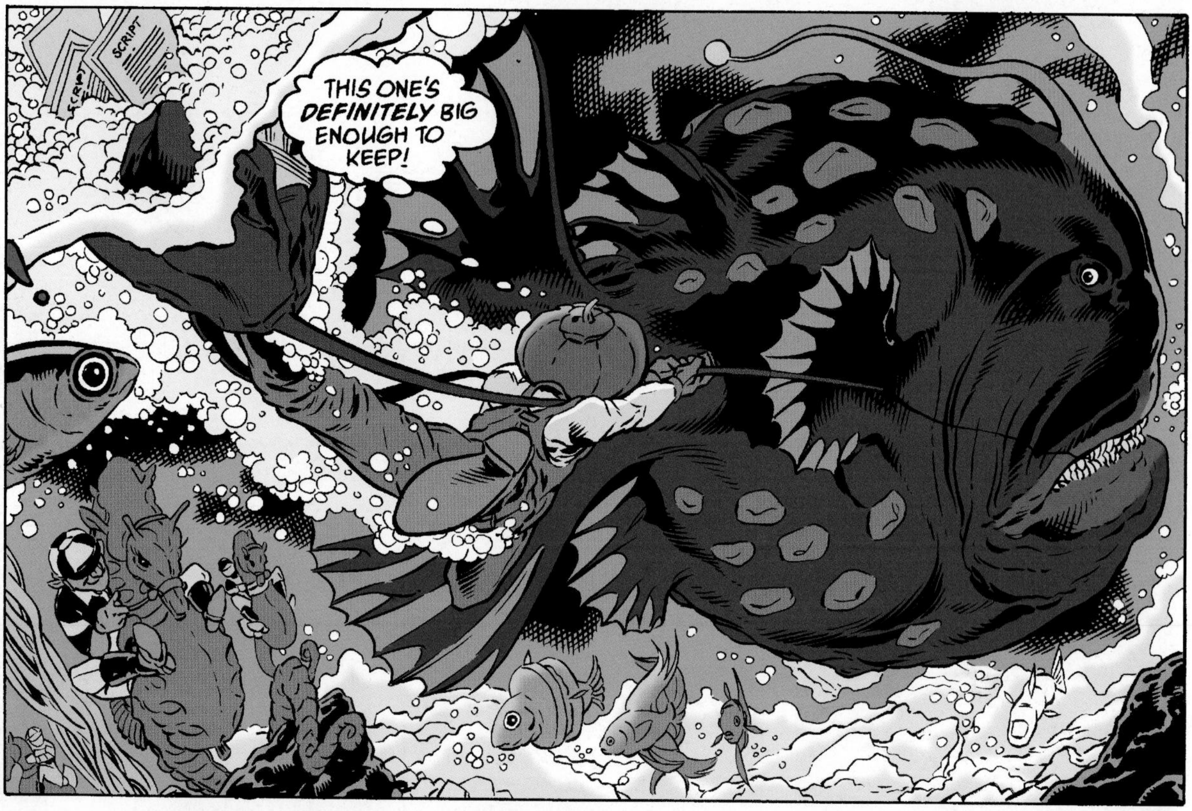
THIS ONE'S DEFINITELY BIG ENOUGH TO KEEP!

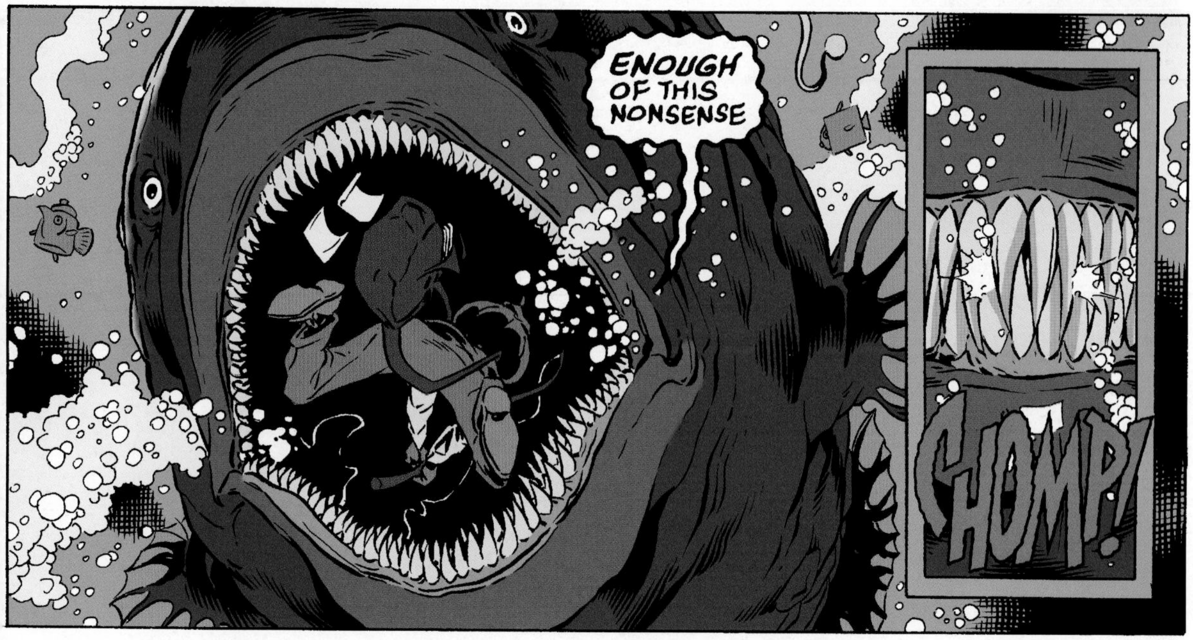
ENOUGH OF THIS NONSENSE
CHOMP!

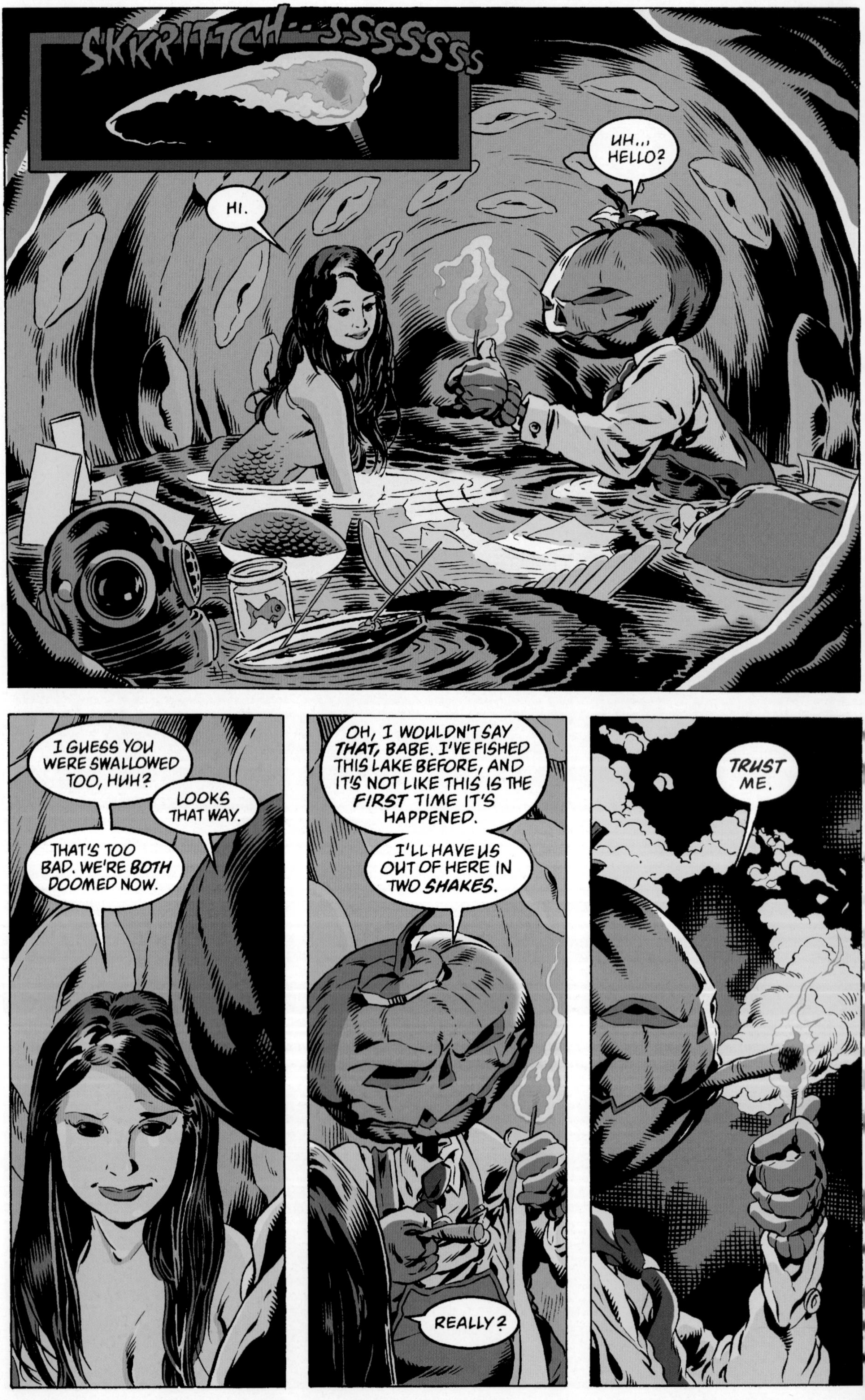
SKKRITTCH--SSSSSSS
HI.
UH.., HELLO?
I GUESS YOU WERE SWALLOWED TOO, HUH?
LOOKS THAT WAY.
THAT'S TOO BAD. WE'RE BOTH DOOMED NOW.
OH, I WOULDN'T SAY THAT, BABE. I'VE FISHED THIS LAKE BEFORE, AND IT'S NOT LIKE THIS IS THE FIRST TIME IT'S HAPPENED.
I'LL HAVE US OUT OF HERE IN TWO SHAKES.
REALLY?
TRUST ME.

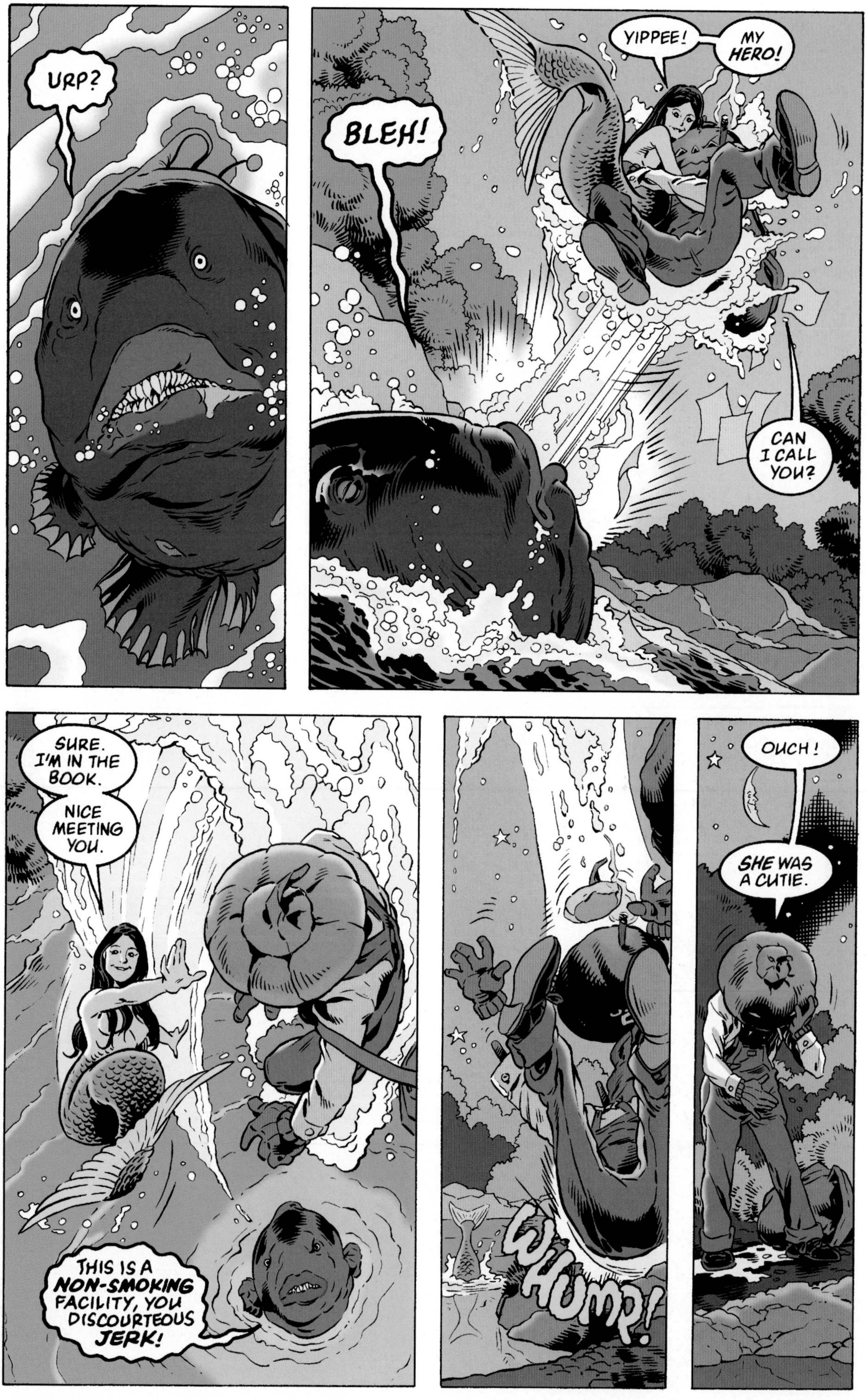
URP?
BLEH!
YIPPEE!
MY HERO!
CAN I CALL YOU?
SURE. I'M IN THE BOOK.
NICE MEETING YOU.
THIS IS A NON-SMOKING FACILITY, YOU DISCOURTEOUS JERK!
WHUMP!
OUCH!
SHE WAS A CUTIE.

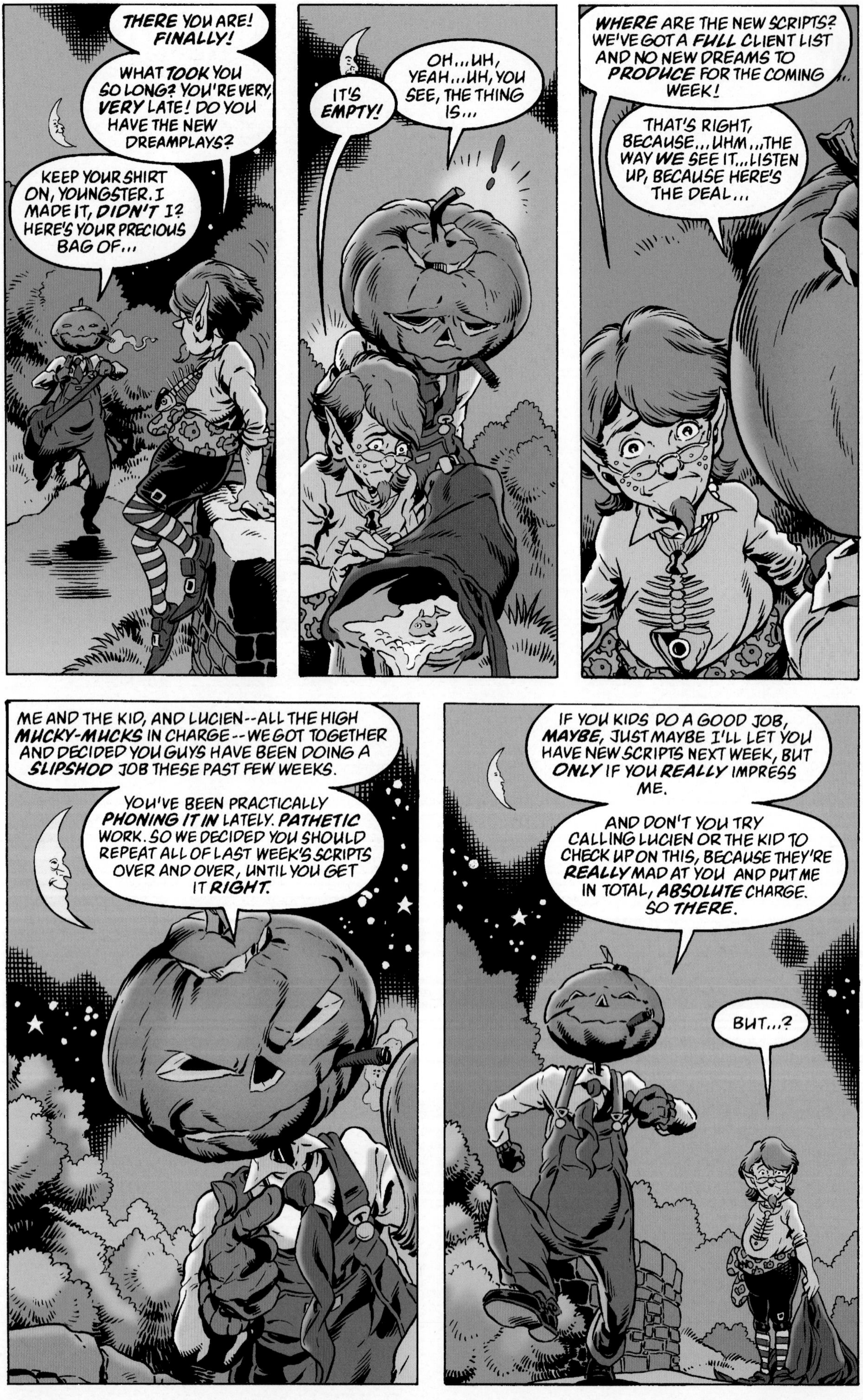
THERE YOU ARE! FINALLY!
WHAT TOOK YOU SO LONG? YOU'RE VERY, VERY LATE! DO YOU HAVE THE NEW DREAMPLAYS?
KEEP YOUR SHIRT ON, YOUNGSTER. I MADE IT, DIDN'T I? HERE'S YOUR PRECIOUS BAG OF...
IT'S EMPTY!
OH...UH, YEAH...UH, YOU SEE, THE THING IS...
!
WHERE ARE THE NEW SCRIPTS? WE'VE GOT A FULL CLIENT LIST AND NO NEW DREAMS TO PRODUCE FOR THE COMING WEEK!
THAT'S RIGHT, BECAUSE...UHM...THE WAY WE SEE IT...LISTEN UP, BECAUSE HERE'S THE DEAL...
ME AND THE KID, AND LUCIEN--ALL THE HIGH MUCKY-MUCKS IN CHARGE--WE GOT TOGETHER AND DECIDED YOU GUYS HAVE BEEN DOING A SLIPSHOD JOB THESE PAST FEW WEEKS.
YOU'VE BEEN PRACTICALLY PHONING IT IN LATELY. PATHETIC WORK. SO WE DECIDED YOU SHOULD REPEAT ALL OF LAST WEEK'S SCRIPTS OVER AND OVER, UNTIL YOU GET IT RIGHT.
IF YOU KIDS DO A GOOD JOB, MAYBE, JUST MAYBE I'LL LET YOU HAVE NEW SCRIPTS NEXT WEEK, BUT ONLY IF YOU REALLY IMPRESS ME.
AND DON'T YOU TRY CALLING LUCIEN OR THE KID TO CHECK UP ON THIS, BECAUSE THEY'RE REALLY MAD AT YOU AND PUT ME IN TOTAL, ABSOLUTE CHARGE. SO THERE.
BUT...?

Are there really universal symbols which occur in 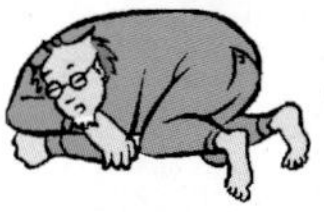 dreams and can be interpreted by experts?

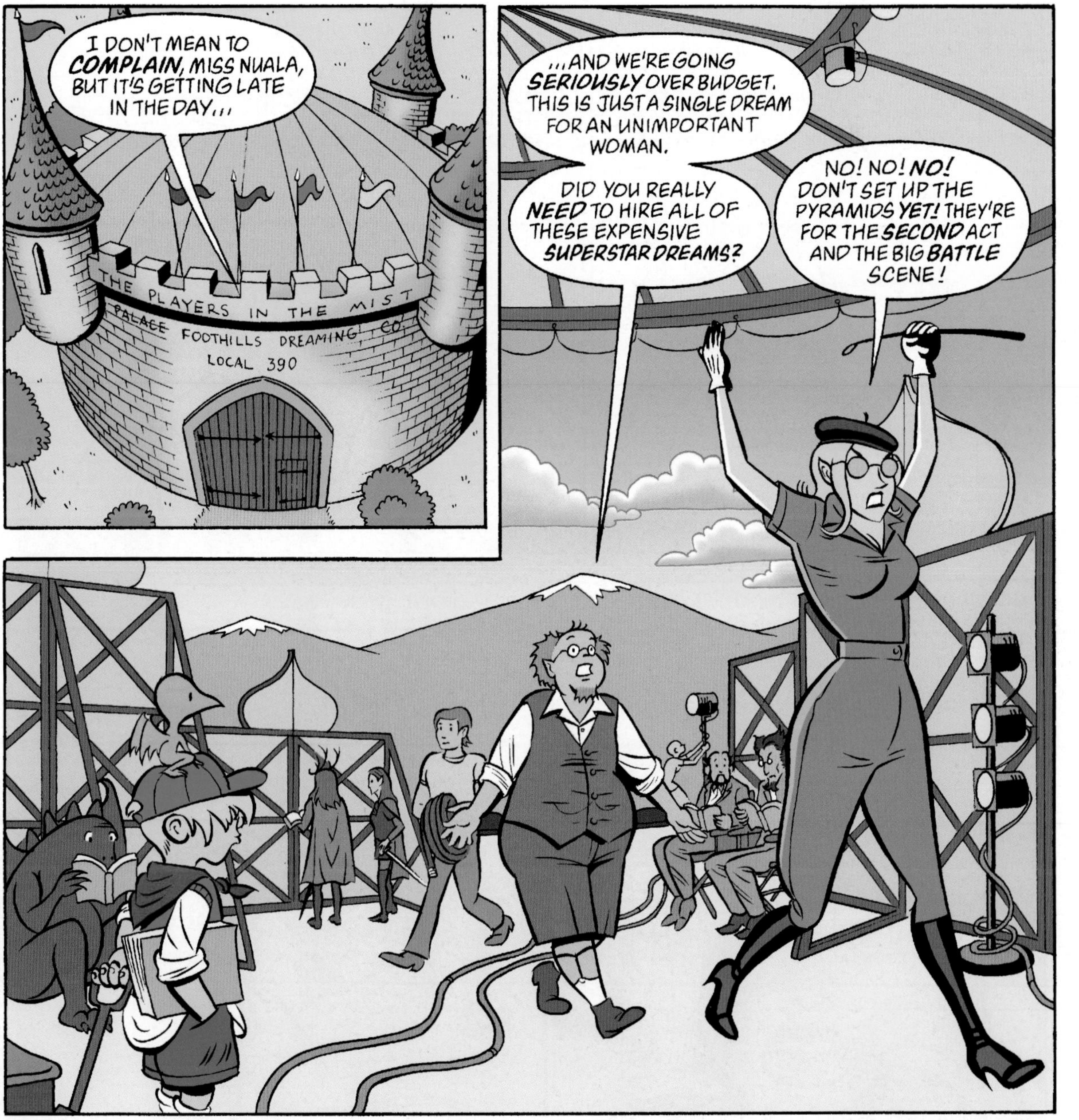
I DON'T MEAN TO COMPLAIN, MISS NUALA, BUT IT'S GETTING LATE IN THE DAY...
THE PLAYERS IN THE MIST
PALACE FOOTHILLS DREAMING CO.
LOCAL 390
...AND WE'RE GOING SERIOUSLY OVER BUDGET. THIS IS JUST A SINGLE DREAM FOR AN UNIMPORTANT WOMAN.
DID YOU REALLY NEED TO HIRE ALL OF THESE EXPENSIVE SUPERSTAR DREAMS?
NO! NO! NO! DON'T SET UP THE PYRAMIDS YET! THEY'RE FOR THE SECOND ACT AND THE BIG BATTLE SCENE!

I'LL **NEVER** BE ABLE TO MEMORIZE ALL OF THIS.

I THINK SHE GAVE YOU MORE **LINES** THAN ME.

I JUST THINK THINGS ARE GETTING OUT OF **HAND.**

YOU DON'T **GET IT,** DO YOU? I'M **NOT** WILLING TO SETTLE FOR SOMETHING **ORDINARY.** I WANT NOTHING **LESS** THAN **THE EXTRAORDINARY.** THIS PRODUCTION IS CERTAIN TO SWEEP THE COVETED **SLEEPY AWARDS** THIS YEAR.

BEST LEADING ACTOR; BEST LEADING ACTRESS; BEST DREAMPLAY; AND, OF COURSE, BEST DIRECTOR.

READ **CAREFULLY,** OLD FRIEND. WE CAN'T AFFORD TO PARTICIPATE IN ANYTHING THAT DOESN'T REFLECT WELL ON THE **LIBRARY CORPS.**

Meep?

CAN'T WE **AT LEAST** TRY TO MOVE ALONG A LITTLE MORE RAPIDLY?

NOT UNTIL WE PIN DOWN THE **EXACT** SYMBOLIC MEANING BEHIND EACH PART OF THE THEMATIC WHOLE.

THIS IS **VITALLY** IMPORTANT. SYMBOLISM IS ALL! **EVERYTHING** DEPENDS ON IT!

THE MAN WITH NO FACE REPRESENTS THE INCREASING DEPERSONALIZATION OF OUR DREAMER'S CULTURE.

THE THIRTY-SEVEN SETS OF SIAMESE TWIN LESBIAN BALLET-DANCING ZOMBIE NUNS IN THE CHICKEN SUITS REPRESENTS THE NEED TO FIND LOVE AMIDST CHAOS.

THE FOUR AND TWENTY BLACKBIRDS, BAKED INTO SEPARATE SINGLE-SERVING PIES, REPRESENTS THE FRACTURING OF... HEY! WHERE **IS** THAT DAMNED BAKERY TRUCK ANYWAY?

NOW, WHERE WAS I?

264

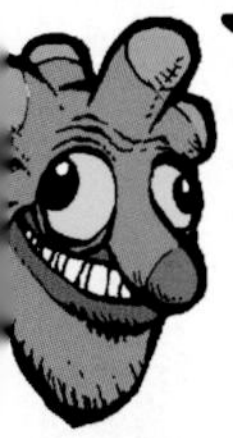

Why aren't you supposed to wake a sleepwalker?

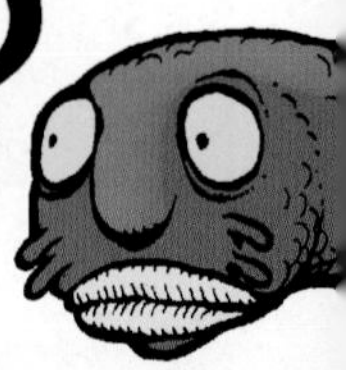

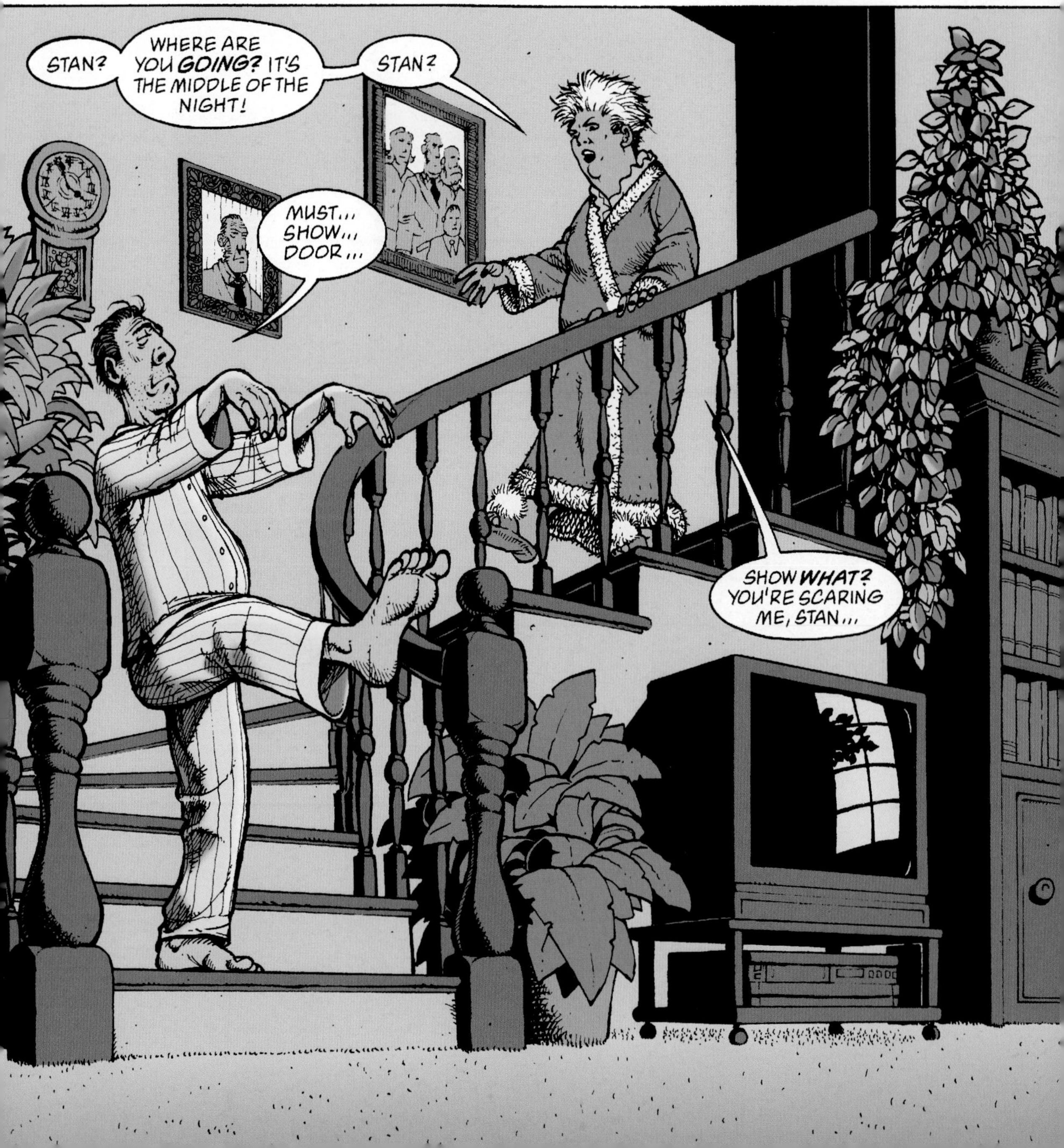
STAN?
WHERE ARE YOU **GOING?** IT'S THE MIDDLE OF THE NIGHT!
STAN?
MUST... SHOW... DOOR...
SHOW **WHAT?** YOU'RE SCARING ME, STAN...

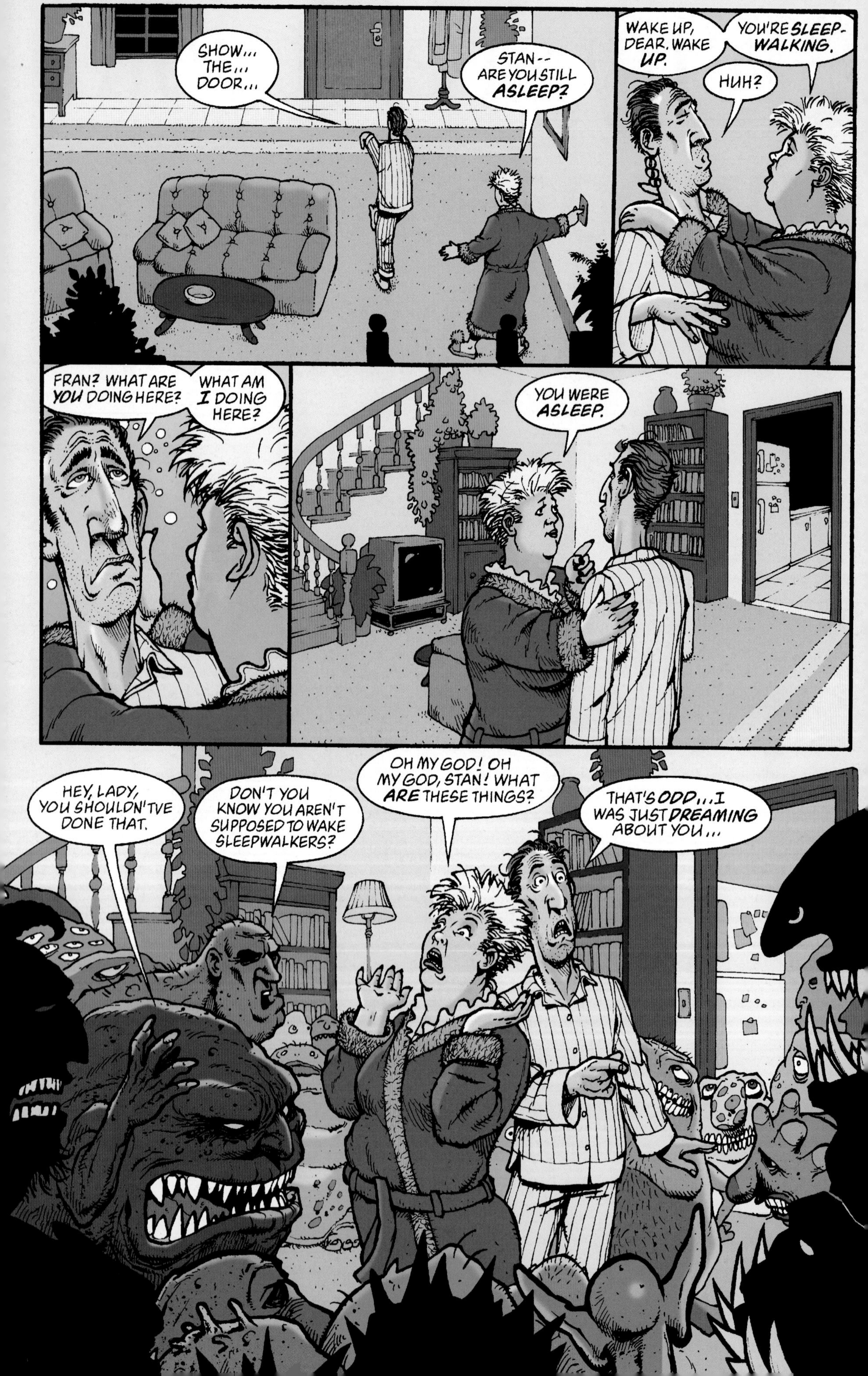
SHOW... THE... DOOR...
STAN-- ARE YOU STILL ASLEEP?
WAKE UP, DEAR. WAKE UP.
YOU'RE SLEEP-WALKING.
HUH?
FRAN? WHAT ARE YOU DOING HERE?
WHAT AM I DOING HERE?
YOU WERE ASLEEP.
HEY, LADY, YOU SHOULDN'T'VE DONE THAT.
DON'T YOU KNOW YOU AREN'T SUPPOSED TO WAKE SLEEPWALKERS?
OH MY GOD! OH MY GOD, STAN! WHAT ARE THESE THINGS?
THAT'S ODD... I WAS JUST DREAMING ABOUT YOU...

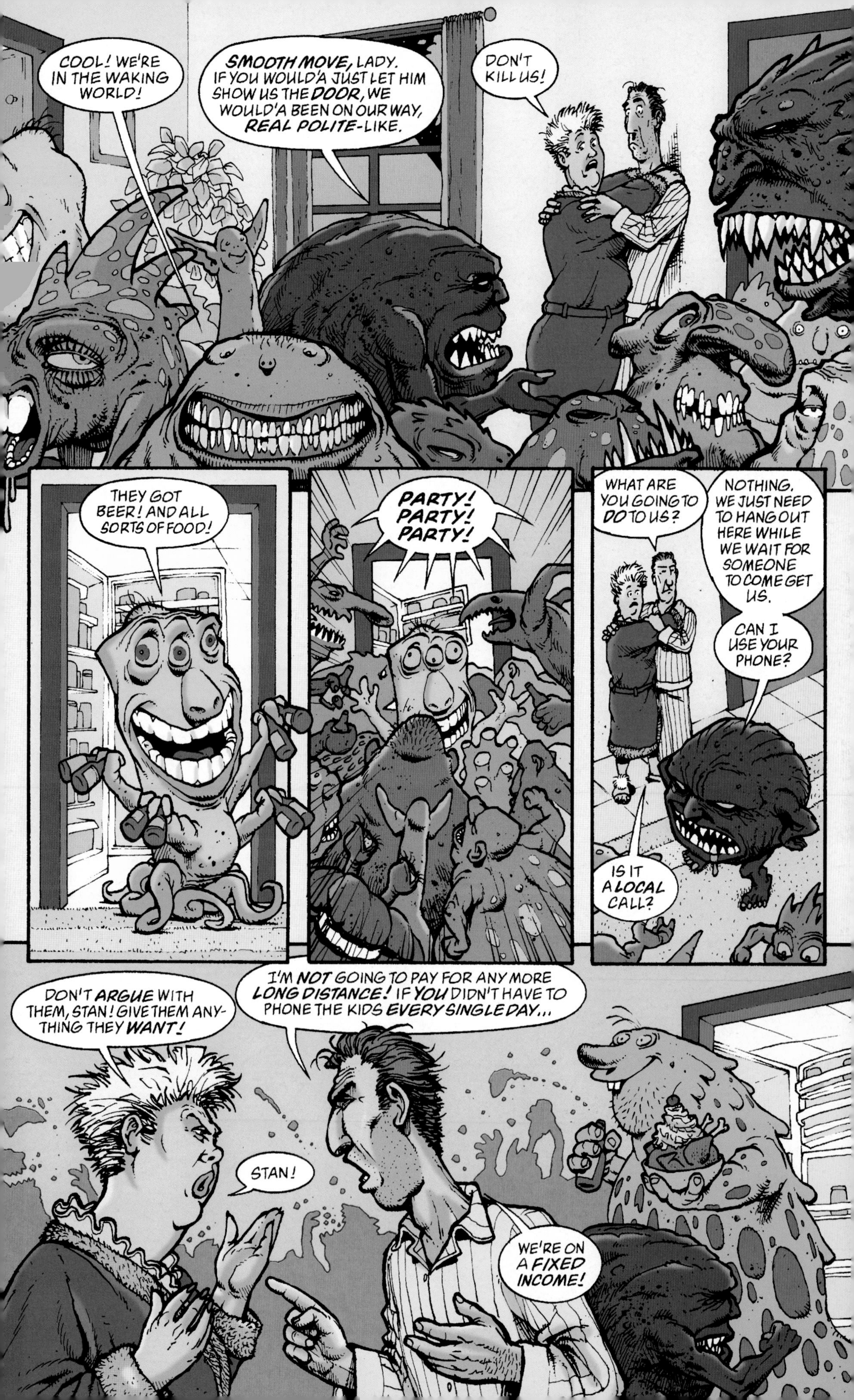
COOL! WE'RE IN THE WAKING WORLD!
SMOOTH MOVE, LADY. IF YOU WOULD'A JUST LET HIM SHOW US THE DOOR, WE WOULD'A BEEN ON OUR WAY, REAL POLITE-LIKE.
DON'T KILL US!
THEY GOT BEER! AND ALL SORTS OF FOOD!
PARTY! PARTY! PARTY!
WHAT ARE YOU GOING TO DO TO US?
NOTHING. WE JUST NEED TO HANG OUT HERE WHILE WE WAIT FOR SOMEONE TO COME GET US.
CAN I USE YOUR PHONE?
IS IT A LOCAL CALL?
DON'T ARGUE WITH THEM, STAN! GIVE THEM ANYTHING THEY WANT!
I'M NOT GOING TO PAY FOR ANY MORE LONG DISTANCE! IF YOU DIDN'T HAVE TO PHONE THE KIDS EVERY SINGLE DAY...
STAN!
WE'RE ON A FIXED INCOME!

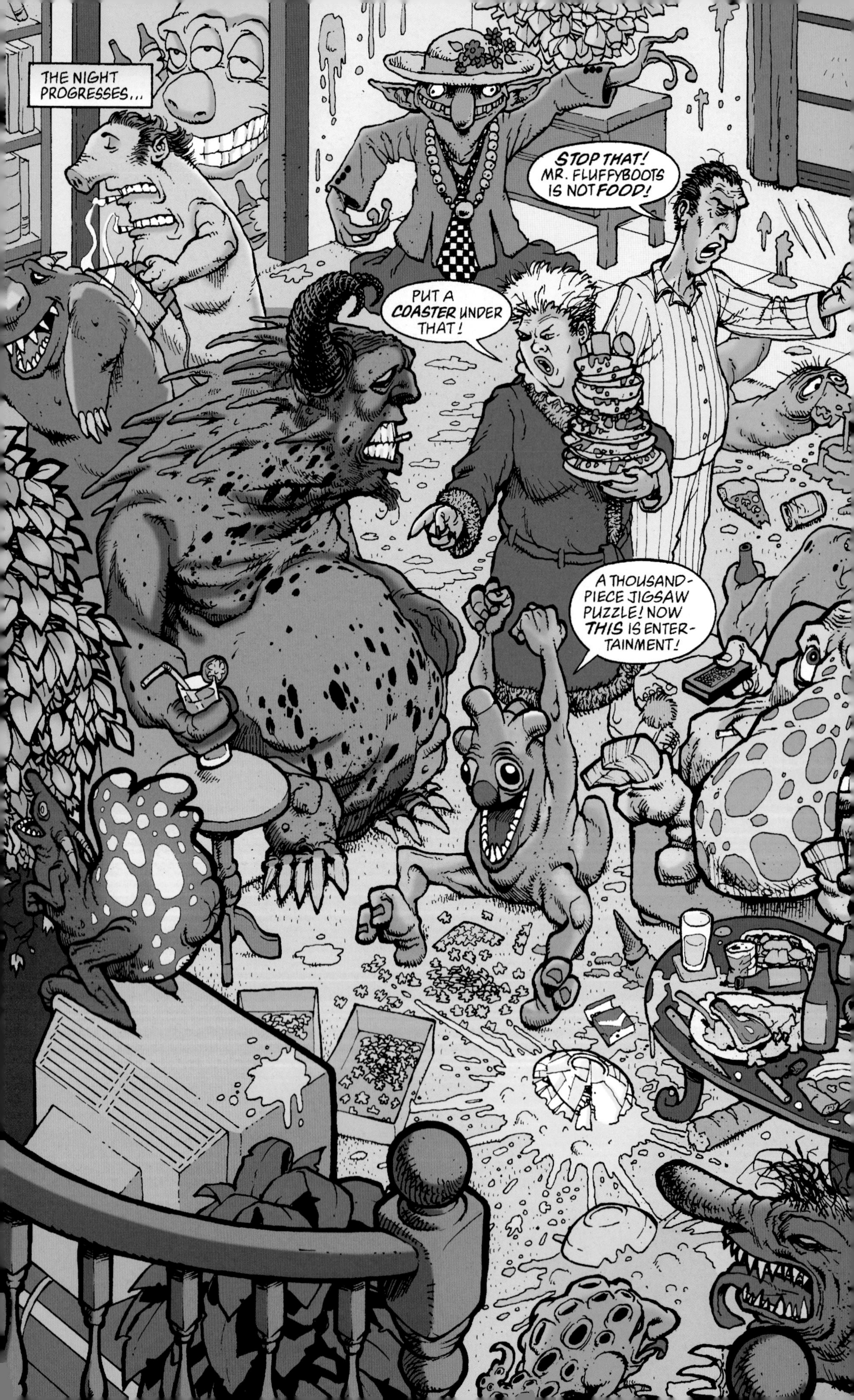
THE NIGHT PROGRESSES...
STOP THAT! MR. FLUFFYBOOTS IS NOT FOOD!
PUT A COASTER UNDER THAT!
A THOUSAND-PIECE JIGSAW PUZZLE! NOW THIS IS ENTERTAINMENT!

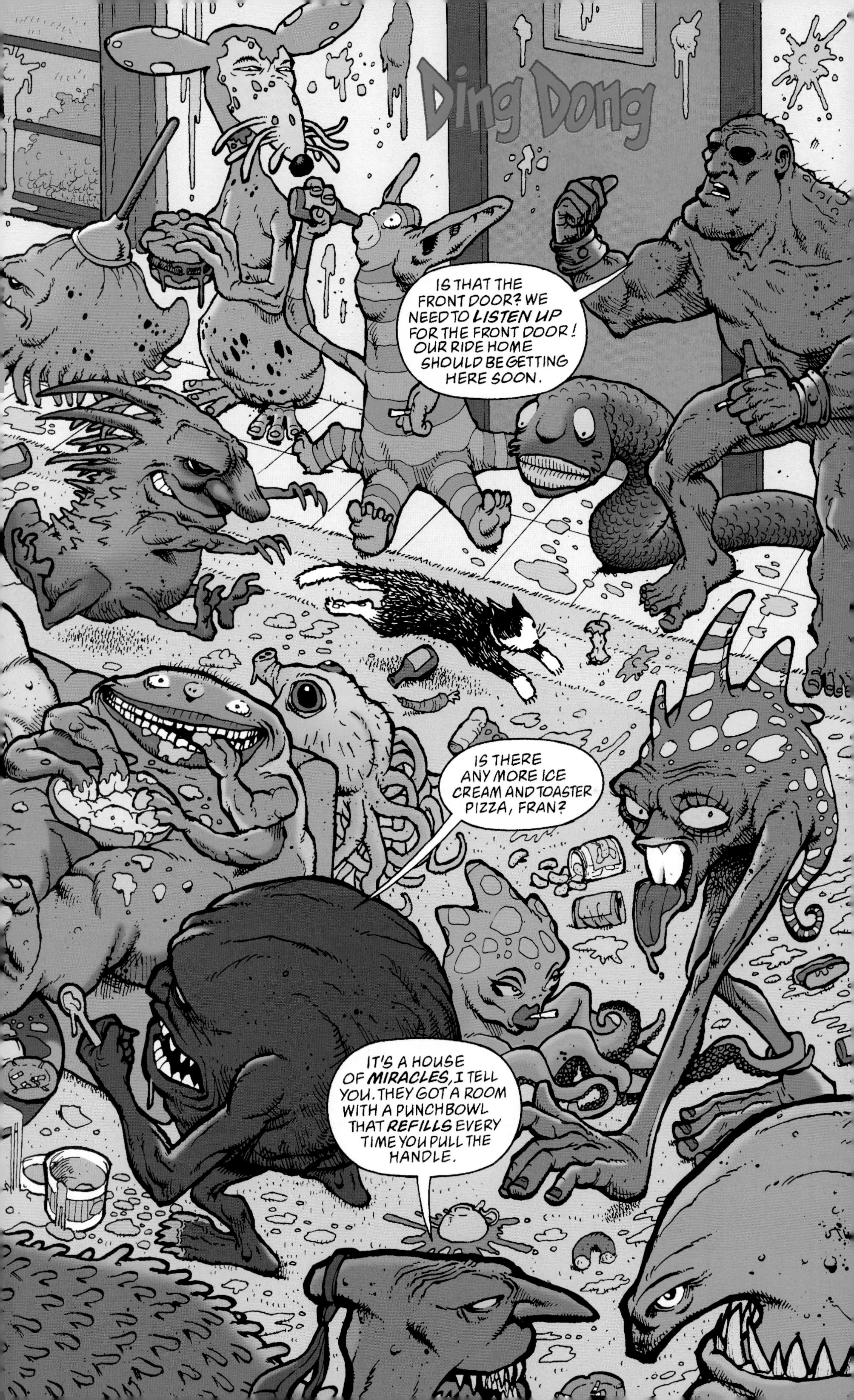
Ding Dong
IS THAT THE FRONT DOOR? WE NEED TO LISTEN UP FOR THE FRONT DOOR! OUR RIDE HOME SHOULD BE GETTING HERE SOON.
IS THERE ANY MORE ICE CREAM AND TOASTER PIZZA, FRAN?
IT'S A HOUSE OF MIRACLES, I TELL YOU. THEY GOT A ROOM WITH A PUNCHBOWL THAT REFILLS EVERY TIME YOU PULL THE HANDLE.

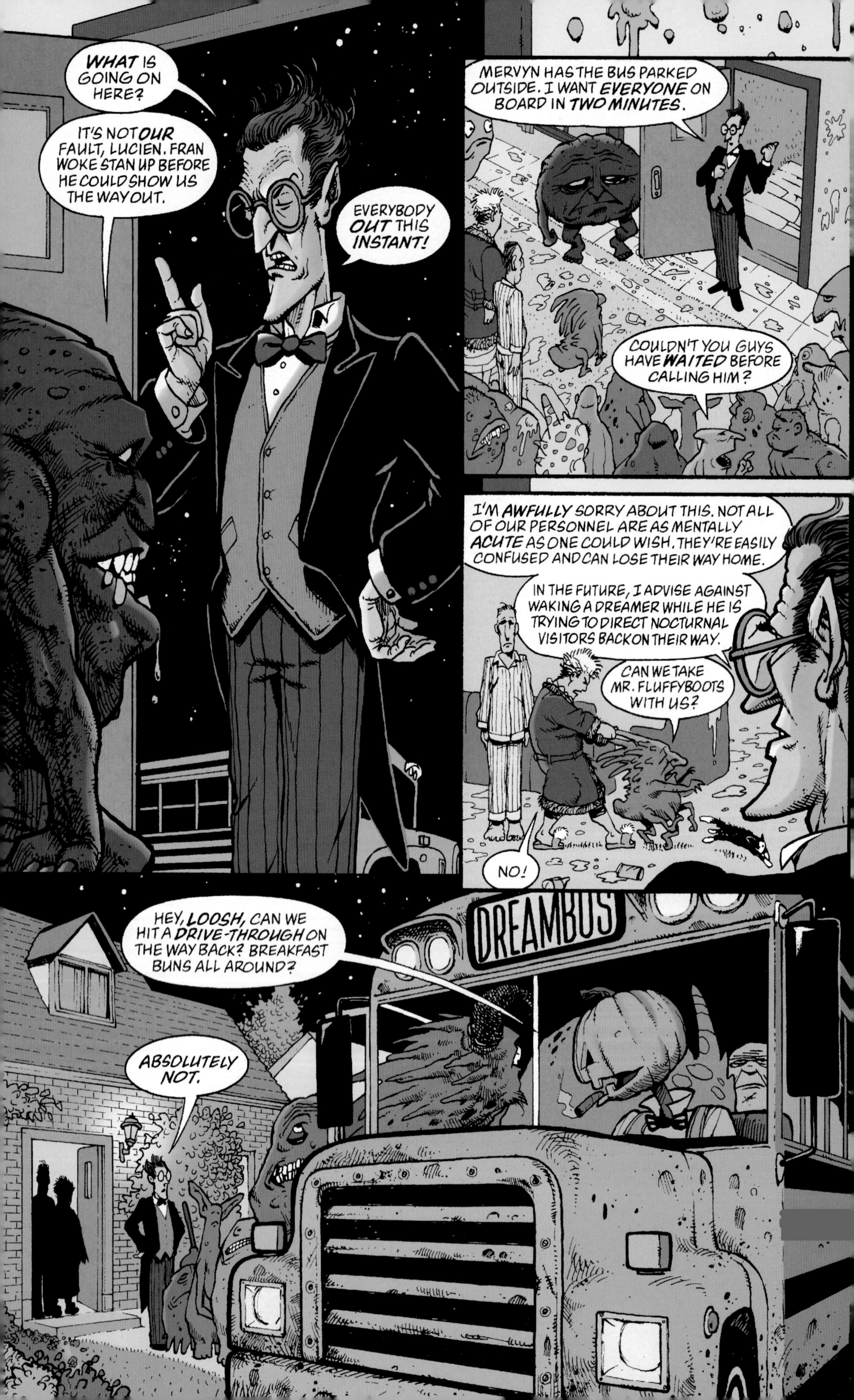
WHAT IS GOING ON HERE?
IT'S NOT OUR FAULT, LUCIEN. FRAN WOKE STAN UP BEFORE HE COULD SHOW US THE WAY OUT.
EVERYBODY OUT THIS INSTANT!
MERVYN HAS THE BUS PARKED OUTSIDE. I WANT EVERYONE ON BOARD IN TWO MINUTES.
COULDN'T YOU GUYS HAVE WAITED BEFORE CALLING HIM?
I'M AWFULLY SORRY ABOUT THIS. NOT ALL OF OUR PERSONNEL ARE AS MENTALLY ACUTE AS ONE COULD WISH. THEY'RE EASILY CONFUSED AND CAN LOSE THEIR WAY HOME.
IN THE FUTURE, I ADVISE AGAINST WAKING A DREAMER WHILE HE IS TRYING TO DIRECT NOCTURNAL VISITORS BACK ON THEIR WAY.
CAN WE TAKE MR. FLUFFYBOOTS WITH US?
NO!
DREAMBUS
HEY, LOOSH, CAN WE HIT A DRIVE-THROUGH ON THE WAY BACK? BREAKFAST BUNS ALL AROUND?
ABSOLUTELY NOT.

Why is it often so hard to remember your dreams?

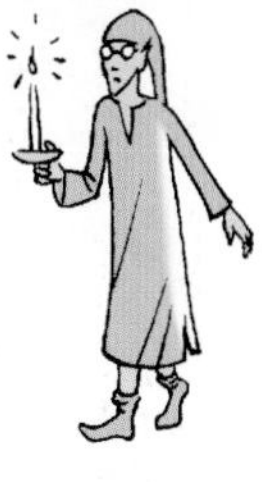

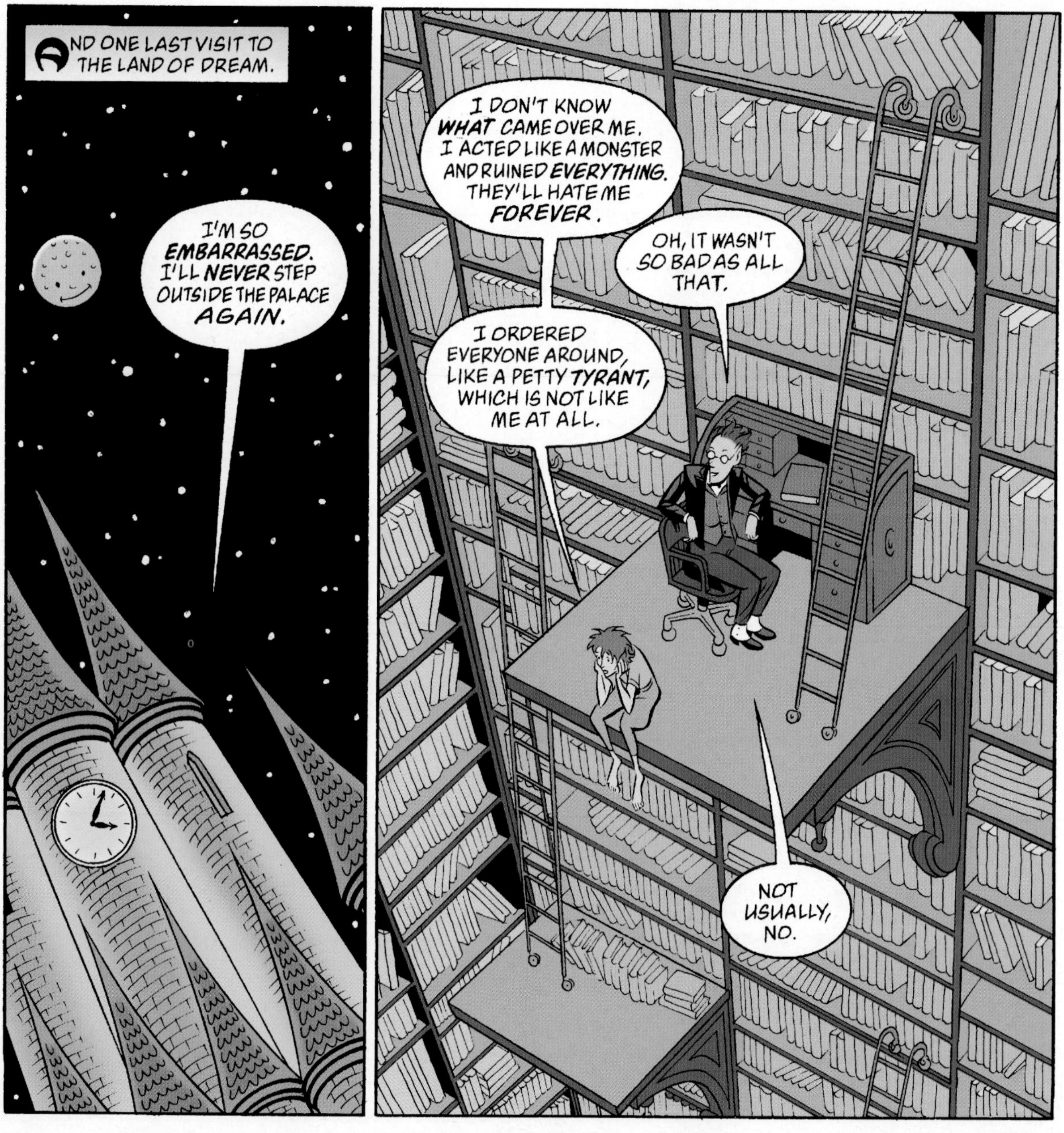

AND ONE LAST VISIT TO THE LAND OF DREAM.
I'M SO EMBARRASSED. I'LL NEVER STEP OUTSIDE THE PALACE AGAIN.
I DON'T KNOW WHAT CAME OVER ME. I ACTED LIKE A MONSTER AND RUINED EVERYTHING. THEY'LL HATE ME FOREVER.
OH, IT WASN'T SO BAD AS ALL THAT.
I ORDERED EVERYONE AROUND, LIKE A PETTY TYRANT, WHICH IS NOT LIKE ME AT ALL.
NOT USUALLY, NO.

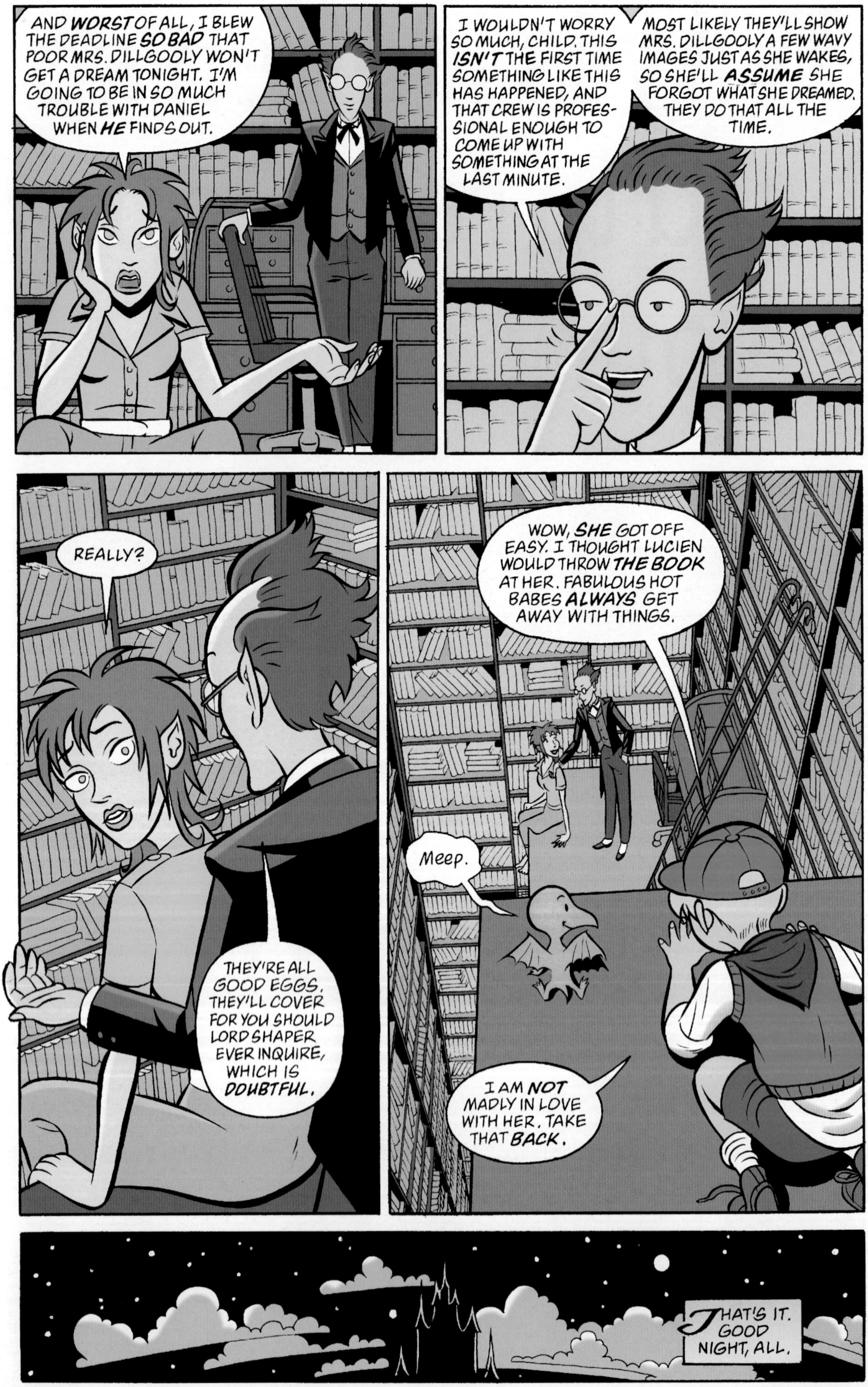
AND WORST OF ALL, I BLEW THE DEADLINE SO BAD THAT POOR MRS. DILLGOOLY WON'T GET A DREAM TONIGHT. I'M GOING TO BE IN SO MUCH TROUBLE WITH DANIEL WHEN HE FINDS OUT.
I WOULDN'T WORRY SO MUCH, CHILD. THIS ISN'T THE FIRST TIME SOMETHING LIKE THIS HAS HAPPENED, AND THAT CREW IS PROFES-SIONAL ENOUGH TO COME UP WITH SOMETHING AT THE LAST MINUTE.
MOST LIKELY THEY'LL SHOW MRS. DILLGOOLY A FEW WAVY IMAGES JUST AS SHE WAKES, SO SHE'LL ASSUME SHE FORGOT WHAT SHE DREAMED. THEY DO THAT ALL THE TIME.
REALLY?
THEY'RE ALL GOOD EGGS. THEY'LL COVER FOR YOU SHOULD LORD SHAPER EVER INQUIRE, WHICH IS DOUBTFUL.
WOW, SHE GOT OFF EASY. I THOUGHT LUCIEN WOULD THROW THE BOOK AT HER. FABULOUS HOT BABES ALWAYS GET AWAY WITH THINGS.
Meep.
I AM NOT MADLY IN LOVE WITH HER. TAKE THAT BACK.
THAT'S IT. GOOD NIGHT, ALL.

the sandman presents

The Thessaliad

Part One:
THE DAUGHTERS OF GARM

Or, Far Too Much About Pie

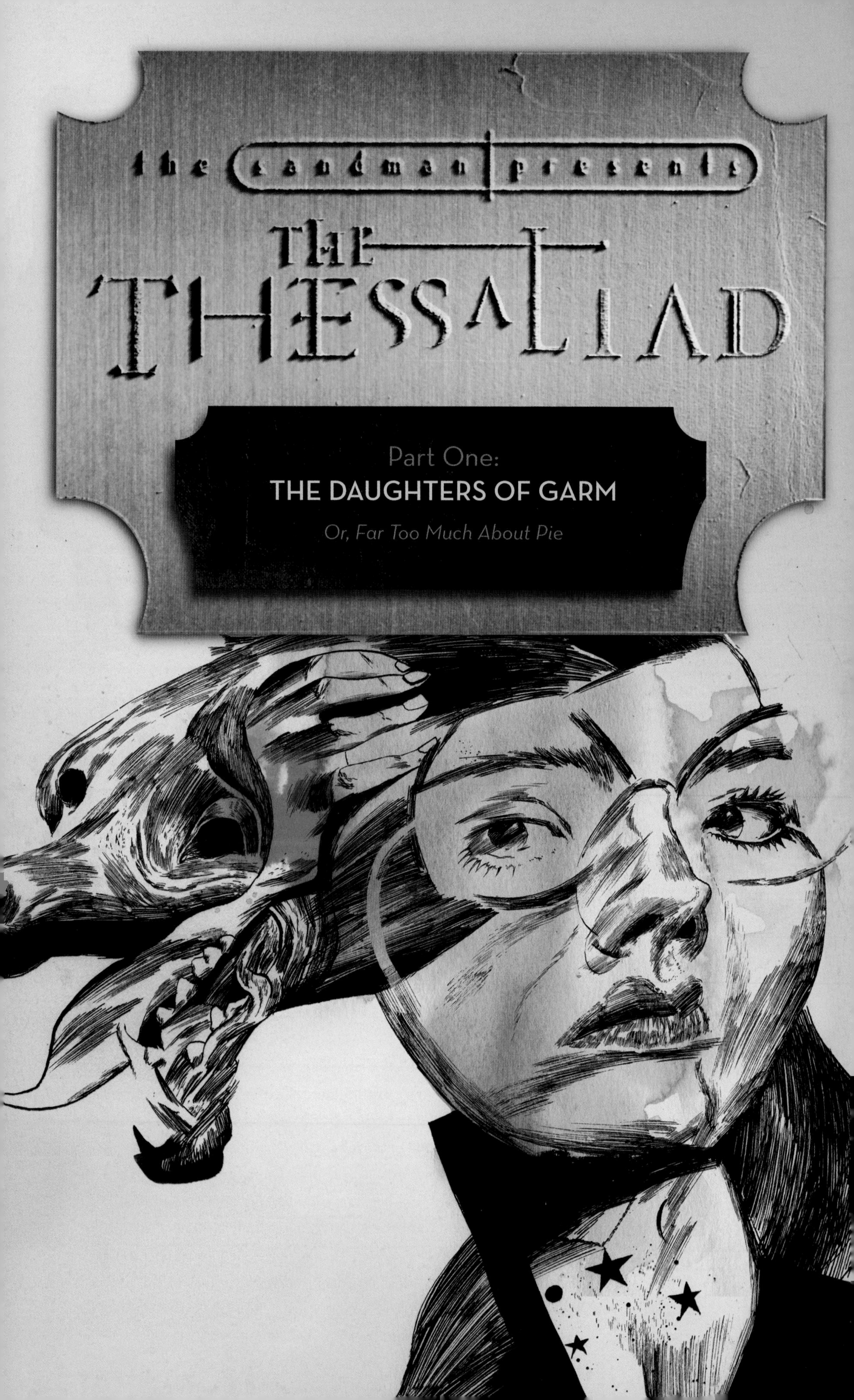

EVERYONE HATED THE TITLE. "THE THESSALIAD? WHAT THE HELL DOES THAT MEAN?" I loved it. In this one instance, everyone else is wrong and I'm right. The story of Thessaly *should* be called the Thessaliad, just as the story of (Troy) Ilium was called the Iliad and Aeneas' story was called the Aeneid. Get it? Too pompous? Trying to show off my (nearly, almost) classical education? Maybe. But as a wise man said, no story is strong enough to survive the mistakes of more than one person, so I dug my heels in and got my way.

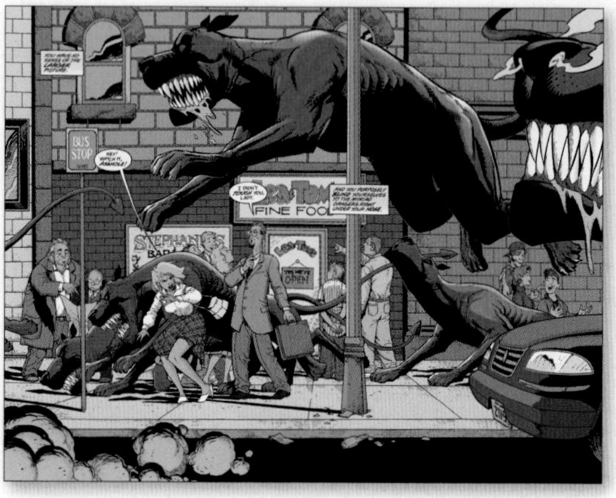
BUS STOP

Continuing my work in the Gaiman vineyards (for which I remain grateful), this four-part tale is yet another foray into the world of story – specifically, the story of the last and most powerful of the Thessalian witches, a woman feared by all the gods. It's about what happens when a character knows the rules and structure of storytelling backwards and forwards, so much so that she can use that knowledge to manipulate its outcome – even though she's part of the story.

I wanted to play with the well-worn tropes of the Heroic Quest in this tale, a staple of fantasy fiction. But what happens when one of the questing party knows all the rules in advance? I thought that might be fun to explore.

I'm old and my memory isn't what it used to be, so I'm not certain that this is the first time I worked with Shawn McManus, but I suspect it was, since Shawn was top-of-the-list for this miniseries based on his being one of the co-creators of Thessaly, the character in THE SANDMAN. This pairing turned out to be quite the boon for me, Shawn being a truly inventive artist (as you're about to discover for yourself, assuming you haven't encountered his work before). He's one of those rare breeds who can draw anything with verve and clarity, no matter how silly or difficult the subject matter. From here I'd go on to work with him again, in FABLES from time to time and in books like the short-lived SHADOWPACT, basically any time both he and I were available. Eventually we were able to force him into a semi-permanent gig as the official CINDERELLA artist, in the two (so far) FABLES spinoffs featuring the world's best secret agent (that Bond fellow only being the world's greatest *male* secret agent).

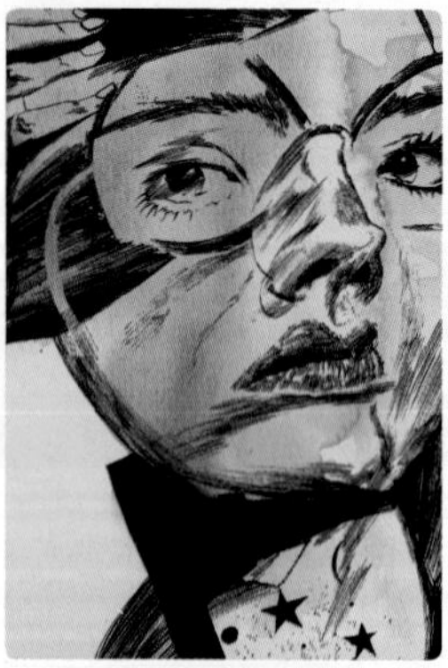

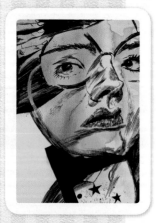

THE THESSALIAD

ART BY
Shawn McManus

COLORS BY
Daniel Vozzo

LETTERS BY
John Costanza

COVER ART BY
Dave McKean

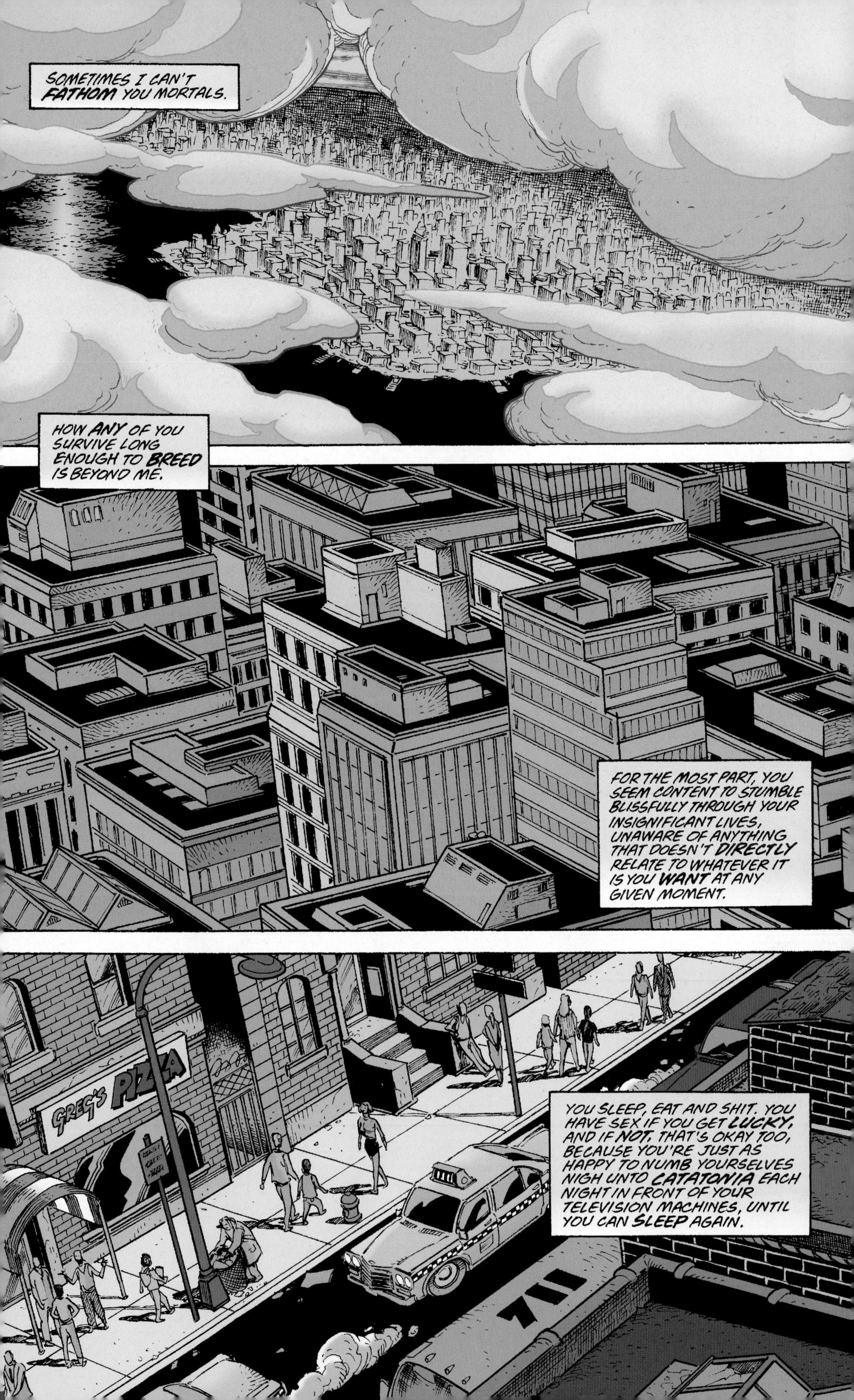
SOMETIMES I CAN'T **FATHOM** YOU MORTALS.
HOW **ANY** OF YOU SURVIVE LONG ENOUGH TO **BREED** IS BEYOND ME.
FOR THE **MOST PART**, YOU SEEM CONTENT TO STUMBLE BLISSFULLY THROUGH YOUR INSIGNIFICANT LIVES, UNAWARE OF ANYTHING THAT DOESN'T **DIRECTLY** RELATE TO WHATEVER IT IS YOU **WANT** AT ANY GIVEN MOMENT.
GREG'S PIZZA
YOU SLEEP, EAT AND SHIT. YOU HAVE SEX IF YOU GET **LUCKY**, AND IF **NOT**, THAT'S OKAY TOO, BECAUSE YOU'RE JUST AS HAPPY TO NUMB YOURSELVES NIGH UNTO **CATATONIA** EACH NIGHT IN FRONT OF YOUR TELEVISION MACHINES, UNTIL YOU CAN **SLEEP** AGAIN.

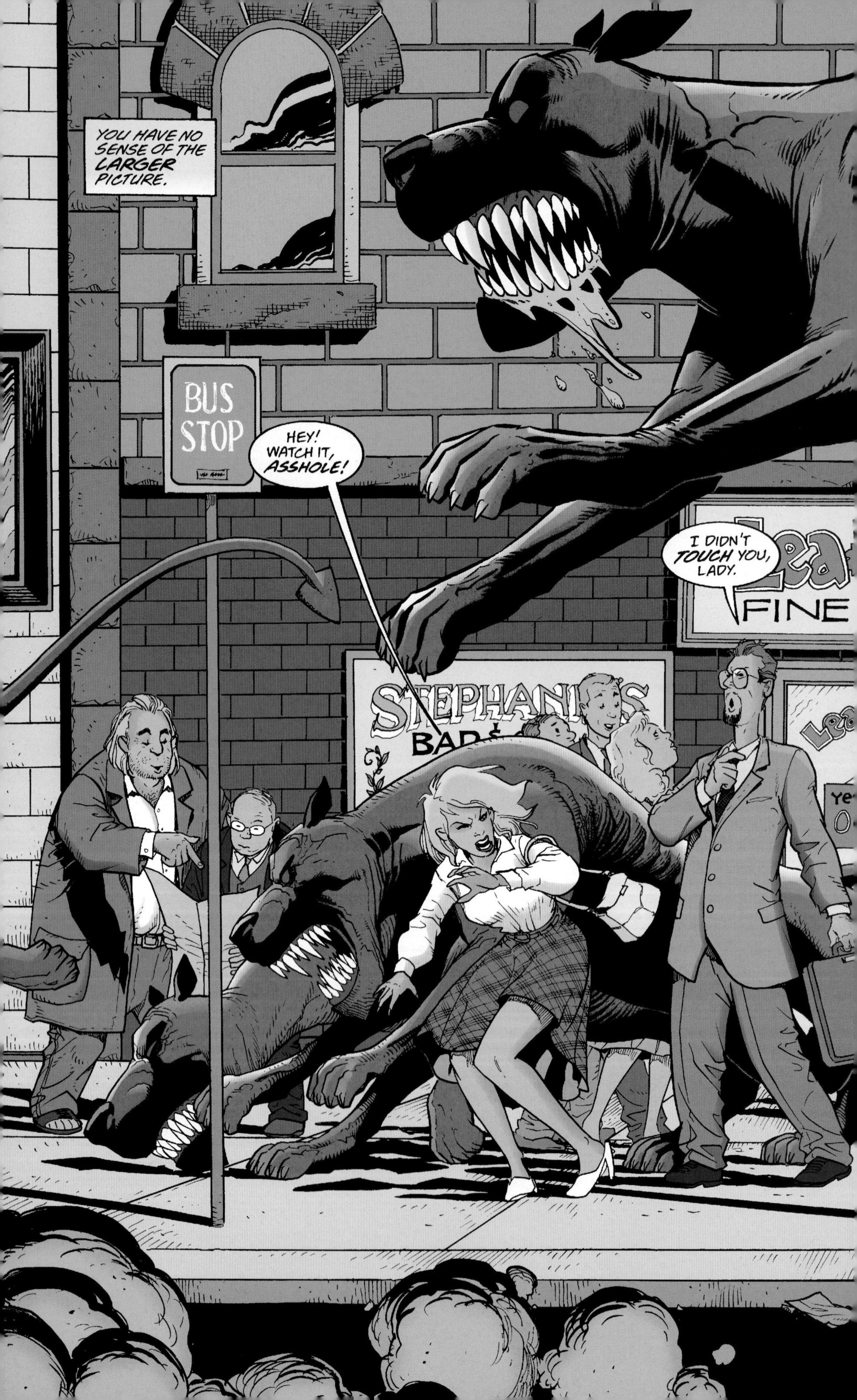
YOU HAVE NO SENSE OF THE LARGER PICTURE.
BUS STOP
HEY! WATCH IT, ASSHOLE!
I DIDN'T TOUCH YOU, LADY.
FINE
STEPHANIE'S
BAR

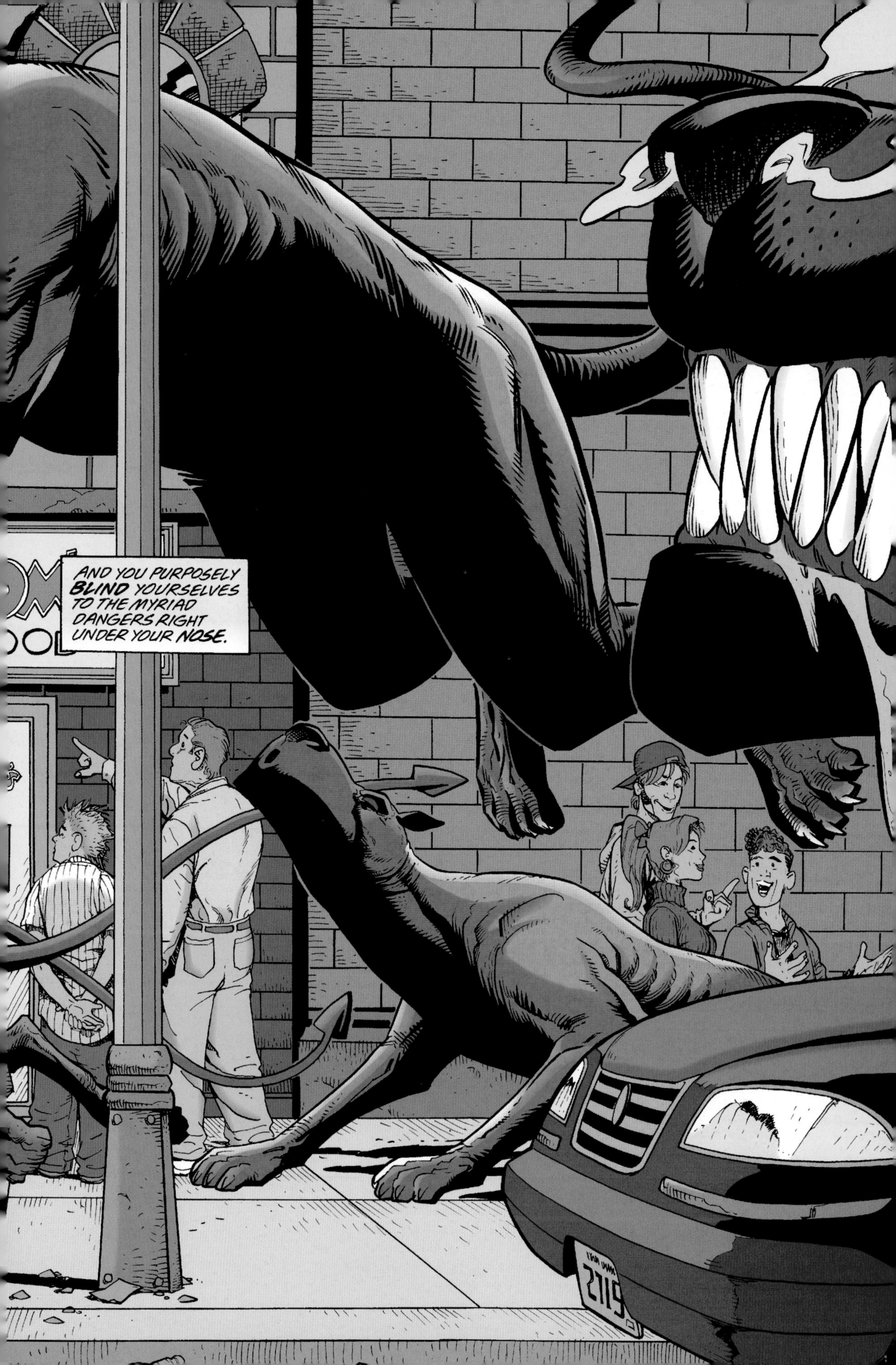
AND YOU PURPOSELY BLIND YOURSELVES TO THE MYRIAD DANGERS RIGHT UNDER YOUR NOSE.

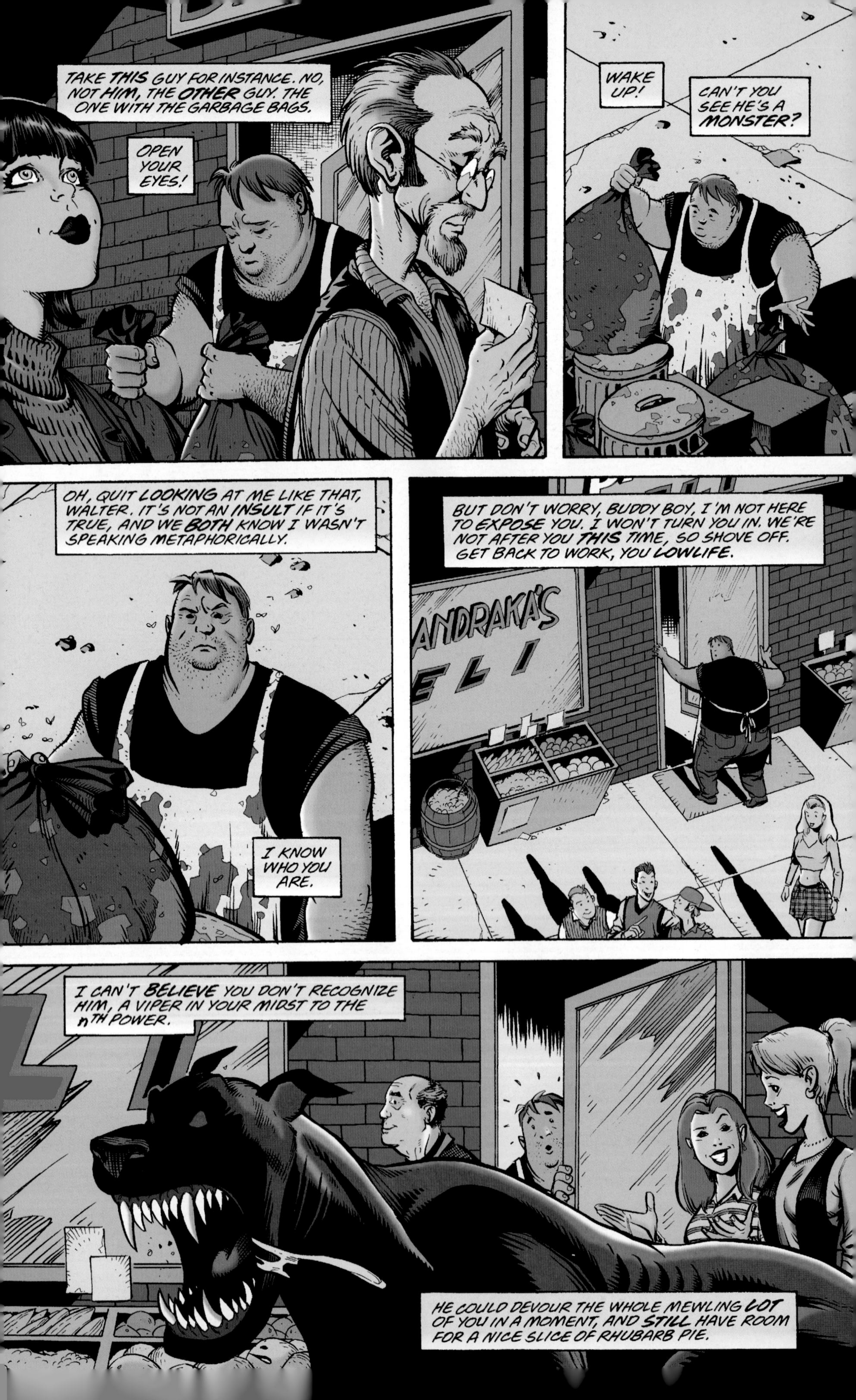
TAKE THIS GUY FOR INSTANCE. NO, NOT HIM, THE OTHER GUY. THE ONE WITH THE GARBAGE BAGS.
OPEN YOUR EYES!
WAKE UP!
CAN'T YOU SEE HE'S A MONSTER?
OH, QUIT LOOKING AT ME LIKE THAT, WALTER. IT'S NOT AN INSULT IF IT'S TRUE, AND WE BOTH KNOW I WASN'T SPEAKING METAPHORICALLY.
I KNOW WHO YOU ARE.
BUT DON'T WORRY, BUDDY BOY, I'M NOT HERE TO EXPOSE YOU. I WON'T TURN YOU IN. WE'RE NOT AFTER YOU THIS TIME, SO SHOVE OFF. GET BACK TO WORK, YOU LOWLIFE.
ANDRAKA'S
ELI
I CAN'T BELIEVE YOU DON'T RECOGNIZE HIM, A VIPER IN YOUR MIDST TO THE nTH POWER.
HE COULD DEVOUR THE WHOLE MEWLING LOT OF YOU IN A MOMENT, AND STILL HAVE ROOM FOR A NICE SLICE OF RHUBARB PIE.

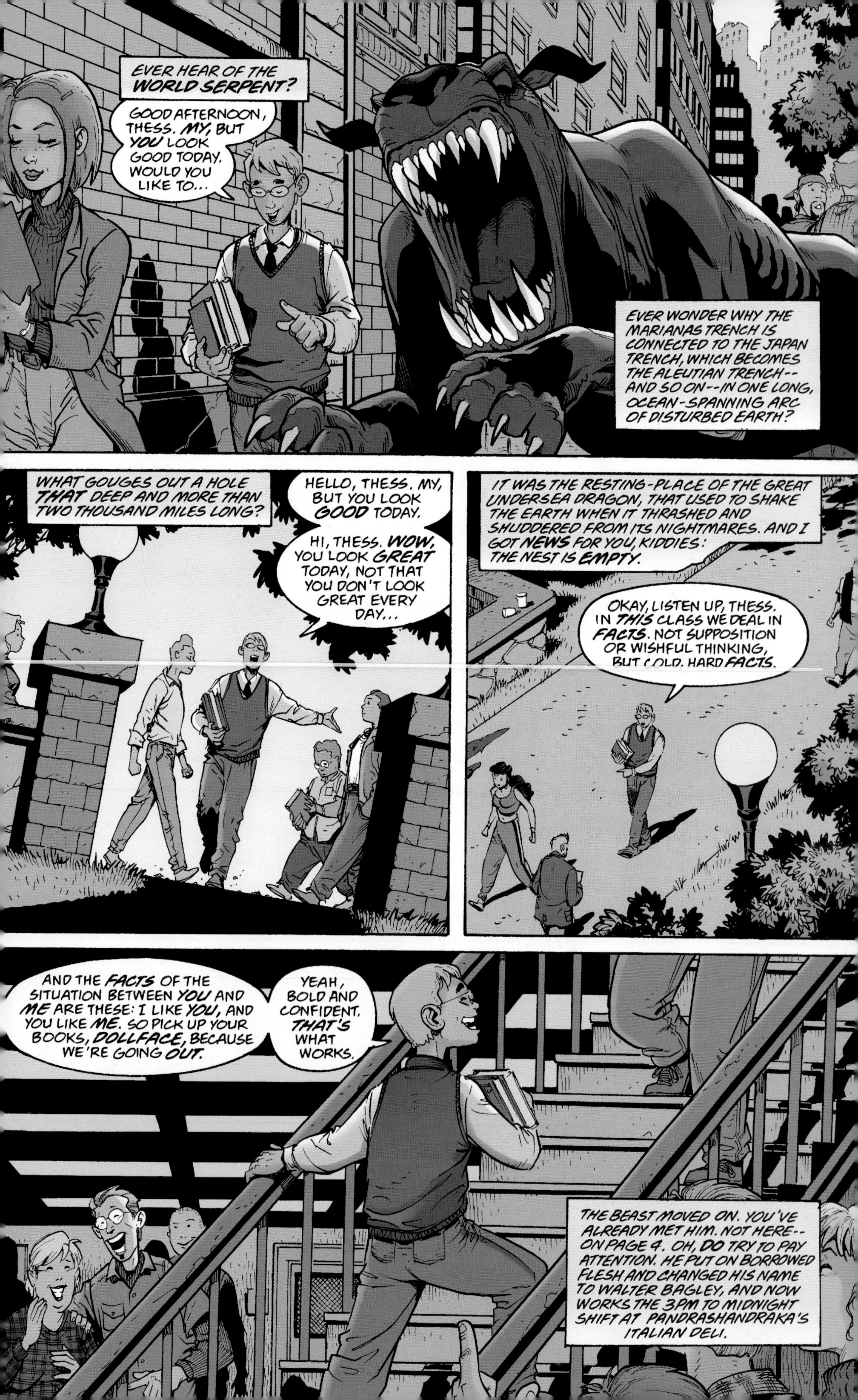
EVER HEAR OF THE WORLD SERPENT?
GOOD AFTERNOON, THESS. MY, BUT YOU LOOK GOOD TODAY. WOULD YOU LIKE TO...
EVER WONDER WHY THE MARIANAS TRENCH IS CONNECTED TO THE JAPAN TRENCH, WHICH BECOMES THE ALEUTIAN TRENCH--AND SO ON--IN ONE LONG, OCEAN-SPANNING ARC OF DISTURBED EARTH?
WHAT GOUGES OUT A HOLE THAT DEEP AND MORE THAN TWO THOUSAND MILES LONG?
HELLO, THESS. MY, BUT YOU LOOK GOOD TODAY.
HI, THESS. WOW, YOU LOOK GREAT TODAY, NOT THAT YOU DON'T LOOK GREAT EVERY DAY...
IT WAS THE RESTING-PLACE OF THE GREAT UNDERSEA DRAGON, THAT USED TO SHAKE THE EARTH WHEN IT THRASHED AND SHUDDERED FROM ITS NIGHTMARES. AND I GOT NEWS FOR YOU, KIDDIES: THE NEST IS EMPTY.
OKAY, LISTEN UP, THESS. IN THIS CLASS WE DEAL IN FACTS. NOT SUPPOSITION OR WISHFUL THINKING, BUT COLD, HARD FACTS.
AND THE FACTS OF THE SITUATION BETWEEN YOU AND ME ARE THESE: I LIKE YOU, AND YOU LIKE ME. SO PICK UP YOUR BOOKS, DOLLFACE, BECAUSE WE'RE GOING OUT.
YEAH, BOLD AND CONFIDENT. THAT'S WHAT WORKS.
THE BEAST MOVED ON. YOU'VE ALREADY MET HIM. NOT HERE--ON PAGE 4. OH, DO TRY TO PAY ATTENTION. HE PUT ON BORROWED FLESH AND CHANGED HIS NAME TO WALTER BAGLEY, AND NOW WORKS THE 3PM TO MIDNIGHT SHIFT AT PANDRASHANDRAKA'S ITALIAN DELI.

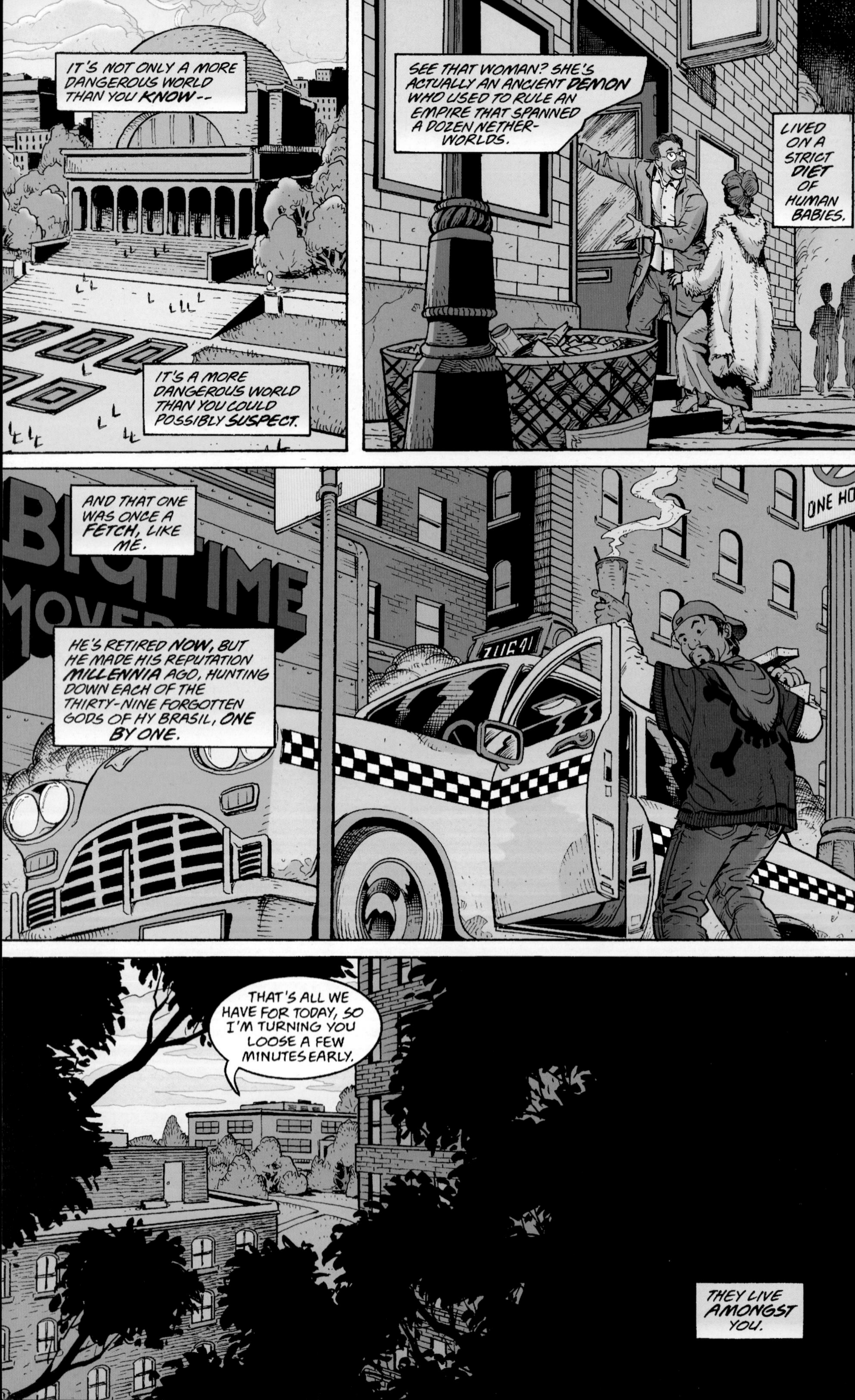
IT'S NOT ONLY A MORE DANGEROUS WORLD THAN YOU KNOW--
IT'S A MORE DANGEROUS WORLD THAN YOU COULD POSSIBLY SUSPECT.
SEE THAT WOMAN? SHE'S ACTUALLY AN ANCIENT DEMON WHO USED TO RULE AN EMPIRE THAT SPANNED A DOZEN NETHER-WORLDS.
LIVED ON A STRICT DIET OF HUMAN BABIES.
BIG TIME MOVER
AND THAT ONE WAS ONCE A FETCH, LIKE ME.
HE'S RETIRED NOW, BUT HE MADE HIS REPUTATION MILLENNIA AGO, HUNTING DOWN EACH OF THE THIRTY-NINE FORGOTTEN GODS OF HY BRASIL, ONE BY ONE.
ONE HO
THAT'S ALL WE HAVE FOR TODAY, SO I'M TURNING YOU LOOSE A FEW MINUTES EARLY.
THEY LIVE AMONGST YOU.

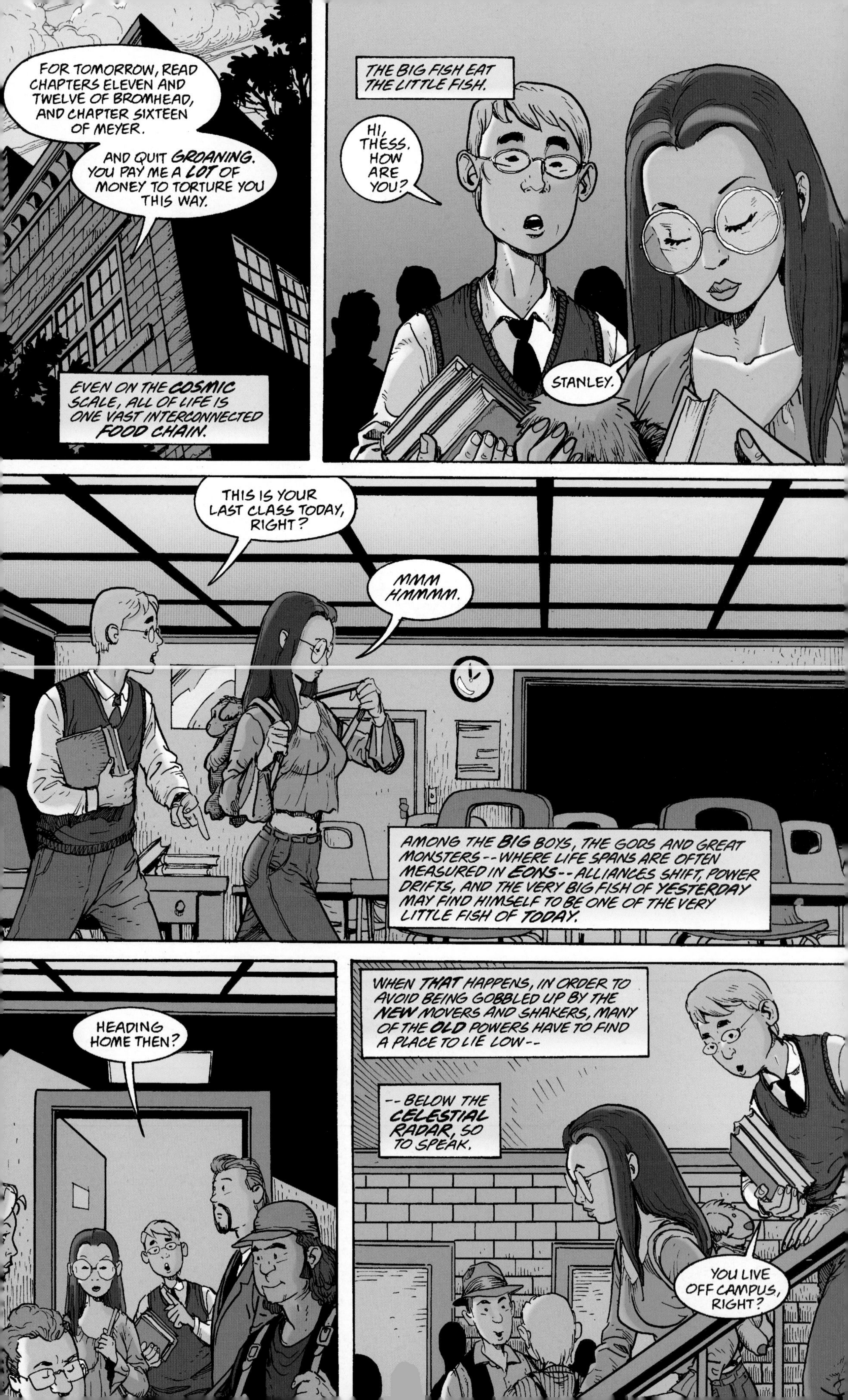
FOR TOMORROW, READ CHAPTERS ELEVEN AND TWELVE OF BROMHEAD, AND CHAPTER SIXTEEN OF MEYER.
AND QUIT GROANING. YOU PAY ME A LOT OF MONEY TO TORTURE YOU THIS WAY.
EVEN ON THE COSMIC SCALE, ALL OF LIFE IS ONE VAST INTERCONNECTED FOOD CHAIN.
THE BIG FISH EAT THE LITTLE FISH.
HI, THESS. HOW ARE YOU?
STANLEY.
THIS IS YOUR LAST CLASS TODAY, RIGHT?
MMM HMMMM.
AMONG THE BIG BOYS, THE GODS AND GREAT MONSTERS--WHERE LIFE SPANS ARE OFTEN MEASURED IN EONS--ALLIANCES SHIFT, POWER DRIFTS, AND THE VERY BIG FISH OF YESTERDAY MAY FIND HIMSELF TO BE ONE OF THE VERY LITTLE FISH OF TODAY.
HEADING HOME THEN?
WHEN THAT HAPPENS, IN ORDER TO AVOID BEING GOBBLED UP BY THE NEW MOVERS AND SHAKERS, MANY OF THE OLD POWERS HAVE TO FIND A PLACE TO LIE LOW--
--BELOW THE CELESTIAL RADAR, SO TO SPEAK.
YOU LIVE OFF CAMPUS, RIGHT?

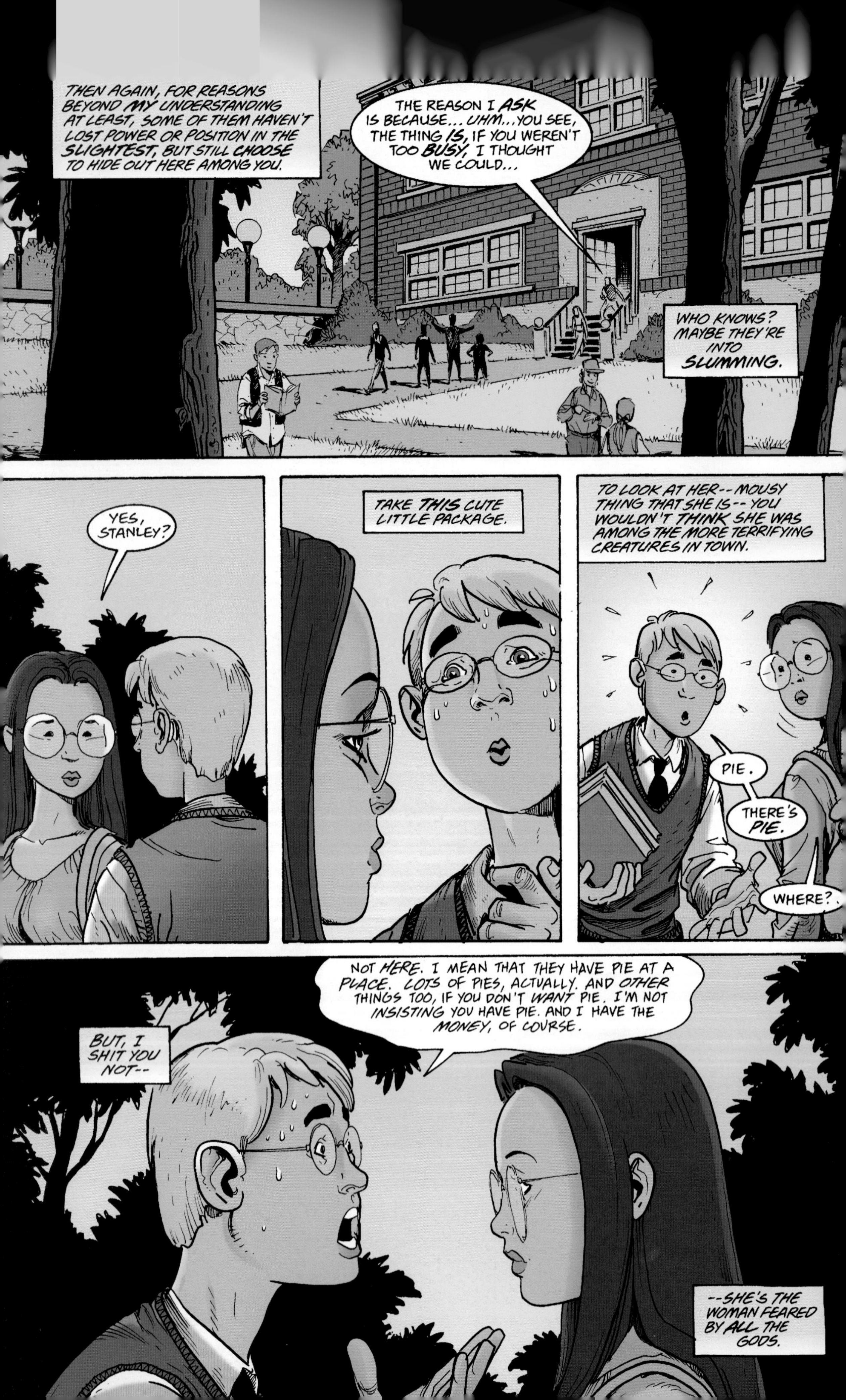
THEN AGAIN, FOR REASONS BEYOND MY UNDERSTANDING AT LEAST, SOME OF THEM HAVEN'T LOST POWER OR POSITION IN THE SLIGHTEST, BUT STILL CHOOSE TO HIDE OUT HERE AMONG YOU.
THE REASON I ASK IS BECAUSE... UHM... YOU SEE, THE THING IS, IF YOU WEREN'T TOO BUSY, I THOUGHT WE COULD...
WHO KNOWS? MAYBE THEY'RE INTO SLUMMING.
YES, STANLEY?
TAKE THIS CUTE LITTLE PACKAGE.
TO LOOK AT HER-- MOUSY THING THAT SHE IS-- YOU WOULDN'T THINK SHE WAS AMONG THE MORE TERRIFYING CREATURES IN TOWN.
PIE.
THERE'S PIE.
WHERE?
BUT, I SHIT YOU NOT--
NOT HERE. I MEAN THAT THEY HAVE PIE AT A PLACE. LOTS OF PIES, ACTUALLY. AND OTHER THINGS TOO, IF YOU DON'T WANT PIE. I'M NOT INSISTING YOU HAVE PIE. AND I HAVE THE MONEY, OF COURSE.
--SHE'S THE WOMAN FEARED BY ALL THE GODS.

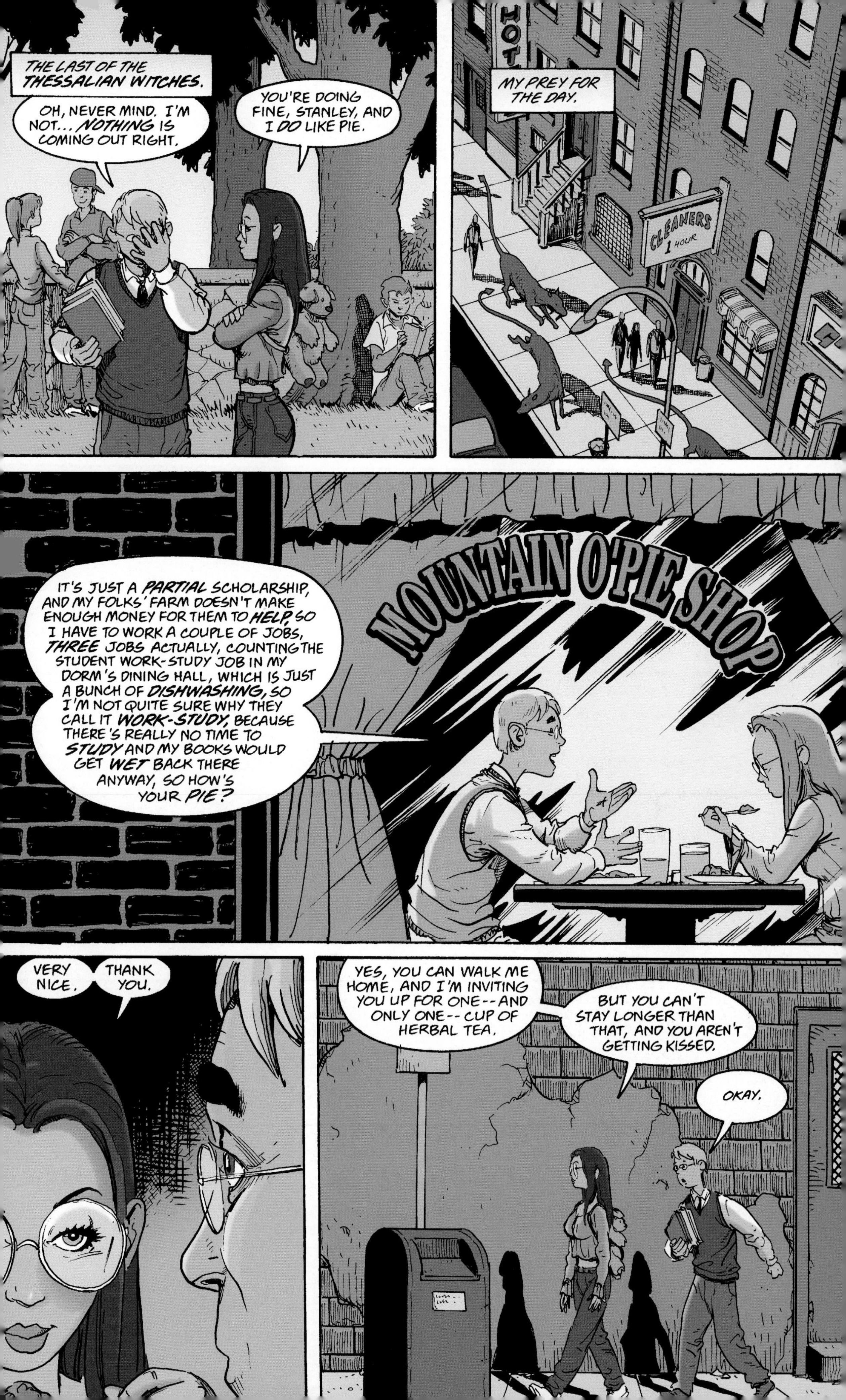
THE LAST OF THE THESSALIAN WITCHES.
OH, NEVER MIND. I'M NOT... NOTHING IS COMING OUT RIGHT.
YOU'RE DOING FINE, STANLEY, AND I DO LIKE PIE.
MY PREY FOR THE DAY.
CLEANERS 1 HOUR
MOUNTAIN O'PIE SHOP
IT'S JUST A PARTIAL SCHOLARSHIP, AND MY FOLKS' FARM DOESN'T MAKE ENOUGH MONEY FOR THEM TO HELP, SO I HAVE TO WORK A COUPLE OF JOBS, THREE JOBS ACTUALLY, COUNTING THE STUDENT WORK-STUDY JOB IN MY DORM'S DINING HALL, WHICH IS JUST A BUNCH OF DISHWASHING, SO I'M NOT QUITE SURE WHY THEY CALL IT WORK-STUDY, BECAUSE THERE'S REALLY NO TIME TO STUDY AND MY BOOKS WOULD GET WET BACK THERE ANYWAY, SO HOW'S YOUR PIE?
VERY NICE.
THANK YOU.
YES, YOU CAN WALK ME HOME, AND I'M INVITING YOU UP FOR ONE--AND ONLY ONE--CUP OF HERBAL TEA.
BUT YOU CAN'T STAY LONGER THAN THAT, AND YOU AREN'T GETTING KISSED.
OKAY.

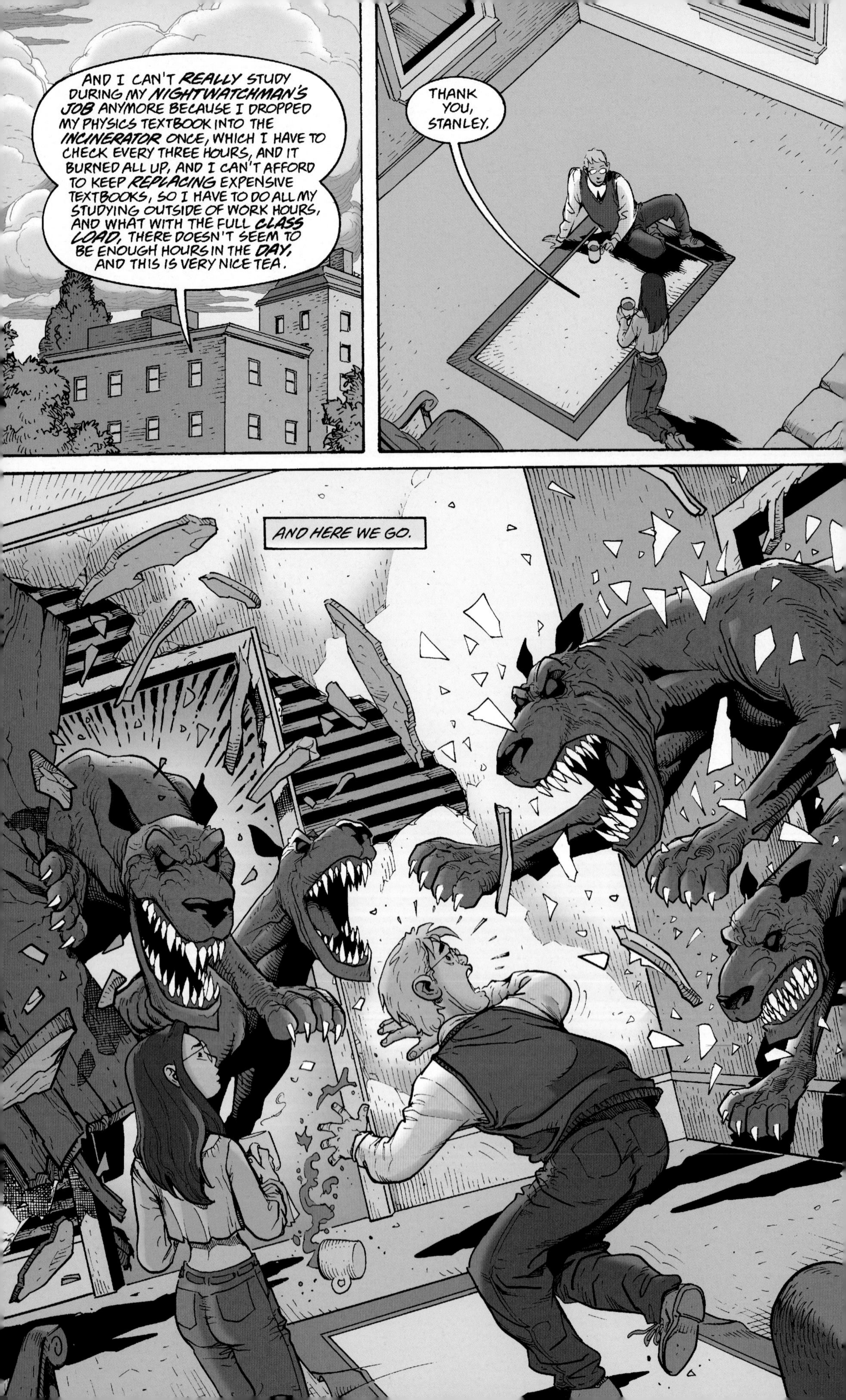
AND I CAN'T REALLY STUDY DURING MY NIGHTWATCHMAN'S JOB ANYMORE BECAUSE I DROPPED MY PHYSICS TEXTBOOK INTO THE INCINERATOR ONCE, WHICH I HAVE TO CHECK EVERY THREE HOURS, AND IT BURNED ALL UP, AND I CAN'T AFFORD TO KEEP REPLACING EXPENSIVE TEXTBOOKS, SO I HAVE TO DO ALL MY STUDYING OUTSIDE OF WORK HOURS, AND WHAT WITH THE FULL CLASS LOAD, THERE DOESN'T SEEM TO BE ENOUGH HOURS IN THE DAY, AND THIS IS VERY NICE TEA.
THANK YOU, STANLEY.
AND HERE WE GO.

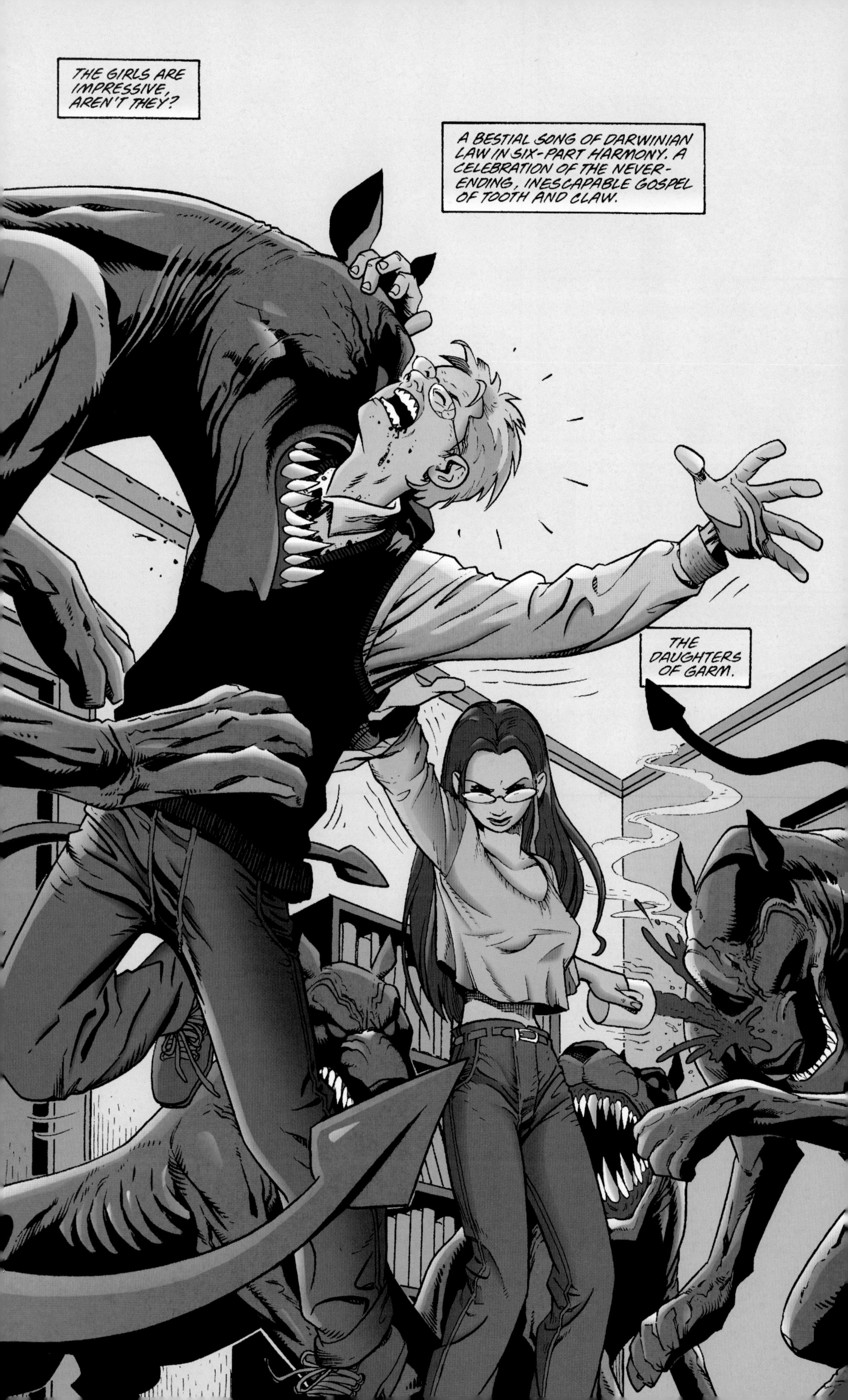
THE GIRLS ARE IMPRESSIVE, AREN'T THEY?
A BESTIAL SONG OF DARWINIAN LAW IN SIX-PART HARMONY. A CELEBRATION OF THE NEVER-ENDING, INESCAPABLE GOSPEL OF TOOTH AND CLAW.
THE DAUGHTERS OF GARM.

BUT FOR ALL THEIR OBVIOUS *TALENT*, I DIDN'T *WANT* TO WORK WITH THEM.

THEY WERE *FORCED* ON ME.

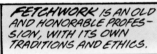

FETCHWORK IS AN OLD AND HONORABLE PROFESSION, WITH ITS OWN TRADITIONS AND ETHICS.

A CERTAIN AMOUNT OF *ELEGANCE* IS EXPECTED, AND--

--IN THE CIRCLES I TRAVEL IN--

--ANY OVERT SHOW OF CLUMSY THUGGISH-NESS IS *DEFINITELY* SOMETHING TO GET YOU TALKED ABOUT.

FOR JUST THAT REASON I *USUALLY* HUNT ALONE, USING *INVESTIGATION* AND *DETECTION* TO TRACK DOWN MY QUARRY.

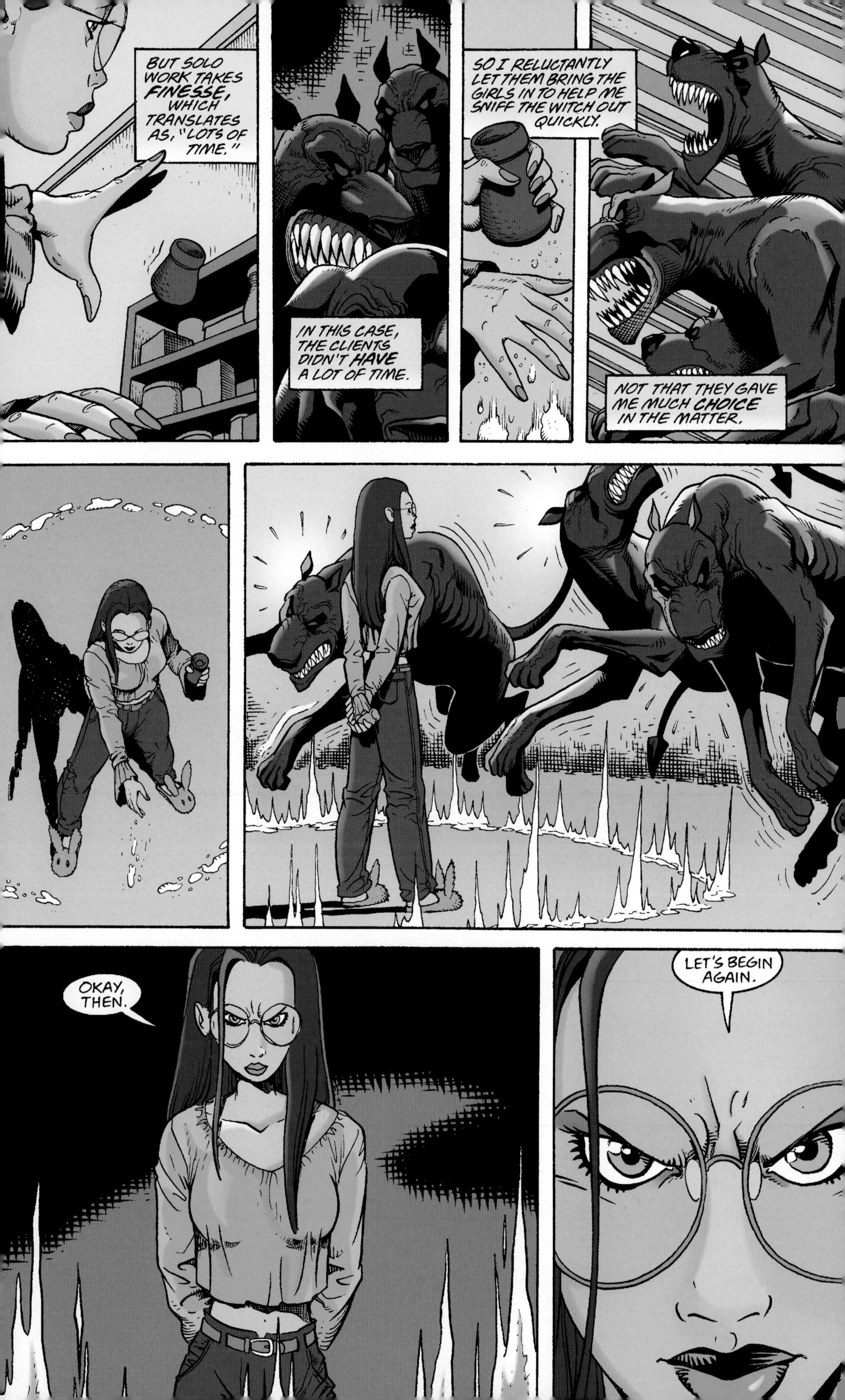
BUT SOLO WORK TAKES FINESSE, WHICH TRANSLATES AS, "LOTS OF TIME."
IN THIS CASE, THE CLIENTS DIDN'T HAVE A LOT OF TIME.
SO I RELUCTANTLY LET THEM BRING THE GIRLS IN TO HELP ME SNIFF THE WITCH OUT QUICKLY.
NOT THAT THEY GAVE ME MUCH CHOICE IN THE MATTER.
OKAY, THEN.
LET'S BEGIN AGAIN.

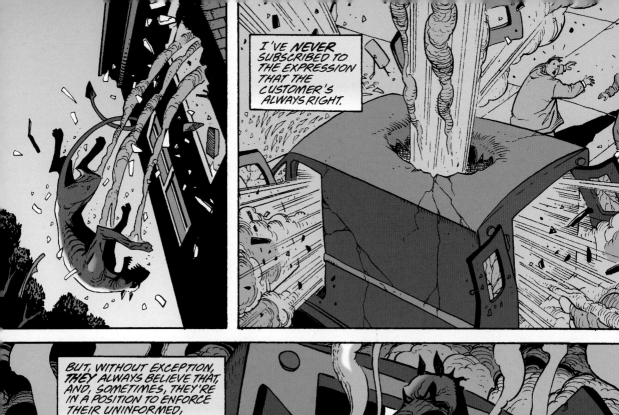

I'VE NEVER SUBSCRIBED TO THE EXPRESSION THAT THE CUSTOMER'S ALWAYS RIGHT.

BUT, WITHOUT EXCEPTION, *THEY* ALWAYS BELIEVE THAT, AND, SOMETIMES, THEY'RE IN A POSITION TO ENFORCE THEIR UNINFORMED, UNTESTED OPINIONS.

TOO BAD, BUT IT'S THE OCCASIONAL PRICE OF DOING BUSINESS.

I'M SUPPOSED TO BE THE PROFESSIONAL THOUGH.

I SHOULD HAVE FOUND A WAY TO CONVINCE THEM *MY* WAY WAS BETTER.

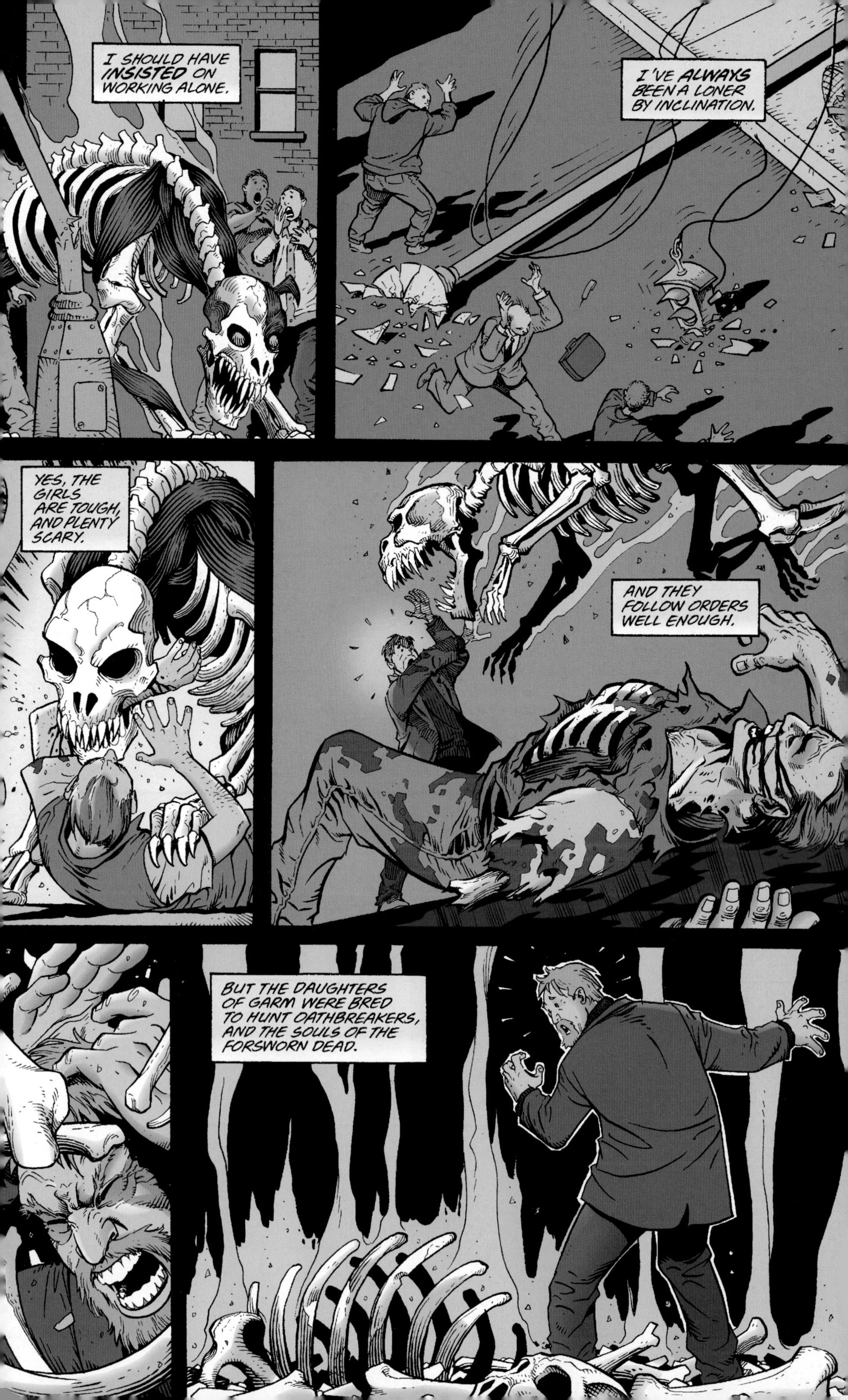
I SHOULD HAVE INSISTED ON WORKING ALONE.
I'VE ALWAYS BEEN A LONER BY INCLINATION.
YES, THE GIRLS ARE TOUGH, AND PLENTY SCARY.
AND THEY FOLLOW ORDERS WELL ENOUGH.
BUT THE DAUGHTERS OF GARM WERE BRED TO HUNT OATHBREAKERS, AND THE SOULS OF THE FORSWORN DEAD.

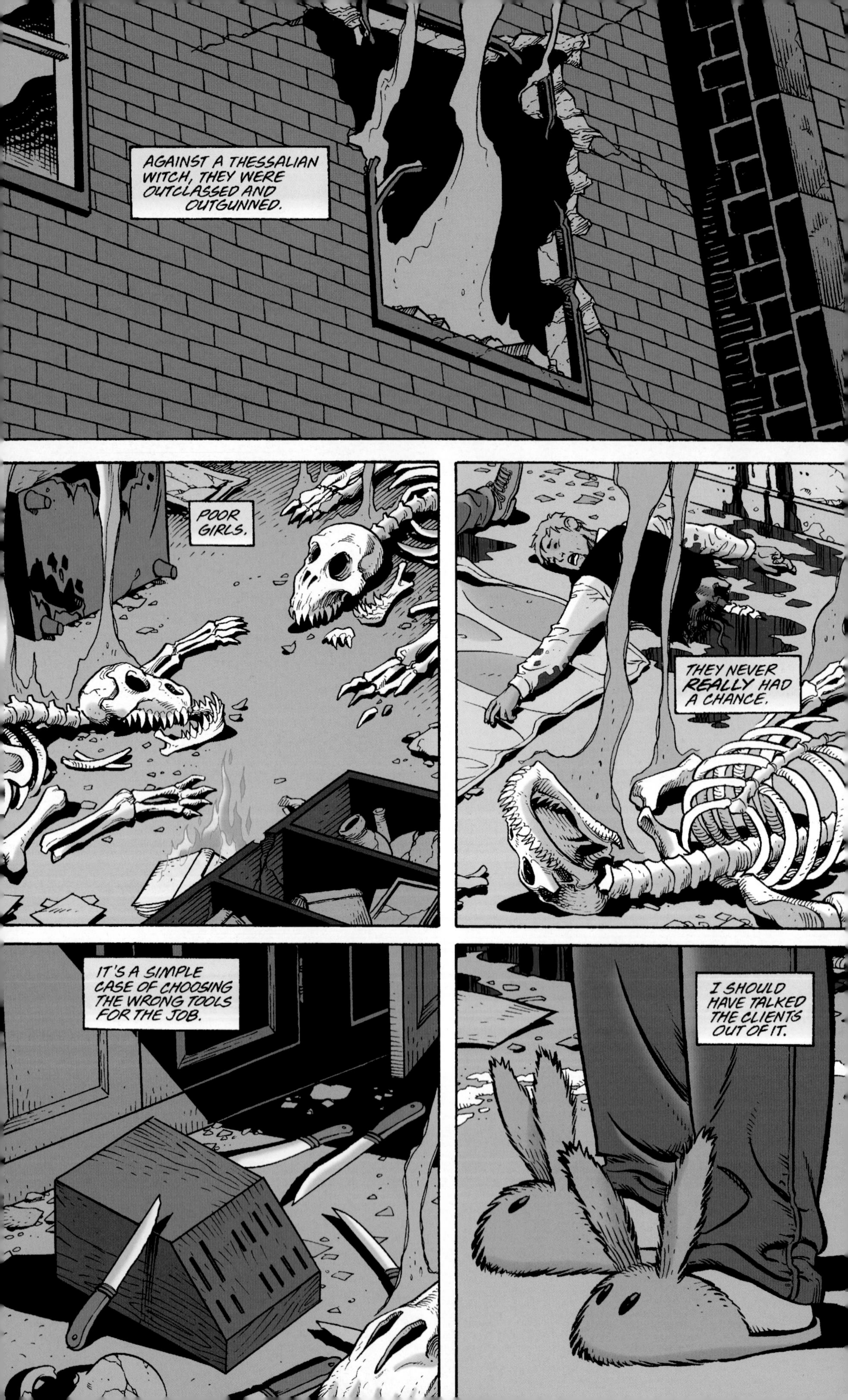
AGAINST A THESSALIAN WITCH, THEY WERE OUTCLASSED AND OUTGUNNED.
POOR GIRLS.
THEY NEVER REALLY HAD A CHANCE.
IT'S A SIMPLE CASE OF CHOOSING THE WRONG TOOLS FOR THE JOB.
I SHOULD HAVE TALKED THE CLIENTS OUT OF IT.

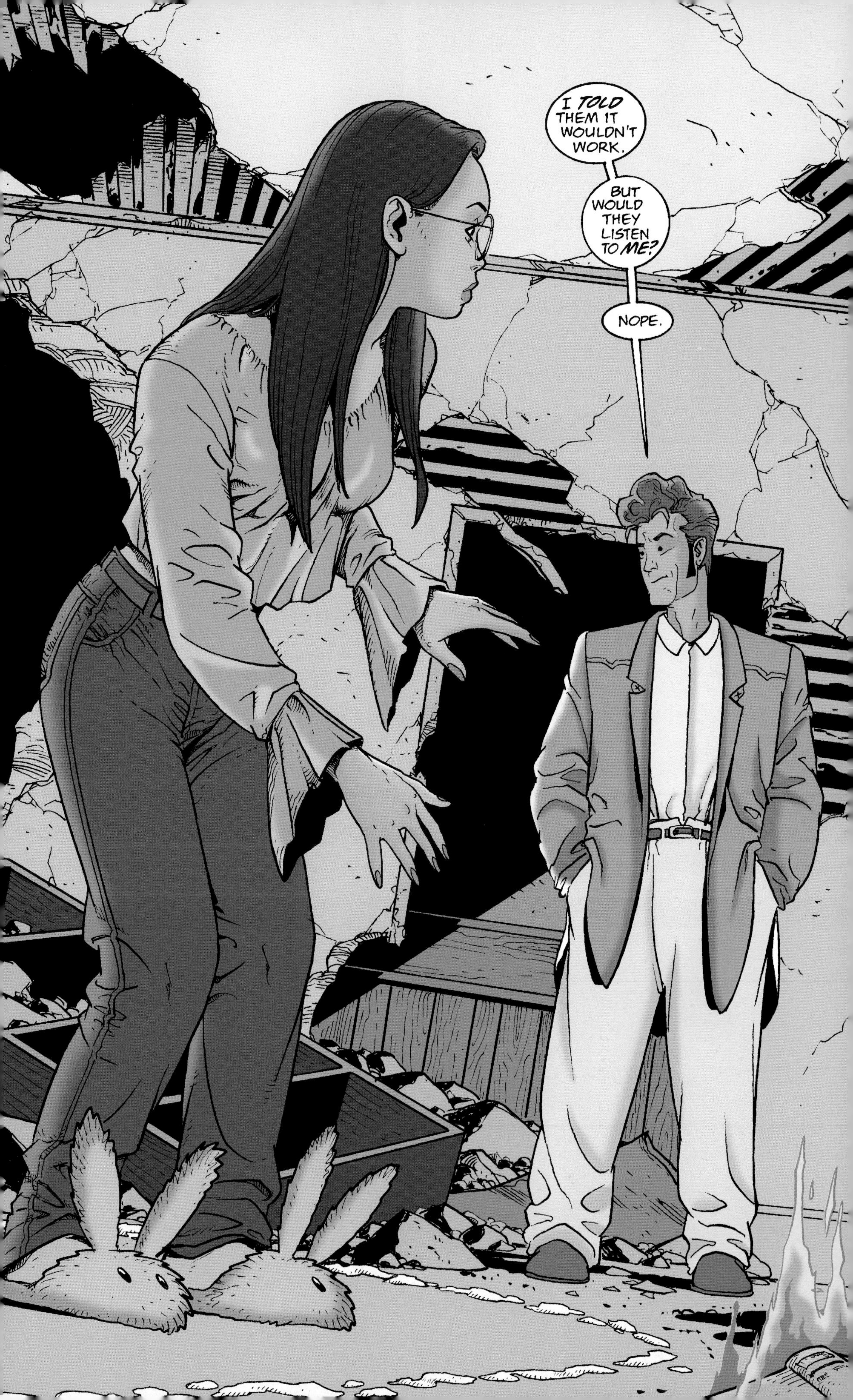
I *TOLD* THEM IT WOULDN'T WORK.
BUT WOULD THEY LISTEN TO *ME?*
NOPE.

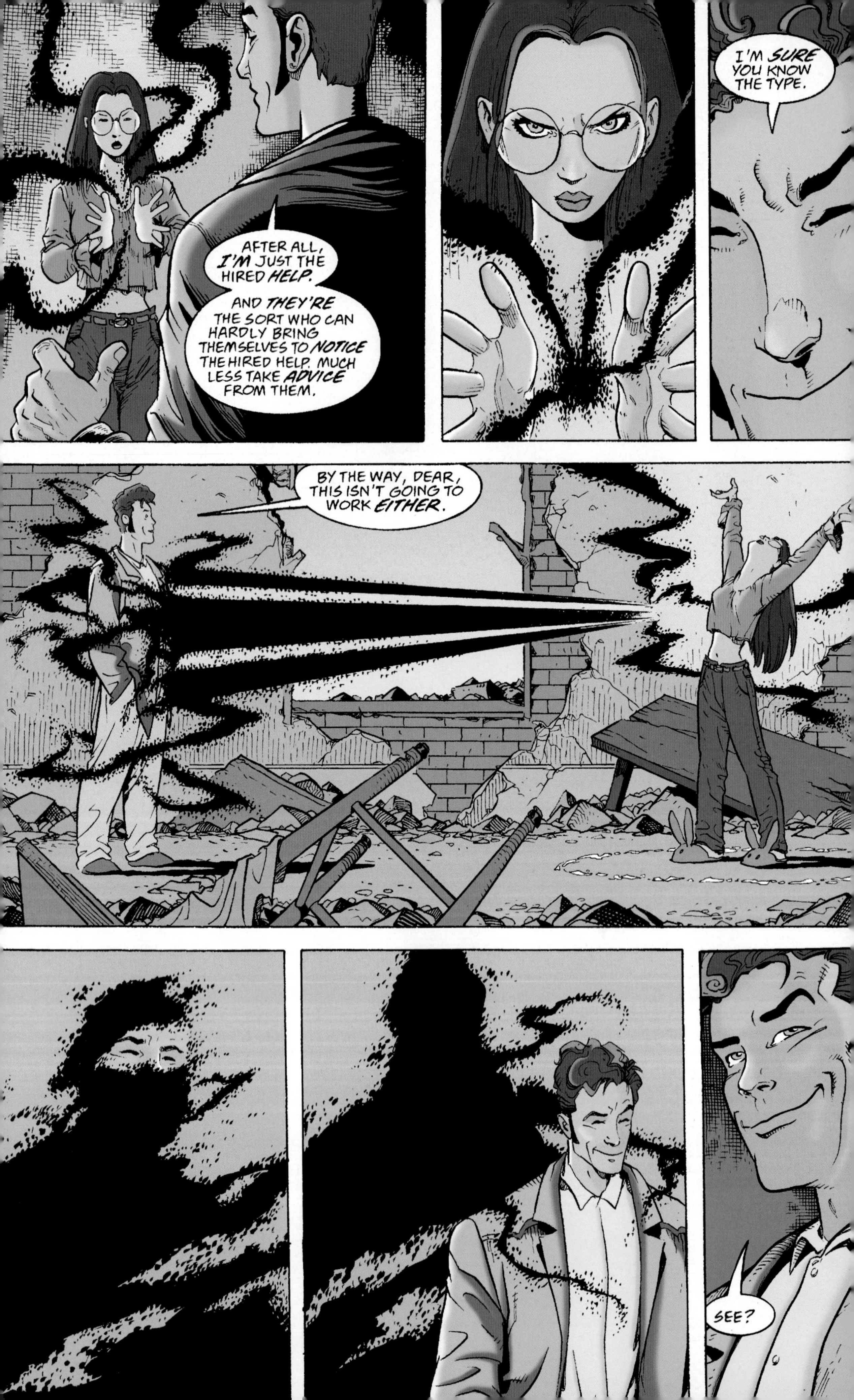
AFTER ALL, I'M JUST THE HIRED HELP.
AND THEY'RE THE SORT WHO CAN HARDLY BRING THEMSELVES TO NOTICE THE HIRED HELP, MUCH LESS TAKE ADVICE FROM THEM.
I'M SURE YOU KNOW THE TYPE.
BY THE WAY, DEAR, THIS ISN'T GOING TO WORK EITHER.
SEE?

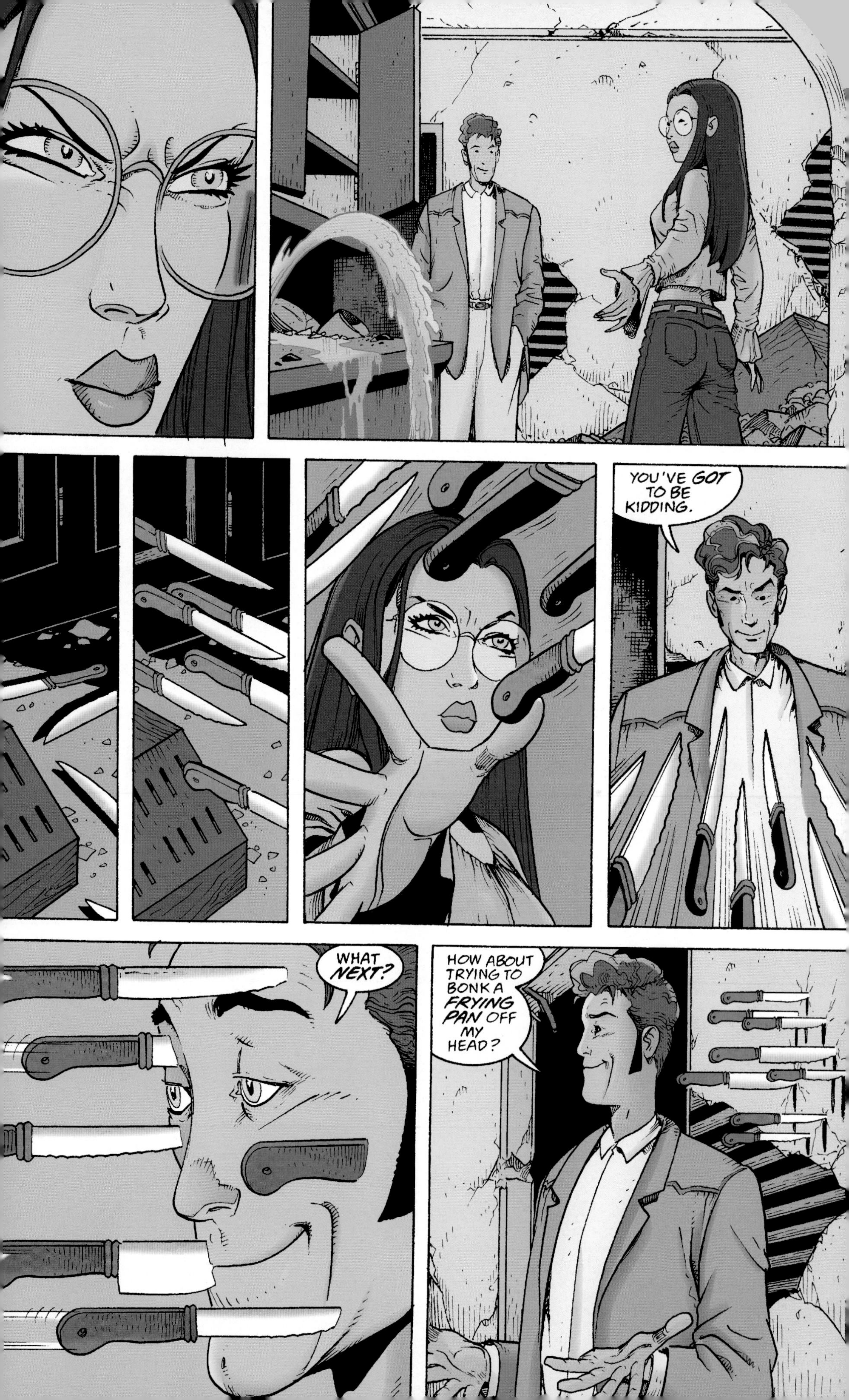
YOU'VE GOT TO BE KIDDING.
WHAT NEXT?
HOW ABOUT TRYING TO BONK A FRYING PAN OFF MY HEAD?

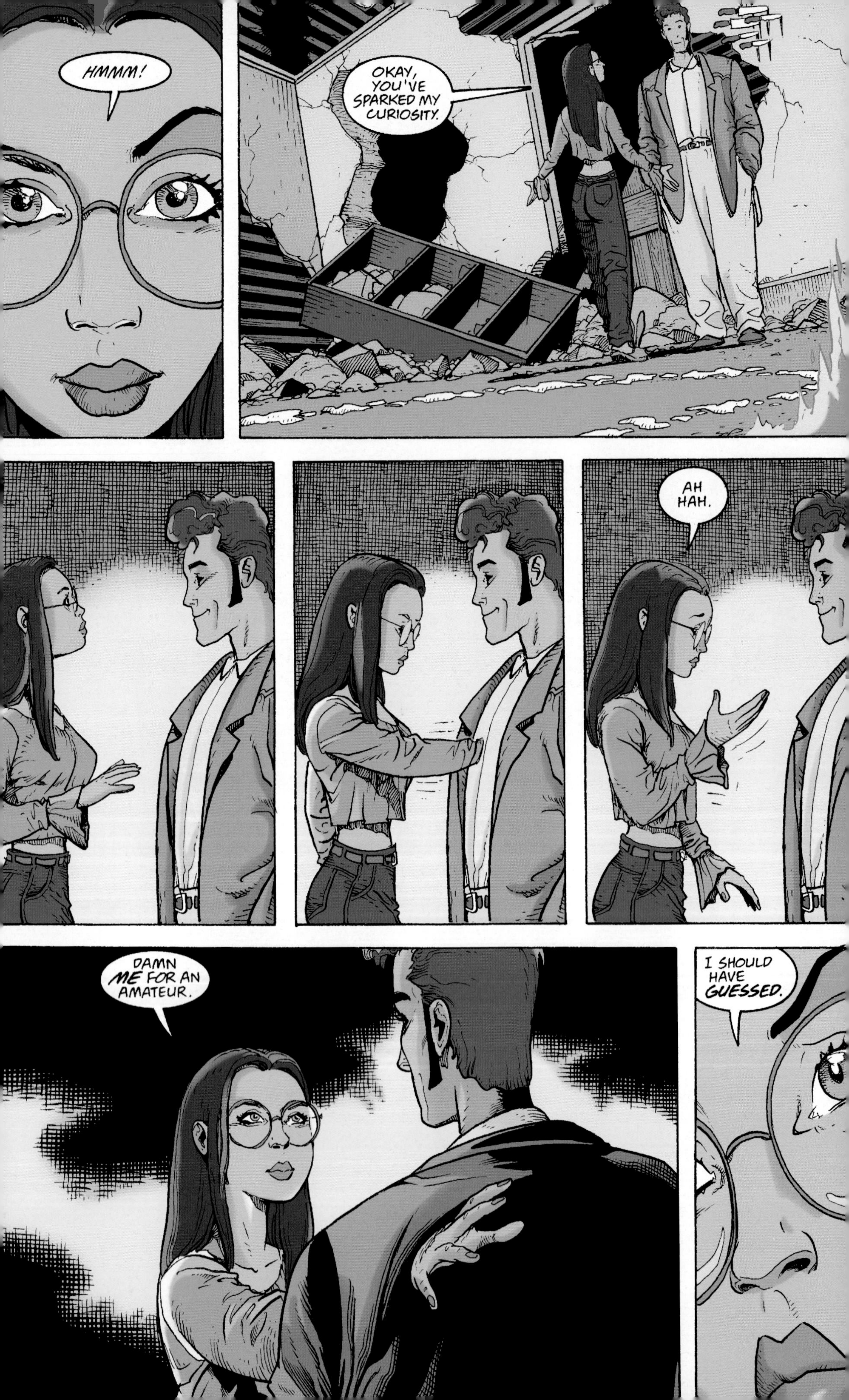
HMMM!
OKAY, YOU'VE SPARKED MY CURIOSITY.
AH HAH.
DAMN ME FOR AN AMATEUR.
I SHOULD HAVE GUESSED.

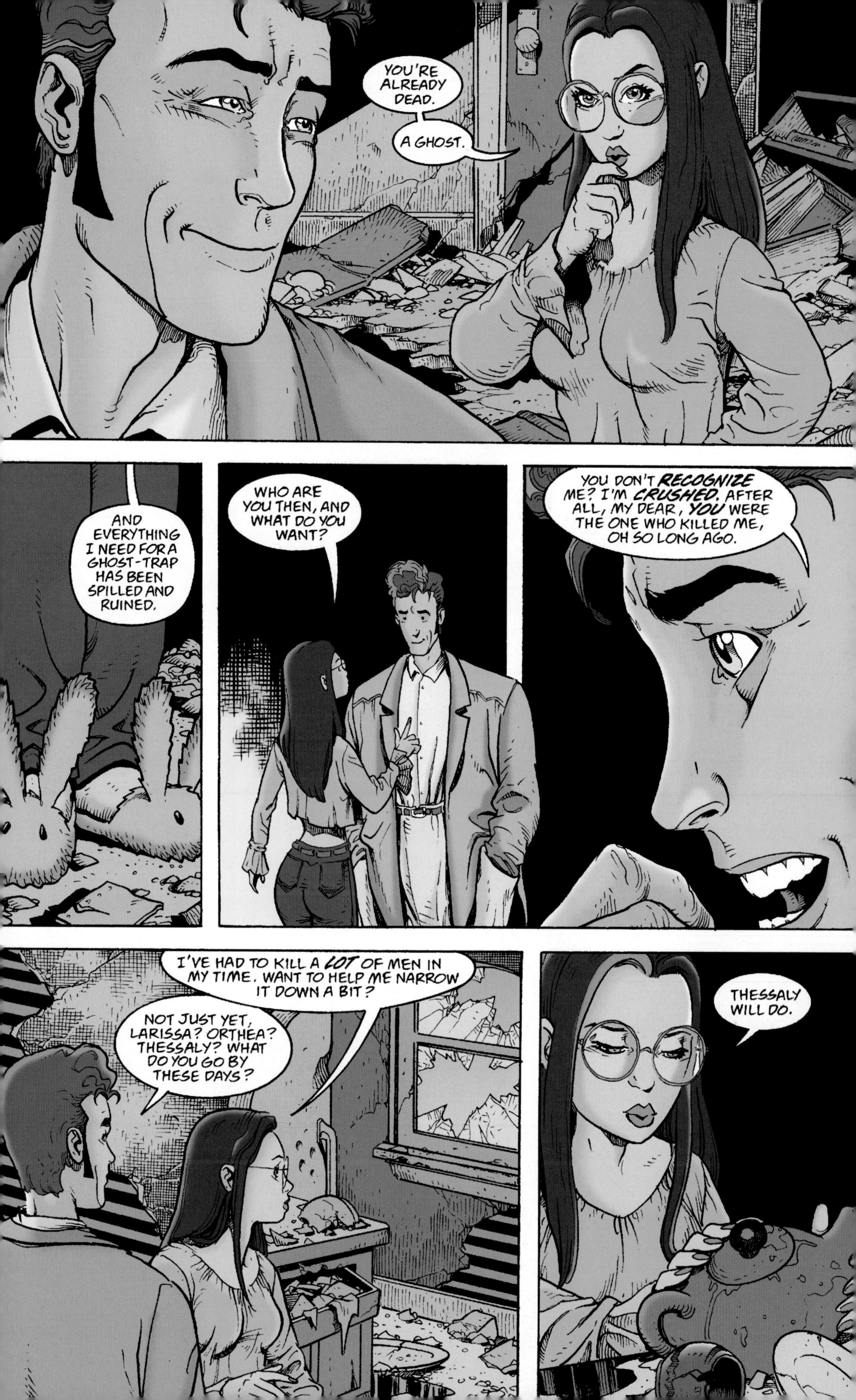
YOU'RE ALREADY DEAD.
A GHOST.
AND EVERYTHING I NEED FOR A GHOST-TRAP HAS BEEN SPILLED AND RUINED.
WHO ARE YOU THEN, AND WHAT DO YOU WANT?
YOU DON'T RECOGNIZE ME? I'M CRUSHED. AFTER ALL, MY DEAR, YOU WERE THE ONE WHO KILLED ME, OH SO LONG AGO.
I'VE HAD TO KILL A LOT OF MEN IN MY TIME. WANT TO HELP ME NARROW IT DOWN A BIT?
NOT JUST YET, LARISSA? ORTHEA? THESSALY? WHAT DO YOU GO BY THESE DAYS?
THESSALY WILL DO.

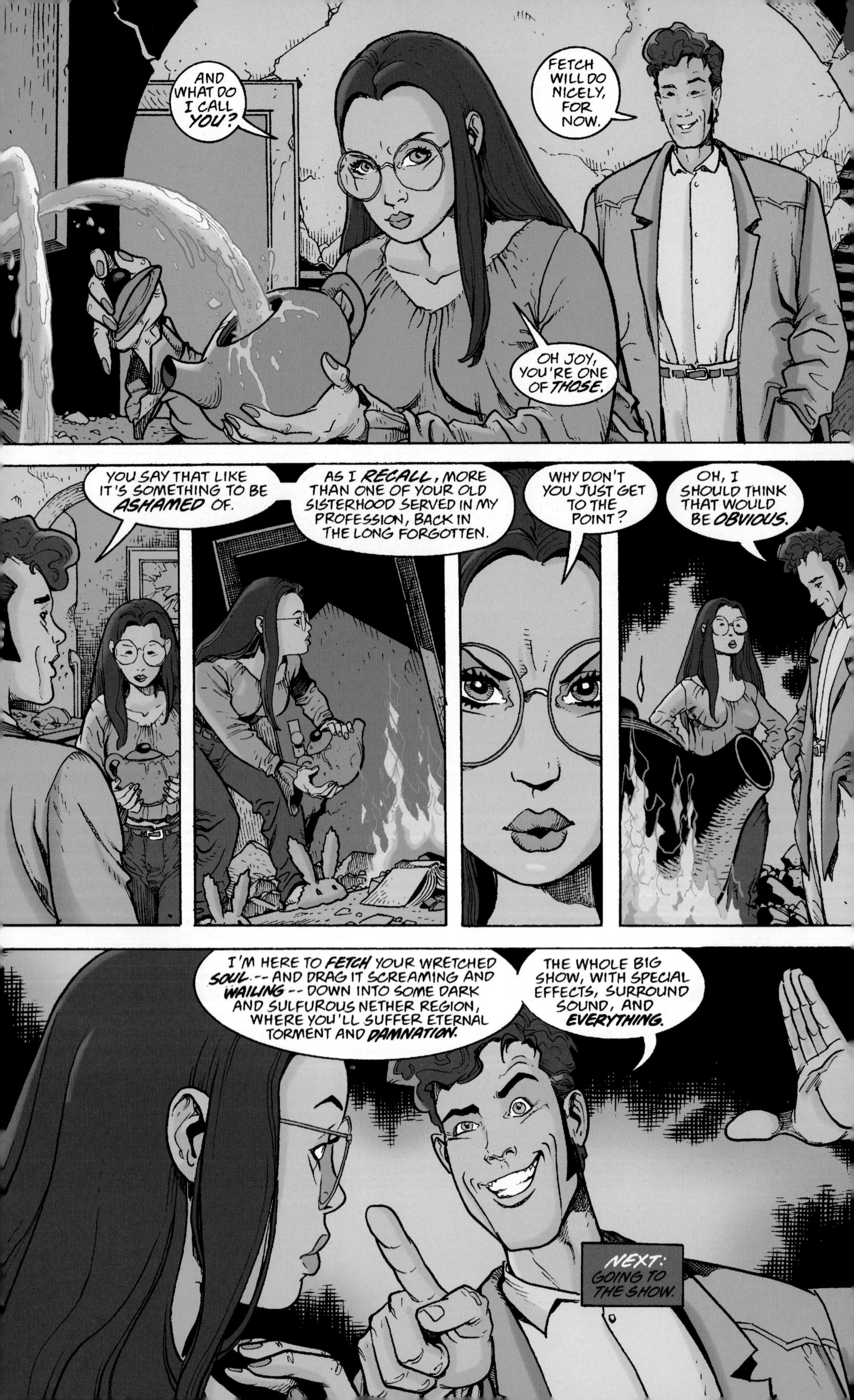
AND WHAT DO I CALL YOU?
FETCH WILL DO NICELY, FOR NOW.
OH JOY, YOU'RE ONE OF THOSE.
YOU SAY THAT LIKE IT'S SOMETHING TO BE ASHAMED OF.
AS I RECALL, MORE THAN ONE OF YOUR OLD SISTERHOOD SERVED IN MY PROFESSION, BACK IN THE LONG FORGOTTEN.
WHY DON'T YOU JUST GET TO THE POINT?
OH, I SHOULD THINK THAT WOULD BE OBVIOUS.
I'M HERE TO FETCH YOUR WRETCHED SOUL.-- AND DRAG IT SCREAMING AND WAILING -- DOWN INTO SOME DARK AND SULFUROUS NETHER REGION, WHERE YOU'LL SUFFER ETERNAL TORMENT AND DAMNATION.
THE WHOLE BIG SHOW, WITH SPECIAL EFFECTS, SURROUND SOUND, AND EVERYTHING.
NEXT: GOING TO THE SHOW.

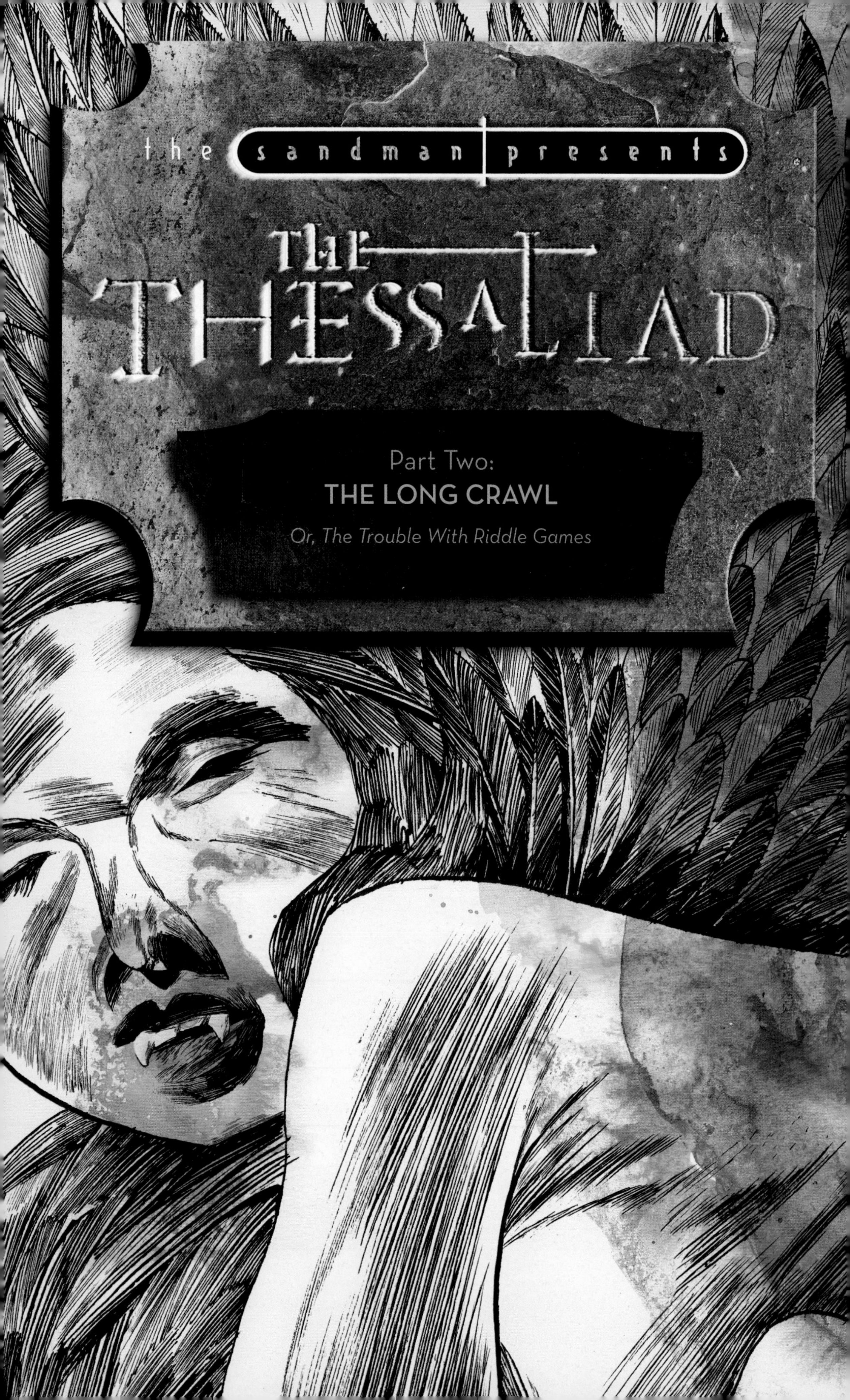
the sandman presents
THE THESSALIAD
Part Two:
THE LONG CRAWL
Or, The Trouble With Riddle Games

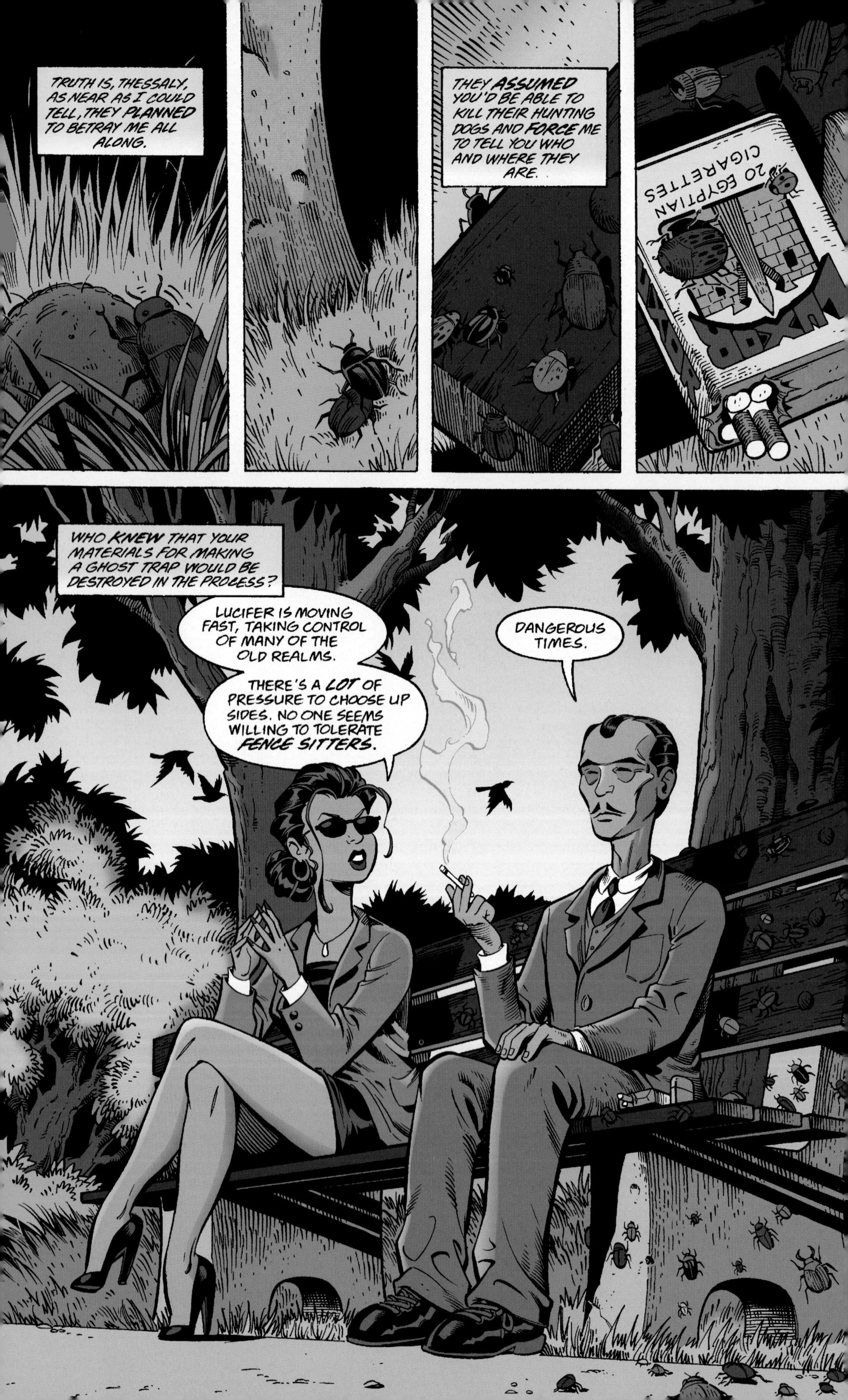
TRUTH IS, THESSALY, AS NEAR AS I COULD TELL, THEY PLANNED TO BETRAY ME ALL ALONG.
THEY ASSUMED YOU'D BE ABLE TO KILL THEIR HUNTING DOGS AND FORCE ME TO TELL YOU WHO AND WHERE THEY ARE.
20 EGYPTIAN CIGARETTES
WHO KNEW THAT YOUR MATERIALS FOR MAKING A GHOST TRAP WOULD BE DESTROYED IN THE PROCESS?
LUCIFER IS MOVING FAST, TAKING CONTROL OF MANY OF THE OLD REALMS.
THERE'S A LOT OF PRESSURE TO CHOOSE UP SIDES. NO ONE SEEMS WILLING TO TOLERATE FENCE SITTERS.
DANGEROUS TIMES.

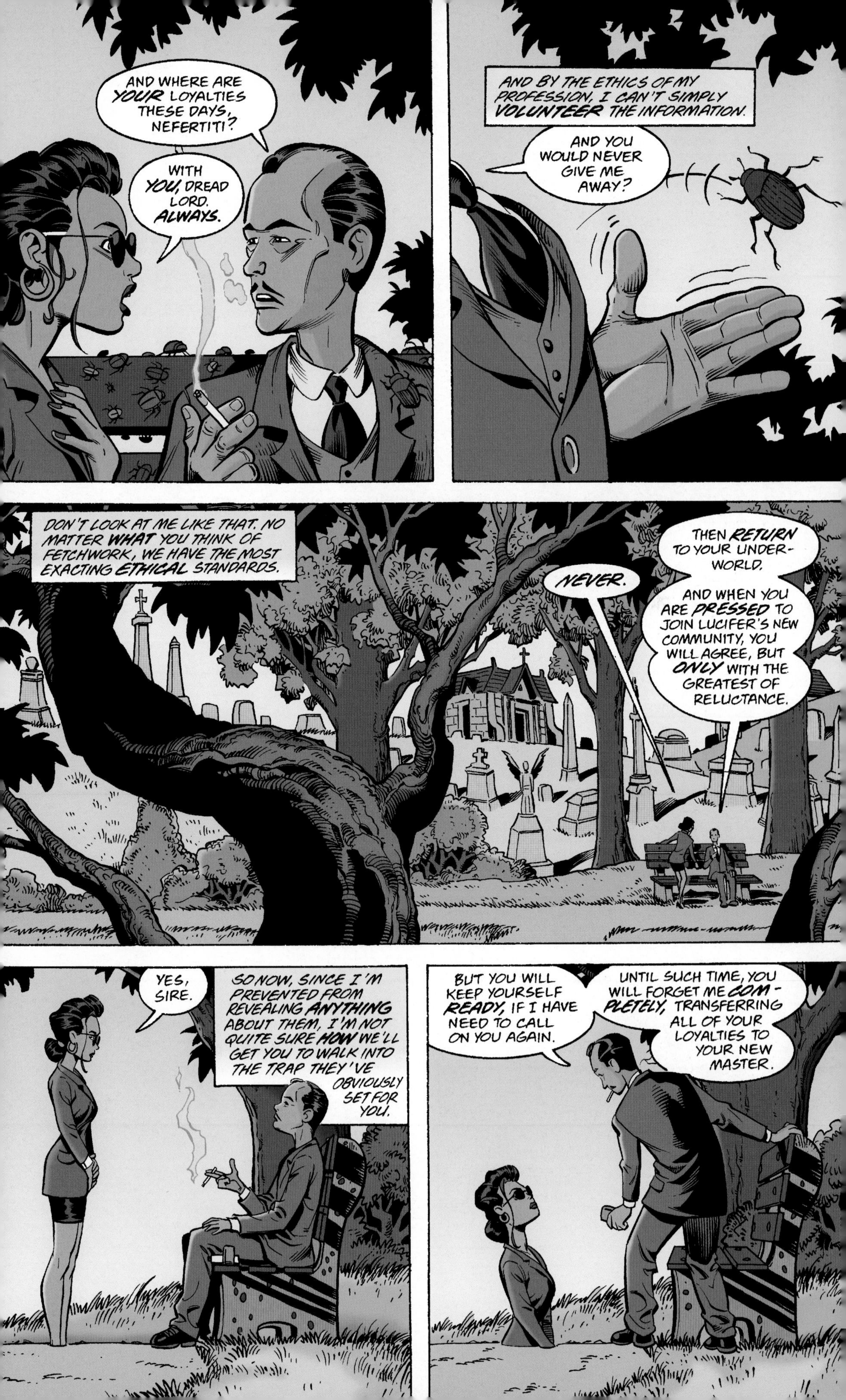
AND WHERE ARE YOUR LOYALTIES THESE DAYS, NEFERTITI?
WITH YOU, DREAD LORD. ALWAYS.
AND BY THE ETHICS OF MY PROFESSION, I CAN'T SIMPLY VOLUNTEER THE INFORMATION.
AND YOU WOULD NEVER GIVE ME AWAY?
DON'T LOOK AT ME LIKE THAT. NO MATTER WHAT YOU THINK OF FETCHWORK, WE HAVE THE MOST EXACTING ETHICAL STANDARDS.
NEVER.
THEN RETURN TO YOUR UNDER-WORLD.
AND WHEN YOU ARE PRESSED TO JOIN LUCIFER'S NEW COMMUNITY, YOU WILL AGREE, BUT ONLY WITH THE GREATEST OF RELUCTANCE.
YES, SIRE.
SO NOW, SINCE I'M PREVENTED FROM REVEALING ANYTHING ABOUT THEM, I'M NOT QUITE SURE HOW WE'LL GET YOU TO WALK INTO THE TRAP THEY'VE OBVIOUSLY SET FOR YOU.
BUT YOU WILL KEEP YOURSELF READY, IF I HAVE NEED TO CALL ON YOU AGAIN.
UNTIL SUCH TIME, YOU WILL FORGET ME COM-PLETELY, TRANSFERRING ALL OF YOUR LOYALTIES TO YOUR NEW MASTER.

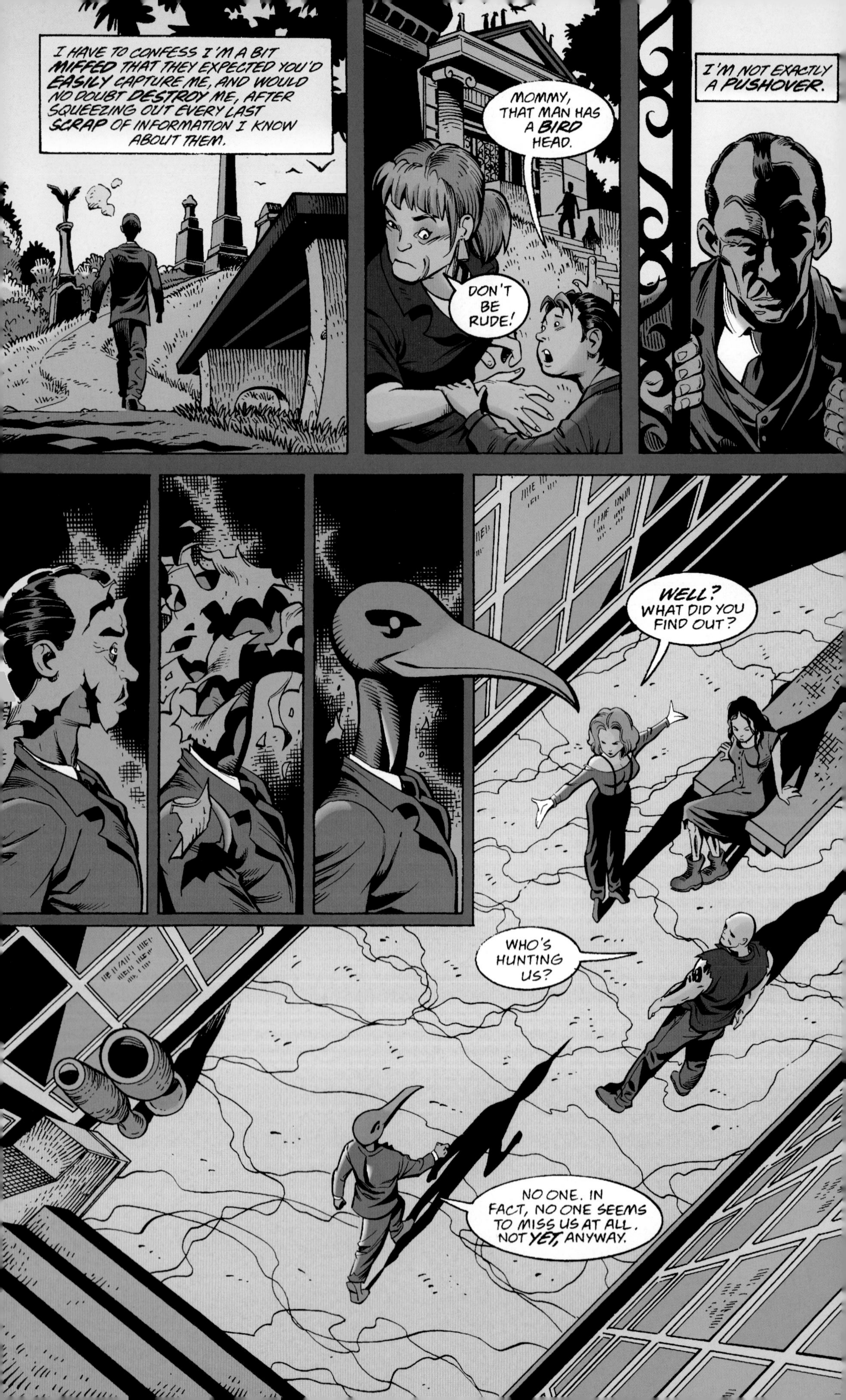
I HAVE TO CONFESS I'M A BIT MIFFED THAT THEY EXPECTED YOU'D EASILY CAPTURE ME, AND WOULD NO DOUBT DESTROY ME, AFTER SQUEEZING OUT EVERY LAST SCRAP OF INFORMATION I KNOW ABOUT THEM.
MOMMY, THAT MAN HAS A BIRD HEAD.
DON'T BE RUDE!
I'M NOT EXACTLY A PUSHOVER.
WELL? WHAT DID YOU FIND OUT?
WHO'S HUNTING US?
NO ONE. IN FACT, NO ONE SEEMS TO MISS US AT ALL. NOT YET, ANYWAY.

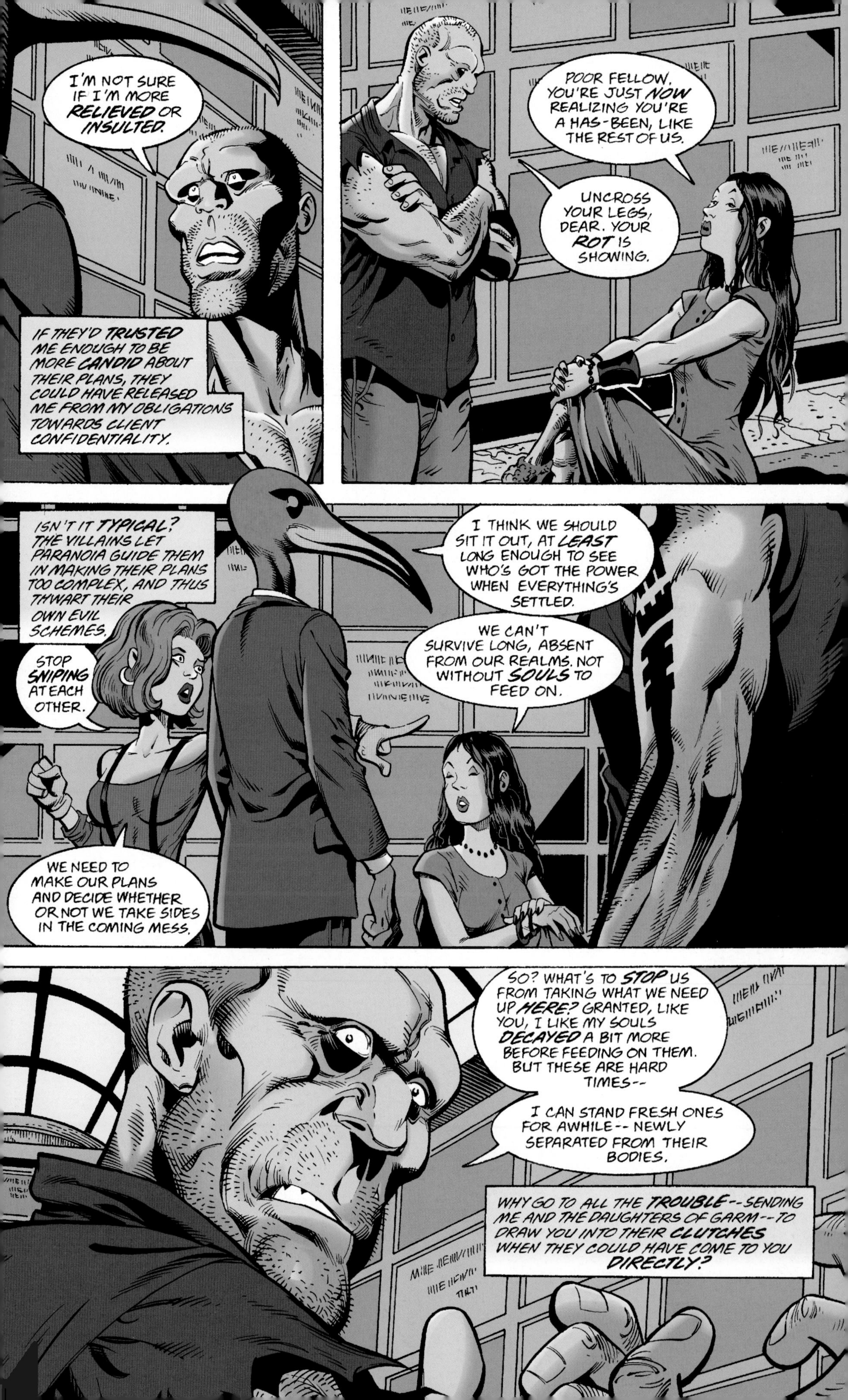
I'M NOT SURE IF I'M MORE RELIEVED OR INSULTED.
IF THEY'D TRUSTED ME ENOUGH TO BE MORE CANDID ABOUT THEIR PLANS, THEY COULD HAVE RELEASED ME FROM MY OBLIGATIONS TOWARDS CLIENT CONFIDENTIALITY.
POOR FELLOW, YOU'RE JUST NOW REALIZING YOU'RE A HAS-BEEN, LIKE THE REST OF US.
UNCROSS YOUR LEGS, DEAR. YOUR ROT IS SHOWING.
ISN'T IT TYPICAL? THE VILLAINS LET PARANOIA GUIDE THEM IN MAKING THEIR PLANS TOO COMPLEX, AND THUS THWART THEIR OWN EVIL SCHEMES.
STOP SNIPING AT EACH OTHER.
WE NEED TO MAKE OUR PLANS AND DECIDE WHETHER OR NOT WE TAKE SIDES IN THE COMING MESS.
I THINK WE SHOULD SIT IT OUT, AT LEAST LONG ENOUGH TO SEE WHO'S GOT THE POWER WHEN EVERYTHING'S SETTLED.
WE CAN'T SURVIVE LONG, ABSENT FROM OUR REALMS. NOT WITHOUT SOULS TO FEED ON.
SO? WHAT'S TO STOP US FROM TAKING WHAT WE NEED UP HERE? GRANTED, LIKE YOU, I LIKE MY SOULS DECAYED A BIT MORE BEFORE FEEDING ON THEM. BUT THESE ARE HARD TIMES--
I CAN STAND FRESH ONES FOR AWHILE-- NEWLY SEPARATED FROM THEIR BODIES.
WHY GO TO ALL THE TROUBLE-- SENDING ME AND THE DAUGHTERS OF GARM-- TO DRAW YOU INTO THEIR CLUTCHES WHEN THEY COULD HAVE COME TO YOU DIRECTLY?

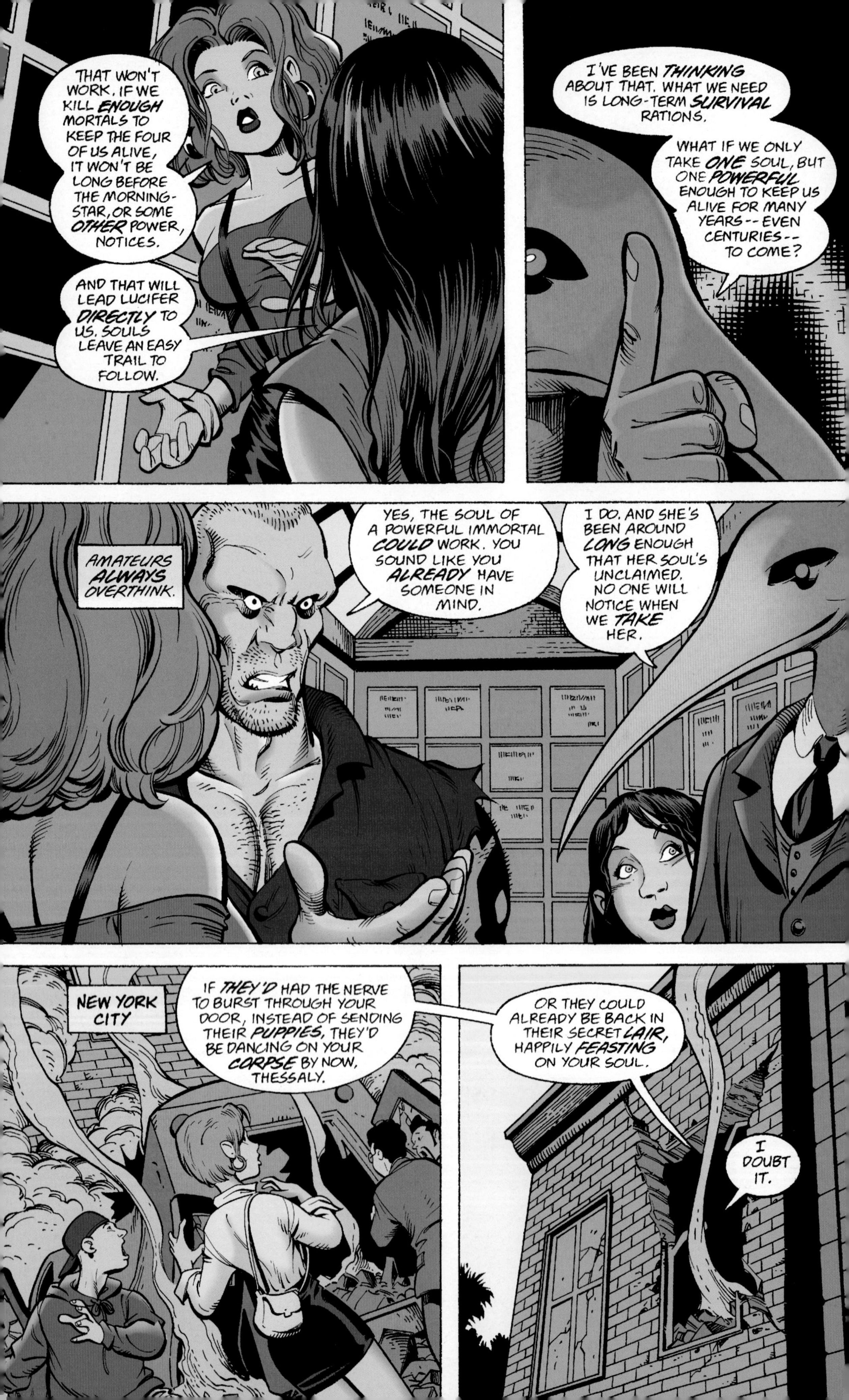
THAT WON'T WORK. IF WE KILL ENOUGH MORTALS TO KEEP THE FOUR OF US ALIVE, IT WON'T BE LONG BEFORE THE MORNING-STAR, OR SOME OTHER POWER, NOTICES.
AND THAT WILL LEAD LUCIFER DIRECTLY TO US. SOULS LEAVE AN EASY TRAIL TO FOLLOW.
I'VE BEEN THINKING ABOUT THAT. WHAT WE NEED IS LONG-TERM SURVIVAL RATIONS.
WHAT IF WE ONLY TAKE ONE SOUL, BUT ONE POWERFUL ENOUGH TO KEEP US ALIVE FOR MANY YEARS -- EVEN CENTURIES -- TO COME?
AMATEURS ALWAYS OVERTHINK.
YES, THE SOUL OF A POWERFUL IMMORTAL COULD WORK. YOU SOUND LIKE YOU ALREADY HAVE SOMEONE IN MIND.
I DO. AND SHE'S BEEN AROUND LONG ENOUGH THAT HER SOUL'S UNCLAIMED. NO ONE WILL NOTICE WHEN WE TAKE HER.
NEW YORK CITY
IF THEY'D HAD THE NERVE TO BURST THROUGH YOUR DOOR, INSTEAD OF SENDING THEIR PUPPIES, THEY'D BE DANCING ON YOUR CORPSE BY NOW, THESSALY.
OR THEY COULD ALREADY BE BACK IN THEIR SECRET LAIR, HAPPILY FEASTING ON YOUR SOUL.
I DOUBT IT.

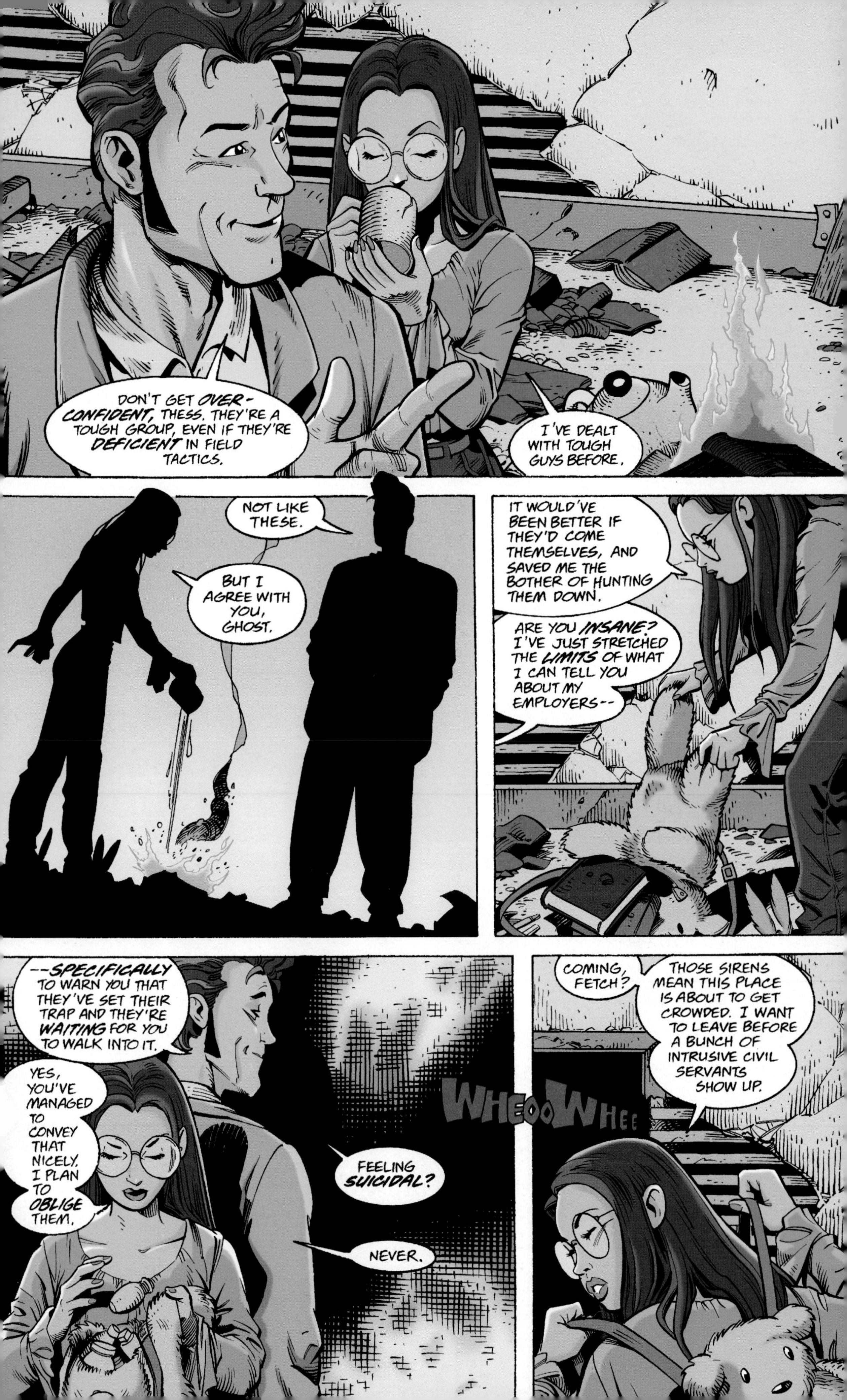
DON'T GET OVER-CONFIDENT, THESS. THEY'RE A TOUGH GROUP, EVEN IF THEY'RE DEFICIENT IN FIELD TACTICS.
I'VE DEALT WITH TOUGH GUYS BEFORE.
NOT LIKE THESE.
BUT I AGREE WITH YOU, GHOST.
IT WOULD'VE BEEN BETTER IF THEY'D COME THEMSELVES, AND SAVED ME THE BOTHER OF HUNTING THEM DOWN.
ARE YOU INSANE? I'VE JUST STRETCHED THE LIMITS OF WHAT I CAN TELL YOU ABOUT MY EMPLOYERS--
--SPECIFICALLY TO WARN YOU THAT THEY'VE SET THEIR TRAP AND THEY'RE WAITING FOR YOU TO WALK INTO IT.
YES, YOU'VE MANAGED TO CONVEY THAT NICELY. I PLAN TO OBLIGE THEM.
FEELING SUICIDAL?
NEVER.
WHEOOWHEE
COMING, FETCH?
THOSE SIRENS MEAN THIS PLACE IS ABOUT TO GET CROWDED. I WANT TO LEAVE BEFORE A BUNCH OF INTRUSIVE CIVIL SERVANTS SHOW UP.

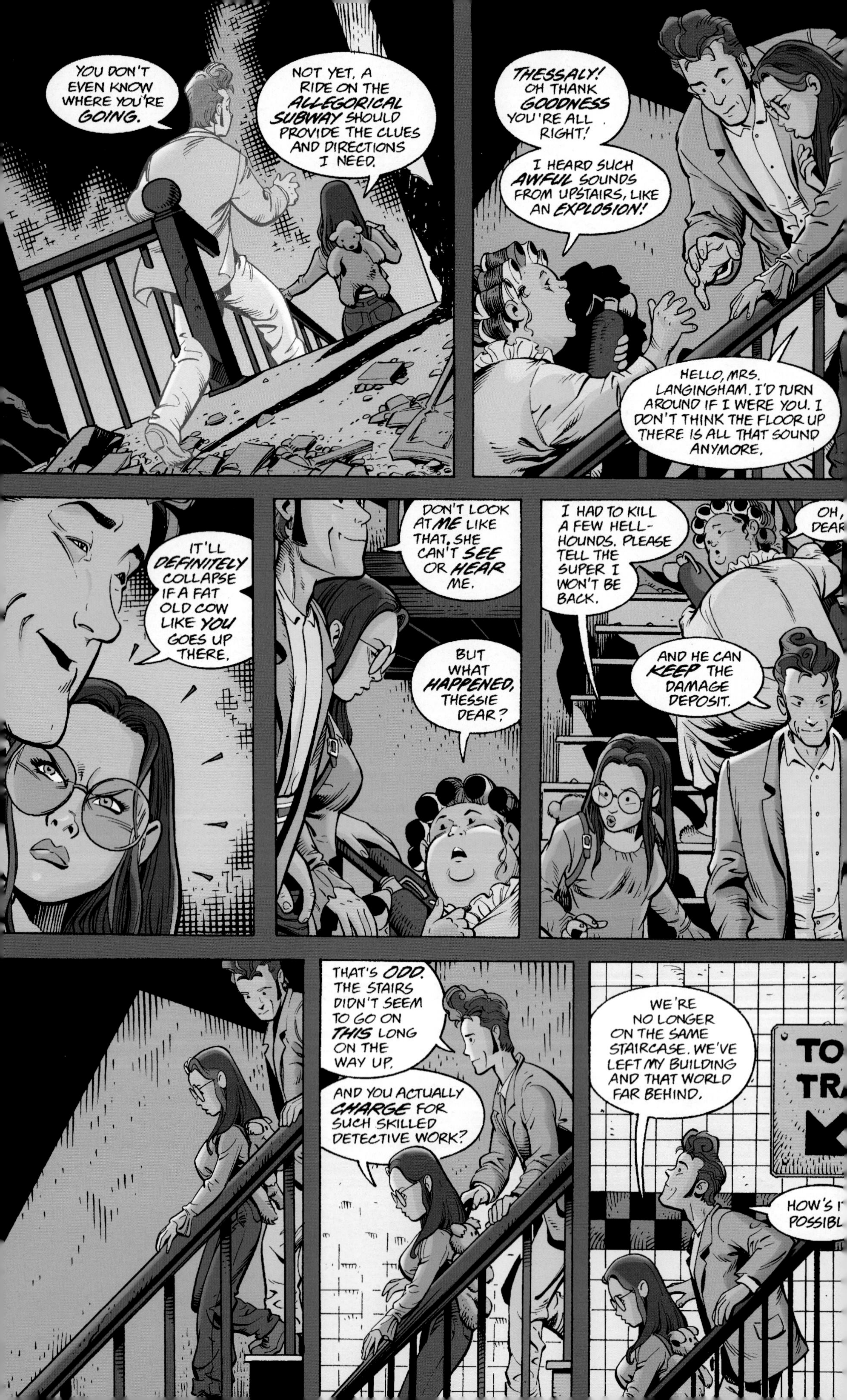
YOU DON'T EVEN KNOW WHERE YOU'RE GOING.
NOT YET. A RIDE ON THE ALLEGORICAL SUBWAY SHOULD PROVIDE THE CLUES AND DIRECTIONS I NEED.
THESSALY! OH THANK GOODNESS YOU'RE ALL RIGHT!
I HEARD SUCH AWFUL SOUNDS FROM UPSTAIRS, LIKE AN EXPLOSION!
HELLO, MRS. LANGINGHAM. I'D TURN AROUND IF I WERE YOU. I DON'T THINK THE FLOOR UP THERE IS ALL THAT SOUND ANYMORE.
IT'LL DEFINITELY COLLAPSE IF A FAT OLD COW LIKE YOU GOES UP THERE.
DON'T LOOK AT ME LIKE THAT. SHE CAN'T SEE OR HEAR ME.
BUT WHAT HAPPENED, THESSIE DEAR?
I HAD TO KILL A FEW HELL-HOUNDS. PLEASE TELL THE SUPER I WON'T BE BACK.
OH, DEAR
AND HE CAN KEEP THE DAMAGE DEPOSIT.
THAT'S ODD. THE STAIRS DIDN'T SEEM TO GO ON THIS LONG ON THE WAY UP.
AND YOU ACTUALLY CHARGE FOR SUCH SKILLED DETECTIVE WORK?
WE'RE NO LONGER ON THE SAME STAIRCASE. WE'VE LEFT MY BUILDING AND THAT WORLD FAR BEHIND.
HOW'S I POSSIBL

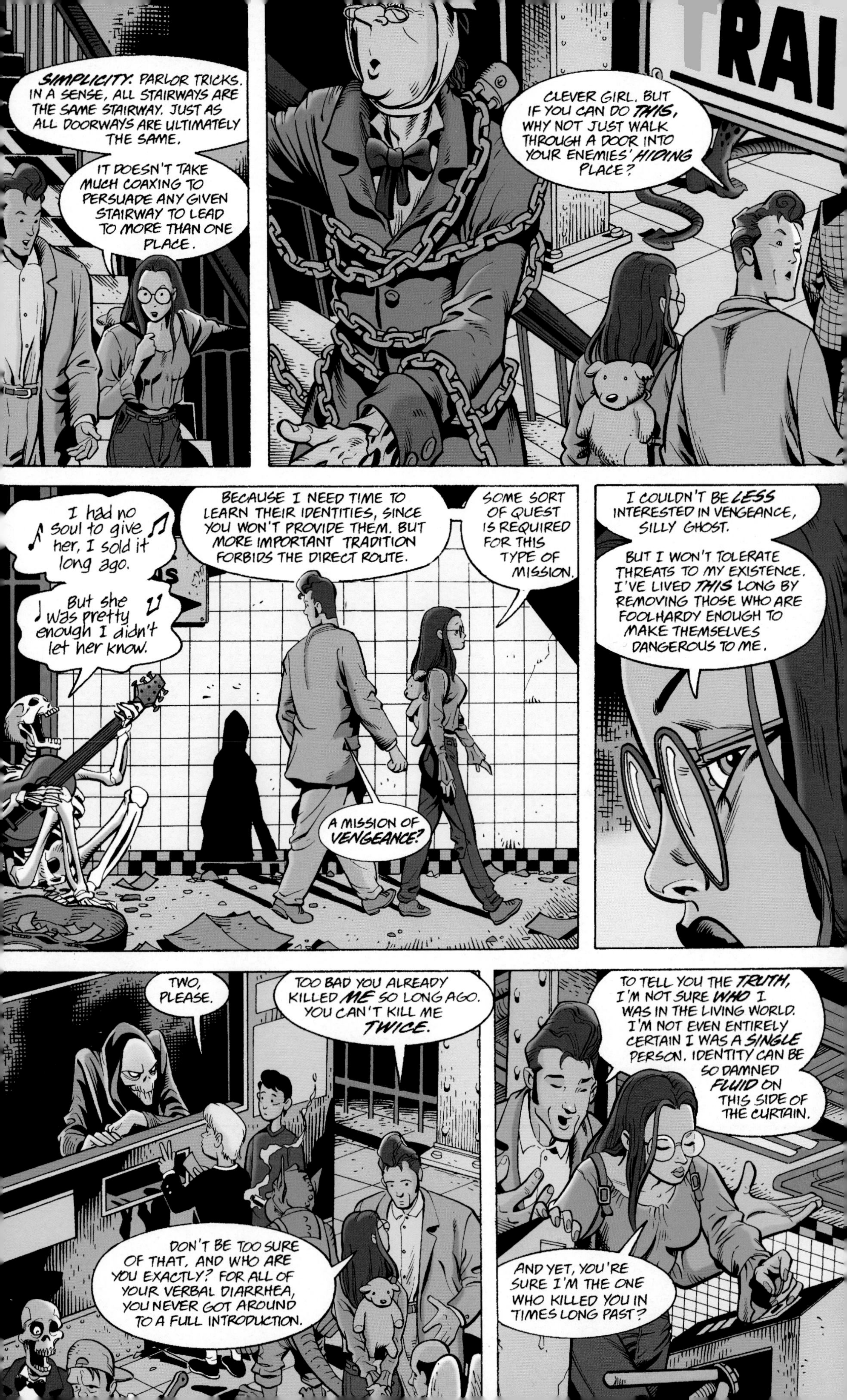

SIMPLICITY. PARLOR TRICKS. IN A SENSE, ALL STAIRWAYS ARE THE SAME STAIRWAY. JUST AS ALL DOORWAYS ARE ULTIMATELY THE SAME.
IT DOESN'T TAKE MUCH COAXING TO PERSUADE ANY GIVEN STAIRWAY TO LEAD TO MORE THAN ONE PLACE.
TRAI
CLEVER GIRL. BUT IF YOU CAN DO THIS, WHY NOT JUST WALK THROUGH A DOOR INTO YOUR ENEMIES' HIDING PLACE?
I had no soul to give her, I sold it long ago.
But she was pretty enough I didn't let her know.
BECAUSE I NEED TIME TO LEARN THEIR IDENTITIES, SINCE YOU WON'T PROVIDE THEM. BUT MORE IMPORTANT TRADITION FORBIDS THE DIRECT ROUTE.
SOME SORT OF QUEST IS REQUIRED FOR THIS TYPE OF MISSION.
A MISSION OF VENGEANCE?
I COULDN'T BE LESS INTERESTED IN VENGEANCE, SILLY GHOST.
BUT I WON'T TOLERATE THREATS TO MY EXISTENCE. I'VE LIVED THIS LONG BY REMOVING THOSE WHO ARE FOOLHARDY ENOUGH TO MAKE THEMSELVES DANGEROUS TO ME.
TWO, PLEASE.
TOO BAD YOU ALREADY KILLED ME SO LONG AGO. YOU CAN'T KILL ME TWICE.
DON'T BE TOO SURE OF THAT. AND WHO ARE YOU EXACTLY? FOR ALL OF YOUR VERBAL DIARRHEA, YOU NEVER GOT AROUND TO A FULL INTRODUCTION.
TO TELL YOU THE TRUTH, I'M NOT SURE WHO I WAS IN THE LIVING WORLD. I'M NOT EVEN ENTIRELY CERTAIN I WAS A SINGLE PERSON. IDENTITY CAN BE SO DAMNED FLUID ON THIS SIDE OF THE CURTAIN.
AND YET, YOU'RE SURE I'M THE ONE WHO KILLED YOU IN TIMES LONG PAST?

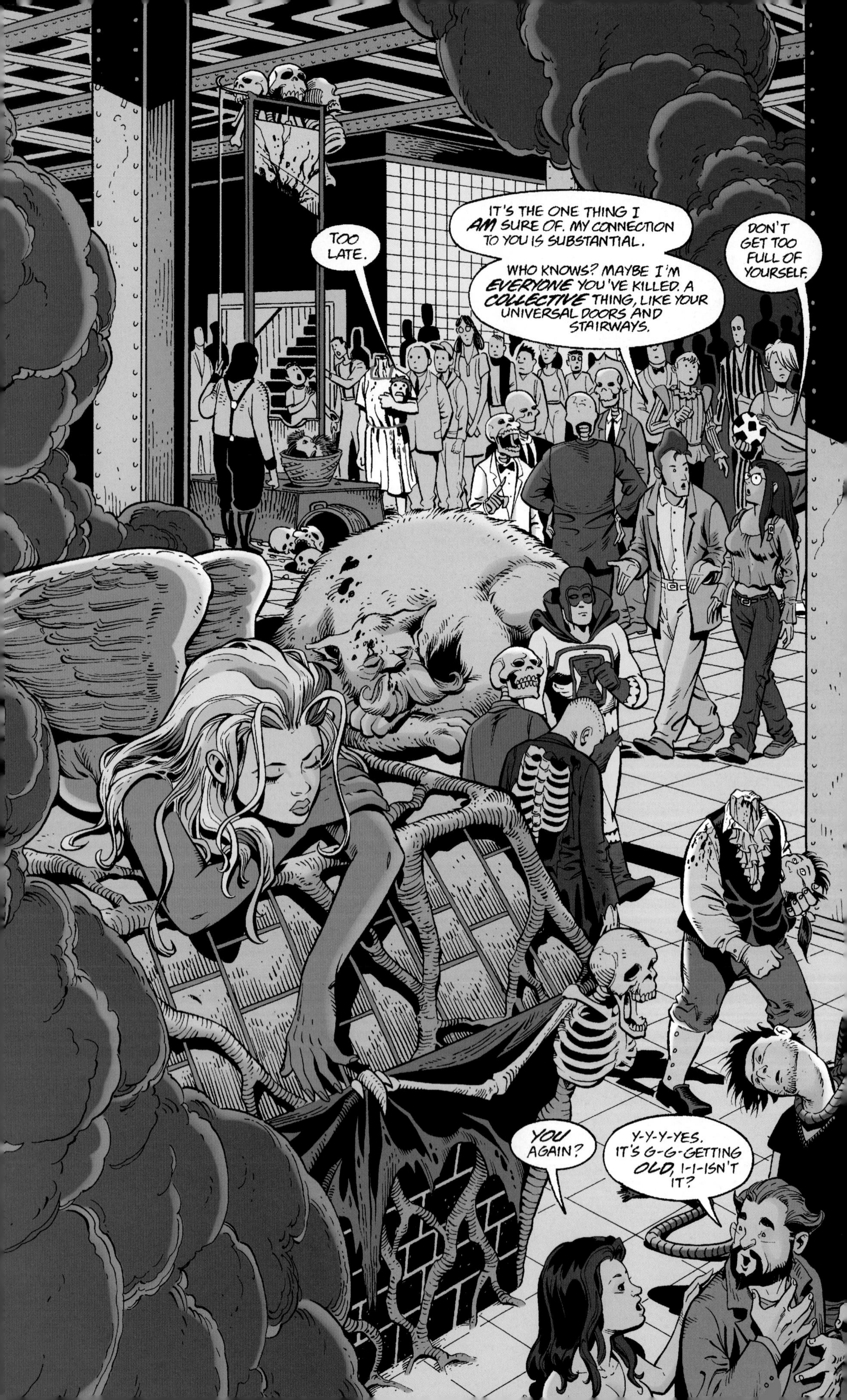
TOO LATE.
IT'S THE ONE THING I AM SURE OF. MY CONNECTION TO YOU IS SUBSTANTIAL.
WHO KNOWS? MAYBE I'M EVERYONE YOU'VE KILLED. A COLLECTIVE THING, LIKE YOUR UNIVERSAL DOORS AND STAIRWAYS.
DON'T GET TOO FULL OF YOURSELF.
YOU AGAIN?
Y-Y-Y-YES. IT'S G-G-GETTING OLD, I-I-ISN'T IT?

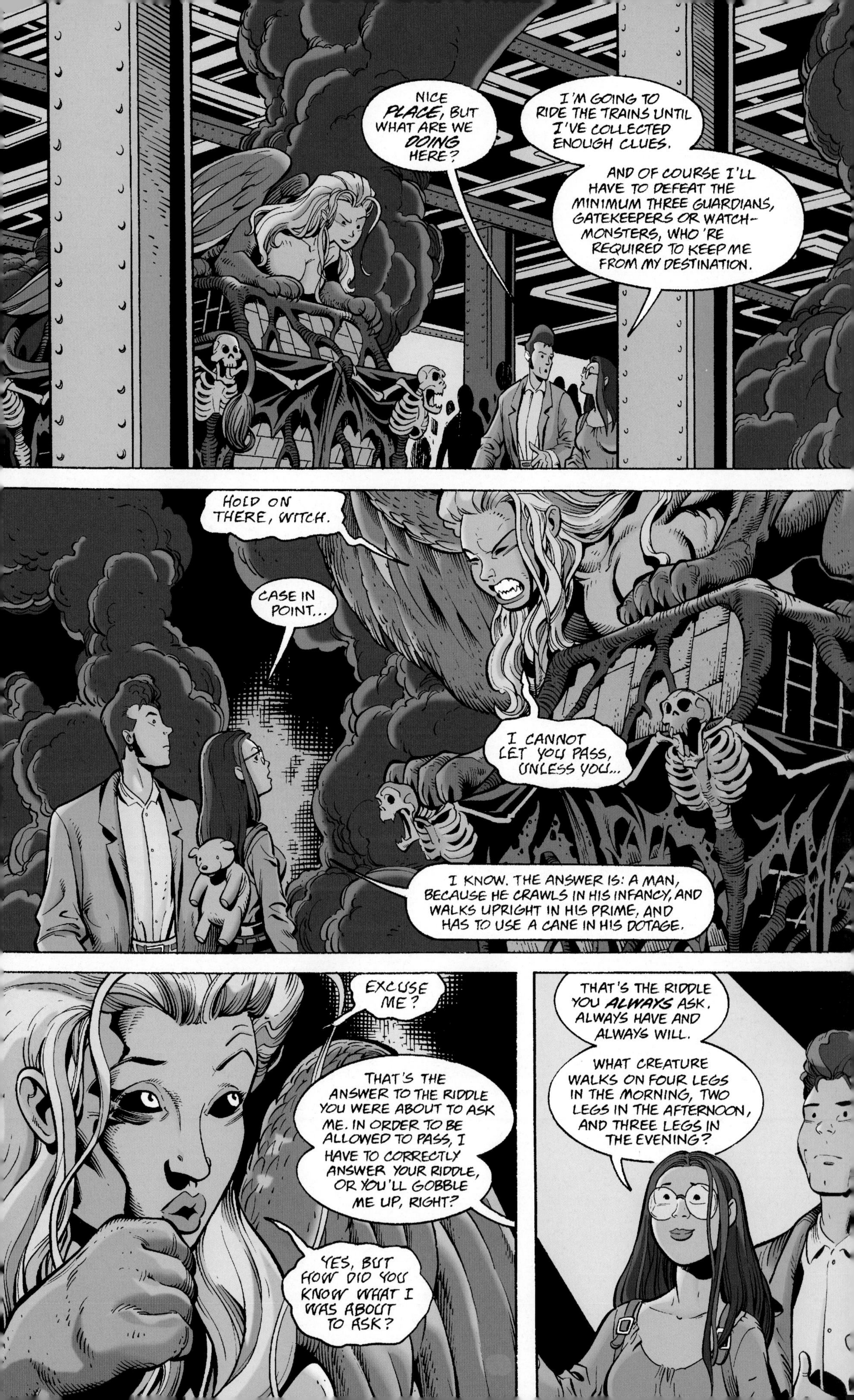
NICE PLACE, BUT WHAT ARE WE DOING HERE?
I'M GOING TO RIDE THE TRAINS UNTIL I'VE COLLECTED ENOUGH CLUES.
AND OF COURSE I'LL HAVE TO DEFEAT THE MINIMUM THREE GUARDIANS, GATEKEEPERS OR WATCH-MONSTERS, WHO'RE REQUIRED TO KEEP ME FROM MY DESTINATION.
HOLD ON THERE, WITCH.
CASE IN POINT...
I CANNOT LET YOU PASS, UNLESS YOU...
I KNOW. THE ANSWER IS: A MAN, BECAUSE HE CRAWLS IN HIS INFANCY, AND WALKS UPRIGHT IN HIS PRIME, AND HAS TO USE A CANE IN HIS DOTAGE.
EXCUSE ME?
THAT'S THE ANSWER TO THE RIDDLE YOU WERE ABOUT TO ASK ME. IN ORDER TO BE ALLOWED TO PASS, I HAVE TO CORRECTLY ANSWER YOUR RIDDLE, OR YOU'LL GOBBLE ME UP, RIGHT?
YES, BUT HOW DID YOU KNOW WHAT I WAS ABOUT TO ASK?
THAT'S THE RIDDLE YOU ALWAYS ASK. ALWAYS HAVE AND ALWAYS WILL.
WHAT CREATURE WALKS ON FOUR LEGS IN THE MORNING, TWO LEGS IN THE AFTERNOON, AND THREE LEGS IN THE EVENING?

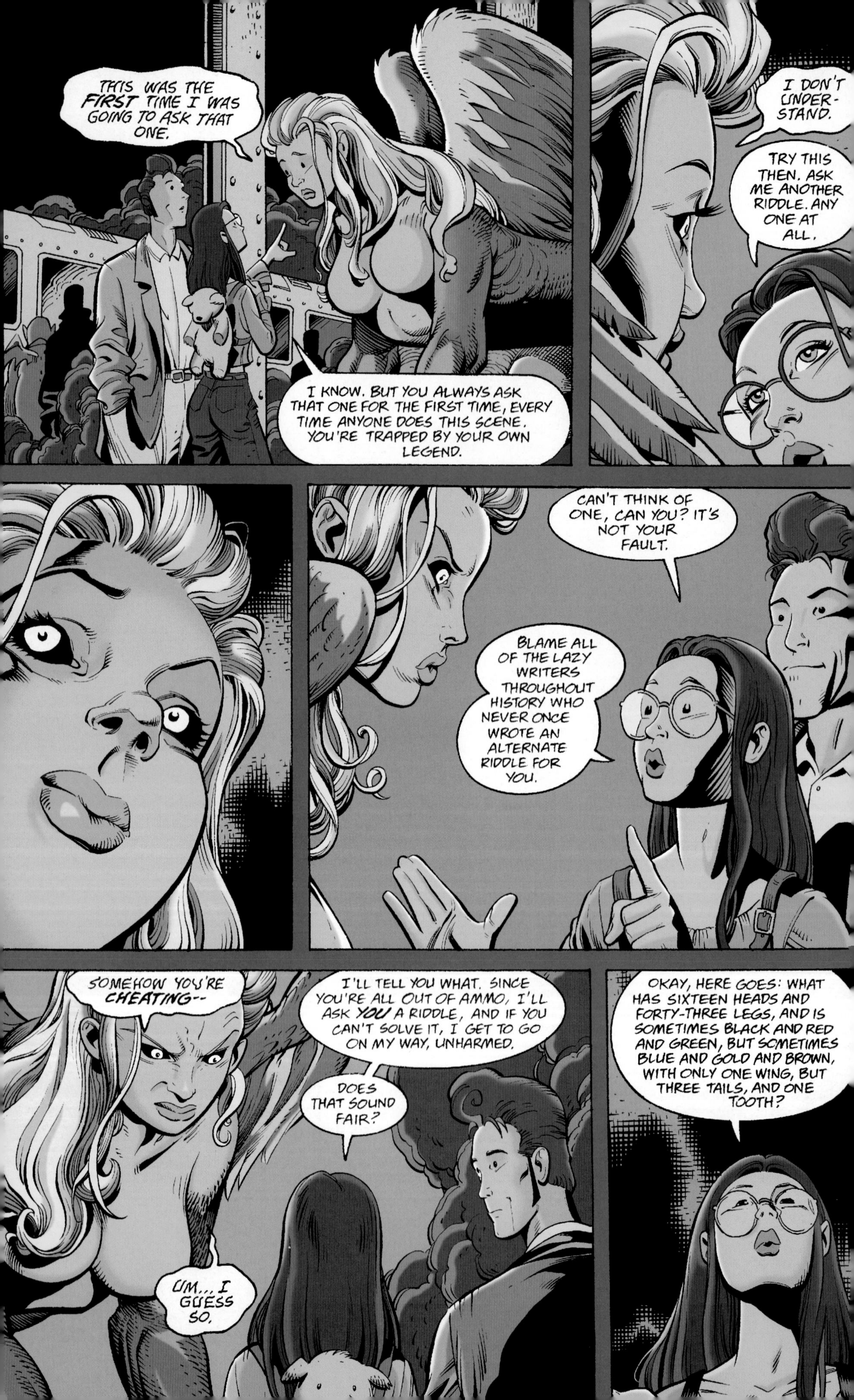
THIS WAS THE FIRST TIME I WAS GOING TO ASK THAT ONE.
I KNOW. BUT YOU ALWAYS ASK THAT ONE FOR THE FIRST TIME, EVERY TIME ANYONE DOES THIS SCENE. YOU'RE TRAPPED BY YOUR OWN LEGEND.
I DON'T UNDER-STAND.
TRY THIS THEN. ASK ME ANOTHER RIDDLE. ANY ONE AT ALL.
CAN'T THINK OF ONE, CAN YOU? IT'S NOT YOUR FAULT.
BLAME ALL OF THE LAZY WRITERS THROUGHOUT HISTORY WHO NEVER ONCE WROTE AN ALTERNATE RIDDLE FOR YOU.
SOMEHOW YOU'RE CHEATING--
I'LL TELL YOU WHAT. SINCE YOU'RE ALL OUT OF AMMO, I'LL ASK YOU A RIDDLE, AND IF YOU CAN'T SOLVE IT, I GET TO GO ON MY WAY, UNHARMED.
DOES THAT SOUND FAIR?
UM... I GUESS SO.
OKAY, HERE GOES: WHAT HAS SIXTEEN HEADS AND FORTY-THREE LEGS, AND IS SOMETIMES BLACK AND RED AND GREEN, BUT SOMETIMES BLUE AND GOLD AND BROWN, WITH ONLY ONE WING, BUT THREE TAILS, AND ONE TOOTH?

I...GIVE UP. I DON'T KNOW.

OKAY, THEN. BETTER LUCK NEXT TIME. BYE BYE.

COME ALONG, FETCH. YOU'RE ABOUT TO MISS THE TRAIN.

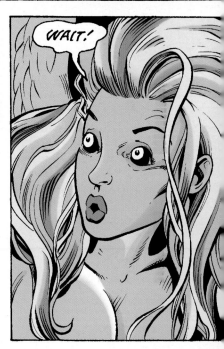

WAIT!

WHAT'S THE ANSWER?

WHO KNOWS? I FOR ONE DON'T HAVE A CLUE.

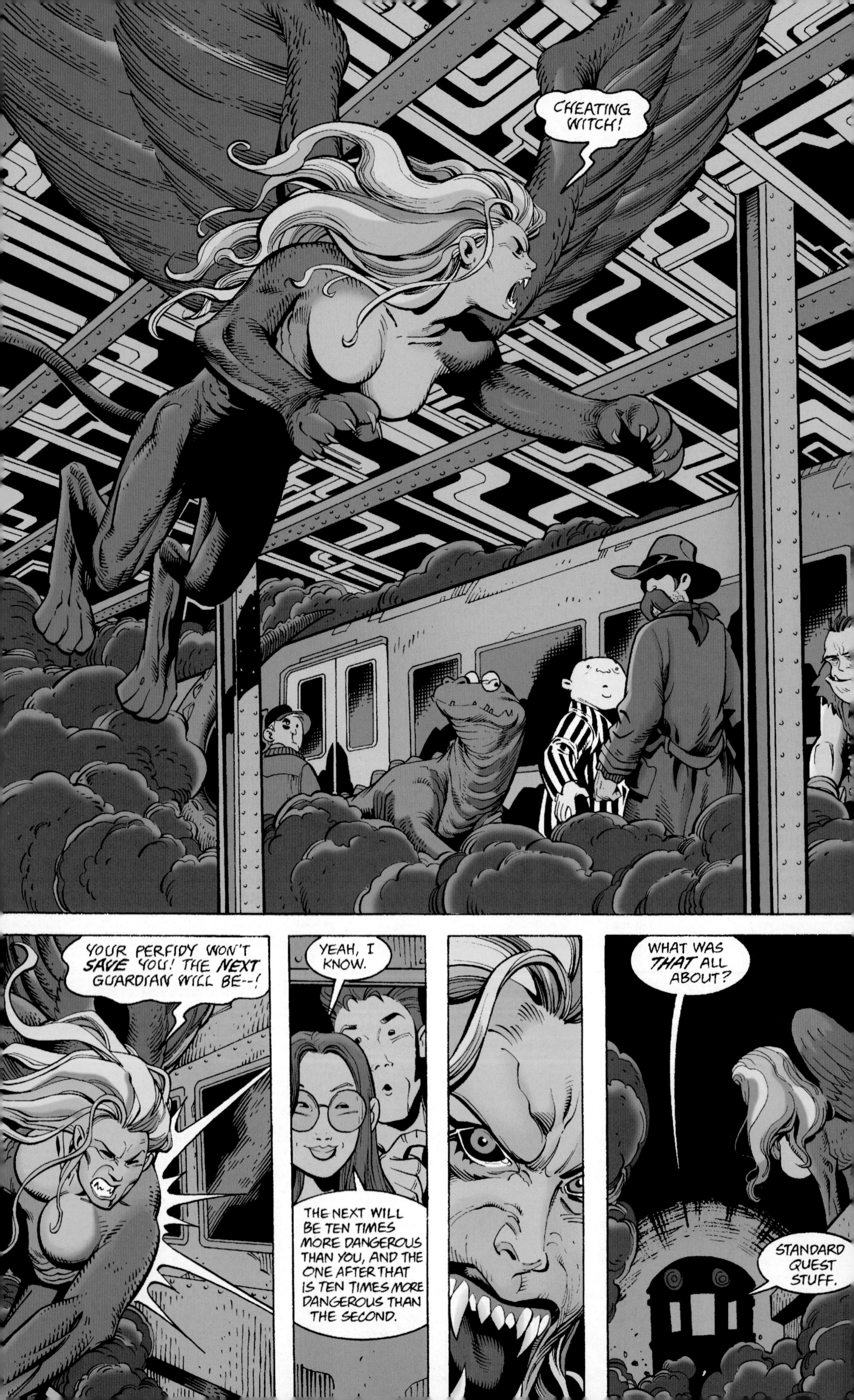
CHEATING WITCH!
YOUR PERFIDY WON'T **SAVE** YOU! THE **NEXT** GUARDIAN WILL BE--!
YEAH, I KNOW.
THE NEXT WILL BE TEN TIMES MORE DANGEROUS THAN YOU, AND THE ONE AFTER THAT IS TEN TIMES MORE DANGEROUS THAN THE SECOND.
WHAT WAS **THAT** ALL ABOUT?
STANDARD QUEST STUFF.

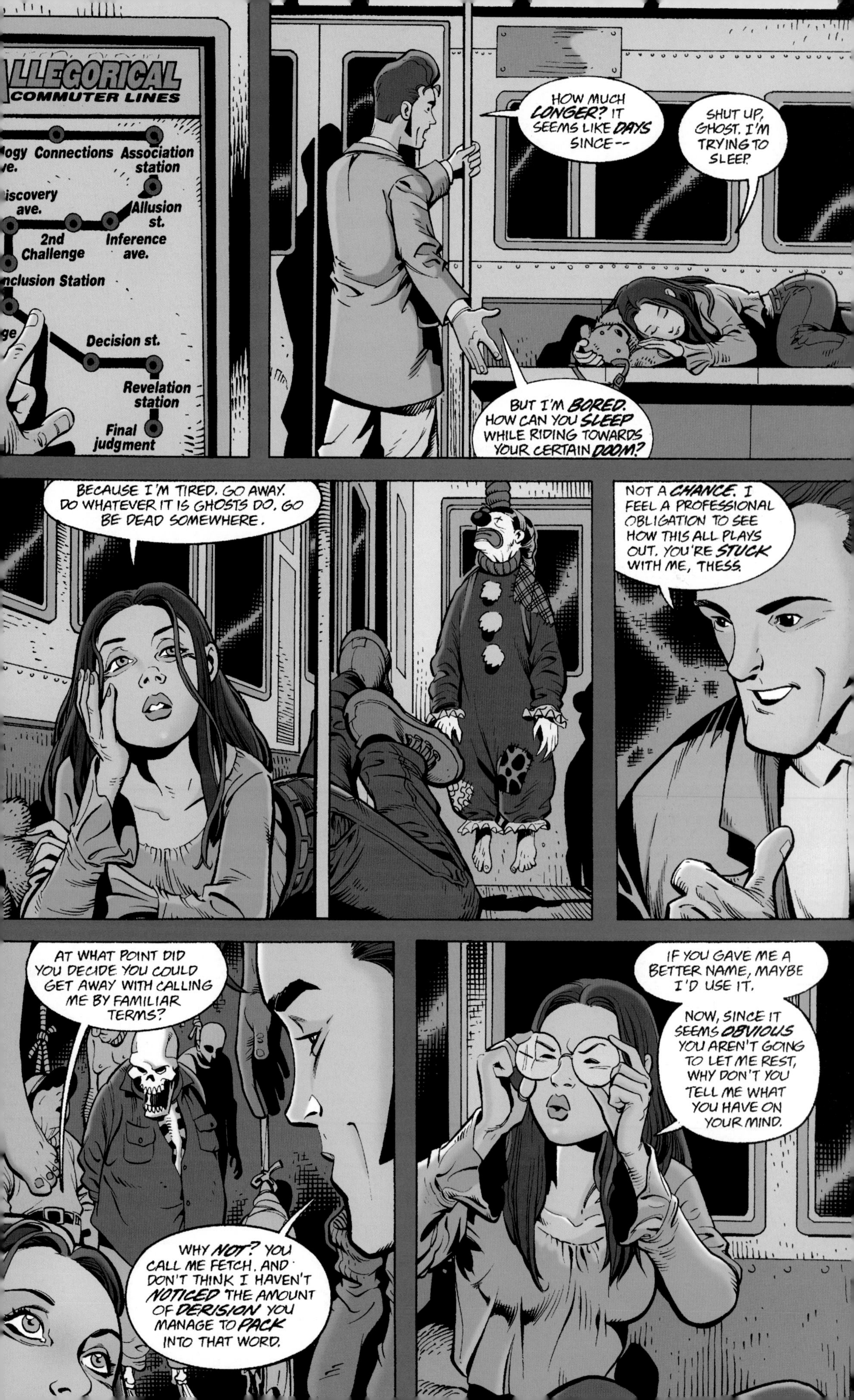

ALLEGORICAL
COMMUTER LINES
Connections
Association station
Discovery ave.
Allusion st.
2nd Challenge
Inference ave.
Decision st.
Revelation station
Final judgment
HOW MUCH LONGER? IT SEEMS LIKE DAYS SINCE--
SHUT UP, GHOST. I'M TRYING TO SLEEP.
BUT I'M BORED. HOW CAN YOU SLEEP WHILE RIDING TOWARDS YOUR CERTAIN DOOM?
BECAUSE I'M TIRED. GO AWAY. DO WHATEVER IT IS GHOSTS DO. GO BE DEAD SOMEWHERE.
NOT A CHANCE. I FEEL A PROFESSIONAL OBLIGATION TO SEE HOW THIS ALL PLAYS OUT. YOU'RE STUCK WITH ME, THESS.
AT WHAT POINT DID YOU DECIDE YOU COULD GET AWAY WITH CALLING ME BY FAMILIAR TERMS?
WHY NOT? YOU CALL ME FETCH. AND DON'T THINK I HAVEN'T NOTICED THE AMOUNT OF DERISION YOU MANAGE TO PACK INTO THAT WORD.
IF YOU GAVE ME A BETTER NAME, MAYBE I'D USE IT.
NOW, SINCE IT SEEMS OBVIOUS YOU AREN'T GOING TO LET ME REST, WHY DON'T YOU TELL ME WHAT YOU HAVE ON YOUR MIND.

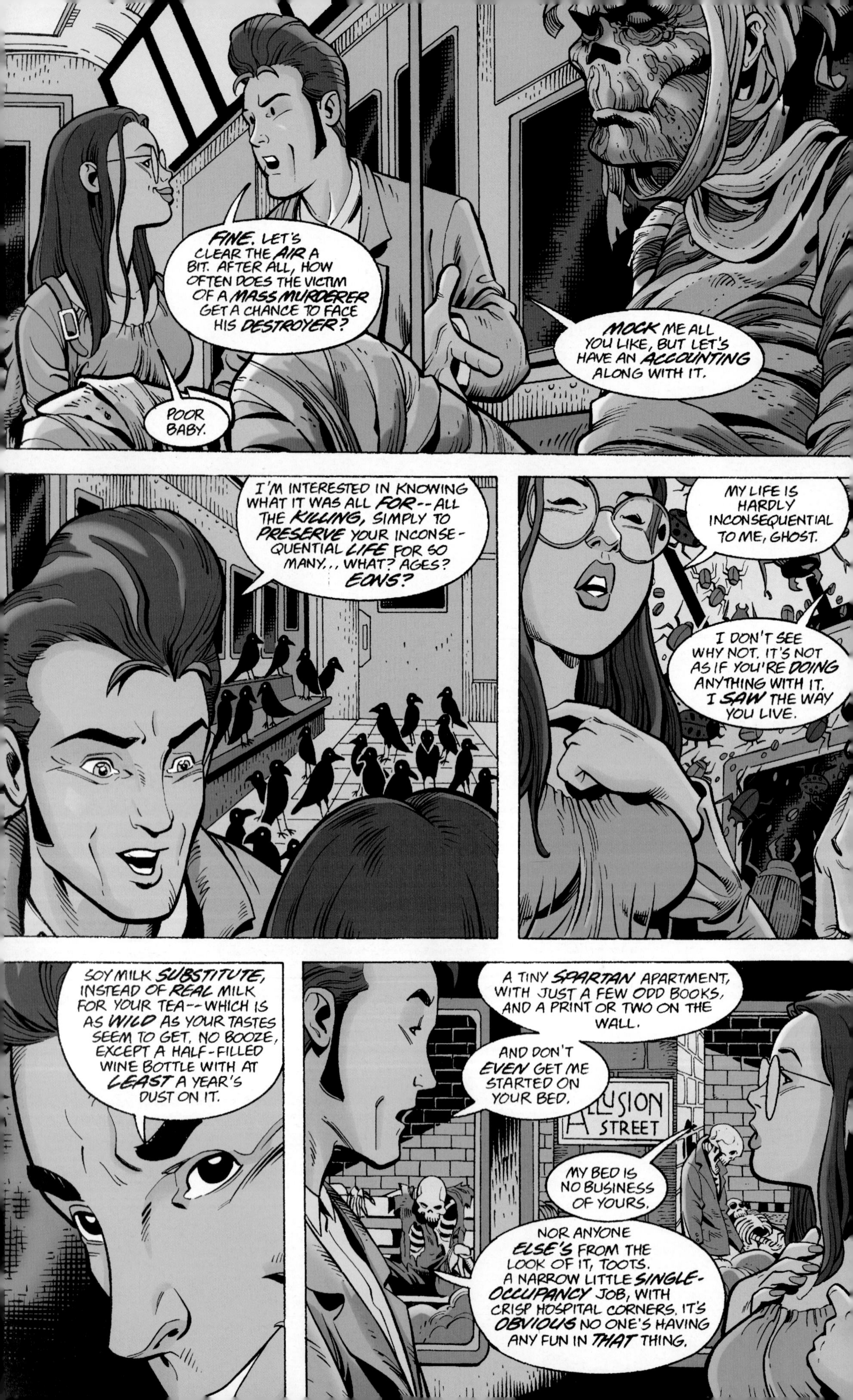
FINE. LET'S CLEAR THE AIR A BIT. AFTER ALL, HOW OFTEN DOES THE VICTIM OF A MASS MURDERER GET A CHANCE TO FACE HIS DESTROYER?
POOR BABY.
MOCK ME ALL YOU LIKE, BUT LET'S HAVE AN ACCOUNTING ALONG WITH IT.
I'M INTERESTED IN KNOWING WHAT IT WAS ALL FOR--ALL THE KILLING, SIMPLY TO PRESERVE YOUR INCONSE-QUENTIAL LIFE FOR SO MANY... WHAT? AGES? EONS?
MY LIFE IS HARDLY INCONSEQUENTIAL TO ME, GHOST.
I DON'T SEE WHY NOT. IT'S NOT AS IF YOU'RE DOING ANYTHING WITH IT. I SAW THE WAY YOU LIVE.
SOY MILK SUBSTITUTE, INSTEAD OF REAL MILK FOR YOUR TEA--WHICH IS AS WILD AS YOUR TASTES SEEM TO GET, NO BOOZE, EXCEPT A HALF-FILLED WINE BOTTLE WITH AT LEAST A YEAR'S DUST ON IT.
A TINY SPARTAN APARTMENT, WITH JUST A FEW ODD BOOKS, AND A PRINT OR TWO ON THE WALL.
AND DON'T EVEN GET ME STARTED ON YOUR BED.
ALLUSION STREET
MY BED IS NO BUSINESS OF YOURS.
NOR ANYONE ELSE'S FROM THE LOOK OF IT, TOOTS. A NARROW LITTLE SINGLE-OCCUPANCY JOB, WITH CRISP HOSPITAL CORNERS. IT'S OBVIOUS NO ONE'S HAVING ANY FUN IN THAT THING.

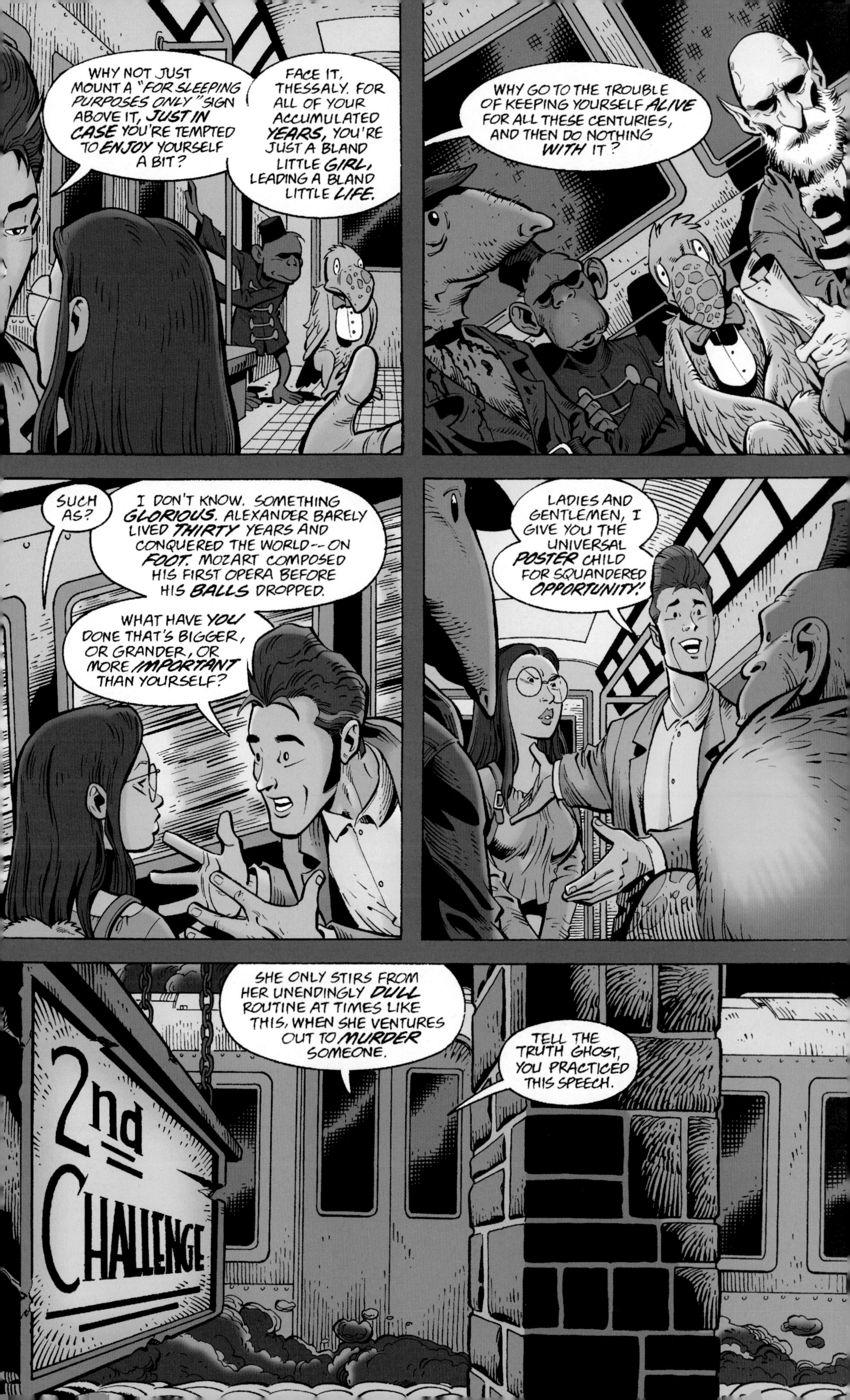
WHY NOT JUST MOUNT A "FOR SLEEPING PURPOSES ONLY" SIGN ABOVE IT, JUST IN CASE YOU'RE TEMPTED TO ENJOY YOURSELF A BIT?
FACE IT, THESSALY. FOR ALL OF YOUR ACCUMULATED YEARS, YOU'RE JUST A BLAND LITTLE GIRL, LEADING A BLAND LITTLE LIFE.
WHY GO TO THE TROUBLE OF KEEPING YOURSELF ALIVE FOR ALL THESE CENTURIES, AND THEN DO NOTHING WITH IT?
SUCH AS?
I DON'T KNOW. SOMETHING GLORIOUS. ALEXANDER BARELY LIVED THIRTY YEARS AND CONQUERED THE WORLD--ON FOOT. MOZART COMPOSED HIS FIRST OPERA BEFORE HIS BALLS DROPPED.
WHAT HAVE YOU DONE THAT'S BIGGER, OR GRANDER, OR MORE IMPORTANT THAN YOURSELF?
LADIES AND GENTLEMEN, I GIVE YOU THE UNIVERSAL POSTER CHILD FOR SQUANDERED OPPORTUNITY!
2nd CHALLENGE
SHE ONLY STIRS FROM HER UNENDINGLY DULL ROUTINE AT TIMES LIKE THIS, WHEN SHE VENTURES OUT TO MURDER SOMEONE.
TELL THE TRUTH GHOST, YOU PRACTICED THIS SPEECH.

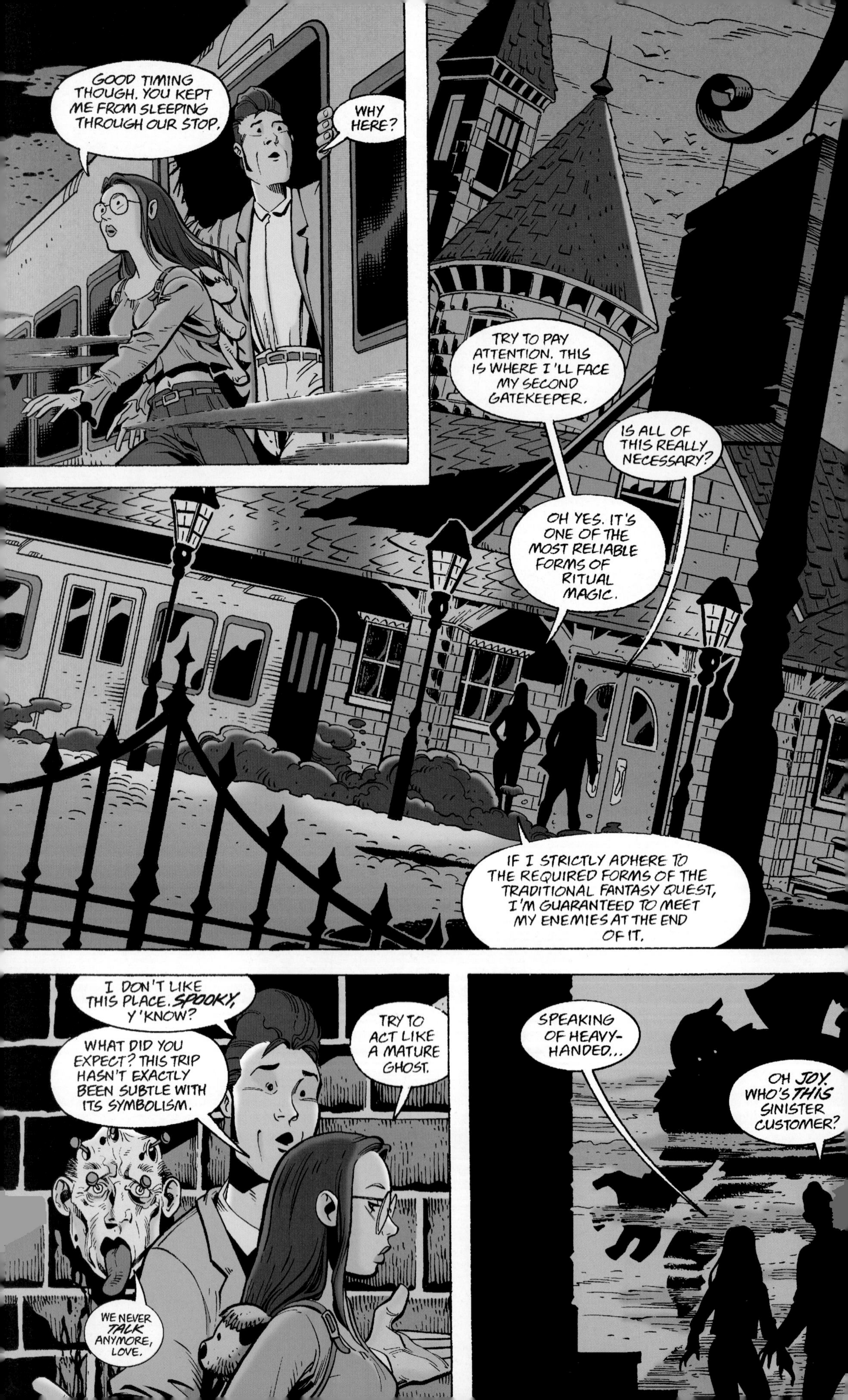
GOOD TIMING THOUGH. YOU KEPT ME FROM SLEEPING THROUGH OUR STOP.
WHY HERE?
TRY TO PAY ATTENTION. THIS IS WHERE I'LL FACE MY SECOND GATEKEEPER.
IS ALL OF THIS REALLY NECESSARY?
OH YES. IT'S ONE OF THE MOST RELIABLE FORMS OF RITUAL MAGIC.
IF I STRICTLY ADHERE TO THE REQUIRED FORMS OF THE TRADITIONAL FANTASY QUEST, I'M GUARANTEED TO MEET MY ENEMIES AT THE END OF IT.
I DON'T LIKE THIS PLACE. *SPOOKY*, Y'KNOW?
WHAT DID YOU EXPECT? THIS TRIP HASN'T EXACTLY BEEN SUBTLE WITH ITS SYMBOLISM.
TRY TO ACT LIKE A MATURE GHOST.
WE NEVER *TALK* ANYMORE, LOVE.
SPEAKING OF HEAVY-HANDED...
OH *JOY*. WHO'S *THIS* SINISTER CUSTOMER?

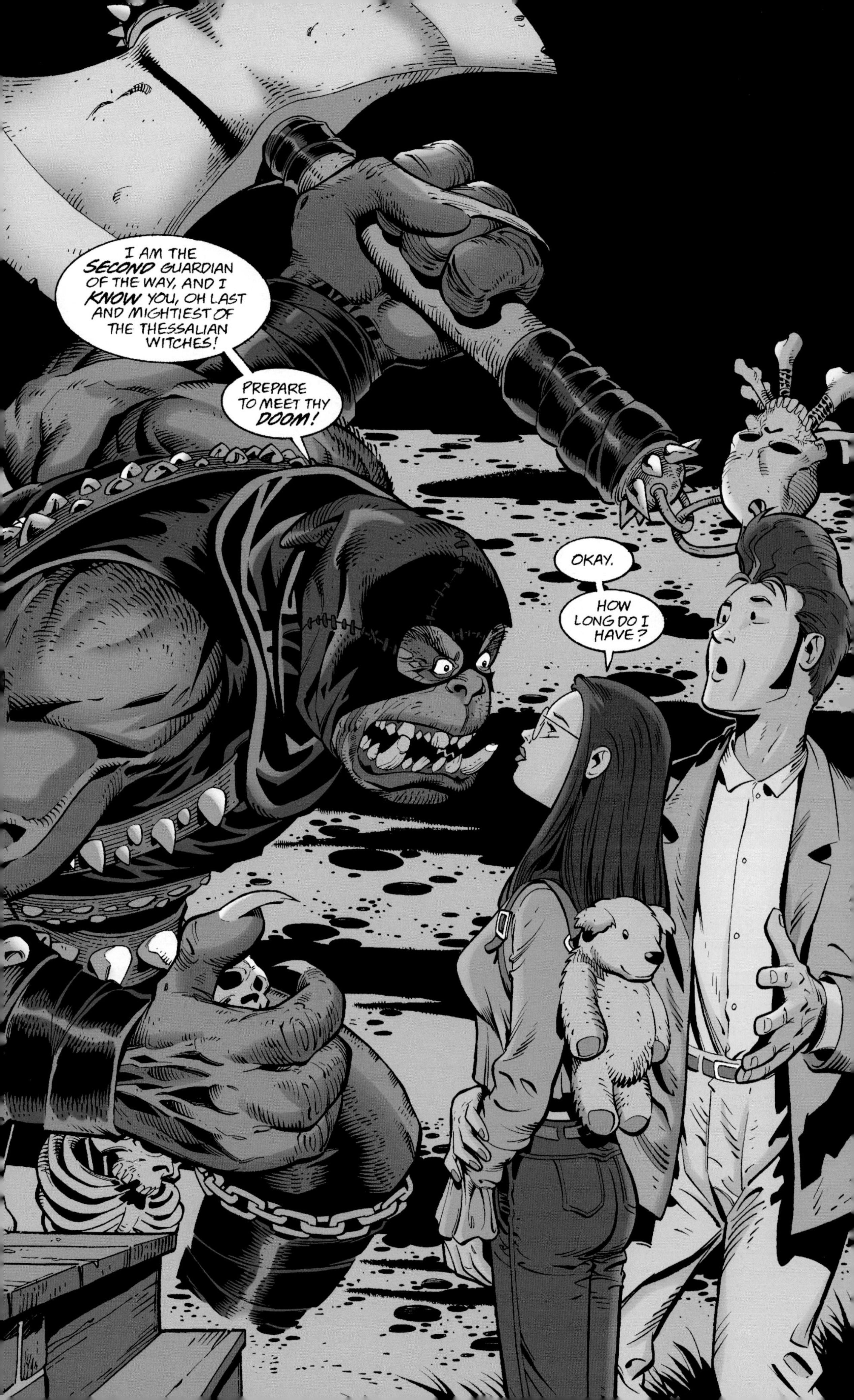
I AM THE SECOND GUARDIAN OF THE WAY, AND I KNOW YOU, OH LAST AND MIGHTIEST OF THE THESSALIAN WITCHES!
PREPARE TO MEET THY DOOM!
OKAY.
HOW LONG DO I HAVE?

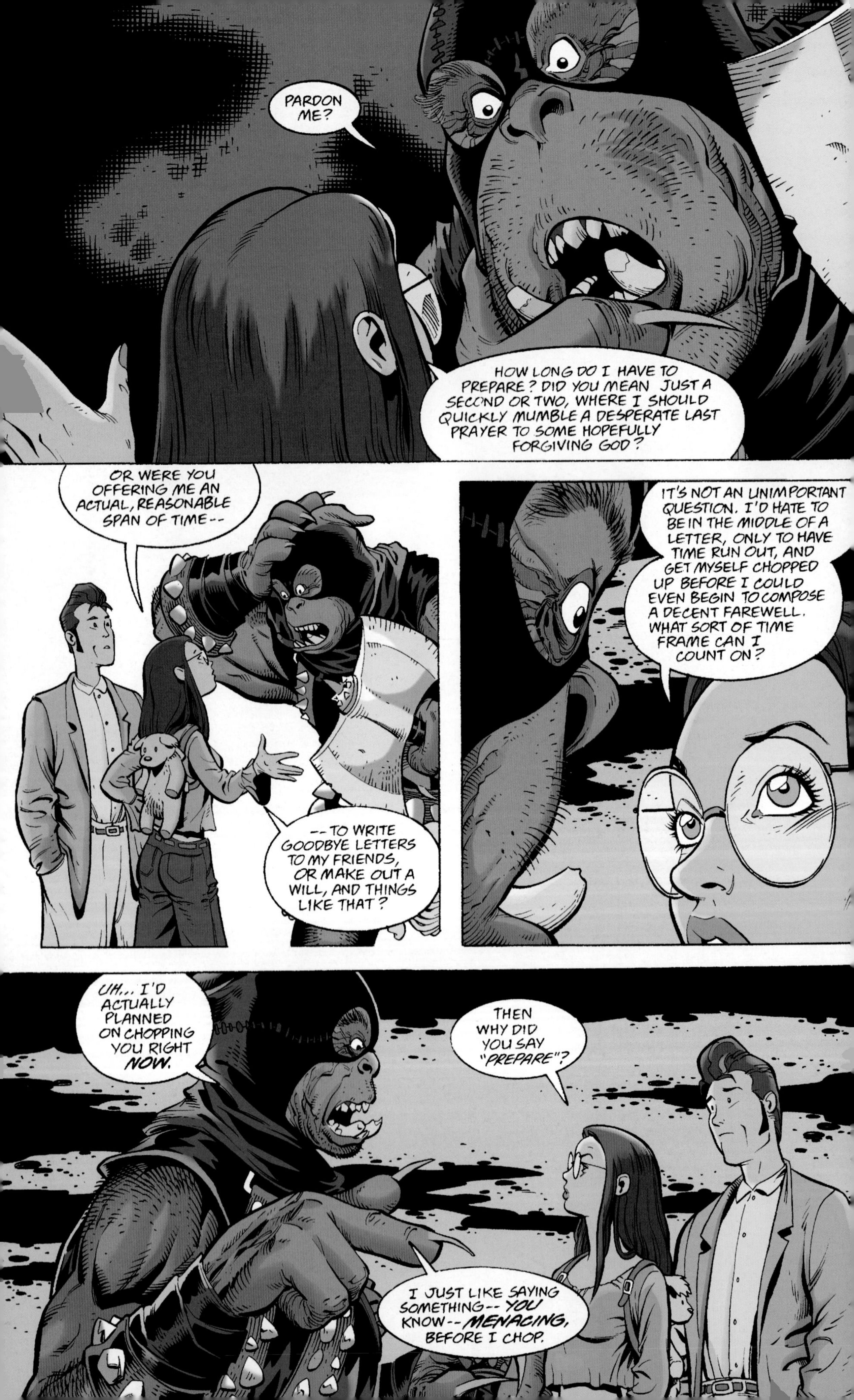
PARDON ME?
HOW LONG DO I HAVE TO PREPARE? DID YOU MEAN JUST A SECOND OR TWO, WHERE I SHOULD QUICKLY MUMBLE A DESPERATE LAST PRAYER TO SOME HOPEFULLY FORGIVING GOD?
OR WERE YOU OFFERING ME AN ACTUAL, REASONABLE SPAN OF TIME--
--TO WRITE GOODBYE LETTERS TO MY FRIENDS, OR MAKE OUT A WILL, AND THINGS LIKE THAT?
IT'S NOT AN UNIMPORTANT QUESTION. I'D HATE TO BE IN THE MIDDLE OF A LETTER, ONLY TO HAVE TIME RUN OUT, AND GET MYSELF CHOPPED UP BEFORE I COULD EVEN BEGIN TO COMPOSE A DECENT FAREWELL. WHAT SORT OF TIME FRAME CAN I COUNT ON?
UH... I'D ACTUALLY PLANNED ON CHOPPING YOU RIGHT NOW.
THEN WHY DID YOU SAY "PREPARE"?
I JUST LIKE SAYING SOMETHING--YOU KNOW--MENACING, BEFORE I CHOP.

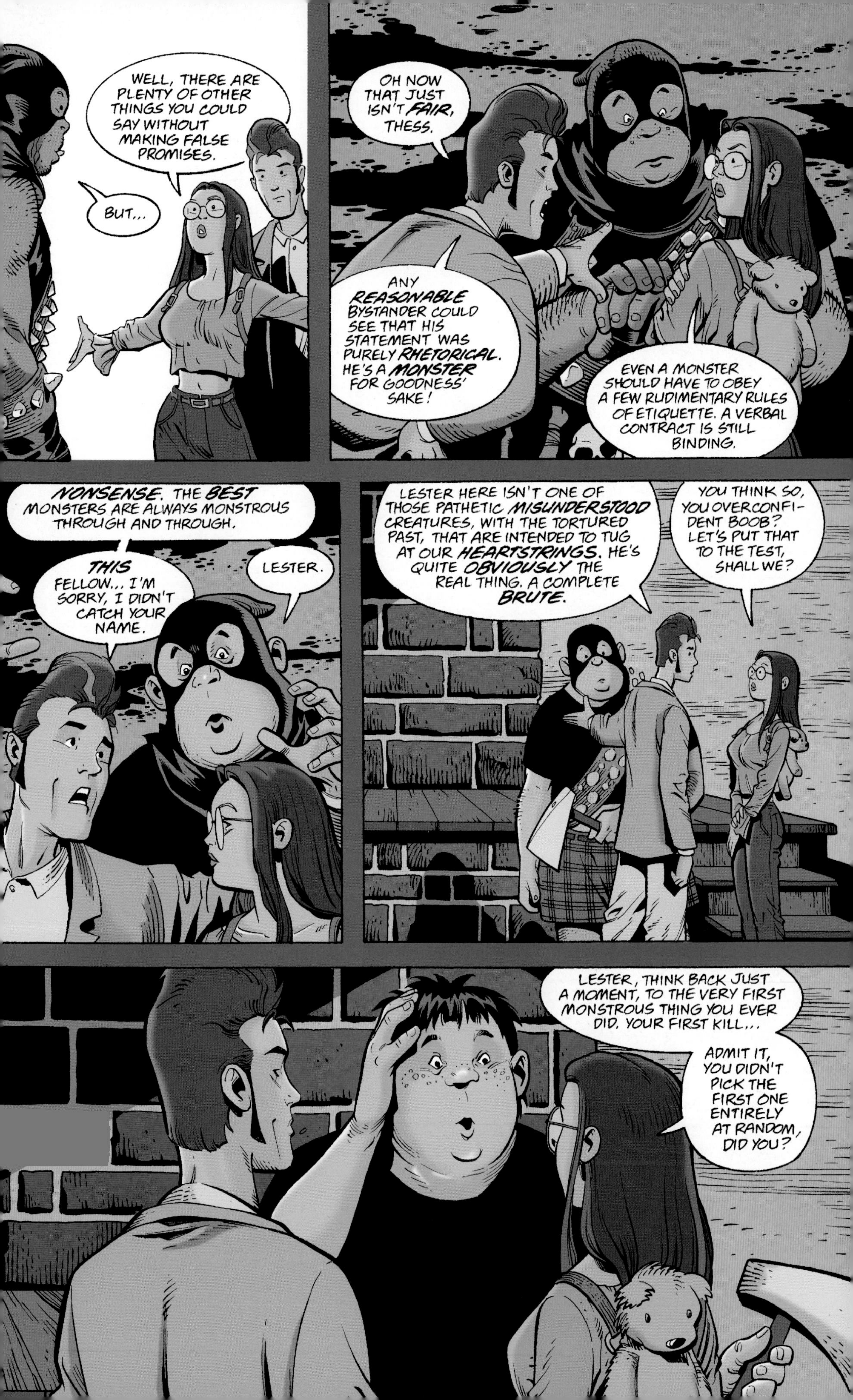

WELL, THERE ARE PLENTY OF OTHER THINGS YOU COULD SAY WITHOUT MAKING FALSE PROMISES.
BUT...
OH NOW THAT JUST ISN'T FAIR, THESS.
ANY REASONABLE BYSTANDER COULD SEE THAT HIS STATEMENT WAS PURELY RHETORICAL. HE'S A MONSTER FOR GOODNESS' SAKE!
EVEN A MONSTER SHOULD HAVE TO OBEY A FEW RUDIMENTARY RULES OF ETIQUETTE. A VERBAL CONTRACT IS STILL BINDING.
NONSENSE. THE BEST MONSTERS ARE ALWAYS MONSTROUS THROUGH AND THROUGH.
THIS FELLOW... I'M SORRY, I DIDN'T CATCH YOUR NAME.
LESTER.
LESTER HERE ISN'T ONE OF THOSE PATHETIC MISUNDERSTOOD CREATURES, WITH THE TORTURED PAST, THAT ARE INTENDED TO TUG AT OUR HEARTSTRINGS. HE'S QUITE OBVIOUSLY THE REAL THING. A COMPLETE BRUTE.
YOU THINK SO, YOU OVERCONFI-DENT BOOB? LET'S PUT THAT TO THE TEST, SHALL WE?
LESTER, THINK BACK JUST A MOMENT, TO THE VERY FIRST MONSTROUS THING YOU EVER DID, YOUR FIRST KILL...
ADMIT IT, YOU DIDN'T PICK THE FIRST ONE ENTIRELY AT RANDOM, DID YOU?

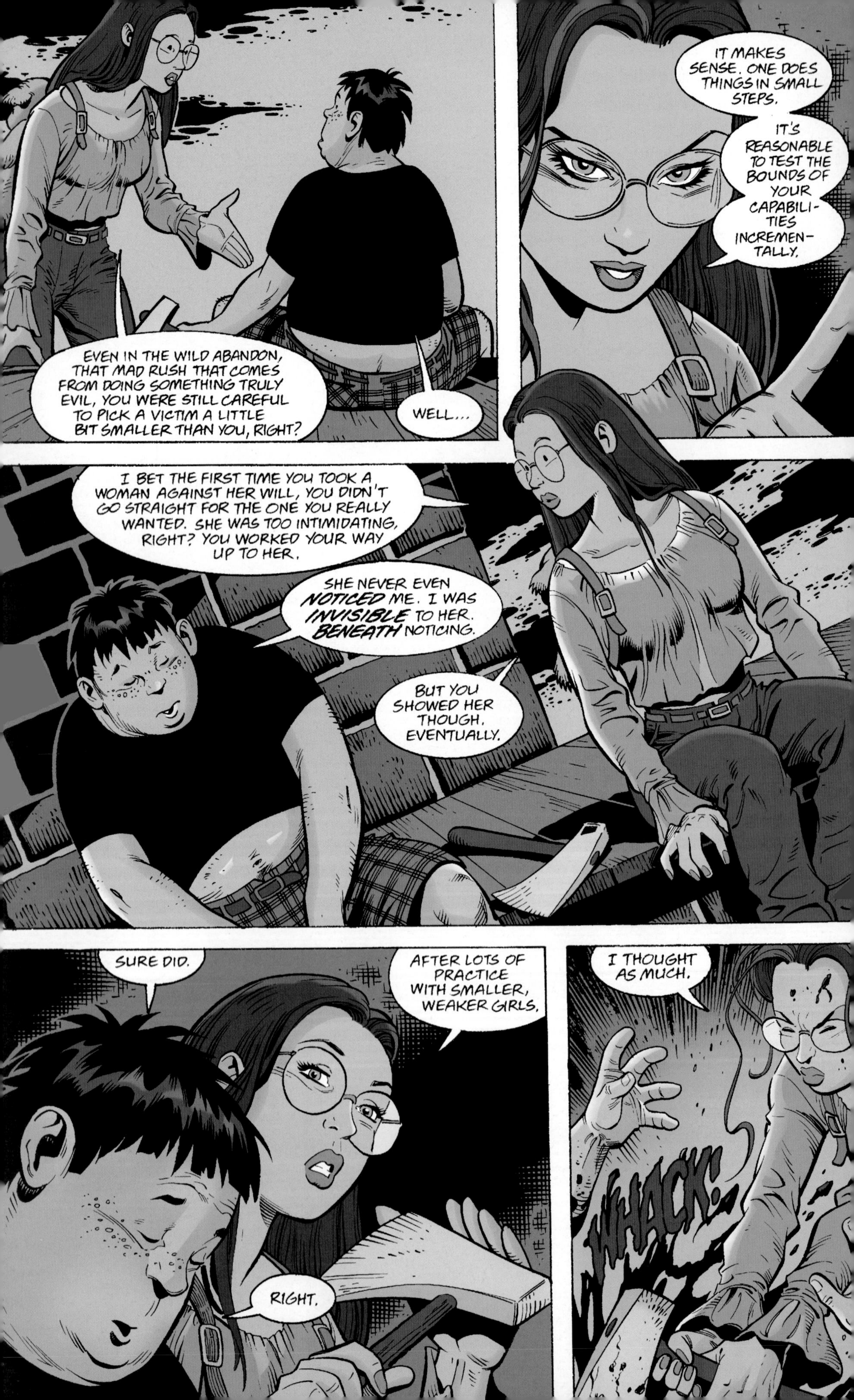
EVEN IN THE WILD ABANDON, THAT MAD RUSH THAT COMES FROM DOING SOMETHING TRULY EVIL, YOU WERE STILL CAREFUL TO PICK A VICTIM A LITTLE BIT SMALLER THAN YOU, RIGHT?
WELL...
IT MAKES SENSE. ONE DOES THINGS IN SMALL STEPS.
IT'S REASONABLE TO TEST THE BOUNDS OF YOUR CAPABILITIES INCREMENTALLY.
I BET THE FIRST TIME YOU TOOK A WOMAN AGAINST HER WILL, YOU DIDN'T GO STRAIGHT FOR THE ONE YOU REALLY WANTED. SHE WAS TOO INTIMIDATING, RIGHT? YOU WORKED YOUR WAY UP TO HER.
SHE NEVER EVEN *NOTICED* ME. I WAS *INVISIBLE* TO HER. *BENEATH* NOTICING.
BUT YOU SHOWED HER THOUGH. EVENTUALLY.
SURE DID.
AFTER LOTS OF PRACTICE WITH SMALLER, WEAKER GIRLS.
RIGHT.
I THOUGHT AS MUCH.
WHACK!

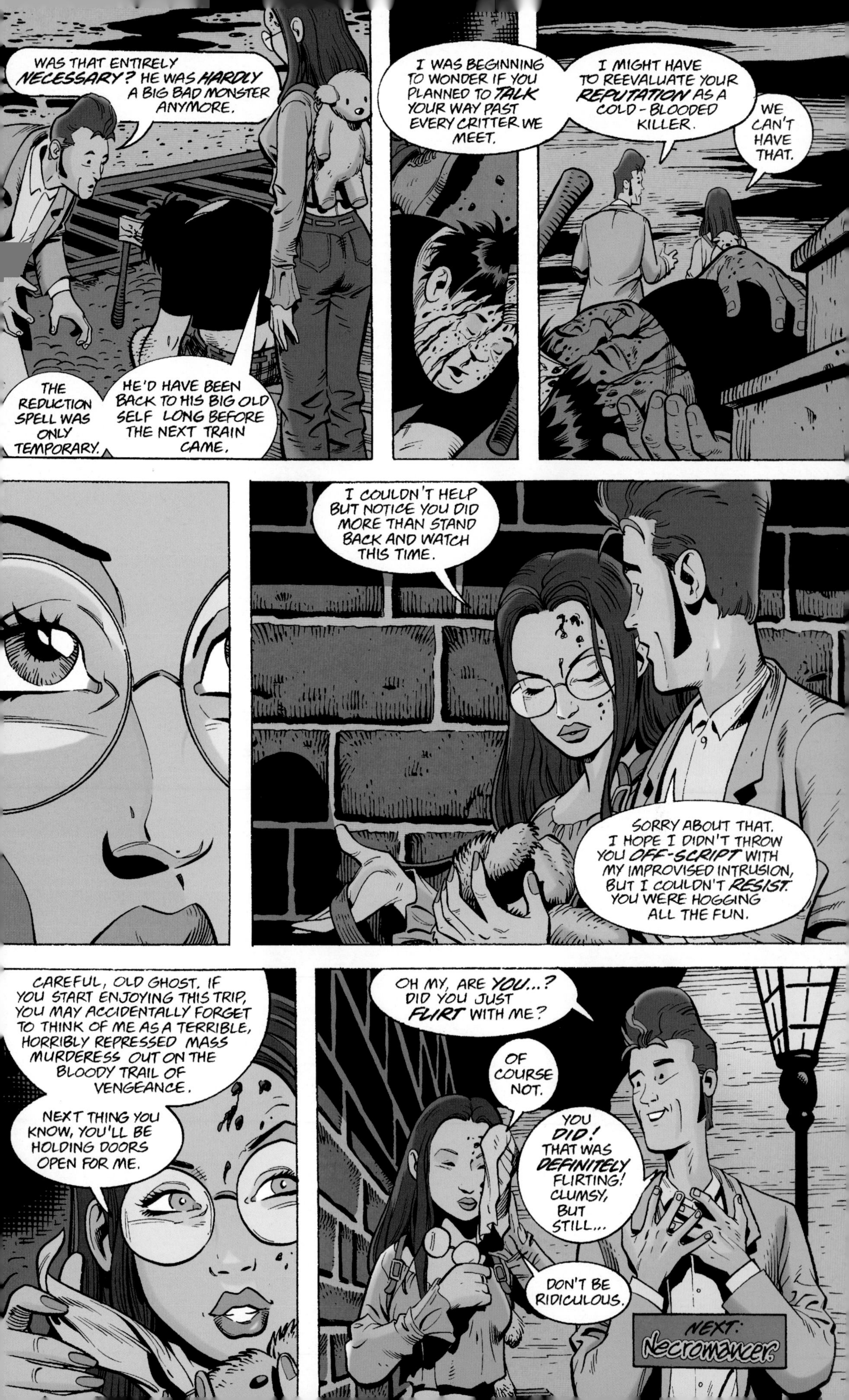
WAS THAT ENTIRELY NECESSARY? HE WAS HARDLY A BIG BAD MONSTER ANYMORE.
THE REDUCTION SPELL WAS ONLY TEMPORARY.
HE'D HAVE BEEN BACK TO HIS BIG OLD SELF LONG BEFORE THE NEXT TRAIN CAME.
I WAS BEGINNING TO WONDER IF YOU PLANNED TO TALK YOUR WAY PAST EVERY CRITTER WE MEET.
I MIGHT HAVE TO REEVALUATE YOUR REPUTATION AS A COLD-BLOODED KILLER.
WE CAN'T HAVE THAT.
I COULDN'T HELP BUT NOTICE YOU DID MORE THAN STAND BACK AND WATCH THIS TIME.
SORRY ABOUT THAT. I HOPE I DIDN'T THROW YOU OFF-SCRIPT WITH MY IMPROVISED INTRUSION, BUT I COULDN'T RESIST. YOU WERE HOGGING ALL THE FUN.
CAREFUL, OLD GHOST. IF YOU START ENJOYING THIS TRIP, YOU MAY ACCIDENTALLY FORGET TO THINK OF ME AS A TERRIBLE, HORRIBLY REPRESSED MASS MURDERESS OUT ON THE BLOODY TRAIL OF VENGEANCE.
NEXT THING YOU KNOW, YOU'LL BE HOLDING DOORS OPEN FOR ME.
OH MY, ARE YOU...? DID YOU JUST FLIRT WITH ME?
OF COURSE NOT.
YOU DID! THAT WAS DEFINITELY FLIRTING! CLUMSY, BUT STILL...
DON'T BE RIDICULOUS.
NEXT: Necromancer.

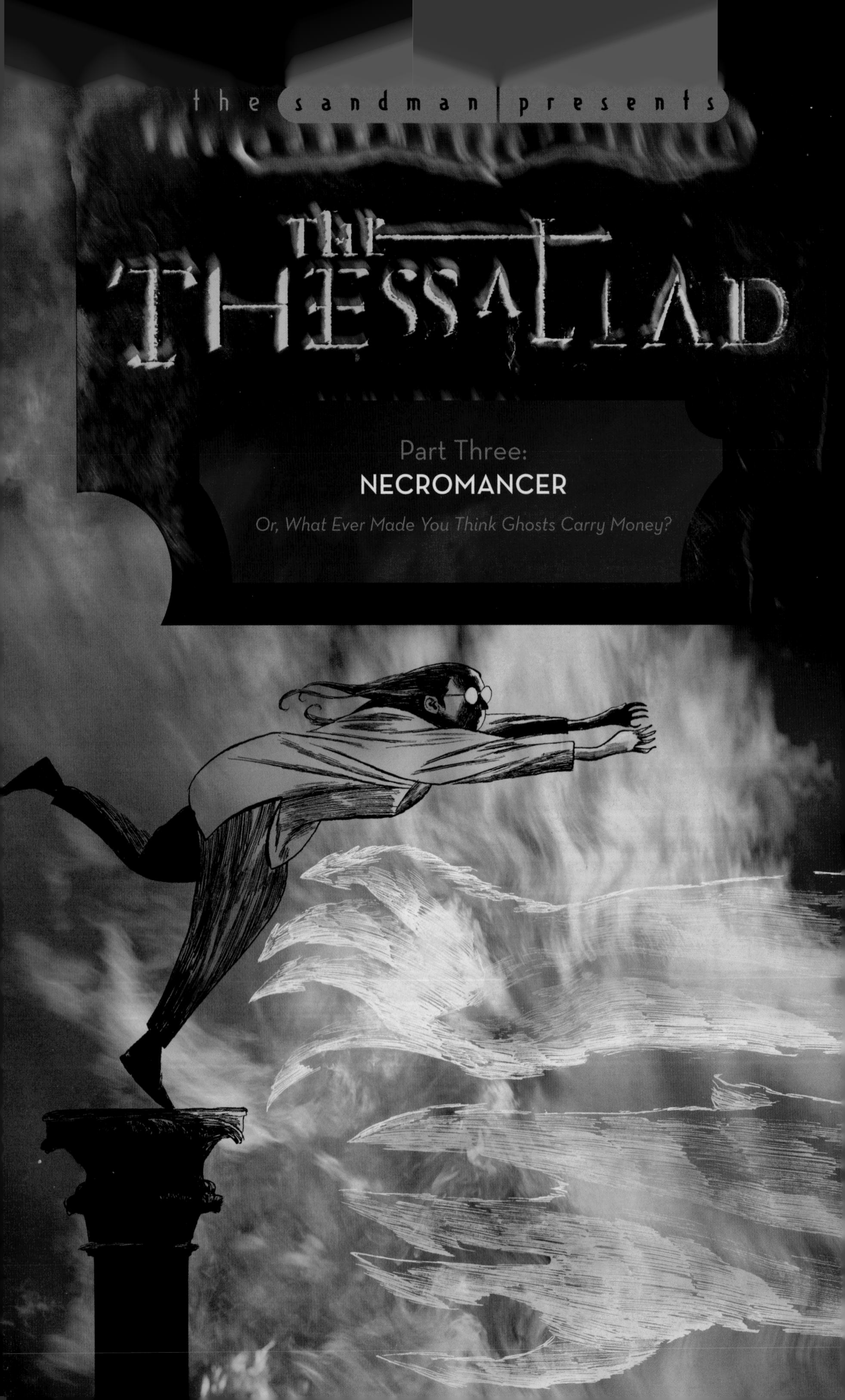
the sandman presents
THE THESSALIAD
Part Three:
NECROMANCER
Or, What Ever Made You Think Ghosts Carry Money?

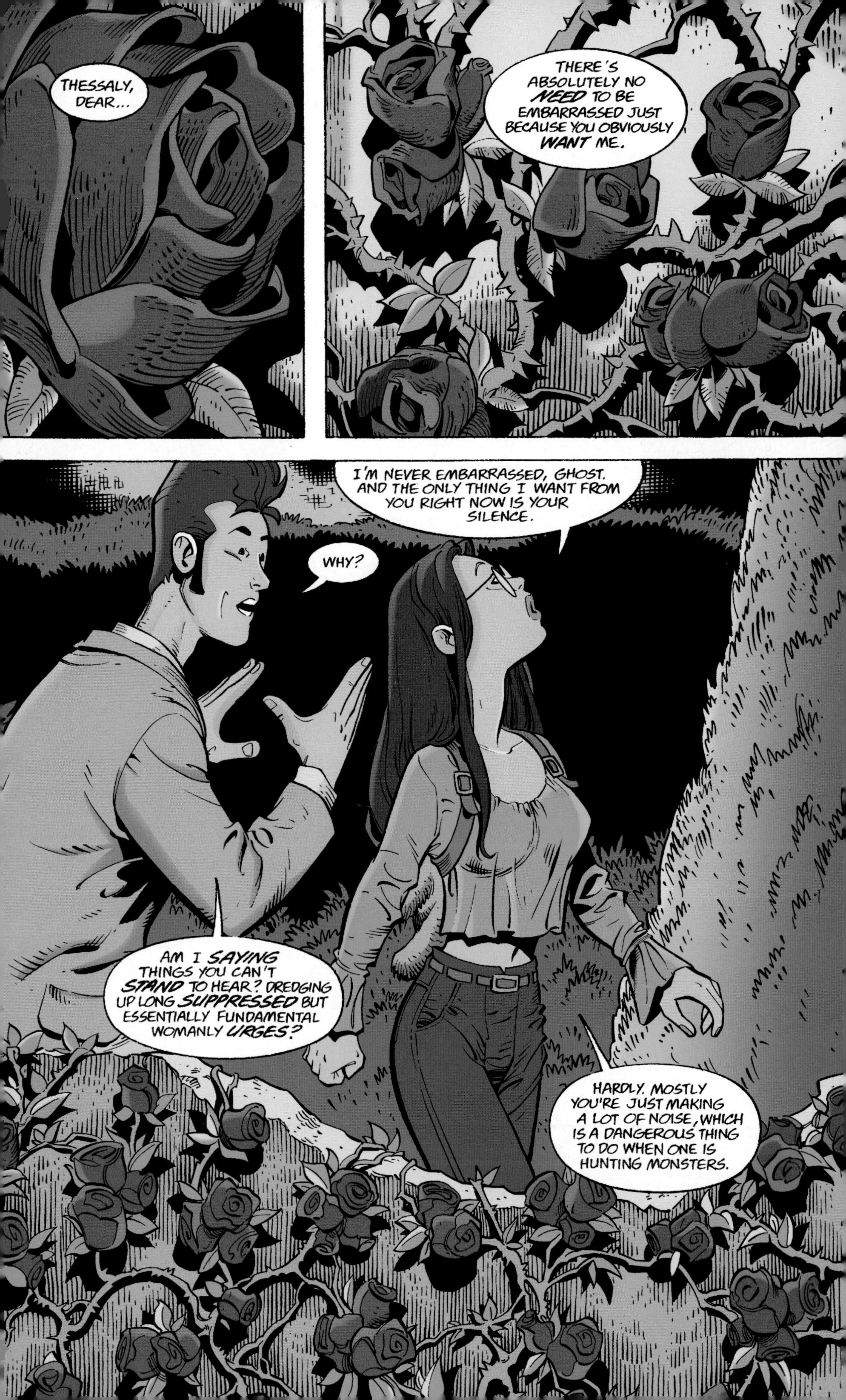
THESSALY, DEAR...
THERE'S ABSOLUTELY NO NEED TO BE EMBARRASSED JUST BECAUSE YOU OBVIOUSLY WANT ME.
I'M NEVER EMBARRASSED, GHOST. AND THE ONLY THING I WANT FROM YOU RIGHT NOW IS YOUR SILENCE.
WHY?
AM I SAYING THINGS YOU CAN'T STAND TO HEAR? DREDGING UP LONG SUPPRESSED BUT ESSENTIALLY FUNDAMENTAL WOMANLY URGES?
HARDLY. MOSTLY YOU'RE JUST MAKING A LOT OF NOISE, WHICH IS A DANGEROUS THING TO DO WHEN ONE IS HUNTING MONSTERS.

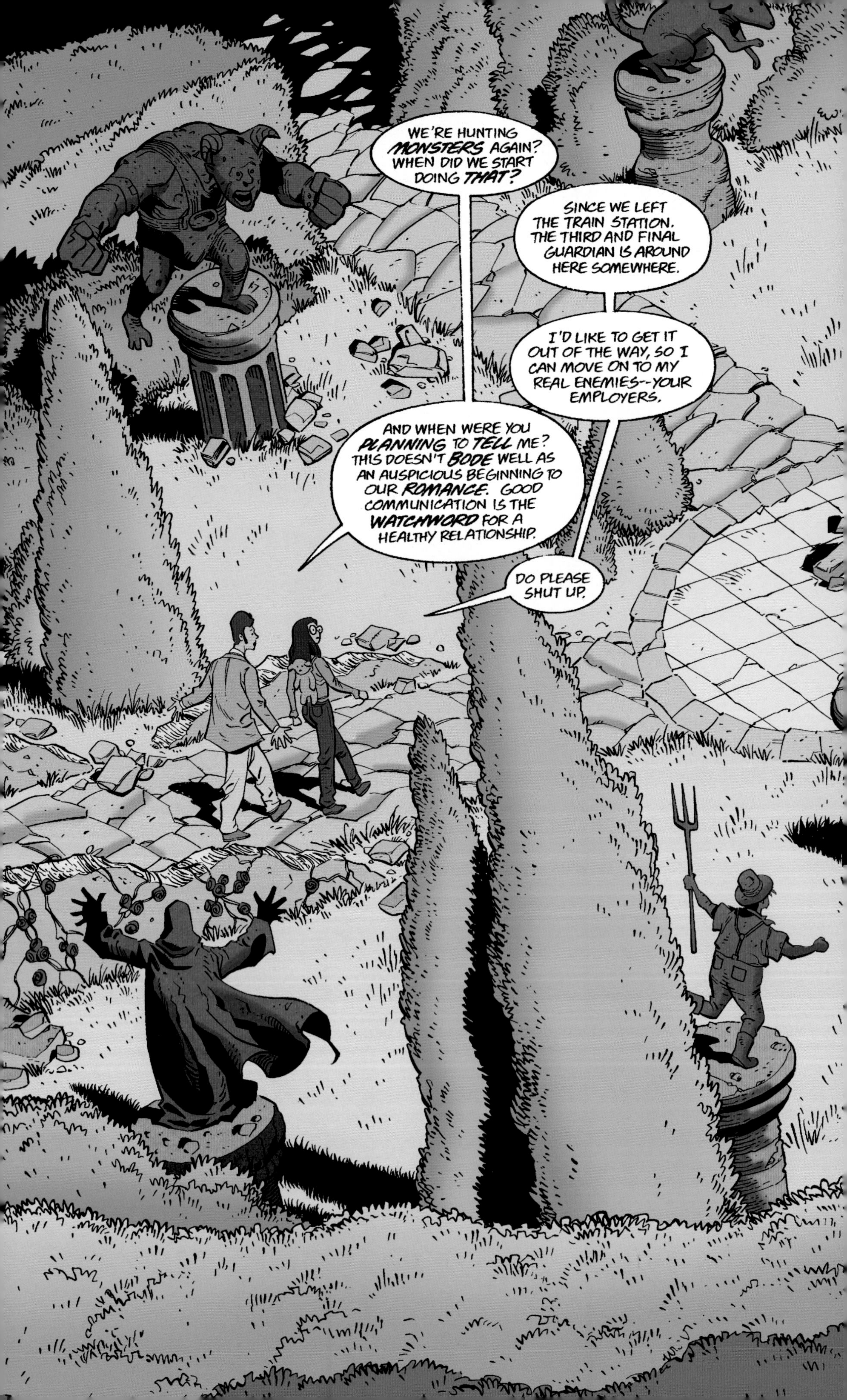
WE'RE HUNTING MONSTERS AGAIN? WHEN DID WE START DOING THAT?
SINCE WE LEFT THE TRAIN STATION. THE THIRD AND FINAL GUARDIAN IS AROUND HERE SOMEWHERE.
I'D LIKE TO GET IT OUT OF THE WAY, SO I CAN MOVE ON TO MY REAL ENEMIES--YOUR EMPLOYERS.
AND WHEN WERE YOU PLANNING TO TELL ME? THIS DOESN'T BODE WELL AS AN AUSPICIOUS BEGINNING TO OUR ROMANCE. GOOD COMMUNICATION IS THE WATCHWORD FOR A HEALTHY RELATIONSHIP.
DO PLEASE SHUT UP.

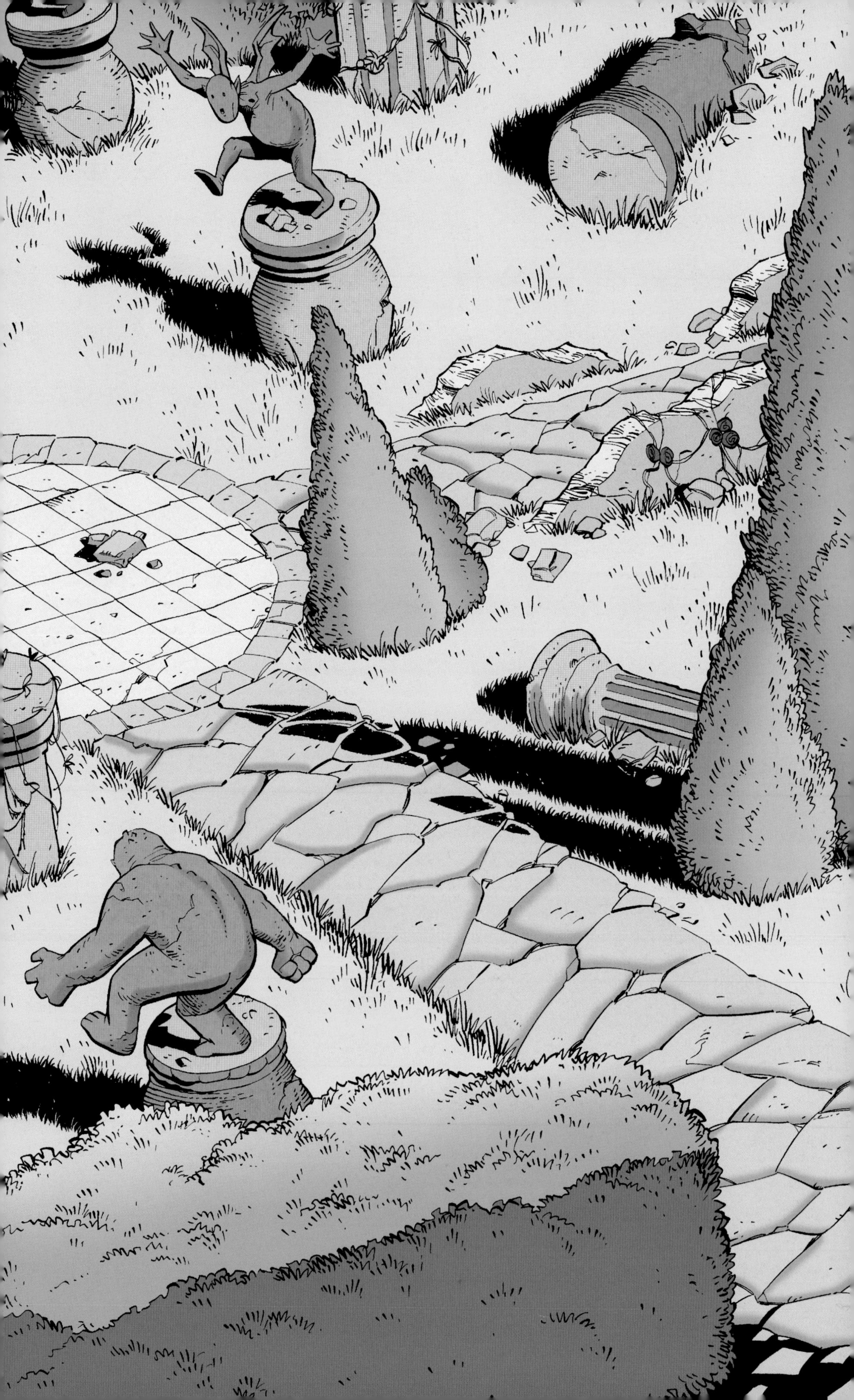

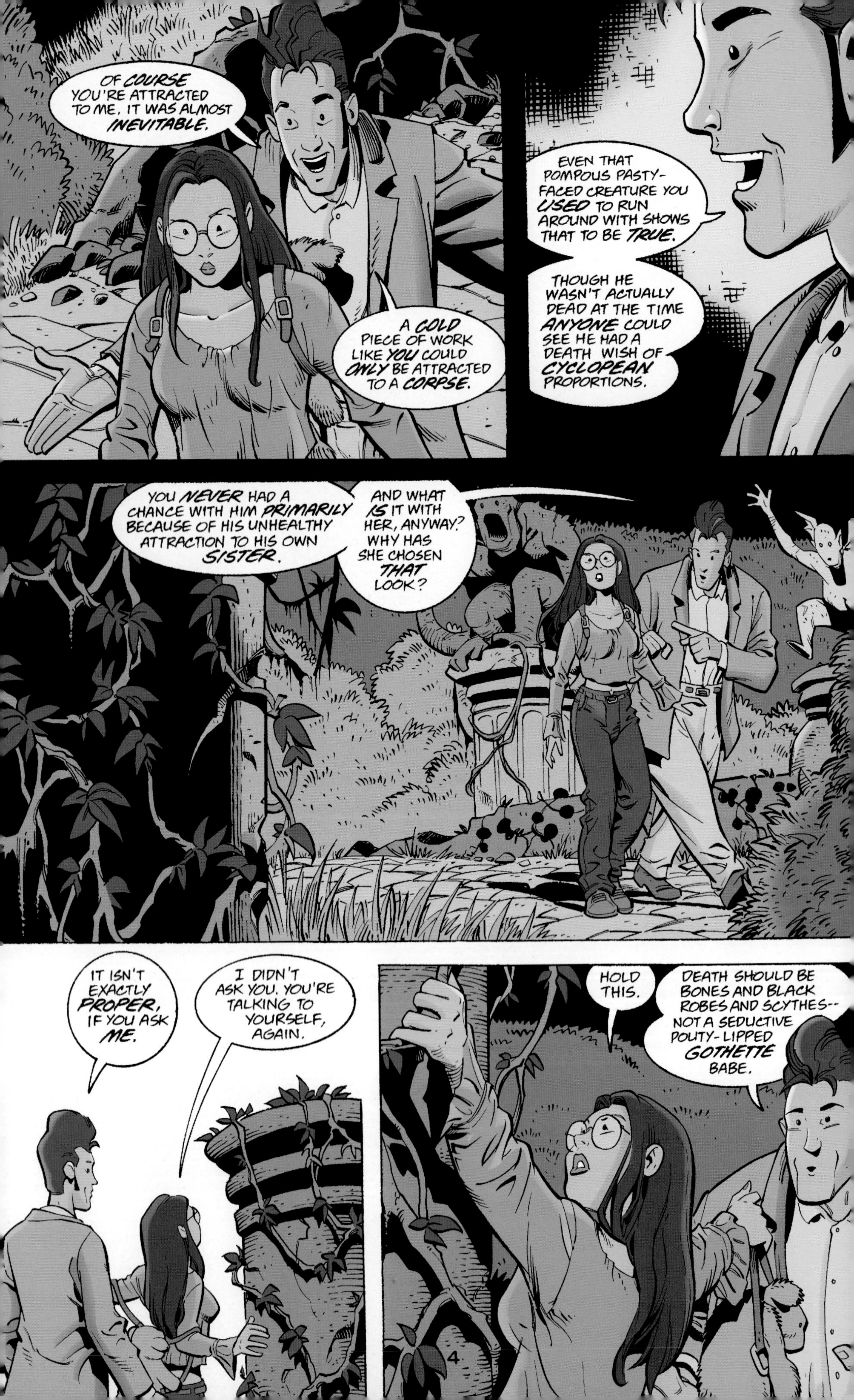

OF COURSE YOU'RE ATTRACTED TO ME. IT WAS ALMOST INEVITABLE.
A COLD PIECE OF WORK LIKE YOU COULD ONLY BE ATTRACTED TO A CORPSE.
EVEN THAT POMPOUS PASTY-FACED CREATURE YOU USED TO RUN AROUND WITH SHOWS THAT TO BE TRUE.
THOUGH HE WASN'T ACTUALLY DEAD AT THE TIME ANYONE COULD SEE HE HAD A DEATH WISH OF CYCLOPEAN PROPORTIONS.
YOU NEVER HAD A CHANCE WITH HIM PRIMARILY BECAUSE OF HIS UNHEALTHY ATTRACTION TO HIS OWN SISTER.
AND WHAT IS IT WITH HER, ANYWAY? WHY HAS SHE CHOSEN THAT LOOK?
IT ISN'T EXACTLY PROPER, IF YOU ASK ME.
I DIDN'T ASK YOU. YOU'RE TALKING TO YOURSELF, AGAIN.
HOLD THIS.
DEATH SHOULD BE BONES AND BLACK ROBES AND SCYTHES-- NOT A SEDUCTIVE POUTY-LIPPED GOTHETTE BABE.

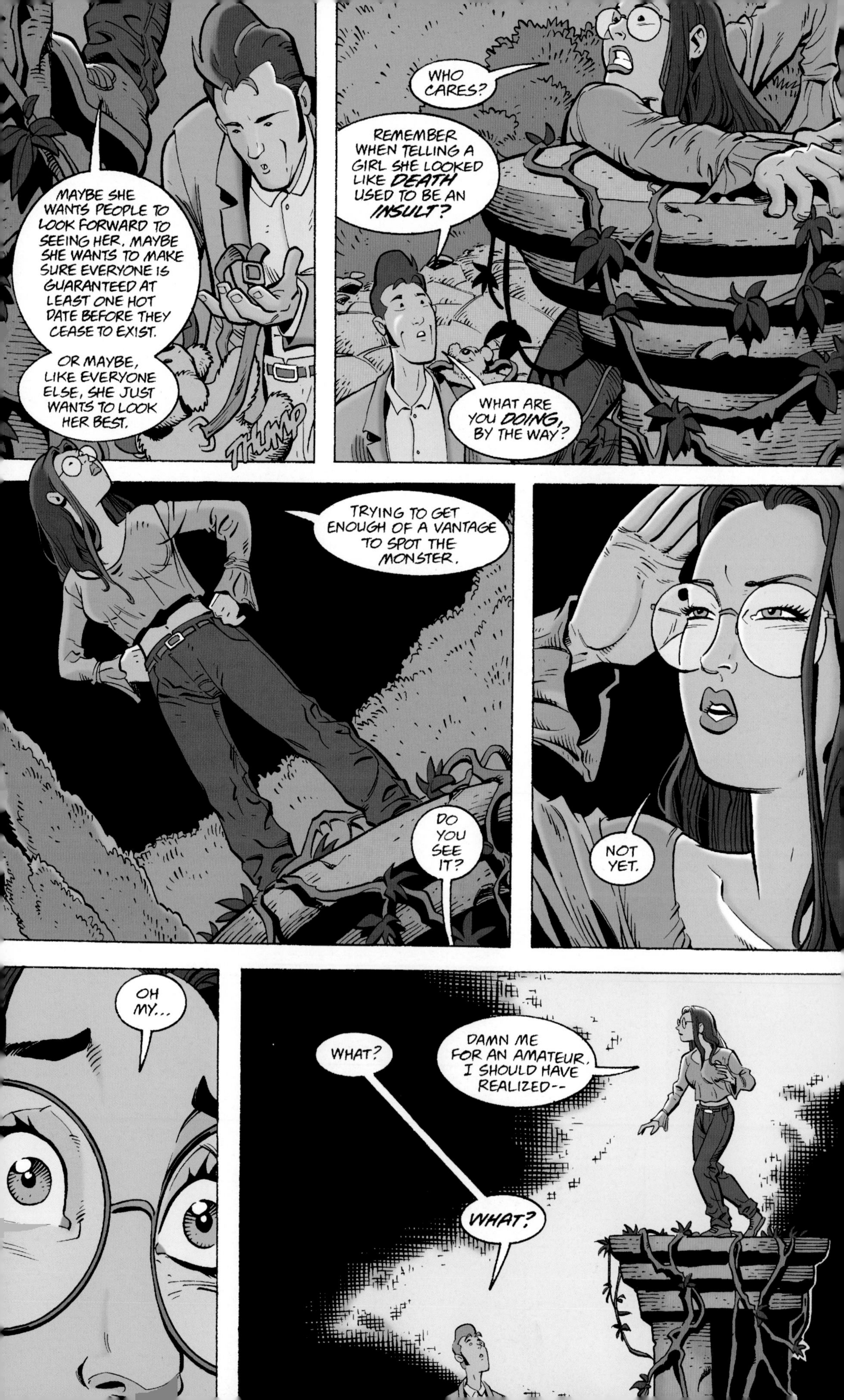
MAYBE SHE WANTS PEOPLE TO LOOK FORWARD TO SEEING HER. MAYBE SHE WANTS TO MAKE SURE EVERYONE IS GUARANTEED AT LEAST ONE HOT DATE BEFORE THEY CEASE TO EXIST.
OR MAYBE, LIKE EVERYONE ELSE, SHE JUST WANTS TO LOOK HER BEST.
THUNK
WHO CARES?
REMEMBER WHEN TELLING A GIRL SHE LOOKED LIKE DEATH USED TO BE AN INSULT?
WHAT ARE YOU DOING, BY THE WAY?
TRYING TO GET ENOUGH OF A VANTAGE TO SPOT THE MONSTER.
DO YOU SEE IT?
NOT YET.
OH MY...
WHAT?
DAMN ME FOR AN AMATEUR. I SHOULD HAVE REALIZED--
WHAT?

THE MONSTER WAS VISIBLE ALL THE TIME.

BASILISK HEDGE--

THESS?

HELLO?

WELL, FUCK ME BLIND.

THIS ISN'T HOW I WANTED THINGS TO TURN OUT.

BEING A GHOST, THERE'S NOT AN AWFUL LOT I CAN DO TO HELP YOU OUT, THESS.

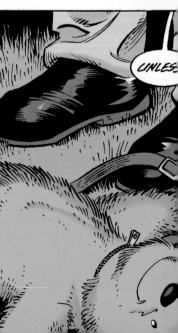

UNLES--

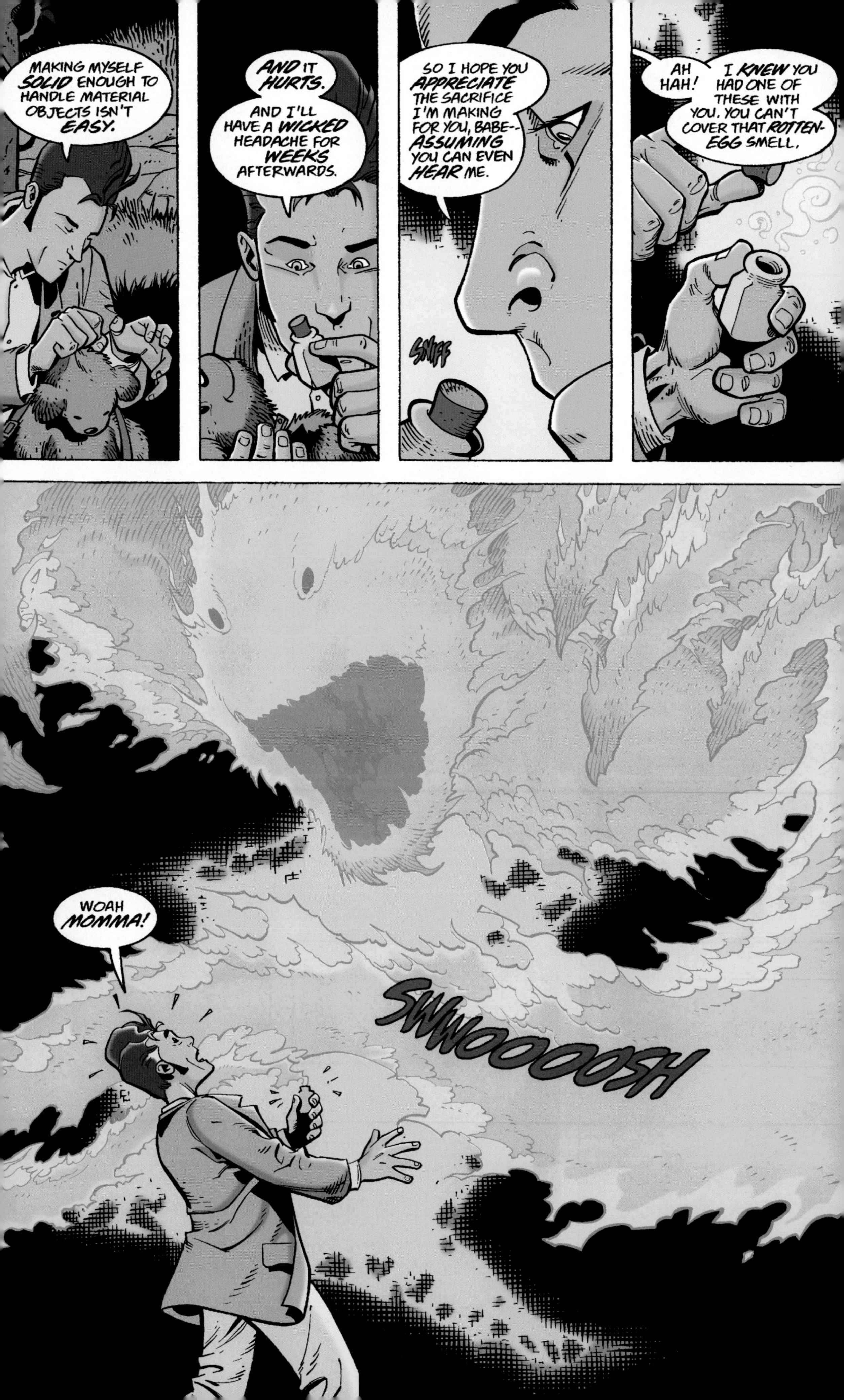
MAKING MYSELF SOLID ENOUGH TO HANDLE MATERIAL OBJECTS ISN'T EASY.
AND IT HURTS.
AND I'LL HAVE A WICKED HEADACHE FOR WEEKS AFTERWARDS.
SO I HOPE YOU APPRECIATE THE SACRIFICE I'M MAKING FOR YOU, BABE-- ASSUMING YOU CAN EVEN HEAR ME.
SNIFF
AH HAH!
I KNEW YOU HAD ONE OF THESE WITH YOU. YOU CAN'T COVER THAT ROTTEN-EGG SMELL.
WOAH MOMMA!
SWWOOOOOSH

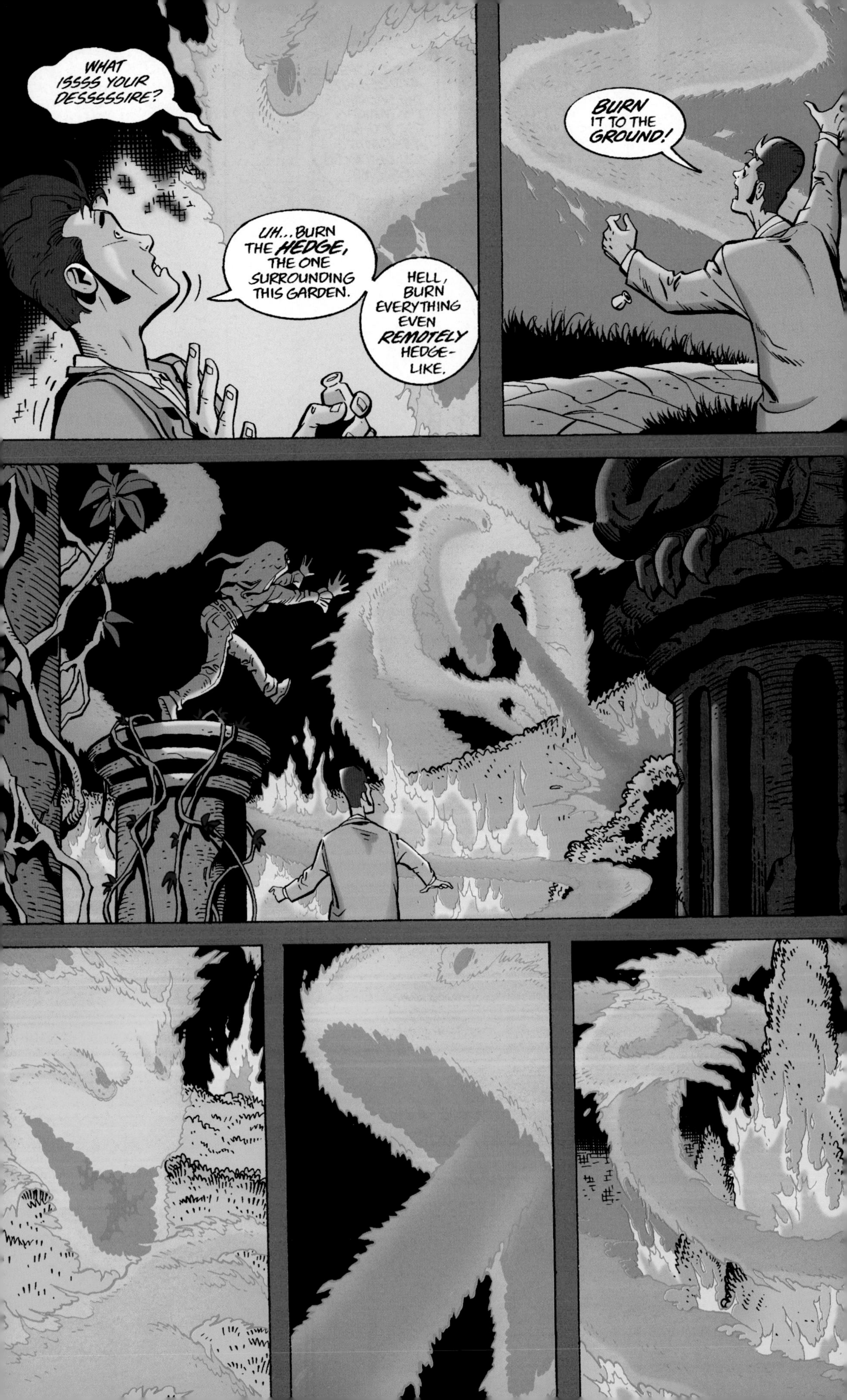
WHAT ISSSS YOUR DESSSSSIRE?
UH...BURN THE HEDGE, THE ONE SURROUNDING THIS GARDEN.
HELL, BURN EVERYTHING EVEN REMOTELY HEDGE-LIKE.
BURN IT TO THE GROUND!

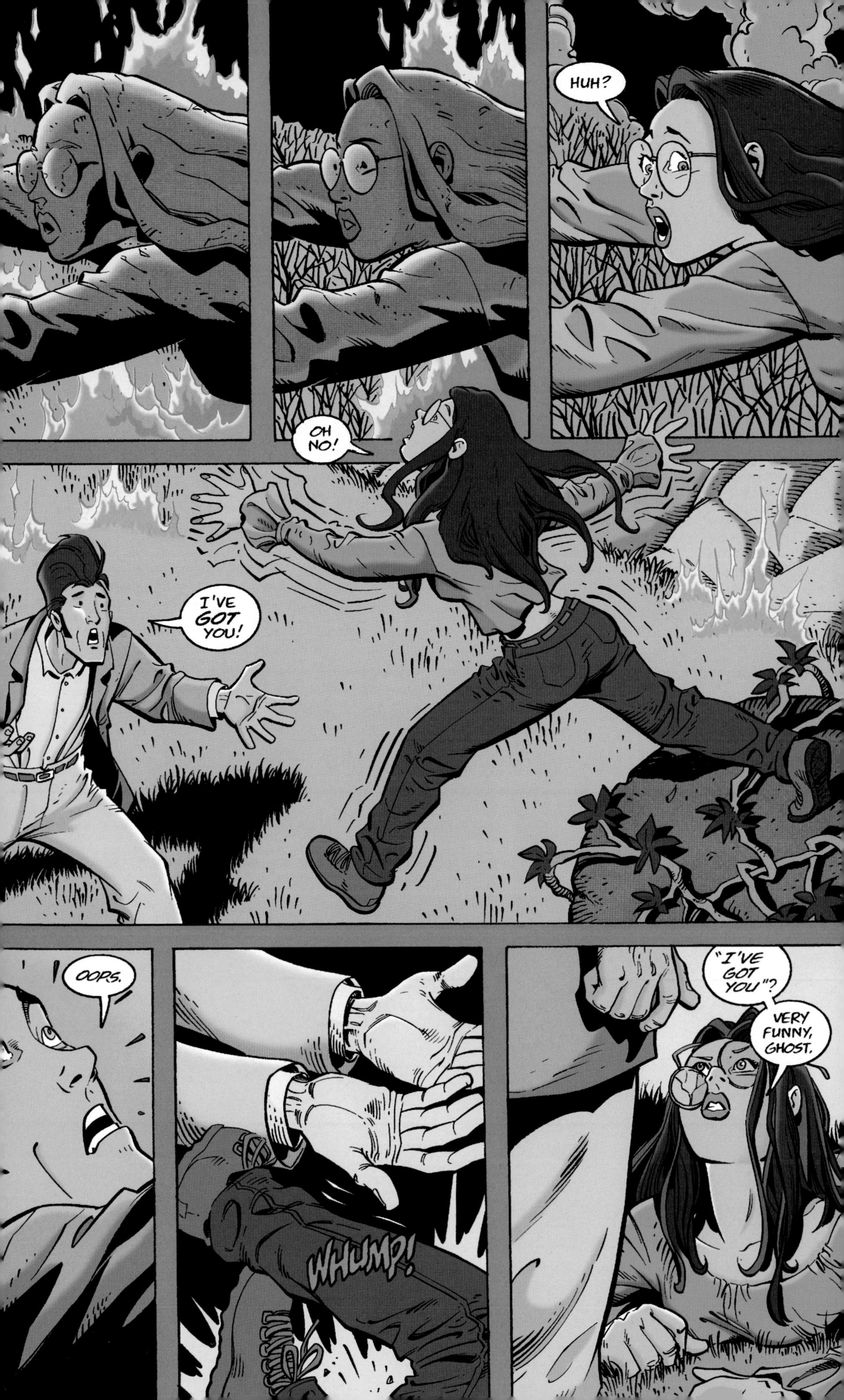
HUH?
OH NO!
I'VE GOT YOU!
OOPS.
WHUMP!
"I'VE GOT YOU"?
VERY FUNNY, GHOST.

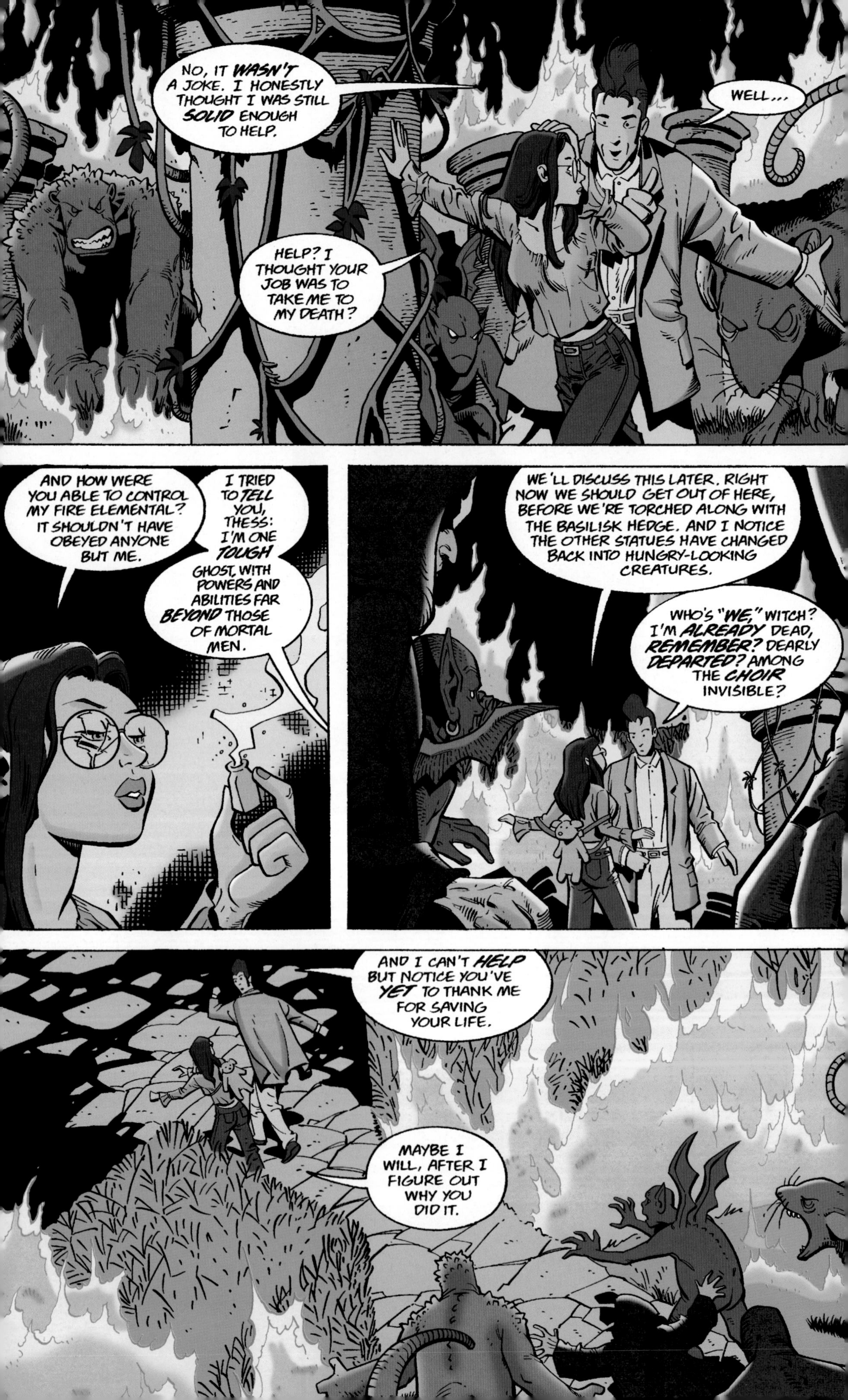
NO, IT WASN'T A JOKE. I HONESTLY THOUGHT I WAS STILL SOLID ENOUGH TO HELP.
WELL...
HELP? I THOUGHT YOUR JOB WAS TO TAKE ME TO MY DEATH?
AND HOW WERE YOU ABLE TO CONTROL MY FIRE ELEMENTAL? IT SHOULDN'T HAVE OBEYED ANYONE BUT ME.
I TRIED TO TELL YOU, THESS: I'M ONE TOUGH GHOST, WITH POWERS AND ABILITIES FAR BEYOND THOSE OF MORTAL MEN.
WE'LL DISCUSS THIS LATER. RIGHT NOW WE SHOULD GET OUT OF HERE, BEFORE WE'RE TORCHED ALONG WITH THE BASILISK HEDGE. AND I NOTICE THE OTHER STATUES HAVE CHANGED BACK INTO HUNGRY-LOOKING CREATURES.
WHO'S "WE," WITCH? I'M ALREADY DEAD, REMEMBER? DEARLY DEPARTED? AMONG THE CHOIR INVISIBLE?
AND I CAN'T HELP BUT NOTICE YOU'VE YET TO THANK ME FOR SAVING YOUR LIFE.
MAYBE I WILL, AFTER I FIGURE OUT WHY YOU DID IT.

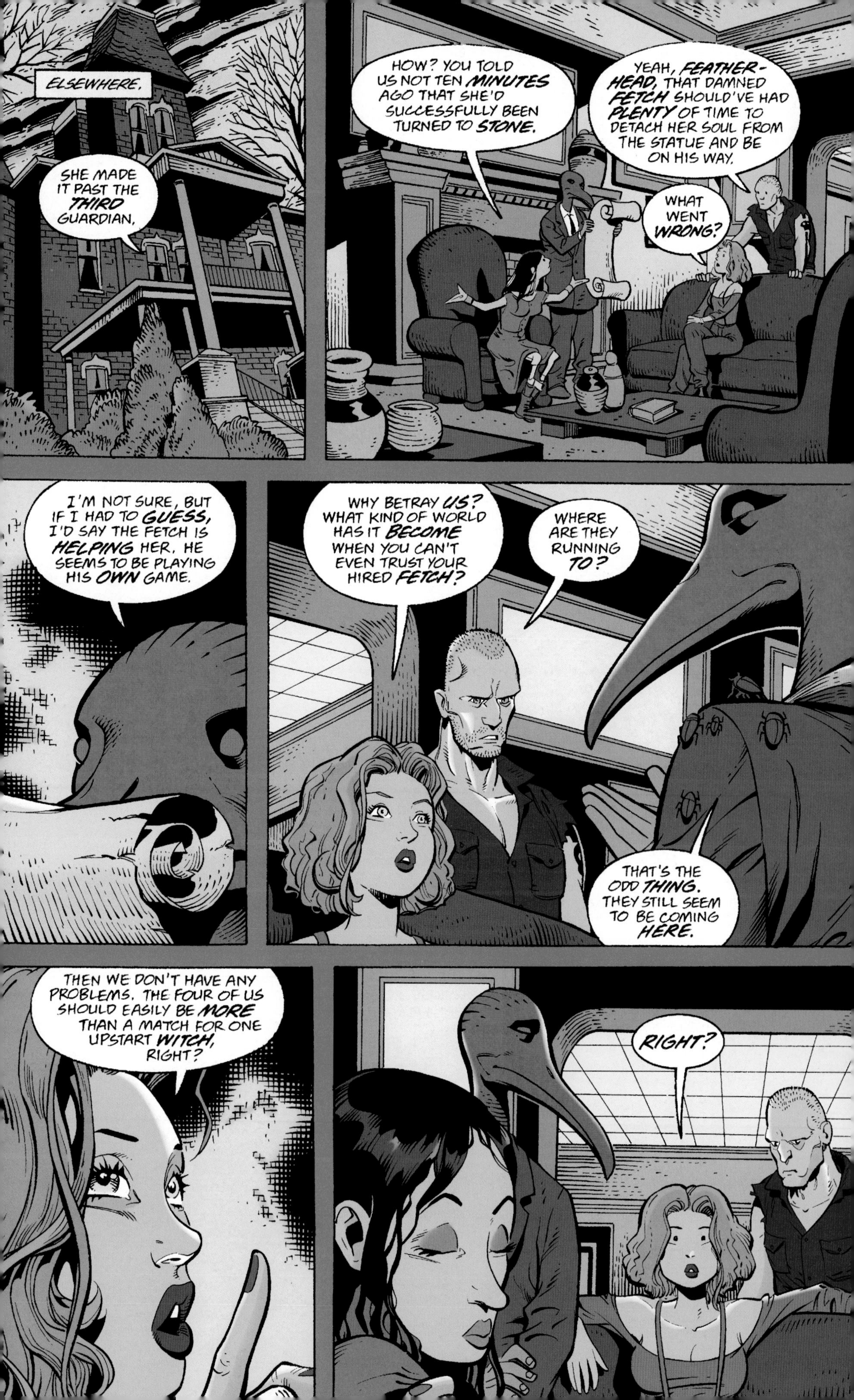
ELSEWHERE.
SHE MADE IT PAST THE THIRD GUARDIAN.
HOW? YOU TOLD US NOT TEN MINUTES AGO THAT SHE'D SUCCESSFULLY BEEN TURNED TO STONE.
YEAH, FEATHER-HEAD, THAT DAMNED FETCH SHOULD'VE HAD PLENTY OF TIME TO DETACH HER SOUL FROM THE STATUE AND BE ON HIS WAY.
WHAT WENT WRONG?
I'M NOT SURE, BUT IF I HAD TO GUESS, I'D SAY THE FETCH IS HELPING HER. HE SEEMS TO BE PLAYING HIS OWN GAME.
WHY BETRAY US? WHAT KIND OF WORLD HAS IT BECOME WHEN YOU CAN'T EVEN TRUST YOUR HIRED FETCH?
WHERE ARE THEY RUNNING TO?
THAT'S THE ODD THING. THEY STILL SEEM TO BE COMING HERE.
THEN WE DON'T HAVE ANY PROBLEMS. THE FOUR OF US SHOULD EASILY BE MORE THAN A MATCH FOR ONE UPSTART WITCH, RIGHT?
RIGHT?

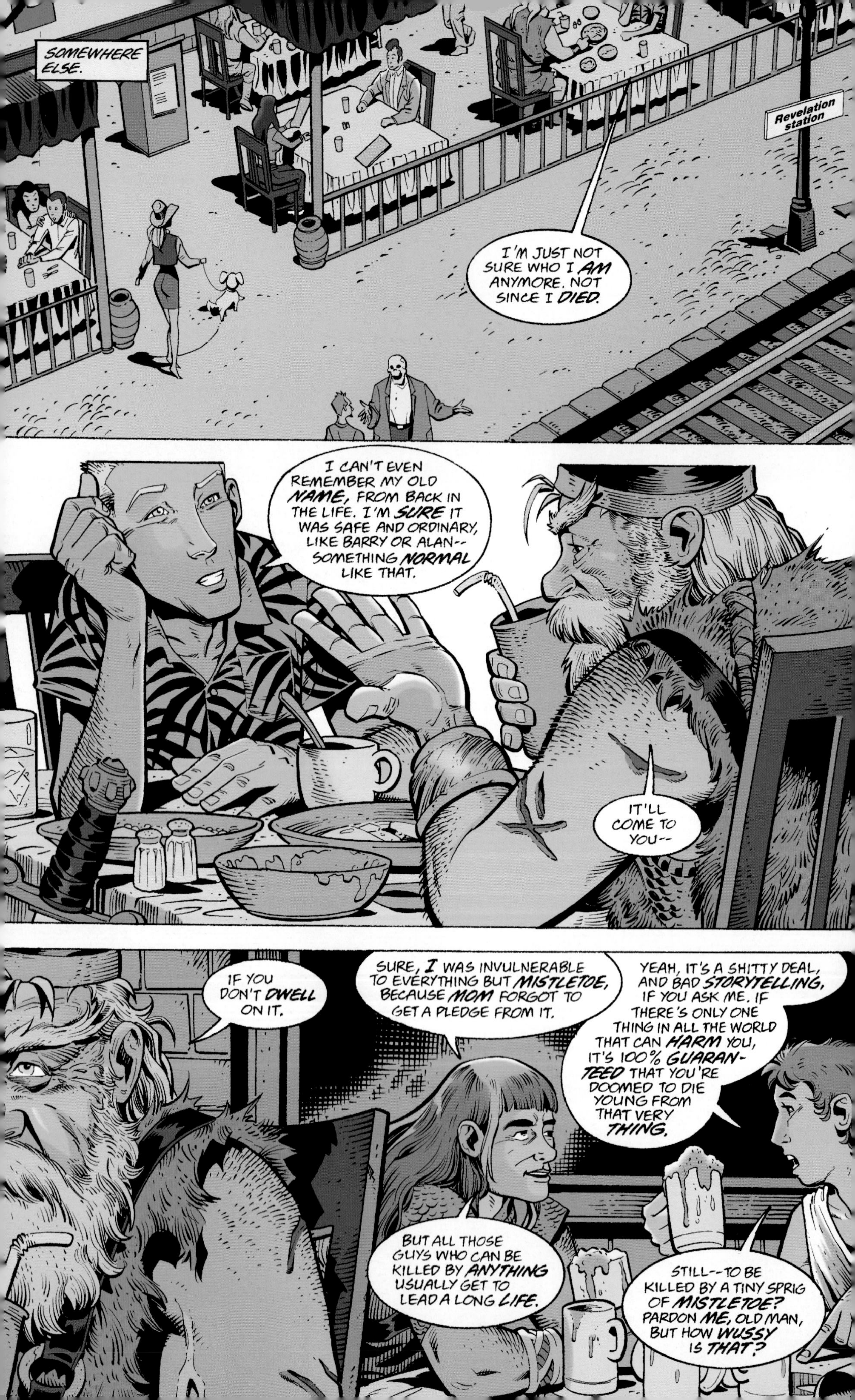
SOMEWHERE ELSE.
Revelation station
I'M JUST NOT SURE WHO I AM ANYMORE. NOT SINCE I DIED.
I CAN'T EVEN REMEMBER MY OLD NAME, FROM BACK IN THE LIFE. I'M SURE IT WAS SAFE AND ORDINARY, LIKE BARRY OR ALAN-- SOMETHING NORMAL LIKE THAT.
IT'LL COME TO YOU--
IF YOU DON'T DWELL ON IT.
SURE, I WAS INVULNERABLE TO EVERYTHING BUT MISTLETOE, BECAUSE MOM FORGOT TO GET A PLEDGE FROM IT.
YEAH, IT'S A SHITTY DEAL, AND BAD STORYTELLING, IF YOU ASK ME. IF THERE'S ONLY ONE THING IN ALL THE WORLD THAT CAN HARM YOU, IT'S 100% GUARANTEED THAT YOU'RE DOOMED TO DIE YOUNG FROM THAT VERY THING.
BUT ALL THOSE GUYS WHO CAN BE KILLED BY ANYTHING USUALLY GET TO LEAD A LONG LIFE.
STILL--TO BE KILLED BY A TINY SPRIG OF MISTLETOE? PARDON ME, OLD MAN, BUT HOW WUSSY IS THAT?

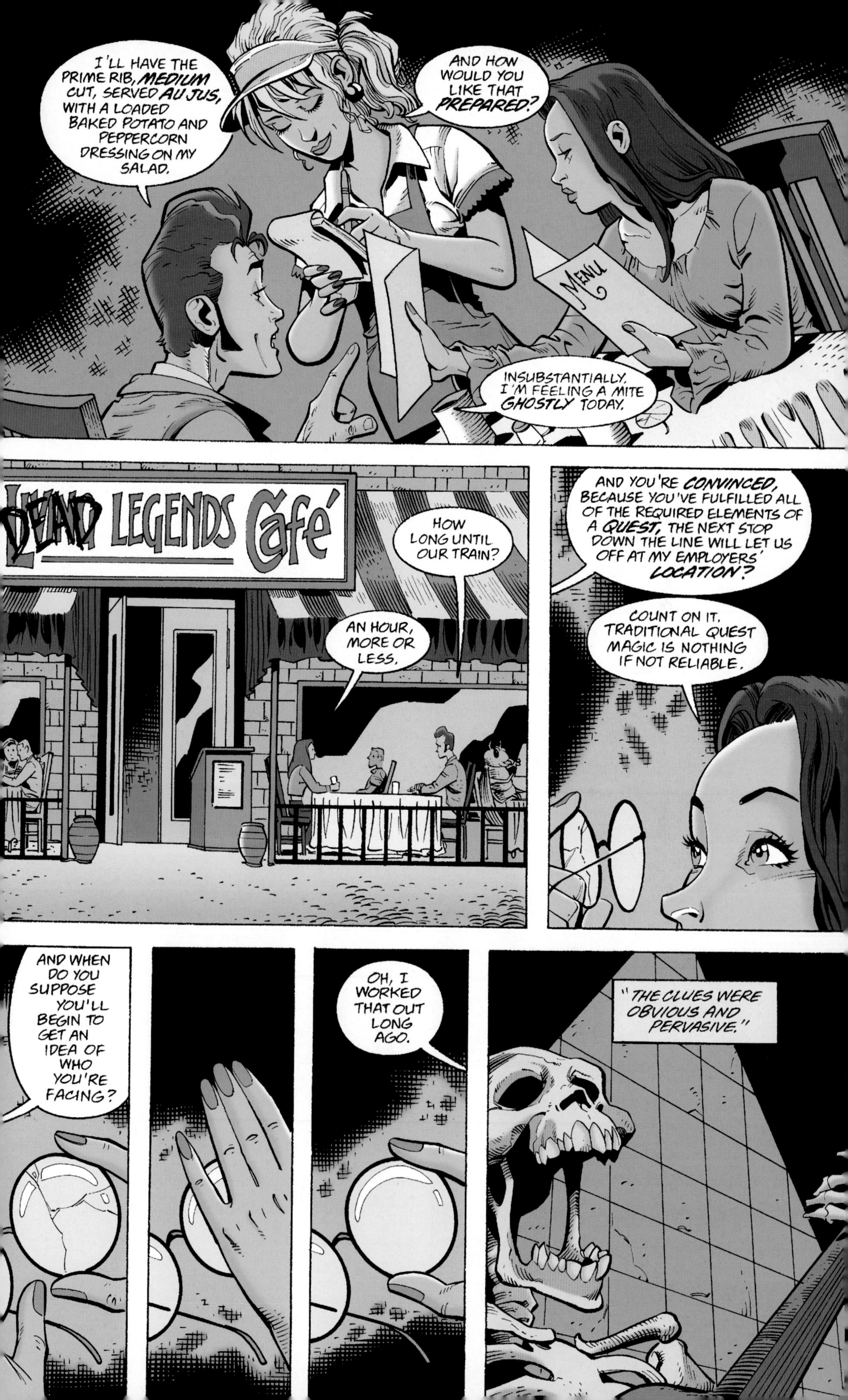
I'LL HAVE THE PRIME RIB, MEDIUM CUT, SERVED AU JUS, WITH A LOADED BAKED POTATO AND PEPPERCORN DRESSING ON MY SALAD.
AND HOW WOULD YOU LIKE THAT PREPARED?
INSUBSTANTIALLY. I'M FEELING A MITE GHOSTLY TODAY.
MENU
DEAD LEGENDS Café
HOW LONG UNTIL OUR TRAIN?
AN HOUR, MORE OR LESS.
AND YOU'RE CONVINCED, BECAUSE YOU'VE FULFILLED ALL OF THE REQUIRED ELEMENTS OF A QUEST, THE NEXT STOP DOWN THE LINE WILL LET US OFF AT MY EMPLOYERS' LOCATION?
COUNT ON IT. TRADITIONAL QUEST MAGIC IS NOTHING IF NOT RELIABLE.
AND WHEN DO YOU SUPPOSE YOU'LL BEGIN TO GET AN IDEA OF WHO YOU'RE FACING?
OH, I WORKED THAT OUT LONG AGO.
"THE CLUES WERE OBVIOUS AND PERVASIVE."

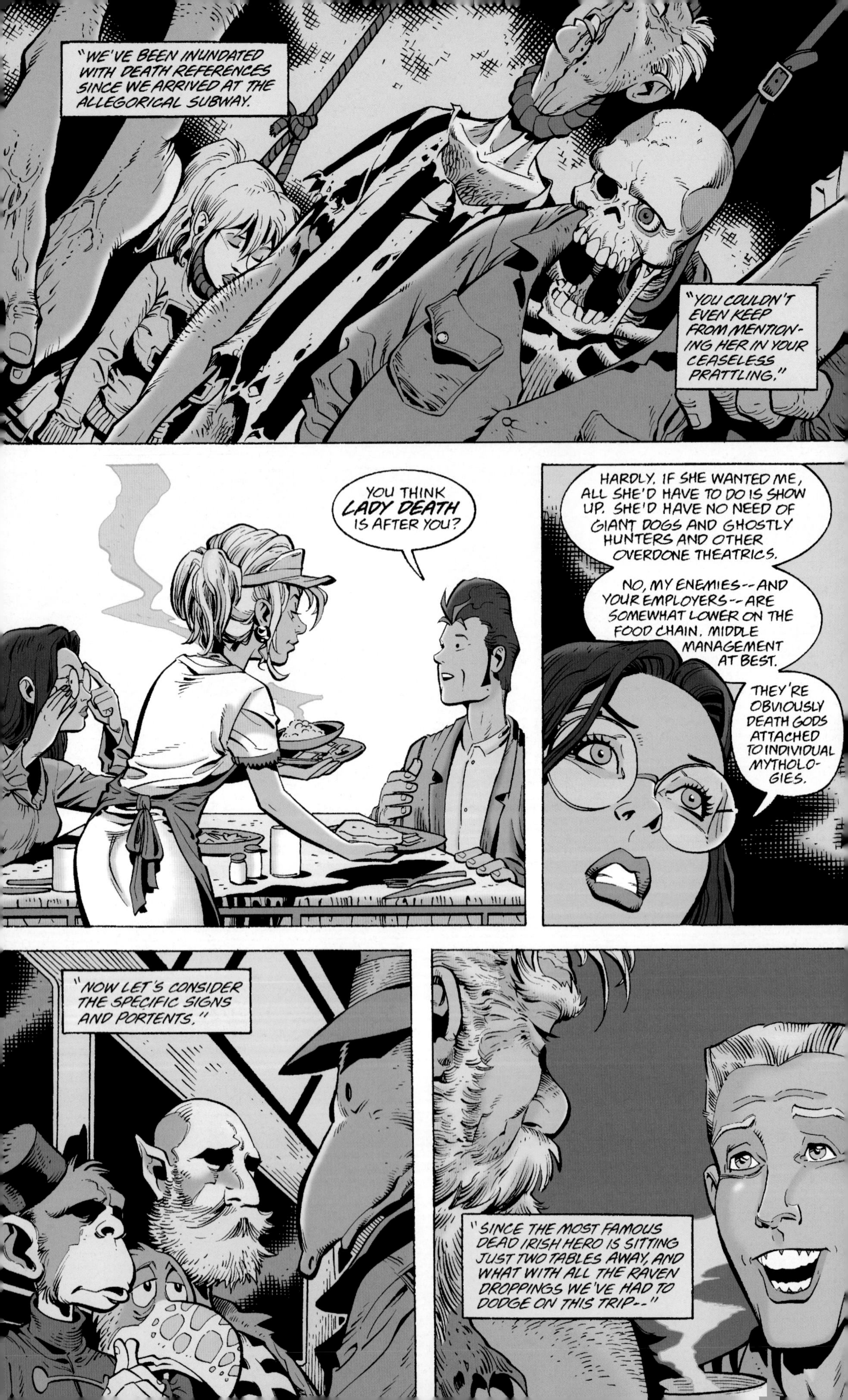
"WE'VE BEEN INUNDATED WITH DEATH REFERENCES SINCE WE ARRIVED AT THE ALLEGORICAL SUBWAY.
"YOU COULDN'T EVEN KEEP FROM MENTIONING HER IN YOUR CEASELESS PRATTLING."
YOU THINK LADY DEATH IS AFTER YOU?
HARDLY. IF SHE WANTED ME, ALL SHE'D HAVE TO DO IS SHOW UP. SHE'D HAVE NO NEED OF GIANT DOGS AND GHOSTLY HUNTERS AND OTHER OVERDONE THEATRICS.
NO, MY ENEMIES--AND YOUR EMPLOYERS--ARE SOMEWHAT LOWER ON THE FOOD CHAIN. MIDDLE MANAGEMENT AT BEST.
THEY'RE OBVIOUSLY DEATH GODS ATTACHED TO INDIVIDUAL MYTHOLOGIES.
"NOW LET'S CONSIDER THE SPECIFIC SIGNS AND PORTENTS."
"SINCE THE MOST FAMOUS DEAD IRISH HERO IS SITTING JUST TWO TABLES AWAY, AND WHAT WITH ALL THE RAVEN DROPPINGS WE'VE HAD TO DODGE ON THIS TRIP--"

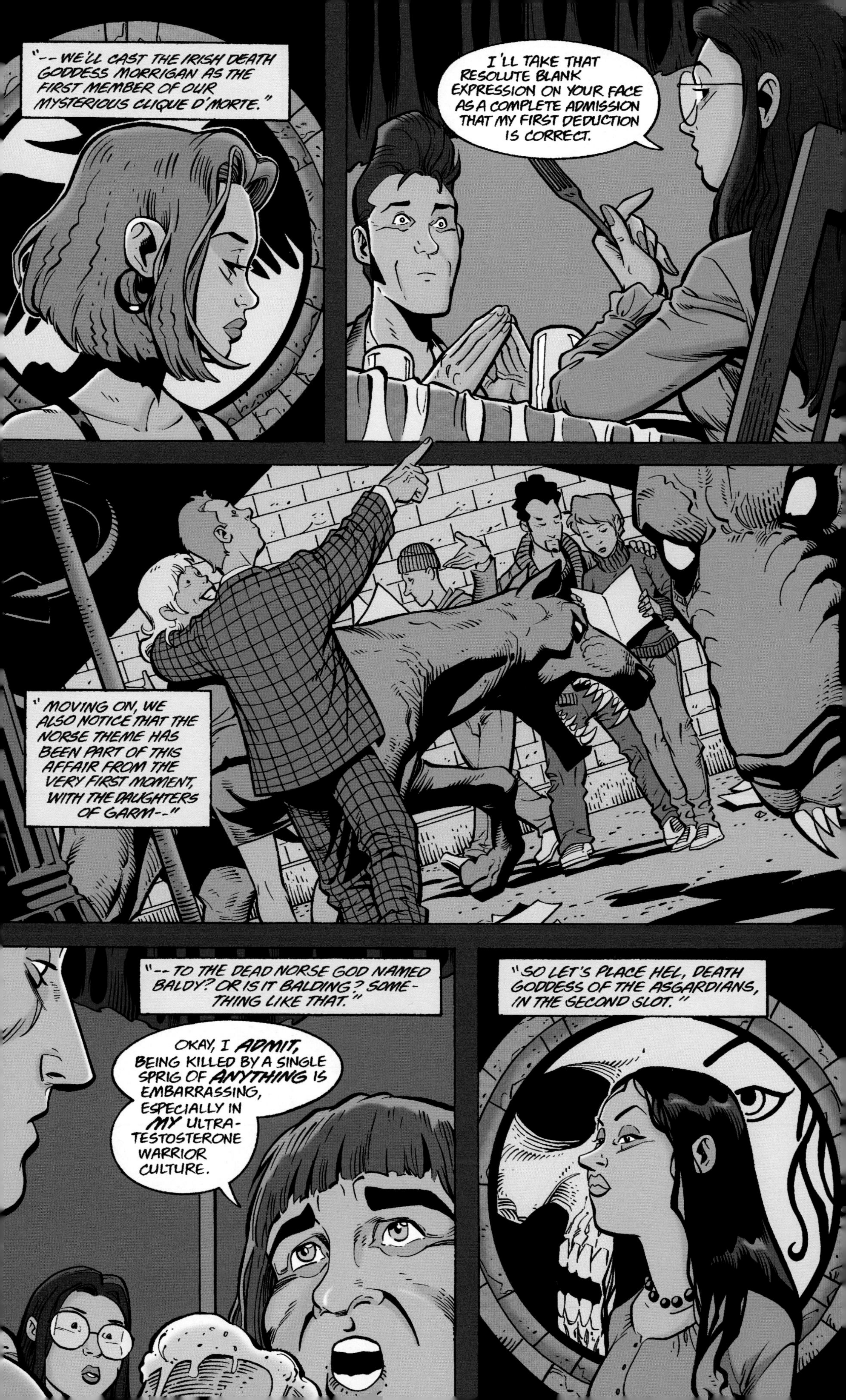
"--WE'LL CAST THE IRISH DEATH GODDESS MORRIGAN AS THE FIRST MEMBER OF OUR MYSTERIOUS CLIQUE D'MORTE."
I'LL TAKE THAT RESOLUTE BLANK EXPRESSION ON YOUR FACE AS A COMPLETE ADMISSION THAT MY FIRST DEDUCTION IS CORRECT.
"MOVING ON, WE ALSO NOTICE THAT THE NORSE THEME HAS BEEN PART OF THIS AFFAIR FROM THE VERY FIRST MOMENT, WITH THE DAUGHTERS OF GARM--"
"--TO THE DEAD NORSE GOD NAMED BALDY? OR IS IT BALDING? SOMETHING LIKE THAT."
OKAY, I ADMIT, BEING KILLED BY A SINGLE SPRIG OF ANYTHING IS EMBARRASSING, ESPECIALLY IN MY ULTRA-TESTOSTERONE WARRIOR CULTURE.
"SO LET'S PLACE HEL, DEATH GODDESS OF THE ASGARDIANS, IN THE SECOND SLOT."

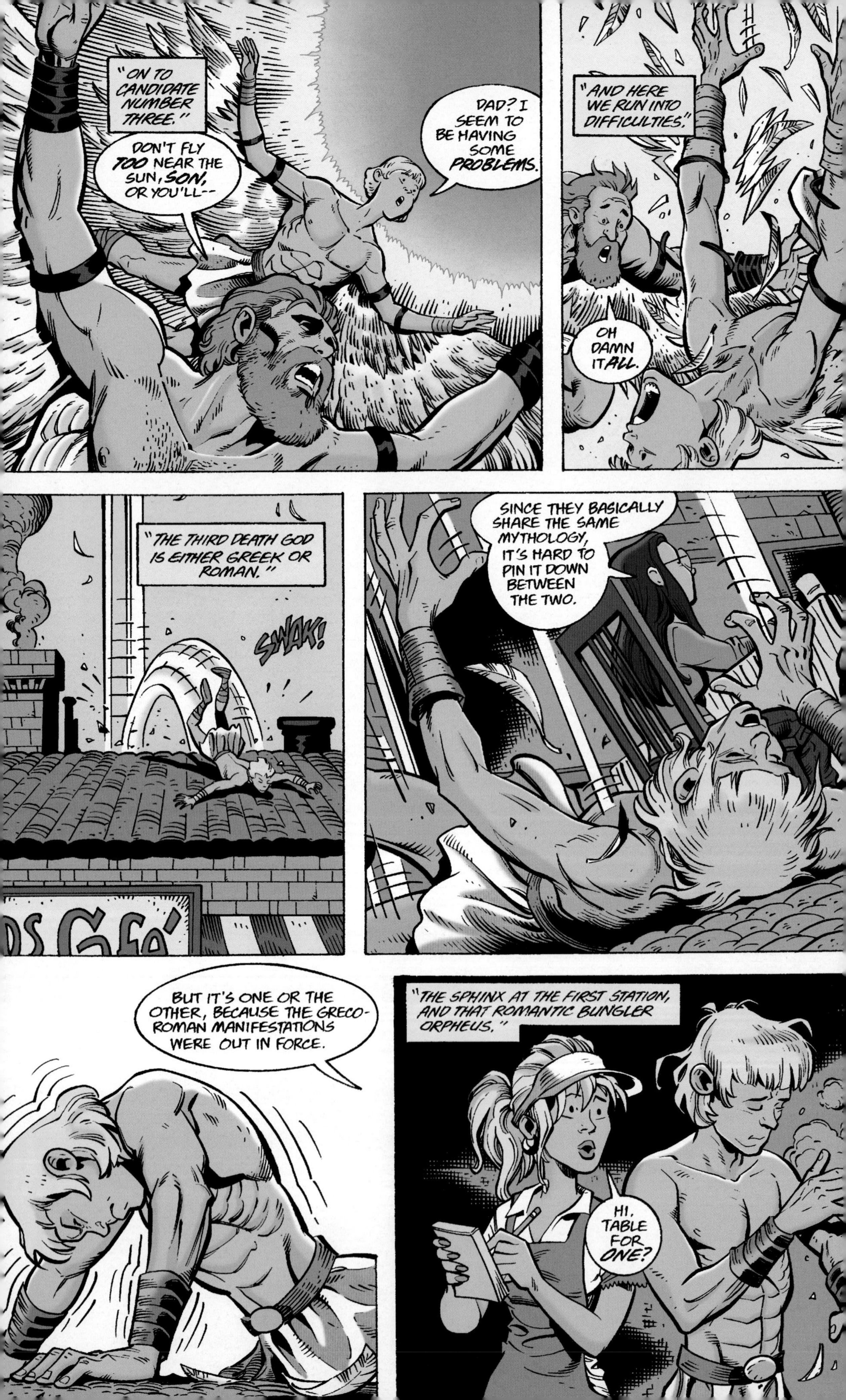
"ON TO CANDIDATE NUMBER THREE."
DON'T FLY TOO NEAR THE SUN, SON, OR YOU'LL--
DAD? I SEEM TO BE HAVING SOME PROBLEMS.
"AND HERE WE RUN INTO DIFFICULTIES."
OH DAMN IT ALL.
"THE THIRD DEATH GOD IS EITHER GREEK OR ROMAN."
SWAK!
SINCE THEY BASICALLY SHARE THE SAME MYTHOLOGY, IT'S HARD TO PIN IT DOWN BETWEEN THE TWO.
BUT IT'S ONE OR THE OTHER, BECAUSE THE GRECO-ROMAN MANIFESTATIONS WERE OUT IN FORCE.
"THE SPHINX AT THE FIRST STATION, AND THAT ROMANTIC BUNGLER ORPHEUS."
HI. TABLE FOR ONE?

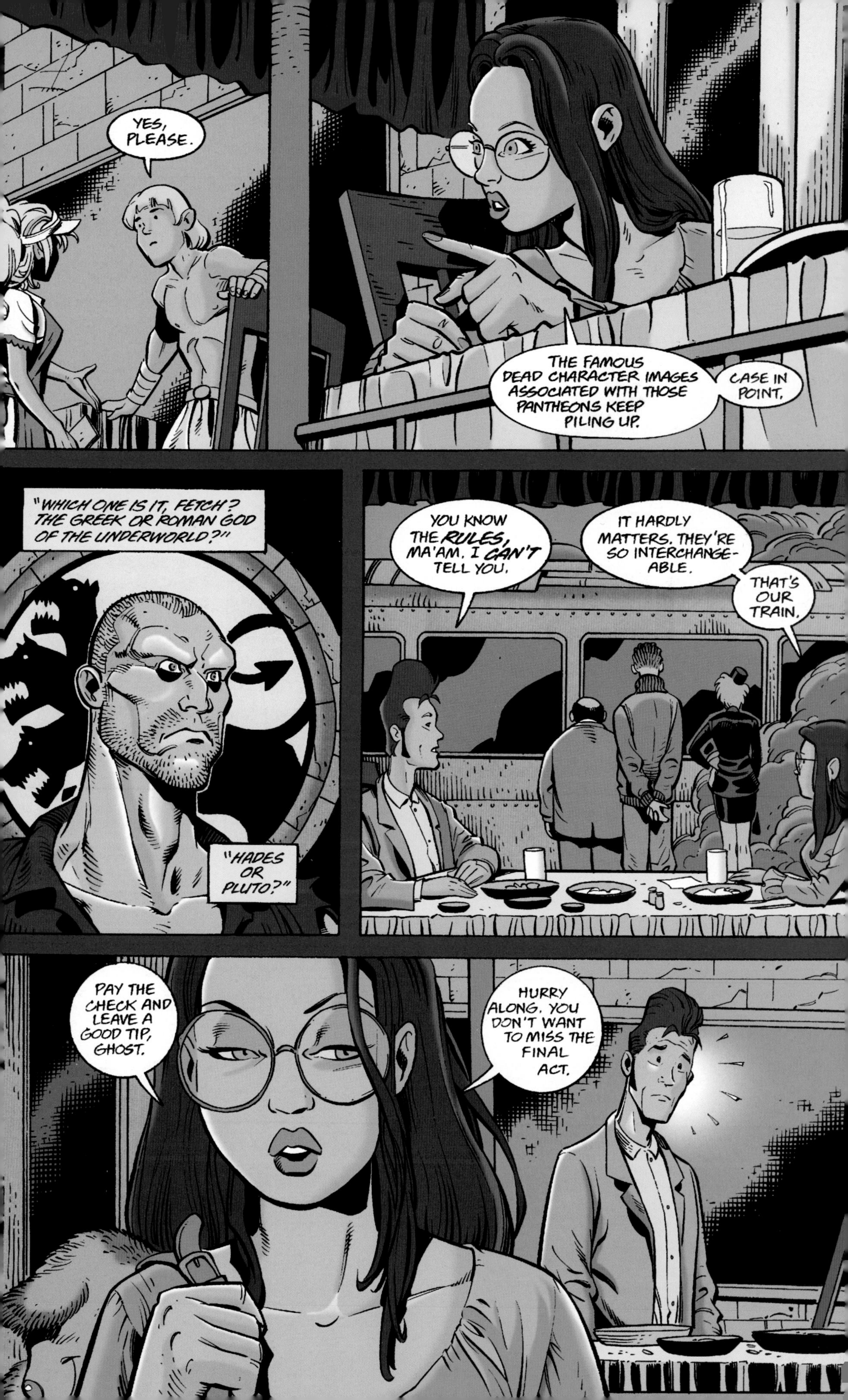
YES, PLEASE.
THE FAMOUS DEAD CHARACTER IMAGES ASSOCIATED WITH THOSE PANTHEONS KEEP PILING UP.
CASE IN POINT.
"WHICH ONE IS IT, FETCH? THE GREEK OR ROMAN GOD OF THE UNDERWORLD?"
"HADES OR PLUTO?"
YOU KNOW THE *RULES*, MA'AM. I *CAN'T* TELL YOU.
IT HARDLY MATTERS. THEY'RE SO INTERCHANGE-ABLE.
THAT'S OUR TRAIN.
PAY THE CHECK AND LEAVE A GOOD TIP, GHOST.
HURRY ALONG. YOU DON'T WANT TO MISS THE FINAL ACT.

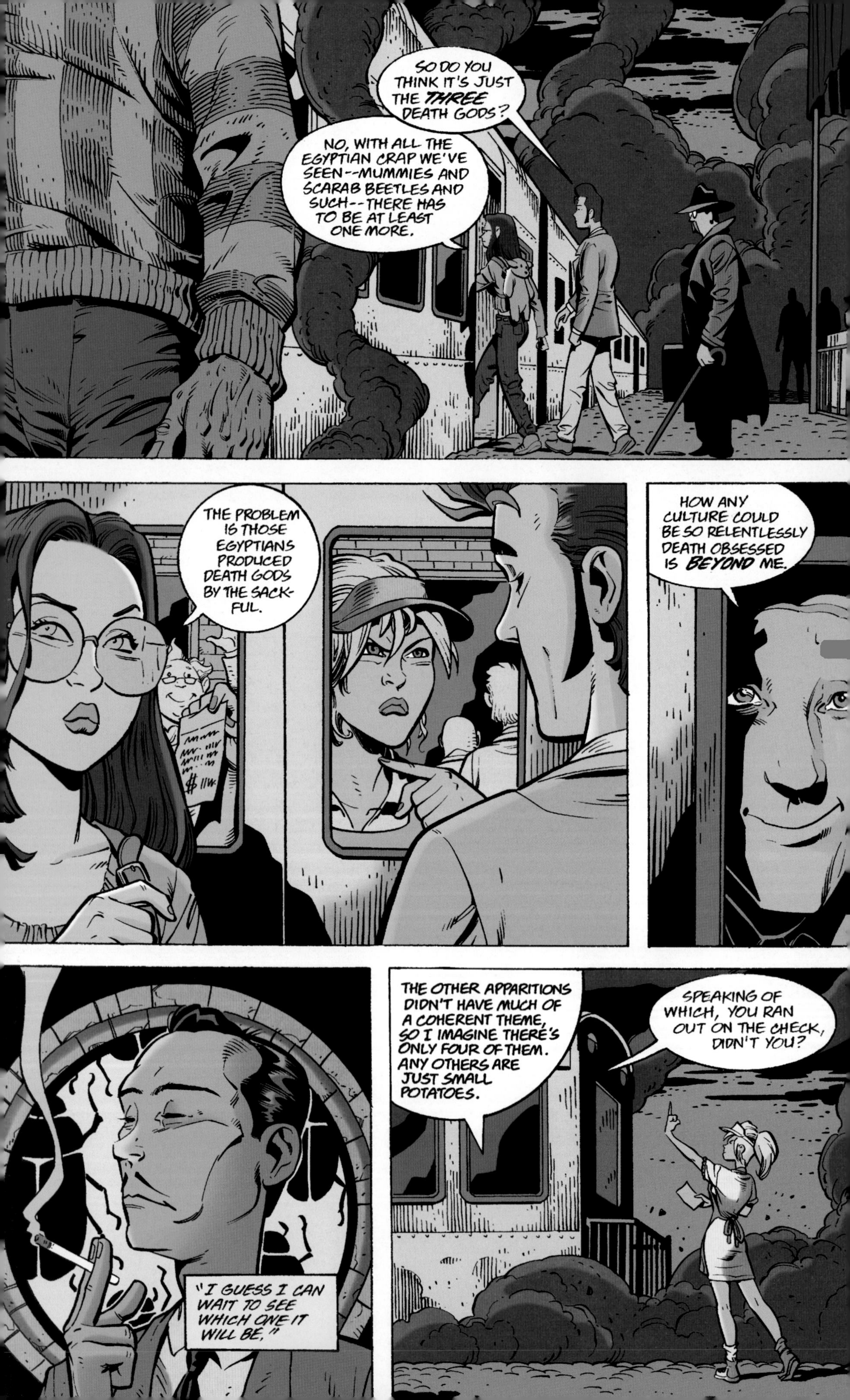

SO DO YOU THINK IT'S JUST THE *THREE* DEATH GODS?
NO, WITH ALL THE EGYPTIAN CRAP WE'VE SEEN--MUMMIES AND SCARAB BEETLES AND SUCH--THERE HAS TO BE AT LEAST ONE MORE.
THE PROBLEM IS THOSE EGYPTIANS PRODUCED DEATH GODS BY THE SACK-FUL.
HOW ANY CULTURE COULD BE SO RELENTLESSLY DEATH OBSESSED IS *BEYOND* ME.
"I GUESS I CAN WAIT TO SEE WHICH ONE IT WILL BE."
THE OTHER APPARITIONS DIDN'T HAVE MUCH OF A COHERENT THEME, SO I IMAGINE THERE'S ONLY FOUR OF THEM. ANY OTHERS ARE JUST SMALL POTATOES.
SPEAKING OF WHICH, YOU RAN OUT ON THE CHECK, DIDN'T YOU?

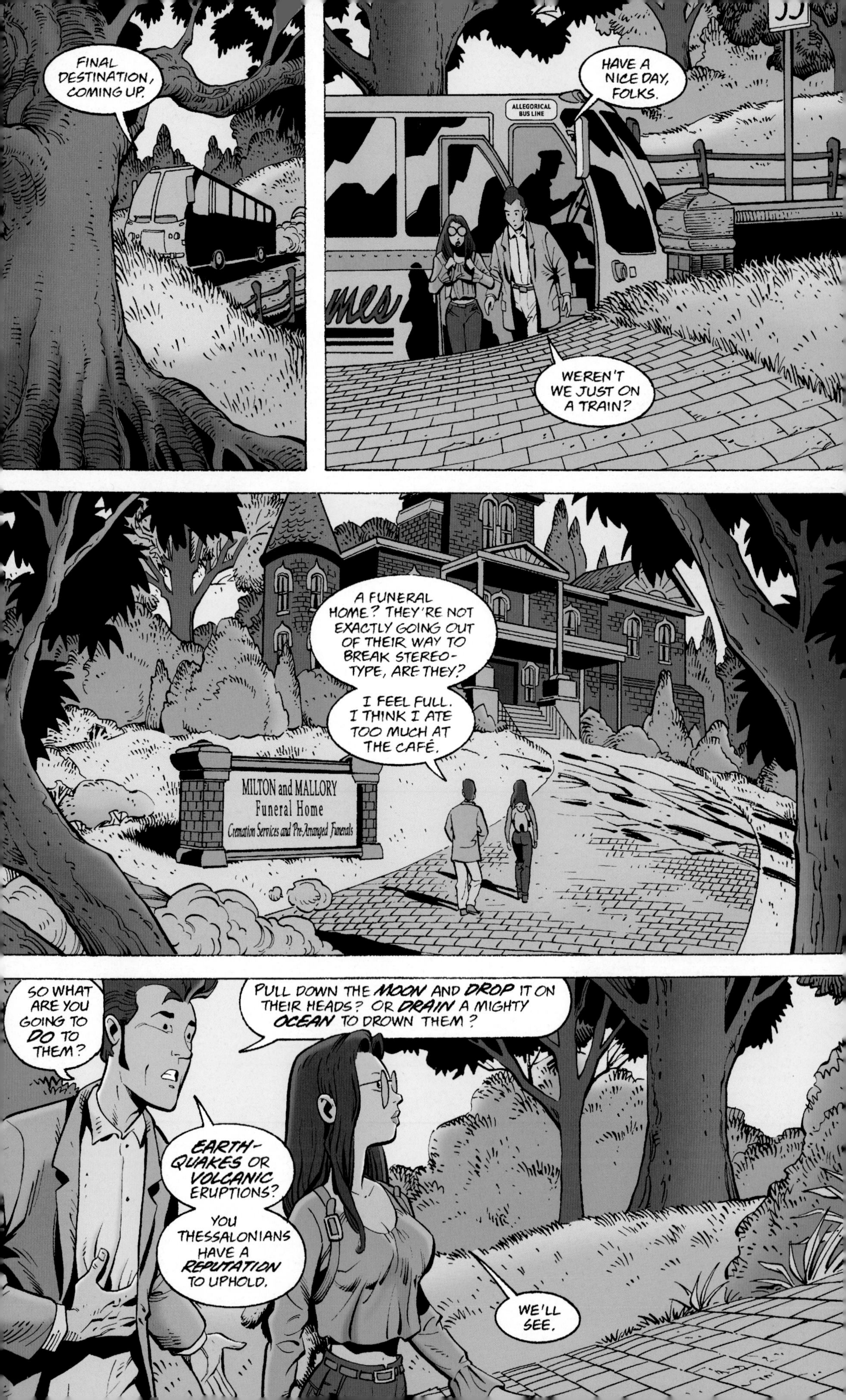
FINAL DESTINATION, COMING UP.
HAVE A NICE DAY, FOLKS.
ALLEGORICAL BUS LINE
WEREN'T WE JUST ON A TRAIN?
A FUNERAL HOME? THEY'RE NOT EXACTLY GOING OUT OF THEIR WAY TO BREAK STEREO-TYPE, ARE THEY?
I FEEL FULL. I THINK I ATE TOO MUCH AT THE CAFÉ.
MILTON and MALLORY Funeral Home Cremation Services and Pre-Arranged Funerals
SO WHAT ARE YOU GOING TO DO TO THEM?
PULL DOWN THE MOON AND DROP IT ON THEIR HEADS? OR DRAIN A MIGHTY OCEAN TO DROWN THEM?
EARTH-QUAKES OR VOLCANIC ERUPTIONS?
YOU THESSALONIANS HAVE A REPUTATION TO UPHOLD.
WE'LL SEE.

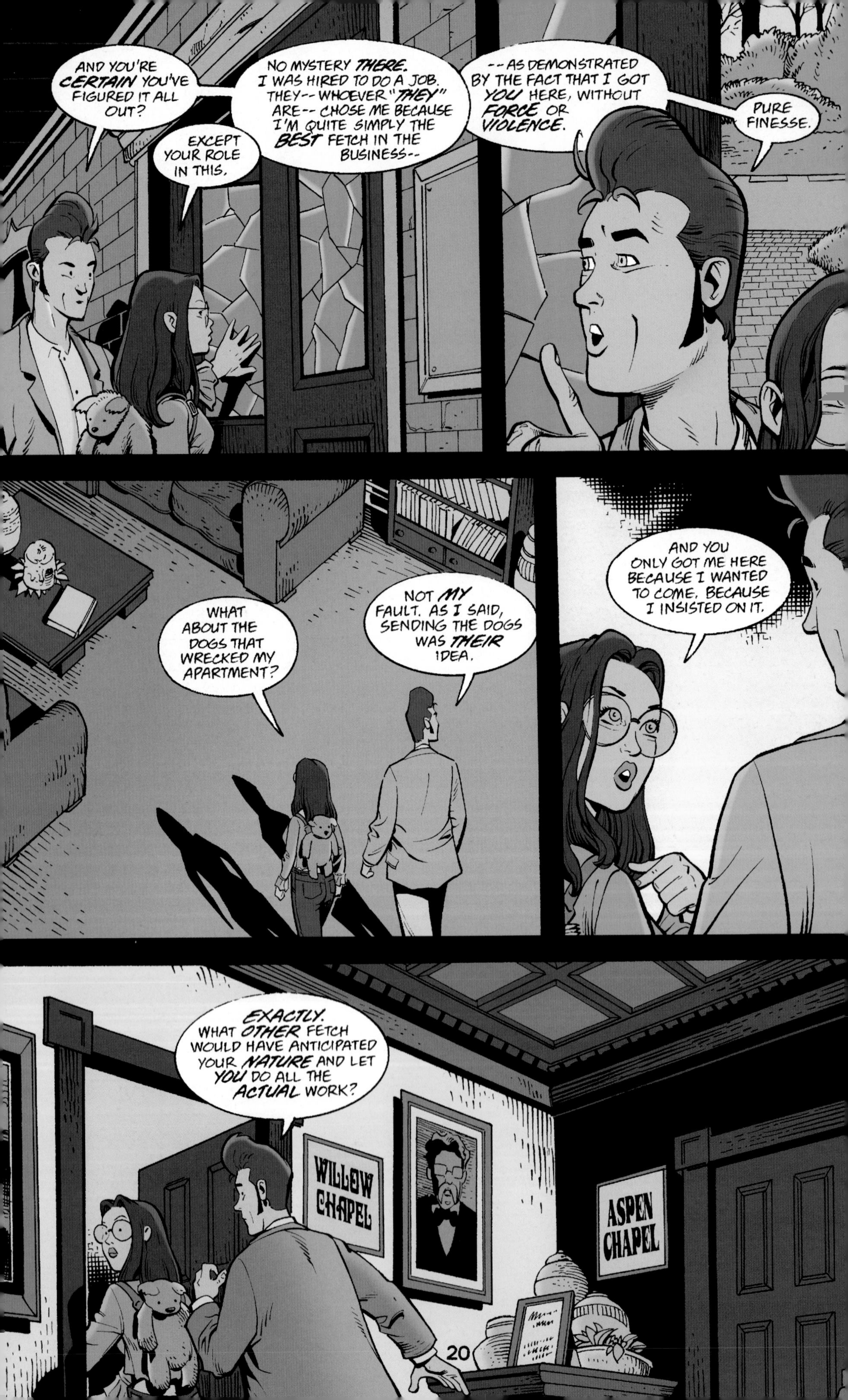
AND YOU'RE CERTAIN YOU'VE FIGURED IT ALL OUT?
EXCEPT YOUR ROLE IN THIS.
NO MYSTERY THERE. I WAS HIRED TO DO A JOB. THEY-- WHOEVER "THEY" ARE-- CHOSE ME BECAUSE I'M QUITE SIMPLY THE BEST FETCH IN THE BUSINESS--
--AS DEMONSTRATED BY THE FACT THAT I GOT YOU HERE, WITHOUT FORCE OR VIOLENCE.
PURE FINESSE.
WHAT ABOUT THE DOGS THAT WRECKED MY APARTMENT?
NOT MY FAULT. AS I SAID, SENDING THE DOGS WAS THEIR IDEA.
AND YOU ONLY GOT ME HERE BECAUSE I WANTED TO COME. BECAUSE I INSISTED ON IT.
EXACTLY. WHAT OTHER FETCH WOULD HAVE ANTICIPATED YOUR NATURE AND LET YOU DO ALL THE ACTUAL WORK?
WILLOW CHAPEL
ASPEN CHAPEL

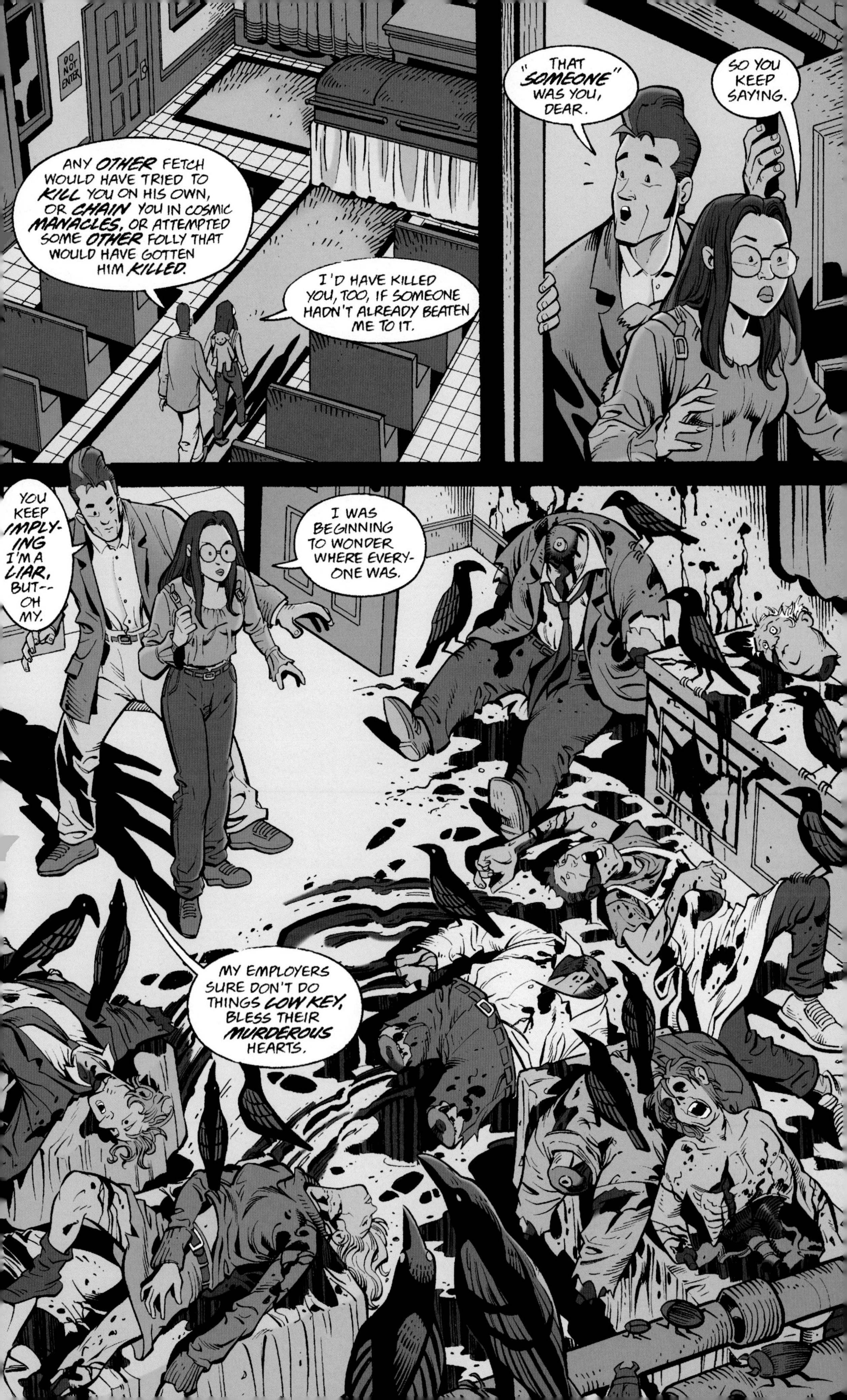
ANY OTHER FETCH WOULD HAVE TRIED TO KILL YOU ON HIS OWN, OR CHAIN YOU IN COSMIC MANACLES, OR ATTEMPTED SOME OTHER FOLLY THAT WOULD HAVE GOTTEN HIM KILLED.
I'D HAVE KILLED YOU, TOO, IF SOMEONE HADN'T ALREADY BEATEN ME TO IT.
"THAT "SOMEONE" WAS YOU, DEAR.
SO YOU KEEP SAYING.
YOU KEEP IMPLY-ING I'M A LIAR, BUT-- OH MY.
I WAS BEGINNING TO WONDER WHERE EVERY-ONE WAS.
MY EMPLOYERS SURE DON'T DO THINGS LOW KEY, BLESS THEIR MURDEROUS HEARTS.
DO NOT ENTER

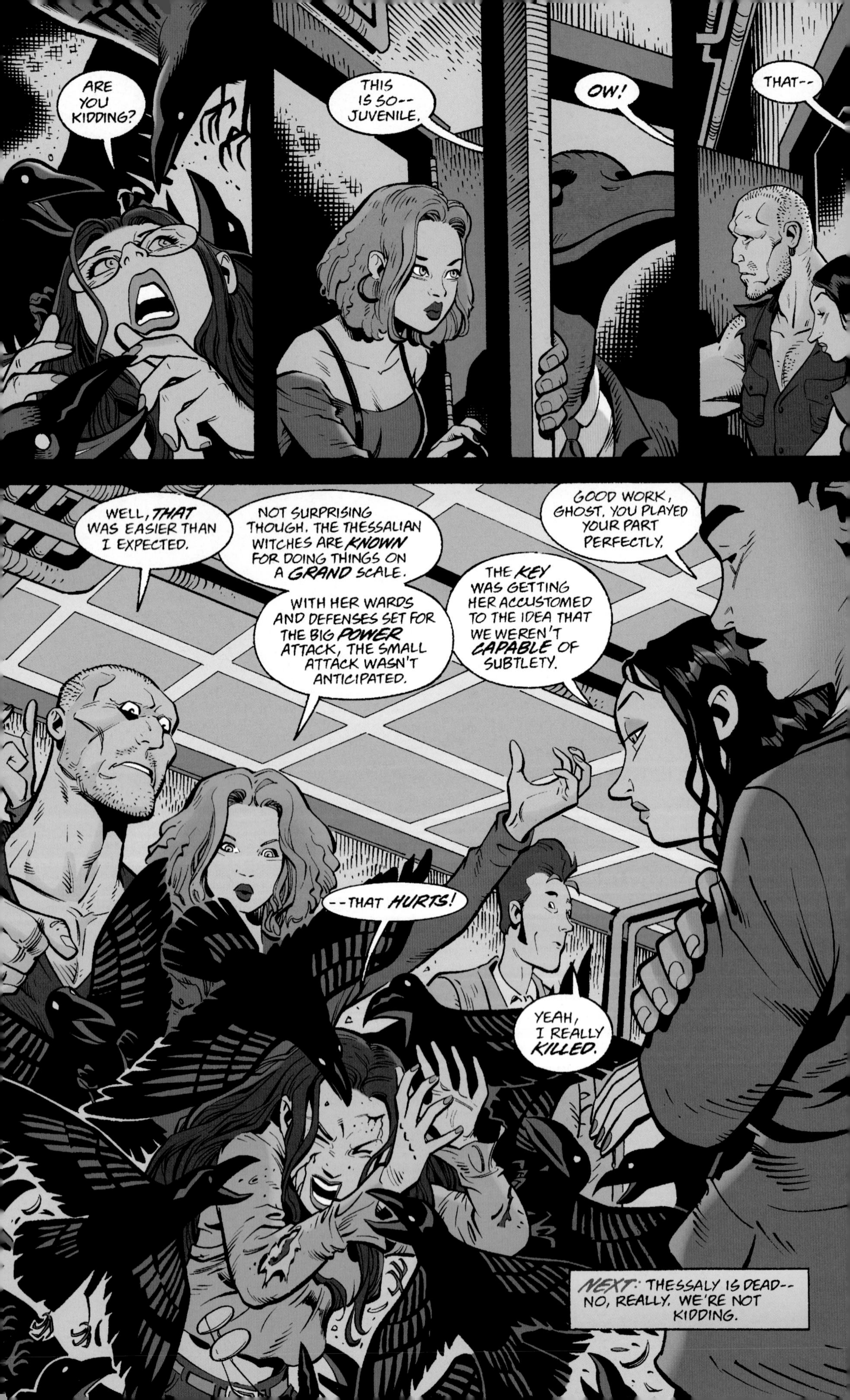
ARE YOU KIDDING?
THIS IS SO-- JUVENILE.
OW!
THAT--
WELL, THAT WAS EASIER THAN I EXPECTED.
NOT SURPRISING THOUGH. THE THESSALIAN WITCHES ARE KNOWN FOR DOING THINGS ON A GRAND SCALE.
WITH HER WARDS AND DEFENSES SET FOR THE BIG POWER ATTACK, THE SMALL ATTACK WASN'T ANTICIPATED.
THE KEY WAS GETTING HER ACCUSTOMED TO THE IDEA THAT WE WEREN'T CAPABLE OF SUBTLETY.
GOOD WORK, GHOST. YOU PLAYED YOUR PART PERFECTLY.
--THAT HURTS!
YEAH, I REALLY KILLED.
NEXT: THESSALY IS DEAD-- NO, REALLY. WE'RE NOT KIDDING.

the sandman presents

The Thessaliad

Part Four:
SOUL FOOD

Or, So Much for Clever Hidden Plans

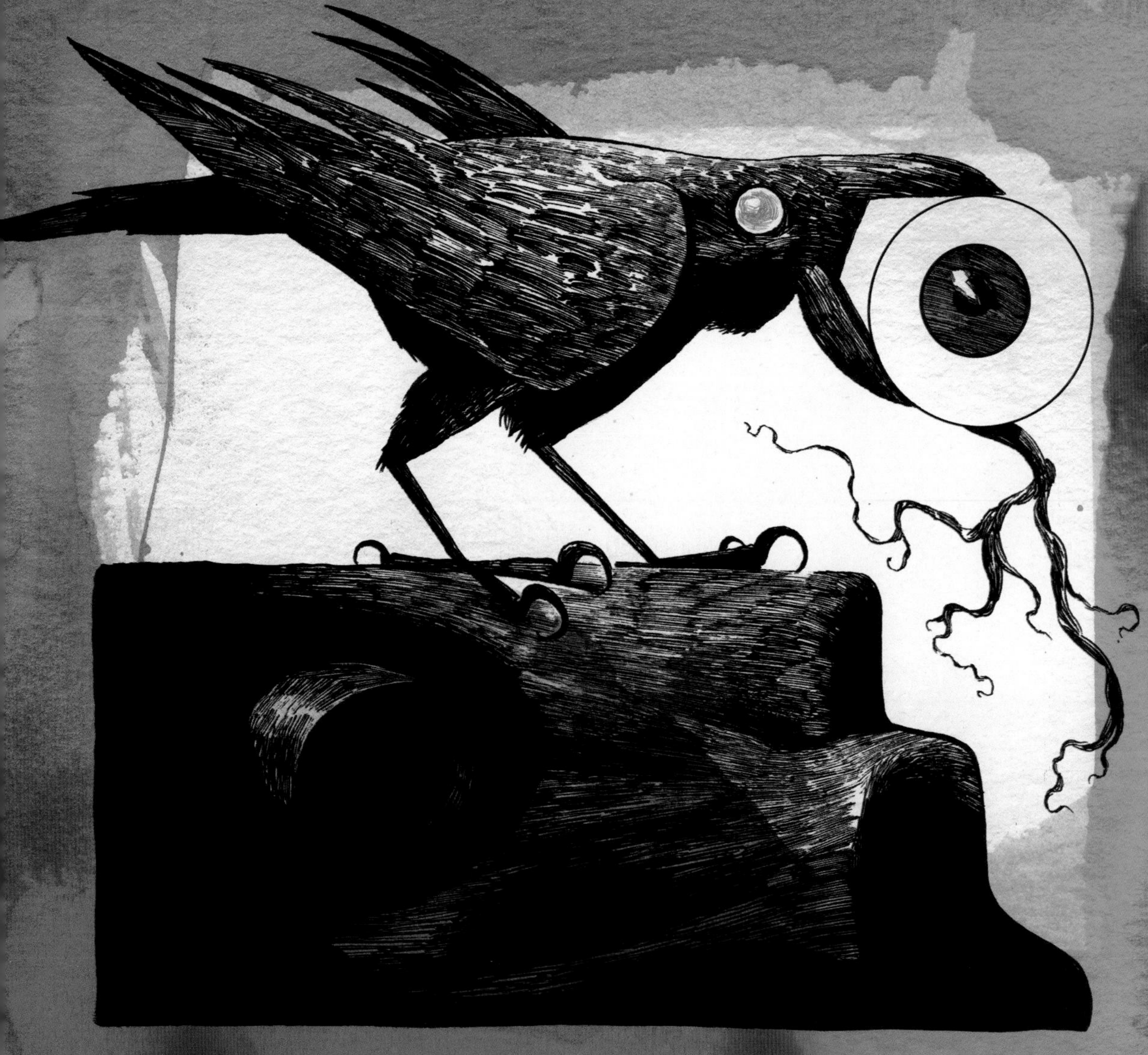

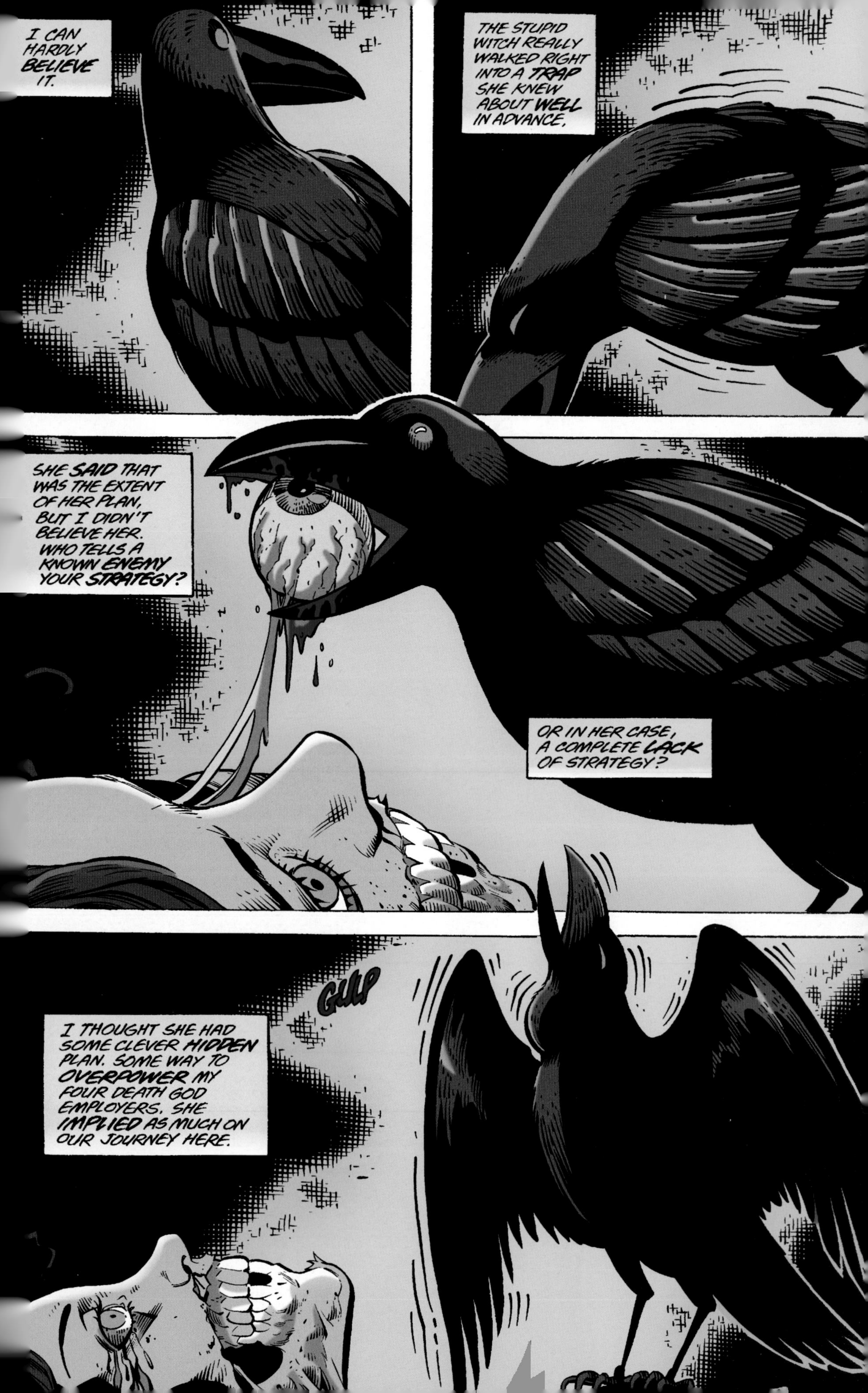
I CAN HARDLY BELIEVE IT.
THE STUPID WITCH REALLY WALKED RIGHT INTO A TRAP SHE KNEW ABOUT WELL IN ADVANCE.
SHE SAID THAT WAS THE EXTENT OF HER PLAN, BUT I DIDN'T BELIEVE HER. WHO TELLS A KNOWN ENEMY YOUR STRATEGY?
OR IN HER CASE, A COMPLETE LACK OF STRATEGY?
GULP
I THOUGHT SHE HAD SOME CLEVER HIDDEN PLAN. SOME WAY TO OVERPOWER MY FOUR DEATH GOD EMPLOYERS. SHE IMPLIED AS MUCH ON OUR JOURNEY HERE.

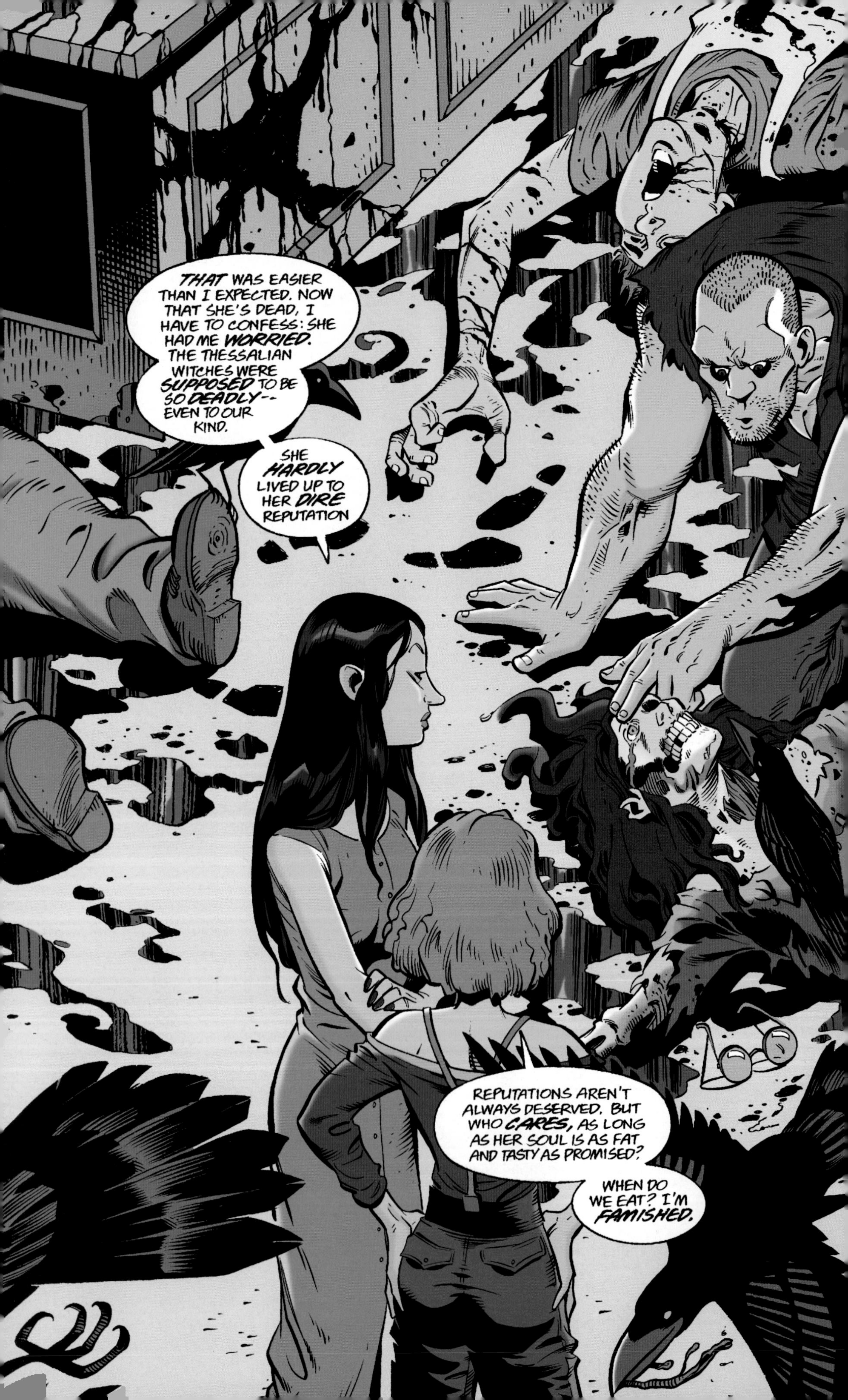
THAT WAS EASIER THAN I EXPECTED. NOW THAT SHE'S DEAD, I HAVE TO CONFESS: SHE HAD ME WORRIED. THE THESSALIAN WITCHES WERE SUPPOSED TO BE SO DEADLY-- EVEN TO OUR KIND.
SHE HARDLY LIVED UP TO HER DIRE REPUTATION
REPUTATIONS AREN'T ALWAYS DESERVED. BUT WHO CARES, AS LONG AS HER SOUL IS AS FAT AND TASTY AS PROMISED?
WHEN DO WE EAT? I'M FAMISHED.

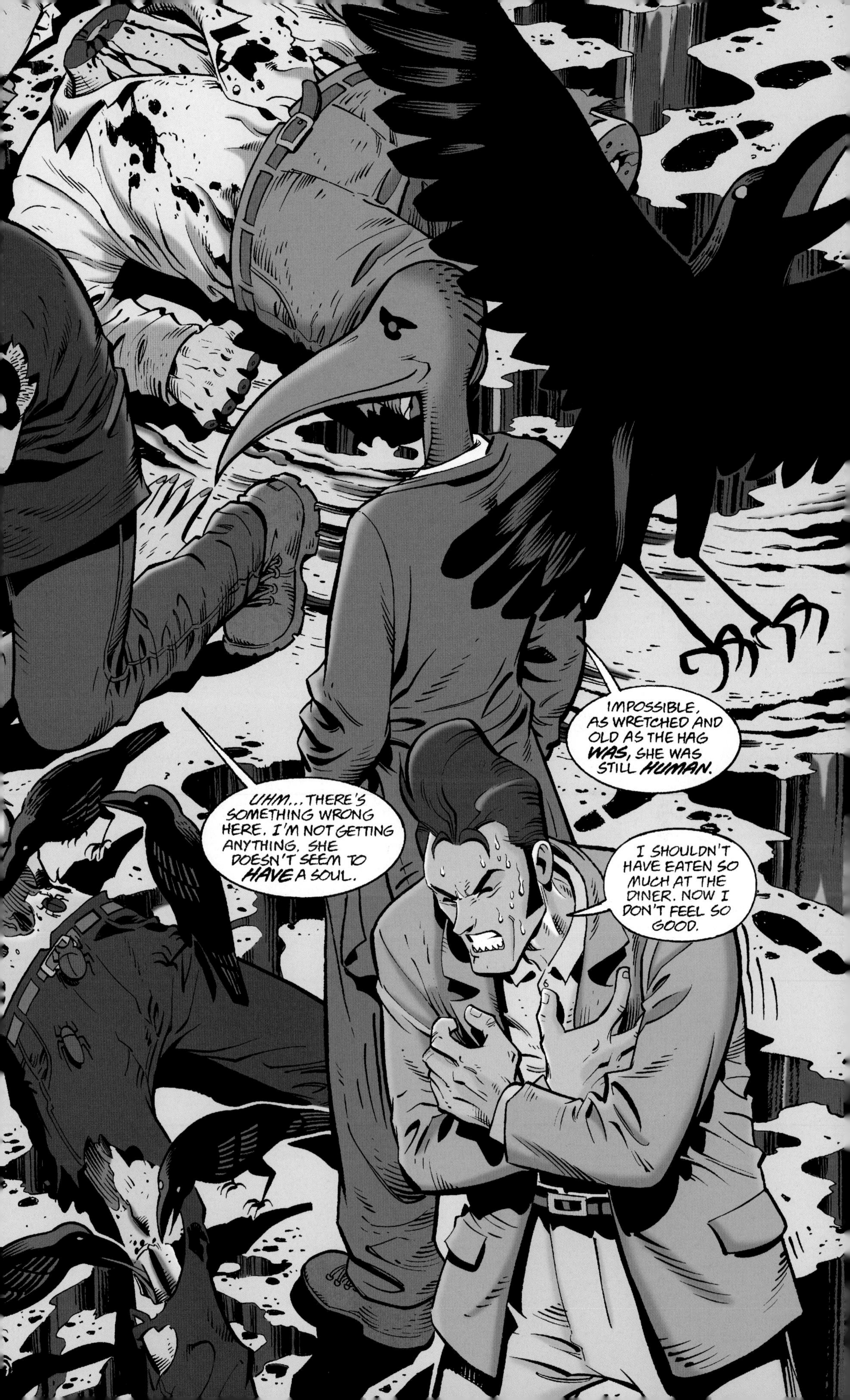
IMPOSSIBLE, AS WRETCHED AND OLD AS THE HAG WAS, SHE WAS STILL HUMAN.
UHM... THERE'S SOMETHING WRONG HERE. I'M NOT GETTING ANYTHING. SHE DOESN'T SEEM TO HAVE A SOUL.
I SHOULDN'T HAVE EATEN SO MUCH AT THE DINER. NOW I DON'T FEEL SO GOOD.

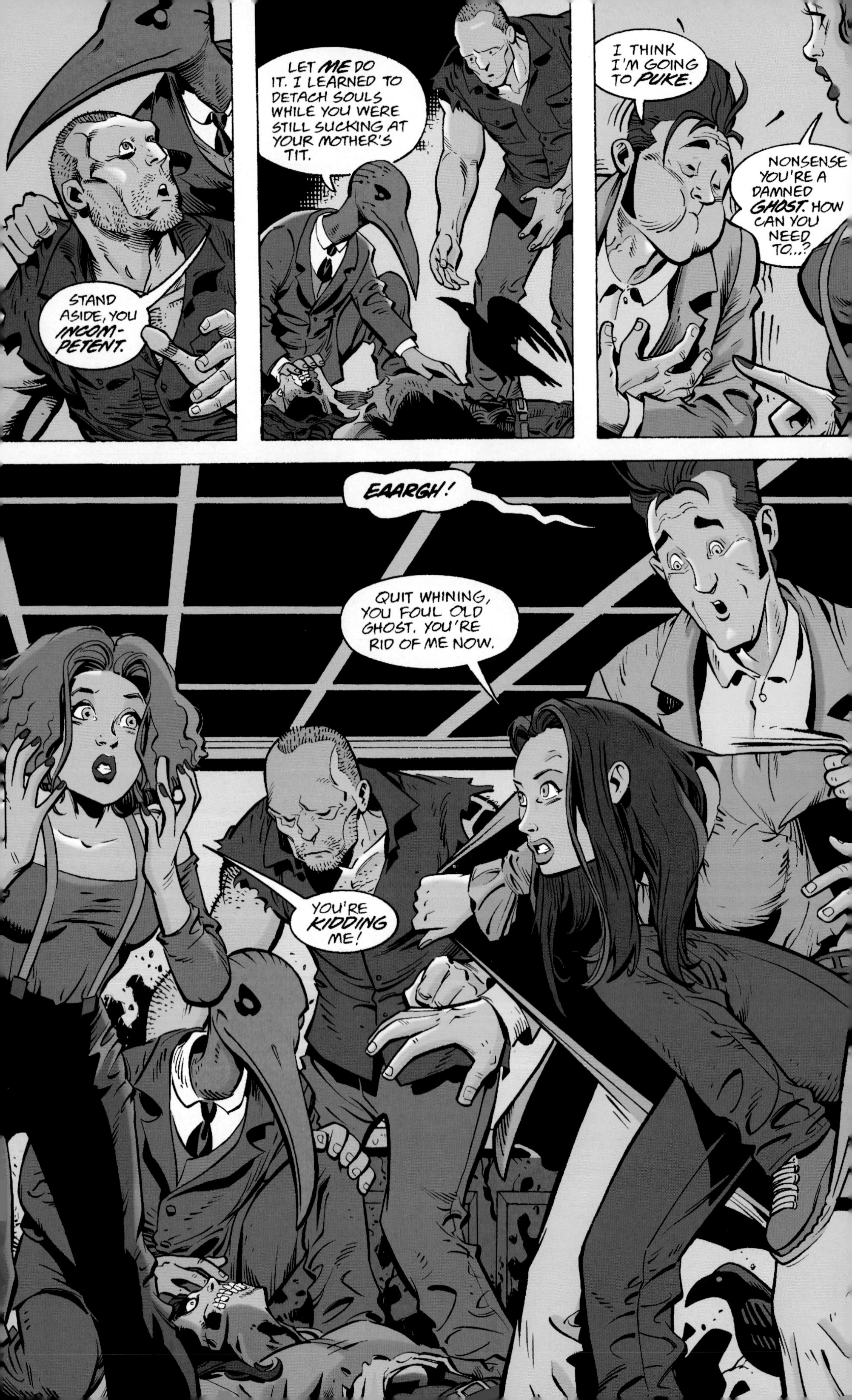
STAND ASIDE, YOU INCOMPETENT.
LET ME DO IT. I LEARNED TO DETACH SOULS WHILE YOU WERE STILL SUCKING AT YOUR MOTHER'S TIT.
I THINK I'M GOING TO PUKE.
NONSENSE YOU'RE A DAMNED GHOST. HOW CAN YOU NEED TO...?
EAARGH!
QUIT WHINING, YOU FOUL OLD GHOST. YOU'RE RID OF ME NOW.
YOU'RE KIDDING ME!

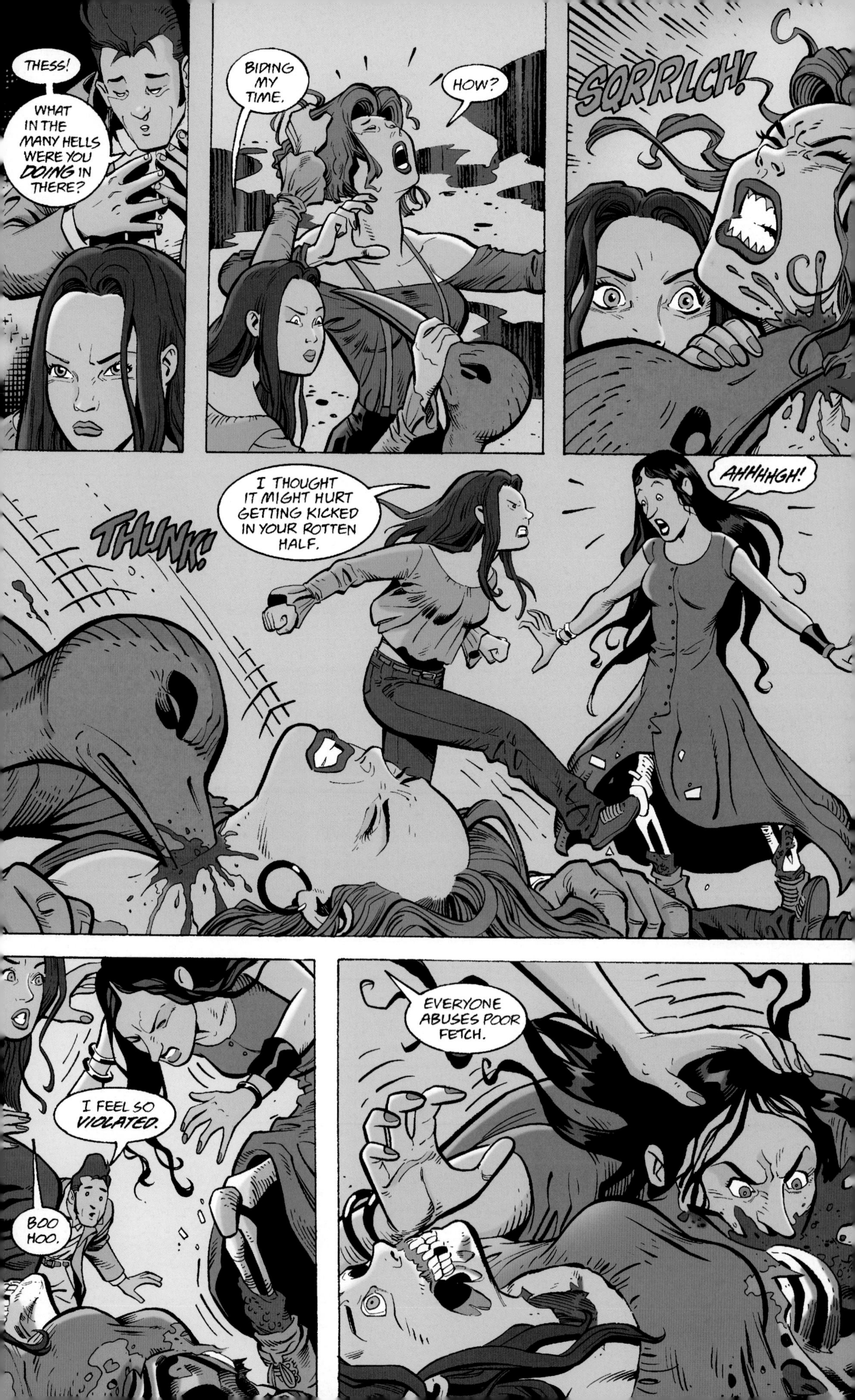
THESS!
WHAT IN THE MANY HELLS WERE YOU *DOING* IN THERE?
BIDING MY TIME.
HOW?
SQRRLCH!
I THOUGHT IT MIGHT HURT GETTING KICKED IN YOUR ROTTEN HALF.
THUNK!
AHHHHGH!
I FEEL SO *VIOLATED*.
BOO HOO.
EVERYONE ABUSES POOR FETCH.

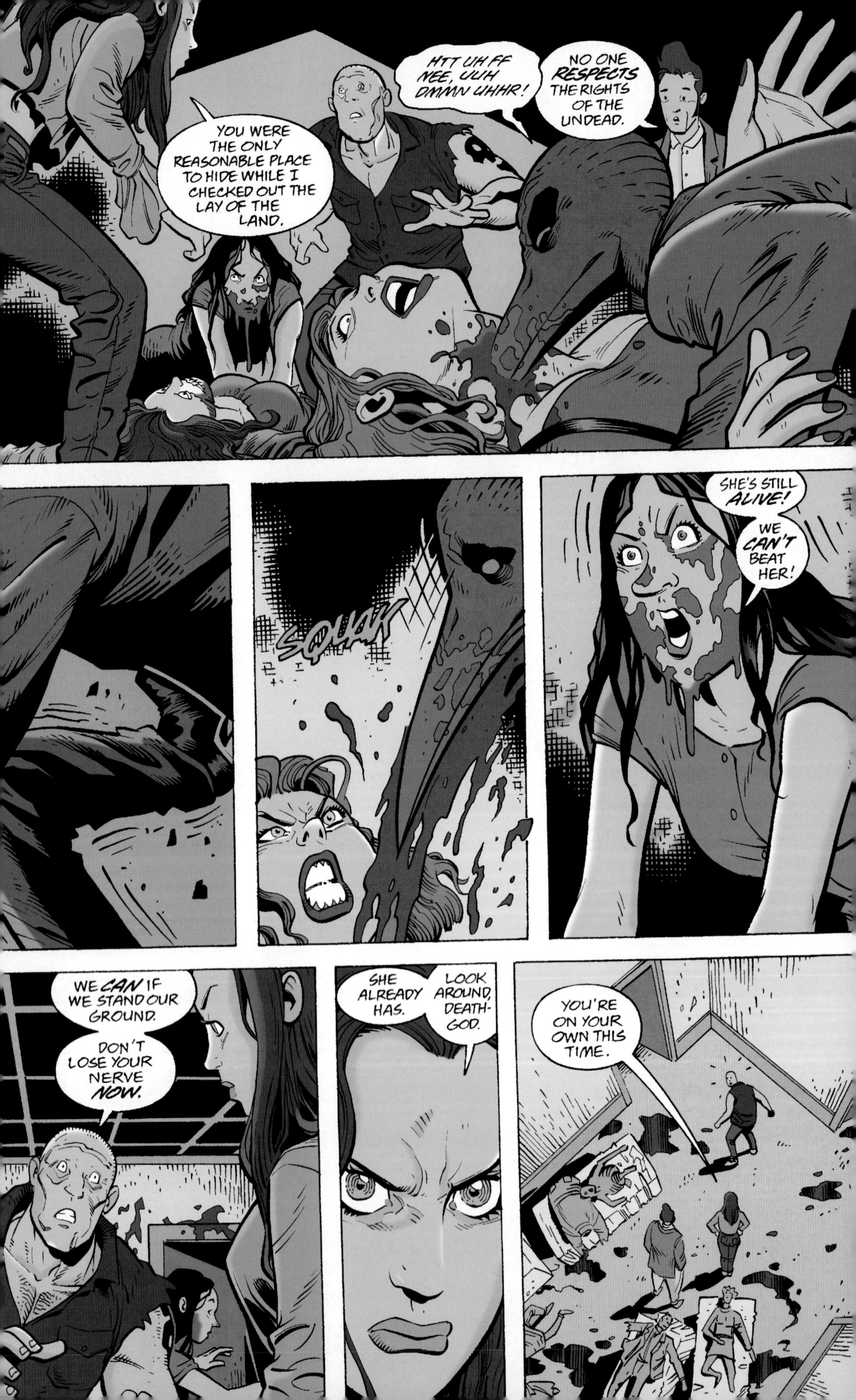
YOU WERE THE ONLY REASONABLE PLACE TO HIDE WHILE I CHECKED OUT THE LAY OF THE LAND.
HTT UH FF NEE, UUH DMMN UHHR!
NO ONE RESPECTS THE RIGHTS OF THE UNDEAD.
SQUAK
SHE'S STILL ALIVE!
WE CAN'T BEAT HER!
WE CAN IF WE STAND OUR GROUND.
DON'T LOSE YOUR NERVE NOW.
SHE ALREADY HAS.
LOOK AROUND, DEATH-GOD.
YOU'RE ON YOUR OWN THIS TIME.

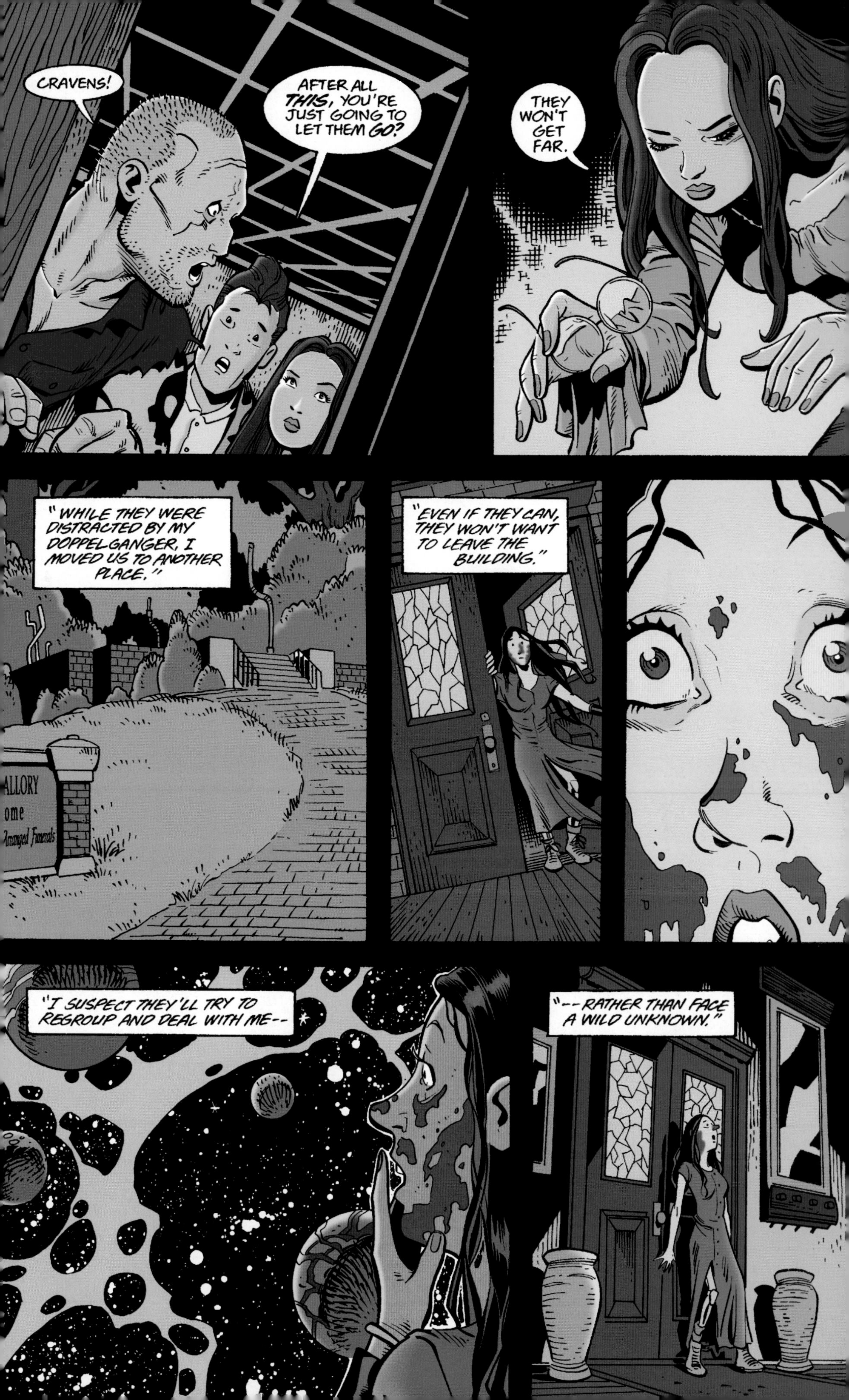
CRAVENS!
AFTER ALL THIS, YOU'RE JUST GOING TO LET THEM GO?
THEY WON'T GET FAR.
"WHILE THEY WERE DISTRACTED BY MY DOPPELGANGER, I MOVED US TO ANOTHER PLACE."
ALLORY
ome
Arranged Funerals
"EVEN IF THEY CAN, THEY WON'T WANT TO LEAVE THE BUILDING."
"I SUSPECT THEY'LL TRY TO REGROUP AND DEAL WITH ME--
"--RATHER THAN FACE A WILD UNKNOWN."

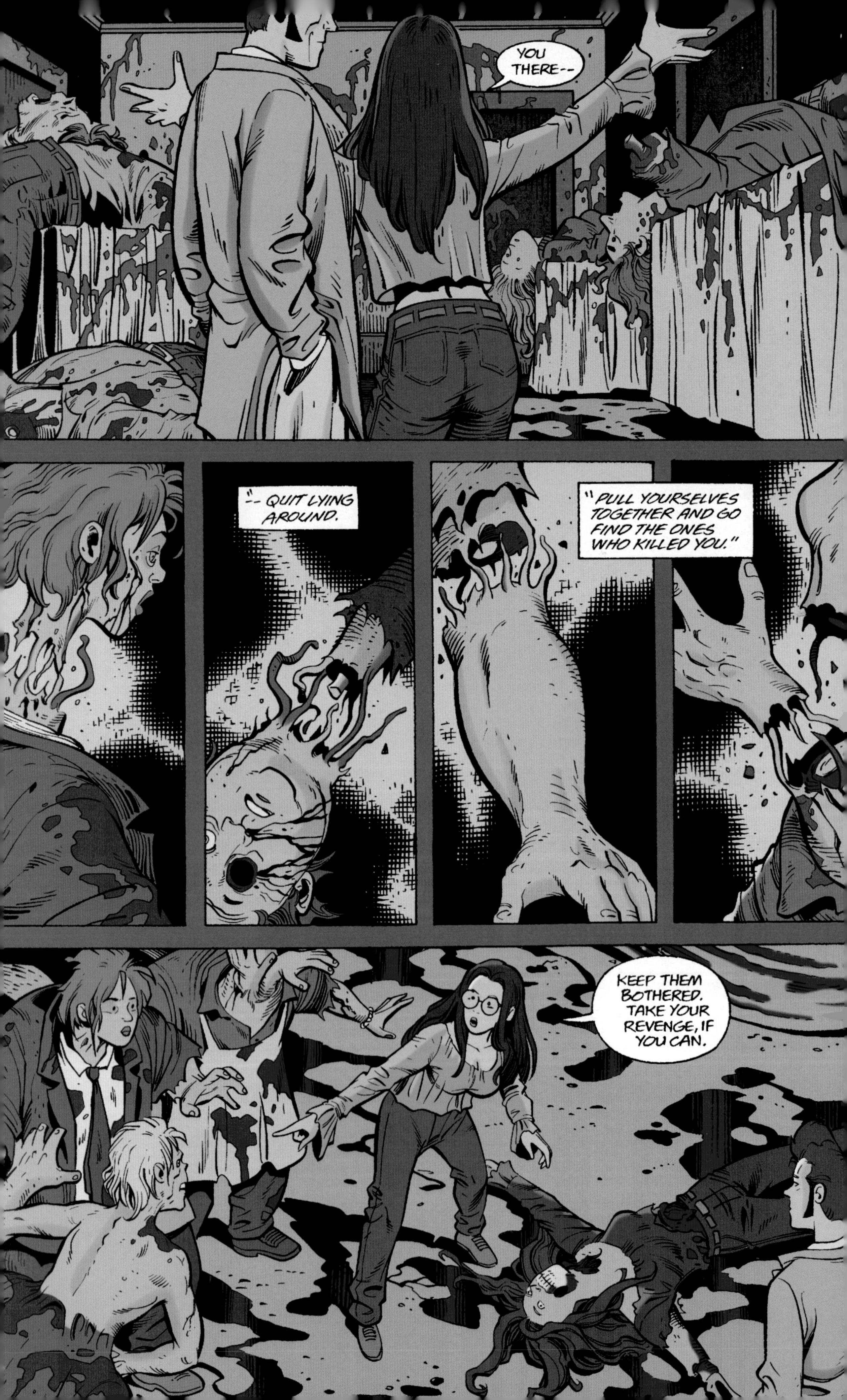
YOU THERE--
"--QUIT LYING AROUND.
"PULL YOURSELVES TOGETHER AND GO FIND THE ONES WHO KILLED YOU."
KEEP THEM BOTHERED. TAKE YOUR REVENGE, IF YOU CAN.

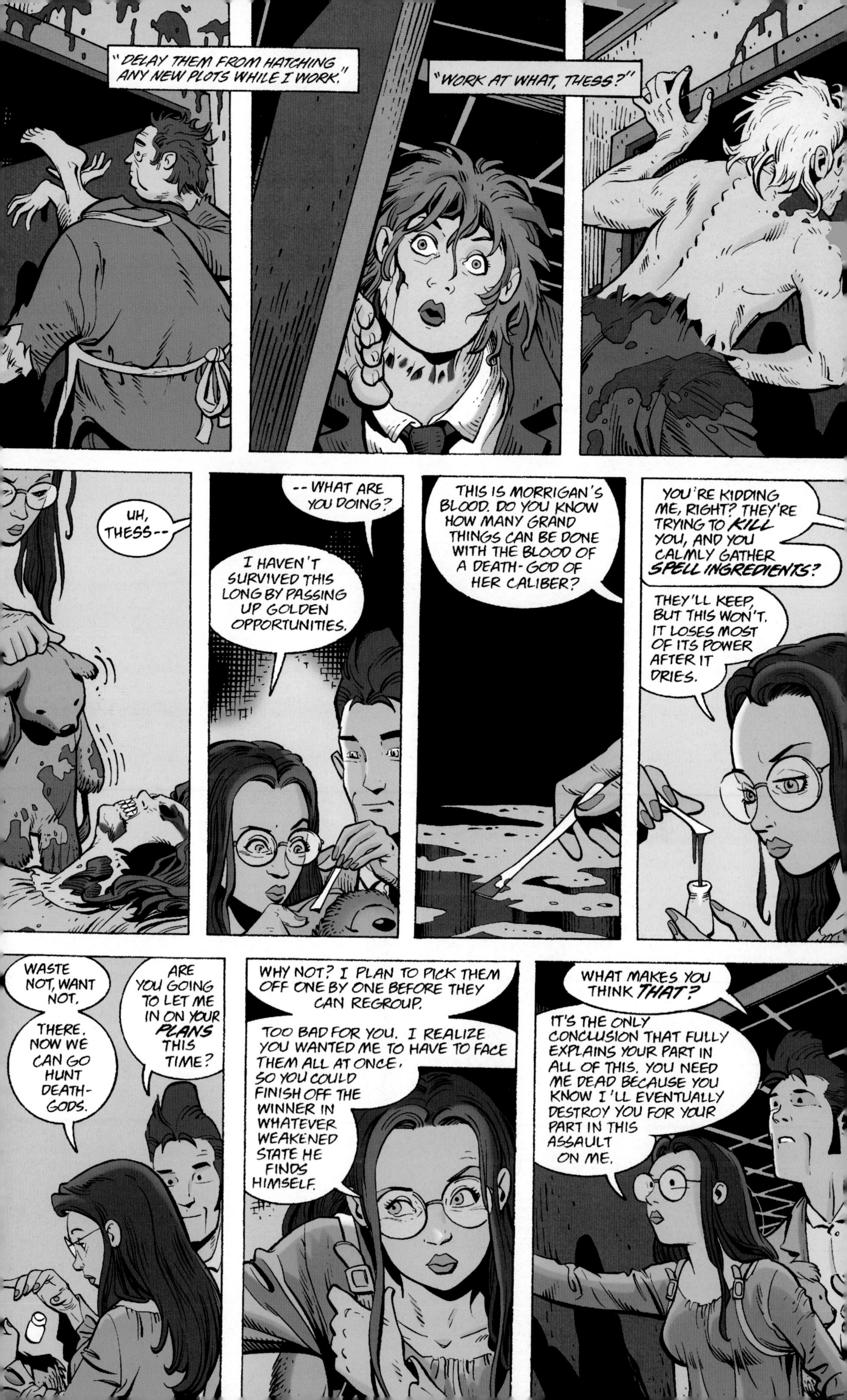
"DELAY THEM FROM HATCHING ANY NEW PLOTS WHILE I WORK."
"WORK AT WHAT, THESS?"
UH, THESS--
--WHAT ARE YOU DOING?
I HAVEN'T SURVIVED THIS LONG BY PASSING UP GOLDEN OPPORTUNITIES.
THIS IS MORRIGAN'S BLOOD. DO YOU KNOW HOW MANY GRAND THINGS CAN BE DONE WITH THE BLOOD OF A DEATH-GOD OF HER CALIBER?
YOU'RE KIDDING ME, RIGHT? THEY'RE TRYING TO KILL YOU, AND YOU CALMLY GATHER SPELL INGREDIENTS?
THEY'LL KEEP, BUT THIS WON'T. IT LOSES MOST OF ITS POWER AFTER IT DRIES.
WASTE NOT, WANT NOT.
THERE. NOW WE CAN GO HUNT DEATH-GODS.
ARE YOU GOING TO LET ME IN ON YOUR PLANS THIS TIME?
WHY NOT? I PLAN TO PICK THEM OFF ONE BY ONE BEFORE THEY CAN REGROUP.
TOO BAD FOR YOU. I REALIZE YOU WANTED ME TO HAVE TO FACE THEM ALL AT ONCE, SO YOU COULD FINISH OFF THE WINNER IN WHATEVER WEAKENED STATE HE FINDS HIMSELF.
WHAT MAKES YOU THINK THAT?
IT'S THE ONLY CONCLUSION THAT FULLY EXPLAINS YOUR PART IN ALL OF THIS. YOU NEED ME DEAD BECAUSE YOU KNOW I'LL EVENTUALLY DESTROY YOU FOR YOUR PART IN THIS ASSAULT ON ME.

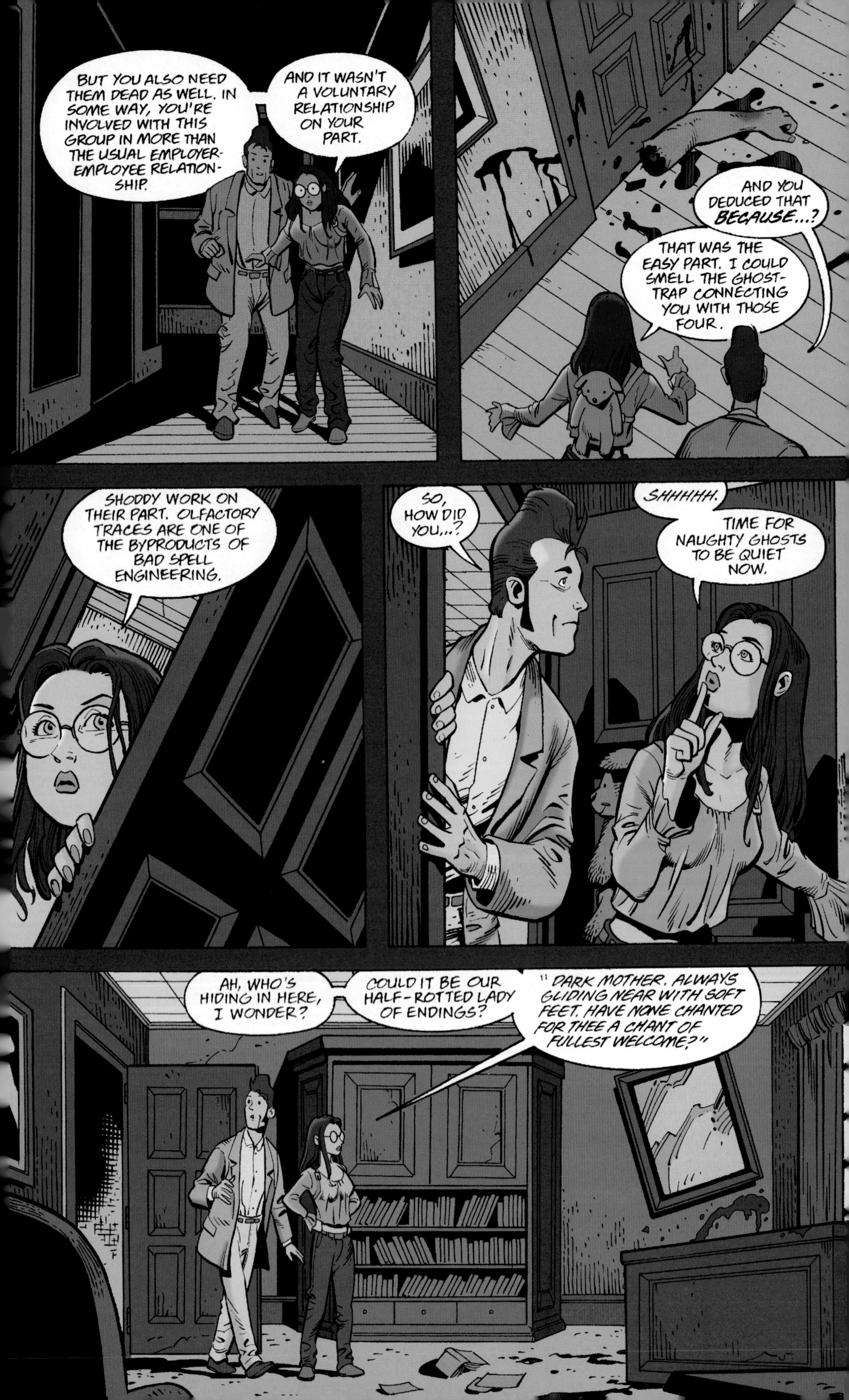
BUT YOU ALSO NEED THEM DEAD AS WELL. IN SOME WAY, YOU'RE INVOLVED WITH THIS GROUP IN MORE THAN THE USUAL EMPLOYER-EMPLOYEE RELATIONSHIP.
AND IT WASN'T A VOLUNTARY RELATIONSHIP ON YOUR PART.
AND YOU DEDUCED THAT BECAUSE...?
THAT WAS THE EASY PART. I COULD SMELL THE GHOST-TRAP CONNECTING YOU WITH THOSE FOUR.
SHODDY WORK ON THEIR PART. OLFACTORY TRACES ARE ONE OF THE BYPRODUCTS OF BAD SPELL ENGINEERING.
SO, HOW DID YOU...?
SHHHHH.
TIME FOR NAUGHTY GHOSTS TO BE QUIET NOW.
AH, WHO'S HIDING IN HERE, I WONDER?
COULD IT BE OUR HALF-ROTTED LADY OF ENDINGS?
"DARK MOTHER. ALWAYS GLIDING NEAR WITH SOFT FEET. HAVE NONE CHANTED FOR THEE A CHANT OF FULLEST WELCOME?"

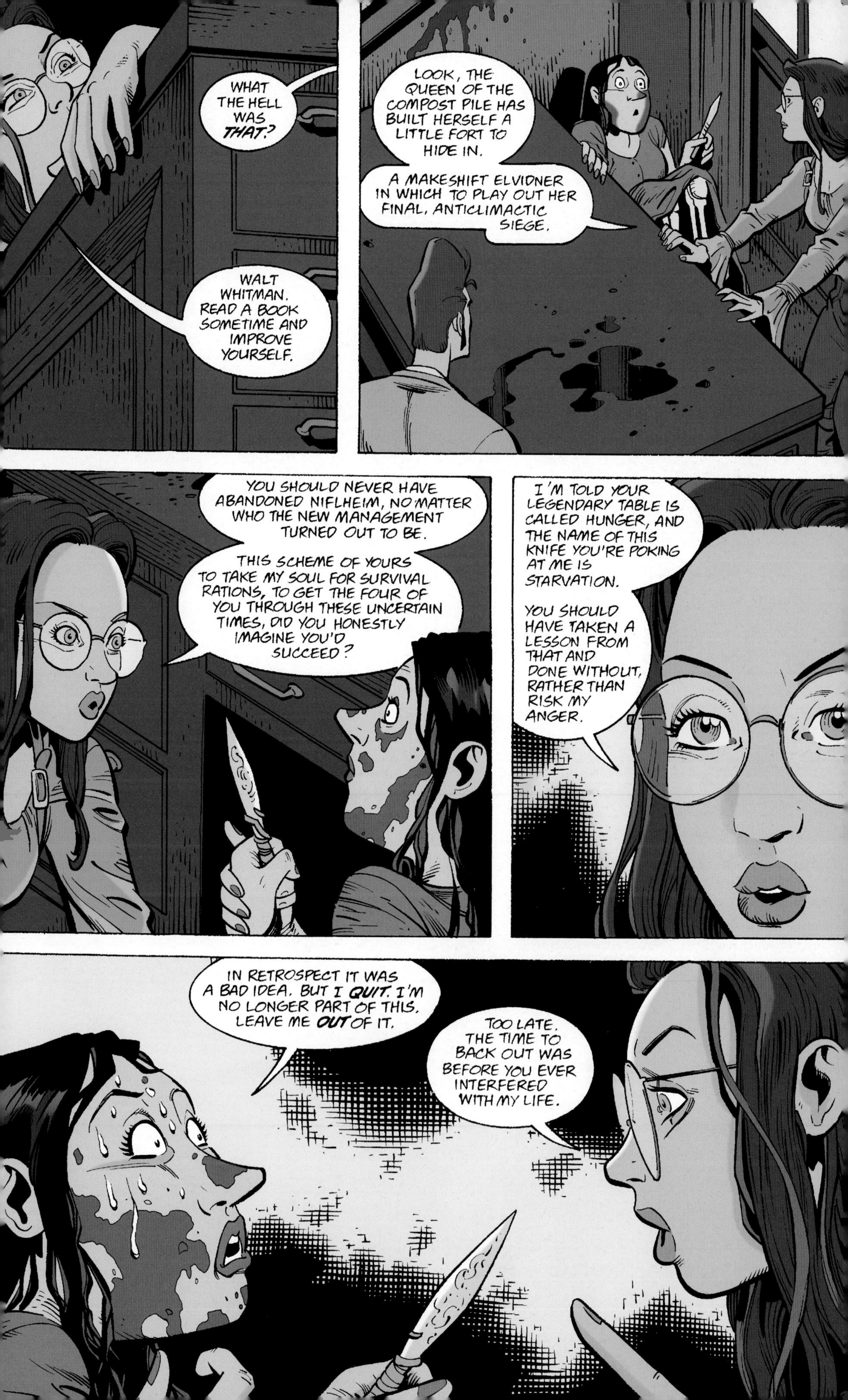

WHAT THE HELL WAS *THAT?*
WALT WHITMAN. READ A BOOK SOMETIME AND IMPROVE YOURSELF.
LOOK, THE QUEEN OF THE COMPOST PILE HAS BUILT HERSELF A LITTLE FORT TO HIDE IN.
A MAKESHIFT ELVIDNER IN WHICH TO PLAY OUT HER FINAL, ANTICLIMACTIC SIEGE.
YOU SHOULD NEVER HAVE ABANDONED NIFLHEIM, NO MATTER WHO THE NEW MANAGEMENT TURNED OUT TO BE.
THIS SCHEME OF YOURS TO TAKE MY SOUL FOR SURVIVAL RATIONS, TO GET THE FOUR OF YOU THROUGH THESE UNCERTAIN TIMES, DID YOU HONESTLY IMAGINE YOU'D SUCCEED?
I'M TOLD YOUR LEGENDARY TABLE IS CALLED HUNGER, AND THE NAME OF THIS KNIFE YOU'RE POKING AT ME IS STARVATION.
YOU SHOULD HAVE TAKEN A LESSON FROM THAT AND DONE WITHOUT, RATHER THAN RISK MY ANGER.
IN RETROSPECT IT WAS A BAD IDEA. BUT I *QUIT.* I'M NO LONGER PART OF THIS. LEAVE ME *OUT* OF IT.
TOO LATE. THE TIME TO BACK OUT WAS BEFORE YOU EVER INTERFERED WITH MY LIFE.

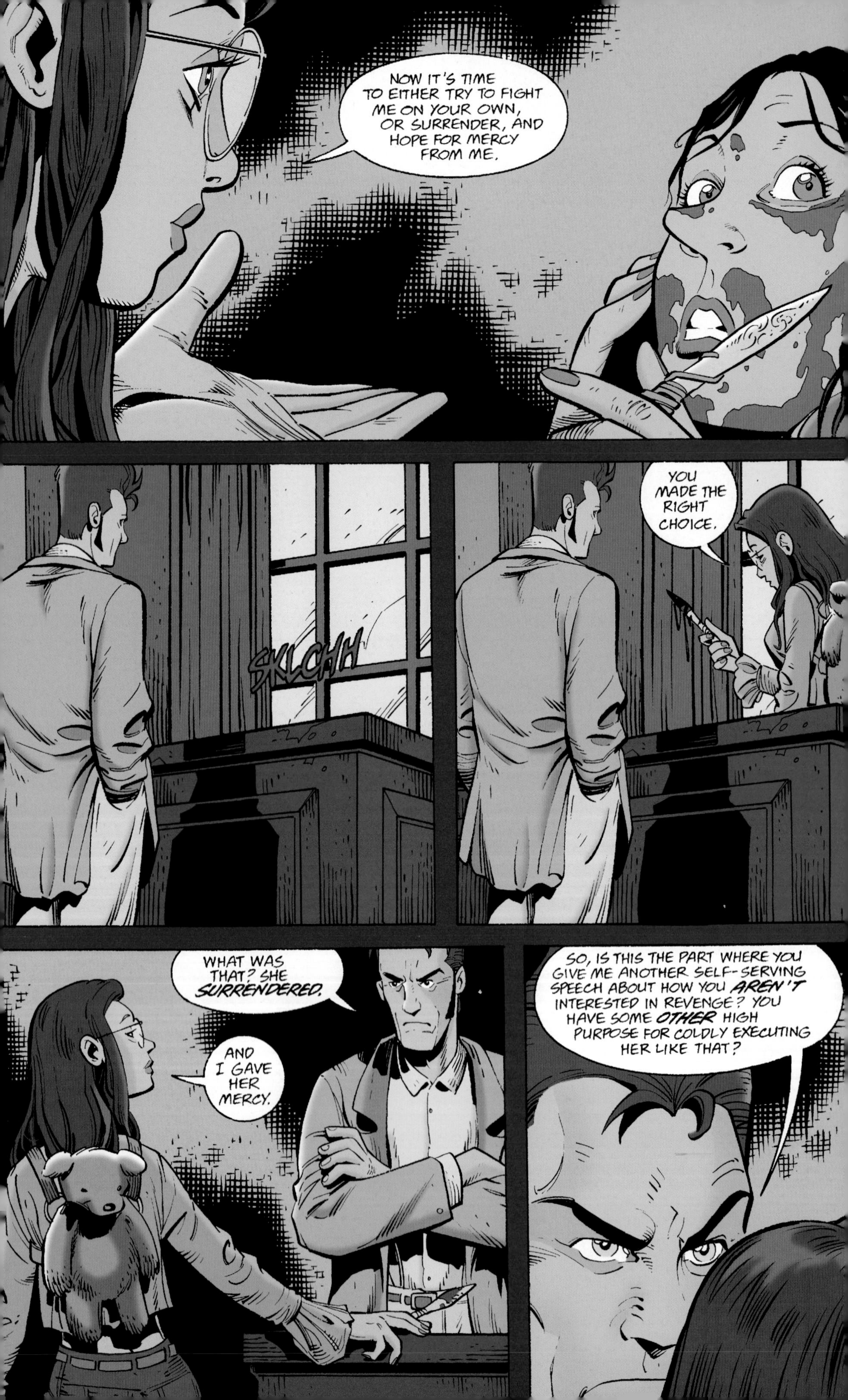
NOW IT'S TIME TO EITHER TRY TO FIGHT ME ON YOUR OWN, OR SURRENDER, AND HOPE FOR MERCY FROM ME.
SKLCHH
YOU MADE THE RIGHT CHOICE.
WHAT WAS THAT? SHE SURRENDERED.
AND I GAVE HER MERCY.
SO, IS THIS THE PART WHERE YOU GIVE ME ANOTHER SELF-SERVING SPEECH ABOUT HOW YOU AREN'T INTERESTED IN REVENGE? YOU HAVE SOME OTHER HIGH PURPOSE FOR COLDLY EXECUTING HER LIKE THAT?

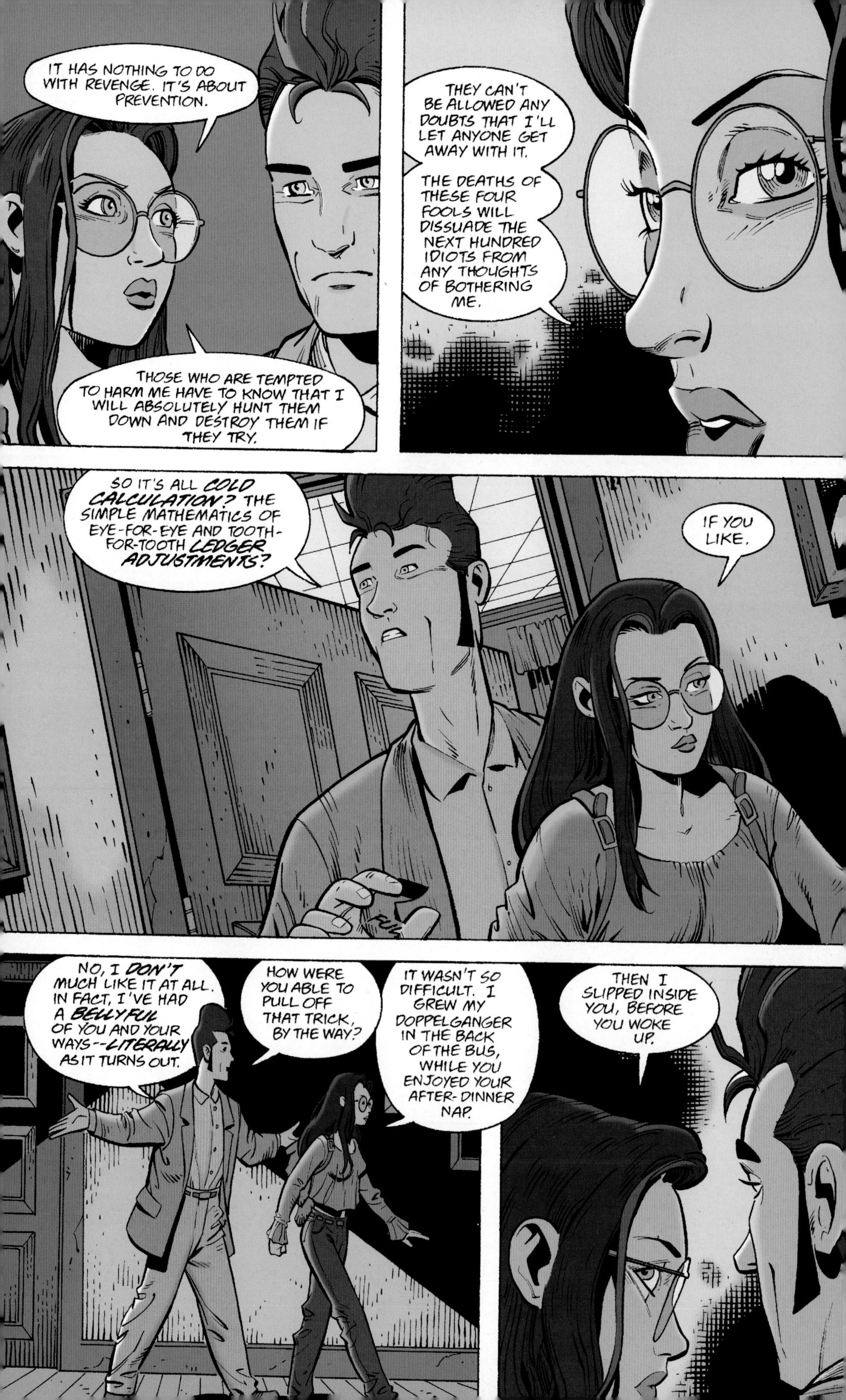
IT HAS NOTHING TO DO WITH REVENGE. IT'S ABOUT PREVENTION.
THOSE WHO ARE TEMPTED TO HARM ME HAVE TO KNOW THAT I WILL ABSOLUTELY HUNT THEM DOWN AND DESTROY THEM IF THEY TRY.
THEY CAN'T BE ALLOWED ANY DOUBTS THAT I'LL LET ANYONE GET AWAY WITH IT.
THE DEATHS OF THESE FOUR FOOLS WILL DISSUADE THE NEXT HUNDRED IDIOTS FROM ANY THOUGHTS OF BOTHERING ME.
SO IT'S ALL *COLD CALCULATION*? THE SIMPLE MATHEMATICS OF EYE-FOR-EYE AND TOOTH-FOR-TOOTH *LEDGER ADJUSTMENTS*?
IF YOU LIKE.
NO, I *DON'T* MUCH LIKE IT AT ALL. IN FACT, I'VE HAD A *BELLYFUL* OF YOU AND YOUR WAYS--*LITERALLY* AS IT TURNS OUT.
HOW WERE YOU ABLE TO PULL OFF THAT TRICK, BY THE WAY?
IT WASN'T SO DIFFICULT. I GREW MY DOPPELGANGER IN THE BACK OF THE BUS, WHILE YOU ENJOYED YOUR AFTER-DINNER NAP.
THEN I SLIPPED INSIDE YOU, BEFORE YOU WOKE UP.

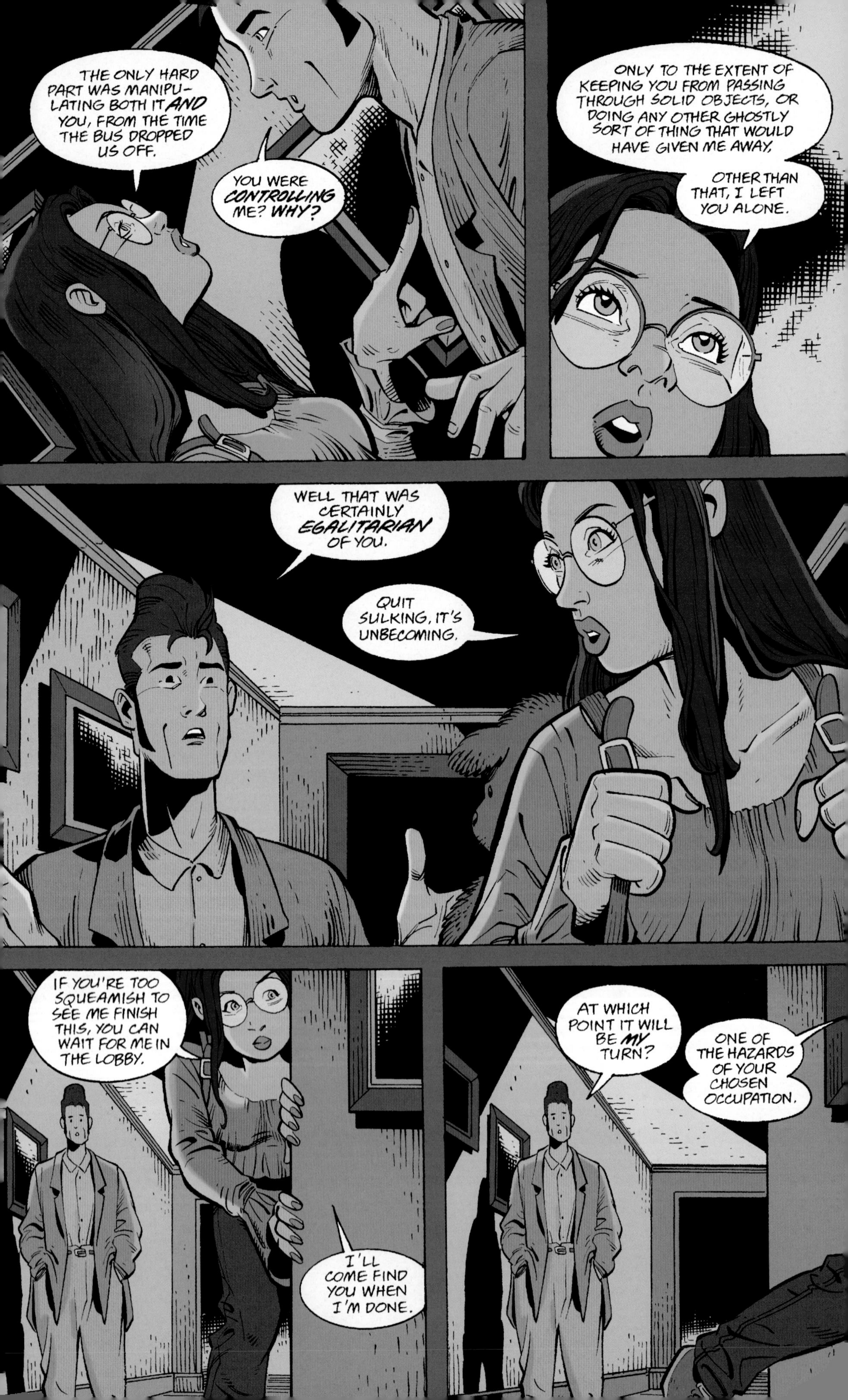
THE ONLY HARD PART WAS MANIPULATING BOTH IT AND YOU, FROM THE TIME THE BUS DROPPED US OFF.
YOU WERE CONTROLLING ME? WHY?
ONLY TO THE EXTENT OF KEEPING YOU FROM PASSING THROUGH SOLID OBJECTS, OR DOING ANY OTHER GHOSTLY SORT OF THING THAT WOULD HAVE GIVEN ME AWAY.
OTHER THAN THAT, I LEFT YOU ALONE.
WELL THAT WAS CERTAINLY EGALITARIAN OF YOU.
QUIT SULKING, IT'S UNBECOMING.
IF YOU'RE TOO SQUEAMISH TO SEE ME FINISH THIS, YOU CAN WAIT FOR ME IN THE LOBBY.
I'LL COME FIND YOU WHEN I'M DONE.
AT WHICH POINT IT WILL BE MY TURN?
ONE OF THE HAZARDS OF YOUR CHOSEN OCCUPATION.

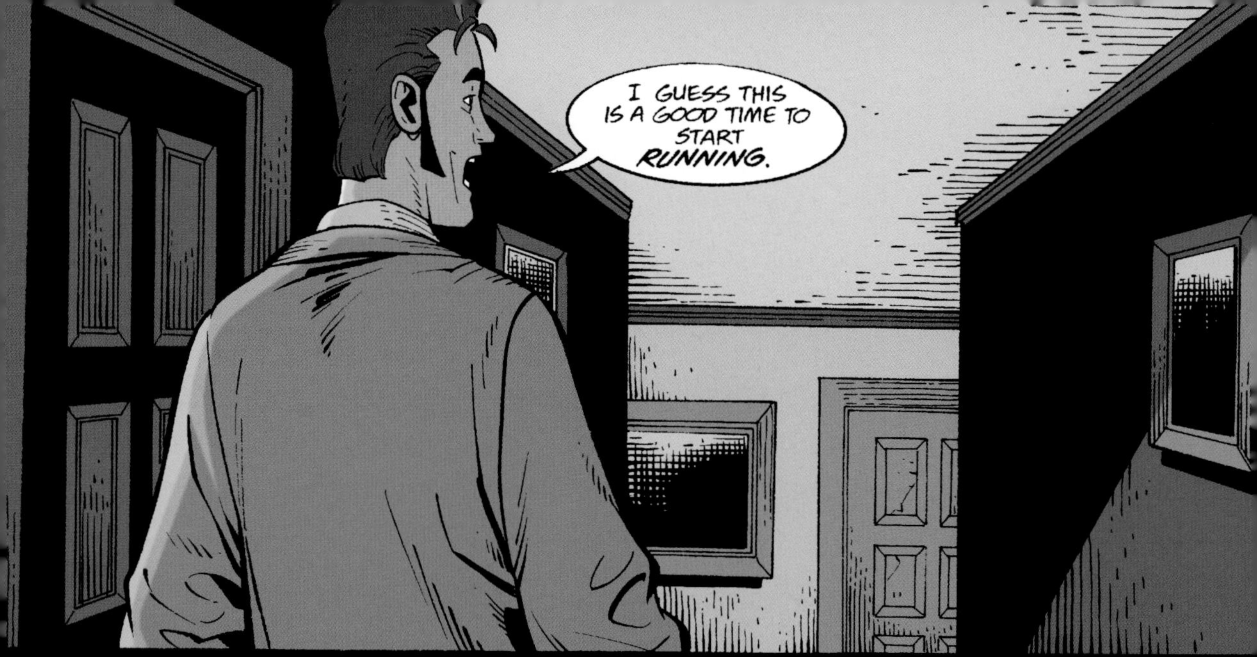
I GUESS THIS IS A GOOD TIME TO START RUNNING.
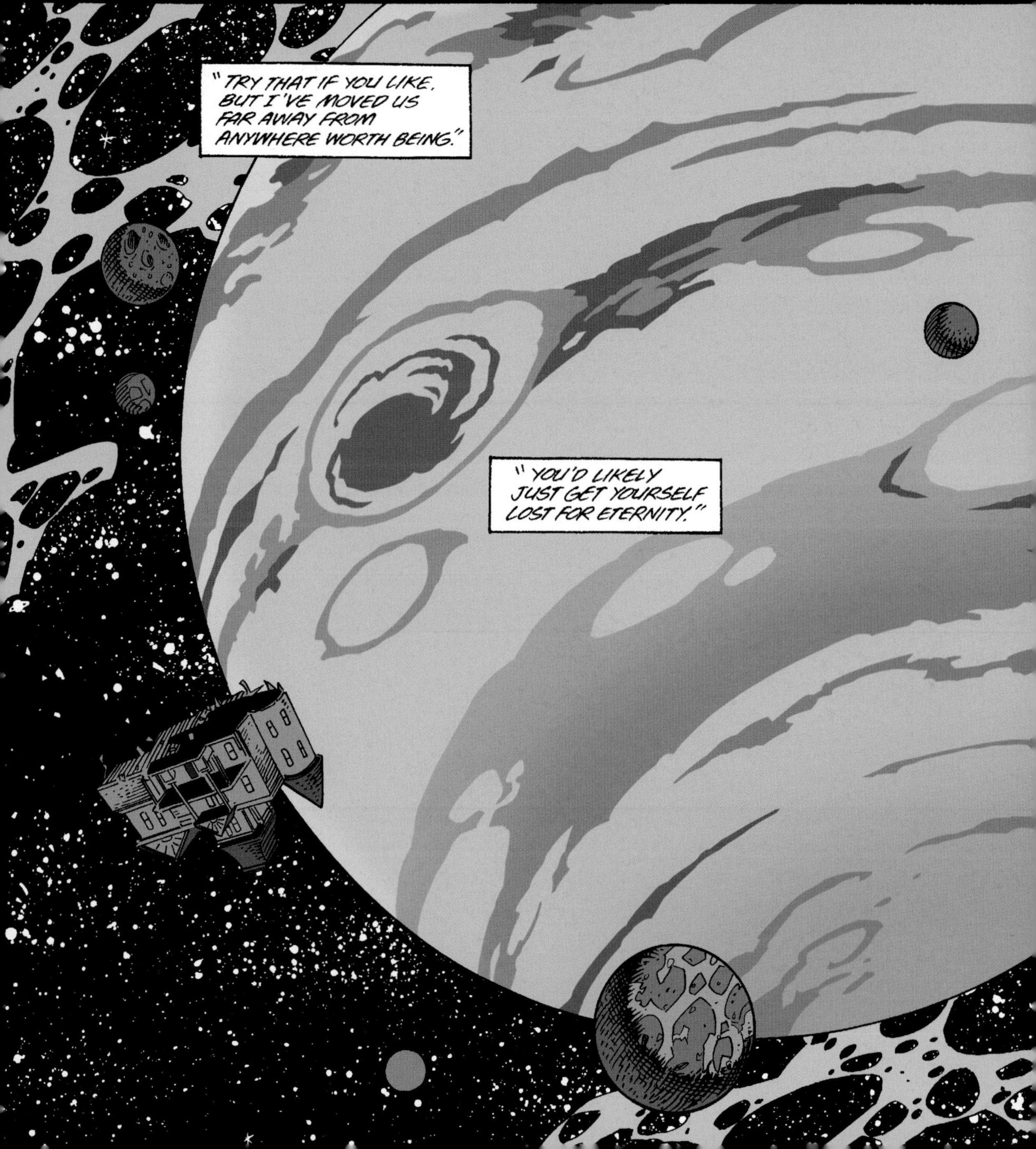
"TRY THAT IF YOU LIKE, BUT I'VE MOVED US FAR AWAY FROM ANYWHERE WORTH BEING."
"YOU'D LIKELY JUST GET YOURSELF LOST FOR ETERNITY."

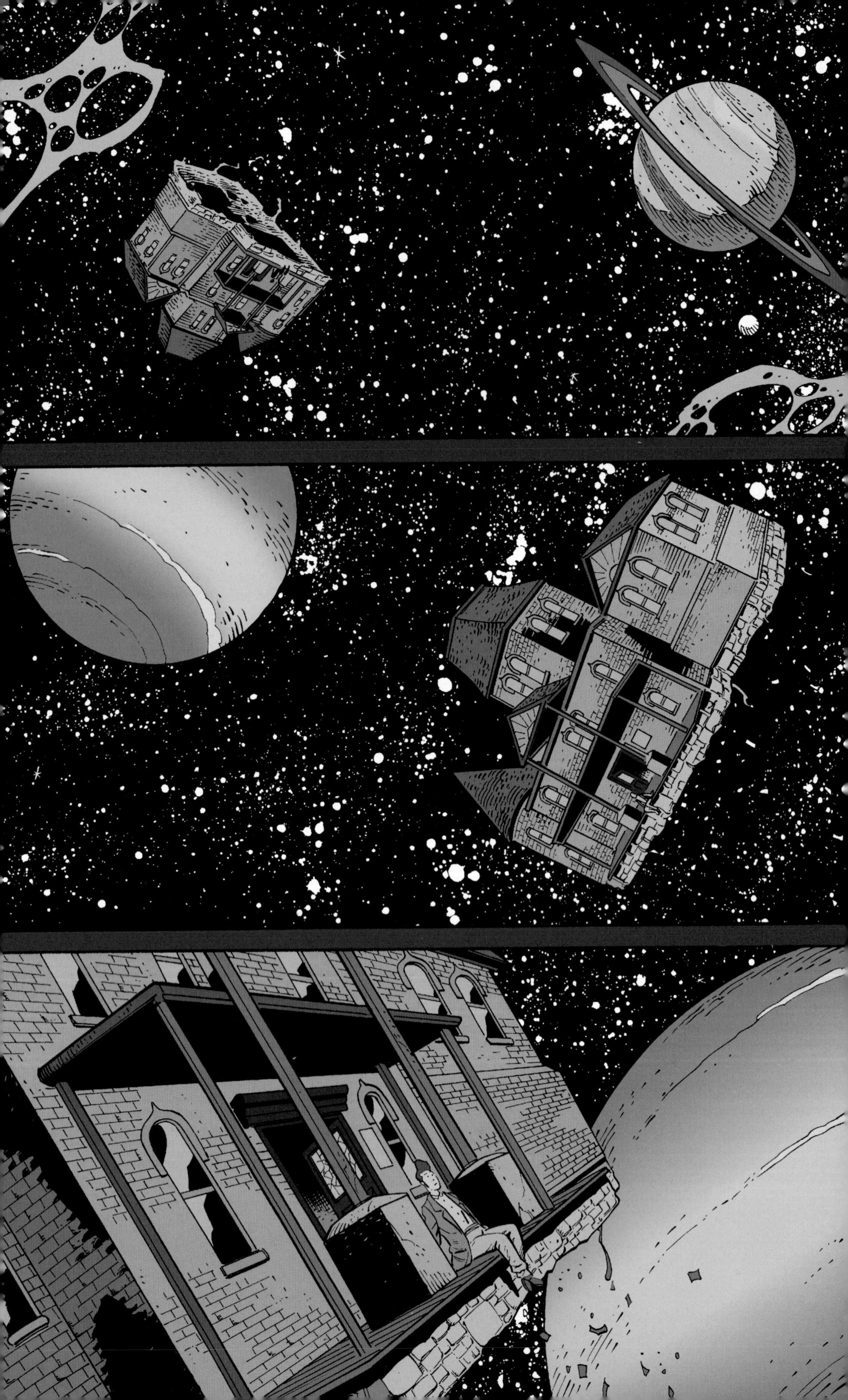

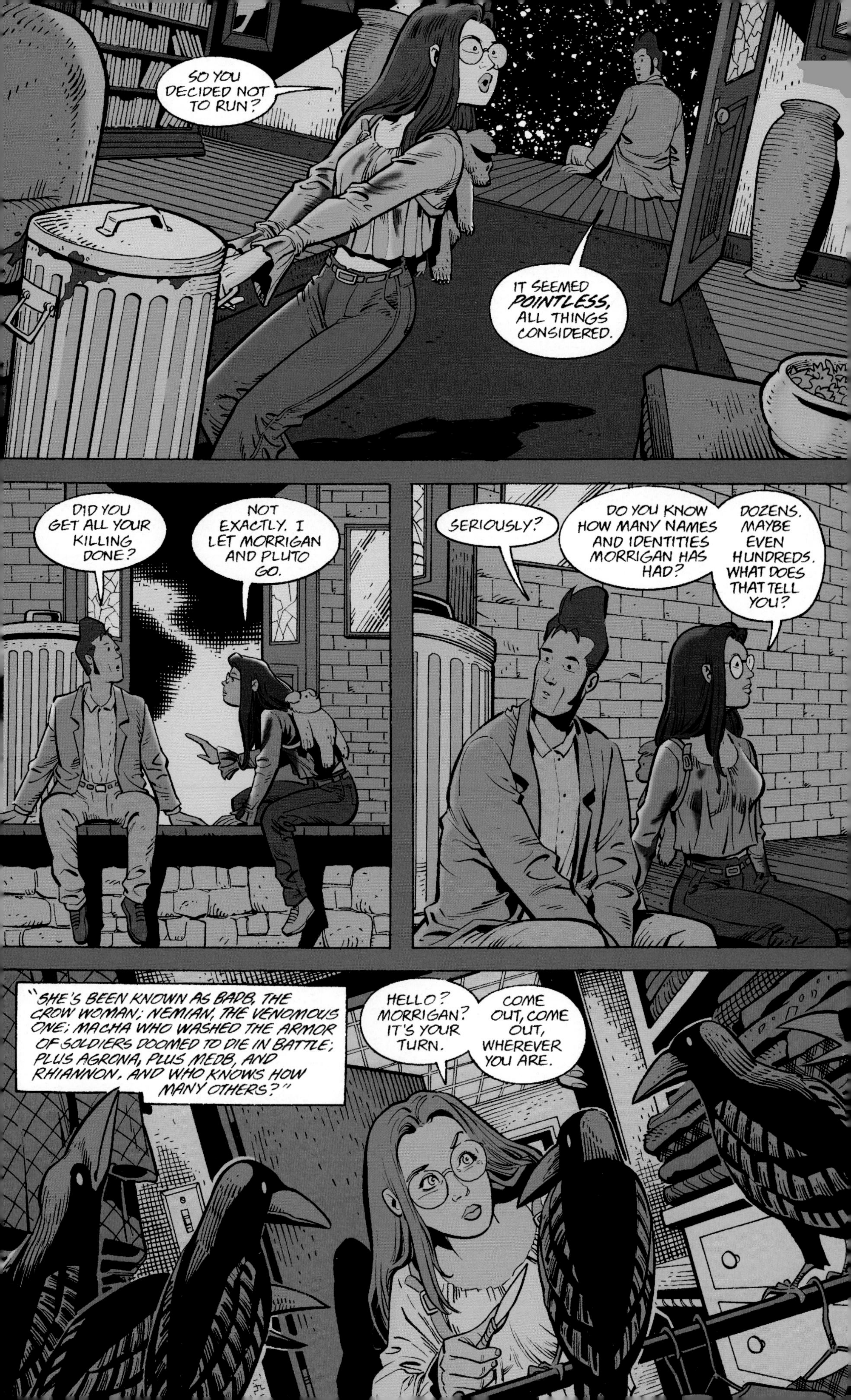
SO YOU DECIDED NOT TO RUN?
IT SEEMED POINTLESS, ALL THINGS CONSIDERED.
DID YOU GET ALL YOUR KILLING DONE?
NOT EXACTLY. I LET MORRIGAN AND PLUTO GO.
SERIOUSLY?
DO YOU KNOW HOW MANY NAMES AND IDENTITIES MORRIGAN HAS HAD?
DOZENS. MAYBE EVEN HUNDREDS. WHAT DOES THAT TELL YOU?
"SHE'S BEEN KNOWN AS BADB, THE CROW WOMAN; NEMIAN, THE VENOMOUS ONE; MACHA WHO WASHED THE ARMOR OF SOLDIERS DOOMED TO DIE IN BATTLE; PLUS AGRONA, PLUS MEDB, AND RHIANNON, AND WHO KNOWS HOW MANY OTHERS?"
HELLO? MORRIGAN? IT'S YOUR TURN.
COME OUT, COME OUT, WHEREVER YOU ARE.

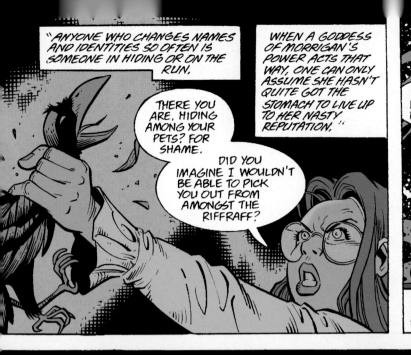

"ANYONE WHO CHANGES NAMES AND IDENTITIES SO OFTEN IS SOMEONE IN HIDING OR ON THE RUN."

THERE YOU ARE, HIDING AMONG YOUR PETS? FOR SHAME.

DID YOU IMAGINE I WOULDN'T BE ABLE TO PICK YOU OUT FROM AMONGST THE RIFFRAFF?

WHEN A GODDESS OF MORRIGAN'S POWER ACTS THAT WAY, ONE CAN ONLY ASSUME SHE HASN'T QUITE GOT THE STOMACH TO LIVE UP TO HER NASTY REPUTATION."

SO SHE'S LIKELY A *COWARD*. WHY DOES THAT TRANSLATE TO LETTING HER GO?

BECAUSE SHE'LL KEEP HER PLEDGE TO STAY FAR AWAY WHILE THE CENTURIES ROLL BY.

NO ONE WHO WALKS THE LANDS I WALK WILL EVER HEAR THAT I LET HER GET AWAY WITH ANYTHING.

"OF COURSE I DIDN'T JUST TAKE HER WORD. I LOCKED HER IN RAVEN FORM FOR A THOUSAND YEARS AND PLANTED A COMPULSION IN HER TO GO FIND OTHER SKIES TO FLY IN."

"AND YOU DID THE SAME FOR LORD PLUTO?"

"SUBSTANTIALLY. HE ALSO LACKED THE TIMBER ALONE THAT HE WAS ABLE TO SUMMON IN GROUPS.

"DID YOU KNOW HE'S A GOD OF WEALTH, IN ADDITION TO HIS DUTIES AS A KEEPER OF THE DEAD? IT SHOULDN'T HAVE SURPRISED ME. THE UNDERWORLD IS PREGNANT WITH PRECIOUS METALS."

I'LL *SHOWER* YOU WITH ALL MANNER OF RICHES!

GOLD? SILVER? RARE GEMSTONES OF EVERY COLOR?

ALL THAT AND *MORE!* ANY *BAUBLE* YOU *DESIRE!*

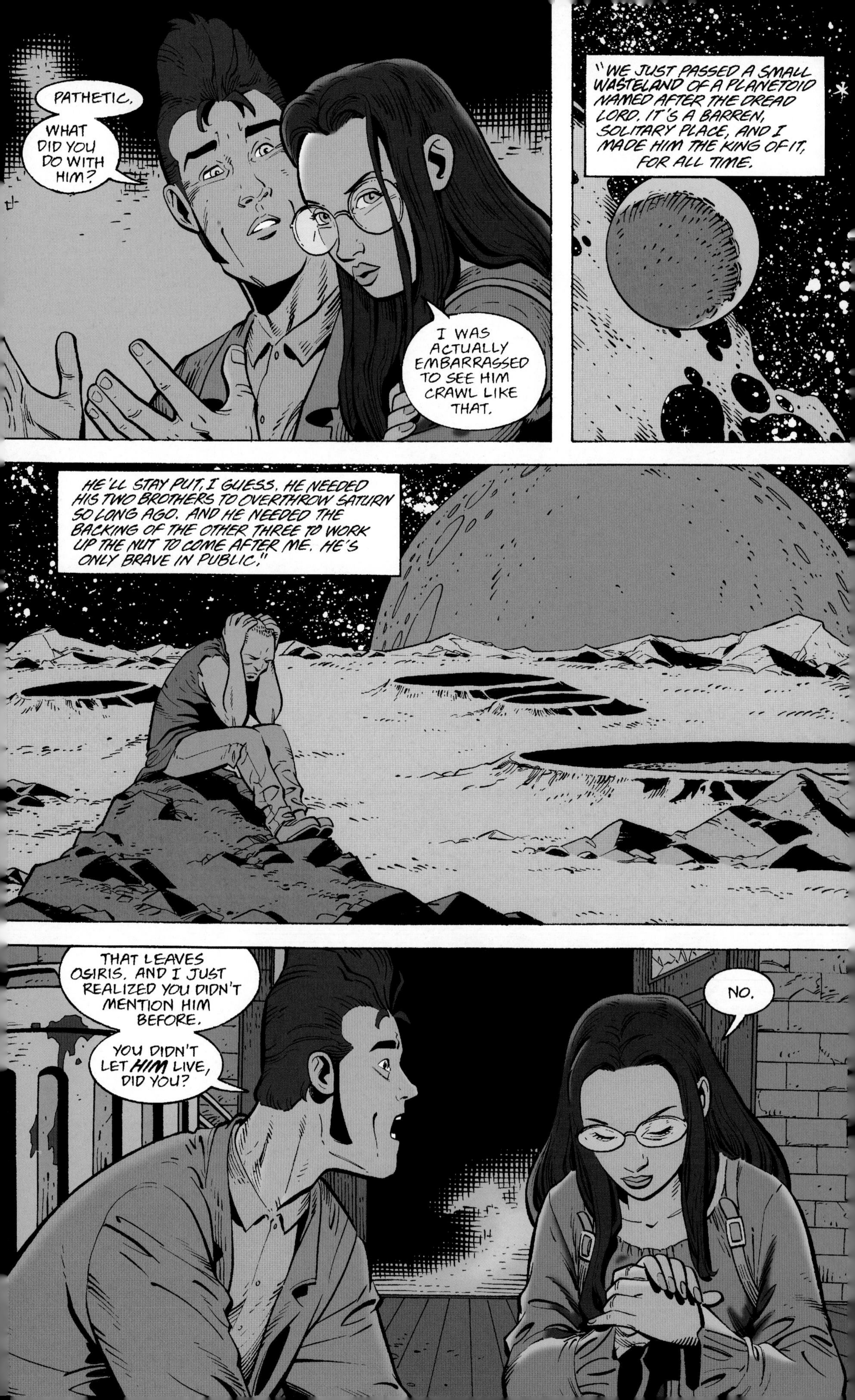
PATHETIC.
WHAT DID YOU DO WITH HIM?
I WAS ACTUALLY EMBARRASSED TO SEE HIM CRAWL LIKE THAT.
"WE JUST PASSED A SMALL WASTELAND OF A PLANETOID NAMED AFTER THE DREAD LORD. IT'S A BARREN, SOLITARY PLACE, AND I MADE HIM THE KING OF IT, FOR ALL TIME.
HE'LL STAY PUT, I GUESS. HE NEEDED HIS TWO BROTHERS TO OVERTHROW SATURN SO LONG AGO. AND HE NEEDED THE BACKING OF THE OTHER THREE TO WORK UP THE NUT TO COME AFTER ME. HE'S ONLY BRAVE IN PUBLIC."
THAT LEAVES OSIRIS. AND I JUST REALIZED YOU DIDN'T MENTION HIM BEFORE.
YOU DIDN'T LET *HIM* LIVE, DID YOU?
NO.

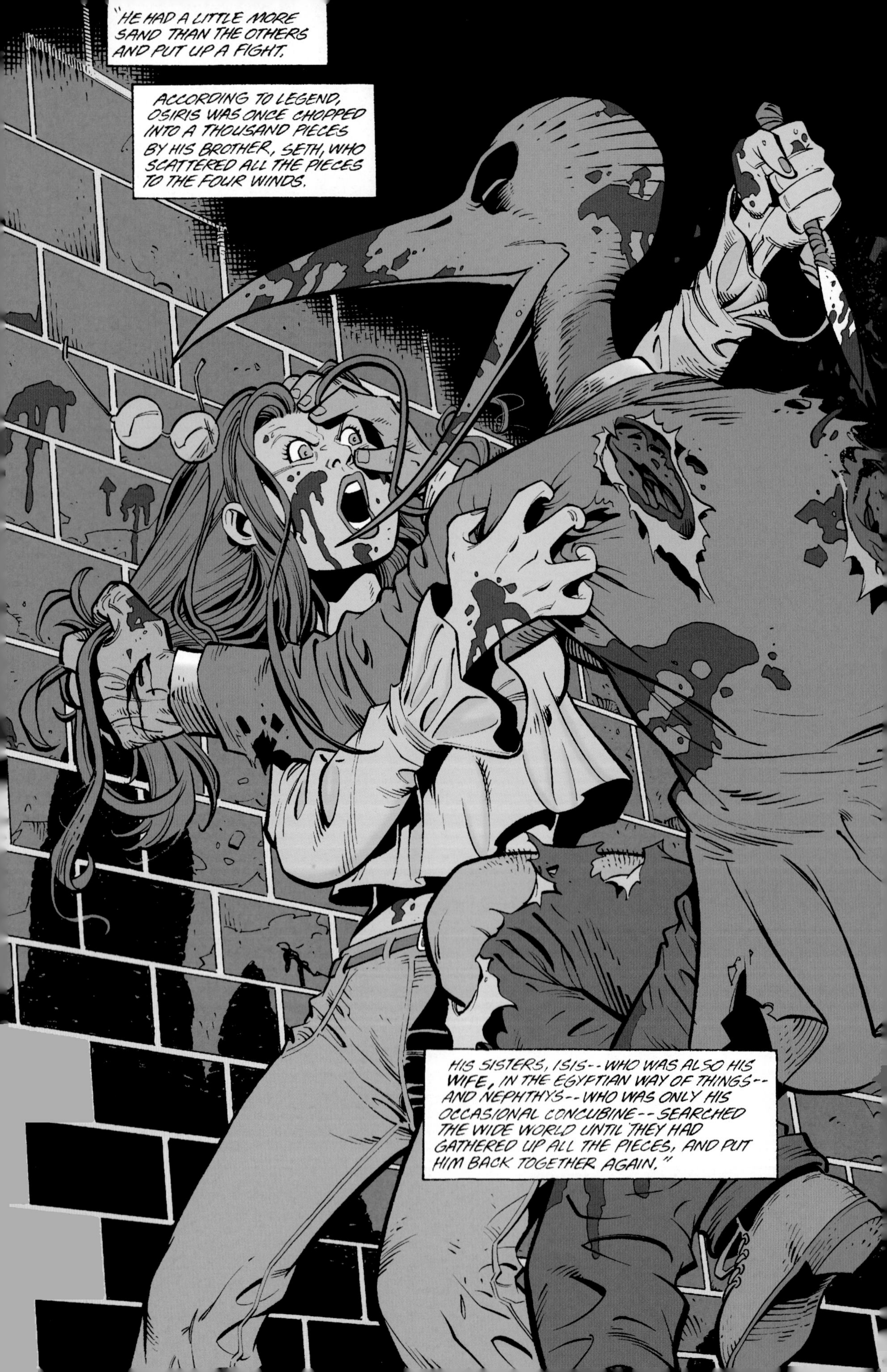
"HE HAD A LITTLE MORE SAND THAN THE OTHERS AND PUT UP A FIGHT.
ACCORDING TO LEGEND, OSIRIS WAS ONCE CHOPPED INTO A THOUSAND PIECES BY HIS BROTHER, SETH, WHO SCATTERED ALL THE PIECES TO THE FOUR WINDS.
HIS SISTERS, ISIS--WHO WAS ALSO HIS WIFE, IN THE EGYPTIAN WAY OF THINGS--AND NEPHTHYS--WHO WAS ONLY HIS OCCASIONAL CONCUBINE--SEARCHED THE WIDE WORLD UNTIL THEY HAD GATHERED UP ALL THE PIECES, AND PUT HIM BACK TOGETHER AGAIN."

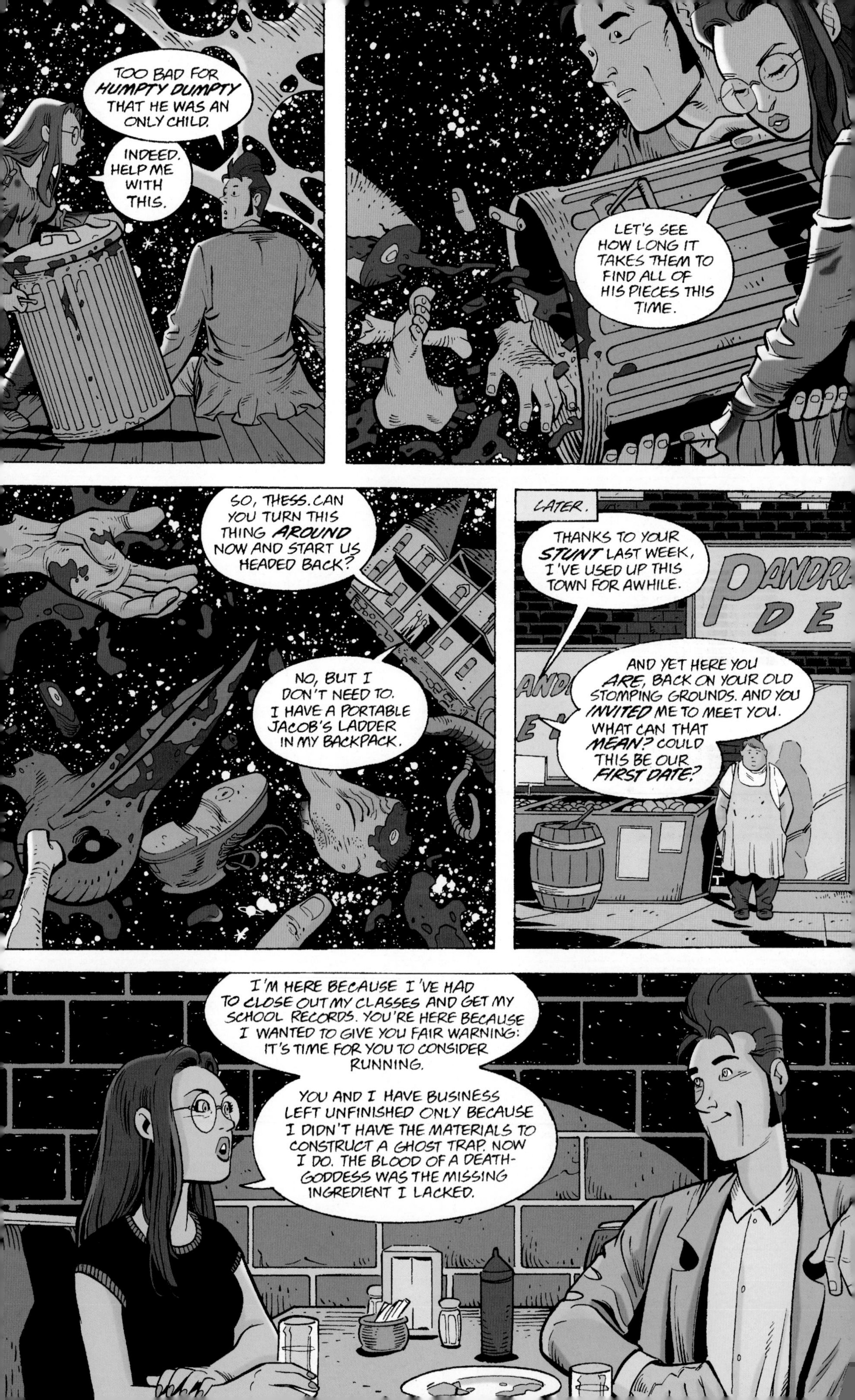
TOO BAD FOR HUMPTY DUMPTY THAT HE WAS AN ONLY CHILD.
INDEED. HELP ME WITH THIS.
LET'S SEE HOW LONG IT TAKES THEM TO FIND ALL OF HIS PIECES THIS TIME.
SO, THESS. CAN YOU TURN THIS THING AROUND NOW AND START US HEADED BACK?
NO, BUT I DON'T NEED TO. I HAVE A PORTABLE JACOB'S LADDER IN MY BACKPACK.
LATER.
THANKS TO YOUR STUNT LAST WEEK, I'VE USED UP THIS TOWN FOR AWHILE.
AND YET HERE YOU ARE, BACK ON YOUR OLD STOMPING GROUNDS. AND YOU INVITED ME TO MEET YOU. WHAT CAN THAT MEAN? COULD THIS BE OUR FIRST DATE?
I'M HERE BECAUSE I'VE HAD TO CLOSE OUT MY CLASSES AND GET MY SCHOOL RECORDS. YOU'RE HERE BECAUSE I WANTED TO GIVE YOU FAIR WARNING: IT'S TIME FOR YOU TO CONSIDER RUNNING.
YOU AND I HAVE BUSINESS LEFT UNFINISHED ONLY BECAUSE I DIDN'T HAVE THE MATERIALS TO CONSTRUCT A GHOST TRAP. NOW I DO. THE BLOOD OF A DEATH-GODDESS WAS THE MISSING INGREDIENT I LACKED.

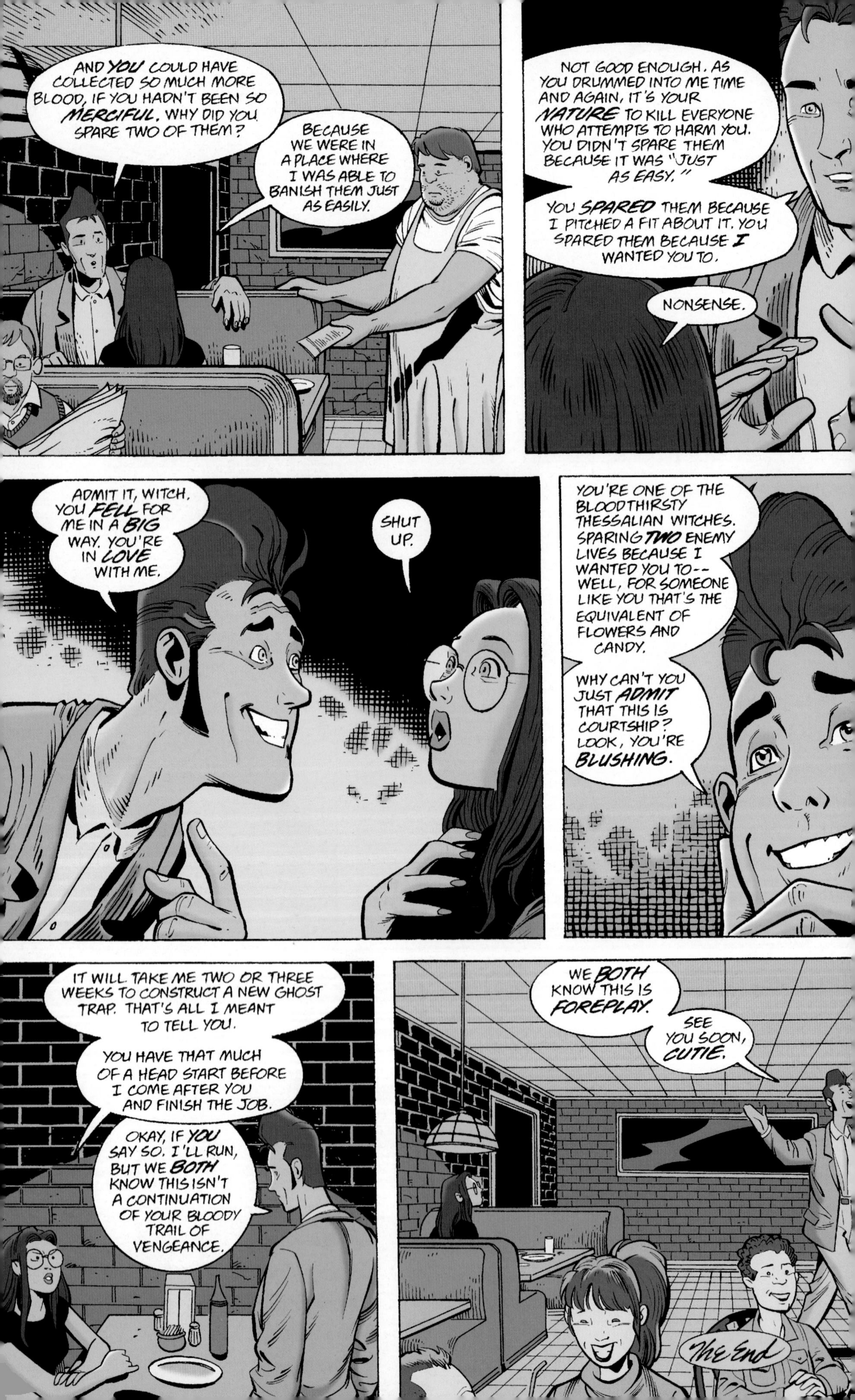
AND YOU COULD HAVE COLLECTED SO MUCH MORE BLOOD, IF YOU HADN'T BEEN SO MERCIFUL. WHY DID YOU SPARE TWO OF THEM?
BECAUSE WE WERE IN A PLACE WHERE I WAS ABLE TO BANISH THEM JUST AS EASILY.
NOT GOOD ENOUGH. AS YOU DRUMMED INTO ME TIME AND AGAIN, IT'S YOUR NATURE TO KILL EVERYONE WHO ATTEMPTS TO HARM YOU. YOU DIDN'T SPARE THEM BECAUSE IT WAS "JUST AS EASY."
YOU SPARED THEM BECAUSE I PITCHED A FIT ABOUT IT. YOU SPARED THEM BECAUSE I WANTED YOU TO.
NONSENSE.
ADMIT IT, WITCH. YOU FELL FOR ME IN A BIG WAY. YOU'RE IN LOVE WITH ME.
SHUT UP.
YOU'RE ONE OF THE BLOODTHIRSTY THESSALIAN WITCHES. SPARING TWO ENEMY LIVES BECAUSE I WANTED YOU TO-- WELL, FOR SOMEONE LIKE YOU THAT'S THE EQUIVALENT OF FLOWERS AND CANDY.
WHY CAN'T YOU JUST ADMIT THAT THIS IS COURTSHIP? LOOK, YOU'RE BLUSHING.
IT WILL TAKE ME TWO OR THREE WEEKS TO CONSTRUCT A NEW GHOST TRAP. THAT'S ALL I MEANT TO TELL YOU.
YOU HAVE THAT MUCH OF A HEAD START BEFORE I COME AFTER YOU AND FINISH THE JOB.
OKAY, IF YOU SAY SO. I'LL RUN, BUT WE BOTH KNOW THIS ISN'T A CONTINUATION OF YOUR BLOODY TRAIL OF VENGEANCE.
WE BOTH KNOW THIS IS FOREPLAY.
SEE YOU SOON, CUTIE.
The End

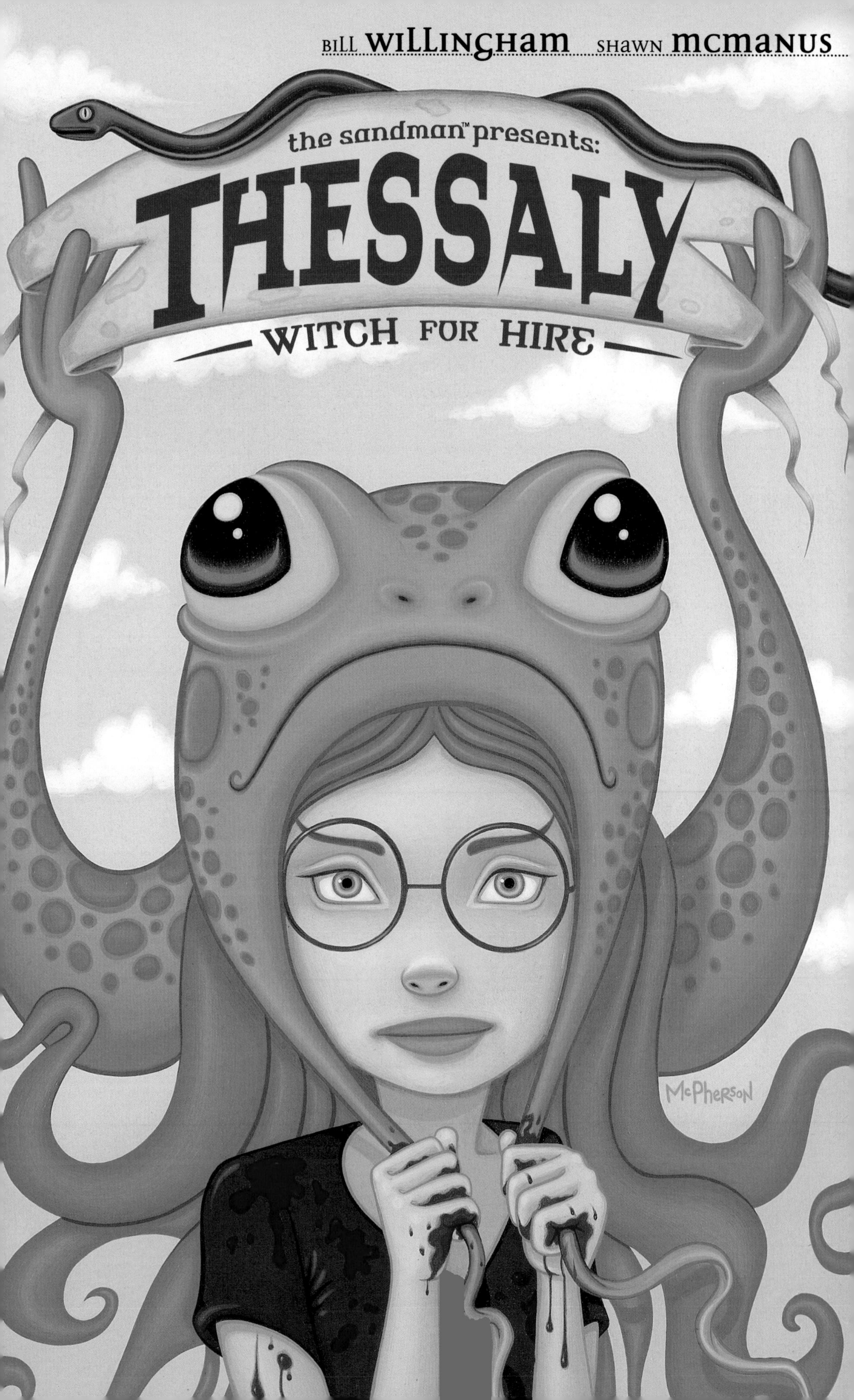

BILL WILLINGHAM SHAWN MCMANUS
the sandman™ presents:
THESSALY
WITCH FOR HIRE
McPHERSON

THE IDEA BEHIND THIS WAS SIMPLE. "Bill," Shelly said over the phone (she was now Shelly *Bond*, officially), "would you be interested in doing another THESSALY miniseries, working with Shawn again on the art?" The universe's smallest measurable fragment of time was how long it took me to think it over.

"Yes," I said.

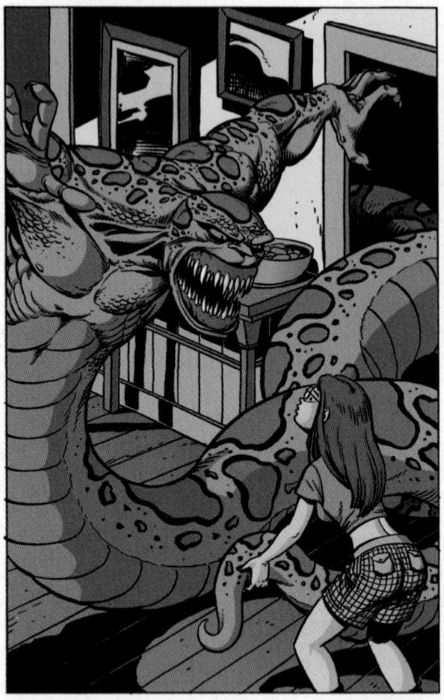

And so, we were once more off to the races.

Of course I wanted to bring back the Fetch character from the previous story. Thessaly would never admit that she and the ghost were friends; she's not the type to admit much of anything. She might even go so far as to say they last parted company as dire enemies, but in this one instance she's wrong.

This is a story about how no one can get you into trouble like a friend — something I fear we can all relate to. Minus the magical trappings, you might say that this is a true story.

For those who like a peek behind the curtain, this miniseries also contains one of the two uses of my family's old warrior housecat as a character in my stories. In this one he appears as Fat Charlie in the third chapter. Later on he appears as McTavish the Monster in my middle-grade novel called *Down the Mysterly River* (which is out now). Yes, I fully expect DC to bill me for the commercial I just cleverly slipped into this introductory note.

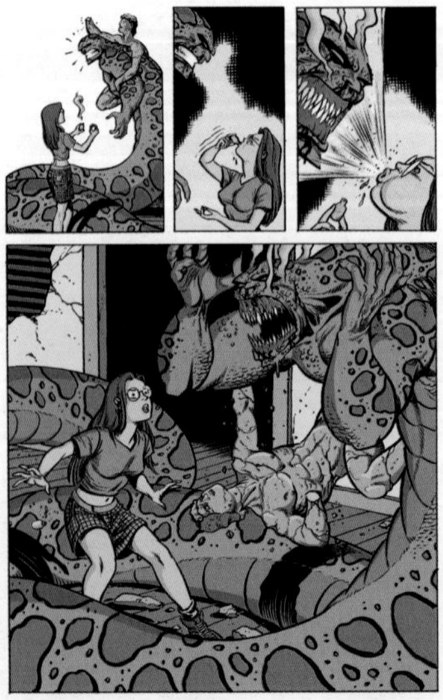

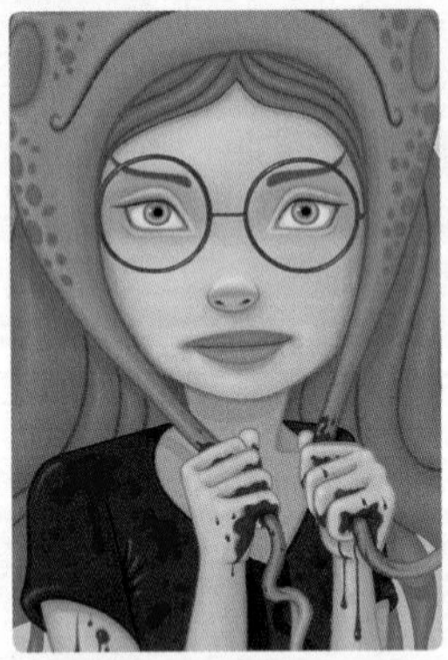

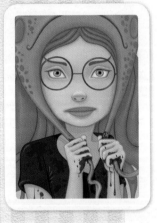

THESSALY—WITCH FOR HIRE

ART BY
Shawn McManus

COLORS BY
Pamela Rambo

LETTERS BY
Nick J. Napolitano *(Part 1)*,
Rob Leigh *(Part 2)*
Phil Balsman *(Parts 3-4)*

COVER ART BY
Tara McPherson

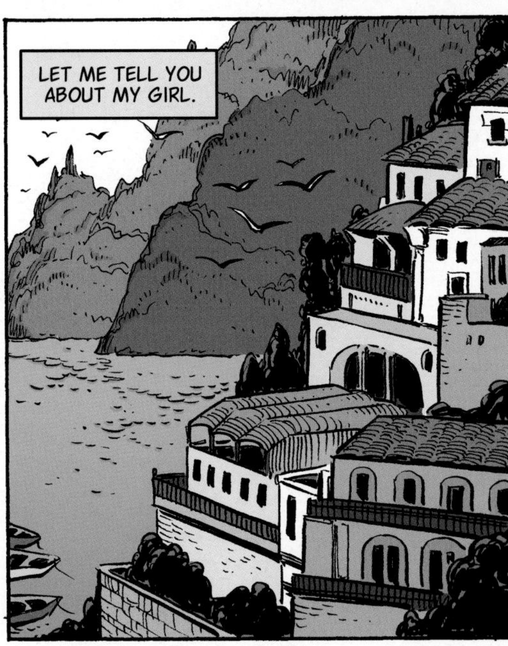
LET ME TELL YOU ABOUT MY GIRL.

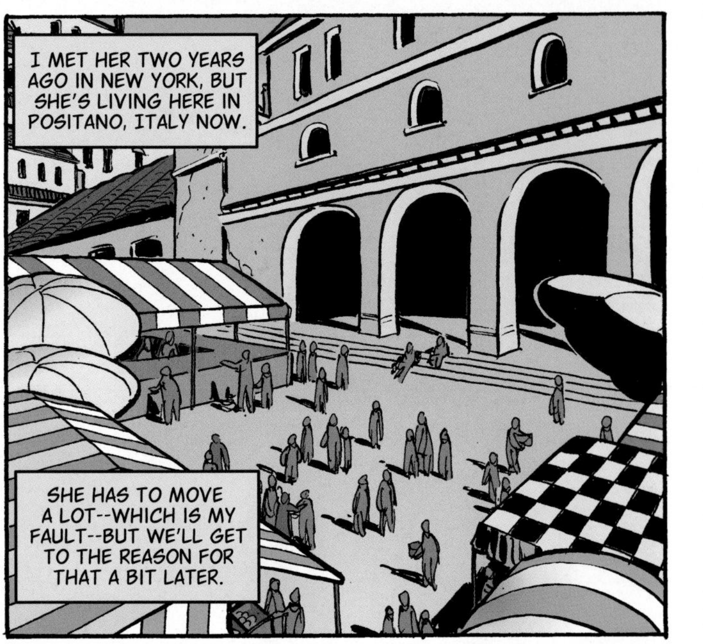
I MET HER TWO YEARS AGO IN NEW YORK, BUT SHE'S LIVING HERE IN POSITANO, ITALY NOW.
SHE HAS TO MOVE A LOT--WHICH IS MY FAULT--BUT WE'LL GET TO THE REASON FOR THAT A BIT LATER.

MY GIRL
OR FAR TOO MUCH ABOUT SNAKES

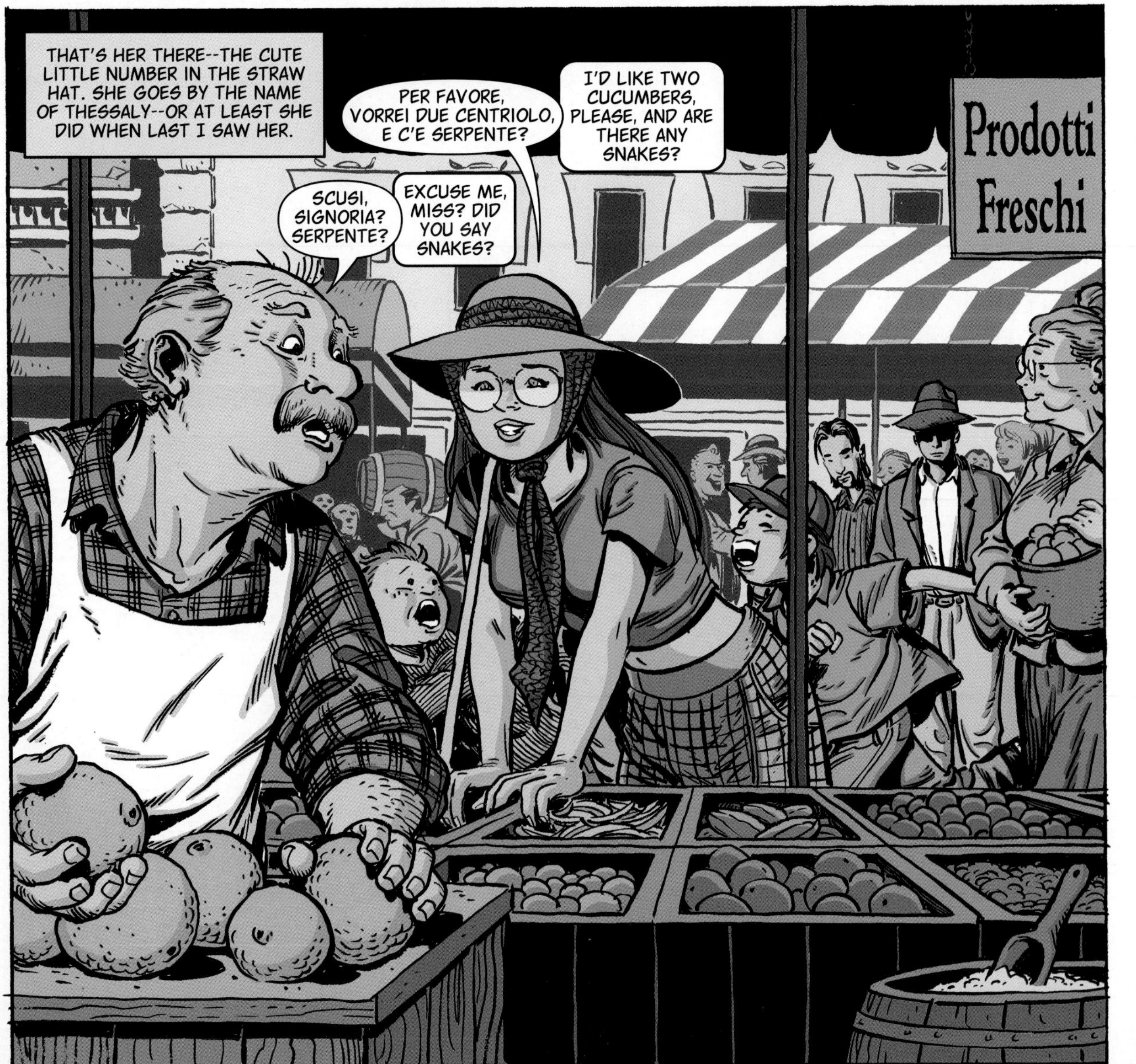
THAT'S HER THERE--THE CUTE LITTLE NUMBER IN THE STRAW HAT. SHE GOES BY THE NAME OF THESSALY--OR AT LEAST SHE DID WHEN LAST I SAW HER.
PER FAVORE, VORREI DUE CENTRIOLO, E C'E SERPENTE?
I'D LIKE TWO CUCUMBERS, PLEASE, AND ARE THERE ANY SNAKES?
Prodotti Freschi
SCUSI, SIGNORIA? SERPENTE?
EXCUSE ME, MISS? DID YOU SAY SNAKES?

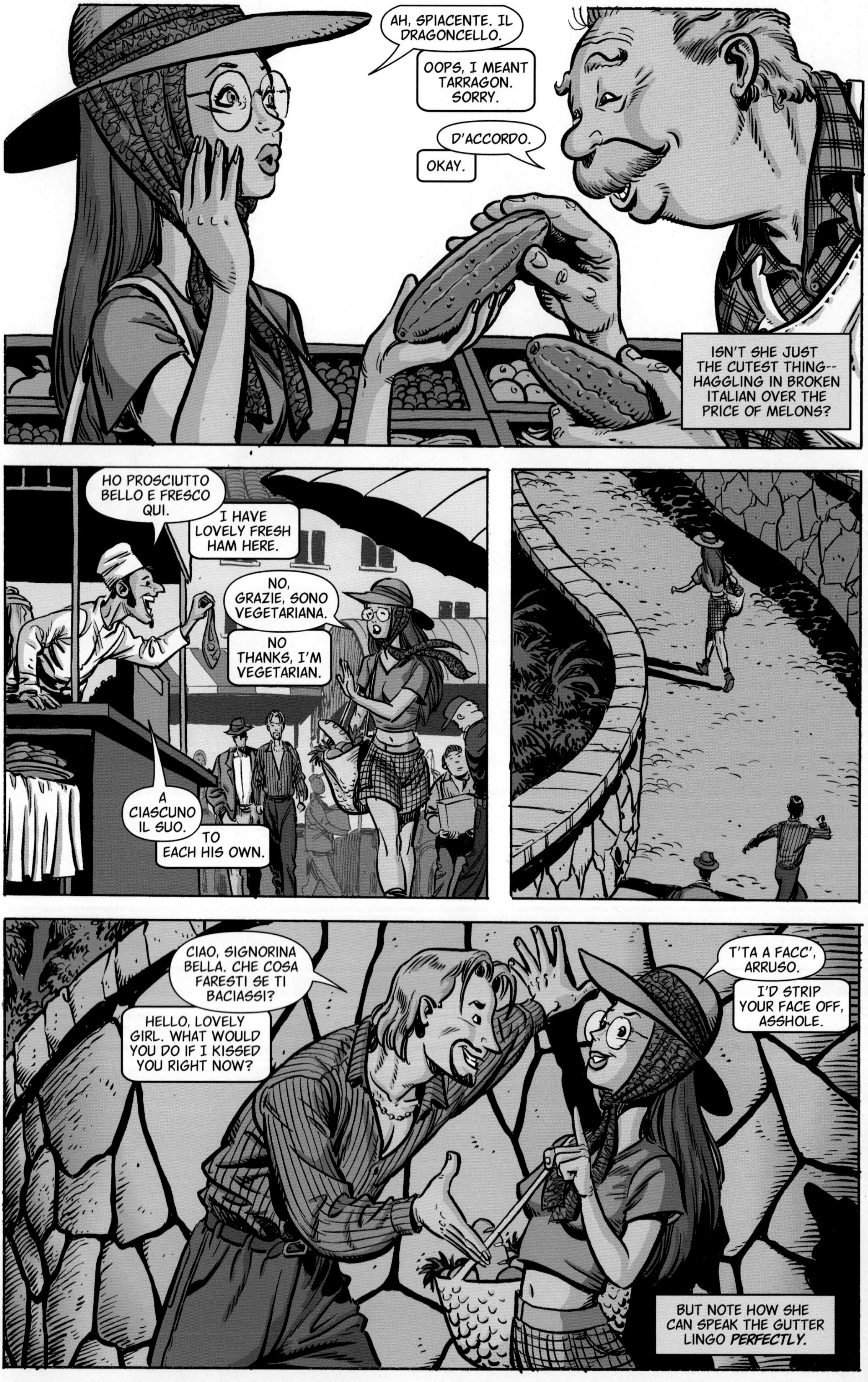
AH, SPIACENTE. IL DRAGONCELLO.
OOPS, I MEANT TARRAGON. SORRY.
D'ACCORDO.
OKAY.
ISN'T SHE JUST THE CUTEST THING-- HAGGLING IN BROKEN ITALIAN OVER THE PRICE OF MELONS?
HO PROSCIUTTO BELLO E FRESCO QUI.
I HAVE LOVELY FRESH HAM HERE.
NO, GRAZIE, SONO VEGETARIANA.
NO THANKS, I'M VEGETARIAN.
A CIASCUNO IL SUO.
TO EACH HIS OWN.
CIAO, SIGNORINA BELLA. CHE COSA FARESTI SE TI BACIASSI?
HELLO, LOVELY GIRL. WHAT WOULD YOU DO IF I KISSED YOU RIGHT NOW?
T'TA A FACC', ARRUSO.
I'D STRIP YOUR FACE OFF, ASSHOLE.
BUT NOTE HOW SHE CAN SPEAK THE GUTTER LINGO *PERFECTLY.*

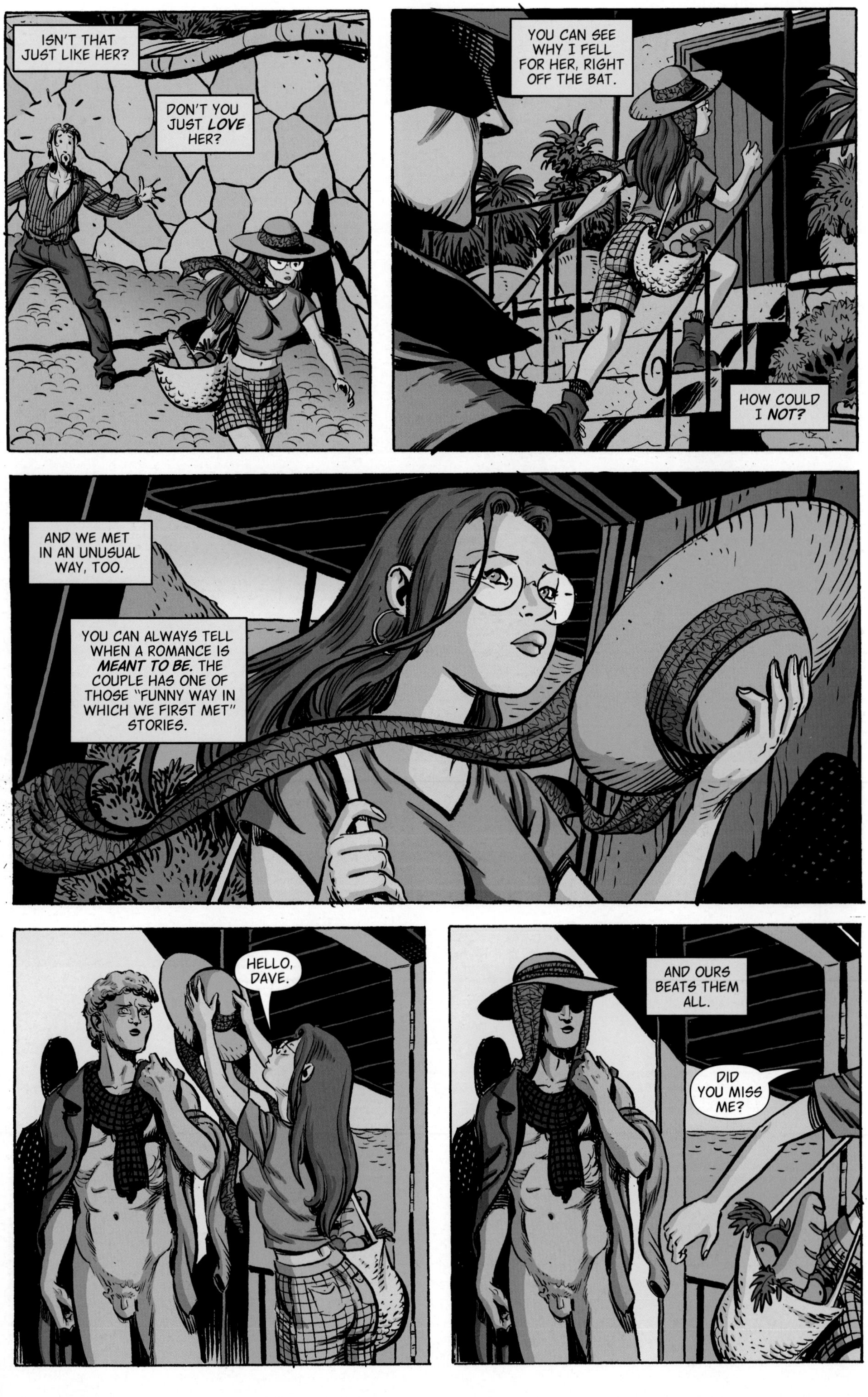
ISN'T THAT JUST LIKE HER?
DON'T YOU JUST LOVE HER?
YOU CAN SEE WHY I FELL FOR HER, RIGHT OFF THE BAT.
HOW COULD I NOT?
AND WE MET IN AN UNUSUAL WAY, TOO.
YOU CAN ALWAYS TELL WHEN A ROMANCE IS MEANT TO BE. THE COUPLE HAS ONE OF THOSE "FUNNY WAY IN WHICH WE FIRST MET" STORIES.
HELLO, DAVE.
AND OURS BEATS THEM ALL.
DID YOU MISS ME?

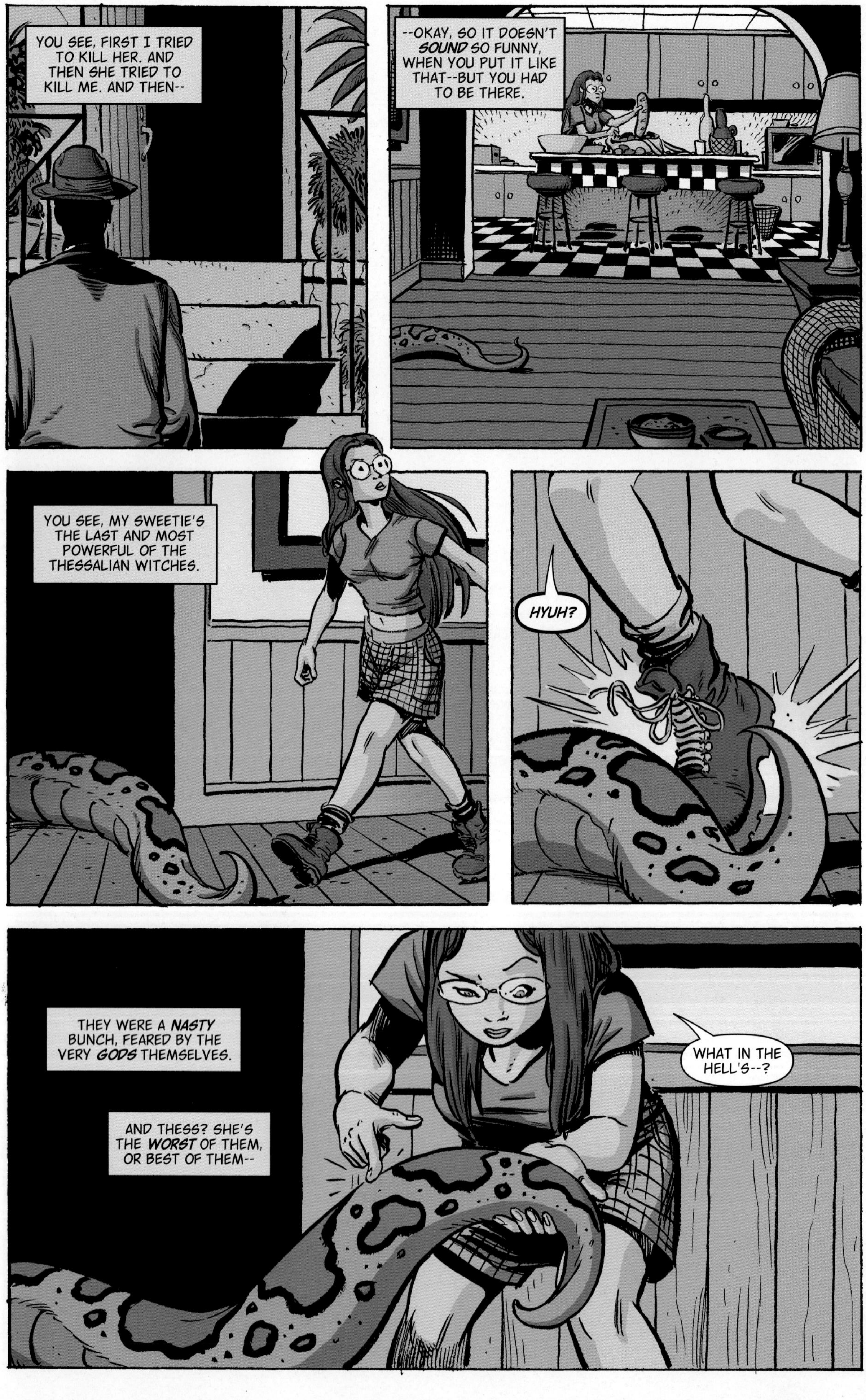
YOU SEE, FIRST I TRIED TO KILL HER. AND THEN SHE TRIED TO KILL ME. AND THEN--
--OKAY, SO IT DOESN'T *SOUND* SO FUNNY, WHEN YOU PUT IT LIKE THAT--BUT YOU HAD TO BE THERE.
YOU SEE, MY SWEETIE'S THE LAST AND MOST POWERFUL OF THE THESSALIAN WITCHES.
HYUH?
THEY WERE A *NASTY* BUNCH, FEARED BY THE VERY *GODS* THEMSELVES.
AND THESS? SHE'S THE *WORST* OF THEM, OR BEST OF THEM--
WHAT IN THE HELL'S--?

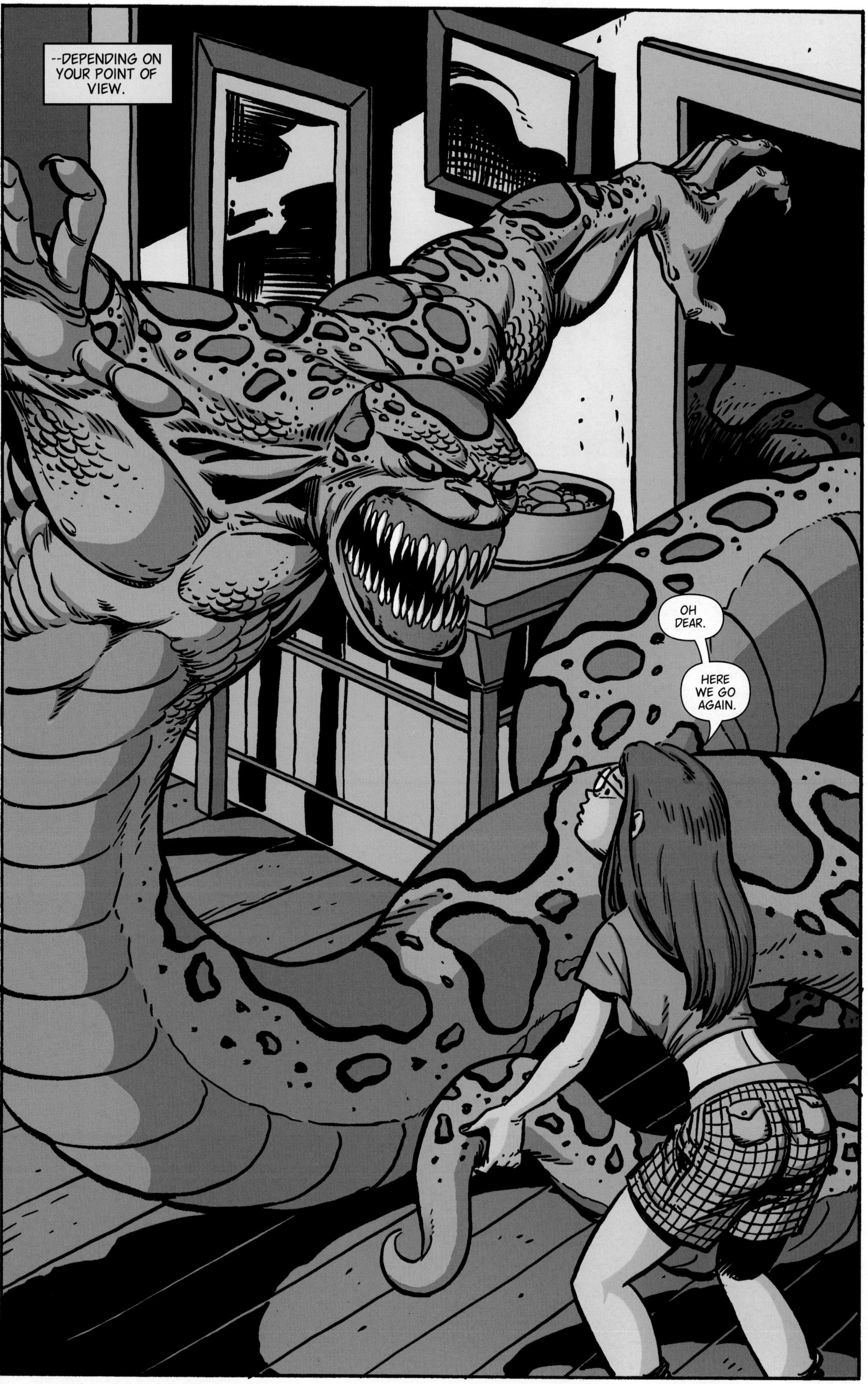
--DEPENDING ON YOUR POINT OF VIEW.
OH DEAR.
HERE WE GO AGAIN.

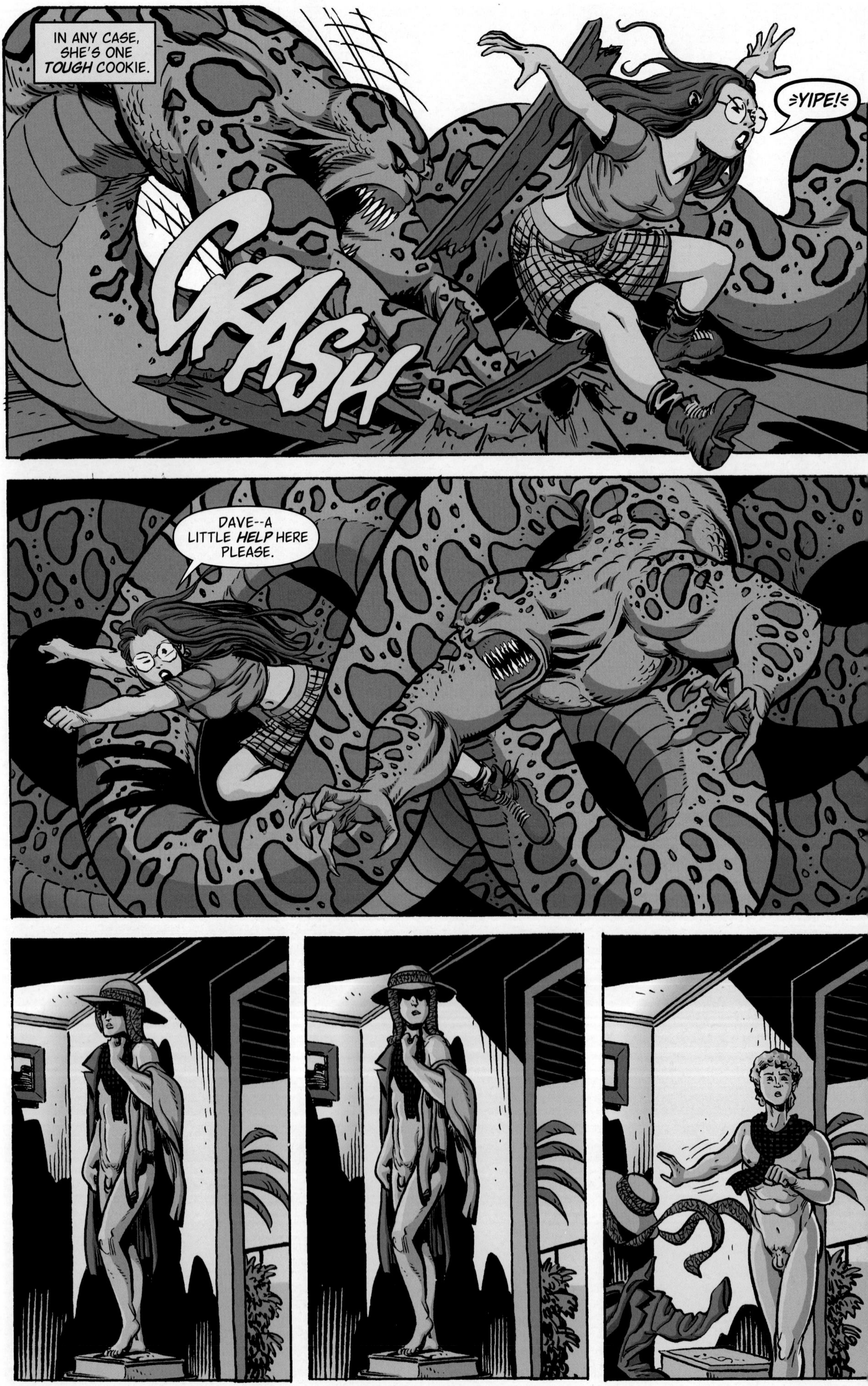
IN ANY CASE, SHE'S ONE TOUGH COOKIE.
YIPE!
CRASH
DAVE--A LITTLE HELP HERE PLEASE.

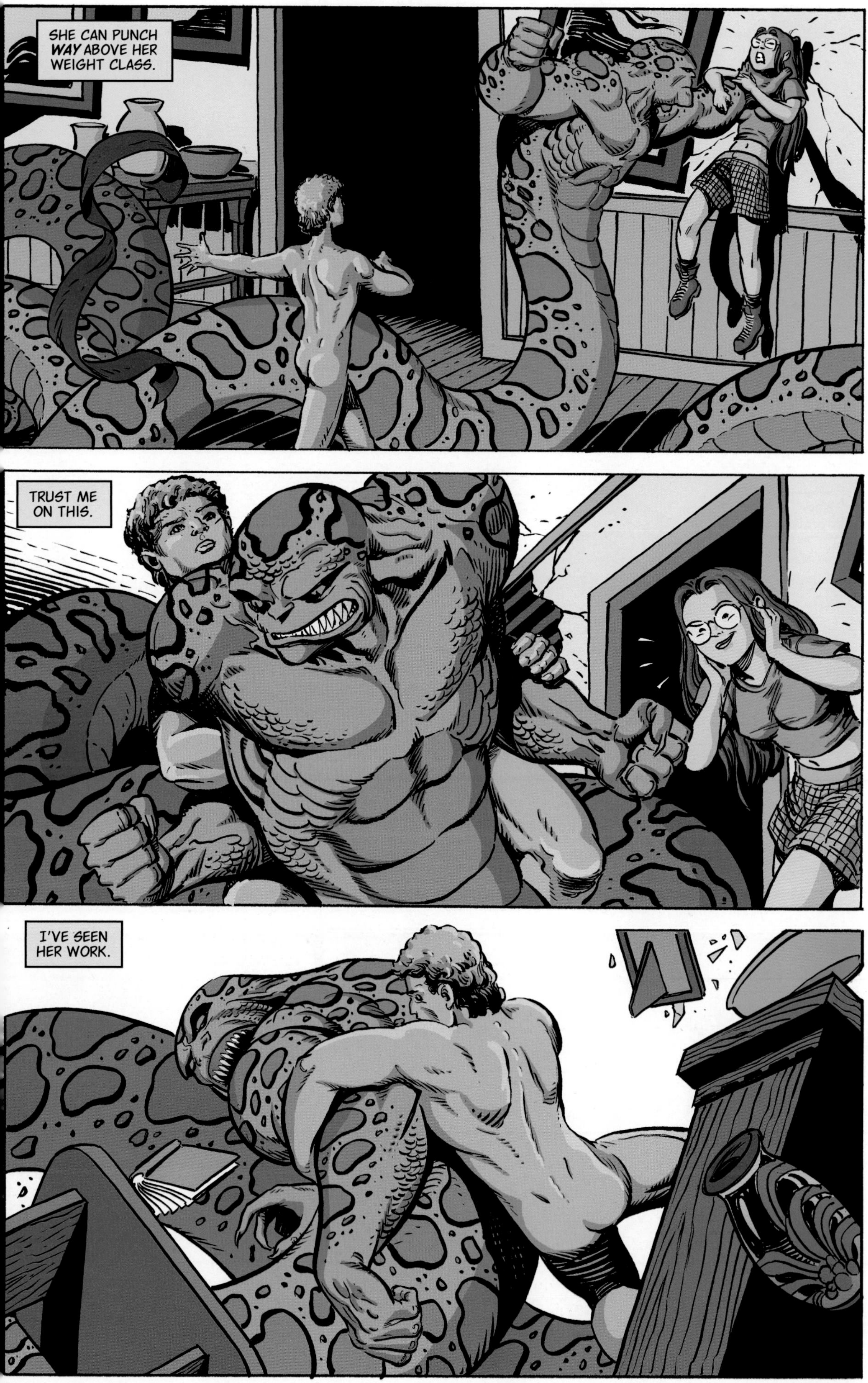
SHE CAN PUNCH WAY ABOVE HER WEIGHT CLASS.
TRUST ME ON THIS.
I'VE SEEN HER WORK.

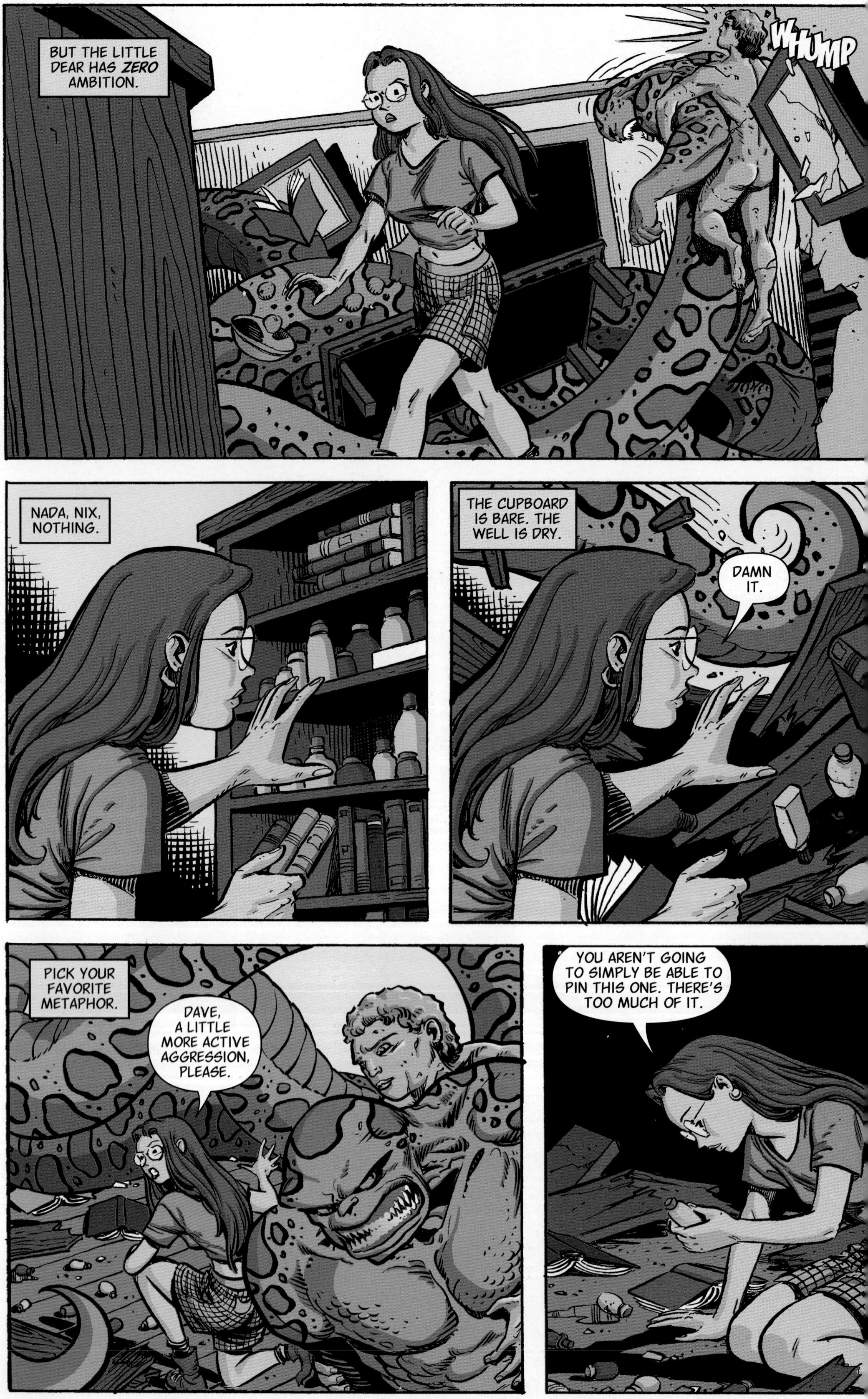

BUT THE LITTLE DEAR HAS ZERO AMBITION.
WHUMP
NADA, NIX, NOTHING.
THE CUPBOARD IS BARE. THE WELL IS DRY.
DAMN IT.
PICK YOUR FAVORITE METAPHOR.
DAVE, A LITTLE MORE ACTIVE AGGRESSION, PLEASE.
YOU AREN'T GOING TO SIMPLY BE ABLE TO PIN THIS ONE. THERE'S TOO MUCH OF IT.

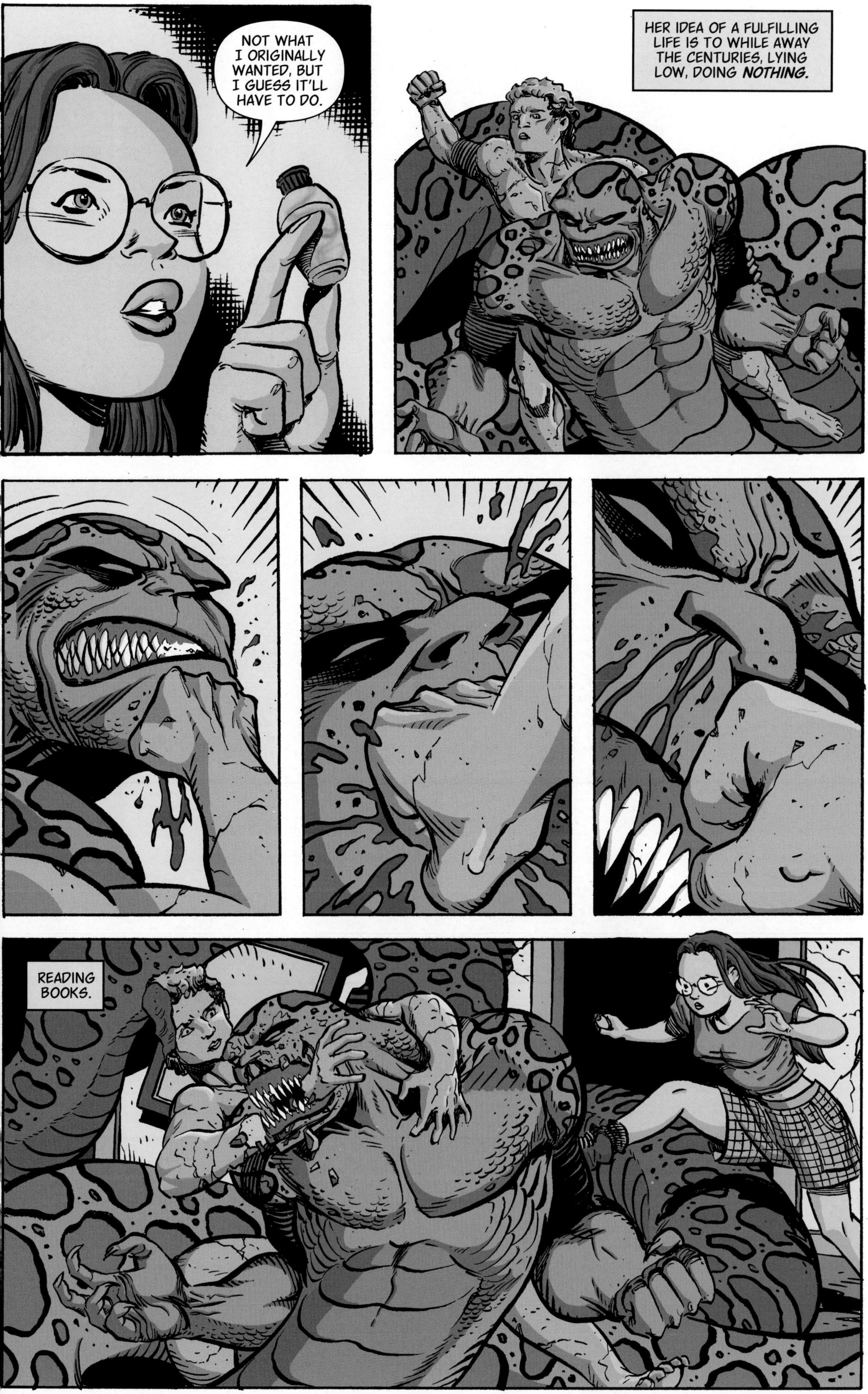
NOT WHAT I ORIGINALLY WANTED, BUT I GUESS IT'LL HAVE TO DO.
HER IDEA OF A FULFILLING LIFE IS TO WHILE AWAY THE CENTURIES, LYING LOW, DOING NOTHING.
READING BOOKS.

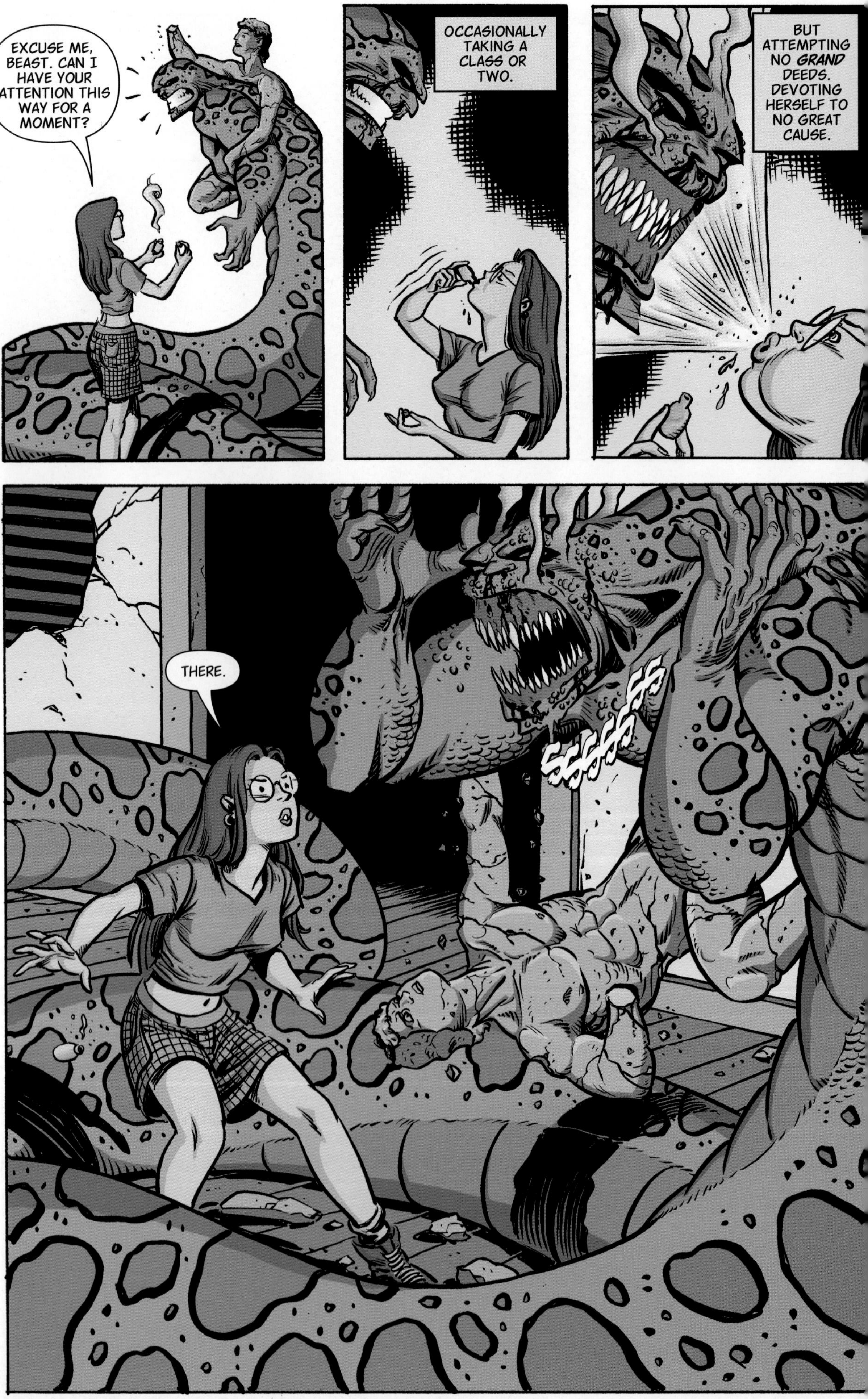
EXCUSE ME, BEAST. CAN I HAVE YOUR ATTENTION THIS WAY FOR A MOMENT?
OCCASIONALLY TAKING A CLASS OR TWO.
BUT ATTEMPTING NO GRAND DEEDS. DEVOTING HERSELF TO NO GREAT CAUSE.
THERE.
SSSSSS

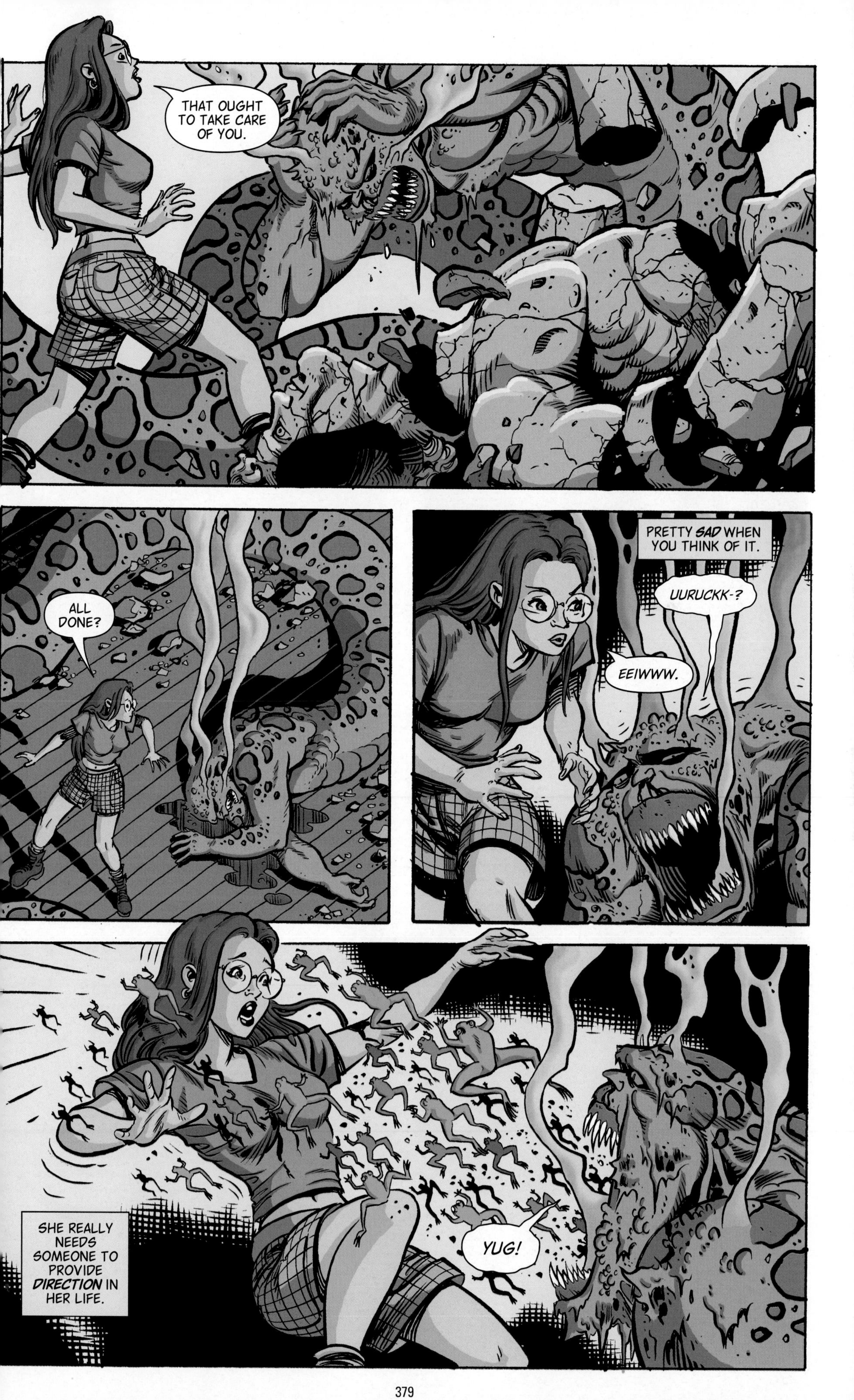
THAT OUGHT TO TAKE CARE OF YOU.
ALL DONE?
PRETTY SAD WHEN YOU THINK OF IT.
UURUCKK-?
EEIWWW.
SHE REALLY NEEDS SOMEONE TO PROVIDE DIRECTION IN HER LIFE.
YUG!

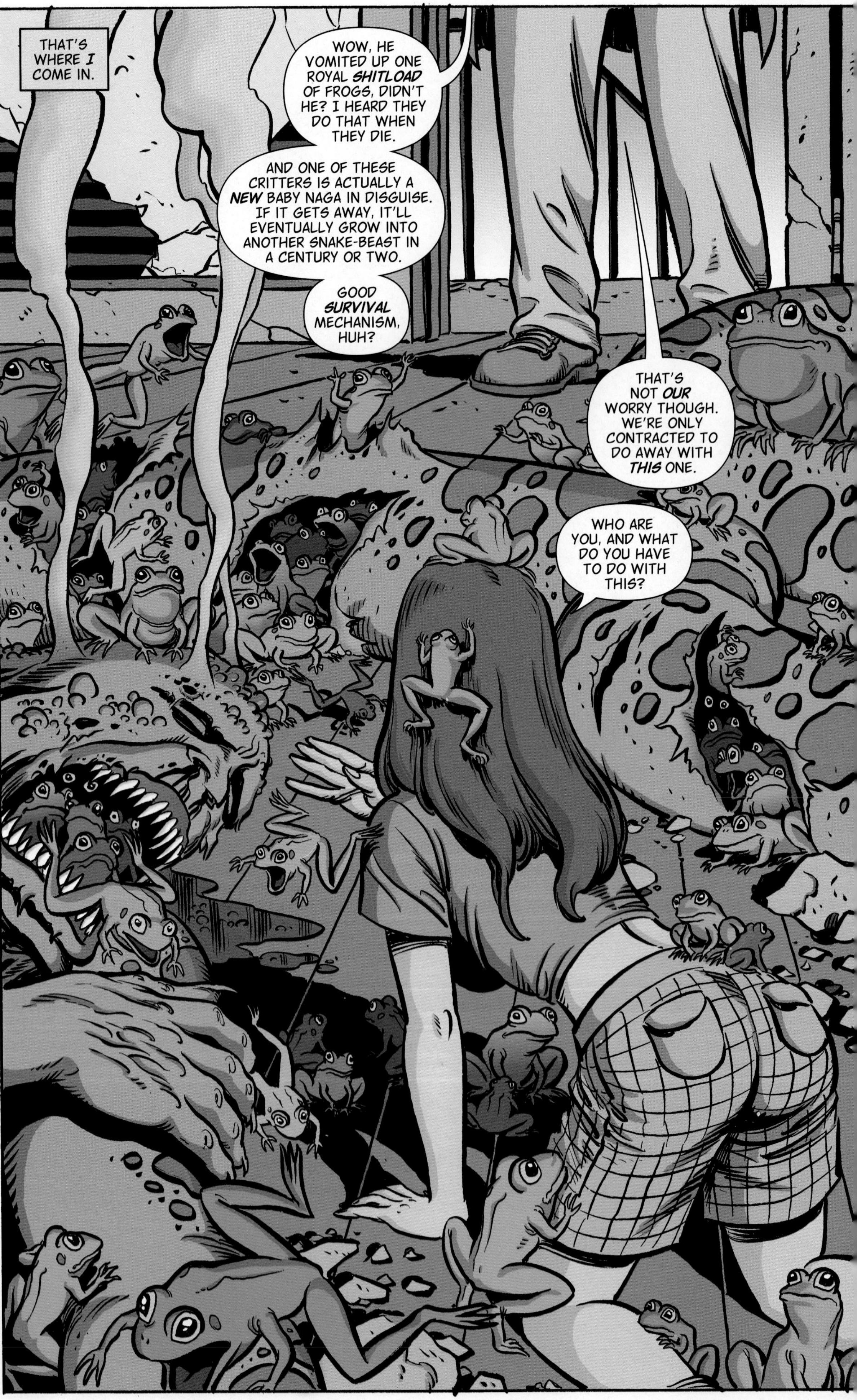

THAT'S WHERE *I* COME IN.
WOW, HE VOMITED UP ONE ROYAL *SHITLOAD* OF FROGS, DIDN'T HE? I HEARD THEY DO THAT WHEN THEY DIE.
AND ONE OF THESE CRITTERS IS ACTUALLY A *NEW* BABY NAGA IN DISGUISE. IF IT GETS AWAY, IT'LL EVENTUALLY GROW INTO ANOTHER SNAKE-BEAST IN A CENTURY OR TWO.
GOOD *SURVIVAL* MECHANISM, HUH?
THAT'S NOT *OUR* WORRY THOUGH. WE'RE ONLY CONTRACTED TO DO AWAY WITH *THIS* ONE.
WHO ARE YOU, AND WHAT DO YOU HAVE TO DO WITH THIS?

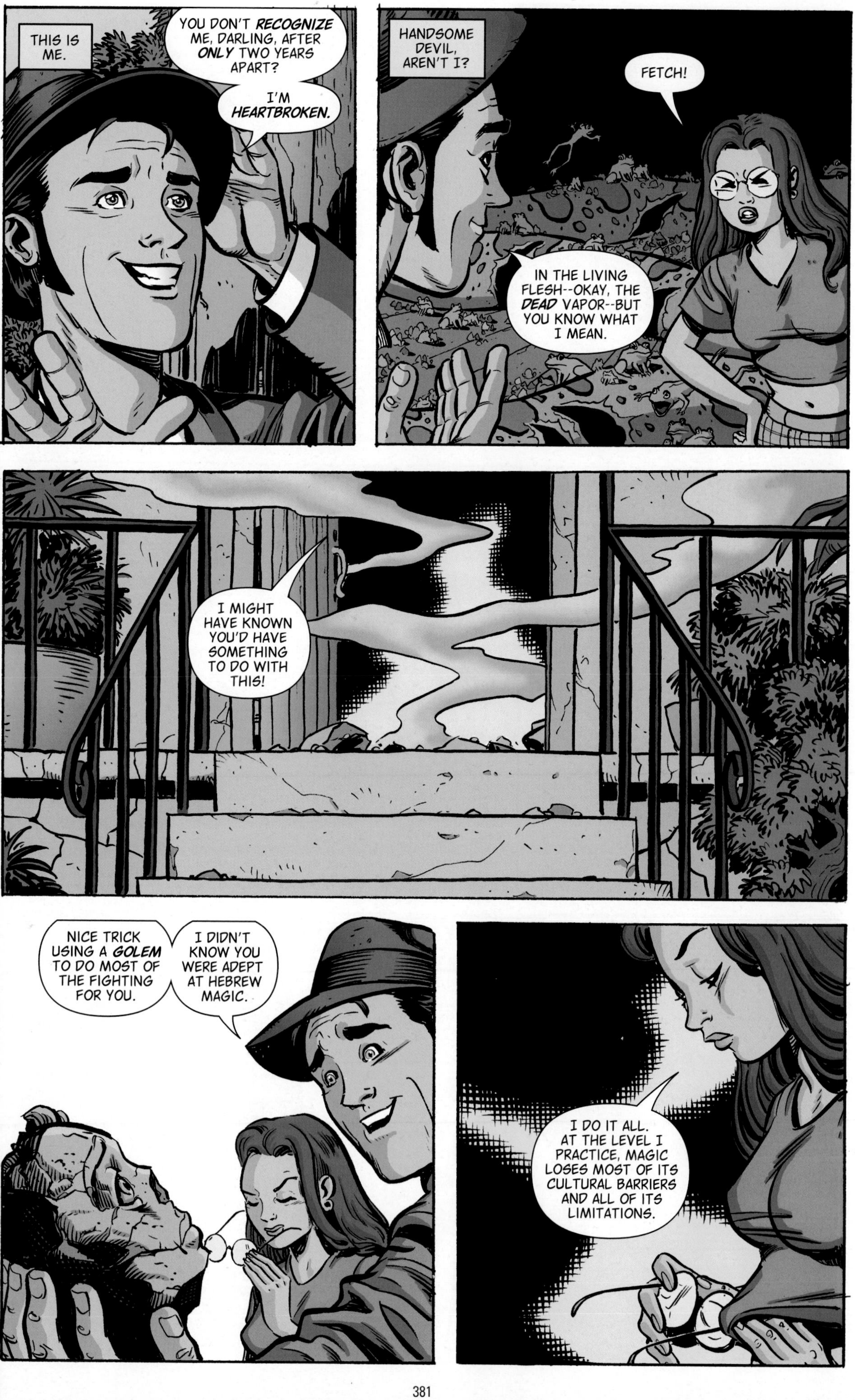
THIS IS ME.
YOU DON'T *RECOGNIZE* ME, DARLING, AFTER *ONLY* TWO YEARS APART?
I'M *HEARTBROKEN.*
HANDSOME DEVIL, AREN'T I?
FETCH!
IN THE LIVING FLESH--OKAY, THE *DEAD* VAPOR--BUT YOU KNOW WHAT I MEAN.
I MIGHT HAVE KNOWN YOU'D HAVE SOMETHING TO DO WITH THIS!
NICE TRICK USING A *GOLEM* TO DO MOST OF THE FIGHTING FOR YOU.
I DIDN'T KNOW YOU WERE ADEPT AT HEBREW MAGIC.
I DO IT ALL. AT THE LEVEL I PRACTICE, MAGIC LOSES MOST OF ITS CULTURAL BARRIERS AND ALL OF ITS LIMITATIONS.

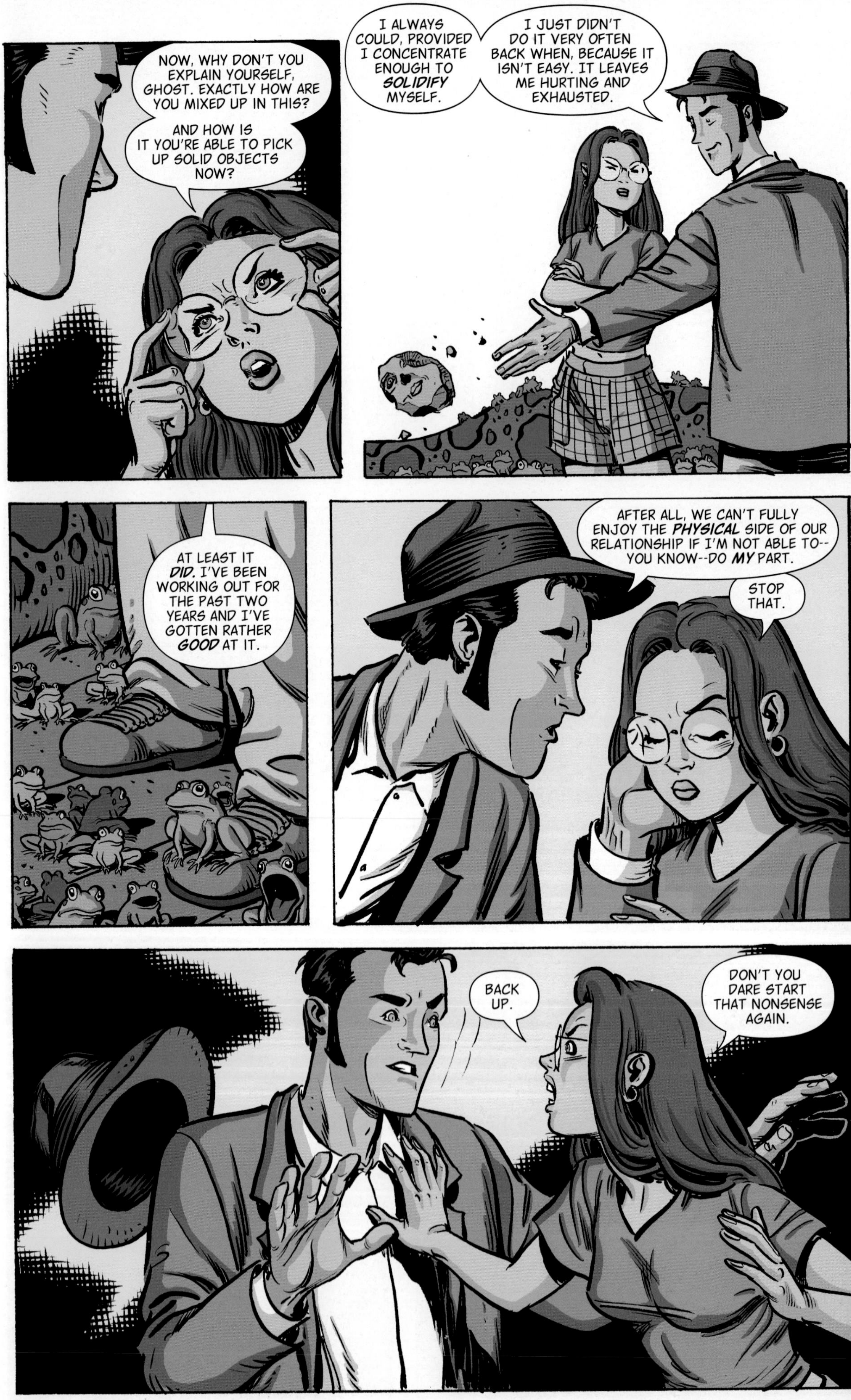
NOW, WHY DON'T YOU EXPLAIN YOURSELF, GHOST. EXACTLY HOW ARE YOU MIXED UP IN THIS?
AND HOW IS IT YOU'RE ABLE TO PICK UP SOLID OBJECTS NOW?
I ALWAYS COULD, PROVIDED I CONCENTRATE ENOUGH TO ***SOLIDIFY*** MYSELF.
I JUST DIDN'T DO IT VERY OFTEN BACK WHEN, BECAUSE IT ISN'T EASY. IT LEAVES ME HURTING AND EXHAUSTED.
AT LEAST IT ***DID.*** I'VE BEEN WORKING OUT FOR THE PAST TWO YEARS AND I'VE GOTTEN RATHER ***GOOD*** AT IT.
AFTER ALL, WE CAN'T FULLY ENJOY THE ***PHYSICAL*** SIDE OF OUR RELATIONSHIP IF I'M NOT ABLE TO--YOU KNOW--DO ***MY*** PART.
STOP THAT.
BACK UP.
DON'T YOU DARE START THAT NONSENSE AGAIN.

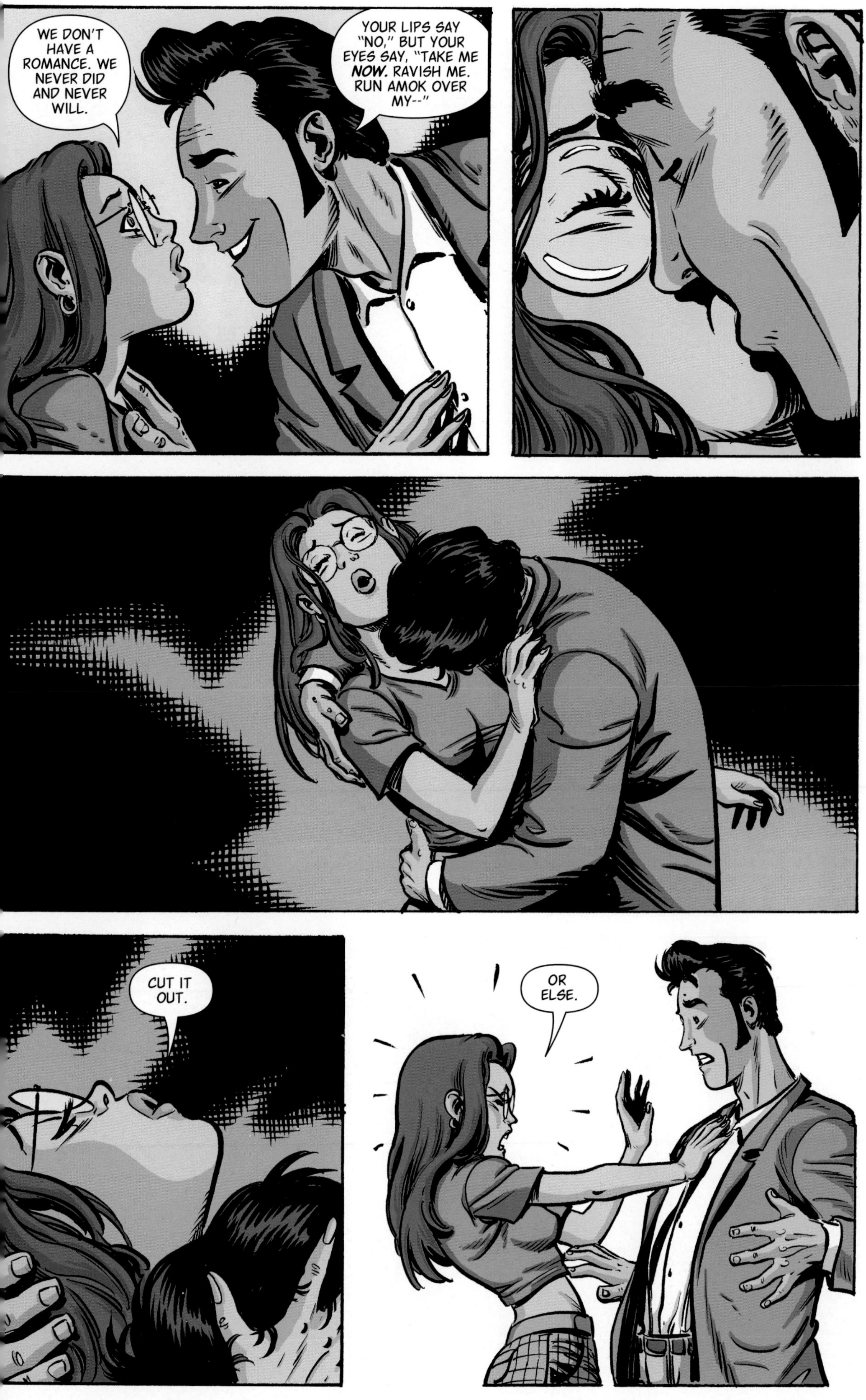
WE DON'T HAVE A ROMANCE. WE NEVER DID AND NEVER WILL.
YOUR LIPS SAY "NO," BUT YOUR EYES SAY, "TAKE ME **NOW.** RAVISH ME. RUN AMOK OVER MY--"
CUT IT OUT.
OR ELSE.

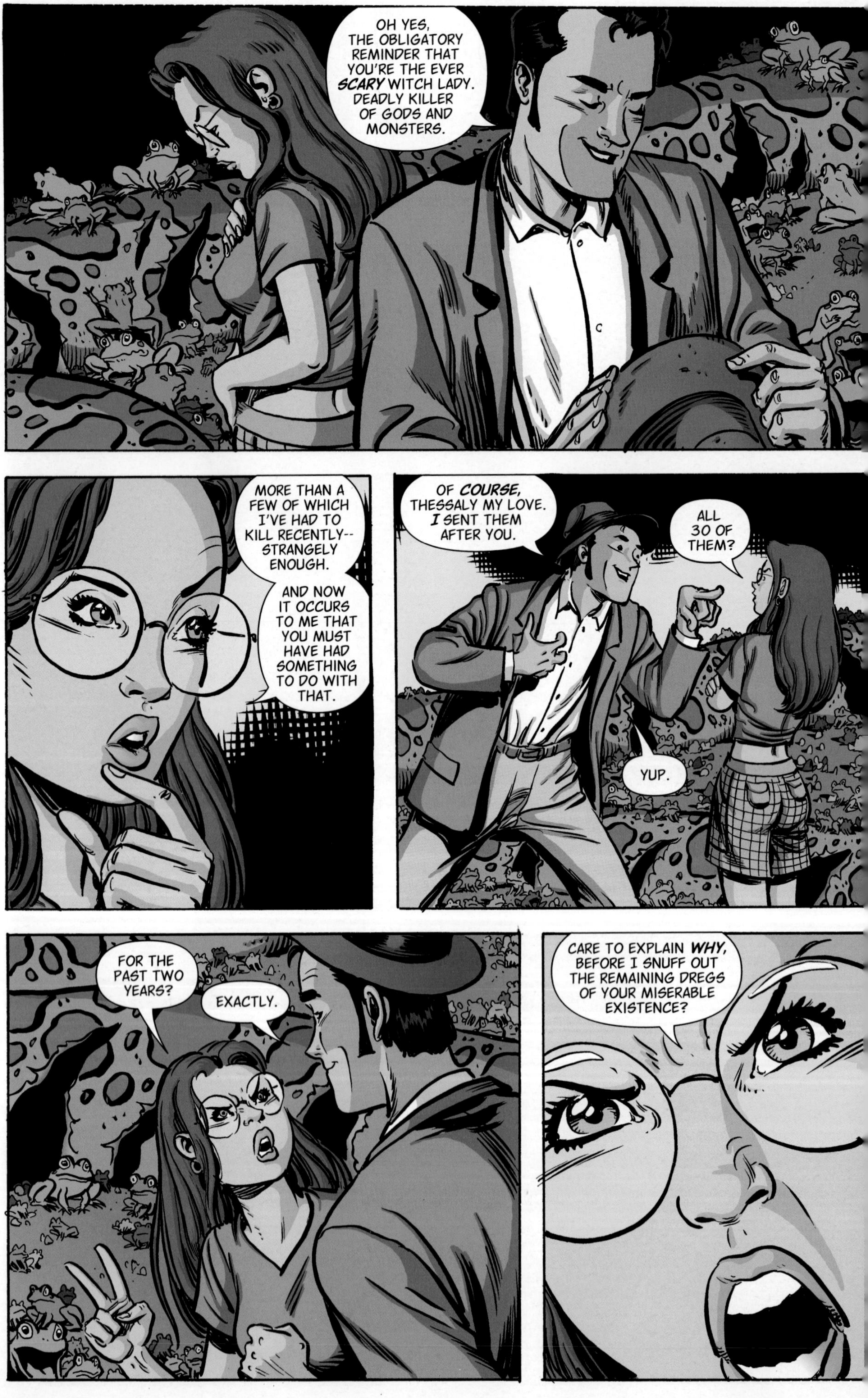
OH YES, THE OBLIGATORY REMINDER THAT YOU'RE THE EVER *SCARY* WITCH LADY. DEADLY KILLER OF GODS AND MONSTERS.
MORE THAN A FEW OF WHICH I'VE HAD TO KILL RECENTLY-- STRANGELY ENOUGH.
AND NOW IT OCCURS TO ME THAT YOU MUST HAVE HAD SOMETHING TO DO WITH THAT.
OF *COURSE,* THESSALY MY LOVE. *I* SENT THEM AFTER YOU.
ALL 30 OF THEM?
YUP.
FOR THE PAST TWO YEARS?
EXACTLY.
CARE TO EXPLAIN *WHY,* BEFORE I SNUFF OUT THE REMAINING DREGS OF YOUR MISERABLE EXISTENCE?

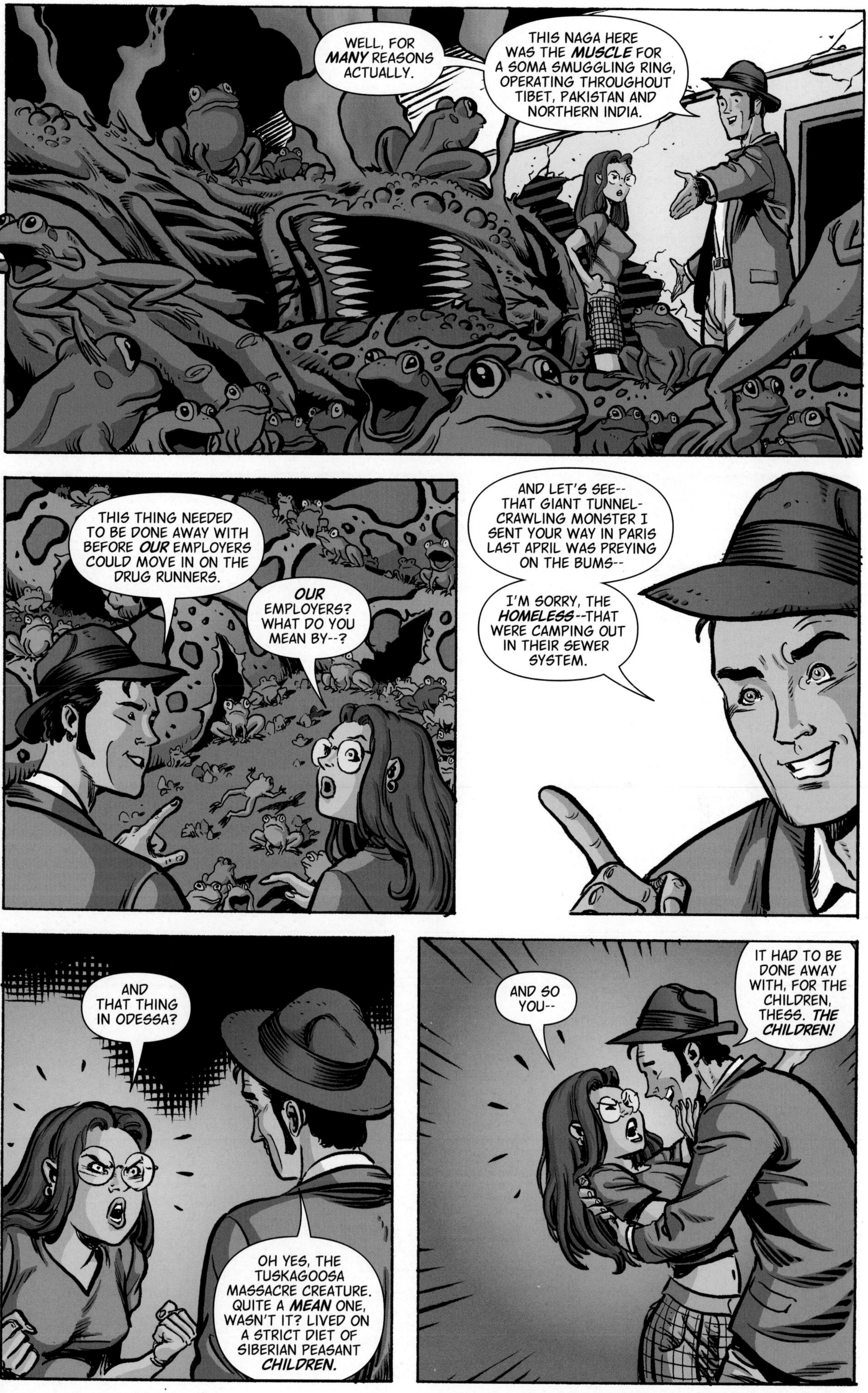
WELL, FOR MANY REASONS ACTUALLY.
THIS NAGA HERE WAS THE MUSCLE FOR A SOMA SMUGGLING RING, OPERATING THROUGHOUT TIBET, PAKISTAN AND NORTHERN INDIA.
THIS THING NEEDED TO BE DONE AWAY WITH BEFORE OUR EMPLOYERS COULD MOVE IN ON THE DRUG RUNNERS.
OUR EMPLOYERS? WHAT DO YOU MEAN BY--?
AND LET'S SEE-- THAT GIANT TUNNEL-CRAWLING MONSTER I SENT YOUR WAY IN PARIS LAST APRIL WAS PREYING ON THE BUMS--
I'M SORRY, THE HOMELESS--THAT WERE CAMPING OUT IN THEIR SEWER SYSTEM.
AND THAT THING IN ODESSA?
OH YES, THE TUSKAGOOSA MASSACRE CREATURE. QUITE A MEAN ONE, WASN'T IT? LIVED ON A STRICT DIET OF SIBERIAN PEASANT CHILDREN.
AND SO YOU--
IT HAD TO BE DONE AWAY WITH, FOR THE CHILDREN, THESS. THE CHILDREN!

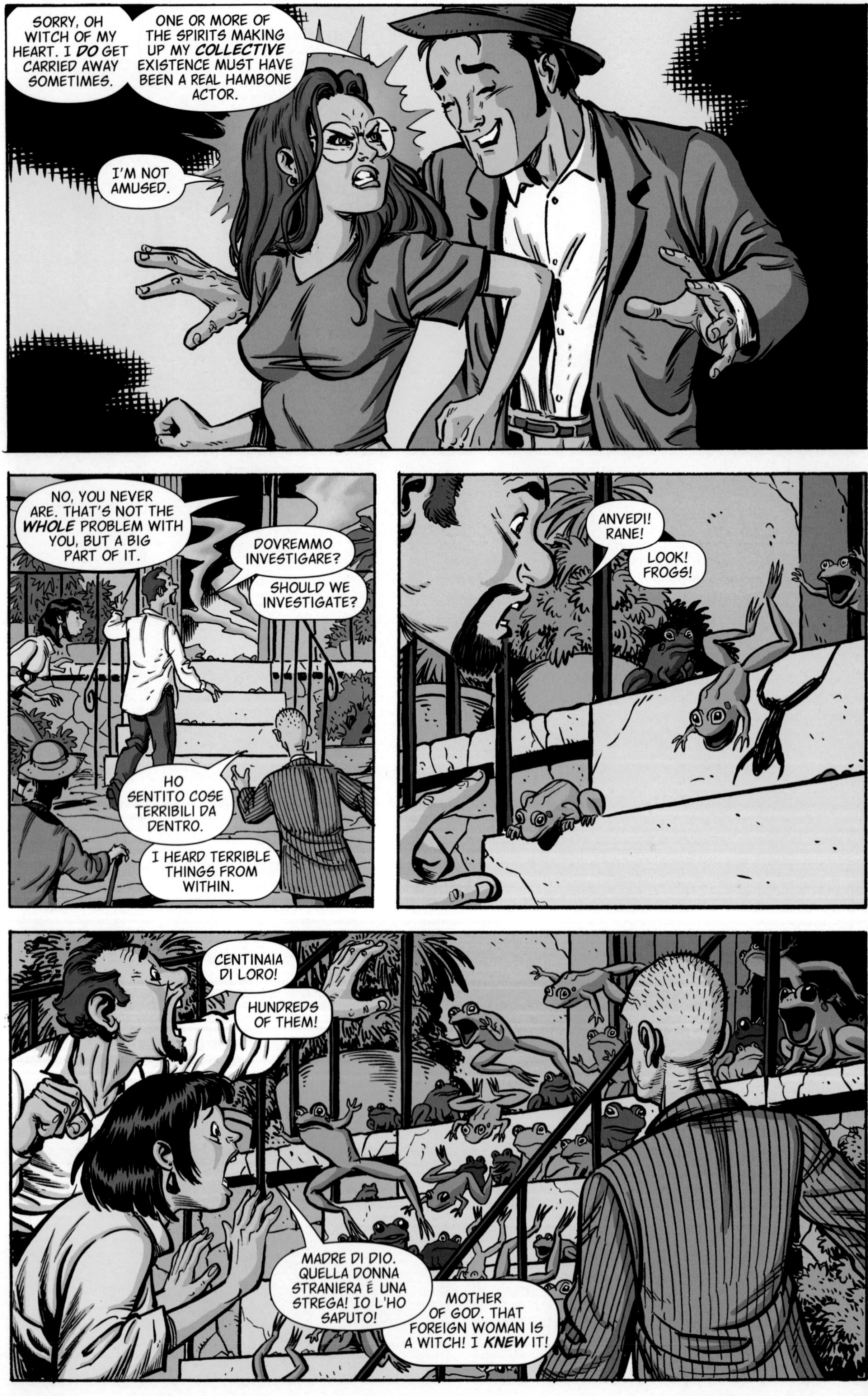
SORRY, OH WITCH OF MY HEART. I DO GET CARRIED AWAY SOMETIMES.
ONE OR MORE OF THE SPIRITS MAKING UP MY COLLECTIVE EXISTENCE MUST HAVE BEEN A REAL HAMBONE ACTOR.
I'M NOT AMUSED.
NO, YOU NEVER ARE. THAT'S NOT THE WHOLE PROBLEM WITH YOU, BUT A BIG PART OF IT.
DOVREMMO INVESTIGARE?
SHOULD WE INVESTIGATE?
HO SENTITO COSE TERRIBILI DA DENTRO.
I HEARD TERRIBLE THINGS FROM WITHIN.
ANVEDI! RANE!
LOOK! FROGS!
CENTINAIA DI LORO!
HUNDREDS OF THEM!
MADRE DI DIO. QUELLA DONNA STRANIERA É UNA STREGA! IO L'HO SAPUTO!
MOTHER OF GOD. THAT FOREIGN WOMAN IS A WITCH! I KNEW IT!

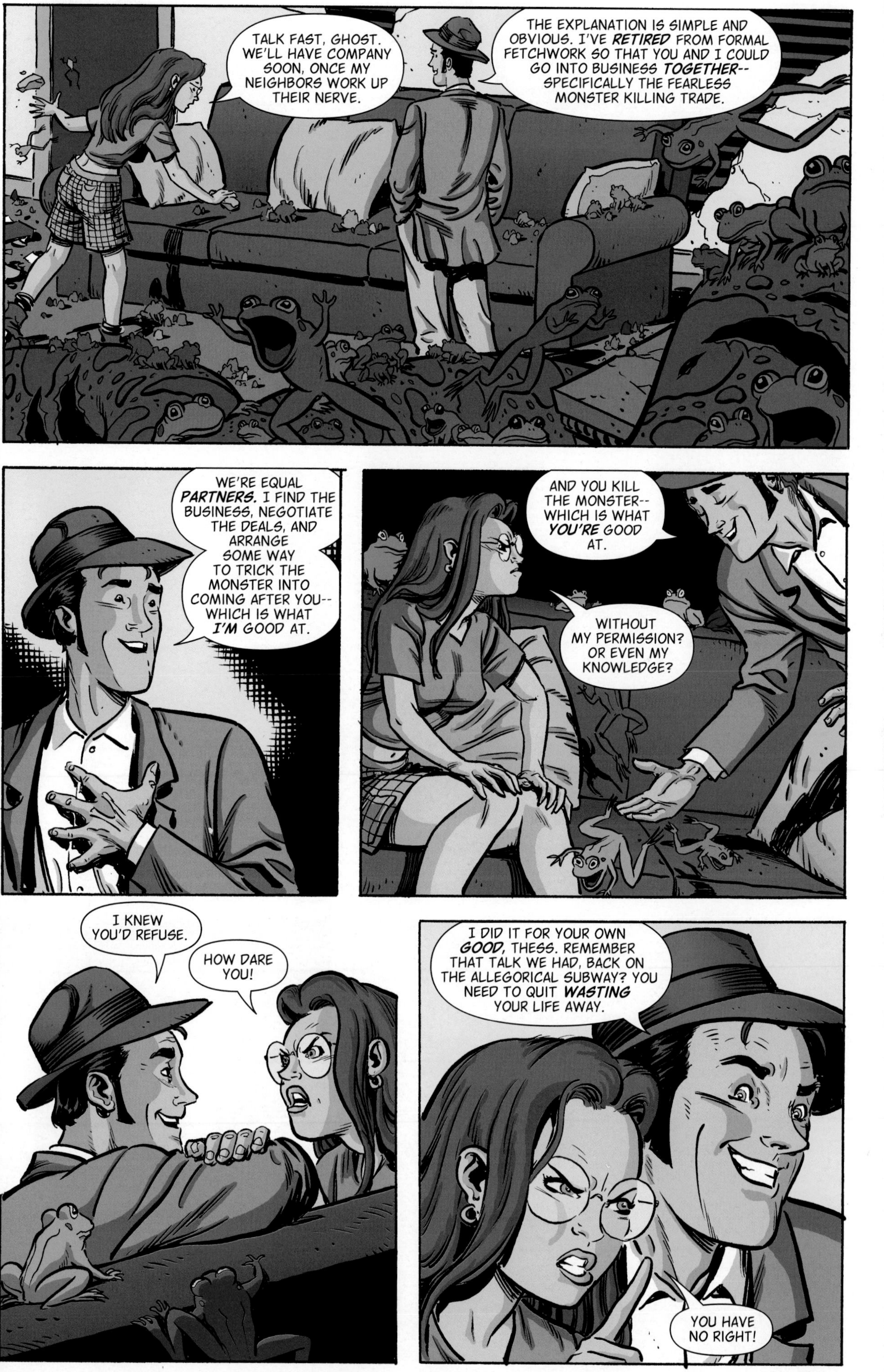
TALK FAST, GHOST. WE'LL HAVE COMPANY SOON, ONCE MY NEIGHBORS WORK UP THEIR NERVE.
THE EXPLANATION IS SIMPLE AND OBVIOUS. I'VE *RETIRED* FROM FORMAL FETCHWORK SO THAT YOU AND I COULD GO INTO BUSINESS *TOGETHER*-- SPECIFICALLY THE FEARLESS MONSTER KILLING TRADE.
WE'RE EQUAL *PARTNERS.* I FIND THE BUSINESS, NEGOTIATE THE DEALS, AND ARRANGE SOME WAY TO TRICK THE MONSTER INTO COMING AFTER YOU-- WHICH IS WHAT *I'M* GOOD AT.
AND YOU KILL THE MONSTER-- WHICH IS WHAT *YOU'RE* GOOD AT.
WITHOUT MY PERMISSION? OR EVEN MY KNOWLEDGE?
I KNEW YOU'D REFUSE.
HOW DARE YOU!
I DID IT FOR YOUR OWN *GOOD*, THESS. REMEMBER THAT TALK WE HAD, BACK ON THE ALLEGORICAL SUBWAY? YOU NEED TO QUIT *WASTING* YOUR LIFE AWAY.
YOU HAVE NO RIGHT!

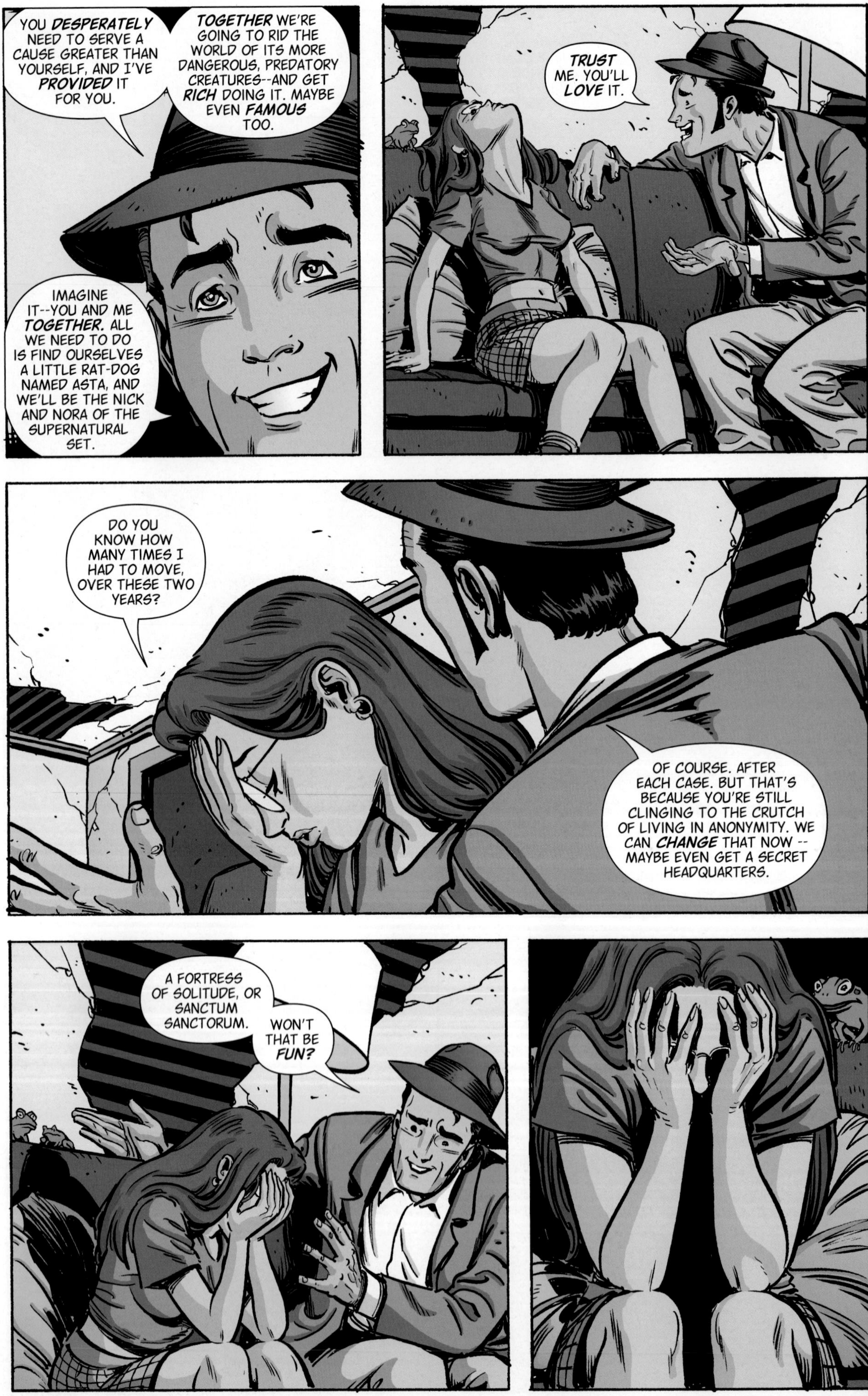
YOU DESPERATELY NEED TO SERVE A CAUSE GREATER THAN YOURSELF, AND I'VE PROVIDED IT FOR YOU.
TOGETHER WE'RE GOING TO RID THE WORLD OF ITS MORE DANGEROUS, PREDATORY CREATURES--AND GET RICH DOING IT. MAYBE EVEN FAMOUS TOO.
IMAGINE IT--YOU AND ME TOGETHER. ALL WE NEED TO DO IS FIND OURSELVES A LITTLE RAT-DOG NAMED ASTA, AND WE'LL BE THE NICK AND NORA OF THE SUPERNATURAL SET.
TRUST ME. YOU'LL LOVE IT.
DO YOU KNOW HOW MANY TIMES I HAD TO MOVE, OVER THESE TWO YEARS?
OF COURSE. AFTER EACH CASE. BUT THAT'S BECAUSE YOU'RE STILL CLINGING TO THE CRUTCH OF LIVING IN ANONYMITY. WE CAN CHANGE THAT NOW -- MAYBE EVEN GET A SECRET HEADQUARTERS.
A FORTRESS OF SOLITUDE, OR SANCTUM SANCTORUM.
WON'T THAT BE FUN?

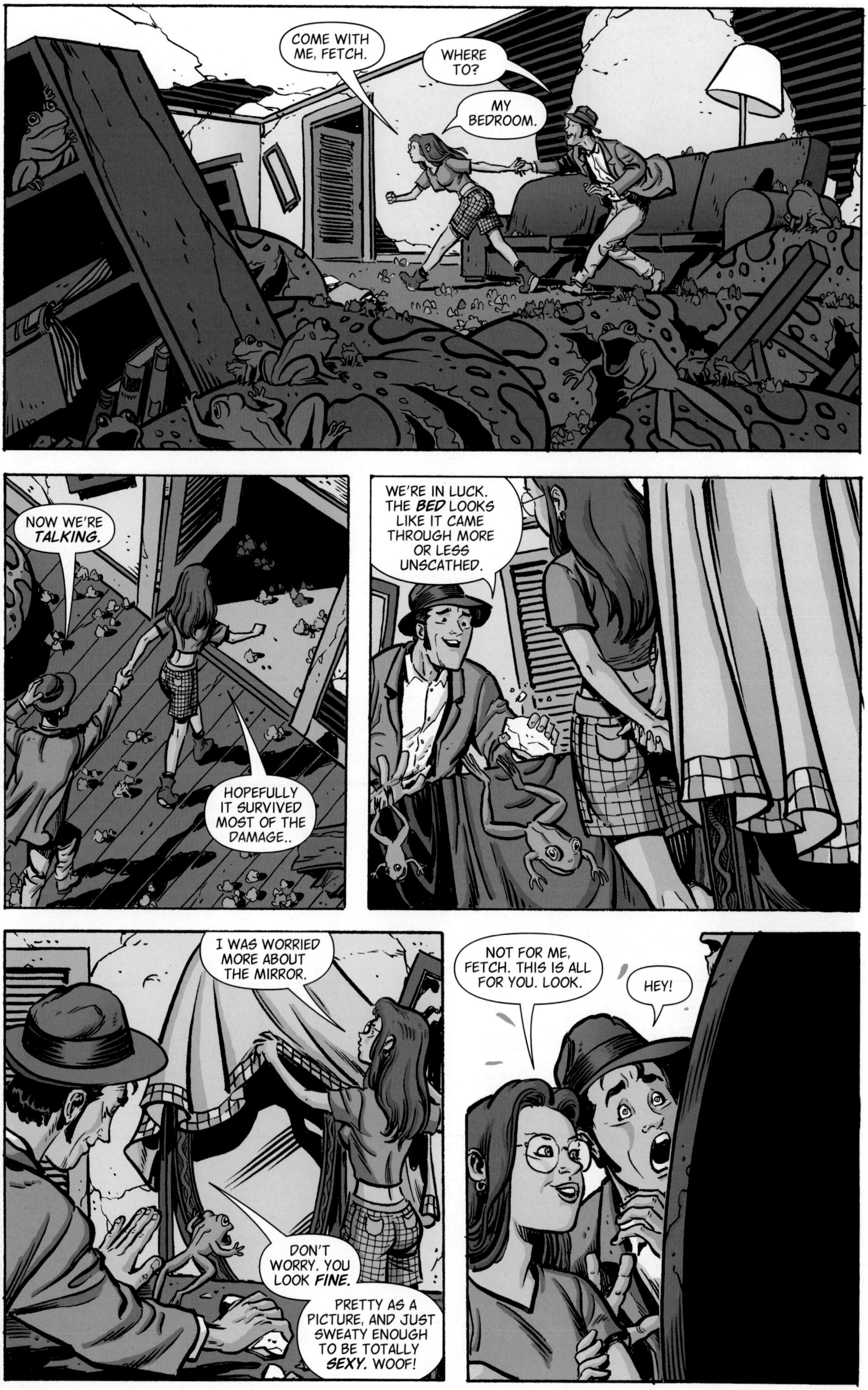

COME WITH ME, FETCH.
WHERE TO?
MY BEDROOM.
NOW WE'RE *TALKING.*
HOPEFULLY IT SURVIVED MOST OF THE DAMAGE..
WE'RE IN LUCK. THE *BED* LOOKS LIKE IT CAME THROUGH MORE OR LESS UNSCATHED.
I WAS WORRIED MORE ABOUT THE MIRROR.
DON'T WORRY. YOU LOOK *FINE.*
PRETTY AS A PICTURE, AND JUST SWEATY ENOUGH TO BE TOTALLY *SEXY.* WOOF!
NOT FOR ME, FETCH. THIS IS ALL FOR YOU. LOOK.
HEY!

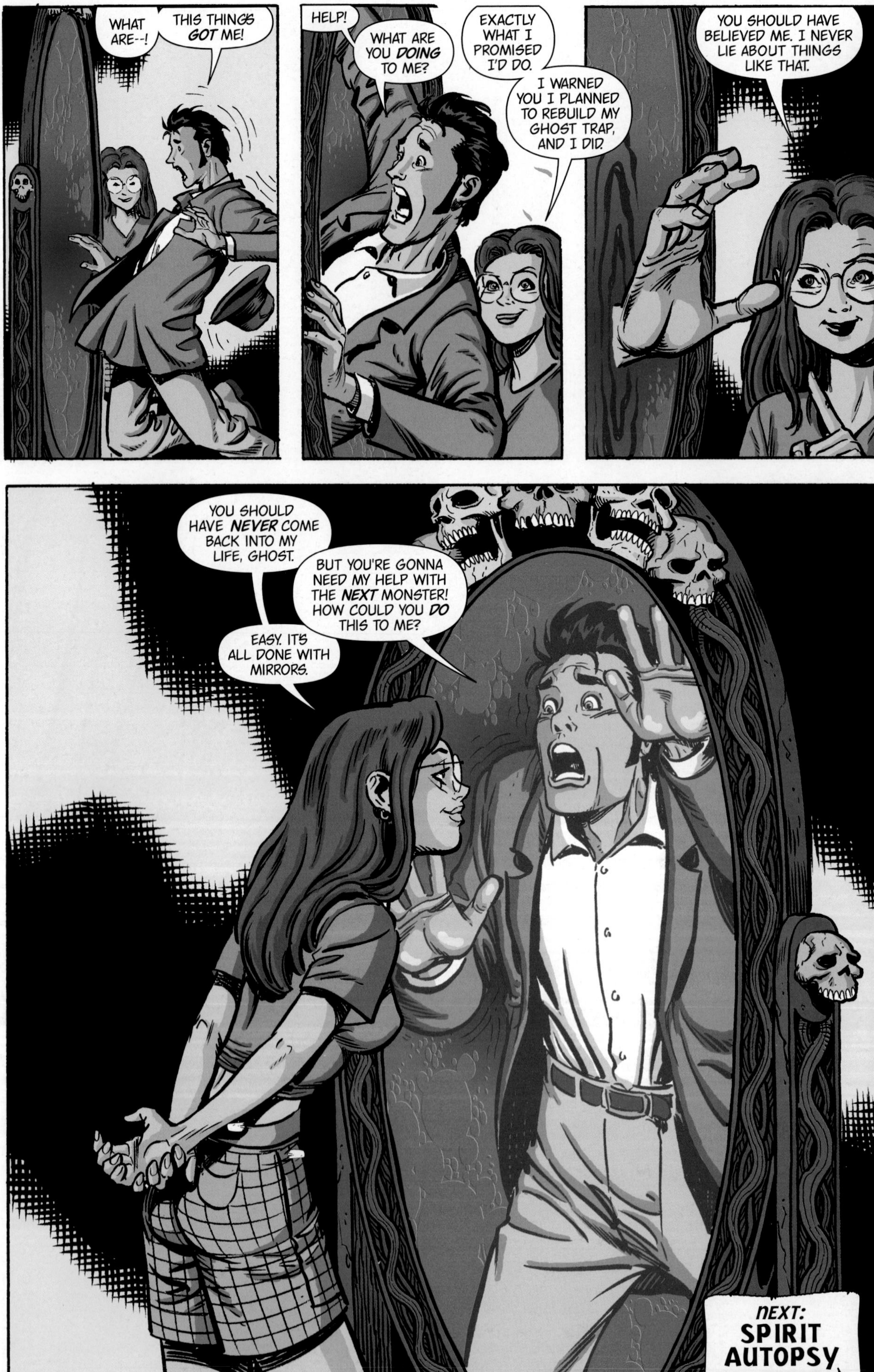
WHAT ARE--!
THIS THING'S GOT ME!
HELP!
WHAT ARE YOU DOING TO ME?
EXACTLY WHAT I PROMISED I'D DO.
I WARNED YOU I PLANNED TO REBUILD MY GHOST TRAP, AND I DID.
YOU SHOULD HAVE BELIEVED ME. I NEVER LIE ABOUT THINGS LIKE THAT.
YOU SHOULD HAVE NEVER COME BACK INTO MY LIFE, GHOST.
BUT YOU'RE GONNA NEED MY HELP WITH THE NEXT MONSTER! HOW COULD YOU DO THIS TO ME?
EASY. IT'S ALL DONE WITH MIRRORS.
NEXT: SPIRIT AUTOPSY

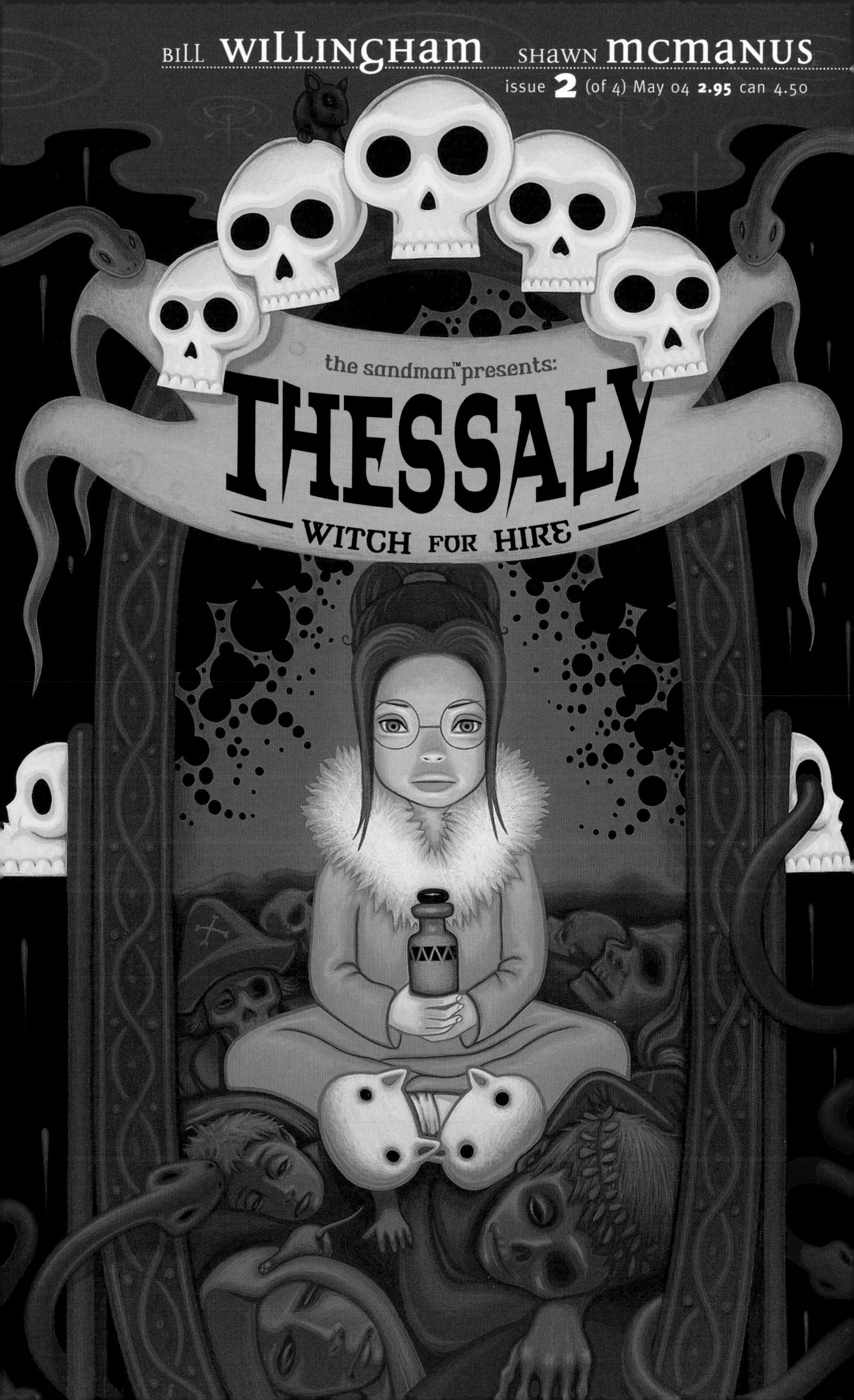
BILL WILLINGHAM SHAWN MCMANUS
issue 2 (of 4) May 04 2.95 can 4.50
the sandman™ presents:
THESSALY
WITCH FOR HIRE

WHERE ARE WE TODAY? HELL IF *I* KNOW. THESS KEEPS ME UNDER A TARP IN THE BACK OF HER *TRUCK*, MOST OF THE TIME.

ON A CLEAR DAY,

I CAN SEE THE DISTANT SAILS OF MY SHIP COMING IN.

BUT IT'S *HOT* AND DUSTY, AND OFF THE BEATEN TRACK.

The Coffee Conspiracy

SUCH A LONG WAY,

AND I'VE WAITED ALL THIS TIME FOR MY LIFE TO BEGIN.

SHE'S *INDOORS* SOMEWHERE, ENJOYING A *LEISURELY* LUNCH, IN AIR-CONDITIONED COMFORT, WHILE I'M *STUCK* OUT IN THE MIDDAY HEAT.

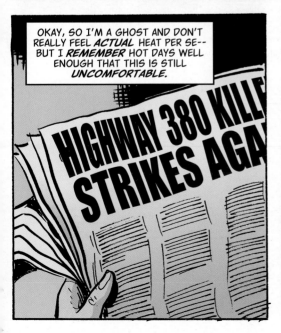

OKAY, SO I'M A GHOST AND DON'T REALLY FEEL *ACTUAL* HEAT PER SE-- BUT I *REMEMBER* HOT DAYS WELL ENOUGH THAT THIS IS STILL *UNCOMFORTABLE*.

HIGHWAY 380 KILLE STRIKES AGA

OKAY, I THINK YOU'D ALL BETTER LEAVE NOW.

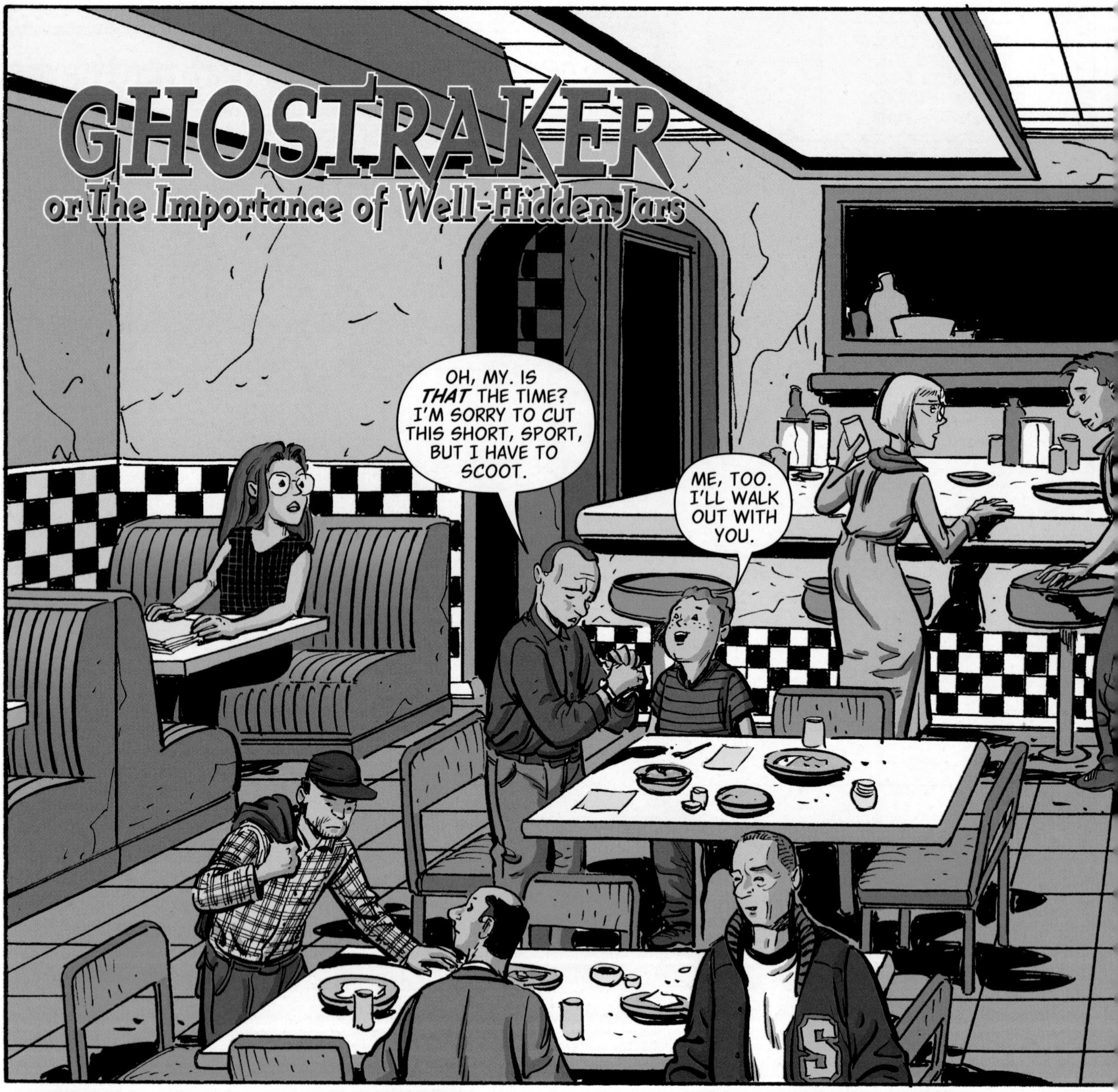
GHOSTRAKER
or The Importance of Well-Hidden Jars
OH, MY. IS *THAT* THE TIME? I'M SORRY TO CUT THIS SHORT, SPORT, BUT I HAVE TO SCOOT.
ME, TOO. I'LL WALK OUT WITH YOU.

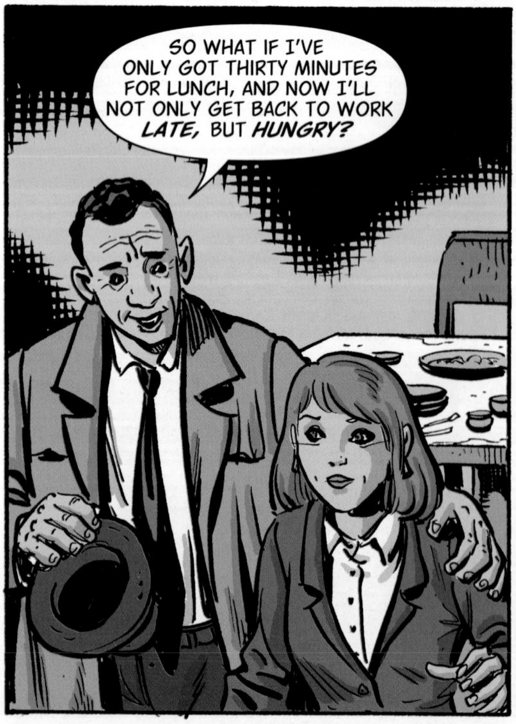
SO WHAT IF I'VE ONLY GOT THIRTY MINUTES FOR LUNCH, AND NOW I'LL NOT ONLY GET BACK TO WORK *LATE,* BUT *HUNGRY?*

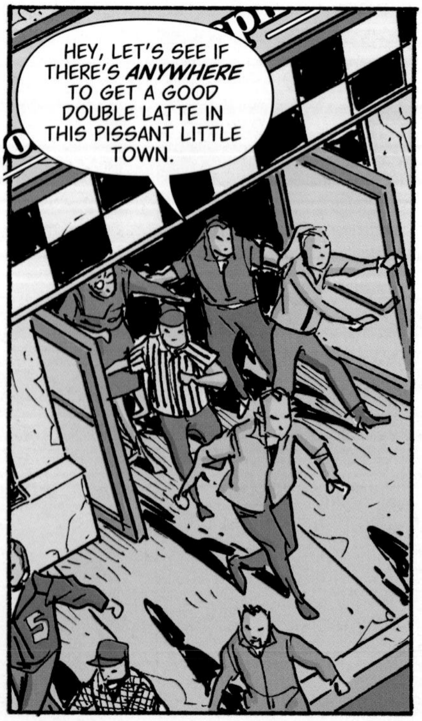
HEY, LET'S SEE IF THERE'S *ANYWHERE* TO GET A GOOD DOUBLE LATTE IN THIS PISSANT LITTLE TOWN.

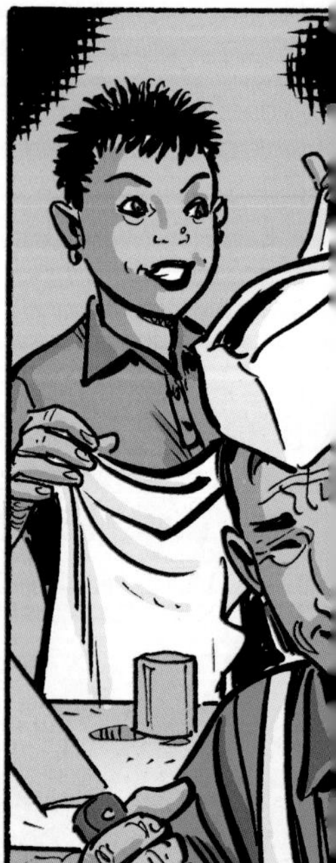

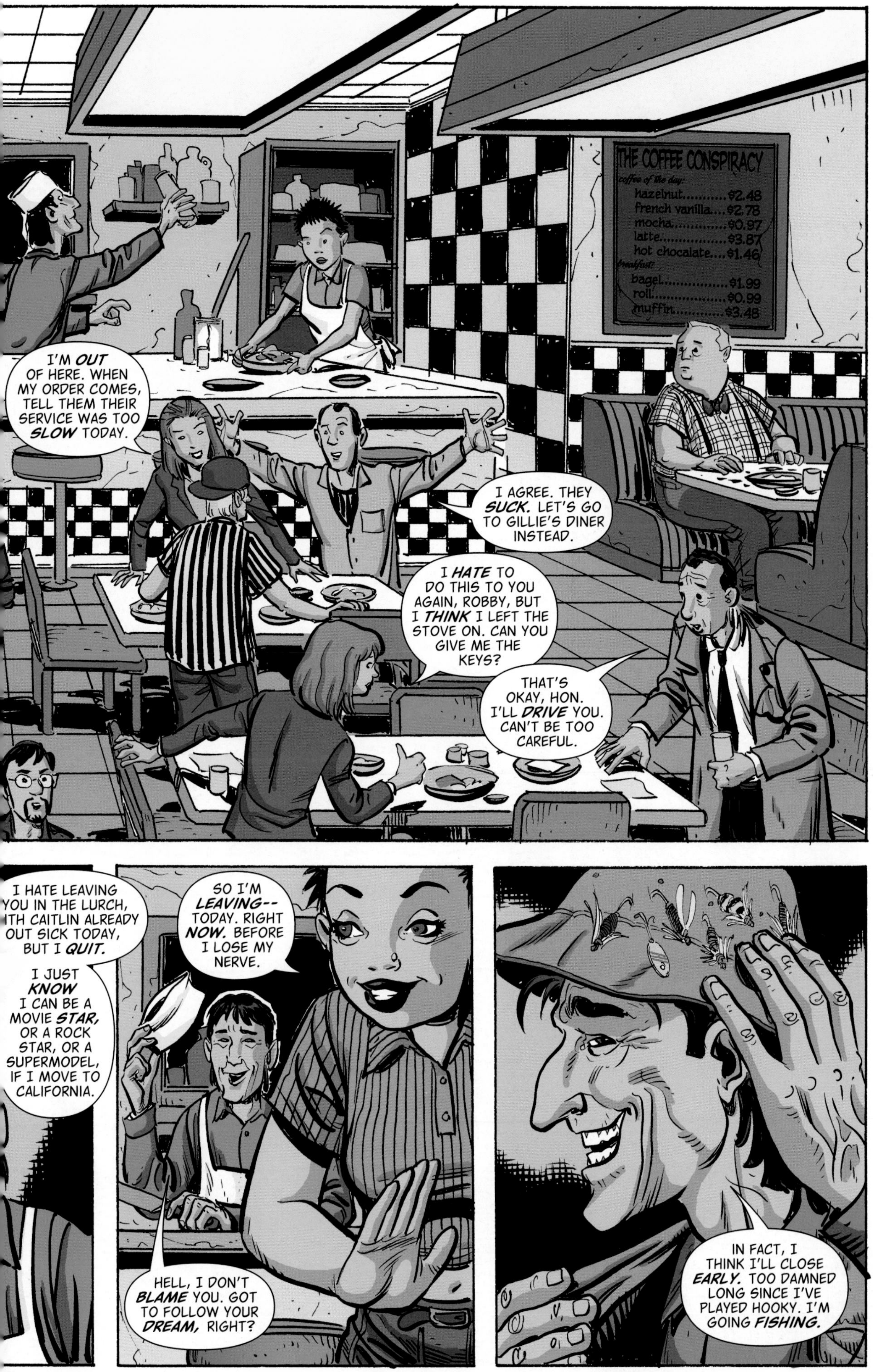
THE COFFEE CONSPIRACY
coffee of the day:
hazelnut..........$2.48
french vanilla....$2.78
mocha.............$0.97
latte.................$3.87
hot chocolate....$1.46
breakfast:
bagel...............$1.99
roll..................$0.99
muffin..............$3.48
I'M OUT OF HERE. WHEN MY ORDER COMES, TELL THEM THEIR SERVICE WAS TOO SLOW TODAY.
I AGREE. THEY SUCK. LET'S GO TO GILLIE'S DINER INSTEAD.
I HATE TO DO THIS TO YOU AGAIN, ROBBY, BUT I THINK I LEFT THE STOVE ON. CAN YOU GIVE ME THE KEYS?
THAT'S OKAY, HON. I'LL DRIVE YOU. CAN'T BE TOO CAREFUL.
I HATE LEAVING YOU IN THE LURCH, ITH CAITLIN ALREADY OUT SICK TODAY, BUT I QUIT.
I JUST KNOW I CAN BE A MOVIE STAR, OR A ROCK STAR, OR A SUPERMODEL, IF I MOVE TO CALIFORNIA.
SO I'M LEAVING-- TODAY. RIGHT NOW. BEFORE I LOSE MY NERVE.
HELL, I DON'T BLAME YOU. GOT TO FOLLOW YOUR DREAM, RIGHT?
IN FACT, I THINK I'LL CLOSE EARLY. TOO DAMNED LONG SINCE I'VE PLAYED HOOKY. I'M GOING FISHING.

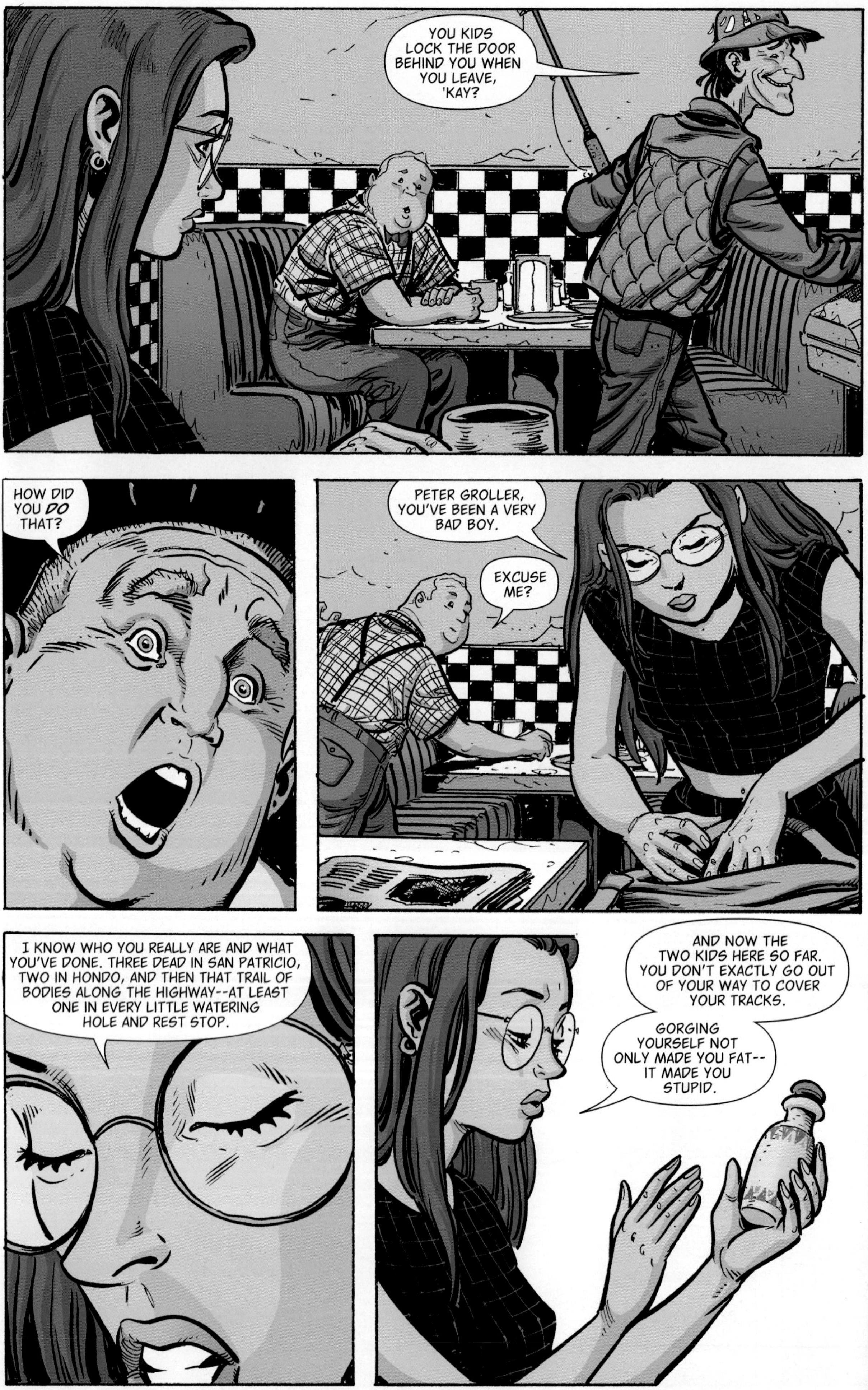
YOU KIDS LOCK THE DOOR BEHIND YOU WHEN YOU LEAVE, 'KAY?
HOW DID YOU *DO* THAT?
PETER GROLLER, YOU'VE BEEN A VERY BAD BOY.
EXCUSE ME?
I KNOW WHO YOU REALLY ARE AND WHAT YOU'VE DONE. THREE DEAD IN SAN PATRICIO, TWO IN HONDO, AND THEN THAT TRAIL OF BODIES ALONG THE HIGHWAY--AT LEAST ONE IN EVERY LITTLE WATERING HOLE AND REST STOP.
AND NOW THE TWO KIDS HERE SO FAR. YOU DON'T EXACTLY GO OUT OF YOUR WAY TO COVER YOUR TRACKS.
GORGING YOURSELF NOT ONLY MADE YOU FAT--IT MADE YOU STUPID.

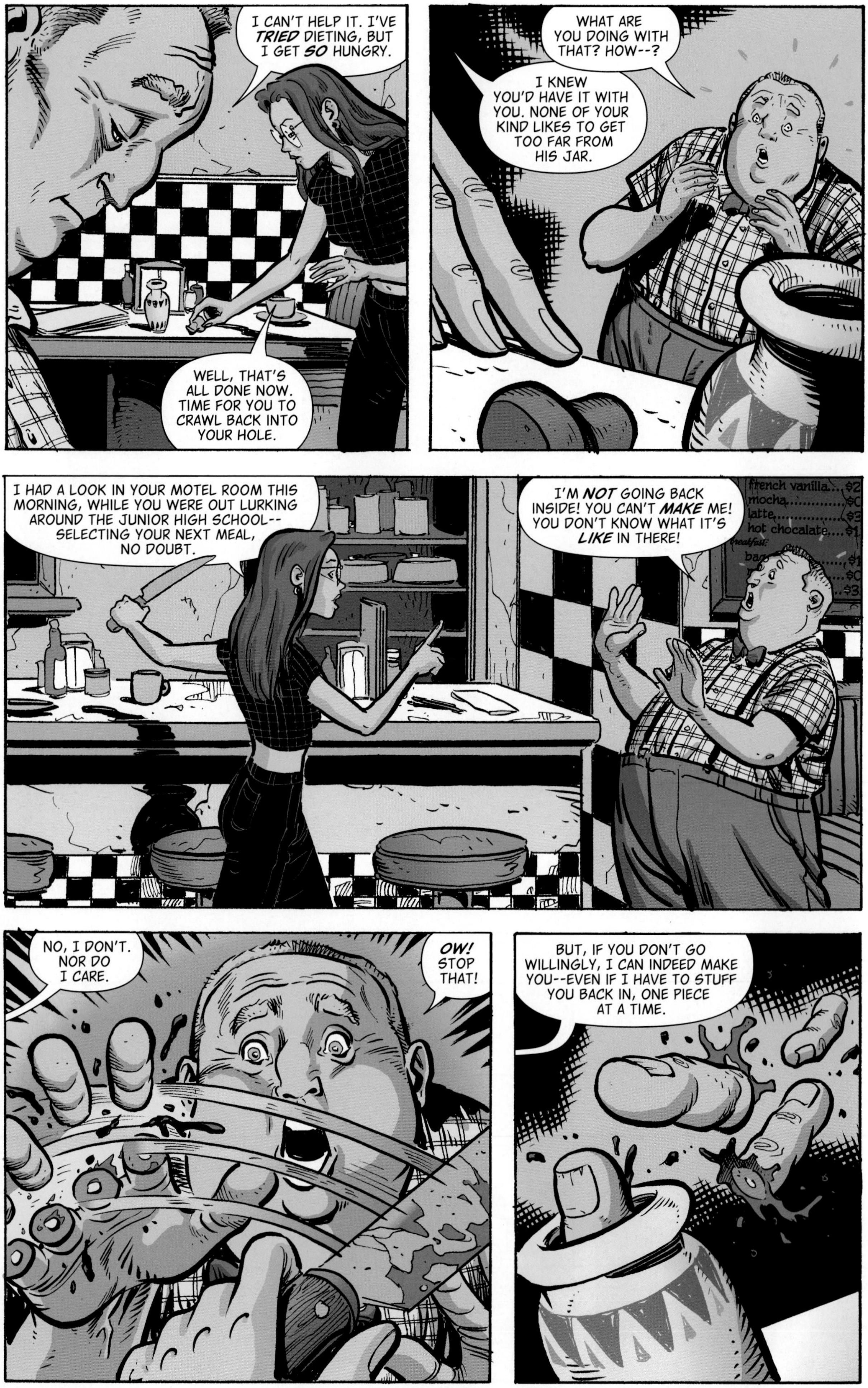

I CAN'T HELP IT. I'VE ***TRIED*** DIETING, BUT I GET ***SO*** HUNGRY.
WELL, THAT'S ALL DONE NOW. TIME FOR YOU TO CRAWL BACK INTO YOUR HOLE.
WHAT ARE YOU DOING WITH THAT? HOW--?
I KNEW YOU'D HAVE IT WITH YOU. NONE OF YOUR KIND LIKES TO GET TOO FAR FROM HIS JAR.
I HAD A LOOK IN YOUR MOTEL ROOM THIS MORNING, WHILE YOU WERE OUT LURKING AROUND THE JUNIOR HIGH SCHOOL-- SELECTING YOUR NEXT MEAL, NO DOUBT.
I'M ***NOT*** GOING BACK INSIDE! YOU CAN'T ***MAKE*** ME! YOU DON'T KNOW WHAT IT'S ***LIKE*** IN THERE!
NO, I DON'T. NOR DO I CARE.
OW! STOP THAT!
BUT, IF YOU DON'T GO WILLINGLY, I CAN INDEED MAKE YOU--EVEN IF I HAVE TO STUFF YOU BACK IN, ONE PIECE AT A TIME.

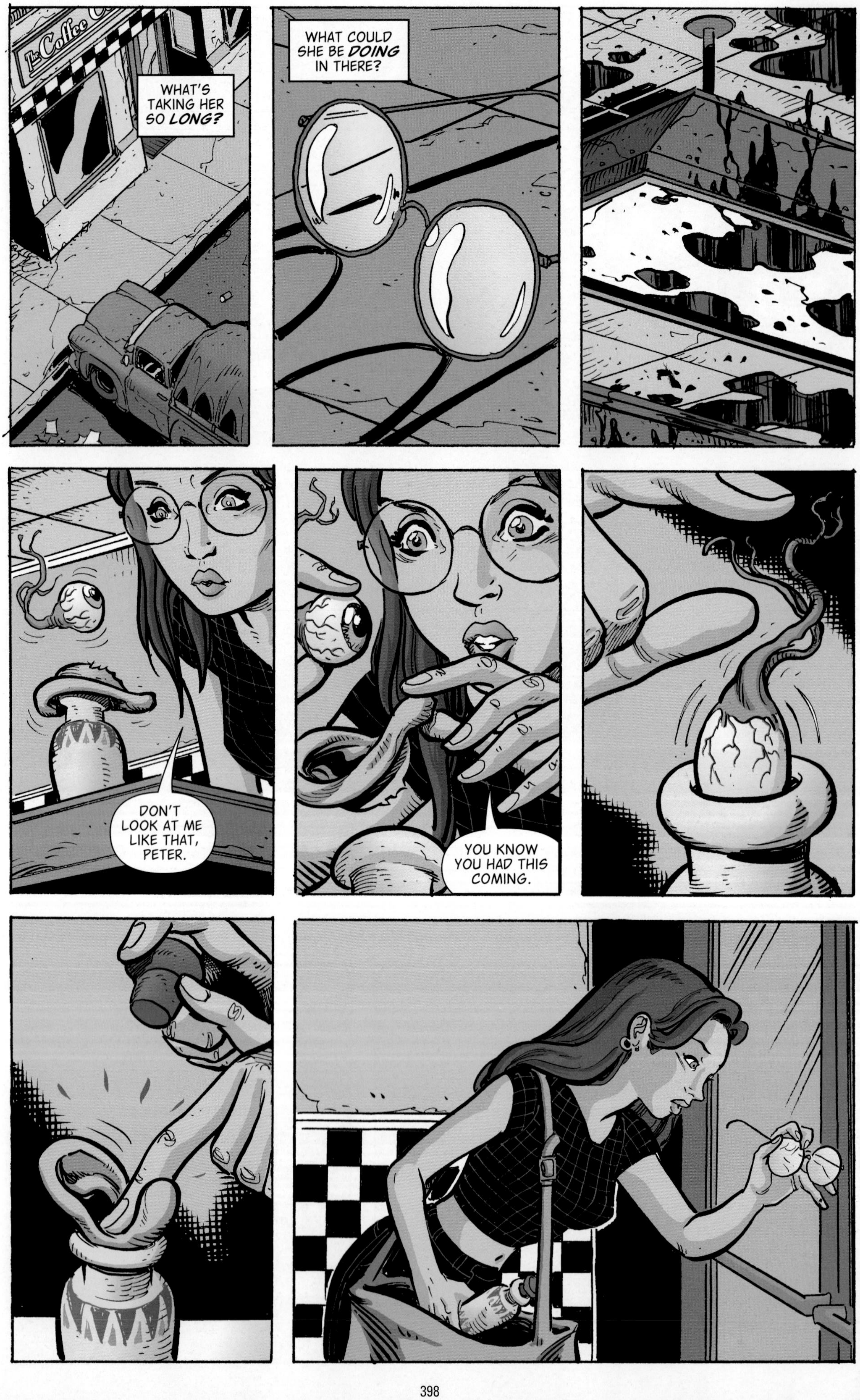
The Coffee
WHAT'S TAKING HER SO LONG?
WHAT COULD SHE BE DOING IN THERE?
DON'T LOOK AT ME LIKE THAT, PETER.
YOU KNOW YOU HAD THIS COMING.

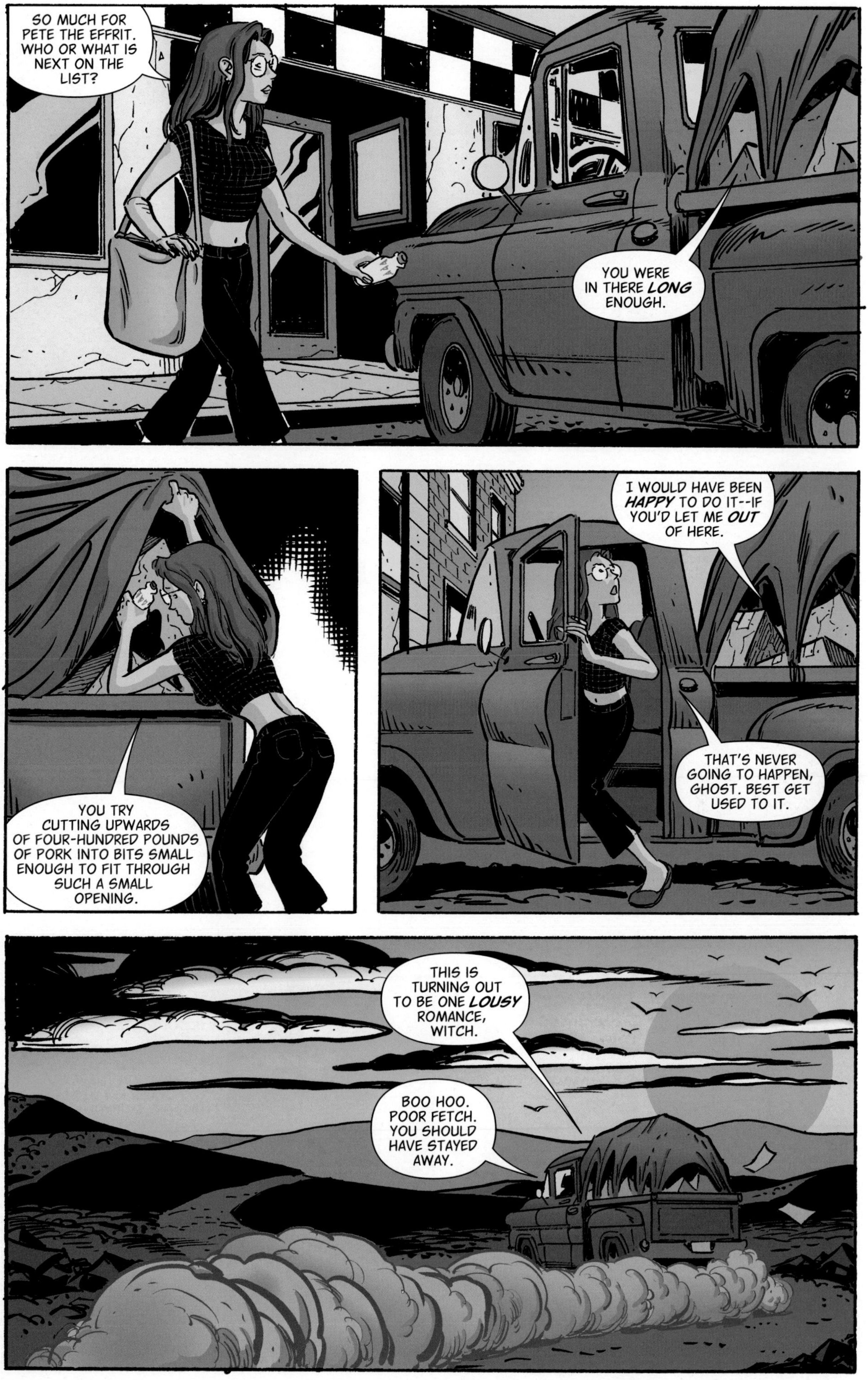
SO MUCH FOR PETE THE EFFRIT. WHO OR WHAT IS NEXT ON THE LIST?
YOU WERE IN THERE LONG ENOUGH.
YOU TRY CUTTING UPWARDS OF FOUR-HUNDRED POUNDS OF PORK INTO BITS SMALL ENOUGH TO FIT THROUGH SUCH A SMALL OPENING.
I WOULD HAVE BEEN HAPPY TO DO IT--IF YOU'D LET ME OUT OF HERE.
THAT'S NEVER GOING TO HAPPEN, GHOST. BEST GET USED TO IT.
THIS IS TURNING OUT TO BE ONE LOUSY ROMANCE, WITCH.
BOO HOO. POOR FETCH. YOU SHOULD HAVE STAYED AWAY.

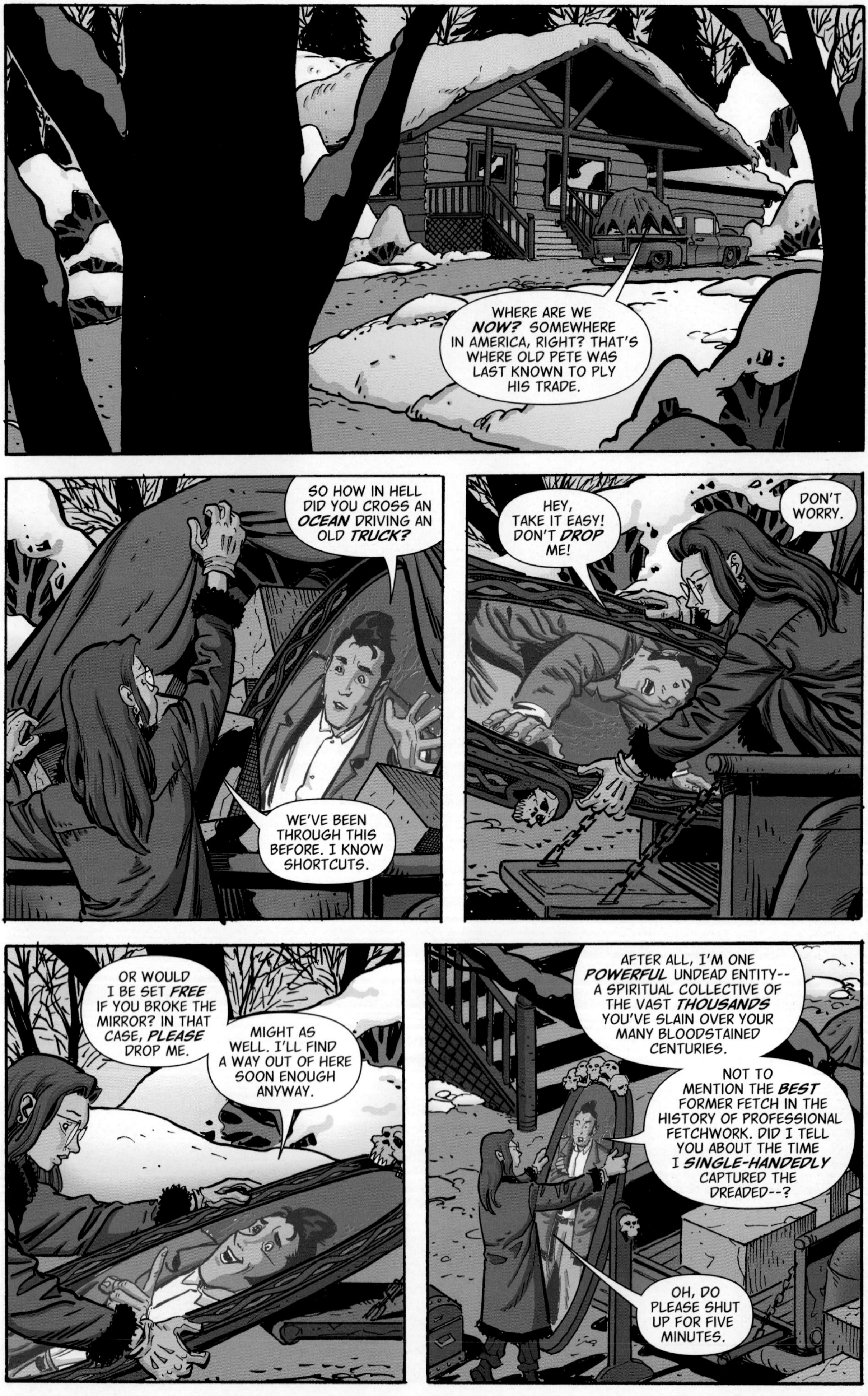
WHERE ARE WE NOW? SOMEWHERE IN AMERICA, RIGHT? THAT'S WHERE OLD PETE WAS LAST KNOWN TO PLY HIS TRADE.
SO HOW IN HELL DID YOU CROSS AN OCEAN DRIVING AN OLD TRUCK?
WE'VE BEEN THROUGH THIS BEFORE. I KNOW SHORTCUTS.
HEY, TAKE IT EASY! DON'T DROP ME!
DON'T WORRY.
OR WOULD I BE SET FREE IF YOU BROKE THE MIRROR? IN THAT CASE, PLEASE DROP ME.
MIGHT AS WELL. I'LL FIND A WAY OUT OF HERE SOON ENOUGH ANYWAY.
AFTER ALL, I'M ONE POWERFUL UNDEAD ENTITY-- A SPIRITUAL COLLECTIVE OF THE VAST THOUSANDS YOU'VE SLAIN OVER YOUR MANY BLOODSTAINED CENTURIES.
NOT TO MENTION THE BEST FORMER FETCH IN THE HISTORY OF PROFESSIONAL FETCHWORK. DID I TELL YOU ABOUT THE TIME I SINGLE-HANDEDLY CAPTURED THE DREADED--?
OH, DO PLEASE SHUT UP FOR FIVE MINUTES.

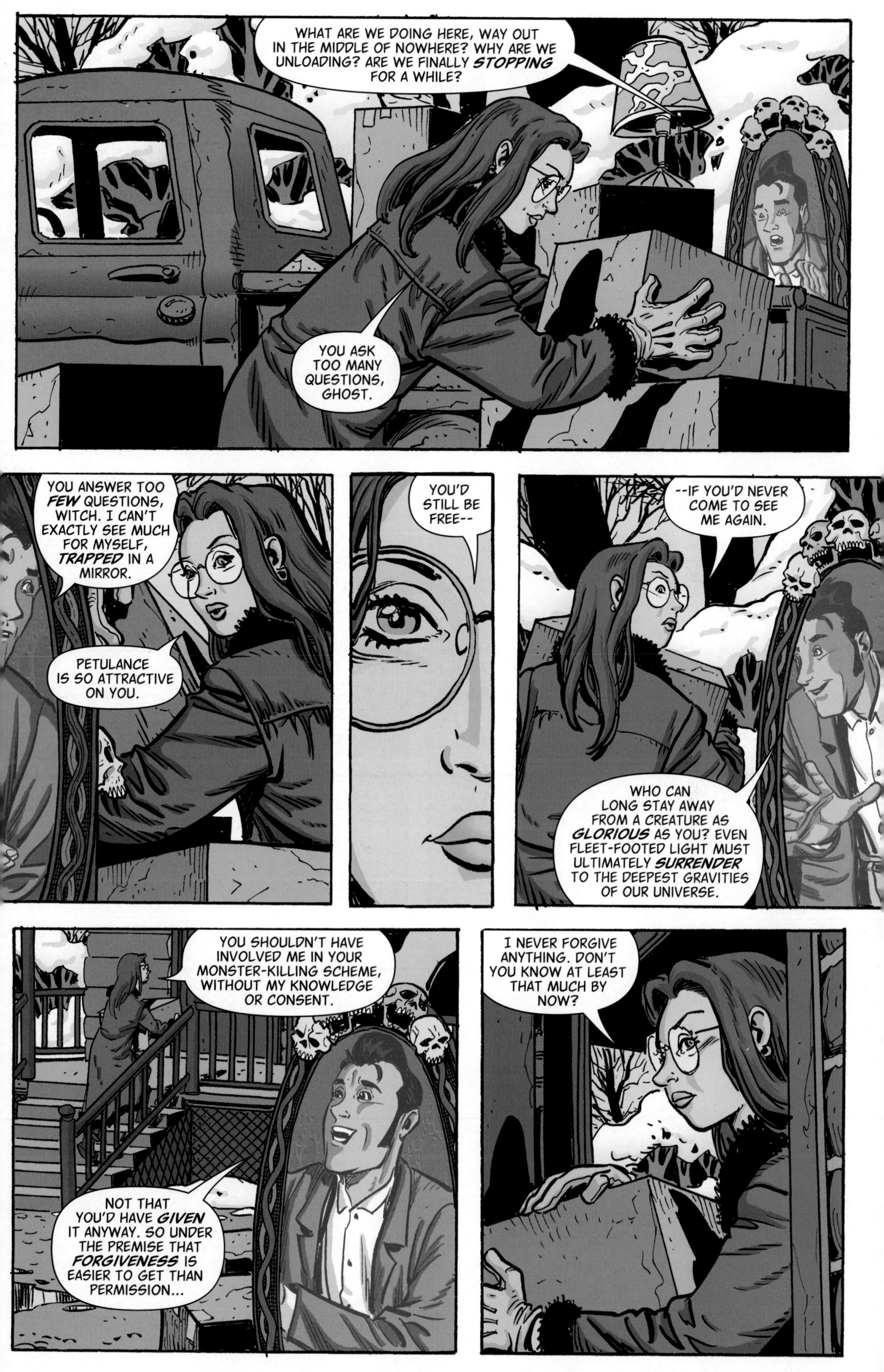
WHAT ARE WE DOING HERE, WAY OUT IN THE MIDDLE OF NOWHERE? WHY ARE WE UNLOADING? ARE WE FINALLY STOPPING FOR A WHILE?
YOU ASK TOO MANY QUESTIONS, GHOST.
YOU ANSWER TOO FEW QUESTIONS, WITCH. I CAN'T EXACTLY SEE MUCH FOR MYSELF, TRAPPED IN A MIRROR.
PETULANCE IS SO ATTRACTIVE ON YOU.
YOU'D STILL BE FREE--
--IF YOU'D NEVER COME TO SEE ME AGAIN.
WHO CAN LONG STAY AWAY FROM A CREATURE AS GLORIOUS AS YOU? EVEN FLEET-FOOTED LIGHT MUST ULTIMATELY SURRENDER TO THE DEEPEST GRAVITIES OF OUR UNIVERSE.
YOU SHOULDN'T HAVE INVOLVED ME IN YOUR MONSTER-KILLING SCHEME, WITHOUT MY KNOWLEDGE OR CONSENT.
NOT THAT YOU'D HAVE GIVEN IT ANYWAY. SO UNDER THE PREMISE THAT FORGIVENESS IS EASIER TO GET THAN PERMISSION...
I NEVER FORGIVE ANYTHING. DON'T YOU KNOW AT LEAST THAT MUCH BY NOW?

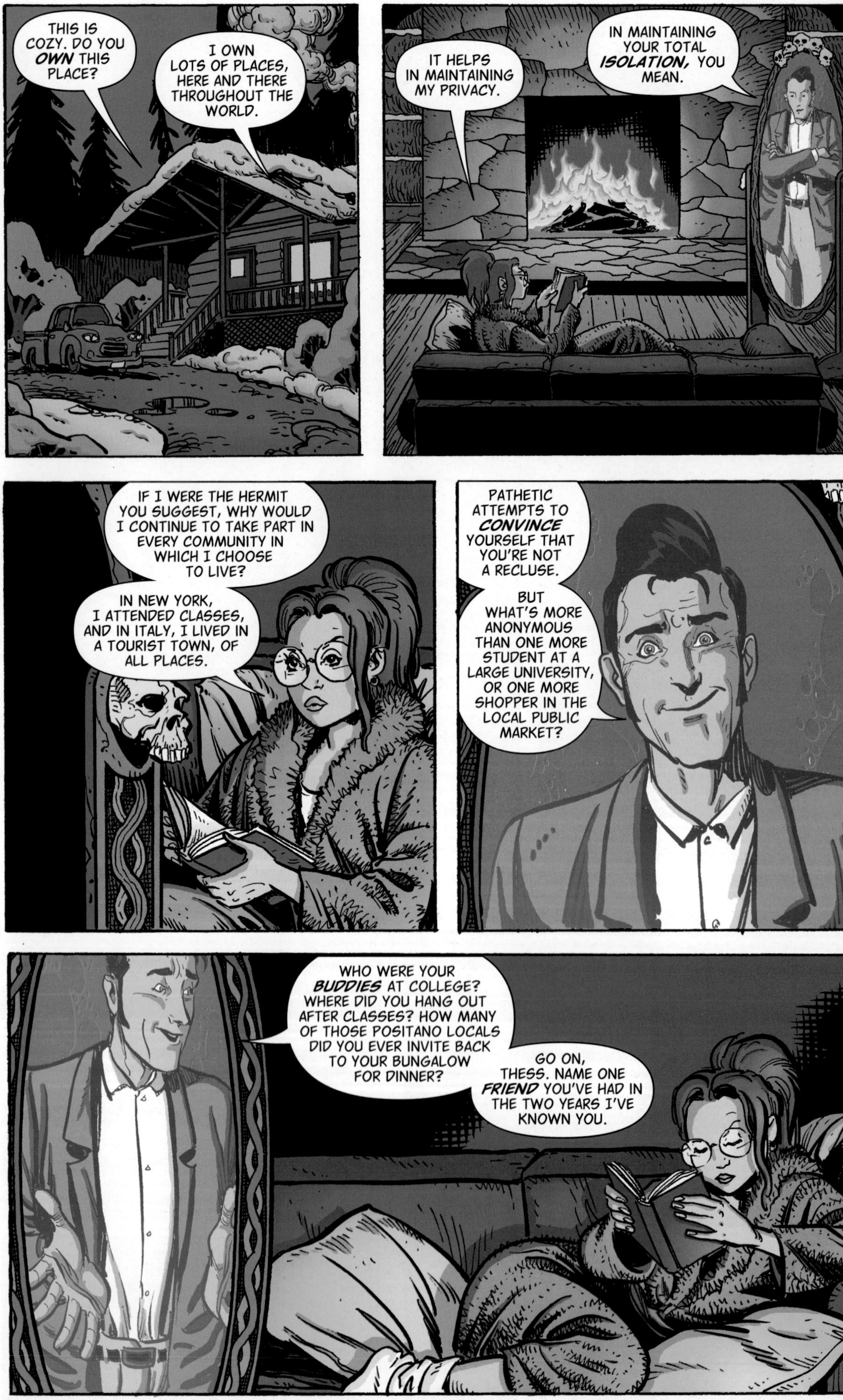
THIS IS COZY. DO YOU *OWN* THIS PLACE?
I OWN LOTS OF PLACES, HERE AND THERE THROUGHOUT THE WORLD.
IT HELPS IN MAINTAINING MY PRIVACY.
IN MAINTAINING YOUR TOTAL *ISOLATION,* YOU MEAN.
IF I WERE THE HERMIT YOU SUGGEST, WHY WOULD I CONTINUE TO TAKE PART IN EVERY COMMUNITY IN WHICH I CHOOSE TO LIVE?
IN NEW YORK, I ATTENDED CLASSES, AND IN ITALY, I LIVED IN A TOURIST TOWN, OF ALL PLACES.
PATHETIC ATTEMPTS TO *CONVINCE* YOURSELF THAT YOU'RE NOT A RECLUSE.
BUT WHAT'S MORE ANONYMOUS THAN ONE MORE STUDENT AT A LARGE UNIVERSITY, OR ONE MORE SHOPPER IN THE LOCAL PUBLIC MARKET?
WHO WERE YOUR *BUDDIES* AT COLLEGE? WHERE DID YOU HANG OUT AFTER CLASSES? HOW MANY OF THOSE POSITANO LOCALS DID YOU EVER INVITE BACK TO YOUR BUNGALOW FOR DINNER?
GO ON, THESS. NAME ONE *FRIEND* YOU'VE HAD IN THE TWO YEARS I'VE KNOWN YOU.

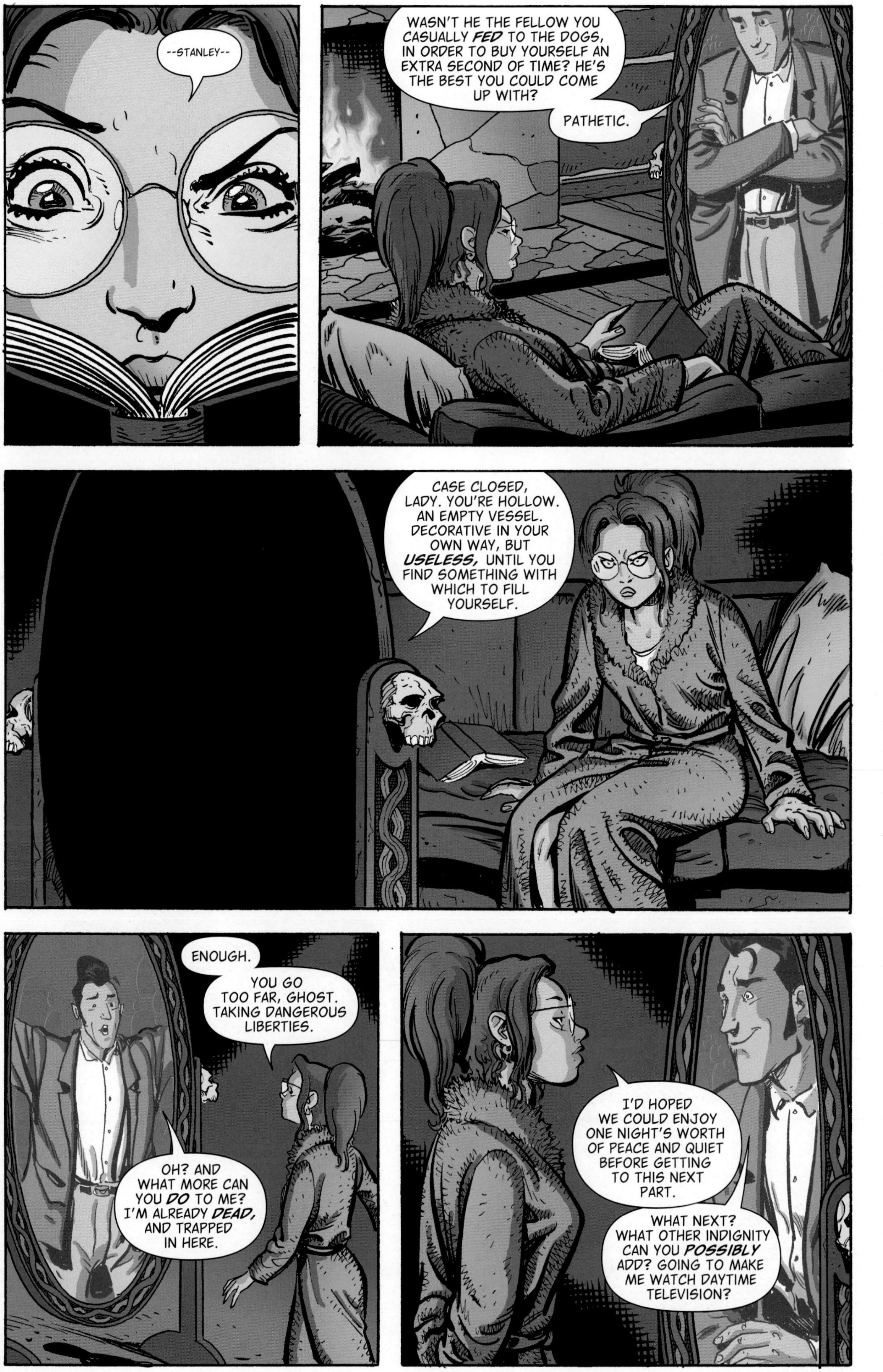
--STANLEY--
WASN'T HE THE FELLOW YOU CASUALLY FED TO THE DOGS, IN ORDER TO BUY YOURSELF AN EXTRA SECOND OF TIME? HE'S THE BEST YOU COULD COME UP WITH?
PATHETIC.
CASE CLOSED, LADY. YOU'RE HOLLOW. AN EMPTY VESSEL. DECORATIVE IN YOUR OWN WAY, BUT USELESS, UNTIL YOU FIND SOMETHING WITH WHICH TO FILL YOURSELF.
ENOUGH.
YOU GO TOO FAR, GHOST. TAKING DANGEROUS LIBERTIES.
OH? AND WHAT MORE CAN YOU DO TO ME? I'M ALREADY DEAD, AND TRAPPED IN HERE.
I'D HOPED WE COULD ENJOY ONE NIGHT'S WORTH OF PEACE AND QUIET BEFORE GETTING TO THIS NEXT PART.
WHAT NEXT? WHAT OTHER INDIGNITY CAN YOU POSSIBLY ADD? GOING TO MAKE ME WATCH DAYTIME TELEVISION?

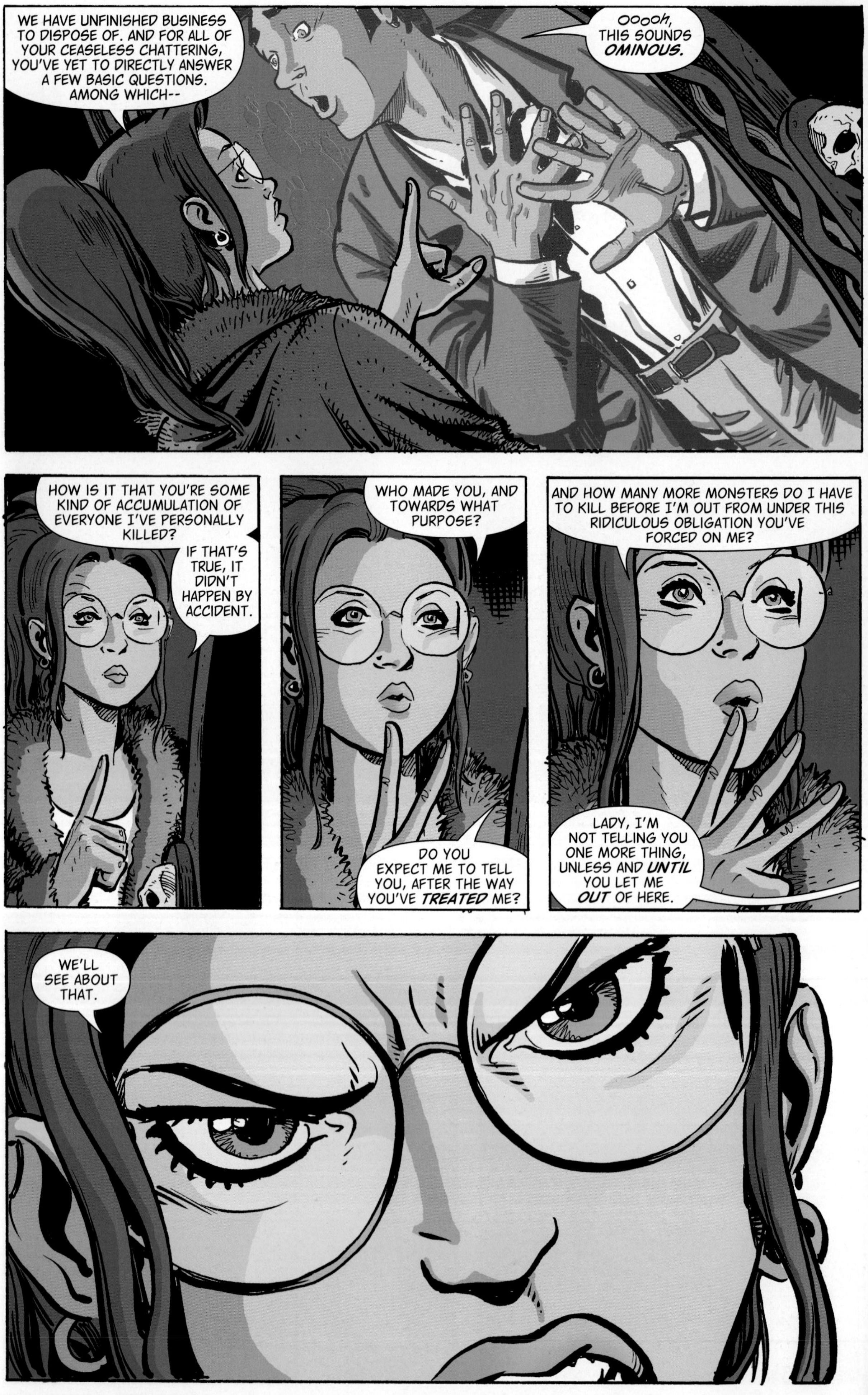
WE HAVE UNFINISHED BUSINESS TO DISPOSE OF. AND FOR ALL OF YOUR CEASELESS CHATTERING, YOU'VE YET TO DIRECTLY ANSWER A FEW BASIC QUESTIONS. AMONG WHICH--
Ooooh, THIS SOUNDS *OMINOUS.*
HOW IS IT THAT YOU'RE SOME KIND OF ACCUMULATION OF EVERYONE I'VE PERSONALLY KILLED?
IF THAT'S TRUE, IT DIDN'T HAPPEN BY ACCIDENT.
WHO MADE YOU, AND TOWARDS WHAT PURPOSE?
DO YOU EXPECT ME TO TELL YOU, AFTER THE WAY YOU'VE *TREATED* ME?
AND HOW MANY MORE MONSTERS DO I HAVE TO KILL BEFORE I'M OUT FROM UNDER THIS RIDICULOUS OBLIGATION YOU'VE FORCED ON ME?
LADY, I'M NOT TELLING YOU ONE MORE THING, UNLESS AND *UNTIL* YOU LET ME *OUT* OF HERE.
WE'LL SEE ABOUT THAT.

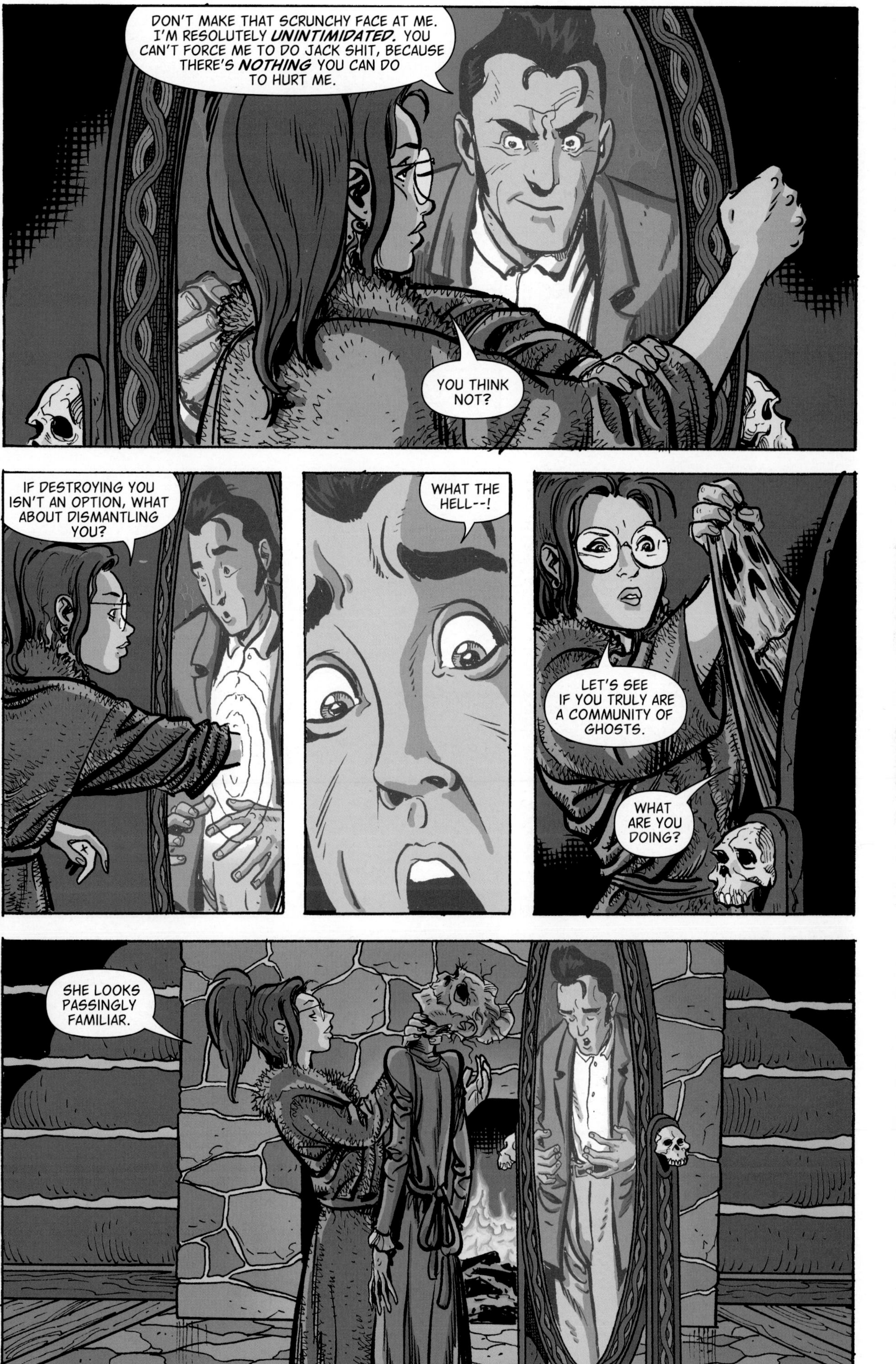
DON'T MAKE THAT SCRUNCHY FACE AT ME. I'M RESOLUTELY UNINTIMIDATED. YOU CAN'T FORCE ME TO DO JACK SHIT, BECAUSE THERE'S NOTHING YOU CAN DO TO HURT ME.
YOU THINK NOT?
IF DESTROYING YOU ISN'T AN OPTION, WHAT ABOUT DISMANTLING YOU?
WHAT THE HELL--!
LET'S SEE IF YOU TRULY ARE A COMMUNITY OF GHOSTS.
WHAT ARE YOU DOING?
SHE LOOKS PASSINGLY FAMILIAR.

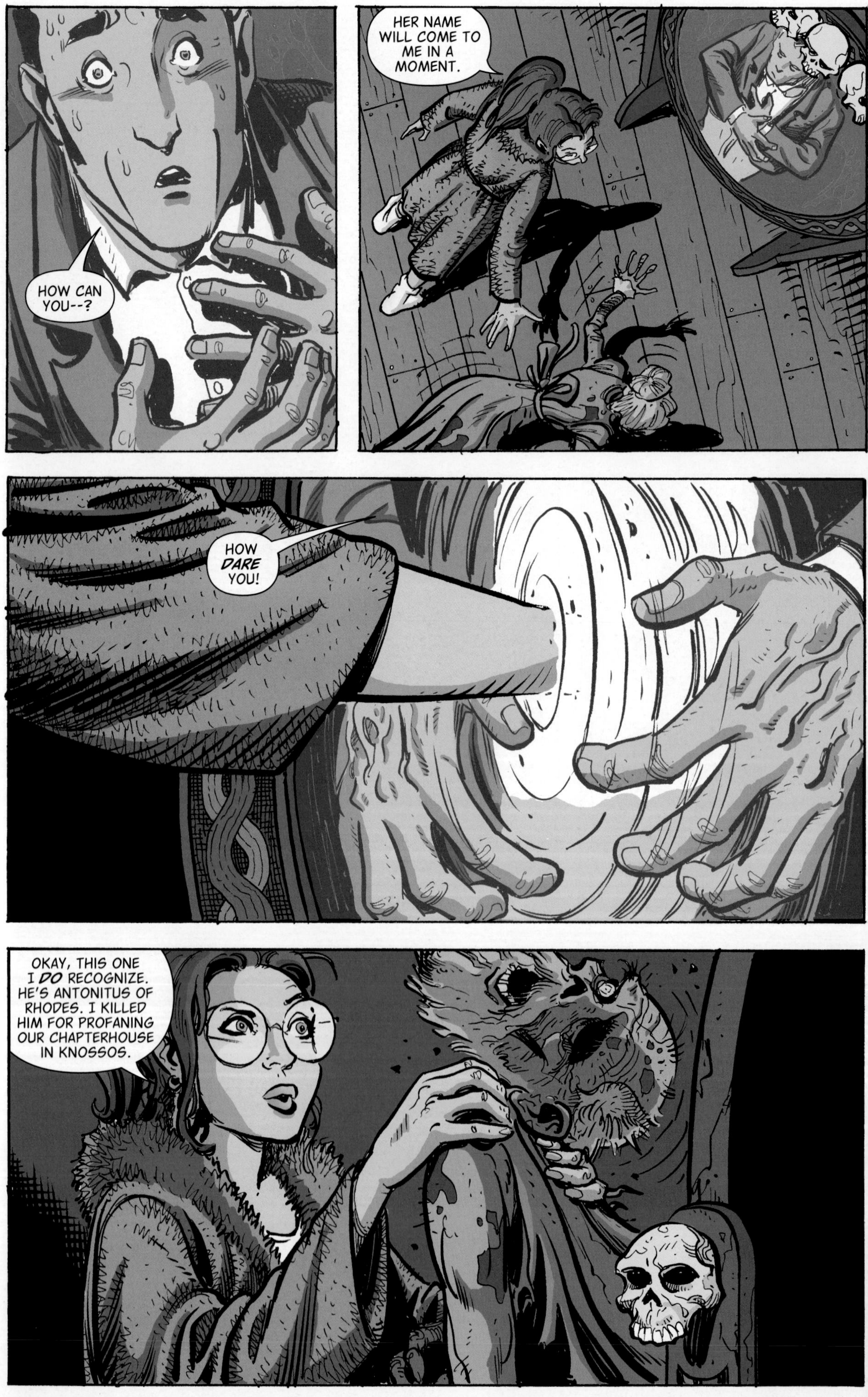
HOW CAN YOU--?
HER NAME WILL COME TO ME IN A MOMENT.
HOW *DARE* YOU!
OKAY, THIS ONE I *DO* RECOGNIZE. HE'S ANTONITUS OF RHODES. I KILLED HIM FOR PROFANING OUR CHAPTERHOUSE IN KNOSSOS.

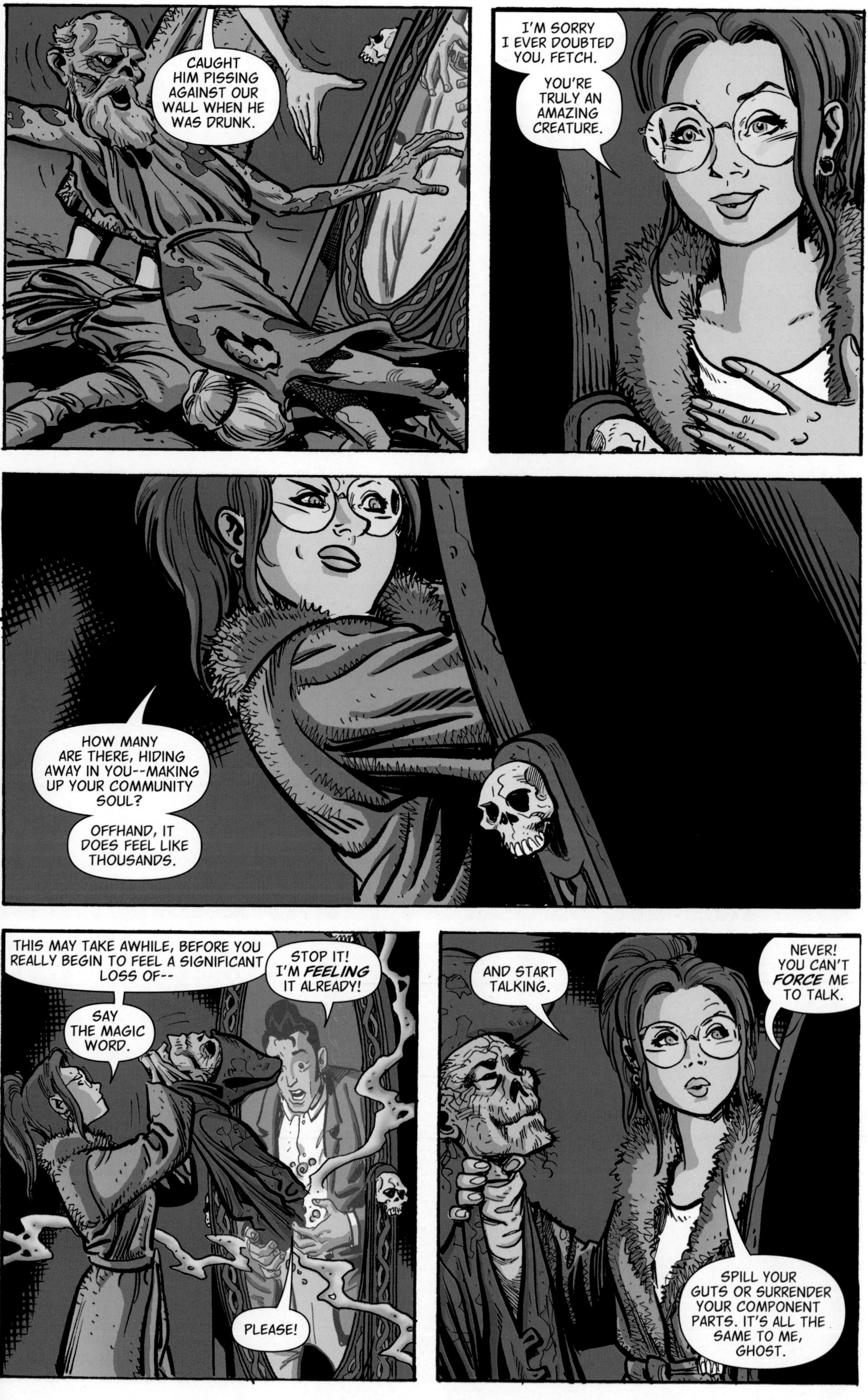

CAUGHT HIM PISSING AGAINST OUR WALL WHEN HE WAS DRUNK.
I'M SORRY I EVER DOUBTED YOU, FETCH.
YOU'RE TRULY AN AMAZING CREATURE.
HOW MANY ARE THERE, HIDING AWAY IN YOU--MAKING UP YOUR COMMUNITY SOUL?
OFFHAND, IT DOES FEEL LIKE THOUSANDS.
THIS MAY TAKE AWHILE, BEFORE YOU REALLY BEGIN TO FEEL A SIGNIFICANT LOSS OF--
STOP IT! I'M *FEELING* IT ALREADY!
SAY THE MAGIC WORD.
PLEASE!
AND START TALKING.
NEVER! YOU CAN'T *FORCE* ME TO TALK.
SPILL YOUR GUTS OR SURRENDER YOUR COMPONENT PARTS. IT'S ALL THE SAME TO ME, GHOST.

LONDON

OKAY, WHY DIDN'T I JUST *TELL* HER AND SAVE MYSELF THE MISERY? REASONABLE QUESTION.

I'VE BEEN BRAVE BEFORE (WHEN OCCASION FORCED IT ON ME) AND I'VE BEEN STUBBORN BEFORE--

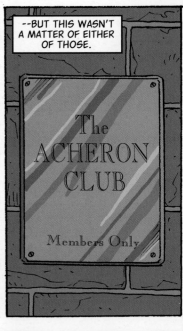

--BUT THIS WASN'T A MATTER OF EITHER OF THOSE.

The ACHERON CLUB

Members Only

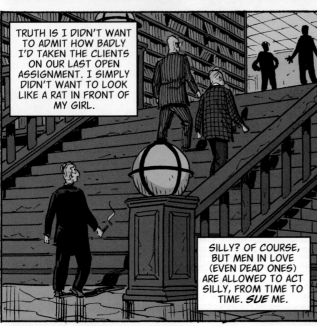

TRUTH IS I DIDN'T WANT TO ADMIT HOW BADLY I'D TAKEN THE CLIENTS ON OUR LAST OPEN ASSIGNMENT. I SIMPLY DIDN'T WANT TO LOOK LIKE A RAT IN FRONT OF MY GIRL.

SILLY? OF COURSE, BUT MEN IN LOVE (EVEN DEAD ONES) ARE ALLOWED TO ACT SILLY, FROM TIME TO TIME. *SUE* ME.

WELL, I'LL BE BUGGERED AND HUNG TO DRY.

GEOFFREY PINDER-SMYTHE, IS THAT *YOU*, OF ALL THE DECREPIT OLD CATAMITES I DIDN'T EXPECT TO SEE TONIGHT? WHAT ARE *YOU* DOING HERE?

CELEBRATING.

SIT, MORGANTHROPE, IF YOU'RE GOING TO JOIN ME. DON'T *HOVER*.

I SHOULD THINK YOU'D BE IN MORE OF A *FUNEREAL* STATE-- CONSIDERING THE FATE *WAITING* FOR YOU IN ONLY A FEW DAYS' TIME. IT *IS* IN JUST A DAY OR TWO, ISN'T IT?

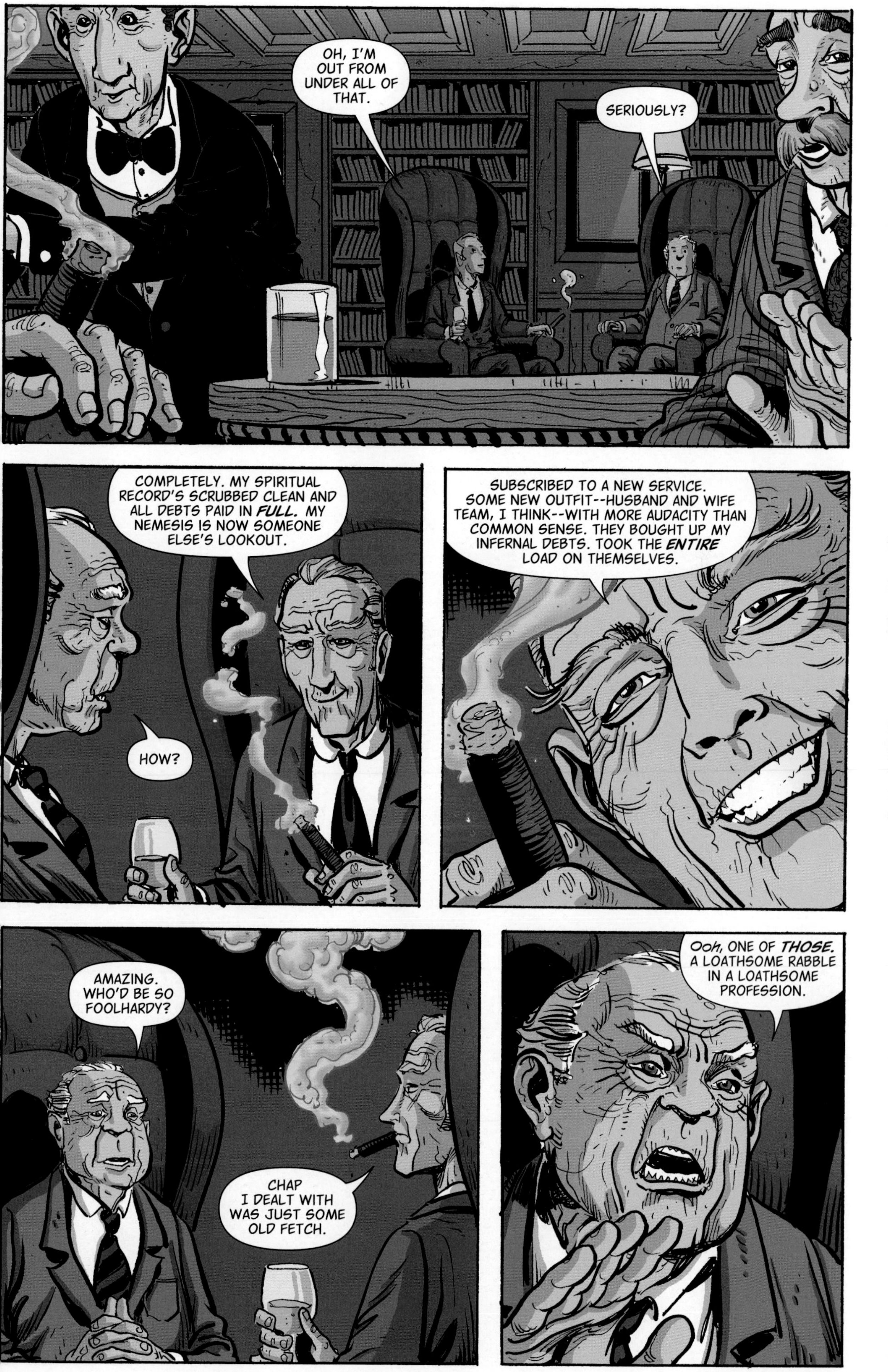
OH, I'M OUT FROM UNDER ALL OF THAT.
SERIOUSLY?
COMPLETELY. MY SPIRITUAL RECORD'S SCRUBBED CLEAN AND ALL DEBTS PAID IN *FULL.* MY NEMESIS IS NOW SOMEONE ELSE'S LOOKOUT.
HOW?
SUBSCRIBED TO A NEW SERVICE. SOME NEW OUTFIT--HUSBAND AND WIFE TEAM, I THINK--WITH MORE AUDACITY THAN COMMON SENSE. THEY BOUGHT UP MY INFERNAL DEBTS. TOOK THE *ENTIRE* LOAD ON THEMSELVES.
AMAZING. WHO'D BE SO FOOLHARDY?
CHAP I DEALT WITH WAS JUST SOME OLD FETCH.
Ooh, ONE OF ***THOSE.*** A LOATHSOME RABBLE IN A LOATHSOME PROFESSION.

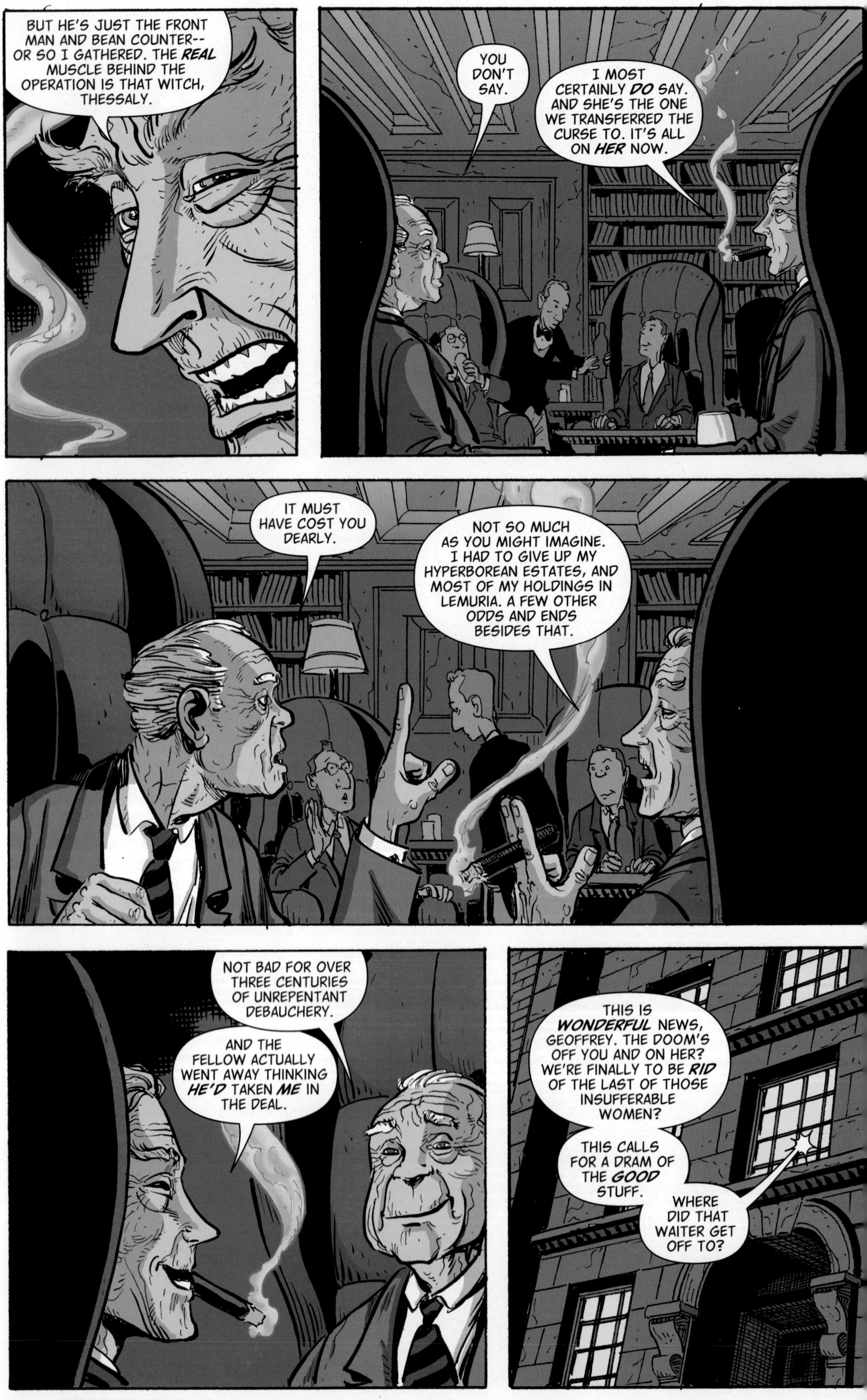
BUT HE'S JUST THE FRONT MAN AND BEAN COUNTER-- OR SO I GATHERED. THE ***REAL*** MUSCLE BEHIND THE OPERATION IS THAT WITCH, THESSALY.
YOU DON'T SAY.
I MOST CERTAINLY ***DO*** SAY. AND SHE'S THE ONE WE TRANSFERRED THE CURSE TO. IT'S ALL ON ***HER*** NOW.
IT MUST HAVE COST YOU DEARLY.
NOT SO MUCH AS YOU MIGHT IMAGINE. I HAD TO GIVE UP MY HYPERBOREAN ESTATES, AND MOST OF MY HOLDINGS IN LEMURIA. A FEW OTHER ODDS AND ENDS BESIDES THAT.
NOT BAD FOR OVER THREE CENTURIES OF UNREPENTANT DEBAUCHERY.
AND THE FELLOW ACTUALLY WENT AWAY THINKING ***HE'D*** TAKEN ***ME*** IN THE DEAL.
THIS IS ***WONDERFUL*** NEWS, GEOFFREY. THE DOOM'S OFF YOU AND ON HER? WE'RE FINALLY TO BE ***RID*** OF THE LAST OF THOSE INSUFFERABLE WOMEN?
THIS CALLS FOR A DRAM OF THE ***GOOD*** STUFF.
WHERE DID THAT WAITER GET OFF TO?

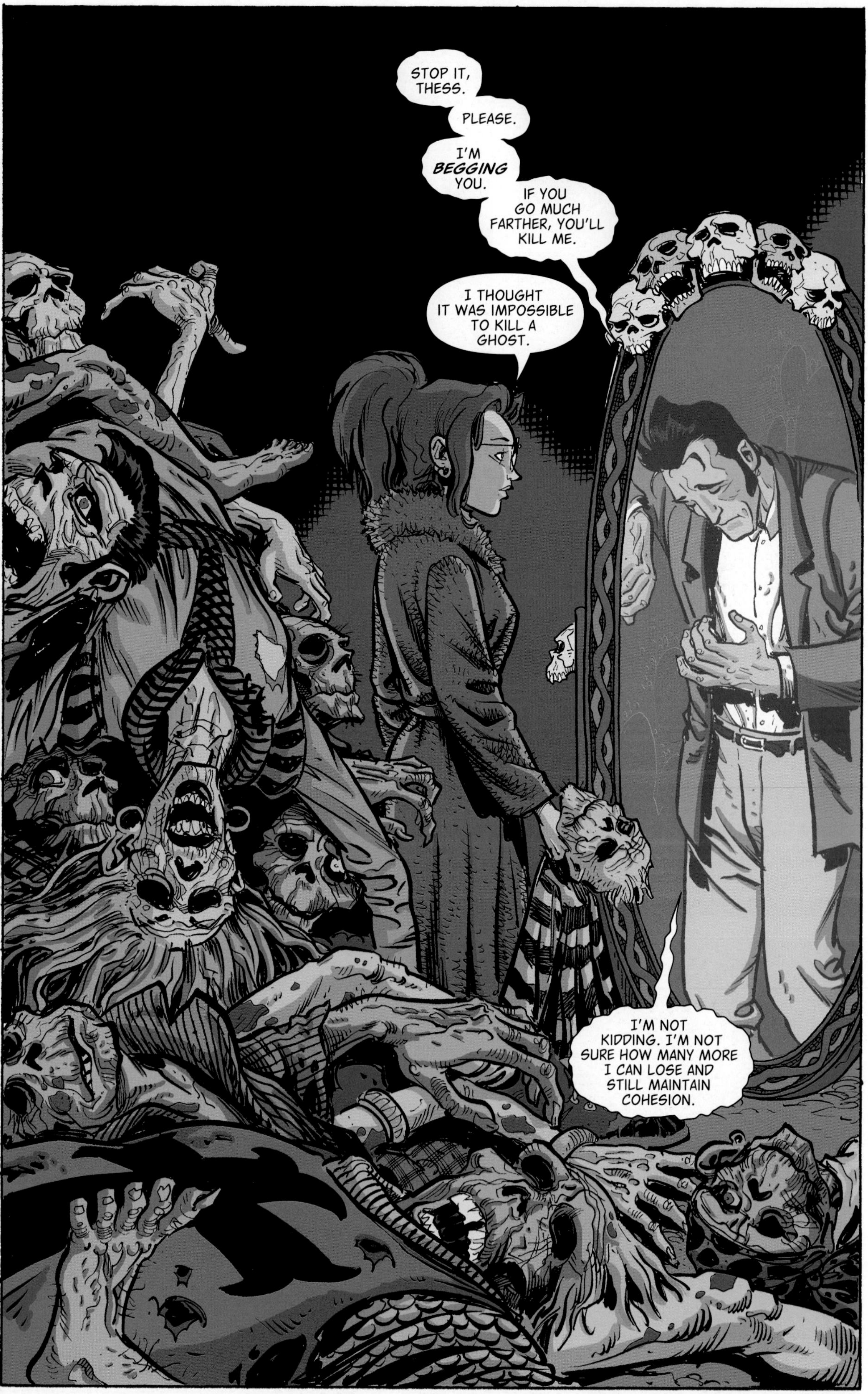
STOP IT, THESS.
PLEASE.
I'M **BEGGING** YOU.
IF YOU GO MUCH FARTHER, YOU'LL KILL ME.
I THOUGHT IT WAS IMPOSSIBLE TO KILL A GHOST.
I'M NOT KIDDING. I'M NOT SURE HOW MANY MORE I CAN LOSE AND STILL MAINTAIN COHESION.

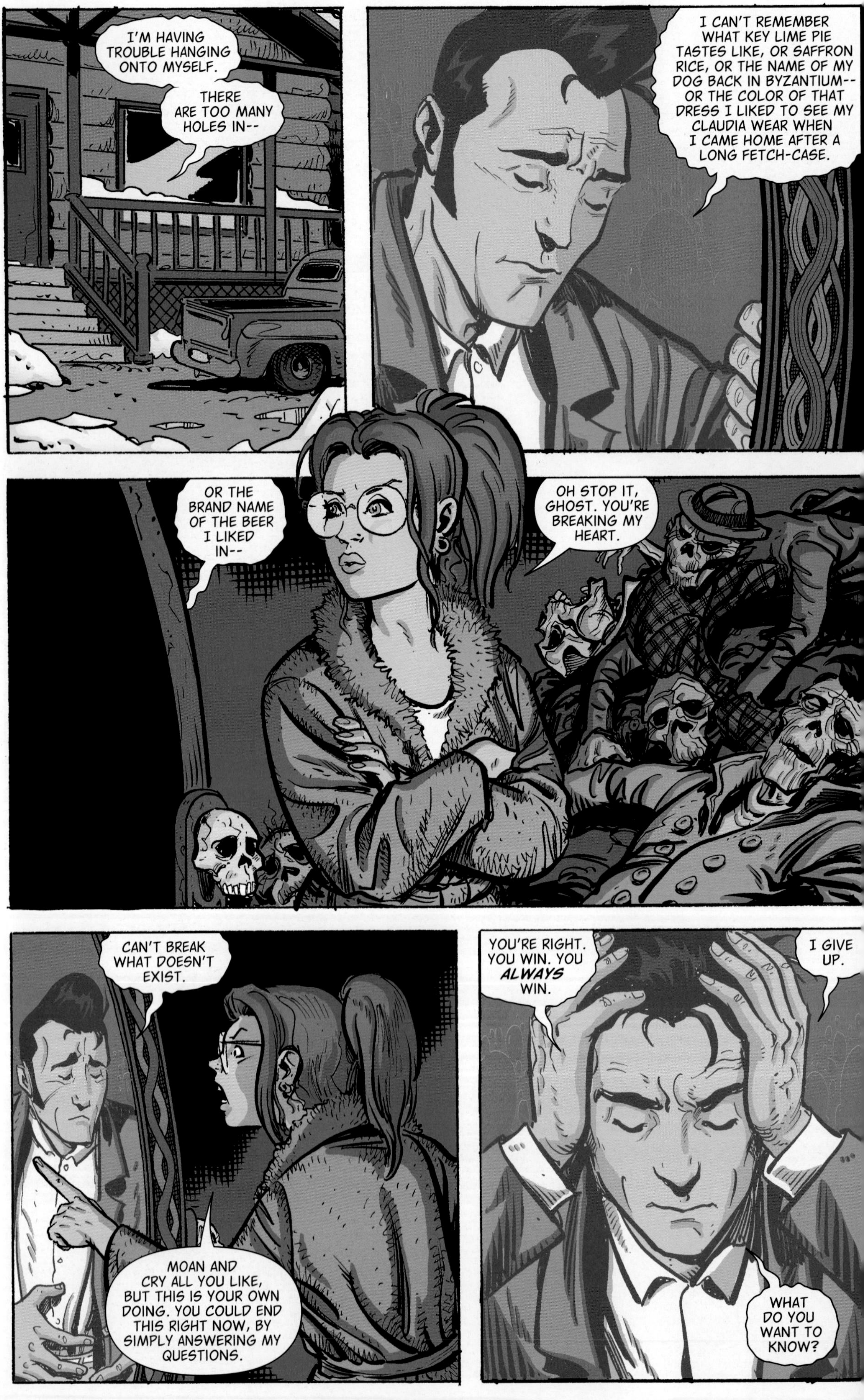
I'M HAVING TROUBLE HANGING ONTO MYSELF.
THERE ARE TOO MANY HOLES IN--
I CAN'T REMEMBER WHAT KEY LIME PIE TASTES LIKE, OR SAFFRON RICE, OR THE NAME OF MY DOG BACK IN BYZANTIUM-- OR THE COLOR OF THAT DRESS I LIKED TO SEE MY CLAUDIA WEAR WHEN I CAME HOME AFTER A LONG FETCH-CASE.
OR THE BRAND NAME OF THE BEER I LIKED IN--
OH STOP IT, GHOST. YOU'RE BREAKING MY HEART.
CAN'T BREAK WHAT DOESN'T EXIST.
MOAN AND CRY ALL YOU LIKE, BUT THIS IS YOUR OWN DOING. YOU COULD END THIS RIGHT NOW, BY SIMPLY ANSWERING MY QUESTIONS.
YOU'RE RIGHT. YOU WIN. YOU *ALWAYS* WIN.
I GIVE UP.
WHAT DO YOU WANT TO KNOW?

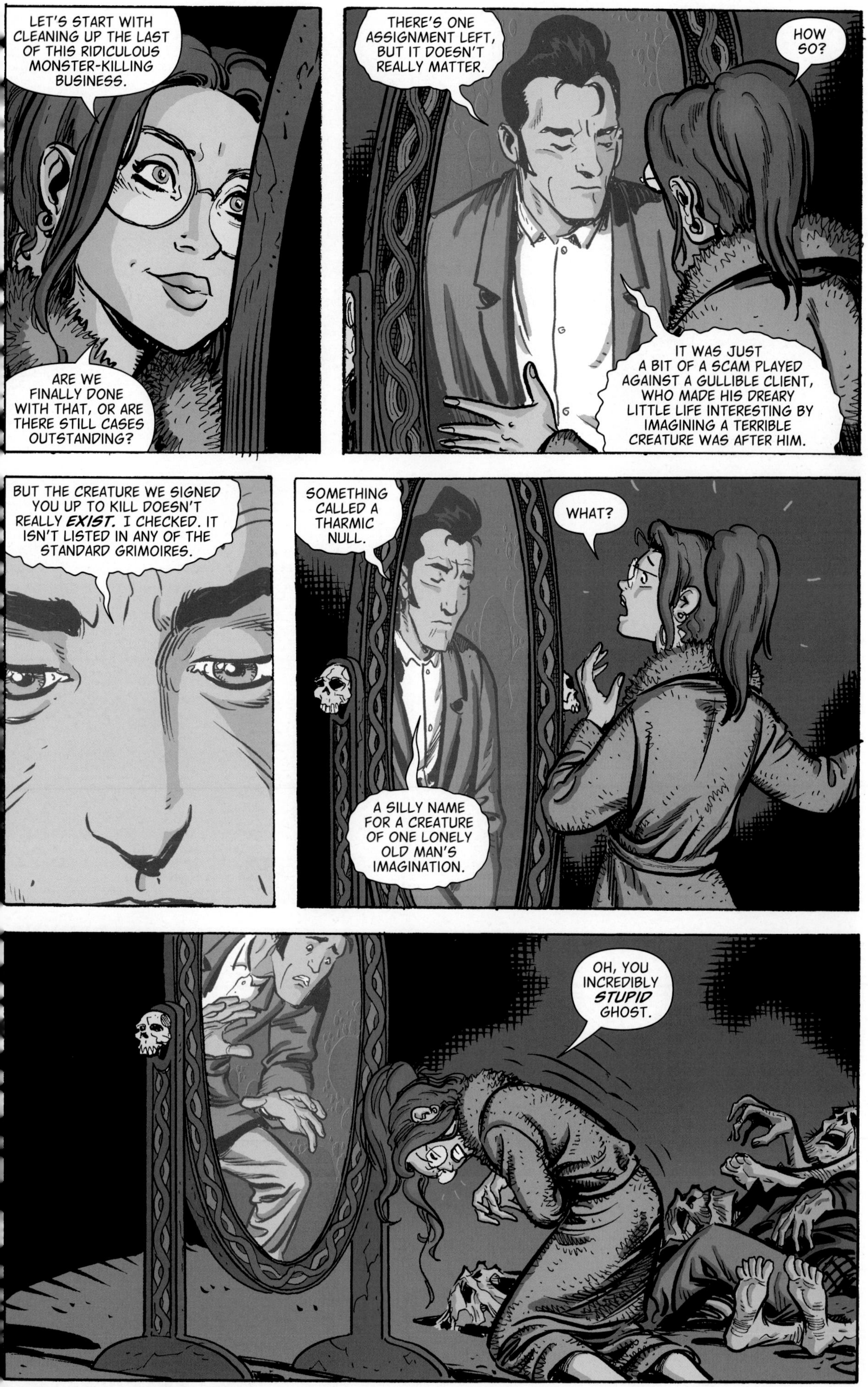
LET'S START WITH CLEANING UP THE LAST OF THIS RIDICULOUS MONSTER-KILLING BUSINESS.
ARE WE FINALLY DONE WITH THAT, OR ARE THERE STILL CASES OUTSTANDING?
THERE'S ONE ASSIGNMENT LEFT, BUT IT DOESN'T REALLY MATTER.
HOW SO?
IT WAS JUST A BIT OF A SCAM PLAYED AGAINST A GULLIBLE CLIENT, WHO MADE HIS DREARY LITTLE LIFE INTERESTING BY IMAGINING A TERRIBLE CREATURE WAS AFTER HIM.
BUT THE CREATURE WE SIGNED YOU UP TO KILL DOESN'T REALLY ***EXIST.*** I CHECKED. IT ISN'T LISTED IN ANY OF THE STANDARD GRIMOIRES.
SOMETHING CALLED A THARMIC NULL.
WHAT?
A SILLY NAME FOR A CREATURE OF ONE LONELY OLD MAN'S IMAGINATION.
OH, YOU INCREDIBLY ***STUPID*** GHOST.

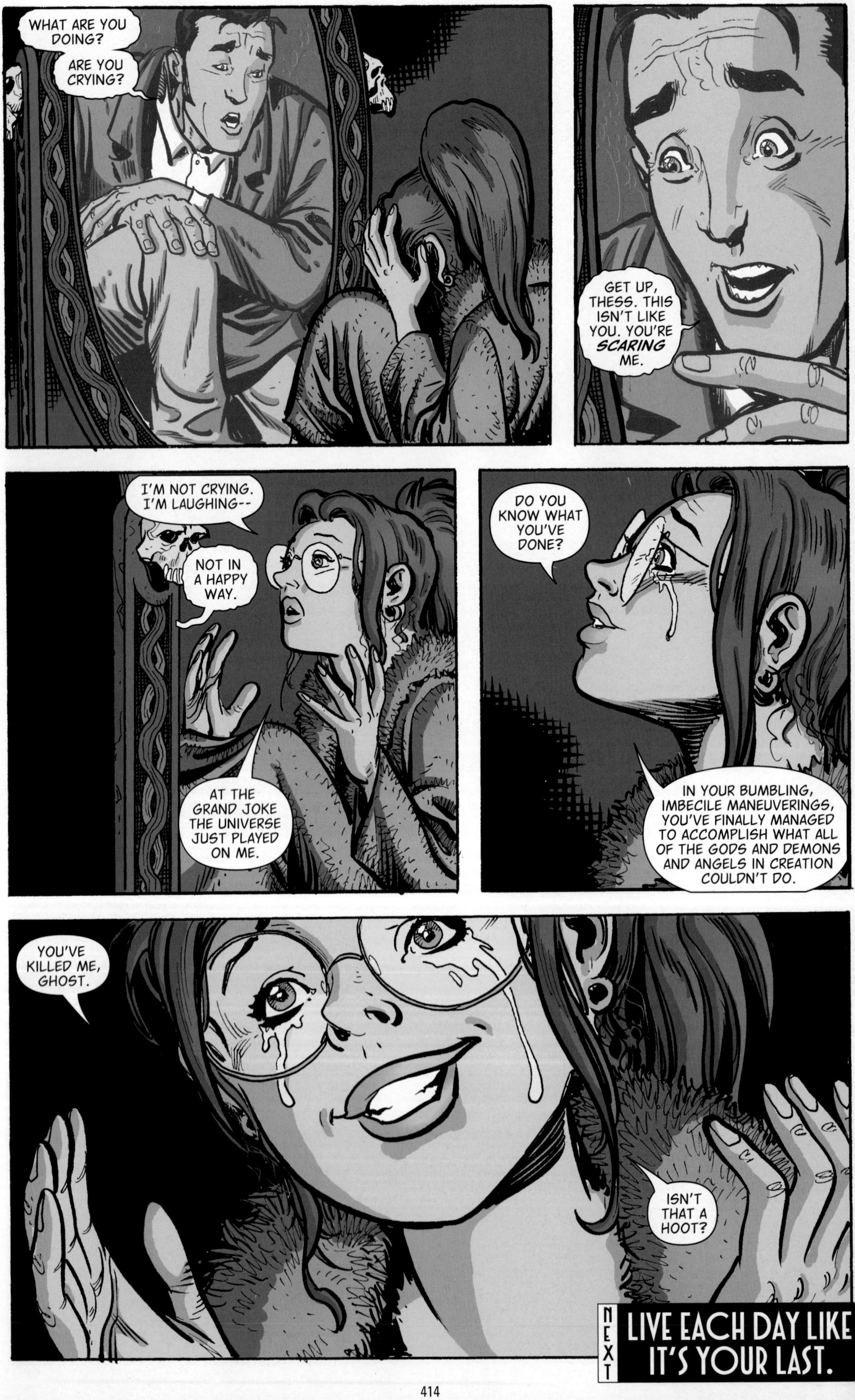

WHAT ARE YOU DOING?
ARE YOU CRYING?
GET UP, THESS. THIS ISN'T LIKE YOU. YOU'RE *SCARING* ME.
I'M NOT CRYING. I'M LAUGHING--
NOT IN A HAPPY WAY.
AT THE GRAND JOKE THE UNIVERSE JUST PLAYED ON ME.
DO YOU KNOW WHAT YOU'VE DONE?
IN YOUR BUMBLING, IMBECILE MANEUVERINGS, YOU'VE FINALLY MANAGED TO ACCOMPLISH WHAT ALL OF THE GODS AND DEMONS AND ANGELS IN CREATION COULDN'T DO.
YOU'VE KILLED ME, GHOST.
ISN'T THAT A HOOT?
NEXT
LIVE EACH DAY LIKE IT'S YOUR LAST.

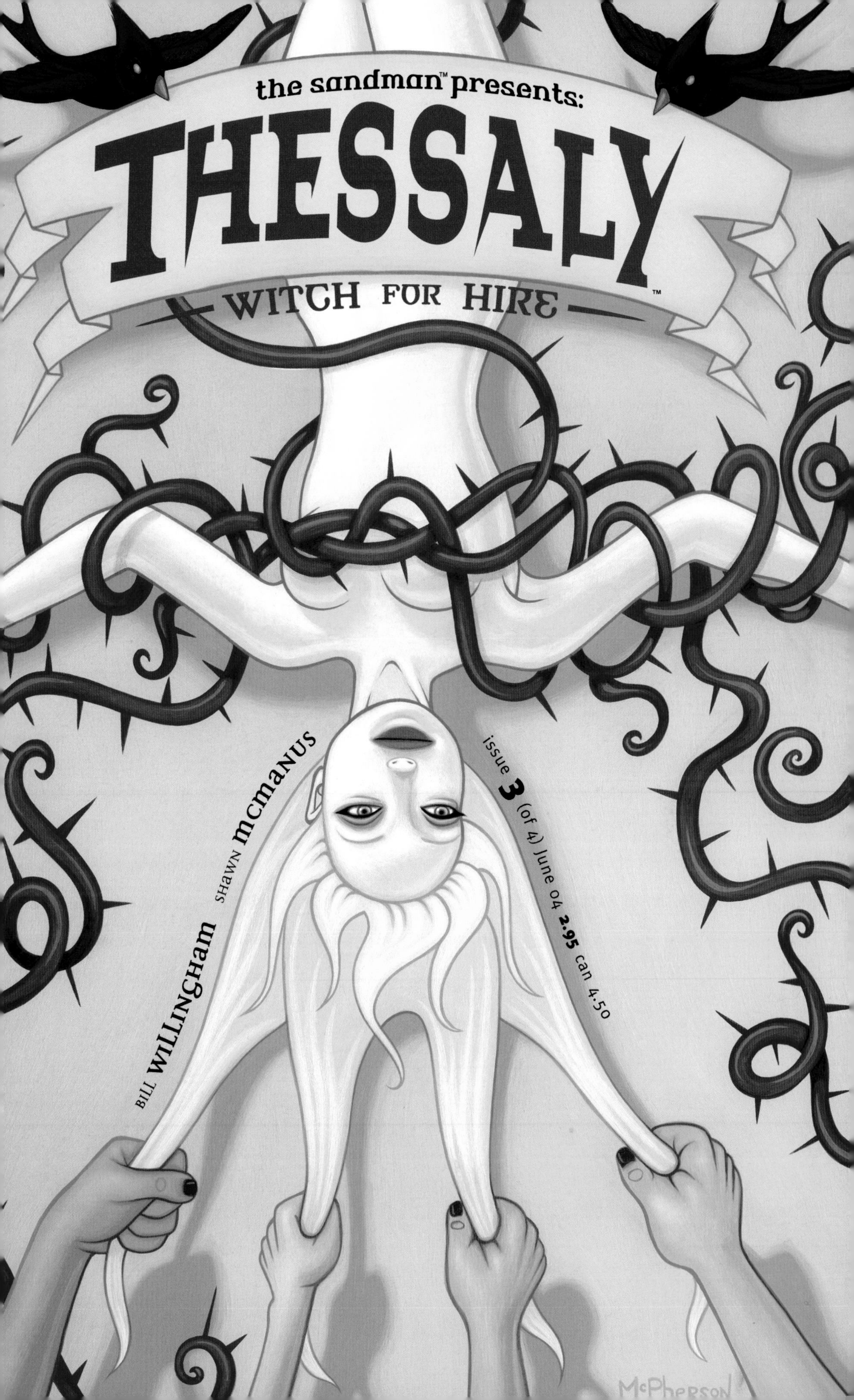
the sandman™ presents:
THESSALY
WITCH FOR HIRE™
BILL WILLINGHAM
SHAWN MCMANUS
issue 3 (of 4) June 04 2.95 can 4.50
McPherson

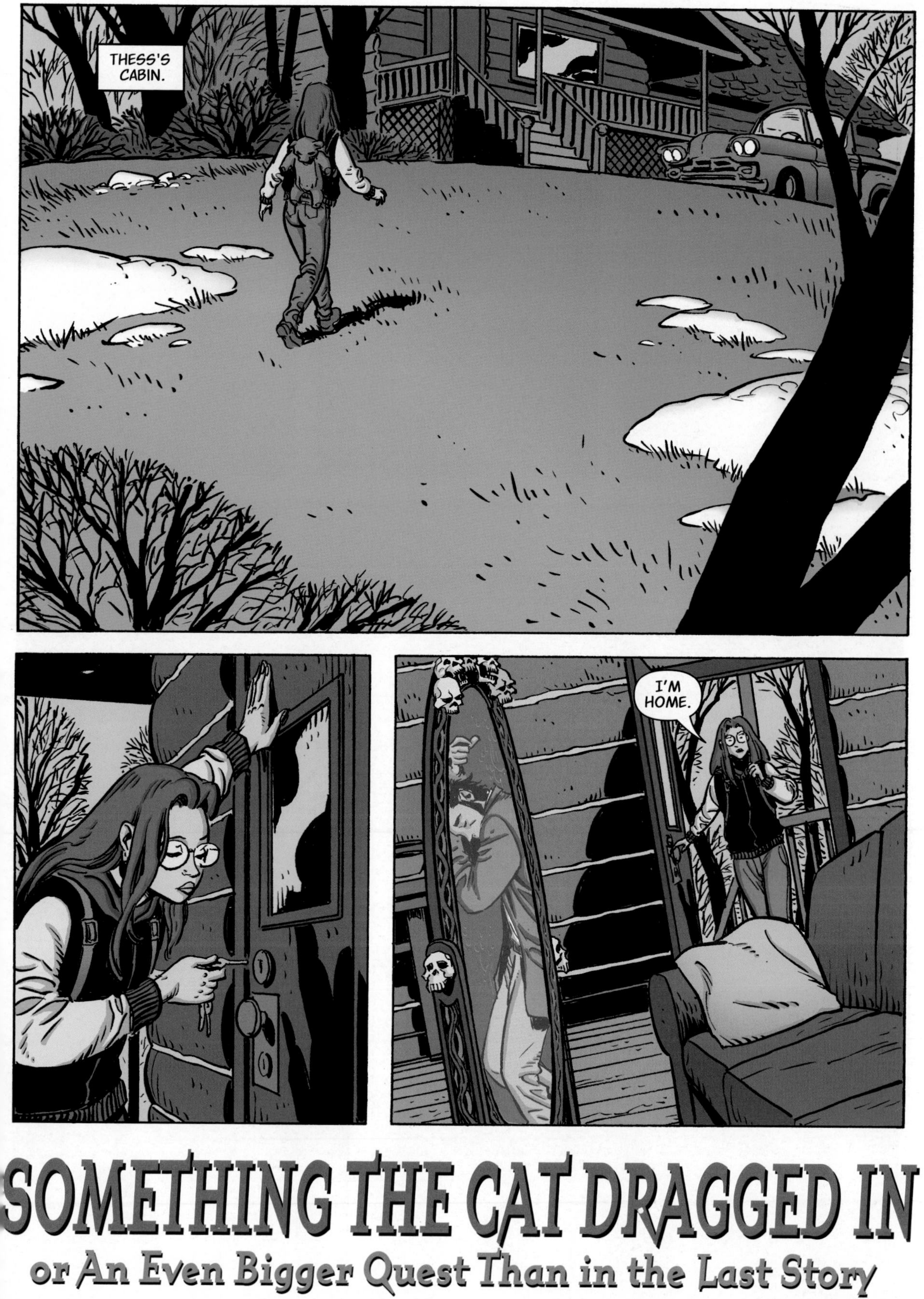
THESS'S CABIN.
I'M HOME.

SOMETHING THE CAT DRAGGED IN

or An Even Bigger Quest Than in the Last Story

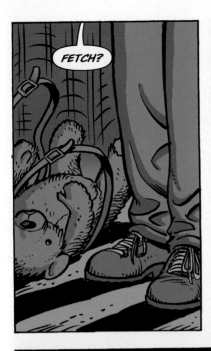

FETCH?

ZZZZZZZZ

HELLO?

WERE YOU SLEEPING?

I DIDN'T KNOW GHOSTS *COULD* SLEEP.

NEITHER DID I.

BUT APPARENTLY WHEN WE GET *BORED* ENOUGH...

...DID YOU HAVE TO LEAVE ME HERE FOR A *WEEK* WITH NOTHING TO DO? COULDN'T YOU HAVE AT *LEAST* TURNED ON THE TV, OR SHOVED SOME DAMN *BOOKS* IN HERE WITH ME?

FIRST: I DON'T HAVE A TELEVISION MACHINE.

SECOND: THE MIRROR ONLY HOLDS GHOSTS.

AND GHOST BOOKS ARE RARE. I OWN A FEW, BUT NOT HERE, AND I'D NEVER LEND THEM TO YOU ANYWAY.

THESSALY, MY PUDDING, YOU LOOK LIKE HELL.

LIKE SOMETHING THE CAT DRAGGED IN.

HAVE A NICE TRIP?

MORE IMPORTANT, DID YOU FIND OUT ANYTHING *USEFUL?*

THE TRIP WASN'T NICE, BY ANY DEFINITION OF THE WORD.

AS FOR USEFUL, WELL--

A GRAND TOUR IS A DIFFICULT UNDERTAKING, NOT TO BE VENTURED LIGHTLY, OR FOR FRIVOLOUS REASONS.

IT'S TOO COSTLY, IN TERMS OF POWER EXPENDED AND DANGERS ENCOUNTERED.

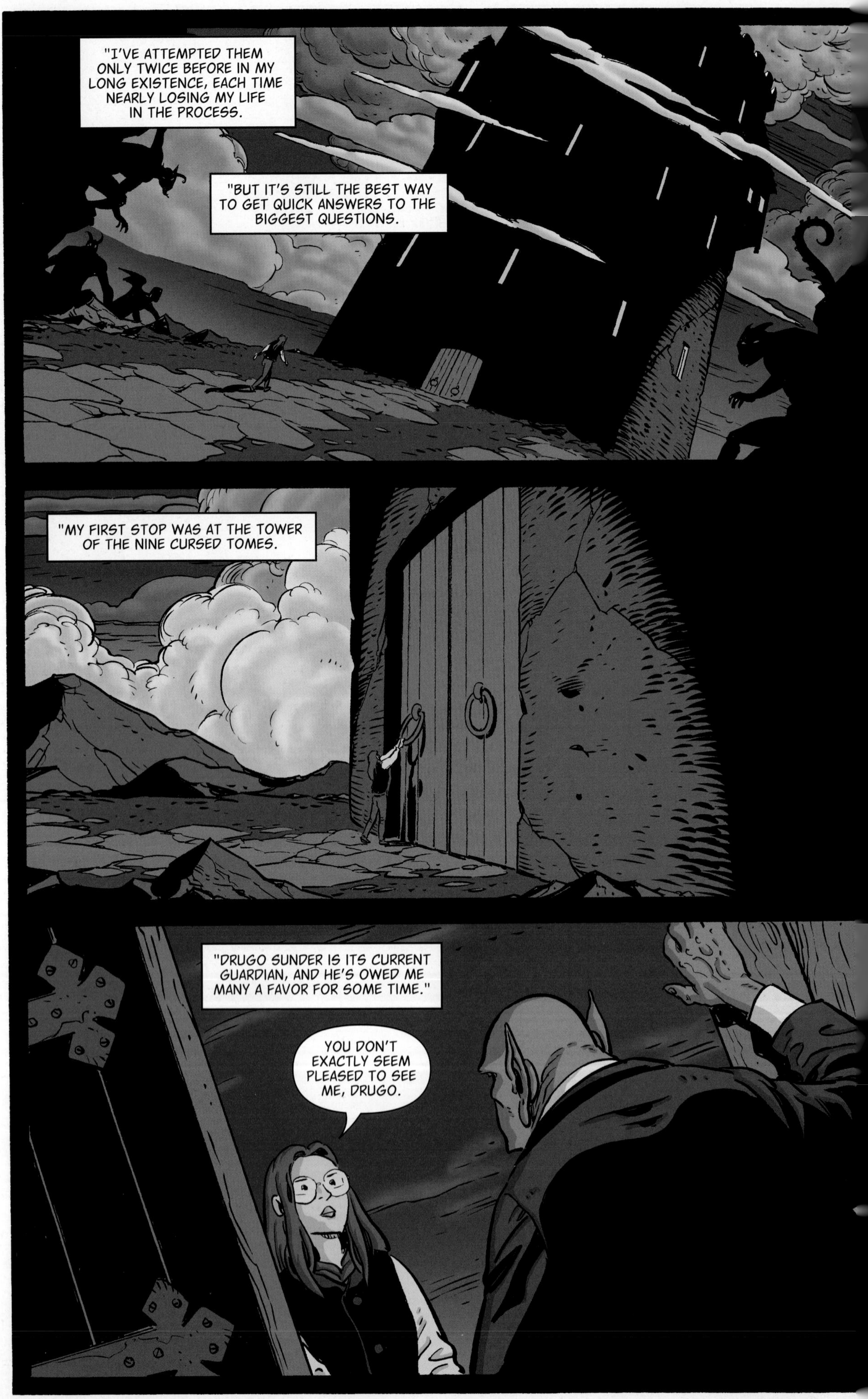
"I'VE ATTEMPTED THEM ONLY TWICE BEFORE IN MY LONG EXISTENCE, EACH TIME NEARLY LOSING MY LIFE IN THE PROCESS.
"BUT IT'S STILL THE BEST WAY TO GET QUICK ANSWERS TO THE BIGGEST QUESTIONS.
"MY FIRST STOP WAS AT THE TOWER OF THE NINE CURSED TOMES.
"DRUGO SUNDER IS ITS CURRENT GUARDIAN, AND HE'S OWED ME MANY A FAVOR FOR SOME TIME."
YOU DON'T EXACTLY SEEM PLEASED TO SEE ME, DRUGO.

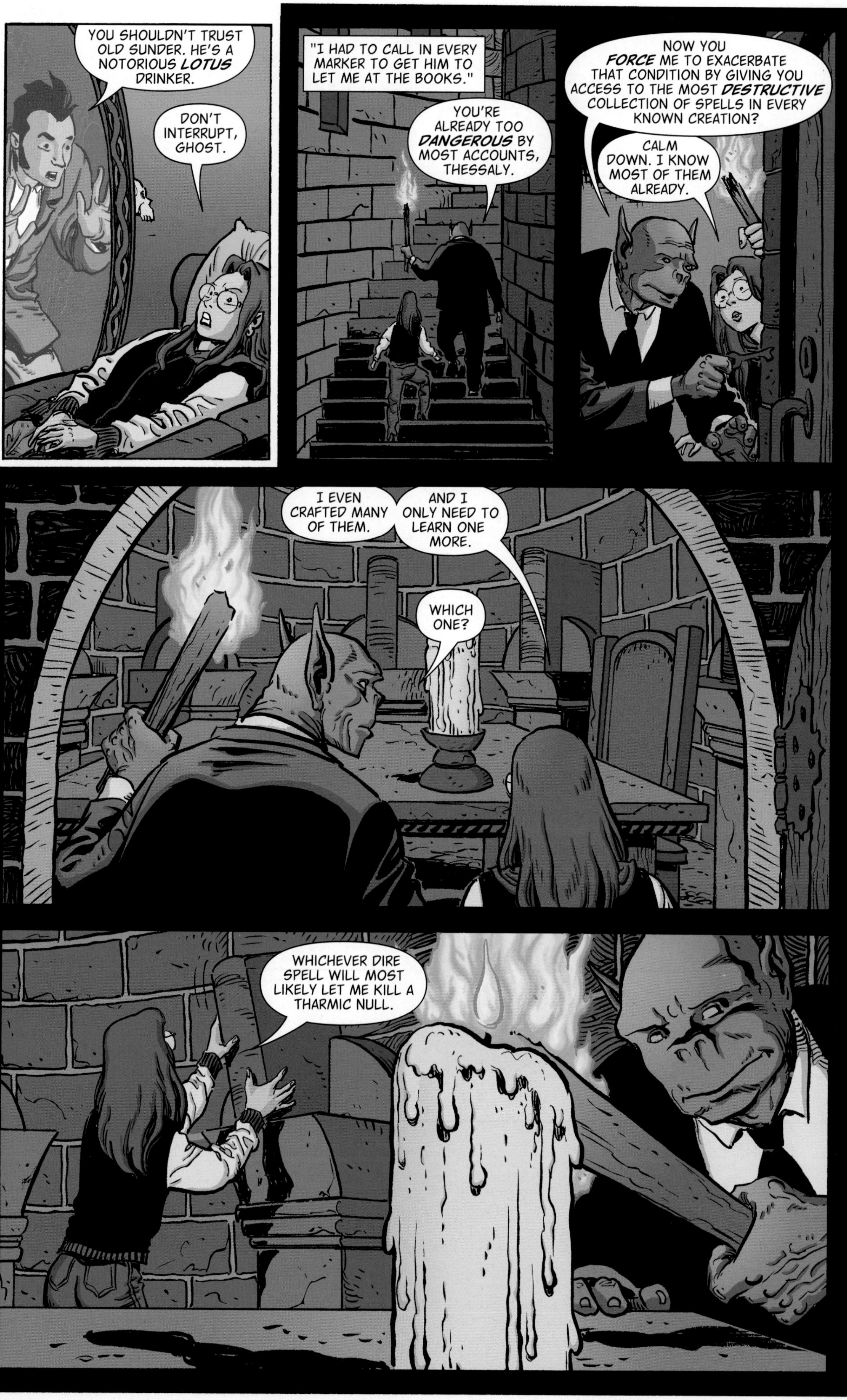

YOU SHOULDN'T TRUST OLD SUNDER. HE'S A NOTORIOUS *LOTUS* DRINKER.
DON'T INTERRUPT, GHOST.
"I HAD TO CALL IN EVERY MARKER TO GET HIM TO LET ME AT THE BOOKS."
YOU'RE ALREADY TOO *DANGEROUS* BY MOST ACCOUNTS, THESSALY.
NOW YOU *FORCE* ME TO EXACERBATE THAT CONDITION BY GIVING YOU ACCESS TO THE MOST *DESTRUCTIVE* COLLECTION OF SPELLS IN EVERY KNOWN CREATION?
CALM DOWN. I KNOW MOST OF THEM ALREADY.
I EVEN CRAFTED MANY OF THEM.
AND I ONLY NEED TO LEARN ONE MORE.
WHICH ONE?
WHICHEVER DIRE SPELL WILL MOST LIKELY LET ME KILL A THARMIC NULL.

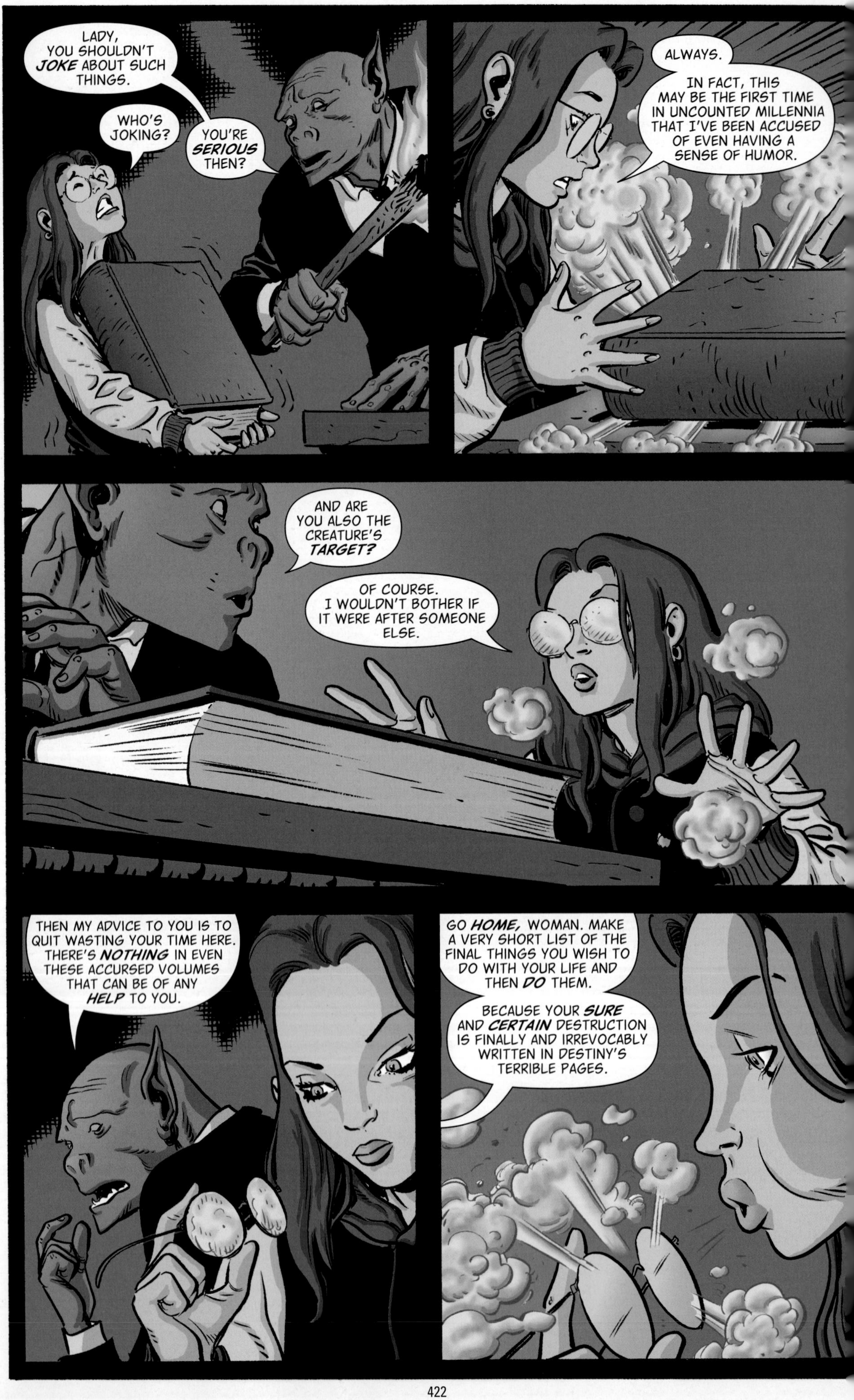
LADY, YOU SHOULDN'T JOKE ABOUT SUCH THINGS.
WHO'S JOKING?
YOU'RE SERIOUS THEN?
ALWAYS.
IN FACT, THIS MAY BE THE FIRST TIME IN UNCOUNTED MILLENNIA THAT I'VE BEEN ACCUSED OF EVEN HAVING A SENSE OF HUMOR.
AND ARE YOU ALSO THE CREATURE'S TARGET?
OF COURSE. I WOULDN'T BOTHER IF IT WERE AFTER SOMEONE ELSE.
THEN MY ADVICE TO YOU IS TO QUIT WASTING YOUR TIME HERE. THERE'S NOTHING IN EVEN THESE ACCURSED VOLUMES THAT CAN BE OF ANY HELP TO YOU.
GO HOME, WOMAN. MAKE A VERY SHORT LIST OF THE FINAL THINGS YOU WISH TO DO WITH YOUR LIFE AND THEN DO THEM.
BECAUSE YOUR SURE AND CERTAIN DESTRUCTION IS FINALLY AND IRREVOCABLY WRITTEN IN DESTINY'S TERRIBLE PAGES.

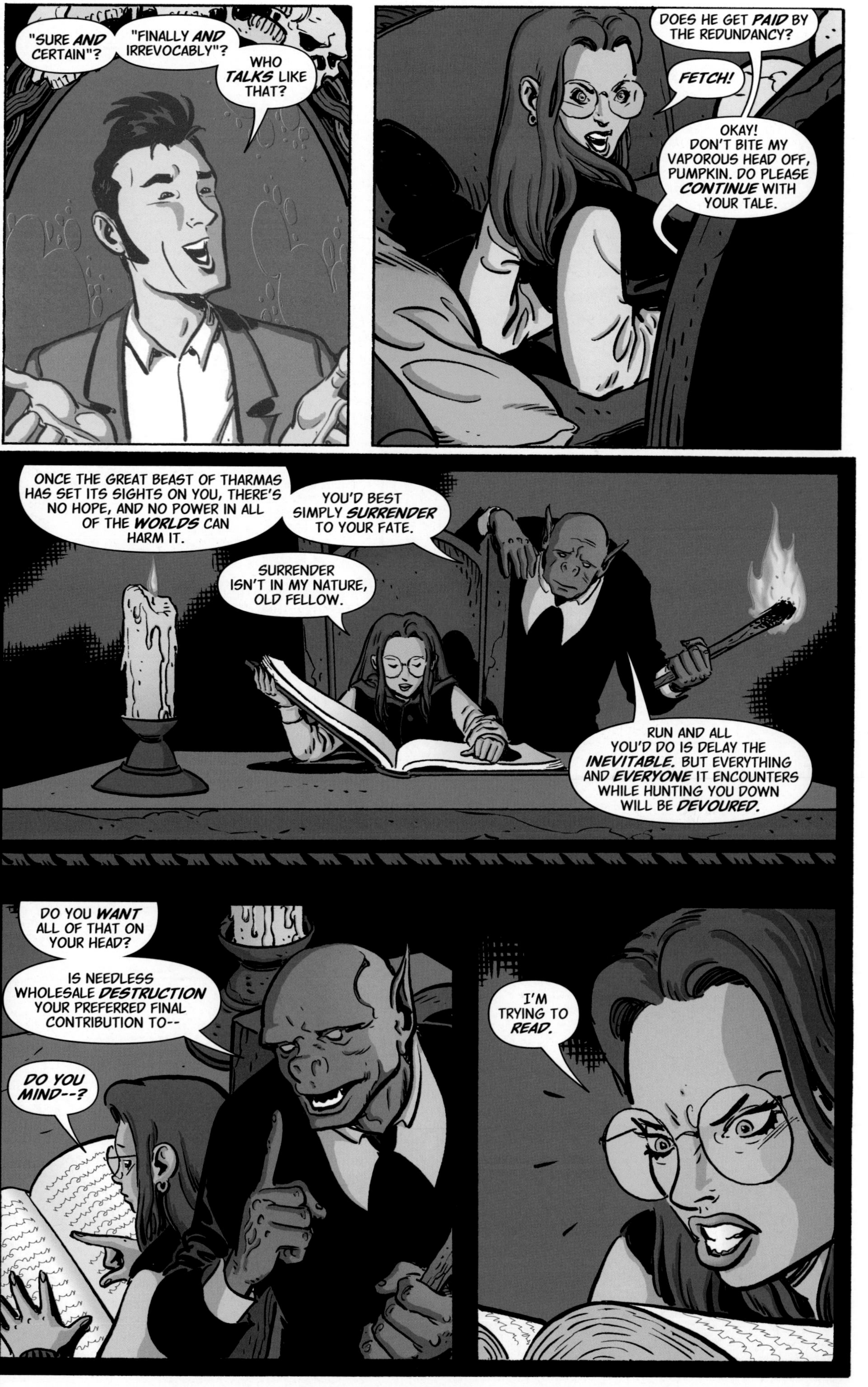
"SURE AND CERTAIN"?
"FINALLY AND IRREVOCABLY"?
WHO TALKS LIKE THAT?
DOES HE GET PAID BY THE REDUNDANCY?
FETCH!
OKAY! DON'T BITE MY VAPOROUS HEAD OFF, PUMPKIN. DO PLEASE CONTINUE WITH YOUR TALE.
ONCE THE GREAT BEAST OF THARMAS HAS SET ITS SIGHTS ON YOU, THERE'S NO HOPE, AND NO POWER IN ALL OF THE WORLDS CAN HARM IT.
YOU'D BEST SIMPLY SURRENDER TO YOUR FATE.
SURRENDER ISN'T IN MY NATURE, OLD FELLOW.
RUN AND ALL YOU'D DO IS DELAY THE INEVITABLE. BUT EVERYTHING AND EVERYONE IT ENCOUNTERS WHILE HUNTING YOU DOWN WILL BE DEVOURED.
DO YOU WANT ALL OF THAT ON YOUR HEAD?
IS NEEDLESS WHOLESALE DESTRUCTION YOUR PREFERRED FINAL CONTRIBUTION TO--
DO YOU MIND--?
I'M TRYING TO READ.

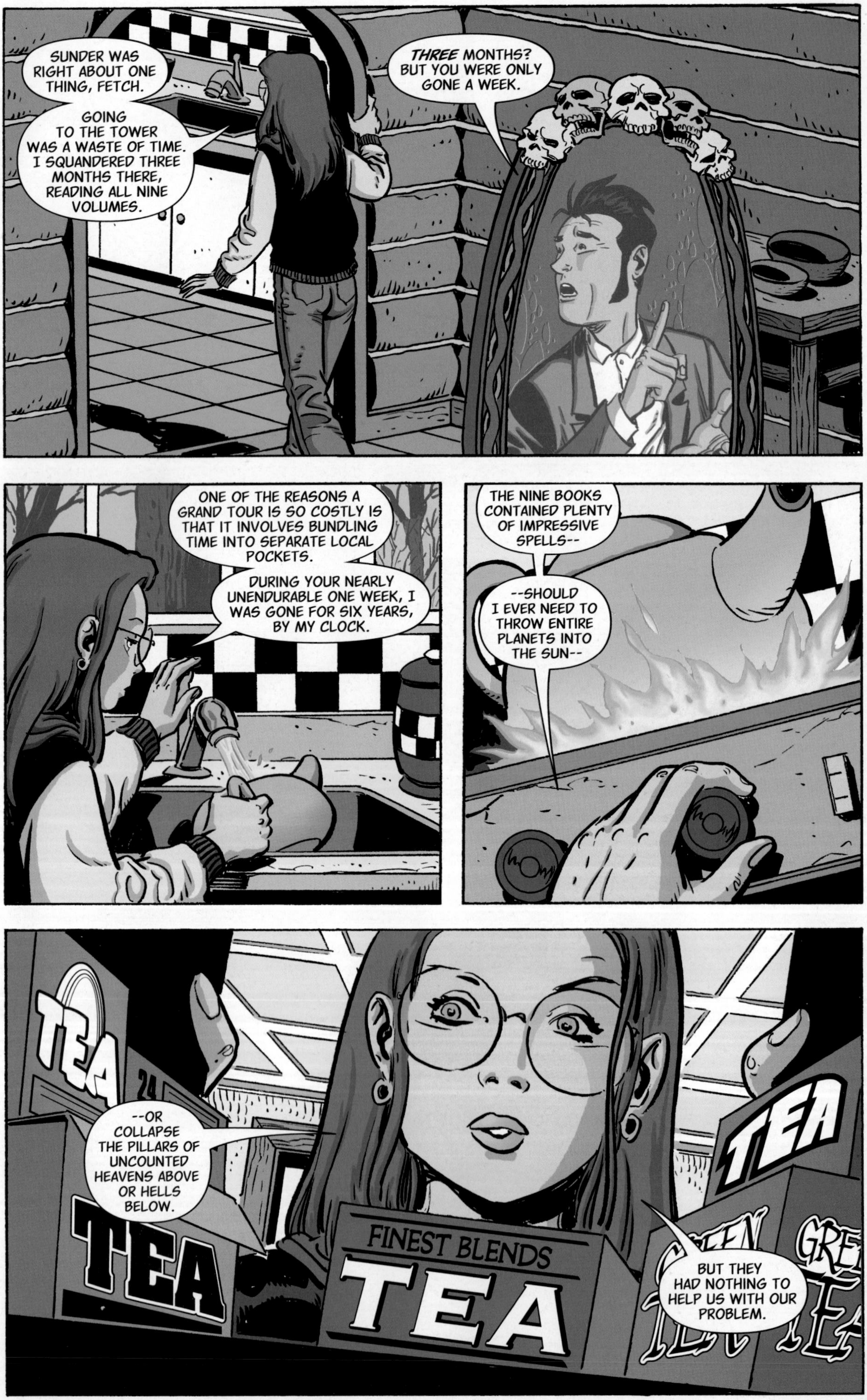
SUNDER WAS RIGHT ABOUT ONE THING, FETCH.
GOING TO THE TOWER WAS A WASTE OF TIME. I SQUANDERED THREE MONTHS THERE, READING ALL NINE VOLUMES.
THREE MONTHS? BUT YOU WERE ONLY GONE A WEEK.
ONE OF THE REASONS A GRAND TOUR IS SO COSTLY IS THAT IT INVOLVES BUNDLING TIME INTO SEPARATE LOCAL POCKETS.
DURING YOUR NEARLY UNENDURABLE ONE WEEK, I WAS GONE FOR SIX YEARS, BY MY CLOCK.
THE NINE BOOKS CONTAINED PLENTY OF IMPRESSIVE SPELLS--
--SHOULD I EVER NEED TO THROW ENTIRE PLANETS INTO THE SUN--
TEA
24
TEA
--OR COLLAPSE THE PILLARS OF UNCOUNTED HEAVENS ABOVE OR HELLS BELOW.
FINEST BLENDS
TEA
TEA
BUT THEY HAD NOTHING TO HELP US WITH OUR PROBLEM.

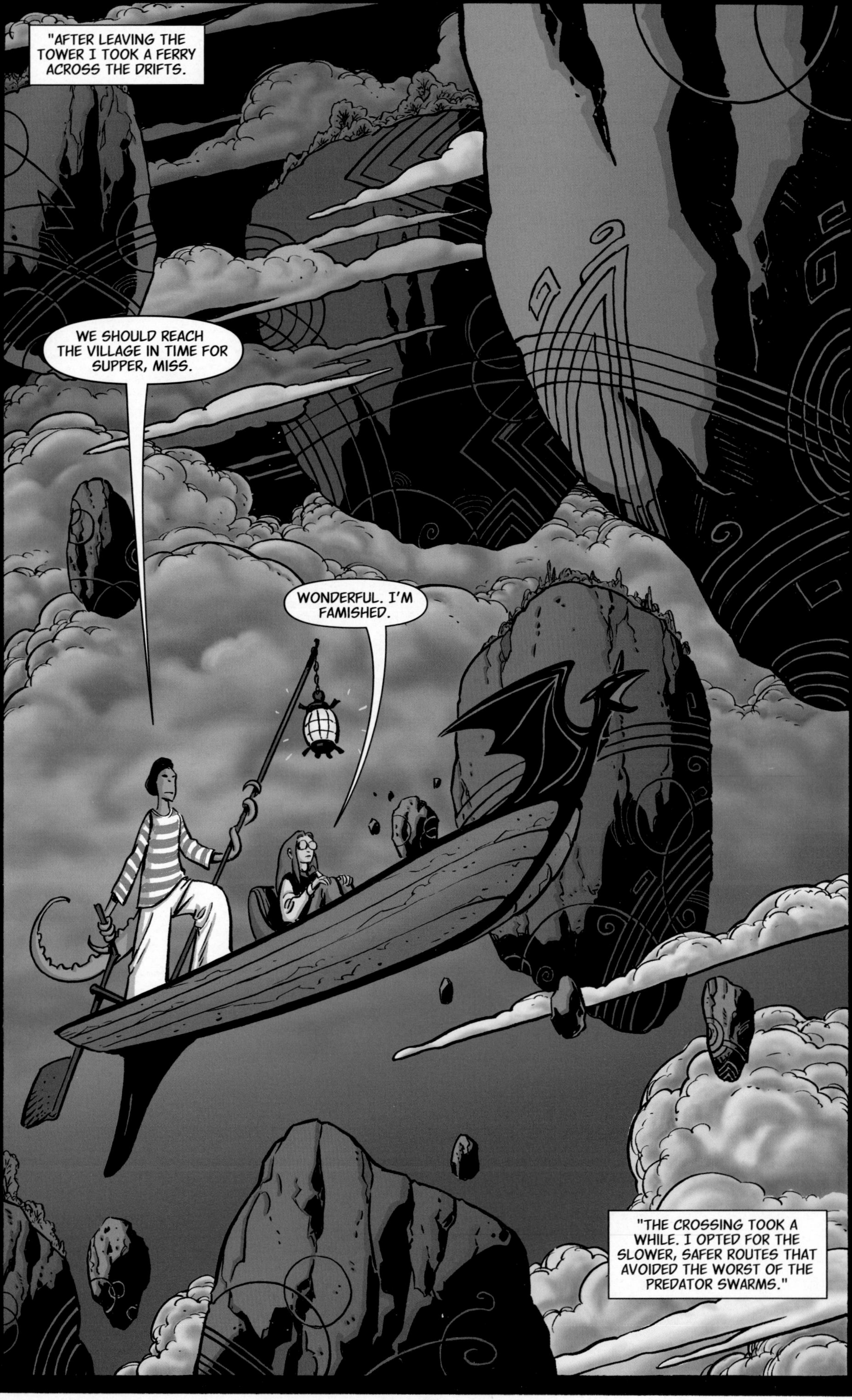
"AFTER LEAVING THE TOWER I TOOK A FERRY ACROSS THE DRIFTS.
WE SHOULD REACH THE VILLAGE IN TIME FOR SUPPER, MISS.
WONDERFUL. I'M FAMISHED.
"THE CROSSING TOOK A WHILE. I OPTED FOR THE SLOWER, SAFER ROUTES THAT AVOIDED THE WORST OF THE PREDATOR SWARMS."

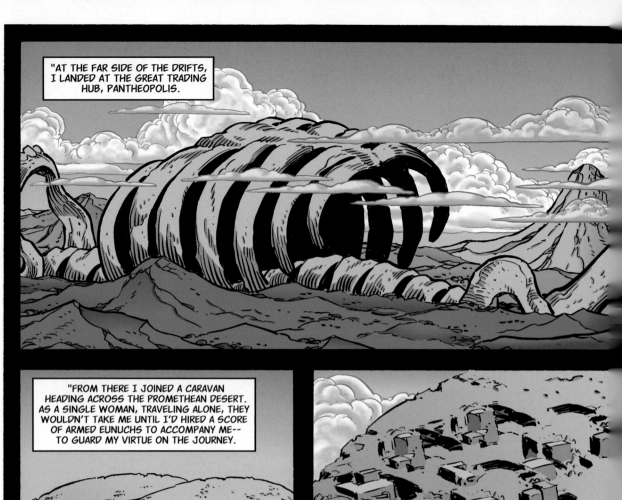

"AT THE FAR SIDE OF THE DRIFTS, I LANDED AT THE GREAT TRADING HUB, PANTHEOPOLIS.

"FROM THERE I JOINED A CARAVAN HEADING ACROSS THE PROMETHEAN DESERT. AS A SINGLE WOMAN, TRAVELING ALONE, THEY WOULDN'T TAKE ME UNTIL I'D HIRED A SCORE OF ARMED EUNUCHS TO ACCOMPANY ME-- TO GUARD MY VIRTUE ON THE JOURNEY.

"BUT EVENTUALLY I MADE IT (VIRTUE MORE OR LESS INTACT) TO THE CITY OF--WELL, I CAN'T REALLY PRONOUNCE IT, BUT IT ROUGHLY TRANSLATES AS 'THE HOUSE OF THE LAST TITAN.'

"IT WAS IMPRESSIVE, TO SAY THE LEAST. ITS POPULATION NUMBERS IN THE HUNDREDS OF MILLIONS. EVEN THE SINGLE TOWERING RIB I VISITED HOUSED OVER A MILLION SOULS."

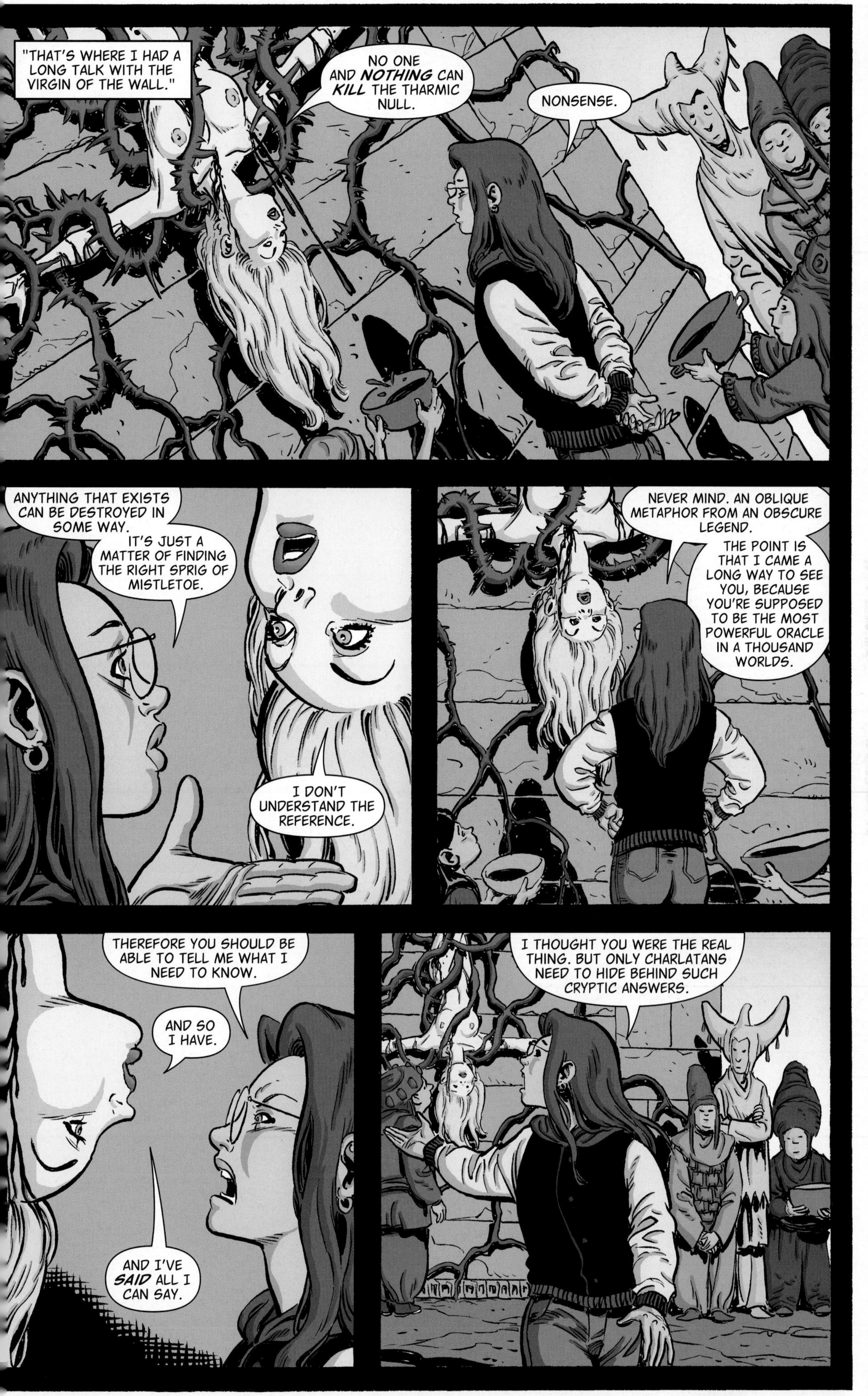
"THAT'S WHERE I HAD A LONG TALK WITH THE VIRGIN OF THE WALL."
NO ONE AND **NOTHING** CAN **KILL** THE THARMIC NULL.
NONSENSE.
ANYTHING THAT EXISTS CAN BE DESTROYED IN SOME WAY.
IT'S JUST A MATTER OF FINDING THE RIGHT SPRIG OF MISTLETOE.
I DON'T UNDERSTAND THE REFERENCE.
NEVER MIND. AN OBLIQUE METAPHOR FROM AN OBSCURE LEGEND.
THE POINT IS THAT I CAME A LONG WAY TO SEE YOU, BECAUSE YOU'RE SUPPOSED TO BE THE MOST POWERFUL ORACLE IN A THOUSAND WORLDS.
THEREFORE YOU SHOULD BE ABLE TO TELL ME WHAT I NEED TO KNOW.
AND SO I HAVE.
AND I'VE **SAID** ALL I CAN SAY.
I THOUGHT YOU WERE THE REAL THING. BUT ONLY CHARLATANS NEED TO HIDE BEHIND SUCH CRYPTIC ANSWERS.

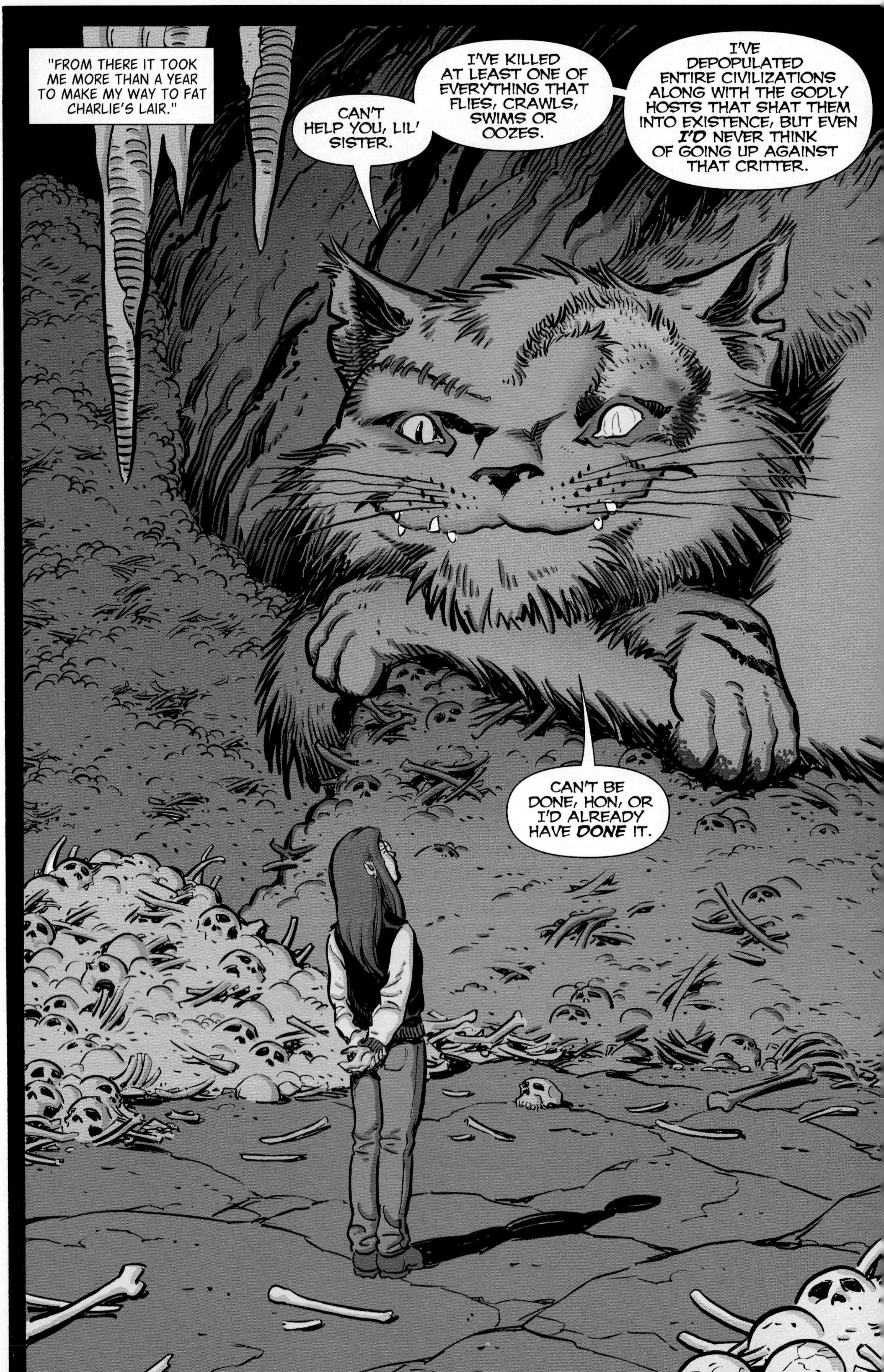
"FROM THERE IT TOOK ME MORE THAN A YEAR TO MAKE MY WAY TO FAT CHARLIE'S LAIR."
CAN'T HELP YOU, LIL' SISTER.
I'VE KILLED AT LEAST ONE OF EVERYTHING THAT FLIES, CRAWLS, SWIMS OR OOZES.
I'VE DEPOPULATED ENTIRE CIVILIZATIONS ALONG WITH THE GODLY HOSTS THAT SHAT THEM INTO EXISTENCE, BUT EVEN *I'D* NEVER THINK OF GOING UP AGAINST THAT CRITTER.
CAN'T BE DONE, HON, OR I'D ALREADY HAVE **DONE** IT.

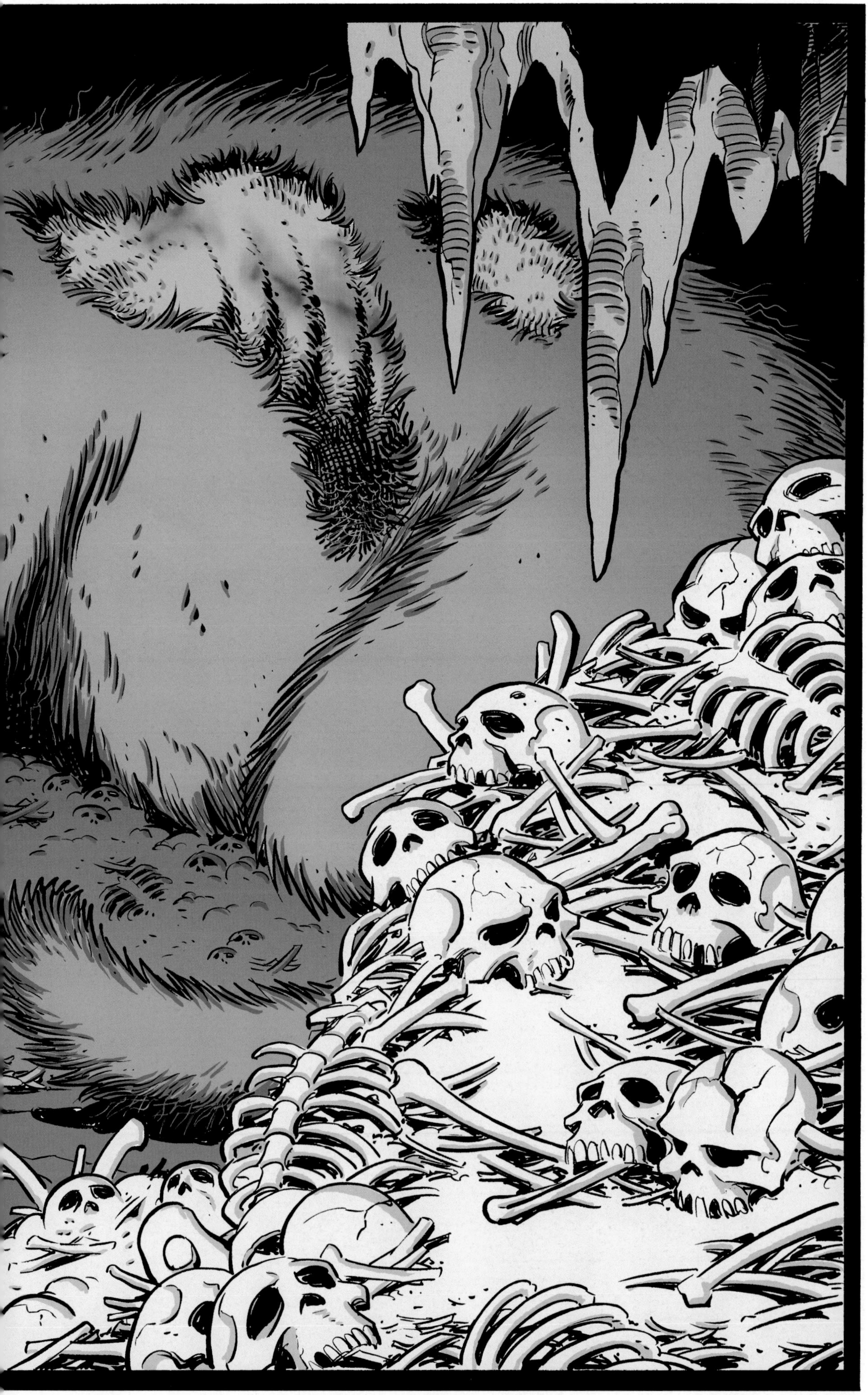

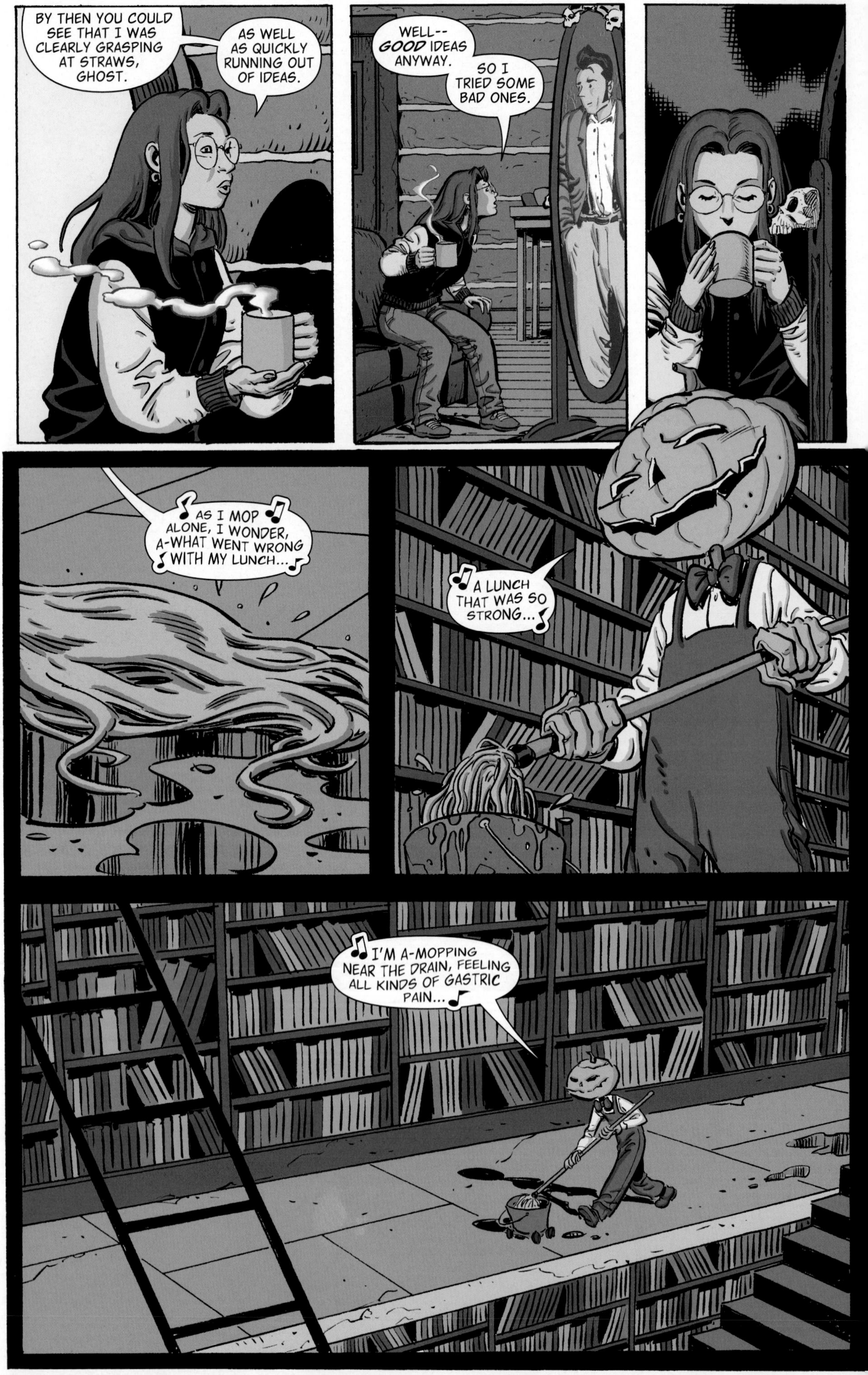
BY THEN YOU COULD SEE THAT I WAS CLEARLY GRASPING AT STRAWS, GHOST.
AS WELL AS QUICKLY RUNNING OUT OF IDEAS.
WELL-- GOOD IDEAS ANYWAY.
SO I TRIED SOME BAD ONES.
AS I MOP ALONE, I WONDER, A-WHAT WENT WRONG WITH MY LUNCH...
A LUNCH THAT WAS SO STRONG...
I'M A-MOPPING NEAR THE DRAIN, FEELING ALL KINDS OF GASTRIC PAIN...

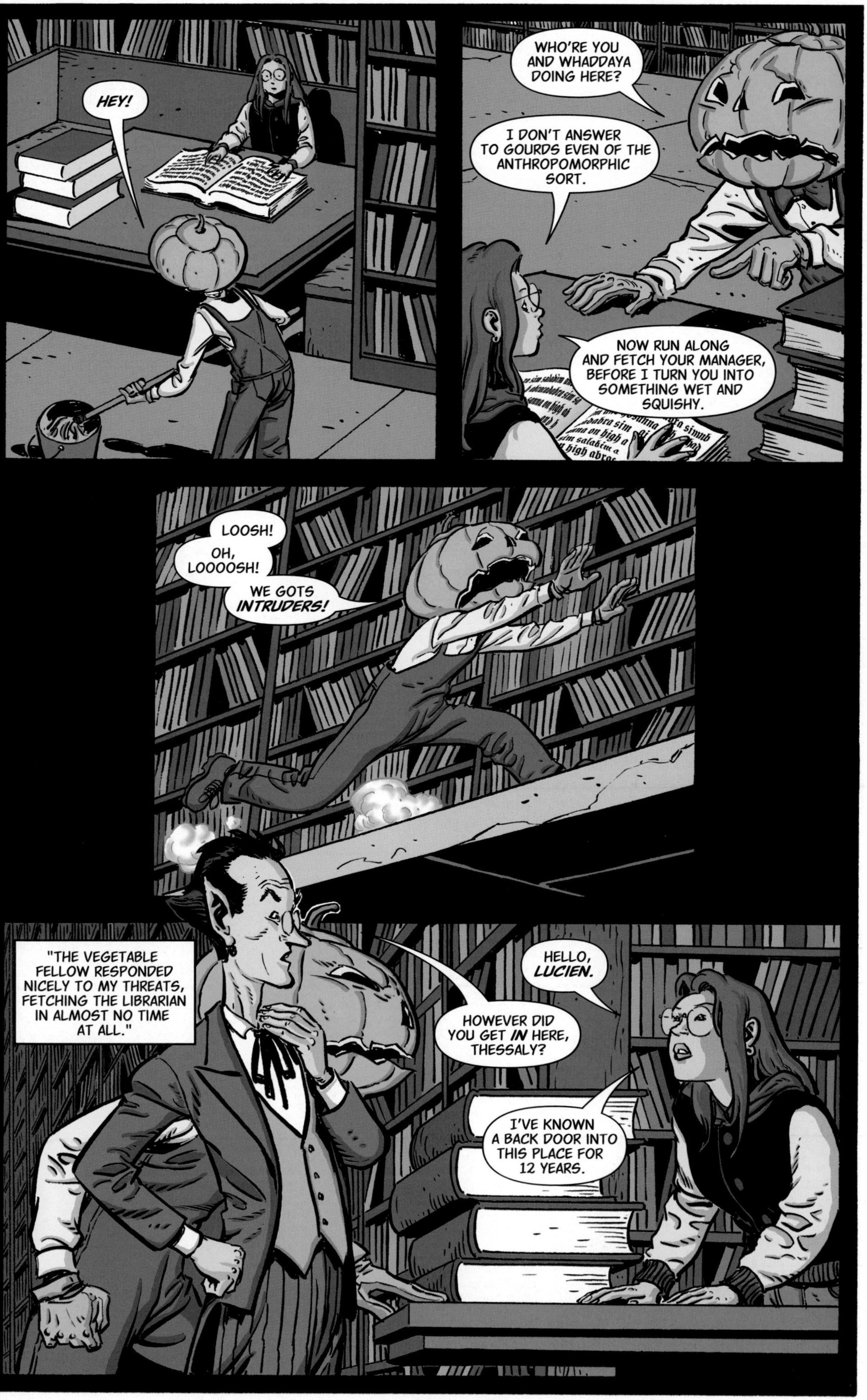
HEY!
WHO'RE YOU AND WHADDAYA DOING HERE?
I DON'T ANSWER TO GOURDS EVEN OF THE ANTHROPOMORPHIC SORT.
NOW RUN ALONG AND FETCH YOUR MANAGER, BEFORE I TURN YOU INTO SOMETHING WET AND SQUISHY.
LOOSH!
OH, LOOOOSH!
WE GOTS *INTRUDERS!*
"THE VEGETABLE FELLOW RESPONDED NICELY TO MY THREATS, FETCHING THE LIBRARIAN IN ALMOST NO TIME AT ALL."
HOWEVER DID YOU GET *IN* HERE, THESSALY?
HELLO, *LUCIEN.*
I'VE KNOWN A BACK DOOR INTO THIS PLACE FOR 12 YEARS.

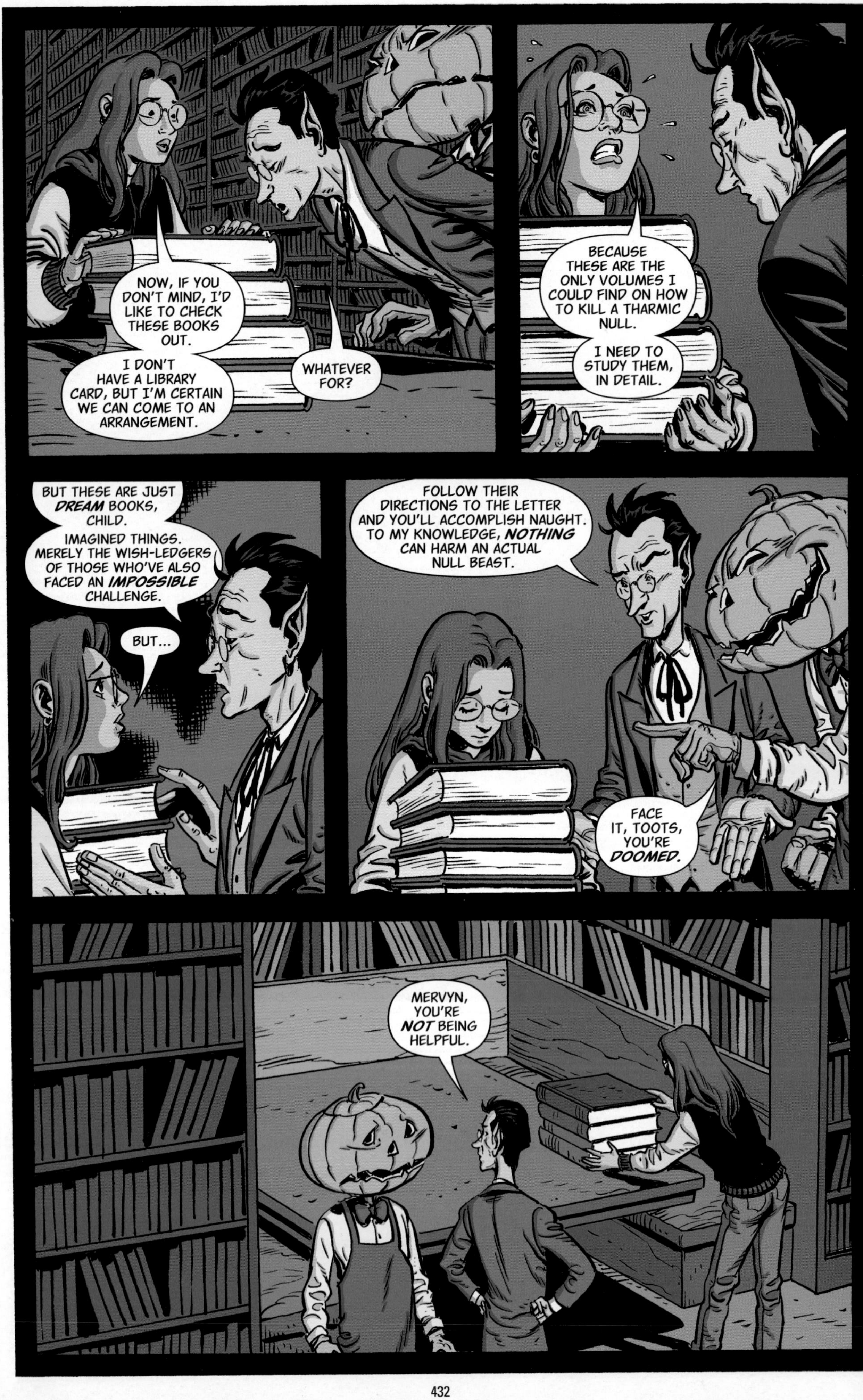
NOW, IF YOU DON'T MIND, I'D LIKE TO CHECK THESE BOOKS OUT.
I DON'T HAVE A LIBRARY CARD, BUT I'M CERTAIN WE CAN COME TO AN ARRANGEMENT.
WHATEVER FOR?
BECAUSE THESE ARE THE ONLY VOLUMES I COULD FIND ON HOW TO KILL A THARMIC NULL.
I NEED TO STUDY THEM, IN DETAIL.
BUT THESE ARE JUST DREAM BOOKS, CHILD.
IMAGINED THINGS. MERELY THE WISH-LEDGERS OF THOSE WHO'VE ALSO FACED AN IMPOSSIBLE CHALLENGE.
BUT...
FOLLOW THEIR DIRECTIONS TO THE LETTER AND YOU'LL ACCOMPLISH NAUGHT. TO MY KNOWLEDGE, NOTHING CAN HARM AN ACTUAL NULL BEAST.
FACE IT, TOOTS, YOU'RE DOOMED.
MERVYN, YOU'RE NOT BEING HELPFUL.

SO, WHAT DO WE DO *NOW?*

NOTHING. SIT HERE AND AWAIT OUR FATES. I'VE RUN OUT OF IDEAS.

NONSENSE. I *REFUSE* TO BE DESTROYED BY SOMETHING I'VE NEVER HEARD OF.

ARE YOU SURE THIS ISN'T SOME ELABORATE *HOAX* YOU COOKED UP, IN ORDER TO TEACH ME A VALUABLE *LIFE* LESSON--WELL, A DEATH LESSON ANYWAY?

IT'S REAL, FETCH, AND EVEN BEING ALREADY DEAD WON'T SAVE YOU.

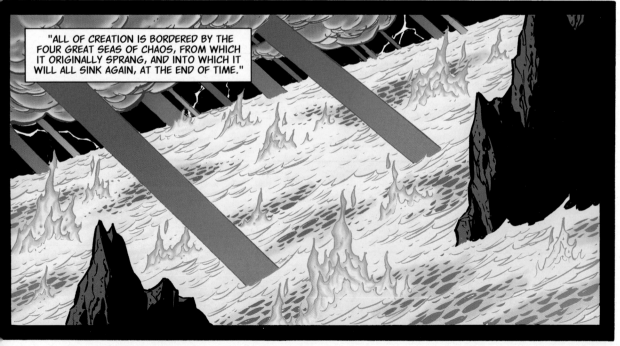

"ALL OF CREATION IS BORDERED BY THE FOUR GREAT SEAS OF CHAOS, FROM WHICH IT ORIGINALLY SPRANG, AND INTO WHICH IT WILL ALL SINK AGAIN, AT THE END OF TIME."

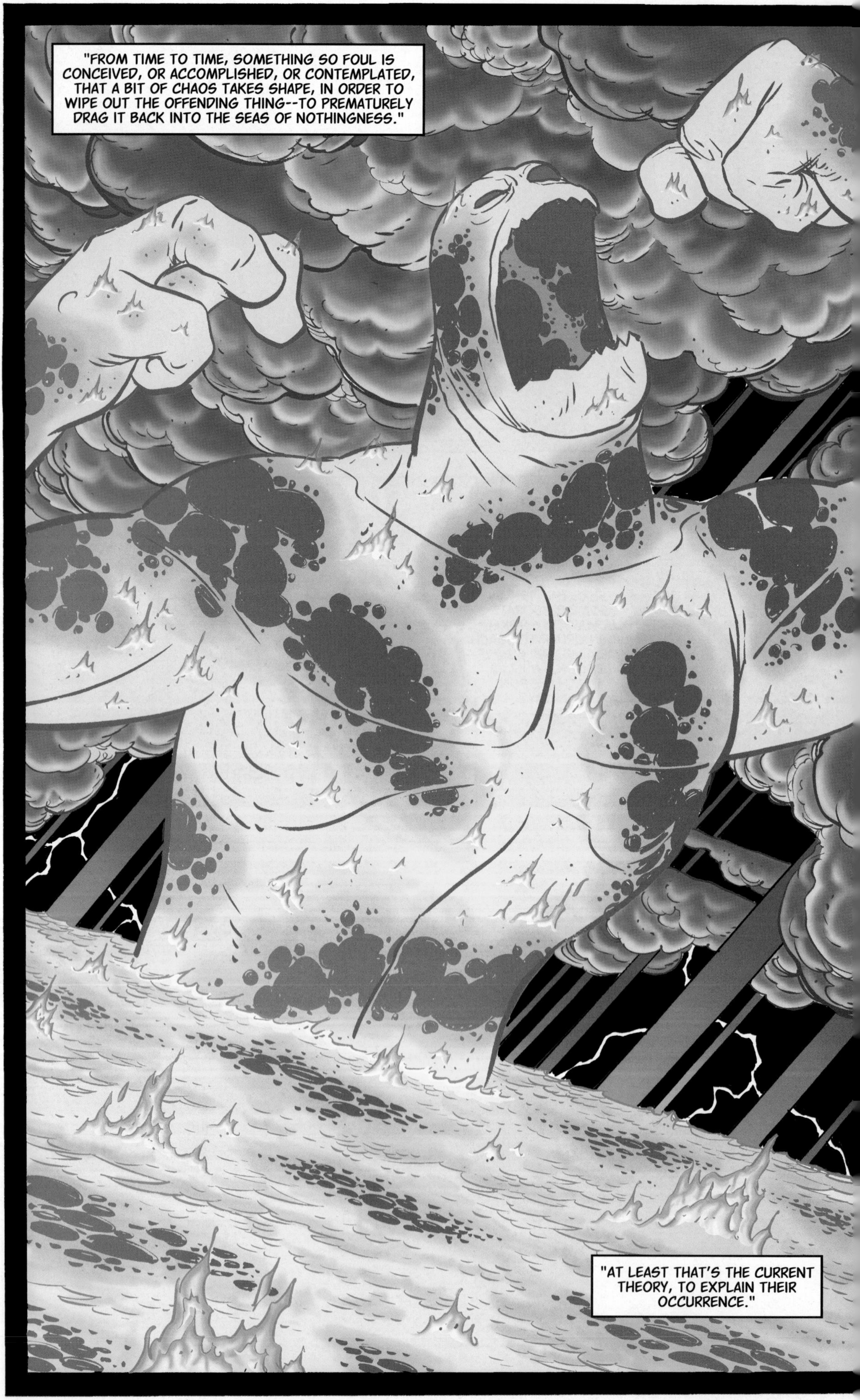
"FROM TIME TO TIME, SOMETHING SO FOUL IS CONCEIVED, OR ACCOMPLISHED, OR CONTEMPLATED, THAT A BIT OF CHAOS TAKES SHAPE, IN ORDER TO WIPE OUT THE OFFENDING THING--TO PREMATURELY DRAG IT BACK INTO THE SEAS OF NOTHINGNESS."
"AT LEAST THAT'S THE CURRENT THEORY, TO EXPLAIN THEIR OCCURRENCE."

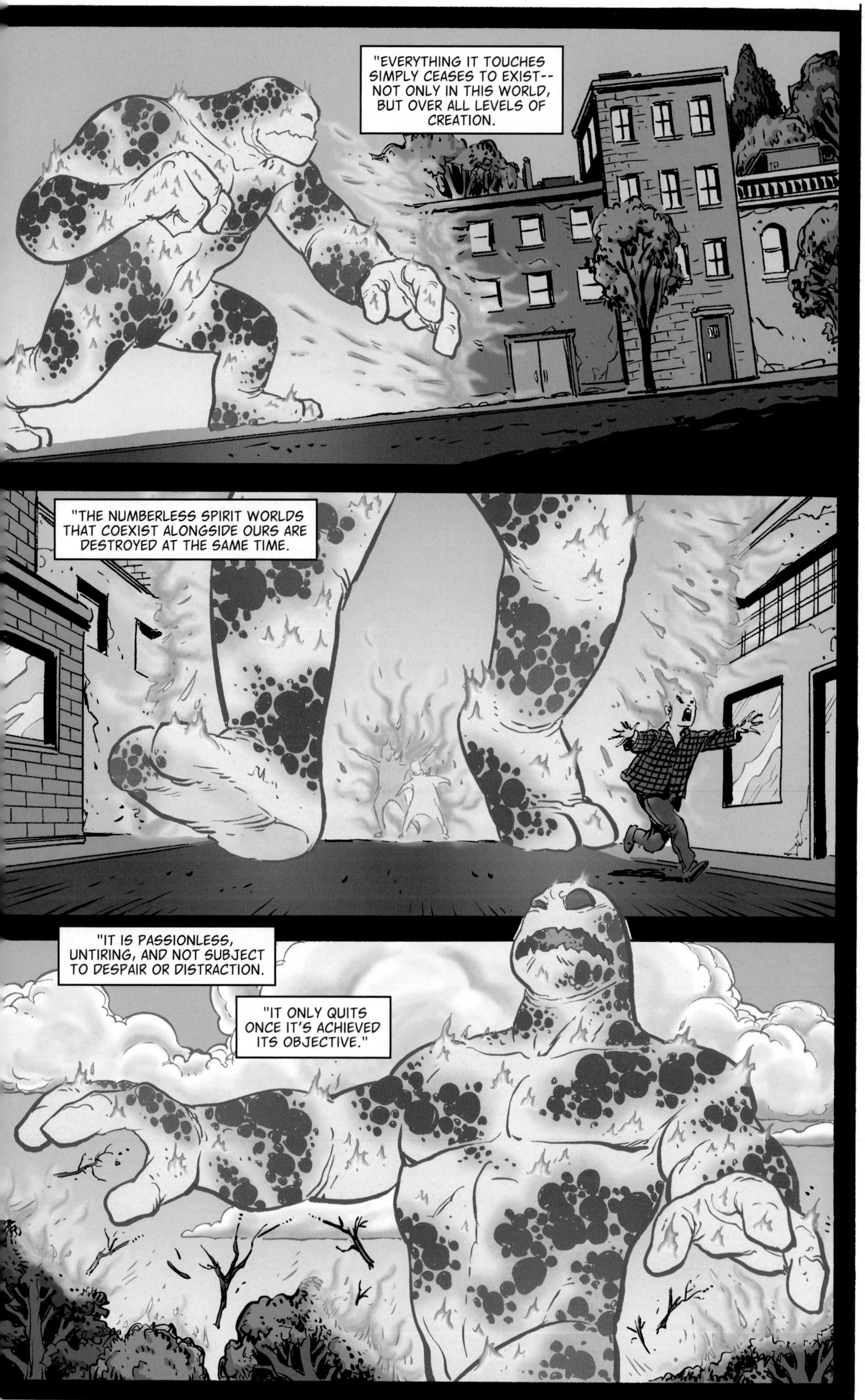
"EVERYTHING IT TOUCHES SIMPLY CEASES TO EXIST-- NOT ONLY IN THIS WORLD, BUT OVER ALL LEVELS OF CREATION.
"THE NUMBERLESS SPIRIT WORLDS THAT COEXIST ALONGSIDE OURS ARE DESTROYED AT THE SAME TIME.
"IT IS PASSIONLESS, UNTIRING, AND NOT SUBJECT TO DESPAIR OR DISTRACTION.
"IT ONLY QUITS ONCE IT'S ACHIEVED ITS OBJECTIVE."

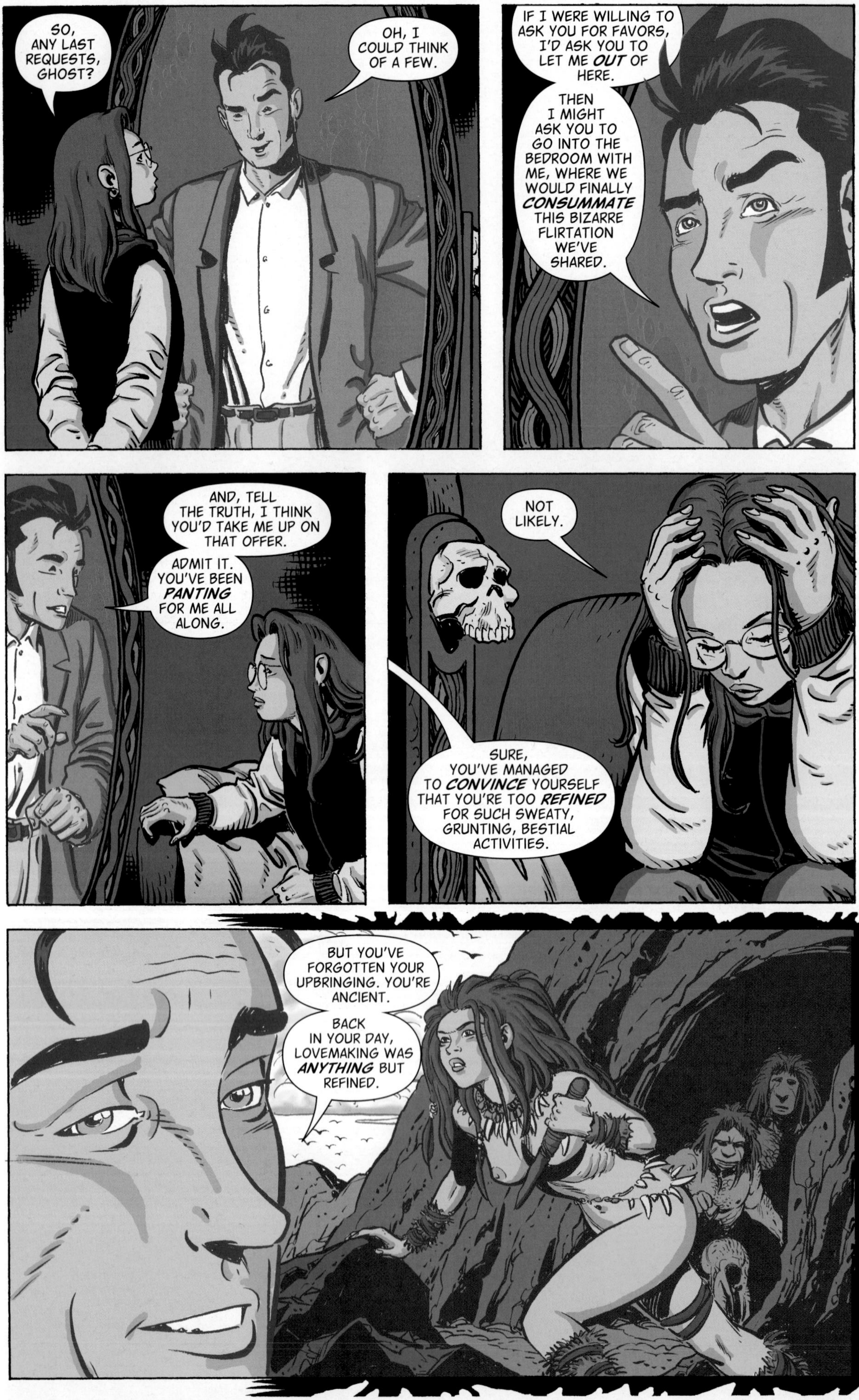
SO, ANY LAST REQUESTS, GHOST?
OH, I COULD THINK OF A FEW.
IF I WERE WILLING TO ASK YOU FOR FAVORS, I'D ASK YOU TO LET ME *OUT* OF HERE.
THEN I MIGHT ASK YOU TO GO INTO THE BEDROOM WITH ME, WHERE WE WOULD FINALLY *CONSUMMATE* THIS BIZARRE FLIRTATION WE'VE SHARED.
AND, TELL THE TRUTH, I THINK YOU'D TAKE ME UP ON THAT OFFER.
ADMIT IT. YOU'VE BEEN *PANTING* FOR ME ALL ALONG.
NOT LIKELY.
SURE, YOU'VE MANAGED TO *CONVINCE* YOURSELF THAT YOU'RE TOO *REFINED* FOR SUCH SWEATY, GRUNTING, BESTIAL ACTIVITIES.
BUT YOU'VE FORGOTTEN YOUR UPBRINGING. YOU'RE ANCIENT.
BACK IN YOUR DAY, LOVEMAKING WAS *ANYTHING* BUT REFINED.

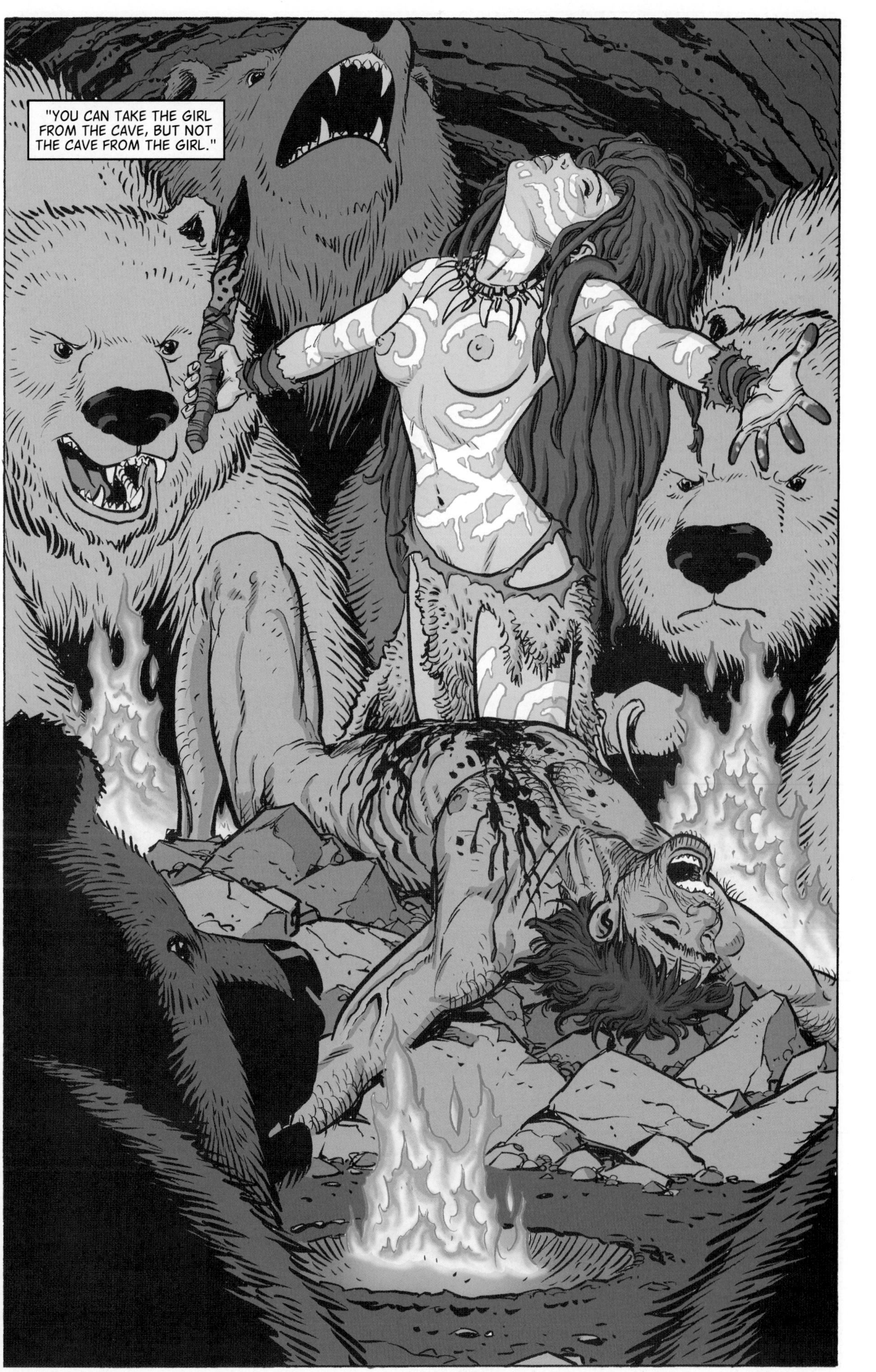
"YOU CAN TAKE THE GIRL FROM THE CAVE, BUT NOT THE CAVE FROM THE GIRL."

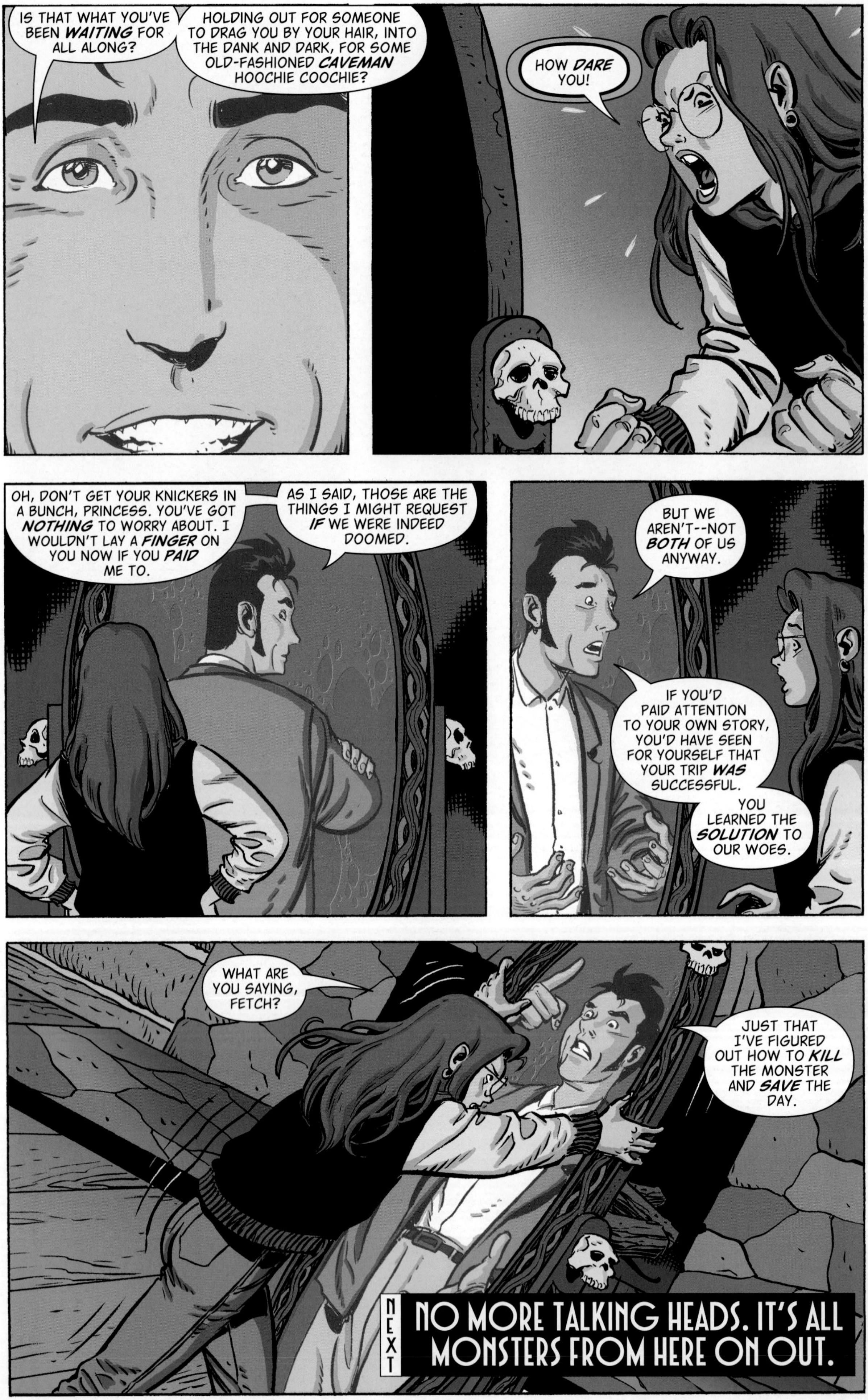
IS THAT WHAT YOU'VE BEEN WAITING FOR ALL ALONG?
HOLDING OUT FOR SOMEONE TO DRAG YOU BY YOUR HAIR, INTO THE DANK AND DARK, FOR SOME OLD-FASHIONED CAVEMAN HOOCHIE COOCHIE?
HOW DARE YOU!
OH, DON'T GET YOUR KNICKERS IN A BUNCH, PRINCESS. YOU'VE GOT NOTHING TO WORRY ABOUT. I WOULDN'T LAY A FINGER ON YOU NOW IF YOU PAID ME TO.
AS I SAID, THOSE ARE THE THINGS I MIGHT REQUEST IF WE WERE INDEED DOOMED.
BUT WE AREN'T--NOT BOTH OF US ANYWAY.
IF YOU'D PAID ATTENTION TO YOUR OWN STORY, YOU'D HAVE SEEN FOR YOURSELF THAT YOUR TRIP WAS SUCCESSFUL.
YOU LEARNED THE SOLUTION TO OUR WOES.
WHAT ARE YOU SAYING, FETCH?
JUST THAT I'VE FIGURED OUT HOW TO KILL THE MONSTER AND SAVE THE DAY.
NEXT
NO MORE TALKING HEADS. IT'S ALL MONSTERS FROM HERE ON OUT.

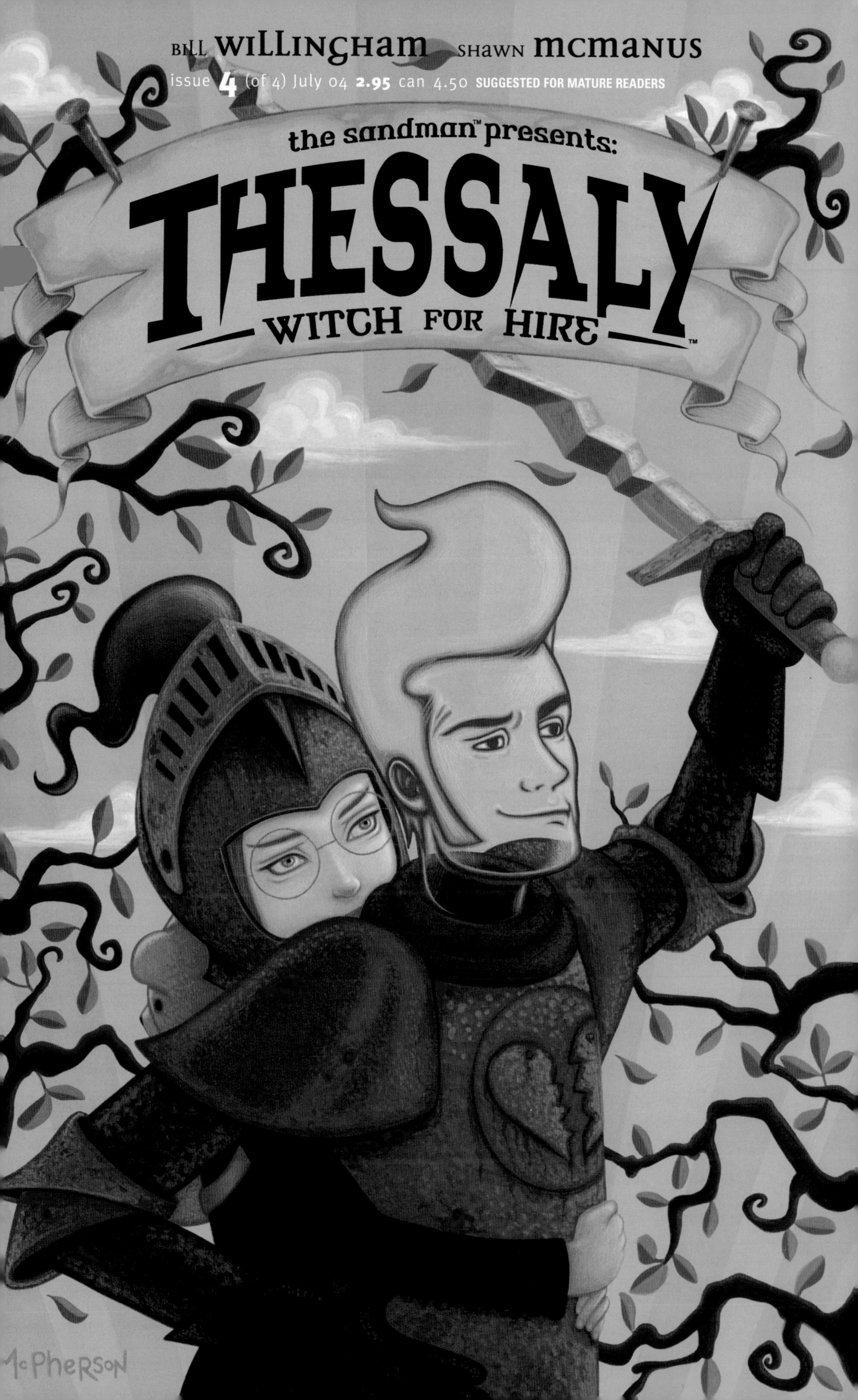

BILL WILLINGHAM SHAWN MCMANUS
issue 4 (of 4) July 04 2.95 can 4.50 SUGGESTED FOR MATURE READERS
the sandman™ presents:
THESSALY
WITCH FOR HIRE™
McPHERSON

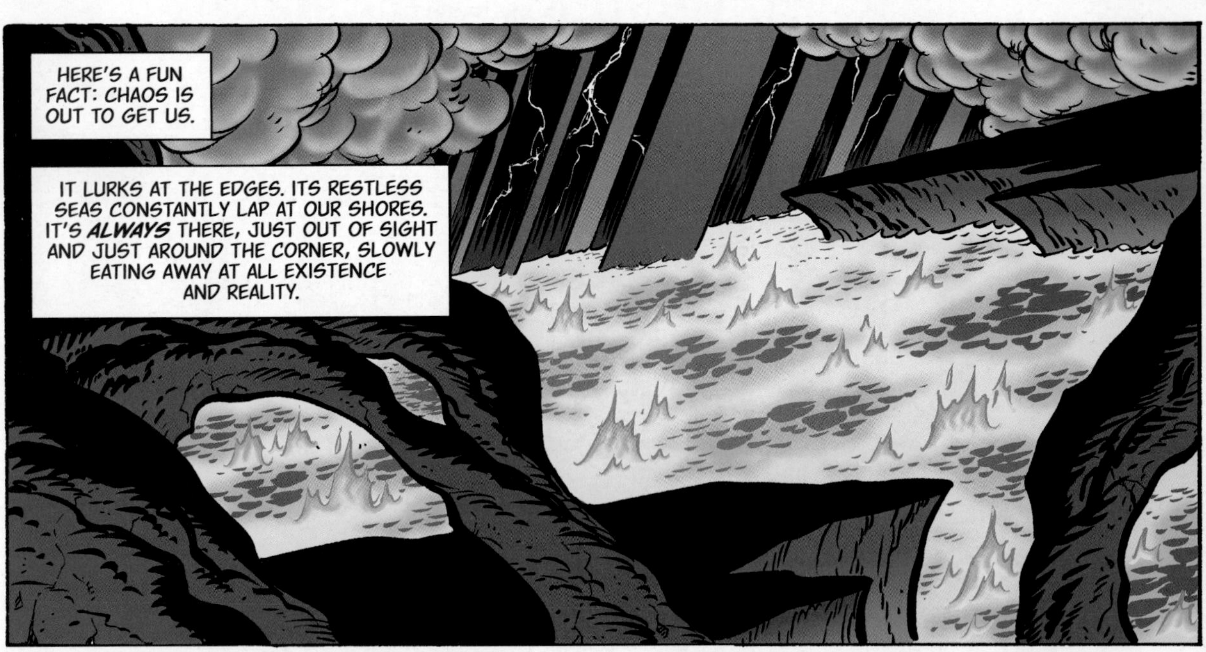
HERE'S A FUN FACT: CHAOS IS OUT TO GET US.
IT LURKS AT THE EDGES. ITS RESTLESS SEAS CONSTANTLY LAP AT OUR SHORES. IT'S *ALWAYS* THERE, JUST OUT OF SIGHT AND JUST AROUND THE CORNER, SLOWLY EATING AWAY AT ALL EXISTENCE AND REALITY.

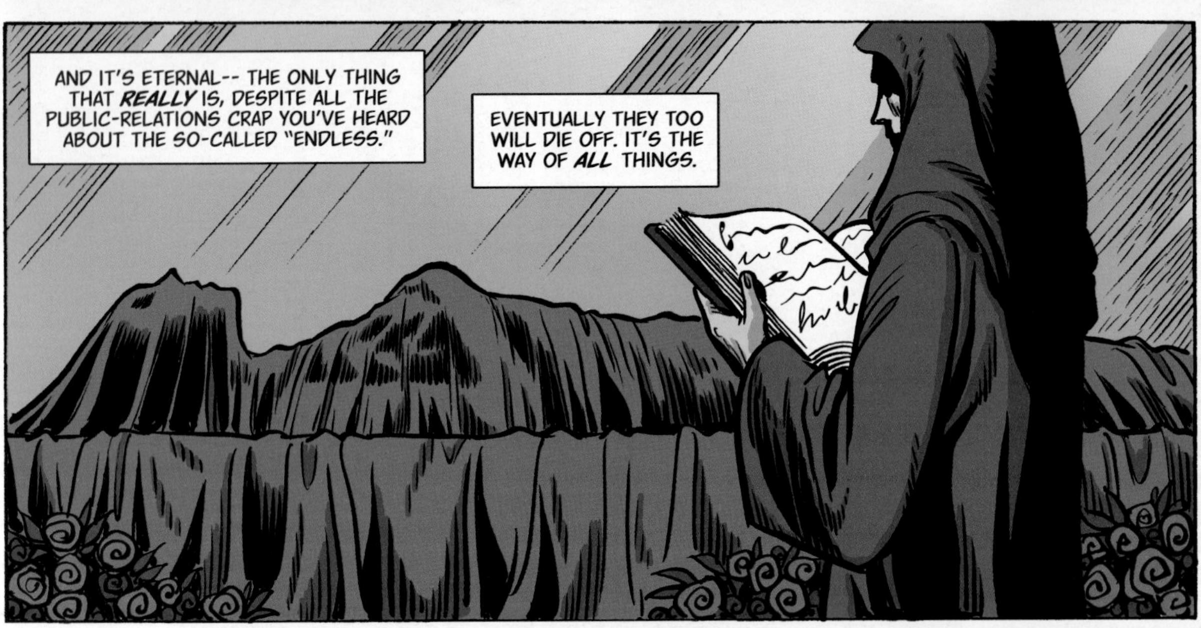
AND IT'S ETERNAL-- THE ONLY THING THAT *REALLY* IS, DESPITE ALL THE PUBLIC-RELATIONS CRAP YOU'VE HEARD ABOUT THE SO-CALLED "ENDLESS."
EVENTUALLY THEY TOO WILL DIE OFF. IT'S THE WAY OF *ALL* THINGS.

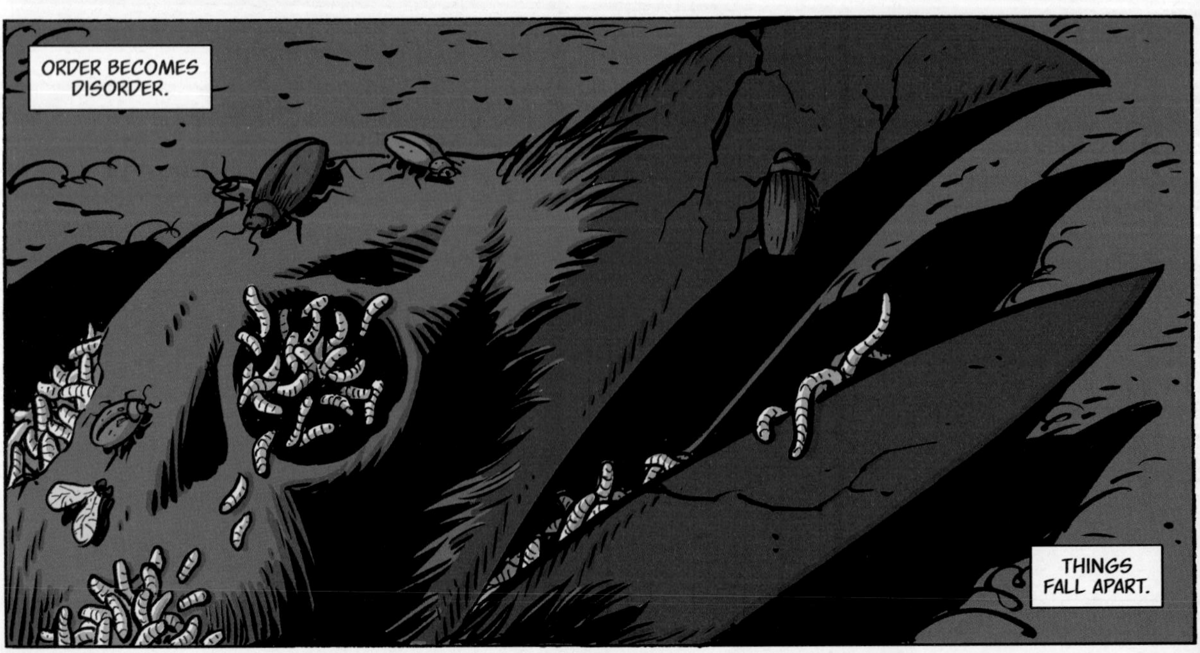
ORDER BECOMES DISORDER.
THINGS FALL APART.

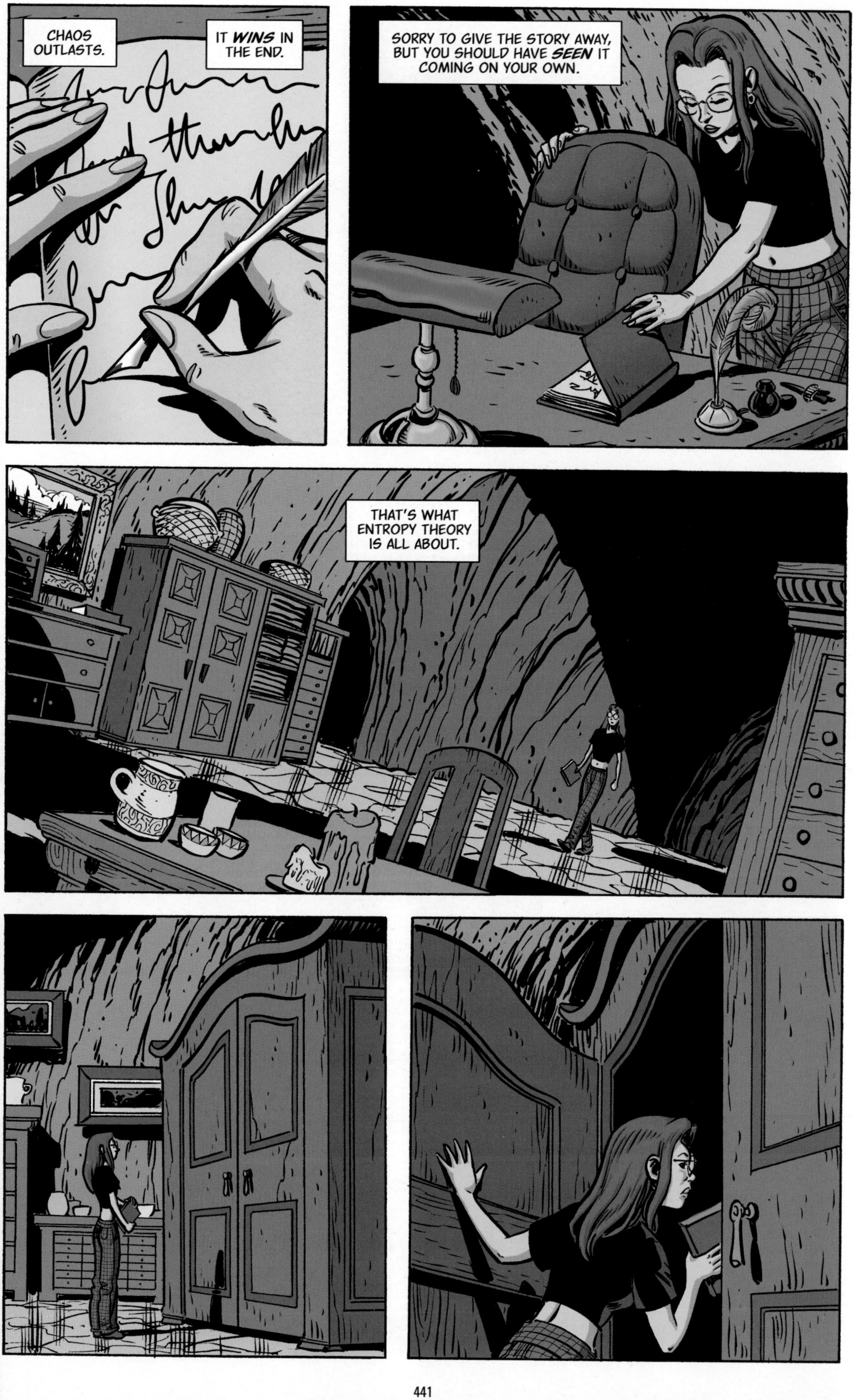
CHAOS OUTLASTS.
IT WINS IN THE END.
SORRY TO GIVE THE STORY AWAY, BUT YOU SHOULD HAVE SEEN IT COMING ON YOUR OWN.
THAT'S WHAT ENTROPY THEORY IS ALL ABOUT.

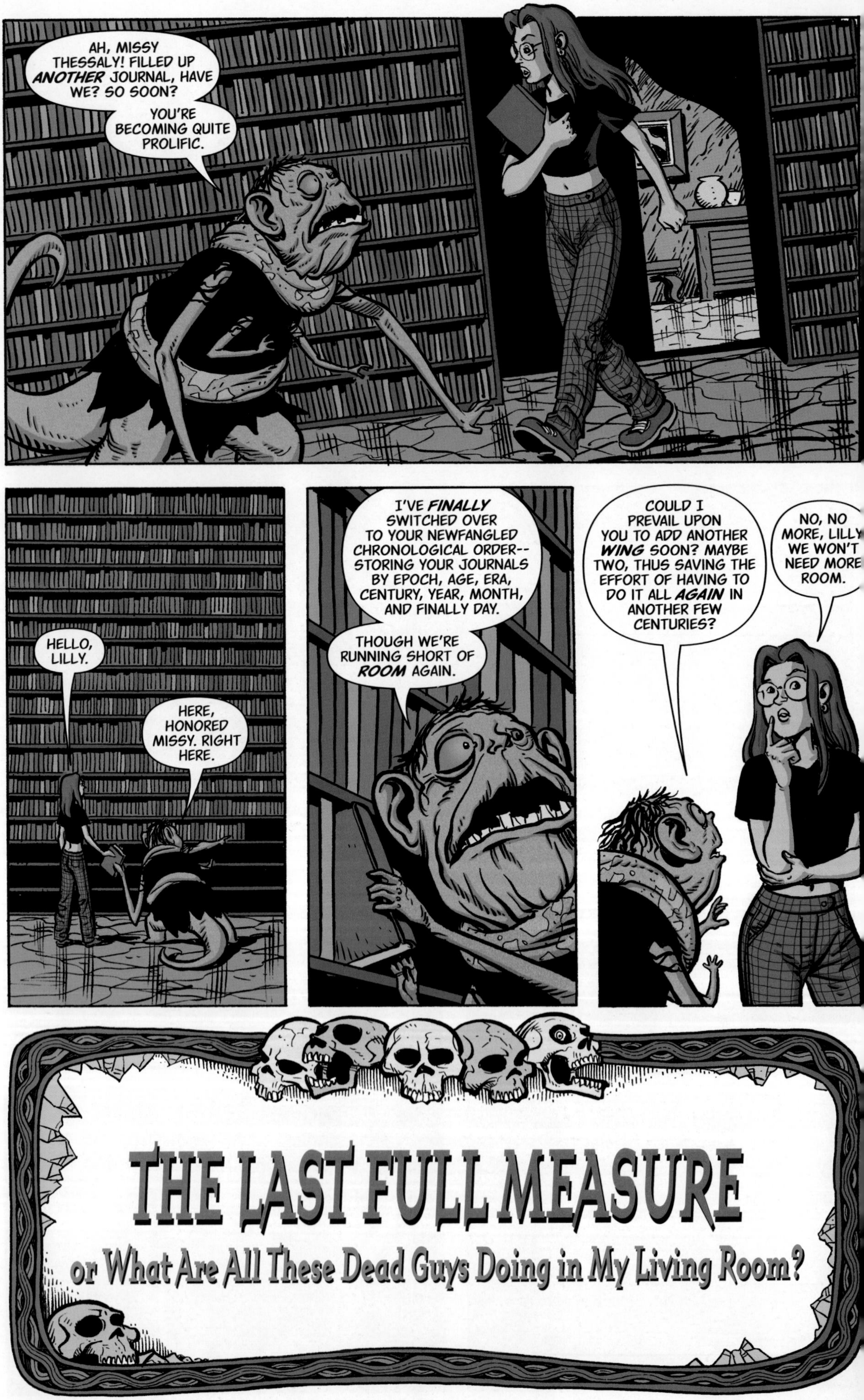

AH, MISSY THESSALY! FILLED UP *ANOTHER* JOURNAL, HAVE WE? SO SOON?
YOU'RE BECOMING QUITE PROLIFIC.
HELLO, LILLY.
HERE, HONORED MISSY. RIGHT HERE.
I'VE *FINALLY* SWITCHED OVER TO YOUR NEWFANGLED CHRONOLOGICAL ORDER-- STORING YOUR JOURNALS BY EPOCH, AGE, ERA, CENTURY, YEAR, MONTH, AND FINALLY DAY.
THOUGH WE'RE RUNNING SHORT OF *ROOM* AGAIN.
COULD I PREVAIL UPON YOU TO ADD ANOTHER *WING* SOON? MAYBE TWO, THUS SAVING THE EFFORT OF HAVING TO DO IT ALL *AGAIN* IN ANOTHER FEW CENTURIES?
NO, NO MORE, LILLY WE WON'T NEED MORE ROOM.
THE LAST FULL MEASURE
or What Are All These Dead Guys Doing in My Living Room?

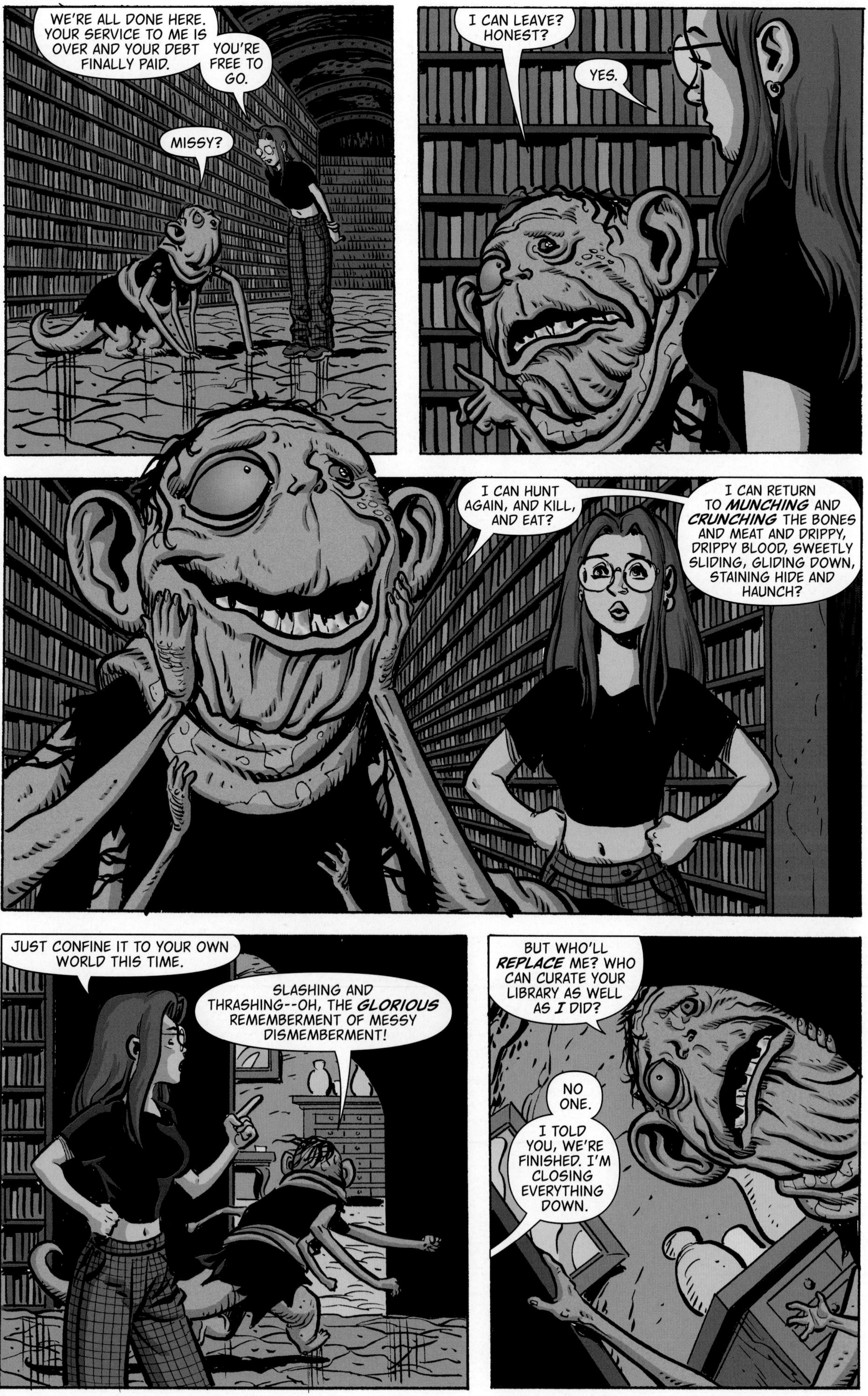
WE'RE ALL DONE HERE. YOUR SERVICE TO ME IS OVER AND YOUR DEBT FINALLY PAID.
YOU'RE FREE TO GO.
MISSY?
I CAN LEAVE? HONEST?
YES.
I CAN HUNT AGAIN, AND KILL, AND EAT?
I CAN RETURN TO MUNCHING AND CRUNCHING THE BONES AND MEAT AND DRIPPY, DRIPPY BLOOD, SWEETLY SLIDING, GLIDING DOWN, STAINING HIDE AND HAUNCH?
JUST CONFINE IT TO YOUR OWN WORLD THIS TIME.
SLASHING AND THRASHING--OH, THE GLORIOUS REMEMBERMENT OF MESSY DISMEMBERMENT!
BUT WHO'LL REPLACE ME? WHO CAN CURATE YOUR LIBRARY AS WELL AS I DID?
NO ONE.
I TOLD YOU, WE'RE FINISHED. I'M CLOSING EVERYTHING DOWN.

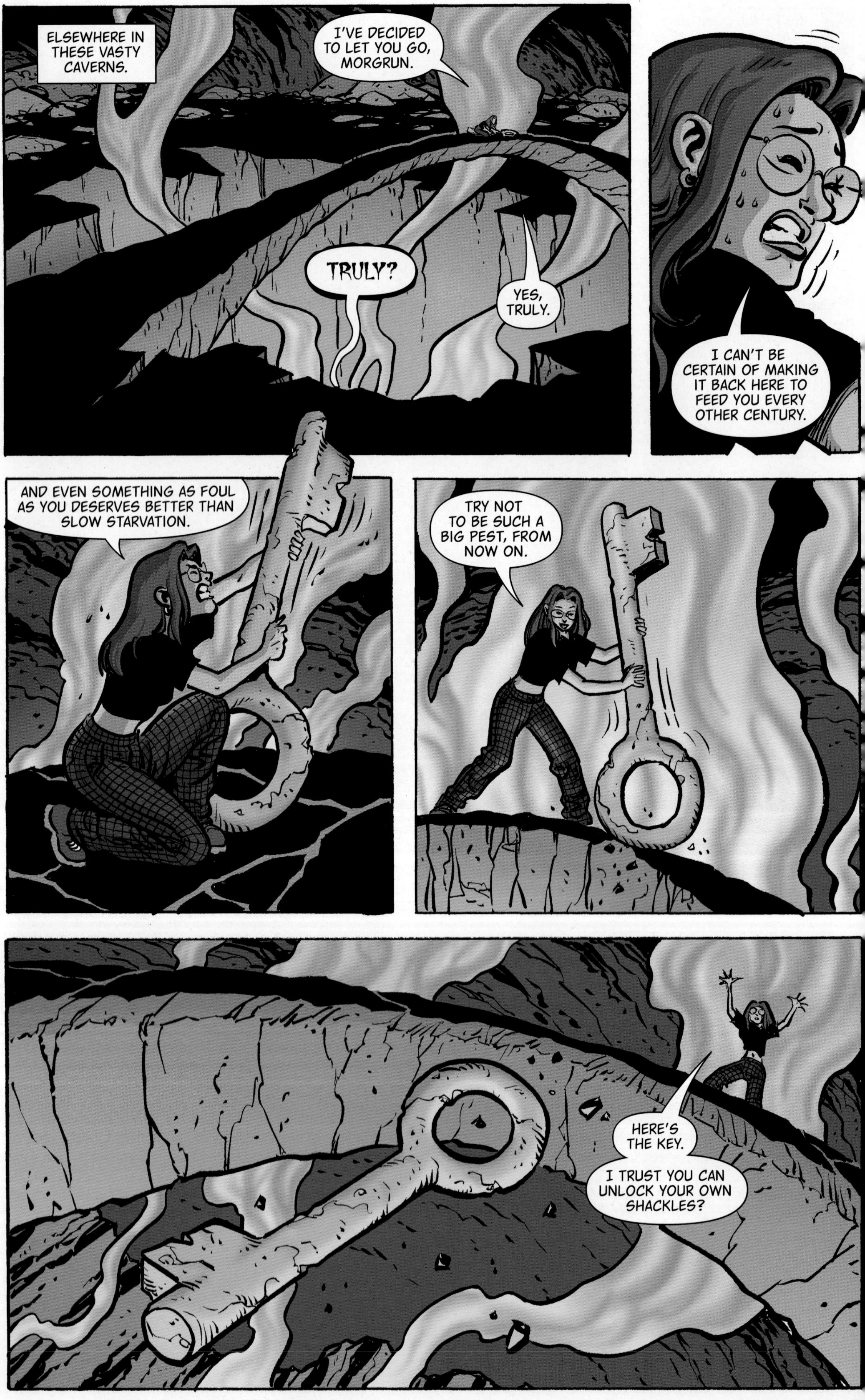
ELSEWHERE IN THESE VASTY CAVERNS.
I'VE DECIDED TO LET YOU GO, MORGRUN.
TRULY?
YES, TRULY.
I CAN'T BE CERTAIN OF MAKING IT BACK HERE TO FEED YOU EVERY OTHER CENTURY.
AND EVEN SOMETHING AS FOUL AS YOU DESERVES BETTER THAN SLOW STARVATION.
TRY NOT TO BE SUCH A BIG PEST, FROM NOW ON.
HERE'S THE KEY.
I TRUST YOU CAN UNLOCK YOUR OWN SHACKLES?

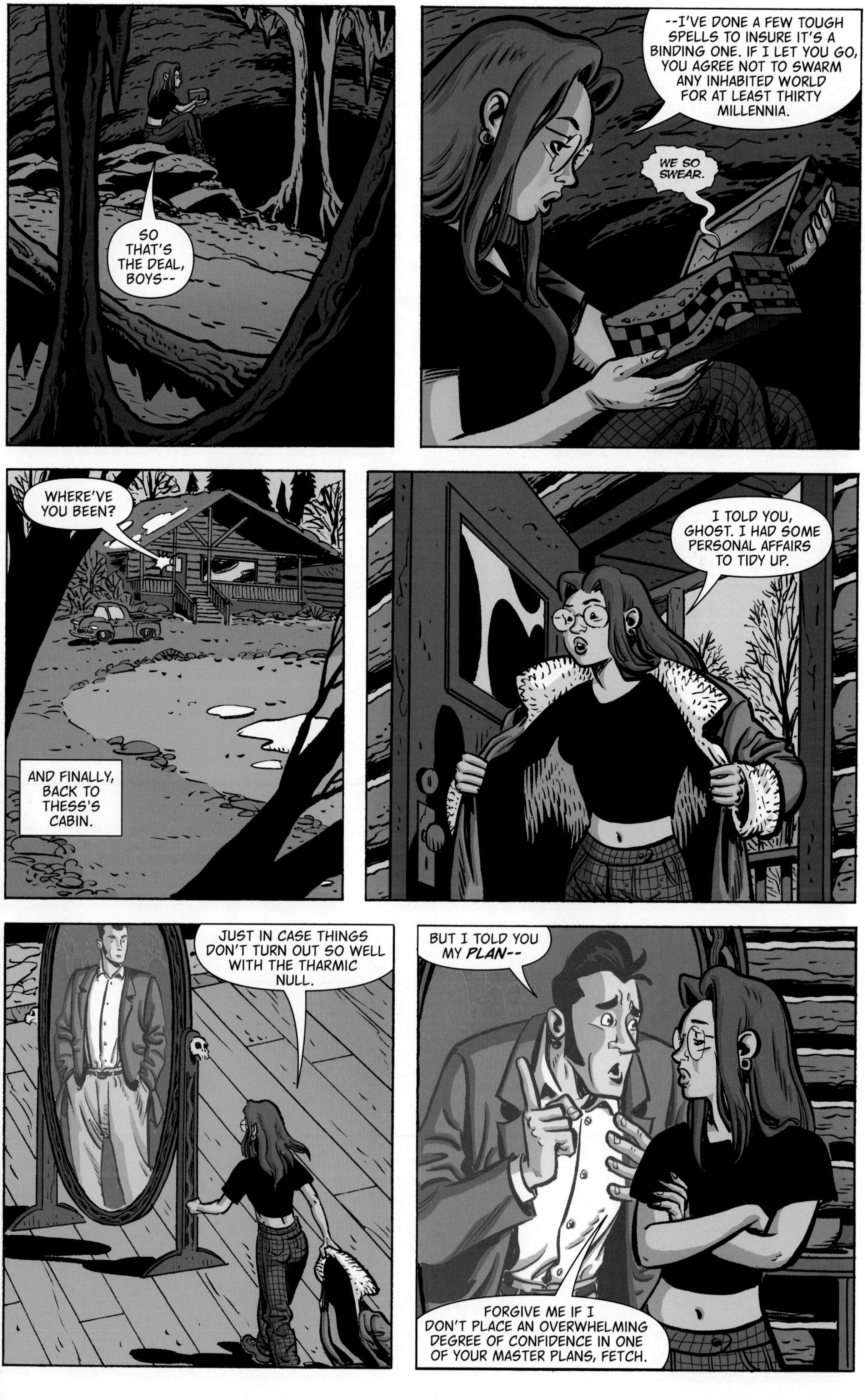
SO THAT'S THE DEAL, BOYS--
--I'VE DONE A FEW TOUGH SPELLS TO INSURE IT'S A BINDING ONE. IF I LET YOU GO, YOU AGREE NOT TO SWARM ANY INHABITED WORLD FOR AT LEAST THIRTY MILLENNIA.
WE SO SWEAR.
WHERE'VE YOU BEEN?
AND FINALLY, BACK TO THESS'S CABIN.
I TOLD YOU, GHOST. I HAD SOME PERSONAL AFFAIRS TO TIDY UP.
JUST IN CASE THINGS DON'T TURN OUT SO WELL WITH THE THARMIC NULL.
BUT I TOLD YOU MY PLAN--
FORGIVE ME IF I DON'T PLACE AN OVERWHELMING DEGREE OF CONFIDENCE IN ONE OF YOUR MASTER PLANS, FETCH.

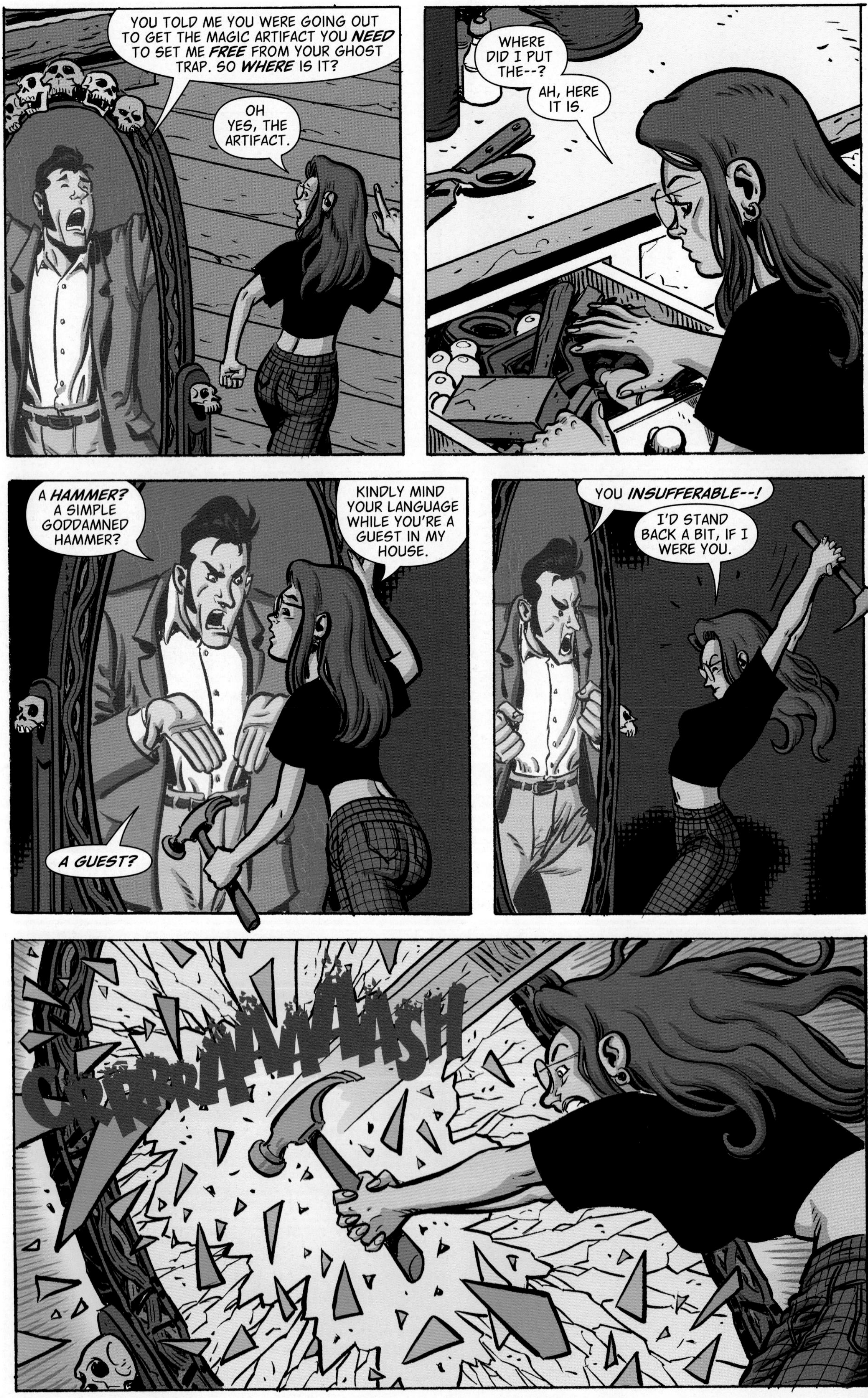
YOU TOLD ME YOU WERE GOING OUT TO GET THE MAGIC ARTIFACT YOU NEED TO SET ME FREE FROM YOUR GHOST TRAP. SO WHERE IS IT?
OH YES, THE ARTIFACT.
WHERE DID I PUT THE--?
AH, HERE IT IS.
A HAMMER? A SIMPLE GODDAMNED HAMMER?
KINDLY MIND YOUR LANGUAGE WHILE YOU'RE A GUEST IN MY HOUSE.
A GUEST?
YOU INSUFFERABLE--!
I'D STAND BACK A BIT, IF I WERE YOU.
CRRRRAAAAASH

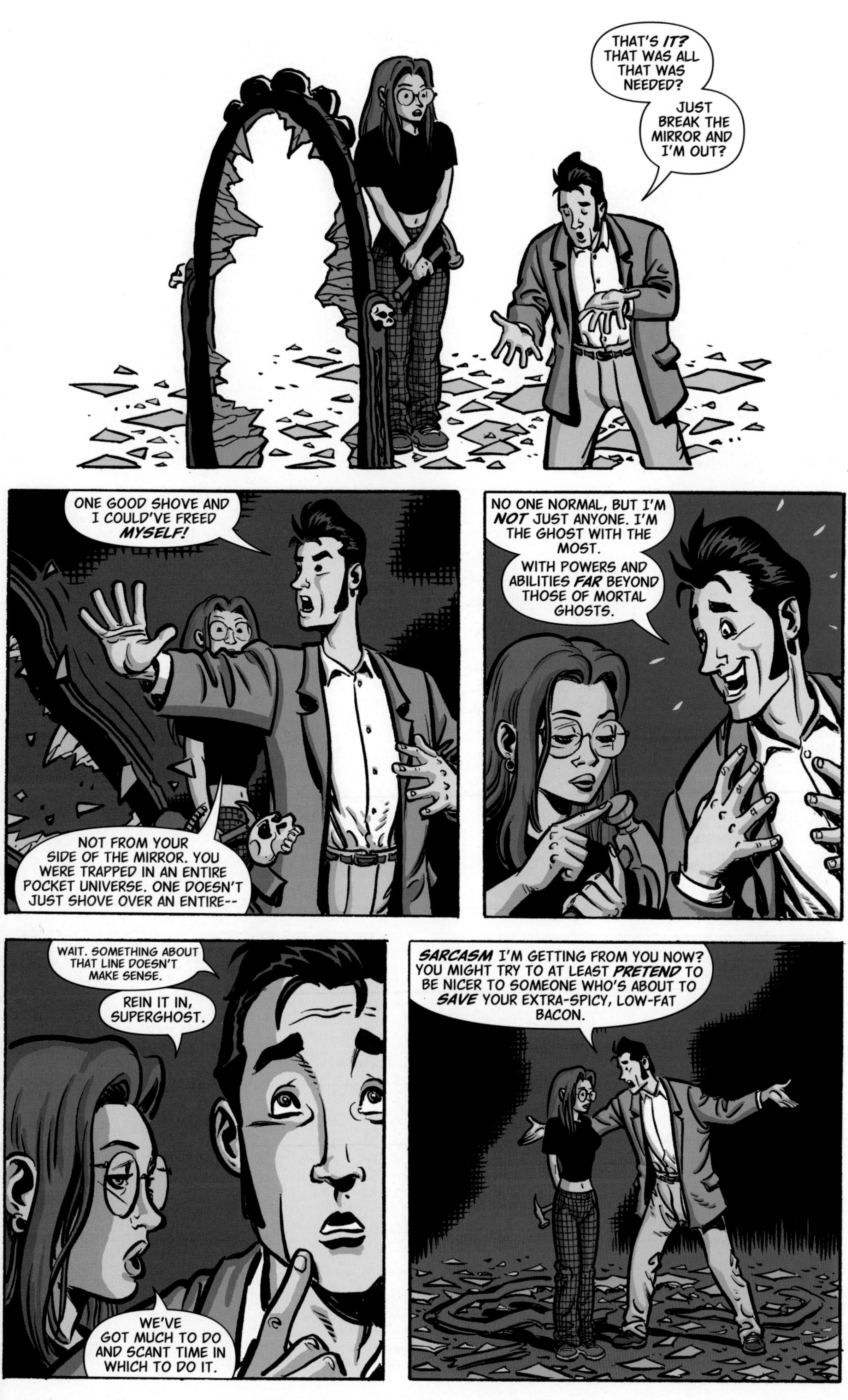
THAT'S *IT?* THAT WAS ALL THAT WAS NEEDED?
JUST BREAK THE MIRROR AND I'M OUT?
ONE GOOD SHOVE AND I COULD'VE FREED *MYSELF!*
NOT FROM YOUR SIDE OF THE MIRROR. YOU WERE TRAPPED IN AN ENTIRE POCKET UNIVERSE. ONE DOESN'T JUST SHOVE OVER AN ENTIRE--
NO ONE NORMAL, BUT I'M *NOT* JUST ANYONE. I'M THE GHOST WITH THE MOST.
WITH POWERS AND ABILITIES *FAR* BEYOND THOSE OF MORTAL GHOSTS.
WAIT. SOMETHING ABOUT THAT LINE DOESN'T MAKE SENSE.
REIN IT IN, SUPERGHOST.
WE'VE GOT MUCH TO DO AND SCANT TIME IN WHICH TO DO IT.
SARCASM I'M GETTING FROM YOU NOW? YOU MIGHT TRY TO AT LEAST *PRETEND* TO BE NICER TO SOMEONE WHO'S ABOUT TO *SAVE* YOUR EXTRA-SPICY, LOW-FAT BACON.

OKAY, YOU'VE BEEN AT THIS FOR HOURS.

WHAT'S TAKING SO LONG?

SHUT UP, GHOST.

IT'S NOT AN EASY CREATURE TO TRACK.

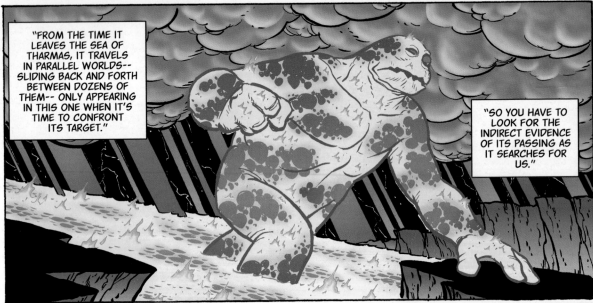

"FROM THE TIME IT LEAVES THE SEA OF THARMAS, IT TRAVELS IN PARALLEL WORLDS-- SLIDING BACK AND FORTH BETWEEN DOZENS OF THEM-- ONLY APPEARING IN THIS ONE WHEN IT'S TIME TO CONFRONT ITS TARGET."

"SO YOU HAVE TO LOOK FOR THE INDIRECT EVIDENCE OF ITS PASSING AS IT SEARCHES FOR US."

"IN THE ITURI CONGO A NEW FLESH-EATING VIRUS DEVASTATES THE ENTIRE POPULATION OF A MANGBELE VILLAGE."

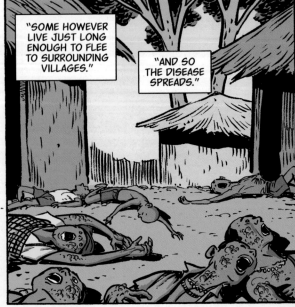

"SOME HOWEVER LIVE JUST LONG ENOUGH TO FLEE TO SURROUNDING VILLAGES."

"AND SO THE DISEASE SPREADS."

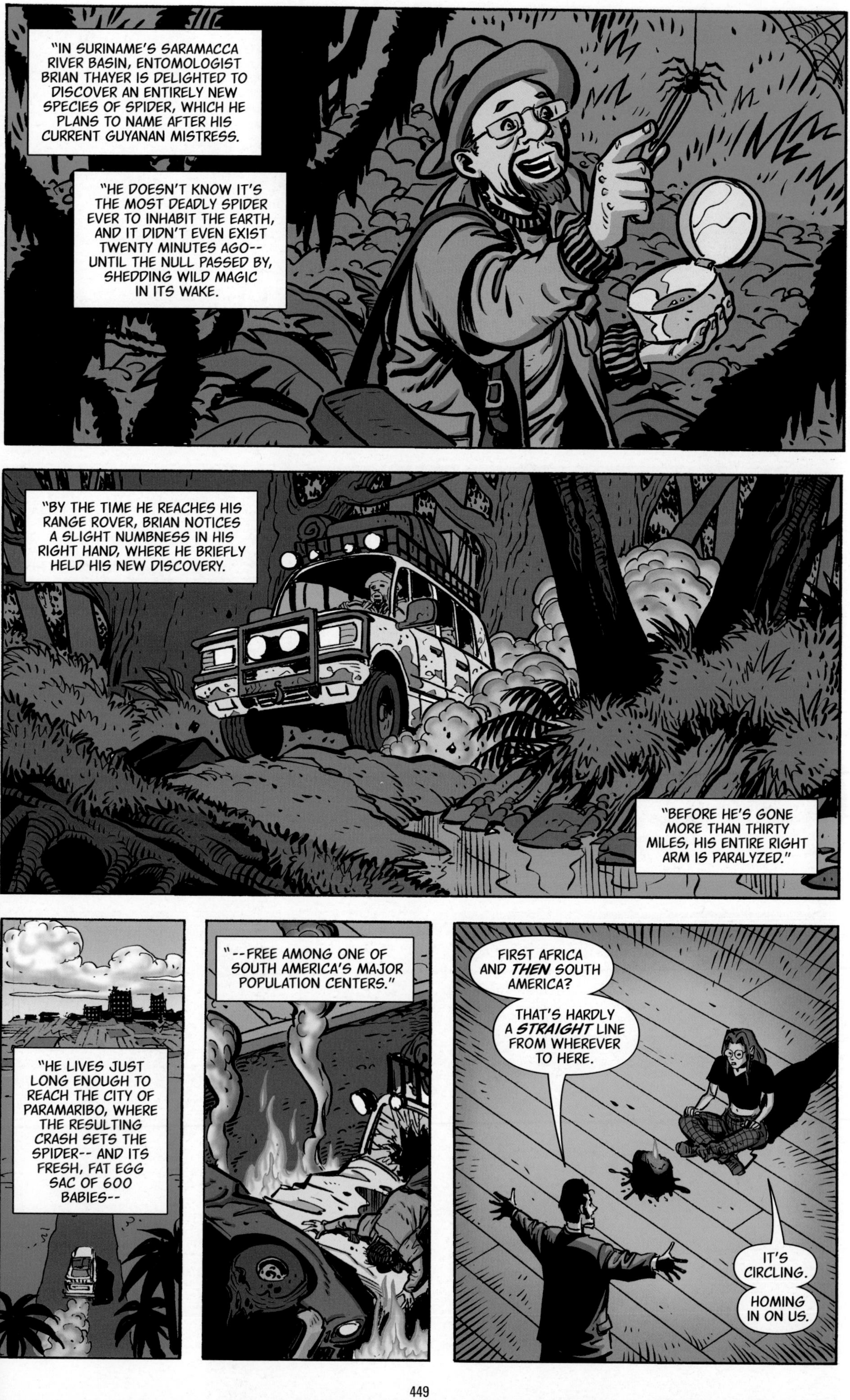
"IN SURINAME'S SARAMACCA RIVER BASIN, ENTOMOLOGIST BRIAN THAYER IS DELIGHTED TO DISCOVER AN ENTIRELY NEW SPECIES OF SPIDER, WHICH HE PLANS TO NAME AFTER HIS CURRENT GUYANAN MISTRESS.
"HE DOESN'T KNOW IT'S THE MOST DEADLY SPIDER EVER TO INHABIT THE EARTH, AND IT DIDN'T EVEN EXIST TWENTY MINUTES AGO-- UNTIL THE NULL PASSED BY, SHEDDING WILD MAGIC IN ITS WAKE.
"BY THE TIME HE REACHES HIS RANGE ROVER, BRIAN NOTICES A SLIGHT NUMBNESS IN HIS RIGHT HAND, WHERE HE BRIEFLY HELD HIS NEW DISCOVERY.
"BEFORE HE'S GONE MORE THAN THIRTY MILES, HIS ENTIRE RIGHT ARM IS PARALYZED."
"HE LIVES JUST LONG ENOUGH TO REACH THE CITY OF PARAMARIBO, WHERE THE RESULTING CRASH SETS THE SPIDER-- AND ITS FRESH, FAT EGG SAC OF 600 BABIES--
"--FREE AMONG ONE OF SOUTH AMERICA'S MAJOR POPULATION CENTERS."
FIRST AFRICA AND ***THEN*** SOUTH AMERICA?
THAT'S HARDLY A ***STRAIGHT*** LINE FROM WHEREVER TO HERE.
IT'S CIRCLING.
HOMING IN ON US.

MAYBE YOU'D BETTER START THE *DISMANTLING*.

NOT YET.

EVEN WITH MY REINFORCING ENCHANTMENTS, WE DON'T KNOW HOW LONG YOU CAN HOLD YOURSELF TOGETHER, LACKING YOUR COMPONENT PARTS.

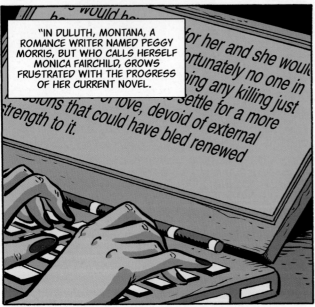

"IN DULUTH, MONTANA, A ROMANCE WRITER NAMED PEGGY MORRIS, BUT WHO CALLS HERSELF MONICA FAIRCHILD, GROWS FRUSTRATED WITH THE PROGRESS OF HER CURRENT NOVEL.

"THEN SHE STARTS THINKING ABOUT ALL OF THE LOVELY KNIVES IN HER KITCHEN, AND HOW MUCH SHE'D DEARLY LIKE TO SLIT THE THROATS OF EVERY ONE OF HER NOISY, ANNOYING, INTRUSIVE NEIGHBORS.

"SHE GOES TO WORK, NOT REALIZING A THOUSAND OTHERS IN TOWN HAVE JUST HAD SIMILAR EPIPHANIES."

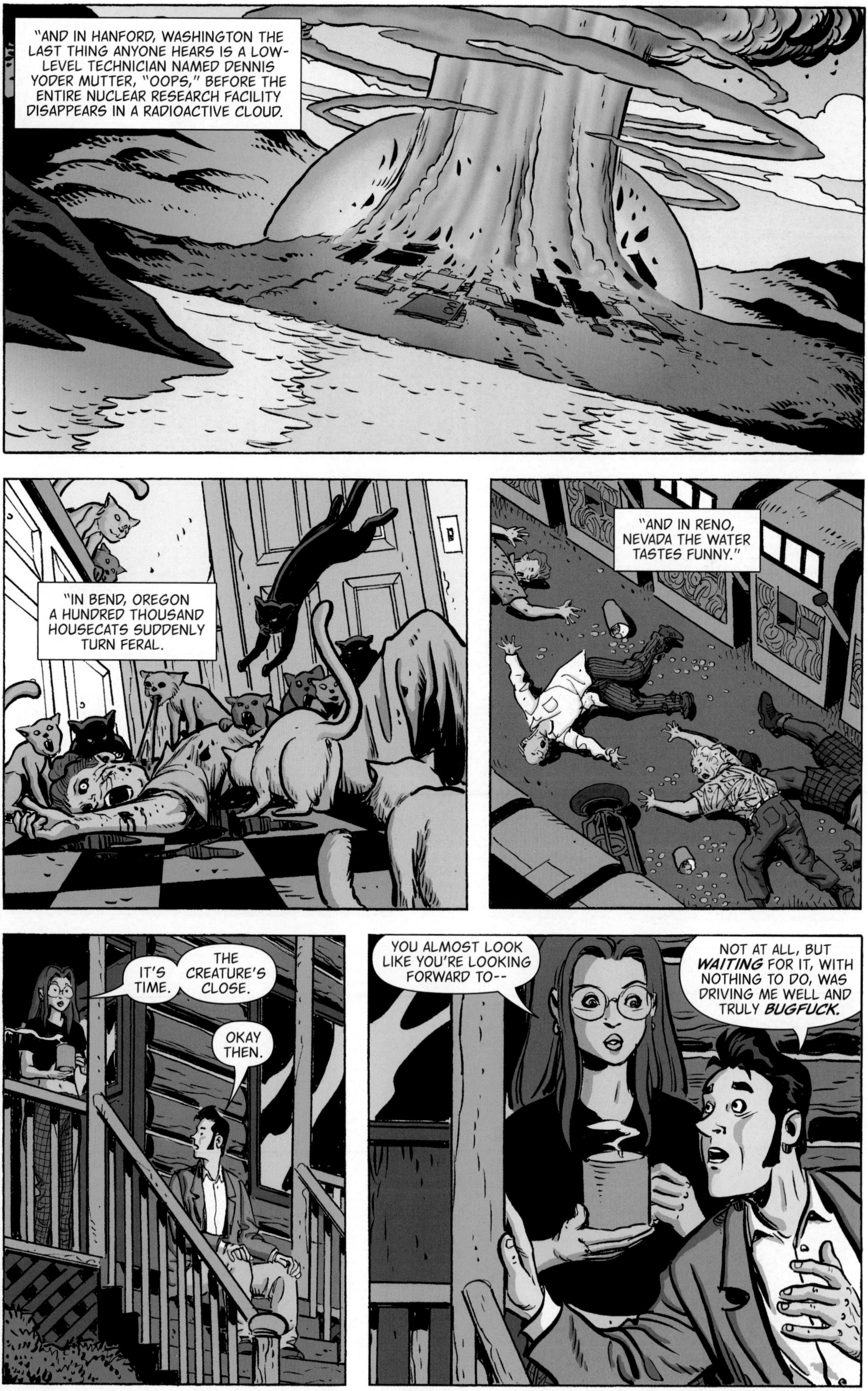
"AND IN HANFORD, WASHINGTON THE LAST THING ANYONE HEARS IS A LOW-LEVEL TECHNICIAN NAMED DENNIS YODER MUTTER, "OOPS," BEFORE THE ENTIRE NUCLEAR RESEARCH FACILITY DISAPPEARS IN A RADIOACTIVE CLOUD.
"IN BEND, OREGON A HUNDRED THOUSAND HOUSECATS SUDDENLY TURN FERAL.
"AND IN RENO, NEVADA THE WATER TASTES FUNNY."
IT'S TIME.
THE CREATURE'S CLOSE.
OKAY THEN.
YOU ALMOST LOOK LIKE YOU'RE LOOKING FORWARD TO--
NOT AT ALL, BUT *WAITING* FOR IT, WITH NOTHING TO DO, WAS DRIVING ME WELL AND TRULY *BUGFUCK.*

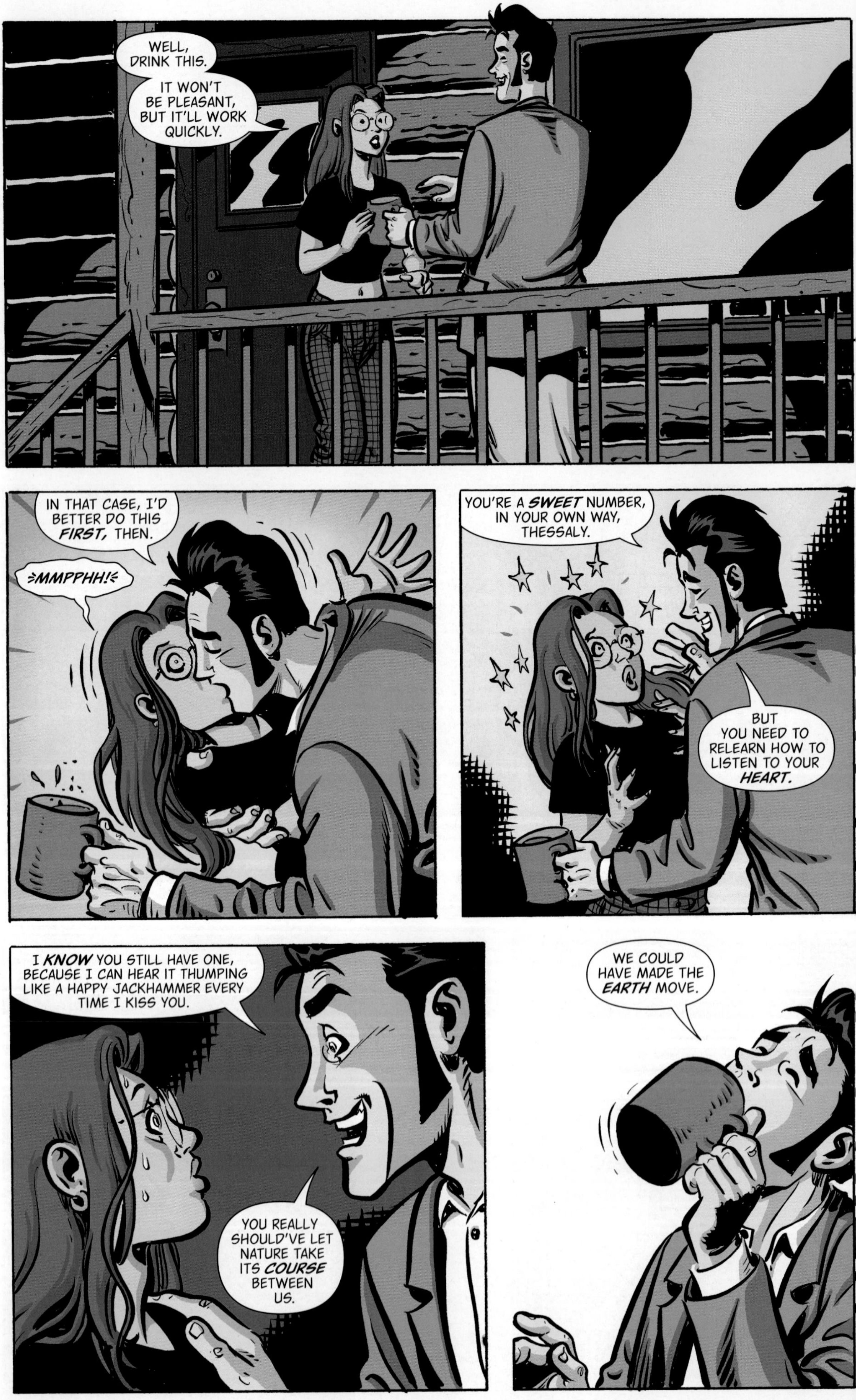
WELL, DRINK THIS.
IT WON'T BE PLEASANT, BUT IT'LL WORK QUICKLY.
IN THAT CASE, I'D BETTER DO THIS *FIRST,* THEN.
MMPPHH!
YOU'RE A *SWEET* NUMBER, IN YOUR OWN WAY, THESSALY.
BUT YOU NEED TO RELEARN HOW TO LISTEN TO YOUR *HEART.*
I *KNOW* YOU STILL HAVE ONE, BECAUSE I CAN HEAR IT THUMPING LIKE A HAPPY JACKHAMMER EVERY TIME I KISS YOU.
YOU REALLY SHOULD'VE LET NATURE TAKE ITS *COURSE* BETWEEN US.
WE COULD HAVE MADE THE *EARTH* MOVE.

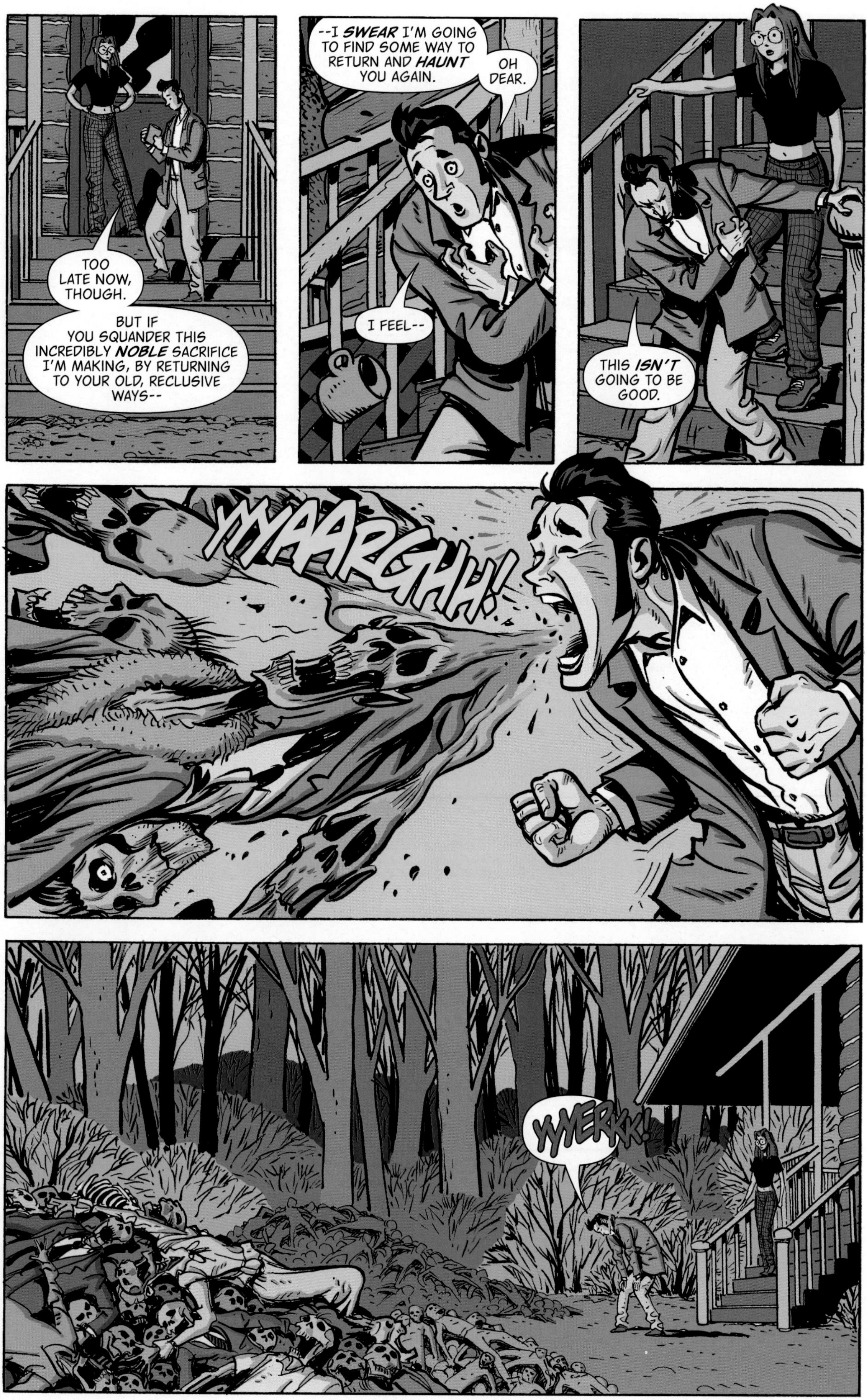
TOO LATE NOW, THOUGH.
BUT IF YOU SQUANDER THIS INCREDIBLY NOBLE SACRIFICE I'M MAKING, BY RETURNING TO YOUR OLD, RECLUSIVE WAYS--
--I SWEAR I'M GOING TO FIND SOME WAY TO RETURN AND HAUNT YOU AGAIN.
OH DEAR.
I FEEL--
THIS ISN'T GOING TO BE GOOD.
YYYAARGHH!
YYYERKK!

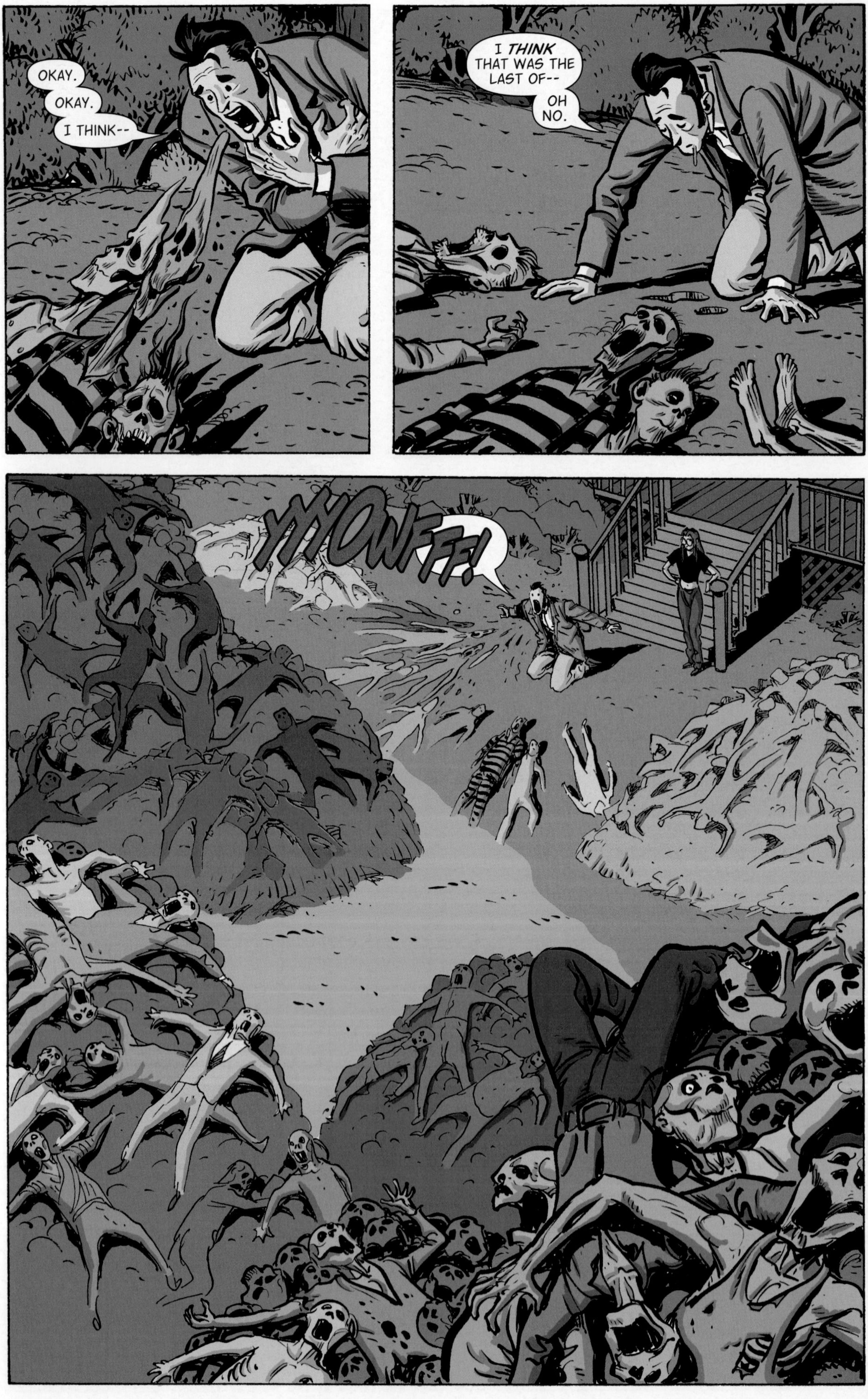
OKAY.
OKAY.
I THINK--
I *THINK* THAT WAS THE LAST OF--
OH NO.
YYYOWFFF!

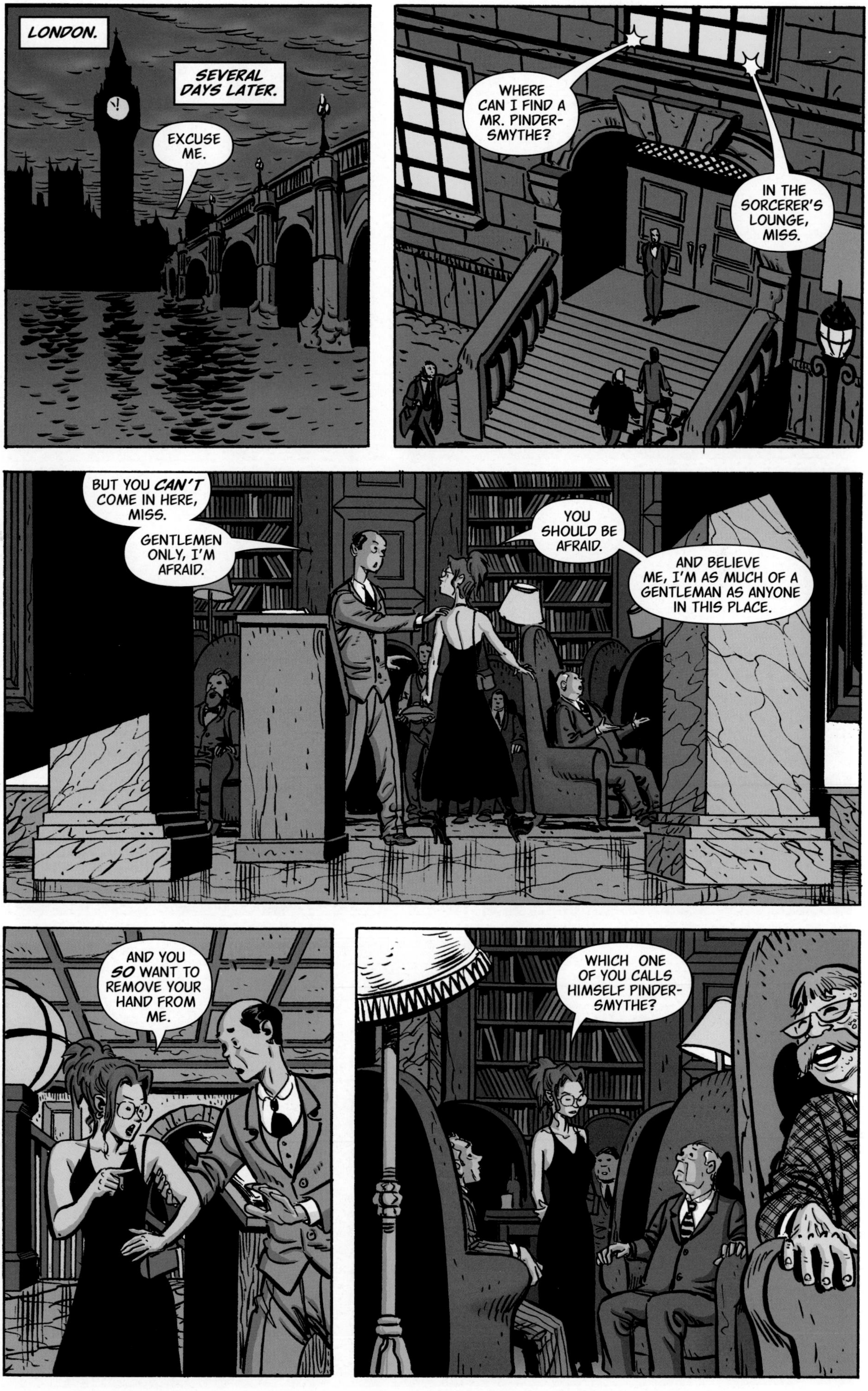
LONDON.
SEVERAL DAYS LATER.
EXCUSE ME.
WHERE CAN I FIND A MR. PINDER-SMYTHE?
IN THE SORCERER'S LOUNGE, MISS.
BUT YOU CAN'T COME IN HERE, MISS.
GENTLEMEN ONLY, I'M AFRAID.
YOU SHOULD BE AFRAID.
AND BELIEVE ME, I'M AS MUCH OF A GENTLEMAN AS ANYONE IN THIS PLACE.
AND YOU SO WANT TO REMOVE YOUR HAND FROM ME.
WHICH ONE OF YOU CALLS HIMSELF PINDER-SMYTHE?

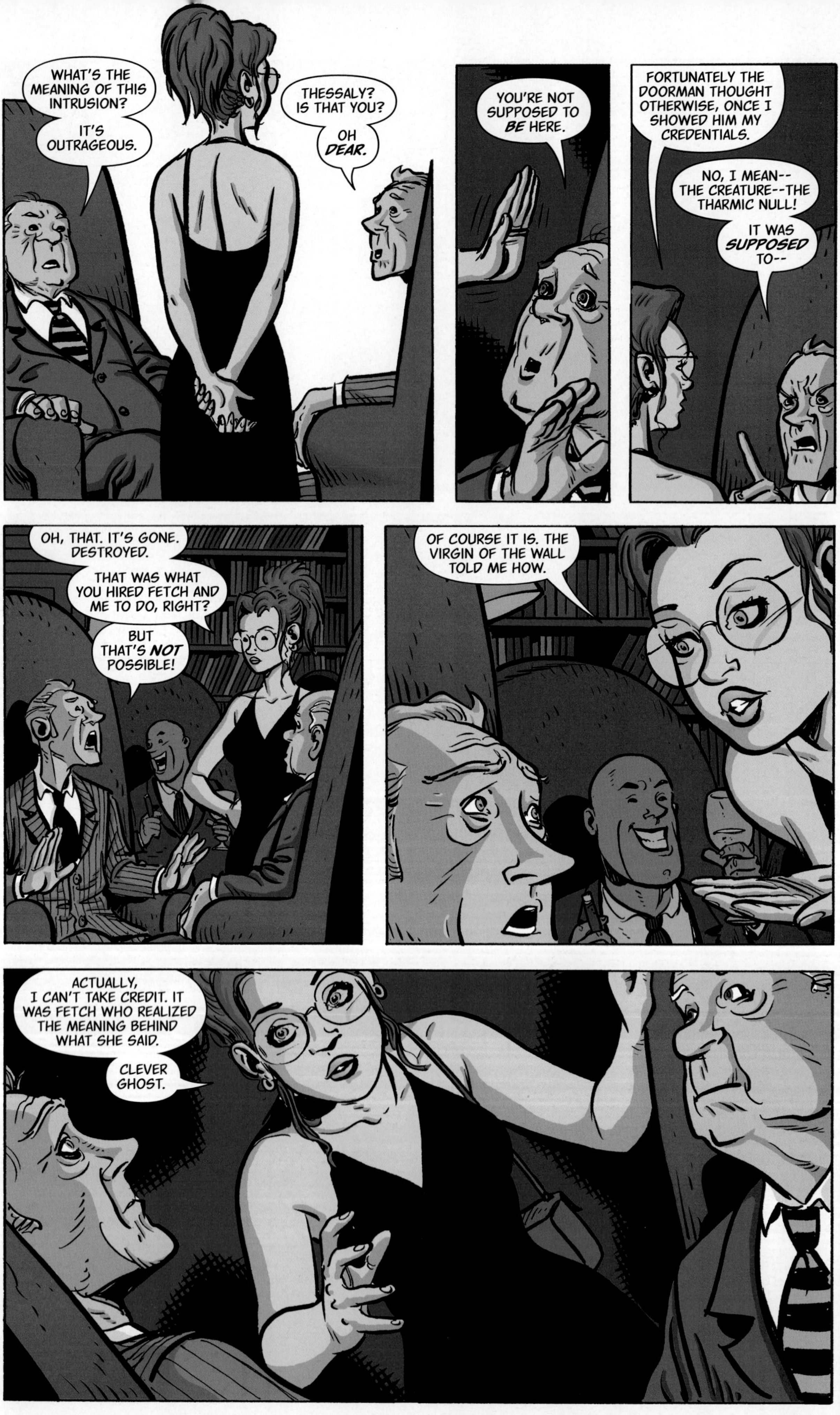

WHAT'S THE MEANING OF THIS INTRUSION?
IT'S OUTRAGEOUS.
THESSALY? IS THAT YOU?
OH *DEAR.*
YOU'RE NOT SUPPOSED TO *BE* HERE.
FORTUNATELY THE DOORMAN THOUGHT OTHERWISE, ONCE I SHOWED HIM MY CREDENTIALS.
NO, I MEAN-- THE CREATURE--THE THARMIC NULL!
IT WAS *SUPPOSED* TO--
OH, THAT. IT'S GONE. DESTROYED.
THAT WAS WHAT YOU HIRED FETCH AND ME TO DO, RIGHT?
BUT THAT'S *NOT* POSSIBLE!
OF COURSE IT IS. THE VIRGIN OF THE WALL TOLD ME HOW.
ACTUALLY, I CAN'T TAKE CREDIT. IT WAS FETCH WHO REALIZED THE MEANING BEHIND WHAT SHE SAID.
CLEVER GHOST.

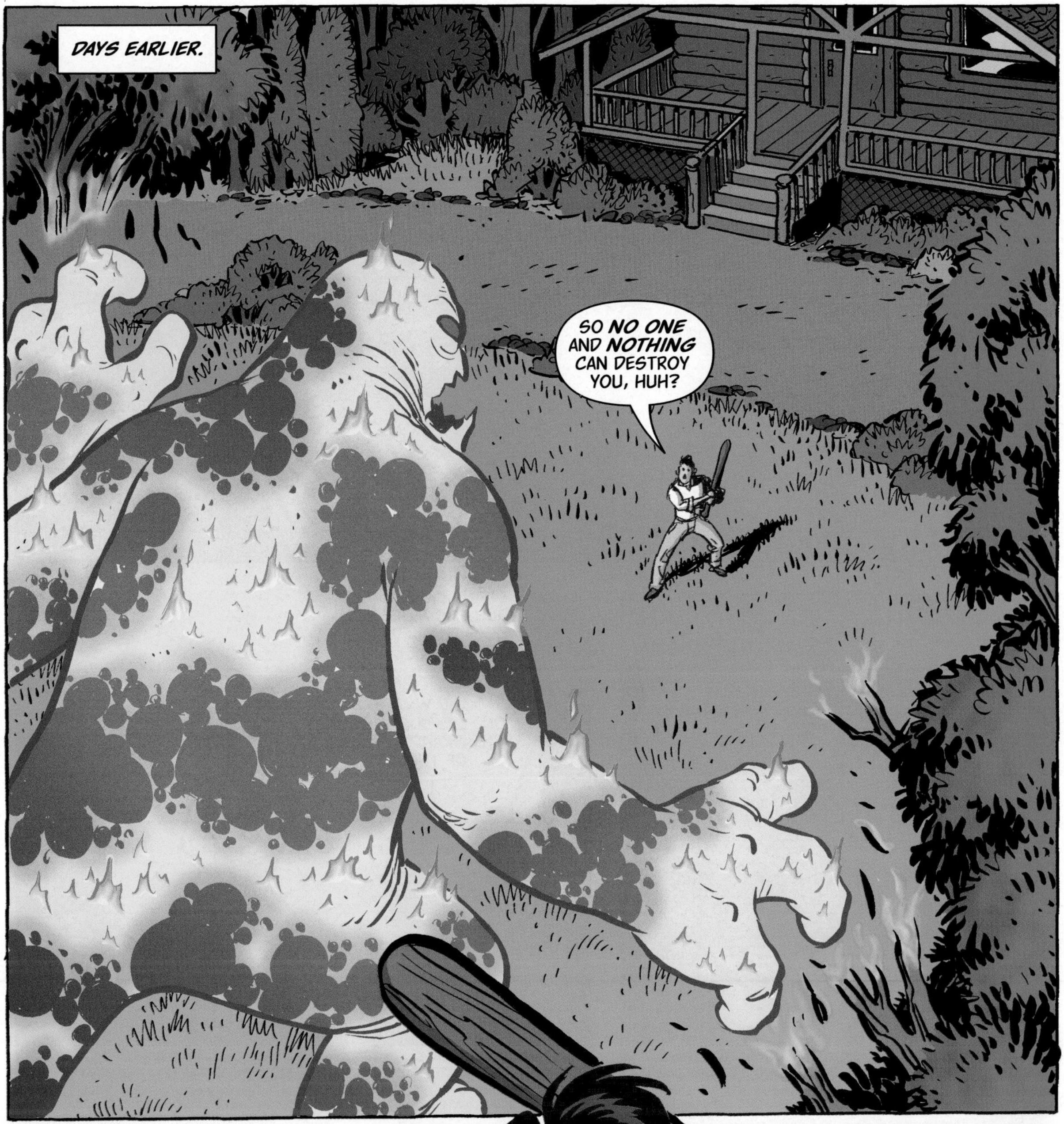
DAYS EARLIER.
SO NO ONE AND NOTHING CAN DESTROY YOU, HUH?

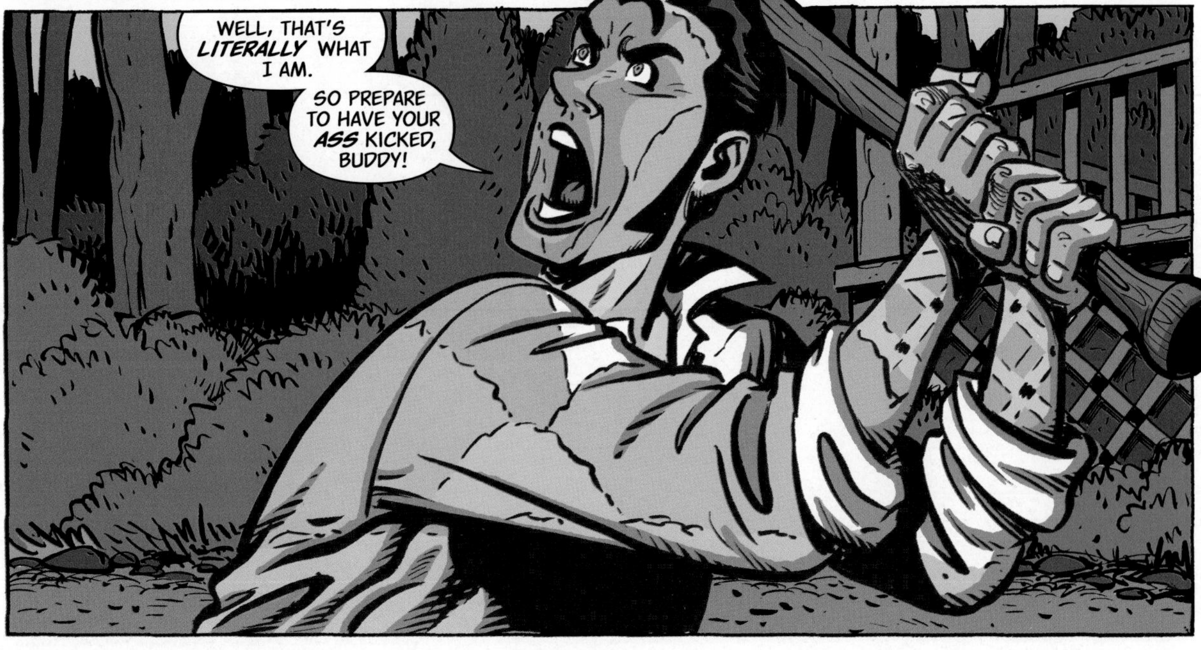
WELL, THAT'S LITERALLY WHAT I AM.
SO PREPARE TO HAVE YOUR ASS KICKED, BUDDY!

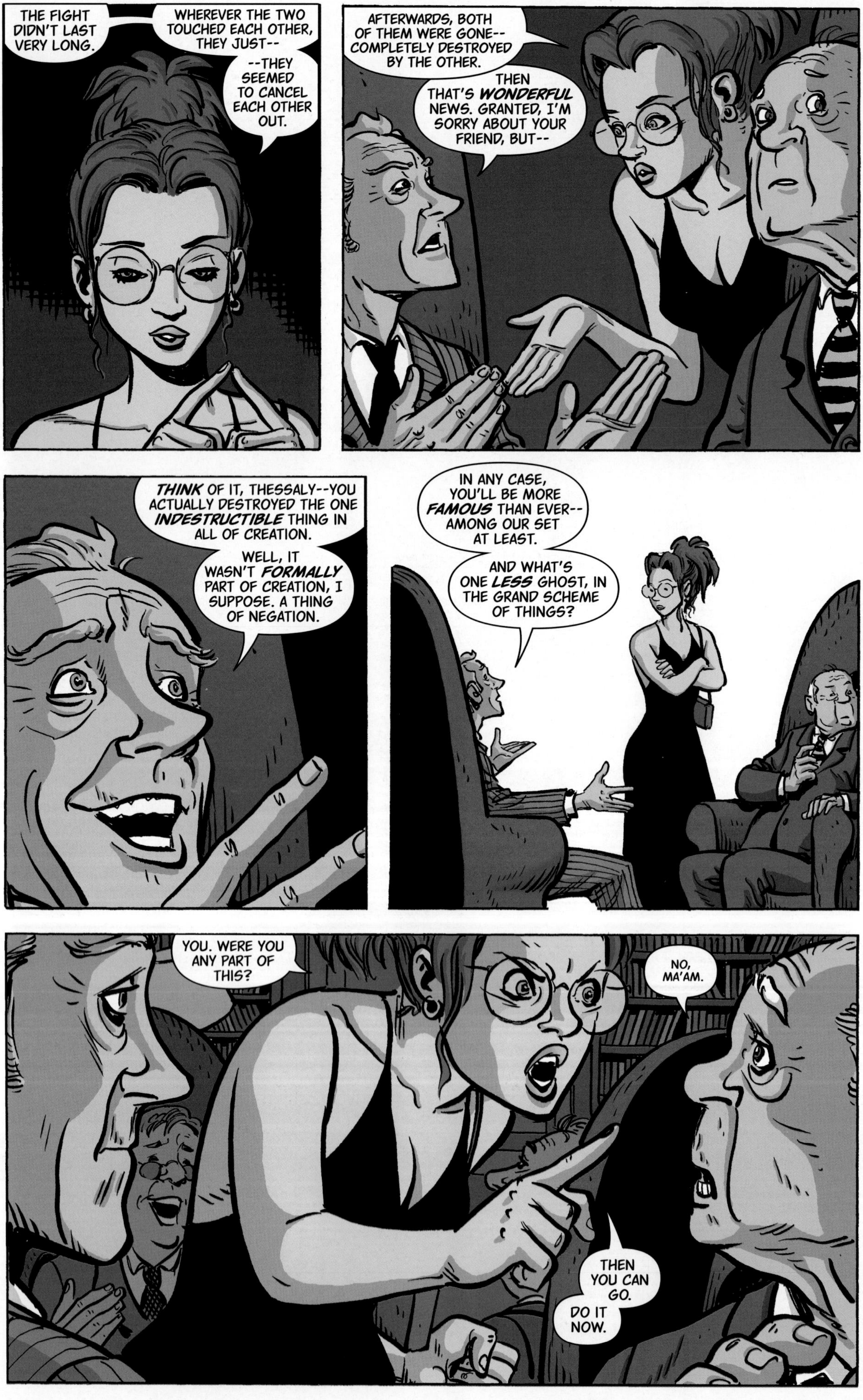
THE FIGHT DIDN'T LAST VERY LONG.
WHEREVER THE TWO TOUCHED EACH OTHER, THEY JUST--
--THEY SEEMED TO CANCEL EACH OTHER OUT.
AFTERWARDS, BOTH OF THEM WERE GONE--COMPLETELY DESTROYED BY THE OTHER.
THEN THAT'S WONDERFUL NEWS. GRANTED, I'M SORRY ABOUT YOUR FRIEND, BUT--
THINK OF IT, THESSALY--YOU ACTUALLY DESTROYED THE ONE INDESTRUCTIBLE THING IN ALL OF CREATION.
WELL, IT WASN'T FORMALLY PART OF CREATION, I SUPPOSE. A THING OF NEGATION.
IN ANY CASE, YOU'LL BE MORE FAMOUS THAN EVER--AMONG OUR SET AT LEAST.
AND WHAT'S ONE LESS GHOST, IN THE GRAND SCHEME OF THINGS?
YOU. WERE YOU ANY PART OF THIS?
NO, MA'AM.
THEN YOU CAN GO.
DO IT NOW.

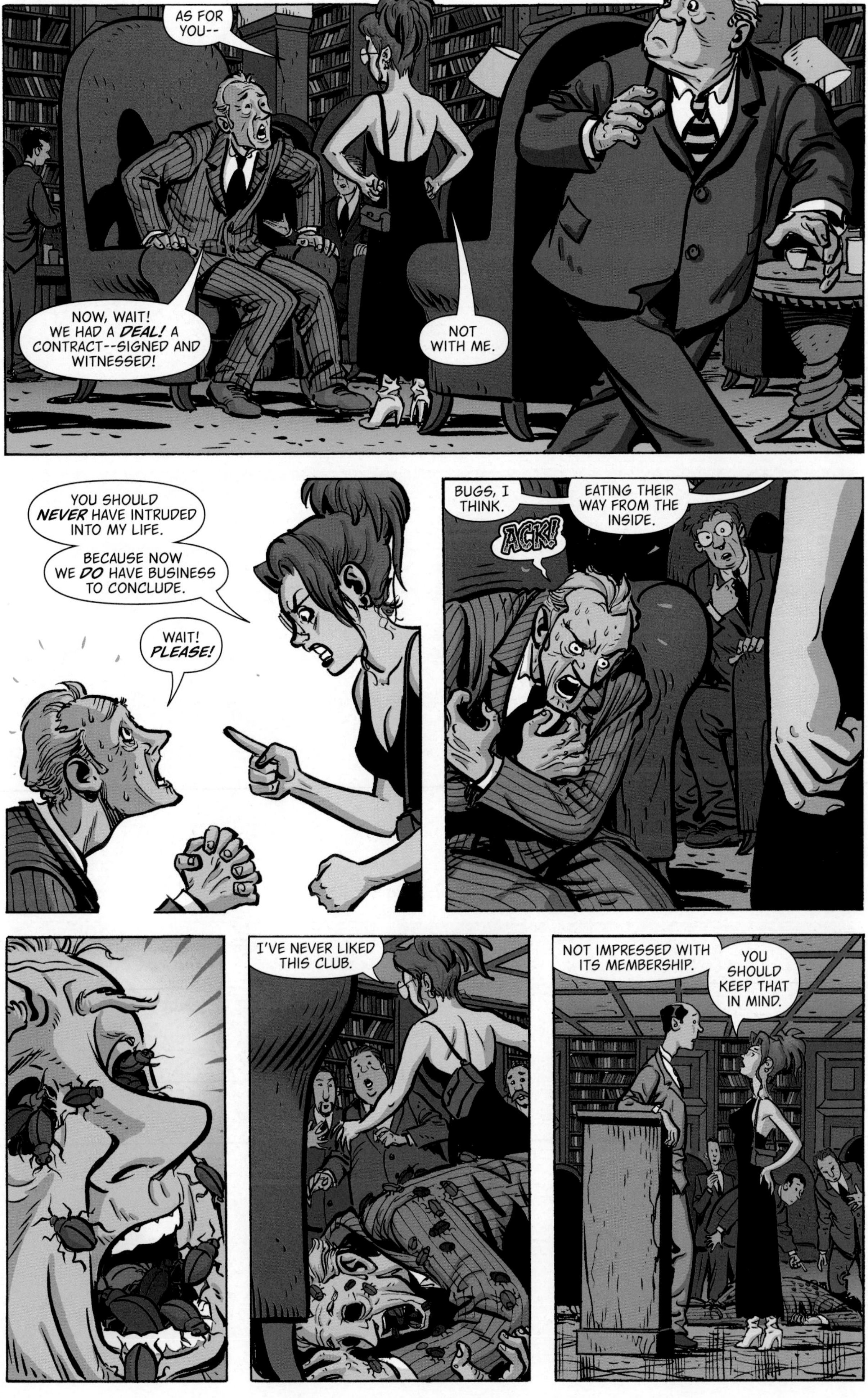
AS FOR YOU--
NOW, WAIT! WE HAD A ***DEAL!*** A CONTRACT--SIGNED AND WITNESSED!
NOT WITH ME.
YOU SHOULD ***NEVER*** HAVE INTRUDED INTO MY LIFE.
BECAUSE NOW WE ***DO*** HAVE BUSINESS TO CONCLUDE.
WAIT! ***PLEASE!***
BUGS, I THINK.
EATING THEIR WAY FROM THE INSIDE.
ACK!
I'VE NEVER LIKED THIS CLUB.
NOT IMPRESSED WITH ITS MEMBERSHIP.
YOU SHOULD KEEP THAT IN MIND.

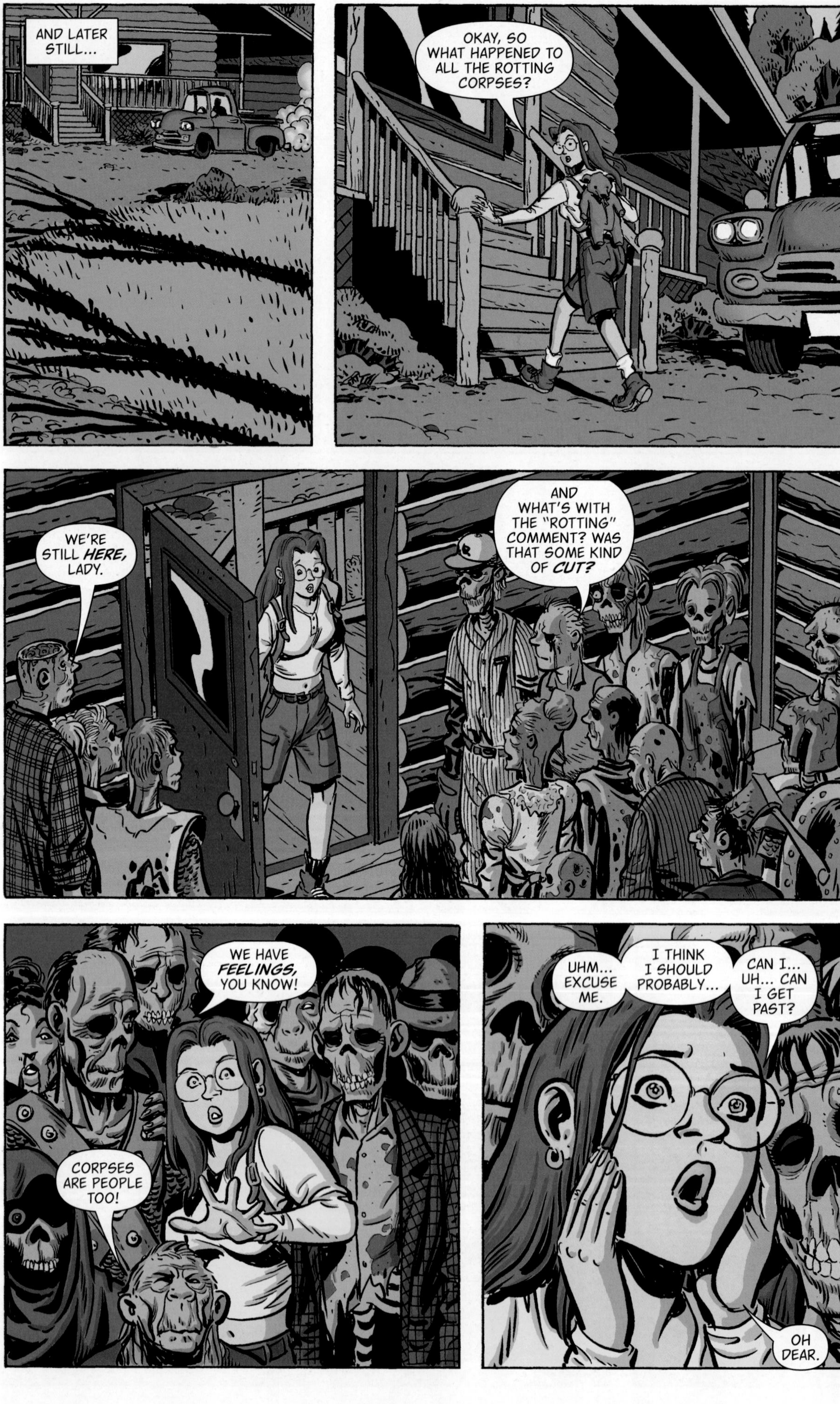
AND LATER STILL...
OKAY, SO WHAT HAPPENED TO ALL THE ROTTING CORPSES?
WE'RE STILL HERE, LADY.
AND WHAT'S WITH THE "ROTTING" COMMENT? WAS THAT SOME KIND OF CUT?
WE HAVE FEELINGS, YOU KNOW!
CORPSES ARE PEOPLE TOO!
UHM... EXCUSE ME.
I THINK I SHOULD PROBABLY...
CAN I... UH... CAN I GET PAST?
OH DEAR.

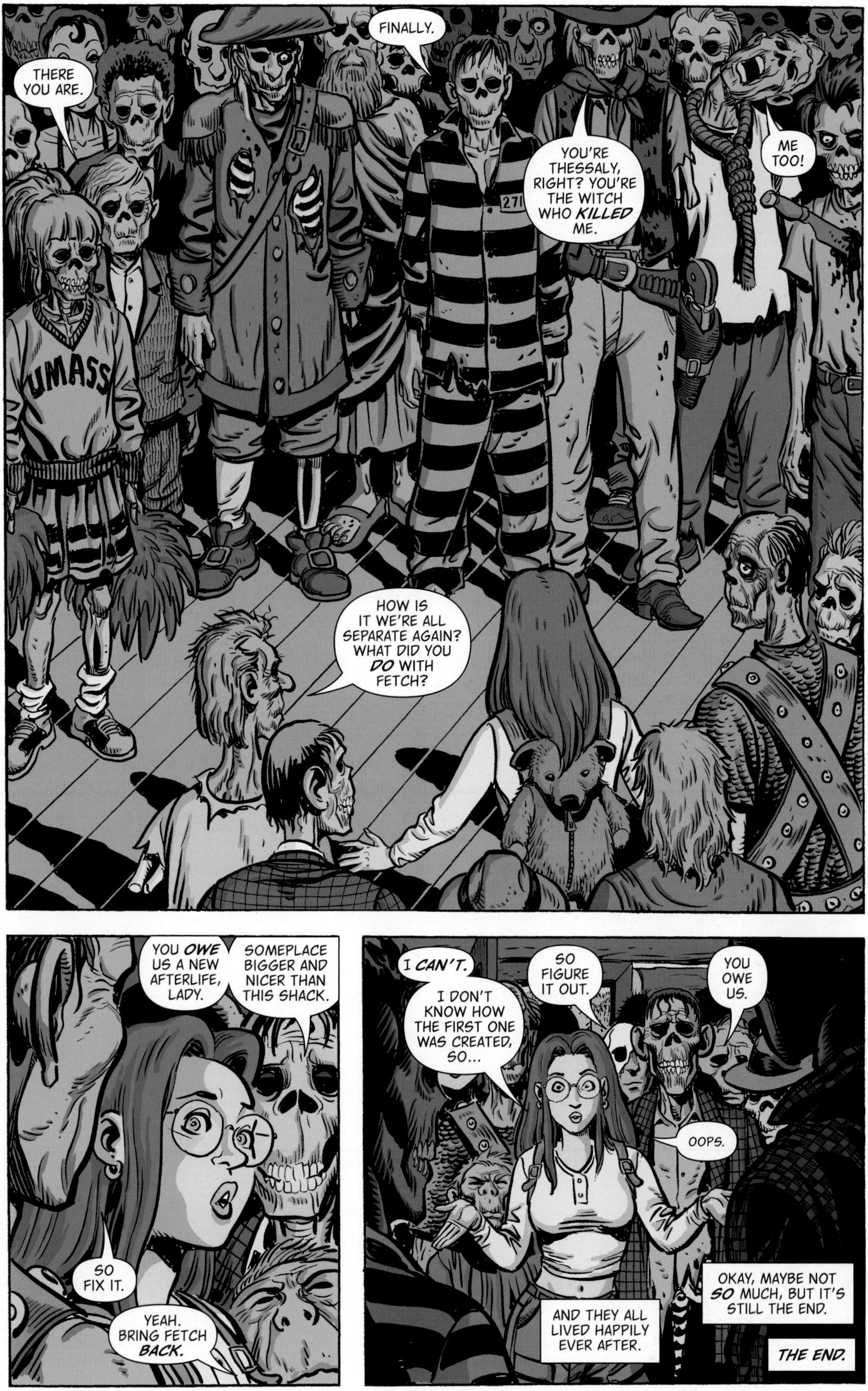
THERE YOU ARE.
FINALLY.
YOU'RE THESSALY, RIGHT? YOU'RE THE WITCH WHO *KILLED* ME.
ME TOO!
HOW IS IT WE'RE ALL SEPARATE AGAIN? WHAT DID YOU *DO* WITH FETCH?
YOU *OWE* US A NEW AFTERLIFE, LADY.
SOMEPLACE BIGGER AND NICER THAN THIS SHACK.
SO FIX IT.
YEAH. BRING FETCH *BACK.*
I *CAN'T.*
I DON'T KNOW HOW THE FIRST ONE WAS CREATED, SO...
SO FIGURE IT OUT.
YOU OWE US.
OOPS.
AND THEY ALL LIVED HAPPILY EVER AFTER.
OKAY, MAYBE NOT *SO* MUCH, BUT IT'S STILL THE END.
THE END.

THIS IS THE FIRST IN A SMALL SERIES OF INSET STORIES I WROTE FOR MATT STURGES'S LONG RUN ON *HOUSE OF MYSTERY*.

I wanted to accomplish two things with this short-short tale. First, I wanted to explore the idea of the hollow woman, which one can find, from time to time, in English, Irish and Scottish fairy tales. They were women who seemed solid and lovely when seen from the front, but turned out to be no more than a hollow mask of a person when viewed from behind. Basically I wanted to float an idea on how and why they got that way.

Second, I wanted to try for once to write a truly creepy and disturbing story, something I wasn't quite able to pull off a decade earlier in that "It Takes a Village" story in FLINCH (if you'll recall, I said we'd get back to this). Judging entirely by the reader reaction, I think that this time I was able to get there.

The idea behind these HOUSE OF MYSTERY stories is that every tale is being told by one of the residents or guests of the house, which is how they pay for drinks and meals in a place that doesn't have any other form of currency. This, then, is a story being told by one of the regulars named Hungry Sally, who eats and eats and eats, but somehow can never quite get full.

"...I wanted to try for once to write a truly creepy and disturbing story..."

THE HOLLOWS

ART BY
Ross Campbell

LETTERS BY
Todd Klein

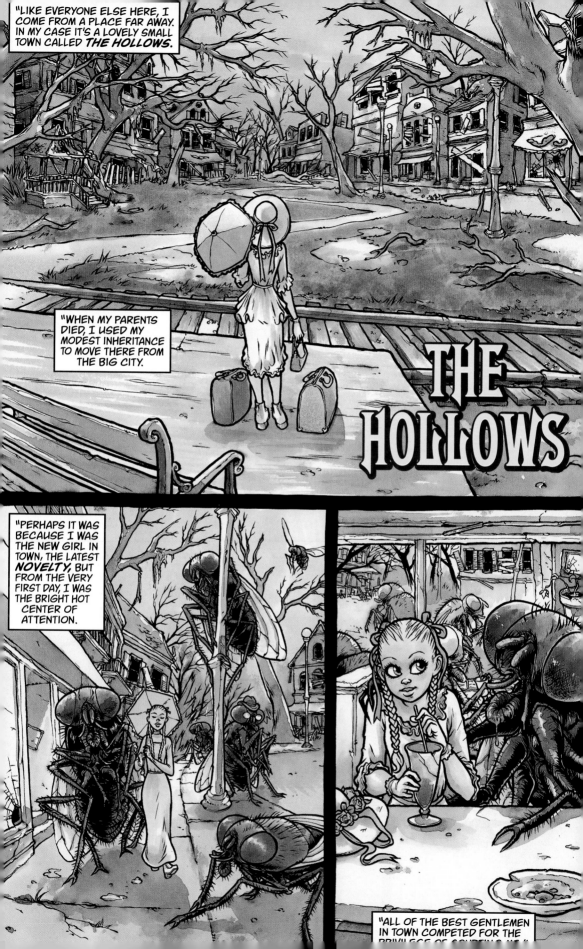

"LIKE EVERYONE ELSE HERE, I COME FROM A PLACE FAR AWAY. IN MY CASE IT'S A LOVELY SMALL TOWN CALLED *THE HOLLOWS.*

"WHEN MY PARENTS DIED, I USED MY MODEST INHERITANCE TO MOVE THERE FROM THE BIG CITY.

THE HOLLOWS

"PERHAPS IT WAS BECAUSE I WAS THE NEW GIRL IN TOWN, THE LATEST *NOVELTY,* BUT FROM THE VERY FIRST DAY, I WAS THE BRIGHT HOT CENTER OF ATTENTION.

"ALL OF THE BEST GENTLEMEN IN TOWN *COMPETED* FOR THE

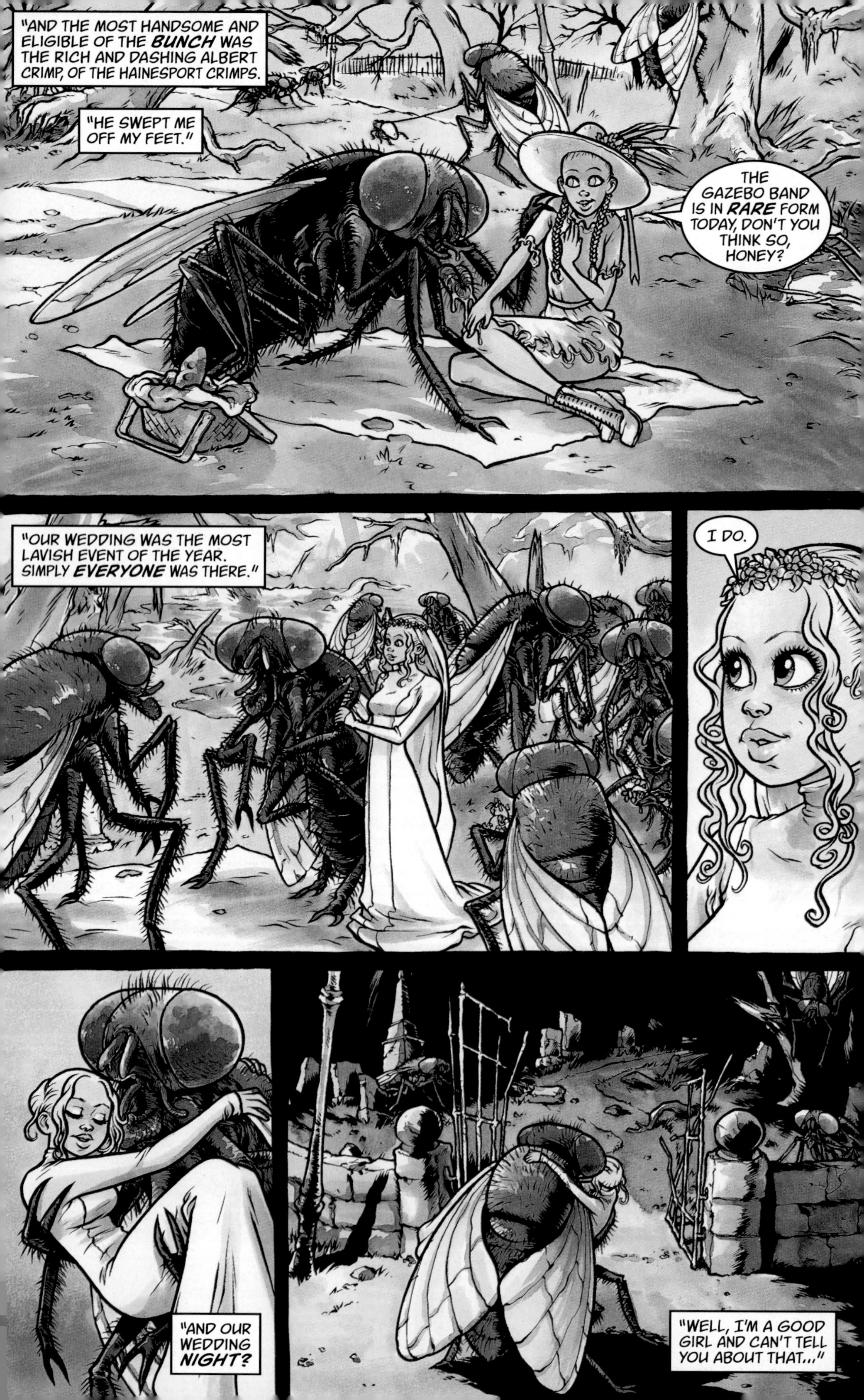
"AND THE MOST HANDSOME AND ELIGIBLE OF THE BUNCH WAS THE RICH AND DASHING ALBERT CRIMP, OF THE HAINESPORT CRIMPS.
"HE SWEPT ME OFF MY FEET."
THE GAZEBO BAND IS IN RARE FORM TODAY, DON'T YOU THINK SO, HONEY?
"OUR WEDDING WAS THE MOST LAVISH EVENT OF THE YEAR. SIMPLY EVERYONE WAS THERE."
I DO.
"AND OUR WEDDING NIGHT?
"WELL, I'M A GOOD GIRL AND CAN'T TELL YOU ABOUT THAT..."

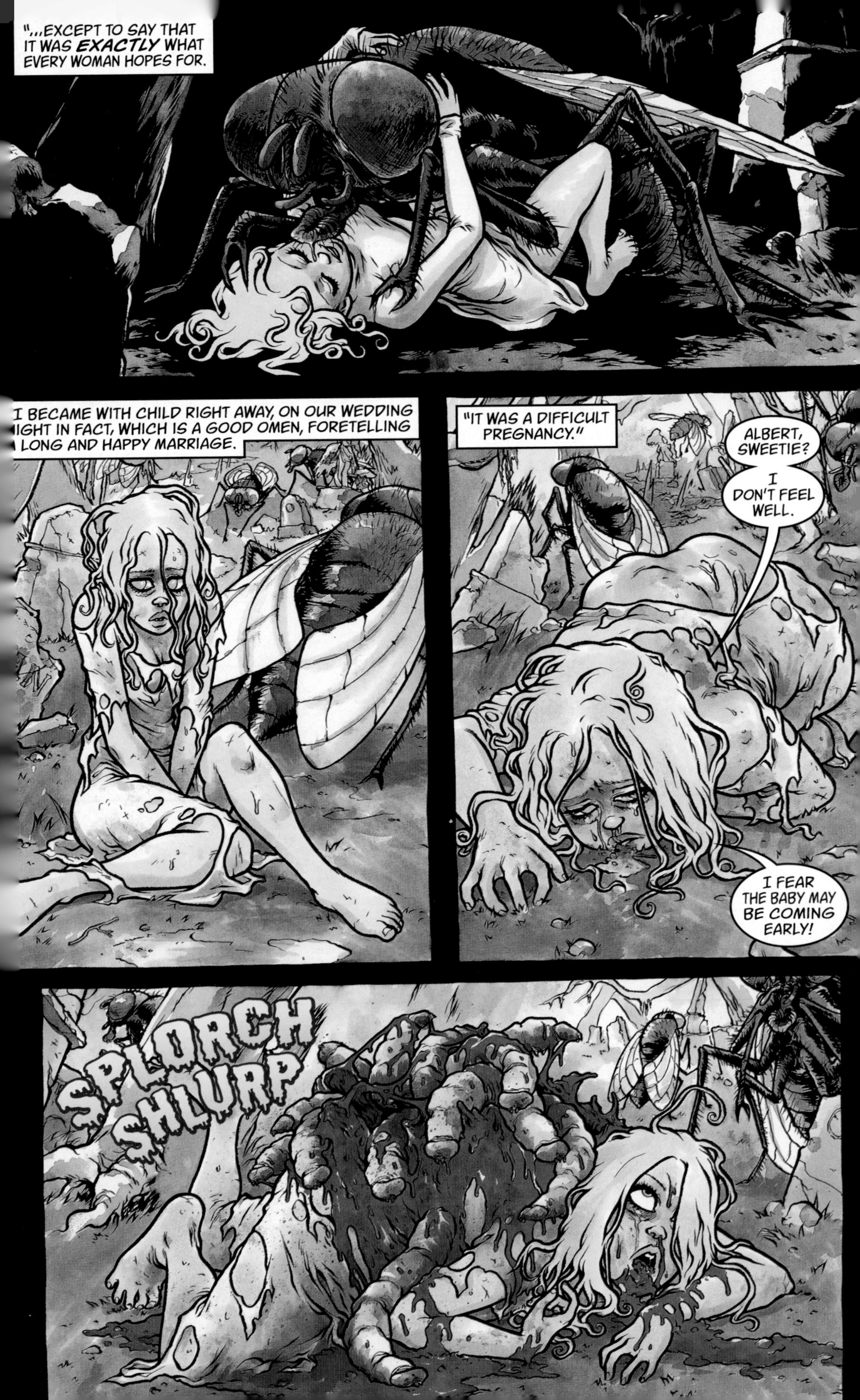
"...EXCEPT TO SAY THAT IT WAS ***EXACTLY*** WHAT EVERY WOMAN HOPES FOR.
I BECAME WITH CHILD RIGHT AWAY, ON OUR WEDDING IGHT IN FACT, WHICH IS A GOOD OMEN, FORETELLING LONG AND HAPPY MARRIAGE.
"IT WAS A DIFFICULT PREGNANCY."
ALBERT, SWEETIE?
I DON'T FEEL WELL.
I FEAR THE BABY MAY BE COMING EARLY!
SPLORCH
SHLURP

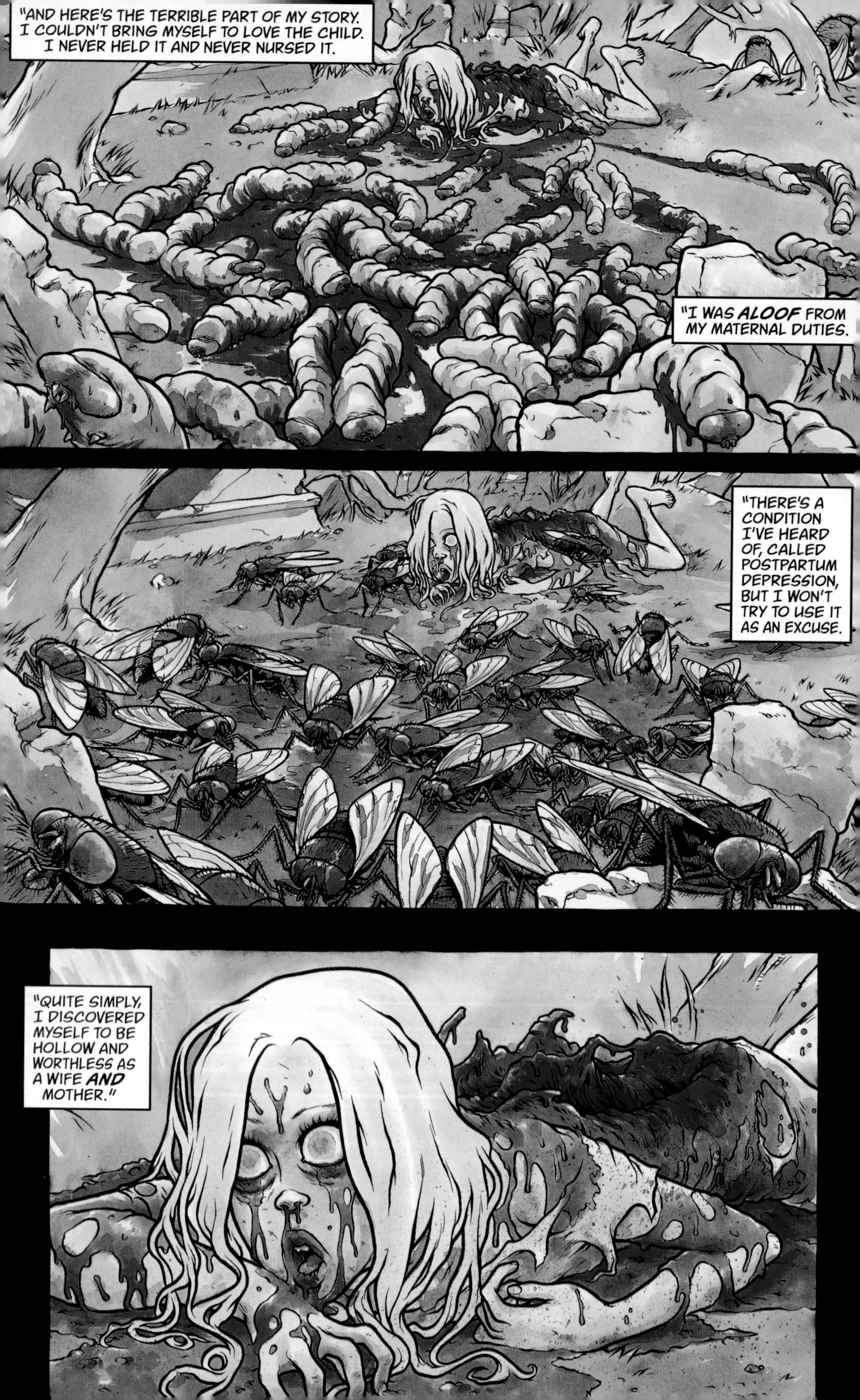
"AND HERE'S THE TERRIBLE PART OF MY STORY. I COULDN'T BRING MYSELF TO LOVE THE CHILD. I NEVER HELD IT AND NEVER NURSED IT.
"I WAS ALOOF FROM MY MATERNAL DUTIES.
"THERE'S A CONDITION I'VE HEARD OF, CALLED POSTPARTUM DEPRESSION, BUT I WON'T TRY TO USE IT AS AN EXCUSE.
"QUITE SIMPLY, I DISCOVERED MYSELF TO BE HOLLOW AND WORTHLESS AS A WIFE AND MOTHER."

IN MY TIME ON THIS EARTH I'VE NOTICED THAT EVERYONE'S PROFESSION CAN BE MYSTERIOUS, WONDERFUL AND EXCITING TO THOSE LOOKING IN FROM THE OUTSIDE. For a writer that effect can be heightened considerably. Assuming I'm not unique, writers often find themselves grilling new acquaintances, or even total strangers, about their life and professions in exacting detail, in ways that no cop would be allowed to pursue without a flood of civil liberties lawyers descending upon him.

I'm embarrassed to say that I've forgotten his name, but a few years back, while attending a convention in Toronto, I was met at the airport by the fellow assigned to drive me to the convention site and then to my hotel. This man, one of several convention driver volunteers, had specifically asked to pick me up so that he could

> *"...writers often find themselves grilling new acquaintances, or even total strangers, about their life and professions in exacting detail..."*

have me all to himself for a time, to grill me about — well, I assume my funnybook work, but we'll never know, since he never got a chance to ask a single question in a drive that took more than an hour.

The reason he never got to ask me anything is that he made the mistake of answering a few of my introductory questions first — questions of the standard "who are you and what do you do" variety that are pretty much required on meeting someone for the first time. Specifically, he made the mistake of mentioning he was a professional process server — one of those guys who serve official court documents (like subpoenas) to folks, most of whom don't want to receive them. As soon as he mentioned this, I needed to know everything I possibly could about this mysterious and wonderful profession. His plans about learning anything at all about me were doomed. I took up the entire drive questioning him about every minor detail of his life.

I felt guilty enough about monopolizing his time that I promised the polite but frustrated young man that I would at least build a future story from our talk. "Perhaps something like the adventures of the world's greatest process server," I said.

I don't know if he believed me, but I was sincere. Here then is the story that I owed to a fine fellow whose name I really am embarrassed to have forgotten.

IN TOO DEEP

Art by
Jill Thompson

Letters by
Todd Klein

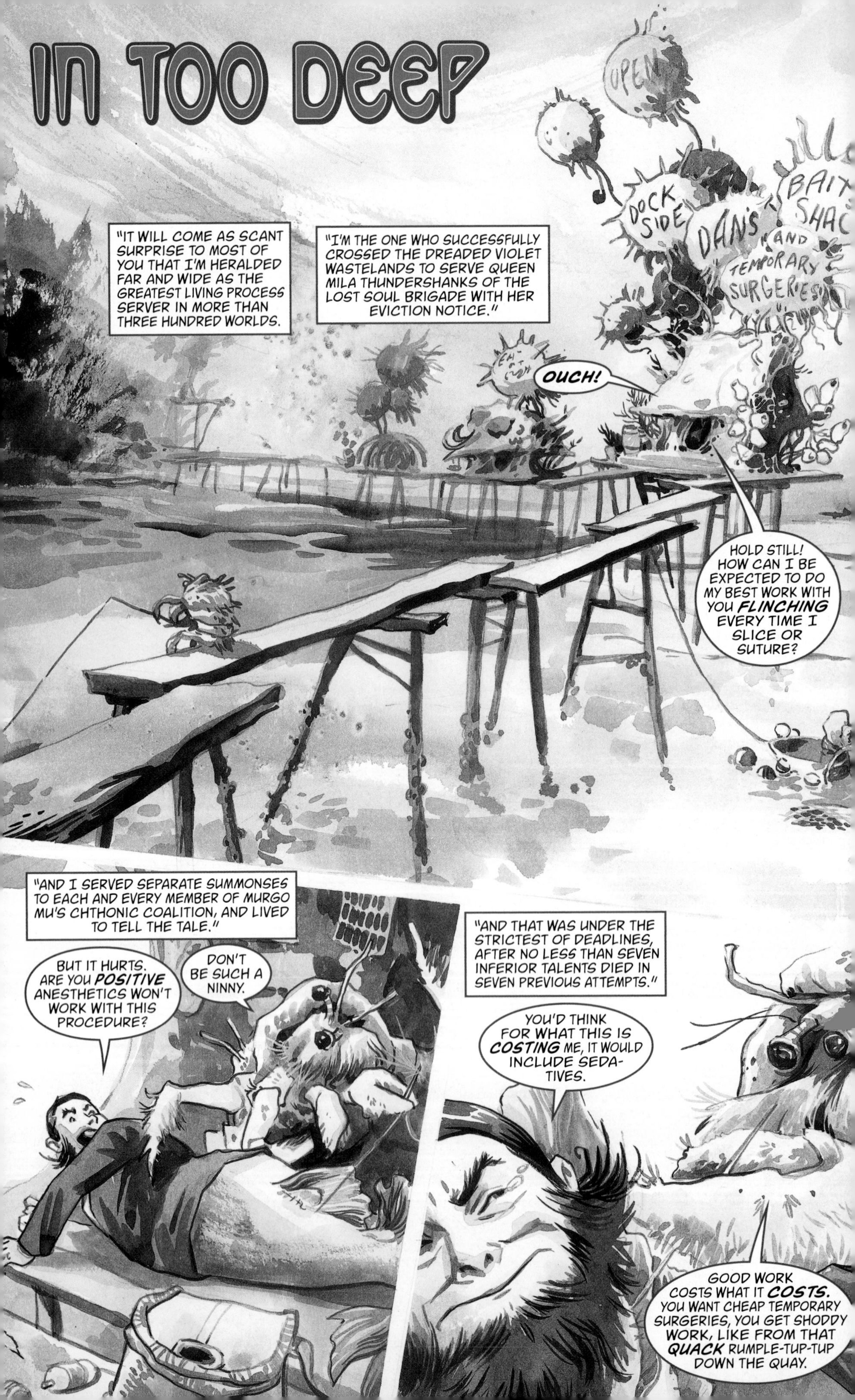
IN TOO DEEP
OPEN
DOCK SIDE
DAN'S BAIT SHAC
AND TEMPORARY SURGERIES
"IT WILL COME AS SCANT SURPRISE TO MOST OF YOU THAT I'M HERALDED FAR AND WIDE AS THE GREATEST LIVING PROCESS SERVER IN MORE THAN THREE HUNDRED WORLDS.
"I'M THE ONE WHO SUCCESSFULLY CROSSED THE DREADED VIOLET WASTELANDS TO SERVE QUEEN MILA THUNDERSHANKS OF THE LOST SOUL BRIGADE WITH HER EVICTION NOTICE."
OUCH!
HOLD STILL! HOW CAN I BE EXPECTED TO DO MY BEST WORK WITH YOU *FLINCHING* EVERY TIME I SLICE OR SUTURE?
"AND I SERVED SEPARATE SUMMONSES TO EACH AND EVERY MEMBER OF MURGO MU'S CHTHONIC COALITION, AND LIVED TO TELL THE TALE."
BUT IT HURTS. ARE YOU *POSITIVE* ANESTHETICS WON'T WORK WITH THIS PROCEDURE?
DON'T BE SUCH A NINNY.
"AND THAT WAS UNDER THE STRICTEST OF DEADLINES, AFTER NO LESS THAN SEVEN INFERIOR TALENTS DIED IN SEVEN PREVIOUS ATTEMPTS."
YOU'D THINK FOR WHAT THIS IS *COSTING* ME, IT WOULD INCLUDE SEDA-TIVES.
GOOD WORK COSTS WHAT IT *COSTS.* YOU WANT CHEAP TEMPORARY SURGERIES, YOU GET SHODDY WORK, LIKE FROM THAT *QUACK* RUMPLE-TUP-TUP DOWN THE QUAY.

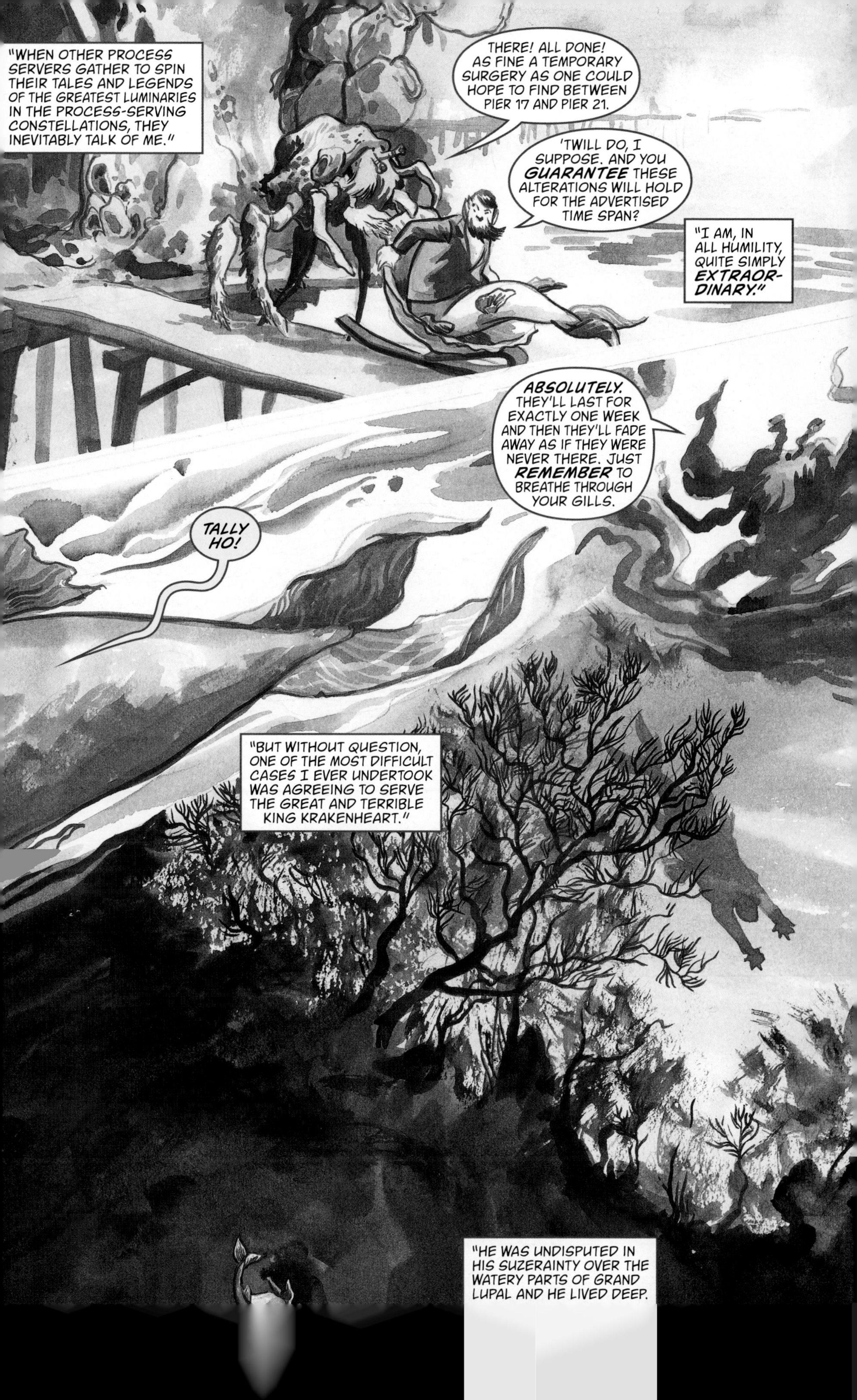
"WHEN OTHER PROCESS SERVERS GATHER TO SPIN THEIR TALES AND LEGENDS OF THE GREATEST LUMINARIES IN THE PROCESS-SERVING CONSTELLATIONS, THEY INEVITABLY TALK OF ME."
THERE! ALL DONE! AS FINE A TEMPORARY SURGERY AS ONE COULD HOPE TO FIND BETWEEN PIER 17 AND PIER 21.
'TWILL DO, I SUPPOSE. AND YOU GUARANTEE THESE ALTERATIONS WILL HOLD FOR THE ADVERTISED TIME SPAN?
"I AM, IN ALL HUMILITY, QUITE SIMPLY EXTRAOR-DINARY."
ABSOLUTELY. THEY'LL LAST FOR EXACTLY ONE WEEK AND THEN THEY'LL FADE AWAY AS IF THEY WERE NEVER THERE. JUST REMEMBER TO BREATHE THROUGH YOUR GILLS.
TALLY HO!
"BUT WITHOUT QUESTION, ONE OF THE MOST DIFFICULT CASES I EVER UNDERTOOK WAS AGREEING TO SERVE THE GREAT AND TERRIBLE KING KRAKENHEART."
"HE WAS UNDISPUTED IN HIS SUZERAINTY OVER THE WATERY PARTS OF GRAND LUPAL AND HE LIVED DEEP.

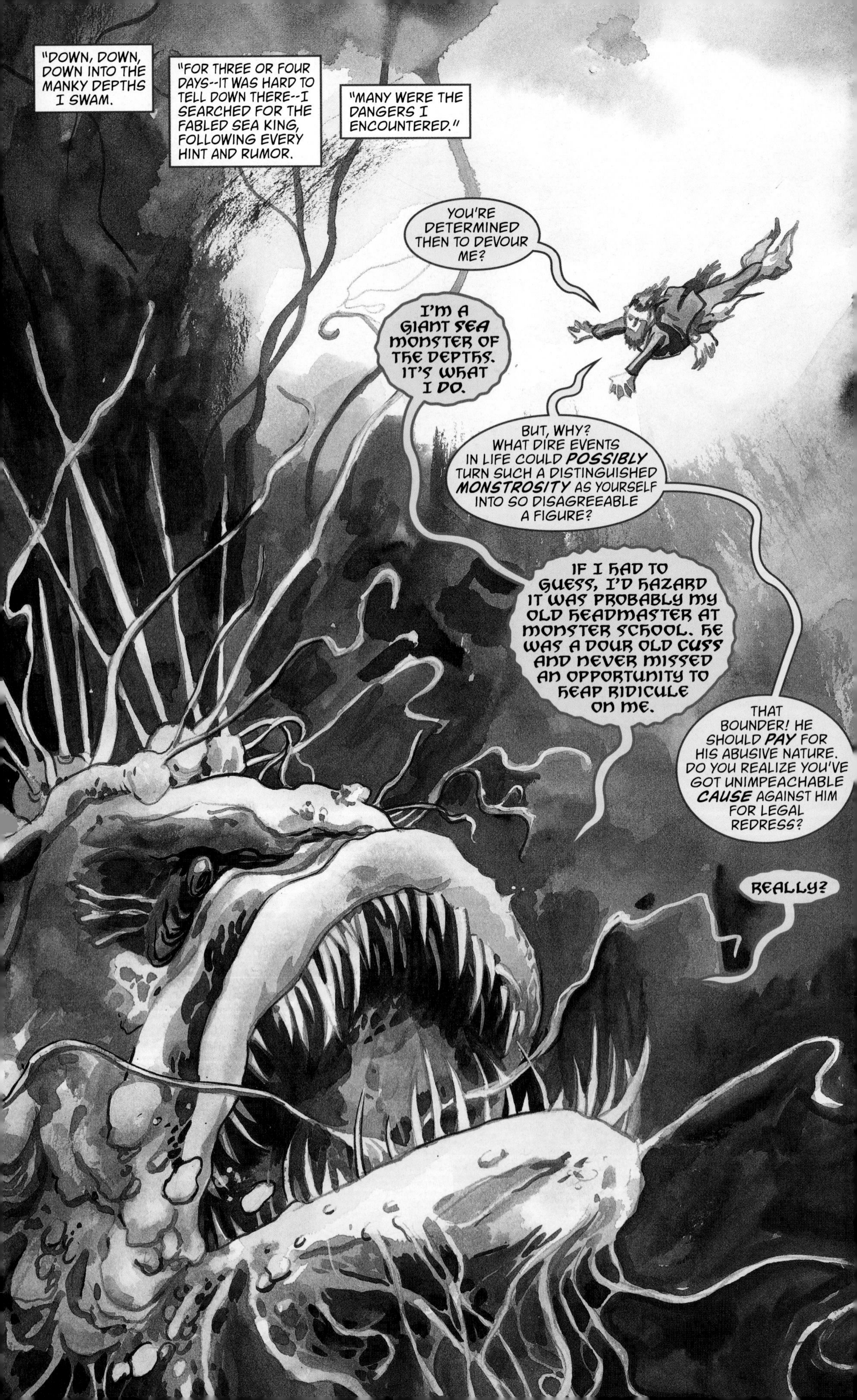
"DOWN, DOWN, DOWN INTO THE MANKY DEPTHS I SWAM.
"FOR THREE OR FOUR DAYS--IT WAS HARD TO TELL DOWN THERE--I SEARCHED FOR THE FABLED SEA KING, FOLLOWING EVERY HINT AND RUMOR.
"MANY WERE THE DANGERS I ENCOUNTERED."
YOU'RE DETERMINED THEN TO DEVOUR ME?
I'M A GIANT SEA MONSTER OF THE DEPTHS. IT'S WHAT I DO.
BUT, WHY? WHAT DIRE EVENTS IN LIFE COULD POSSIBLY TURN SUCH A DISTINGUISHED MONSTROSITY AS YOURSELF INTO SO DISAGREEABLE A FIGURE?
IF I HAD TO GUESS, I'D HAZARD IT WAS PROBABLY MY OLD HEADMASTER AT MONSTER SCHOOL. HE WAS A DOUR OLD CUSS AND NEVER MISSED AN OPPORTUNITY TO HEAP RIDICULE ON ME.
THAT BOUNDER! HE SHOULD PAY FOR HIS ABUSIVE NATURE. DO YOU REALIZE YOU'VE GOT UNIMPEACHABLE CAUSE AGAINST HIM FOR LEGAL REDRESS?
REALLY?

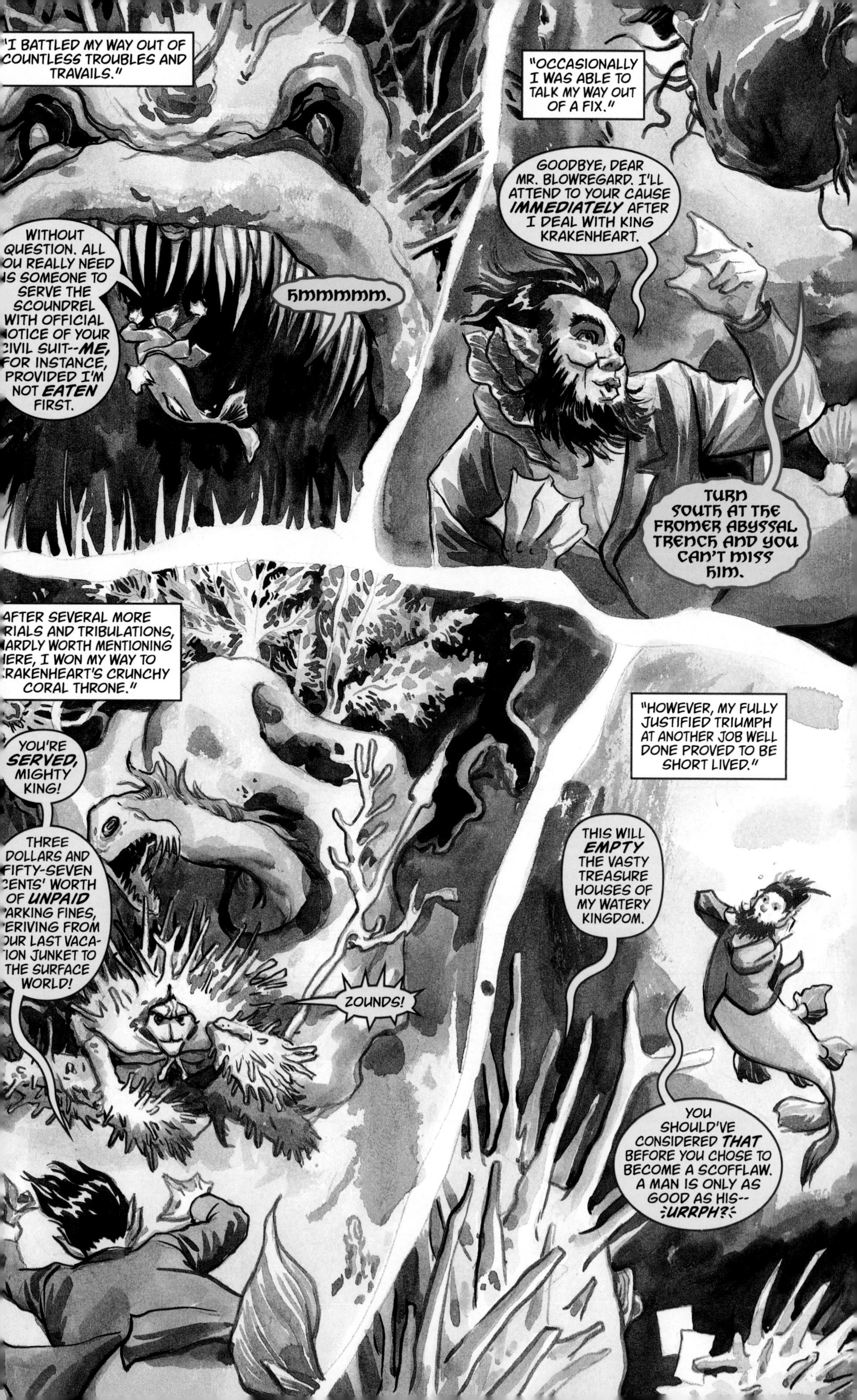
"I BATTLED MY WAY OUT OF COUNTLESS TROUBLES AND TRAVAILS."
WITHOUT QUESTION. ALL OU REALLY NEED IS SOMEONE TO SERVE THE SCOUNDREL WITH OFFICIAL IOTICE OF YOUR CIVIL SUIT--**ME,** FOR INSTANCE, PROVIDED I'M NOT **EATEN** FIRST.
HMMMMM.
"OCCASIONALLY I WAS ABLE TO TALK MY WAY OUT OF A FIX."
GOODBYE, DEAR MR. BLOWREGARD. I'LL ATTEND TO YOUR CAUSE **IMMEDIATELY** AFTER I DEAL WITH KING KRAKENHEART.
TURN SOUTH AT THE FROMER ABYSSAL TRENCH AND YOU CAN'T MISS HIM.
AFTER SEVERAL MORE RIALS AND TRIBULATIONS, IARDLY WORTH MENTIONING IERE, I WON MY WAY TO RAKENHEART'S CRUNCHY CORAL THRONE."
YOU'RE **SERVED,** MIGHTY KING!
THREE DOLLARS AND FIFTY-SEVEN CENTS' WORTH OF **UNPAID** PARKING FINES, ERIVING FROM OUR LAST VACA-ION JUNKET TO THE SURFACE WORLD!
ZOUNDS!
"HOWEVER, MY FULLY JUSTIFIED TRIUMPH AT ANOTHER JOB WELL DONE PROVED TO BE SHORT LIVED."
THIS WILL **EMPTY** THE VASTY TREASURE HOUSES OF MY WATERY KINGDOM.
YOU SHOULD'VE CONSIDERED **THAT** BEFORE YOU CHOSE TO BECOME A SCOFFLAW. A MAN IS ONLY AS GOOD AS HIS-- **URRPH?**

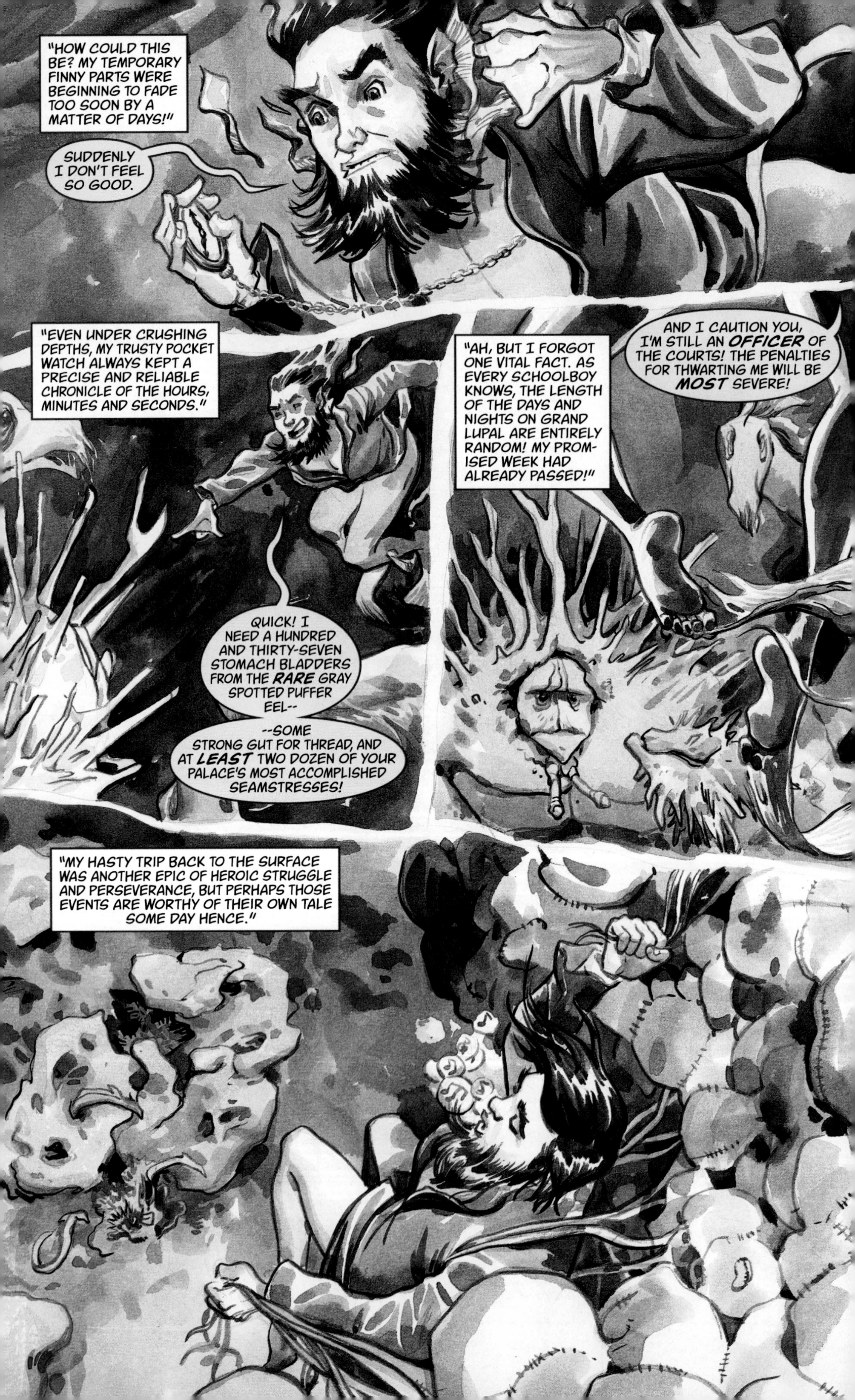
"HOW COULD THIS BE? MY TEMPORARY FINNY PARTS WERE BEGINNING TO FADE TOO SOON BY A MATTER OF DAYS!"
SUDDENLY I DON'T FEEL SO GOOD.
"EVEN UNDER CRUSHING DEPTHS, MY TRUSTY POCKET WATCH ALWAYS KEPT A PRECISE AND RELIABLE CHRONICLE OF THE HOURS, MINUTES AND SECONDS."
QUICK! I NEED A HUNDRED AND THIRTY-SEVEN STOMACH BLADDERS FROM THE *RARE* GRAY SPOTTED PUFFER EEL--
--SOME STRONG GUT FOR THREAD, AND AT *LEAST* TWO DOZEN OF YOUR PALACE'S MOST ACCOMPLISHED SEAMSTRESSES!
"AH, BUT I FORGOT ONE VITAL FACT. AS EVERY SCHOOLBOY KNOWS, THE LENGTH OF THE DAYS AND NIGHTS ON GRAND LUPAL ARE ENTIRELY RANDOM! MY PROMISED WEEK HAD ALREADY PASSED!"
AND I CAUTION YOU, I'M STILL AN *OFFICER* OF THE COURTS! THE PENALTIES FOR THWARTING ME WILL BE *MOST* SEVERE!
"MY HASTY TRIP BACK TO THE SURFACE WAS ANOTHER EPIC OF HEROIC STRUGGLE AND PERSEVERANCE, BUT PERHAPS THOSE EVENTS ARE WORTHY OF THEIR OWN TALE SOME DAY HENCE."

O NE OF THE ADVANTAGES OF BELONGING TO A GROUP OF WRITERS (in my case it's the Clockwork Storybook group, the second greatest writing group in the history of English letters) is that when you're stuck on some aspect of a story, you can pick up the phone and call

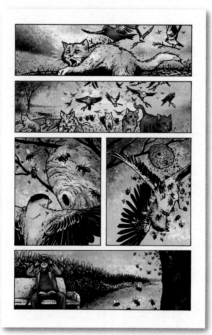

on one of your writing group comrades to talk it out — to try to work through the logjam of whatever it is that has you stuck.

One of the disadvantages of belonging to a writing group is that when one of the other writers calls you up, needing help in working through a stuck story, you're pretty much obligated to take the time to help. After all, that's the major point of the writing group's existence.

So, when I was stuck on one of the short stories I was supposed to be writing for Matt Sturges's HOUSE OF MYSTERY, and since Matt was also a member of our writing group, he had no choice but to spend some time talking me through it, even though in this case I could tell there were other things he needed to be doing.

The trouble was I didn't even have the first idea of a story.

We talked for some time, during which Matt tossed random ideas at me. But nothing seemed to click, until he said, in an exasperated voice, "This is going nowhere. So let's try a completely different tack. What is it you see around you, right now?"

I was visiting a friend at the time, and was out on their back porch, so I described what I saw. "There are birds coming and going from the bird feeder and the cat is trying to sneak up on them."

"Then that's your story," Matt said. "Do a war between cats and birds."

My first reaction was that's a silly idea, and Matt clearly wants to go do other things. My second reaction was the story you see here.

THE WAR

ART BY
David Petersen

LETTERS BY
Todd Klein

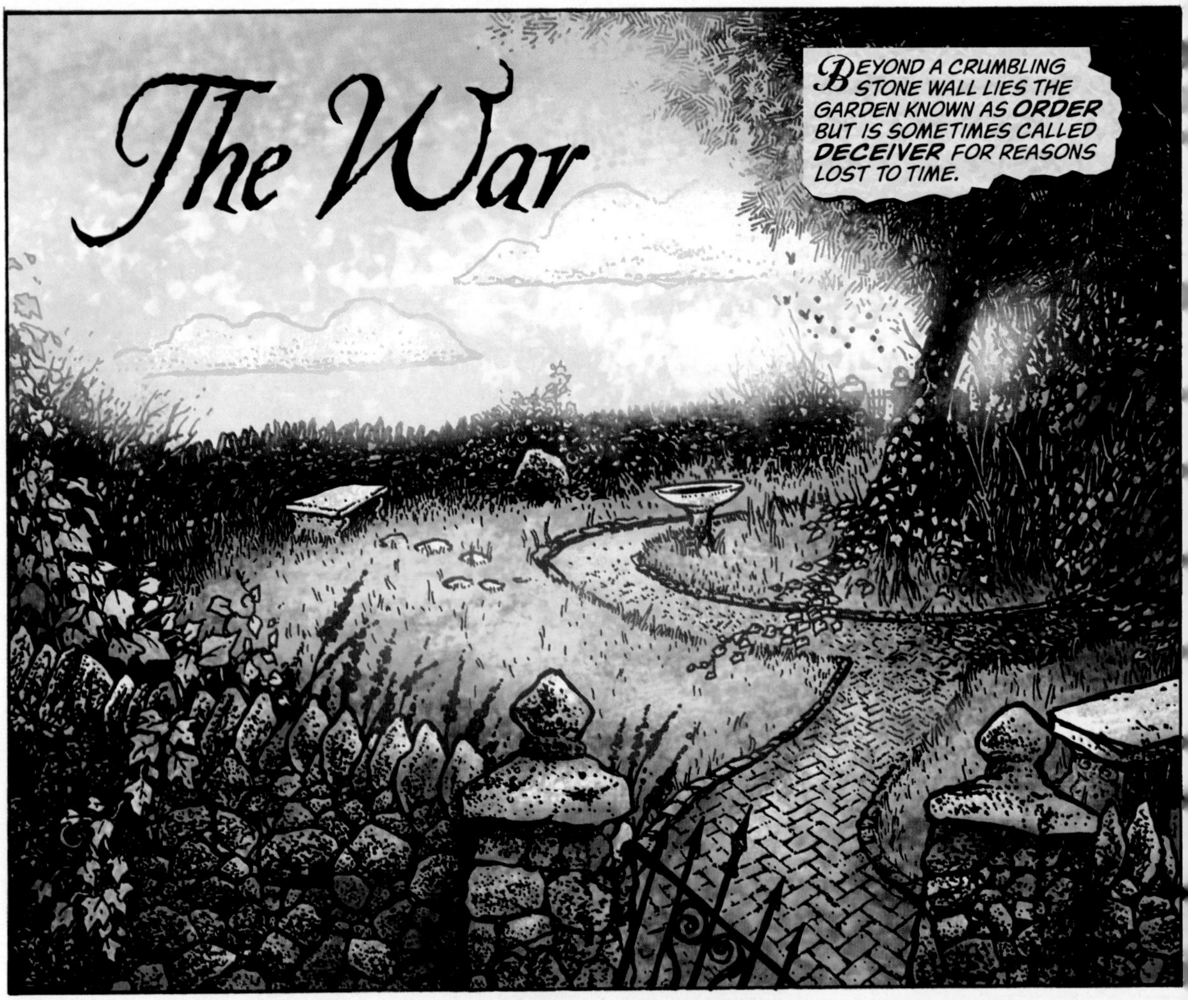
The War
BEYOND A CRUMBLING STONE WALL LIES THE GARDEN KNOWN AS **ORDER** BUT IS SOMETIMES CALLED **DECEIVER** FOR REASONS LOST TO TIME.

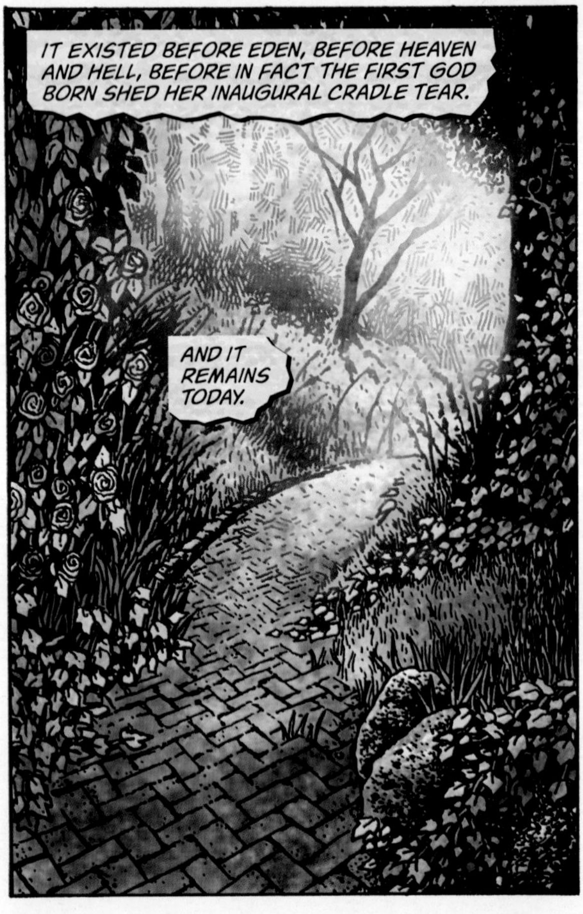
IT EXISTED BEFORE EDEN, BEFORE HEAVEN AND HELL, BEFORE IN FACT THE FIRST GOD BORN SHED HER INAUGURAL CRADLE TEAR.
AND IT REMAINS TODAY.

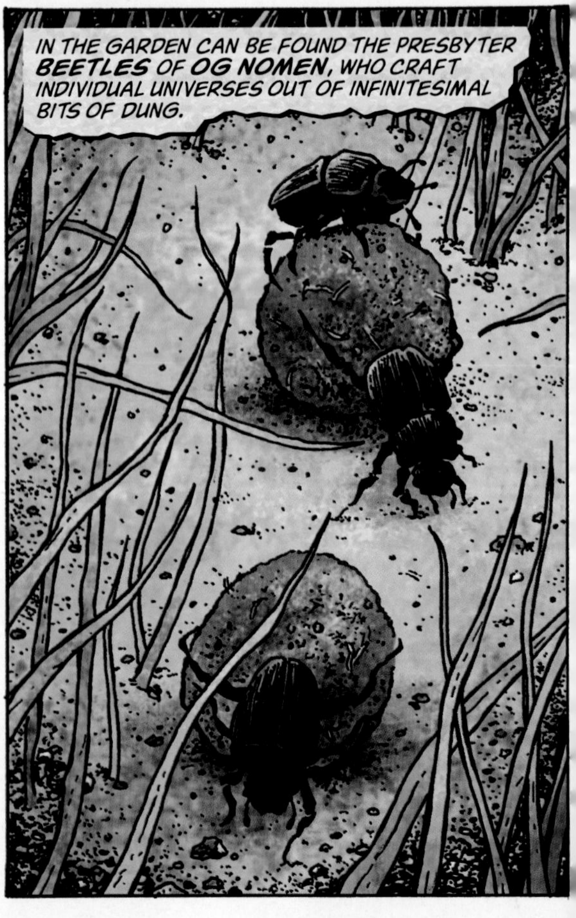
IN THE GARDEN CAN BE FOUND THE PRESBYTER **BEETLES** OF **OG NOMEN**, WHO CRAFT INDIVIDUAL UNIVERSES OUT OF INFINITESIMAL BITS OF DUNG.

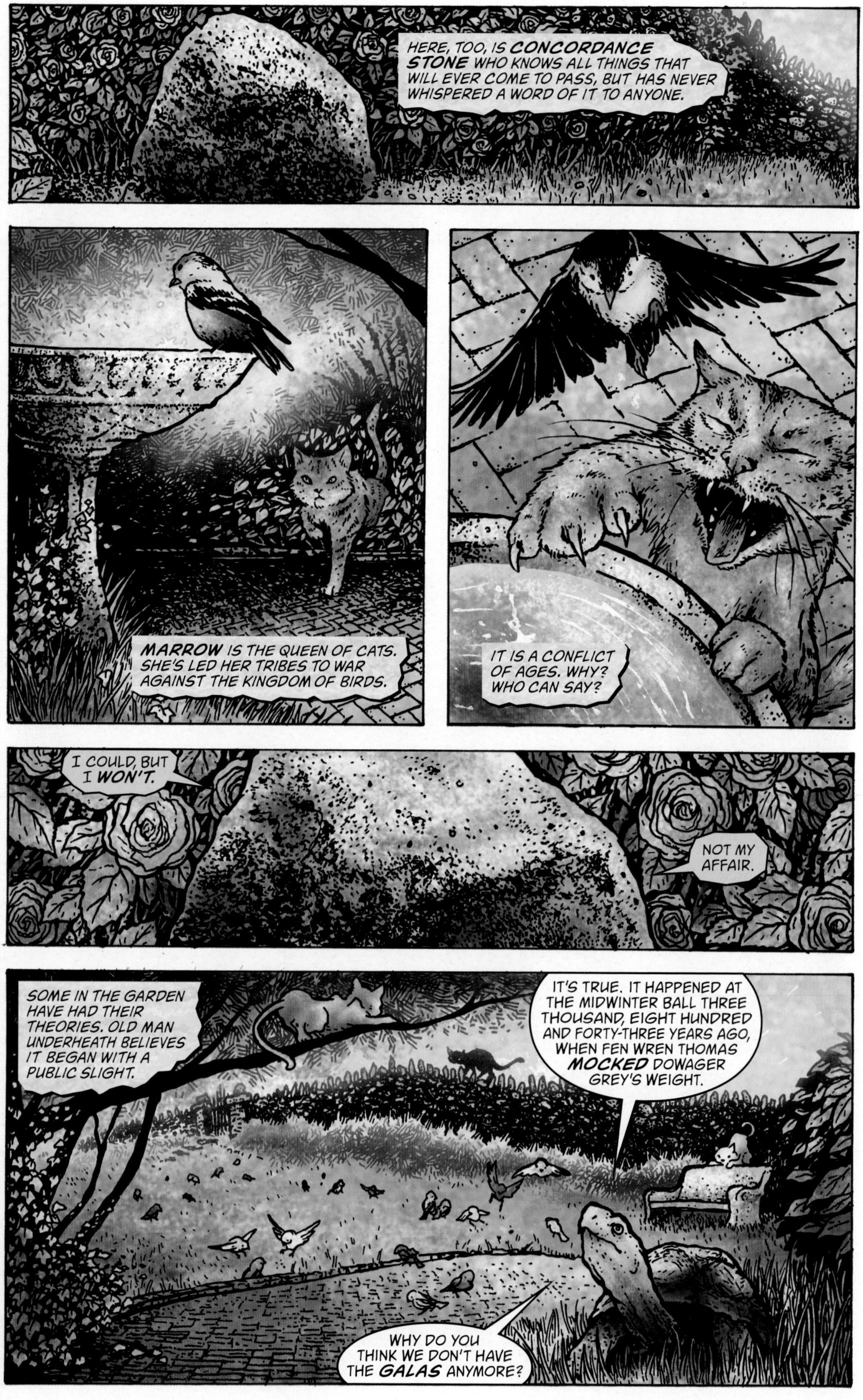
HERE, TOO, IS CONCORDANCE STONE WHO KNOWS ALL THINGS THAT WILL EVER COME TO PASS, BUT HAS NEVER WHISPERED A WORD OF IT TO ANYONE.
MARROW IS THE QUEEN OF CATS. SHE'S LED HER TRIBES TO WAR AGAINST THE KINGDOM OF BIRDS.
IT IS A CONFLICT OF AGES. WHY? WHO CAN SAY?
I COULD, BUT I WON'T.
NOT MY AFFAIR.
SOME IN THE GARDEN HAVE HAD THEIR THEORIES. OLD MAN UNDERHEATH BELIEVES IT BEGAN WITH A PUBLIC SLIGHT.
IT'S TRUE. IT HAPPENED AT THE MIDWINTER BALL THREE THOUSAND, EIGHT HUNDRED AND FORTY-THREE YEARS AGO, WHEN FEN WREN THOMAS MOCKED DOWAGER GREY'S WEIGHT.
WHY DO YOU THINK WE DON'T HAVE THE GALAS ANYMORE?

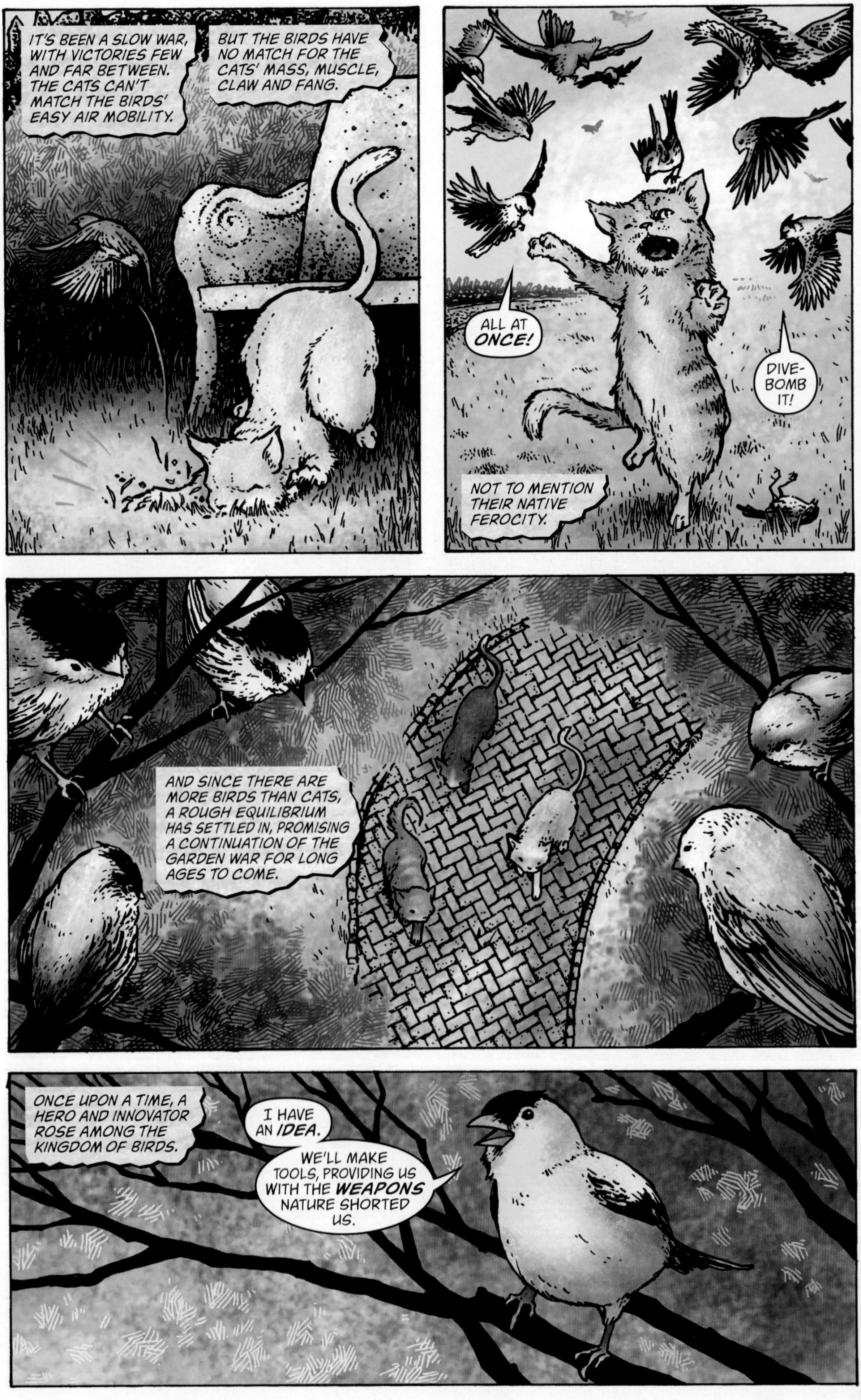
IT'S BEEN A SLOW WAR, WITH VICTORIES FEW AND FAR BETWEEN. THE CATS CAN'T MATCH THE BIRDS' EASY AIR MOBILITY.
BUT THE BIRDS HAVE NO MATCH FOR THE CATS' MASS, MUSCLE, CLAW AND FANG.
ALL AT ONCE!
DIVE-BOMB IT!
NOT TO MENTION THEIR NATIVE FEROCITY.
AND SINCE THERE ARE MORE BIRDS THAN CATS, A ROUGH EQUILIBRIUM HAS SETTLED IN, PROMISING A CONTINUATION OF THE GARDEN WAR FOR LONG AGES TO COME.
ONCE UPON A TIME, A HERO AND INNOVATOR ROSE AMONG THE KINGDOM OF BIRDS.
I HAVE AN IDEA.
WE'LL MAKE TOOLS, PROVIDING US WITH THE WEAPONS NATURE SHORTED US.

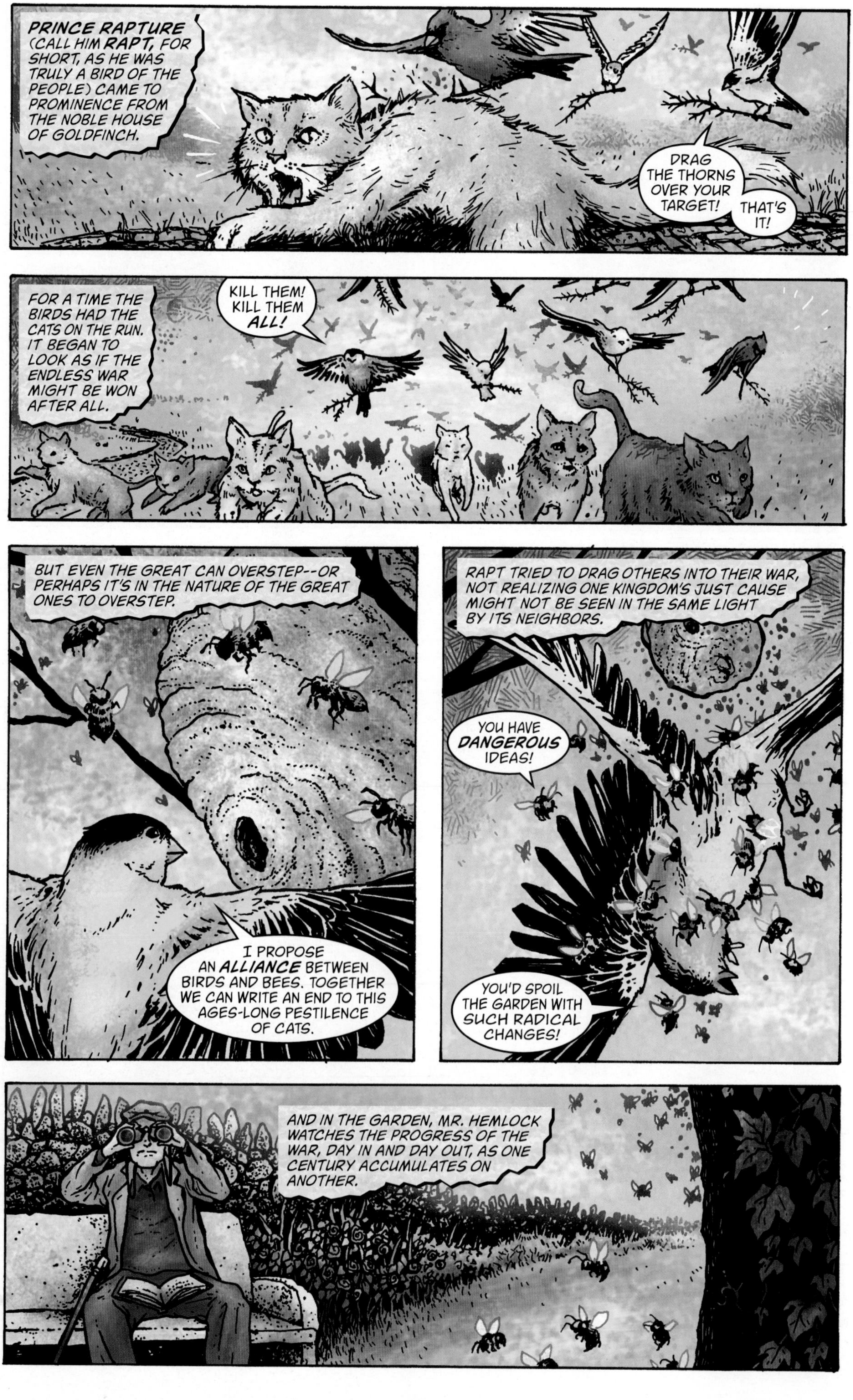
PRINCE RAPTURE (CALL HIM RAPT, FOR SHORT, AS HE WAS TRULY A BIRD OF THE PEOPLE) CAME TO PROMINENCE FROM THE NOBLE HOUSE OF GOLDFINCH.
DRAG THE THORNS OVER YOUR TARGET!
THAT'S IT!
FOR A TIME THE BIRDS HAD THE CATS ON THE RUN. IT BEGAN TO LOOK AS IF THE ENDLESS WAR MIGHT BE WON AFTER ALL.
KILL THEM! KILL THEM ALL!
BUT EVEN THE GREAT CAN OVERSTEP--OR PERHAPS IT'S IN THE NATURE OF THE GREAT ONES TO OVERSTEP.
I PROPOSE AN ALLIANCE BETWEEN BIRDS AND BEES. TOGETHER WE CAN WRITE AN END TO THIS AGES-LONG PESTILENCE OF CATS.
RAPT TRIED TO DRAG OTHERS INTO THEIR WAR, NOT REALIZING ONE KINGDOM'S JUST CAUSE MIGHT NOT BE SEEN IN THE SAME LIGHT BY ITS NEIGHBORS.
YOU HAVE DANGEROUS IDEAS!
YOU'D SPOIL THE GARDEN WITH SUCH RADICAL CHANGES!
AND IN THE GARDEN, MR. HEMLOCK WATCHES THE PROGRESS OF THE WAR, DAY IN AND DAY OUT, AS ONE CENTURY ACCUMULATES ON ANOTHER.

HE WATCHES, HE TAKES NOTES, AND HE KEEPS A CAREFUL TALLY OF THE DEAD. WHY DOES HE DO THIS?

BECAUSE MR. HEMLOCK IS THE THIRTEENTH SON OF FATE (WHO ALSO HAS NINE DAUGHTERS, THANK YOU FOR ASKING) AND THIS IS HIS PART OF THE FAMILY BUSINESS.

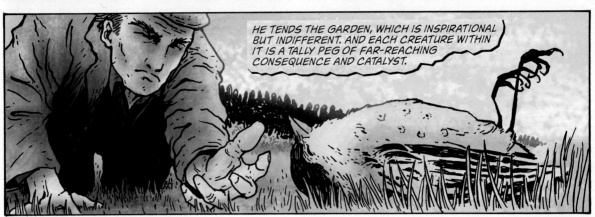

HE TENDS THE GARDEN, WHICH IS INSPIRATIONAL BUT INDIFFERENT. AND EACH CREATURE WITHIN IT IS A TALLY PEG OF FAR-REACHING CONSEQUENCE AND CATALYST.

HE KNOWS THAT IF THE BIRDS EVER WIN THE WAR, POETRY WILL DISAPPEAR FROM THE COUNTLESS UNIVERSES OUTSIDE THE GARDEN.

AND IF THE CATS WIN, SECOND THOUGHTS WILL DIE, LEAVING ONLY FIRST IMPULSE.

THIS IS TRULY A WAR OF MOMENT, THEN. BUT HEMLOCK IS READY TO STEP IN, SHOULD IT EVER LOOK AS IF ONE SIDE IS ABOUT TO GAIN THE UPPER HAND.

GOOD JOB, GENTLEBEES. GRANDLY *DONE*. THANK YOU FOR HELPING ME OUT.

OUR PLEASURE, SIR, AS *ALWAYS*.

THERE'S THAT LIST I SPOKE OF EARLIER — THE LIST OF ALL THE INCREDIBLE COMICS ARTISTS I COULD ONLY HOPE AND DREAM OF GETTING TO WORK WITH ONE DAY. To say that the immortal Bernie Wrightson was high on my list would be a criminal understatement. When he became available to do one of the HOUSE OF MYSTERY stories I was in hog heaven. The intrepid Shelly Bond set up a call between us.

"What do you want to draw?" I asked, hoping he couldn't detect how intimidated I was to be talking to him. "Or what are you tired unto death of drawing? Either way, I'm confident I can provide a story to suit."

"I was going to ask the same of you," he said. "What did you have in mind to write?"

This turned into a discourse on his life and work. Perhaps a bit too enthusiastically, I spoke of each and every one of his past projects, including his much loved *Monsters* coloring book and my favorite of all of his paintings: *Bad Doings at Knuckledown Lonesome*, depicting a group of desperate villagers trying to put a vampire a bit more resolutely into his grave (which also inspired my choice of title for this collection).

"Let's do that then," Wrightson said. "Let's do an old-fashioned monster rally."

And so we did.

GOTHIC ROMANCE

Art by
Bernie Wrightson

Colors by
Lee Loughridge

Letters by
Todd Klein

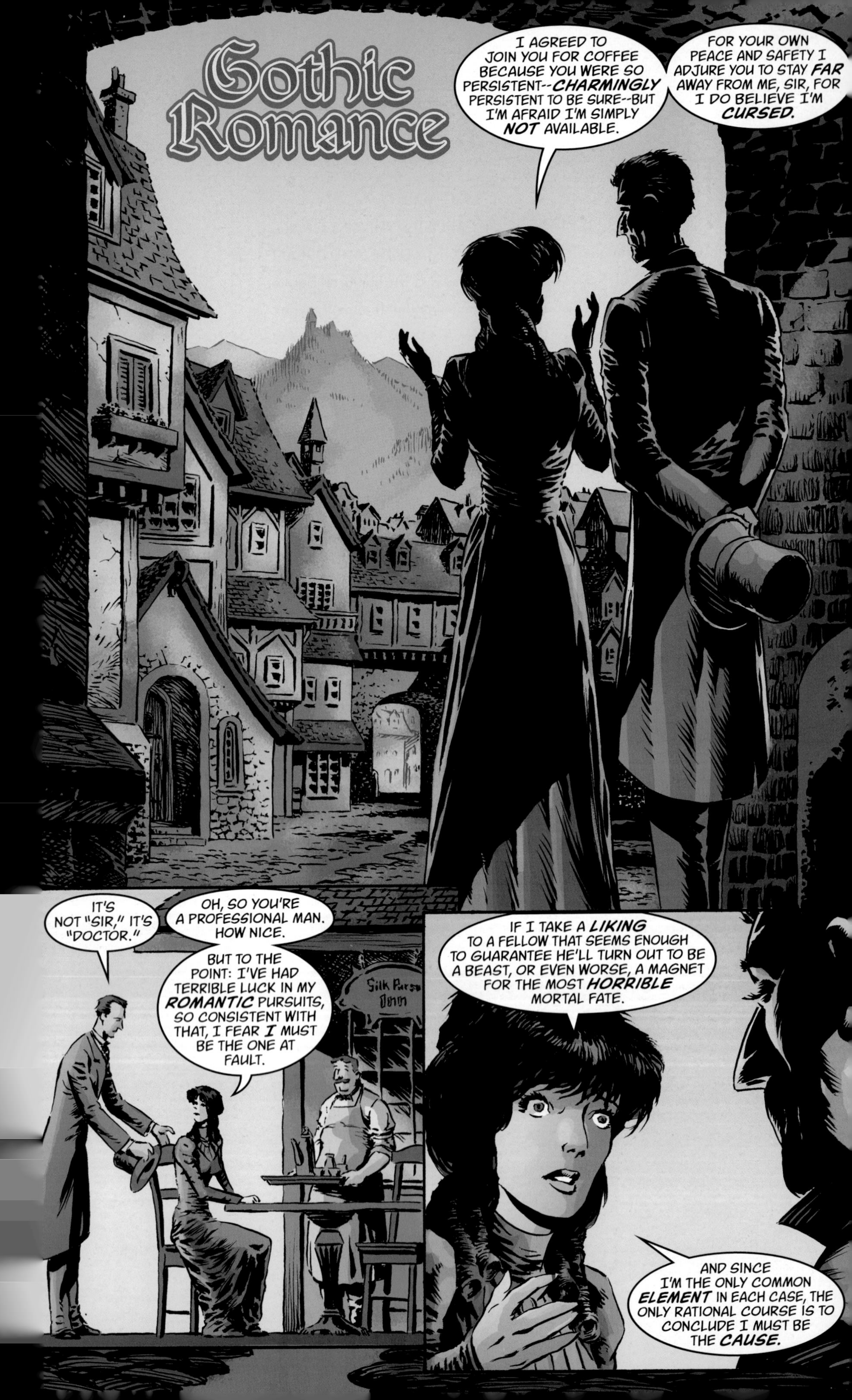
Gothic Romance
I AGREED TO JOIN YOU FOR COFFEE BECAUSE YOU WERE SO PERSISTENT--CHARMINGLY PERSISTENT TO BE SURE--BUT I'M AFRAID I'M SIMPLY NOT AVAILABLE.
FOR YOUR OWN PEACE AND SAFETY I ADJURE YOU TO STAY FAR AWAY FROM ME, SIR, FOR I DO BELIEVE I'M CURSED.
IT'S NOT "SIR," IT'S "DOCTOR."
OH, SO YOU'RE A PROFESSIONAL MAN. HOW NICE.
BUT TO THE POINT: I'VE HAD TERRIBLE LUCK IN MY ROMANTIC PURSUITS, SO CONSISTENT WITH THAT, I FEAR I MUST BE THE ONE AT FAULT.
IF I TAKE A LIKING TO A FELLOW THAT SEEMS ENOUGH TO GUARANTEE HE'LL TURN OUT TO BE A BEAST, OR EVEN WORSE, A MAGNET FOR THE MOST HORRIBLE MORTAL FATE.
AND SINCE I'M THE ONLY COMMON ELEMENT IN EACH CASE, THE ONLY RATIONAL COURSE IS TO CONCLUDE I MUST BE THE CAUSE.

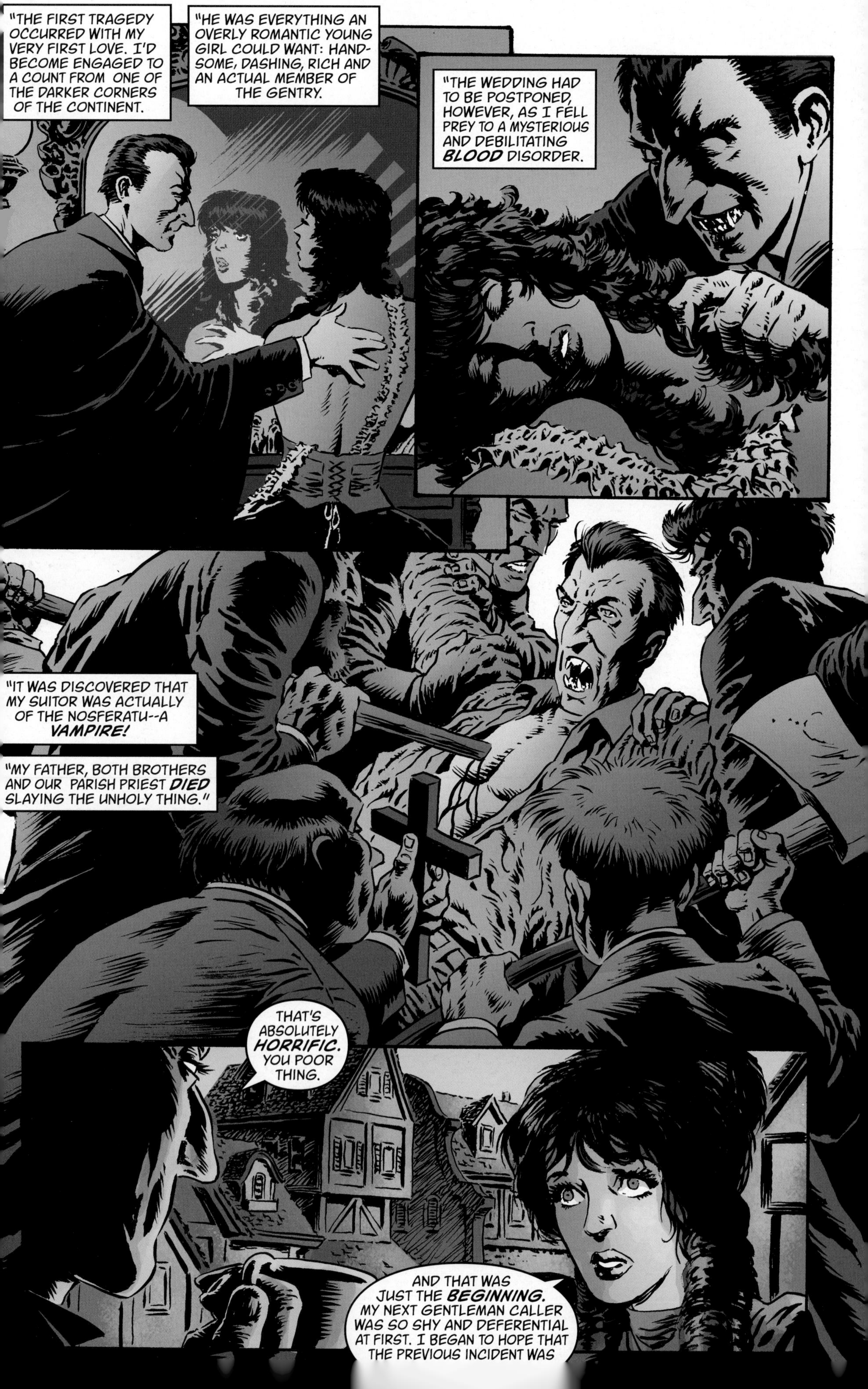
"THE FIRST TRAGEDY OCCURRED WITH MY VERY FIRST LOVE. I'D BECOME ENGAGED TO A COUNT FROM ONE OF THE DARKER CORNERS OF THE CONTINENT.
"HE WAS EVERYTHING AN OVERLY ROMANTIC YOUNG GIRL COULD WANT: HANDSOME, DASHING, RICH AND AN ACTUAL MEMBER OF THE GENTRY.
"THE WEDDING HAD TO BE POSTPONED, HOWEVER, AS I FELL PREY TO A MYSTERIOUS AND DEBILITATING ***BLOOD*** DISORDER.
"IT WAS DISCOVERED THAT MY SUITOR WAS ACTUALLY OF THE NOSFERATU--A ***VAMPIRE!***
"MY FATHER, BOTH BROTHERS AND OUR PARISH PRIEST ***DIED*** SLAYING THE UNHOLY THING."
THAT'S ABSOLUTELY ***HORRIFIC.*** YOU POOR THING.
AND THAT WAS JUST THE ***BEGINNING.*** MY NEXT GENTLEMAN CALLER WAS SO SHY AND DEFERENTIAL AT FIRST. I BEGAN TO HOPE THAT THE PREVIOUS INCIDENT WAS

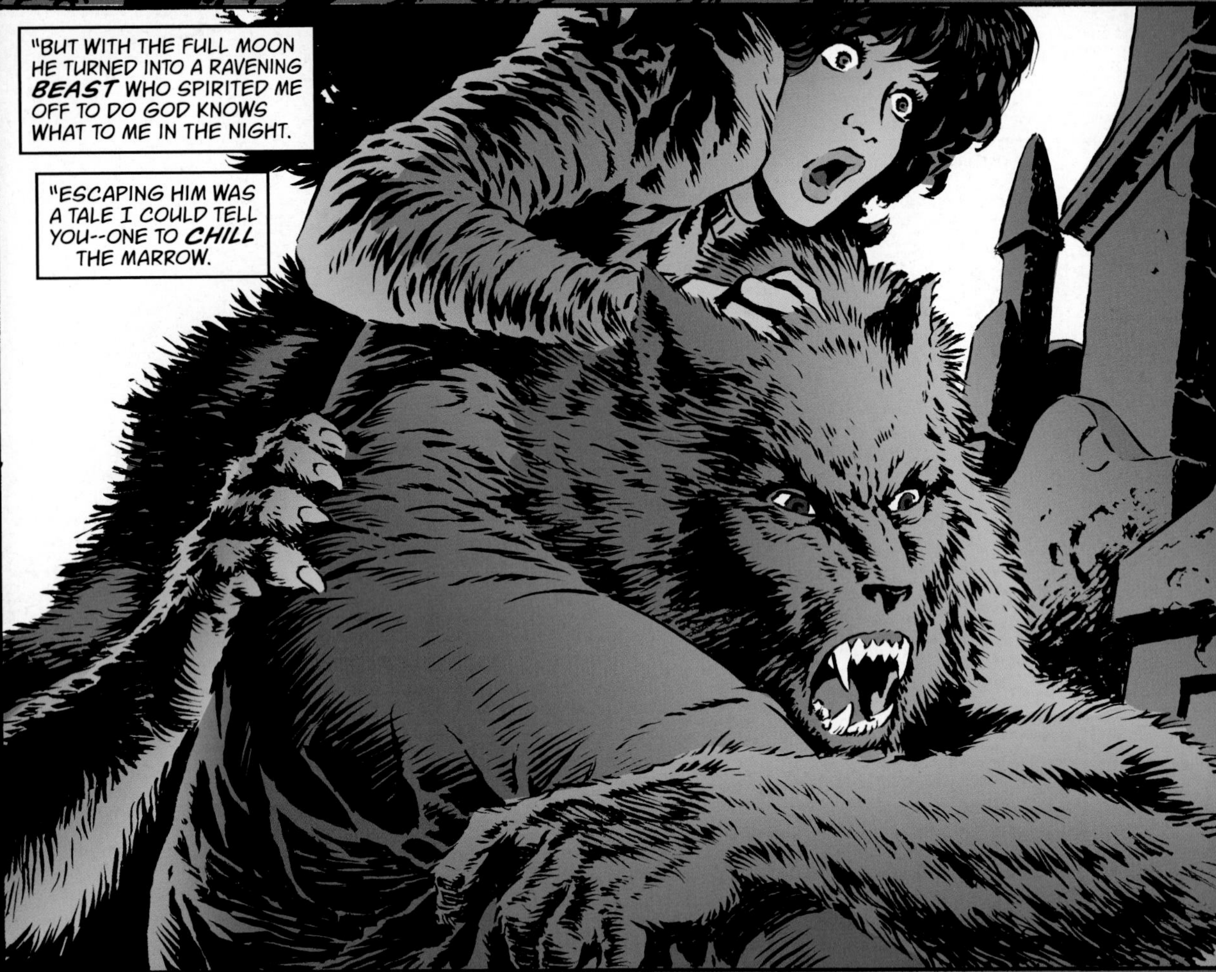
"BUT WITH THE FULL MOON HE TURNED INTO A RAVENING BEAST WHO SPIRITED ME OFF TO DO GOD KNOWS WHAT TO ME IN THE NIGHT.
"ESCAPING HIM WAS A TALE I COULD TELL YOU--ONE TO CHILL THE MARROW.
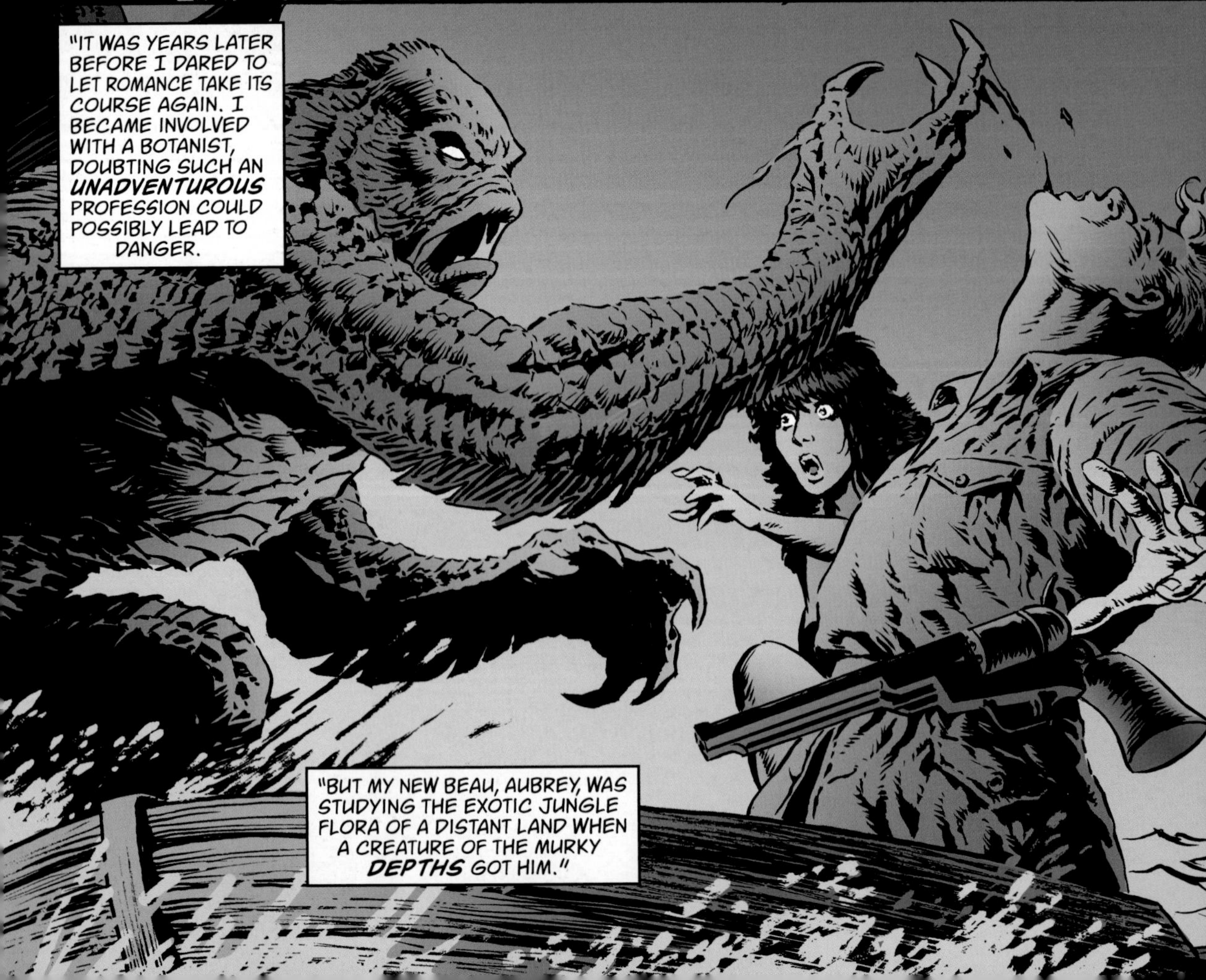
"IT WAS YEARS LATER BEFORE I DARED TO LET ROMANCE TAKE ITS COURSE AGAIN. I BECAME INVOLVED WITH A BOTANIST, DOUBTING SUCH AN UNADVENTUROUS PROFESSION COULD POSSIBLY LEAD TO DANGER.
"BUT MY NEW BEAU, AUBREY, WAS STUDYING THE EXOTIC JUNGLE FLORA OF A DISTANT LAND WHEN A CREATURE OF THE MURKY DEPTHS GOT HIM."

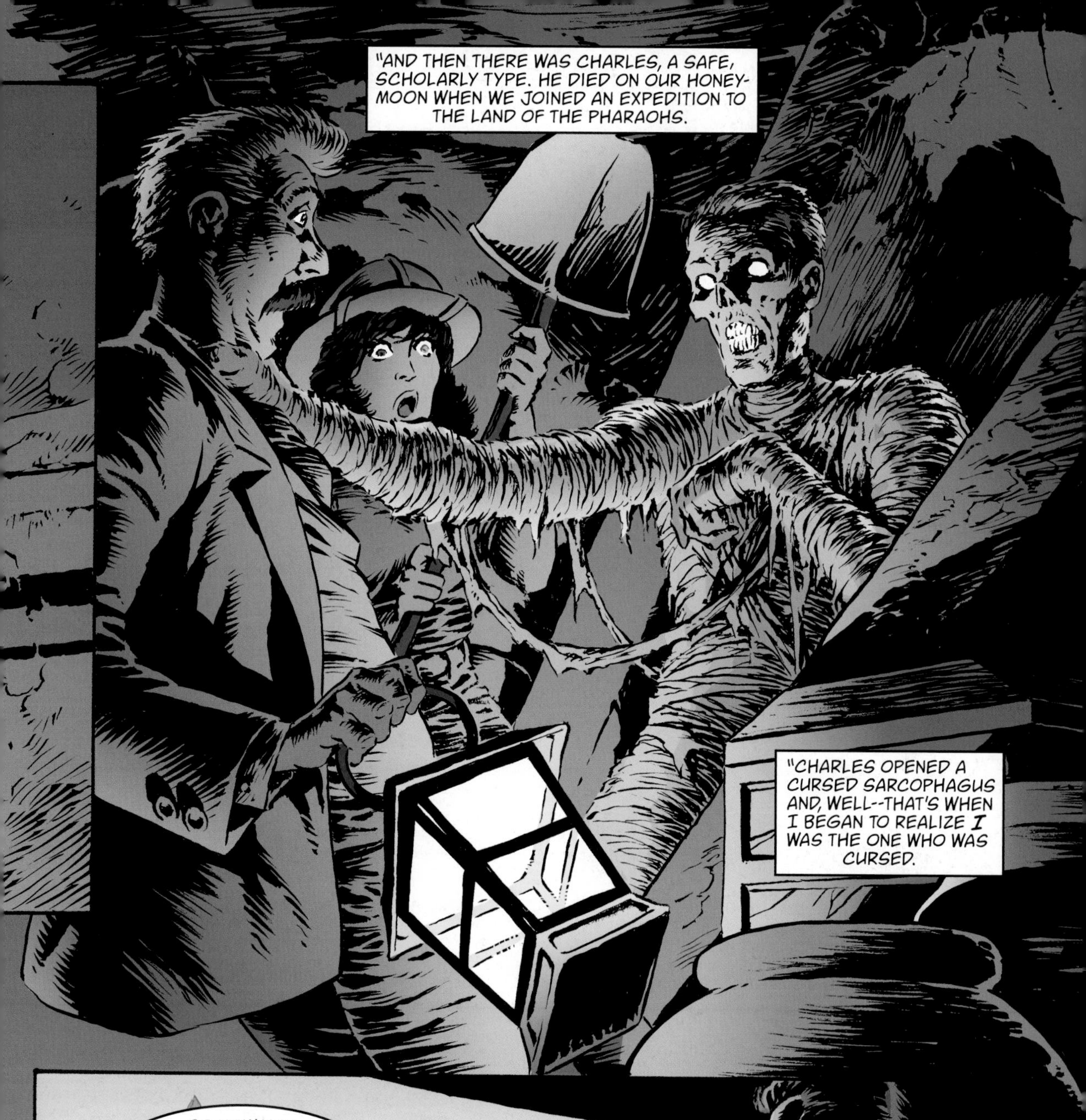
"AND THEN THERE WAS CHARLES, A SAFE, SCHOLARLY TYPE. HE DIED ON OUR HONEY-MOON WHEN WE JOINED AN EXPEDITION TO THE LAND OF THE PHARAOHS.
"CHARLES OPENED A CURSED SARCOPHAGUS AND, WELL--THAT'S WHEN I BEGAN TO REALIZE *I* WAS THE ONE WHO WAS CURSED.

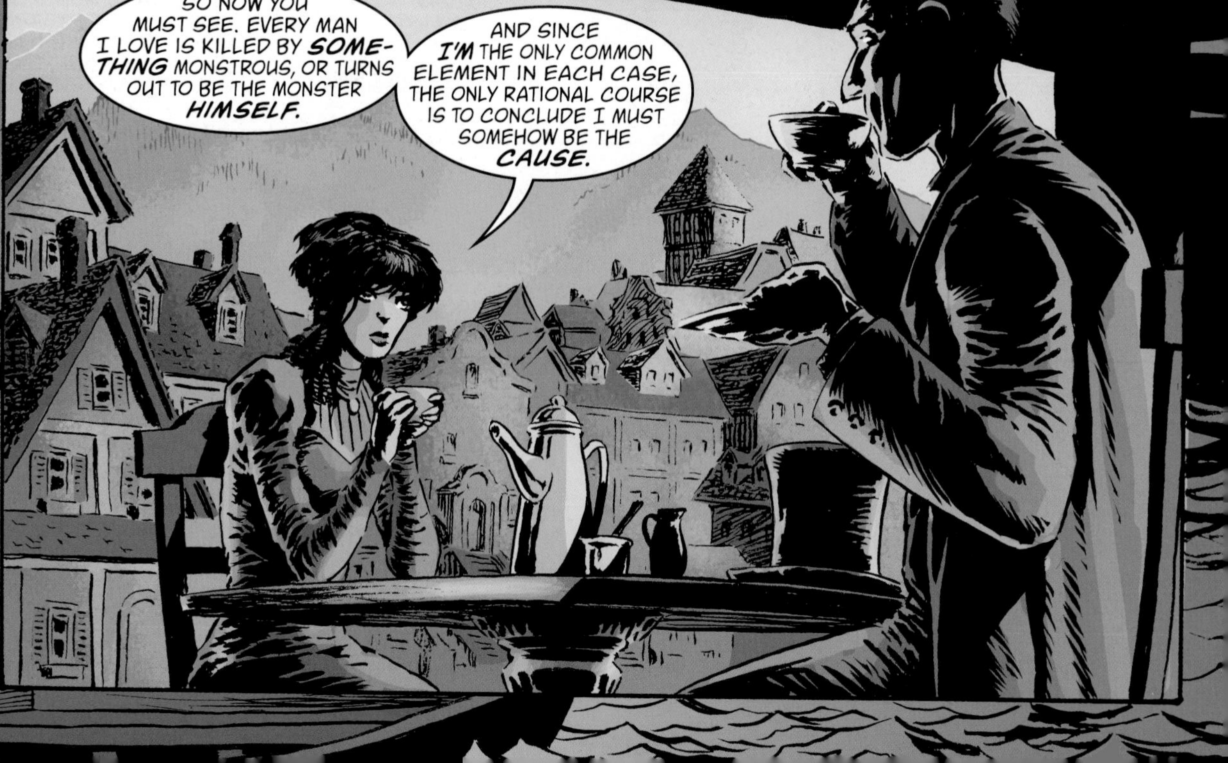
SO NOW YOU MUST SEE. EVERY MAN I LOVE IS KILLED BY ***SOME-THING*** MONSTROUS, OR TURNS OUT TO BE THE MONSTER ***HIMSELF.***
AND SINCE ***I'M*** THE ONLY COMMON ELEMENT IN EACH CASE, THE ONLY RATIONAL COURSE IS TO CONCLUDE I MUST SOMEHOW BE THE ***CAUSE.***

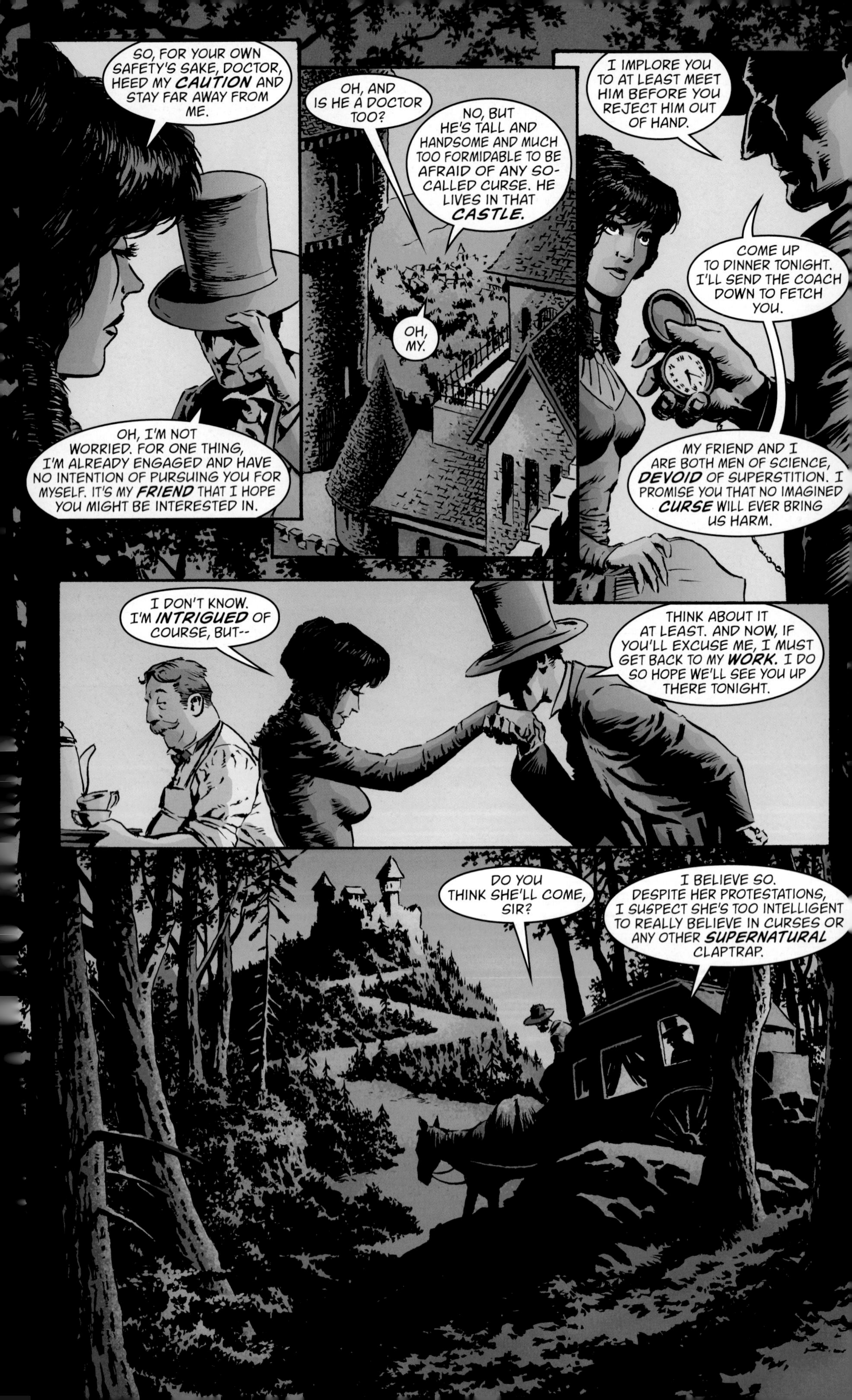
SO, FOR YOUR OWN SAFETY'S SAKE, DOCTOR, HEED MY **CAUTION** AND STAY FAR AWAY FROM ME.
OH, I'M NOT WORRIED. FOR ONE THING, I'M ALREADY ENGAGED AND HAVE NO INTENTION OF PURSUING YOU FOR MYSELF. IT'S MY **FRIEND** THAT I HOPE YOU MIGHT BE INTERESTED IN.
OH, AND IS HE A DOCTOR TOO?
NO, BUT HE'S TALL AND HANDSOME AND MUCH TOO FORMIDABLE TO BE AFRAID OF ANY SO-CALLED CURSE. HE LIVES IN THAT **CASTLE.**
OH, MY.
I IMPLORE YOU TO AT LEAST MEET HIM BEFORE YOU REJECT HIM OUT OF HAND.
COME UP TO DINNER TONIGHT. I'LL SEND THE COACH DOWN TO FETCH YOU.
MY FRIEND AND I ARE BOTH MEN OF SCIENCE, **DEVOID** OF SUPERSTITION. I PROMISE YOU THAT NO IMAGINED **CURSE** WILL EVER BRING US HARM.
I DON'T KNOW. I'M **INTRIGUED** OF COURSE, BUT--
THINK ABOUT IT AT LEAST. AND NOW, IF YOU'LL EXCUSE ME, I MUST GET BACK TO MY **WORK.** I DO SO HOPE WE'LL SEE YOU UP THERE TONIGHT.
DO YOU THINK SHE'LL COME, SIR?
I BELIEVE SO. DESPITE HER PROTESTATIONS, I SUSPECT SHE'S TOO INTELLIGENT TO REALLY BELIEVE IN CURSES OR ANY OTHER **SUPERNATURAL** CLAPTRAP.

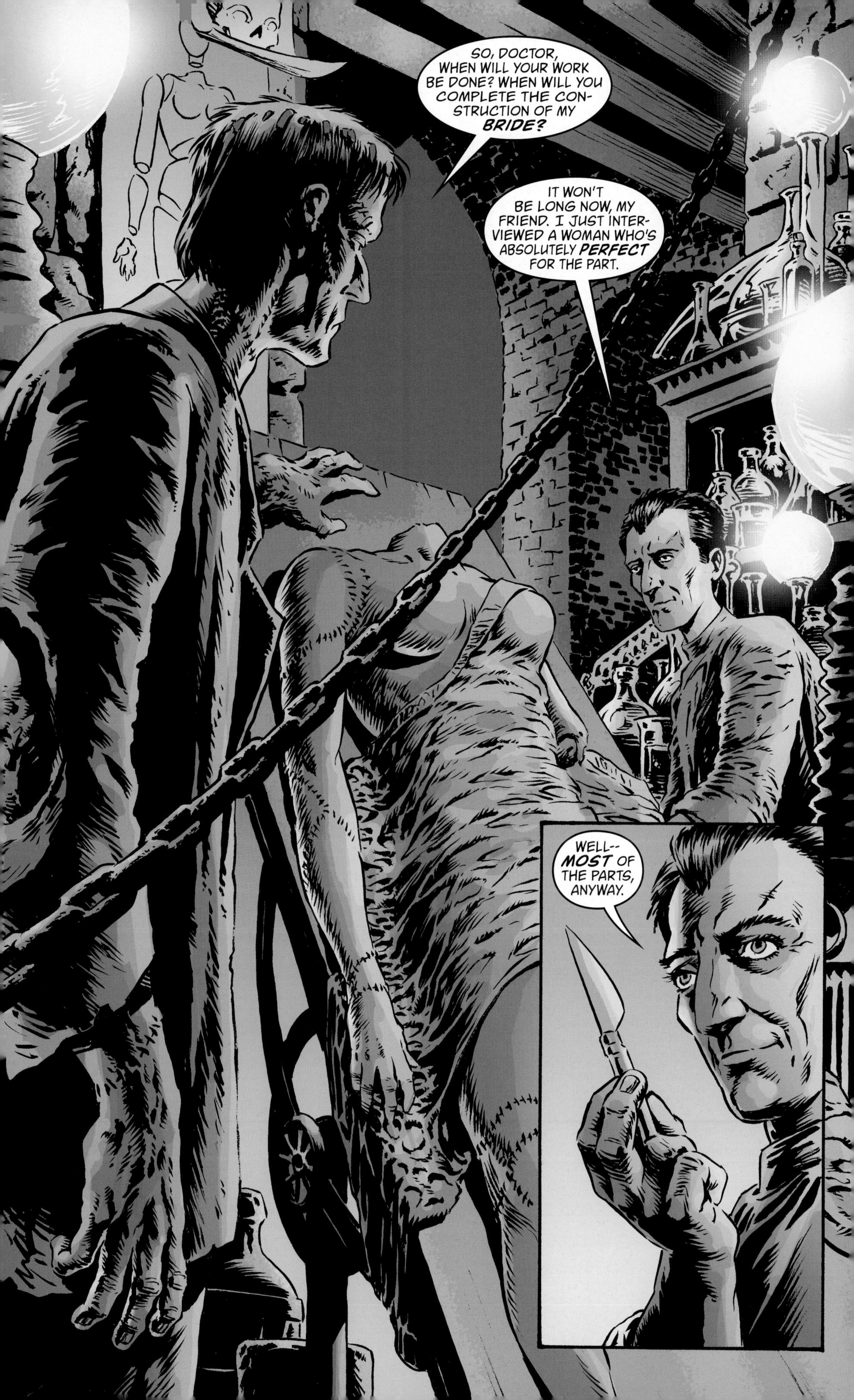
SO, DOCTOR, WHEN WILL YOUR WORK BE DONE? WHEN WILL YOU COMPLETE THE CON-STRUCTION OF MY ***BRIDE?***
IT WON'T BE LONG NOW, MY FRIEND. I JUST INTER-VIEWED A WOMAN WHO'S ABSOLUTELY ***PERFECT*** FOR THE PART.
WELL-- ***MOST*** OF THE PARTS, ANYWAY.

THIS WAS THE LUCKY 13TH ISSUE OF *HOUSE OF MYSTERY* and the idea was that every story within it would be, in some manner or other, a rumination on the number thirteen. I've often stated, as a point of personal philosophy, "If it's worth doing, it's worth overdoing." And so it was.

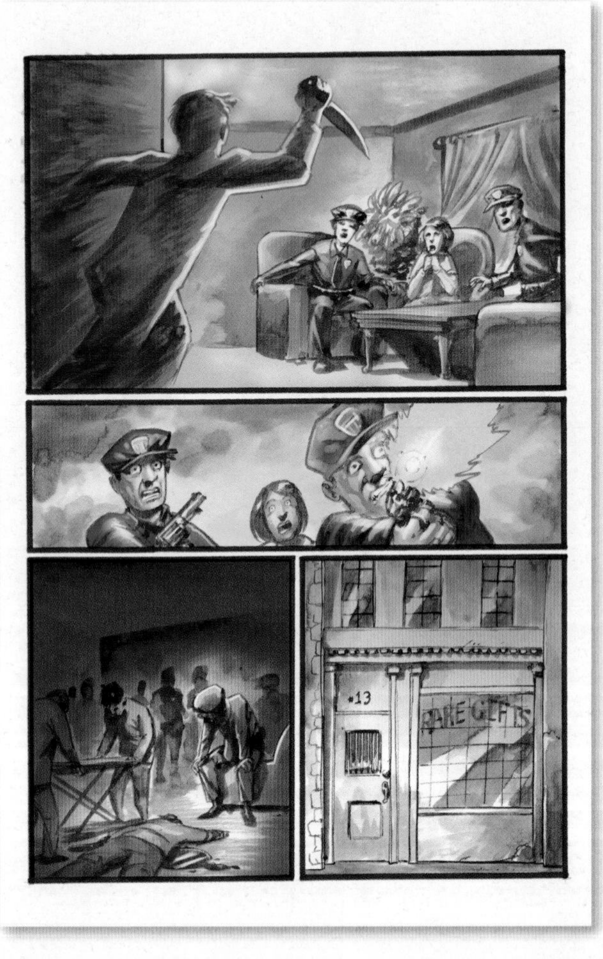
RARE GIFTS

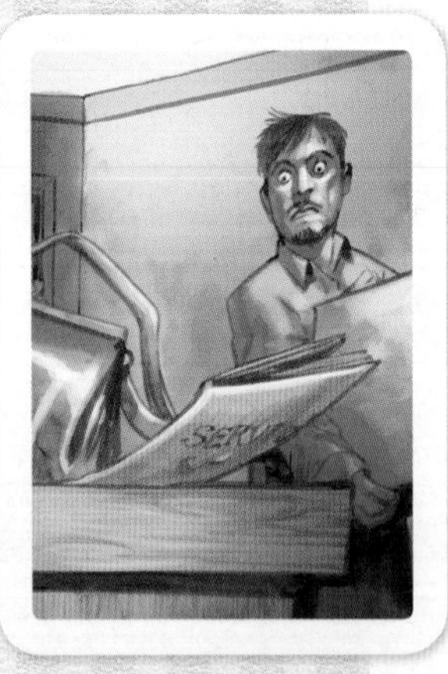

THE LACE ANNIVERSARY

ART BY
Eric Powell

LETTERS BY
Todd Klein

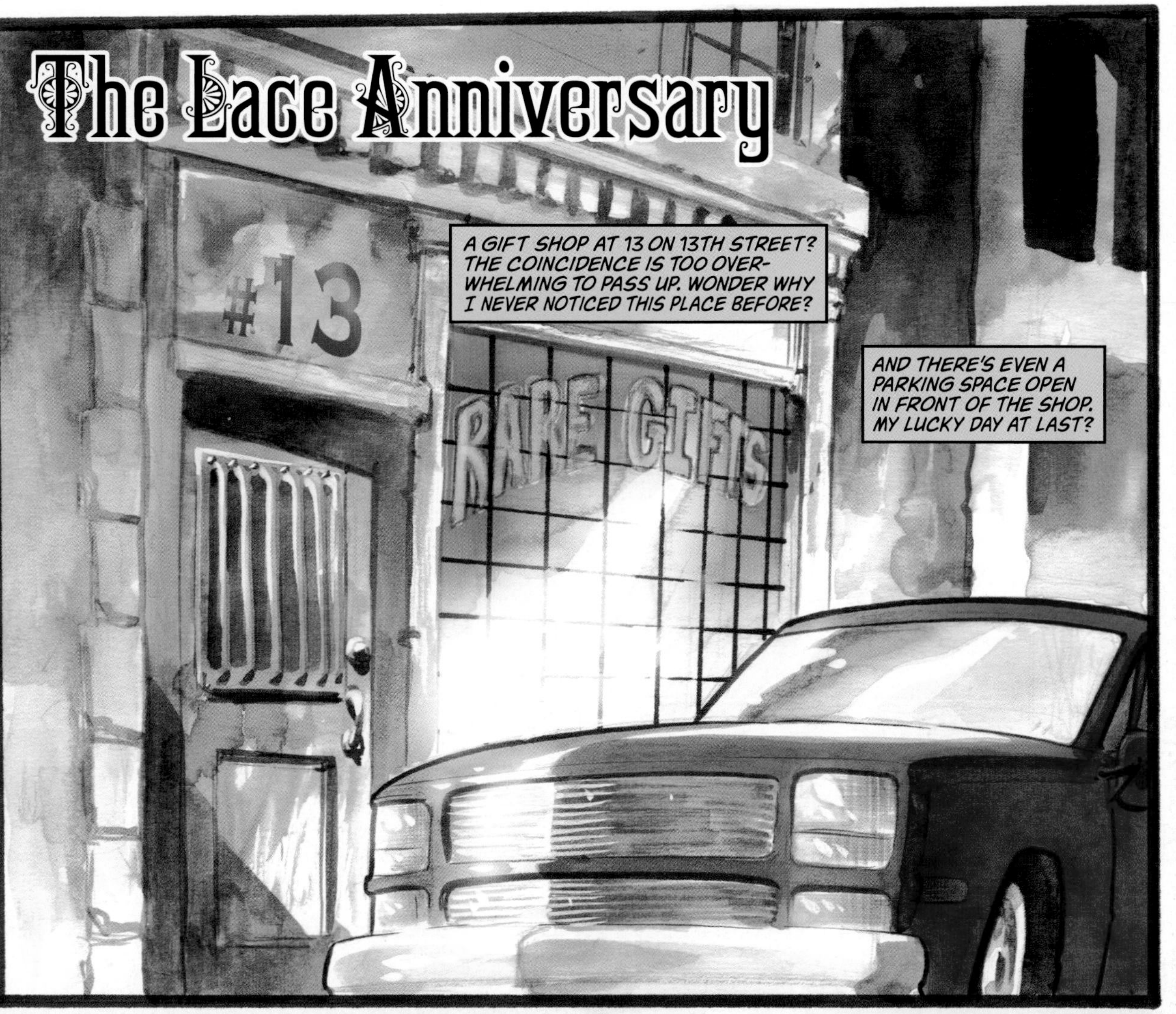
The Lace Anniversary
A GIFT SHOP AT 13 ON 13TH STREET? THE COINCIDENCE IS TOO OVER-WHELMING TO PASS UP. WONDER WHY I NEVER NOTICED THIS PLACE BEFORE?
#13
RARE GIFTS
AND THERE'S EVEN A PARKING SPACE OPEN IN FRONT OF THE SHOP. MY LUCKY DAY AT LAST?

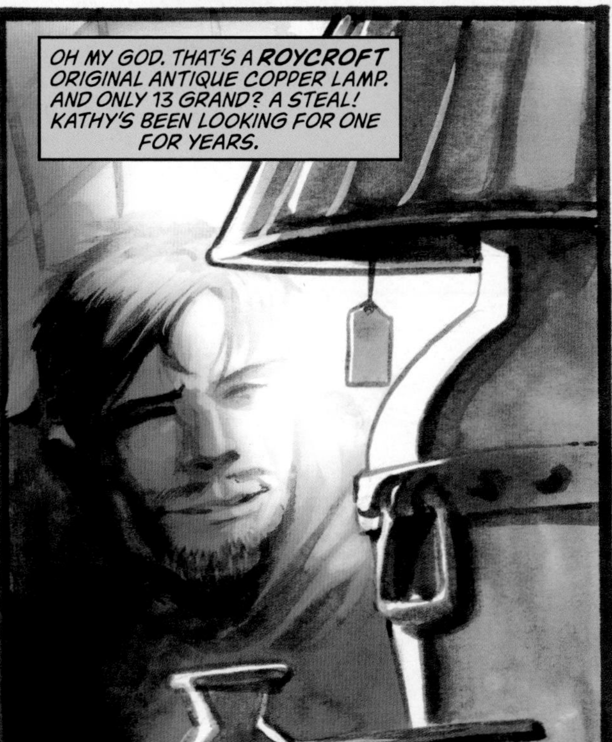
OH MY GOD. THAT'S A ROYCROFT ORIGINAL ANTIQUE COPPER LAMP. AND ONLY 13 GRAND? A STEAL! KATHY'S BEEN LOOKING FOR ONE FOR YEARS.

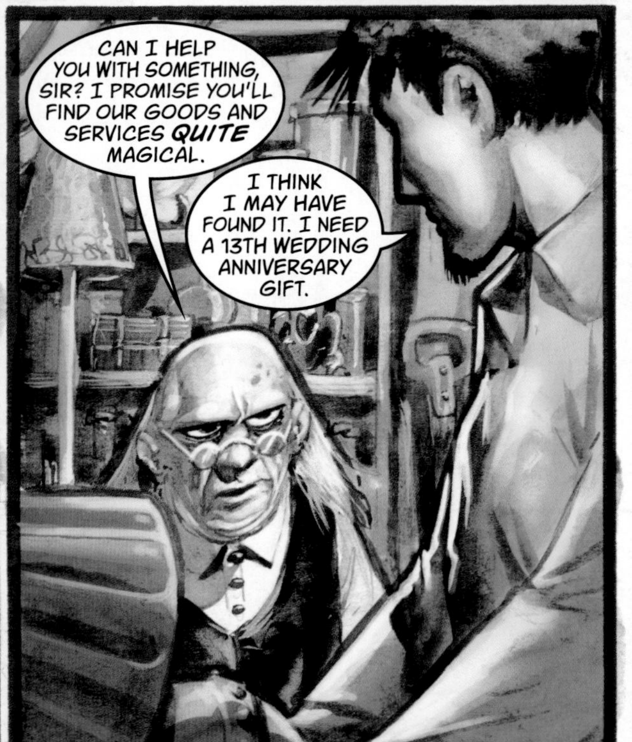
CAN I HELP YOU WITH SOMETHING, SIR? I PROMISE YOU'LL FIND OUR GOODS AND SERVICES QUITE MAGICAL.
I THINK I MAY HAVE FOUND IT. I NEED A 13TH WEDDING ANNIVERSARY GIFT.
13

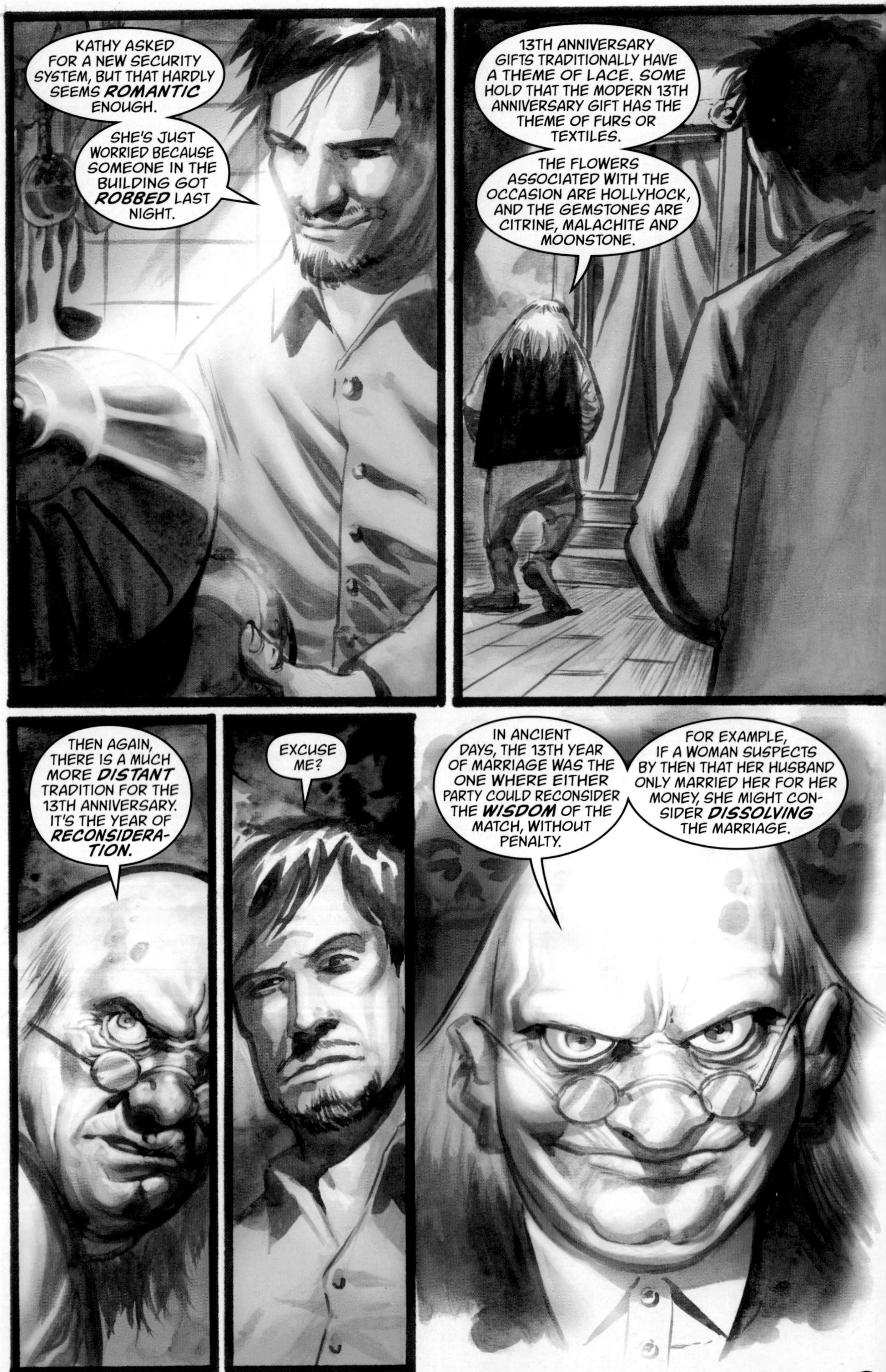
KATHY ASKED FOR A NEW SECURITY SYSTEM, BUT THAT HARDLY SEEMS ROMANTIC ENOUGH.
SHE'S JUST WORRIED BECAUSE SOMEONE IN THE BUILDING GOT ROBBED LAST NIGHT.
13TH ANNIVERSARY GIFTS TRADITIONALLY HAVE A THEME OF LACE. SOME HOLD THAT THE MODERN 13TH ANNIVERSARY GIFT HAS THE THEME OF FURS OR TEXTILES.
THE FLOWERS ASSOCIATED WITH THE OCCASION ARE HOLLYHOCK, AND THE GEMSTONES ARE CITRINE, MALACHITE AND MOONSTONE.
THEN AGAIN, THERE IS A MUCH MORE DISTANT TRADITION FOR THE 13TH ANNIVERSARY. IT'S THE YEAR OF RECONSIDERA-TION.
EXCUSE ME?
IN ANCIENT DAYS, THE 13TH YEAR OF MARRIAGE WAS THE ONE WHERE EITHER PARTY COULD RECONSIDER THE WISDOM OF THE MATCH, WITHOUT PENALTY.
FOR EXAMPLE, IF A WOMAN SUSPECTS BY THEN THAT HER HUSBAND ONLY MARRIED HER FOR HER MONEY, SHE MIGHT CON-SIDER DISSOLVING THE MARRIAGE.
13

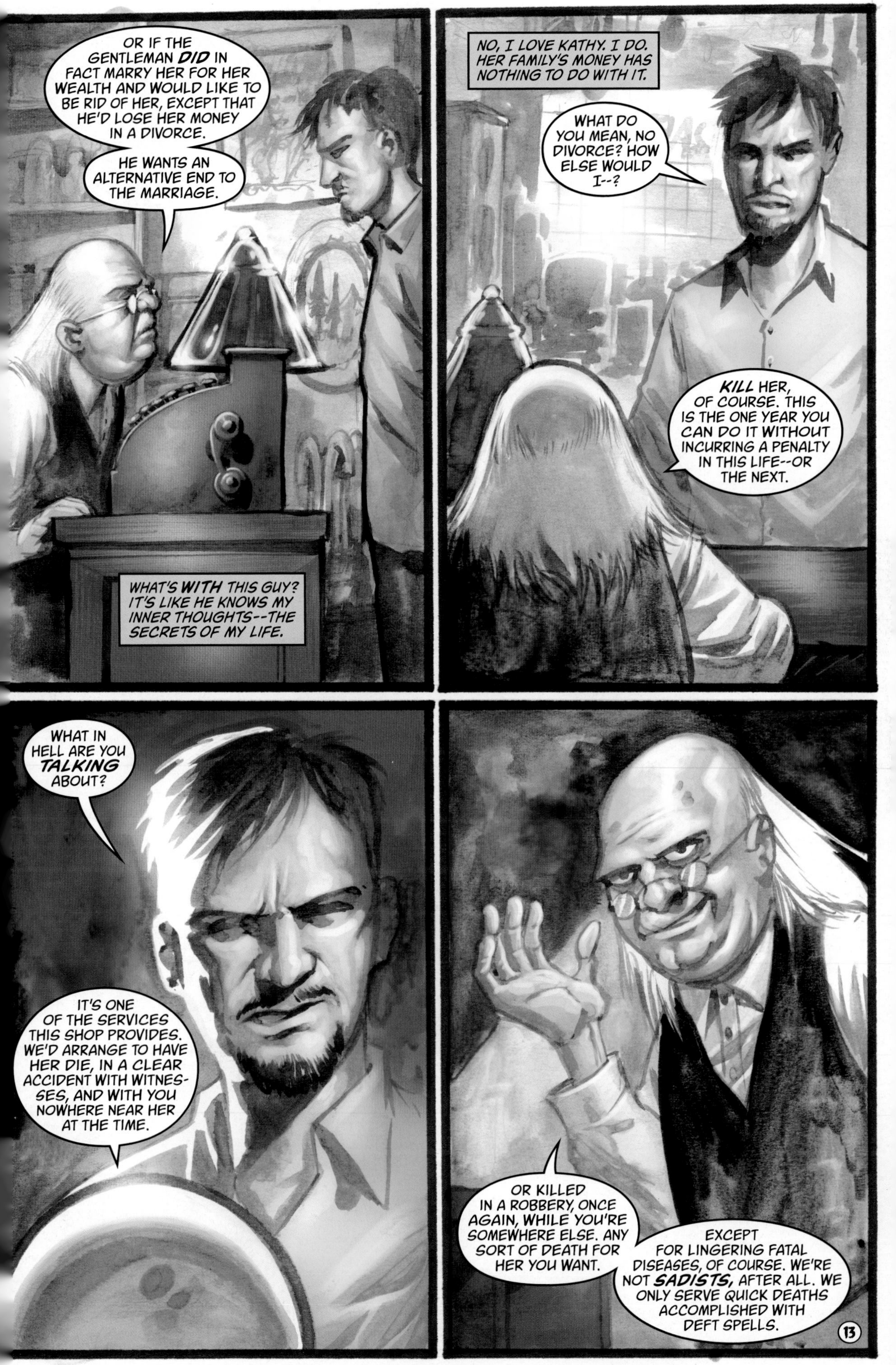
OR IF THE GENTLEMAN DID IN FACT MARRY HER FOR HER WEALTH AND WOULD LIKE TO BE RID OF HER, EXCEPT THAT HE'D LOSE HER MONEY IN A DIVORCE.
HE WANTS AN ALTERNATIVE END TO THE MARRIAGE.
WHAT'S WITH THIS GUY? IT'S LIKE HE KNOWS MY INNER THOUGHTS--THE SECRETS OF MY LIFE.
NO, I LOVE KATHY. I DO. HER FAMILY'S MONEY HAS NOTHING TO DO WITH IT.
WHAT DO YOU MEAN, NO DIVORCE? HOW ELSE WOULD I--?
KILL HER, OF COURSE. THIS IS THE ONE YEAR YOU CAN DO IT WITHOUT INCURRING A PENALTY IN THIS LIFE--OR THE NEXT.
WHAT IN HELL ARE YOU TALKING ABOUT?
IT'S ONE OF THE SERVICES THIS SHOP PROVIDES. WE'D ARRANGE TO HAVE HER DIE, IN A CLEAR ACCIDENT WITH WITNESSES, AND WITH YOU NOWHERE NEAR HER AT THE TIME.
OR KILLED IN A ROBBERY, ONCE AGAIN, WHILE YOU'RE SOMEWHERE ELSE. ANY SORT OF DEATH FOR HER YOU WANT.
EXCEPT FOR LINGERING FATAL DISEASES, OF COURSE. WE'RE NOT SADISTS, AFTER ALL. WE ONLY SERVE QUICK DEATHS ACCOMPLISHED WITH DEFT SPELLS.
13

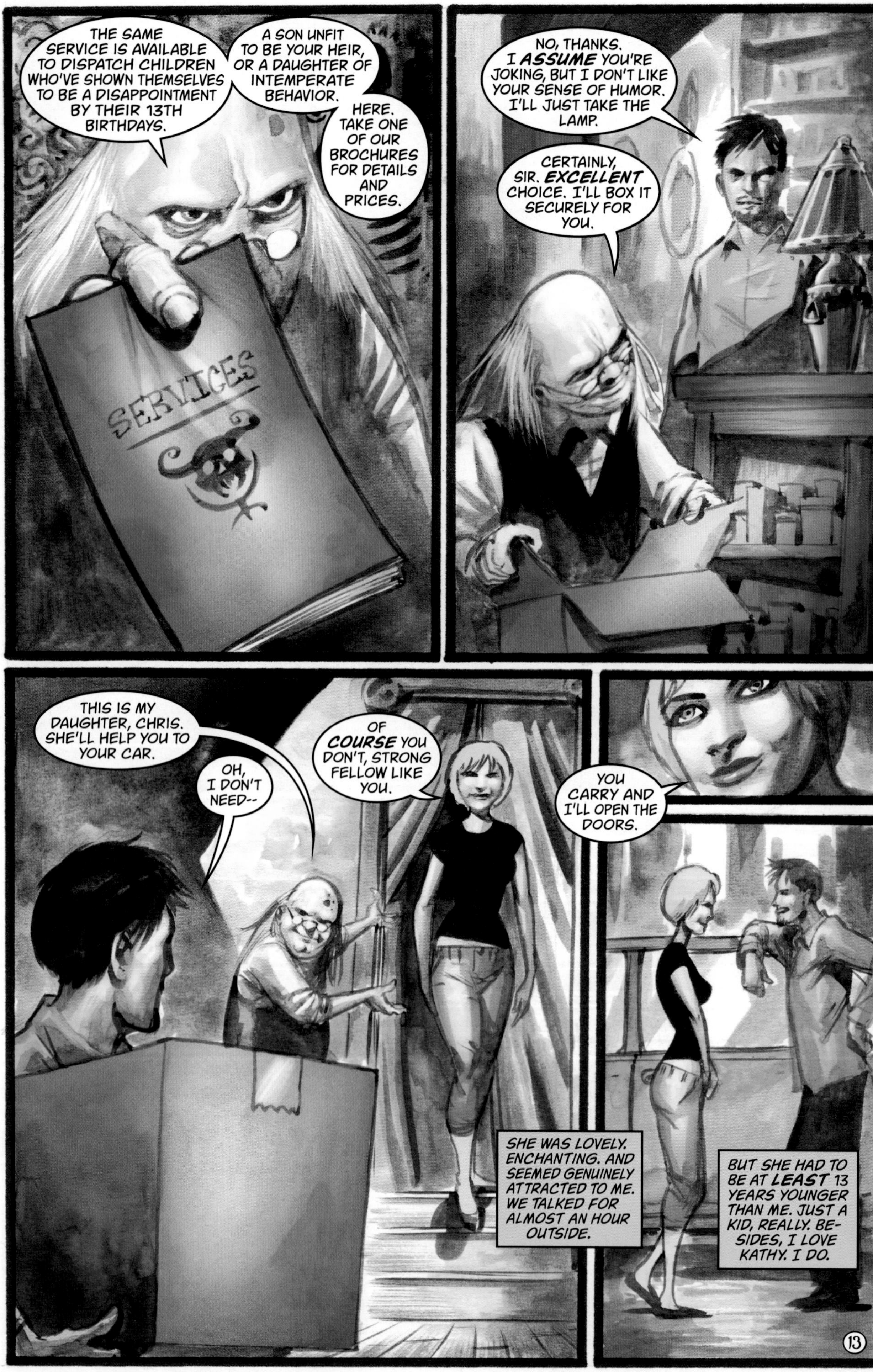
THE SAME SERVICE IS AVAILABLE TO DISPATCH CHILDREN WHO'VE SHOWN THEMSELVES TO BE A DISAPPOINTMENT BY THEIR 13TH BIRTHDAYS.
A SON UNFIT TO BE YOUR HEIR, OR A DAUGHTER OF INTEMPERATE BEHAVIOR.
HERE. TAKE ONE OF OUR BROCHURES FOR DETAILS AND PRICES.
SERVICES
NO, THANKS. I ASSUME YOU'RE JOKING, BUT I DON'T LIKE YOUR SENSE OF HUMOR. I'LL JUST TAKE THE LAMP.
CERTAINLY, SIR. EXCELLENT CHOICE. I'LL BOX IT SECURELY FOR YOU.
THIS IS MY DAUGHTER, CHRIS. SHE'LL HELP YOU TO YOUR CAR.
OH, I DON'T NEED--
OF COURSE YOU DON'T, STRONG FELLOW LIKE YOU.
SHE WAS LOVELY. ENCHANTING. AND SEEMED GENUINELY ATTRACTED TO ME. WE TALKED FOR ALMOST AN HOUR OUTSIDE.
YOU CARRY AND I'LL OPEN THE DOORS.
BUT SHE HAD TO BE AT LEAST 13 YEARS YOUNGER THAN ME. JUST A KID, REALLY. BESIDES, I LOVE KATHY. I DO.
13

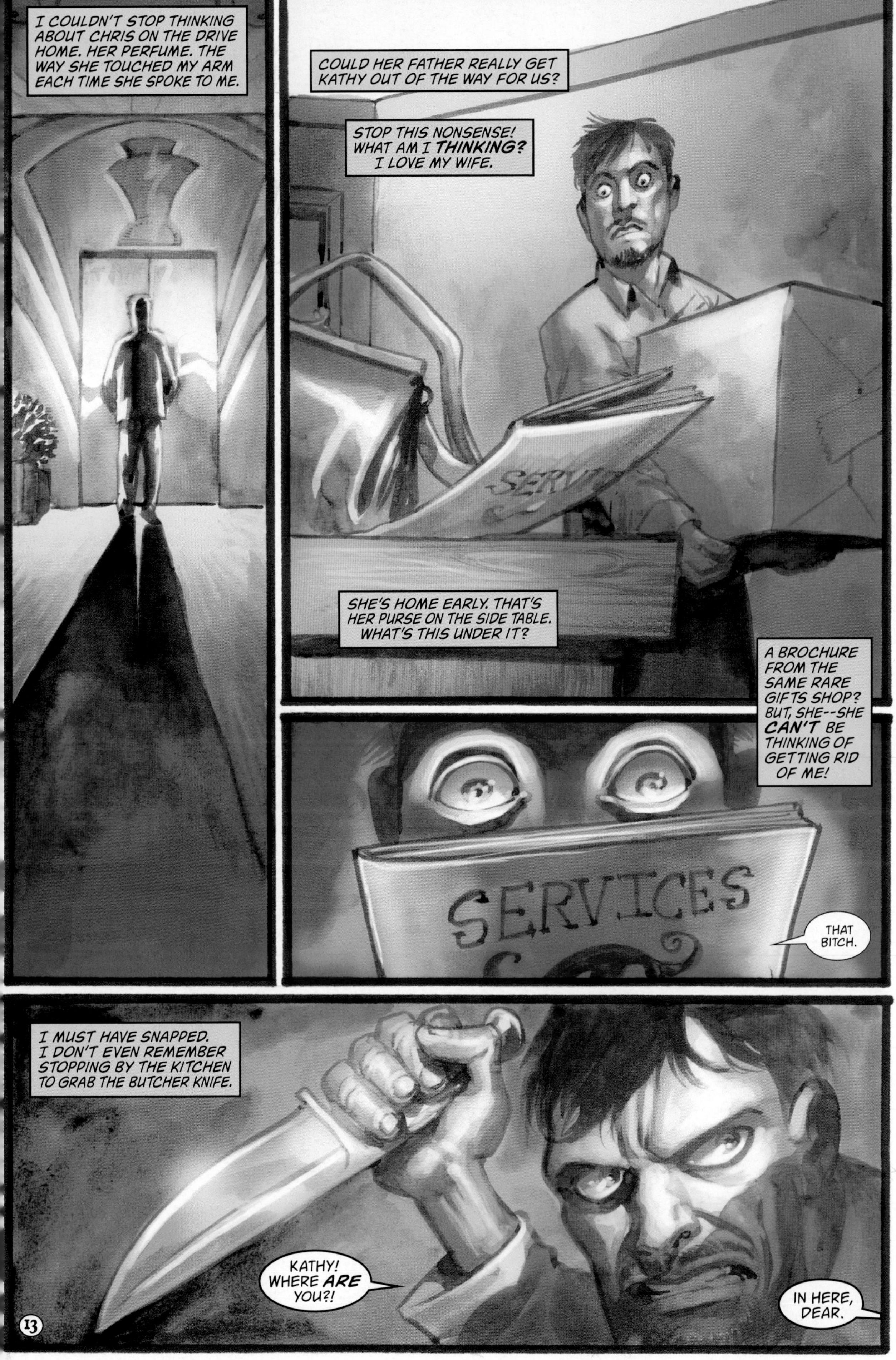
I COULDN'T STOP THINKING ABOUT CHRIS ON THE DRIVE HOME. HER PERFUME. THE WAY SHE TOUCHED MY ARM EACH TIME SHE SPOKE TO ME.
COULD HER FATHER REALLY GET KATHY OUT OF THE WAY FOR US?
STOP THIS NONSENSE! WHAT AM I **THINKING?** I LOVE MY WIFE.
SERVIC
SHE'S HOME EARLY. THAT'S HER PURSE ON THE SIDE TABLE. WHAT'S THIS UNDER IT?
A BROCHURE FROM THE SAME RARE GIFTS SHOP? BUT, SHE--SHE **CAN'T** BE THINKING OF GETTING RID OF ME!
SERVICES
THAT BITCH.
I MUST HAVE SNAPPED. I DON'T EVEN REMEMBER STOPPING BY THE KITCHEN TO GRAB THE BUTCHER KNIFE.
KATHY! WHERE **ARE** YOU?!
IN HERE, DEAR.
13

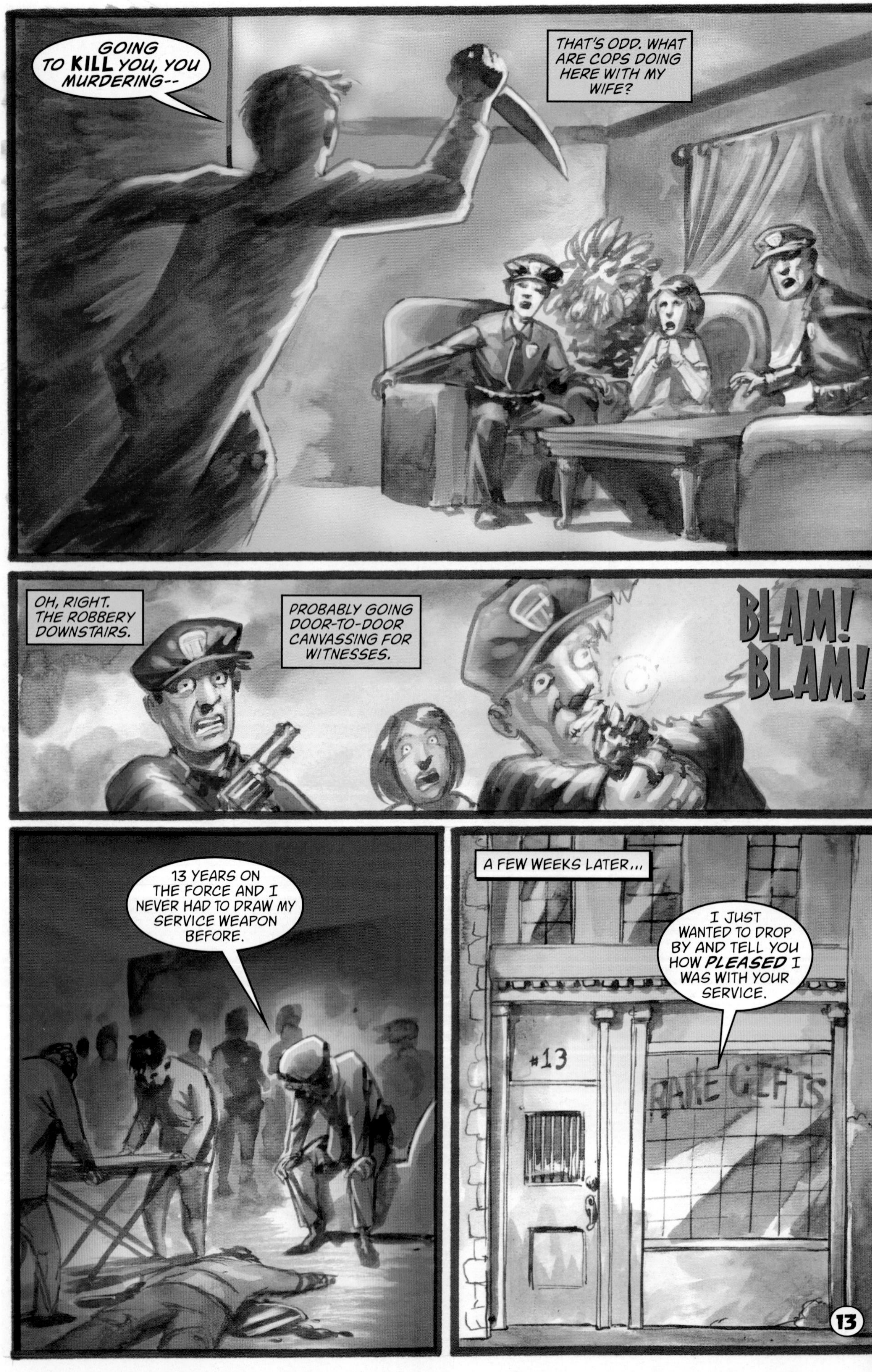
GOING TO KILL YOU, YOU MURDERING--
THAT'S ODD. WHAT ARE COPS DOING HERE WITH MY WIFE?
OH, RIGHT. THE ROBBERY DOWNSTAIRS.
PROBABLY GOING DOOR-TO-DOOR CANVASSING FOR WITNESSES.
BLAM! BLAM!
13 YEARS ON THE FORCE AND I NEVER HAD TO DRAW MY SERVICE WEAPON BEFORE.
A FEW WEEKS LATER...
I JUST WANTED TO DROP BY AND TELL YOU HOW PLEASED I WAS WITH YOUR SERVICE.
#13
RARE GIFTS
13

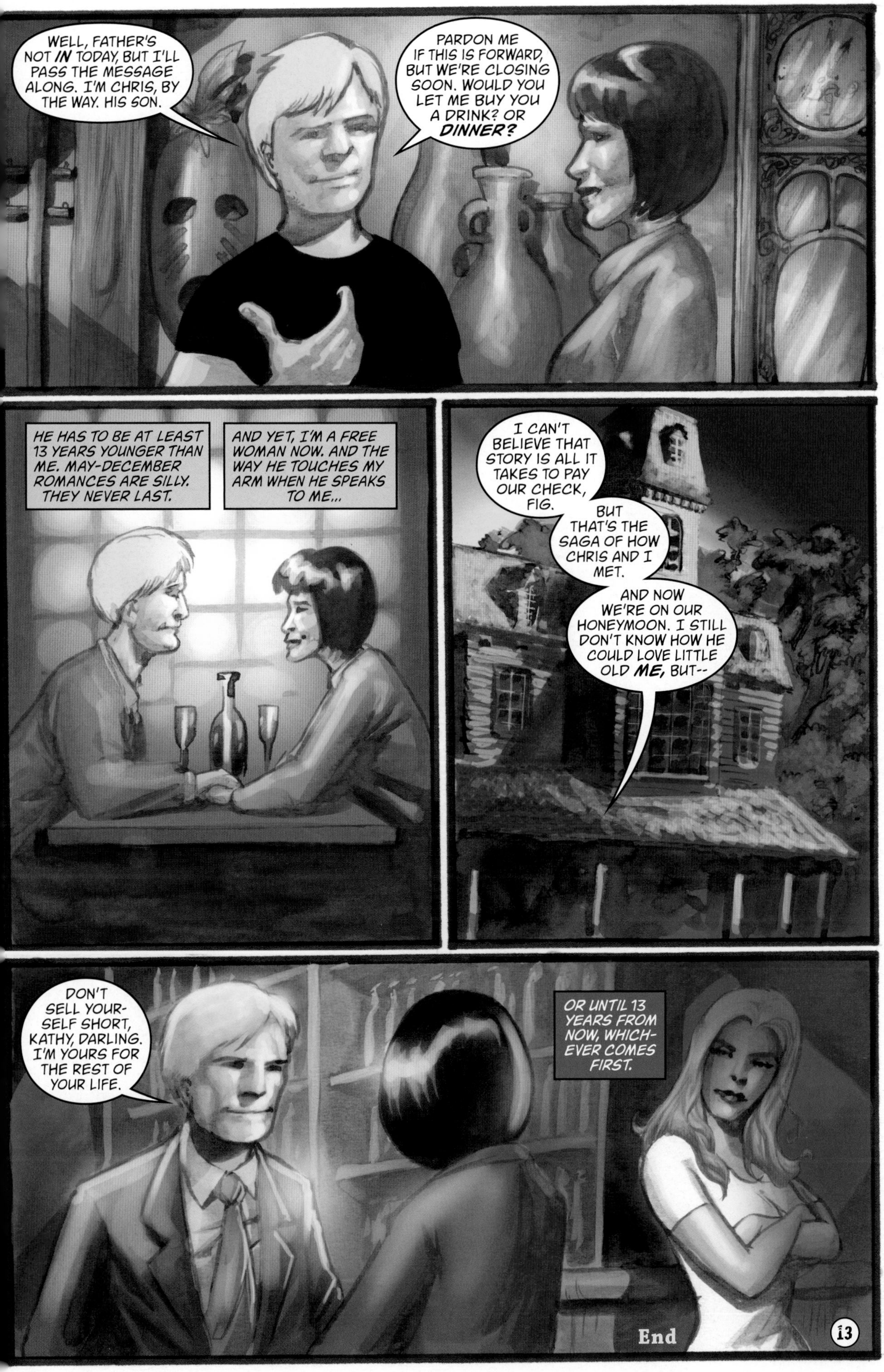
WELL, FATHER'S NOT ***IN*** TODAY, BUT I'LL PASS THE MESSAGE ALONG. I'M CHRIS, BY THE WAY. HIS SON.
PARDON ME IF THIS IS FORWARD, BUT WE'RE CLOSING SOON. WOULD YOU LET ME BUY YOU A DRINK? OR ***DINNER?***
HE HAS TO BE AT LEAST 13 YEARS YOUNGER THAN ME. MAY-DECEMBER ROMANCES ARE SILLY. THEY NEVER LAST.
AND YET, I'M A FREE WOMAN NOW. AND THE WAY HE TOUCHES MY ARM WHEN HE SPEAKS TO ME...
I CAN'T BELIEVE THAT STORY IS ALL IT TAKES TO PAY OUR CHECK, FIG.
BUT THAT'S THE SAGA OF HOW CHRIS AND I MET.
AND NOW WE'RE ON OUR HONEYMOON. I STILL DON'T KNOW HOW HE COULD LOVE LITTLE OLD ***ME,*** BUT--
DON'T SELL YOURSELF SHORT, KATHY, DARLING. I'M YOURS FOR THE REST OF YOUR LIFE.
OR UNTIL 13 YEARS FROM NOW, WHICHEVER COMES FIRST.
End
13

ONE OF MY CAUTIONARY RULES, when considering my wish list of those I hope to work with someday, is not to get greedy with the Fates. Whenever I get a chance to work with one of the comic book legends, I have to assume it will be the only chance I'll ever get. Therefore I endeavor not to waste the opportunity. With Bernie Wrightson, in hindsight it was clear that "an old-fashioned monster rally" was the only thing we could possibly do.

And now here comes Richard Corben willing to let me pen a story for him? Well, of course it has to be a gothic-y, Edgar Allan Poe-type tale. There was really no other choice.

THE HOUNDS OF TITUS ROAN

Art by
Richard Corben

Letters by
Todd Klein

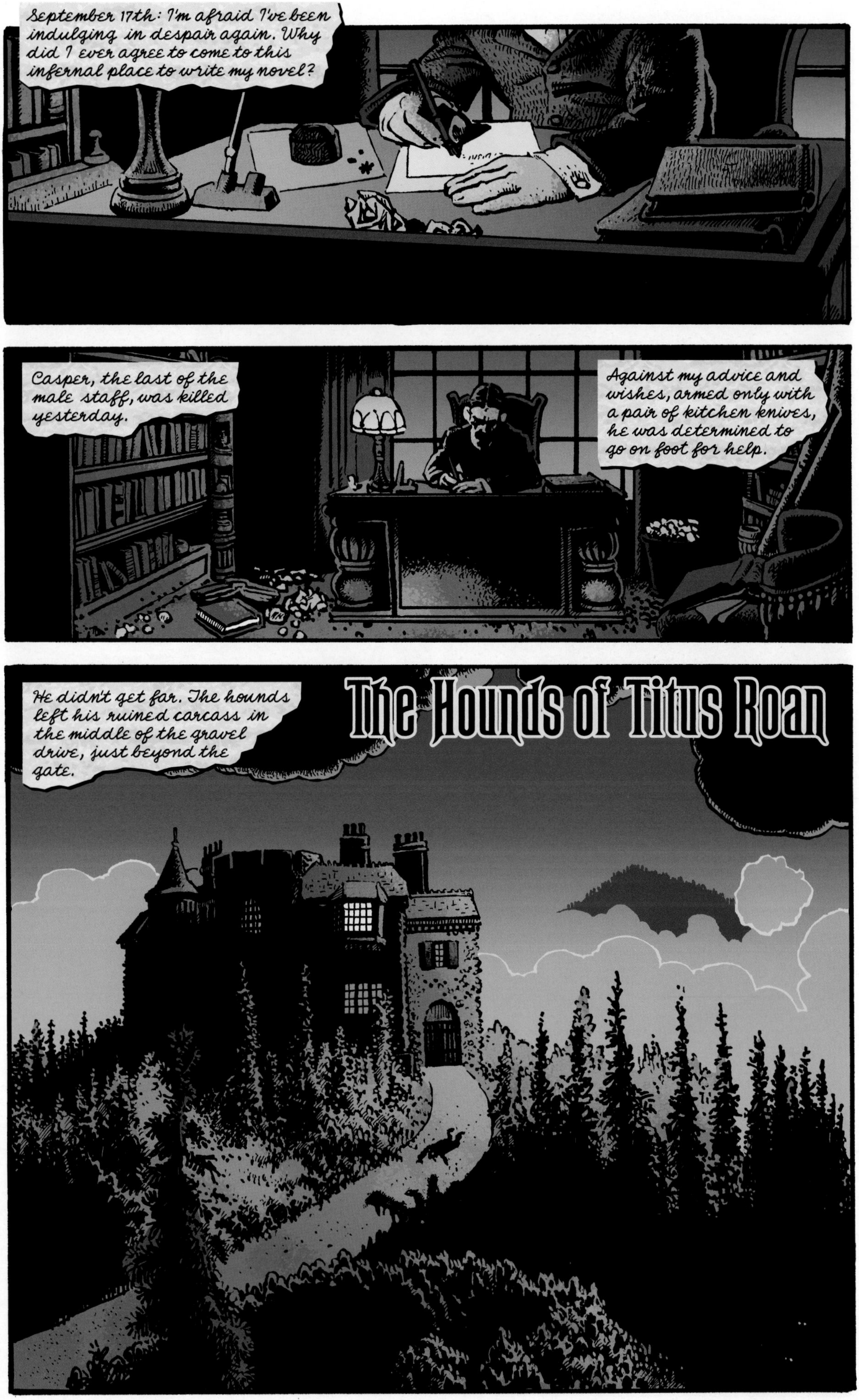
September 17th: I'm afraid I've been indulging in despair again. Why did I ever agree to come to this infernal place to write my novel?
Casper, the last of the male staff, was killed yesterday.
Against my advice and wishes, armed only with a pair of kitchen knives, he was determined to go on foot for help.
He didn't get far. The hounds left his ruined carcass in the middle of the gravel drive, just beyond the gate.
The Hounds of Titus Roan

Now I am trapped here alone, with young Betty, the only surviving member of the staff.

ARE WE LOCKED UP SECURE FOR THE EVENING?

YES, SIR.

I'm far from certain, but I believe she was one of the linen maids, or some such.

I TRUST WE CAN DISPENSE WITH *FORMALITIES* FROM NOW ON, BETTY. WE'RE THE LAST TWO TOGETHER, YOU AND I.

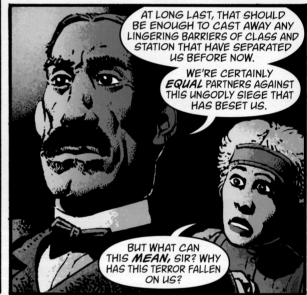

AT LONG LAST, THAT SHOULD BE ENOUGH TO CAST AWAY ANY LINGERING BARRIERS OF CLASS AND STATION THAT HAVE SEPARATED US BEFORE NOW.

WE'RE CERTAINLY *EQUAL* PARTNERS AGAINST THIS UNGODLY SIEGE THAT HAS BESET US.

BUT WHAT CAN THIS *MEAN*, SIR? WHY HAS THIS TERROR FALLEN ON US?

CALL ME DAVID--PLEASE. AND I CONFESS I CAN'T EVEN *GUESS* AT THE ANSWER TO YOUR QUESTION.

NOW, HELP ME FIND SOMETHING TO MAKE OUR SUPPER. YOU PROBABLY KNOW YOUR WAY AROUND THE LARDER BETTER THAN I.

WE *MUST* KEEP OURSELVES FORTIFIED AGAINST THE CONTINUING ORDEAL.

September 20th: Has the murder of poor Casper satisfied the creatures' bloodlust at long last? They've left us alone for the past three days.

I'M HAPPY TO HELP, SIR, BUT I DON'T UNDERSTAND WHAT WE'RE DOING.

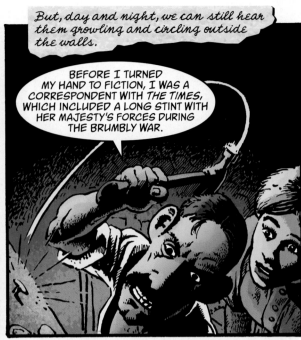

But, day and night, we can still hear them growling and circling outside the walls.

BEFORE I TURNED MY HAND TO FICTION, I WAS A CORRESPONDENT WITH *THE TIMES*, WHICH INCLUDED A LONG STINT WITH HER MAJESTY'S FORCES DURING THE BRUMBLY WAR.

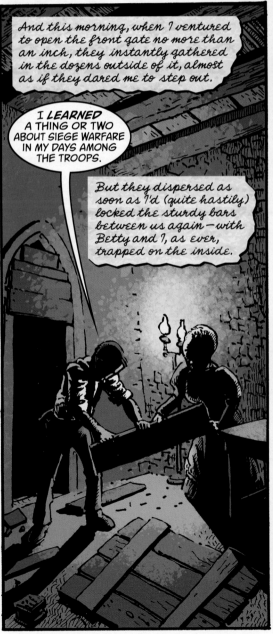

And this morning, when I ventured to open the front gate no more than an inch, they instantly gathered in the dozens outside of it, almost as if they dared me to step out.

I *LEARNED* A THING OR TWO ABOUT SIEGE WARFARE IN MY DAYS AMONG THE TROOPS.

But they dispersed as soon as I'd (quite hastily) locked the sturdy bars between us again — with Betty and I, as ever, trapped on the inside.

SUCH AS THE IMPORTANCE OF CREATING DEFENSIBLE *FALLBACK* POSITIONS.

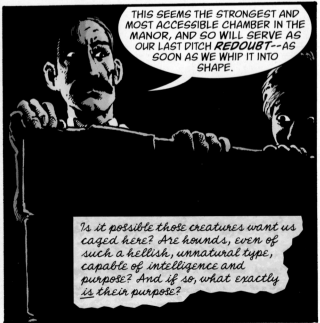

THIS SEEMS THE STRONGEST AND MOST ACCESSIBLE CHAMBER IN THE MANOR, AND SO WILL SERVE AS OUR LAST DITCH *REDOUBT*--AS SOON AS WE WHIP IT INTO SHAPE.

Is it possible those creatures want us caged here? Are hounds, even of such a hellish, unnatural type, capable of intelligence and purpose? And if so, what exactly is their purpose?

WELL? WHAT ARE YOU WAITING FOR?

September 29th: Why don't they attack us? I know the walls and gate can't be keeping them out, because they've made it over the walls before.

When they first appeared last month, they got in and killed seven in the courtyard. They've incredible powers not to be found in benevolent nature.

COME *KILL* US OR GO AWAY! BUT, FOR GOD'S SAKE, DON'T KEEP US HERE WAITING, DAY AFTER DAY!

They commenced their predations the day after I arrived here, at the remote and luxurious Villa at Titus Roan—almost as if they were waiting for me.

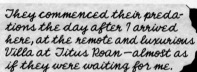

WELL?

DAVID, COME BACK INSIDE.

I could never have afforded to engage these lodgings on my own, but an anonymous benefactor—a fan of my novels—secured it for me for the season.

THEY JUST PROWL BACK AND FORTH OUTSIDE THE WALLS, BETTY. WHY? WHAT DO THEY *WANT?*

WHO CAN KNOW THE MIND AND WILL OF MONSTERS? CERTAINLY NOT I.

Now I wonder if some infernal scheme has been undertaken against me. Of course that's impossible. But why don't the hounds attack?

COME TO BED NOW. IT'S LATE AND YOU'LL CATCH A *CHILL* OUT HERE.

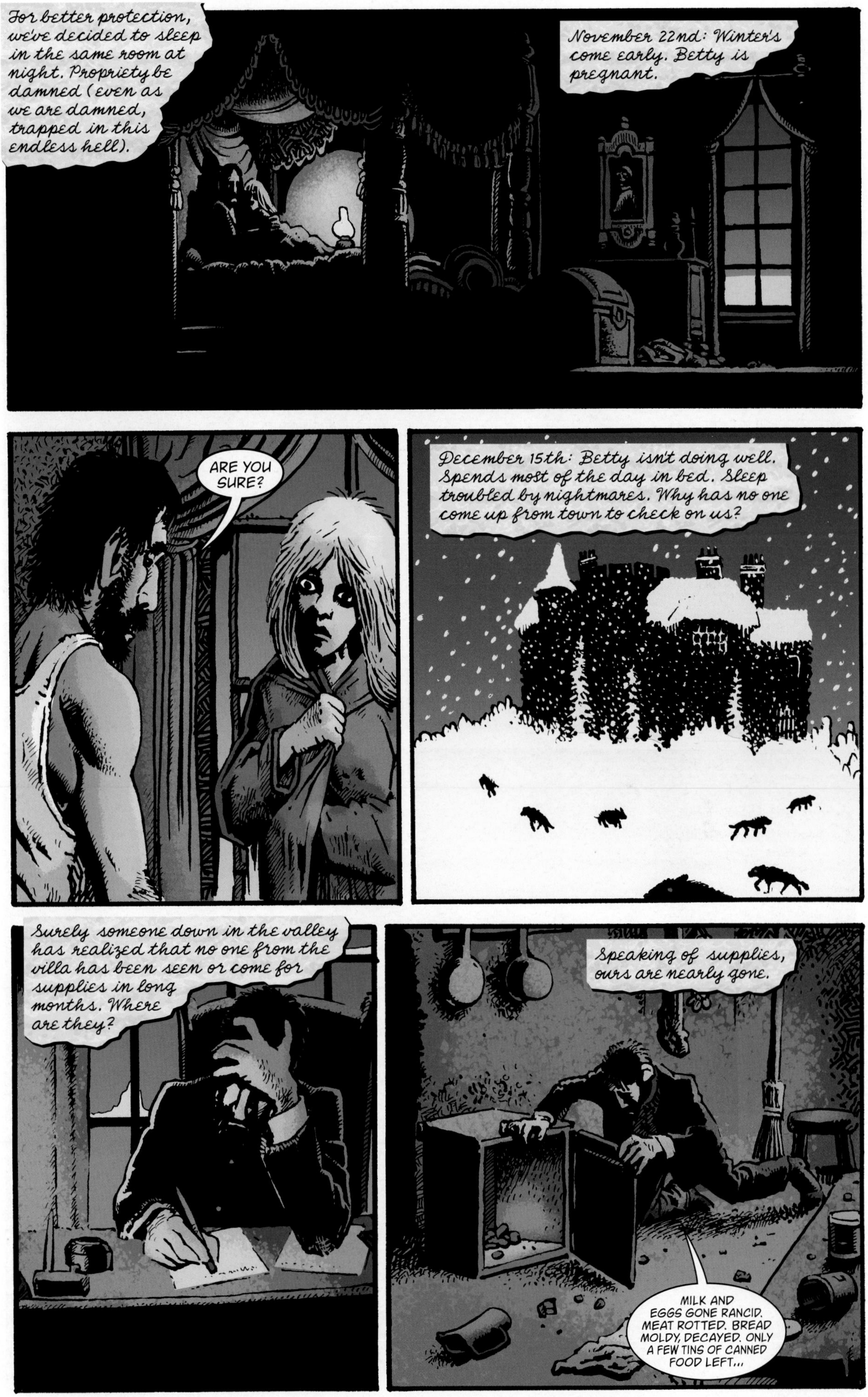

For better protection, we've decided to sleep in the same room at night. Propriety be damned (even as we are damned, trapped in this endless hell).
November 22nd: Winter's come early. Betty is pregnant.
ARE YOU SURE?
December 15th: Betty isn't doing well. Spends most of the day in bed. Sleep troubled by nightmares. Why has no one come up from town to check on us?
Surely someone down in the valley has realized that no one from the villa has been seen or come for supplies in long months. Where are they?
Speaking of supplies, ours are nearly gone.
MILK AND EGGS GONE RANCID. MEAT ROTTED. BREAD MOLDY, DECAYED. ONLY A FEW TINS OF CANNED FOOD LEFT...

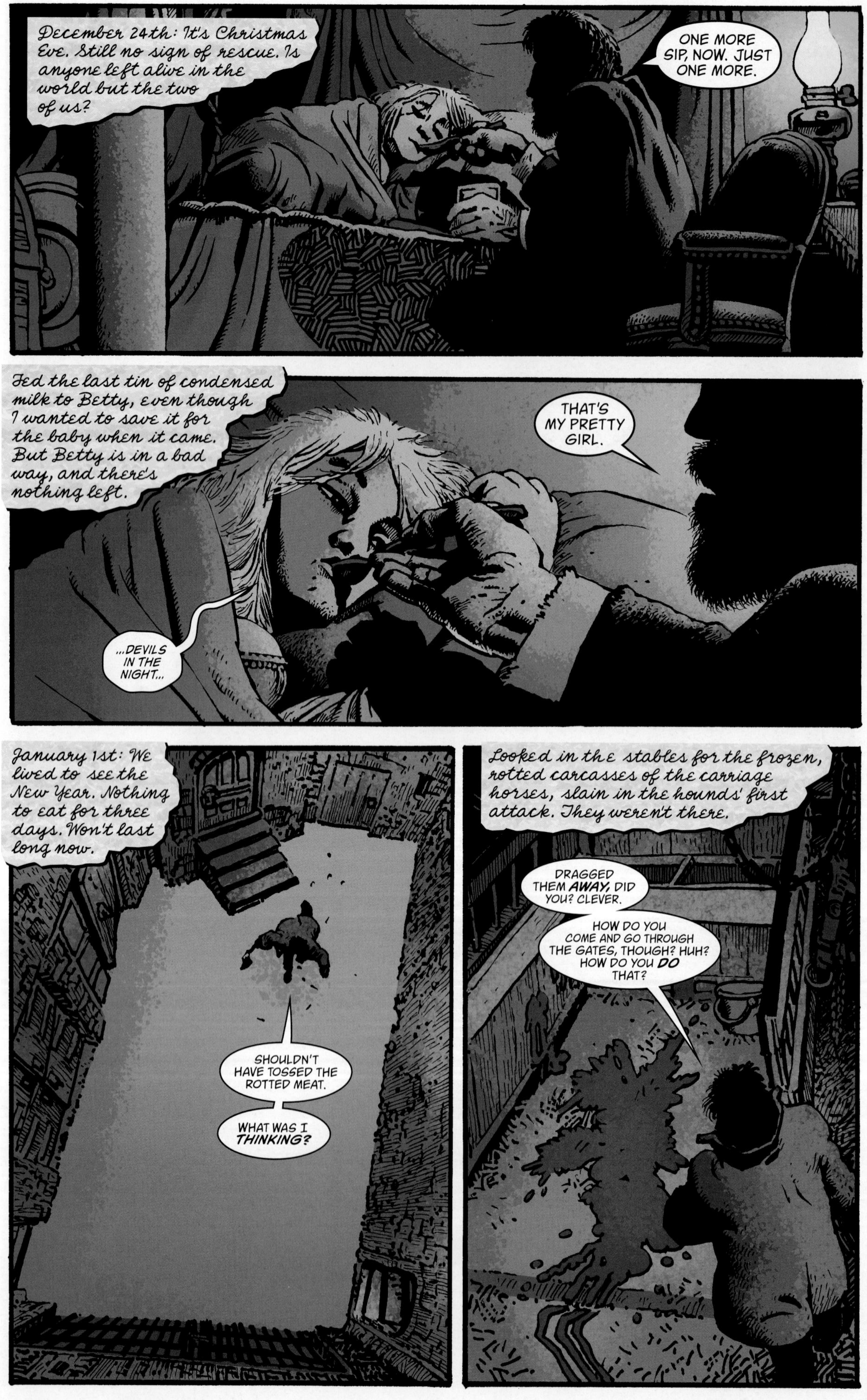
December 24th: It's Christmas Eve. Still no sign of rescue. Is anyone left alive in the world but the two of us?
ONE MORE SIP, NOW. JUST ONE MORE.
Fed the last tin of condensed milk to Betty, even though I wanted to save it for the baby when it came. But Betty is in a bad way, and there's nothing left.
THAT'S MY PRETTY GIRL.
...DEVILS IN THE NIGHT...
January 1st: We lived to see the New Year. Nothing to eat for three days. Won't last long now.
SHOULDN'T HAVE TOSSED THE ROTTED MEAT.
WHAT WAS I THINKING?
Looked in the stables for the frozen, rotted carcasses of the carriage horses, slain in the hounds' first attack. They weren't there.
DRAGGED THEM AWAY, DID YOU? CLEVER.
HOW DO YOU COME AND GO THROUGH THE GATES, THOUGH? HUH? HOW DO YOU DO THAT?

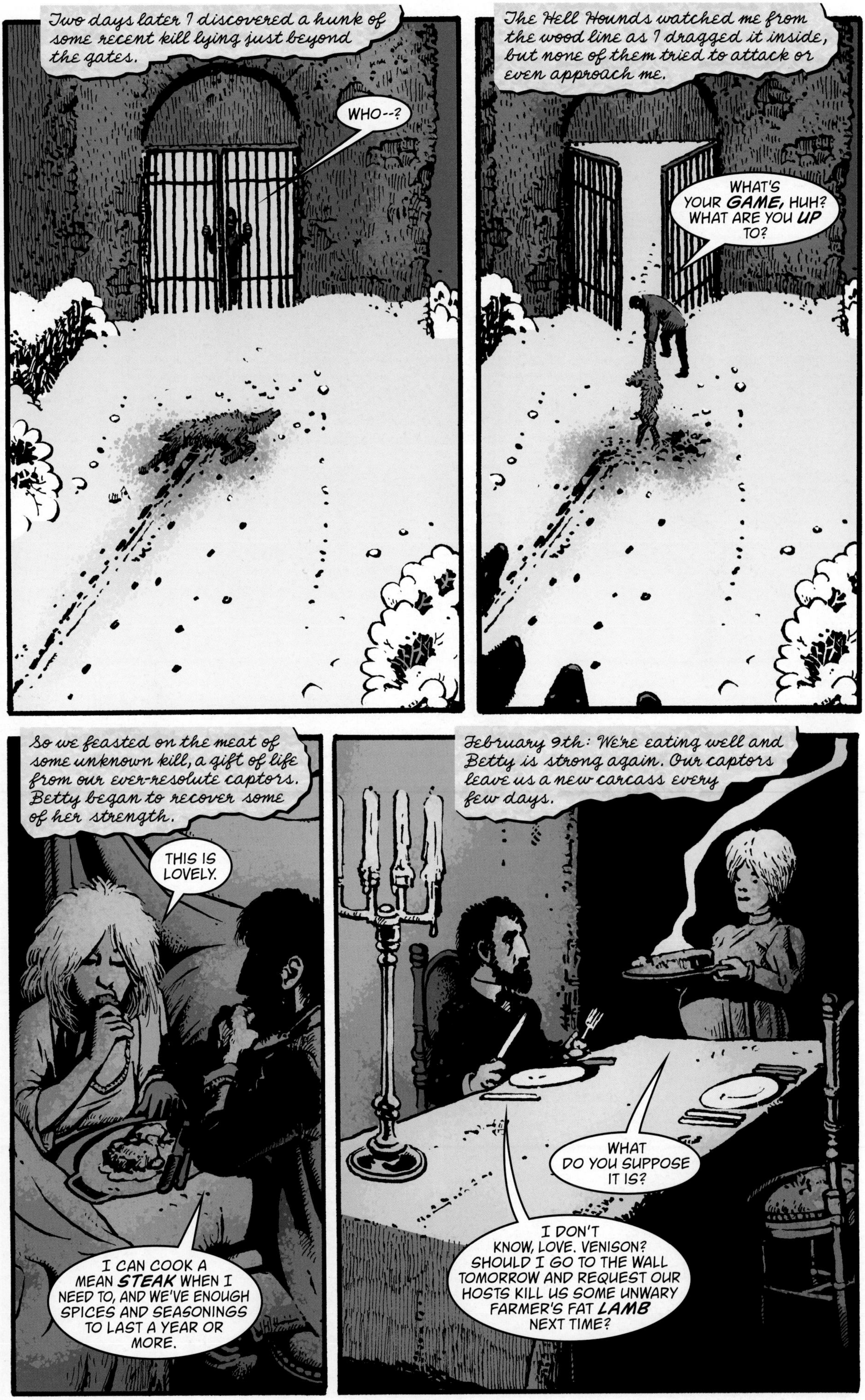
Two days later I discovered a hunk of some recent kill lying just beyond the gates.
WHO--?
The Hell Hounds watched me from the wood line as I dragged it inside, but none of them tried to attack or even approach me.
WHAT'S YOUR GAME, HUH? WHAT ARE YOU UP TO?
So we feasted on the meat of some unknown kill, a gift of life from our ever-resolute captors. Betty began to recover some of her strength.
THIS IS LOVELY.
I CAN COOK A MEAN STEAK WHEN I NEED TO, AND WE'VE ENOUGH SPICES AND SEASONINGS TO LAST A YEAR OR MORE.
February 9th: We're eating well and Betty is strong again. Our captors leave us a new carcass every few days.
WHAT DO YOU SUPPOSE IT IS?
I DON'T KNOW, LOVE. VENISON? SHOULD I GO TO THE WALL TOMORROW AND REQUEST OUR HOSTS KILL US SOME UNWARY FARMER'S FAT LAMB NEXT TIME?

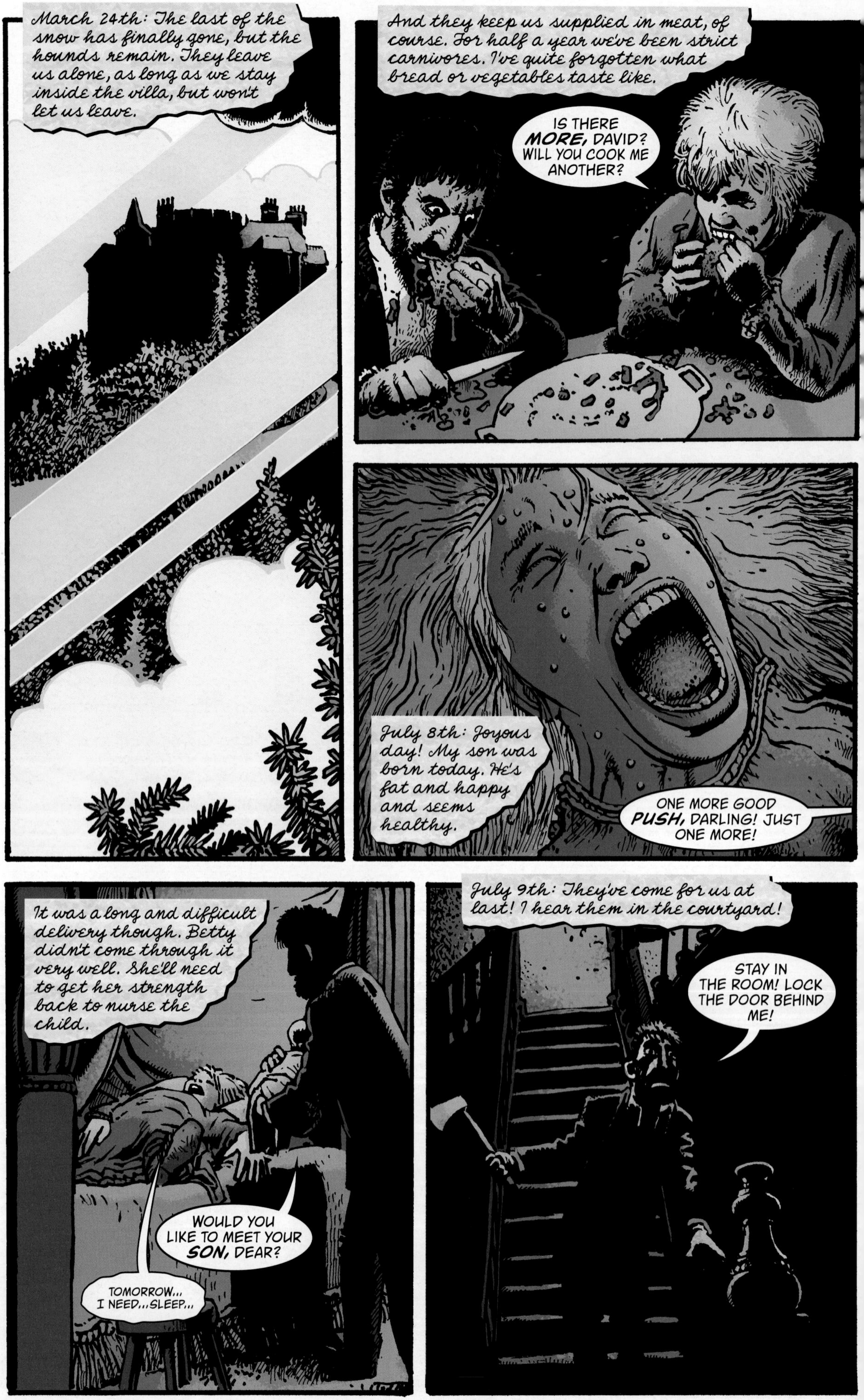
March 24th: The last of the snow has finally gone, but the hounds remain. They leave us alone, as long as we stay inside the villa, but won't let us leave.
And they keep us supplied in meat, of course. For half a year we've been strict carnivores. I've quite forgotten what bread or vegetables taste like.
IS THERE MORE, DAVID? WILL YOU COOK ME ANOTHER?
July 8th: Joyous day! My son was born today. He's fat and happy and seems healthy.
ONE MORE GOOD PUSH, DARLING! JUST ONE MORE!
It was a long and difficult delivery though. Betty didn't come through it very well. She'll need to get her strength back to nurse the child.
WOULD YOU LIKE TO MEET YOUR SON, DEAR?
TOMORROW... I NEED...SLEEP...
July 9th: They've come for us at last! I hear them in the courtyard!
STAY IN THE ROOM! LOCK THE DOOR BEHIND ME!

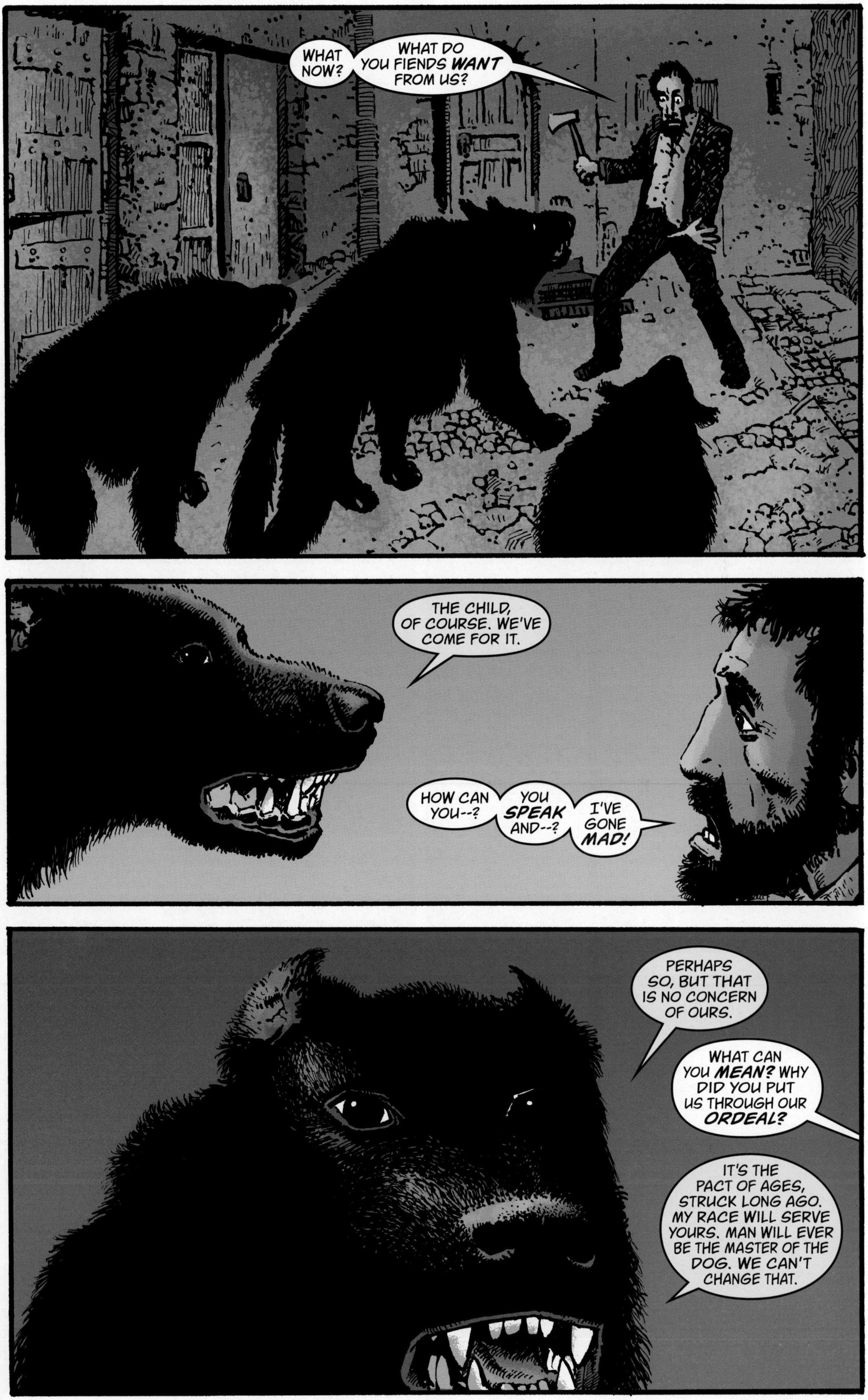
WHAT NOW?
WHAT DO YOU FIENDS WANT FROM US?
THE CHILD, OF COURSE. WE'VE COME FOR IT.
HOW CAN YOU--?
YOU SPEAK AND--?
I'VE GONE MAD!
PERHAPS SO, BUT THAT IS NO CONCERN OF OURS.
WHAT CAN YOU MEAN? WHY DID YOU PUT US THROUGH OUR ORDEAL?
IT'S THE PACT OF AGES, STRUCK LONG AGO. MY RACE WILL SERVE YOURS. MAN WILL EVER BE THE MASTER OF THE DOG. WE CAN'T CHANGE THAT.

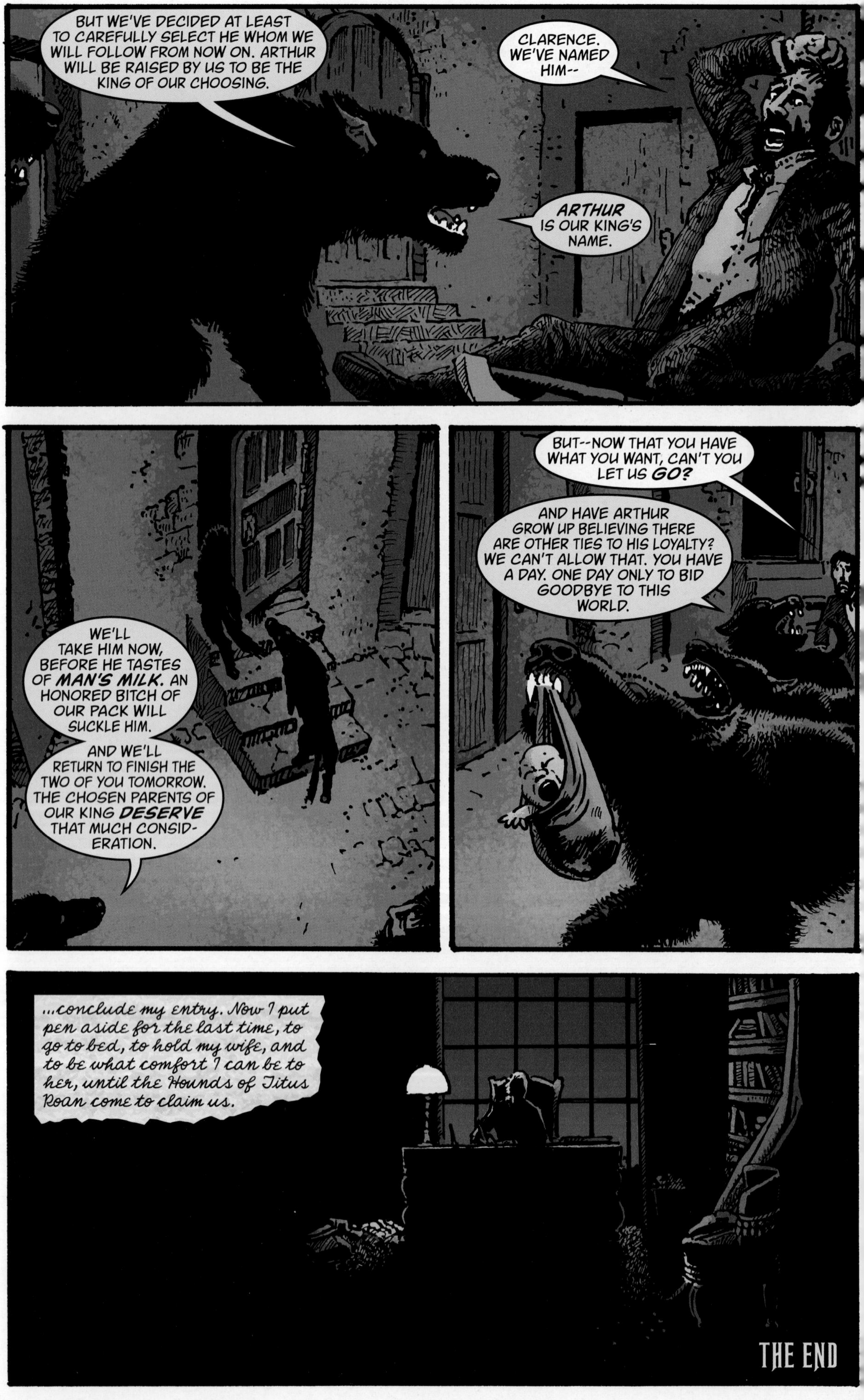
BUT WE'VE DECIDED AT LEAST TO CAREFULLY SELECT HE WHOM WE WILL FOLLOW FROM NOW ON. ARTHUR WILL BE RAISED BY US TO BE THE KING OF OUR CHOOSING.
CLARENCE. WE'VE NAMED HIM--
ARTHUR IS OUR KING'S NAME.
WE'LL TAKE HIM NOW, BEFORE HE TASTES OF MAN'S MILK. AN HONORED BITCH OF OUR PACK WILL SUCKLE HIM.
AND WE'LL RETURN TO FINISH THE TWO OF YOU TOMORROW. THE CHOSEN PARENTS OF OUR KING DESERVE THAT MUCH CONSIDERATION.
BUT--NOW THAT YOU HAVE WHAT YOU WANT, CAN'T YOU LET US GO?
AND HAVE ARTHUR GROW UP BELIEVING THERE ARE OTHER TIES TO HIS LOYALTY? WE CAN'T ALLOW THAT. YOU HAVE A DAY. ONE DAY ONLY TO BID GOODBYE TO THIS WORLD.
...conclude my entry. Now I put pen aside for the last time, to go to bed, to hold my wife, and to be what comfort I can be to her, until the Hounds of Titus Roan come to claim us.
THE END

AND SO HERE WE ARE AT THE FINAL STORY IN THIS COLLECTION. And considering that he's the best artist I've ever had the privilege to work with (among a truly Olympian pantheon of incredible artists, so don't imagine for an instant that this is a trivial statement), I think it's fitting that we end with another collaboration between Mark Buckingham and myself.

But here's a confession. Mark is a great writer, too. Even though my name appears in the credits (and to be fair, I did contribute a wee bit here and there), this is primarily Mark's story. He came up with the ideas, he drew it, and then he provided most of the writing, too.

My greatest fear is that Mark will someday realize that he doesn't need me in order to craft great stories, and he'll leave me to do what he can so ably do on his own. So please don't tell him I said this.

For the record, my second greatest fear involves being dropped into a slippery-sided tub full of snakes, sharks, 'gators and the odd ninja assassin or two, but since that hardly ever happens anymore, it's really not germane to our discussion.

Seeing as we're nearly done here, let me take a line or two to thank you for coming along on this walk through some of the more interesting byways of my storytelling life. Thanks also for your help in telling these stories — for filling in the many important details between panels, in this most terse of all the story mediums. I hope to see you again, in other fictional lands, where we can pass an afternoon swapping interesting lies with each other.

— BILL WILLINGHAM

August 2011

HIGH SPIRITS

PENCILS BY
Mark Buckingham

INKS BY
Kevin Nowlan

COLORS BY
Lee Loughridge

LETTERS BY
Todd Klein

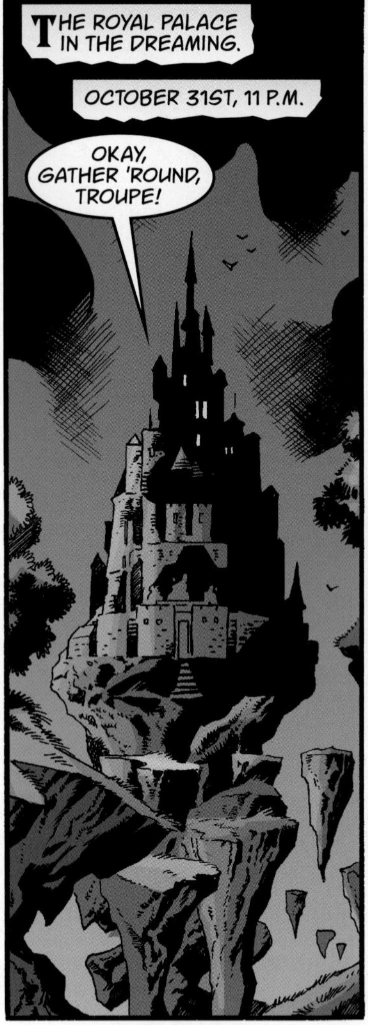
THE ROYAL PALACE IN THE DREAMING.
OCTOBER 31ST, 11 P.M.
OKAY, GATHER 'ROUND, TROUPE!

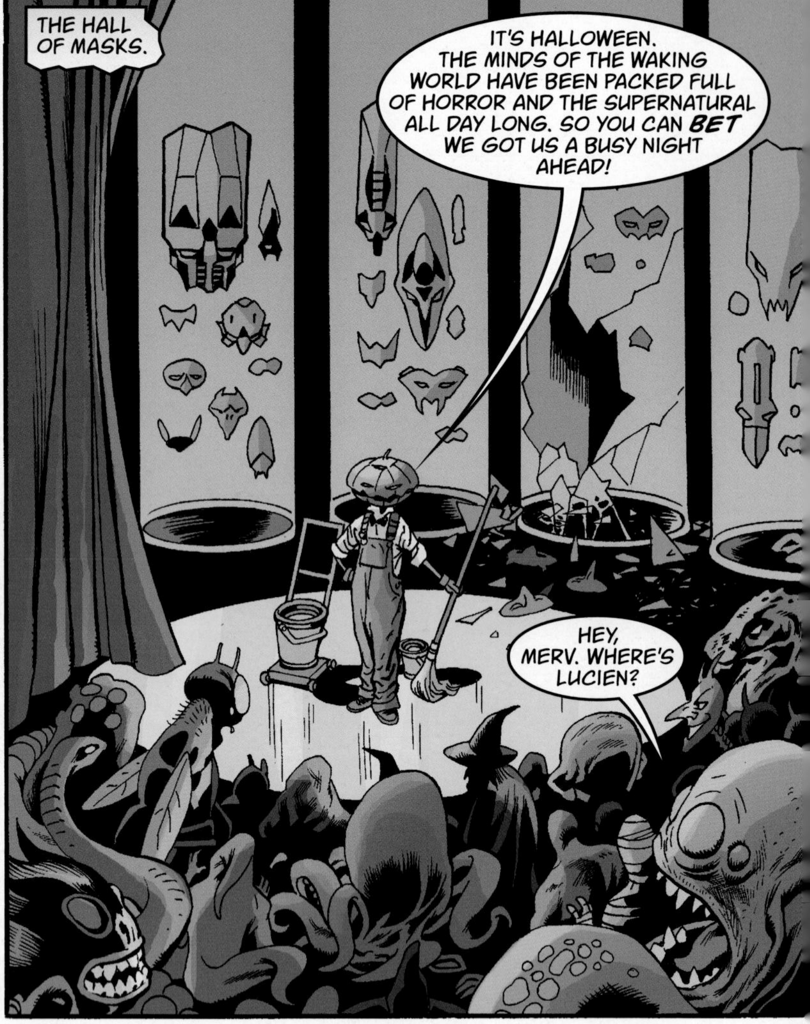
THE HALL OF MASKS.
IT'S HALLOWEEN. THE MINDS OF THE WAKING WORLD HAVE BEEN PACKED FULL OF HORROR AND THE SUPERNATURAL ALL DAY LONG. SO YOU CAN BET WE GOT US A BUSY NIGHT AHEAD!
HEY, MERV. WHERE'S LUCIEN?

HIGH SPIRITS

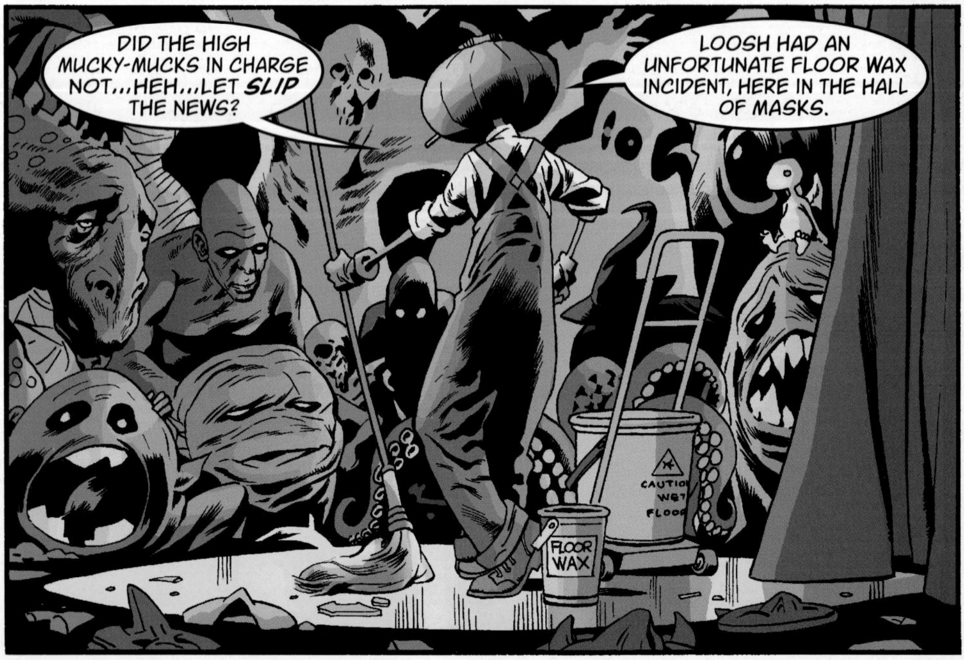
DID THE HIGH MUCKY-MUCKS IN CHARGE NOT...HEH...LET SLIP THE NEWS?
LOOSH HAD AN UNFORTUNATE FLOOR WAX INCIDENT, HERE IN THE HALL OF MASKS.
CAUTION WET FLOOR
FLOOR WAX

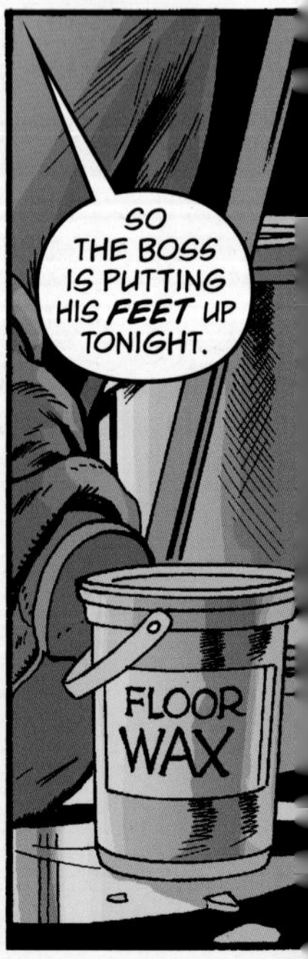
SO THE BOSS IS PUTTING HIS FEET UP TONIGHT.
FLOOR WAX

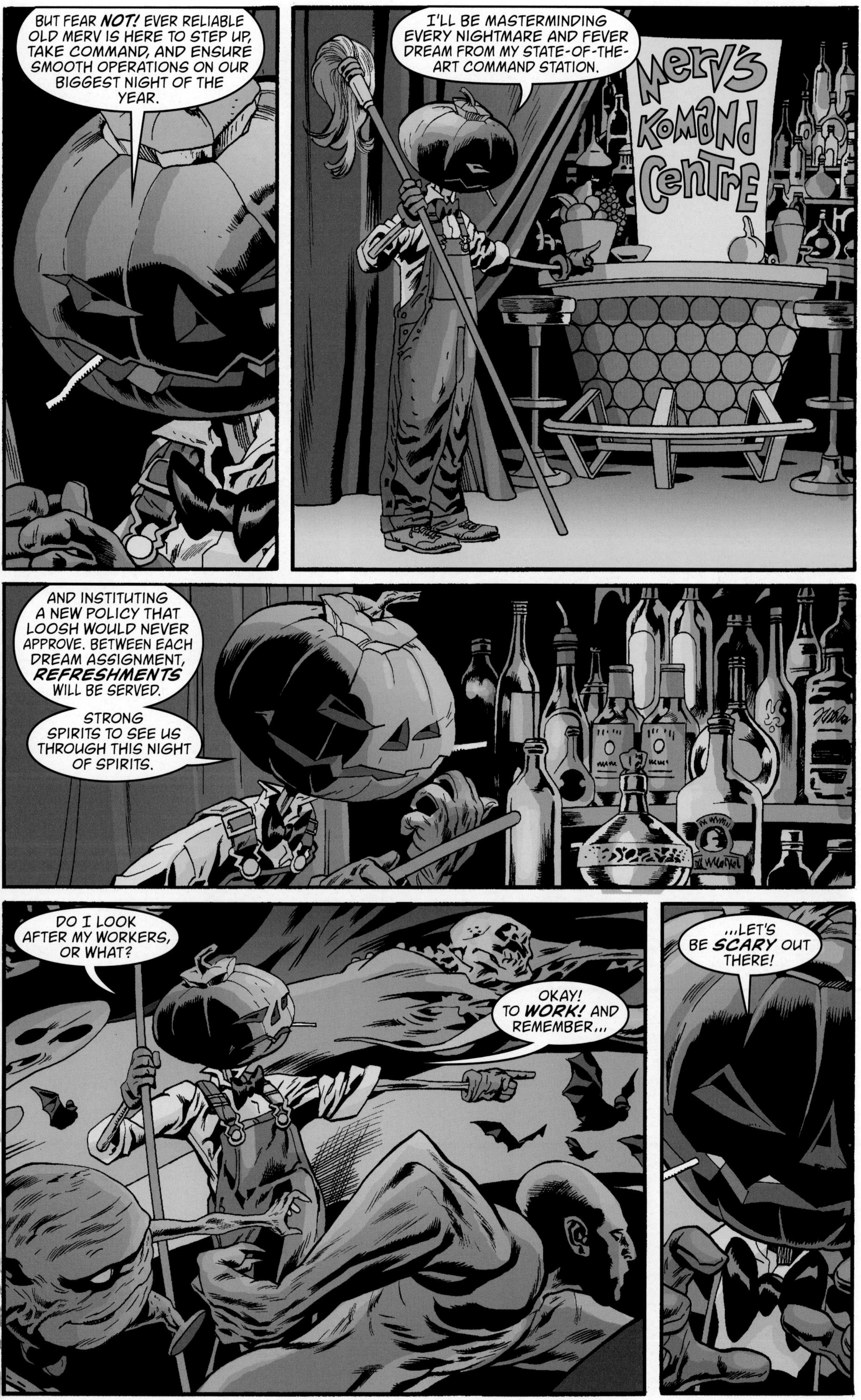
BUT FEAR *NOT!* EVER RELIABLE OLD MERV IS HERE TO STEP UP, TAKE COMMAND, AND ENSURE SMOOTH OPERATIONS ON OUR BIGGEST NIGHT OF THE YEAR.
I'LL BE MASTERMINDING EVERY NIGHTMARE AND FEVER DREAM FROM MY STATE-OF-THE-ART COMMAND STATION.
MERV'S KOMAND CENTRE
AND INSTITUTING A NEW POLICY THAT LOOSH WOULD NEVER APPROVE. BETWEEN EACH DREAM ASSIGNMENT, ***REFRESHMENTS*** WILL BE SERVED.
STRONG SPIRITS TO SEE US THROUGH THIS NIGHT OF SPIRITS.
DO I LOOK AFTER MY WORKERS, OR WHAT?
OKAY! TO ***WORK!*** AND REMEMBER...
...LET'S BE ***SCARY*** OUT THERE!

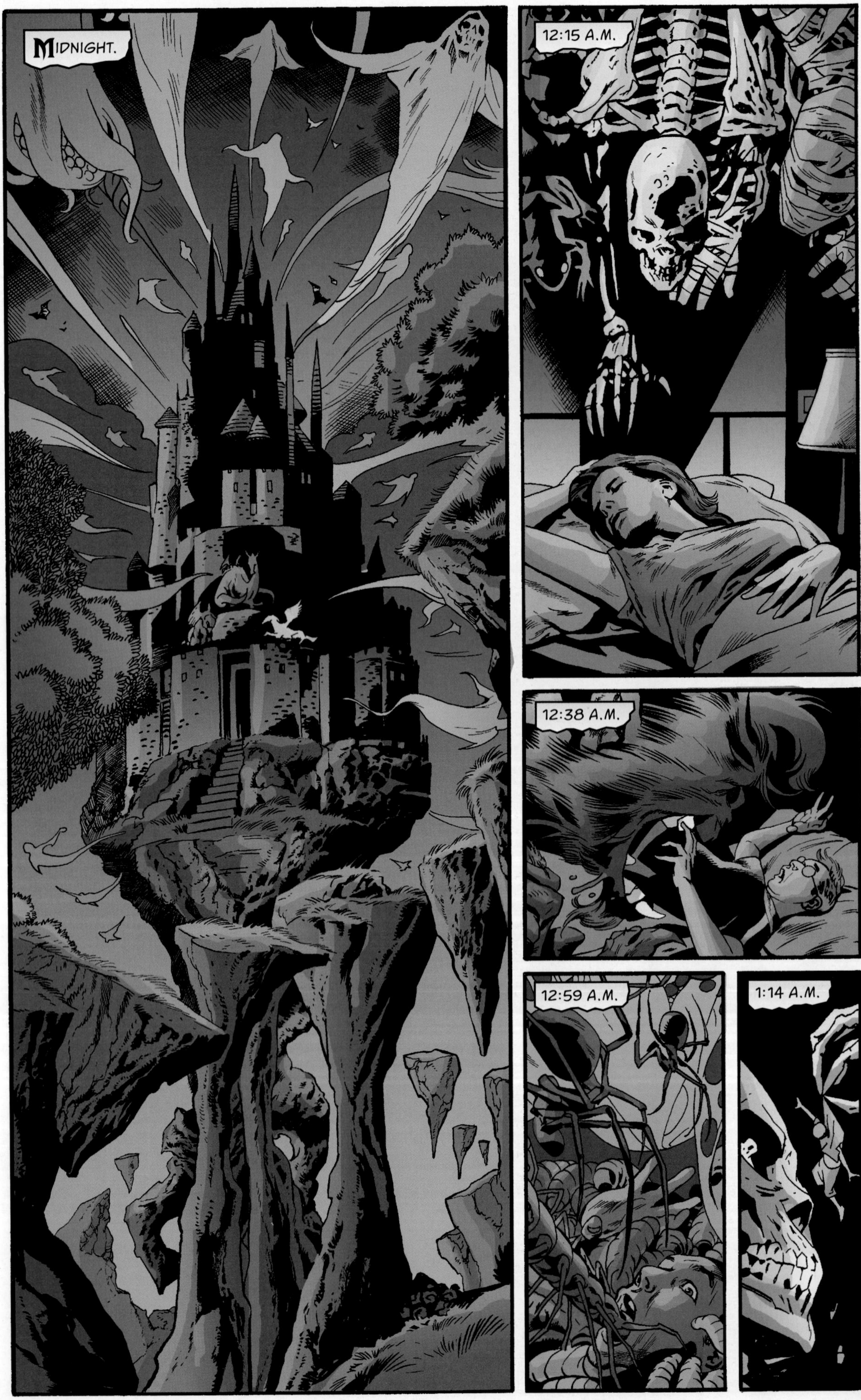
MIDNIGHT.
12:15 A.M.
12:38 A.M.
12:59 A.M.
1:14 A.M.

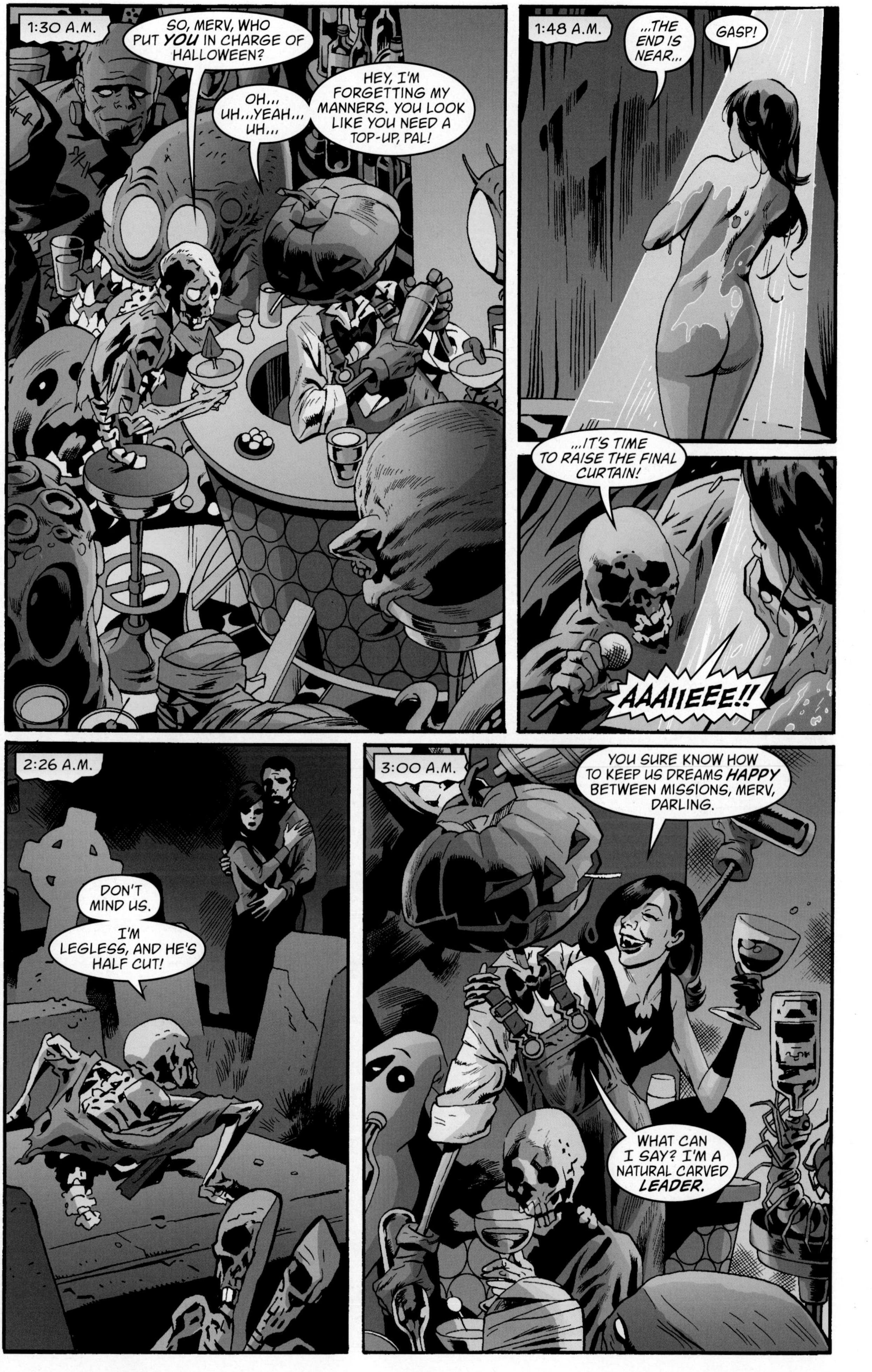
1:30 A.M.
SO, MERV, WHO PUT *YOU* IN CHARGE OF HALLOWEEN?
OH... UH...YEAH... UH...
HEY, I'M FORGETTING MY MANNERS. YOU LOOK LIKE YOU NEED A TOP-UP, PAL!
1:48 A.M.
...THE END IS NEAR...
GASP!
...IT'S TIME TO RAISE THE FINAL CURTAIN!
AAAIIEEE!!
2:26 A.M.
DON'T MIND US.
I'M LEGLESS, AND HE'S HALF CUT!
3:00 A.M.
YOU SURE KNOW HOW TO KEEP US DREAMS *HAPPY* BETWEEN MISSIONS, MERV, DARLING.
WHAT CAN I SAY? I'M A NATURAL CARVED *LEADER*.

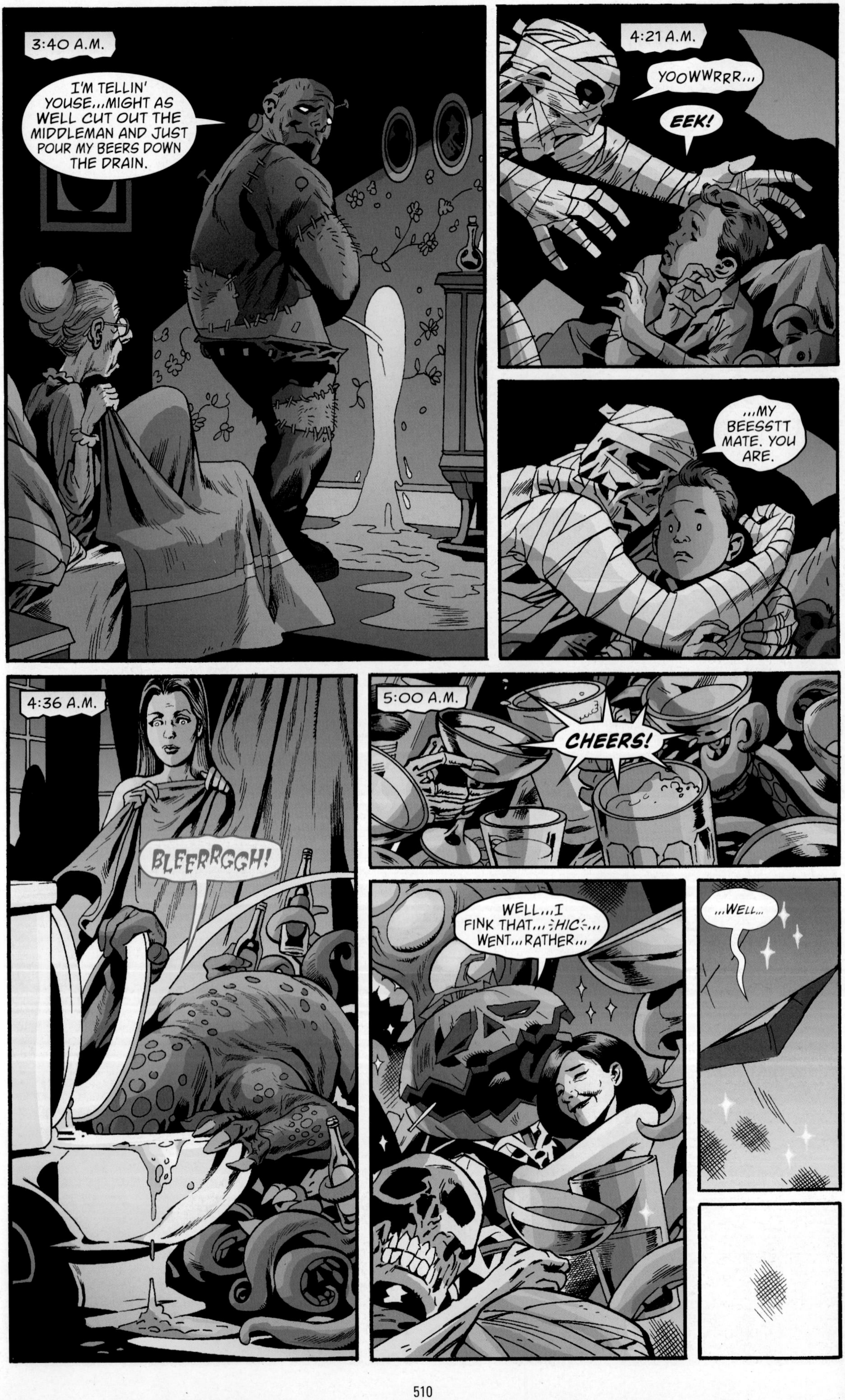
3:40 A.M.
I'M TELLIN' YOUSE...MIGHT AS WELL CUT OUT THE MIDDLEMAN AND JUST POUR MY BEERS DOWN THE DRAIN.
4:21 A.M.
YOOWWRRR...
EEK!
...MY BEESSTT MATE. YOU ARE.
4:36 A.M.
BLEERRGGH!
5:00 A.M.
CHEERS!
WELL...I FINK THAT...HIC...WENT...RATHER...
...WELL...

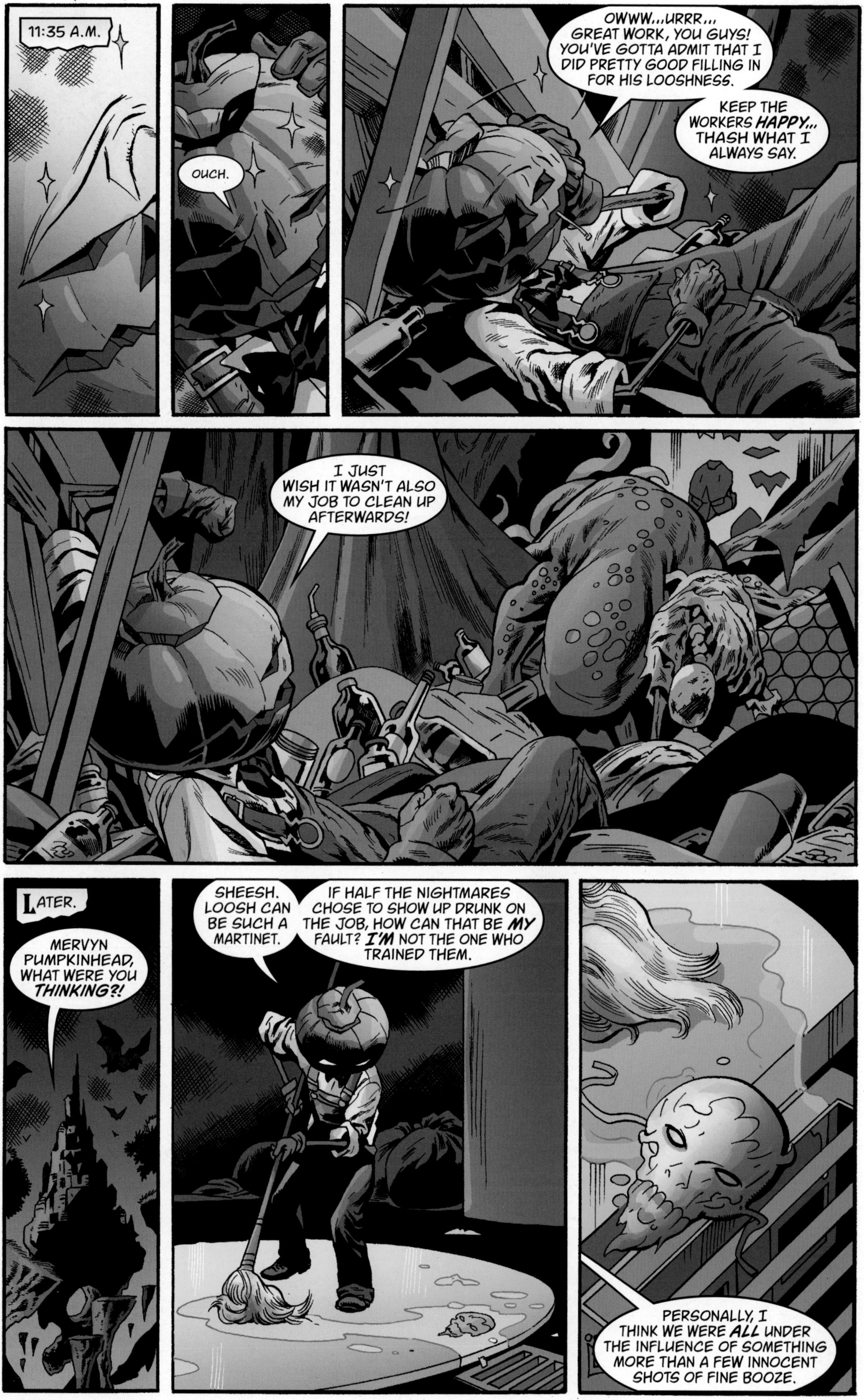
11:35 A.M.
OUCH.
OWWW...URRR... GREAT WORK, YOU GUYS! YOU'VE GOTTA ADMIT THAT I DID PRETTY GOOD FILLING IN FOR HIS LOOSHNESS.
KEEP THE WORKERS HAPPY... THASH WHAT I ALWAYS SAY.
I JUST WISH IT WASN'T ALSO MY JOB TO CLEAN UP AFTERWARDS!
LATER.
MERVYN PUMPKINHEAD, WHAT WERE YOU THINKING?!
SHEESH. LOOSH CAN BE SUCH A MARTINET.
IF HALF THE NIGHTMARES CHOSE TO SHOW UP DRUNK ON THE JOB, HOW CAN THAT BE MY FAULT? I'M NOT THE ONE WHO TRAINED THEM.
PERSONALLY, I THINK WE WERE ALL UNDER THE INFLUENCE OF SOMETHING MORE THAN A FEW INNOCENT SHOTS OF FINE BOOZE.